Landmarks of the American Revolution

SECOND EDITION

Library of Military History

Editorial Board

Landmarks of the American Revolution

SECOND EDITON

Library of Military History

Mark M. Boatner III
Introduction by Barnet Schecter

CHARLES SCRIBNER'S SONS
An imprint of Thomson Gale, a part of The Thomson Corporation

Detroit • New York • San Francisco • San Diego • New Haven, Conn. • Waterville, Maine • London • Munich

Landmarks of the American Revolution, Second Edition
Library of Military History

Mark M. Boatner III
Introduction by Barnet Schecter

For more information, contact
Thomson Gale
27500 Drake Rd.
Farmington Hills, MI 48331-3535
Or you can visit our Internet site at
http://www.gale.com

LIBRARY OF CONGRESS CATALOGING-IN-PUBLICATION DATA

Boatner, Mark Mayo, 1921-
Landmarks of the American Revolution : library of military history / Mark M. Boatner ; foreword by Barnet Schecter. – 2nd ed.
p. cm.
Includes bibliographical references and index.
ISBN 0-684-31473-8 (hardcover : alk. paper)
1. Historic sites – United States – Guidebooks. 2. United States – History – Revolution, 1775-1783. I. Title.
E159.B67 2006
917.304'931—dc22

2006002325

This title is also available as an e-book and as a three volume set with the *Encyclopedia of the American Revolution*
E-book ISBN 0-684-31546-7
Three volume set ISBN 0-684-31470-3
Contact your Gale sales representative for ordering information.

Printed in the United States of America
10 9 8 7 6 5 4 3 2 1

Editorial and Production Staff

PROJECT EDITOR

Stephen Cusack

EDITORIAL SUPPORT

Erin Bealmear
Kristin Hart

IMAGING

Randy Bassett
Dean Dauphinais
Lezlie Light
Mike Logusz
Christine O'Bryan

COPYEDITORS

Ann Davidson

CAPTION WRITER

Judith Culligan

PROOFREADER

Michael Levine

CARTOGRAPHER

XNR Productions (Madison, Wisconsin)

INDEXER

Wendy Allex

COVER & PAGE DESIGNER

Kate Scheibel

PERMISSIONS

Margaret Chamberlain-Gaston
Shalice Shah-Caldwell
Lori Hines

MANAGER, COMPOSITION

Mary Beth Trimper

ASSISTANT MANAGER, COMPOSITION

Evi Seoud

MANUFACTURING

Wendy Blurton

SENIOR EDITOR

Stephen Wasserstein

EXECUTIVE VICE PRESIDENT AND PUBLISHER

Frank Menchaca

Contents

Preface

Books, television, and the Internet provide a wealth of images and information relating to the landmarks of the American Revolution, but there is still no substitute for being there. Whether one makes the pilgrimage to Concord's North Bridge on a glorious autumn day, walks the ramparts of Fort Ticonderoga, or soaks up the atmosphere of Philadelphia's Independence Hall, the sites that together constitute the birthplace of the United States offer a living connection to a great watershed in human history. This revised, expanded, and updated edition of Mark Boatner's *Landmarks of the American Revolution* is an invitation, in his words, to discover "America's outdoor archives, the new dimensions of history that lie in seeing, smelling, touching, and walking through famous places."

Even where these sites have been paved over, a bronze tablet or steel panel marking the spot—and the guidance of this book—can enable us to marvel at the contrast between the modern urban fabric and the bucolic landscape directly beneath the asphalt, where the Revolutionary War once raged. Reading a plaque at Park Avenue and 37th Street in Manhattan, once the center of a rural estate where Mary Murray served cakes and Madeira to the invading British generals in 1776, one imagines the roar of the subway underfoot to be the British naval bombardment at Kips Bay a few blocks to the east. Did the patriotic Mrs. Murray really interrupt the invasion and save thousands of American soldiers? *Landmarks*, in conjunction with the two companion volumes that make up the *Encyclopedia of the American Revolution*, sorts out military history from colorful lore, providing a definitive guide to locating and knowing what happened at the sites of independence.

When Boatner set out to write *Landmarks* in 1968, nothing so comprehensive had been attempted since 1848, when Benson Lossing embarked on an 8,000 mile journey through the original thirteen states and Canada gathering local history and lore from elderly eye-witnesses of the Revolution and producing more than 1,000 drawings of relevant scenery and buildings for his monumental *Pictorial Field-Book of the Revolution.* With the benefit of Lossing's opus and in the same spirit, Boatner produced a book he described as part travel guide, part regional history, and part geographical dictionary. In writing *Landmarks*, Boatner also relied on the in-depth entries about people, places and events in his own *Encyclopedia of the American Revolution*, first published in 1966. Revised, expanded, and updated, the one-volume encyclopedia now constitutes the two companion volumes to this set.

Determined not to omit an important site "merely because it had been destroyed by real estate development or ignored by earlier writers of historic guides," Boatner compiled his long list of landmarks from general histories of the Revolution and then plotted them onto modern maps. Relying on primary sources, the expertise of regional historians, and visits to the sites, Boatner pinpointed skirmish and battle sites, as well as taverns, bridges, graves, historic houses, churches, and monuments. He included well-established tourist attractions like the Saratoga and Yorktown battlefields, architectural treasures such as the Chew Mansion and Mount Vernon, and historic districts in Annapolis, Philadelphia, and Schenectady. However, he also examined an extraordinary variety of less traveled routes, including the trail of Benedict Arnold's expedition through Maine and Canada and the network of settlements in Tennessee where Patriots gathered to march into the Carolinas in support of the local militia, leading to the pivotal victory at Kings Mountain. He even tracked down sites that had ended up on private property or were unknown to local residents.

Urging readers not to confuse history with patriotism, Boatner examined Florida's role in the Revolution, neglected by most guidebooks because British and Loyalist leaders dominated events there. If we "shake our nationalistic vanities and concede that we should be interested in what happened in both camps during the Revolution," Boatner wrote, "there is more to be found . . . than you might have suspected." Similarly, Boatner includes the Simsbury Copper Mines in Connecticut, where the Americans kept prisoners of war and Loyalists in dismal underground cells, in retaliation for the horrific conditions on British prison ships in Brooklyn's Wallabout Bay, and in New York City's jails. With the same vigor he applied to tracking down the sites of American victories, Boatner located the scenes of disastrous American defeats, including the Brier Creek battlefield in Georgia, where "the amateur American generals" were overwhelmed by "the British professionals" and their classic maneuvers.

Published in 1971, *Landmarks* evaluated local efforts to preserve and mark historic sites and served as Boatner's pulpit for exhorting federal, state, and local authorities to prepare for the bicentennial of the Declaration of Independence by improving their management of tourism information and destinations. At the same time, Boatner condemned an "epidemic of skyscraper building" in one part of the country and "a land development orgy of record proportions" in another. A soldier-scholar and ardent preservationist, Boatner was acutely concerned about overdevelopment and the disappearance of landmarks. A native of Virginia, Mark M. Boatner III is a descendant of prominent statesmen and soldiers of the Revolution. After graduating from West Point in 1943, he served as a combat infantryman in Italy and Korea before earning a masters degree in international affairs from George Washington University. His other books, *Military Customs and Traditions*, *Civil War Dictionary*, and *Encyclopedia of the American Revolution*, were all published before he retired from the Army in 1969.

A groundbreaking project, *Landmarks* catalogued and described places connected to the Revolution across an area that now encompasses twenty-seven states, Washington, D.C., and Canada. Picking up where Boatner left off, this expanded and updated version of *Landmarks* includes the work of various scholars and researchers enlisted by Stephen Wasserstein, Scribner senior editor, and by historian Harold Selesky, editor of the two companion volumes, the *Encyclopedia of the American Revolution.*

An extensive chapter on the Caribbean by Andrew O'Shaughnessy, Saunders Director of the Robert H. Smith International Center for Jefferson Studies near Monticello, is a new and unusual feature of the present volume which identifies the wealth of surviving landmarks in this important theater of the American Revolution.

Writer and journalist Donald Lowe put his skills to work in the service of the entire volume, painstakingly bringing the chapters up to date by contacting local historical societies, museums, tourism directors, and town clerks to check on the current condition of each landmark and any change of ownership. Lowe also provides new contact information for government agencies and historic sites, including telephone numbers, websites, street addresses, and local directions.

Honoring Boatner's careful eye for the details of landscape, Lowe checked, for example, if a particular tree was still standing on a given site. In the case of Battlefield State Park in Princeton, New Jersey, Lowe discovered that after nearly 300 years, the solitary white oak, known since the Revolution as the Mercer Oak, had collapsed in 2001. It was to this tree, according to legend, that the mortally wounded General Hugh Mercer was brought after the battle. In Bucks County, Pennsylvania, tourists might simply pass by the Greene Inn on Durham Road, home of Edna's Antiques, with its yard full of old radiators and bathtubs, not knowing, as Lowe informs us, that this was General Nathanael Greene's headquarters before the attack on Trenton in December 1776.

This new edition of *Landmarks* provides a great deal of additional information about the role of African Americans and Native Americans in the Revolution as well as resources for exploring these topics further. Lowe points out, for example, that the members of the Old First Church near the Bennington Battle Monument in Vermont, were early opponents of slavery and supporters of racial equality. In 1780 they became the first white congregation in American history to have an African American minister, Revolutionary War veteran Reverend Lemuel Haynes.

Most of the numerous gaps in coverage of Native Americans and African Americans were filled by historian Michael Bellesilles, author of *Revolutionary Outlaws: Ethan Allen and the Struggle for Independence on the Early American Frontier*, who was enlisted to edit and update material throughout *Landmarks*, particularly the chapter on Vermont. One of his most striking additions is the Black Heritage Trail in Boston, which includes the home of George Middleton, the leader of an all-black militia company that received a flag from John Hancock for its outstanding service in the Revolutionary War. Also on this trail is the African Meeting House, the oldest surviving black church in America.

Along with a heightened awareness of American diversity among historians (and greater diversity in the ranks of the profession), much has changed in the field of historic preservation since *Landmarks* was first written in 1971, when the preservation movement had not fully picked up steam. The destruction of Pennsylvania Station in 1963 was a catalyst for New York City's formation of a Landmarks Preservation Commission, which became a model for others around the country. First Lady Ladybird Johnson's report, "With Heritage So Rich," warned that historic sites were vanishing under the onslaught of overdevelopment and led to the passage of the National Historic Preservation Act in 1966. Without adequate funding, the law's impact was not immediate, however, and the criteria for inclusion in a National Register of Historic Places were developed gradually.

The movement gained momentum in the late sixties and early seventies. The National Environmental Protection Act of 1969 gave teeth to the 1966 law by creating fines for violators. An executive order signed by President Richard Nixon, followed in 1974 by the Moss–Bennett Act and in 1979 by the Archeological Resources Protection Act, unleashed an explosion of research and preservation activity. State Historic Preservation Offices were established and provided with matching funds by the federal government. Through grants to researchers, the National Park Service expanded its focus and mission to take stock of battlefields and their condition, as did the Department of Defense. Private sector archeologists also joined the effort to inventory the nation's military heritage sites.

At the same time, however, relic collectors, armed since the 1950s with increasingly sophisticated metal detectors, were combing through Revolutionary and Civil War battle sites, taking home bullets, swords, and buttons. More recently, these artifacts have entered the Internet marketplace through E-Bay. Only in the last few years have archeologists, who once shunned such collectors, begun enlisting them as partners, interviewing them about the precise locations where artifacts were discovered and using that knowledge to map entire battlefields.

In the late 1990s, the American Battlefields Protection Program, run by the National Park Service, launched a broad effort to make a national inventory of Civil War sites and a report on their condition. By 2001—the 225th anniversary of the Declaration of Independence—Congress had mandated a similar effort for Revolutionary War sites through the ABPP, and grants were awarded to finance site visits. Without systematic physical inspection, and a central database, the government did not know if a particular site had become a state park or had been buried under a shopping mall. Along with the National Register of Historic Places, Boatner's *Landmarks* guided the panel of park service officials and scholars that compiled the list of Revolutionary War sites.

In the twenty-first century, the discovery and analysis of Revolutionary War battlefields continue to reshape our perception of the nation's history. Public-private partnerships to acquire and protect sites, along with advances in archeological techniques, play a major role. The latter include global positioning systems, which use satellites to locate artifacts and map battle sites; computerized, ground-penetrating radar, which finds graves and other disturbances in the soil; and the electronic surveyor's transit, a laser-equipped device that makes short work of measuring a piece of ground.

At the Camden battlefield in South Carolina, for example, archeologists have combined these tools with old-fashioned shovel work, eyewitness accounts, and information from relic collectors to expand the borders of the 300-acre site and to revise the accepted location of the front lines 700 yards to the south. Such work may eventually earn National Park status for the Camden battlefield, and South Carolina is turning to archeologists in other initiatives, including the creation of a Francis Marion Trail, marking the campsites and battlefields associated with the indomitable "Swamp Fox." New York has also been active in developing a Revolutionary War trail throughout the state, devoting significant resources to archeological work, for example, at Fort Montgomery on the Hudson River.

Beyond the condensed narrative developed for schoolchildren and for textbooks to encapsulate the complex eight-year war—Lexington, Concord, Bunker Hill, Trenton, Saratoga, Yorktown—*Landmarks* offers a fuller picture of the American struggle for independence, fleshing out, geographically, the bare bones of the traditional story. Shunning any regional bias, Boatner arranged the chapters in alphabetical order, by state, following the same encyclopedic impulse that had led to his classic one-volume *Encyclopedia of the American Revolution* (1966), the basis for the two companion volumes in this set. The result is a guidebook proportioned by the quantity of historical markers on the ground in a given state, more accurately reflecting where the military action was concentrated during the course of the war.

New York State, for example, has the longest chapter, because almost one third of the fighting took place within its borders. Before the Revolutionary War, until the transfer to Massachusetts prompted by the Boston Tea Party, the headquarters of the British military had been in New York City, and after its recapture in the summer and fall of 1776, the city resumed that role for seven years—the rest of the war. Moreover, control of the Hudson River–Lake Champlain corridor, traversing the state from Canada to New York Harbor, was the focus of Britain's grand strategy for dividing the colonies and ending the rebellion.

The revision of the section on New York City's landmarks draws on three years of research for *The Battle for New York: The City at the Heart of the American Revolution*, during which I spent several weeks exploring the five boroughs by subway, ferry, and on foot, locating the events of the Revolution and the markers commemorating them amid the modern cityscape. Among the local experts I relied on were Dr. Laurence Simpson of the Sons of the American Revolution in the State of New York; Nathan Hale scholar Richard Mooney; William Parry, Herb Yellin, and John Gallagher at the Old Stone House Historic Interpretive Center; Jonathan Kuhn of the Parks Department; and Savona Bailey McClain of the West Harlem Art Fund.

Like New York, New Jersey also receives more attention than usual in *Landmarks*. While Americans are generally familiar with Washington's victories at Trenton and Princeton, the entire state, located between the rebel capital at Philadelphia and the main British base in

New York, was the scene of extensive military operations and clashes. Washington encamped in the Watchung Mountains at Morristown in order to keep an eye on the roads to Philadelphia and intercept the British.

Rhode Island, the smallest state, nonetheless receives a long chapter because of its active resistance to the crown in the run-up to the war and because it was occupied by the British, and headquarters to the French fleet, producing a rich fabric of Revolutionary sites and markers that have been well preserved. The state has more colonial-era houses than all of the other former colonies combined. In Rhode Island, the first regiment of African American troops to fight for the United States distinguished itself in battle, and this chapter, like the others in this revised edition of *Landmarks*, provides additional information about the service of these troops, the prevalence of slavery in colonial life, including in the North, and resources for learning more about black history in the state.

Unlike Rhode Island, South Carolina was the scene of intense fighting. Some 180 battles and skirmishes were triggered by British proclamations that forced Patriots and Loyalists actively to choose sides, producing an atmosphere of civil war. The British attempted to create a second hub for their operations by capturing Charleston, South Carolina in 1780. The ensuing war in the southern states resulted in the British defeat at Yorktown in 1781, commonly remembered as the end of the Revolutionary War.

However, the conflict lasted for two more years. On his way back to continue the American vigil around New York City, Washington warned Congress that complacency after the allied victory was the country's worst enemy. Indeed, ever since their defeat at Saratoga and the advent of the Franco-American alliance, the British had begun shifting their focus to include the Caribbean, and in a major naval battle there in 1782, Admiral de Grasse, the victor of Yorktown, was captured and his fleet badly damaged.

Andrew O'Shaughnessy's chapter on the Caribbean is a reminder that the American Revolution was a global war, a clash of superpowers (the British and the French) in a contest not only for North America but for the profitable sugar-producing islands of the Caribbean as well. The picturesque forts of St. Barts and San Juan also attest to the Dutch and Spanish presence in the area over the centuries and their supporting roles in the effort to undermine Britain's grip on the hemisphere. Additionally, American privateers prowled the Caribbean, preying on British shipping.

However, the ruined fortresses overlooking aquamarine harbors and the sun-drenched sugar plantations with their sprawling great houses and cramped slave huts reveal the moral shadows and contradictions of America's "Glorious Cause." While Americans protested their political enslavement to Parliament and a tyrannical King George III, they made the enslavement of Africans and African Americans the centerpiece of their economy, not only in the South, but in the northern states as well. The West Indies were an enormous slave market, because of the demand for labor to harvest sugarcane. During the colonial period, New York and New England earned bills of exchange, redeemable in England, by exporting food to the islands, freeing up land to cultivate the cash crop exclusively. Sugar and molasses were turned into rum in New England and exported to buy more slaves.

In adopting the Constitution in 1787, the United States would include protections for slaveholders' rights, a devil's bargain in the eyes of abolitionists, but a necessary compromise according to Federalists bent on keeping sectional differences from shattering the country. To its credit, Congress banned slavery in the Northwest territories, the modern Midwest, areas which George Rogers Clark conquered during the Revolution, clearing the way for American settlement of the region. *Landmarks* includes Michigan, Illinois, Indiana, and Ohio, illuminating another important theaters of the war and its impact on the future of the United States.

The campaigns in the Old Northwest also introduce the role of Native Americans in the Revolution, as they formed alliances with both sides and were drawn into the frontier fighting. This revision of *Landmarks* includes more detail about a massacre of Moravian

Indians by American forces in 1782 in eastern Ohio, "one of the most horrific scenes in American military history," and the memorial to its victims. Also included throughout this edition is more information about tourism sites that preserve Native American culture and history through authentically reconstructed buildings, costumed interpretation, and craft demonstrations. The updated chapter on Connecticut notes that the Pequot tribe, decimated by white settlers in the seventeenth century, has made a comeback, ironically through its wildly successful gambling casinos, the bane of preservationists in various states trying to save historic landmarks.

While economic development threatens historic sites, recent scholarship has eroded the saintly image of America's Founding Fathers. Some owned slaves and are known to have sired children out of wedlock, sometimes with those very slaves. Indeed the colonial economy, both North and South, was heavily dependent on African American slave labor and the profits of the slave trade. The launch of the greatest democratic experiment in human history in 1776 was also accompanied by the officially sanctioned slaughter or removal of Native American tribes.

On the other hand, while the American Revolution excluded Native Americans, blacks, poor whites, and women from its credo of human equality, it created a society in which meaningful protest and reform were possible. The United States remains a work-in-progress, still struggling with deep divisions of race and class. As we balance in our minds these two versions of America's founding—the celebratory and the critical—the more we learn about the Revolutionary generation as real people rather than icons, and the more compelling it becomes to preserve and to visit the homes, statehouses, and battlefields where they lived, worked, and died for the "Glorious Cause" of self-government.

Barnet Schecter, New York City

List of Articles

ALABAMA

What is now the state of Alabama was an area where many national interests competed from the earliest period of European exploration and colonization. The region was home to the Alabama, Cherokee, Chickasaw, Choctaw, Koasati, and Muskogee, or Creek, nations. In the sixteenth century both the Spanish and English claimed the Gulf Coast area, though the French established the first European settlements in the vicinity of modern Mobile. The French pushed north along the wide rivers and established a number of outposts among the Indians. Meanwhile, the grant of Georgia to Oglethorpe in 1732 included part of what is now northern Alabama, bringing into the region additional competitors, many of whom mixed freely with the Indians, producing a number of famous leaders (see MCGILLIVRAY PLANTATION SITE).

Under the Treaty of 1763 ending the Seven Years' War, France gave Britain rights to all its territory east of the Mississippi except the Isle of Orleans, and much of today's state of Alabama was then in British West Florida. During the Revolution this region was a refuge for Loyalists, a base for Indian raids against the American frontier, and the objective of Spanish expeditions from Louisiana. The capture of Mobile by the Spanish in 1780 was part of a program to establish a claim on the vast territory of British Florida. The Treaty of 1783 put the northern boundary of Spanish West Florida at the thirty-first parallel, but until 1798 Spain persisted in claiming a boundary on the parallel running through today's Vicksburg (at the mouth of the Yazoo River). To protect its interests Spain also undertook intrigues with American settlers in the Ohio Valley to establish independent governments that would be a buffer between Spanish colonies and the newly created United States. The so-called Spanish Conspiracy, 1786 to 1809, involved many men who had been officers on the Patriot side during the Revolution. During the War of 1812, Alabama was the site of U.S. actions against the Spanish in Mobile as well as against the Creek Indians.

Tourist information is issued by the Alabama Bureau of Tourism and Travel, 401 Adams Avenue Suite 126, P.O. Box 4927, Montgomery, Ala. 36103. Website: www.touralabama.org; phone: (334) 242-4169. The Alabama Department of Archives and History is at 624 Washington Avenue, Montgomery, Ala. 36130. Phone: (334) 242-4435.

Fort Tombigbee Site, Tombigbee River, Sumter County. The French built a fort here in 1735 as an advance base during the Chickasaw War. It developed into a supply depot, permanent trading post, and outpost against British encroachment. The British took over in 1763 and renamed the place Fort York, but abandoned it five years later. Spain claimed that its northern boundary of West Florida, fixed at the thirty-first parallel by the Treaty of 1783, should be recognized as running much farther north (through modern Vicksburg), and pushed beyond this line to build Fort Confederation on the site of Forts Tombigbee and York. Occupying this place during the brief period 1794 to 1797, the Spanish finally accepted United States title to the Mississippi Territory and withdrew. Fort Confederation became an American post but lost its importance and fell into ruins after being the site of final negotiations with the Indians (1802–1803) for surrender of their lands in the region. The marked location of the forts is just off U.S. 11 near Epes.

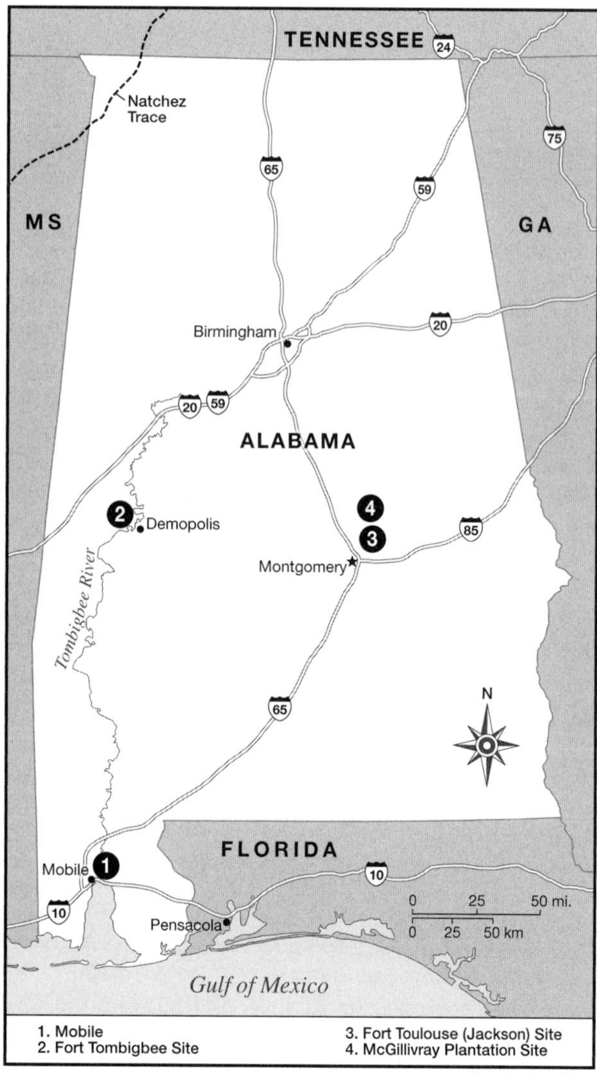

MAP BY XNR PRODUCTIONS. THE GALE GROUP.

Fort Toulouse (Jackson) State Park, near Wetumpka in Montgomery County. The French built this fort in 1717 and surrendered it in 1763 to the British, who held it until the end of the Revolution. At the head of the Alabama River and on the edge of Creek country near the site of Montgomery, it was of little significance as a British outpost but important during the War of 1812. General Andrew Jackson built a strong fort on its site in 1814, making his peace treaty here with the Creeks in August of that year. A Registered National Historic Landmark relating primarily to the French period, the a 6-acre tract in the park has remains of the fort. The Alabama Historic Commission owns the entire 165-acre park. Adjoining private property has a large Indian mound and the site of a prehistoric village. Another adjoining tract includes the Isaac Ross Cemetery, which contains many graves dating from the War of 1812 (about two hundred of these were relocated to the national cemetery in Mobile in 1897); there may be some French graves. Proper archaeological exploration began in 1971 and continued for fifteen years. That exploration resumed in 2001, and more is planned as remains of the fort and adjoining farmsteads are being discovered. Phone: (334) 567-3002. The Alabama Historical Commission can be contacted by phone at (334) 242-3184.

McGillivray Plantation Site, near Wetumpka, Elmore County, also known as Little Tallassee Plantation. The Creek leader Alexander McGillivray is important enough to merit a long sketch in the *Dictionary of American Biography,* but this colorful and influential man is little remembered. He was born about 1759, son of a prominent trader and Georgia politician by a French-Creek wife. After spending his first fourteen years at his father's trading post on the Tallapoosa River, he then lived in Charleston and Savannah. Father and son became Loyalists, losing their property by confiscation, after which the father returned to his native Scotland and Alexander became a renowned chief among his mother's people. During the Revolution, Alexander was a British agent, sending out war parties to attack the frontier settlements. He also formed ties with Panton and Leslie and Company (see PENSACOLA under Florida), and after the Revolution was a power in the complex politics of the Old Southwest. When he died at Mobile of stomach trouble and pneumonia he was in his early thirties. Better educated by far than most Americans of the region, he left three plantations and about sixty slaves.

During the period of his greatest influence he lived on a plantation whose site is marked on County Road 47 about 4 miles north of Wetumpka. Here, on privately owned farmland, where no traces of the plantation buildings remain, is a commemorative plaque on a boulder. Interestingly, an internet site on lost treasures lists the McGillivray Plantation as a possible cache for gold coins and other treasure loot.

Mobile, Mobile Bay. Founded in 1702 by the French, originally at Twenty-seven Mile Bluff about 20 miles up the Mobile River from the present site, Mobile was the seat of French government in the province of Louisiana until 1720 (when it was transferred to Biloxi). Meanwhile, the French had also established a short-lived settlement on Dauphin Island, the sand spit at the mouth of Mobile Bay, and had built Fort Condé (1711) in Mobile. The British acquired Mobile in 1763, established a garrison, and renamed the French work Fort Charlotte. During the Revolution, Mobile and Pensacola were subsidiary to Jamaica as bases for military operations, both of the unhealthful outposts being in the backwaters of the war.

Governor Bernardo de Galvez took Mobile with a small force on 14 March 1780, capturing the British garrison of about three hundred men. Spain's possession was confirmed in the Treaty of 1783, and the United States seized the city in 1813.

Across the bay from Mobile on the eastern approach to the city and in the place now called Spanish Fort is Old Spanish Fort, built by Galvez after taking Mobile in 1780. The site of the French, British, and Spanish works known successively as Forts Condé, Charlotte, and Carlotta is occupied by the Fort Condé-Charlotte House (open) on Theatre Street between St. Emanuel and Royal Streets. Here a jail and courthouse were built in the early 1700s. The colonial structure was blown up in 1819 and the rubble was used to fill the marsh nearby. Picturesque little Bienville Square, in the business district, preserves the name of Mobile's founder and has a French and a British cannon from the forts mentioned above.

At the entrance to Mobile Bay are Fort Morgan State Park and the state monument on Dauphin Island. These places continued to figure prominently in the defenses of Mobile after the colonial and Revolutionary eras, but some of the early landmarks survive. In the 410-acre Fort Morgan State Park are remains of the Spanish fort built in 1559 by colonists under Tristan de Luna. Phone: (251) 540-5257. Fort Gaines was begun in 1821, figured prominently in the Civil War Battle of Mobile Bay, and is being restored. But Dauphin Island, where it is located, was a landmark in the history of French settlement of the Gulf Coast; here the French set up their first colony in the Louisiana Territory. The island is reached by a bridge and is a popular recreational area. Phone: (334) 861-5524.

The Fort Conde Historic Museum, which shares space with the Mobile Welcome Center, is the partial reconstruction of the 1724 French fort which the British captured during the Seven Years' War. Located in downtown Mobile, the fort offers period-costumed guides and demonstrations of cannon and musket firing. The fort is operated by the Museum of Mobile; admission is free. It is located at 150 South Royal Street, Mobile, Ala. 36652. Phone: (251) 208-7569; website: http://www.museumofmobile.com. (Mobile Historic Development Commission, Box 1827, Mobile, Ala. 36601. Phone: (251) 208-7965.

CANADA

A handful of British heroes frustrated all American efforts during the Revolution to bring Canada into the Patriot camp. Royal Governor Guy Carleton (1724–1808), who took over his duties in 1767 after having distinguished himself as an army officer, was primarily responsible for the enlightened political policies that kept the French Canadians loyal, although he badly erred in assuming that these people would extend this loyalty to active military support. Carleton's brilliant defense of Canada in 1775 to 1776 against the mismanaged American invasion was achieved with a handful of regulars, including naval personnel, and the recently raised Royal Highland Emigrants under Allan Maclean.

Patriot forces endured incredible hardships in Canada before being driven back in confusion, a disease-ridden skeleton of an army. Two fine American generals were left behind in Canadian graves, Richard Montgomery at Quebec and John Thomas at Fort Chambly. Among the many Patriots in Canadian jails were Ethan Allen (captured at Montreal) and Dan Morgan (taken prisoner at Quebec).

Canada subsequently was the base for major counteroffensives along the Lake Champlain waterway and for the sustained frontier warfare waged by the Loyalists and Indians throughout the Revolution. The "fourteenth colony" also became the new home not only for Iroquois refugees from western New York but also for most of the estimated 100,000 Loyalists who left the Thirteen Colonies, many of them to escape persecution by the Patriots. A Canadian historian has written that these fugitives were "the makers of Canada," a claim that is certainly extreme and would lead one to expect that in modern Canada there would be many interesting landmarks associated with these Loyalists. But this is not the case. Some will be found in the Great Lakes region and many in the Maritime Provinces. With the exception of places associated with Loyalists and Indians displaced by the American Revolution, most Revolutionary War sites in Canada are in the province of Quebec.

The United Empire Loyalists' (UEL) Association of Canada appears to be oriented toward genealogy and social activity. The UEL has branches throughout Canada, with a museum at Adolphustown, Ontario. Its headquarters is located in the historic George Brown House in Toronto, 50 Baldwin Street, Suite 202, Toronto, Canada M5T 1L4. Phone: (416) 591-1783.

Tourism is a major industry in Canada, and an abundance of well-organized and beautifully presented information for visitors is available on the Canadian Tourism Commission website at www.travelcanada.ca. This commission is located at 55 Metcalfe Street, Suite 600, Ottawa, Ontario K1P 6L5, and it provides information on every aspect of travel in Canada, including historic sites. The Canadian government administers the historic sites and designations under the Parks Canada Agency. Its office is located in Gatineau, Quebec at 25 Eddy Street. A good website for obtaining further information is at http://www.pc.gc.ca.

Similar to the state of Maine, much of Canada's Revolutionary War history deals with Arnold's March to Quebec. Any of the books cited in the entry on Maine will serve this entry well as extra reference material. The Arnold Expedition Society is still functioning, although less so than when it did valuable research on the Arnold Trail in preparation for the American bicentennial. The Society is difficult to contact, and information on the Canadian portion of the Arnold Trail is not easily accessed via the internet. Consequently, the aforementioned books may be the best source for garnering information on this captivating, albeit ill-fated, trek north led by Benedict Arnold.

The Abenaki Museum in Odanak, Quebec, is devoted to the history and culture of the Abenaki people, who once lived in northern New England. Driven further north by the British in the early eighteenth century, the Abenaki had settled mostly around what is now the United States / Canada border and sided with the French in the various colonial wars aimed at halting British expansion. With the Revolution, though, the Abenaki mostly sided with the British, leading to their expulsion from the United States. The museum includes the reconstruction of an eighteenth-century frontier fort. The museum is located west of the St. Francois bridge at Pierreville on Highway 226, and is open every day. Phone: (514) 568-2600.

Annapolis Royal (PORT ROYAL), Nova Scotia. *See* FORT ANNE and PORT ROYAL HABITATION National Historic Parks.

Arnold Trail. The section on the Arnold Trail in the entry on Maine, and its numerous cross-references, traces the route of the Arnold Expedition of 1775 to the Canadian border. The final leg of the trip is covered below under Chaudière River.

Historic sites in the Lake Megantic area have not yet been located with certainty, but the Arnold Expedition Historical Society (AEHS) has done a considerable amount of field work in conjunction with a few Canadian members of the Society. Major landmarks such as Lake Megantic and Spider Lake (Lac aux Araignées) preserve their original names and can be easily found on modern maps. The "Beautiful Meadow," as it was called by Arnold's men when they made their first camp in Canada after crossing "Height of Land," can be viewed from Route 34 about a mile north of Woburn and to the east. Large-scale modern maps show a house in this area that may have been used by Arnold's troops and where the AEHS hopes to conduct a thorough archaeological search.

A view of the Height of Land from the Canadian side is of particular interest for reasons given in the Maine entry. For the closest view from a major road, follow Route 34 north from Woburn a few miles to the point where this road shows on highway maps as a sharp right-angle turn from east-west to north-south. From this point and in the direction east-southeast (i.e., slightly south of east), at a range of about a mile, is the low saddle in the Height of Land through which the Arnold expedition probably passed.

Brantford, Ontario. One of the most intriguing men of the Revolutionary period was Joseph Brant (Thayendanegea), the scholarly Mohawk warrior. An influential leader among the Iroquois, he brought the Mohawk, Cayuga, Seneca, and Onondaga to the British side, leading Indian contingents in some of the fiercest battles of the Revolution. With the end of the war, as the victorious United States seized more and more Iroquois land, Brant led many of his people into British Canada, settling primarily along the Grand River in modern Ontario. In the town of Brantford, at the ford of the Grand River, Brant built the Chapel of the Mohawks, the oldest existing Protestant Church in Ontario and the only "Royal Indian Chapel" in the world. Brant's tomb is next to the church. The church is on Mohawk Street, southwest of the town center. Further up the street is the Woodland Indian Cultural Centre, dedicated to the history and culture of the Iroquois Indians and home to the Indian Hall of Fame. The Centre is open every day; phone: (519) 729-2650. Thirty miles east on Lake Ontario (via Highway 403), in the town of Burlington, is the Joseph Brant Museum, a reconstruction of the house where he spent his last seven years translating the Bible into Mohawk. The house contains artifacts from Brant's life as well as displays on Iroquois culture. The Museum is located at 1240 North Shore Boulevard East, south of Highway 403, and is open Tuesday to Friday, 10 A.M. to 4:30 P.M., and Sunday, 1 P.M. to 4:30 P.M. Phone: (416) 634-3556.

The Cedars (Les Cèdres), about 25 miles above Montreal on the north bank of the St. Lawrence. An American outpost at this place surrendered in mid-May 1776 without putting up any real resistance to a force of about 650 British and Indians. A relief column walked into an ambush about 4 miles from the Cedars a day or so later, and one hundred men surrendered after holding out for less than an hour. When General Benedict Arnold approached with a larger relief force, he was informed that the captured American commander at the Cedars, Major Isaac Butterfield, had agreed to give up the post in return for a guarantee that the prisoners would be protected from the Indians. After some negotiating, Arnold agreed to take the captured Americans back to Montreal for later exchange, and there was no further fighting.

Little research has been done into this interesting affair, and not even the dates are known for sure. Les Cèdres remains a little dot on today's highway maps. It is on Route 2 between Pointe des Cascades and Coteau du Lac a few miles southeast of Autoroute 20. Coteau du Lac, 40 miles southwest of Montreal, was a major portage site for the Native Americans that bypassed the Coteau Rapids between Lake St. François and Lake St. Louis, the narrowest section of the St. Lawrence River. In 1779 the King's Royal Regiment of New York, a Loyalist unit commanded by William Twiss, began work on the first lock canal in North America. Completed in 1781, the canal had three locks over a space of 100 meters, facilitating transport to the

Great Lakes. This rock-hewn canal is beautifully sited and worth a detour. A blockhouse was built on the site in 1813 in anticipation of invasion from the United States and is open to the public 14 May to 9 October.

Chaudière River. Route 24 follows the Chaudière from Lake Megantic to Jersey Mills, where the Rivière du Loup (now Rivière Linière) joins the St. Lawrence. The drive provides a good view of the river along which the Americans struggled in their few surviving bateaux. In forming an opinion of what the river was like when Arnold's famished and exhausted troops followed this route in November 1775, during a winter of exceptional cold and immediately after a hurricane of record-breaking proportions, the visitor should bear in mind that the present water level may be far different from what the American expedition experienced. The falls that caused such difficulties are around the mouth of Stafford Creek, and they stretch for almost a mile from a point about 2.5 miles above the center of the village of Le Grand Sault.

The village of Sartigan mentioned in contemporary journals of the expedition, the first little settlement reached in Canada, was at the mouth of the Rivière Famine. The latter shows on modern highway maps a short distance down the Chaudière from St.-Georges. In 1775 the place had very few French settlers, some traders, and an Indian village. But this was the edge of the wilderness from which the Americans had finally emerged, and Arnold was waiting at Sartigan with provisions assembled by his advance detachment. Three men died after an orgy of stuffing themselves with cooked food. It was here that the mysterious Nantais joined Arnold's force, and about fifty local Indians also were enlisted with their canoes for the remainder of the journey.

Arnold's force remained strung out for several more days as it struggled on to the place that is still called Ste.-Marie. Adjoining the Chapelle de Ste.-Anne, 0.75 mile northwest of the center of town and near the motel called La Seigneurie de Ste.-Marie, is a handsome house dating from 1809. Still in the family of the original seigneur, it is on the site of the one visited by Arnold's troops on their march to Quebec and looted by them later in the winter. Other surviving structures in the area were built after the Americans passed through, but the site of the existing village remains an important landmark of the Arnold Expedition. Here they rallied before leaving the Chaudière and striking out overland through the snow, mud, and knee-deep water toward Point Levis.

Deschambault, St. Lawrence River. The puny American army that besieged Quebec was forced to withdraw early in May 1776 when British reinforcements were able to resume navigation. Without waiting for all these fresh troops to arrive, General Guy Carleton made a sortie from his fortress

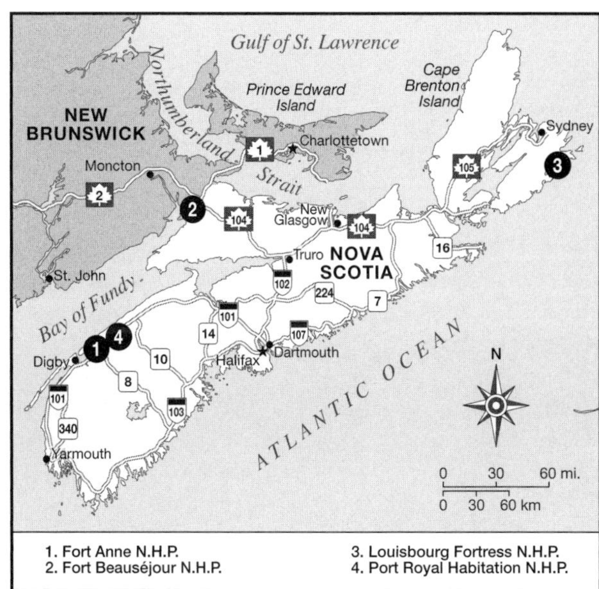

MAP BY XNR PRODUCTIONS. THE GALE GROUP.

on 6 May. The Americans under General John Thomas mustered only 250 effectives, and these retreated in disorder to Deschambault, 40 miles upstream from Quebec, before Thomas could rally them for the march back to Sorel. The name of the old French settlement is preserved in the picturesque modern village of Deschambault. The village dates back to 1674 and has several noteworthy historic sites (unrelated to the Revolutionary War) in addition to an extremely scenic countryside.

Fort Anne National Historic Park, Annapolis Royal, Nova Scotia. Open 15 May through October. Phone: (902) 532-2397. Scots settlers founded Nova Scotia near this site, then were replaced in the 1630s by the French, who made Port Royal the capital of Acadia and constructed a fort on the current location. The British captured the fort in 1710 during the War of the Spanish Succession, renamed it Annapolis Royal, and restored the colony's name of Nova Scotia. British troops occupied the fort until 1854. The deportation of the Acadians in 1755 was orchestrated from the fort, which became Fort Anne in the early nineteenth century. Operations against American privateers were conducted from the fort during the Revolution.The earthen ramparts of the seventeenth-century fort, to which additions were made by the British after taking the place in 1710, are part of the site restored by the Canadian government. A large building dating from 1797, originally the officers' quarters, has been renovated, preserving the floor plan but using modern materials to make the structure as nearly fireproof as possible. In addition to the office of the park superintendent it includes a fine historical library and museum exhibits pertaining to the stormy past of this region.

Fort Chambly. *Built in the early 1700s on the banks of the Richelieu River in Quebec, Fort Chambly protected New France from attacks by the British. The fort was surrendered to the British in 1760, and briefly came under the control of American forces at the start of the Revolutionary War.* © EARL & NAZIMA KOWALL/CORBIS.

Fort Beauséjour is located at the head of the Bay of Fundy near Aulac, New Brunswick. Built by the French in 1751 in response to the British Fort Lawrence in Nova Scotia, Fort Beauséjour fell to the British in 1755. Many Acadians passed through the fort in the next few years during their forced deportation. Renamed Fort Cumberland, the fort was attacked by an alliance of local English- and French-speaking settlers and a small force of New England patriots in 1776. The British defeated the rebels, taking many prisoners. Expanded during the War of 1812, the fort was abandoned in 1835 and declared a National Historic Site in 1926. It is open 9 A.M. to 5 P.M. from 1 June to 15 October.

Fort Chambly National Historic Park, Chambly Rapids, Richelieu River near the junction of Highways 112 and 223, province of Quebec. Phone: (450) 658-1585. Probably the first historic site to be preserved by the Canadian government, this is now an exceptionally attractive and interesting landmark. Alterations made during the long period of occupation by French and British forces have materially changed the original appearance, but vestiges remain of the stone fort built around 1710. The cemetery a short distance to the southwest has many old graves, including that of General John Thomas (see below). A display room and audiovisual program interpret the history of the site.

The first French fort here was built of logs in 1665 by four companies of regulars commanded by a young captain, Jacques de Chambly. He was later granted a seigneury, on which he established the settlement that grew into the modern town bearing his name. Fort Chambly had been created because it controlled a critical point on the strategic waterway through Lake Champlain from the St. Lawrence to the Hudson River. Long before the French and British arrived to fight over their colonial frontiers the Hurons and Iroquois had sent war parties past the rapids at Chambly. Samuel de Champlain opened a new era by accompanying a Huron expedition up the Richelieu River in 1609 to give the Iroquois their first taste of European warfare, but the effect was unfortunate: for the next half-century the Iroquois so thoroughly ravaged the Canadian frontier that Huron power was destroyed and

French settlements on the St. Lawrence almost wiped out. What is now the Richelieu was better known then as "la rivière des Iroquoisè." Establishment of Fort Chambly in 1665 brought two decades of relative security from Iroquois raids, but in 1687 the nineteen-man garrison of the fort and about eighty local settlers fought off 150 Mohawks.

After a disastrous fire in 1702 the wooden fort was rebuilt in stone. The surrounding settlement prospered for half a century, undisturbed by major military operations. In 1760 the fort surrendered to superior British forces, and all of Canada passed to British control shortly thereafter.

At the start of the American Revolution the British lacked the strength in Canada to man the extensive system of frontier fortifications. General Guy Carleton concentrated the bulk of his few regulars about 10 miles south of Chambly at Fort St.-Jean. The latter fell after a heroic defense, but only after the American invaders had slipped past in two bateaux and quickly captured Chambly. In one of the "most discreditable" surrenders in the history of the British army, the local commander not only failed to put up a proper fight but also, more importantly, failed to destroy his stores. Large stocks of food and much important matériel were captured, enabling the invaders to renew successfully their siege of St.-Jean.

Chambly was a base for the Americans during the next months of their ill-fated invasion of Canada. The American commander in chief, Major General John Thomas (1724–1776), died of smallpox at Chambly during the retreat (2 June); as mentioned above, he lies in the cemetery near the fort. In the ensuing British counteroffensive Chambly became an important logistical base, a function it served again during the War of 1812. But by this time the fort itself was deteriorating. By 1882 the federal government had started making efforts to preserve what survived of the crumbling walls. In 1921 the 2.5-acre national park was created. The high stone walls have been rebuilt on three sides; on the river side only the buttresses of the wall have been restored. Remarkably good judgment and taste have been exercised in creating a park of beauty and recreational value (a great spot for local fishermen) that is also of exceptional historic interest. Restoration is ongoing, and several buildings within the site are refurbished and restored.

Fort Prince of Wales, Churchill Harbor, Hudson Bay, Manitoba. Phone: (204) 675-8863. Open daily 1 P.M. to 5 P.M. and 6 P.M. to 9 P.M. from June through 10 November. A large masonry work measuring about 300 feet between the tips of the four corner bastions, this fort was built by the Hudson's Bay Company between 1733 and 1771. It surrendered on 8 August 1782 to three French warships without firing a shot; the thirty-nine-man garrison was not only unaware that there was a war on in their part of the world (where a French ship had not been seen in more than forty years) but also unprepared to defend a fortress designed for about four hundred men. The French spent two days destroying as much as they could, burning the wooden buildings, using demolitions to destroy the forty-two cannon and to blow in the walls of the stone barracks, but doing little damage to the outer walls, which measured up to 40 feet thick. The fort is being restored by the Canadian government as a National Historic Site, and visitors are greeted by a costumed staff. Interpretive programs and guided tours are available. Perhaps the most powerful fortification in North America and certainly its most northerly one, Fort Prince of Wales is across the harbor from the town of Churchill. It can be visited by boat in summer and by dogsled and over-snow vehicles in winter. The Canadian army base of Fort Churchill is about 6 miles down the coast.

Fortress of Louisbourg National Historic Park, Cape Breton Island, Nova Scotia. The history of the ill-fated French fortress of Louisbourg belongs to the colonial era exclusively. Construction was started in 1720 and completed in 1745 after many difficulties; from that time until its demolition by the British in 1760 the "impregnable fortress" was fighting a losing battle against the elements even more than against the Anglo-Saxons. Badly sited, built by unskilled workmen and corrupt contractors, and lacking adequate naval support, Louisbourg was captured by a New England expedition in 1745 and by a British expedition in 1758.

In 1928 the Canadian government designated the fortress area a National Historic Site. In 1961 it undertook a remarkable program of restoring the fortress to its 1745 condition. The undertaking began with the idea of providing work for unemployed coal miners of the region. But a tremendous amount of research by archivists and archaeologists had to be done before actual reconstruction could be started. The result is a valuable collection of some 350,000 items in the Louisbourg archives excavated from the site. About fifty buildings and massive defensive works are included in what is now (2005) the largest reconstructed eighteenth-century French fortified town in North America. The park was fully operational in 1972, by which time the Citadel and Magazin Général had been reconstructed.

Fortress of Louisbourg National Historic Park is therefore of exceptional interest in the field of historic preservation. Having trained a local workforce in such crafts as stonecutting, stone masonry, wrought iron work, carpentry, timber hewing, and slating, the project managers have since developed a costume department that produces authentic garments of the period. Many of the staff are adorned in these costumes as they perform living histories and lead tour groups.

About 23 square miles are included in the park. A reception center has an orientation program, and buses leave from this point on tours of the fortress area. From Sydney the park is 26 miles to the southeast on Route 22 through the town of Louisbourg; it is about a mile farther on the same highway to the reception center. Phone: (902) 733-2280; website: http://www.louisbourg.ca/fort/.

Halifax, Nova Scotia, was the headquarters of British naval operations during the American Revolution. Central to these defensive operations was the massive Halifax Citadel. There have been forts on this site overlooking the city and harbor since 1749, though the current fortifications, intended to defend Halifax from a possible United States invasion, were completed in 1856 after nearly thirty years of construction. The Army Museum, dedicated to Canadian military history, is located in the Cavalier Building. The grounds are open year round, 9 A.M. to 5 P.M.; the museum, guided tours, living-history displays, and orientation film are offered from 7 May to 3 October. Phone: (902) 426-5080.

L'Île-aux-Noix, Richelieu River, province of Quebec. A swampy island in the river between the outlet of Lake Champlain and St.-Jean was the logical place for defensive works in this strategic route between Canada and the English colonies to the south. But the site presented several problems. First, it was horribly unhealthful because of poor drainage and malarial swamps. Second, it could be easily bypassed or attacked by troops moving overland.

The island was uninhabited until a mustered-out French soldier leased it in 1753 for an annual rent of one bag of walnuts (*noix*), from which the 210-acre island derived its name. A year later the French decided to fortify the island, but they lacked the troops to garrison the major work they wanted to build there. When the British advanced for their final conquest of Canada, forcing the overextended French defenders to abandon Ticonderoga and Crown Point (see under NEW YORK), l'Île-aux-Noix was little more than a patrol base.

But 3,000 troops under General François de Bourlamaque arrived on 5 August 1759 to organize the defenses of the island. Less than four months later he had completed a star-shaped earthwork covering about half the island. The energetic and ingenious Frenchman handled the problem of defense against amphibious attack by putting log barriers across the channels on both sides of the island. These not only served as physical barriers but also raised the water level so that many potential landing sites were denied to an enemy approaching downstream from the outlet of Lake Champlain, 12 miles away.

The final work at l'Île-aux-Noix was directed by a man whose name would gain world fame in other fields, Colonel (later Admiral) Louis Antoine de Bougainville. (He made an important voyage of exploration around the world in 1767 to 1769. The largest island of the Solomon group, two straits, and the Bougainvillaea genus of vines are named for him.) But l'Île-aux-Noix proved to be untenable in the Seven Years' War. Soon after Bougainville took command in the spring of 1760 his troops helped frustrate two attempts by Major Robert Rogers and his Rangers to surprise Fort St.-Jean, about 12 miles down the river from the island.

The long-expected British attack started on 16 August, when seven thousand men and forty cannon commanded by Colonel William de Haviland invested Bougainville's isolated position. After four days and nights of an artillery duel Bougainville complied with orders to abandon the position to save his troops. The withdrawal to the west bank was successful, but Bougainville reached Montreal, only to surrender with the rest of the French troops in Canada on 8 September 1760.

The British destroyed the works on l'Île-aux-Noix. When American troops made it their base in 1775 as they advanced toward Montreal, the desolate island had a single farm. Nature had reclaimed what the British had left of the fortifications, and the island's trees presumably had been razed for construction of the latter. The horrors of the American occupation of the island, particularly during the Rebels' retreat from Canada in June 1776, are dramatically portrayed in histories and novels of the Revolution. Some eight thousand haggard troops were crowded on the island, which then was about 400 yards wide and a mile long. Smallpox, malaria, and dysentery killed up to twenty men a day.

In July 1776 a detachment of Hessians occupied the island, which became a fortified British base for subsequent counteroffensives into New York. Work on stone fortifications was started by four thousand troops in 1782 but soon was discontinued.

L'Île-aux-Noix became an important naval base in the War of 1812. During the years 1819 to 1828 Fort Lennox was built to protect the vital shipyard that had evolved. Fort Lennox National Historic Park preserves massive stone structures and other landmarks of the years following the American Revolution, but the site remains important and interesting for its associations with that war. A museum has exhibits of the colonial and Revolutionary periods. It is located at 1 61st Avenue, Saint-Paul-de-l'Île-aux-Noix, Quebec, Canada JOJ 1GO. Phone: (450) 291-5700.

Sir John Johnson's House in Williamstown, Ontario. Johnson was a prominent leader of the Loyalists during the Revolution and played a pivotal role in persuading many of them to settle in Ontario after the war ended. As commander of the King's Regiment of New York,

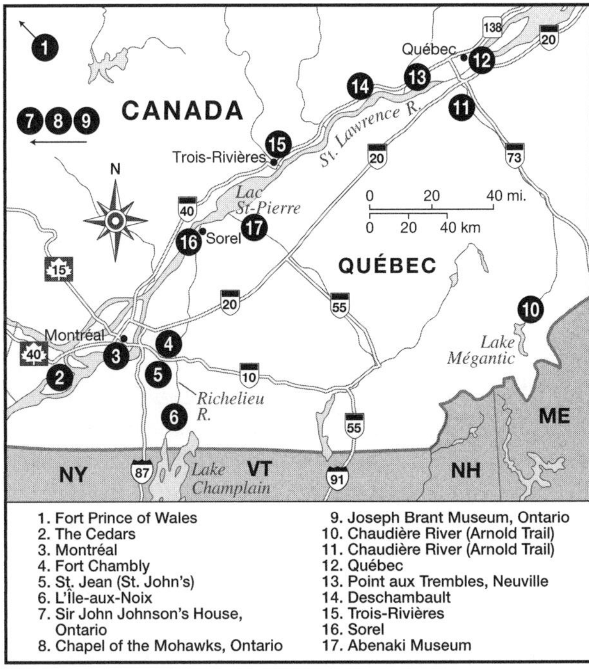

MAP BY XNR PRODUCTIONS. THE GALE GROUP.

Johnson led a number of military actions against the rebels, losing all his possessions in New York as a consequence. A general by the end of the war, Johnson worked to settle Loyalists in the St. Lawrence River valley and along the north shore of Lake Ontario. He founded the town of Williamstown, named for his father, beginning construction of his home there in 1784. The house is off County Road 17 and is open during the summer from 10:00 A.M. to 4:00 P.M. Phone: (613) 925-2896.

Montreal (Montréal), St. Lawrence River. At the head of ocean navigation nearly 1,000 miles up the St. Lawrence, Montreal is also near the head of the strategic waterway through Lake Champlain to the Hudson River. Montreal's growth was favored not only by its importance as a natural communications hub and its climate, which is less harsh than elsewhere in Quebec, but also by its unusual arrangement of two wide terraces. Formerly beaches of an inland sea, these terraces protect the city from flooding while giving easy access to the river. But the outstanding topographic feature is the 753-foot-high Mount Royal, whose crest is only 2 miles from the riverbank; it gives the city its name. An exceptionally large Indian village called Hochelaga was located on the northern slope of this mountain when Jacques Cartier discovered it in 1535. The village had disappeared by the time Samuel de Champlain arrived three-quarters of a century later to establish a trading post (1611). After careful prior planning, including selection of the first colonists on the basis of their good character as well as their qualifications as skilled workers, the first permanent settlement of Montreal was established in 1642. The first Iroquois attack came a year later, and others followed for many decades. But Montreal's population was about two thousand at the turn of the century, when the Indians finally made peace (1701). The natural advantages of the location as a gateway to the west then overshadowed the disadvantage of being easily accessible to Iroquois war parties.

Despite its many natural defensive features and its economic importance, Montreal was never a military stronghold. It was taken by the British in 1760. American troops met little resistance in occupying the city in mid-November 1775, and they stayed seven months.

Old Montreal is a section of the present city where the original settlement, Ville Marie, was located. This 95-acre historic area should be visited on foot. The most important landmark pertaining to the American Revolution is the little Château de Ramezay, 280–290 Notre Dame Street East. Phone: (514) 861-3708. Built in 1705 by Governor Claude de Ramezay, the one-and-one-half-story stone structure qualifies as a château only in the most basic definition of that French word: "habitation royale ou seigneuriale." But it is certainly an important American landmark, having been used by the top French, English, American, and Canadian authorities in the city. It was headquarters of the American occupying force (see above). The "Congressional Committee to Canada," composed of Benjamin Franklin, Samuel Chase, and Charles Carroll, used the building for several weeks in the spring of 1776 before returning to Philadelphia in early June to report on the "shocking mismanagement" of military operations. Now an attractive and important historical museum, the Château de Ramezay has scores of portraits spanning three centuries and exhibits pertaining to the colonial and Revolutionary era.

Old Fort in Ste. Hélène's Island Park is the site of early French military works. In the surviving facilities, dating from 1822, drill exhibitions are presented frequently by La Compagnie Franche de la Marine and the Fraser Highlanders. (The latter regiment figured prominently in battles of the Colonial Wars and the Revolution.) Canadian military history over an extensive period is represented in the collections of the Montreal Military and Maritime Museum in the arsenal.

Other historic landmarks of cultural importance if not of direct relevance to the subject of this guide are the Maison St. Gabriel (1698), Notre Dame de Bon Secours (1771), the Seminary of St. Sulpice (1710), the Hôtel Dieu (a hospital founded in 1644), the Grey Nuns' Mother House and Museum (1738), and Mount Royal Park.

Sites of several important skirmishes with the Iroquois are marked in and around Montreal. Longueuil, a name familiar to students of the period, is a maze of autoroute interchanges and a metro stop on today's maps. No mention is made in current popular guides of sites associated with the abortive American attack of 24 to 25 Sepember 1775 by Ethan Allen and John Brown. The latter did not manage to get across the river for the proposed double envelopment (that delight of amateur strategists), but Allen shuttled his 110 troops over in canoes during the night and was captured along with forty men. The much-dreaded Walter Butler played a decisive role in both the Allen-Brown attack and the operations connected with the Cedars (see CEDARS, THE, above, and BUTLERSBURY under New York).

A good website for information on touring Montreal is www.tourisme-montreal.org.

Pointe Aux Trembles (Neuville), St. Lawrence River. On the north bank of the river about 20 miles upstream from Quebec, this is the place to which General Benedict Arnold's seven hundred troops withdrew from the Plains of Abraham on 19 November 1775. Here Arnold waited for General Richard Montgomery's column, which arrived from Montreal on 2 December. Three days later the combined force of about one thousand Americans resumed the siege of Quebec. Interesting to students of the American Revolution only as a map location, Pointe aux Trembles is now the village of Neuville on Route 2, which follows the old road used by the Americans in marching between Montreal and Quebec in 1775 to 1776.

Port Royal Habitation National Historic Park, near Annapolis Royal, Nova Scotia. After founding Canada's oldest European settlement in 1605 at what became Annapolis Royal, the French pioneers under the Sieur de Monts constructed the Habitation. This group of buildings around a central courtyard has been reconstructed on the original foundations with scrupulous fidelity by the Canadian government (1938–1939). In 1985 a monument was erected honoring Membertou, the heroic Mi'kmaq chief who aided the French settlers and converted to Christianity in 1610. Phone: (902) 532-2898.

Quebec (Québec), St. Lawrence River. Although few man-made structures of the eighteenth century remain standing in the picturesque city of Quebec, the topography of this historic place is virtually unchanged. Although such now-famous and dominating landmarks as the Citadel and the ramparts overlooking the lower town (not to mention the hotel Château Frontenac) are post-eighteenth-century features of the city, they are generally in consonance with the original character of the colonial stronghold that guarded the front door to Canada.

The so-called Diorama of Quebec Military History, a brief presentation involving a 400-square-foot model of the city and its outskirts, is the logical starting place for a tour of Quebec. The diorama is upstairs in the Musée du Fort, 10 rue Ste.-Anne (opposite Château Frontenac). Phone: (418) 692-1759. Programs are presented continually (alternately in French and English) throughout the year, and you may have a long wait to get in during the summer. A taped narrative covers "the six sieges of Quebec." More than 5 miles of wiring, 2,000 tiny light bulbs, slide projections, dramatic sound effects including music, and miniature smoke ejectors are used. Events of the American Revolution, including the night attacks by Benedict Arnold and Richard Montgomery on New Year's Eve of 1775, pass swiftly at the end of this interesting program. There is nothing to be learned here about this abortive military action of the Revolution other than that it took place. But there is much for the serious student of the Revolution to learn from the splendid panoramic model of the city as it appeared in the eighteenth century. Remarkable historical accuracy is possible because of the scale model constructed between 1806 and 1808 by the Quebecois military engineer, Jean-Baptiste Duberger.

With the Duberger model in mind, let's move immediately to the landmarks associated with the Arnold-Montgomery assault. The spot where the latter was killed is at the base of the bluff on which the Citadel (1822–1823) now stands. Boulevard Champlain now runs along the river edge, and on the rocky face of the bluff is a plaque indicating the location of the Près-de-Ville Barricade, where Montgomery died at the head of the column from Cape Diamond (Plains of Abraham) that was to link up in the lower town with Arnold's column. This ended the promising career of the man who had left the British army and come to America only two years before the Revolution started. He had bought a 67-acre farm at Kings Bridge, New York, and married the daughter (Janet) of Robert R. Livingston. With great reluctance he left his happy personal affairs to join General Philip Schuyler's wing of the Patriot invasion of Canada. As a brigadier general he took over from Schuyler when ill health forced the latter to drop out. Montgomery showed first-class military ability in leading his low-quality troops and squabbling subordinate officers forward, capturing St. Jean and Montreal, then pushing down the St. Lawrence to link up with Arnold at Quebec. Montgomery probably was better known to the British than to his own new countrymen, and they buried him with respect. In 1818 his body was moved from the St. Louis Bastion (where there is a marker) to St. Paul's Chapel in New York City.

Arnold's column (see CHAUDIÈRE RIVER) approached the lower town from the north. The wonderful name "Sault au Matelot" was applied from earliest colonial times to the northeastern tip of the bluff overlooking the mouth of the St. Charles River. The Duberger model shows that some twenty-five years after Arnold's attack there was a narrow street extending the entire distance around the east and north shorelines that was the American line of advance. But the Sault au Matelot Street in which Arnold's column was trapped and forced to surrender could not have included the stretch now bearing that name between St. James and St. Paul Streets.

The place where the Americans encountered (and overcame) the first barricade, at what was then the head of Sault au Matelot Street, is marked at the junction of St. Jacques and Sous le Cap Streets, a few feet west of today's Sault au Matelot Street. Here Arnold was seriously wounded in the leg. Dan Morgan succeeded Arnold as overall commander of the desperate enterprise, personally leading his troops over the barricade, taking a large number of prisoners, and entering Sault au Matelot Street. They proceeded only a few hundred yards before encountering a second defensive position that barred the way to Mountain Hill, the road to the upper town. Although this could have been taken, Morgan permitted subordinates to talk him into delaying until stragglers closed up and Montgomery's column made contact from the opposite direction. The British recovered from their brief setback, stiffening their resistance and sending out a large force through the Palace Gate to cut off Morgan's retreat. Montgomery's column had turned back after he was killed, and Morgan's men realized too late that they were trapped.

The British took more than four hundred prisoners with a loss of fewer than twenty killed and wounded on their own side. The thirty officers and five "gentlemen volunteers" were confined in the upper floors of the North Tower of the Bishop's Palace. Later, the central structure around which the Seminary and Laval University were developed, the Bishop's Palace, was badly damaged by a fire, in 1865. The rooms were rearranged and a fifth floor added in the subsequent reconstruction; so it is not certain exactly where the American officers were held.

American journals report that enlisted men were imprisoned first in the Recollects Monastery and later in the Dauphin Jail. The former site is now occupied by the English (Anglican) Cathedral on the Place d'Armes. The second is said to have been about 150 yards from St. John's Gate, which the prisoners were able to study on moonlit nights while planning their unsuccessful escape attempt in mid-March 1776. Presumably the site is where the Morrin College building was put up (c. 1810–1812).

The Plains of Abraham as recently as 1908 were defaced by a jail and a rifle factory. Since then the extensive and handsome Parc des Champs de Bataille has been developed. Wolfe's Cove has been obliterated by landfills extending several hundred yards into the river, but the site is easy to locate, being a major road junction on Boulevard Champlain; it is almost 2 miles southwest of the lower town. General James Wolfe met with a bloody defeat about 6 miles northeast of Quebec at Montmorency Falls when he made a frontal attack against the French on 31 July 1759. He then surprised the defenders of the strongly fortified city of Quebec by landing during the night of 12 to 13 September at several places along the river and using a small, virtually undefended path to reach the Plains of Abraham. (British troops landed at three places, on a fairly wide front, between the Anse des Mères, where the Notre Dame de la Garde is now located on Boulevard Champlain opposite the Transatlantic Wharf, and the Anse du Foulon, since called Wolfe's Cove.) A landscaped roadway now traces Wolfe's general route up the bluff. Large monuments mark the spots where Wolfe died and where Montcalm was mortally wounded. Other monuments and eighteen historic tablets are located in the 235-acre park. Panoramic views of the St. Lawrence are provided at several points along the drive that follows the edge of the bluff. On Cape Diamond southeast of the Citadel are vestiges of earthworks built in 1783.

The house in the suburb of Ste.-Foy used by General Montgomery survived in altered form for many years as Holland House. Its site is near Bellemont Cemetery. The site of the Intendant's Palace, destroyed by bombardment after Benedict Arnold tried to use it for troops quarters, is privately owned. Outside the palace gate, this was where Intendant Talon had vaults constructed in about 1670 to establish a brewery. The worthy enterprise did not prosper, and the official residence of the intendant of New France was subsequently built on the Talon Vaults. Three centuries later the site serves its originally intended purpose.

Standard tourist guides lead visitors to Notre Dame des Victoires (1688), the Old Jesuit House (c. 1700), and other important landmarks outside the scope of this guide.

Much remains to be done in locating all the sites associated with the Arnold-Montgomery expedition. The author is indebted to the Abbé Honorius Provost, archivist of the Séminaire de Québec and past-president of the Société Historique de Québec, for sympathetic assistance.

As the only remaining walled city in North America, a tour of Quebec's fortifications is well worthwhile. A guided walking tour covering the nearly 3 miles of remaining walls and adjacent fortifications lasting ninety minutes can be taken from the Fortifications of Québec Interpretation Centre, 1 June to 9 October. The center is located at 100 Saint-Louis Street; phone: (800) 463-6769.

A fine extant example of eighteenth-century architecture is the Maillou House, 17 Saint-Louis Street, built in 1736. Also of note is the Artillery Park, 2 D'Auteuil Street, Québec, which includes the Arsenal Foundry, Officers' Quarters, and Dauphine Redoubt. The buttresses of the latter structure were built in 1712; most of the rest of the site was reconstructed in the nineteenth century. These buildings were central to Quebec's defense throughout the eighteenth century. The site is open every day from 1 April to 9 October, 10 A.M. to 5 P.M. Phone: (800) 463-6769.

The official website of Quebec tourism is www.bonjourquebec.com. Toll-free phone: (877) BONJOUR.

St. Johns (St.-Jean), Richelieu River. General Guy Carleton's decision to adopt a "forward strategy" in defending Canada against the American invasion of 1775 resulted in the concentration of most of his regulars at this place. From their base on l'Île-aux-Noix the Americans needed two months to take the position, which was finally surrendered by Major Charles Preston on 2 November 1775. This delaying action cost Carleton most of his best troops, but it may well have been decisive in saving Canada.

St. Johns, as it is known in American accounts, was strategically located near the head of navigation from Lake Champlain. A marker on Champlain Street says the original fort was built here in 1666. (Most authorities give a later date for establishment of the first true military fortification.) Montcalm had work done here in 1758, and Carleton enlarged and strengthened the place in 1775. By that time St. Johns comprised a barracks, some brick buildings, and a stone house with two redoubts located to guard the approaches to the complex.

The first Revolutionary War action here occurred in May 1775 when Colonel Benedict Arnold, with fifty men in the schooner *Liberty*, a vessel captured at Skenesboro, surprised the fifteen-man British garrison. (This was seven days after the American capture of Ticonderoga, New York.) Arnold destroyed five bateaux and withdrew with the large sloop *George III*, four bateaux, the fifteen prisoners, and some supplies. Colonel Ethan Allen had followed Arnold from Ticonderoga with about sixty men in bateaux. Meeting Arnold as the latter withdrew from his highly successful raid, Allen foolishly decided to occupy and hold St. Johns. He was driven back by the British relief column from Chambly (see FORT CHAMBLY NATIONAL HISTORIC PARK).

When the American column under General Philip Schuyler approached St. Johns in September 1775 the place was defended by 500 British regulars of the Seventh and Twenty-sixth Foot Regiments, later reinforced by an ensign and 12 sailors, 100 Canadian militia, and 70 men of the newly raised unit of Royal Highland Emigrants. Lieutenant John André was among the prisoners taken by the Americans when they captured the fort. (He was exchanged a year later after spending his period of parole in Pennsylvania.)

All that remains of historic interest in the modern industrial city of St.-Jean is a vestige of the old fort on the campus of the military college.

Sorel, St. Lawrence River at the mouth of the Richelieu River. Named after the first commander of the French fort built here in 1665 to guard the northern terminus of the strategic waterway through Lake Champlain to the Hudson River, Sorel was an important point during the Colonial Wars and the first years of the American Revolution. Subsequent development as a manufacturing and shipbuilding center has eradicated historic landmarks of the eighteenth century.

Trois Rivières, St. Lawrence River. Now a thriving industrial metropolis, Trois Rivières is the second oldest European city in Canada. It was founded in 1634 as an outpost on the Iroquois frontier. During the eighteenth century it was famous for its iron works, the site of which is now a public campground on the Maurice River about 8 miles from the center of town. Although a National Historic Site, Vieilles Forges is difficult to find and is not worth the effort. A major American defeat took place on 8 June 1776 when 2,000 troops under General William Thompson attempted to take Trois Rivières. Believing the settlement to be defended by only 800 troops, the Patriots discovered too late that General John Burgoyne's regulars had started arriving there, and that about 6,000 men under General Simon Fraser were already on the ground. Thompson landed about 3 miles upstream of the town, about where the huge bridge now spans the river from Trois Rivières Ouest. Leaving a guard of 250 men with the bateaux and with a native guide who failed (perhaps intentionally) to lead them under cover of darkness to the river road, the Americans were quickly in trouble. But Thompson and his four regimental commanders—Arthur St. Clair, William Irvine, William Maxwell, and Anthony Wayne—happened to be outstanding military leaders. Still unaware of the odds, they defied the fire of three British vessels in the river and pressed on. Wayne routed a superior force on the outskirts of Trois Rivières, but the Americans were soon stopped by superior forces defending from behind entrenchments and supported by artillery. General Guy Carleton, the British commander in Canada, could have cut off and captured the entire force, but declined to do so because he did not want the burden of so many prisoners. The 1,100 survivors of this expedition got back to Sorel only after surviving great physical hardship and the danger of ambush in the swamps. (The boat guard made off with the bateaux.) Total American losses in this operation were about 400, including General Thompson and 235 others taken prisoner. The British lost fewer than 20 killed and wounded.

Several historic buildings survive in the older section of the city. The Anglican Church, at the east end of Notre Dame Street, evolved from the Recollet Monastery (1699). Generals Richard Montgomery and Benedict Arnold are said to have used the building in their operations from Montreal to Quebec (1775) and Arnold used it again during the subsequent retreat (1776). The nearby Ursuline Convent on Rue des Ursulines (open on a limited schedule) dates from 1697.

CARIBBEAN

The Caribbean was a major theater of the American Revolutionary War. This was because the islands were economically important as the principal market for the slave trade in the Americas and as the primary source of sugar and rum consumed in Europe and America. Furthermore, they were divided among the colonial powers of Britain, France, Spain, and the Netherlands, which were all belligerents at some stage of the Revolutionary War. The French, Spanish, and Dutch islands were vital sources of the military supplies and gunpowder that sustained the Continental army. The American flag was first saluted in the Danish and Dutch islands of the Caribbean. American privateers swarmed these seas and were likened to an infestation of fleas by the British.

The Caribbean was also the location of critical naval battles that had major implications for the war in North America, and the defense of the British colonies in the Caribbean deflected military resources from the British commanders in America. The islands were all variously affected by the war, with large-scale military preparations and economic disruption. However, the small islands of the eastern Caribbean were the scenes of the most dramatic military events, and are therefore given particular consideration here. American Loyalists from Georgia and South Carolina settled in the Bahamas, Jamaica, Dominica, the Turks and Caicos Islands, and Belize. Alexander Hamilton, George Washington, Crispus Attucks, and John Paul Jones all spent time in the Caribbean before 1776. The war's surviving relics in the Caribbean convey the interconnection between the history of the islands and the revolutionary history of the United States.

ANTIGUA

Antigua was a British colony between 1632 and 1981. The 108-square-mile island had close ties with America before the Revolutionary War. Benjamin Franklin sent his nephew, Benjamin Meacom, to set up a printing press in Antigua. The captain of one of the ships whose cargo was destroyed in the Boston Tea Party was involved in a bar fight in Antigua after leaving Boston. The island had relied on food imports from North America before 1775, and the war caused severe shortages that led to the deaths of an estimated one-fifth of the slave population. Antigua led the other Caribbean islands, together with Tortola, in fitting out privateers against the Americans, beginning with the sloop *Reprisal,* which had captured three American vessels by January 1777, and whose owners declared that they were "zealously disposed to assist in reducing his Majesty's rebellious colonies in America to lawfull obedience." Antigua alone among the British Leeward Islands escaped conquest by the French. Its defense was a high priority owing to the presence of English Harbour, which was the main British naval base in the eastern Caribbean. Like Virginia, Antigua had strong royalist ties during the English Civil War, and the local rum is called "Cavalier."

Clarence House, overlooking English Habour, was built for Prince William Henry, a younger son of George III who later became duke of Clarence and King William IV. He had served in the Caribbean and visited New York during the American Revolution. He was captain of the *Pegasus* when he visited Antigua in 1787. Clarence House is now the official residence of the governor-general of Antigua, and it is open to visitors when he is not in residence.

Falmouth is at the foot of Monk's Hill. St. Paul's Church has a graveyard with the tomb of the Honorable James Charles Pitt, son of the earl of Chatham and commander of H.M.S *Hornet,* who died at the age of twenty at English Harbour on 13 November 1780. The epitaph reads: "The genius that inspired / and the virtues that adorned the parent / were revived in the son / whose dawning merit / bespoke a meridian splendor / worthy of the name Pitt." St. Paul's, originally fortified in 1676, was the first church building on the island. It doubled as a courthouse.

Fig Tree Hill commands views of Guadeloupe, Montserrat, Nevis, and St. Kitts.

Fort Barrington on Goat Hill is on the promontory at the northern beach side of Deep Bay. It was named after Admiral Sir Samuel Barrington and was completed on the site of an earlier structure in 1779. It was a signal station which reported movements of ships by flag and light signals to Rat Island. It has views of St. John's Harbour, St. Kitts, and Nevis. It is accessible via Five Islands near the Royal Antiguan Resort.

Fort James is on a promontory at the northern end of St. John's, and was first fortified in 1704 to 1705. It contained barracks for about seventy-five men for the regiment of British troops stationed on the island since the 1730s. The walls are in good condition and there is a kitchen building with a seventeenth-century open-fire range. Ten of the original cannon with 5.5-inch bores remain. They weigh 2.5 tons, have a range of 100 yards, and fired 4-pound shot. They were manned by a team of twelve. The fort commands an extensive view of the harbor of St. John's. It can be reached from Fort Road.

Monks Hill and Fort George overlook English Harbour and Falmouth. The fortress was erected on the 669-foot summit of the hill between 1689 and 1705. The outer walls surrounded an area of about 7 acres which were intended as a refuge for the inhabitants in the event of an invasion. They are largely intact, together with the ruins of powder magazines, including the west magazine built in 1731, the original gun sites for thirty-two cannon, a water cistern, and a stone inscription to King George II. It was too large and exposed to be defended as a regular fort. It is accessible by car by following signs from Liberta off the main road through the village of Table Hill Gordon. It can also be reached by foot from Cobbs Cross at Falmouth Harbour. Further west is the fort on Johnstone Point.

Nelson's Dockyard National Park at English Harbour was perfectly situated—in landlocked basins formed from a volcano cone—to afford ships protection. It was used by the Royal Navy to refit, careen, and shelter warships between 1725 and 1889. It was expanded during the American Revolution to become the primary British base in the eastern Caribbean, and occasionally it repaired ships from the British fleet in North America during the Revolutionary War. It was more important than Port Royal at Jamaica because of the location and the prevailing wind directions from east to west. It is today a wonderfully preserved Georgian dockyard built principally between 1778 and 1792 that includes the Copper and Lumber Store (1789); the Capstan House; the Boat and Joiner's Loft (1778); the Cordage and Canvas Store (1778–1784); the Seaman's Galley (1778); and the Saw Pit and Saw Pit Cabin (1769). Among the many artisans who worked at the dockyard was a caulker called John Baxter who arrived from Chatham in 1778 and opened the first Methodist Chapel in Antigua in 1783. Horatio Nelson spent time here while he commanded H.M.S. *Boreas* on the Leeward Island Station between 1784 and 1787. There is a museum with an emphasis on naval history at the Admiral's House at Nelson's Dockyard and an interpretation center at Dow's Hill which also offers a panoramic view of Nelson's Dockyard. The ruins of Fort Berkley are located on the long spit at the other end of the harbor which it protected. Fort Charlotte was built to the north of Fort Berkeley in 1745.

Plantation Houses. Betty's Hope, south of the village of Pares in the parish of St. Peter, was established in about 1674 and was owned for three hundred years by the Codrington family of Gloucestershire in England. The word "hope" meant an enclosed piece of land, and Betty's Hope was named after the daughter of the founder, Sir Christopher Codrington. It is a restored plantation which includes a working seventeenth-century windmill together with exhibits and demonstrations of the manufacture of sugar and rum. The Codrington family also owned the neighboring island of Barbuda, where their slaves grew provisions for their plantations in Antigua. Parham Hill Plantation's great house dates from 1722.

Rat Island in St. John's Harbour is joined to the mainland by an isthmus. It was first fortified in 1741 and contained barracks for the regular British army regiment stationed on the island from the 1730s.

St. John's, Antigua's capital, is situated in the north of the leeward coast at the head of a harbor with the same name. It was defended on the south by Fort Barrington and the north by Fort James, and also by the fortifications on Rat Island. The walls are in good condition and some guns remain. The Old Court House on Long and Market Streets was built in 1747 and was designed by the English-born American architect Peter Harrison. It was extensively rebuilt, with the addition of the cast-iron pillars, after the earthquake of 1843. The law courts met on the ground floor and the legislature on the floor above. The building now houses the Historical and Archaeological Society of Antigua and Barbuda (HAS), which has a specialist library, and the Museum of Antigua and Barbuda. It used to contain the historical records of the island but these are now stored, about a third of a mile to the east, in a purpose-built National Archives Building opposite the sport field called the Antigua Recreation Ground. The Police Station (1750s) and guardhouse (1754) in Newgate Street were formerly an arsenal, now surrounded by railings composed of firelocks and bayonets. St. John's Anglican Cathedral between Long and Newgate Streets has many interesting eighteenth-century memorial tablets and graves. It was built in 1683 and rebuilt in 1745 and 1847. Government House was once frequented by great admirals such as Lord Hood and Lord Nelson. It was the private home of the merchant Thomas Kerby in 1750, and is now the residence of the governor-general. The barracks building was erected in 1735. The Historic Redcliffe Quay, also known as Pickett's Wharf, is on the waterfront of St. John's. It was a trading center with warehouses, taverns, and docks, which are now converted into restaurants and shops. At the time of the American Revolution it was owned by Charles Kerr, a merchant of Scottish descent who had many commercial interests including a shipyard; he was chief supplier to the navy in 1781. The district was extensively damaged by the fire of 1841.

Shirley Heights is part of national park which comprises Nelson's Dockyard. It was built during the governorship of Sir Thomas Shirley. The fortifications mostly postdate the American Revolution, although they were begun in 1781. The postwar years were a major period for the construction of fortifications throughout the British Caribbean. The investment was largely a response to the experiences of the American Revolution in which an island might hold out for several weeks with a small garrison and strong fortifications, as did St. Kitts in January 1781. There are today the ruins of barracks, batteries, cisterns, and powder magazines. The ordnance building is now used as a restaurant. A weathered stone on the front of the main building at the west end records that the First West India Regiment was stationed there more than thirty years after the barracks were built. This regiment originated in the South Carolina Black Corps, which was created during the American Revolution, drawing upon slaves who were given their freedom in return for serving in the British army, and then sent to the West Indies. Shirley Heights has a magnificent view of English Harbour, Montserrat, and Redonda.

For further information contact the following: the Antigua and Barbuda Department of Tourism, 610 Fifth Avenue, Suite 311, New York, N.Y. 10020; phone: (888) 268–4227 (toll-free) or (212) 541-4117; fax: (212) 541-4789; email: info@antigua-barbuda.org; the Antigua and Barbuda Department of Tourism, Government Complex, Queen Elizabeth Highway, St. John's, Antigua, West Indies; phone: (268) 462-0408; fax: (268) 462-2483; email: deptourism@antigua.gov.ag; the Antigua and Barbuda Historical and Archaeological Society, Church Street, P.O. Box 103, English Harbour, Antigua; phone: (268) 463–1060; the Historical and Archaeological Society, Museum of Antigua and Barbuda, Box 2103, St. John's, Antigua, West Indies; phone: (268) 462-4930; fax (268) 462-1469; email: museum@candw.ag; website: www.antiguanice.com. At Nelson's Dockyard National Park contact the chairperson of the NPA, Ms. Valerie Hodge, the parks commissioner, Mrs. A. Martin, and the onsite archaeologist, Dr. Reg A. Murphy, at P.O. Box 1283, St. John's, Antigua, West Indies; phone: (268) 460-1379; fax: (268) 460-1516; email: natpark@candw.ag. Christopher Codrington has created a website, "Historic Antigua and Barbuda," with information relating to the history, archaeology, and genealogy of the island at idt.net/~coopcod, or email him at coopcod@villages.ios.com. The National Archives are located at Rappaport Centre, Factory Road, St. Johns; phone: (268) 462-3946.

BAHAMAS

The Bahamas were a British colony included in a grant by Charles I to Sir Robert Heath, then attorney general of England, on 30 October 1629. During the American Revolution the islands were the scene of the first deployment of marines from North America. On 3 March 1776 an American fleet commanded by Esek Hopkins attacked Nassau. They remained on the island for two weeks, during which time they dismantled the forts to obtain the ammunition and guns. During the war the Bahamas fitted out privateers which captured 124 American ships, together with 15 Spanish and 31 French ships, between 1777 and 1782. In January 1778 another party of American marines attacked and held the island for two days while they spiked the remaining guns at Nassau. The Spanish retook Nassau in 1782 with the help of the *South Carolina*, the largest and most powerful American ship to serve in the war, under the command of Commodore Alexander Gillon. The French seized the Turks Islands and defended them against a counterattack by Captain Horatio Nelson of the H.M.S. *Albermarle* in 1783. It was a group of American Loyalists led by Andrew

Deveaux, a lieutenant colonel of the South Carolina militia, who retook the Bahamas from the Spanish on 18 September 1783. The Bahamas were transformed by the Revolutionary War when their population doubled with the arrival of Loyalist refugees and their slaves from Georgia and the Carolinas.

Cat Island contains the ruins of the American Loyalist Andrew Deveaux's mansion, built in 1783 in Port Howe. He led the expedition that reconquered the island from the Spanish.

Nassau, the capital of New Providence, dates from 1729. Fort Charlotte commands the western entrance to the harbor. It was named after Queen Charlotte, the wife of George III, and was built between 1787 and 1794 on the orders of John Murray, the fourth earl of Dunmore, who had been governor of Virginia at the outbreak of the American Revolution and was also a former governor of New York. Fort Montagu, built in 1742, commanded the eastern end of the harbor overlooking the narrows between Hog and Athol Islands. It was briefly captured by the Americans in 1776. The fort is named after the duke of Montagu of the Royal Foresters of South Carolina, who launched a bold attack to repossess the island from the Spanish on 14 April 1783. Montagu financed the expedition, despite having lost much of his fortune in the war, assembling 220 men with only 150 muskets. He cleverly deceived his opponents regarding his actual numbers. The Deanery is a private residence dating from 1710. The kitchen and former slave quarters are in a one-story building to the west of the house. The Priory (1787) was the official residence of Governor Dunmore. The Vendue House is now the Pompey Museum. It was a slave auction house built some time before 1769. Blackbeard's Tower, northeast of Nassau, allegedly dates from the late 1600s. Also in New Providence there is a late-seventeenth-century fort at Northwest Point and the ruins of a fort at South Ocean Beach.

For further information contact: the Bahamas Ministry of Tourism, P.O. Box N-3701, Nassau, Bahamas; phone: (242) 322-7500; fax: (242) 328-0945; email: tourism@bahamas.com; the Department of Archives, P.O. Box SS-6341, Nassau, N. P., Bahamas; phone: (242) 393-2175, 393-2855; fax: (242) 393-2855; email: archives@batelnet.bs; website: www.bahamasnationalarchives.bs; the Bahamas Public Library, Rawson Square, Nassau, Bahamas. At the College of the Bahamas Library you may contact Ms. Williamae Johnson at Oakes Field, P.O. Box N1645, Nassau, Bahamas; phone: (242) 323-7930 ext. 227; fax: 242 323 7834; email: williamar@cob.edu.bs. Also helpful are the Bahamas National Trust, The Retreat, Village Road, P.O. Box N-4105, Nassau, New Providence, Bahamas; phone: (242) 393-1317; fax: (242) 393-4978; and the Bahamas Historical Society, Elizabeth Avenue/Shirley Street, P.O. Box 55-6833, Nassau, Bahamas; phone: (242) 322-4231.

BARBADOS

Barbados was a British colony between 1627 and 1966. The 166-square-mile island had close links with British North America before 1775. A group of adventurers from the island led the settlement of South Carolina, whose original slave code was closely modeled on that of Barbados. Benjamin Franklin was first apprenticed in Philadelphia to Samuel Keimer, who later became a printer in Barbados. George Washington made his only trip abroad in 1751 to Barbados when he visited the island in the hope of finding a remedy for his ill half-brother Lawrence Washington, from whom he later inherited Mount Vernon. He kept a diary during his visit to the island between 28 September and 3 November. He became ill himself during the trip, and very nearly died of smallpox. His brother was related through marriage to Gedney Clarke, a local merchant, who was a member of the council, collector of customs, and owner of the Bell Plantation. Clarke greeted the Washingtons on their arrival in Barbados. Crispus Attucks, one of the victims of the Boston Massacre in 1770, and Prince Hall, a member of a British Army Lodge of Freemasons in Boston in 1775 and the founder of the first African Grand Lodge in Boston, were both from Barbados. During the American Revolution the island suffered severe food shortages in the early stages of the war, having previously relied upon imports of fish, corn, and rice from North America. General Sir John Vaughan made the island his command headquarters when he arrived with the Eighty-ninth Regiment in February 1780. The island was devastated by a hurricane the following October. Benjamin Franklin gave American privateers orders for ships to be allowed to pass without molestation to relieve the island.

Bridgetown is the capital of Barbados. Few buildings survived the destruction of the hurricanes of 1780 and 1831, and the fire of 1860. The Law Courts are housed in a building completed between 1730 and 1732, which was the place where the assembly met between 1729 and 1784. It was the oldest assembly in the British Caribbean, having been founded in 1639, twenty years after the assembly in Virginia, which was the first in North America. During the American Revolution the building also doubled as a jail for confining prisoners of war, including Captain John Manley and his crew of the American privateer *Cumberland* who escaped, clearly with inside help, in 1779. The Nichols Building (now the law offices of Harford Chambers), on the corner of Lucas and James, with its curvilinear gables, is Bridgetown's oldest surviving building, thought to predate 1700. The Government House, approached from Trafalgar Square by Constitution Road and Government Hill, was leased as the residence of the governors of the island in 1703 and purchased in 1736. It was known as Pilgrim after the first resident, the Quaker John Pilgrim, and was rebuilt in 1755. It is not open to the public because it is now the official residence of the governor-general. Literary Row, connecting Lake's Folly with Cheapside, is named after the Literary Society, founded in August 1777. Queen's Park contains the King's (now Queen's) House, which became the residence of General Sir John Vaughan in 1780. It was destroyed by a hurricane the same year. Major General Gabriel Christie demolished the remnants of the original structure to build the present one, ordered the purchase of the land, and added some barracks on the west side of the house. The current structure was built in 1783 to be the residence of the commanding officer of the British army in the eastern Caribbean (Barbados and the Windward and Leeward Islands). Today the main building is used as a theater and gallery.

Carlisle Bay was named after the earl of Carlisle, to whom Charles I granted the island in 1627. Barbados lacks a natural harbor, and the British fleet was therefore stationed at Antigua. Nevertheless, the navy frequently moored in Carlisle Bay during the American Revolution. The British expedition against St. Lucia sailed from Barbados on 12 December 1778. It included five thousand troops who had served under Sir Henry Clinton in North America. The Careenage, a harbor of modest dimensions, is a basin on the lower reaches of the old Constitution River, which terminates in the Molehead. In December 1772 work commenced on dredging the water and rebuilding the wharves, necessitating the removal of 5,760 tons of rubbish. It was sufficiently successful to enable vessels of a draught of 9 or 10 feet to enter the channel by April 1773, but the achievement was reversed by the effects of the hurricane of October 1780. The Careenage was defended by Charles Fort on Needham's Point, which dated from 1650, but was completely rebuilt in 1811 to 1812, and is now located in the grounds of the Hilton Hotel.

Codrington College was a school at the time of the American Revolution and a plantation owned by the Society for the Propagation of the Gospel in Foreign Parts (SPG). It is a very impressive building with its avenue of tall cabbage-palm trees lining the drive of the approach and its view of the Atlantic Ocean. It was founded by Christopher Codrington, the governor-general of the Leeward Islands, who bequeathed two sugar plantations for the education of scholars and for the religious instruction of the slaves to the SPG by his will of 1710. It opened as a grammar school in 1745 and a theological college in 1830. The Principal's Lodge, or Consett's House, was the original great house of the plantation where Christopher Codrington lived; it predates 1700 but was gutted by fire in 1926. The college buildings were completed in 1743. They feature a triple-arched open portico through which the visitor glimpses the sea. There are 5 acres of woodland and a large lily pond which dominates the garden in front of the college. It is indicative of the poverty of the educational infrastructure of the islands in this period that the school was closed between 1775 and 1796.

Fort George was a redoubt about 2.5 miles east of Bridgetown which was under construction in 1779. It was never completed, but a few traces remain.

The Morgan Lewis Mill was originally built by Dutch Jews from Brazil. It is still functional and is now preserved by the Barbados National Trust. As on St. Kitts and Antigua, there are towers of eighteenth-century sugar mills throughout Barbados. There are additional displays of the operation of the sugar industry at St. Nicholas Abbey and the Sir Frank Hutson Sugar Machinery Museum.

Plantation Houses. Drax Hall, together with St. Nicholas Abbey, is one of two remaining Jacobean houses in Barbados. It is not open to the public, but the exterior is sufficient testimony of the immense prosperity of the island in the late seventeenth century. Sunbury Plantation House and Museum in St. Philip was built in the 1660s and much expanded around 1770. It was severely damaged in a fire in 1995. It is the only plantation house that can be toured throughout, with period furnishings and estate tools. There still survive a large number of houses which either predate or were contemporaneous with the American Revolution: Aberdare in Christ Church; Alleyndale Hall in St. Peter (c. 1720); Bagatelle (Parham House); Bath in St. John; the Bay Mansion in St. Michael (pre-1784); Brighton in St. George (1652); Clifton Hall in St. John; Halton in St. Philip; Harmony Hall in St. Michael (pre-1700); Holders House in St. James (pre-1700); Malvern in St. John; Newcastle in St. John; Hopfield in Christ Church; Porters in St. James (pre-1700, and owned for more than two hundred years by the Alleyne family); Warrens in St. Thomas (1683); and Wildey House in St. Michael (1760s).

St. Ann's Fort in Bridgetown was established during the reign of Queen Anne and contains some seventy buildings of historical and architectural interest which were all part of the former military garrison. The buildings mostly postdate the American Revolution, although the expansion of the site began with the arrival of a British garrison under the command of General Sir John Vaughan in 1780. The early-eighteenth-century shot tower in the center of the fort still exists; it is a sexagonal building which was used for making lead shot. The Savannah was a military parade ground which is used for sporting and ceremonial events. It is surrounded by the largest collection of seventeenth-century English artillery in existence, including one of only two surviving cannon of Oliver Cromwell's army. The Barbados Museum and Historical Society has been housed in the Military Prison (1817–1818) since 1933. It contains a large collection of artifacts and paintings from the eighteenth century, as well as a reference library above the ground floor.

St. George's Parish Church contains a painting of the Resurrection by the Pennsylvanian painter Benjamin West, who became president of the Royal Academy and was the favorite artist of George III. It was commissioned for the church by the president of the council, the Honorable Henry Frere of Lower Estate, and it was exhibited at the Royal Academy in 1786, labeled "Not For Sale." However, it was another thirty years before it was placed in the church because of a disagreement between the rector and Frere. During the period of opposition to the Townshend Duties in America in 1768, Frere had written a pamphlet to show that "Barbados hath always preserved a uniform and steady attachment to great Britain." St. Nicholas Abbey, St. Peter was one of the finest homes in seventeenth-century English America, built around 1650 to 1660. Sir John Yeamans, the second owner of the house, led a pioneer expedition to South Carolina, where he became governor in 1672. During the American Revolution it was the home of Sir John Gay Alleyne, who acquired the house through his wife in 1746 and who for thirty years was the speaker of the House of Assembly. Mount Gay, one of the best and oldest brands of rum in the Caribbean, was named after Alleyne. He likely added the triple-arcaded portico at the entrance, together with the interior moldings and sash windows. The house is remarkably well preserved.

Speightstown, St. Peter is 12 miles from Bridgetown. It was a port defended by five batteries and forts. There are still visible ruins of Denmark Fort, Orange Fort, Dover Fort, Coconut Fort, and the Heywood Battery. There are also fortress ruins near Maycock's Bay. On 12 June 1777 American privateers took fishing boats and slaves off the coast, with losses estimated at £2,000. The town contains today many fine examples of early colonial architecture, such as the three-story, late-seventeenth-century Arlington House.

Washington House (Bush Hill House), situated at the top of Bush Hill to the north of the Garrison Savannah and Main Guard, was the residence where the nineteen-year-old George Washington stayed during his seven-week visit in 1751. It was purchased by the British Ordnance Department in 1789 and became the quarters of the commanding engineer and/or commanding officer of St. Ann's Garrison.

A reference library is available for research on the island's history and genealogy at the Barbados Museum and Historical Society, St. Ann's Garrison, St. Michael; phone: (246) 427-0201; fax: (246) 429-5946; email: admin@barbmuse.org.bb; website: http://www.Barbmuse.org.bb. Also useful is the Barbados National Trust, Wildey House, Widley, St. Michael, Barbados; phone: (246) 426-2421 / 436-9033; fax: (246) 429-9055; website: http://www.sunbeach.net.trust. You can reach the National Archives via phone: (246) 425-1380 or fax: (246) 425-5911. For a guide to historic places visit http://www.barbados.org/historic.htm. Also contact the Barbados Tourism Authority, Harbour Road, Bridgetown, Barbados; phone: (246) 427-2623; fax (246) 426-4080; email: btainfo@barbados.org; website: http://barbados.org/; and the Barbados Tourism Authority, USA/New York Office, 800 Second Avenue, New York, N.Y. 10017; phone: (212) 986-6516 / (800) 221-9831; fax: (212) 573-9850; email: btany@barbados.org; website: http://barbados.org/usa.

BRITISH VIRGIN ISLANDS

The Virgin Islands were part of the British federal colony of the Leeward Islands after 1672 and are still a British colony. They comprise a group of twenty islands including Tortola, Virgin Gorda, Anegada, Jost van Dyke, Peter's Island, and Salt Islands.

Tortola is the largest of this group of islands. In response to the threat of American privateers, the local merchants fitted out pirateers, or "pickaroons," which carried anywhere between 4 to 68 guns with crews of between 20 and 309 men. They were sufficiently successful to incur the wrath of the United States. As late as 1782, Congress made plans for a retaliatory raid against Tortola. There are still the remains of the home of Dr. William Thornton, who was born in the Virgin Islands and who designed the Capitol in Washington, D.C., and who was chosen by Thomas Jefferson to design some of the buildings at the University of Virginia. The ruins of Fort George, Fort Charlotte, and Fort Shirley mostly date from the 1790s. Fort Recovery in the west of the island was built by the Dutch between 1648 and 1660.

For further information contact: Library Services Department, Flemming Street, Road Town, Tortola, British Virgin Islands; phone: (284) 494-3428; the British Virgin Islands Tourist Board, 3390 Peachtree Road N.E., Atlanta, Ga. 30326; phone: (404) 240-8018; fax: (404) 233-2318; or the British Virgin Islands National Parks Trust, c/o Ministry of Natural Resources Road Town, Tortola, BVI.

CUBA

Cuba is the largest island in the Caribbean with a total area of 42,860 square miles, and it was a Spanish colony between 1492 and 1898. It was the assembly point for the silver fleets to Spain. Charles III initiated a major expansion of the navy and of the fortifications of the islands in the decade before the American Revolution. The impetus for strengthening the defenses of the Spanish islands was partly a response to British successes during the Seven Years' War, when the British had conquered Havana (1762) and the Floridas. Spain consequently built the formidable fortress of Fortaleza in Havana between 1763 and 1774. The British never attempted to attack the island following the entry of Spain into the Revolutionary War in 1779. The Spanish were cautious in their support of the American Revolution. They allied themselves with France but never formally with the United States. They opened the ports of Cuba to American trade in 1780. The highest-ranking prisoner in Havana during the war was Major General John Campbell, the former commander of British forces at Pensacola.

Havana. There are almost 350 surving buildings in the city which date from between 1512 and 1800. El Castillo de la Real Fuerza (the Castle of Royal Force), commanding the harbor mouth, was commissioned by Philip II and built in 1558 to 1577 on a site of an earlier fortress of Hernando de Soto. The bell tower was added in 1630 to 1634. The fortress was the residence of the captain general between 1577 and 1762 and was used as a barracks during the American Revolution. The Castillo de los Tres Reyes del Morro, at the mouth of the harbor, was built in 1579 and overwhelmed after a forty-four-day siege by the British in 1762. There are still sixty cannon pointing out to sea. The polygon structure is at the center of the UNESCO World Heritage program for the restoration of Old Havana. It faces, across the harbor, the Castillo de la Punta on the Malecón promenade, which was completed in 1600. The Fortaleza San Carlos de la Cabaña was begun in 1763 and completed in 1774, and occupies about a tenth of the surface area of Old Havana. It could accommodate five thousand troops. It was the largest fort built on the Spanish Main and, together with the rebuilding of El Morro, it illustrates the major improvements to the defenses of the Spanish islands which were undertaken in the decade before the American Revolution. The Cabaña is now a historical study center and a museum of military history, and part of the Morro-Cabaña Historic Park. The Plaza Carlos Manuel de Céspedes (Plaza de la Iglesia), the oldest square in the city, was expanded to its present size in 1776. The government buildings are particularly impressive, especially the Captain General's Palace, with its façade of ten grand columns, which was built between 1776 and 1791. It was the residence of the colonial governors and is now the Municipal Museum. The palaces include the Palacio del Segundo Cob, built between 1772 and 1776; the Mateo Pedroso y Florencia House, which dates from 1780; the Palacio del Conde Lombillo, built as the home of the royal treasurer in 1737 and reconstructed in 1762; and the Palacio de los Condes de Casa-Bayona (1720). There are numerous former private residences, such as the Zambrana House at 117-19 Calle Obispo, which is the oldest house in Havana, dating from 1570; the Hostal Valencia on Calle Officios, south of the Plaza de Armas, a mansion dating from the mid-eighteenth century, and now a hotel; and El Patio, opposite the cathedral, built in 1775. Like Santo Domingo and Puerto Rico, Cuba has many early religious buildings, including the Santa Clara of Assisi Convent, which was built between 1636 and 1643; the San Cristóbal Cathedral, built between 1748 and 1777; the Seminario de San Carlos and San Ambrosio, behind the cathedral, which dates from 1772; the Church and Convent of Nuestra Senor de Belén (1718); La Merced (1755–1792); and the San Francisco de Paula Church (1745). The boundary of Old Havana is marked by a shaded boulevard, the Paseo, or Prado, built in 1772.

Santiago de Cuba is Cuba's second major city after Havana. The Castillo del Morr was built about 1663 and expanded in 1710. It retains its moat, drawbridge, ramparts, cannon, dungeons, barracks, and chapel. It was built on the site of an earlier fort which was destroyed in 1662 by the English pirate and later governor of Jamaica, Henry Morgan. The home of Diego Velázquez is the oldest villa in Cuba, built between 1516 and 1530.

For further information contact: the Canadian Board of Cuban Tourism, 1200 Bay Street, Suite 305, Toronto, Ontario M5R 2A5; phone: (416) 362-0700; fax: (416) 362-6799; email: info@gocuba.ca. An alternate address is 2075, rue University, Bureau 460, Montréal, Québec H3A 2L1; phone: (514) 875-8004; fax: (514) 875-8006; email: montreal@gocuba.ca. Other useful contacts are: Archivo Nacional (National Archive), Compostela esq. San Isidro, La Habana 1, Cuba; Biblioteca Nacional (National Library), Plaza de la Revolución José Martí, Apartado Oficial 3, La Habana, Cuba; Cuban Genealogical Society, P.O. Box 2650, Salt Lake City, Utah 84110-2650; Cuban Index, c/o Peter E. Carr, P.O. Box 15839, San Luis Obispo, Calif. 93406-5839; Oficina del Historiador Ciudad de La Habana, Tacon No. 1, La Habana Vieja, Ciudad de la Habana 10100, Republica de Cuba; phone: (53-7) 2876 / 5062 / 5001; fax: 33 8183.

Trinidad de Cuba was founded in 1514 and is now a UNESCO World Heritage Site. The Plaza Mayor

(Antigua Plaza de Trinidad) was laid out in 1522. The Inquisitor's House (Lara House) was the home of the head of the Spanish Inquisition and dates from 1732. The Guamuhaya Archaeological Museum is in a house built in 1732, and the Museum of Colonial Architecture is in a house built in 1735.

The Valle de Los Ingenios is a valley with the remains of numerous plantations, slave burial sites, mills, and great houses. It is designated a UNESCO World Heritage Site. It includes the San Alejo de Manaca Iznaga Villa, a hacienda and plantation great house, built in 1750. Cuba's sugar industry developed later than that of the British and French islands in the Caribbean, so most of the island's sugar plantations date from the nineteenth century.

CURAÇAO

The Dutch captured Curaçao from the Spanish in 1634. The 171-square-mile island was a center for the slave trade and illicit commerce with the Spanish Main. The island possesses the earliest synagogue in the Western Hemisphere and seventeenth-century tombstones of Jewish settlers.

Plantations (*landhuis*) and Great Houses. There are several historically interesting buildings on Curaçao: the Civil Service Registration Office, a pre-1740 mansion; Jan Kock, a great house on a salt mining estate built around 1750 to 1764; Brievengat Landhuis (1750) and Ascension (1700), which were restored by the Curaçao Foundation for Preserving Ancient Monuments; Casa Venezolana (1750); Daniel Lanhuis (1750); Groot Santa Marta House, which has late-seventeenth-century features; Hato Landhuis, the home of an eighteenth-century director of the Dutch West Indies Company; Klein Santa Maria (1700); Knip Landhuis (late 1600s); Savonet (1662 and rebuilt 1806), which houses a museum; and Stroomzigt (1780).

Willemstad, the capital and chief port of Curaçao, is really two cities, Punda and Otrabanda, surrounding the narrows of St. Anna Bay. On the Punda side is the Herrenstraat, which predates 1700. St. Anna's Catholic Church was built in 1751, and the Mikvé Israel-Emanuel Synagogue around 1730 to 1732. There is a ceremonial bath in the 1780 courtyard museum. The Beth Haim Cemetery was established by Sephardic Jews, with more than 2,500 tombs dating from 1668. The Penha House, on the corner of Handelskade and Heerenstraat, dates from 1708. The Fortkerk, the old Dutch Reformed Church which faces into Wilhelminaplein, was constructed in 1763 and rebuilt in 1796. Fort Amsterdam was constructed between 1642 and 1675. It was built according to a seventeenth-century design and retains the arched entrance to the original governor's residence (1642). Rif Fort, or Riffort, south of Brionplein, dates from 1768, and protected the harbor with Water Fort, built in 1634. The Curaçao Museum is further west of Bironplein in a nineteenth-century great house in Otrabanda.

For further information contact: Curaçao Tourist Board, Pietermaai 19, P.O. Box 3266, Curaçao Netherlands Antilles; phone: 599 9 434 82 00; fax: 599 9 461 50 17/ 461 23 05; email: ctdbcur@ctdb.net; Curaçao Monument Council, Inter regional Committee Action, Willemstad (ICAW), Monument Bureau, Scharlooweg 51, Willemstad, Curaçao; phone: 599 9 465 46 88; fax: 599 9 465 45 91; Corporation for Urban Revitalization, Monument Conservation Foundation Belvederestraat 43/45, P.O. Box 2042, Willemstat, Curaçao; phone: 599 9 462 86 80; fax: 599 9 462 72 75. In the United States contact Joel Grossman at Tourism Solutions, 7951 Sixth Street S.W., Suite 216, Plantation, Fla. 33145; phone: (954) 370-5887 / (800) 328-7222; fax: (954) 723-7949; email: jbgrossman@aol.com.

DOMINICA (THE COMMONWEALTH OF DOMINICA)

Dominica was one of the last islands to be formally colonized by Europeans. With its very mountainous and richly forested terrain, the 290-square-mile island has some of the best natural features in the Caribbean. In 1607 Captain John Smith and a group of colonists stopped at the island on their way to settle Jamestown. French settlers began arriving during the eighteenth century, but the island remained independent until its conquest by the British in 1761 and formal cession in 1763. During the American Revolution the French seized the initiative in the Caribbean when the marquis de Bouillé captured Dominica from the British on 7 September 1778. Admiral Sir Samuel Barrington had secret orders not to leave Barbados, but to await an expedition from North America which was destined for St. Lucia. The French retained the island for the rest of the war, but it was returned to the British in the peace treaty of 1783. Maroons (runaway slaves) waged an internal guerrilla war against the British which began during the American Revolution in 1780 and lasted until 1814. They were assisted by the forested, mountainous, and rugged terrain of the island, together with the small size of the army garrison. The island was nevertheless a popular destination for American Loyalists. Dominica became an independent republic in 1978.

The Cabrits National Park contains Prince Rupert's Garrison, where some fifty different military structures were constructed between 1770 and 1815. These included Fort Shirley, overlooking Prince Rupert's Bay, with its

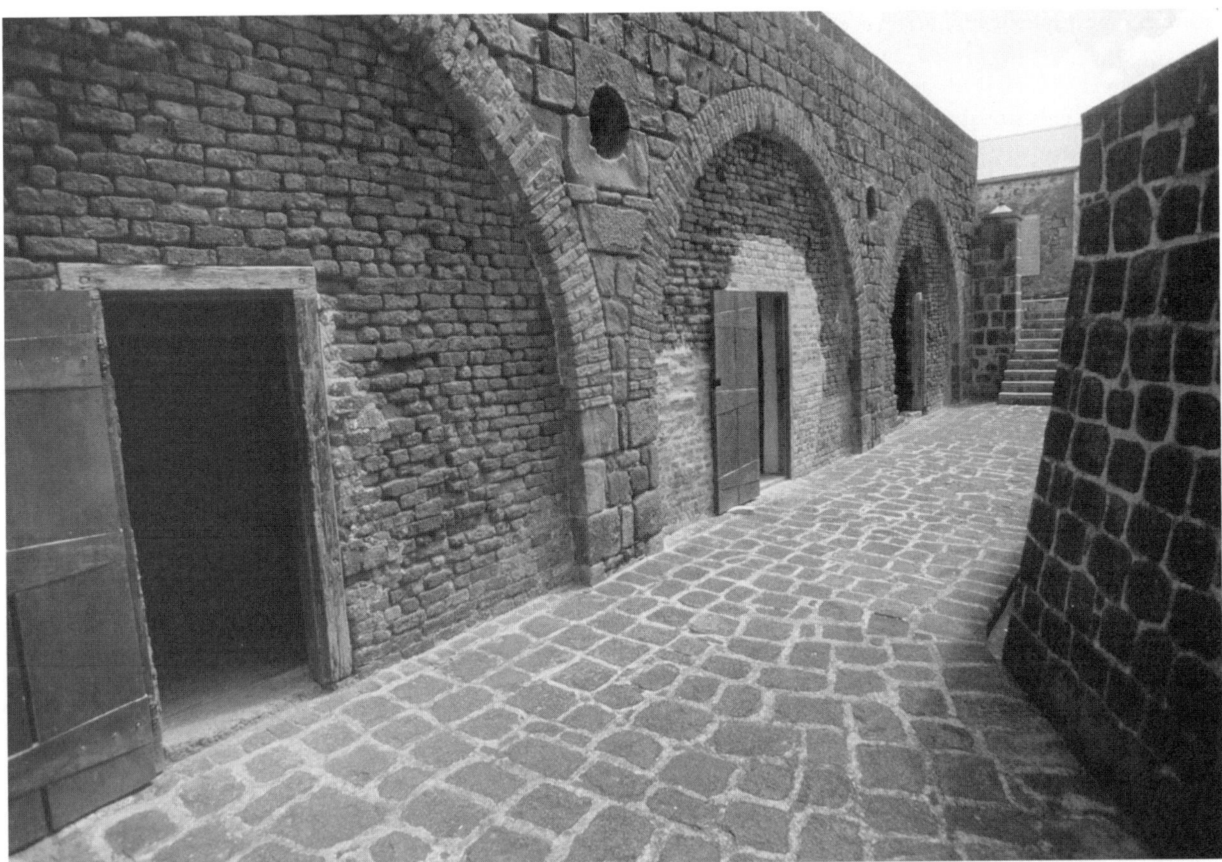

Fort Shirley. *The Cabrits National Park near Portsmouth, Dominica, contains Prince Rupert's Garrison, where some fifty military structures were built between 1770 and 1815. These include Fort Shirley, a restored stone structure that overlooks Prince Rupert's Bay.*

seven-gun batteries, seven cisterns, powder magazines, storehouses, a guardhouse, a parade ground, engineers' quarters, officers' quarters, two hospitals, a commandant's house, and barracks for six hundred men. The structures were mostly built by the British, although there were some additions made by the French during their occupation in 1778 to 1783. They were abandoned as a military post in 1854. There is a museum in the old powder magazine. The site was formed by the twin peaks of volcanoes overlooking Prince Rupert's Bay and Portsmouth, and is surrounded on three sides by water. The park has views of the French islands of Les Saintes, where Rodney won his victory in 1782, and Guadeloupe.

Carib Territory. Dominica is unusual in that some of the indigenous people who predated Columbus and who were decimated elsewhere in the Caribbean survived here. The British surveyed and divided the island into lots in 1763, reserving only 23 acres of mountainous land and rocky shoreline at Salybia for the Caribs. Their descendants continue to live in the region.

Fort Cashacrou, Scotts Head. Overlooking Soufriere Bay, this was the site where the invading French fought the British en route to Pointe Michel on 7 September 1778. It was the first fort captured by the marquis de Bouillé. The ruins of the fort remain, although much of it was destroyed by erosion and fell into the sea. It has a view of Martinique.

Old Mill Cultural Centre at Canefield has a small museum with displays of pre-Columbian artifacts, as well as exhibits of local art and handicrafts.

Prince Rupert's Bay, Portsmouth is a fine natural harbor protected by two hills, the Cabrits. Nelson frequently visited the harbor for wood and water while commanding the H.M.S. *Boreas.*

Rodney's Rock, on the leeward side of the island, was named after Admiral Sir George Rodney and is associated with many legends connected with him. It was supposedly the site where one of the French ships was wrecked following the Battle of the Saintes.

Roseau, the capital. The original town of Roseau was largely destroyed by fire during the occupation of the French in 1778 and 1781, and again in 1795 and 1805. The streets were named after the royal family and contemporary statesmen, including Lord Hillsborough, who held the newly created position of British secretary of state for America after 1768; Great George, after George III; and Hanover, after the house of Hanover. Fort Young Hotel, which defended the harbor, began construction in 1770 on the orders of the first governor Sir William Young and was completed during the French occupation in 1783. It was much damaged in the hurricane of 1979. The House of Assembly stands on the site of the original assembly created in 1765. Fort Morene Bruce was fortified during the eighteenth century with batteries, barracks, and blockhouses. It is accessible via a path called Jack's Walk, named after James Bruce, the British army engineer who designed the fort. The barracks continue to be used for government residences and police training. The fort has good views of the town and Botanical Gardens.

For further information contact: the Dominica Tourist Board, National Development Corporation, P.O. Box 293, Roseau, Commonwealth of Dominica; phone: (767) 448-2045; fax: (767) 448-5840. In the United States contact Steve Johnson at the United States Post Office, 110-64 Queens Boulevard, P.O. Box 42, Forest Hills, N.Y. 11375-6347; phone: (718) 261-9615 / (888) 645-5637; fax: (718) 261-0702; email: dominicany@dominica.dm; website: http://www.dominica.dm.

DOMINICAN REPUBLIC (SANTO DOMINGO)

The Dominican Republic shares the island of Hispaniola with Haiti (formerly St. Domingue). The 18,816-square-mile country was a Spanish colony until 1822 and, following a period of occupation by Haiti, became independent in 1844. It was sacked by Sir Francis Drake in 1586. It was after a failed attack on the island in 1655 that William Penn chose instead to conquer Jamaica. Admiral José de Solano was governor of the island between 1771 and 1778 before becoming commander of the Spanish navy stationed at Havana.

Puerto Plata contains the oldest fort in the New World, the Fortaleza de San Felipe, built between 1520 and 1585. The central keep is now a museum.

For further information contact: Archivo General de la Nación (National Archive), Calle M. East Daz, Santo Domingo, La República Dominicana; Biblioteca Nacional (National Library), César Nicolás Penson 91, Plaza de la Cultura, Santo Domingo, La República Dominicana; Instituto Dominicano de Genealogía, Inc. (Dominican Genealogy Institute, Inc.) P.O. Box 3350, Calle Mercedes, #204, Santo Domingo, República Dominicana; phone: (809) 687-3992; fax: (809) 687-0027; Secretaría de Estado de Turismo, Av. Mèxico esq. C/ 30 de Marzo, Oficinas Gubernamentales Bloque D, Santo Domingo, República Dominicana; phone: (809) 221-4660; fax: (809) 682-3806.

Santo Domingo de Guzmán. The old city was founded by the brother of Christopher Columbus in 1498 and is now a UNESCO Site of World Heritage. The city plan became the blueprint for cities throughout Spanish America. The Cathedral de Santa María de Menor was built in 1523 to 1540 and is located in the center of the Old Town. The Las Mercedes Church dates from 1555. There is a museum in the sixteenth-century Casa de Tostado that includes displays of furnishings and militaria. There are similar displays in the Casa del Cordón, built in 1503 by a patron of the Franciscan Order. The Universidad da San Tomas de Aquina is the oldest university in the Americas (1538). The old city wall contains the remains of the Fort San Felipe and the city gate, the Puerta de San Diego (1540–1555). The Forteleza Ozama dates from 1507. It includes the Casa Batidas (1512) and the Torre del Homenaje (Tower of Homage), built between the sixteenth and eighteenth centuries, where Columbus's son Diego stayed on his arrival in Santo Domingo. The town contains a rich array of palaces and official buildings, including the House of Cord, where Diego Columbus lived while awaiting the building of the Alcázar de Cólon. The Alcázar (1510–1514), sometimes called Columbus Palace, was the home of the Columbus family until 1577 and is now the Viceroyalty Museum. It is adjacent to a group of eight buildings known as Ataranzana, which was the warehouse district, with a sixteenth-century chandlery, a royal armory, and customhouses, and now the home of the Naval Underwater Archaeology Museum. The Calle de las Damas is the oldest street in the city, where there are several noteworthy buildings, including the Casa Francia, which was the home of the conquistador Hernán Cortés, and the Ovando House (1510–1515). The Casas Reales, built in the early sixteenth century, was the headquarters of the governor, the captains general, the Audiencia, the Treasury, and the Supreme Court. It now contains a museum.

GRENADA

Grenada was a British colony from its capture from the French in 1762 until 1974 (except for the brief interval of French occupation between 1779 and 1784). On 4 July 1779 Admiral d'Estaing seized the 120-square-mile island, which was then the largest sugar producer after Jamaica in the British West Indies. Governor Lord Macartney attempted to defend the island with a force of only 150 regulars and 300 militia against 3,000 French troops. The free blacks and free coloreds who were French hastened his surrender by deserting the garrison. The French captured thirty richly laden merchant ships in the port, and d'Estaing sacked the town of St. George because the governor refused to surrender. The British admiral John Byron did not reach the island until 6 July, and his inferior fleet fought an indecisive sea battle against d'Estaing's fleet off the coast of Grenada. Byron then returned to St. Kitts with 183 killed and 340 wounded, as well as considerable damage to the masts and rigging, and six ships disabled. Hurricane Ivan leveled most of the buildings on the island in 2004.

Hospital Hill, overlooking St. George, was stormed and captured by a force of some 3,000 men under the command of Count Dillon and Admiral d'Estaing during the conquest in July 1779. Lord Macartney made a final attempt to resist the invasion with a total force of no more than 500 men, who entrenched themselves at the summit of the hill. The French sustained heavy losses during their successful attack, with some 300 killed and another 200 wounded.

Richmond Hill was the site of four forts. It was the scene of much construction during the American Revolution, including that of Fort Frederick, which was built by the French in 1779 to 1780 and completed by the British in 1784 to 1791, and Fort Mathew, which dates from between 1779 and 1783.

St. George's is the capital town, which was established by the French in 1705 and originally called Fort Royal, but renamed after George III by Governor Robert Melville (1764–1771). The town surrounds a landlocked bay known as the Carenage, or inner harbor, which was used by the British and French fleets during the American Revolution. Many of the original buildings were lost in the fires of 1771 and 1775. Fort St. George was established in about the 1680s and rebuilt in 1705 to 1706. It commands a particularly attractive view of the town. In 1779 Lord Macartney withdrew to the fort and finally surrendered after a bombardment by the guns from Hospital Hill. Until recently the fort contained one of the earliest barracks in the Caribbean, which were built before 1762. It has subterranean passages, one redoubt of the original three, and a small military museum. The hospital (Morne de l'Hopital) was built in the early eighteenth century. Fort Mathew, at the top of Richmond Heights, was once the officers' quarters and mess hall. It had an elaborate kitchen which was still in use in the 1970s. Fort Frederick, above the citadel, survived as a partial ruin.

For further information contact: Grenada Board of Tourism, Burns Point, P.O. Box 293, St. George's, Grenada, West Indies; phone: (473) 440-2279 / 2001 / 3377; fax: (473) 440-6637; email: gbt@caribsurf.com; Grenada Board of Tourism, 317 Madison Avenue, Suite 1704, New York, N.Y. 10017; phone: (212) 687-9554 / (800) 927-9554; fax: (212) 573-9731; email: noel@rfcp.com; Public Library / National Archives, 2 Carenage, St. George's, Grenada; phone: (473) 440-2506.

GUADELOUPE

Guadeloupe is composed of two islands, Basse-Terre and Grande-Terre, which have a combined surface area of 582 square miles. It was settled by the French in 1635 and, apart from two interludes of British occupation in 1759 to 1763 and in 1810, it has remained French.

Basse-Terre, capital of the two islands, contains Fort St. Charles (Fort Louis) and dates from 1643. It is the site of a museum and is well preserved. There are the ruins of batteries at Pointe Allègre and at Deshaies. Vieux Habitants is one of the earliest settlements on Basse-Terre. The stone church was consecrated in 1666. The churchyard has some early tombstones.

Grande-Terre has the eighteenth-century fortress Fort Fleur d'Epée, built on a hillside with a moat and drawbridge. There are many ruins of eighteenth-century sugar mills on both islands.

For further information contact: Office du Tourisme, Syndicat d'Initiative du Moule, Boulevard maritime Damencourt, 97160 Le Moule; phone: 590 (0)5 90 23 89 03; fax: 590 (0)5 90 23 03 58 ;email: info@ot-lemoule.com; Archives Départementales de la Guadeloupe (Guadeloupe Departmental Archive), P.O. Box 74, 97102 Basse-Terre Cedex; Archives Départementales de la Guadeloupe, B.P. 74, 97120 Basse Terre, Cedex, Guadeloupe; French Government Tourist Office, 444 Madison Avenue, 16th Floor, New York, N.Y. 10022; phone: (410) 286-8310; fax: (202) 331-1528; website: http://www.guadeloupe-info.com/index-gb.htm; Archives Départementales de la Guyane, Place Leopold Heder, 97302 Cayenne, Cedex, Guadeloupe.

HAITI (ST. DOMINGUE)

The colony Haiti was ceded to France by the Treaty of Ryswick in 1697, thus splitting the island of Hispaniola with the Spanish colony of Santo Domingo (now the Dominican Republic). On the eve of the American Revolution the island was producing more sugar than the entire produce of all the British islands. It was a major conduit of illicit trade to America during the Revolutionary War. St. Domingue exploited its neutral status before France formally entered the war in 1778, and as early as September 1775, it was the source of large quantities of gunpowder to the rebellion, providing a conduit between France and America. Caron de Beaumarchais, better known as the playwright who wrote *The Marriage of Figaro,* used the guise of a merchant firm called Roderigue Hortalez and Company to establish a regular trade between Europe and America via St. Domingue. The first shipment sailed towards the end of 1776. Beaumarchais kept an agent on the island to oversee the operations of the company called Carabas. Congress also had agents on the island, Richard Harrison at Cap Français and Nicholas Rogers at Port-au-Prince. In addition, there were purchasing agents from America, including Stephen Ceronio at Cap Français and John Dupuy at the Môle St. Nicholas. The island was the base of operations for Admiral D' Estaing's expedition against Savannah, Georgia in 1779. The free colored people and black troops who participated in the campaign included some future leaders of the Haitian Revolution. The island was the intended rendezvous for the combined operation of the French and Spanish fleets against Jamaica in 1782. Admiral de Grasse was on his way from Martinique to St. Domingue when he was intercepted and captured by Admiral Rodney at the Battle of the Saintes. St. Domingue was the scene of the second major revolution in the Americas. After thirteen years of war and a successful slave revolt, it became an independent black republic in 1804. There are few remaining buildings dating from the colonial period.

Cap Hatïen, known in the eighteenth century as Cap Français, La Cap, or by the English as the Cape, is the oldest city in Haiti. In 1781 Admiral de Grasse sailed from here for the Chesapeake, where he played a critical role in preventing the British fleet from relieving the army of Lord Cornwallis. The façade of the city's cathedral dates from the eighteenth century. Fort Picolet, possibly built by Louis XIV's great military architect, Vauban, commands the only navigable channel to the harbor of Cap Hatïen. Fort Magny and Fort St. Joseph are eighteenth century in origin.

Fort Liberté, a town on the north coast, was the location of five forts that guarded the bay, including Fort Dauphin, which dates from 1730. The blockhouse and ruins of the barracks are still visible.

Môle St. Nicholas, in the northeast of the island, was the great naval stronghold commanding the Windward Passage. The harbor, fort, and town are located in a landlocked bay.

Port au Prince. The Ancienne Cathédral Catholique, now very dilapidated, dates from 1720. Fort Nationale, northeast of St. Trinité, dates from the late seventeenth century.

For further information contact: Rehabiliter le Patrimoine Naturel et Historique, 26 Rue Ducoste, Port-au-Prince, République d'Haiti, phone: 509 22 1219; Haitian American Historical Society, Daniel Fils-Aimé, Sr., Chairman, 8340 Northeast Second Avenue, Suite 222, Miami, Fla. 33138; phone: (786) 621-0035; email: hahs@haitianhistory.org; Haitian American Historical Society, P.O. Box 531033, Miami, Fla. 33153; Consulate General of Haiti Tourist Office, 271 Madison Avenue, 17th Floor, New York, N.Y. 10016; phone: (212) 697-9767; fax: (212) 681-6991; website: www.haiti.org. You may also search the database of the civil registers of the Archives Nationales d'Haïti.

JAMAICA

Conquered by the British from the Spanish in 1655 in an expedition led by Admiral Penn and General Venables, the 4,411-square-mile island was the largest and most valuable colony in the British Caribbean until it became independent in 1962. Admiral Penn's son was rewarded with the patent for Pennsylvania by Charles II, largely in gratitude for his father's capture of Jamaica. In 1776 a slave rebellion broke out in Hanover Parish and quickly spread to other parts of the island before being suppressed by British troops on their way to serve in North America. It resulted in the trial of 135 slaves, of whom 17 were executed, 45 transported, and 11 subjected to corporal punishment. The defense of the island was a major priority of the British government during the Revolutionary War. American privateers launched raids such as the one repelled by the fort at St. Ann's Bay in 1777. After their entry into the war, France and Spain planned combined operations against Jamaica. There was a frenzy of military construction following the French invasion threat in late 1778. A series of redoubts were built at intervals up the Cane River Valley, with the first at Drummond's Hill, just south of Newsted, across the track joining the two roads on either side of the Mammee River. In the summer of 1779, when the island was gripped by an invasion scare, Sir Henry Clinton embarked Lord Cornwallis and 4,000 British troops for Jamaica. The crisis illustrated the willingness of Britain to defend the island at all costs, even at the risk of sacrificing the war for America. The economic problems caused by the war were aggravated by one of the worst recorded series of hurricanes (six) in the history of the island, in which an estimated 15,000 slaves perished. Jamaica was the most popular destination in the Caribbean for American Loyalists. As many as 400 white families, together with 5,000 slaves, arrived following the British evacuation of Savannah, Georgia, in July 1782; and another 1,278 whites and 2,613 blacks arrived following the British departure from Charleston, South Carolina the following December.

Apostles' Battery, to the west of Port Royal, was built in the 1740s to protect the south channel into Kingston Harbour. It was a heavily fortified line of twelve guns known as the Twelve Apostles, including nine 42-pounders and three 32-pounders. A stone parapet and paved platform, together with a cistern for 3,000 gallons of water, were added before 1757. There remains the outline of the platform, the northern retaining wall, the cistern, and the magazine. The other buildings were largely removed for a nineteenth-century gun emplacement.

Bath, in the parish of St. Thomas contains hot and cold springs discovered in the 1690s. The buildings are gone except for the foundation plaque, which is set in the wall of the modern bathhouse. The Botanic Garden was established during the American Revolution in 1779. The first breadfruit seedling from the Pacific was transplanted by the H.M.S. *Bounty* to Bath in 1793.

Cockpit Country is an area which stretches across the parishes of Trelawany, St. Elizabeth, and St. James. It was the sanctuary of the maroons, the runaway slaves who fought two major wars with the British, in the 1690s to the 1730s and again in the 1790s. It was ideal territory for maroons because of its rugged terrain, which was difficult to traverse. The white limestone formation produces a series of irregular circular arenas that look like inverted cones from the air, and terminate in most cases in a sinkhole in the apex. The British feared that the maroons might support a foreign enemy, and this made them the subject of much suspicion among the whites during the American Revolution. Their main historic towns are Trelawny Town (now Maroon Town) in St. James and Accompong in St. Elizabeth. Trelawny Town still contains barracks built by the British during the Maroon Wars of the 1690s to 1730s.

Falmouth in the parish of Trelawny was laid out in the 1770s following the creation of the new parish in 1770, which was named after Governor Sir William Trelawny, who died in office in 1772. It is a remarkable survival of a Georgian town in the Caribbean, although most of the buildings are now dilapidated. They date from between 1790 and 1830.

Fort Augusta guarded the narrows into Kingston Harbour and faces across the bay opposite Port Royal. It can be reached by the Portmore Causeway. The construction began in 1740 with the outbreak of war with Spain. It was named in honor of the mother of George III and completed in the mid-1750s. Three hundred people died from an explosion in the powder magazine when lightning struck three thousand barrels of powder in 1763. There remain important features of the fort, including the curtain and redan guarding the western approach. The magazine is now used as a chapel. The rest is used as a prison.

Fort Haldane has a commanding view of the town and harbor of Port Maria in the parish of St. Mary. It was named after General Haldane, the governor in 1759. It originally contained an officers' house, barracks, and kitchen. A battery and brick pitched-roof powder magazine are all that survive.

Kingston, with its harbor and backdrop of the Blue Mountains, was the largest town in the British West Indies in the eighteenth century and the commercial center of Jamaica. It was at Kingston that the Boston-born Eliphalet Fitch obtained the military supplies for Francisco Miranda that were used by the Spanish in the invasion of the Bahamas in 1782. Miranda was then a visiting Spanish official arranging a prisoner exchange under a flag of truce, but was later to become a revolutionary leader in Venezuela. Kingston was severely damaged by fire and an earthquake in 1907. Headquarters House, built by a merchant in 1750, is now the offices of the Jamaica National Trust. The Institute of Jamaica is at East Street. It houses the National Library, which possesses the finest collection of manuscripts and books pertaining to Jamaica and, more generally, to the West Indies. The Kingston Synagogue has some very early gravestones. The approaches to Kingston and its harbor were protected by Port Royal, Fort Augusta, Fort Johnston, Fort Small (Fort Clarence), and Rockfort.

Lucea is a port town in the parish of Hanover on the northwest coast of Jamaica. Fort Charlotte was one of the larger fortresses in the island, mounting twenty-two to twenty-five guns, of which three survive on rotary carriages. It is situated on a peninsula overlooking the harbor of the town. It was probably built around 1752. The walls were 6 feet thick and were built in 1761. The north of the island was particularly vulnerable to attacks by pirates and privateers. The admiral commanding the Jamaica station at Port Royal sent two ships to Lucea to help quell the slave rebellion that broke out in Hanover in 1776.

Montego Bay, in the parish of St. James, was the chief north-coast port for much of the eighteenth century. It was protected by Fort Montego (Fort Frederick), which had a regular garrison of British troops and was built in 1750. It had gun embrasures, barracks, and a hospital. It mounted two 24-pounders and eight 18-pounders in 1764. A cannon exploded in the face of a gunner during a gun salute to celebrate the surrender of Havana in 1760. The foundation stone of the parish church of St. James was laid the year of the Battle of Bunker Hill in 1775, and the building was completed in 1782. Today there are remains of a large powder magazine.

Ocho Rios has the remains of a fort dating from about 1777 to 1780 and restored in the 1970s. It still has four cannon.

Plantation Houses. There are number of plantation houses of the period. Rose Hall, constructed between 1770 and 1780 near Montego Bay, is one of the grandest great houses in the Caribbean. It is open to the public. Although it is very impressive, only the original pavilion of the house remains. It had 12 bedrooms, 52 doors, and 365 windows. Greenwood Plantation House was built between 1780 and 1800 and is associated with the family of Elizabeth Barrett Browning. It houses the largest plantation library on the island and has one of the finest museum and antique collections. Other great houses include Bellfied, near Montego Bay, which is a restored 1735 great house on the Barnett estate open to the public and still a functioning plantation; Cardiff Hall (c. 1765); Colbeck Castle near Old Harbour, St. Catherine, which was built as a fortified house in the late 1660s; Drax Hall in St. Ann (established 1690); Good Hope in Trelawny (c. 1755), which contains furniture original to the house; Green Park in Trelawny; Hampstead and Retreat estates, which belonged to a colored woman, Jane Stone, who died at the age of eighty in 1774; Halse Hall, a seventeenth-century fortified home in the Rio Minho Valley; Minard in St. Ann; Seville in St. Ann (1745); Fairfield in St. James, built in 1776; Stewart Castle, near Falmouth, a fortified home dating from the early eighteenth century; and Stokes Hall in St. Thomas, which was one of the earliest seventeenth-century plantations and is now a ruin maintained by the National Trust. There are examples of slave hospitals at Orange Valley in Trelawny and Kenilworth in Hanover.

Port Antonio in Portland is one of the finest ports in Jamaica, with a backdrop of the Blue Mountains. Fort George is located on a peninsula called Upper Titchfield. It was designed by Charles Lilly, who was for many years the chief military engineer in Jamaica. He began the fort when he was nearly seventy, following his return to the island in 1728. It contained embrasures for twenty-two guns in a 10-foot-thick wall, which remains together with the original parade ground, bastion, and old barracks. It is now Titchfield High School. The courthouse dates from the eighteenth century.

Port Henderson (New Brighton), St. Catherine, is a seaside village about 4 miles from Passage Fort and 6 miles from Spanish Town. It became the sea link to the capital, Spanish Town, with the silting up of the Rio Cobre, and provided much of the stone for the fortifications of the island. It contains the Long House, a hotel erected about 1780 by the entrepreneur John Henderson. A small redoubt was constructed during the frenzy of the invasion scare of 1778. The semicircular platform can still be seen about 20 feet up the hillside near thc junction of the Fort Augusta Road. It probably contained about half a dozen guns to prevent landings by small boats. Rodney's Lookout, a signal station, was built on the crest of Port Henderson in response to invasion scares in the early 1780s and was damaged by the earthquake of 1782. The ruins are on the top of a flight of steps near the Apostle's Battery. It was probably renamed following Rodney's victory at the Saintes. The British feared that an invasion might be accomplished by a landing in the Hellshire Hills, where the enemy might evade the guns of Kingston Harbour and enter Spanish Town. The British built two forts with semicircular platforms, both of which survive. Fort Small (renamed Fort Clarence in 1799) was built on the end of Port Henderson Hill. It was heavily armed, to prevent ships supporting an enemy landing, with eight 24-pounders and one 10-inch mortar. Five of the 24-pounders remain, on their original platform with the carriages rotted away, together with the magazine and platform. Fort Johnston was built on the plain that separates Port Henderson Hill from the Hellshire Hump ridge. It was more lightly armed than the other forts, with the intention of resisting infantry troops rather than ships. The magazine is lost, but the barracks and platform remain with all the original cannon, four 12-pounders and five 6-pounders.

Port Morant is a port town 7 miles from Morant Bay that was protected by Fort Lindsay. The fort is on the opposite side of the bay from the town. It was fortified in the mid-eighteenth century, replacing an earlier fort, Fort William, that was abandoned due to erosion. There are remnants, but the battery is gone.

Port Royal was a British naval base for the Jamaican squadron located in Kingston Harbour on a 7-mile peninsula known as the Palisadoes. The dockyard is next to the site of a sunken city that was once the second-largest town in English America after Boston, until two-thirds of the original town was destroyed by an earthquake and a tidal wave on 7 June 1692. The dockyard supplied, refitted, and watered ships of the Royal Navy between 1735 and 1905. Admiral Sir George Rodney did much to develop the facility when he was the resident commander between 1771 and 1774. Sir Peter Parker, who had collaborated with Sir Henry Clinton in the ill-fated attempt on Charleston, South Carolina, in 1776, commanded the

Jamaican fleet at Port Royal between 1778 and 1782. Horatio Nelson first visited the dockyard in May 1777 at the age of nineteen, and he commanded the batteries at Fort Charles in 1779. He shared quarters with Captain William Cornwallis, the brother of the general Lord Charles Cornwallis, who surrendered at Yorktown. After returning to Jamaica from an expedition to Nicaragua in 1780, Nelson was nursed back to life by the colored proprietress of his lodging house, who was called Cubah, or Couba Cornwallis. The dockyard was defended by a group of fortresses that included Fort Charles, renamed after Charles II, which was built between 1660 and 1696. It alone among the fortresses encircling the harbor survived the hurricane of 1692. It was rebuilt in its present form in 1722 to 1724. The wooden walkway in Fort Charles is now called Nelson's Quarterdeck. The batteries on the sea front had a double tier of guns that numbered 104 in 1767. The fort now contains a maritime museum. St. Peter's Church, built in 1725 to 1726, contains many naval and military monuments. There are some remains of a fort erected at the eastern end of Port Royal which was called "Prince William Henry's Polygon" when it was completed in 1783, and which was much damaged by the hurricane of 1787. The northern bastion is located outside the eastern wall enclosing Morgan's Harbour beach club. There is a museum with archaeological artifacts of the sunken city of Port Royal in the Royal Naval Hospital (1818–1819).

Rio Bueno contains the deepest harbor in the island. Columbus anchored his ships for three days here on his first visit to Jamaica in 1494. Fort Dundas was built during the American Revolution and dates from 1778.

Rockfort dates from 1729. It was designed to protect the eastern routes to Kingston. It is largely intact with its large bastion to the south, its entrance gate, its magazine, and its northern curtain dug into the Long Mountain. It was capable of mounting seventeen guns. The sites of the guardhouse and barracks are visible. There is a track to a redoubt, about 100 feet high and 200 yards east of the fort, on Long Mountain.

St. Andrew. The Parish Church dates from 1700, although there were earlier structures, and the parish registers date back to 1666. It contains many impressive monuments of the eighteenth century. Stony Hill had a garrison and barracks. There is a small magazine that survives. It was to be a last refuge in the hills in the event of an invasion in which the enemy seized the Liguanea plain. Three redoubts were constructed in 1778. The first, with a 24-pounder and four 6-pounder cannon, was on the site of the present Fort Belle, just to the north of the bridge and over the gully on the main road out of Kingston. A smaller, second battery was constructed a few hundred yards northward on the site of the present location of 34 Stilwell Road. The third battery, designed for four guns, remains intact at Bridgemont Heights.

Spanish Town, also known as St. Jago de la Vega, was capital of Jamaica until 1870. The impressive buildings around the main square indicate the economic importance of Jamaica to Britain. The King's House, the residence of the governor, was begun during the administration of Lieutenant Governor Henry Moore in 1759 to 1762; he later became governor of New York during the Stamp Act crisis. The house was completed in 1762 to 1765 following the arrival of Governor William Henry Lyttleton, who was a former governor of South Carolina. The dimensions are much larger than those of the governor's palace at Williamsburg, the capital of the largest colony in North America (Virginia). Unfortunately, only the façade survives today following a fire that gutted the building in 1925. There is an archaeological museum next to the house and the Jamaican People's Museum of Craft and Technology. The House of the Assembly on the east side of the square took some twenty years to complete from the time it was started around 1762. In December 1774 the assembly members composed a petition to George III sympathetic to the Americans that elicited the thanks of Congress and the Connecticut House of Representatives. The Rodney Memorial on the north side of the square was commissioned by the island assembly to celebrate the victory of Admiral Sir George Rodney against de Grasse at the battle of the Saintes in 1782. The statue was designed by John Bacon, the leading contemporary English sculptor, who portrayed Rodney in classical garb. The Anglican Cathedral of St. James was built as the parish church of St. Catherine in 1714. It contains numerous monuments, including one by Bacon and a memorial to Sir Basil Keith, who died during his tenure as governor in 1777. Spanish Town contained a barracks for one of the two peacetime regiments of the British army, but the current structure dates from 1791. The Jamaica Archives are housed in the building behind the Rodney Memorial.

For further information contact: Jamaica Tourist Board, 3530 Ashford Dunwoody Road N.E., Box 304, Atlanta, Ga. 30319; phone: (770) 452-7799; fax: (770) 452-0220; and Jamaica Historical Society, c/o Department of History, University of the West Indies, Mona Campus, Kingston 7, Jamaica. At the National Library Institute of Jamaica, advance permission to use the library's resources is recommended. You can find the library at 12 East Street, 6 Kingston, Jamaica, or via telephone at (809) 922-0620. The Jamaica Archives are located in Spanish Town, Jamaica and can be contacted at (809) 984-2581. At the Registrar General records of births, baptisms, deaths, burials, and marriages are available. The registrar is located at

Vital Records Information, Twickenham Park, Spanish Town, St. Catherine, Jamaica, and can also be reached at (876) 984–3041 / 5, http://www.rgd.gov.jm, or information @rgd.gov.jm.

MARTINIQUE

Martinique was the headquarters of the French navy in the Caribbean. It was the base of the French admirals associated with key events in the Revolutionary War—d'Estaing and de Grasse. The 425-square-mile island was settled by the French in 1635 and it remains under French government as an overseas department. In 1776 Congress sent the twenty-four-year-old William Bingham as an agent to the island with instructions to procure munitions for the Continental army and to encourage a French alliance against the British. He held court with the captains of American privateers and issued blank commissions for privateers in the American Coffee House in Fort-de-France. The protection given by the island to American privateers became a major issue between the British government and the court of France. In January 1779 Admiral John Byron blockaded d'Estaing's French fleet for five months at Fort Royal. In 1781 Sir Samuel Hood unsuccessfully attempted to prevent the entry of de Grasse into Martinique before his junction with additional ships in the harbor and his departure for Yorktown.

Fort-de France, formerly known as Fort Royal, has been the capital of Martinique since 1680. Fort St. Louis gave shelter to the fleet and dates from 1638. It is still used by the army, and it has its original ramparts and dungeons. Jacques Dyel du Parquet began construction on the rocky peninsula in the bay in 1640. It was attacked by the Dutch in 1674 and captured by the English in 1673 (as well as in 1794 and 1809). It was much strengthened in the early eighteenth century according to the classic system of Vauban. It had a moat, which was filled in to become the Boulevard of the Chevalier de Ste.-Marthe. The town was nearly destroyed by a fire in 1890.

La Pagerie is a sugar plantation near Trois-Islets on the southern shore of Fort de France Bay. It was associated with the future Empress Marie Joséphine Rose Tasher de la Pagerie, who was born in 1766 and married Napoleon in 1796. The kitchen, a single stone building, remains from her time; it is now a museum. Joséphine was baptized at Trois Ilets in an eighteenth-century church which still exists, but she lived most of her first eight years on St. Lucia.

Plantations and Plantation Houses. Leyritz Plantation dates from the early 1700s, when it was built for a cavalry officer, Michel de Leryritz, who was a native of Bordeaux. The 250-acre sugar plantation borders the Altantic Coast and has a backdrop to the west of Mount Pelée. It contains a great house, granary, chapel, sugar factory, and original slave huts. Other plantation houses on Martinique include the Dominican Fond Saint-Jacques Estate, built in 1658 and rebuilt in 1769; Pécoul (1760); La Frégate, a seventeenth-century house; and La Gaoulé, located at La Diament on the south coast, which dates from 1740. The St. James plantation house is now a museum of the history and production of rum.

Pointe du Diamant (Diamond Rock) is off the southern tip of the western coast and had a fortress. It is visible from Pigeon Island on St. Lucia.

La Poterie, a large clay factory, was established in 1694 at Trois Ilets. It includes the manager's house, slave cottages, kilns, stores, administration, and ancillary building.

St. Pierre was leveled and thirty thousand people killed by the eruption of Mont Pelé in 1902.

For further information contact: Bureau du Patrimoine, 43 bis rue Jacques Cazotte, 97200 Fort-de-France, Martinique; phone: 596 63 85 55; French Government Tourist Office, Martinique, 444 Madison Ave, 16th Floor, New York, N.Y. 10022; phone: (900) 990-0040 / (202) 659-7779 / (800) 391-4909; website: www.martinique.org; Saba Tourist Bureau, phone: 011 599 416 2231; Archives Départinentales de la Martinique, B.P. 720 Boulevard du Chevalier de Sainte-Marie, 97262 Fort de France, Martinique; Université des Antilles et de la Guyane, Bibliotheque Universitaire, Campus Universitaire, BP7210 Schoelcher, Martinique; Archives Départementales de la Martinique (Martinique Departmental Archive), P.O. Box 649, 97262 Fort-de-France Cedex.

MONTSERRAT

Montserrat was one of the four principal islands in the colony of the British Leeward Islands at the time of the American Revolution. Following French entry into the American Revolution in 1778, it constantly faced the peril of a French attack, especially during the voyages of Admiral d'Estaing in the spring of 1779. On 28 and 29 April of that year the governor expected an imminent invasion by five French ships of the line off the island. In July the French fleet was in sight for three days, during which time the ships exchanged fire with the batteries around Plymouth. Their aim was the surrender of the island. Following the surrender of St. Kitts in 1782, Montserrat also submitted to the French, but was restored to Britain by the peace in 1783. The island was severely damaged by a volcanic eruption of the Soufriere Hills on 18 July 1995 which destroyed the capital town of Plymouth. The island is beginning to attract tourists back, but a large area affected by the volcano is prohibited to both visitors and residents in an exclusion zone. The boundary for the exclusion zone is from Plymouth and southwards to St. Patrick's through Windy Hill and Harris, and down to the east coast at the site of W. H. Bramble Airport.

NEVIS

Nevis was a British colony that was first settled by the English in 1628 and that became independent, in a federation with St. Kitts, in 1983. It is separated by a strait of 2 miles from St. Kitts. Alexander Hamilton, the aide-de-camp to George Washington during the Revolutionary War and the secretary of the treasury in the first administration of Washington, was born on Nevis. There were riots in Nevis against the Stamp Act in 1765. Following the entry of France into the American Revolution, this 35-square-mile island was constantly threatened with invasion, especially by Admiral d'Estaing in 1779. On 27 April of that year, five of his ships came down in a direct line of battle off Charlestown. The headmost ship, of 84 guns, came within reach of cannon fire. The inhabitants expected an attack at every minute, but the ships tacked and stood to windward. On 3 May, Admiral Byron was off Nevis looking for de Grasse with 20 ships of the line and 2 frigates. On 22 July the French fleet again passed very near to the forts. In February 1782 the island submitted to the French following the surrender of St. Kitts, but was restored to the British by the peace of 1783.

Bath House was built by John Huggins in 1778. It is located near sulphur springs which were believed to have medicinal qualities. As early as 1625, the waters were recommended in an account by Robert Harcourt of Stanton Harcourt near Oxford. The bathhouse continues to function, but the hotel, which once had a ballroom and was intended to accommodate fifty guests, is in ruins. It commands a pleasant view of St. Kitts and St. Eustatius.

Charlestown became the capital after an earthquake damaged Jamestown in 1660. Many of the original buildings, including the Court House, were destroyed in the earthquake of 1843. It was the scene of Stamp Act riots on 1 November 1765 after the collector of stamps fled from St. Kitts following riots on the night of 31 October. In Charlestown the "Sons of Liberty" burnt two houses and loaded the stamps on to a navy longboat which they then set on fire. The Museum of Nevis History is located in Hamilton House, which is built on the foundations of the birthplace of Alexander Hamilton. He was born out of wedlock some time between 1755 and 1757 (most probably in January of the latter year). His origins were always a cause of embarrassment to him, and the jest of his political opponents in the United States. He lived on the island until the age of nine, then moved to St. Croix with his mother. The two-story building was constructed around 1680, destroyed in an earthquake in 1840, and then restored in 1983. Prince William Street commemorates the 1787 royal visit of Prince William, a younger son of George III. He served in the Royal Navy in the Caribbean during the later years of the American Revolution. There is a Jewish cemetery in Government Road with nineteen tombstones dating from 1654 to 1768.

Fort Charles guarded the southern entrance to Charlestown and was built in 1680. It once enclosed six acres, with thirteen cannon, two bastions facing out to sea, two ramparts, and moats on the leeward side. The perimeter wall, the cistern, and the powder magazine survive, together with dismounted guns with "G.R." on the barrel, for "Georgius Rex" (King George), and "W.C." on the other other side, for the makers Walder & Co. of Rotherham, England. This was the site where the Nevis Council and President John Herbert met to sign the capitulation terms to the French in February 1782. There are also some remains of fortifications at Mosquito Point and a battery at Saddle Hill (1740).

Montpelier was the location of the marriage of Horatio Nelson and Frances Nisbet on 11 March 1787. She was the widow of a local doctor, and he was captain of the H.M.S. *Boreas.* Prince William Henry, the future King William IV, gave the bride away. The plantation belonged to her uncle, John Herbert, the president of the council of Nevis. It was the largest house on the island at the time. Nelson was in Nevis enforcing the Navigation Acts against illicit trade between the island and the United States. He was virtually prisoner at one time on board his own ship, facing suits from planters who opposed restrictions on the trade with the newly independent United States.

Mount Nevis, or Nevis Peak (3,596 feet), has views from the summit of Barbuda, Redonda, St. Kitts, St. Eustatius, and Saba.

The Nelson Museum is located near Government House. Originally, the collection belonged to Robert Abrahams, a lawyer and author from Philadelphia, who exhibited it at his residence at Morning Star. It includes memorabilia from the life of Admiral Horatio Nelson, including parts of the set of the Royal Worcester china plates commissioned for Nelson's wedding in Nevis. Nelson spent much of his career in the Caribbean during the American Revolutionary War.

Plantation Houses. The Eden Brown Estate was built in 1740. It was never occupied, but is an impressive ruin.

Hamilton House. *Alexander Hamilton was born in Charlestown on Nevis around 1757 in a house that was destroyed by an earthquake in 1840. Hamilton House was later built on its foundation, and now houses the Museum of Nevis History.* © TONY ARRUZA/CORBIS.

Other estate houses include Mount Pleasant, which dates from the 1770s; Mountravers, which has a slave prison, and dates from the 1770s; the Nisbet Plantation House, which has a mill dating to about 1778; and the Old Manor estate house, near Clay Ghaut, which dates from the late seventeenth century.

St. John's Fig Tree Church. The parish register contains an entry for the marriage of Horatio Nelson to Frances Nisbet in 1787. There are tombstones in the graveyard dating from 1682.

For further contact information see ST. KITTS.

PUERTO RICO

The 3,340-square-mile island was a Spanish colony between 1508 and 1898, when it was ceded to the United States. During the American Revolution there was much discussion among the British about invading Puerto Rico. It was an object advocated by the governor of the Leeward Islands, William Mathew Burt. Major General John Vaughan drew up plans for such an expedition in December 1779, but the British had too few troops and were largely on the defensive in the Caribbean. Furthermore, like Cuba and the Dominican Republic, the defenses of Puerto Rico were greatly strengthened in the decade before the American Revolution as part of the naval and colonial defense program initiated by Charles III. The reform of the garrison and improvement in the defenses was implemented by Alejandro O'Reilly and Tomas O'Daly, who were both descendants of "Wild Geese" Irishmen who served with the Spanish army after fleeing the British in Ireland. O'Reilly later presided over the transfer of New Orleans from France to Spain in 1769 and became governor of Louisiana (1766–1770).

Fort San Cristobal is half a mile east of El Morro on Avenida Muñoz Rivera leading into the Plaza de Colon. The original batteries were greatly strengthened between 1765 and 1772 by an engineer named Tomas O'Daly.

Fort de San Gerónimo del Boquerón in the Condado Lagoon was begun in the sixteenth century. It contains a museum relating to the military history of Puerto Rico.

San Juan was named by the conquistador Juan Ponce de León. It has some eight hundred historic structures and six monuments designated a UNESCO World Heritage Site. It was primarily a military town because the port served the ships sailing between Spain and its colonies in the Americas. La Fortaleza is the city's oldest fortress, built about 1520, with a tower and gate that date from 1540. It became a storehouse for bullion and the residence of governors, and it has remained so for four hundred years. The major fortress, the San Felipe del Morro, dates from 1539 but it was redesigned during the American Revolution and completed in 1783. The six fortified levels rise 140 feet above sea level. It protected the entrances to the bay and repelled an attack of Drake and Hawkins in 1595. The castle has a panoramic view of San Juan. El Canuelo is a small fort in the harbor. The old city is surrounded by the original wall, which dates from 1630. The Castillo San Cristóbal was built in the decade before the American Revolution, between 1766 and 1772, and was modified in 1783. There is a military museum in the Fort San Jerónimo (1788–1797). The Dominican Convent, El Convento Dominicano, was begun in 1523 on land donated by Ponce de León. The seventeenth-century Carmelite convent is now a hotel called El Convento. The Casa del Callejón is an eighteenth-century mansion on Calle Fortaleza. It is now a museum which has exhibits on colonial architecture in the old city. The Cathedral of San Juan de Bautista is at Cristo and Luna. It was founded by the Dominicans in 1523 and contains the tomb of Ponce de León. Casa Blanca (1523) was the fortified mansion overlooking Juan Bay which was occupied by the family of Ponce de León. It is now a museum.

For further information contact: Archivo General de Puerto Rico, Instituto de Cultura, P.O. Box 9024184, San Juan, PR 00902-4184; phone: (787) 722-2113; Archivo Historico de Caguas, Departamento de Desarrollo Cultural Municipio de Caguas, P.O. Box 907, Caguas, PR 00726; phone: (787) 258-0070; Archivo Historico de Mayaguez, Municipio de Mayaguez, P.O. Box 447, Mayaguez, PR 00681; phone: (787) 833-5195; Archivo Historico Municipal, Municipio de San German, P.O. Box 85, San German, PR 00683; phone: (787) 892-7979; Biblioteca Regional del Caribe (Caribbean Regional Library) y de Estudios Latinoamericanos, P.O. Box 21927, San Juan, P.R. 00931-1927; phone: (787) 764-0000; email: vtorres@upracd.upr.clu.edu or cromero@upracd.upr.clu.edua; Archivo General de Puerto Rico (Puerto Rico General Archive), Apartado 4184, San Juan, PR 00905-4184; Registro de Propiédad (Property Registrar), Sección 2, Apartado 2551, Ponce, PR 00733-2551; Sociédad Puertorriqueña de Genealogía (Puerto Rican Genealogical Society), 103 Avenida Universidad, Ste. 239, Río Piedras, PR 00925; Puerto Rico Institute of Culture, Museums, and Parks; phone: (787) 724-5477.

ST. BARTHÉLÉMEW (ST. BARTHOLOMEW, ST. BARTS, OR ST. BARTH)

St. Bartholomew is an island of only 8 square miles which was occupied by France in 1648. It was briefly captured by the British in January 1779 and recaptured by the French on 28 February 1779. The French ceded the island in 1784 to Sweden in exchange for trading rights at Gothenburg. It was restored to France in 1877.

For further information contact: St. Barthelemy (St. Barts), French Government Tourist Office, 444 Madison Avenue, 16th Floor; New York, N.Y. 10022; phone: (212) 838-7800; fax: (212) 838-7855; website: www.st-barths.com; www.caribbean-direct.com.

ST. CROIX

St. Croix was the largest Danish colony in the Virgin Islands from 1733 until its sale to the United States in 1917. At the age of nine Alexander Hamilton moved to the 82-square-mile island with his mother, and there, years later, published his first article, in the *Royal Danish American Gazette.* A native of St. Croix, Abram Markoe, organized the first troop of Light Horse in Philadelphia. The flag he commissioned for them was a forerunner of the Stars and Stripes. (He later gave his property for the site of the first presidential house in the United States.) On 25 October 1776 Frederiksted in St. Croix became the first foreign port to salute the American flag, but it was unofficial, occurring when the ship was leaving the port with a small cargo of gunpowder. The first official salute is therefore usually attributed to St. Eustatius, in the following November.

Christiansted was founded in 1734 by the Danish West India and Guinea Company. Alexander Hamilton, together with his mother and brother, lived in a two-story house at 34 Company Street next to the Anglican church after they were abandoned by James Hamilton in 1766. His mother ran a shop on the ground floor. She bought some of her merchandise from the New York merchants David Beekman and Nicholas Cruger, who were to become the patrons of the young Alexander Hamilton. She suddenly died on 19 Feburary 1768, and her small inheritance was claimed by the son by her first marriage, which meant that there was nothing for her two boys by James Hamilton. The boys were then placed under the guardianship of their first cousin, Peter Lytton. On 16 July he committed suicide. His father arrived to adopt the boys but died shortly afterwards, leaving them again orphaned and alone. Alexander then began to clerk for Beekman and Cruger. He became conversant in several languages and in dealing with different currencies, and traded throughout the Leeward Islands. He moved to the home of Thomas Stevens, a well-respected merchant, in King Street, and also found a mentor in the pastor of the Scottish Presbyterian church, Hugh Knox, who had moved to the island from Saba. It was through this connection that Hamilton left to study at the Elizabethtown Academy in New Jersey. The Alexander Hamilton House at 55 King Street was built in the 1750s, then rebuilt following a fire in the 1970s. On the same street, 52 King Street is an early-eighteenth-century residence. The old West India and Guinea Company warehouse was built in 1749 and is now the post office. The Steeple Building (1753) was the first Lutheran church. Fort Christiansvaern (1734 and partly rebuilt in 1772) and Government House (built between 1747 and 1830) are located on the waterfront of Christiansted; they are a National Historic Site. The fort is well preserved, with barracks, dungeon, powder magazine, officers, kitchen, battery, battlements, a double entrance staircase, and sally port.

Frederiksted lost many of its original buildings owing to a tidal wave in 1867 and a fire in 1878. Along the waterfront was the warehouse of Nicholas Cruger, the New York employer of Alexander Hamilton. Fort Frederik, begun in 1752, was the site of the (unofficial) first foreign salute of the American flag. The fort retains its garrison, barracks, arsenal, canteen, stables, courtyard, and commandants' quarters (1760).

The Grange was the plantation of the maternal aunt of Alexander Hamilton, Ann Faucette, and her husband James Lytton, located outside the capital Christiansted. The couple had left Nevis for St. Croix. They hosted Hamilton's mother, Rachel Faucette, and grandmother, Mary Faucette, who also left Nevis for St. Croix. Hamilton's mother had her ill-fated wedding at the age of sixteen to Johann Michael Lavien in St. Croix. Her husband later had her imprisoned for adultery in the fort, Christiansvaern. Following her release after three to five months in prison she fled the island, leaving behind a son by her marriage, and sought refuge in St. Kitts in 1750. Lavien succeeded in obtaining a formal divorce in 1759 when Rachel moved to Nevis, where she gave birth to Alexander, whose father was James Hamilton. Lavien referred in the divorce papers to her "whore-children" born after her departure from St. Croix. In April 1765 Rachel returned to St. Croix when James Hamilton was representing Archibald Ingram of St. Kitts in a debt-collection case against Alexander Moir in Christiansted. James Hamilton absconded upon the completion of the case, abandoning his wife and children in St. Croix. Her sister and brother-in-law, who owned the Grange, had already left the island, sold the plantation, and returned to Nevis. There is a monument erected in her memory by Gertrude Atherton.

For further information contact: United States Virgin Islands Department of Tourism, P.O. Box 4538, Christiansted, St. Croix, Virgin Islands 00822; phone: (340) 773-0495; fax: (340) 773-5074.

ST. DOMINGUE. *See* HAITI.

ST. EUSTATIUS (STATIA)

An island of only 9 square miles, St. Eustatius was settled by the Dutch in 1635. During the American Revolution it was able to exploit the neutrality of the Netherlands (until 1781) to become the leading source of supplies and gunpowder to the Patriots in North America. The island was so wealthy that it was known as the "Golden Rock." On 16 November 1776 Fort Oranje fired what is often regarded as the first official salute of the American flag at the *Andrew Doria*, a ship of the Continental navy which was carrying a copy of the Declaration of Independence. The British observed the scene from 8 miles away at Brimstone Hill in St. Kitts. The date of the event is now a national holiday. Sir George Rodney and General John Vaughan captured the island on 3 February 1781. They carried out the attack before the inhabitants were even aware of the outbreak of war between Britain and the Netherlands. Rodney ordered that the Dutch flag remain flying and surprised many ships. Rodney proceeded to plunder the island and auction the proceeds. But the capture proved a fiasco: Rodney failed to intercept de Grasse's fleet en route from France to Yorktown, where it played a critical role in the defeat of the British. Rodney sailed home rather than follow de Grasse, pleading ill health, but his first priority on returning to Britain was to defend his behavior at St. Eustatius against his critics in Parliament. The fleet carrying the prizes from St. Eustatius back to England was captured by the French. On 26 November the marquis de Bouillé, the French governor of Martinique, surprised the garrison and retook the island from the British. The British officer in command was later court-martialed and found guilty of neglect. The French seized 2 million livres, including the pay for the British troops in North America.

Fort Amsterdam, more correctly named Concordia, was located at the northeast of the island facing the Atlantic Ocean, near a cliff overlooking the Bargine Bay and Great Bay. It is marked on a French map of 1781.

Fort Oranje (Fort Orange) in Oranjestad was built in 1629 by the French. It was rebuilt, enlarged, and named by the Zeelanders in 1636. It was constructed around a plaza facing the sea, and had sixteen cannon. Abraham Revené lived in the commander's house when he

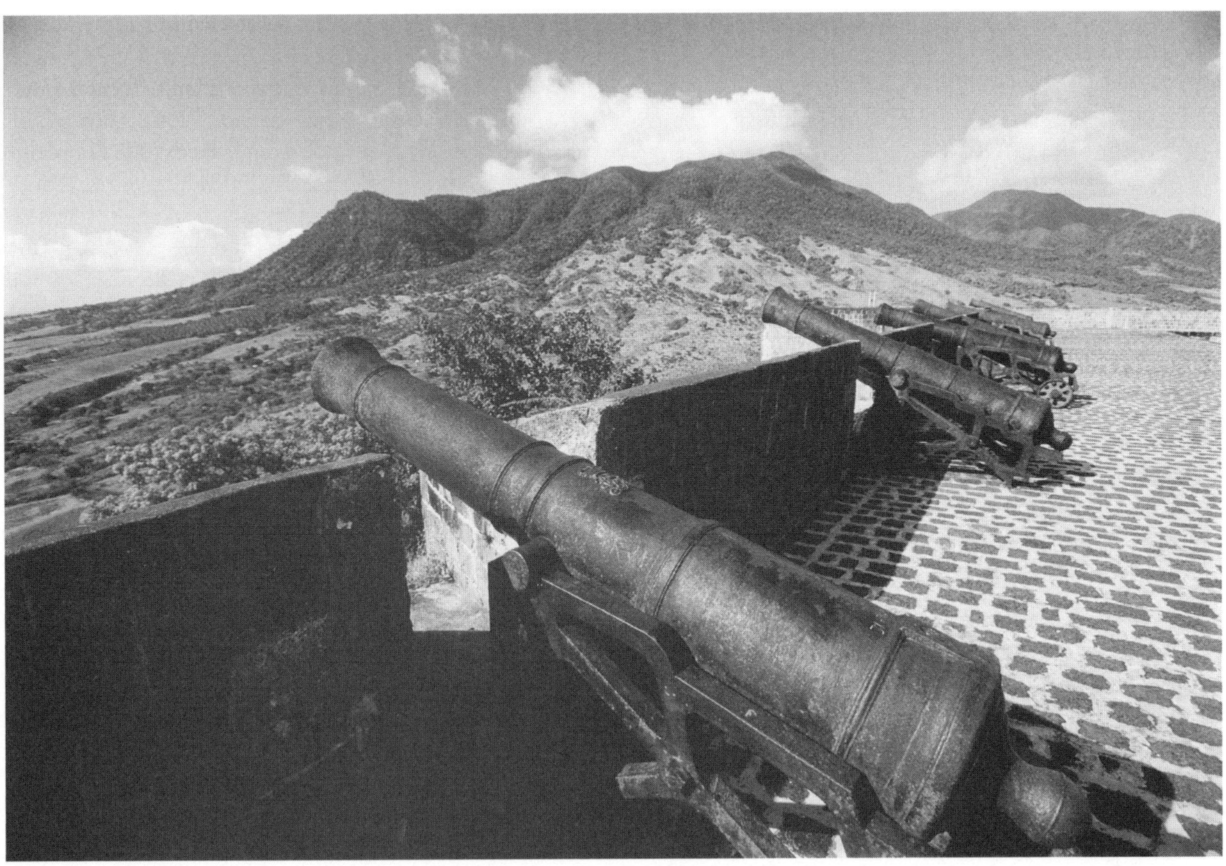

Battlements at Brimstone Hill Fortress. *Dubbed the Gibraltar of the West Indies, Brimstone Hill on the southwest coast of Saint Kitts was first fortified in 1690 and remained in regular use until the withdrawal of the last garrison in 1853.* © BOB KRIST/CORBIS.

performed the salute in reply to the thirteen-gun salute by Isaiah Robinson, the commander of the *Andrew Doria.* There is a plaque in the courtyard commemorating the salute of the American flag on 16 November 1776, presented by President Franklin D. Roosevelt on 12 December 1939.

Forts and Batteries. In addition to Fort Oranje and Fort Amsterdam, there are numerous remnants of former military installations dating from the period of the American Revolution. These include Fort de Windt, which is believed to date from the governorship of Jan de Windt, between September 1753 and January 1775; Bourbon's Battery, or Four Gun Battery (1780s); Fort Amsterdam, or Waterfort, from the late seventeenth century; Royal Battery (1780s); Tumble Down Dick Battery (early eighteenth century); Jenkin's Bay Battery (1780s); Stronghold at Venus Bay (1780s); Jussac's Battery (1780s); Fort Panga, or Signal Hill (1780s); Battery St. Louis (1780s); Battery Corre (1780s); Battery de Windt, or Lisbourne's Battery (third quarter of the eighteenth century); Frederick's Battery; Nassau's Battery (third quarter of the eighteenth century); Fort Dolijn, also called a Have's Batter (early eighteenth century); and Bouillé's Battery (1780s).

Lynch Plantation Museum is a museum dedicated to domestic life on the island, with a collection of household artifacts and antiques. It is located on the northeastern side of the island.

Oranjestad contains ruins and evidence of the commercial vitality of the town during the period of the American Revolution, especially in Lower Town around the bay where building began in the 1750s. The St. Eustatius Historical Foundation Museum is located in one of the oldest and most attractive houses in the Upper Town, the Simon Doncker House Museum. Sir George Rodney made it his headquarters after he captured the island in 1781. The date of the building is not known, but the house is marked on a plantation map of 1775. The Government Guesthouse is an eighteenth-century building which was restored and officially opened by Queen Beatrix on 16 November 1992. The Dutch Reformed Church in Oranjestad was built in 1755. It was in ruins until the tower was restored in 1981 and subsequent work was performed in 2000.

Synagogue "Honen Dalim" in Oranjestad, built in 1739 but now in ruins, is the second-oldest synagogue in the Western Hemisphere. The cemetery has graves dating back to 1742. Rodney selected the Jews for particularly harsh punishment, accusing them of aiding the American Revolution, when he sacked the island in 1781. The graves of several traders from New England, particularly Rhode Island, are located near the cemetery, where the names are mostly Portuguese, being primarily Sephardic Jews from Brazil.

For more information contact: St. Eustatius Historical Foundation, P.O. Box 71, Oranjestad A25, St. Eustatius, Netherland Antilles; St. Eustatius Tourism Development Foundation, Fort Oranje, Oranjestad, St. Eustatius, Netherlands Antilles, Dutch Caribbean; phone: (599-3) 182433; fax (599-3) 182433; email: euxtour@goldenrock.net; website: www. statiatourism.com.

ST. JOHN

St. John was a Danish colony from 1718 until its sale to the United States in 1917. About two-thirds of the 20-square-mile island was designated a National Park in 1956. Annaberg Estate dates from the 1780s. The U.S. National Park Service here gives demonstrations of the operations of a plantation. Frederik's Fort, at the east end of the island at Coral Bay, was built on the site of an earlier fortress on Fortsberg Hill in 1736, partly in response to the slave rebellion of 1733. It therefore contained defenses directed inland as well as towards the sea, such as the battery at Cruz Bay. There is also a coastal battery facing the entrance to Coral Bay lower down on Fortsberg Hill. Reef Bay plantation has a great house dating from before 1780.

For further information contact: United States Virgin Islands Department of Tourism, P.O. Box 200, Cruz Bay, St. John, USVI 00831; phone: (340) 776-6450; fax: (340) 779-4097; Virgin Islands National Park, Cruz Bay Visitor Center, phone: (340) 776-6201 ext. 238.

ST. KITTS (ALSO KNOWN AS ST. CHRISTOPHER)

St. Kitts was the oldest British colony in the Caribbean from the time of the first English settlement in 1623; it became independent in 1983. The 68-square-mile island was divided with the French for much of the time between 1627 and 1713. Alexander Hamilton's parents met in St. Kitts in the 1750s. His father, James Hamilton, the younger son of a prominent Scottish family, had left Scotland to seek his fortune in the West Indies. He evidently had little success, because he was listed in the council minutes in 1748 as a watchman for the port of Basseterre. The two were unable to marry because Rachel was technically still married to a failed planter in St. Croix. St. Kitts was the scene of the most ferocious Stamp Act riots in the British Caribbean in 1765. During the Revolutionary War the island was under constant threat of attack by the French. Throughout much of the month of February 1779, Admiral d'Estaing hovered menacingly off the island with five ships of the line. On 3 February, Fig Tree Fort fired on the ships and hit the deck of the *Iphegenic*. On 6 March the *Governor Trumbull*, one of the most successful American privateers in the Caribbean, was taken off St. Kitts after a pursuit of several hours. In May d'Estaing was able to take St. Vincent after Admiral Byron hurriedly left St. Lucia, fearing for the safety of St. Kitts. On 15 July, Byron returned to St. Kitts with his badly damaged, blood-drenched ships following a naval battle off Grenada with d'Estaing. The French again appeared off Basseterre with twenty-six sail of the line, one large frigate, and five thousand men. A battle seemed imminent, with the two fleets almost in gunshot range. D'Estaing instead sailed to Cap François and then prepared to cooperate with American land forces at Savannah, Georgia. On 11 January 1782, accompanied by the same victorious French army and commanders who fought at Yorktown, Admiral de Grasse landed unopposed in St. Kitts with eight thousand troops commanded by the governor of Martinique, the marquis de Bouillé, who immediately captured the capital city of Basseterre. He then proceeded to besiege Brimstone Hill. Almost two weeks after the start of the siege, Admiral Hood arrived with a relief expedition of twenty-two ships from Barbados against the superior fleet of twenty-nine ships under de Grasse. In a brilliant maneuver, Hood managed to lure the French fleet from its moorings and to displace it with his own fleet, but apart from an exchange of messages on the first day, he was unable to communicate with the besieged garrison. He succeeded in landing troops off Frigate Bay under General Robert Prescott, who engaged in an intense action for which both sides claimed victory. On 12 February, after almost five weeks of resistance, the sick and exhausted garrison on Brimstone Hill, depleted of ammunition and provisions, with only five hundred men left in defense, finally submitted to the French, giving them full possession of St. Kitts and the neighboring island of Nevis. St. Kitts was returned to Britain by the peace terms of 1783.

Basseterre was the capital of St. Kitts. The area around Independence Square with its central gardens was laid out on land purchased in 1750. The town suffered major fires in 1776 (and again in 1867). There are few of the original buildings from the time of the American Revolution. The town was the scene of Stamp Act riots in 1765 contemporaneous with those of Boston. On the evening of 31 October a crowd of three to four hundred people assembled at Noland's Tavern. They seized the stamp official and paraded him through the public market. They knocked him down, and he claimed that they were ready to murder him but for the intervention of "some negroes" who knew him. The crowd continued on the rampage, forcing the collector to flee to Nevis. On 5 November the crowd assembled again, burning effigies of the stamp master and his deputy. They finished the evening with a dinner and toasts to "Liberty, Property and no Stamps." During the American Revolutionary War, Basseterre was the port where the convoys gathered from the British colonies in the eastern Caribbean for the "homeward" voyage to Britain. The bay was protected by Fort Smith, of which nothing now remains, and Fort Thomas, named after Governor George Thomas, which stands in the grounds of a hotel of the same name. Fort Street was the site of a third fort, which stood in the center of the waterfront. The Anglican church of St. George, like most ecclesiastical buildings in the islands, has been repeatedly rebuilt since its construction in 1670. The churchyard, also in common with the churches throughout the islands, has gravestones from the early eighteenth century.

Brimstone Hill Fortress National Park is a UNESCO World Heritage Site. Dubbed the Gibraltar of the West Indies, Brimstone Hill (779 feet high) was first fortified in 1690 by Sir Timothy Thornhill, and it remained in regular use until the withdrawal of the last garrison in 1853. The site consists of bastions, barracks, offices, storerooms, and magazines, spread across 30 acres. There is a museum relating the history of the island which is housed in some of the barrack rooms in the citadel. The citadel on the summit and the large bastion just below were added in the late eighteenth century. The fortress has views of the western side of the island, as well as of Nevis, St. Eustatius, Saba, St. Martin, and St. Barthélémy. The landing of the French at Basseterre in January 1781 forced the twelve thousand British military regulars and militia to retreat to a defensive position 9 miles away in the formidable fortifications at Brimstone Hill, against which the French began siege operations. The garrison submitted after almost five weeks of resistance.

Charles Fort, Sandy Point, situated on Cleverly's Hill under Brimstone Hill and named after King Charles II, was a military post from 1670 until it was abandoned in 1854. Some forty years later, in 1890, it was used as a Hansen home (leper asylum). The home was closed in 1996. The point was a suitable site to protect and deflect ships making for Sandy Point Road.

Frigate Bay. Fort Tyson overlooks the bay where British troops landed from Hood's ships on 18 February 1782, commanded by General Robert Prescott.

Plantation Houses. St. Kitts' plantations include Belmont Estate Yard; Fairview Inn (1698–1701); Lodge Great House; and Shadwell Great House, built in the second quarter of the eighteenth century.

For more information contact: St. Kitts–Nevis Tourist Board, Church Street, P.O. Box 132, Basseterre, phone: (809) 465–2620; National Archives, Government Headquarters, Church Street, Box 186, Basseterre, St. Kitts; phone: (869) 465-2521. Researchers should contact the archivist before visiting because research space is limited. Also useful are: St. Christopher Heritage Society, Bank Street, P.O. Box 338, Basseterre, St. Kitts; phone: (869) 465-5584; St. Kitts and Nevis Department of Tourism, 414 East 75th Street, 5th Floor, New York, N.Y. 10021; phone: (800) 582-6208; fax: (212) 734-6511; website: www.stkitts-nevis.com.

ST. LUCIA

The 238-square-mile island was a French colony at the beginning of the American Revolutionary War. It was captured by the British in an expedition commanded by Admiral Samuel Barrington and Major General James Grant on 13 December 1778. Britain gave up Philadelphia partly to free five thousand troops for the conquest of St. Lucia. Sir Henry Clinton, the British commander in chief in North America, attributed his failure to wage a more aggressive war to the loss of these troops and the failure of the government to replace them with additional reinforcements. Sir George Rodney had persuaded the government of the necessity of taking the island in order to provide a base for the British navy to shadow the French navy at Martinique. The British gave the island priority second only to Antigua and Jamaica. The French made several unsuccessful attempts to recapture St. Lucia, which was restored to France by the peace of 1783. The high quality local rum is appropriately called Admiral Rodney and is sold in boxes commemorating the battle of the Saintes.

Castries (Petit Carenage). During the British occupation it was called Carenage Town, and only acquired its present name after the French reoccupation in 1784. It possessed one of the finest harbors in the Caribbean. The town has few original buildings from the period of the American Revolution owing to the damage caused by the hurricane of 1780, together with the fires of 1796, 1812, 1948, and 1951.

Grand Cul-du-Sac Bay was the landing place of the British invasion under the command of General Meadows and Brigadier General Prescott on 13 December 1778 with five thousand men. It was also the scene of an ensuing engagement between Admiral Sir Samuel Barrington and

Count d'Estaing. The latter had arrived too late from North America to deflect the British.

Gros Islet (Rodney Bay), in the northeast, was regarded by Rodney as the finest bay in the Caribbean. It was the place where the French landed their forces in 1778. Rodney sailed from the bay to his victory over de Grasse at the Battle of the Saintes.

Marigot Bay is one of the most beautiful coves in the Caribbean. In 1778 Admiral Samuel Barrington sailed into the harbor and camouflaged his ships by tying large palm fronds to the mast to escape the pursuit of Admiral d'Estaing.

Morne Fortuné (Good Luck Hill), 850 feet above sea level, was the site of fortifications overlooking Castries. The ruins of a guardroom, three cells, and stables are located near the entrance to Radio St. Lucia Studios, and date from the late 1770s. Some of the rings for tethering horses can still be seen in the walls. The Halfmoon Battery was built in 1752 and renamed in about 1797. It was at one time a gun emplacement for three 18-pounders and two 24-pounders. A short-oven, built about 1780, was moved from another location in the recent past. The Prevost's Redoubt is among the best-preserved gun emplacements, and was built in 1782. The military cemetery has graves of French and British soldiers dating from 1782. The site has excellent views of the Pitons, the interior of the island, and Martinique.

Moule à Chique, a mountain peak on the southern peninsula, has a view of the neighboring island of St. Vincent, located 20 miles away.

Paix Bouche, in the northeast of the island, was associated with Joséphine Tascher de la Pagerie, future wife of Napoleon and empress of France. The family lived on the island from 1763 until 1771. The ruins of the estate are still visible.

Pigeon Island National Park, overlooking Gros Islet Bay, has two hills north of Castries which were fortified by the British in 1778. The fortifications were strengthened under the personal supervision of Rodney between 1780 and 1782. Fort Rodney was on the lower hill (221 feet). There remains a two-gun battery, guns slides, barracks, garrisons and a powder magazine, hospital, cooperage, kitchen, bakery, officers' quarters, and a signal station, built between 1778 and 1780. The signal station was of great importance for relaying information regarding the movements of the French ships around Fort-de-France (Fort Royal), Martinique. The highest hill (334 feet) is called the Vigie (Lookout). It was the scene of intense fighting when d'Estaing attempted to recapture the island in 1778. With five thousand men, jointly commanded by Lowendahl and de Bouillé, he attempted to storm the lines of General Meadows. He lost some seventy men in the first attack when the British used their bayonets to resist. Two further attempts were repulsed by the British. There is a former military cemetery which dates from 1781. Pigeon Island is now joined to the mainland by a causeway and is a national park with a museum and restaurant. The museum is located in the old officers' quarters and run by the St. Lucia Archaeological and Historical Society.

The Pitons, or peaks, were for generations landmarks for mariners. Gros Piton is 2,619 feet and Petit Piton is 2,481 feet.

Plantation Houses. Most of St. Lucia's plantation homes were destroyed in the French Revolution. There are the remains of six estates in the area of Soufrière: Malmaison, which was the home of the future empress Joséphine, the wife of Napoleon; Diamond, which has a pre-1745 windmill; Anse Mamin; Palmiste; and Rabot and Union Vale. In the area of Micoud, there are the plantations of Beauchamps, Fond, and Trouassee. To the south of Vieux Fort, there is Giraudy House and Savannes. Near Dauphin is the Morne Paix Bouche estate and Marquis, which was the home of the governors of St. Lucia. The Mamicou estate on the midwestern coast was the home of the chevalier de Micoud, who defended the island against the British in 1778. Around the southwest coast, there is Choiseul, Laborie, and River Doree. Between Castries and Gros Islet Bay are Cap House and Grand Rivière.

Rat Island in Choc Bay was fortified by the British during the American Revolution.

Vieux Fort, situated on the south coast of a peninsula called Moule-a-Chique, was the first part of the island to be settled by Europeans. It was the district where the British first introduced sugar in 1765, and it became the center of the sugar estates in the eighteenth century. It is now an industrial area, near the main airport, which has a museum about the history and culture of St. Lucia.

For further information contact: National Archives, P.O. Box 3060, Clarke Street, Vigie, Castries, St. Lucia; phone: (758) 452-1654; email: stlunatarch_mt@candw.lc; website: http://www.geocities.com/sluarchives/index.html; St. Lucia National Trust, P.O. Box 525, Castries, St. Lucia; phone: (758) 452-5005; fax: (758) 453–2791; St. Lucia Tourist Board; phone: (800) 456–3984; website: www.stlucia.org.

ST. MARTIN/ST. MAARTEN

The 36-square-mile island was divided between France and the Netherlands after 1648. It was named after Sieur St. Martin, who claimed the island for Louis XIII. The two colonial powers continued to contest the island and to drive one another out. On 5 January 1779 a British expedition from Anguilla took the French northern half of the island, which had a good harbor and the potential for sugar crops. In March 1780 it was recaptured by the French. Rodney did much damage to the Dutch half of the island following his capture of St. Eustatius in 1781.

Marigot is the capital and a port in the French half of the island (St. Martin), where the main fortress was Point Blanche, St. Louis (Fort St. Louis), built on the edges of the town in 1760. It is in ruins, with several cannons and decaying walls and ramparts.

Philipsburg is the capital of the Dutch half of the island (St. Maarten), where the main fortress was Fort Amsterdam, founded in 1631 and substantially rebuilt and modified in 1633 and 1648; it was used as a signal station until the 1950s. It is now in ruins. The town contains seventeenth- and eighteenth-century remains of a synagogue.

For further information contact: Dutch St.Maarten Tourist Office, 675 Third Ave, Suite 1806, New York, N.Y. 10017; phone: (800) 786-2278; fax: (212) 953–2145; Cultural Centre of Philipsburg, Back Street, Philipsburg, St. Maarten; phone: 5995 22056; French St. Martin Tourism; phone: (877) 956-1234; website: www.st-martin.org; Office du Tourisme, Route de Sandy Ground, 97150 Marigot, St. Martin; phone: 590 875721; fax: 590 875643; email: sxmto@aol.com; St. Martin Tourist Office, 675 Third Avenue, Suite 1807, New York, N.Y. 10017; phone: (212) 475-8970 / (877) 956-1234; email: sxmtony@msn.com.

ST. THOMAS

The 30-square-mile island was a Danish colony in the Virgin Islands between 1672 and 1917. The inhabitants colonized St. Croix and St. John, which were sold by Denmark to the United States to become the American Virgin Islands. After Rodney's capture of St. Eustatius in January 1781, St. Thomas became a major source of supplies to the Americans.

Charlotte Amalie, the capital and a port town, suffered six fires between 1804 and 1832. The fortifications are the most impressive structures remaining. Fort Christian, although much altered since its erection in the 1670s, retains parts of the original structure and early-eighteenth-century additions. It houses the Virgin Islands Museum. The facing hills also needed to be fortified because they could be used by an invading enemy to attack the fort. There are two round towers, known as Bluebeard's Castle (Frederik's Fort) on Smithberg, a hill east of the harbor, which was completed in 1689, and Blackbeard's Castle (Trygborg), built in the early 1680s by the Danish West India Company. Prince Frederik's Battery was built to protect the west side of the harbor entrance in 1780. The Virgin Islands legislature meets in the former eighteenth-century military barracks south of Fort Christian. The military ward of a hospital dating from the last quarter of the eighteenth century is now a private residence called the Adams House. Crown House dates from 1750. It has eighteenth-century furnishings and interiors. The Frederick Lutheran Church claims to be the second-oldest Lutheran Church in the Americas, and has a parsonage that dates from about 1776. The town was a refuge for large numbers of Jews escaping St. Eustatius following the attack by Rodney in 1782.

New Herrnhut Moravian Church was the original church established in the Caribbean by the Moravians, who began their mission at St. Thomas in 1732 and purchased the plantation on which the church is located in 1738. The Moravians originated among the followers of John Hus, the Bohemian priest who was burnt for heresy in 1415. In the eighteenth century Count Nicholas Ludwig von Zinzendorf of Saxony first granted Moravians asylum and then played a key role in revitalizing the denomination. They were notable for their preaching among the slave population. They became active throughout the Caribbean, including in Jamaica (1754), Antigua (1756), Barbados (1765), and St. Kitts (1774), and in North America, where they were particularly active in North Carolina and Pennsylvania before the American Revolution. Count von Zinzendorf visited St. Thomas in support of the Moravians' earliest mission to the Caribbean. Augustus Gottlieb Spangenberg of Bethlehem, Pennsylvania, preached his first sermons under the ceiba at the Moravian Mission at Nisky near Crown Bay. The seminary and school next to the ruins of the church were built in 1777.

Sail Rock was supposedly mistaken by a French frigate for a British ship during the American Revolution. The French ship fired a broadside at the rock, whose ricochet gave the impression of return fire. The cannonade continued throughout the night.

For further information contact: United States Virgin Islands Department of Tourism, P.O. Box 6400, St. Thomas, Virgin Islands 00804; phone: (340) 774-8784; fax: (340) 774-4390.

ST. VINCENT

St. Vincent was a British colony following its conquest by General Robert Monckton in 1762; it became independent in 1969. The 239-square-mile island was inhabited principally by Caribs, who were descendants of the original peoples of the Caribbean at the time of Columbus. They mostly intermarried with runaway slaves and are therefore often called the Black Caribs. They resisted British expansion and fought a war with British troops in 1772 to 1773 which necessitated the removal of troops from Boston and was widely condemned among the opposition parties in Britain. The war did not result in a clear victory, which some Patriot newspapers in North America interpreted as evidence of the weakness of Britain. During the American Revolution the Black Caribs remained a constant source of anxiety to the British, and were believed to be in league with the French. On 16 June 1779 the island was captured by Admiral d'Estaing and 400 men under the command of the chevalier du Romain. Valentine Morris, British governor of the island, managed to assemble in opposition only 44 regulars and 35 militia. The island was returned to the British by the terms of the peace of 1783. James Hamilton, the indebted father of Alexander Hamilton who had abandoned his wife and family in St. Croix, died in St. Vincent on 3 June 1799. He had lived for nine years on the island, and previously on the nearby island of Bequia. He and his son exchanged some correspondence, but never met in thirty-five years.

Botanic Gardens. Reputed to be the oldest in the Western Hemisphere, they occupy 20 acres of land 1 mile outside of Kingstown. The collection includes tropical trees, palms, lilies, hibiscus, and bougainvillea, as well as preserved rare species. It was here that the notorious Captain Bligh planted a Tahitian breadfruit tree in 1797 in hopes that it would prove a useful food source for the Caribbean islands. (His first attempt to collect breadfruit trees from Tahiti in 1787 was thwarted by the mutiny aboard his ship, the *Bounty.*) The gardens contain the Archaeological Museum (for which visitors should check opening times in advance).

Dorsetshire Hill used to have barracks and was the scene of intense fighting between the British, French, and Caribs. The fortifications, which only consisted of earthworks, no longer exist.

Kingstown is the capital. It was protected by batteries, with Can Garden Point to the south and to the northwest by Fort Charlotte (the current building dates from 1796–1806), named after George III's wife, Queen Charlotte. The former soldiers' quarters are now a museum. St. George's Anglican Church graveyard contains the tomb of Governor William Leyborne, who died in office in 1775, and men from the Seventieth Regiment stationed at Fort Charlotte.

Young Island, off Calliaqua Bay in the south of the island, has the adjacent Fort Duvernette, or Fort Rock, at 260 feet above sea level. It dates from 1800 but has guns from the reign of George II. It protected the entrance to Kingstown.

For further information contact: St. Vincent and the Grenadines Archives Department, Cotton Ginnery Compound, Frenches, Kingstown, St. Vincent and the Grenadines; phone: (784) 456-1689; email: document @caribsurf.com: Director of Libraries, Kingstown, St. Vincent, phone: (784) 457-2292; Kingstown Public Library, Lower Middle Street, Kingstown, St. Vincent; phone: (784) 457-2022; the National Trust (St. Vincent and the Grenadines), c/o CARIPEDA, P.O. Box 1132, Arnos Vale, St. Vincent and the Grenadines; Registrar General, Government Buildings, Kingstown, St. Vincent; phone: (784) 457-1424; Yulu Griffith, Chief Archivist, Archives Department, Cotton Ginnery Compound, Frenches, Kingstown, St. Vincent and the Grenadines, West Indies.

THE SAINTES

The Saintes are group of eight islands located 7 miles to the south of Guadeloupe, which were the scene of Sir George Rodney's victory against the French on 12 April 1782. For further contact information see GUADELOUPE.

TOBAGO

Tobago was a British colony between 1762 and 1962. The 116-square-mile island was part of the government of Grenada during the American Revolution. Patrick Ferguson, the British commander killed at King's Mountain (1780) who invented the first repeating rifle used in the British army (1776), had joined the Seventieth Regiment in 1768 in Tobago, where he was involved in the suppression of slave revolts in 1770 to 1771. John Paul Jones, the Scottish-born American naval hero, was master of the *Betsy* when he fled Tobago for America after killing a sailor in 1773. During the Revolutionary War, Tobago was twice raided by the crews of American privateers, first after a landing at Bloody Spike on 30 December 1777 and second (in an attack by fifty men) on 17 January 1779. Before leaving the Caribbean for his decisive intervention in the British defeat at Yorktown, Admiral de Grasse captured the island in 1781. It was the only British colony in the Caribbean to be ceded to France in the Peace of Paris in 1783. It returned to British rule in 1793.

Caldedonia, "the Retreat," is the country house where Lieutenant Governor George Ferguson surrendered to the French in 1781. It was formerly the property of a soldier, James Clark, whose grave is at Fort Granby guarding Georgetown.

Concordia, on the north side of the island, is a plateau with a good view of Scarborough. Lieutenant Governor Ferguson made his last stand against the French at this point in 1781.

Crown Point is in the low-lying region of Tobago. Fort Milford, close to the shore, was built by the British between 1771 and 1781. It has one French and five British cannon, and fine seaward views.

Mount St. George was originally known by the British as George Town. Studley Park House was formerly the courthouse, built around 1788. Fort Granby at Granby Point was erected by the Sixty-second Regiment in 1765 to guard Barbados Bay—the harbor of Mount St. George. The ruins of the barracks and two tombstones are still visible.

Plymouth, also called Soldier's Barrack, was the major port of entry to Tobago and regarded as a safe harbor. It is the site of Fort James, built by the British in 1768 to 1777, which overlooks Great Courland Bay and today is maintained by the Tobago House of Assembly Tourism Division. The barracks and four mounted cannon are all that remain. Nearby is the mysterious tombstone of Betty Stiven (Stevens), dated 25 November 1783 with the inscription, "She was a mother without knowing it, and a Wife without letting her Husband know it, except by her kind indulgences to him." The town was the site where the French captured the island from the British in 1781.

Scarborough is the capital and principal town in Tobago. Its Fort King George was built between 1770 and 1786. There are still pieces of cannon, a powder magazine, a bell, and a fresh-water tank. It guarded the harbor and today offers a panoramic view. The Tobago Museum is in the Barrack Guard House.

For further information contact: Trinidad and Tobago Tourism Office, Keating Communications, 350 Fifth Avenue, Suite 6316, New York, N.Y. 10118; phone: (800) 748-4224 / (868) 623-6022; fax: (212) 760-6402; website: www.tidco.co.tt; National Archives, 105 St. Vincent Street, P.O. Box 763, Port of Spain, Trinidad; phone: (868) 625–2689; Tobago Heritage Committee, Tobago, West Indies; Head Librarian, National Heritage Library, 8 Knox Street, Port of Spain, Trinidad, West Indies; phone: (868) 623-6124; email: heritage@trinidad.net; website: http://www.nalis.gov.tt/Heritage.html; University Libraries, University of the West Indies, St. Augustine, Trinidad and Tobago; phone: (868) 662-2002; fax: (868) 662-9238; email: mainlib @library.uwi.tt.

VIRGIN ISLANDS (U.S.). *See* ST. CROIX, ST. JOHN, and ST. THOMAS.

Andrew Jackson O'Shaughnessy

CONNECTICUT

In the colonial era and during the events leading to the Revolution, Connecticut had a vital political role. During the Revolution it became known as "the Provision State" for its preeminence in giving logistical support. Because of this Connecticut suffered three major punitive expeditions; its native son Benedict Arnold was the hero of the first (see DANBURY) and the villain of the last (see NEW LONDON). The large number of Connecticut settlers in Ohio is a direct result of these raids, the Western Reserve being "reserved" by Connecticut for settlement by its people when it surrendered claims to all other western lands in 1786. The 500,000-acre tract in this reserve known as the Fire Lands was used to compensate citizens of Danbury, Fairfield, Norwalk, New Haven, and New London for their losses in British raids. But although Connecticut saw little fighting on its own soil, it sent a great many of its men off to serve in the Continental army, and for some, their absence from Connecticut helps to explain why the local militia showed so little valor in defending home and hearth. But most scholars note that the majority of Connecticut's Continental soldiers were reluctant enlistees, as was true for soldiers from most states.

Industrial prosperity since the Revolution has eliminated many of Connecticut's historical landmarks. Unfortunately, there is no published guide to historical markers. The inventory of 1962, presumably the most recent, lists 139 historical signs restricted to about 50 towns and containing minimal information. The following listing identifies the major historical landmarks in Connecticut, omitting a good many of purely architectural importance. Agencies with statewide responsibility are identified at the end of the section on Hartford.

Bridgeport, Fairfield County. Now a city of 141,000 people, Bridgeport—then called Newfield—was in the path of Governor Tryon's raid of 1779. The Grovers Hill Fort site on Black Rock Drive is where a protected gun emplacement was erected in 1776 to overlook a small harbor. From there Captains Daniel Hawley and Samuel Lockwood departed with twenty-five men in a whaleboat to capture Thomas Jones (1731–1792) at his home, Fort Neck, South Oyster Bay, Long Island. This happened on 6 November 1779. The Patriots seized the much-persecuted Judge Jones, who wrote a history of the Revolution from the Loyalist viewpoint (*History of New York during the Revolutionary War*, published in 1879), with the idea of exchanging him for General Gold Selleck Silliman. The latter had been a student at Yale, was chief of military activities in Fairfield County, and had been kidnapped earlier in the year by the Loyalists.

In April 1780 the two hostages were exchanged. The Gold Selleck Silliman home remains standing in Fairfield. Judge Jones's house, called Tryon Hall in honor of the governor, survived until modern times but has since disappeared. The unmarked site is on Merrick Road west of Cartwright Avenue in Massapequa, New York on Long Island. In the Library of Congress there are eighteen measured drawings of the house made from data gathered in 1934 by the Historic American Buildings Survey.

(Bridgeport Public Library Historical Collections, 925 Broad Street, Bridgeport, Conn. 06604; phone: (203) 576-7417. Website: www.bridgeportpubliclibrary.org.)

Compo Beach, Long Island Sound between Norwalk and Bridgeport. A force of two thousand British and Loyalist raiders landed in this vicinity on 25 April 1777 and debarked three days later after burning Danbury, fighting their way through a blocking position at Ridgefield, and launching a vigorous spoiling attack from Compo Hill to permit their safe withdrawal. The expedition had been escorted from New York by two frigates. Compo Road leads south from U.S. 1 in Westport Township to the present community of Compo Beach, which features a 29-acre park in the general area of the British landing and re-embarkation.

Danbury, Fairfield County. Emigrants from Norwalk settled this region of wooded foothills of the Berkshires in 1684. Good waterpower helped make Danbury an important manufacturing center from colonial days. The British mercantile system discouraged production in America of goods that would compete with English manufacturing, and the growing hat industry in the colonies led to passage in 1732 of the Hat Act, which imposed restrictions including export of hats from one colony to another. Danbury's long preeminence as a center of the felt industry dates from the beginning of felt hat manufacture in 1780.

The village was also an important supply depot for the Patriot forces in the Revolution, and consequently the objective of a devastating enemy raid in April 1777. General William Tryon, former royal governor of North Carolina and later of New York, led about 2,000 British and Loyalist troops from Compo Beach to reach Danbury, unopposed, on 23 April. The 150 Continental troops stationed in the area evacuated the small quantity of military supplies from the Episcopal church (see below), but the raiders, unimpeded by patriotic heroism, burned about 20 homes and twice that number of barns and storehouses, and destroyed military clothing and provisions, including a supply of about 1,700 tents.

General Benedict Arnold happened to be in the area, tending to his neglected personal affairs in New Haven and thoroughly disgusted with the failure of Congress to recognize his military accomplishments. Washington was urging Congress to promote Arnold to major general, and urging Arnold to stay in the service. The Danbury raid brought the "Whirlwind Hero" into the field, and the British met their first real resistance at Ridgefield. General David Wooster was mortally wounded in pursuing the British. He died five days later (2 May 1777), and is buried here in Wooster Cemetery on Ellsworth Avenue. Congress gave Arnold a horse and a promotion and voted Wooster a monument, but never got around to putting it up. The Masons erected one in 1854.

Enoch Crosby, the famous Patriot spy, was living in Danbury when the Revolution started (see FISHKILL VILLAGE, NEW YORK). The Early Episcopal Church site is now occupied by the South Street School at Main and South Streets. The old church was spared by the raiders of 1777 because most of its members were Loyalists, but Danbury got even by neglecting the structure, then moving it to the southwest corner of South Street and Mountainville Avenue, where it became a tenement house and finally was destroyed. The Colonel Joseph Platt Cooke House of 1770 at 342 Main Street was torn down in 1972 to make way for a bank. Having survived the British raid of 1777 (it was only partially burned), its visitors during the Revolution included Washington, Lafayette, and Rochambeau.

The Danbury Scott-Fanton Museum and Historical Society, formed in 1947 by a merger of older organizations, has preserved four old structures: the John Rider House (c. 1785), the John Dodd House and Hat Shop (1790), the Charles Ives Homestead (c. 1780), and the King Street One-Room School. The first two are house museums adjoining Huntington Hall, a modern administrative building and museum, in downtown Danbury at 43-45 Main Street. The other buildings are being restored on property owned by the Society adjacent to Rogers Park.

(Danbury Museum and Historical Society, 43 Main Street, Danbury, Conn. 06810; phone: (203) 743-5200; website: www.danburyhistorical.org.)

Fairfield, Fairfield County. Roger Ludlow took part in the Swamp Fight of 1637 that wiped out what remained of the Pequot Indians. (Their population, estimated at three thousand, was nearly depleted. However, the Western Pequots received federal recognition as a tribe in 1983 and emerged as a powerful economic force in southeastern Connecticut when their casinos, which opened in 1992, prospered.) The battle site is just east of the presently settled area of Fairfield, Connecticut.

Attracted to the real-estate development possibilities of the site, Ludlow settled Fairfield in 1639, although he first took interest in the area after his success in battling the Pequots. The town prospered, giving its name to the county, but was virtually destroyed by British raiders during the Revolution. Abandoned on the approach of General Tryon's expedition in July 1779, Fairfield was occupied by the British on 8 July. Four small houses were spared, apparently because the British used them during their brief stay, but the rest were burned. The Patriots reported the loss of 83 homes, 54 barns, 47 storehouses, 2 schools, 2 churches, and the courthouse. Nearby Bridgeport outstripped Fairfield after the Revolution, but the latter is nevertheless a thriving town of about 57,000 people today.

Marked historic sites in Fairfield are McKenzies Point, off which the British anchored in July 1779; the beach where they landed and Beach Road, which they used in occupying the town; and the green, where Tryon posted the proclamation calling for inhabitants to swear allegiance to King George III. The Town Hall, rebuilt on the green in 1794, has records dating from 1648. Opposite the green at 636 Old Post Road is the Fairfield Historical Society, a venerable institution dating from 1903 and active today. The Society has a museum, archives, and library.

The Gold Selleck Silliman House (1756) is still standing. Privately owned, this large, clapboard structure with a central chimney has been somewhat remodeled. The house is historic not only as the home of a prominent Patriot general but as the site of his kidnapping on 1 May 1779 by Loyalists. The Patriots retaliated by kidnapping Judge Thomas Jones (see BRIDGEPORT) and holding him a few days at the Silliman house before taking him to Middletown. Mrs. Silliman fled to Trumbull, where she stayed at a tavern on Daniels Farm Road; there on 8 August 1779 she gave birth to Benjamin Silliman, who became a prominent and influential scientist of the first half of the next century. (The historic tavern has been destroyed.) The Gold Selleck Silliman House is at 506 Jennings Road in Fairfield, about 200 yards east of the Black Rock Turnpike.

(Fairfield Historical Society, 636 Old Post Road, Fairfield, Conn. 06430; phone: (203) 259-1598; email: info@fairfieldhs.org.)

Farmington, Hartford County. In 1640 this area was established as Tunxis Plantation, a frontier trading center about 10 miles west of Hartford and Wethersfield. Rochambeau's French army camped here in the summer of 1781 en route to join Washington's forces for an attack on New York City. The site is marked by a plaque on a boulder in the small park at Main Street and Farmington Avenue. The Stanley-Whitman House at 37 High Street, a two-and-a-half-story saltbox with a great center chimney and a long sloping rear roof, was built about 1720 and is of exceptional architectural interest (framed overhang with pendants). A National Historic Landmark, in 1935 it opened as the Farmington Museum, displaying seventeenth- and eighteenth-century objects of particular note. Now a town of about twenty-three thousand, Farmington is perhaps best known for Miss Porter's School for Girls (established 1843).

Fort Griswold State Park, Fort and Thames Streets, Groton, New London County. The New London raid by Benedict Arnold on 6 September 1781 included reduction of two forts defending the mouth of the Thames River: Fort Trumbull on the west and Fort Griswold on Groton Heights. The latter, defended by Lieutenant Colonel William Ledyard with about 140 militia, was a square fort with stone walls 12 feet high, a fraised ditch, and outworks. (A fraise is a form of palisade, but the pointed timbers are slanted horizontally toward the front.) Fort Trumbull was not designed for defense against an attack by land, so its small garrison of twenty-four men under Captain Adam Shapley delivered one volley of musket and cannon, spiked their eight guns, and reinforced Fort Griswold.

Cannon Mounts at Fort Griswold. *Groton's Fort Griswold, a square structure with thick stone walls, was attacked in 1781 by British forces led by Benedict Arnold.* © LEE SNIDER/PHOTO IMAGES/CORBIS.

The British attack on the latter position was led by Lieutenant Colonel Edmund Eyre, who landed on the east side of the river with two British battalions, the Third Battalion of New Jersey Loyalists, a detachment of German light infantry (*jaegers*), and some artillery. Total strength was about eight hundred.

Fort Griswold resisted repeated assaults for about forty minutes. Eyre was mortally wounded in the first attack, and his second in command, Major Montgomery, was killed on the parapet while leading another effort. A bas-relief at Old Fort Griswold, used as the frontispiece of Benjamin Quarles's study, *The Negro in the American Revolution*

(1961), shows the barefoot black servant of the fort commander killing Montgomery with a spear. (This man, Jordan Freeman, and another black orderly, Lambo Lathan, were killed later in this action.) Christopher Ward, in his standard work on the Revolution, *The War of the Revolution*, says Montgomery was killed by Captain Shapley, but sources remain divided.

The odds were too great, however, for the Patriots. How the subsequent massacre occurred is not known. It is said that Ledyard was stabbed with his own sword after surrendering it to a Loyalist officer, whereupon an American officer stabbed the latter, after which the victors bayoneted a great many of the vanquished.

Benedict Arnold reported 85 Patriots killed at Fort Griswold and 60 wounded, most of them mortally. The Americans reported about 75 killed, only 3 of them before the surrender. None of these figures are reliable, but Arnold's own losses of about 50 killed and 150 wounded indicate the severity of the fighting around Fort Griswold.

The 860-acre state park contains portions of the stone fortification and earthworks. A 135-foot monument on the hill near the fort was dedicated in 1830 to the victims of the massacre and lists their names, reflecting the racism of the era by listing the African American victims last under "Colored Men," and giving Lambert Latham, who had fought heroically in the battle, the first name "Sambo." The site provides an excellent point of observation. The nearby Monument House, operated by the Daughters of the American Revolution, has relics of the battle, period furniture, china, and other exhibits. The Fort Griswold State Park is located at 57 Fort Street, Groton, Conn. 06340; phone: (860) 445-1729. Information about Fort Griswold is available from the Connecticut Department of Environmental Protection (DEP); phone: (860) 424-3200; email: dep.stateparks @po.state.ct.us.

Greens Farms, Long Island Sound, Westport Township, Fairfield County. Governor William Tryon's Connecticut Coast raid of July 1779 reached this place on 9 July and destroyed more than two hundred buildings, according to one report (though most accounts put the figure at about 30). The punitive expedition had previously ravaged Fairfield, and it ended at Norwalk. The name of the colonial settlement is preserved in the present village, which shows on highway maps.

Guilford, Long Island Sound, New Haven County. Because it was not among the many shore towns destroyed by British punitive expeditions, Guilford, settled in 1639 by English Puritans under Reverend Henry Whitfield, has three surviving houses of the early colonial era. What may be the oldest stone dwelling in New England stands as the Whitfield House, on Whitfield Street, built in 1639 and used as a fort, church, and meeting hall. The massive two-and-a-half-story structure with steeply pitched roof and huge end chimneys was restored in 1936—perhaps too well for architectural historians to accept—and is a state museum. The Hyland House (1660) at 84 Boston Street and Griswold House (1735) at 171 Boston Street are National Historic Landmarks, both open to the public.

Guilford was the starting point for the highly successful raid led by Colonel Return Jonathan Meigs (see MEIGS HOUSE SITE) in May 1777. There is historical confusion about this operation, which followed Governor Tryon's raid on Danbury by about a month. Most authorities give 23 to 24 May as the dates, but some have it taking place on 12 or 29 May.

Whatever the exact time, about 170 men under Meigs left Guilford in 13 whaleboats escorted by 2 armed sloops, rowed from Sachem Head through British warships in the Sound without being detected in the night, and surprised and defeated Lieutenant Colonel Stephen De Lancey's "battalion" of 70 Loyalists at Sag Harbor, Long Island (see under NEW YORK), killing 6 and capturing the rest. Meigs then burned 100 tons of hay, 10 transports, and the wharves. He was back at Guilford by noon, having covered almost 100 miles in 18 hours without losing a man. Congress voted him "an elegant sword."

(Dorothy Whitfield Historic Society, 84 Boston Street [Hyland House]; Guilford Keeping Society, 171 Boston Street [Griswold House], phone: (203) 453-3176; and Henry Whitfield State Historical Museum, 248 Old Whitfield Street, phone: (203) 453-2457; all in Guilford, Conn. 06437.)

Hale (Nathan) Birth Site, near Coventry, Tolland County. The house in which Nathan Hale was born (6 June 1755) was pulled down after the new family home was built adjacent to it. According to local tradition, the newer house incorporates a part of the one in which Nathan was born. Hale was executed as a spy on 22 September 1776, more than a month before the family moved into the new structure, and he never saw it. The Nathan Hale Homestead, as it is called, has been restored and furnished handsomely by the Antiquarian and Landmark Society of Connecticut (Hartford) (255 Main Street, Hartford, Conn. 06103).

The site is 4.5 miles from the village of Coventry at 2229 South Street, Coventry, Connecticut. The phone number is (860) 742-6917. From the junction of Conn. State Highway 31 (from South Coventry) and U.S. Highway 44A in Coventry, go west 0.5 mile on U.S. 44A, turn south on Silver Street, follow this south to South Street, and turn east to the site. State highway markers are on U.S. 6 near Andover and at the junction

Nathan Hale Schoolhouse. *This schoolhouse in New London, Connecticut, is where Hale taught from March 1774 until July 1775, when he left to become a lieutenant in the 7th Connecticut Militia.* © TODD GIPSTEIN/CORBIS.

of the road that runs to the site along the southwest side of Wamgumbaug Lake near South Coventry.

Hale (Nathan) Schoolhouse, East Haddam. On a bluff overlooking the Connecticut River, behind St. Stephen's Episcopal Church, is the first school in which Nathan Hale taught for one season after graduating from Yale (1773) and before moving to teach in New London. The school originally stood on the town green at the junction of Main Street and Norwich Road. In 1799 it ceased to be used as a school and was moved up to the front yard of what became St. Stephen's in the 1890s. Here it was a dwelling for one hundred years. Saved then from demolition, it was moved to its present location behind the church at 29 Main Street and it has recently been furnished with desks and a fireplace to restore its colonial appearance. Owned by the Sons of the American Revolution, it is open on weekends. The graves of General Joseph Spencer (1714–1789) and his wife are in the nearby churchyard.

(East Haddam Historical Society, 264 Town Street, East Haddam, Conn. 06423.)

Hartford, Connecticut River. No dramatic military action occurred here in the capital of Connecticut during the Revolution to give it "historic landmarks" for today's tourist to visit. But the place, first occupied by the Dutch in 1633 and settled a few years later by Englishmen from around Cambridge, Massachusetts, had a large political role in colonial and federalist politics. The Treaty of Hartford in 1650 established the boundary between New Amsterdam and the New England colonies (a line running due north of Greenwich, and diagonally across Long Island from Oyster Bay). The *Hartford Courant,* founded in 1764 and still publishing (285 Broad Street), is one of more than one hundred periodicals established in Hartford, and is America's oldest newspaper with a continuous circulation under the same name; it was very influential in the critical years before and after the Revolution in shaping public opinion.

The old town square, laid out in 1637, is now called City Hall Square. Here is the Old State House, an outstanding example of colonial architecture designed by Charles Bulfinch (its construction supervised by John Trumbull), completed in 1796, used as one of the state's two capitols until 1873 (sharing the honor with the capitol in New Haven), and then the sole capitol until 1879 (when the new building was completed). It is a National Historic Landmark. The present State Capitol (1880) is embellished with historic art inside and out. Relics include Israel Putnam's tombstone and Lafayette's camp bed. The State Library and Court Building contains a full-length portrait of George Washington by Gilbert Stuart and the original charter of 1662 (or a duplicate signed also by Charles II the same year). The Connecticut Historical Society's museum has Israel Putnam's sword, Nathan Hale's diary, and a piece of the original charter of 1662.

(Antiquarian and Landmarks Society of Connecticut, 255 Main Street, Hartford, Conn. 06106; phone: (860) 247-8996. Connecticut Historical Commission, 59 South Prospect Street, Hartford, Conn. 06106; phone: (860) 566-3005. Connecticut Historical Society, 1 Elizabeth Street, Hartford, Conn. 06105. Connecticut State Library, 231 Capitol Avenue, Hartford, Conn. 06115; phone: (860) 253-7412.)

Litchfield Historic District, Litchfield County. The 250th anniversary of Litchfield, a pretty little town of about 1,400 people, was celebrated in 1969. Although no fighting took place in the region during the Revolution, Litchfield was an important communications hub, with routes to New York City and Albany from Boston, Hartford, and New Haven. The town was a military depot and workshop for the Continental army in the north. More than five hundred Litchfield men went away to serve in the war, among them four companies of Sheldon's Horse, recruited in the vicinity by Benjamin Tallmadge. Ethan Allen's birthplace also survives in Litchfield. Another local man who left for the war was Aaron Burr, brother-in-law of Tapping Reeve and the latter's first law student.

About forty structures and other landmarks are within the relatively small Litchfield Historic District. The most important are listed below; all but the first are private homes today and not open to the public.

The Judge Tapping Reeve House (1773) and Law School Building (1784) are on South Street and Wolcott Street, a block from the green. Judge Reeve quickly became famous as a teacher of law and is generally credited with founding the country's first law school (1774). Ten years later he found it necessary to erect the small frame structure in his side yard. Judge Reeve's graduates make impressive statistics: 101 members of Congress, 34 chief justices of states, 40 judges of higher state courts, 28 United States senators, 14 governors of states, 6 cabinet members, and 3 justices of the United States Supreme Court. Two (Aaron Burr and John C. Calhoun) became vice presidents of the United States. (Aaron Burr, whose father was the second president of Princeton, had graduated from that college with distinction at age sixteen. His sister Sally married Reeve, who was also a Princetonian. Aaron was Reeve's first student and was nineteen when he left to become an "unattached volunteer" on Benedict Arnold's march to Quebec.) The houses are open to the public and operated by the Litchfield Historical Society, which also has a museum on the green and a research library.

The Ethan Allen Birthplace, a small, gambrel-roofed house on Old South Road, is believed to date from 1736 (scratched on a fireplace), which would make it the oldest in the village.

Sheldon's Tavern on North Street dates from 1760. The *WPA Guide* says it was designed by William Spratt, a London architect serving in the British army, and that Spratt added the ornamental railing on the roof in 1790 when the inn became a private residence. Other authorities say that Spratt only designed the elaborate entrance portico and palladian window added after 1760. George Washington's diary records his spending a night here.

The Benjamin Tallmadge House of 1775 is next to Sheldon's Tavern. Colonel Tallmadge (whose original home was in Setauket, New York), one of Washington's most esteemed subordinates and companions during the Revolution, became a businessman in Litchfield after the war. He added the second-story porticos after seeing Mount Vernon, to which the house bears a marked resemblance. The so-called Colonel Tallmadge House of 1784 was built by him as a store just south of his home. In 1801 it was moved to its present location across North Street and a few doors farther north.

Oliver Wolcott the Older was a signer of the Declaration of Independence, and governor of Connecticut from 1796 until his death the next year. The family has a remarkable record for filling this office, best summarized by the fact that the senior Oliver Wolcott's sister Ursula had the distinction of having a father, brother, husband, son, and nephew (Oliver, Jr.) who were governors of Connecticut. The Older Oliver Wolcott House is presently owned by a direct descendant of the man who built it in 1753 to 1754. Part of the statue of George III from Bowling Green (see under NEW YORK CITY: MANHATTAN) was molded into bullets by local ladies working in the side yard of this house. It is a simple frame structure of two and one-half stories with a gable roof and central chimney. Located on South Street opposite the Tapping Reeve House, it is near the handsome house of 1799 owned at one time by Oliver Wolcott, Jr. A contemporary building to the rear of the latter structure houses the Oliver Wolcott Library.

(Litchfield Historical Society, 7 South Street, Litchfield, Conn. 06759; phone: (860) 567-4501.)

Meigs (Return Jonathan) House Site, Middletown, Middlesex County. The house itself was torn down in 1936; the site is at 64 Crescent Street in a town of some 43,000 people, first settled in 1650. Son of a hatter, Colonel Return Jonathan Meigs (1740–1823) is interesting not only because of his remarkable Revolutionary War record as a combat commander but also for his delightful name, which was handed down from his father, who had been so named by his own father. As the story goes, Meigs's grandfather was courting a Quaker lady who had just about rejected him as a prospective husband when she suddenly relented and called out "Return, Jonathan!"; the overjoyed suitor vowed to make those sweet words his firstborn son's name.

Colonel Meigs of the Revolution started as a lieutenant in 1772, was a captain when he led a company to Boston, and was a major (second in command to the controversial Roger Enos) during Arnold's March to Quebec. One of the valuable journals of this expedition was kept by Meigs. Captured after scaling the walls of Quebec, he was on parole until exchanged a little more than a year later (10 January 1777). Promoted to lieutenant colonel, he conducted a brilliant raid from Guilford to Sag Harbor, Long Island (see under NEW YORK). He later had a major role in the capture of Stony Point, New York, and in stopping the mutiny of Connecticut troops in May 1780. When Arnold's treason was discovered, Meigs's Sixth Connecticut ("Leather Cap") Regiment was the first sent to defend the West Point area from the expected British offensive. The Connecticut regiments were reorganized shortly thereafter, and Meigs retired from military service (1 January 1781). After the war he became a surveyor for the Ohio Company of Associates, a leader in settling the region, and later an Indian agent.

Colonel Meigs's son and namesake became governor of Ohio. Another namesake (1801–1891), a nephew, was a prominent lawyer.

(Middlesex County Historical Society, 151 Main Street, Middletown, Conn. 06457; phone: (860) 349-0665.)

Mystic, New London County. The 37-acre Mystic Seaport Village recreates a coastal village of the nineteenth century, the time when famous clipper ships were built here. Among the dwellings is the Samuel Buckingham House (1768). The others date from after the Revolution, a total of nearly sixty structures of various sorts. Historic ships are exhibited at the wharves.

The Denison Homestead (1717), on Pequot-Sepos Road about 1.5 miles from Mystic, is on the 200-acre site of the original "mansion house" built by Captain George Denison, commander of Connecticut troops in King Philip's War. It is restored to show how eleven generations lived here. (Address inquiries to Denison Society, Pequot-Sepos Rd. P.O. Box 42, Mystic, Conn. 06355; phone: (860) 536-9248.)

Newgate Prison and Granby Copper Mines, East Granby, Hartford County. Often called the Simsbury mines, these were first worked in 1707. "Granby coppers" were common currency after 1737. By 1773 the mines were no longer productive, and they became Connecticut's jail for burglars, horse thieves, robbers, and—appropriately—counterfeiters. The place was named for Newgate Prison in London. During the Revolution it housed Loyalists and prisoners of war, acquiring an even more evil reputation than its namesake. In 1827 the newly completed prison at Wethersfield replaced Newgate. The aboveground structures, dating mostly from the early nineteenth century, had fallen into ruin when the Connecticut Historical Commission acquired the site in 1968. These have been restored, and the site was opened to the public in 1972. In 1976 Newgate Prison was declared a National Historic Landmark. Presently visitors can tour the 70-foot mine, where underground cells are preserved. A museum interprets Newgate's history as a prison and as probably the first copper mine developed in British America.

Take Exit 40 off I-91, heading West on Route 20. Proceed for approximately 8 miles until you come to the intersection of Routes 187 and 20. Continue up the hill, take a right at the signal light. Head north on Newgate Road for 2.3 miles; Olde New-Gate Prison is on the left.

(Connecticut Historical Commission, 59 South Prospect Street, Hartford, Conn. 06106.)

New Haven, New Haven Bay. A band of recently arrived English Puritans established the town and colony at this choice location in 1637. A few years later it was expanded into the New Haven Jurisdiction to include the towns of New Haven, Guilford, Milford, Stamford, Bramford, and (across the Sound on Long Island) Southold. This "jurisdiction" dissolved in 1664.

The older portion of the modern city preserves the original layout of square blocks around the 16-acre green, the first such city plan in America. In about 1750 New Haven started its period of greatest prosperity, becoming a major port for the expanding trade with other American colonies and the West Indies. Benedict Arnold moved here as a young man of twenty-ome to open a shop to sell drugs and books, and soon became a successful merchant sailing his own ships to Canada and the West Indies. New Haven was notorious as a center for illicit trade, and consequently a hotbed of Revolutionary sentiment from the start of the resistance to British authority.

The prime objective of General Sir Henry Clinton's punitive expedition along the Connecticut Coast in July

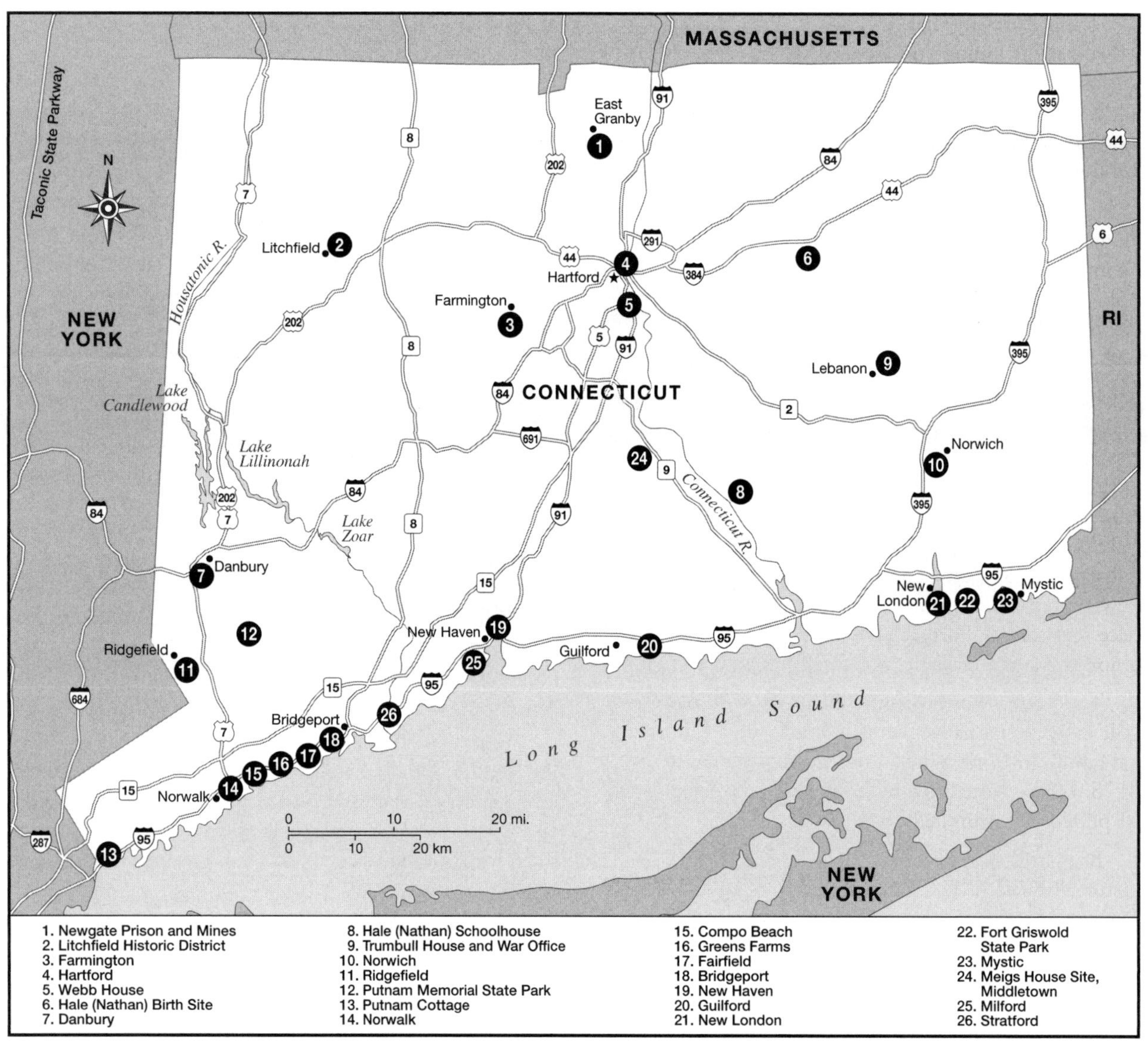

MAP BY XNR PRODUCTIONS. THE GALE GROUP.

1779 was New Haven. Brigadier Garth's division of his force attacked the place on 5 July. It was delayed briefly at a bridge across West River by a small body of volunteers including Yale students, but the raiders detoured along Milford Hill to the Derby Road and entered the town about noon. Reinforcements from the second division landed on the east side of the harbor and attacked the small position at Black Rock, now preserved as Fort Hale Park (see below). Garth intended to burn the town the next day, as soon as he had secured his position. But the local militia was massing in such strength that Garth withdrew from the town without being able to organize what he called "the conflagration it so richly deserved." The town did not suffer the fate of Fairfield, Greens Farms, and Norwalk, which were burned during the next few days.

The most important historical landmark surviving in New Haven is Connecticut Hall (1752), all that is left of Old Brick Row of Yale College. This dormitory has the room occupied by Nathan Hale as a student.

New Haven Green is where Captain Benedict Arnold assembled his Second Company, Connecticut Governor's Foot Guard, on 22 April 1775, two days after the bloodshed at Lexington and Concord, and forced the New Haven selectmen to surrender the keys to the municipal powder house.

The old burial ground of the First Church of Christ, part of which is covered by the present structure (the fourth on the site) is on Temple Street in the middle of the green. The oldest of the 137 historic gravestones dates from 1687.

Yale University has several notable libraries and museums, including the Beinecke Rare Book and Manuscript Library (which houses a Gutenberg Bible and books from the college library of 1742), the Peabody Museum of Natural History, Sterling Memorial Library, and the Yale Collection of Musical Instruments.

East Rock Park, which starts about a mile northeast of the green, preserves a point used by the Indians for signaling and the place where many inhabitants of New Haven took refuge during the British raid. The 426-acre park encompasses a rock that is 359 feet high and 1.5 miles long.

Fort Hale Park overlooks the harbor from the east. Here Governor Tryon's division of the punitive expedition, mainly Loyalists and Germans, overcame a small garrison and three guns that had caused them considerable annoyance during their landing a short distance south at Lighthouse Point (so called after 1840). Tryon reembarked from Fort Hale when Garth withdrew from New Haven and continued his raid to the south. The place was called Fort Rock before being renamed in honor of Nathan Hale after the Revolution.

The Pardee Morris House, 325 Lighthouse Road, was built in 1685, partially destroyed during the Revolution, and rebuilt in 1780. With period furnishings, it is among the "Sites Also Noted" by the National Survey and open to the public (hours limited).

Back in the center of town, the New Haven Colony Historical Society, 114 Whitney Avenue, has a regional museum.

(New Haven Preservation Trust, 900 Chapel Street, Box 1671, New Haven, Conn. 06510; phone: (203) 562-5919.)

New London, Thames River, New London County. About 3 miles from where the river enters Long Island Sound, and a good natural harbor, the site was settled in 1646 by John Winthrop the Younger with Puritans from Massachusetts. In 1658 it adopted the name New London, having been called Nameaug, and the Thames lost its Indian name at the same time. Colonial landmarks surviving in the present city of 26,000 are the Antientist burial ground laid out in 1653, the Old Town Mill built about 1650 and rebuilt in 1712, the Joshua Hempsted House of 1678 (open to the public), and the lighthouse of 1909 on the spot where the original one was put up in 1760.

Benedict Arnold's raid of 6 September 1781 destroyed about 150 buildings, including 65 private dwellings, and did damage valued by a committee after the war at $486,000. The "Fire Lands," a 500,000-acre tract in the Western Reserve (now in Ohio), was used to repay Connecticut citizens for war losses in New London and other towns raided by the British.

New London was picked for this raid because the traitor Arnold knew the terrain from his childhood, Connecticut was a vital source of supplies for the Continental army, and New London was an important naval base. Some twenty privateers had been fitted out in the three years after the congressional resolution of March 1776 permitted their use against "enemies of these United Colonies." (Arnold destroyed about twelve ships; fifteen escaped upriver.) Another purpose of the New London raid was to divert Patriot strength from the force marching to Yorktown. The principal military action of the raid (and one of the last battles of the Revolution in the north) took place on the site of Fort Griswold State Park.

Benedict Arnold claimed that most of the destruction in New London was caused by accidental fires, which his troops made every effort to control. The Patriots accused him of viewing the scene from the old cemetery (on Hempstead Street north of Bulkeley Square) "with the apparent satisfaction of a Nero." The cemetery has about one hundred graves of Revolutionary War veterans.

Several other historic sites exist in today's New London. Fort Trumbull State Park, rebuilt by the United States Navy in the late 1830s, opened to the public in 2002. Located at 90 Walbach Street, it sits on the same grounds as the original Fort Trumbull made famous in Benedict Arnold's raid on Fort Griswold. Only one building remains from its Revolutionary War days: the Nathan Hale Schoolhouse, which is now located at Union Plaza in downtown New London. The historic building, referred to as "the traveling schoolhouse" by local historians for its many locales, is where the Patriot spy taught from March 1774 until July 1775, when he left his career as a teacher to become a lieutenant in the Seventh Connecticut Militia. In Williams Park, facing Broad Street, is a duplicate of the Nathan Hale statue located in New York City's City Hall Park. The Nathaniel Shaw House, 11 Blinman Street, was the home of the marine agent responsible for equipping the state's naval vessels, giving sailing orders, and overseeing disposal of privateersmen's prizes. The New London County Historical Society, founded in 1870, has occupied the Shaw House since 1907. The phone number is (860) 443-1209.

(New London Landmarks, 49 Washington Street, New London, Conn. 06320; phone: (860) 442-0003.)

Norwalk, Fairfield County. The site was bought from the Indians by Roger Ludlow and Daniel Patrick, then settled in 1651 by a small company from Hartford. Many legends are associated with the place. The home of Colonel Thomas Fitch, an officer of the Seven Years' War, is called the "Yankee Doodle House" because he is said to have inspired the song (see also FORT CRAILO under

New York). A memorial fountain was erected by the DAR in memory of Nathan Hale, who obtained his schoolmaster disguise here before heading for Long Island on his fatal mission. The chair in which Governor Tryon sat on Grumman's Hill to watch his troops burn the town in July 1779 has been preserved. (This ended his Connecticut Coast raid, which started at New Haven on 5 July and passed through Fairfield and Greens Farms before reaching Norwalk on 11 July.) Otherwise, the landmarks of the Revolution have been obliterated in a modern industrial city of over eighty thousand people.

Norwich, head of the Thames River, New London County. Uncas the Mohegan, famous friend of the white settlers, defeated his Narragansett sachem counterpart 3 miles north of the present city in 1643. The original settlement of Europeans, established in 1659 and called Mohegan until 1662, was an important port during the eighteenth century. Benedict Arnold's home was here from his birth in 1741 until he sold the family property on the death of his parents twenty-one years later and went to live with his sister Hannah in New Haven. Norwich was the home of the Huntington family: Benjamin (1736–1800) was a member of the Continental Congress, a judge, and the first mayor of the town (1784–1796); Jabez (1719–1786) a Patriot leader and militia general during the Revolution; his son Jedediah (1743–1818) a general in the Continental Army; and another son, Ebenezer (1754–1834), a soldier during the Revolution and later a congressman. Samuel Huntington (1731–1796), in another line of the family, settled in Norwich after being admitted to the bar in 1758. He was prominent in the politics leading to the break with England, a member of the Continental Congress throughout the war, a signer of the Declaration of Independence, and president of the Congress for almost two years (29 September 1779 to 6 July 1781). During the last ten years of his life he was governor of Connecticut.

Leffingwell Inn is a well-restored structure dating from 1675, opened as an inn by Norwich's most prominent founding father, Thomas Leffingwell, and operated during the Revolutionary era by Colonel Christopher Leffingwell. Still known as "Thomas Leffingwell's publique house" after Thomas himself ceased to be active, under Christopher's management it was an important center of Revolutionary politics. George Washington was entertained at the inn. The structure reflects the colonial practice of making a mansion by joining two small houses and adding ells. Leffingwell Inn is restored, furnished with seventeenth- and eighteenth-century pieces, and open to the public at odd hours, and it displays a number of rare items. It is at the junction of Connecticut Highways 2, 32, and 169 (Turnpike Exit 81), at 348 Washington Street (Society of the Founders of Norwich, Connecticut, P.O. Box 13, 405 Washington Street, Norwich, Conn. 06360; phone: (203) 889-9440.)

Norwichtown Green, center of the original settlement, has been designated a historic district. The Royal Mohegan Burial Ground, near the junction of Sachem and Washington Streeets, has the grave of Uncas, who died about 1682.

Putnam Cottage, Greenwich, Fairfield County. From this little house, which dates from about 1730, the sixty-one-year-old Israel Putnam is reputed to have made his legendary flight (26 February 1779) to escape capture by a patrol of British dragoons. Although the story should not be given much credence, Putnam Cottage is on the list of "Sites Also Noted" by the National Survey of Historic Sites and Buildings in 1964. A highway marker on U.S. 1 at 243 Putnam Avenue in Greenwich is in front of the "cottage," formerly Knapp's Tavern. Under the care of the local Daughters of the American Revolution chapter since 1906, it has two rooms restored in the style of the seventeenth century and various historical relics. The marker mentions the "famous ride down 'Put's Hill.'" The Post Road is cut through the rock at about the place where the general would have ridden down to the valley.

Putnam Memorial State Park, just north of Redding, Fairfield County. The encampment of several Continental brigades under the overall command of General Israel Putnam during the exceptionally severe winter of 1778 to 1779 is preserved in this 183-acre state park. The blockhouses and palisade have been restored, a museum has relics of "Connecticut's Valley Forge," and traces of original buildings are preserved. Recreational facilities include picnicking, pond fishing, and hiking.

"Old Put" rode from here to inspect outposts around Greenwich (see PUTNAM COTTAGE). The site of his legendary killing of a wolf in its den during the winter of 1742 to 1743 is in Wolf Den State Park, between Pomfret and Brooklyn, Windham County. The legendary hero of the Colonial Wars who became known in the Revolution as "Old Put" had moved into the latter area of Connecticut around 1740, when in his early twenties. The great-grandson of an English immigrant to Massachusetts (1634), he was a cousin of General Rufus Putnam and granduncle of the founder of Putnam's Sons publishers.

Ridgefield Battle Site, Fairfield County. Governor William Tryon's two thousand British and Tory raiders returning to their ships after burning Danbury on 26 April 1777 were blocked the next afternoon by a force of Continentals and militia under Generals Benedict

Arnold and G. S. Silliman around Ridgefield (15 miles south of Danbury). General David Wooster nipped at Tryon's heels with two hundred militia, snapping up about forty prisoners before he was mortally wounded. About midafternoon the raiders hit the blocking position at Ridgefield and forced Arnold to withdraw. A highway marker on a little hill on Main Street south of the junction of the Danbury Road reads "Battle of Ridgefield, April 27, 1777. The Third and Chief Engagement Occurred on This Ridge."

The British camped a mile away. A Loyalist guided them the next morning around another delaying position established by Arnold on the route to Compo Beach. The raiders then debarked after conducting a four-hundred-man spoiling attack that disrupted an intended American assault.

Congress was finally forced to recognize Arnold's exceptional merit and promote him to major general. He had had one horse killed beneath him, another wounded, and had narrowly escaped capture. Wooster died five days after the action at Ridgefield and is buried in Danbury.

Still standing in Ridgefield is the Keeler Tavern, where the British emplaced a gun after driving Arnold from the barricade mentioned above. A cannonball remains embedded in a corner post of the tavern, fired by Tryon after the battle of Ridgefield. The house had been shelled by the British earlier, and a man climbing its stairs had a cannonball pass between his legs. "I'm killed! I'm a dead man!" he is reported to have shouted after falling to the foot of the stairs and insisting that both legs were gone. "As soon as he was undeceived," as Benson Lossing told the story after visiting the tavern in 1848, "he put them [the legs] in requisition, and fled, as fast as they could carry him. . . ." The Keeler Tavern Preservation Society opened the Keeler Tavern as a museum in 1966. It is located on Main Street (Route 35) in Ridgefield.

(Ridgefield Library and Historical Association, 472 Main Street, Ridgefield, Conn. 06877; phone: (203) 438-2282. The Ridgefield Historical Society, The Scott House, 4 Sunset Lane, Ridgefield, Conn. 06877; phone: (203) 438-5821; website: www.ridgefieldhistoricalsociety.org.)

Stratford. The Captain David Judson House, 967 Academy Hill, is most interesting for the slave quarters in the basement. The house has been restored to how it probably looked in 1775, when the Judsons owned seven slaves. The house is owned by the Stratford Historical Society, which also operates the Catherine Bunnell Mitchell Museum next door. An exhibit in the latter explores slavery and the role of African American soldiers during the Revolution. There are also a number of documents relevant to the Revolutionary period and an account by the slave Jack Arabas, who successfully sued for his freedom after his owner reneged on a promise to free him if he joined the Continental army. The House and Museum are open from June through October on Wednesday, Saturday, and Sunday, 11 A.M. to 4 P.M. Take Exit 53 from the Merritt Parkway south to Main Street and then continue 5 miles to Academy Hill. Phone: (203) 378-0630.

(National Society of Colonial Dames in Connecticut, 211 Main Street, and the Wethersfield Historical Society, 150 Main Street; phone: (860) 529-7656. Both addresses are in Wethersfield, Conn. 06109.)

Trumbull House and War Office, Lebanon, New London County. Jonathan Trumbull the Elder (1710–1785) became governor of Connecticut in 1769 and held this office until his voluntary retirement after the Revolution, a year before his death. He was the only governor on the Patriot side when the Revolution started. Connecticut being the principle source of food, clothing, and munitions for Washington's army, Trumbull's most important activity was managing this support. More than 1,200 meetings of the Connecticut Council of Safety were held in the converted Trumbull store next to his home, many of them pertaining to supply. The appellation "Brother Jonathan," which the British used as early as March 1776 to designate Americans, may have originated from Washington's alleged remark "We must consult Brother Jonathan" when faced with a particularly tough problem; he would have been referring to the elder Jonathan Trumbull. (The latter's son and namesake was paymaster general of the Northern Department while his brother Joseph was commissary general of the army.)

The sites are marked on Lebanon Commons. Trumbull's house, built by his father in 1740, is the property of the DAR. The store, built probably in 1732, was restored in 1891 when acquired by the Sons of the American Revolution. Both buildings have been moved, and the "War Office" is no longer next to the Trumbull home, but diagonally across the green.

(Lebanon Historical Society, 856 Trumbull Highway, on the Historic Lebanon Green, P.O. Box 151, Lebanon, Conn. 06249; phone: (860) 642-6579.)

Webb Deane Stevens Museum, 211 Main Street, Wethersfield, Hartford County. The historic Wethersfield Conference on 21 to 22 May 1781 between Washington and Rochambeau in the Webb House, a handsome old frame house, has long been accepted as laying the strategic groundwork for the triumph at Yorktown. "Many secondary accounts erroneously state that at the Wethersfield conference (22 May 1781) Washington was told by the French that Admiral de Grasse was definitely coming north to cooperate with the allies . . .," writes Don Higginbotham in *The War of American Independence* (1971). "Though

Rochambeau did have advance notice of de Grasse's plans, he felt obliged by his instructions not to disclose the information at that time. . . . Several very recent works, failing to consult Fitzpatrick or Freeman on this point, repeat the mistake" (p. 388 n50).

The Joseph Webb House was declared a National Historic Landmark in 1961. (Also in Wethersfield is the Buttolph-Williams House of 1692.)

Readers who wish to corroborate this question for themselves can check the two well-known sources cited by Higginbotham: Fitzpatrick, ed., *Writings of Washington,* XX, pp. 103–104, and D. S. Freeman, *Washington,* V, p. 296 n87.

There is no historical doubt as of this writing that Washington spent several days in May 1781 in the Webb House. He arrived on 19 May, rode to Hartford on 21 May to meet Count Rochambeau and returned with him to the Webb House, and the next day had a conference that broadly outlined the plans for a combined Franco-American offensive against New York City. Virginia figured in the discussion only in that Washington hoped British troops there would ease their pressure on Lafayette if weakened by detachments sent to defend New York.

The house built by Joseph Webb in 1752, meanwhile, is a well-preserved two-story structure of considerable architectural interest. Its setting is enhanced by the broad street of old trees and old homes on which it stands today. One of these is the home of Silas Deane, America's first diplomat abroad; south of the Webb House, it was built in 1776.

The other namesake house was built in 1788 by Isaac Stevens for his bride, Sarah Wright. The Milford Cemetery, just off Cherry Street near the center of Milford, was established in 1642. This historic cemetery contains the graves of several African American Revolutionary War soldiers. Even more unusual, there is a plaque honoring these soldiers on the town green.

DELAWARE

The little state of Delaware produced a disproportionate number of men who loomed large in the Revolution: the important political theorist John Dickinson; Caesar and Thomas Rodney; and "the American Diomed," Robert Kirkwood, killed in action as a sixty-two-year-old captain after the Revolution, "the thirty-third time he had risked his life for his country" (wrote "Light Horse Harry" Lee in his *Memoirs*). Only the Dickinson House survives in modern Delaware as a landmark associated with the lives of these men. Their names are honored in other states: the town of Rodney in Jefferson County, Missouri, where Thomas acquired land after the Revolution; and the Kirkwood subdivision of Camden, South Carolina, one of the many places where Captain Kirkwood distinguished himself as a leader of the "Blue Hen Chickens."

The single regiment of Delaware Continentals was one of the smartest-looking and best-equipped units to take the field at the start of the Revolution, and its men turned out also to be probably the best fighters. The nickname comes from a legendary brood of Delaware gamecocks. There was almost no fighting on Delaware soil (only at Cooch's Bridge), but the Delaware Continentals fought with conspicuous gallantry and irreplaceable losses from the first major battle in New York (Long Island) to the last major battle in the South (Eutaw Springs), missing few in between. Their memorials are therefore almost everywhere except in Delaware itself.

A primary source of information is the Historical Society of Delaware, founded in 1864, which is located at 505 Market Street at the intersection of Sixth and Market Streets, Wilmington, Del. 19801. It maintains the Delaware History Museum, a research library, and three historic sites. Phone: (302) 655-7161. Another source is the state tourism office at 99 Kings Highway, in Dover. It is accessible via the internet at www. visitdelaware.net, or by phone at (302) 739-4271. Additionally, the Division of Historical and Cultural Affairs and the Delaware State Museum, which administers the Delaware State Visitors Center, has a reliable assortment of brochures and guidebooks to help the curious find their way through a state that is directly, over the last thirty years, recovering its Revolutionary War past. The visitors' center is at 406 Federal Street, Dover, Del. 19901. Website: www. destatemuseums.org; phone: (302) 739-4266.

Cooch's Bridge Battlefield. After failing to oppose the British landing at Head of Elk (see under MARYLAND), American forces then fought an unsuccessful delaying action that started on Iron Hill and passed by the place now known as Cooch's Bridge. The latter is about a mile south of Newark on Old Baltimore Turnpike. The Cooch House, briefly used by Cornwallis, survives in today's Cooch's Bridge, and is occupied by the Cooch family. A large granite marker on the highway at the entrance to the property points out that the fighting took place in this vicinity, the only Revolutionary War battle in Delaware and (allegedly) the first in which the Stars and Stripes were carried.

The Cooch House is in an excellent state of repair, the large brown structure standing on well-tended grounds about 100 yards from the highway. It is the private home of a direct descendent of Colonel Cooch. In 2005 plans to renovate the site, the bridge, the gristmill, and the encompassing 200-acre grounds are underway. The battlefield is presently marked by four cannon from the War of 1812 loaned from the Brooklyn Navy Yard.

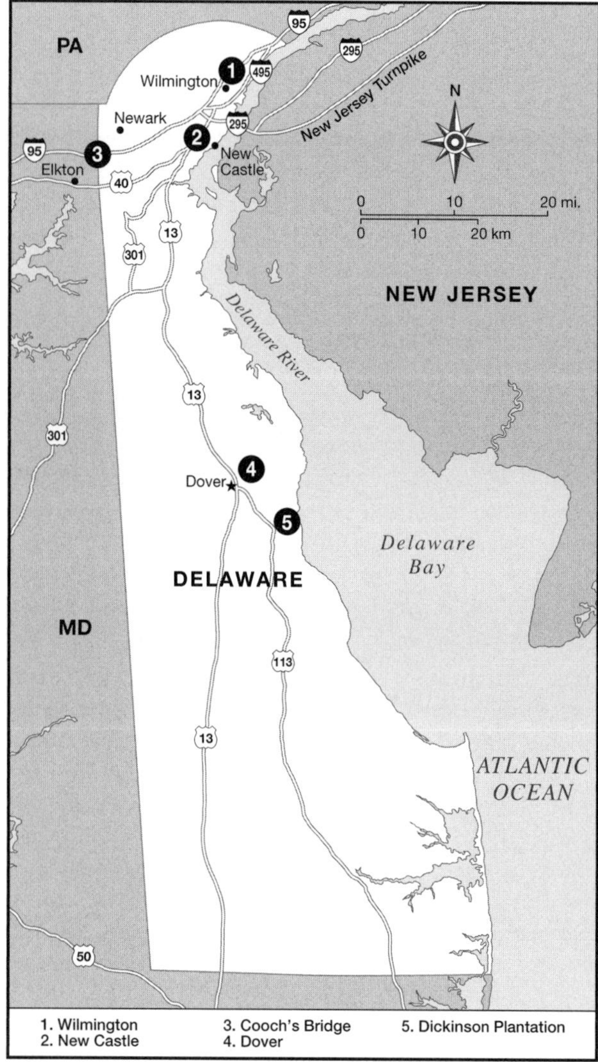

MAP BY XNR PRODUCTIONS. THE GALE GROUP.

John Dickinson Plantation, 340 Kitts Kummock Road, near Dover. Phone: (302) 739-3277. Threatened with destruction in 1952, the home of John Dickinson, "Penman of the Revolution," was saved by the National Society of Colonial Dames of America. The state matched the latter organization's donation of $25,000, and the property has been restored with state funds and private gifts. It is maintained by the state's Department of Historic and Cultural Affairs.

One authority has said that in the literature of the American Revolution the position of John Dickinson was comparable to that of George Washington in military affairs, Benjamin Franklin in diplomacy, and Robert Morris in finance. Born in Maryland in 1732, Dickinson was raised in this house built by his father in 1740. He studied law in Philadelphia before spending another three years at the Middle Temple in London. During the Stamp Act controversy he did most of the work in drafting the "Declaration of Rights and Grievances" (1765), and later, the "Petition to the King" (1771). Meanwhile, he presented constitutional objections to the Townshend Acts in fourteen essays in the *Pennsylvania Chronicle* (1767–1768) that became famous as "The Farmer's Letters." In pamphlet form they were titled "Letters from a Farmer in Pennsylvania to the Inhabitants of the British Colonies." Dickinson argued that Parliament had authority only to regulate colonial trade but not to tax them for revenue.

During the Revolution he was active in Congress as leader of the conservative faction. He was one of only two congressmen who immediately took the field for military duty when the fighting started, although he had voted against the Declaration of Independence. John Dickinson continued his strenuous public career until his death in 1808.

The house built by his father burned in 1804, with little surviving except the brick walls. Dickinson rebuilt it as a tenant house. The structure consists of two stories, a gable roof replacing the original hip roof, and a small kitchen wing added after 1804. The present reconstruction, based on Dickinson's records of 1804 to 1806, has been open to the public since 1956. The National Survey calls it "one of the most interesting architectural examples of the plantation house of the region" and comments that with its setting of cultivated fields it looks much as it did originally. A garden near the house has also been restored. Though the slave quarters are no longer extant, the plantation tour does include information about the Dickinsons' slaveholding and attitude toward manumission. More information on the generally avoided topic of slavery during the War for Independence can be gleaned at the Afro-American Historical Society of Delaware, 512 East Fourth Street, Wilmington, Del.; phone: (302) 571-9300.

The Dickinson House is reached by driving 6 miles south from Dover on U.S. 113 and 0.5 mile east on Kitts Hummock Road.

Dover. The state capital since 1777, Dover was established in 1683. The Delaware State Museum manages eight museums, each addressing different aspects of the state's history. Information on these museums is accessible through the previously referenced contact at the beginning of this entry. Of particular note is the State House Museum, located on the green in Dover and open Tuesday through Saturday, 10 A.M. to 4:30 P.M., and Sunday 1:30 to 4:30 P.M. The Georgian-style building has been restored to its 1792 appearance. The museum has a great deal of information about Delaware in the Revolution and early republic, as well as a special exhibit on slavery and free blacks in the eighteenth century.

John Dickinson Plantation. *This dirt-floor dwelling on the grounds of the Dickinson Plantation near Dover, Delaware, was inhabited by plantation slaves or tenant farmers. The enclosed plots were used to grow vegetables and herbs.* © KEVIN FLEMING/CORBIS.

The Nanticoke Museum preserves the history of the Nanticoke, the original inhabitants of the Delmarva Peninsula. In 1742 the Delaware government accused them of conspiracy and denied them the right to choose a chief. They eventually requested and obtained permission to join the Iroquois, and followed most of that people into exile in Canada at the end of the Revolution. A small remnant of the Nanticoke people hung on in a community on Angola Neck, finally gaining official recognition in 1922. Their museum is north of Millsboro on Del. Route 24 and open Tuesday to Thursday, 9 A.M. to 4 P.M., and Saturday, noon to 4 P.M. Phone: (302) 945-7022.

New Castle, Delaware River. The historic section of the city survives as an exceptionally picturesque area containing several structures of great architectural importance and spanning a long period of Dutch, Swedish, and English occupation. New Castle was founded in 1651 by Peter Stuyvesant and was the seat of Dutch government on the South (Delaware) River. A large section of the village green (marketplace) laid out by Stuyvesant has been preserved in the heart of the historic district. After being held briefly by the Swedes the town was seized by the British (1664) and given to William Penn in 1682. A marker at Delaware Street and the Strand indicates the place where Penn first set foot on American soil. The National Survey identifies the following surviving eighteenth-century structures as being of special importance: the Old Court House (also known as the State House), the Amstel House, Immanuel Episcopal Church (1703), the Gunning-Bedford House, and the Presbyterian Church, all dating from before 1730. The Amstel House serves as one of the three museums and the headquarters for the New Castle Historical Society, 2 East Fourth Street. Phone: (302) 322-2794. Its website, www.newcastlehistory.org, provides a virtual tour and interesting facts about some of these buildings.

The Old Court House on 211 Delaware Street was built in 1732 to house the colonial assembly, which met here until 1777. It was here that an acrimonious sesssion debated and finally approved the Declaration of Independence. Guided tours address Delaware's early history; Tuesday to Saturday, 10 A.M. to 4:30 P.M., Sunday 1:30 P.M. to 4:30 P.M. Phone: (302) 323-5319.

Wilmington. A port city whose harbor is formed by the mouths of Brandywine and Christina Creeks about a mile from the Delaware River, this place was settled by the Swedes in 1638. Holy Trinity, or Old Swedes Church, dates from 1698, and is "probably the oldest church in the United States which has been in continuous use" ("Wilmington," *Encyclopaedia Britannica*, 11th ed.). The old First Presbyterian Meeting House was built in 1740 and is located at Tenth and Market Streets; the Wilmington Friends' School (1748) at 101 School Road in North Wilmington; and Old Town Hall (1798) at 500 Block Market Street. In a 1976 response to the historic buildings falling victim to urban decay, the city moved five houses listed on the National Register of Historic Places to the 500 block of Market Street. They are: the Cook-Simms House (1778); the Coxe House (1801); the Jacobs House (1748); and the Jacob and Obidiah Dingee Houses (1771) and (1773). This area is named Wilmington Square, and all of the homes can be viewed from the outside. Other tour arrangements can be made by calling Wilmington Square at (302) 655-7161.

In colonial times Wilmington was famous for its flour mills, and water-powered mills of many types were located along the Brandywine. E. I. du Pont began building his powder industry 3 miles north of the city in 1802.

The Patriot army was concentrated around Wilmington before the Battle of the Brandywine. The city was occupied by the British several months later when the Delaware River forts finally were reduced, but few landmarks associated with the Revolutionary War have survived the economic development of the region. The other side of the coin is nearby New Castle.

DISTRICT OF COLUMBIA

Until about a decade after the end of the American Revolution the 69-square-mile area now comprising the District of Columbia was a wilderness relieved only by the little village of Georgetown. The only National Historic Landmark of the Revolution in the nation's capital is the Gundelo *Philadelphia* (below). But Washington has many important museums, libraries, and other attractions for persons interested in the American Revolution. Help with locating these is available through the Washington, D.C. Convention and Tourism Corporation. It is located at 901 Seventh Street N.W., 4th Floor, 20001. Website: www.washington.org; phone: (202) 789–7000.

In addition to the Gundelo *Philadelphia*, the city's boundary markers of the original district going back to the mid-eighteenth century were added to the National Register of Historic Places in 1996.

There are some museums of particular note to students of the American Revolution. The Daughters of the American Revolution Museum at 1776 D Street N.W. features thirty-two period rooms and a library of great use to genealogists. The museum is open Monday to Friday 9:30 A.M. to 4:00 P.M. and Saturday 9:00 A.M. to 5:00 P.M.; the library Monday to Friday 8:30 A.M. to 4:00 P.M. and Saturday 9:00 A.M. to 5:00 P.M.; period room tours are available Monday to Friday 10:00 A.M. to 2:30 P.M. and Saturday 9:00 A.M. to 4:30 P.M. Phone: (202) 628-1776.

The Navy Museum, operated by the Department of the Navy in the Washington Navy Yard, 805 Kidder Breese S.E., is one of the few museums in the country to devote much attention to the role of the navy during the Revolution. Its exhibits trace the American naval effort in its three components: the Continental navy, state navies, and privateers. In addition, the museum examines the key role of the French navy in obtaining ultimate victory for the Americans. There are many intriguing artifacts from the first years of the United States Navy. Unfortunately, increased fear has led the Department of Defense to require that those interested call ahead for an appointment: (202) 433-4882.

No historical guide can fail to include the need for a visit to the National Archives. Among its many treasures are the original Declaration of Independence and Constitution. Its holdings and those of the Library of Congress form the cornerstone of American historical research. The National Archives Building is located at 700 Pennsylvania Avenue N.W., and is open Monday and Wednesday 8:45 A.M. to 5:00 P.M.; Tuesday, Thursday, and Friday 8:45 A.M. to 9:00 P.M.; and Saturday 8:45 A.M. to 4:45 P.M. For more information, check their website: http://www.archives.gov/dc-metro/.

The Library of Congress occupies three buildings on Capitol Hill: the Thomas Jefferson Building (1897), the John Adams Building (1938), and the James Madison Memorial Building (1981). The main entrance is 101 Independence Avenue, S.E. The library is open Monday to Friday, 8:30 A.M. to 9:30 P.M., and Saturday, 8:30 A.M. to 6:30 P.M. Guided tours are available from the Great Hall of the Thomas Jefferson Building, Monday to Friday, 10:30 and 11:30 A.M. and 1:30, 2:30, and 3:30 P.M., and Saturday, 10:30 and 11:30 A.M. and 1:30 and 2:30 P.M. For more information, check their website: http://www.loc.gov/. The Library of Congress also hosts the incredibly valuable American Memory website: http://memory.loc.gov/ammem/.

Gundelo ***Philadelphia,*** Smithsonian Institution, Museum of History and Technology, 14th Street and Constitution Avenue. The exceptionally well-preserved hulk of the U.S. gundelo *Philadelphia* is a National Historic Landmark. Part of Benedict Arnold's hastily built fleet, it was sunk in the Battle of Valcour Island, New York, on 11 October 1776 and recovered in 1935. After being exhibited at various places in New York, in 1960 the remarkable relic was placed in the Smithsonian.

Beautifully displayed for viewing from all angles (a catwalk is provided parallel to one gunwale), the craft is 54 feet long, 15 feet in beam, and about 5 feet deep. The 36-foot mast has only the top section missing, and the hull timbers remain in place. Three shot holes are visible, one with the ball remaining lodged. Hundreds of objects were found with the boat and many are arranged as they might have been originally on the deck.

FLORIDA

The role of East and West Florida in the Revolution has been brushed off as being peripheral and inconsequential, even by those who might be expected to have a parochial interest in stressing it. One reason may be that history is confused with patriotism: the Revolutionary events in the Floridas were dominated not by American patriots but by British and Loyalist leaders. The Floridas were a refuge for southern Loyalists and hostile Indians, and patriot politicians of Georgia and the Carolinas made a fiasco of three attempted military expeditions against St. Augustine. But if we shake our nationalistic vanities and concede that we should be interested in what happened in both camps during the Revolution, there is more to be found in Florida pertaining to the American Revolution than you might have suspected.

It so happens that British and Loyalist leaders in Florida during the Revolution were exceptionally able men. Unfortunately there are virtually no architectural landmarks standing to remind the modern visitor of these men, but at least they should be named.

The first British governor of East Florida was James Grant, appointed in 1764 and invalided home in 1771. A professional soldier, veteran of several colonial campaigns, prisoner of war in Montreal with Andrew Lewis of Virginia, and commander of the Cherokee Expedition of 1761 in the Carolinas, he was well known in America before the Revolution. During this service he developed a profound contempt for the martial qualities of his provincial associates of the Colonial Wars and is alleged to have told the House of Commons in February 1775 that he "would undertake to march from one end of the [American] continent to the other with five thousand men." This slander was uttered within hearing of an American, William Alexander (Lord Stirling, so-called), whom he would meet on the battlefield of Long Island, New York, a few months later. Grant went on to play a prominent role in battles against Washington's army until detached to the West Indies with a force of about six thousand troops. In Florida he was an excellent governor. (Alden, *The South in the Revolution*, p. 122.)

Grant's deputy and temporary governor after his departure was Dr. John Moultrie, Loyalist brother of the South Carolina hero William Moultrie.

Patrick Tonyn arrived on 1 March 1774 to take over as governor, remaining for the duration of the Revolution. A lieutenant colonel in 1761, promoted to full colonel in August 1777, and jumped to major general on 19 October 1781, he rose after the Revolution to full general. John Moultrie remained as lieutenant governor to Tonyn, sailing for England in 1784.

The Swiss brothers Augustine and Marc Prevost performed brilliantly as British officers in Florida and later in Georgia. They probably were sons of the officer who had raised the Royal American Regiment (or Sixtieth Foot), during the Colonial Wars. Augustine was a fifty-two-year-old veteran when the Revolution started, and was promoted soon thereafter to colonel and to the local rank of major general in February 1779, when he led British troops from East Florida into Georgia. His younger brother, Marc, figured prominently in skirmishes in Florida (especially Alligator Bridge) before distinguishing himself at Brier Creek (see under GEORGIA.)

Indian agent John Stuart, the Sir William Johnson of the South, had held his post thirteen years before the Revolution. From St. Augustine and Pensacola he continued his important duties in Florida. After the Revolution

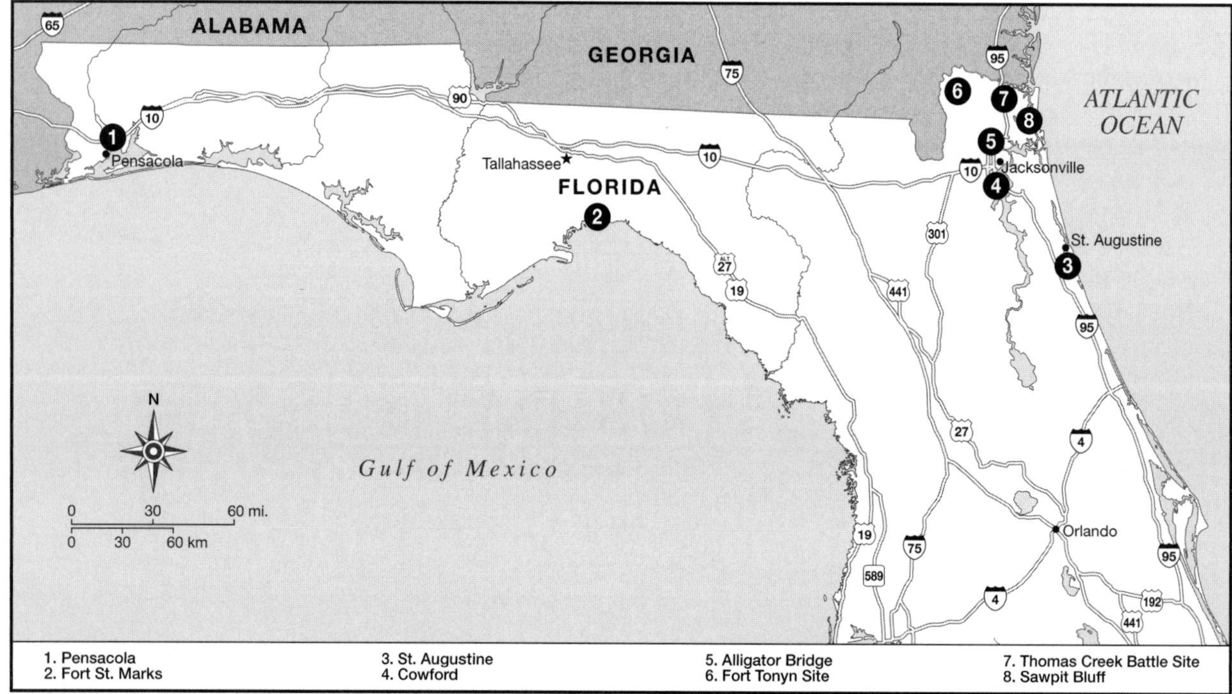

MAP BY XNR PRODUCTIONS. THE GALE GROUP.

this interesting man had a prominent role in the Napoleonic Wars.

John Brown was the great Loyalist commander, reaching Florida after being run out of Augusta, Georgia, to become lieutenant colonel of the King's Rangers and superintendent of Indian affairs for the Eastern Division of H. M. Southern Indian Department. He was conspicuously effective in Revolutionary War actions in East Florida and Georgia.

The tourism industry is extremely strong and diverse in Florida. It appears, consequently, that Revolutionary War landmarks information receives smaller focus here than in other states, and can be difficult to find on a state-agency level. A state tourism website, www.visitflorida.com, offers some degree of colonial landmark information. Other reliable sources include local historical societies, and they are listed when possible within sections on the appropriate landmarks.

Alligator Bridge, Alligator Creek, Nassau County. Historians still debate the battle's exact location, some saying it was east of the little town of Callahan, others quite certain that it was central Callahan, where a marker has been placed. The attack by Colonel Elijah Clark with three hundred mounted Georgia militia here on 30 June 1778 against a much larger force of British regulars, Loyalists, and Indians was the major engagement of the third unsuccessful attempt by the Americans to conquer East Florida. As in previous failures, southern politicians refused to subordinate their militia to the command of Continental army officers. So while General Robert Howe camped 15 miles north at Fort Tonyn with some four hundred regular troops and waited for Georgia governor John Houstoun and South Carolina general Andrew Williamson to catch up with their militia, Elijah Clark pursued the enemy detachment that had been routed from an outpost just west of Fort Tonyn. (The King's Rangers of Colonel Thomas Brown had been driven from around the Captain Taylor House near King's Ferry. Retreating south into Cabbage Swamp, they had been saved by a column of some two hundred British regulars sent north from the defensive position being hastily organized at Alligator Bridge.)

In hasty field fortifications established by Major Marc Prevost were 500 British regulars. Outside the works were another 200 regulars plus about 100 Rangers under Brown and a Colonel McGirth.

Clark attacked with a detachment of mounted men, expecting to break through a weak point in the British field works and pour the rest of his three hundred troops into the breach. The horses had trouble getting through the obstacles of logs and brush put out for precisely this purpose, then reached the ditch dug with the same general idea in mind. This was too wide for the horses to jump, and at this dramatic moment the Redcoats started shooting and shouting. Clark was wounded and almost captured, after which recall was sounded. According to other accounts the decisive maneuver was a counterattack by the British troops posted outside their works. But Clark withdrew, having had nine killed in action.

Hunger and sickness did the rest, and the invasion of 1778 collapsed.

A marker in the middle of modern Callahan says this was the site of Alligator Bridge. Archaeological efforts have not significantly proven it to be in open land much farther east, but some historians reason that the creek is not wide enough at Callahan for a bridge, and that King's Highway, where the action occurred, probably crossed the creek farther east.

Cowford, St. Johns River in Jacksonville. (Cowford was the original name of what is now Jacksonville.) This was the headquarters of British defensive efforts against the three Patriot campaigns to conquer East Florida. Earlier it was where Governor Tonyn held negotiations with some of the Lower Creek Indians (later Seminoles) to conclude an alliance; the Treaty of Cowford was drawn up in December 1775.

A year later a skirmish took place at Cowford when a small force of Patriots advanced this far south before being driven back across St. Marys River by Britain's Indian allies. "I must acknowledge that they are very intelligent, and usefull Spies in observing the movements of the Rebels," said Tonyn in a letter of 27 January 1777 touching on this otherwise unreported action.

The site is on the north side of the St. Johns around the west end of the I-95 bridge.

Fort St. Marks (San Marcos de Apalache), at the junction of the Wakulla and St. Marks Rivers, near the village of St. Marks, Wakulla County. During the British occupation of Florida, 1763 to 1783, an important Indian trading post was founded here by Panton, Leslie and Company. The company remained when the Spanish came back in 1787, and San Marcos became even busier as a trading center. General Andrew Jackson captured the fort and settlement in 1818 during the Seminole campaign. His execution of two British traders in the area brought on a diplomatic crisis that led Spain to sign the treaty ceding Florida to the United States. Three Spanish forts of wood had been built here during the period 1565 to 1763. A portion of the stonework for the Spanish fort started in 1763 (but not completed) is still standing in a heavily wooded tract that is now a state historic memorial and state park called San Marcos de Apalache State Historic Site. A museum, open 9 A.M. to 5 P.M. (Thursday through Monday), houses artifacts from the site and exhibits. This National Historic Landmark is on Fla. 363 about 2 miles south of U.S. 98 on Old Fort Road. Phone: (850) 922-6007.

Fort Tonyn Site, Nassau County. General Patrick Tonyn having been governor of East Florida from 1774 until the end of the American Revolution, it would be logical to assume that more than one fort bore his name during this period. A Georgia historical marker on the west edge of St. Marys says "East of here, at the junction of Peter Creek and St. Marys River, the British built Fort Tonyn in 1776. . . . It appears that in the War of 1812, Fort Pickering was built on the Fort Tonyn site." The National Survey includes under "Sites Also Noted" (for inclusion in the National Register) "Fort Tonyn, Nassau County [Florida]." In his pamphlet "Southernmost Battlefields of the Revolution" (1970), Charles E. Bennett writes: "the author once believed Fort Tonyn was on Amelia Island, as previous published maps and accounts so stated; however, a manuscript map in the Library of Congress and a careful reading of the Grimké journal and of the order book of Robert Howe indicate it was near, and to the east of, Mills's Ferry. The usual road north, which became King's Road, was apparently at that time through Mills's Ferry instead of its later location in the vicinity of Coleraine" (p. 70). This puts the site within a mile to the east of where U.S. 1 (King's Road) crosses St. Marys River, and on the south bank. Apart from the pretty little town of Mills's (formerly King's) Ferry there is nothing to see here. No exploration of the site has yet been undertaken. The "King" for whom the ferry and road were named, incidentally, was not His Royal Highness but the provincial entrepreneur who owned property here. It is not clear from all highway maps, but the general trace of King's Road in this region is followed by U.S. 23 and 301 as well as U.S. 1.

General Robert Howe found the fort unoccupied when he arrived on 28 June 1778 in the course of the third unsuccessful attempt by the Patriots to win control of East Florida. While Howe camped here with some four hundred Continental troops, Colonel Elijah Clark led his mounted Georgia militia to defeat at Alligator Bridge.

Pensacola, Pensacola Bay. Ponce de Leon and Panfilo de Narvaez may have visited this place in 1513 and 1528. It was later De Soto's base for exploring the interior (1539–1542). The Spanish did not establish a permanent settlement until 1696, when the place appears to have acquired its present name and Fort San Carlos was built about where Fort Barrancas later stood in the War of 1812.

Pensacola changed hands three times in 1719, and finally was destroyed by the French. When Spain regained control in 1723 the Spanish colonists moved the settlement to the west end of Santa Rosa Island. After a destructive hurricane in 1752 they returned to the mainland and started building a town.

East and West Florida were ceded to the British in 1763, and most of Pensacola's Spanish citizens moved to Mexico and Cuba.

A Spanish attempt to seize the British outpost in the spring of 1780 was frustrated by a British squadron. But almost exactly a year later, on 9 March 1781, a Spanish squadron appeared with an army commanded by the capable young governor of Louisiana, Bernardo de Galvez (1746–1786). After leisurely preparations, building up a land and sea force that outnumbered the British by about ten to one, Galvez was forced to undertake formal siege operations and a long bombardment. The British under Brigadier John Campbell continued to have hopes of holding out. But on 8 May a Spanish shell detonated their principal magazine, inflicting more than 100 casualties and demolishing a principal redoubt. After the garrison repulsed the first assault, Galvez got a foothold in the damaged fort and the British position became untenable. Campbell surrendered 650 survivors of a garrison that had numbered about 900 initially. British troops at Pensacola included Provincials raised in Maryland and Pennsylvania; it is said that one of these men deserted and gave Galvez information that enabled his gunners to hit the British magazine.

Locations of the Spanish and British forts involved in the siege are marked. Fort Bernardo, built by Galvez for this operation, was in the block now formed by Brainerd, Spring, Gonzales, and Barcelona Streets. The site of Fort George (built 1763) was acquired in 1924 for construction of the Knights of Columbus Home; the marker is at Palafox and Jackson Streets, eight blocks south and two east of the Spanish fort site.

The Panton, Leslie and Company warehouse site at Main and Baylen Streets comes close to meeting all criteria as a National Historic Landmark. William Panton was a Scot who established a trading empire with outposts from western Tennessee (Chickasaw Bluffs) through Creek, Chicasaw, and Cherokee country, and with bases in Havana, Nassau, New Orleans, and Mobile (see FORT ST. MARKS). Ruins of his Pensacola warehouse were removed in the 1940s. The city erected a replica on a smaller scale on the site, which is marked. Also marked is the approximate location of the grave of the Creek leader Alexander McGillivray, who was buried in Panton's garden with Masonic honors in 1793. Panton's warehouse was on the waterfront, the land south of Main Street having been reclaimed.

The Hispanic Museum at 120 Church Street in Pensacola is where the first permanent Spanish settlement was located and the site of British barracks during the Revolution. Two centuries of Spanish culture in the region are depicted in the well-conceived museum. Phone: (850) 595-5985.

Many other historic landmarks and a number of important architectural attractions of the post-Revolutionary period are in Pensacola. On nearby Santa Rosa Island is a cross commemorating the mass celebrated in 1559 by Dominicans in Tristan de Luna's short-lived settlement. Some of these are maintained by the Historic Pensacola District, which summarizes them in brochures and guides. Its website, www.historicpensacola.org, offers a virtual tour. Phone: (850) 595-5985. Historic Pensacola also operates the T. T. Wentworth Jr. Florida State Museum, located at 830 South Jefferson Street in Pensacola. The Pensacola Historical Society oversees the Pensacola Historical Museum, located at 115 East Zaragossa Street. It contains exhibits on early Indian and military history. The Society keeps a genealogy and reference library there. Phone: (850) 434-5455.

St. Augustine, St. Johns County. Ponce de Leon made the first landing here in 1513, serving the claim that St Augustine is "America's oldest city." Spain claimed possession and founded the first settlement in 1565, making St. Augustine the oldest European settlement north of Mexico. During the Colonial Wars the place changed hands many times, and it was the base for Spain's last efforts to maintain a foothold on the Atlantic coast. One of the purposes of settling Georgia was to establish an outpost from which to drive the Spanish from East Florida (see DARIEN, GEORGIA, and ST. SIMONS ISLAND, GEORGIA).

During the Revolution, St. Augustine was a Loyalist and slave refuge and a base for military operations into Georgia and South Carolina. The Castillo de San Marcos (begun in 1672) was the British headquarters. Through most of the eighteenth century American slaves who made it to the Castillo were granted their freedom, first by the Spanish governor and then, after 1775, by the British. After the fall of Charleston in May 1780 Lieutenant Governor Christopher Gadsden and seventy-seven other prominent Patriots were taken to St. Augustine, where Governor Tonyn offered them parole within the area. All but the elderly Gadsden accepted, and he spent ten months in the Castillo dungeon before being exchanged. After the Revolution, St. Augustine was reoccupied by a Spanish garrison, 1783 to 1821. Florida was then ceded to the United States.

Despite the serious fire of 1914, many colonial structures have survived from the Spanish, British, and American periods of this historic city's existence. The Castillo is the most famous attraction. The Castillo de San Marcos National Monument, located at 1 Castillo Drive, St. Augustine 32084, is a 25-acre park that includes the masonry structure and the surrounding grounds. It is open to the public daily from 8:45 A.M. to 4:45 P.M. Phone: (904) 829-6506, ext. 234.

Sawpit Bluff, mouth of Nassau River, Duval County. A plantation at this scenic spot was the proposed rendezvous for Patriot forces from Sunbury, Georgia in May 1777 (see THOMAS CREEK BATTLE SITE). Part of a tabby wall in

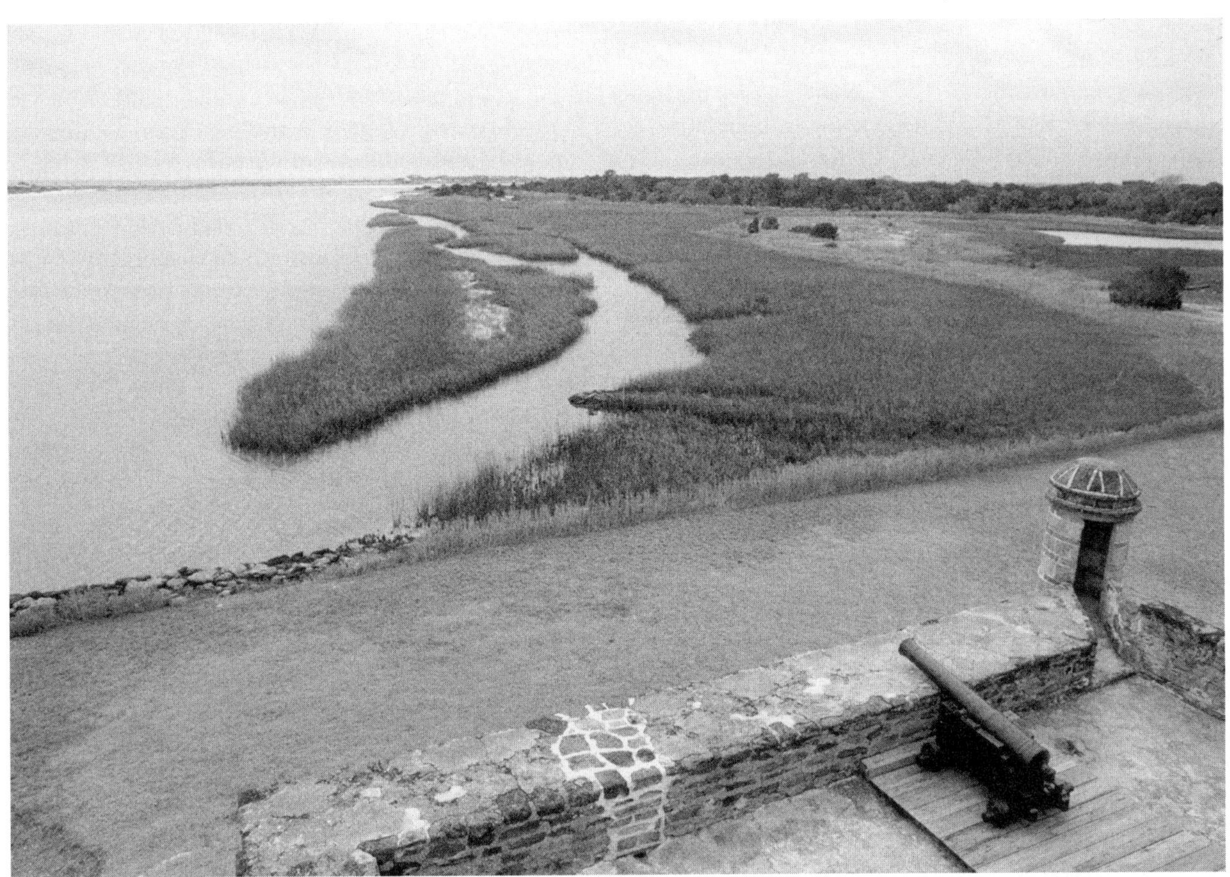

Coastline at Fort Matanzas. Fort Matanzas, built on an inlet south of St. Augustine, Florida, was an outpost of Castillo de San Marcos, which served as a British base during the Revolutionary War. © NIK WHEELER/CORBIS.

the driveway of a private home is all that remains of the Revolutionary War settlement, but the site is picturesque. It is on the south end of the bridge across the Nassau to the southern tip of Amelia Island.

Thomas Creek Battle Site, Duval County. The Patriot defeat here on 17 May 1777 ended the second of three mismanaged attempts by American forces to invade East Florida. Colonel John Baker had marched south from Sunbury, Georgia with about one hundred mounted Georgia militia to link up at Sawpit Bluff with four hundred Continental troops under Lieutenant Colonel Samuel Elbert who were being transported by water from Sunbury. As usual, Georgia Loyalists had kept the British informed of Patriot movements. Baker's camp at Sawpit was raided the night of 14 to 15 May by Indians, who got away with forty horses. These were recovered the next morning after a skirmish in which one Indian was killed. British Governor Tonyn's after-action report of 18 June said the rebels mutilated the body of the Indian, "which greatly exasperated the Savages."

Baker began to worry about the delay of the seaborne force from Sunbury and moved west to find a better strategic location. A British column of Loyalists, Indians, and regulars had meanwhile started north from the St. Johns River to deal with this invasion. Scouts brought the British leaders information the night of 16 to 17 May that the Americans were camped a short distance away.

In accordance with a careful plan, Lieutenant Colonel Thomas Brown advanced with his Rangers and Indians to engage the Rebels while the main body of British regulars under Major Marc Prevost came up in three columns to surround them. At 9 A.M. the British advance guard saw the mounted column of Georgia militia, and Brown set up an ambuscade. His troops delivered a surprise fire at 50 yards from the front and flank, turning Baker's column in the direction of Prevost's expected appearance. Already shaken by this sudden fire, the Patriots were quickly overwhelmed by superior numbers of British regulars advancing through the heavy underbrush. About half of the Georgia militia fled at the sight of the British bayonets, and their commander did not wait long to follow with a handful of supporters. Captain Ignatius Few, a Captain Williams, and about forty men surrendered. A British eyewitness wrote in his memoirs: "The prisoners were all put to death except 16, among whom was Captain Few, saved with difficulty by Major Prevost and the [regular] troops from the fury of the Black Creek Factor," the latter being the Indians involved in the action two days earlier and "greatly exasperated" by the mutilation of their fallen comrade. From British reports it would appear that no Americans were killed in action, but that all deaths occurred after surrender or while trying to escape.

The amphibious force under Elbert did not reach Florida until two days after the Battle of Thomas Creek, and a day later (20 May) it landed on the north end of Amelia Island. Here they were joined by eighteen survivors of Baker's militia, who told the story of their defeat. Elbert decided to abandon the attempt to invade Florida.

This fiasco faded away in a storm of recrimination. The regulars blamed the militia for lacking subordination. General Lachlan McIntosh, who had mortally wounded Button Gwinnett in a duel in Savannah the day before the battle in Florida, wrote about a month later: "Our late Don quixot Expedition to Augustine proved abortive as I expected," and he blamed the regular, Elbert, saying he never had thought this officer the man best qualified to command the operation.

In 1778 the Americans made their third attempt to invade Florida and failed again because Patriot politicians and congressionally appointed military commanders in Georgia could not team up, even to win a war (see ALLIGATOR BRIDGE).

According to the federal government's information regarding its Timucuan Ecological and Historic Preserve, the exact location of the Thomas Creek Battle Site is yet to be determined. However, it notes that the battle site is part of the Timucuan Preserve and is possibly located at the intersection of U.S. 17 and the Nassau River.

GEORGIA

Only Texas (11,000) and New York (2,800) have more historical markers than Georgia, which has erected nearly 2,600 of them. The state's markers most often pertain to the Civil War, but they also cover a broad range of other historical topics, including events and places from the American Revolution. The marker program began in 1952 by the state appointed Historical Commission. The Historical Commission was abolished in 1973 in favor of the Georgia Department of Natural Resources, and then, after a brief try at privatizing the maintenance and erection of historical markers, the state transferred the responsibility to the Georgia Historical Society in 1997. The Society is located at 501 Whitaker Street in Savannah and serves the state as the main authority on Georgia's history. In addition to housing a museum and archives, it sells a variety of publications through its website that offer insight into the state's colonial and Revolutionary era past. (Website: www.georgiahistory.com; phone: (912) 651-2125.) Another state agency responsible for matters pertaining to historical sites is the Georgia Department of Archives and History, 5800 Jonesboro Road, Morrow, Ga. 30260; phone: (678) 364-3700.

Altamaha River. *See* DARIEN.

Augusta. At the head of navigation of the Savannah River (240 miles by water from the port of Savannah, half that distance by road), the site of Augusta was a natural communications hub long before the white man arrived. Carolina colonists had a trading post in the area before Oglethorpe established the town of Augusta in 1735 to 1736 and named it for the Princess of Wales. Fort Augusta, built in 1736 about 100 yards from the river, was enlarged by the British invaders in 1780 to 1781 and renamed Fort Cornwallis.

On the eve of the Revolution, Augusta was the center of the most heavily settled area of Georgia and the most important inland trading center in the southeast. Some six hundred men and two thousand pack horses came each spring for goods. But as in so many other backcountry regions of the South, the people were predominantly Loyalist.

The British marched up the river in January 1779 and occupied Augusta but were forced to withdraw after two weeks because of Patriot military operations described in the sections on Kettle Creek and Brier Creek battlegrounds. With Savannah in enemy hands, Augusta became Georgia's temporary capital until the Patriots were run out again in mid-June 1780. Shortly before, Charleston had fallen, and the British were undertaking the conquest of the entire South. Part of their strategy was to establish strong Loyalist bases in the backcountry, notably at Ninety Six, South Carolina, and Augusta.

Colonel Thomas Brown was the Loyalist commander in Augusta. A native of East Riding in Yorkshire, from a family of wealthy merchants, he had come to Georgia after 1773 to take up 5,000 acres near the confluence of the Broad and Savannah Rivers as a family investment. Understandably, he was unsympathetic to the Whigs, who advocated revolution, but he made himself the object of their wrath by publicly ridiculing their cause. For this he was tarred and feathered, publicly exposed in a cart, and forced to profess support of the Whigs. They had picked on the wrong man. Brown made his way into the backcountry of South Carolina, where he joined the Loyalists. Later he became a redoubtable leader of militia under the

British in East Florida and proved to have an exceptional talent for recruiting Indians. The British commissioned him superintendent of Indian affairs for the region and lieutenant colonel of the King's Rangers, an organization which he recruited and led.

Thomas Brown returned to Georgia with the British invaders and led Colonel Archibald Campbell's column to Augusta in January 1779. He withdrew with Campbell the next month (see BRIER CREEK), but returned in June 1780 as commander of the occupation forces in Augusta. On 14 September he was suddenly attacked by Patriot militia under Colonel Elijah Clark, 350 of the latter's troops and 80 recruited by Lieutenant Colonel James McCall. Clark had hoped to raise a much larger force but nevertheless went ahead with this misguided attempt to liberate Augusta.

The Patriots achieved surprise, but accidentally and for a most peculiar reason. They approached in three columns, one hitting the Indian camp on the outskirts of town and then the trading center around the Mackay House. Most of the Augusta garrison rushed to defend the latter place, stripping Fort Grierson to a small guard detachment, not realizing that two other Patriot columns were advancing to attack that place. The little fort was easily captured. Clark invested the Mackay House, cutting off its water supply and blocking an effort by Brown's fifty Cherokee allies to reinforce him.

The beleaguered Loyalists had meanwhile reported their situation to Colonel John Cruger at Ninety Six, some 45 miles due north, and, confident that a relief column would arrive from Ninety Six, held out despite great suffering from lack of water. Clark lacked the strength for an assault, and after maintaining the siege for four days he was forced to retreat on the approach of Cruger with five hundred troops from Ninety Six.

"It was a reckless, ill-advised expedition," concluded Sydney G. Fisher in his *Struggle for American Independence* (II, p. 347). Not only did it fail to accomplish any military purpose, but it precipitated a wave of Loyalist vindictiveness that made earlier atrocities seem mild. The Patriot hero Elijah Clark abandoned twenty-nine of his wounded. Thirteen rebels were hanged, most of them on the open-air staircase of the Mackay House. The rest of the prisoners were cruelly disposed of by the Indians.

Until this time Brown had offered lenient terms to Whigs of the area and had reported to his British superiors that he was leaning over backwards to conciliate the backcountry people. After Clark's attack in mid-September 1780 he turned vindictive. His troops revisited homes of their Whig enemies with such vengeance that four hundred women and children were forced to flee for protection in Clark's camp.

When General Nathanael Greene's army moved south to drive the British from the Carolinas, Patriot militia again besieged Augusta. By this time Fort Cornwallis had been completed about a mile east of Fort Grierson. (Fort Cornwallis did not figure in the earlier action, not then being in service.) Brown's Rangers, about 265 officers and men, held Fort Cornwallis and may have been reinforced by other troops. Some eighty militia under Colonel James Grierson garrisoned Fort Grierson, and about three hundred Creek Indians completed Brown's command. About twice that total number of Patriot militia were around Augusta when the operation started on 16 April 1781. Clark was back on the scene, and General Andrew Pickens was there with his newly recruited regiment of "state regulars" from South Carolina (his men were paid in plunder taken from Loyalists). Also on hand was a detachment of Over Mountain Men under Colonel Isaac Shelby (see SYCAMORE SHOALS AND FORT WATAUGA SITES under Tennessee).

After scoring a number of local successes, cutting off Loyalist relief columns and capturing enemy outposts (see BEECH ISLAND and FORT GALPHIN under South Carolina), the militia leaders convinced Greene that Augusta could be taken by assault. Greene therefore detached "Light Horse Harry" Lee with his legion to Augusta. The Continentals arrived on 23 May, and Fort Grierson was quickly taken. Proving that the Loyalists had no monopoly on committing atrocities, the Patriots killed thirty of the eighty defenders as they tried to fight their way back to Fort Cornwallis. Most of the fifty prisoners were wounded, and Colonel Grierson was murdered. (Captain Samuel Alexander of the Georgia militia is generally blamed, but this is disputed.)

Their resistance strengthened by the ruthlessness of the Patriots, the defenders of Fort Cornwallis held out for almost two weeks. The besiegers undertook "regular approaches," but were hampered by a lack of heavy artillery. Construction of a Maham tower was started (see FORT WATSON under South Carolina for the first use of this device). Brown made several sorties and tried to destroy the tower by blowing up a nearby house in which he had secretly hidden powder. On 1 June the Patriots started delivering an effective fire from their tower into Fort Cornwallis, but it was not until three days later that Brown offered to negotiate. The expected relief was not in sight (Ninety Six was also besieged), and the Loyalists lacked the strength to fight off the assault that was forming.

It was sound military practice to parole the garrison of a fortress in return for its surrender, thereby sparing the attacker casualties and time, and this is what the Patriots finally agreed to do. Brown and his 334 survivors were marched off under heavy guard (primarily for their own protection) to Savannah, where they were paroled. About fifty Loyalists and forty Patriots were buried at Augusta.

A memorial cross in the churchyard of St. Paul's marks the site of Forts Augusta and Cornwallis. Benson Lossing reported seeing remains of the ditch and embankments as late as 1849.

What has long been called the Mackay House was discovered to be in fact the Ezekiel Harris House, built in 1797. The actual Mackay House was largely destroyed during the battle that occurred there, fell into disrepair, and was destroyed a few years later. The Harris House, at 1822 Broad Street, has been called "the finest example of colonial frame residential architecture south of the Potomac," though it is in fact not from the colonial period, and has several unique features for this section of the South. The Harris House has eighteenth-century furnishings on the first floor, Revolutionary War exhibits on the second, and exhibits of the Indian trade on the third. The house, which is now correctly listed in the National Register of Historic Places, is open Tuesday to Saturday, 10 A.M. to 4:30 P.M., and has an excellent tour which discusses how the erroneous identification saved the building from destruction. Phone: (760) 737-2820. The house is owned by the Augusta Museum of History at 560 Reynolds Street; phone: (706) 722-8454.

Brier (Briar) Creek Battlefield and vicinity. In late 1778 and early 1779 British troops converged on Georgia from New York and Florida, conquering coastal Georgia with ease and pushing up the Savannah River to establish a base at Augusta. Patriot militia turned out to swell the forces commanded by General Benjamin Lincoln, and the portly commander from Massachusetts soon felt he could undertake a counteroffensive. As the initial move he ordered General John Ashe with about 1,500 men to join forces with the 1,200 under General Andrew Williamson near Augusta.

The night of 13 to 14 February 1779 the British hurriedly evacuated Augusta in the face of this threat from the South Carolina side. On 25 February General Ashe crossed the river and followed the route taken by the British in their retreat to General Prevost's fortified camp at Hudson's Ferry (east and slightly north of modern Newington, where there is a highway marker).

In Screven County the Savannah River and Brier Creek form a pocket. Into this marched Ashe, following the old Augusta road that paralleled the swamp-lined river, and near the end of this pocket he was stopped by the demolished bridge across the creek. Ashe was camped in the immediate vicinity of the bridge and making preparations to repair it for a continuation of his advance south when he was called to a council of war at Black Swamp, South Carolina. The decision was made at this meeting on 1 March for all the other generals to mass their scattered forces around Augusta and then to join Ashe on Brier Creek. This would involve a march of 80 miles for Lincoln's troops at Purrysburg to Augusta, picking up General Griffith Rutherford's 700 North Carolinians at Black Swamp and Williamson's 1,200 South Carolinians near Augusta. This combined force would then have to march another 50 miles to reach Brier Creek.

While the amateur American generals concluded their deliberations, the British professionals already were marching to execute a classic example of "defeat in detail." Under cover of darkness on the night of 1 to 2 March, two columns left their camp at Hudson's Ferry. One of these, a diversionary effort under Major McPherson, moved back up the old Augusta road to Buck Creek, about 3 miles south of the destroyed bridge on Brier Creek. Here the First Battalion of the Seventy-first Highlanders and 150 Loyalists would make a feint to distract attention from the main attack.

The latter were commanded by General Prevost's younger brother, Lieutenant Colonel Marc Prevost. Marc Prevost had a well-balanced force of about 900 troops, regular infantry, light infantry, dragoons, grenadiers, Florida rangers and militia, and five pieces of field artillery.

Early on the morning of 2 March, having covered 30 miles along the general route of modern Ga. 24, Prevost reached Paris Mill (now Millhaven), about 14 miles to the rear of the American camp. Here he was delayed in improvising a crossing because the Americans had destroyed the bridge. Mobile forces, light infantry, and dragoons got over the creek that evening and moved swiftly to defeat the outposts and cut the supply lines between Paris Mill and the Savannah River. To complete their good fortune, the British captured the messenger sent to inform Ashe of this unexpected threat to his rear.

The Patriot general had returned to his headquarters around noon on 2 March. He ordered a strong cavalry patrol under Major Ross to reconnoiter in the direction of Hudson's Ferry the next morning in preparation for the attack that Ashe hoped to make when reinforcements arrived from South Carolina. Major Ross, not otherwise identified, had joined the Patriots on Brier Creek just a day earlier, and he emerges as a major offender in this comedy of errors because he did not inform Ashe when he made contact with the enemy a mere 3 miles to the south on Buck Creek. At a time when the Patriots badly needed reconnaissance forces to the north, Ross remained inactive and silent to the south.

As Ross was moving south, Prevost was advancing on the Patriot camp. About 2:30 P.M., minutes before the enemy came into sight, General Ashe received a warning message from the commander of his baggage train (at Burton's Ferry, about where U.S. 301 now crosses the Savannah). Prevost deployed astride the road in a line extending from the creek to the river. Reduced to an effective strength of only 800 because detachments were off on other missions, shaken by the sudden appearance of enemies in force to their rear, and with many men waiting to receive ammunition, the Americans were quickly routed. Only the left flank, sixty Georgia Continentals and 150 militia commanded by General Samuel Elbert and Lieutenant Colonel John McIntosh, put up a real fight before being overwhelmed.

Elbert's life was spared, it is said, when a British officer recognized the Masonic distress sign (one of many such incidents reported in many wars). The McIntosh involved here is the "Come and take it" McIntosh of Fort Morris fame (see SUNBURY SITE AND FORT MORRIS).

Between 150 and 200 Americans were killed in action or drowned in trying to swim the Savannah. With a loss of about 16 killed and wounded, the British took 170 prisoners, 7 guns, and 500 stands of arms in addition to a quantity of ammunition, provisions, and baggage.

The disaster is unusually well documented because the record of the court of inquiry has been preserved in the memoirs of General William Moultrie, who was president of the court. In a remarkably brief opinion (seventy-eight words), the court concluded "that General Ashe did not take all the necessary precautions . . . to secure his camp and obtain timely intelligence" but that he showed no lack of personal courage "and remained in the field as long as prudence and duty required."

Freeman's Old Bridge was never rebuilt, and the old Augusta road was rerouted over Brannen's Bridge about a mile upstream. Here a roadside park features a large historic marker with an excellent map showing troop dispositions and movements involved in the battle. The late Clyde D. Hollingsworth of nearby Sylvania did most of the research for this marker.

An elevated highway on a dirt causeway has obliterated the portion of the battlefield where the British and American lines met, but the rest of the landscape has changed little since 1779. Brier Creek is dark and deep where it runs past the roadside park near the modern bridge. There are only a few homes and fishing camps in the area where the southern Patriots were roundly trounced.

The best route to the battlefield is from the center of Sylvania along East Ogeechee Street. (From the picturesque old county clerk's office this street is between two modern banks.) Follow this route for 11 miles through the countryside to the roadside creek and historical marker. A side road to Buck Creek Church (the crossroad is about 1.5 miles short of Brier Creek Bridge) leads to the area where the British diversionary effort was made and where Major Ross was located.

Cherokee Ford, Savannah River (Abbeville County, South Carolina; Elbert County, Georgia). In mid-February 1779 a Patriot blockhouse at Cherokee Ford, defended by an eight-man detachment commanded by a lieutenant and armed with two swivel guns, barred the passage of Colonel Boyd and his 800 Loyalists. Boyd declined to fight his way across into Georgia, marched about 5 miles upstream, and put his mounted troops across the Savannah at several points. Captain Robert Anderson had been moving up the Georgia side of the river to oppose Boyd's crossing. Although outnumbered and forced to deal with several enemy columns, the Patriots attacked through heavy canebrakes along the riverbank and inflicted one hundred casualties, losing about a third that number themselves. Boyd marched on to Kettle Creek, Georgia (see KETTLE CREEK BATTLEFIELD).

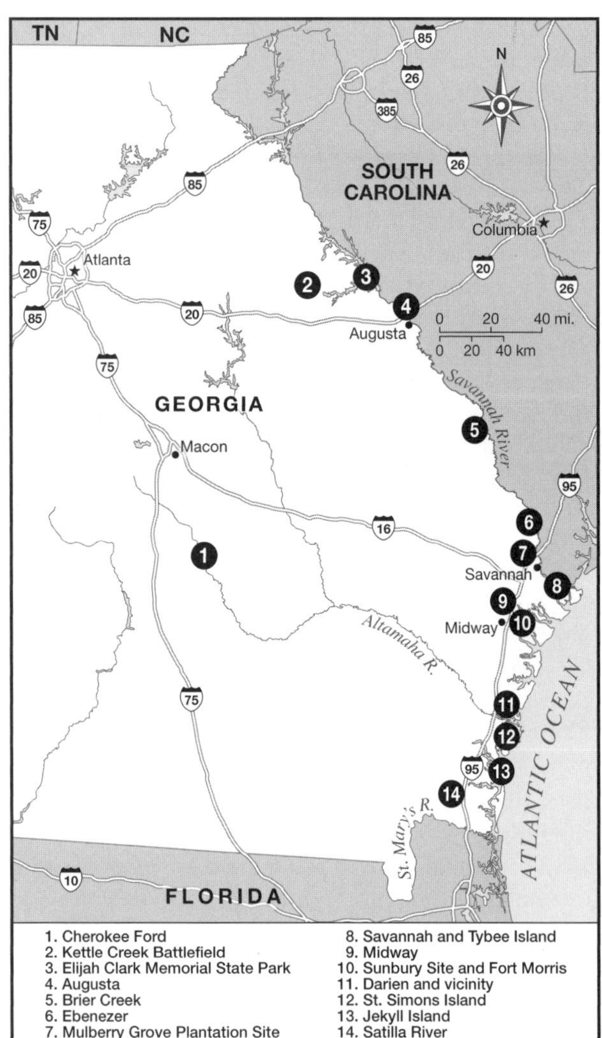

MAP BY XNR PRODUCTIONS. THE GALE GROUP.

Cherokee Ford was at the mouth of Rocky Creek, about a mile north of where State Highway 72 crosses the Savannah River. A railroad bridge spans the river at this point, which can be reached by an unimproved road off S.C. 72 just west of Calhoun Falls.

Elijah Clark Memorial State Park, on Clark Hill Reservoir of the Savannah River, in Lincoln County, 7 miles northeast of Lincolnton on U.S. 378 and Ga. 43.

"After 125 or more years," reads a wonderfully wry sentence in the brochure of the Department of State Parks, "Georgia has realized that the shortcomings of [Elijah] Clark were outweighed by the great service he rendered the state." The highlight of Clark's great service as a partisan leader during the Revolution was his part in the morale-building victory at Kettle Creek (see KETTLE CREEK BATTLEFIELD).

Authorities disagree on various details of his career, including his military genius, but there can be no doubt about Clark being a tough partisan leader throughout the Revolution. His postwar career included Indian fighting, involvement in the schemes of French minister Genêt against Spain, illegal establishment of the "Trans-Oconee State" in Creek territory, and alleged involvement in the Yazoo Land Fraud. But he was a popular hero in Georgia when he died in 1799, and now he is an official hero.

The state park features conjectural reconstructions of the simple log buildings erected by this "Hero of Hornet's Nest." The larger one is a two-room cabin with an extra-wide dogtrot in the center and chimneys on each end. Copies of uniforms and documents are displayed and the cabin is featured as a museum. The smaller structure in the rear is furnished as a kitchen. In the park are the graves of Clark, his wife, and several of their children, moved here from their original site in the county.

Recreational facilities in the 447-acre park include cabins, family camping, fishing and swimming. For full information call the park at (800) 864-7275.

Darien and vicinity, Altamaha River, McIntosh County. On U.S. 17 and Interstate 95, the country around modern Darien was of great strategic importance from the earliest colonial days until the end of the Revolution. It is the center of the delta of the Altamaha River, which was a natural barrier between Spanish settlements in Florida and English colonies along the Atlantic coast. When the French pushed along the Mississippi and the Gulf of Mexico, they had hopes of colonizing the line of the Altamaha to form a corridor to the Atlantic Ocean.

The site of Fort King George, the state's oldest standing fort, about a mile east of modern Darien, has been beautifully developed by the Georgia Historical Commission with a splendid little museum that interprets the history of the site from prehistoric times and its early occupation by the Spanish (1650–1686). On special occasions that vary from year to year, the Fort King George site offers reenactments and living histories. Phone (912) 437-4770.

Fort King George was established in 1721 and garrisoned by provincial troops before being taken over by an independent company of Royal soldiers. Bessie Lewis, who has long searched the archives on both sides of the Atlantic for the history of Fort King George, found documentary evidence to prove that many of the garrison were Swiss. After enduring the hardships of battle and disease for six years, during which time they buried 140 of their comrades and had to repair the damages of a nearly disastrous fire, the garrison was moved to Port Royal, South Carolina. Two lookouts were maintained at Fort King George from 1727 to 1733, until the permanent English settlement was established at Savannah by Oglethorpe.

Three years later a colony of Scots Highlanders under John McIntosh Mohr settled near Fort King George, building a new fort for defense against the Spanish colonists in Florida and a town where modern Darien still stands. When the Spanish threat ended, the fort fell into ruins, but at the start of the Revolution it was rebuilt.

Darien figured in the abortive efforts of the southern colonists to mount an offensive into Spanish Florida, but it was not the scene of any specific action of significance. Among the settlers who achieved importance in the war was Lachlan McIntosh (1725–1806), who had come to Darien with his parents in 1736. His nephew John McIntosh (1755–1826) became famous for his successful defense of Sunbury (see SUNBURY SITE AND FORT MORRIS) and had a long military career.

The site of Fort Darien has not been precisely located, but the state has developed 12 acres around Fort King George into a scenic archaeological landmark. The authorities have made the economical decision not to reconstruct the British fortification of 1721 to 1727, even though there is more than adequate information as to its appearance. A visitor to the museum can reconstruct in his mind's eye this frontier post on the Lower Bluff of the strategic Altamaha River of Georgia.

Ebenezer, Savannah River, Effingham County. When the British took Savannah in December 1778 and prepared to conquer the rest of Georgia and South Carolina, General Prevost (see SUNBURY SITE AND FORT MORRIS) first massed at Ebenezer. From a base here he sent Colonel Archibald Campbell up the river to take Augusta, and from here he himself led the raid to Charleston.

Ebenezer's claim to fame transcends the role it played in the Revolution. The two hundred Salzburg Lutherans who settled here in 1736 built the second church in Georgia (1741, replaced in 1769 by the brick structure that survives) and the first gristmill and sawmill, and their rice mill probably was the first in America. Silk culture was their most successful industry. But British occupation destroyed the promising settlement, driving out the inhabitants who had come to the New World to escape the evils of the Old. Unable to recover after the British left, it gradually faded into oblivion. The official highway map of the state of Georgia, as of this writing, does not show it, although Ga. 275 dead-ends there.

The site of New Ebenezer, as it was originally called, is overgrown with timber except for a few open spots. The only remaining building is Jerusalem Church (1769), the oldest standing public building in Georgia. A large brick structure (60 by 80 feet) with an interior balcony, it is topped by a frame belfry. The brick walls are 23 inches thick. Modern Salzburgers have done their architectural heritage no favor by building their new parish house so close to the beautifully simple old church. This structure of 1958, connected by a short covered passage to the renovated church, includes a small museum. The Georgia Salzburger Society meets at the church on 12 March and Labor Day. Lutheran services are held every Sunday and services are sometimes held in German.

Just before reaching the church, visitors will see the old cemetery on the left. It is well maintained within the modern burial ground, but few old headstones have survived. A few hundred feet beyond the church is a picturesque overlook on the bluff of the Savannah River.

Fort Frederica National Monument. *See* ST. SIMONS ISLAND.

Jekyll Island, Brunswick County. Nine miles long, 1.25 miles wide, with 11 miles of beach, Jekyll Island was first a hunting and fishing ground of the Guale Indians, then a Spanish stronghold and pirate base (from about 1566 to 1732, when Georgia was founded as an English colony). Oglethorpe named the island for a family that contributed to his colonization of Georgia. Spanish commissioners were entertained in 1736 by Major William Horton, first English resident of the island, while Oglethorpe paraded the garrison of nearby St. Simons to indicate a greater military strength than he actually had there. The deception delayed Spanish efforts to reassert their claim to this region until 1742, when they were defeated on St. Simons Island. After this final repulse the Spaniards burned the buildings on Jekyll Island and withdrew to Florida. The tabby remains of Horton's house are on the north end of the island, and the road he cut from his house to the beach still bears his name.

For fifty-six years (1886–1942) the island was the exclusive vacation site of a group of America's wealthiest millionaires, who selected this island after searching the world for the ideal spot. They bought it for $125,000 from the du Bignon family, who became founding members of the Jekyll Island Club. The du Bignons had owned the island since the Revolution, building a great fortune in cotton, and their burial ground has been preserved.

In 1947 the state of Georgia acquired Jekyll Island for $675,000 (which works out to about $10 per acre) and made it a state park. This purchase by court condemnation decree during the tenure of an acting governor is noted on a historical marker at the entrance of the island of Riverview Drive, where ten other markers are located.

Most of the tourist attractions on Jekyll Island are identified with the tenure of the millionaires, but there are places of interest pertaining to the Sea Island cotton and Civil War era. In 2000 the Jekyll Island Foundation was formed to preserve the natural and historical riches of the area. Website: www.jekyllislandfoundation.org; phone: (912) 635-4053.

Kettle Creek Battlefield, located off Highway 44, 8 miles southwest of Washington, Wilkes County. Here on 14 February 1779 a Patriot force of about 450 under Andrew Pickens, John Dooly, and Elijah Clark surprised and defeated 600 Loyalists commanded by Colonel James Boyd, an Irishman from Raeburn Creek, South Carolina. The victory prevented a dangerous linkup of Carolina and Georgia Loyalists. It also was a rare example of coordination among Patriot military leaders.

Half a page is devoted to Kettle Creek Battlefield in the 1964 report of The National Survey, *Colonials and Patriots: Historic Places Commemorating our Forebears, 1700–1783,* which points out that the site "appears much as it did at the time of the battle." In 1930 the Daughters of the American Revolution, who owned 12 acres of the battlefield on the north side of Kettle Creek, gave the federal government an easement to erect a monument on so-called Battle Hill. (In point of fact, the decisive action of the battle took place on the south side of the creek, although the Loyalists were camped on the north side and some fighting took place there.) Now Wilkes County has acquired title to the 12 acres from the DAR. Guided tours of the site are offered through the Washington-Wilkes Chamber of Commerce. Phone: (706) 678-2013.

Because the history of the Kettle Creek campaign is not well known outside of Georgia, where it is often called "the state's favorite battle," a brief sketch is included here. British forces from Florida and New York converged in the last days of 1778 to take Savannah, all of coastal Georgia, and then establish a base at Augusta. From the latter place they were fanning out through the backcountry, using veteran Loyalist units from Florida and rallying others from Georgia and the Carolinas. Patriot militia leaders were trying to organize resistance.

The main enemy threat soon crystallized in the form of about seven hundred Loyalists led by Colonel Boyd. Starting with a nucleus of troops from Anson County, North Carolina, Boyd marched south, gathering strength and spreading destruction through South Carolina as he headed for a proposed rendezvous in Georgia with five hundred Loyalists under Colonel Daniel McGirth. The linkup was supposed to take place on Little River, the southern boundary of modern Wilkes County and about 6 miles north of where the Battle of Kettle Creek took place.

Boyd's crossing of the Savannah River above Augusta was opposed by Patriot forces moving up both banks to attack him. Frustrated at Cherokee Ford, he moved about 5 miles upstream and succeeded in crossing on a broad front, but because of effective resistance he lost about 100 troops (including deserters). With his remaining 600 men, Boyd first marched westward to shake off pursuit. Then he cut south toward the rendezvous. Around a farm on the north side of Kettle Creek he went into camp on the afternoon of 13 February (a Saturday). Boyd's men and horses were tired after three days of arduous campaigning, and it looked as if the worst was over, so the Loyalist leader put his horses out to graze and let his men settle down to prepare their first hot food in several days.

Three separate Patriot forces had joined in the pursuit. Colonel John Dooly, a North Carolinian who had settled in Georgia, could have claimed the overall command because of seniority. But Colonel Andrew Pickens had 250 troops to Dooly's 100, so Dooly waived his seniority to give Pickens command of their combined forces. Colonel Elijah Clark joined later with 100 mounted infantry. The Whigs crossed the Broad River at Fishdam Ford, about 5 miles downstream from where the Tories had crossed (later Webb's Ferry), and camped at Clarke's Creek, within 4 miles of the enemy.

The next morning (14 February) Pickens advanced cautiously on Boyd's position without being detected. After a brief reconnaissance he formed for action with Dooly on the right, himself in the center, and Clark's dragoons on the left. Alerted only when his pickets opened fire on the advancing Patriots, Boyd reacted quickly and well. He moved forward with about 100 men to establish a delaying position while the rest of his command formed to defend their camp.

The Patriot center under Pickens attacked aggressively, and Boyd was mortally wounded when he rejoined the main body with his delaying force, but he had bought valuable time. Dooly and Clark, on the flanks, were seriously impeded by canebrakes, but when they finally came on line the Loyalists were forced across the creek. Here the fighting was renewed. Some authorities believe the entire action lasted an hour and three-quarters; others say it ended in less than an hour. But only about half of the 600 Loyalists engaged in the action escaped to join the garrison in Augusta. Boyd and nineteen of his men were killed, and another twenty-two taken prisoner; the rest fled, some to Augusta, most to their homes. The Patriots lost seven men. Five Loyalist prisoners were hanged as traitors. Boyd died game, having led his troops bravely after making the cardinal military mistake of underestimating his enemies and allowing himself to be surprised.

Much work remains to be done by historians and archaeologists in reconstructing the Battle of Kettle Creek. The terrain is virtually undisturbed, and an excellent topographic map in the 1:24,000 series is available from the U.S. Geological Survey. ("Philomath Quad., Ga., 7.5'" is the identification.)

The site is open at all times, and is 11.5 miles southwest of Washington, Georgia, off Highway 44 on Warhill Road. A virtual tour of the battlefield is available at http://www.rootsweb.com/~gawilkes/kettlecreek.htm.

Midway, Liberty County on U.S. 17 and near Interstate 95. A handsome frame church, a reconstructed eighteenth-century home, and a clutch of historical markers alert the traveler to the fact that Midway is of exceptional historical interest. The Midway Society was organized here in 1754 to settle a grant of 32,000 acres. Its members were substantial people of New England and South Carolinian origins from Dorchester, South Carolina, where a Congregationalist community had been founded in 1695. They were seeking better land and relief from overcrowding in Old Dorchester. The pioneers prospered as cultivators of rice, indigo, and other crops. Politically active in their newly formed Parish of St. Johns (1758), they espoused the Patriot cause at the start of the Revolution when the majority of the Georgia colonists were reluctant to cast in their lot with rebels to the north. The Midway Society had undertaken to establish other settlements throughout the parish, serving these with associate pastors from the main meeting house at Midway. The port town of Sunbury, about 10 miles east, was the most important of these, and Button Gwinnett's enthusiastic leadership of the "Sunbury faction" during his brief tenure as governor in the spring of 1777 led to his fatal duel with General Lachlan McIntosh of Darien (see SAVANNAH).

Gwinnett and Dr. Lyman Hall are the two signers of the Declaration of Independence of which St. James Parish is so proud, although neither was a member of the congregation (as has been persistently claimed). The two men had homes in Sunbury as well as at Midway. (The so-called Button Gwinnett Home on St. Catherine's Island was built long after his death, according to its present owners and the Georgia Historical Society.)

When the British shifted their military efforts to the South in the last months of 1778, two columns from Florida converged on St. James Parish. Lieutenant Colonel Marc Prevost, brilliant younger brother of the British commander in Florida, marched toward Midway while an amphibious force under Lieutenant Colonel L. V. Fuser sailed to attack Sunbury. Colonel John White of North Carolina, commander of the Fourth Georgia Continentals, posted his two hundred regulars and their two cannon to defend a breastwork just south of Midway

Church. When Brigadier General James Screven arrived with about twenty militia the Patriots advanced a mile and a half south to set up a new defensive line.

Screven was mortally wounded and captured in the skirmish that followed (24 November 1778). White withdrew in good order through the town in the face of superior force, but Prevost learned that Fuser had not yet reached Sunbury and that a strong Rebel force was rallying for a defense of Ogeechee Ferry. Burning Midway Church and other buildings, the four hundred British, Loyalists, and Indians retreated to Florida. The next day, 25 November, an outnumbered Patriot force defied Fuser's demand to surrender Fort Morris (see SUNBURY SITE AND FORT MORRIS).

Midway Church was reconstructed in 1792, and the town prospered until again ravaged by war in 1864. But the community boasts a remarkable record of producing famous Americans: eighty-six ministers including the fathers of Oliver Wendell Holmes and Samuel F. B. Morse, as well as several governors, congressmen, and cabinet members. A great-grandfather of Theodore Roosevelt was General Daniel Stewart of Midway.

Midway Museum, a few yards behind the church, is a house museum in the privately-owned custody of Midway Museum, Inc. The structure is a reconstruction in the raised-cottage style prevalent in the area during the eighteenth century. Completely furnished, it has a detached kitchen and a few exhibits pertaining to the history of the region through the Civil War. A diorama shows Colonel John McIntosh in full Highland regalia rejecting the British demand to surrender Fort Morris, and this exhibit gives an indication of what the fort and surrounding area looked like at the time. The museum and its grounds are open every day except Monday. Phone: (927) 884-5837.

Mulberry Grove Plantation, Savannah River, Chatham County. About 10 miles above Savannah on 2,200 acres of the best bottomland in Georgia, the confiscated estate of Royal Lieutenant Governor John Graham became the home of General Nathanael Greene. Here he died suddenly (of sunstroke) at the age of forty-four, shortly after taking up permanent residence, and his young son was drowned at Mulberry Plantation. (See Colonial Park Cemetery, SAVANNAH, for the story of their lost tomb.)

The twenty-six-year-old Eli Whitney met the widow of General Greene and her plantation manager while travelling to Savannah, and it was while staying as a guest at Mulberry Grove that he invented the cotton gin.

The plantation house was burned in late 1864 or early 1865 by Sherman's troops. The restored mansion was wrecked by a storm in the early 1900s and not rebuilt.

A highway marker is on U.S. 17 at the City Hall in Port Wentworth. Mulberry Grove is located about 2 miles northeast of that marker and is owned by the Georgia Port Authority, which intends to make it into a parking lot for shipping containers.

St. Simons Island, Brunswick County. Landmarks of the pre-Columbian and colonial era are numerous. Vestiges of the Spanish missions remain in the Old Spanish Garden (marker at Ocean Boulevard on Demere Road). At Gascoigne Bluff, where the highway bridge now arrives from the mainland, the Indians had a village and the first English settlers landed in 1736.

Fort Frederica National Monument is a National Historic Landmark (established 1936) whose story is told by its tabby ruins, excavated building foundations, and modern museum. This 247-acre park is located about 12 miles from Brunswick on St. Simons Island along U.S. 17. Established in 1736 by Oglethorpe, Fort Frederica was his base for the unsuccessful attack on St. Augustine three years later. From the fort he led a band of Highlanders to defeat two hundred Spanish raiders near Christ Church in 1742. The raiders were annihilated in a pursuit that ended at Bloody Marsh. Both sites are marked. As a national park, Fort Frederica is known for its bird watching in addition to guided historical tours of the preserved grounds. During the summer there are historical recreations of eighteenth-century British garrison life. Most interesting is the annual lime-burning festival in August, when the staff makes the tabby, from which many of these coastal forts are built, by burning oyster shells in a kiln. Phone: (912) 638-3639.

Oglethorpe's defeat of the Spaniards was significant in American history because it ended the efforts of Spain to regain Georgia by force. The Treaty of Aix-la-Chapelle in 1748 ended Fort Frederica's strategic importance, and its gradual abandonment was hastened by a fire ten years later.

Among the other sites marked on the island is the place where Charles Wesley had religious services on 14 March 1736, the first Sunday after his arrival in Georgia. On the wall of Christ Church (whose present building dates from 1884) is a cross made from the great oak long designated as the tree under which Wesley preached to Oglethorpe and about twenty others on this occasion. Portions of the old military road and sites of colonial forts are marked.

Satilla River, Camden County. The first major river barrier north of St. Marys River, which divides the present states of Georgia and Florida, the Satilla figured prominently in military operations of the colonial and Revolutionary era. It is now noted as the last of Georgia's wild and scenic rivers. Experienced canoeists can enjoy campsites and other facilities along a 149-mile

Fort Frederica. *The story of Fort Frederica on St. Simon's Island in Georgia is told by its tabby ruins and excavated building foundations.* © LEE SNIDER/PHOTO IMAGES/CORBIS.

stretch of the river between Woodbine (U.S. 17) and the vicinity of Waycross (U.S. 82).

Savannah. If you know where to look you will find an obscure plaque in a wall alongside a busy street in an area of abandoned railroad buildings. "Upon this spot stood the Spring Hill Redoubt," it reads. "Here on October 9, 1779, one of the bloodiest engagements of the Revolutionary War was fought, when repeated assaults were made by the Allied troops of Georgia, South Carolina and France in an effort to retake Savannah from the British." The marker is on the intersection of West Broad Street and Liberty in front of the visitors center in Savannah. In 2004 the Coastal Heritage Society, in conjunction with the city of Savannah, commemorated the Spring Hill Redoubt in its 225th anniversary of the Battle of Savannah. Yet, historians to this day question as to why this battle, deemed one of the American Revolution's most fiercely fought, continues to receive short shrift in terms of writings and remembrance.

The British had captured Savannah on 29 December 1778, a force from New York under Lieutenant Colonel Archibald Campbell landing at Girardeau's Plantation (now the railroad docks of the Seaboard Coast Line, about a mile below the city). The British advanced generally along the line of modern Wheaton Street. A marker at the end of East Liberty Street tells of the British turning movement that forced General Robert Howe to retreat into South Carolina and abandon Savannah.

Admiral comte Charles-Hector Théodat d'Estaing appeared off the Georgia coast in the fall of 1779 with about 40 warships and 4,000 troops to collaborate with the Americans in a powerful effort to retake Savannah. The Patriot force, under General Benjamin Lincoln, numbered 600 Continentals, 200 cavalry under Count Casimir Pulaski, and 750 militia. The British garrison, under the veteran Swiss, General Augustine Prevost, was composed largely of Loyalists and numbered only 2,400 initially. Ranks of the defenders were swelled by 800 men when Lieutenant Colonel John Maitland arrived from Beaufort after a remarkable movement through the coastal swamps that eluded Allied land and sea forces. Two other exceptional enemy commanders—the New York Loyalist and son-in-law of Oliver De Lancey, Lieutenant Colonel

John Cruger, and British Captain James Moncrieff—figured prominently in the defense of the city. Leading roles in the attack were played by Colonels John Laurens and Francis Marion and Sergeant William Jasper, all of South Carolina. Among the senior American officers were General William Moultrie of South Carolina and Lachlan McIntosh of Georgia. Major Thomas Pinckney, later famous as a diplomat, was assigned as aide-de-camp to d'Estaing. And in the back ranks of this stellar cast of characters was the future king of Haiti, Henri Christophe.

Allied generalship was bungling from the start, while British defensive efforts were managed with exceptional competence. The experienced Prevost, veteran of more than twenty years of campaigning in America, anticipated that the main attack would be against the Spring Hill Redoubt, and he made his dispositions accordingly. Moncrieff, whose engineering experience in North America started in 1762, distinguished himself in planning and building the fortifications that ringed Savannah. More than a month after reaching Georgia, d'Estaing finally launched his long-expected attack. Diversionary efforts were made against the eastern and western flanks, but the main attack was from the southwest against the Spring Hill Redoubt. D'Estaing personally led the first piecemeal attack without waiting for two other French columns on his left to get into their assigned positions. In a gallant but uncoordinated series of charges the French lost many men without making any significant gains. To the west the Americans circled through the low ground where the Springfield Canal was later dug and attacked in two columns. The Crescent Flag of Marion's Second South Carolina Continentals and the Lillies of France were planted on the Spring Hill Redoubt, but they could not be kept there. After three American officers and one of d'Estaing's aides had been shot down with the flags, Sergeant William Jasper of Fort Moultrie fame was mortally wounded trying to put them up again.

As the South Carolinians were starting to pull back, the British counterattacked with a crack force of grenadiers and marines to sweep the ditches of the Spring Hill Redoubt and its adjacent artillery position clean. Count Pulaski was mortally wounded in a gallant but foolhardy attempt to lead his cavalry through the abatis just north of the Spring Hill Redoubt. Franco-American coordination had been bad at the start of the operation, and it got worse as the wounded d'Estaing tried to renew the assault. A fresh American column on the left under McIntosh was diverted into the swamps on the western side of Savannah because the French did not want them to interfere with their reorganization in front of the Spring Hill Redoubt. The battle finally ground to a halt in the heavy fog of dawn; but for this poor visibility Prevost could have counterattacked and turned the Allied defeat into a greater disaster.

The Allies lost more than 1,000 killed and wounded. Prevost reported that he buried 203 Allied dead around Spring Hill and another 28 on his left. The French lost 20 percent of their total strength and about 50 percent of those engaged around the Spring Hill Redoubt. American authorities put British losses at about 150, of whom about 40 were killed. (Casualty figures for this action vary wildly.)

In 1833 the Central of Georgia Railway built its tracks along the old Louisville Road and erected its roundhouse, shops, and other buildings over a 14-acre tract of the Spring Hill battlefield. Another 20 acres to the south, through which the attackers advanced and where the Jewish Burial Ground has survived from its dedication in 1773, has succumbed to urban development. In 1990 the Costal Heritage Society opened the Savannah History Museum in the passenger building of the old Central of Georgia Railway. The Battle of Savannah is detailed here through exhibits and among their ten thousand historical artifacts. Phone: (912) 651-6825. Presently the Coastal Heritage Society is working to fulfill the longtime wishes of many American Revolution preservationists by creating a Battlefield Park. In 2004 the state of Georgia approved a $6 million bond to help fund the project, which is now in the post-planning phase. The Coastal Heritage Society offices are located at 303 Martin Luther King Jr. Boulevard in Savannah. Phone: (921) 651-6840.

Savannah of the Revolution occupied the area now bounded on the south by Oglethorpe Avenue, on the east by Lincoln Street, and on the west by Jefferson Street. There were about 430 houses (badly damaged in the Franco-American siege), and six public squares relieving the monotony of founder James Oglethorpe's grid of parallel streets intersecting at right angles. Little remains to remind the visitor of Savannah's eighteenth-century history except the beautiful Colonial Park Cemetery (see below) and the monuments to colonial and Revolutionary heroes in the city squares.

Colonial Park Cemetery is rich in historical associations in addition to being a place of unique beauty in a modern city. Shaded by old trees festooned with Spanish moss and covering about 7 acres between Abercorn and Habersham Streets on Oglethorpe Avenue, the cemetery was used from about 1750 to 1853, when it was closed to burials. There are more than six hundred markers standing, but according to local experts, many of the dates on them are not to be believed. Local lore has it that the Union troops during the Civil War grazed their horses in the cemetery and, being "mischievous" by nature, took time to alter the dates as well as perform other high jinks on the markers. Large brick vaults include remains of such famous families as the Habershams and the McIntoshes. Button Gwinnett is almost certainly buried here, and the one eyesore in the otherwise tastefully restored and maintained park is the modern monument over the spot where some believe his bones lie. The bronze marker includes a facsimile of the rare signature that in recent years has fetched $150,000 in the autograph market. The controversial Gwinnett was a signer of the Declaration of Independence, a military place-seeker in the abortive efforts to organize the defense of the southern colonies before the British got around to conquering them, and for about two months in the spring of 1777 governor and commander in chief of Georgia troops. In this position he antagonized the conservatives by pressing the extreme views of his supporters around Sunbury (see SUNBURY SITE AND FORT MORRIS) and was publicly denounced by the equally controversial Lachlan McIntosh. This led to a duel on the outskirts of Savannah in which both men were wounded. Gwinnett died three days later. He has no known descendants, there is no trustworthy portrait, and only thirty-six of his autographs have survived.

As you come in the central gate of the cemetery from Oglethorpe Avenue, the four so-called colonial vaults are a short distance to the right front. Markers identify the second one as the Graham Vault and tell the visitor that the body of Lieutenant Colonel John Maitland was briefly interred here (he died of malaria a few days after ending his important duties in the defense of Savannah in 1779). Of more interest, however, is the information that the body of General Nathanael Greene lay here for more than a century. But you should know the whole story about the "lost grave" of the officer who was second only to George Washington as a Patriot military hero.

Greene came south to take command of military operations in the Carolinas and Georgia in December 1781. The great Rhode Islander was naturally a hero of the South when the war ended, and the state of Georgia gave him the confiscated plantation of Royal Lieutenant Governor John Graham. Having spent two years traveling between Georgia and Rhode Island, Greene finally sold his property in the North and established his home permanently on his Georgia estate near Savannah in 1785. The next year he died suddenly of sunstroke at the age of only forty-four. With great civic ceremony he was buried in Savannah's Colonial Park Cemetery. Logically, he would have been put to rest in the Graham Vault, but newspaper accounts of the interment did not specify the location. One of Greene's biographers was told insistently by the man who read the burial service that the body was in the Jones Vault, one of the four "colonial vaults" standing in a row near today's Oglethorpe Avenue gate.

Some efforts were made in 1820 and 1840 to clear up what was already becoming a mystery, but Greene's body was not found. Greene's family had meanwhile left the region and witnesses of the burial had died off. High-spirited but ghoulish troops of Sherman's conquering Civil War armies entertained themselves by desecrating colonial graves, opening many tombs and altering epitaphs. It was known also that bodies of the Jones family had been removed by a descendant for reburial elsewhere, and the story sprang up that Greene's bones had also been moved.

In 1901 the Rhode Island Society of the Cincinnati resolved to make a proper effort to find the remains of their hero. After getting all the necessary permissions and the cooperation of local patriot societies, and witnessed by a large crowd, the searchers opened the colonial vaults one by one and quickly found what they were seeking. Unmistakably identifiable by a metal plaque and vestiges of a major general's uniform, and with the remains of Greene's young son who drowned in 1793, was the body that had been lost for more than a century. The explanation was very simply that what had for years been called the Graham Vault was actually the Jones Vault, and the real Graham Vault had never been opened for investigation. In 1902 General Greene and his son were reinterred in the monument erected to the general in Johnson Square after the cornerstone was laid by Lafayette in 1825.

Large-scale street maps of Savannah's historic area are distributed by the city's tourist agencies. A virtual tour website of Savannah that includes many of the Revolutionary War landmarks is www.ourcoast.com.

Jasper Spring is buried under the new intersection of the Westside Bypass (Ga. 26 Loop) and U.S. 17–80. This is where the famous Sergeant William Jasper and a companion surprised a British escort and liberated a number of Patriot prisoners being taken to Savannah for trial and probably for execution. A heroic statue of Jasper is in Madison Square (Bull Street between Charlton and Harris Streets), where two cannon also mark the junction of the colonial roads from Augusta and Darien.

A few blocks east of Madison Square, roughly in the section now covered by Troup and Lafayette Squares, is the area where the French "regular approaches" were dug in 1779 and where most of the French siege artillery was emplaced.

The site of Tondee's Tavern, where the Rebels raised the Liberty Pole and convened the Provincial Congress in the summer of 1775, is at the northwest corner of Broughton and Whitaker Streets. Governor Wright's house, where he was held prisoner for nearly a month in early 1776 before escaping to a British warship, was at the northeast corner of today's State and Jefferson Streets, where the Telfair Academy now stands. Opposite the Davenport House (1821–1822) at 10 East State Street is where the British barracks were built in 1777; they were torn down in 1916.

The Old Dunning House at 24 East Broughton Street was Prevost's headquarters in 1779. The place from which the Rebels first fired a cannon at the British in Georgia waters on 3 March 1776 is in the middle of Montgomery Street just north of Bay Street.

Identified in tourist literature are many interesting landmarks dating from the colonial era. Among these are the recently restored area of the Trustees' Garden, where the Herb House of 1734 stands as Georgia's oldest building and the Pirates' House of 1754 has been restored as a restaurant.

The Georgia Historical Society, 501 Whitaker Street, (912) 651-2125, has a fine collection of books, manuscripts, early Savannah newspapers, and portraits of famous Georgians. On exhibit is the round shot removed from the body of Pulaski. As mentioned earlier, he was wounded in the attack of 9 October 1779 around the Spring Hill Redoubt. He died about two days later aboard an American warship, the *Wasp*, after a surgeon had been unable to remove a projectile of this type from his groin. Presumably this is the fatal missile, extracted during the postmortem examination. One of the mysteries of Revolutionary War history is whether Pulaski was buried at sea, on St. Helena's Island (off Beaufort, South Carolina), or in Greenwich, Georgia, though military records indicate he was buried at sea on 15 October 1779.

Literature on points of historical interest is available from the Convention and Visitors Bureau of the Savannah Area Chamber of Commerce, Savannah 31401. Website: www.savannahchamber.com; phone: (912) 644-6400.

Sunbury Site and Fort Morris, Liberty County. About 11 miles east of Midway on the Midway River and off Exit 76 of Interstate 95 is the 70-acre state park and site of a dead town that once had 496 house lots, three large public squares, five wharves, and a fort. Park office phone: (912) 884-5999.

Sunbury was one of the settlements established by the founders of Midway. The reiterated claim that it grew into a port rivaling Savannah is an exaggeration, but from its founding in 1758 it did become an important place in remarkably short order. On the eve of the Revolution 317 of the lots had been sold, two of them to Lyman Hall, and the population of the town was about 1,000.

Dr. Lyman Hall was one of the New Englanders who had gone to Midway from Dorchester, South Carolina. A graduate of Yale (1747), he was an ordained minister before turning to medicine. As colonial protest against British rule mounted, Dr. Hall became a leader of the radical Patriot faction in Sunbury and was sent to represent St. Johns Parish in the Continental Congress before Georgia got around to electing an official delegation. He and Button Gwinnett, whose plantation was on nearby St. Catherine's Island and who was a justice of the peace in Sunbury (1767–1768), gained provincial immortality by signing the Declaration of Independence. (There is speculation that Gwinnett is buried at Sunbury, but the greater evidence is that he lies in the Colonial Park Cemetery in Savannah.)

After the outbreak of the Revolution a large earthwork was built with slave labor on a bluff overlooking the salt marshes of the river on the southern outskirts of Sunbury. It was manned by fewer than 200 men under Colonel John McIntosh (nephew of General Lachlan McIntosh) when Lieutenant Colonel L. V. Fuser's much stronger force from Florida arrived by ship on 25 November 1778 and demanded its surrender. "Come and take it," was McIntosh's reply. The British declined the invitation and withdrew. (See MIDWAY.)

A few weeks later, when the southern army of General Robert Howe went to meet the greater threat against Savannah, leaving about 200 Continentals at Sunbury, General Augustine Prevost captured Fort Morris with the loss of only one British soldier killed. The American commander had disobeyed his orders to evacuate the fort after the fall of Savannah, eleven days earlier. In addition to the 159 Continentals and 45 militia captured, the Patriots lost 24 guns and a quantity of supplies.

With the decline of its political and commercial importance Sunbury became an educational center, the famous Sunbury Academy being established in 1788 and remaining in operation for at least five years after the retirement of its distinguished principal, Dr. William McWhir, in 1824. A number of misfortunes had meanwhile struck the town: the county seat was moved away in 1797 and hurricanes inflicted great damage in 1804 and 1824. By 1850 the place was deserted, and cornfields covered the house sites until these were taken over by pines. The long-neglected burial ground has a marker that starts, ironically, with the words: "In this Cemetery are buried men and women whose lives contributed much to the early history of Georgia."

As for directions to the cemetery, it must be reported that this author was unable to find the site, and it was not for lack of trying. The modern topographical map shows two cemeteries. Several websites mention the cemetery, some confusing it with the Midway Church cemetery and others referring correctly to it, but giving no details as to its whereabouts. A local resident informed the author that the northernmost of these was the colonial burying ground, but the director of the Georgia Historical Society expressed the opinion that it was the one 1,300 feet farther south.

The remains of Fort Morris are picturesque and interesting. The earthworks have been cleared of underbrush but are covered by widely spaced trees. The central parade, about an acre in extent, shows evidence of recent archaeological exploration. From the long face of the quadrangular fort, which measures almost 100 yards, you can see how guns on the parapet would command the river and how the salt marshes would make attack from three directions virtually impossible. The park is home to a number of historical recreations, including an annual "Come and Take It!" day every November.

A cannon excavated from the site in 1940 is on the courthouse lawn at Hinesville.

To reach Fort Morris and Sunbury, proceed as follows. From U.S. 17 in Midway or Exit 76 on Interstate 95 (3.7 miles east of Midway) drive east on Ga. 38. The turn-off to Sunbury from Ga. 38 is on the left about 4.2 miles from Interstate 95. Old Sunbury is 3 miles away, where a group of historical markers is situated. Fort Morris State Park is 7 miles from the interstate on Fort Morris Road and well marked with directional signs.

Tybee Island, mouth of Savannah River off U.S. 80, 18 miles east of Savannah. Probably the first naval capture of the Revolution was made off Tybee Island on 10 July 1775 when a schooner, the first vessel chartered by the Continental Congress, commanded by Captain Oliver Bowen, seized a British ship and 14,000 pounds of powder. When the British sailed from New York to take Savannah in 1778, they anchored off Tybee (23 December) before proceeding to Girardeau's Plantation. The island became a popular bathing resort and is now part of the Tybee National Wildlife Refuge. A museum operated by the Tybee Island Historical Society includes exhibits pertaining to the early history of the island although, like so many of Georgia's historical attractions, it focuses largely on the Civil War. Phone: (912) 786-5801.

ILLINOIS

"Illinois country" during the colonial period meant all of the Old Northwest between the Wabash and the Mississippi Rivers, the country of the powerful Illinois confederation of Indians. Lake Michigan was then known as Lac des Illinois, connected by the Chicago Portage to the Illinois River, which entered the Mississippi near the mouth of the Missouri. The first permanent French settlement in the Mississippi Valley was established in 1699 at Cahokia, followed the next year by Kaskaskia (see FORT KASKASKIA STATE PARK). The oldest surviving building in the Mississippi Valley is probably the one in Cahokia, although some authorities believe the Melliere House in Prairie du Rocher is older. Across the river the French settlement at St. Louis (1764) was to be renamed by the Spanish with their version of "Illinois," which they spelled "Ylinoises."

The Revolution within the present state of Illinois was notable for the tremendously important campaign waged by George Rogers Clark. Landmarks made famous by his operations have almost all survived to the extent that the names remain on the map and the places can be visited on the ground. Other historic sites of the period of French exploration and settlement have also been preserved. Many in both categories are in state parks.

The Koster archaeological site near Kampsville, called the Center for American Archeology, where digging started in 1968, contains some of the most important archaeological discoveries in the United States. The Koster site, located in Greene County, is open for guided tours during the summer and sponsors student digs and other educational programs. There is a museum and visitors' center. The site is expanded and now joined by a second site, Koster South. Phone: (618) 653-4316.

The state has a number of historic routes that can be traced today on foot and by water—the routes of George Rogers Clark from Louisville, Kentucky, to Kaskaskia, and his route from that place to Vincennes, Indiana, for example. The various portage routes from the Great Lakes to the Ohio and Mississippi Valleys are other historic routes.

Illinois Prairie Path is a 61-mile limestone trail on an abandoned railroad bed across DuPage County, west of Chicago. It has a variety of terrain for hiking, bicycling, and horseback riding. For trail guides and other information, write Illinois Prairie Path, Box 1086, Wheaton, Ill. 60187. Phone: (847) 229-7882. The Forest Preserve District of Cook County administers 150 miles of trails for hikers, bicyclists, and horseback riders on over 21,000 acres. Available on each of the nine divisional areas is a booklet that includes a map and details of the historical and natural history attractions. For information write: Forest Preserve General Headquarters, 536 North Harlem Avenue, River Forest, Ill. 60305.

The Abraham Lincoln Presidential Library, formerly the Illinois State Historical Library in Springfield, features excellent collections in the colonial and Revolutionary War periods. It is located at 112 North Sixth Street, Springfield, Ill. 62701. Phone: (217) 524-7216. The library is the administration office of several landmark sites and important state agencies dealing with the state's early history. Two of those are the Illinois Historic Preservation Agency and the Illinois Association of Museums.

Independent of this library, another useful state site is the Illinois State Historical Society located in Springfield at 210½ South Sixth Street. Phone: (217) 525-2781.

The society offers two publications, *Illinois Heritage,* a glossy bimonthly subscription publication, and the *Journal of the Illinois State Historical Society,* an academic history journal.

Cahokia, Mississippi River opposite St. Louis, St. Clair County. Established by the French in 1699, a year before Kaskaskia, Cahokia was the first settlement in Illinois. The charming little cabin built about 1737 by Jean Baptiste Saucier is still standing and is believed to be the oldest surviving structure in the entire Mississippi Valley outside of New Orleans, Louisiana. (Some authorities believe the Melliere House in Prairie du Rocher may be older.) The Saucier House, built in the French Colonial style with vertical squared logs chinked with wide bands of clay, and with the roof suggesting African influence, is of the type seen throughout the West Indies and in some parts of the American South, but it is an architectural curiosity in the upper Mississippi. In 1793 the cabin became the Cahokia County courthouse and jail. During the early part of the twentieth century this architectural treasure was dismantled several times and reconstructed for exhibition, first at the Louisiana Purchase Exhibition in St. Louis (1904), and then in Jackson Park in Chicago. In 1938 it was reconstructed on its original foundation as the Cahokia Courthouse State Memorial. This state historic site is open 9 A.M. to 5 P.M., Wednesday through Sunday. Phone: (618) 332-1782.

Now a suburb of St. Louis, Cahokia is in the narrow strip of exceptionally fertile flood plain between the mouth of the Missouri River and the Kaskaskia River known in the literature of westward expansion as the American Bottom. The 2,200-acre Cahokia Mounds State Park, 5.5 miles east of East St. Louis on U.S. 40 Business Route, is evidence of the region's importance from prehistoric times. The French settlement was among those in the region that joined the American cause after George Rogers Clark's surprise capture of Fort Gage at Kaskaskia (see FORT KASKASKIA STATE PARK). Cahokia is remembered also for the death of Pontiac, who was assassinated near the center of the village in 1769 by a member of the Peoria tribe opposed to his ever more belligerent rhetoric. The park is managed by the Illinois Historic Preservation Agency. The park's phone for general information: (618) 346-5160. Museum phone: (618) 344-7316. Its website, www.cahokiamounds.com, offers a virtual tour of the site.

Chicago Portage, Cook County. Returning from their exploration of the upper Mississippi (to the Arkansas River) in 1673, Louis Jolliet and Father Jacques Marquette learned from friendly Indians of an ancient shortcut to Lake Michigan. The Chicago Portage, as this was later called, was one of the natural arteries connecting the water routes of the St. Lawrence and Great Lakes system with the Mississippi Valley. During the driest periods it involved an arduous overland portage of about 80 miles from today's La Salle (see STARVED ROCK) on the Illinois River. Ordinarily, however, the Portage Road of about 12 miles along the South Branch of the Chicago River was the only stretch involving a portage. At least forty-eight days of the year, during flood periods, travel by canoe and bateau was possible over the entire route from Des Plaines River through Mud Lake (a swampy vestige of glacial Lake Chicago), along South Branch and the Chicago River into Lake Michigan.

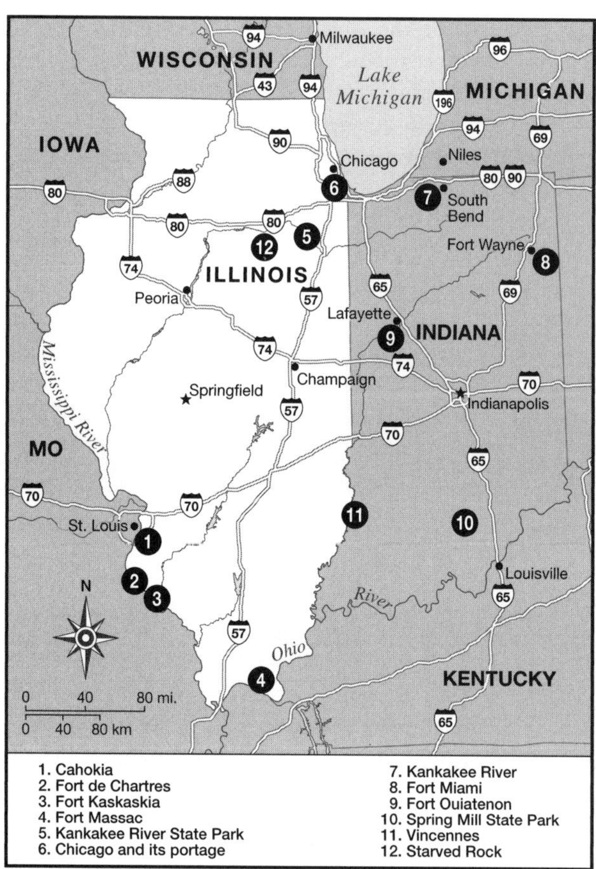

MAP BY XNR PRODUCTIONS. THE GALE GROUP.

Another strategically important portage linked about midway between the sites of La Salle and Chicago. This was the Miami's Portage, which linked the Kankakee River route (see KANKAKEE RIVER STATE PARK) to the St. Joseph (Miamis) River in the vicinity of Fort St. Joseph, Michigan. The Lake Erie–Ohio River portages were thus integrated into the system. (See Scribner's *Atlas of America History,* plates 32, 40, and 41, for an excellent presentation of this network.)

The Miami had a settlement here until the 1650s, returning in the 1690s to establish a village of an estimated 2,500 people at the mouth of the Chicago River. By 1710 they had left for the Maumee and Wabash Valleys in Indiana, and other tribes began to hunt in the area. In the 1740s the Potawatomis constructed a village here, and were joined over the next decade by Ottawas and Chippewas.

La Salle and Tonty were the next Europeans to leave a record of using the Chicago Portage, and many other French explorers traveled it until about 1700. The extended French conflict with the Fox or Mesquakie Indians closed the region to white men until 1740, when French traders returned to the area.

The Treaty of Greenville in 1795, following "Mad Anthony" Wayne's successful campaigns in the Old Northwest, gave the United States a large piece of Indian territory at the mouth of the Chicago River. Until this time there had been no permanent white settlement of real significance on the site of one of the world's great modern cities. It is known that Father Marquette lived briefly in a cabin here in 1674. (The approximate site is marked by a tablet at the north end of Damen Avenue bridge at 26th Street in Chicago.) In 1679 the Sieur de La Salle had established a fort he called Crèvecoeur ("heartbreak") and which the Indians called Checagou, but although this is the first recorded use of a word sounding like Chicago, it was not located near the present metropolis of that name, but near Peoria.

A map of 1683 shows "Fort Checagou" where the city of Chicago is now located. But no development of significance occurred here under French rule other than the short-lived Guardian Angel Mission of 1696 to 1700. (The site is marked in Bowmanville on the North Branch at Foster Avenue.)

The British found no reason to establish a fort or settlement at Chicago after acquiring control of French territory in 1763. It was not until 1803 that the United States moved into the region with the establishment of Fort Dearborn by Captain John Whistler, grandfather of the famous painter. In 1812 the commandant was ordered by General William Hull to evacuate Fort Dearborn and march his garrison and its families to Fort Wayne, Indiana. The Potawatomi massacred most of the men, women, and children and burned the abandoned fort. This was rebuilt in 1816. After various ups and downs the second Fort Dearborn's last vestiges were consumed in the Great Fire of 1871. Its site is marked by a tablet on the Stone Container Building (formerly the London Guarantee and Accident Building), 360 North Michigan Avenue at Wacker Drive. The site of the Fort Dearborn Massacre (15 August 1812) is marked at Calumet Avenue and 18th Street.

Jean Baptiste Point de Sable, a Haitian with French and African parents who established a string of fur-trading stations along Lake Michigan, is usually credited as being modern Chicago's first permanent resident. In 1779 the British arrested him because of his French connections. De Sable was held briefly at Michilimackinac (see MACKINAW CITY and MICHILIMACKINAC STATE PARK under Michigan), but in the same year of his arrest (at Michigan City), he put up a cabin on the site of Chicago and started rebuilding a profitable business. Much of his trade was with the Spanish west of the Mississippi when the Revolution ended. Goods from the Michilimackinac region passed through de Sable's establishment on their way westward across the Chicago Portage, and back came furs in exchange. A settlement grew up around de Sable's station, remaining after his departure in 1800 and evolving into the present city. The original cabin, 22 feet by 40, gave way in 1784 to the house of John Kinzie, where Chicago's first white child was born in 1805. The "Kinzie Mansion" site is marked in two different locations—at opposite ends of the Michigan Avenue Bridge across the Chicago River. Some authorities contend that the house was on the south side of the river, about where Wacker Drive and Michigan Avenue now intersect. The majority favor the location across the river, opposite the site of Fort Dearborn, at Pioneer Court, in front of the Equitable Building, 401 North Michigan Avenue. The Du Sable Museum of African American History, which houses an extensive collection of documents and artifacts on African American history and culture, is located at 740 East 56th Place (near the corner of 57th Street and Cottage Grove Avenue). Phone: (312) 947-0600.

The grave of David Kenison, thought to be the last survivor of the Boston Tea Party, is marked by a boulder in Lincoln Park, near the intersection of Clark and Wisconsin Streets.

Exceptionally fine mosaics depicting the early history of Chicago are in the mezzanine balcony of the Marquette Building, 140 South Dearborn Street.

The Chicago Portage National Historic Site was so designated in 1952, comprising the Old Chicago Portage Forest Preserve and the National Historic Site. This is one of the few national historic sites authorized by the Historic Sites Act of 1935 to be administered by nonfederal owners with the cooperation of the Department of the Interior. The landmark is at the western end of the Portage Road on Des Plaines River and Portage Creek (which ran west from Mud Lake). Although crowded by industry and topographically altered by diversion of the river and canalization of South Branch, the forest preserve remains an area of marsh and hills. A boulder marks the spot where the portage began. Because the bronze plaque had been stolen countless times, a large storyboard has been erected to depict the route and history of the portage. Adjacent portions of the Salt Creek Division of Cook County's Forest Preserve District have sites associated with the Old Laughton Trading Post (established 1828) and Indian trails through the portage area. The portage is part of the Chicago Portage Canoe Trail, a water route running 14 miles on the Des Plaines River. The historic site is just southwest of Chicago in Cook

County, at 536 North Harlem Avenue, just south of 47th Street and the Santa Fe Railroad. The Friends of the Chicago Portage (2001) formed to raise awareness and funding to help maintain the site and plan to make it into an historic park. Portage Days, a historical interpretation tour that began in 2004, is presented 1–9 May every year. Historical information on this site and for the city of Chicago is best accessed through the previously listed Illinois Historic Preservation Agency. Phone: (312) 771-1130.

Fort de Chartres and Prairie du Rocher, Mississippi River between Cahokia and Fort Kaskaskia State Park. One of the first French settlements in the extremely fertile flood plain from Kaskaskia north to Cahokia was Prairie du Rocher. In this vicinity the first stockaded defensive work was erected about 1709, followed by wooden forts in 1720 and about 1736, after which a strong stone fort was built in 1753. Named Fort de Chartres for the son of the French regent, it was the major military work in the upper Mississippi Valley. The British acquired it in 1763, bestowing the new name Fort Cavendish, but abandoned it in 1772, one reason being that the river was eating into the thick outer walls. A portion of the remaining works has been restored within an attractive state park, Fort de Chartres State Historic Site, that includes an interpretive center, provision for guided tours, and picnic facilities. Phone: (618) 284-7230. Four miles to the east is the village that perpetuates the name of the French settlement, Prairie du Rocher, established here in 1721. Still standing are several homes of the French era, including the Melliere House, which may be older than the famous one in Cahokia.

Fort Kaskaskia State Park, overlooking the Mississippi River below the mouth of Kaskaskia River, near Ellis Grove, Randolph County. The French fort here was erected in 1736 and twice rebuilt before the end of the Seven Years' War in 1763. At this time Kaskaskia was the largest French settlement in the Illinois region, having eighty well-built houses, most of them stone. The town was on the west bank of the Kaskaskia River about 6 miles from the Mississippi, which has since shifted its bed into that of the Kaskaskia and eaten the site of the old village. Between Kaskaskia and St. Louis, Missouri, were other settlements at Prairie du Rocher, Ste. Anne, St. Phillipe, Bellefontaine, and Cahokia. The British gained control of the French territory east of the Mississippi in 1763, finding Fort Kaskaskia demolished, but fortifying the Jesuit mission in the village of Kaskaskia and naming it Fort Gage.

When the Revolution broke out the twenty-three-year-old George Rogers Clark, already a veteran explorer of the Ohio country, saw the possibilities of gaining military control over the vast territory of the Old Northwest. His agents visited the French settlements and brought back information that the British garrison had been withdrawn to Detroit, the region was virtually undefended, and the *habitants* could be won over. In recommending to Governor Patrick Henry of Virginia the invasion of the distant region, Clark pointed out the advantages of opening the line of the Mississippi and the Ohio to Spanish supplies from New Orleans and the possibilities of gaining control over Indians of the region.

Clark's bold strategic conception was matched by his subsequent execution of his plans. With fewer than two hundred men he moved down the Ohio, spent some time whipping his little expedition into shape near today's Louisville, Kentucky, and landed at the site of Fort Massac (see FORT MASSAC STATE PARK). Leaving here on 29 June 1778, he spent the next five days covering the remaining 120 miles north to Kaskaskia, moving overland to avoid sacrificing surprise. The local militia had been alerted that something was up, but Clark's approach was so well managed that the defenders relaxed their vigilance when patrols from Kaskaskia failed to confirm the presence of American invaders. Clark collected enough boats to cross the Kaskaskia River after dark, surrounded the town with part of his command, and led the party that surprised the commandant in his quarters. The Chevalier de Rocheblave, a French veteran who had remained to serve in the British army, quite sensibly surrendered the town; not a shot had been fired.

The local French were won over by Clark's diplomacy, readily shifted their allegiance to Virginia, and proved to be a source of strength in Clark's subsequent operations. The fort captured by Clark was a stockaded stone house in the village of Kaskaskia, which has been obliterated by the Mississippi. The present Fort Kaskaskia State Park preserves the site of an older fort that was not in use at the time of Clark's invasion. Across the Kaskaskia and northeast of the old French settlement (now in the Mississippi), Old Fort was built on the bluff with a commanding view of the lower Kaskaskia Valley. Now that the Mississippi River has taken over the latter for its own bed, keep in mind that Old Fort and the lost site of Kaskaskia village were about 6 miles from the Mississippi in the eighteenth century. The fort whose site is preserved in the 233-acre Fort Kaskaskia State Park was a wooden stockade when first erected in 1736. The French rebuilt it in 1761 and destroyed it six years later when they surrendered sovereignty of this region to the British. Garrison Hill Cemetery and the Pierre Menard House (1802) are near the site of the fort.

Fort Kaskaskia State Park is off Ill. 3, at 4372 Park Road in Ellis Grove, about 10 miles north of Chester. Recreational facilities include camping, picnicking, hunting, and fishing. Open Wednesday through Sunday, 9 A.M. to 5 P.M. Phone: (618) 859-3741.

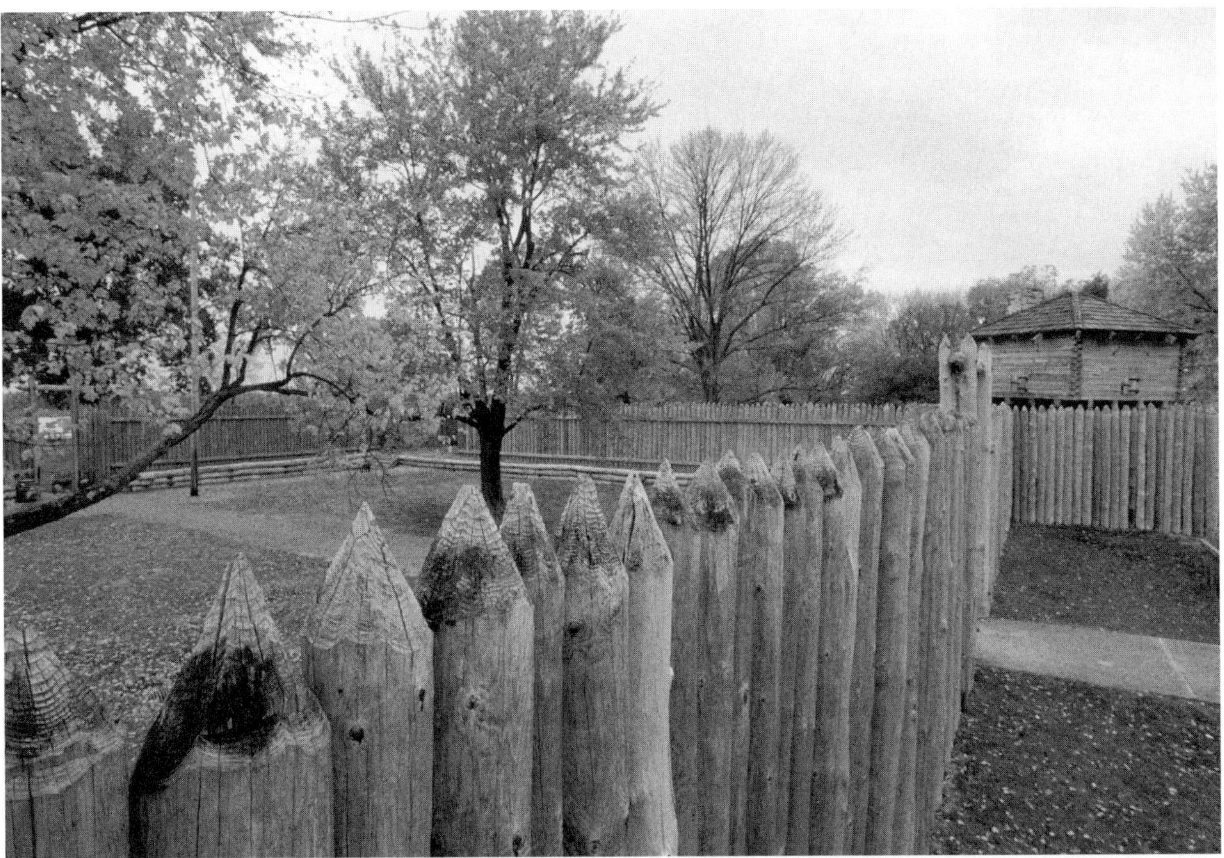

Fort Massac. *This reconstruction of Fort Massac on the Ohio River in Metropolis, Illinois, stands near the site where George Rogers Clark landed after moving down the Ohio River.* © RICHARD HAMILTON SMITH/CORBIS.

Fort Massac State Park, Ohio River, near Metropolis, Massac County. In 1757 the French built an earthwork here named Fort Ascension, then Fort Massiac (for the minister of the navy; the current spelling, Massac, is an anglicized form of the original French name). Long abandoned in 1778, it was near where George Rogers Clark landed after moving down the Ohio, and his point of departure for the arduous overland march to capture Kaskaskia (see FORT KASKASKIA STATE PARK). The state park of about 1,450 acres has a statue of Clark amidst the barely discernible bastions and ditches of the fort. The American fort of 1796 had been restored within the park but was taken down in 2002 in favor of constructing a replica of a fort from 1802. An interpretive museum is on site. Open all year. Take Exit 37 off Interstate 24 and follow the signs into the park. Phone: (618) 524-4712.

Kankakee River State Park. Important in the intricate system of water routes between the Great Lakes and the Ohio and Mississippi Rivers was the Kankakee River. It tied in with the Chicago Portage. Other portages permitted inland water travel along the routes of the St. Joseph and St. Joseph of Maumee Rivers to Fort Miami, thence into Lake Erie. The name and a portion of the terrain are preserved in a 4,000-acre state park where Ill. 102 borders the north side and Ill. 113 the south, about 8 miles northwest of Kankakee. Phone: (815) 933-1383.

La Salle. *See* STARVED ROCK.

Prairie du Rocher. *See* FORT DE CHARTRES AND PRAIRIE DU ROCHER.

Starved Rock (Fort St. Louis site), 5 miles east of La Salle off Ill. 71. As part of his campaign of protecting friendly Indians of the region from the hostile Iroquois, La Salle built Fort St. Louis in 1682 on the 125-foot-high outcropping of sandstone rock that is preserved in Starved Rock State Park. Fort St. Louis was abandoned by the French about five years after being established. The name Starved Rock dates from

1769, when a band of Illinois took refuge there to escape Indian enemies and died of thirst and starvation. The present recreation park is a 2,114-acre area of wooded bluff; excursion boats operate on the Illinois River from the park, and there are winter sports in season. Phone: (815) 667-4726.

About 7 miles southeast of La Salle, off Ill. 178, is Matthiessen State Park Nature Area (1,463 acres), featuring prehistoric stone sculptures in a setting of canyon trails, caves, and waterfalls. The park has walking paths, picnic facilities, and many other outdoor activities, including horseback riding. Phone: (815) 667-4868.

INDIANA

Through most of the eighteenth century Indiana was part of what the historian Richard White has labeled "the Middle Ground," the territory under Indian control, though claimed by European nations, where many cultures met, fought, and traded. Until 1763 it was known to Europeans as "Illinois country," an area of overlap between French Canada and French Louisiana. Vincennes remained for many years under control of French and Spanish authorities in New Orleans even after all the Illinois country east of the Mississippi became British (1763). The only major action in modern Indiana during the Revolution was George Rogers Clark's remarkable victory at Vincennes. But this was critical in winning for the United States a useful claim to the whole vast region between the Ohio and the upper Mississippi. "Indiana Territory" as created in 1800 comprised virtually all of the Old Northwest except what is now Ohio. "Illinois Territory" was not revived as a geographical designation until 1809, when it was used for the country west of the Wabash and the longitude of Vincennes. In 1816 the present boundaries of Indiana were fixed when it was admitted as a state.

Tourist information is available from the Indiana Department of Tourism, 1 North Capitol, Suite 700, Indianapolis, Ind. 46204. Phone: (317) 232-8860. In the latter city also are the Indiana Historical Bureau, State Library, and Historical Building, 140 North Senate Avenue. Phone: (317) 232-2535. The Indiana Historical Society is located at 450 West Ohio Street. Phone: (317) 232-1882.

Fort Miami, the present city of Fort Wayne, near confluence of Maumee, St. Joseph of Maumee, and St. Marys Rivers, Allen County. A map showing the network of river and portage routes between the Great Lakes and the Ohio-Mississippi waterways make the strategic importance of this place apparent. From here it was possible to travel northeast down the Maumee to Lake Erie, north and west to Lake Michigan and the Chicago Portage, southwest to the Wabash, or southeast and then south on the Miami to the Ohio (see Scribner's *Atlas of American History,* plates 40 and 41).

When the French had established their forts on the Great Lakes and started linking these with the Mississippi Valley, Fort Miami was built first, sometime before 1712. It was among those posts taken over by the British in 1761, occupied first by a detachment of Robert Rogers's Rangers. In October of that year it was permanently garrisoned by fifteen British troops under Ensign Robert Holmes. On 27 May 1763 Fort Miami became the third fort to fall in Pontiac's Rebellion (after Sandusky, near the present town of that name in Ohio, and Fort St. Joseph, Michigan). Ensign Holmes was aware that Indian trouble of some sort was brewing. The local Miami Indians realized they could not follow the plan, so successful elsewhere, of surprising the garrison after being invited inside the fort. But they discovered that Holmes's Indian mistress was willing to betray him. This unnamed heroine asked the British officer to visit a cabin about 300 yards outside the fort where another woman needed medical attention. Holmes walked innocently into the ambush, was immediately shot twice and killed, and his sergeant was seized when he ran out to investigate. Unknown to Holmes and the garrison, three soldiers from the fort had been captured two days earlier. The remaining eleven soldiers prepared to defend themselves but quickly agreed to accept the offer that their lives would be spared if they surrendered. Four were taken to Pontiac (who was besieging Detroit); the fate of the others is not known.

The large modern city of Fort Wayne grew up around the fort of the same name built here in 1794 during General "Mad Anthony" Wayne's final conquest of the tribes of the Old Northwest. The site of Fort Miami has been preserved. A good source for historical information on the eighteenth century in this region is the Allen County–Fort Wayne Historical Society. It maintains a museum called the History Center in which a prized exhibit is kept: a camp bed used by General Wayne. It is located at 302 East Berry Street, Fort Wayne, Ind. 46802. Phone: (260) 426-2882.

Fort Ouiatenon, Wabash River below Lafayette, Tippecanoe County. The second military post established in Indiana (after Fort Miami) was at the bend in the Wabash 4 miles below today's city of Lafayette. The name derives from that of the Wea tribe, which came in turn from *wawiiatanong*, "where the current goes round." The French started building a fort here about 1719. This was taken over by the British in 1761 and garrisoned by twenty troops under Lieutenant Edward Jenkins. Arrival of a war belt in this vicinity was the prearranged signal for the start of Pontiac's Rebellion in 1763. On 1 June of that year the Indians invited Jenkins to a meeting outside the fort, seized him and several soldiers, and told him unless he surrendered the garrison all the British would be killed. Jenkins did the reasonable thing and lived to tell about it; he and his twenty men were held captive a month, then sent to Fort de Chartres (see under ILLINOIS), whence the lieutenant eventually made his way via New Orleans to New York.

Ouiatenon was on the border of the Louisiana territory surrendered by France to Britain in 1763, and English control was slow in moving farther down the Wabash to Vincennes. Fort Ouiatenon did not figure in the Revolution except as the principal center of Indian population in the region. According to the British commander at Vincennes, Ouiatenon and the Kickapoo town on the opposite side of the river contained one thousand fighting men between them in 1778. It was destroyed in 1791 by United States troops, and the famous battle of 1811 is commemorated 11 miles to the north (7 miles north of Lafayette) by the Tippecanoe Battlefield State Memorial.

The site of Fort Ouiatenon is preserved on the south bank of the Wabash on South River Road about 3 miles southwest of West Lafayette. The latter is on Ind. 25 about 4 miles southwest of Lafayette. Both sites are maintained by the Tippecanoe County Historical Association located at 1001 South Street, Lafayette, Ind. 47901. Phone: (765) 476-8411.

Kankakee River, northwest corner of state. An important route of canoe and portage travel between the Great Lakes and the Mississippi Valley, this river starts in one corner of modern Michigan (see FORT ST. JOSEPH) and cuts through a corner of Indiana into Illinois (see KANKAKEE RIVER STATE PARK). Portions of the historic passage preserved in Indiana are the LaSalle State Fish and Game Area in Lake County, and the Kankakee State Fish and Wildlife Area on the Laporte-Starke county line.

Spring Mill State Park, near Mitchell, Lawrence County. About 100 acres of primeval forest survive in this 1,300-acre park. This tract of land, Donaldson's Woods, features a hiking trail through trees more than three hundred years old. The park is of historical importance in providing a view of the woodland so familiar to American frontier settlers and an isolated settlement of the type that disappeared rapidly in the westward expansion that followed the Revolutionary era. A frontier trading post dating from about 1815 has been discovered and is partially restored. Phone: (812) 849-4129.

Vincennes, Wabash River, Knox County. To constitute another link in their chain of forts between the Great Lakes and the Louisiana territory, the French built a military post here in 1731, and a permanent settlement grew up in the next few years. It was named for the builder and first commander, the Sieur de Vincennes. When Britain acquired a claim to this region from France in 1763, Vincennes was a village of about eighty-five French families. Not until 1777 did the British assert their sovereignty in Vincennes, sending a garrison and renaming the place Fort Sackville.

But the British had withdrawn their troops to Detroit when the expedition under George Rogers Clark started taking over the Illinois country, where the French *habitants* looked on American control as slightly preferable to British and were easily won over by Clark's little show of force.

Frenchmen from the Kaskaskia region who visited Vincennes reported that the inhabitants had shifted their allegiance to Virginia, and Captain Leonard Helm of Clark's expedition promptly moved in to take command of the militia. Lieutenant Colonel Henry Hamilton in Detroit responded by rounding up about 175 white troops, mostly Frenchmen, and 60 Indians for the long march in midwinter to regain control of Vincennes. Leaving Detroit in early October (1778) and picking up Indian allies until his force finally numbered about 500, Hamilton made an extremely arduous advance to enter Vincennes seventy-one days later (17 December). Captain Helm's security patrols were captured, and the French militia refused to fight, so Hamilton's bag of prisoners totaled two Americans: Helm and one soldier who stood by him.

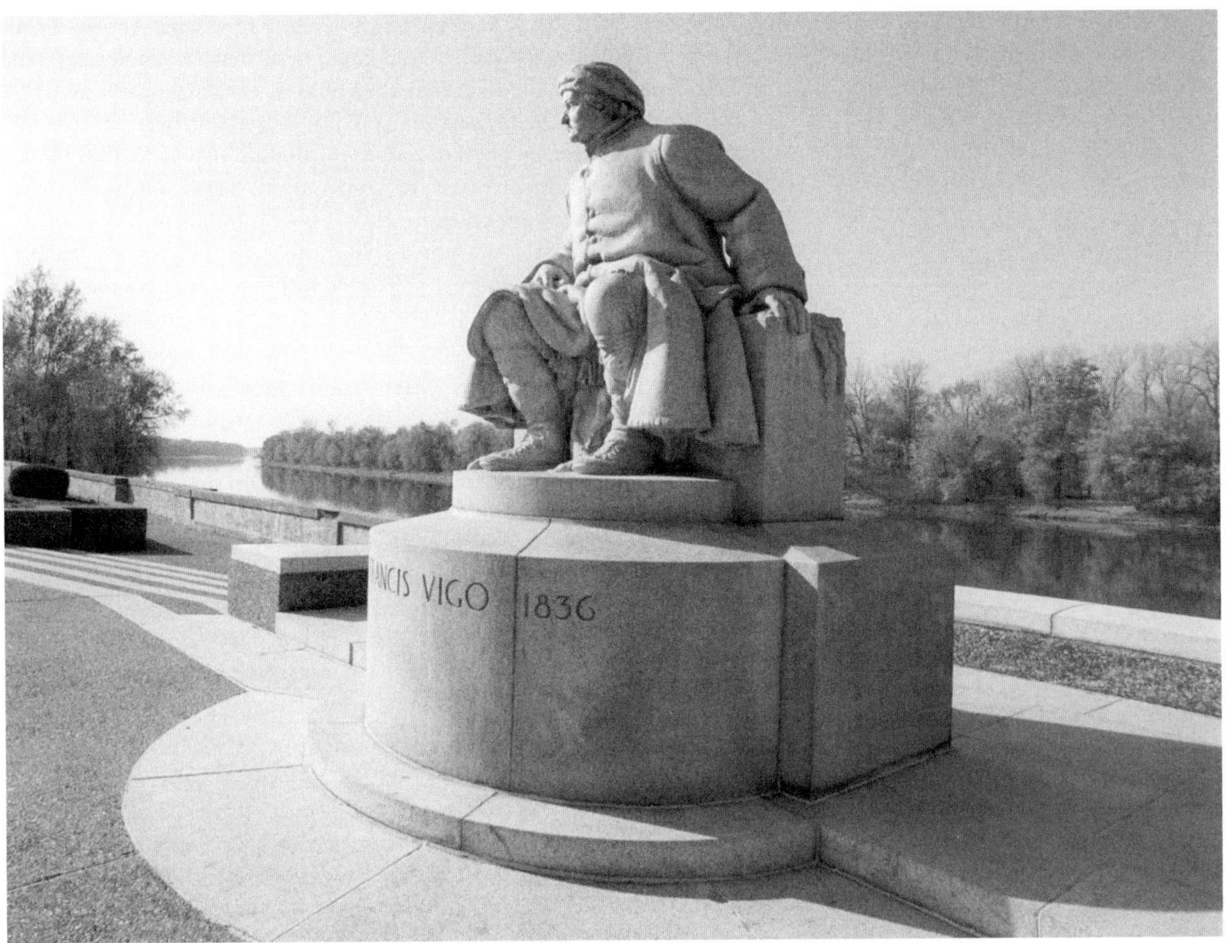

Francis Vigo. *This granite statue of Francis Vigo by sculptor John Angel was placed in 1936 near the George Rogers Clark Memorial in Vincennes, Indiana. Vigo was a St. Louis merchant and trader who provided vital support to Clark's campaign.* AP/WIDE WORLD PHOTOS.

Clark left Kaskaskia on 6 February 1779 with about 200 men for a heroic attempt to retake Vincennes. "I know the case is desperate," he wrote to Governor Patrick Henry a few days earlier, "but, Sir, we must either quit the cuntrey or attact mr. Hamilton." Weather was Clark's main enemy, as it had been Hamilton's; the winter of 1778 to 1779 was exceptionally severe, a fact which made Hamilton's march remarkable, but the early thaw was Clark's problem. The first 100 miles were relatively easy. Within 10 miles of Vincennes, however, the Americans found the country flooded, so they had to wade through icy water, up to their shoulders in places. Game, on which they depended, had been driven off by the waters. The famished troops struggled on for five days before collapsing on reaching high ground within sight of their objective, but they had succeeded in achieving surprise.

Much of Clark's success in the Illinois country had come from his skill in winning over the *habitants*. Hamilton (known as "the Hair Buyer" for his bounty on scalps), on the other hand, could not conceal his contempt for the French settlers. The young American commander planned his strategy accordingly.

Having learned that about a third of the British garrison was temporarily detached on a supply mission up the Wabash, Clark realized that his only chance was to capture Fort Sackville in a quick operation. He lacked the strength to assault it, and he could not spend more than a few days besieging the fort because the British detachment would assemble Indian support and launch a counter-attack with which the Americans could not cope. So Clark sent a captured Frenchman back to Vincennes with a message telling the settlers that he planned to attack and expected friends of the Americans to stay out of the way while "those in the British interest . . . repair to the fort and fight for their King."

Concealing from the prisoner the small size of his force, Clark let him return to Vincennes. But Clark timed things so that the released *habitant* would spread his message just as the invaders put on a well-managed show of force. In the failing light the Americans displayed flags and marched around in such a manner as to appear to number about one thousand troops. When Clark's force reached the village they found that most of the townspeople had taken the advice to stay out of the fight and that recently arrived Indian allies of Hamilton had deserted.

During the night of 23 to 24 February the Americans sniped at the apertures of Fort Sackville. About 9 A.M. Hamilton refused the first surrender summons, but three hours later he sent Captain Helm out with an offer to surrender with the honors of war. Clark refused, but offered to parley. That evening the British commander signed the capitulation, and the next day, 25 February, he surrendered Fort Sackville with its eighty defenders. Captain Helm marked his return to American military service by leading a detachment out to capture the forty-man detachment up the river.

Vincennes remained in American hands—the fort renamed for Patrick Henry—and was capital of the Indiana Territory from 1800 to 1813. It is the oldest city in Indiana. The site of the fort was marked in 1905 by a granite shaft. In 1931 to 1932 the federal government erected the George Rogers Clark Memorial, which is now part of the 26-acre George Rogers Clark National Historical Park. Seven large murals (created on 16-foot by 28-foot Belgium linen) in this Doric temple depict the life of Clark and the winning of the Old Northwest. A bronze statue of Clark is in the rotunda. The visitors center offers a movie on the life of Clark. During the summer there are historical recreations of camp life on the eighteenth-century frontier and firearms demonstrations. On Memorial Day there is a "rendezvous" recreating the annual meetings essential to trade in the Middle Ground. The park is open daily, 9 A.M. to 5 P.M., and can be reached from the Sixth Street or Willow Street Exits on I-50. The entrance is on Second Street. Phone: (812) 882-1776.

Also preserved in Vincennes are the first capitol (c. 1800), Old Cathedral (1826) on the site of the first log church, and the William Henry Harrison Mansion (1804). Harrison was the youngest son of Virginia's Benjamin Harrison of Berkeley Plantation; the house in Vincennes, "Grouseland," now at 3 West Scott Street at Park and Scott Streets, was his home as first governor of the Indiana Territory. Website: www.grouselandfoundation.org; phone: (812) 882-2096. William Henry Harrison went on to become ninth president of the United States, and his grandson, Benjamin, was the twenty-third president (1889–1893).

KENTUCKY

During the colonial era the British attempted to limit westward settlement to the headwaters of rivers flowing into the Atlantic (the Proclamation Line of 1763), but with no success. Only the perils of the wilderness and the actual inahbitants of the region, the Indians, kept the whites from moving west even faster. Five Indian nations had settlements within the region that is now Kentucky: the Cherokee, Chickasaw, Mosopelea, Yuchi, and especially the Shawnee. However, the center of each of these nations lay outside of this contested region. The first permanent white settlement was established at Harrodsburg in 1775, followed the next year by Boonesborough and St. Aspah (Logan's Fort).

The American Revolution in Kentucky was the struggle of these and later settlements to survive the sporadic efforts of British-supported Indian and Loyalist raiders. The colonists' victory at Point Pleasant (now in West Virginia) in 1774 permitted the first real surge of settlement. British-supported raids in 1778 wiped out all but three strongpoints (those mentioned above); then the victories of George Rogers Clark in the Old Northwest in 1778 to 1779 prompted a new wave of immigration, mainly along Boone's Wilderness Trail from Cumberland Gap, but some down the Ohio from Fort Pitt.

In 1776 Virginia formed Kentucky County to encompass virtually all the present state of Kentucky. But the Old Dominion had too many troubles east of the mountains to give the Kentuckians much military support or an adequate system of local government. On the other hand, the frontier settlements in Kentucky, which may mean "dark and bloody ground," did not have the large number of skirmishes that occurred during the Revolution in New York, Pennsylvania, and the southern colonies. Hence there are fewer historic sites of the Revolution in Kentucky than one might suspect. Most of these are now state parks or "shrines" and are identified below.

The Kentucky Historical Highway Marker Program, which includes more than 1,750 markers of various historical topics, is administered by the Kentucky Historical Society. It sells a guide to these markers, *Roadside History: A Guide to Kentucky Highway Markers* (2002). The book is available through the University Press of Kentucky and can be ordered online or by calling (800) 839-6855. The Kentucky Historical Society publishes a number of other books as well, some of which pertain to the state's colonial history. The Society is located at 100 West Broadway, Frankfort, Ky., 40601. Phone: (502) 564-1792.

Tourist literature is available from the Kentucky Department of Tourism at the following address: Capitol Plaza Tower, 22nd floor, 500 Mero Street, Frankfort, Ky. 40601. Website: www.kentuckytourism.com; phone: (502) 564-4930. The Department of Tourism has several brochures and maps obtainable online or by calling the agency directly.

Blue Licks Battlefield, U.S. 68 at crossing of Licking River, near village of Blue Lick Springs, Nicholas County. Often and incorrectly called the last battle of the Revolution, this was a victory of the ferocious Simon Girty over a bunch of foolish frontiersmen on 19 August 1782. A party of Loyalist and Indian raiders threatened Wheeling,West Virginia, in July and then tried, unsuccessfully, to surprise Bryan's Station, just north of modern Lexington. Three days later, 18 August, they started withdrawing slowly to the northeast. Frontiersmen including Daniel Boone and Benjamin Logan started converging on Bryan's Station a few hours

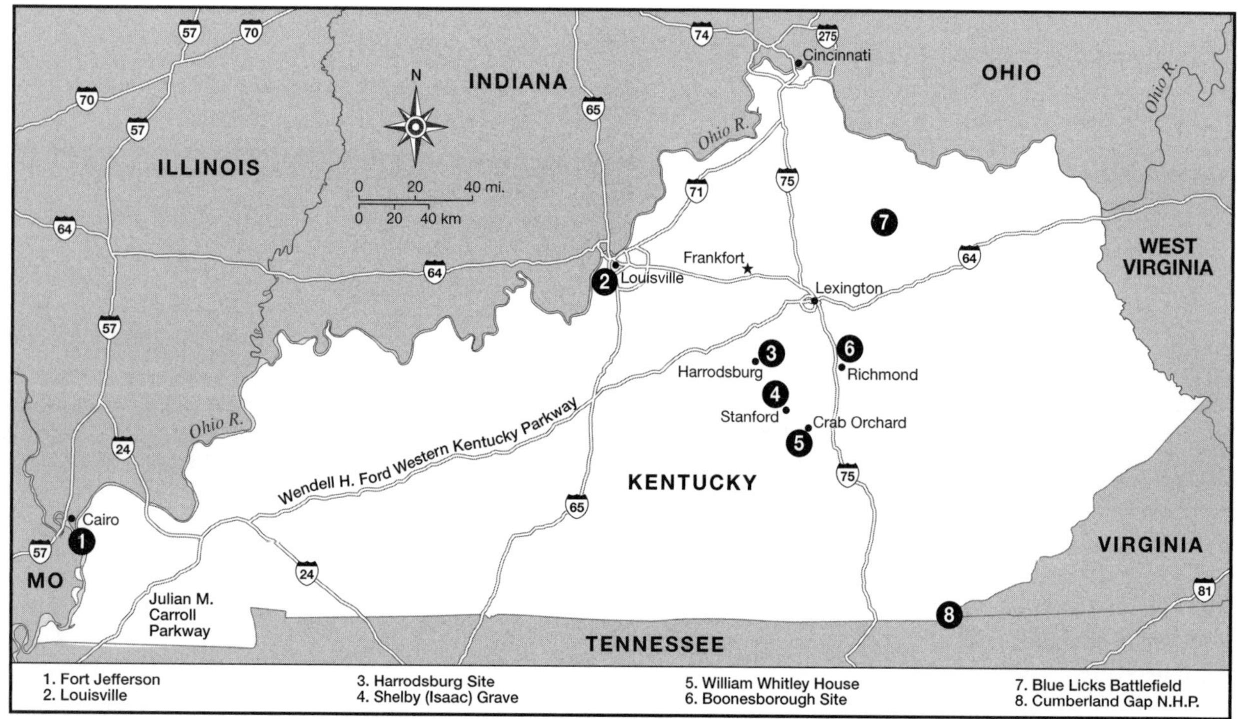

MAP BY XNR PRODUCTIONS. THE GALE GROUP.

after the enemy left the vicinity, and the next morning about 180 of them caught up with Girty's force. Daniel Boone and others advocated waiting until Logan closed up with a large force, but hotter heads prevailed. Simon Girty was waiting with superior numbers (about 250 men) when the Kentuckians made a disorganized charge through the deep ford on a fork of the Licking River.

The tactical lesson ended in a few minutes; then the slaughter began. The Patriots lost about seventy killed and captured, and Daniel Boone's son Israel was among the dead.

Most of the battlefield is included in the 150-acre Blue Licks Battlefield State Park. It is in an attractive section of the state well worth visiting just to enjoy the scenery. But the state park is exceptionally well developed, with landmarks of the battle marked and an interpretive museum that includes a small relief model of the field. Recreational facilities (campsites, picnic areas, playground, and a community pool) are open in season; the museum, souvenir shop, and battlefield are open year-round. Phone: (800) 443-7008.

Boonesborough, 9 miles north of Richmond, Exit 95 off Interstate 75 on Ky. Route 627, Madison County. Daniel Boone explored extensively in 1769 to 1771 through Cumberland Gap into the center of what is now the state of Kentucky. He returned in 1775 as an agent of the Transylvania Company, led his thirty axmen to this spot, and started construction of a fort. When completed in July 1776, at which time Indian hostilities were on the upswing, Boone's fort had four blockhouses and a palisade. Settlers arrived before the fort was completed, using the Wilderness Road through Cumberland Gap that Boone's axmen had opened. In September 1778 Boonesborough and nearby Harrodsburg withstood a sustained Indian campaign that wiped out all but one of the other Kentucky settlements. When the operations of George Rogers Clark in 1778 to 1779 established control in the Old Northwest, new settlers streamed into Kentucky (a county of Virginia from the fall of 1776), making Boonesborough a boom town. A short time later it went into a decline and soon disappeared.

No trace of the fort remains, but there are markers erected by the DAR and the Transylvanians of Henderson, Kentucky. The 108-acre Fort Boonesborough State Park includes the site of the settlement and the Kentucky River Museum. In addition, there are building reconstructions, a gift shop, hiking trails, and a variety of outdoor recreational activities available. Phone: (859) 527-3131. The site of the original Fort Boonesborough was designated a National Historic Landmark in 1996.

Cumberland Gap National Historical Park. The more than 20,000 acres of this park cover parts of Kentucky, Tennessee, and Virginia, with the visitors' center just south of Middlesboro, Kentucky. P.O. Box 1848, Middlesboro, Ky. 40965. Phone: (606) 248-2817.

Long before the white man reached America, Indian war and hunting parties followed Warrior's Path through the natural passage named Cave Gap by Dr. Thomas Walker of Castle Hill, Virginia in 1750. His expedition spent two months exploring the region, but did not get much farther west than the river they named the Cumberland.

John Finley had visited the fabled Bluegrass region of central Kentucky that Walker's party was unable to find, and in 1769 he convinced Daniel Boone, a fellow soldier of the Seven Years' War (1754–1763), that this could be reached through Cumberland Gap. With only four companions, Boone and Finley spent nearly four years exploring the Bluegrass. In September 1773 Boone led an unsuccessful effort to establish a settlement, but three years later he founded Boonesborough.

During the Revolution the Gap was frequently unpassable because of the Indians, but after George Rogers Clark's victories in the Old Northwest in 1778 to 1779, settlers surged through. By the end of the war some twelve thousand people had entered the promised land of Caintuck, most of them through Cumberland Gap (the others down the Ohio, the route used for establishment of the first settlement in 1775 at Harrodsburg). The Wilderness Road was improved for wagon traffic in 1796, but by 1825 it had lost importance except for driving cattle to eastern markets.

About 2 miles of the road remains in the national historical park. In addition to the wilderness scenery and spectacular views from Tri-State Peak and the Pinnacle, the park has ruins of an early iron furnace and Civil War fortifications.

Fort Jefferson, Mississippi River near Wickliffe, Ballard County. This westernmost American base was established by George Rogers Clark after his conquest of the Illinois Country in 1779. The next year it successfully withstood six days of attack by Chickasaws and Choctaws, but in June 1781 it was abandoned as untenable. A blockhouse similar to the one at Fort Jefferson has been reconstructed in the Columbus-Belmont Memorial State Park, site of the Civil War works some 15 miles south of where Fort Jefferson stood. Phone: (270) 667-2327.

Harrodsburg Site, Lexington and Warwick Streets, Harrodsburg, Mercer County. In flagrant defiance of the Proclamation of 1763 limiting westward expansion of white settlers to the watershed of the Alleghenies, three settlements were established in central Kentucky just before the American Revolution.

The oldest permanent one is the present Harrodsburg. James Harrod (1742–1793) was a Pennsylvania frontiersman in the heroic mold, a skilled marksman with a remarkable mastery of woodcraft. During the Seven Years' Wars he served as a private under General John Forbes, and later he explored the Kentucky region. In 1774 he and thirty men picked the site of Harrodsburg and started building cabins, but because of the Indian troubles that culminated in Dunmore's War of that year they had to abandon this initial effort. Harrod took part in the Battle of Point Pleasant, West Virginia, then in 1775 resumed the work that made him famous as founder of Kentucky's first permanent settlement.

Harrod unsuccessfully opposed the ambitious schemes of Richard Henderson's Transylvania Company, whose first settlement, Boonesborough, was established in 1775 only 30 miles northeast of Harrodsburg. Harrod had an active part in the Revolution, building his fort in 1777, escorting military supplies from Virginia to the Ohio River, and taking part in a number of expeditions against the Indians. His settlement and Boonesborough were among the few that survived the Indian attacks of September 1778. After the Revolution the forts at both places disappeared, having outlived their usefulness (no mean trick on the frontier). Harrod himself was not so lucky: he disappeared in 1793 under mysterious circumstances and is believed to have been murdered by an enemy who lured him from home in search of a fabled silver mine.

Development of the area surrounding the site of Old Fort Harrod into the Pioneer Memorial State Park was undertaken in the 1920s. A 28-acre state park now includes a reconstruction of the fort on a slightly reduced scale. The original spring is still flowing inside a 12-foot-high palisade that connects the blockhouses and cabins. Old Fort Harrod State Park is open all year. Phone: (859) 734-3314. Park staff in period costume present an interpretive history. "The Legend of Daniel Boone" is a musical performed in the park during the summer. Another musical, this one from the Shawnee perspective, "Shadows in the Forest," is performed in repertory with the Daniel Boone show.

Louisville, Falls of the Ohio. At this point navigation of the mighty Ohio is interrupted by falls and rapids along a 2-mile stretch where the water drops 26 feet. For 6 miles above this obstacle the Ohio is calm and about a mile wide. The Falls of the Ohio probably were visited by La Salle around 1670. They subsequently became a major landmark in the operations of George Rogers Clark in the Old Northwest during the Revolution. Captain Thomas Bullitt, a military companion of George Washington during the Seven Years' War, surveyed 2,000 acres in the area of today's Louisville in 1773, laid out a town, and attempted to start a permanent settlement. Bullitt was unable to get the necessary approval for his initial survey, and Governor Dunmore meanwhile conveyed the tract to his notorious friend Dr. John Connolly (see also FORKS OF THE OHIO, PENNSYLVANIA, and POINT PLEASANT, WEST VIRGINIA).

A spit of land above the falls later called Corn Island (and since eaten by the river) was where George Rogers Clark established a fortified camp in the summer of 1778 before undertaking the remarkable operations in the Old Northwest (see VINCENNES under Indiana). About twenty English, Scottish, and Irish families had come along with Clark, "much against my inclination," as he wrote later, but he admitted that they proved to be of service in guarding a blockhouse built on the island for his supplies. When Clark's expedition of some two hundred troops moved on (26 June 1778)—shooting the rapids during a total eclipse of the sun—the twenty families remained. During the next winter the settlers built Fort Nelson on the mainland (where Seventh and Main Streets now intersect) and established a town government. Called "the Falls of the Ohio" initially, in 1780 the place was named Louisburg for Louis XVI (whose aid was already recognized as being critical in winning American independence). At this time (14 May 1780) the Virginia legislature declared that Dr. Connolly's title was forfeited. In 1828 Louisville was chartered as a city.

Meanwhile, the "Conqueror of the Old Northwest," whose achievements with a handful of men had done so much to give the United States legal claim to Kentucky and the vast Illinois country, had spent the last nine years of his life in a handsome brick home, Locust Grove, that has been preserved in Louisville. His brother-in-law, Major William Croghan, started building this two-story house in 1802. Clark's personal fortunes had declined after 1786, and since 1803 he had been living across the river from Louisville in a cabin, operating a grist mill, and deteriorating physically. After suffering a stroke of paralysis and having a leg amputated, Clark moved to his sister's home in 1809. He died there in 1818, and his grave was at Locust Grove until moved in 1869 to Cave Hill Cemetery, at Broadway and Baxter Avenue. "A red brick house of architectural distinction," as the National Survey calls it, Locust Grove (c. 1790) is preserved in northeast Louisville and is part of the 55-acre George Rogers Clark Park (561 Blankenbaker Lane). It is designated a National Historic Landmark. Phone: (502) 897-9845.

Shelby (Isaac) Grave, Shelby City, Lincoln County. The military exploits of this second-generation frontiersman spanned many states and are associated prominently with many of the most important sites covered in this book. But Kentucky claims him as its first governor. Elected in 1792, he declined the office in 1796, but again became governor in 1812. His grave is in the half-acre Isaac Shelby Cemetery State Historic Site, located 6 miles south of Danville on Highway 127.

William Whitley House. *Built between 1787 and 1794, the William Whitley house in Stanford, Kentucky, is believed to be the oldest brick residence west of the Allegheny Mountains.* © G.E. KIDDER SMITH/CORBIS.

William Whitley House (Sportsman's Hill), off U.S. 150 on William Whitley Road about 9 miles southeast of Stanford, near Crab Orchard, Lincoln County. Often called the oldest brick residence west of the Alleghenies (which it is not), built between 1787 and 1794, the architecturally important two-and-a-half-story structure with handsome paneling was the home of a remarkable warrior. The state's tourism department bills it as "the first brick home in Kentucky." Whitley came to Kentucky from Virginia in 1775 and took part in Revolutionary War events, but was most famous for protecting emigrant parties from Indian attack along the Wilderness Road. As an elderly man he enlisted as a private in the War of 1812 and died in the Battle of the Thames (1813). The William Whitley State Historic Site was able to purchase about 30 acres of an adjacent farm in 2004 and add to its then 10-acre site. The use for that extra tract is yet to be established, although hiking trails are already formed. This historic site is open all year and has picnic areas. Phone: (606) 355-2881.

LOUISIANA

The "Louisiana Territory" claimed by France during the colonial era was the entire Mississippi Valley. Just before accepting defeat in its imperial struggle with Great Britain in North America, France gave Spain (by the first secret treaty of San Ildefonso, 1762) all its claims west of the Mississippi and the "Isle of Orleans." The latter comprised the town of New Orleans and the surrounding area east of the Mississippi bounded on the north by Bayou Manchac and the chain of lakes. In the treaty of 1763 ending the Seven Years' War, Britain received France's claim to all of the Louisiana Territory east of the Mississippi, including West Florida but excluding the Isle of Orleans, which the French pretended still to want but which they immediately turned over to Spain in accordance with the secret treaty.

During the Revolution, New Orleans was first a source of covert Spanish logistical support for the colonists. After Spain's declaration of war on Great Britain, it was a base for Governor de Galvez's expeditions to capture British posts up the Mississippi to Natchez and along the Gulf of Mexico to Pensacola. All this was to strengthen Spain's subsequent claim to much more of "West Florida" than even the most enthusiastic Spaniard could have hoped to get. (Subsequent events are traced briefly in the introduction to the section on ALABAMA.)

In addition to colonial sites in Baton Rouge and New Orleans (covered below separately), there are several sites of historical interest in other parts of Louisiana. In the present village of Phoenix, on the left bank of the Mississippi on State Highway 39, some 38 miles below New Orleans, is the site of Fort Iberville (1700), also known as Fort de la Boulaye, in Plaquemines Parish. In the American Cemetery in Natchitoches, head of navigation of the Red River, the site of the ruins of Fort Saint-Jean Baptiste (1714) is a State Historic Site. After painstaking archaeological work, the state turned the site into a replica of the original fort. Fort Saint-Jean Baptiste State Historic Site features a church, a trading warehouse, a powder magazine, slave quarters, the commandant's house, barracks, a guardhouse, bastions, and assorted huts. Phone: (318) 356-5555. Near Robeline is a historic park preserving the site of the Presidio de Nuestra Señora del Pillar de Los Adais, built in 1721 to protect Spanish territory from the French and capital of the province of Texas until 1773.

The Louisiana Office of Tourism offers free travel brochures and roadmaps, which are obtainable from its helpful website, www.louisianatravel.com, or by calling (225) 342-8100. The Louisiana Historical Association is located in Lafayette. Phone: (337) 482-6027.

Baton Rouge, Mississippi River. One of the earliest French settlements in the Mississippi Valley, Baton Rouge was a link in the chain of posts along the river from New Orleans to Natchez. Its military importance was overshadowed by Fort Manchac, a few miles downstream, but Baton Rouge was a major trading post and depot. As part of West Florida it passed to the British in 1763, then to the Spanish twenty years later. Spanish rule was overthrown and the Spanish governor killed in a local uprising in September 1810, when the lone-star flag of the Republic of West Florida was raised over Fort San Carlos. About a month later the United States formally declared West Florida to be United States territory as part of the Louisiana Purchase. Under the sixth flag in the history of Baton Rouge to that date (to come were two more, during the Civil War), a major military post of the United States was established. It was maintained, with a temporary

The Cabildo. *Built during the 1790s, the Cabildo in New Orleans was the seat of government in the Louisiana Territory. It now forms part of the Louisiana State Museum.* © PHILIP GOULD/CORBIS.

change in management in 1861 to 1862, until 1879. By 1825 the Pentagon Buildings and an arsenal had been completed on the site of Fort San Carlos. After Louisiana State University was given the land by the federal government in 1902 the Pentagon Buildings were converted into dormitories, then into apartment houses when the university moved to its present location in the southern part of the city. A marble tablet on Building D of the Pentagon Buildings is inscribed: "On this site stood the Spanish fort captured by the Republic of West Florida, September 23, 1810." The Old Arsenal Museum is nearby on the grounds of the Huey Long State Capitol skyscraper. Phone: (225) 342-0401.

New Orleans. Controlling the mouth of the Mississippi River, although more than 100 miles from the Gulf of Mexico, New Orleans soon became the capital of French Louisiana. (The capital was at Mobile, Alabama, then Biloxi, Mississippi, before being established in New Orleans in 1723.) The town had been founded in 1718 by Jean Baptiste Lemoyne, Sieur de Bienville, and it was a sorry place of about one hundred hovels in a malarious patch of swampy ground. In the early years of the American Revolution New Orleans was an important source of supplies for the Patriot cause. The remarkable Oliver Pollock (c. 1737–1823) had the covert help of Spanish authorities in sending gunpowder and other items first to Fort Pitt, and later to George Rogers Clark in the Old Northwest.

Pollock's supply role became less critical when the French and Spanish allied themselves openly with America (in May 1778 and June 1779, respectively), but in July 1779 he raised $300,000 by mortgaging his private property to buy supplies for the colonists. Prior to this he had forwarded $70,000 worth of supplies on his own credit. After the Revolution, Pollock spent eighteen months in custody for failure to satisfy his creditors. After being repaid by state and United States authorities, he left New Orleans to end his long life in Cumberland County, Pennsylvania.

Of architectural interest are Casa Hove, 723 Toulouse Street, and Madame John's Legacy, 632 Dumaine Street, both dating from the 1720s and vying for distinction as the oldest house in the Mississippi Valley. (A fire destroyed most of the city in 1788.) Part of the original Ursuline

Convent, completed in 1734, is preserved in the rectory of St. Mary's Italian Church. The Place D'Armes, transformed in 1856 from a dusty parade ground into the garden park called (Andrew) Jackson Square, is faced by the Basilica of St. Louis (1794) and the Cabildo (1795). Both are the third structures on the same site.

Rampart Street's name comes from the ramparts between Forts St. Jean and Bourgogne, between Barracks and Iberville Streets. Fort St. Ferdinand was built during the Spanish occupation in what is now Beauregard (originally Congo) Square. These and other fortifications were destroyed in 1803 to eradicate suspected causes of the periodic epidemics of yellow fever that swept this subtropical metropolis. On Lake Pontchartrain at the mouth of Bayou St. John are the foundations of Spanish Fort, the first fort in the immediate area of New Orleans. Only a redoubt at first, it was enlarged by the Spanish as a brick structure and garrisoned by Andrew Jackson's troops in the War of 1812.

Jean Lafitte National Historical Park and Preserve focuses attention on the the multiracial culture of eighteenth-century New Orleans. The visitors center, located in the Customs House in the old French Quarter, offers films on the various cultures that created New Orleans, as well as programs on folklore and traditional crafts. The park also includes three Acadian Cultural Centers that examine the Acadians who settled this region in the eighteenth century, including the famous smuggler and pirate Jean Lafitte; the Barataria Unit, which seeks to preserve what is left of the ecology and wildlife of the bayous; and the Chalmette Battlefield, celebrating the United States victory over the British in the War of 1812. The Faubourg Promenade Walk takes the visitor through the historic Garden District as well as to the "City of the Dead" in St. Louis Cemetery. These tours require reservations; phone: (504) 589-2326.

Start at the visitors center, which is down a passageway behind the French Market on the 900 block of Decatur Street. Phone: (504) 589-3882; http://www.nps.gov/jela/.

The Jackson Barracks Military Museum, 6400 St. Claude Avenue, contains weapons, uniforms, and other military items from the Revolutionary War. Phone: (504) 278-8242.

MAINE

Maine's historic sites, most of them coastal forts, are maintained by Maine's Bureau of Parks and Land. This state agency has pertinent information on nearly all of the historic areas concerning Maine during the American Revolution and is a practical place to begin a specific search. The feature "Find Parks and Lands" on its website is particularly useful for obtaining information. The Bureau of Parks and Land is headquartered at 22 State House Station, 18 Elkins Lane, Augusta, Maine 04333. Phone: (207) 287-3821; website: www.state.me.us/doc/parks/. Another good general source is the Maine Office of Tourism. It publishes a helpful travel guide, *Maine Invites You*, which is billed as the state's "official travel planner" and includes information on numerous historic areas. Phone: (888) 624-6345; website: www.visitmaine.com. The Maine Historical Society, located at 489 Congress Street in Portland, offers a wealth of information on the state's role in the Revolutionary War. It maintains a well-staffed research library and displays a variety of museum exhibits and historical programs. Phone: (207) 774-1822; website: www.mainehistory.org.

State highways, 201, 4, and 17 are now designated as National Scenic Byways and dozens of interpretive panels, most of which pertain to the American Revolution, can be viewed. Designed by Nancy Montgomery, they are usually located at rest areas and road pullouts.

There are many books written on the American Revolution in the fourteen states, such as James S. Leamon's outstanding *Revolution Downeast: The War for American Independence in Maine* (Amherst: University of Massachusetts Press, 1993). With Maine, however, attention has focused particularly on Benedict Arnold's expedition to Quebec in 1775. Kenneth Lewis Roberts, author of the popular 1933 novel *Arundel*, collected diaries and letters from the expedition in *March to Quebec* (New York: Doubleday, 1940). Stephen Clark's *Following in Their Footsteps: A Travel Guide and History of the 1775 Secret Expedition to Capture Quebec* (Shapleigh, Maine: Clark Books, 2003) provides a description of the landmarks and topography of Arnold's march while also providing canoeing and hiking maps for anyone willing to duplicate his incredible journey. Thomas Desjardin has written a narrative of the expedition, *Through a Howling Wilderness*, due from St. Martin's Press in 2006.

Agry Point, Kennebec River, short loop of old Maine 27 about 2 miles south of the Gardiner-Randolph bridge. The site is clearly visible from the river for those fortunate enough to have this means of sightseeing. Motorists should start at the point about 2 miles south of the Kennebec River bridge between Gardiner and Randolph. Here the landmarks are Arnold Road coming in from the east to new Maine 27 and a loop of old Maine 27 going off to the west.

Easily spotted on the right of old Route 27 as you drive north is a cemetery close to the road. The most conspicuous monument is to Major Reuben Colburn, whose home and shipyard site you will come to in a moment. He happened to be at Cambridge (Washington's headquarters during the siege of Boston) when the Arnold Expedition was planned. Within a period of eighteen days he made the trip home and had two hundred bateaux built and waiting for the Arnold Expedition when it arrived here by ship on 22 September 1775. (Another twenty were requested by Arnold after his arrival and were promptly built.) In addition, Colburn assembled flour and meat, packed these provisions in kegs, sent two scouts to reconnoiter the route, and furnished Arnold with fifty artificers to accompany the expedition.

A short distance north of the cemetery and near the road is the Colburn House on the left. Acquired by the state in 1972, it is leased by the Arnold Expedition Historical Society (AEHS) and serves as its headquarters. The AEHS is not as active nowadays as it has been in the past, but it does provide tours by appointment during the weekend in July and August. Phone: (207) 582-7080. The Colburn House, built in 1765, is a simple, two-story frame structure of traditional New England design with a central chimney, ridged roof, and large attic. The clapboard siding is painted brown, and the tall, narrow windows trimmed in white. Down the hill from the Colburn House and slightly south is a flat area along the river where the bateaux were built. The attractive little white house that looks like a national historic landmark is modern. Behind it and on somewhat higher ground is a frame building that was a tavern when the thirsty bateaux builders were at work and when Arnold's troops bivouacked here. In an overgrown area of higher ground just to the north of the tavern is a cemetery where the grave of Thomas Agry can be found.

Arnold Trail. Many of the principal landmarks of the march led by Colonel Benedict Arnold through Maine in September and October of 1775 can be found along U.S. 201 and Maine 16 and 27. The Appalachian Trail goes by the three Carry Ponds along the general route followed by Arnold, although the portion of the hiking trail from Caratunk to the East Carry Pond was not Arnold's route. Meanwhile, the road-bound traveler must backtrack from the vicinity of Bingham, start of the Great Carry, to Solon, take Alternate U.S. 201 to North Anson, and Maine 16 north to Stratton. Here one may pick up Arnold's trail on the portion of Dead River not flooded by Flagstaff Lake, and on Maine 27 can follow the general route to the vicinity of Coburn Gore, on the Canadian border.

The line of time-worn Indian trails, portages, and waterways followed by the Arnold Expedition in 1775 had been explored by a number of men in colonial days. A British army engineer, Captain John Montresor, reconnoitered it in 1761 and submitted a report that it was a militarily feasible route. The Patriots followed Montresor's route. In retracing their steps historians have been aided by the fact that so many of Arnold's officers and men kept diaries and journals.

Washington himself conceived the plan of sending a battalion of crack Continental troops over Montresor's route to seize Quebec by a surprise attack before the British could organize its defenses and while they were coping with the major effort being made along the Lake Champlain avenue of approach into Canada. Colonel Benedict Arnold had already impressed Washington and other authorities as being the kind of leader for such a desperate venture, and events proved that he was the ideal commander in this case. But they did not give him much time for preparations before the great white cold descended. As luck would have it, a Kennebec boatbuilder named Reuben Colburn happened to be in Cambridge, Massachusetts when initial preparations were being made in Washington's headquarters, and he agreed to furnish Arnold with two hundred light bateaux on short order. (A bateaux was a flat-bottomed boat with tapering ends used on rivers for carrying heavy and bulky loads.) Colburn sped ahead to start their construction at his shipyard (see AGRY POINT).

A call for volunteers was meanwhile issued among the lines of bored Patriot troops besieging Boston, and a good many venturesome soldiers stepped forward. Washington's order specified that all volunteers be "active woodsmen and well acquainted with batteaux." As things happen in military service, many of Arnold's men did not have these qualifications, but foolish optimism was not a shortcoming of the first American commander in chief, and Washington had directed that men be ordered to fill the ranks of the expedition if not enough volunteered.

About 1,100 men sailed with Arnold from Newburyport, Massachusetts in "dirty coasters and fish boats," as one described it. After a day and a night of stormy weather they reached the mouth of the Kennebec on 20 September, picking up the pilot near Fort Popham (see FORT POPHAM HISTORIC SITE). Modern development has somewhat changed the 35 miles of the beautiful Kennebec River through which they wound their way to Colburn's shipyard from the way Arnold's men saw it in 1775. Yet, some of the original natural splendor remains, and visitors stand a very good chance of spotting an eagle.

At Agry Point, a short distance south of modern Gardiner, the bateaux and provisions were waiting. Subsequent landmarks of the Arnold Trail are covered under the following headings: OLD FORT WESTERN, FORT HALIFAX, SKOWHEGAN FALLS, SOLON FALLS PORTAGE SITE, CROSS OVER PLACE, GREAT CARRY SITES, CATHEDRAL PINES HISTORIC SITE, and HEIGHT OF LAND. See ARNOLD TRAIL under Canada to continue the trip.

Among the landmarks obliterated by dams along the Kennebec are Ticonic Falls, Five Mile Falls, and almost all of the "fearsome" Norridgewock Falls just above Skowhegan. What the diarists and subsequent writers commonly call "falls," incidentally, were rapids rather than true falls, except at Skowhegan and Solon. A reasonable facsimile of the rapids negotiated by the Arnold Expedition is furnished by the Carrabassett River at North Anson.

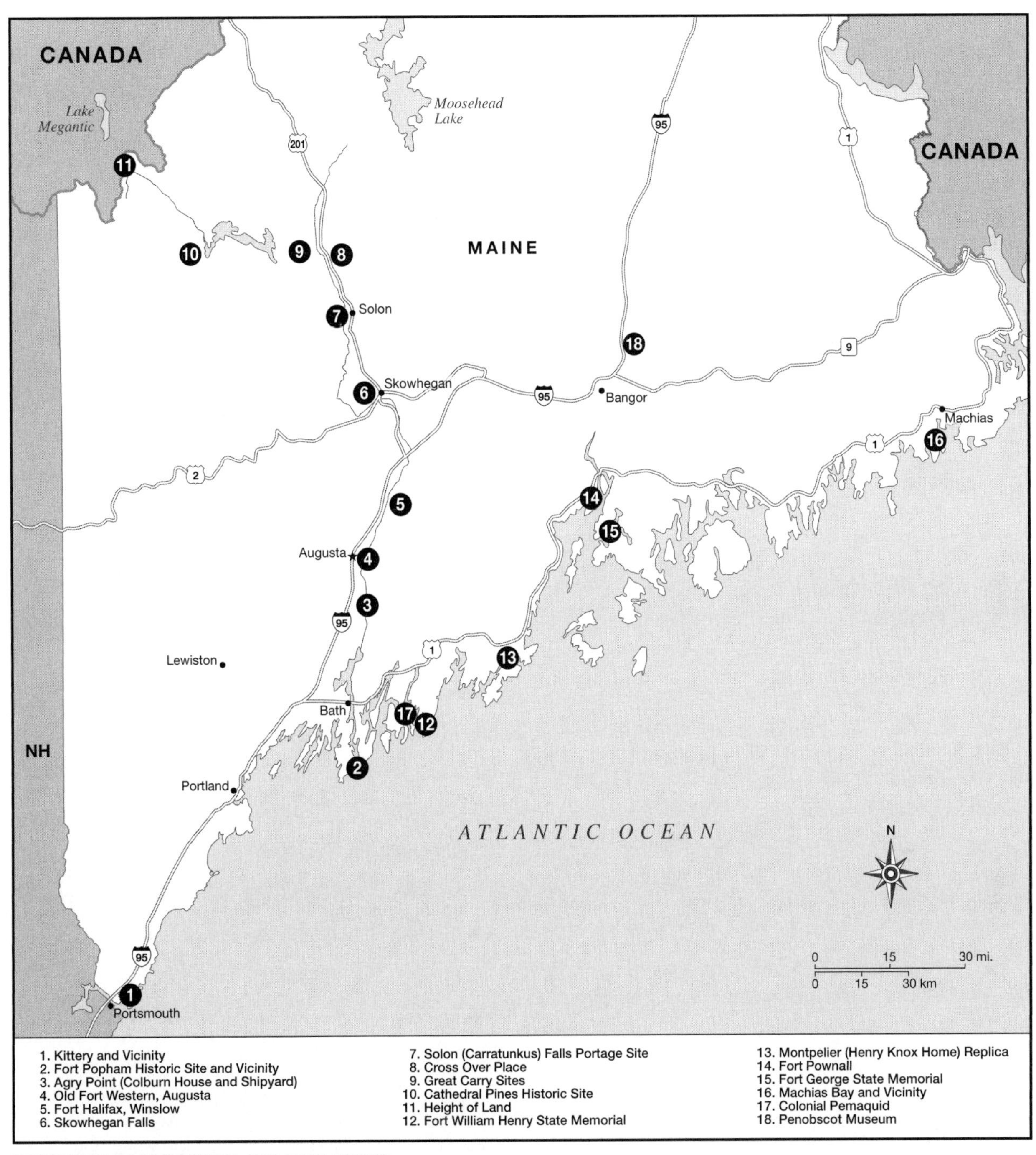

MAP BY XNR PRODUCTIONS. THE GALE GROUP.

As you retrace this route remember that Arnold had the misfortune not only of starting too late in the season and of underestimating his distance (see below), but also of encountering one of the most severe winters in Maine history.

Arnold had figured 180 miles from Agry Point to Quebec, whereas the route was 300 miles. He estimated that the march would take twenty days and started with food for forty-five. The expedition took forty-six days to get from Fort Western to Quebec, but because of spoilage and losses the men were on starvation rations at the end of a month. At this time, 25 October, Arnold stripped his command of all but those who could be given fifteen days' provisions. About seven hundred men made the last leg of the journey across Height of Land and on to Quebec.

The romance and travail of the Arnold Expedition can be experienced two centuries after the event because so much of the primary source material is in print and because most of the terrain is as the Patriots saw it in 1775. Literature is available from official agencies of the state of Maine. Readers with more than a casual interest should get in touch with the Arnold Expedition Historical Society (AEHS), or refer to either Desjardin's or Clark's above-mentioned books.

Cathedral Pines Historic Site, Arnold Trail on Dead River (Flagstaff Lake). A great stand of Norway pines overlooked a curve of Dead River when the Arnold Expedition came this way in 1775. Flagstaff Lake has flooded about 20 miles of his route along the river, including the Indian village that was the home of the mysterious Nantais. Arnold landed at the latter place and erected a flag, and the white settlement subsequently established there was named Flagstaff. A historical marker was moved about 9 miles west to New Flagstaff (part of Eustis) in 1948 when old Flagstaff village was flooded, and is now in front of the Flagstaff Memorial Chapel, just north of Cathedral Pines Park.

The latter site, about 4 miles north of Stratton on Maine 27 and about 2 miles south of Eustis, has a number of plaques commemorating the Arnold Expedition. One honors Colonel Timothy Bigelow (1739–1790), a battalion major who climbed a 4,150-foot mountain in the area for Arnold to find out whether Quebec was in sight. It wasn't, but the mountain bears Bigelow's name. The Appalachian Trail runs over the top of Mount Bigelow.

There had been 4 inches of snow around the Carry Ponds when the Patriots came through; then it started raining heavily, the temperature dropped further, and a tremendous hurricane struck on 21 October after they reached Dead River. So called because of its slow, meandering character most of the time, Dead River was flooded to a width of 200 yards soon after Arnold's men started battling their way up it.

For today's traveler, however, the most scenic portion of Arnold's trail is along Maine 27 from Cathedral Pines to the Canadian border. The highway closely parallels the historic trail, passing running water and the picturesque Chain of Ponds to the Height of Land.

Colonial Pemaquid State Historical Site, Pemaquid River mouth, about a mile west of New Harbor, which is about 13 miles south of Damariscotta on Maine 129 and 130. A large circular stone tower was reconstructed in 1908 as a replica of the third and fourth forts (of 1692 and 1729) on this picturesque coastal point. At its top, the stone tower has, along with a gorgeous view of John's Bay, a fascinating artifact display. Around the masonry wall on the second floor are thirteen exhibits giving the history of the site and surrounding area. The center well is encircled by displays of colonial tools and utensils, including artifacts found in archaeological explorations of a settlement just north of Fort William Henry, which is now reconstructed. (Excavated cellars at the "Pemaquid Diggings" may be visited.) Some authorities believe this community dates back to about 1620, and that it achieved considerable importance. The site of Fort William Henry was first occupied by Fort Pemaquid, a stockade built around 1630 as a defense against pirates. In 1632 it was captured by the pirate Dixie Bull. The second fort, a wooden structure called Fort Charles, was put up in 1677 and destroyed in 1689 by the Penobscot Indians. Sir William Phips had Fort William Henry built in 1692, at which time it was the largest and strongest stone fort in America. French and Indian forces under Baron de Castine and d'Iberville flattened this one in 1696, their attack being supported by three men-of-war. In 1729 Fort Frederick was built on this embattled site, and the Patriots themselves destroyed this one in 1775 to keep it from being taken over by the British during the Revolution.

Colonial Pemaquid State Historic Site features a recently repaired Fort House that holds an archeology lab and a research library. The site's visitors' center has a museum with hundreds of Revolutionary War and prewar artifacts. It is open to the public from 9 A.M. to 5 P.M. daily from Memorial Day through Labor Day. Admission for adults is $2. Phone: (207) 677-2423. The site also has a public boat-launch facility.

Cross Over Place, Kennebec River. A scenic and historic site turnout and small picnic area is at the point on the Kennebec where the Arnold Expedition left the river and started the Great Carry (see GREAT CARRY SITES). This wayside park is midway between Bingham and Caratunk on scenic U.S. 201. A plaque erected by the DAR commemorating the episode can be found there. Approximately a mile up the highway is a rest area, and one of the interpretive panels referenced earlier can be found. Bear in mind, however, that the river as it was in 1775 has been transformed into a lake by the Wyman Dam, built in the 1920s. Also, the terrain over which the marching column of Arnold's Expedition approached the bank from the east has been altered by the construction of U.S. 201.

Fort George State Memorial, Penobscot Bay, Castine. The British fort of 1779, a large rectangular work covering about 3 acres (with a softball field located unceremoniously in the middle of it), is in an area of exceptional beauty and interest. The site is state owned; however, the town of Castine manages it. French, Dutch, and English flags have flown over this picturesque piece of American territory, and it was visited by famous European explorers, perhaps even the Vikings, before it became a bone of imperial contention in the Colonial Wars. During the Revolution the British built Fort George, gave the Patriots a humiliating beating in the Penobscot River, and held the fort until 1783. They reoccupied it during the War of 1812. Castine has more than one hundred historical markers and many old houses in addition to its beautiful coastal scenery and recreational facilities.

The French settlement called Pentegoet was here in 1625. The eventual name was bestowed in honor of Vincent de St. Castine, one of the many French explorers of Penobscot. When the British acquired the region by the Treaty of 1763 Castine became the northernmost settlement of any significance on the seaboard of the Thirteen Colonies.

In the summer of 1779 a British force of about 750 troops under General Francis McLean and three sloops of war arrived at Castine from Nova Scotia and started building Fort George. The area was a source of timber, which the British needed for their shipyards at Halifax. Fort George was also to be a base for the forward defense of Nova Scotia and for operations against American coastal waters. The Massachusetts authorities reacted quickly. Without consulting Congress or the Continental army they mounted the largest amphibious operation of the Revolution: about 20 fighting ships and 2,000 militia troops aboard 20 trading vessels. The roster of commanders included some of the proudest names in New England. Generals Solomon Lovell and Peleg Wadsworth (grandfather of Henry Wadsworth Longfellow) commanded the militia. Lieutenant Colonel Paul Revere had charge of the American artillery. Captain Dudley Saltonstall of the Continental navy was overall naval commander.

This amateur effort failed to achieve surprise, and the God of War called Strike One. The Patriots then failed to make a coordinated attack with sea and land forces, which should have succeeded because the British had only their three sloops, and Fort George had not been completed. For almost three weeks the Patriot force made elaborate preparations to attack, and Strike Two was called. At the worst possible moment, just as the ground troops had debarked for their attack, the British relief force arrived. From Sandy Hook with 10 vessels, including a 64-gun ship, and 1,600 men came Captain Sir George Collier (1738–1795). Collier was a brilliant naval commander, but he needed no particular genius to destroy the entire American flotilla. Saltonstall, who had favored aggressive action against the three British sloops and the incomplete fort on 25 July, did not have a chance on 12 August. The troops scrambled back aboard, and the fleet made a show of resistance before heading up the river, beaching their ships, and escaping into the brush. It was Strike Three and out.

The Massachusetts legislators struck back by blaming Saltonstall for the fiasco, praising their militia generals, and putting in a claim to Congress for part of the $7 million the affair had cost them. (Congress awarded Massachusetts $2 million.) Saltonstall was dismissed from the Continental Navy and returned to his business as a privateer and merchant captain. Paul Revere was accused of disobedience, unsoldierly conduct, and cowardice. More than two years later his case was tried and the court-martial acquitted him of all charges.

During the War of 1812 the British took possession of all of the present state of Maine east of the Penobscot River. They repaired Fort George, and Castine was a popular town for the British forces and a bustling center of trade. On 25 April 1815, almost four months after the Treaty of Ghent ended the war, the British blew up the works and decamped for the last time. The Castine Historical Society serves as an additional source of this town's rich Revolutionary War past. Phone: (207) 326-4118.

Fort Halifax, Winslow, Kennebec County, on U.S. 201 a mile south of the Winslow-Waterville bridge. The oldest blockhouse standing in the United States (1754) rests where Arnold's Expedition saw it in 1775. A 1987 flood disassembled the blockhouse, but the state reassembled it one year later, piece by piece, not unlike a giant jigsaw puzzle. The quality of its reconstruction is evident by the site's ability to retain its National Historic Landmark status. The site comprises about half an acre of level grass and a steep wooded slope down to the creek. However, it is surrounded by a mostly urban setting. Fort Halifax had been established as an outpost for early warning during the French and Indian War. It was a way station for Arnold's Expedition, which took two days to pole its bateaux 18 miles up the Kennebec to this point from Fort Western. The Fort Halifax site is open free to the public from Memorial Day to Labor Day. Phone: (207) 941-4014.

Fort McClary State Memorial. *See* KITTERY.

Fort O'Brien. *See* MACHIAS BAY and vicinity.

Fort Popham Historic Site and vicinity, near Popham Beach State Park (follow signs) about 15 miles south of Bath on Maine 209. The Arnold Expedition of 1775 picked up a pilot here for its trip up the Kennebec to Colburn's shipyard at Agry Point. Civil War Fort Popham (1861) is on the site of a Revolutionary War post at Hunniwell's Point. Whether it was fortified in 1775 is not known, but a wooden blockhouse mounting a 4-pounder, which had been an alarm gun at Fort Frankfort, was there not long after the Revolution started.

Cox's Head, just to the north, and other high ground provided good lookouts to sea, and the post at Hunniwell's Point was maintained primarily to give early warning of British naval threats.

The Popham colonists of 1607 built their fort on Sabino Head, just west of Hunniwell's Point. The Popham Memorial (not to be confused with Fort Popham) marks the site of this first (although unsuccessful) English colony in New England. The settlers took formal possession on 29 August 1607 and built themselves a large earthwork of wood-revetted walls some 450 yards in total length. This was named Fort St. George. Within its walls they put up a storehouse, church, and about fifteen houses for the 120 or so men who would spend the first winter. In addition, they built a ship, the *Virginia.* But the fates were not kind. The weather was unusually harsh, the storehouse burned, their leader, Captain George Popham, died, and the colonists learned that their sponsor back in England, Chief Justice Sir John Popham, also was dead. The Popham colony was abandoned less than a year after its beginning.

The Kennebec River's lower portion has changed somewhat due to increased development; however, one can still get a sense of the way it appeared to the men of Arnold's Expedition. The highway south from Bath, Route 209, generally follows the river and is one of the most scenic in Maine.

Fort Pownall, Penobscot River, about 3.5 miles from Stockton Springs (U.S. 1). Governor Thomas Pownall of Massachusetts selected the location and directed the construction of this fort, which was completed in 1758 or 1759. Its purpose was not only to guard the mouth of the Penobscot north of the embattled works where the Fort George State Memorial now stands, but also to control the valuable traffic with the Indians. After French power in Canada was eliminated, the small garrison of Fort Pownall was reduced to a guard detachment. In March 1775 the British took all the heavy guns and ammunition from the place and set fire to the wooden fortification. During the fiasco of 1779 at Fort George the works were destroyed by the retreating Patriots. The earthworks have survived, and an archaeological dig uprooted many historical items, most of which are held at the Maine State Museum.

Great Carry Sites, Arnold Trail. The Middle and West Carry Ponds are not accessible by roads open to the public. All three ponds, their natural beauty unspoiled, are on the Appalachian Trail. Moose are plentiful. The start of the Great Carry on the Kennebec at the Cross Over Place is easily reached by road, and East Carry Pond can be found by car in good weather, although at some risk to the crankcase. The roads do not show on most highway maps, having been put in by paper companies and private landowners, but at least as far as the Cross Over Place on the west bank there is a splendid highway. The entire length of the Great Carry Sites is about 12 miles, and almost all of the land is owned by a paper company.

From Bingham on the Kennebec drive west across the bridge and turn north. Almost exactly 4 miles from the bridge on this road, turn right at a junction where signs indicate that the Carry Ponds are 11 miles in that direction.

At 7.8 miles is a modern logging trail leading down the riverbank to the right (east). This is the vicinity of Carry Place Stream, where Arnold's bateaux were taken out of the Kennebec to start the carry to Dead River and where a log storehouse was built. The lower ground to the south of the modern road is where the Arnold Trail ran. It followed the ancient Indian route and was used by subsequent generations of settlers and loggers in this region after the Revolution, which is why the trace has survived the centuries.

To reach the East Carry Pond (and others when they are opened to the public), continue north for 0.9 mile and turn left. This leads to a private resort on East Carry Pond at a distance of about 2.5 miles. There is nothing wrong with the road, unless it is covered with snow, except that the clearance at many points is low. The Arnold Trail crosses back and forth across this modern route. At 1.7 miles from the road you will cross a stretch of smooth rock ledges that are mentioned in the journals of the Arnold Expedition, confirming that this is the way they came. (This rock formation is common in many other parts of the country but quite unusual in this part of Maine.) At exactly 2 miles is the junction of the Appalachian Trail and a road fork; the road to the left (west) leads to Middle Carry Pond. Taking the right branch for about 0.1 mile you come to a collection of resort cabins where Arnold launched into the first carrying pond. One of his two launching sites is at the point closest to the main house of this resort colony.

Height of Land, Arnold Trail, vicinity of Coburn Gore (on Canadian border). "The Terrible Carrying Place," as Arnold's men dubbed it, was a 4.25-mile portage through snow and over granite ledges to get from the Chain of Ponds to Lake Megantic. Having sent to the rear all the bateaux except one per company, the Americans headed due north from what is now called Arnold Pond, passed through a saddle of the mountain range, and then went generally westward to Great Meadows in Canada. They were following the route reconnoitered by Captain John Montresor in 1761.

Montresor's map shows "Height of Land" as a long, narrow ridge generally along the present border between Canada and Maine. The name leads one to the conclusion that it is a formidable mountain barrier, whereas the route followed through it by Arnold's men was a rather low saddle. For troops in good physical condition the Height of Land would have presented little challenge. Associates of the Forest Ranger Headquarters at Eustis, who have explored this route with members of the Arnold Expedition Historical Society, believe that Arnold's men had trouble primarily because of their starved and exhausted condition. As for physical obstacles, it is thought that they had to lift their bateaux over several rock strata and had snow to contend with, but that Montresor's route was otherwise an easy one here. People may wonder why they wouldn't have taken the route of today's highway, for it looks to be a much easier way to go. The answer probably lies in the fact that it would have been much longer, and that the route probably had many obstacles since cleared by modern construction equipment.

When you cross from Maine and look back you will see that Height of Land makes sense as a geographical term to travelers approaching it from the flat terrain of Canada, if not to those coming north through the mountains of Maine.

Arnold's exact route through Height of Land is not completely known. The region has many logging roads and trails, but, according to experts, none of these correspond with Arnold's route. It is interesting and instructive to study the modern, large-scale topographic maps of this region that are available from the United States and Canadian official map services. (The United States map sheets are the "Arnold Pond" and "Chain of Ponds" quadrangles. The Canadian maps are "21E/7 West and East WOBURN" and "21E/10 West and East MEGANTIC." See the introduction, above, for addresses and instructions on ordering.) The saddle due north of Arnold's Pond through which the expedition is believed to have passed is at coordinates 580300. Arnold's first camp due west of here was around the surviving house at coordinates 548276, northeast of Woburn; this area was known as Great Meadows or Beautiful Meadow.

Kittery and vicinity. Just across the state line on U.S. 1 is the John Paul Jones Memorial (1924) near the place where the *U.S.S. Ranger* was built. Flying the new Stars and Stripes created by a congressional resolution on the day he was given command of the *Ranger*, Jones sailed for France from Badger's Island in early November 1777. The *Ranger* carried the news of Burgoyne's surrender at Saratoga. On 14 February 1778 in Quiberon Bay the new American flag gained its first formal recognition by a foreign power when the French fleet there was induced to exchange salutes with the *Ranger* (American ships had received salutes from foreign craft since the Dutch fired a salute at St. Eustatius in the West Indies on 16 November 1776). Two months later Jones took the *Ranger* on an audacious and highly successful raid into British waters, giving the Stars and Stripes its baptism of fire (Quaife, Weig, Appleman, *History of the U.S. Flag*, pp. 29, 33, 42).

For more on the naval history of the Revolution and shipbuilding in Maine, visit the Maine Maritime Museum in Bath, open daily 9:30 A.M. to 5:00 P.M., at 243 Washington Street. Phone: (207) 443-1316; website: http://www.bathmaine.com.

Around Kittery Point (take Maine 103) are several homes from the colonial era. The John Bray House (1662) is the oldest in Maine. The house built in 1682 by Bray's son-in-law William Pepperrell, and birthplace of Sir William Pepperrell (1696–1759), is still standing. The house built about 1760 by Lady Pepperrell, widow of Sir William, is of particular architectural significance and qualifies as a Registered National Historic Landmark. Privately owned, it was listed for sale in 2005 by a prominent real estate company for $1.5 million. Opposite it are the First Congregational Church and old parsonage, dating from 1730.

The Fort McClary State Historical Site is on land once owned by Colonel William Pepperrell. The original fortification here, probably a breastwork on which cannons could be mounted, appears to have been erected around 1722. First named Fort William, it went through various transformations. After the Battle of Bunker Hill it was renamed for the senior officer killed in that action, Major Andrew McClary. As reconstructed, Fort McClary features a six-sided blockhouse that was reconstructed in 1986. The blockhouse features a granite base and wooden second story, as it probably looked around 1846. The site commands an impressive view of the Portsmouth Navy Yard, the Isles of Shoals (9 miles southward), the Fort Point Light, and other famous naval landmarks. The state of Maine opens the site to the public from Memorial Day to Labor Day. Phone: (207) 384-5160.

The Maine Information Center at the junction of U.S. 1 and the Maine Turnpike should have travel literature on all these places.

Machias Bay and vicinity, Washington County. Near the eastern end of the Maine coast, the historic seaport of Machias started as a trading post of the French and English. Well over a century later, in 1763, an American settlement was established. An outstanding example of a colonial inn is Burnham Tavern at High and Free Streets in Machias. In good condition, it is now a museum and open to the public from the middle of June until early September. Phone: (207) 255-4432.

The spirit of revolt here was strong. Maine's first Liberty Pole is claimed by civic boosters, and Machias calls itself the birthplace of the American navy (as does Whitehall, New York). "The Lexington of the Sea" is the

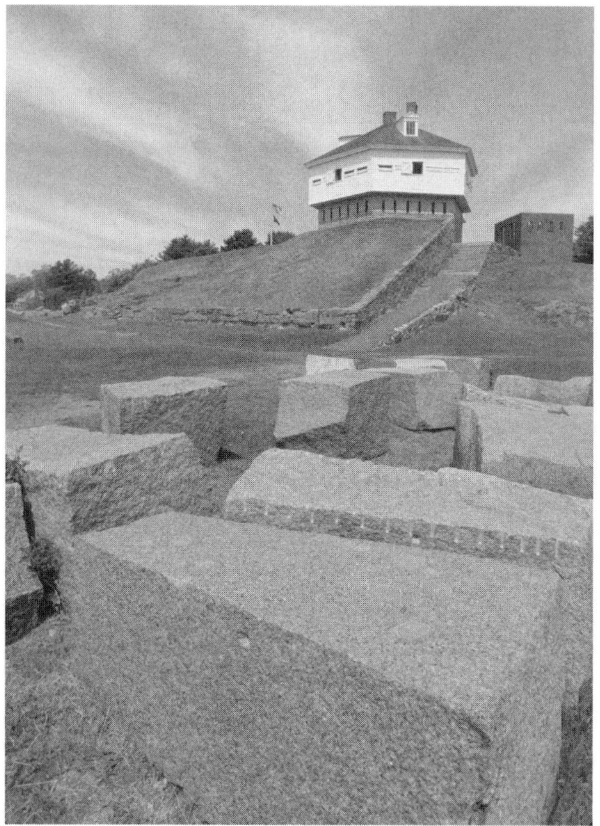

Fort McClary. *This fort at Kittery Point, Maine, features a six-sided blockhouse with a granite base. The blockhouse commands an impressive view of the Portsmouth Navy Yard, the Isles of Shoals, the Fort Point Light, and other famous naval landmarks.* © **ROBERT HOLMES/CORBIS.**

name that has been applied, with some exaggeration, to "the first naval battle of the American Revolution" in a portion of Machias Bay overlooked by the Fort O'Brien State Historic Memorial on Maine 92, 5 miles southeast of Machias. Only breastworks remain here of the place first called Fort Machias when erected in 1775. Although the capture of a four-gun schooner does not constitute a "battle," there was initiative, personal heroism, and historical significance aplenty in the little affair on Machias Bay, and here are the basic facts.

The British schooner *Margaretta* (four guns) escorted two sloops, *Polly* and *Unity*, into the port of Machias on 2 June 1775 to get lumber for the troops in Boston. The Revolution had started a few weeks earlier at Lexington and Concord (19 April), and local Patriots whipped up a scheme to capture the British ships by surprise while the captain of the *Margaretta* and his officers were in church, but this attempt was aborted and the three enemy ships headed for sea. Jeremiah O'Brien and Joseph Wheaton then threw together a force that pursued and captured the *Unity* (on 11 June) and the *Margaretta* (on 12 June). Total losses were seven men killed and wounded on each side.

O'Brien was given command of the *Unity*, renamed the *Machias Liberty* and armed with the *Margaretta*'s four guns. A few weeks later he captured the British naval schooner *Diligent* and its tender off Machias without firing a shot. These two schooners, under O'Brien's command, became the nucleus of the Massachusetts navy (not the Continental navy), and they took a few prizes before being put out of commission in the fall of 1776. Jeremiah O'Brien (1744–1818) had been born in Kittery. He had moved with his family to Machias in 1765. After commanding privateers in the Revolution, interrupted by imprisonment and escape from British prisons, he spent his last seven years as collector of customs at Machias.

Montpelier (Knox Home) Replica, 7 miles east of Thomaston on U.S. 1. This landmark is unique in that it went from state ownership back to private ownership. The Friends of Montpelier now own and manage the site, which is open to the public from 10 A.M. to 4 P.M. Tuesday through Saturday. The Friends of Montpelier are a very active group and they offer a variety of special events, programs, and classes throughout the year. Phone: (207) 354-8062. The house itself is a replica of the handsome mansion built in 1793, during the ten years after the Revolution when Henry Knox was the first United States secretary of war. The original house was razed in 1871.

Old Fort Western, Augusta, east bank of the Kennebec just south of City Hall near at Bowman Street at 16 Cony Street. In a now urban setting is an unprepossessing structure of great historical significance, the surviving garrison house of the New Plymouth Trading Post. The post was established in 1626, but the building dates from 1754. A long, low structure with cedar shake siding, it is a museum depicting colonial living. A few feet in front of the building, along the high bank of the river, are two blockhouses connected by a stockade. These are replicas of the original fortifications. One touch of landscaping is provided by a marker in a small fenced area of grass, where a bronze plaque on a boulder identifies the scene. Adjacent to the site is the Augusta City Center.

The Arnold Expedition was just getting under way when it paused at Fort Western. On Maine 201 about 2 miles south of Augusta are three pictorial panels marked by a highway sign: "Historical Site, Arnold Trail." There is a good view up and down the Kennebec from this spot, and the panels give highlights of the expedition's experiences in this portion of the route. Just north of Fort Western at the fork of U.S. 201 and 202 (Bangor Street and North Belfast Avenue) is a cemetery where a few early settlers are buried. Some of these settlers' remains may have come from the Howard Cemetery, originally located on the actual fort grounds. It is presently a supermarket parking lot. In this cemetery (or possibly in the earlier mentioned cemetery, if his remains were moved) lies the grave of a soldier from the Arnold expedition named Rueben Bishop. The death of Bishop was apparently a significant event, as almost every diarist on the march made serious mention of it. A hotheaded fellow named John McCormack, who had earlier been offended for some unknown reason, burst through the door of the soldier's barracks and fired a shot. Bishop was the unlucky recipient of that ball. He died a few days later. McCormack was tried, found guilty, and sentenced to die the next day at 3 P.M. by hanging. Interestingly, minutes before his execution, Arnold pardoned the killer and sent him off to Washington, and McCormack eventually died in prison. Many of the diarists noted that Bishop died a tormented death, not because of the pain, but because he, unlike most of his comrades, had not fully embraced the ways of Calvinism, and was very agitated over his uncertain afterlife possibilities. Phone: (207) 626-2385.

Pepperrell Family Sites. *See* KITTERY.

Skowhegan Falls, Kennebec River, fork of U.S. 201 and 201A. The Arnold Expedition's bateaux approached these seemingly insurmountable falls over half a mile of dangerous rapids. They then came to the small island that splits the Kennebec here, and through a crevice in the steep rock they lifted and dragged their awkward, 400-pound bateaux.

A Central Maine Power Company substation and dam has pretty well destroyed the natural features of this site, but for the informed visitor enough is left to make a short walk rewarding. You will spot the site easily while crossing the river on U.S. 201 going north. Walk to the left corner of this structure as you face it (generally behind the fire station) and a remnant of the rock ledge that formed the falls will be visible. (Skowhegan means "a place to watch" for salmon.) Blasted out and buried under the power station is the crevice through which countless generations of Indians had lifted their birch canoes and through which Arnold's men cursed their way in 1775.

Solon (Carratunkas) Falls Portage Site, Kennebec River. Solon and its dam are on the highway maps, but there are no signs pointing to the place where Arnold made his portage in this area.

On U.S. 201 just north of the main highway junction in little Solon is a white frame church with a conspicuous spire. After another 0.4 mile north, turn left (west) onto Falls Road, which goes a short distance before ending in a recreation area alongside the river where Solon Dam is located. A DAR marker is on an isolated boulder where you can readily spot it, and it carries a vague message to the effect that Arnold's Expedition passed this way in 1775.

To find the portage, walk back from the boulder about 40 yards along the road you followed in. A trail coming in to the right is probably the portage route of 1775. Follow it south about 200 yards through the woods and you will see where the ground starts dropping off to the flat stretch of riverbank where the bateaux were beached. In its undeveloped condition the area has a wild charm that could be destroyed by misguided efforts to "improve" it as a tourist attraction.

The original inhabitants of Maine were the Abnaki, almost all of whom sided with the British during the Revolution and settled permanently in Canada after the war as the United States expropriated their lands. The exception was the Penobscot of coastal Maine, who were confined to Indian Island in the Penobscot River. The Penobscot National Historical Society Museum is devoted to their history and culture. It is located on the island on Highway 2 just north of Old Town and is open Monday through Friday, 10 A.M. to 4 P.M. Phone: (207) 827-6544.

MARYLAND

There may be several hundred colonial houses still standing in Maryland, a large number being in the Annapolis Historic District. A remarkable archaeological site from the earliest colonial period is at St. Marys. Maryland contributed a number of outstanding Patriot leaders during the Revolution and was famous for the quality of its troops in the Continental army.

The fugitive Continental Congress suffered through a few months of temporary accommodations in Baltimore. Columns of troops came through en route to Virginia and the Carolinas; Washington spent one night in the Hollingsworth Tavern, now an office building in Elkton, and nearby Head of Elk was a point of debarkation and embarkation.

Although Maryland has experienced significant population growth over the last two decades, some of the state remains agricultural. Tourist literature points to a number of oldest-in-continuous-operation places (churches, businesses, ferries, mills, and so on).

General sources of information are the Maryland Office of Tourism, 217 East Redwood Street, Baltimore, Md. 21202; website: www.visitmaryland.org; phone: (888) 639-3526; and the Maryland Historical Society, 201 West Monument Street, Baltimore, Md. 21201; website: www.mdhs.org; phone: (410) 685-3750.

Annapolis, Chesapeake Bay and Severn River. Anne Arundel Town became the Maryland capital in 1694, was renamed Annapolis (for Princess Anne) the next year, and was chartered as a city in 1708. One of the United States oldest cities, it has the oldest state house still in daily use. For about nine months it was the capitol of the United States (27 November 1783 to 13 August 1784).

Colonial Annapolis Historic District, a Registered National Historic Landmark since 1965, has more colonial brick buildings than any other United States city. Much of the original town, one of America's first planned cities, is within the historic district. The preservation effort, due primarily to the Historic Annapolis Foundation, has been exemplary. As pointed out by the National Survey, however, the buildings historic value relate primarily to architecture and to the development of commerce and industry. Several guided walking tours are offered by the Historic Annapolis Foundation. The Foundation has also embarked on a Historical Building Markers endeavor to further aid interested spectators in viewing colonial sites. The Historic Annapolis Foundation is located on 18 Pinkney Street; website: www.annapolis.org; phone: (410) 267-7619.

During the Revolution, Annapolis was a port of embarkation for troops and heavy matériel moving down the Chesapeake for operations in Virginia and the Carolinas. In early March 1781 Lafayette reached Annapolis from Head of Elk with about 1,200 Continentals en route to Virginia, where Benedict Arnold was then ravaging the Old Dominion with a force of British raiders. Lafayette was supposed to link up in the Chesapeake with a French naval expedition under Admiral Destouches, but the latter withdrew to Newport, Rhode Island, after being beaten off the Virginia Capes by a pursuing British fleet. (Lafayette continued to Virginia on foot via Baltimore.) In mid-September 1781 the combined armies of Washington and Rochambeau moved toward Yorktown by ship from Head of Elk, Baltimore, and Annapolis.

Sarcophagus of John Paul Jones. *Located in the chapel of the U.S. Naval Academy in Annapolis, Maryland, this sarcophagus allegedly contains the remains of John Paul Jones, who died in Paris in 1792.* © PAUL A. SOUDERS/CORBIS.

This was about the only large-scale military activity in Annapolis during the Revolution, though a great number of ships involved in the war effort moved in and out of its busy port. Two museums devote some attention to this naval activity. The best known is the United States Naval Academy Museum in Preble Hall just inside the Maryland Avenue gate of the Naval Academy. This museum is open to the public Monday to Saturday, 9 A.M. to 5 P.M., and Sunday, 11 A.M. to 5 P.M. Phone: (410) 293-2108; website: http://www.usna.edu/Museum/. The Annapolis Maritime Museum was heavily damaged by Hurricane Isabel in 2003, so it is best to verify hours and events beforehand. Phone: (410) 295-0104; website: http://www.annapolismaritimemuseum.org/.

The following places are of special significance from the standpoint of Revolutionary War associations:

The John Paul Jones Crypt. This heads the list because it is likely to be ignored in the conventional tourist guides. Located in the chapel of the United States Naval Academy, it allegedly contains the remains of the great naval hero. He died in Paris at the age of forty-two in 1792 and was buried in the old St. Louis Cemetery for foreign Protestants. About half a century later a proposal to rebury him in the United States was blocked by his relatives in Scotland. When Horace Porter was ambassador to France around the turn of the century he undertook a six-year search for the body in the cemetery, which had been covered by houses. In 1905 he found the remains that have been identified as those of John Paul Jones, although Porter's proof is still disputed. The remains were escorted back to the United States by a naval squadron in 1905 and in 1913 placed in their present location, with Horace Porter making the oration at the dedication. (General Porter, a long-time aide to General Ulysses S. Grant, had performed the same function at Grant's Tomb in New York after presiding over the movement to have this monument erected.) Public viewing hours are from 10 A.M. to 4 P.M. Monday through Saturday, and from 1 P.M. to 4 P.M. on Sunday.

The Maryland State House. Located at State Circle, this large brick structure was started in early 1772, when the last royal governor officiated at the cornerstone laying. The name of the architect and completion date are unknown. A massive octagonal dome is the most distinctive feature of this historic building in which the Treaty of Paris was ratified, ending the Revolutionary War, and where Washington officially resigned as commander in chief. In 1786 the Annapolis Convention met in the statehouse and took the decisive step toward formulation of a federal government. (This led to the Constitutional Convention in Philadelphia the next year.) The Maryland State House was designated a National Historic Landmark in 1960. Guided tours of the building, its grounds, memorials, and historical paintings are provided from 9 A.M. to 5 P.M. on weekdays and from 10 P.M. to 4 P.M. on weekends. Visitors should note that intense security procedures are in place and proper identification will be required. Phone: (410) 974-3400.

The Old Treasury Building (1735). This one-story brick structure in State Circle is the oldest public building in Maryland. Open by appointment only. Phone: (410) 267-7619.

St. John's College. The campus covers a large area a few blocks north on College Avenue. The Charles Carroll the Barrister House (1722–1723) on King George Street is a two-story house where the barrister was born. (There were many in this prominent family of the same name, the most famous being Charles Carroll of Carrolton. See BALTIMORE.) Now containing the admissions offices, the house was moved to this location in 1955. It is open to the public. McDowell Hall, now used for classrooms and offices, was started in 1744 as the mansion for colonial governor Thomas Bladen but not finished until 1789. The College had been founded in 1696 as King William's School, was chartered in 1784, and moved into McDowell Hall a year later. Until 1999 an ancient tulip poplar, the Liberty Tree, grew on the campus. It is said to be where the Sons of Liberty met, and a plaque at the tree's base listed its age to be over six hundred years old, although many experts believe it to have been closer to four hundred. The magnificent tree went down during Hurricane Floyd.

Chase-Lloyd (1769) and ***Hammond-Harwood (1774) Houses.*** Of exceptional architectural merit, these houses are located at 22 and 19 Maryland Avenue (King George Street intersection). Both are attributed to architect William Buckland, the former house was the home of signer Samuel Chase. The latter is one of the finest Georgian houses in America, beautifully preserved with original interior woodwork and much original furniture. Both are National Historic Landmarks and open to the public.

The Brice House. This outstanding example of Georgian architecture at Prince George and East Streets was begun in 1766 and is virtually unaltered. Its thirty-five rooms are notable for individual distinction in a harmonious relationship. Built of oversize brick on a fieldstone foundation, the house is 186 feet long with 90-foot chimneys rising above a steep-pitched roof. It was acquired in 1953 by a private owner who has restored it with great fidelity and care. Some authorities believe the architect was William Buckland. Although omitted from most tourist guides because it is not open to the public, Brice House meets most of the criteria for registration as a National Historic Landmark. Dominating its present neighborhood, the elegant old giant can be seen from the street. It underwent another renovation in 1999 and serves as a private library.

The Quynn-Brewer House (1734). The house, at 26 West Street, is restored and furnished in the Queen Anne period.

Baltimore. Founded in 1729 and an important point in the primitive network of early American transportation, Baltimore was a place of no charm when the Continental Congress was forced to take up temporary working facilities here after fleeing Philadelphia in mid-December 1776. "This dirty boggy hole beggars all description," wrote one delegate. "The weather was rainy, and the streets the muddiest I ever saw," John Adams jotted in his diary on 7 February 1778. "This is the dirtiest place in the world."

Industrial achievement has not enhanced Baltimore's allure in the succeeding two centuries, the traffic and air pollution being a questionable exchange for the elimination of muddy streets. But Baltimore is trying hard to be attractive to visitors and in the 1990s undertook and successfully completed considerable urban renewal. The Greater Baltimore Cultural Alliance maintains a service called the Baltimore Fun Guide that serves as a good information source for local sites. Website: www.baltimorefunguide.com; phone: (410) 821-3055.

Baltimore was on the line of march and water movement of Continental troops to Virginia and the Carolinas from the North. Lafayette marched his column through here from Annapolis, and frigates took some of the Allied troops of Washington and Rochambeau from Baltimore to Virginia in the Yorktown campaign. During one of the darkest periods of the Revolution, when the British had overrun much of New York and most of New Jersey, the Continental Congress carried on from Baltimore (20 December 1776 to 4 March 1777). Not more than twenty-five delegates actually appeared for business. Their rented meeting place was the three-story brick house of Henry Fite that stood near today's Baltimore Street at Liberty Street. Many privateers were fitted out in Baltimore during the Revolution and the War of 1812. Fortifications were built where Fort McHenry now stands.

Fells Point Historic District contains many houses left when the town incorporated into Baltimore in 1773. Most date from the maritime prosperity that came after the Revolution.

The Carroll Mansion (about 1812), 800 Lombard Street at Front and Lombard Streets, was the last home of Charles Carroll of Carrolton. He lived there for about ten years before his death in 1832, "envied by many as the wealthiest citizen of the United States and revered by every one as the last surviving signer of the Declaration of Independence" (*Dictionary of American Biography*). Some authorities date the house from 1812; the National Survey concludes it was erected in 1823 on land given by Carroll to his daughter Mary and her husband. The three-and-a-half-story brick mansion has exceptional trim inside and out. It is now a museum owned and operated by Carroll Museums Incorporated. Phone: (410) 605-2964.

Mount Claire (1754), in Carroll Park, is Baltimore's only mansion of the pre-Revolutionary period. It was the elegant plantation house of Charles Carroll the Barrister (see ANNAPOLIS). Wings have been added, but the house is otherwise unaltered. Many of the furnishings are original, and portraits of the Carrolls by Charles Willson Peale are in the drawing room. The house museum is open to the public from Tuesday through Saturday, although calling before visiting is recommended. Phone: (410) 837-3262.

The attractive Flag House and Star-Spangled Banner Museum, 844 East Pratt Street, is the birthplace and home (1973) of Mary Young Pickersgill, the lady who made the 30-foot by 42-foot flag seen "by the dawn's early light" by Francis Scott Key on 14 September 1814. The house museum includes a portrait of Colonel Benjamin Flower, who commanded one of the Continental army's only two regiments of artificers (soldier mechanics who supported the artillery and engineers). The portrait, believed to be by Charles Willson Peale, has in the background a rare view of the Revolutionary War fort just outside Carlisle, Pennsylvania. The Flag House is located in Baltimore's Little Italy section and is open to the public from Tuesday through Saturday, 10 A.M. to 4 P.M. Phone: (410) 837-1793.

The frigate *Constellation* (1797) and Fort McHenry National Monument are historic landmarks of the period immediately following the Revolution. Important museums are operated by the Maryland Historical Society.

Cresap's Fort Site, Oldtown, Potomac River, Alleghany County. Appearing on many colonial maps, Thomas Cresap's stockaded house and trading post was established in 1740 at Shawanese Oldtown. It was on the old Indian trail between the Iroquois country in the north and the Cherokee country in the Carolinas. Cresap was the first white settler in the region, but it was not long until his place was closely associated with the westward route of white exploration and land speculation. Young George Washington spent four days here in 1748, when he was surveying for Lord Fairfax. Braddock's expedition came through in 1755 on the way to disaster at the Forks of the Ohio. Indian marauders killed settlers in the vicinity during Pontiac's Rebellion in 1763. Meanwhile, the name Cresap had become known from Canada to the Carolinas, and from Annapolis far into the Old Northwest.

Thomas Cresap was a Yorkshireman who had come to Maryland around 1717 at the age of fifteen. Two years after his marriage, about ten years later, he moved from the Havre de Grace area into the disputed territory around what is now Wrightsville, Pennsylvania. Here he became the leader of Maryland militia in a bloody and losing war with Pennsylvanians claiming title to the region. The dispute ended with Captain Cresap's being burned out, quite literally, in November 1736. Four years later he was Maryland's westernmost pioneer, the role for which he is remembered in history.

Before long he was a valuable intermediary between the Maryland government and the warring Iroquois and Cherokee. A charter member of the Ohio Company (1749), Cresap and his Indian friend Nemacolin marked and improved the 60 miles of trail from Fort Cumberland to the Monongahela at the site of Redstone Old Fort (today's Brownsville, Pennsylvania on U.S. 40). Cresap was a commissary during the Seven Years' War. His son Michael (1742–1775) was blamed for the Logan Massacre (see under WEST VIRGINIA) that touched off Dunmore's War of 1774. During the Revolution, Colonel Thomas Cresap was active on the home front, even though he was in his early seventies when the war started.

Michael Cresap had a commission from Virginia in 1774 and took part in the war he was accused of starting—it was called Cresap's War by some. Seriously ill in the following winter, he recovered enough to accept a commission from Maryland to raise a company of riflemen to join Washington's army around Boston. Young Cresap marched his command 550 miles in twenty-two days. Two months later he started home from Boston, hoping to recover his health, but died en route in New York City.

The ruins of a stone chimney mark the site of Cresap's Fort, which the National Survey of Historic Sites and Buildings puts in the category of "Sites Also Noted."

Fort Cumberland (lost site), Potomac River at Wills Creek, Alleghany County. In the present city of Cumberland the probable site of Washington's Fort Mount Pleasant (1754) and its successor on the same spot, Fort Cumberland (1755), is on a hill overlooking Washington and Green Streets.

This historic spot of the colonial period was commonly known as "the post at Wills Creek." It was established in 1750 by the Ohio Company. Washington built the first fort on returning from his defeat at Fort Necessity, now in Pennsylvania. Colonel James Inness expanded and renamed the fort the next year. Here Braddock assembled two thousand men before marching to his famous defeat in 1755. Washington was commander at Fort Cumberland for about two years during the Seven Years' War that

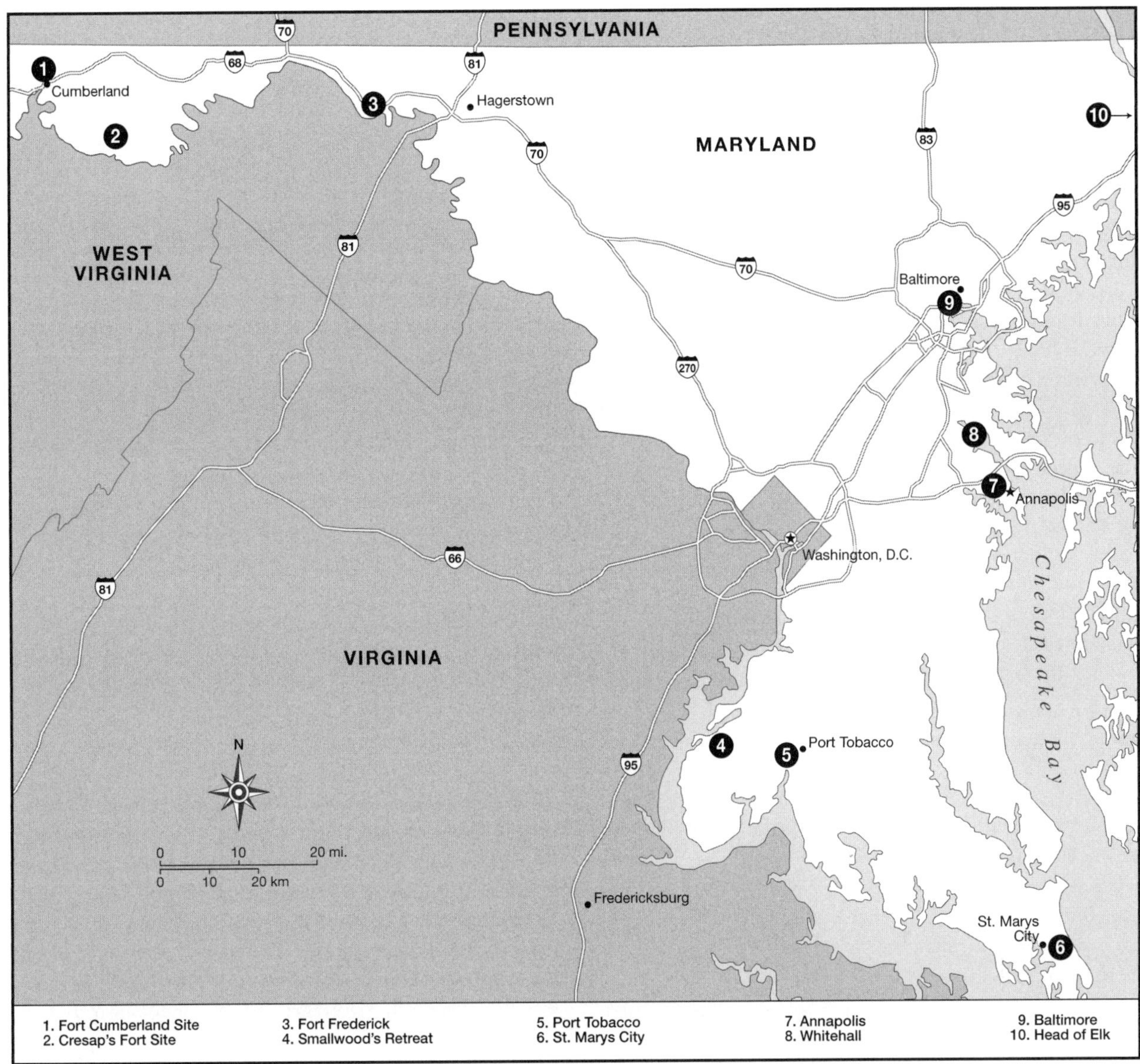

MAP BY XNR PRODUCTIONS. THE GALE GROUP.

followed, but the place was never attacked, and in 1765 it was abandoned. In the Whiskey Rebellion, Fort Cumberland was briefly reoccupied, Washington making his final visit to review troops here in 1794. Meanwhile, a town had been laid out in 1785 near the long-abandoned one. First called Washington Town, it was renamed Cumberland in 1787. It became the eastern terminus of the National Road, authorized in 1806 and started in 1811. Cumberland prospered as construction pushed westward and settlers came through from Baltimore and Pennsylvania. Delay in completion of the Chesapeake and Ohio Canal, of which Cumberland was a terminus, deprived the town of greater prosperity; the Baltimore and Ohio Railroad arrived about eight years before the canal. Cumberland lost its significance as a critical point in the western movement.

Fort Frederick, Potomac River near Clear Spring, Washington County. Braddock's defeat inspired a certain amount of new military construction on the frontier. In the spring of 1756 the Maryland assembly provided for the construction of Fort Frederick, a stone quadrangle with corner bastions erected that year. It was named for Frederick Calvert, sixth Lord of Baltimore. It was garrisoned until 1763, the end of the Seven Years' War, but had no major role. During the Revolution it was used as a prison camp, and it was garrisoned in the Civil War. The state of Maryland acquired it, conducted archaeological research, and reconstructed or restored the walls and other features as part of a 279-acre park with a museum and recreational facilities. It is off U.S. 40, 5 miles south of Clear Spring at 11100 Fort Frederick Road. Phone: (301) 842-2155.

Head of Elk. So called because it was at the head of navigation on the Elk River, this place was of strategic importance because it was the closest point in the Chesapeake Bay for amphibious operations directed against Philadelphia by the British. It was also the closest point from which Patriot forces in the central states could debark for water movement down the Chesapeake. In August 1777 a large British expedition from Staten Island landed at Head of Elk, and four militia companies posted to oppose the expected debarkation scattered without firing a shot. After observing the invasion force from a nearby hill, Washington concentrated his army along White Clay Creek in the vicinity of modern Newark, Delaware. After the action at Cooch's Bridge, Delaware, the Patriots withdrew to defensive positions in Pennsylvania along the Brandywine.

The British used Head of Elk as their port of debarkation for about three months until the Delaware River forts could be reduced and a new line of communications opened up the Delaware to Philadelphia. When American troops started moving south to oppose British operations there, Head of Elk became an embarkation point. General Kalb's Continentals came through in April 1780, Lafayette led his column through Head of Elk about a year later, and the combined American-French expedition of Washington and Rochambeau marched to this place en route to Yorktown.

The historic area is a short distance south of today's Elkton. It is in open country, surrounded by farm and dairy country, but unmarked and difficult to visit without trespassing on private land.

Mason and Dixon Line, boundary between Maryland and Pennsylvania. Although the fortieth parallel apparently was intended to be the boundary between the grants to the Baltimores (1632) and the Penns (1681), a protracted dispute grew. This ended with a boundary survey by Charles Mason and Jeremiah Dixon between 1763 and 1767. Marking stones were erected every mile, each fifth one bearing the arms of Baltimore and Penn on opposite sides. Most are still in place. Although the names of the English surveyors are commonly associated only with the Maryland-Pennsylvania boundary, they also marked the Delaware line.

Port Tobacco, Port Tobacco River, Charles County. "Potobac" is the name of the site on Captain John Smith's map of 1612. Before the Revolution, Port Tobacco covered 60 acres and was an important port and trading center. By 1800 the harbor was silting up, and for various other economic reasons, Port Tobacco gradually faded away. The 2000 census listed twenty residents in the town, although it is featured on several heritage and scenic driving tours. Its courthouse was reconstructed, and there are also four eighteenth-century homes in the area. The Port Tobacco Courthouse phone number is (301) 934-4313.

Within a few miles are several surviving colonial houses. One is the home built about 1760 by Dr. James Craik (1730–1814), chief physician of the Continental army and long-time associate of George Washington. It is noted for fireplaces with large mantels in each room, a solid walnut stairway, and massive locks. Another is the home of John Hanson (1721–1783), active Patriot in the events leading to the Revolution and first president of the Congress of the Confederation (for a one-year term starting 5 November 1781). Other landmarks are the Stag House (1732), Chimney House (1765), and Boswell-Compton House (1770). The Society for the Restoration of Port Tobacco (available at the courthouse phone number) started a fund-raising program of annual house tours in 1968 and remains active.

St. Marys City, St. Marys River, St. Marys County. The history of Maryland starts here, as might be suspected from the names. In November 1633, the year after Charles I granted the charter to George Calvert, first Lord Baltimore, Leonard Calvert established this settlement. (George Calvert died before the charter had passed the great seal, but it was then issued to his eldest son, Cecilius. Leonard, a younger son, was made governor of the new province.)

Maryland's proprietor was a Catholic. He wanted to establish the province as a haven for persecuted Catholics, but he also wanted Protestant colonists, so from the beginning he promised religious tolerance. St. Marys consequently became famous for adoption in 1649 of the historic Toleration Act, although this was limited to Trinitarian Christians. In 1694 the capital was moved from this first settlement to Annapolis.

A replica was built in 1934 of the old state house of 1676. Bricks of the original structure were used to build Trinity Church in 1829. The Leonard Calvert Monument is on the site of Leonard Calvert's negotiations with King Yaocomico for purchase of the colony's land. At Church Point is the site of the town laid out by Leonard Calvert.

The entire area has been designated a historic district, where the foundations of about sixty structures of the seventeenth century have survived undisturbed. This is probably the only site of a major seventeenth-century town in North America that possesses such archaeological importance other than Jamestown, in Virginia.

The site has been developed into Historic St. Mary's City, an interactive living history museum with costumed interpreters engaging visitors into the past of Maryland's first capital city. It features exhibits of the many archaeological finds, and also has a visitors' center and a gift shop. The site is open from mid-March until November and one can take a virtual tour via internet through its website, www.stmaryscity.org. Phone: (800) 762-1634.

Smallwood's Retreat, Potomac River, Charles County. One of the most distinguished military units of the Revolution was Smallwood's Maryland Regiment. "Men of honor, family, and fortune," as their major, Mordecai Gist, put it, they sported fine uniforms and equipment. But they quickly became famous for fighting. Hardly seven months after it was raised, Gist commanded the regiment in the heroic defense of the Patriot right flank in the Battle of Long Island. Under a grubby Brooklyn street today is the mass grave of Marylanders killed there, and in nearby Prospect Park is their monument. (See CORTELYOU HOUSE and PROSPECT PARK under Brooklyn, New York.) Maintaining their outstanding combat record, Smallwood's Regiment went south when the major fighting ended up north. As part of General Nathanael Greene's army they accumulated additional honors in the Carolinas.

General William Smallwood (1732–1792) is remembered more for his contribution to the war as a recruiter and administrator. He was absent on court-martial duty when his troops distinguished themselves on Long Island, although he did rush over from Manhattan to play an important role in covering the American retreat. He was wounded in leading the regiment at White Plains, New York. While recovering, he missed the campaign in New Jersey. In 1780 he marched south with General Kalb's column into the Carolinas, succeeding him as a division commander after the Battle of Camden, South Carolina, and being promoted to major general.

But when the Maryland aristocrat found himself temporarily subordinated to General von Steuben after General Gates was recalled, he refused to serve under a foreigner. Washington and Congress were willing to accept his resignation, but General Greene—Gates's successor—solved the problem by sending Smallwood home to recruit and raise supplies. Remaining in uniform until the end of 1783, he was elected governor in 1785 and served three consecutive one-year terms.

The old bachelor's home, which was coined "Smallwood's Retreat" (probably what the general himself named it) in the National Survey, has been restored in the 628-acre Smallwood State Park. It is open to the public on Sundays from 1 P.M. to 5 P.M., May through September. The park offers hiking, fishing, camping, and a boat marina. Phone: (301) 743-7613. On Md. 224 west of Pisgah and southwest of Mason Springs, the park is east of the United States Naval Proving Grounds.

Whitehall, off St. Margaret's Road on the outskirts of Annapolis, Anne Arundel County. About ten years after coming to America as governor of Maryland (1753–1769), the bachelor Horatio Sharpe built a retreat and entertainment pavilion overlooking Chesapeake Bay. Shortly thereafter he enlarged this into a five-part brick house of Palladian style almost 200 feet in length. "Superlatives become Whitehall," says the 1964 report of the National Survey, "not alone for its distinction of being the first colonial dwelling with temple-type portico, and as an exemplar of eighteenth-century 'country life' in America, but also as an embodiment of a great many composite factors that contribute luster to a building and a site" (*Colonials and Patriots*, p. 89). Whitehall's exterior was restored in 1957 on the basis of careful scholarship.

MASSACHUSETTS

Politically and economically, Massachusetts dominated the movement that led to the American Revolution. In and around Boston are many sites associated with the men and events of the decisive years 1763 to 1775. After the day of Lexington and Concord, the Battle of Bunker Hill, and the final evacuation of Boston by the British on 17 March 1776, Massachusetts was left outside the theater of military operations.

The following pages do not deal with the surviving landmarks of Massachusetts's cultural history and the many places such as Old Deerfield, Plymouth, and Salem where there is much for the visitor to see today. Massachusetts would warrant more pages in this guide if the author had included all major landmarks of the colonial era and all structures of outstanding architectural importance. They were not included because a wealth of literature already exists on historical landmarks in New England in general and the Boston area in particular.

To an extent greater than in almost any other of the original colonies, widespread urban development has obliterated eighteenth-century villages of historic importance and interest in Massachusetts. They are virtually unrecognizable in the Boston area. However, the tourist trade in Massachusetts is long established, and the solid scholarship of regional historians of an older generation is reflected in the material distributed to visitors. Information centers are maintained at a variety of locations, particularly in the Boston area. In addition, a number of websites exist that are very helpful in disseminating information on landmarks. Walking tours are set up in many areas. The Massachusetts Office of Tourism provides a helpful travel booklet, "Massachusetts Getaway Guide," that is obtainable through their informative website, www.massvacation.com. Phone: (617) 973-8500.

Two other agencies with statewide responsibilities are the Massachusetts Historical Commission, 220 Morrissey Boulevard, Boston, Mass. 02125; website: www.sec.state.ma.us; phone: (617) 727-8470; and the Massachusetts Historical Society, 1154 Boylston Street, Boston, Mass. 02215; website: www.masshist.org; phone: (617) 536-1608.

Adams Family Homes. *See* QUINCY.

Arlington (Old Menotomy). *See* RUSSELL (JASON) HOUSE.

Bedford Flag, Bedford. An early militia flag, traditionally associated with the fight at Old North Bridge in Concord and sometimes claimed to be America's oldest surviving flag (it dates to the early eighteenth century), is displayed in the Bedford Free Public Library on 7 Mudge Way just off Great Road in Bedford. Phone: (781) 275-9440. Individuals are able to view the 27" by 29" flag by contacting the librarian and leaving a driver's license or some other manner of deposit in exchange for a magnetic key to the special room in which the flag is stored. Only five people maximum may be in the room at any time.

Boston and vicinity. This is where it all started. Two centuries later, Boston retains in the midst of its commercial bustle a delightful vestige of colonial color and historical allure. Landmarks have been respected in the sustained period of economic prosperity (the traditional archenemy of historic preservation) and the recent epidemic of skyscraper building. The Old North End district still carries an Italian flair, although the neighborhood is becoming more and more homogenized as time goes on. At the other pole from this Little Italy, where Boston still throbs with human vitality, is the loneliness of Dorchester Heights. Cambridge, the address for venerable Harvard College, offers another sharp contrast.

The waterfront in and around Boston has been altered beyond recognition. The site of the Boston Tea Party is high, dry, and far from the beaten tourist track. The famous Necks of Boston and Charlestown, the Back Bay, and the old shoreline of Cambridge have long since been obliterated. Dorchester Heights is discernible for those who know where to look—a slight elevation rising above South Boston's masonry and showing a fringe of trees discernible from the expressway leading north into Boston (see separate article on DORCHESTER HEIGHTS).

Tourism having long been one of Boston's best-organized civic activities, and many outstanding guides to historic landmarks being locally available, this article is restricted to the places of outstanding importance, particularly those that tend to be neglected. "The Freedom Trail" guides the casual tourist to major landmarks from an information center on the Common, and offers free literature, but as an educated British journalist commented, "Take a comprehensive guidebook, for you are left almost entirely to your own devices. . . ." However, in deference to that remark, the Freedom Trail Foundation serves as an excellent resource. Website:www.thefreedomtrail.org; phone: (617) 357-8300.

Overlapping in part with the Freedom Trail is the Black Heritage Trail. Black slaves were first brought to Boston in 1638, and by the time of the Revolution there were several hundred slaves and free blacks living in the city and its environs. This mile and a half trail passes fifteen sites, including the Boston Massacre Site, the Old Granary Burying Ground, and the home of Revolutionary veteran George Middleton, leader of the all-black company called "The Bucks of America" who may have served at Bunker Hill. Walking tour maps and guides are available at the African Meeting House, 8 Smith Court, the oldest extant African American church. The Meeting House is open year-round from Monday to Saturday, 10:00 A.M. to 4:00 P.M. Guided tours are available from Memorial Day weekend through Labor Day weekend. Phone: (617) 742-5415.

Below in alphabetical order are the chief historic landmarks of Revolutionary War Boston, some of them merely sites on the sidewalk or in the street, others structures of great architectural interest and importance:

Beacon Hill derives its name from the beacon erected in 1635, a few years after Boston was settled from Charlestown. A new beacon erected in 1768 was blown down in 1789. The next year a tall monument was erected to commemorate the location of the primitive signal (never used for its intended purpose of warning of invasion), which had long been shown on plans of the town. This monument was taken down in 1811 when Beacon and Copp's Hills were graded to provide fill for the Mill Pond, Beacon Hill being lowered 110 feet by this operation. The Beacon Hill Historic District, north of the Common (Beacon Street) and east of the Charles River embankment, is a National Historic Landmark of the late eighteenth and the nineteenth centuries.

Boston Common is the same plot of some 50 acres purchased by the original settlers in 1634 from the first white inhabitant, William Blackstone. It is the oldest public park in the country, still owned by all the people of Boston, as it was more than three centuries ago. The Common originally fronted on Back Bay, and the British expedition to Lexington and Concord left in boats from the southwest tip of the Common, now the junction of Charles and Boylston Streets.

Boston Massacre Site is marked by a circle of paving stones in State Street at its intersection with Congress Street, just east of the Old State House. Here on 5 March 1770 a British guard of some ten regulars opened fire on a crowd of about sixty men. Three citizens were killed on the spot and two were mortally wounded. John Adams and Josiah Quincy defended the regulars, five of whom were acquitted and two convicted of manslaughter but not seriously punished. The Patriots did all they could to exploit the "massacre" as propaganda, most famously in Paul Revere's dramatic engraving. All five victims were buried together in the Granary Burying Ground (see below) just to the right of the entrance. In 1888 the citizens of Boston erected the Crispus Attucks Monument on the Boston Commons facing Tremont Street to commemorate the former slave who fell to a British bullet during the massacre. The monument has a copy of Revere's famous engraving with Attucks in the foreground. It is worth noting that most recreations of this illustration make Attucks white.

Boston Tea Party Site, marked by a plaque on the Sheraton Building on Atlantic Avenue northeast of Congress Street, was Griffin's Wharf, where, on 16 December 1773, a band of colonists boarded three tea ships and threw £10,000 worth of tea into the water. The British reacted by invoking punitive action, the Intolerable Acts, one of which closed the port of Boston. This led the Patriots to call the first Continental Congress to consider united resistance by all the colonies.

Castle William was on Castle Island, now the tip of a peninsula in South Boston. Castle Island (so called because it looked like a castle to Governor John Winthrop and his exploring party) was fortified in the early 1630s. Castle William never performed the role for which it was best

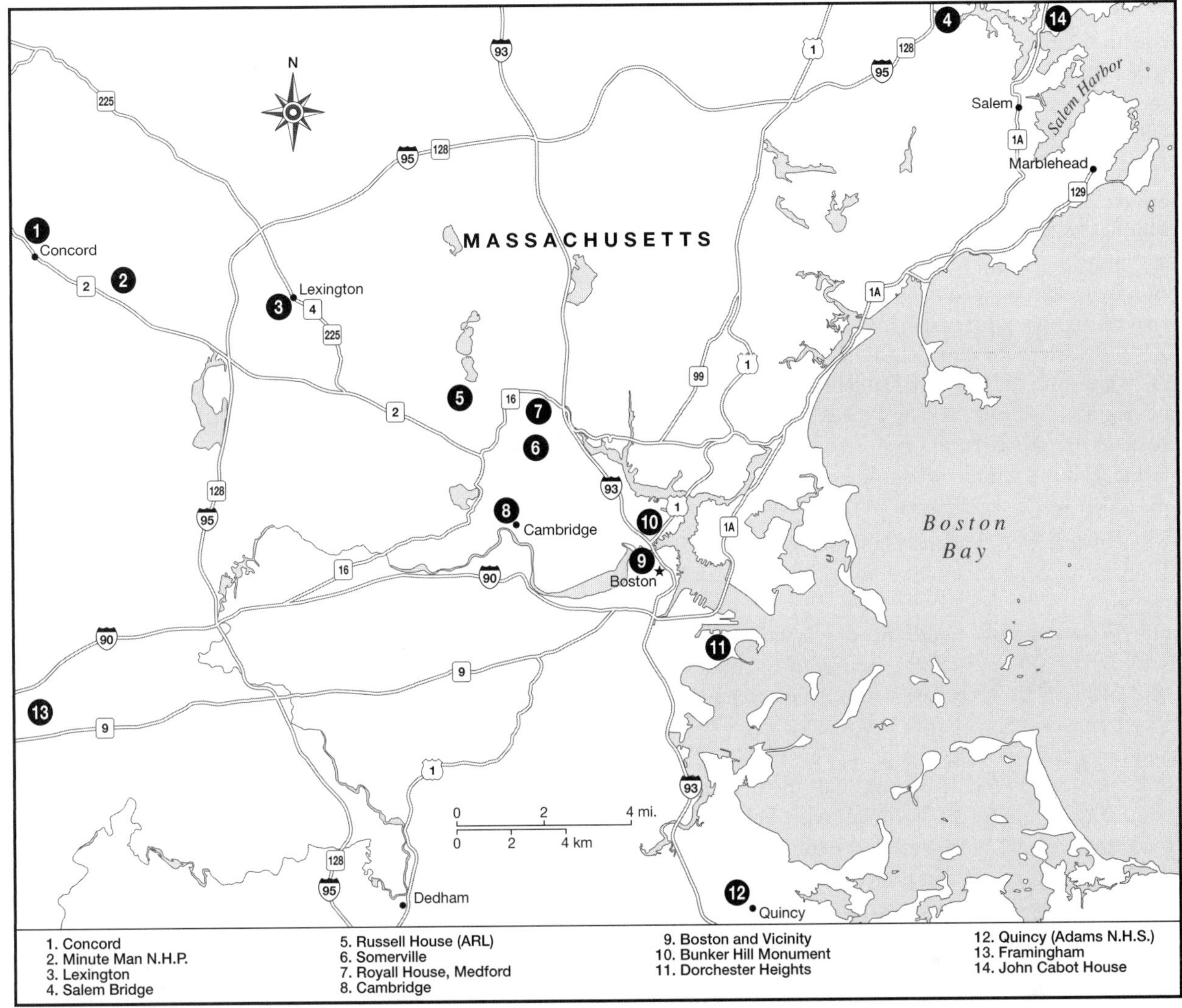

MAP BY XNR PRODUCTIONS. THE GALE GROUP.

suited, defending the entrance to Boston's inner harbor, but it was a refuge for British authorities during the troubled period leading to the Revolution. The British soldiers were withdrawn here after the Boston Massacre. Before this, town authorities defied the Quartering Act by refusing to provide troop quarters in Boston so long as the barracks on Castle Island were empty, but the British finally succeeded in getting accommodations for most of their garrison in the town. The Sixty-fourth Regiment ended up being posted on the island, leaving from here on its expedition to Salem and Salem Bridge. When the Patriots occupied the island after the British evacuated Boston, they renamed it Fort Independence. Paul Revere was in command of the post in 1778 to 1779 as a lieutenant colonel of militia, being relieved after the disastrous Penobscot Expedition in 1779 (see FORT GEORGE under Maine). A new fort built in 1801 (where Edgar Allan Poe served as a soldier in 1827) was abandoned in 1880, eventually becoming part of Marine Park. Guided tours of the castle are available on weekends in June through August, from noon to 3:30 P.M. The site is at the end of Gardner Way, South Boston.

Copp's Hill was one of Boston's original three hills (the others being Beacon Hill and Fort Hill). It was the site of a windmill as early as 1632 and a burial ground from 1659. During the Battle of Bunker Hill the British bombarded Charlestown from here, setting the fires that virtually destroyed the old town. An earthwork was hastily thrown up near the southwest corner of the cemetery for the battery, and another was dug to the rear for the supporting infantry. Traces remained until 1807, when Copp's Hill was cut down several feet to get dirt for filling in Mill Pond. Many ancient slate tombstones, including those of Cotton Mather and Edward Hartt, builder of the

U.S.S. *Constitution*, remain on the hilltop, which is reached by climbing Hull Street from Old North Church. Through the large buildings that mask most of the view you can see parts of Charlestown, including the Bunker Hill Monument.

Copp's Hill Burying Ground, Hull and Snowhill Streets. Just uphill from the Old North Church, Copp's Hill has been a cemetery since 1659, making it second in age only to King's Chapel, founded in 1630. General Burgoyne commanded the British artillery from the cemetery during the bombardment of Charlestown, 17 June 1775. British soldiers practiced their shooting by aiming at the tombstone of Captain Daniel Malcom with its bold inscription, "A true Son of Liberty." Among the many veterans of the Revolution buried here is Prince Hall, founder of the African Masonic Lodge in 1787, which is the oldest black organization in the United States.

Faneuil Hall, Faneuil Hall Square, was first built in 1742 with a long room above the marketplace to be used for public meetings. It remains vital to Boston as a museum, marketplace, and meeting hall. Little could the designer have forecast what momentous debates would take place in the structure whose primary purpose had been to provide Boston with a central market. The original building had been destroyed, except for the walls, by a fire in January 1761, and dedication of the new hall coincided with the beginning of the break with Britain. A town meeting here on 2 November 1772 adopted Sam Adams's motion to appoint "a committee of correspondence . . . to state the rights of the Colonists . . . as men, as Christians, and as Subjects; and to communicate the same to the several towns and to the world." History has few examples of "committee effort" leading to more dramatic action than the Committees of Correspondence created throughout the colonies to follow this lead by Boston. When the British garrison was established in Boston in 1768 some troops were permitted to use Faneuil Hall as temporary quarters (the rest camping temporarily on the Common). During the siege of Boston (April 1775 to March 1776) British officers and Loyalist ladies presented amateur theatricals in the hall. In 1805 to 1806 the building was tripled in size by increasing its three bays to seven and adding a third story. Architect Charles Bullfinch preserved the general appearance of the exterior but moved to the east end of the building the large cupola with its famous grasshopper weather vane. The fourth floor, lighted by dormers, is the armory of the Ancient and Honorable Artillery Company, a militia unit organized in 1638 and the country's oldest surviving military formation. Faneuil Hall is still a thriving market on the building's first floor. In the attic is a collection of items dating from colonial days, and in the great hall on the second floor, often used as a city government meeting place, is a collection of paintings including copies of portraits whose originals are in safer quarters at the Boston Museum of Fine Arts. Reconstructed in 1898 to 1899 with modern materials replacing wood to the extent possible, this National Historic Landmark, is owned and administered by the city.

Fort Hill Square, off Oliver Street, is the vestige of Corn Hill, where one of Boston's first fortifications was erected in the early 1630s. At the foot of the hill was South Battery, called the Sconce. The colonial fort was abandoned long before the Revolution, but was occupied by a regiment of regulars when the British garrison was established in 1768. The Royal Welch Fusiliers manned the position in 1774. After the British evacuation, Fort Hill was strengthened by the Americans, but in 1779 its heavy guns were moved to the Hudson Highlands. In 1797 the fort was leveled and the hill converted into a mall. Later the hill was graded to provide fill for the new dock area (1869–1872).

Franklin's Birthplace is indicated by a marker at 17 Milk Street, nearly opposite Old South Meeting House (see below). The location was controversial for a short time after it was revealed that Franklin once stated that he was born in his father's small house at the southwest corner of Hanover and Union Streets. However, further evidence convinced scholars that Franklin was mistaken.

Granary Burying Ground, Tremont Street at the head of Bromfield Street and adjoining the Common, has many old graves, including those of the Boston Massacre victims, Peter Faneuil, the parents of Benjamin Franklin (marked by a conspicuous monument), and three signers of the Declaration of Independence: John Hancock, Sam Adams, and Robert Treat Paine. The grave of James Otis is at eyeball level through the fence from the Tremont Street sidewalk.

Green Dragon Tavern site, on Blackstone Street just east of Marshall Street, is indicated by a marker. This is famous as the meeting place of the Caucus Club, which dominated Boston politics perhaps fifty years before the Revolution and reached the height of its influence as the break with England approached. An early leader was Deacon John Adams, whose son Sam took over to become the leading politician of Revolutionary Boston. The Green Dragon has therefore been called the "Headquarters of the Revolution."

King's Chapel and Burying Ground, School and Tremont Streets, is a short distance northeast of the Common and in the heart of old Boston. Virtually unaltered since its construction in 1749 to 1754, this "superb example of the work of Peter Harrison" (the judgment of the National Survey) is well preserved and in good condition. The architect intended that the blocky structure be topped by a lofty spire in the style of London's churches of the period. But the spire was never built, and it is most unfortunate that some courageous architectural historian has not prevailed on Boston to do Harrison the courtesy of adding this badly needed feature. Perhaps the neglect is intentional; perhaps Boston wants this squat stone structure to remain ugly. Built to serve British officers, it was highly unpopular in Puritan Boston as its first Anglican church. Because of continued antiroyalist sentiment even after the Revolution, it was long called Stone Chapel rather than King's Chapel. In 1789 it became the first avowedly Unitarian church in the United States, and it is active today as one of 1,100 churches and fellowships of that faith in America. The massive walls of Quincy granite were erected around an earlier wooden structure which was used until the time came to take it apart and pass the pieces through the arched windows of the new structure. In the courtyard and to the left as you enter is the interesting monument erected in 1917 to the memory of the Chevalier de St. Sauveur, killed by a Boston mob in 1778 when he attempted to interfere with their pilfering of a bakery established by the French fleet. Three or four French sailors also were killed about this time in riots against the French in Charlestown. Admiral d'Estaing managed to conceal his feelings, and the Massachusetts House of Delegates passed a resolution to erect a monument over young St. Sauveur's grave. In 1917 they finally got around to it. The twenty-four-line inscription starts in English and then has sixteen lines in French, prepared by d'Estaing. The chevalier's grave is believed to be in the crypt of the chapel.

The burying ground of about half an acre adjoining the chapel is maintained by Boston's Parks and Recreation Department. Established in 1630, according to the marker, its graves include those of Mayflower passenger Mary Chilton (who died in 1679) and William Dawes, Jr. (1745–1799), the little-publicized messenger who rode from Boston the same night as Paul Revere to warn the countryside that the British were headed for Lexington and Concord. Visiting hours are 9 A.M. to 5 P.M., Monday through Friday. Phone: (617) 523-1749.

Liberty Tree site is on Washington at Essex Street, near the end of Boylston Street (the latter being the southern edge of the Common). The elm was already about 120 years old in 1765 when it became the country's first Liberty Tree and inspired the fashion of such symbols throughout the colonies. British troops cut it down for firewood in 1775.

Old North Church, 193 Salem Street, has architectural and historical distinctions that make it one of the country's most important landmarks. The lantern signal from its belfry, "One, if by land, and two, if by sea," as the historically garbled poem by Longfellow put it, was arranged by Paul Revere on the eve of his historic ride to Lexington. Built in 1723, topped by a 191-foot wooden steeple in 1740, it has survived fires and hurricanes (the last one in 1954 blowing down the second tower of 1806). The interior, carefully and thoroughly restored in 1912 to 1914, is of particular importance in the history of American church design. Among the one thousand or more persons buried in thirty-eight tombs under the church is Major John Pitcairn of the Royal Marines, who figured prominently in the events at Lexington and Concord and was mortally wounded while leading the final assault on Bunker Hill. Paul Revere as a young boy assisted in organizing a guild to ring the church's famous peal of eight bells, cast in 1744 and still used. General Thomas Gage, who occupied pew 62, not far from pew 54 of Paul Revere's son, is said to have watched the Battle of Bunker Hill from the steeple (and he logically would also have visited the British battery nearby on Copp's Hill). The setting of Old North Church is unfortunately crowded on three sides, but this is relieved somewhat by Paul Revere Mall (established 1933) to the southeast. An attractive walled garden easily overlooked on the northeast side of the church and a terraced approach to the back give the handsome brick structure some breathing space and fire protection. Old North Church is owned and administered by the Corporation of Christ Church in the City of Boston. It is open Monday through Friday from 9 A.M. to 5 P.M., and Episcopalian services are given on Sundays at 9 A.M. and 11 A.M. Phone: (617) 523-6676.

Old North Square survives only as a vestigial plot opposite the Paul Revere House (see below). An asphalt-paved area of about a third of an acre is marked by a plaque erected in 1946: "Here in North Square lived Paul Revere and his wife," the visitor is informed. "Here lived Major Pitcairn of the soldiery occupying Boston in 1775. . . ." At the time of the Revolution the square was near the waterfront.

Old South Meeting House, Milk and Washington Streets, shares with the Old State House and Faneuil Hall the fame of being a place of public assembly in the tumultuous days leading to the Revolution. Large for its day, Old South was built in 1729 to 1730 and then called Third Church (serving Boston's third body of Congregationalists). It was shortly thereafter named Old South to distinguish it from another body of Congregationalists calling themselves "New South Church." During the British occupation a cavalry riding school was operated in Old South, most of its interior furnishings and the parsonage having been used by the soldiers for firewood. In 1783 the congregation restored the interior much as it had been. A century later the structure was saved by public sentiment from demolition. Since that time it has been owned and administered by the Old South Association, which turned it into a museum and headquarters for its organization. The slave poet Phillis Wheatley belonged to this church during the Revolutionary period. On the wall is a copy of Washington's will ordering freedom for his slaves. The Old South Meeting House is utilized for public debates, panel discussions, and events with colonial and Revolutionary themes, including reenactments. Every December it stages a dramatization of the debate that led to the Boston Tea Party. Phone: (617) 482-6439.

Old State House (Second Boston Town House), Washington and State Streets, has been called "the scene of proceedings of greater moment than those at any other building in the Thirteen Colonies" (*Colonials and Patriots,* p. 109). Here James Otis delivered his famous speech in 1761 challenging the legality of writs of assistance. The walls are those built originally in 1712 to 1713, having survived the fire of 1747 that destroyed the rest of the structure. Unfortunate internal changes were made first in 1830 and perpetuated when the building was rescued in 1882 and rededicated, so only the exterior appearance survives from its important period 1766 to 1776. Towering office buildings have destroyed the setting, and the basement has become the entrance and exit of a subway station, but the Old State House with its large lion and unicorn figures has genuine colonial allure. The building is owned by the city, with custody vested in the Bostonian Society, and serves as the Society's museum. Website: www.bostonhistory.org. Relics displayed include works of Paul Revere and tea from the Boston Tea Party. It is open daily from 9 A.M. to 5 P.M. Phone: (617) 720-1713.

Paul Revere House, 19 North Street, is a rare example of Stuart-era architecture in America and is Boston's only surviving building of the seventeenth century. The original portion was built soon after the Boston fire of 1676 on the site of the Increase Mather Parsonage. When Paul Revere took possession almost a century later, the simple two-and-a-half-story frame house with an end chimney probably had been enlarged to three full stories. After his death in 1818 it degenerated into a tenement and store, being considerably altered but miraculously spared from destruction. In 1908 it was carefully restored. Well maintained and open to the public, the house is important not only for its association with the famous Patriot and craftsman but also as a rare specimen of a seventeenth-century urban home. Website: www.paulreverehouse.org. Phone: (617) 523-2338.

Bunker Hill Monument, Charlestown, Greater Boston. The battle of Bunker Hill has been well nigh overwhelmed by the history of the Bunker Hill Monument Association. In 1825 this organization owned 18 acres of the battlefield, but in 1834 it sold most of this land to raise funds for building a huge monument. Now a 221-foot obelisk stands in a 4-acre rectangle of worn grass where there might have been a properly conceived historic park and some much-needed relief in the urban monotony of modern Boston. In giving less than a full page to this landmark, the National Survey comments: "The monument itself possesses considerable interest as an example of early historical monumentation" (*Colonials and Patriots,* p. 93). Unfortunately, "the monument is much in need of rehabilitation and development, particularly in regard to its interpretation of the battle story" (ibid.).

The cornerstone was laid on 17 June 1825, the fiftieth anniversary of the battle, with Daniel Webster delivering the oration in the presence of the Marquis de Lafayette. Construction of the dressed granite obelisk was not completed until 1843. By 1919 the Association was no longer able to cope with administration of the monument, so the task was assumed by the Commonwealth of Massachusetts, delegated to the Metropolitan District Commission. It was designated a National Historic Site in 1962 it and is open daily from 9 A.M. to 5 P.M. at no charge. The top of the obelisk is reachable by climbing 294 steps (no elevator). Renovations of the monument and the entire site are currently in progress. Phone: (617) 242-5641. A primitive museum and a statue of Colonel William Prescott are current features. Monument Park is approached from the southwest by rather steep streets that preserve some feeling of the slope up which the British attacked.

The original topography having been altered tremendously by landfills, the grading of hills, and high-density urbanization, landmarks of the battle are gone except for Breed's Hill. The granite obelisk marks the approximate center of the American redoubt that repulsed two attacks before falling to the third. Moulton's Point, where the British landed unopposed at about 1 P.M. to make their first attack along the low ground northeast of Breed's Hill, has been extended to form the United States Navy Yard (where the U.S.S. *Constitution,* "Old Ironsides," is exhibited). But the portion of old Charlestown generally southwest of Monument Square has many interesting structures surviving from the period right after the Revolution. (The old town was almost totally destroyed in the British bombardment of 1775.) The picturesque Old Burying Ground on Phipps Street has more than one hundred graves dating from before 1700.

The oldest building is the General Joseph Warren Tavern, 105 Main Street, in the Thompson Triangle Development. Nearby are the Benjamin Thompson House (started in 1777), and others of a few years later.

The John Cabot House, 117 Cabot Street, in Beverly, was owned by a Revolutionary War privateer. It is the headquarters of the Beverly Historical Society and displays a number of military and maritime items. Open Tuesday through Saturday 10 A.M. to 4 P.M. Phone: (978) 922-1186.

Cambridge, Charles River (Greater Boston). The township, now almost entirely built over, originally contained several separate villages. Newton and Lexington were

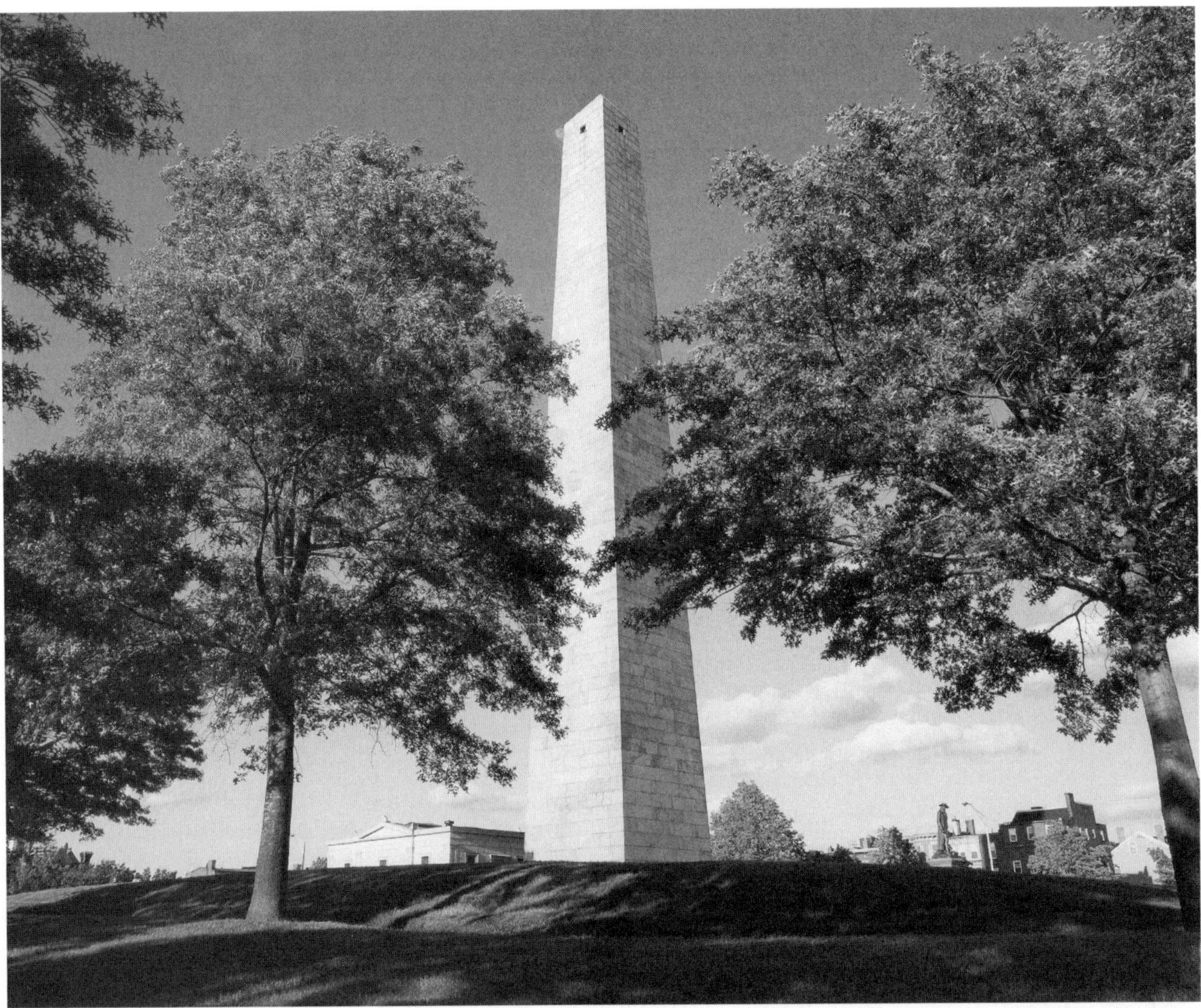

Bunker Hill Monument. *The cornerstone of Boston's Bunker Hill Monument was laid on 17 June 1825, the fiftieth anniversary of the battle. The 221-foot granite obelisk marks the approximate center of the American redoubt that repulsed two British attacks before falling to the third.* © ROYALTY-FREE/CORBIS.

detached in 1691 and 1713; Brighton and Arlington (originally Menotomy) were detached in 1837 and 1867. When the site was selected in 1630 for defensive works protecting the Massachusetts Bay Colony, the plan was for the settlement here to become the capital. Boston won out because of its geographical advantages for commerce as well as for protection from the Indians. First known simply as the New Towne, Cambridge was named in 1638 for Cambridge, England. Harvard College was founded at Cambridge in 1636, and the town quickly became an important intellectual center. The first printing press in British North America was set up here in 1639. (Boston had none until 1676.) Many of the leaders in the Revolution were educated at Harvard.

One of the most important surviving landmarks of the Revolution near Cambridge is the Old Powder House at Somerville, the town that adjoins Cambridge to the north but is sometimes referred to erroneously as being part of Cambridge. While the British raid on the powder house was taking place on 1 September 1774 another detachment marched from Boston and confiscated two field pieces recently procured by the Cambridge militia. John Richard Alden points out in his *General Gage in America* (p. 213) that Governor Gage had every legal right to take this property "but the brief march of the regulars aroused the whole colony." Men flew to arms on the assumption that similar raids would follow, and thousands of aroused citizens gathered in Cambridge. Mob violence was directed against Crown officials, and three more members of the council, including Lieutenant Governor Thomas Oliver, were frightened into resigning. Gage was sufficiently alarmed to start fortifying Boston Neck and restrict his regulars to the city.

The only surviving earthwork of the 10-mile string built in Cambridge and Charlestown for the Boston siege of 1775 to 1776 is a three-gun battery in what is now called Fort Washington Park. Buried deep in a commercial area behind the northwest corner of the Massachusetts Institute of Technology (MIT), the site was originally on the riverbank. The semicircular earthwork with three embrasures has been rebuilt and three cannon emplaced. (They date from after the Revolution.) About an acre of grass is enclosed by an attractive metal fence of cannon and halbert posts and vertical bars. The site is near the tracks of the Boston and Albany Railroad on Waverley Street just northeast of the corner of Chestnut Street. (The latter crosses Brookline Street a few blocks northwest of Waverly and runs between Massachusetts Avenue and the Essex Street Bridge. From Harvard Bridge the site is reached by driving through MIT on Massachusetts Avenue, crossing the railroad, and turning left on Albany Street, then left on Waverley to the park.)

Washington's headquarters during the siege of Boston was the Vassall-Craigie-Longfellow House (Longfellow National Historic Site), 105 Brattle Street. A fine Georgian house built by Major John Vassall in 1759, it is a well-preserved two-story frame structure on a large fenced lot. Henry Wadsworth Longfellow lived here for forty-five years (1837–1882), and the house was conscientiously preserved by the Longfellow House Trust until it transferred responsibility to the National Park Service, which has managed the house since 1974. The house was designated a National Historic Landmark in 1962 and a National Historic Site in 1972. As of 2005 the house is closed to the public except for tours by appointment. Phone: (617) 876-491.

The tour group Lively Lore guides visitors through Harvard Square and offers a "lively" look at where Washington took command of the Continental army and where most of his troops camped. The site of the Washington Elm, under which Washington took command of the Continental army on 3 July 1775, is marked in the north end of the Common. Christ Church, on Garden Street opposite the George Washington Memorial Gateway, faces the Common. Designed and built by Peter Harrison in 1759 to 1761, it was taken over by the Patriots for barracks. Martha Washington, who joined her husband in December 1775, had it returned to its proper use. Burgoyne's Convention army was in Cambridge briefly after its final defeat at Saratoga in October 1777. A Patriot mob enraged by the fact that funeral services for a young British officer were held in the church so heavily damaged the building that services were not resumed until 1790. The organ loft is the finest original feature in the well-restored National Historic Landmark. Plaques mark Washington's pew and one of the bullet holes said to date from the period of his army's encampment.

Massachusetts Hall on the Harvard campus was completed in 1720. The oldest surviving building of the college founded almost a century earlier, it was originally a dormitory with thirty-two chambers and small private studies for its sixty-four occupants. As quarters for 640 soldiers during the siege of Boston, it lost much of the interior woodwork and hardware. Wadsworth House (1726) was used temporarily by Washington after his arrival in Cambridge in 1775. Just inside the Widener Library (1913) are two panoramic models depicting in great detail the original and the modern appearance of Harvard and Cambridge. The phone number for Lively Lore is (617) 354-3344. The Cambridge Historical Society, located at 159 Brattle Street, is very helpful in offering information on Revolutionary War landmarks. Phone: (617) 547-4252. Another good Cambridge source is the state-sponsored Cambridge Historical Commission. Phone: (617) 349-4683.

Charlestown. *See* BUNKER HILL MONUMENT.

Concord and vicinity, Concord County. One of the first two settlements in Massachusetts back from the coast (Dedham being the other), Concord was incorporated as a township in 1635. A county convention here in August 1774 recommended calling for a provincial congress. When Governor Thomas Gage issued instructions for the General Court to meet in his new capital in Salem but then withdrew his summons because the Patriots had gained control of the lower house, the delegates adjourned to Concord in October 1774. Having already proposed (in June) that a continental congress be held, they meanwhile established a revolutionary government in Concord. During the winter of 1774 to 1775 they started forming an armed force and accumulating military stores. London authorities ordered Gage to take positive action to reassert royal authority, suggesting that he arrest the leaders of the illegal congress in Concord. Adjournment of the latter was scheduled for 15 April 1775, the day after Gage got his instructions, but the British commander in chief had already made plans to destroy the Rebel supplies known to be in the Concord area.

This therefore became the objective of the forces sent out from Boston on 19 April. The numerous historical sites associated with the Battle of Lexington and Concord are exhibited at Minute Man National Historical Park, located off Exit 30b on Interstate 95. Phone: (978) 369-6993.

The Barrett Farm turned out to be the ultimate objective of the British on the fateful day. Although

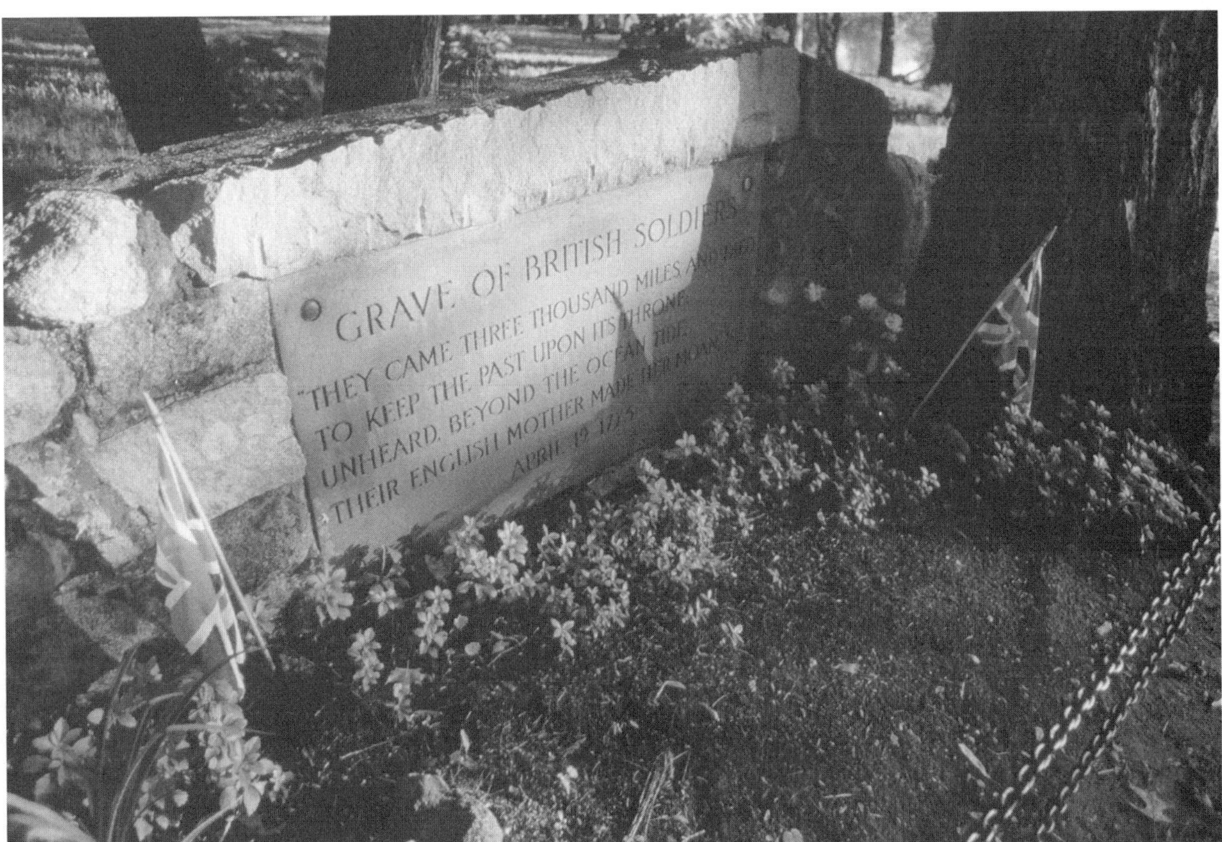

The Grave of a British Soldier. *A tombstone near the Old North Bridge in Concord, Massachusetts, marks the final resting place of an unidentified British soldier who died in the Revolutionary War.* © KELLY-MOONEY PHOTOGRAPHY/CORBIS.

Colonel James Barrett's farmhouse is among the surviving landmarks, it tends to be neglected in summaries of historic sites in the Concord area. Listed in the National Register of Historic Places, today it is one of the few remaining farms in Cambridge. The upkeep of privately owned historical sites is always a challenge, and efforts are underway to help fund a much-needed overhaul of the farm. The two-story frame house is standing about 30 feet from Barrett's Mill Road in a setting little altered by the passage of two centuries. Behind it is the ridge where some of the stores were hidden, and in front of it is the bottomland, still being farmed, where other matériel was plowed under. The site is about 2 miles east of the North Bridge Visitors Center, reached by following Barnes Mill Road, which turns into Barrett's Mill Road on crossing Lowell Road. (The latter runs southeast to Concord.) It may be reached also from the traffic circle on Mass. 2A about 3 miles northwest of Concord.

Retracing the Battle Road from Barrett's Farm, one comes to the well-preserved area around North Bridge. Colonel Barrett's militia made its first contact with the enemy just east of Concord village around 7 A.M. Barrett had just returned from supervising the work of hiding or removing the stores around his farm, and the sixty-five-year-old Patriot leader decided to withdraw his troops across North Bridge to mass on Punkatasset Hill and wait there for reinforcements. The North Bridge Visitors Center provides taped narratives, slide shows, and exhibits that sketch in the history of what happened here and how this action relates to the entire day's operations. An overlook in the gardens of a post-Revolutionary mansion provides a view of picturesque Concord River and the area of the reconstructed North Bridge. Near the bridge stands the Old Manse, or the Reverend William Emerson House. Built in 1770 by the grandfather of Ralph Waldo Emerson, it was the home from 1842 to 1846 of Nathaniel Hawthorne, whose description in *Mosses from an Old Manse* gave it the former name. The Emerson family watched from an upper window while the militia confronted British troops around North Bridge in 1775.

Modern Concord has half the population of today's Lexington, and considerably more small-town charm. The village green has been cut down to the dimensions of a dividing strip on a thruway; it is an island of grass with a large monument in the center and the Colonial Inn facing one end. At the opposite end and across Main Street

(Mass. 2A) is Wright's Tavern. Meeting the criteria for registration as a National Historic Landmark, the two-story frame house with a double-hipped (or monitor) roof and red clapboard siding was built in 1747. In 1751 Amos Wright took over its management as a tavern, hence the present name. Situated in the center of the village between the public meetinghouse and the militia training ground, Wright's Tavern played an important role in events leading to the Revolution. Here the militia assembled on 19 April when the courthouse bell sounded the alarm, and British officers soon arrived to establish their command post and take refreshments. Now owned by the Society of the First Parish, Wright's Tavern serves as church office space and is the home for the Wright Tavern Center for Spiritual Renewal. Classes, seminars and spiritual discussion groups are regularly scheduled. Phone: (973) 369-9602.

The First Parish Meeting House (1901) is on the site of the building in which John Hancock presided over the three hundred delegates to the Provincial Congress in October 1774.

On the ridge across Lexington Road (Mass. 2A) is the Old Hill Burying Ground, with slate headstones and brick tombs from 1677. The most famous of the elaborate inscriptions is on the grave of the African-born slave John Jack, who died in 1773. It reads, in part: "Though born in a land of slavery, he was born free. Though he lived in a land of liberty, he lived a slave."

This ridge played a role in the fighting at Concord. To the northeast is the swath of broad meadow along which the Patriots moved in defilade between North Bridge and Meriam's Corner, where they gave the retreating British the first taste of what was to be continued over the next 16 miles to Boston. From Meriam's Corner (on Mass. 2A, Battle Road) the visitor should detour a few hundred yards north, passing the Meriam House on the right, to look back over this great meadow through which the militia made their envelopment.

The business center of Concord today covers the old mill dam and pond that were the distinctive topographical features of the colonial village. Behind Wright's Tavern is a slight depression left after the area was filled.

Antiquarian House on Lexington Road is a museum with fourteen period rooms from 1685 to 1870 and exhibits pertaining to the Revolution. The Concord Antiquarian Society (1886) operates the museum and has offices and its library here. (Chamber of Commerce, Concord, Mass. 01742.)

Dorchester Heights, South Boston. The significance of this National Historic Site has been so lost that not even the name is preserved on street maps. The original shoreline of Dorchester Neck has been bloated beyond recognition, particularly in the South Bay area. The historic heights now show on city maps as Telegraph Hill in Thomas Park.

The place is interesting and important because its surprise occupation and fortification by Washington's troops on the night of 4 to 5 March 1776 was quickly followed by the British evacuation of Boston (17 March). They had long planned to get out, and the occupation of Dorchester Heights merely accelerated the British departure; yet this detracts nothing from the brilliance of Washington's military achievement. It would not have been possible without Knox's "Noble Train of Artillery" hauled to the Boston lines from Fort Ticonderoga, New York. Nor could it have been achieved without the exceptionally good staff work and leadership that followed. The problem was not only to occupy the heights overnight without being opposed by British troops, but also to get heavy guns in position and fortified during the same night. The ground was still frozen, which meant that digging would be slow, and Rufus Putnam is credited with the plan of using precut heavy timbers for rapid construction of fortifications above ground. A refinement of this novel concept was to take up barrels that could be filled with earth, not only to be emplaced so as to make the works look stronger than they actually were, but also to be rolled down on the British assault troops should they appear. Another problem solved by the planners was collecting enough gunpowder, most of which came from European sources.

The British detected activity on the hill at about 10 P.M. but took no action. When the works became visible the next morning General Howe is said to have commented that the Rebels had done more in one night than his troops could have done in months. His estimate of the number of Americans engaged was ten times the actual number. A proposed counterattack was called off shortly before it was scheduled to start on the evening of 5 March. Washington tried to extend his position about half a mile north to Nook's Hill, but British artillery quickly made this ground untenable.

Dorchester Peninsula had four hills, only two of which were occupied in the operation we have been considering. Called the Twin Hills on some contemporary maps, they were Forster Hill, later designated Telegraph Hill, and Signal Tree Hill, to the southeast. What was generally called Nook's Hill was officially Dorchester Hill. Farthest to the northeast was Bush Tree Hill, which did not figure in Washington's strategy.

A white marble monument was dedicated in 1902 on the 126th anniversary of the British evacuation. A steeple in the style of a colonial meetinghouse tops a tower, the total elevation being 115 feet above Telegraph Hill. The roughly oval park, with high retaining walls on the north, west, and south sides, is named for General John Thomas, who commanded the operation on Dorchester Heights.

Already past his fiftieth birthday, the distinguished-looking Thomas, grandson of an early settler, had started his military service in 1746 as a surgeon and had risen to command of a regiment in Amherst's advance along Lake Champlain to Montreal in 1760. His promotion to major general was dated 6 March 1776. About two weeks later he left Roxbury, reaching Quebec to take command of the Patriot forces in this vicinity. During the subsequent retreat up the St. Lawrence he came down with smallpox and died at Sorel (2 June 1776).

Tall residential buildings mask most of the view from Thomas Park, but the north-south streets provide restricted vistas that give some idea of the place's strategic importance in 1776. In 1951 it was designated the Dorchester Heights National Historic Site by an agreement between the secretary of the interior and the mayor of Boston. The somewhat neglected monument and park, once under the jurisdiction of Boston's Department of Parks, is now run by the National Park Service. The grounds are open free to the public year-round.

Visible from along a several-mile stretch of the Southeast Expressway into Boston, the site can be reached by taking Telegraph Street due east from Dorchester Street at Eighth Street in South Boston. Expressway Exit 16 is the one for Dorchester Street.

Lexington, Lexington County. A modern building of colonial style houses the visitors' center operated by the Lexington Chamber of Commerce. Half a block east of Lexington Green, it is open year-round and a visit should begin here for those who need to have their knowledge of history refreshed. (See MINUTE MAN NATIONAL HISTORICAL PARK, below.)

Lexington Green and nearby ***Buckman Tavern*** have been preserved since the Revolution as historic sites. At the southwest corner of the green is the Revolutionary Monument erected in 1799 to honor the eight minutemen killed here on the historic morning of 19 April 1775. To the rear is a tomb containing the remains of these men. The site of the old belfry, a landmark of the skirmish, is marked by a boulder. Another inscribed boulder indicates one flank of Captain John Parker's line of minutemen.

Buckman Tavern, on Hancock Street opposite the east side of the green, was the place where Parker's men assembled in the cold morning hours of the fateful day before making their stand. Built about 1690, with some structural changes made before 1775, the two-story white clapboard building remains virtually unaltered since the latter date. Its walls bear marks left by British musket balls.

The ***Hancock-Clarke House,*** 35 Hancock Street, sheltered John Hancock and Sam Adams when Paul Revere clattered up at midnight to warn that the British were coming. The provincial government had been established in Concord during the winter of 1774 to 1775, and these two Patriot leaders had been living in the house for almost a month. Hancock wanted to fall out with the Lexington militia, but when Revere got back to the house after being captured on his way to Concord he accompanied Hancock and Adams on their way out of town before returning to watch the shooting on the green. The house was built by the grandfather of John Hancock, and the latter spent seven years here as a boy. The earlier part dates from 1698, the more modern portion from 1734. In 1896 it was moved across the road to its present location. Among the historical treasures on display are the pistols of Major John Pitcairn, commander of the British advance guard engaged on Lexington Green. They were carried into the American lines in the saddle holsters of Pitcairn's horse during the action at Fiske Hill, where Pitcairn was thrown from his horse. General Israel Putnam used them during the Revolution.

Munroe Tavern, 1332 Massachusetts Avenue, was Lord Percy's command post while his forces were deployed in the area to cover the withdrawal of the British from Concord through Lexington. It served also as an aid station during this brief period. The clapboarded structure is southeast of the high ground on which Percy's two cannon were positioned astride the road from Lexington. Although the neighborhood is built up, large trees have survived around the tavern, and its tactical importance in this covering force action remains apparent. The older part of the building dates from 1695. An ell added a few years before the Revolution was removed later.

The three historic houses are administered by the Lexington Historical Society, and they schedule tours at varying times, so it is important to call ahead. Phone: (781) 862-2480.

The ***Old Burying Ground,*** beyond the green and near the Unitarian Church, has the grave of Captain John Parker. A reproduction of the Old Belfry is off Clarke Street, south of the green. The original stood here until 1668, when it was moved to the green, where it survived until 1909.

Menotomy. Detached from Cambridge after the Revolution, this village evolved into the crowded Boston suburb of Arlington. See RUSSELL (JASON) HOUSE.

Minute Man National Historical Park, Lexington, Lincoln, and Concord counties. Phone: (978) 369-6993. Many landmarks of the running battle that started the American Revolution on 19 April 1775 have long been cherished historic sites in the relatively unspoiled New England countryside west of metropolitan Boston. Since the early 1990s these have been integrated into a 970-acre national historical park. Visitor information centers of various types, museums, interpretive displays, and signs have been established.

Buckman Tavern. *John Parker's company of minutemen gathered at Buckman Tavern in Lexington, Massachusetts, in the cold morning hours of 19 April 1775, to await the arrival of British troops.* © KEVIN FLEMING/CORBIS.

The North Bridge Visitors Center, located near the North Bridge that arched the flood just outside Concord village, has exhibits and a sound-slide program that will bolster one's previous knowledge of what happened here to touch off the shot heard round the world. It houses the famous Hancock Cannon, which may have been one of the cannons stolen from the British in September 1774.

The Minute Man Visitors' Center has informational services and literature, and features a multimedia theatric presentation, *The Road To Revolution*, which plays every thirty minutes.

The Battle Road unit of the park is the location of the Battle Road Trail, a 5-mile trail that connects the area's history with markers along the way. Hartwell Tavern is on the trail and is staffed as a living history center from May through October.

In a few hours on the ground you will learn more about the fighting at Lexington and Concord than you could by hours of reading, thanks primarily to the excellent orientation programs and special exhibits mentioned above. Landmarks of the momentous day are not restricted to the actions at Lexington and Concord, but they are best preserved in this area. Major sites are covered in the separate articles on LEXINGTON and CONCORD. Moving back toward Boston over the routes of Paul Revere and William Dawes (who spread the alarm) and over the routes of British advance and retreat, you are in the built-up area of Greater Boston. The colonial topography is buried under streets and modern construction. The village of Menotomy has been renamed Arlington in becoming a suburb of modern Boston, but most other geographical names survive. (Mistic had changed to Medford by 1775.)

Shorelines of 1775 have long since disappeared, eliminating Boston Neck, over which Dawes rode, and Charlestown Neck, over which Revere rode and the British retreated. British embarkation and debarkation points for their movement across Back Bay from Boston Commons to Phips' Point are high and dry. Today's Massachusetts Avenue through Arlington and the northern half of Cambridge follows the colonial road along which the British moved out and back. At Somerville village they feinted as if going toward Boston Neck, then headed for Charlestown Neck.

An exceptionally good guide is *Battle Road,* by Maurice R. Cullen, Jr., with numerous sketch maps and other drawings by Howard L. Rich. The fifty-page paperback is available at the park's information centers.

The Old Burying Ground in Framingham (near Buckminster Square) contains the grave of Peter Salem, who received his freedom when he joined the Continental army. Salem is credited with shooting Major John Pitcairn at the Battle of Bunker Hill. Salem's tombstone sits off by itself in an isolated corner, a segregated graveyard of one.

The Parting Ways Archeological Site, Plymouth, investigates the site of a small community of black Continental soldiers led by Cato Howe. A small museum displays the dig's findings. The site is on Plympton Road just off Mass. 80. Call for an appointment, (617) 746-6028.

Quincy, Norfolk County. The Adams National Historical Park, the John Adams Birthplace, and the John Quincy Adams Birthplace are National Historic Landmarks. Phone: (617) 770-1175. The first, featuring the Adams Mansion, is a memorial to the family that produced two presidents of the United States, the minister to Great Britain during the Civil War, and two distinguished historians. All resided at various times in what they called simply the Old House, now the Adams Mansion. The oldest part was built in 1731 by Major Leonard Vassall. John Adams bought it in 1787. During his presidency he added the large gabled ell and upstairs study. His son, grandson, and two great-grandsons made other additions. In 1946 the Adams Memorial Society donated the house and about five surrounding acres to the federal government.

About a mile south are the other Adams houses, which the Adams Memorial Society also donated to the federal government (National Park Service) in the mid-1970s. Neither of the typical saltboxes is architecturally significant, but both are historically important for their associations with the distinguished family.

The association of the Adamses with the three houses mentioned above is pertinent. The John Adams Birthplace, 133 Franklin Street, is the original homestead where John Adams was born and raised. In 1764 he married and moved into the adjoining house, now known as the John Quincy Adams Birthplace, 141 Franklin Street. Here Abigail and their son remained until after the Revolution, when they joined John Adams in Europe (1783–1788). After this they lived in the Old House, which is now called the Adams Mansion, bought in September 1787 before their return to the United States from England. John Quincy Adams bought both birthplaces from his father in 1803, living in his own birthplace house from 1805 to 1807.

John Adams retired from the presidency in 1801 and spent the rest of his years in the Old House, living to see his son elected president in 1826, on the fourth of July. By some strange numerology this was the fiftieth anniversary of the Declaration of Independence, and his last words are said to have been "Thomas Jefferson still survives." But by even stranger coincidence, Jefferson had died a few hours earlier at Monticello.

John Quincy Adams and his son Charles Francis (1807–1886) made the Old House their summer home. The latter's sons Henry (1838–1918) and Brooks (1848–1927) spent many of their summers there. The visitors center for the Adams National Historic Park is located in Quincy and features some interpretive material in addition to a gift shop. A trolley leaves from there and takes passengers for the forty-five-minute tour of the Adams's houses and a one-hour tour of the Old House. Phone: (617) 770-1175.

Royall (Isaac) House, Medford. Architecturally this is one of America's finest and most interesting colonial houses. It is on the site of a house built about 1637 by Governor John Winthrop. Isaac Royall, a wealthy merchant of Antigua, and his son, a Loyalist who fled the country in 1775, made the extensive modifications of an older brick house that resulted in the handsome three-story structure. Their work dates from the periods 1733 to 1737 and 1747 to 1750; the original house with which they started was built around 1692.

Historically the Royall House is interesting for its association with several famous officers of the Revolution who used it during the siege of Boston. Colonel John Stark occupied the house while his regiment was camped in Medford before the Battle of Bunker Hill. General Washington was a frequent visitor after his arrival to take command of the Continental army.

In 1908 the Royall House Association acquired the property, which has been expertly restored. Outbuildings include brick slave quarters, built before 1737, and probably the only such structures still standing in Massachusetts. Among the historic objects displayed is a tea chest from the Boston Tea Party of 1773, one of the two or three surviving. The Royall House is open to the public for touring from 1 May to 1 October. For details write Royall House Association, 15 George Street, Medford, Mass. 02155.

Russell (Jason) House, 7 Jason Street, Arlington. The present town of 54,000 was the village of Menotomy in 1775. The traffic is bad today between Boston and Lexington, but on 19 April 1775 it was even more dangerous. Past the home of the fifty-eight-year-old Jason Russell clattered Paul Revere and William Dawes in their midnight rides to warn that the British were coming. The lame Russell escorted his family to safety and then returned to set up a barricade of shingles behind his gate, from which position he proposed to shoot the retreating British. The latter were pretty well fed up with this sort of thing by the time they got to Menotomy. Further, their flank security detachments were able to work effectively in the flat plain here, and the militia were not alert to this new development in their running fight. A body of Essex militia, flushed by British patrols moving to clear the flanks of the main column, headed for Russell's house. Russell fell dead in his doorway and eleven militiamen were killed in the house, but eight held out successfully in the basement.

The gray clapboard house of about 1680 was occupied by Russell's descendants until 1890. Turned around and moved back from the road, it was saved in 1923 by the Arlington Historical Society, carefully restored, and made into a house museum. Four rooms are furnished, two in the seventeenth- and the others in the eighteenth-century style. The Arlington Historical Society is located at 11 Academy Street, Arlington; phone: (703) 892-4204.

Salem and Salem Bridge, Essex County. The "shot heard round the world" might well have been fired here several weeks before Lexington and Concord, but the crisis was averted in an episode remembered primarily for its humorous aspect (if remembered at all). General Gage ordered an expedition from Boston to destroy nineteen brass cannon that were being fitted with carriages at Captain Robert Foster's forge near the North River Bridge. (This is what actually was going on there. Gage sent out the expedition on orders from London, where the authorities had information that cannon had been shipped to Salem from Europe.)

Lieutenant Colonel Alexander Leslie sailed with two hundred men of his Sixty-fourth Foot from Castle William to Marblehead Bay. About 2 P.M. on Sunday, 26 February 1775, the regulars started a 5-mile march to Salem. Colonel Timothy Pickering was alerted by a horseman, called his men out of church, and sent forty minutemen to remove the cannon from the forge. The British arrived on the scene to find the militia and a large crowd of hostile citizens on the far bank. A heroic Patriot knocked the bottom out of the only boat the British were able to secure, and the draw of the bridge leading to the forge had been opened. A Loyalist minister and the militia captain came up with an ingenious suggestion that would enable Leslie to carry out his orders without bloodshed: the British troops would be allowed to cross the bridge if they would then withdraw peacefully. The cannon had been hauled away; so Leslie went along with the plan and then retraced his route to Boston.

The affair is generally known by the name of Salem Bridge, but the cannon were hidden in the Salem "North Fields." The latter have long been covered by North Salem, all colonial structures being obliterated in the process. The present bridge carries North Street (Mass. 114) over railroad tracks and several industrial streets in a rundown section of Salem before crossing the tidal inlet of Salem Harbor that is North River. A bronze marker on the present bridge indicates the general location of the original structure. It is a site best visited by map.

Salem was settled in 1626 as a commercial venture, partly agricultural and partly as a wintering place for fishermen. After 1670 it was an important port, and Salem privateers were active in the Colonial Wars as well as the Revolution. When General Gage was appointed governor of the province in 1774 and instructed to put an end to the civil disorder that had been growing at an alarming rate, he tried to establish a new capital at Salem. Here the General Assembly met on 17 June of that year, protesting the move of their seat from Boston and locking the door against Gage's order to dissolve. In the complex political maneuvering that followed, the Patriot faction won out over the royal governor's efforts to establish a loyal body of legislators in Salem, and seated its own partisans in the lower house on 5 October 1774, the date set by Gage for the General Court to convene there. After waiting two days for the governor to arrive and open the session, which Gage refused to do, the Patriots adjourned to Concord and formed a revolutionary government.

Today Salem is a city where many historic sites have been preserved, although most of these are associated with the history of the city before and after the Revolution. The Salem Maritime Historic Site includes the house built in 1762 for Elias Hasket Derby and Derby Wharf. The Pioneers' Village in Forest River Park is a reproduction of a Puritan settlement. The House of Seven Gables (1668) at 54 Turner Street and the Witch House (1642) at 310½ Essex Street are famous landmarks. The Peabody Museum, 161 Essex Street, has important collections including ship models and relics of the colonial and Revolutionary periods. Essex Institute (founded 1848) at 132 Essex Street has one of America's most important historical libraries and museums of the colonial and federal periods, including more than four hundred portraits. The Institute has four historic houses that are open to the public, two of these, near the museum, having been built long before the Revolution. The museum is open to the public year-round. Phone: (978) 744-3390.

Somerville (formerly part of Charlestown), Greater Boston area. The Old Powder House still stands in a park just south of the busy traffic rotary at Broadway, College Avenue, and Powder House Boulevard, southeast of Tufts University. Here on Quarry Hill a stone windmill was built about 1703. In 1747 this was sold to become a gunpowder magazine for the colony, serving this purpose during the period 1756 to 1822. As signs of open rebellion in the countryside became increasingly evident, Governor Thomas Gage sent regulars from Boston to seize the 250 half-barrels of powder at Somerville (then Charlestown). While one detachment marched to Cambridge to confiscate two cannons there, another of about 250 troops went by boat from Boston's Long Wharf to Charlestown. The operations started at dawn on 1 September 1774 and were quickly performed, without incident. But the countryside was aroused, with results described in the section on CAMBRIDGE.

The Old Powder House is a cylindrical tower about 30 feet tall with a beehive-shaped top. The blue stone walls are 2 feet thick, with the inner structure of brick. The tower stands on a rock outcropping in a small park known as Nathan Tufts Park.

Winter Hill and Prospect Hill survive only in place-names, whereas Ploughed Hill and Cobble Hill have not left even this trace.

The Springfield Armory National Historic Site, operated by the National Park Service, contains the world's largest firearms collection, including many weapons from the Revolutionary War. The armory, the first gun manufactory in North America, opened in 1794 and ceased production in 1968. It is open year-round from Tuesday to Saturday, 10:00 A.M. to 5:00 P.M., and is located on impressive grounds on Federal Street in Springfield. Phone: (413)734-8551.

Stockbridge, Berkshire County. The Reverend John Sergeant in 1734 began his missionary work among the Housatonic tribe of the Mahican confederacy near where the village of Stockbridge was established about the same year. Several bands of the tribe were collected on a tract reserved for their use by the colonial government, and they became known as Stockbridge Indians. Many joined the British army in the Seven Years' War, which proved to be a disaster; their town suffered from raids that reduced the population to only two hundred. Yet they offered to form a company of minutemen when the Revolution started; the Massachusetts Provincial Congress accepted in March 1775, and the Stockbridge thus became the first Indians to enlist on either side in this war. They took part in several actions on the northern frontier, including the Battle of Bennington. Their elderly chief, Nimham, and seventeen warriors were killed in action on 31 August 1778 near Van Cortlandt Mansion, New York (see this heading under NEW YORK CITY: THE BRONX).

Several landmarks of the Revolution may be seen in the little town. The latter does not include descendants of the Stockbridge Indians, who abandoned their village during the period 1785 to 1787 and moved to a new Stockbridge in Madison County, New York. (Here their number grew to 300 by 1796, but in 1833 they moved to Green Bay, Wisconsin, whence they scattered.)

The home built in 1739 by John Sergeant, Mission House, is a museum on 19 Main Street. The museum and gift shop are open from Memorial Day to Columbus Day and guided house and garden tours are available. Phone: (413) 298-3239. A mile west is a large mound with an obelisk inscribed: "The Ancient Burial Place of the Stockbridge Indians, Friends of our Fathers." The site of the Indian mission is marked by the Field Chime Tower (1878), and the Stockbridge Library museum has tribal artifacts.

MICHIGAN

French explorers, missionaries, traders, and soldiers traveled the Great Lakes during the colonial era. The first European settlement was established in 1688 by Father Jacques Marquette on the site of Sault Ste. Marie. He replaced this three years later by a mission a few miles south in Mackinac Straits. Antoine de la Mothe Cadillac founded Detroit in 1701. The region of the Great Lakes passed to British control in 1763, and the famous Robert Rogers, accompanied by Lieutenants John Stark and Israel Putnam, moved west from Montreal to receive the surrender of Detroit. Indian displeasure over this change in empire management led almost immediately to Pontiac's Rebellion, a remarkable uprising that wiped out almost all the newly acquired British posts in the Old Northwest. Detroit held out, primarily because its line of communications by water remained unbroken. British regulars, with little support from the provincials, reconquered the region.

During the Revolution the little British post at Detroit was a continuing source of trouble to American frontiersmen. Lieutenant Colonel Henry Hamilton had only a few regulars at Detroit, but he was terribly effective in exploiting Indian hostility toward white settlers and in enlisting the support of Loyalists in leading their raids. When George Rogers Clark undertook his conquest of the Old Northwest, his orders included the capture of Detroit if possible. Clark never was given the necessary means for this latter enterprise, but he did capture Hamilton at Vincennes, now in Indiana, and sent him back to grace the jail at Williamsburg, Virginia.

Detroit continued to be the base for devastating Loyalist-Indian raids until the end of the Revolution. Most historic landmarks in Michigan pertain to the periods before and after the Revolution, many being associated with the campaigns to eliminate the British hold on the western outposts after the Peace of 1783.

Sources of tourist publications and information are: the Historical Society of Michigan, 1305 Abbott Road, East Lansing, Mich. 48823, phone: (517) 324-1828; the Department of History, Arts and Libraries (HAL), phone: (517) 373-2486; the Michigan Historical Center, 702 West Kalamazoo Street, Lansing, Mich. 48909, phone (517) 373-0510; and the Michigan Economic Development Corporation (Tourism), 300 North Washington Square, Lansing, Mich. 48913, phone: (800) 644-2489. Two helpful websites are www.Michigan.org and www.michigan.gov.

Detroit. The strategic importance of the straits on the 27-mile-long waterway north from Lake Erie toward the three Great Lakes to the west was recognized early in the period of French exploration. From its founding in 1701 Detroit was a focus of economic and military rivalry in the Old Northwest.

A century after the first American Revolution another one was precipitated in Detroit by Henry Ford. Quite apart from what this has done to the world at large, it transformed Detroit into a throbbing industrial center with little room for the preservation of historic landmarks of its forebears.

Fort Pontchartrain was a stockaded village and fort of about 200 feet square built by Antoine Laumet de la Mothe Cadillac in 1701, when he founded Detroit. Located south of present Jefferson Avenue between Griswold and Shelby Streets, it was enlarged three times during the 1750s and was a formidable place when turned over to British forces under Robert Rogers in 1760. The name was changed to Fort Detroit. The British garrison held it successfully for fifteen months during Pontiac's War, and Henry Hamilton, known as "the Hair Buyer" because he followed the well-established policy of paying for enemy scalps, operated from Fort Detroit as lieutenant governor of Canada. From Detroit he marched on 7 October 1778 with about two hundred whites and Indians on an arduous trek of seventy-one days in the dead of winter to Vincennes, Indiana. Here he was later surprised by George Rogers Clark and forced to surrender his garrison on 25 February 1779.

Meanwhile, at Detroit the new commander, Major Richard Lernault, built a new fort in 1778 not far from the old one. From here the British operated for the remaining years of the Revolution, continuing to send out powerful raiding parties into the Ohio Valley. Fort Lernault was not surrendered to United States authorities until 11 January 1796, when it was renamed Fort Shelby; in 1802 it was incorporated as the town of Detroit and renamed Fort Detroit. In 1826 the fort, which General William Hull had surrendered to the British during the War of 1812, was given to the city. Within a few months it was leveled to make way for extension of streets over the site, which is marked only by a plaque in the lobby of the Hotel Pontchartrain, 2 Washington Boulevard, Detroit.

The Detroit Historical Commission operates an outstanding museum that traces the city's evolution from prehistoric times; the address of the commission and the museum is 5401 Woodward Avenue, Detroit, Mich. 48202. Website: www.detroithistorical.org; phone: (313) 833-1805 (closed on Mondays).

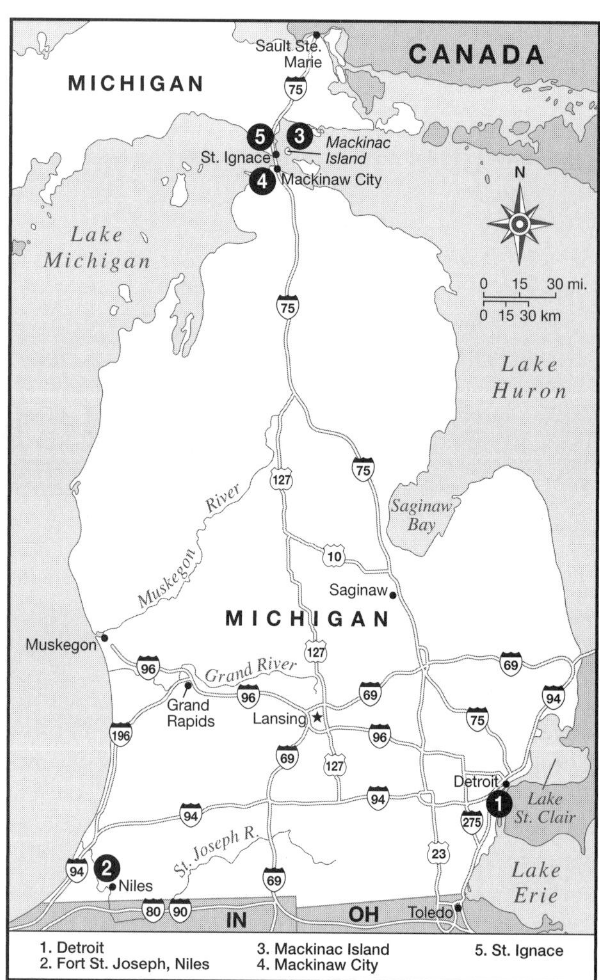

MAP BY XNR PRODUCTIONS. THE GALE GROUP.

Fort St. Joseph, Niles, Berrien County. The French built two posts of this name, one now the city of Port Huron and the other in modern Niles. The former was established by fur traders in 1686 but was destroyed by fire and abandoned two years later. The latter was built in 1697, turned over to the British at the end of the Seven Years' War, captured during Pontiac's uprising (on 25 May 1763), and subsequently returned to the British but not garrisoned until the Revolution. After the British expedition from Fort Michilimackinac (now Mackinaw City) attacked the Spanish settlement on the site of St. Louis, Missouri, the Spanish retaliated by moving against Detroit. Captain Eugenio Pourré with about 120 troops, half of them Indians, surprised Fort St. Joseph in January 1781, and the British surrendered immediately. Pourré held the position twenty-four hours, enabling his government to claim the valleys of the St. Joseph and Illinois Rivers "by right of conquest."

The Fort St. Joseph Historical Museum, 508 East Main Street, Niles, has artifacts from the fort and important Indian collections. Most of the artifacts are on display, but many are stored. These stored artifacts are viewable by contacting the museum and scheduling an appointment. Fort St. Joseph Historical Museum is open Wednesday through Saturday from 10 A.M. to 5 P.M. Phone: (616) 683-4702, ext. 236.

Mackinac Island, Upper Peninsula (end of Lake Huron). "Historically considered," says a note in the splendid *Atlas of American History* (Scribner's, 1943), "the name Michilimackinac applies not only to the Strait, but to the region on either side of the Strait [between Lakes Huron and Michigan] and to the Mackinac Island." The word means "place of the big wounded (or lame) person," according to the Smithsonian Institution's *Handbook of American Indians* (1907), a name applied at various times to the island, the village on this island, to the village and the fort on Point St. Ignace, and "at an early period to a considerable extent of territory in the upper part of the lower peninsula of Michigan. It is derived from the name of a supposed extinct Algonquian tribe" (ibid., I, 857).

Lip-lazy Anglo-Saxons have tried to dismiss all this by changing the word to Mackinac (pronouncing it "mackinaw") and remained fuzzy about what specific geographic spot, general area, or fort they mean when using the word. For example, "Fort Michilimackinac" has been applied to the three successive forts at St. Ignace, at what is today's Mackinaw City, and on Mackinac Island.

Mackinac Island, to use the official name for what the French called Île Michilimackinac, qualifies as a National Historic Landmark. It was here that the Jesuits Claude Dablon and Jacques Marquette planted the first mission settlement in the region in 1671. The next year they moved it to the mainland on the north side of the straits, where the city of St. Ignace now stands. (Their fort here was called Fort De Buade originally, then Fort Michilimackinac.) In 1698 the French abandoned the area, returning in 1715 to build the second Fort Michilimackinac on the south side of the straits. This third French site was taken over by the British in 1761. On 4 June 1763 the Ottawa tricked the British into coming out and watching a game of ball—it was the king's birthday—and then suddenly attacked. The Indians killed twenty-one and captured seventeen of the garrison. The next year the British reestablished the post, having put down Pontiac's Rebellion, of which the sneak attack had been a part. In 1781 they moved to Mackinac Island after becoming alarmed by the success of George Rogers Clark in the Ohio Country (see MACKINAW CITY). The elaborate fortification was still under construction when, in 1796, the British finally withdrew from the region under the terms of Jay's Treaty of 1794.

During the War of 1812 the British again occupied the position. John Jacob Astor took over Mackinac Island for the headquarters of his American Fur Company as soon as the British left. The flourishing fur trade had moved farther west by 1830, depriving the straits of their commercial advantage, and Astor sold his interest in the company a few years later (1834). In 1857 the island became a national park, which was turned over to Michigan in 1895 for development as a state park. Some of the island remains in private ownership, but almost all the historic features are on state land. These include the remains of the stone fort started by the British in 1780 and taken over by United States forces in 1796; still called Fort Mackinac, its original stonework remains as solid as when built two centuries ago. On higher ground is the 1936 reconstruction of the War of 1812 fort, which the British called Fort George and the Americans renamed for Major Andrew Holmes, who was killed in the unsuccessful effort of 4 August 1814 to take the island. Many original buildings remain, and others have been reconstructed.

No automobiles are permitted on Mackinac Island (except for administrative and emergency vehicles). Passenger ferry service runs from St. Ignace and Mackinaw City during the summer only. With most of its shoreline rising in cliffs, the irregularly shaped island (about 3 miles long and 2 miles wide) has many interesting rock formations and has long been a popular summer resort. Further information is available through the Mackinac Island Tourism Bureau, P.O. Box 451, Mackinac Island, Mich. 49757. Website: www.mackinacisland.org; phone (800) 454-5227.

Mackinaw City and Mackinac State Historic Parks, Straits of Mackinac. The preceding article on Mackinac Island deals with the general history of this region and the three variations of the name. Mackinaw City is on one end of the 5-mile-long suspension bridge across the Straits of St. Ignace. This state park encompasses six living-history parks, including the restored Colonial Michilimackinac Historic State Park. Fort Michilimackinac was built originally in 1715 by the French, taken over in 1761 by the British, lost in the massacre of 1763, reoccupied the next year and rebuilt, then moved across the ice to Mackinac Island in 1781.

A National Historic Landmark, the restored buildings include the blockhouses, barracks, French church, storehouse, and British trader's house. The history of the fort and its restoration are depicted. The surprise attack of 1763, precipitated under the pretext of retrieving a fly ball tossed by the Indians into the fort during a game of baggataway (lacrosse), is reenacted annually. The other parks include Fort Mackinac, Historic Downtown, Mackinac Island State Park, Historic Mill Creek, and Old Mackinac Lighthouse. A virtual tour is available via the internet at www.mackinacparks.com. Phone: (231) 436-5563.

St. Ignace, Straits of Mackinac, Upper Peninsula. The history of this place as part of the Michilimackinac region is sketched in the article on nearby MACKINAC ISLAND. The Father Marquette Memorial (1957) at Marquette and State Streets marks the grave of the missionary explorer, moved here in 1677 two years after his death at Ludington. (At the latter place, the site of the original grave is marked by a huge, illuminated cross.) Marquette Park, in which the memorial and grave are located, is the site of St. Ignace Mission, a National Historic Landmark. Phone: (906) 643-8620. Adjacent to the park is the Museum of Ojibwa Culture, which is open daily 10 A.M. to 8 P.M. from Memorial Day to Labor Day, and the rest of the year Tuesday through Saturday, 1 P.M. to 5 P.M. Phone: (906) 643-9161. The fort built nearby to protect the mission was originally named Fort De Buade but soon became known as Fort Michilimackinac. (The two later forts on the site of

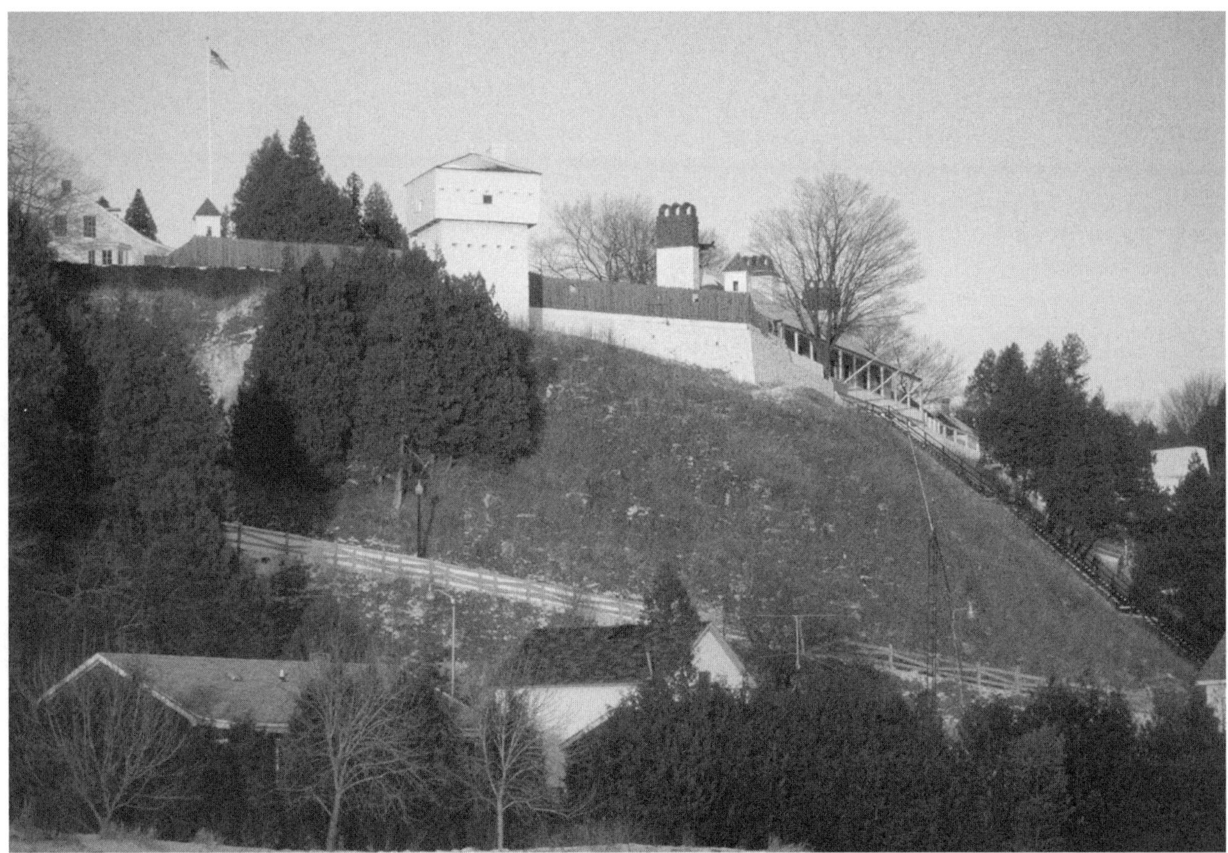

Fort Mackinac. *Fort Mackinac on Mackinac Island in Michigan was built by the British during the Revolutionary War.*
© LAYNE KENNEDY/CORBIS.

today's Mackinaw City and on Mackinac Island were also called by this name, among others.) Four miles north of St. Ignace are Castle Rock (a nearly 200-foot-high Indian lookout) and the Algonquin Museum, a reproduction housing Indian, pioneer, and logging relics. Visitors can climb Castle Rock for a fee of 50 cents and get a splendid view of Mackinac Island and Lake Huron. Phone: (906) 643-8268.

MISSISSIPPI

Until 1795 the Spanish claimed that the northern boundary of their Mississippi territory, acquired by the Treaty of 1783, was an east-west line from today's Vicksburg to the Chattahoochee. (See also the introduction to ALABAMA.) The French established their first permanent settlement near Biloxi in 1699, then moved across the bay in 1719 to build a town where today's city stands. Biloxi was the capital of French Louisiana from then until 1723, when New Orleans took over the role. (The first capital was Mobile, Alabama.)

Mississippi has a number of important prehistoric sites and a great many pertaining to the Civil War, but few related to the American Revolution. Sources of information are Mississippi State Department of Archives and History, 200 North Street, Jackson, Miss. 39201, phone: (601) 576-6850; and the Mississippi Development Authority (Division of Tourism), P.O. Box 849, Jackson, Miss. 39205, website: www.visitmississippi.org, phone: (601) 359-3297. The Division of Tourism offers state maps, organizers, and travel brochures that are available by calling (800) 733-6477.

Natchez, Mississippi River, Adams County. For protection of warehouses here the French built Fort Rosalie with willing help from the Natchez Indians in 1716, naming the fort for the Duchess of Pontchartrain. Once the Natchez realized that the French came as conquerors, relations worsened. In 1729 the Indians rebelled against the French, killing more than two hundred, capturing about the same number of soldiers and settlers, and destroying the fort. The French retaliated, driving the Natchez from the area. The region passed under British control in the Treaty of 1763, but it was not until 1778 that Fort Rosalie was rebuilt, garrisoned, and renamed Fort Panmure. Spain declared war on Great Britain the next year, and Governor de Galvez promptly moved up the river to take Manchac, Baton Rouge, and Natchez. Fort Panmure changed hands several times more before being abandoned. The site is at the foot of South Broadway, on the bluff, directly behind one of the antebellum houses, Rosalie (1820), for which Natchez is now famous. Rosalie is owned and maintained by the local DAR and guided tours are offered on the hour. Phone: (601) 446-5676.

The Grand Village of the Natchez has been reconstructed with a museum chronicling the history of the Natchez and displaying artifacts from this archeological site. Take U.S. 61 south from the center of Natchez to 400 Jefferson Davis Boulevard. The site is open Monday to Saturday, 9 A.M. to 5 P.M., and Sunday 1:30 P.M. to 5 P.M. Phone: (601) 446-6502. The Natchez Historical Society is a recommended source for local colonial history and produces a mixture of historical programs. Reach the society by mail at P.O. Box 49, Natchez, Miss. 39121, or by email at: info@natchezhistoricalsociety.org.

Natchez Trace. The 444-mile Natchez Trace Parkway, which runs between Natchez and Nashville, Tennessee, follows the general route of the famous Indian trail dating from prehistoric times. Called the Chickasaw-Choctaw Trail during the period of French domination and the Path to the Choctaw Nation after the British gained control, it subsequently became known as the Natchez Trace. Before conflicts between European interests and Indian troubles ended in about 1820,

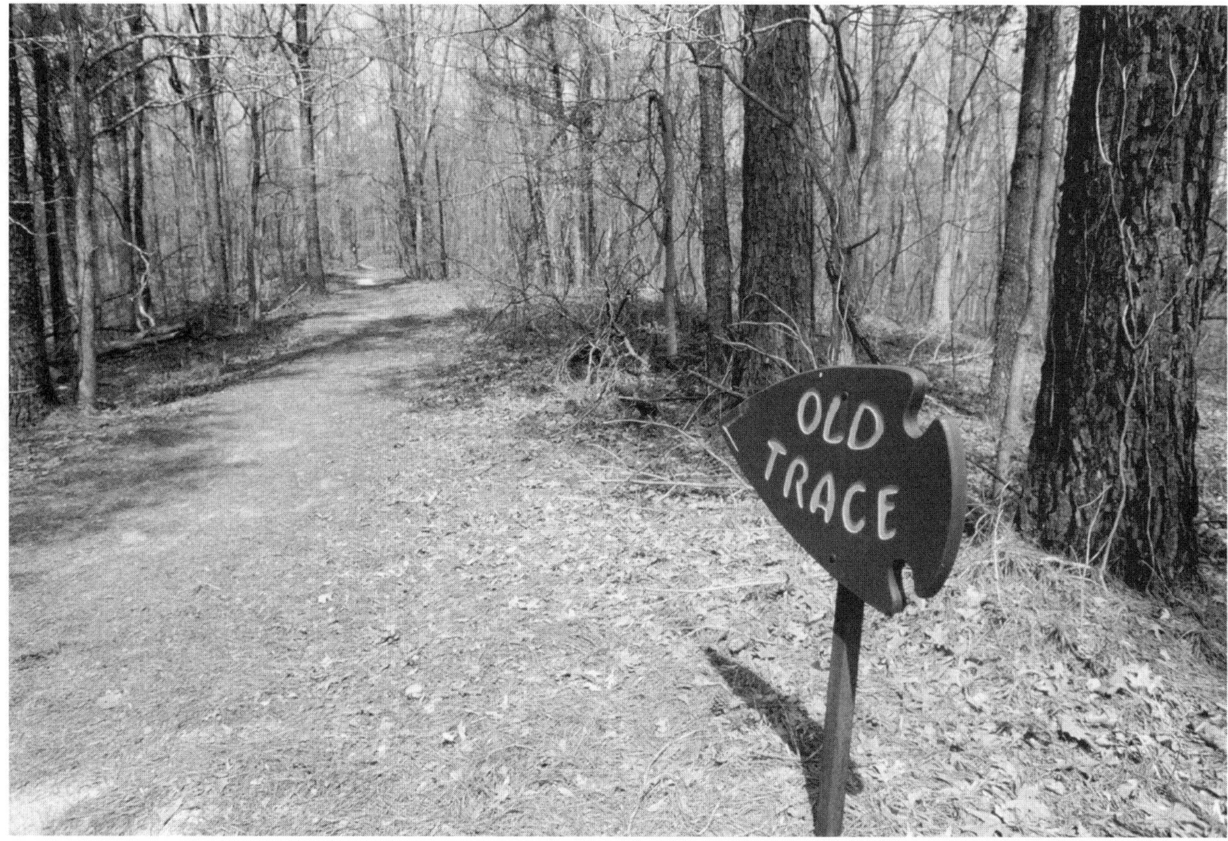

Natchez Trace. *Before conflicts between European interests ended in about 1820, opening the Mississippi River to steamboat traffic, the Natchez Trace, which runs between Nashville and Natchez, was the most heavily traveled road in the region.* © BUDDY MAYS/CORBIS.

opening the Mississippi to the new steamboat traffic, the Natchez Trace was the most traveled road in the Old Southwest.

Historic sites along the Natchez Trace Parkway are indicated by markers, and a number of interpretive exhibits point out their significance. The main visitor center is at Tupelo, Mississippi at Parkway milepost 266, and is open year-round from 8:00 A.M. to 5:00 P.M. Its mailing address is 2680 Natchez Trace Parkway, Tupelo, Miss. 38804. Phone: (800) 305-7417.

Just off the Parkway northwest of Tupelo between U.S. 78 and Miss. 6 is the site of an eighteenth-century Chickasaw fortified village with audio displays telling the history of the Chickasaw.

MISSOURI

The earliest French explorers, Jolliet and Marquette in 1673 and La Salle in 1679, visited the eastern fringe of modern Missouri as they moved along the Mississippi River. Bourgmont's explorations of 1714 to 1724 took him up the Missouri River to the vicinity of modern Leavenworth, Kansas, through Osage territory, and he was followed by trappers and hunters long before the first French settlements were established at Ste. Genevieve (1735), St. Louis (1764), and St. Charles (1769). Fort Orleans was built far up the Missouri in 1720, near the mouth of Grand River (now the boundary between Carroll and Chariton Counties), but its existence was brief. France ceded the region to Spain in 1762.

The only military action of the Revolution took place in St. Louis, but the Missouri region was of some significance during the war as a colony still predominantly French (and hence largely anti-British) and under the administration of Spain, a country hostile to the British and consequently helpful to the American Patriots.

In the complicated diplomacy of the western frontier that followed the Revolution, the Spanish presence in Missouri achieved greater importance. Many Americans came in as settlers after 1796, receiving large land grants because the Spanish wanted to protect the region from possible British offensives from Canada. In 1804 the region was formally transferred to United States administration as part of the Louisiana Purchase. No historic structures of the American Revolution survive in Missouri, but there are several of architectural importance that are associated with the periods before and after the Revolution.

Promotional literature is available from the Missouri Division of Tourism. Website: www.visitmo.com; phone: (573) 751-4133. It publishes a yearly updated free travel guide available through the website or by calling (800) 519-2000. The State Historical Society's address is 1020 Lowry Street, Columbia, Mo. 65201. Phone: (573) 882-7083.

Boone Home, near Defiance, St. Charles County. Daniel Boone (1734–1820) spent many of his later years in this two-story, L-shaped stone house. It was built by his son Nathan during the period 1803 to 1811. With wide halls, the house has three rooms downstairs and four upstairs. Walnut doors, handmade locks, and fireplace mantels carved by the famous frontiersman are features of the interior. Many of the furnishings belonged to Daniel Boone, and the rest are family pieces or others appropriate to the period. Near the house is a museum exhibiting items of pioneer days, and Boonesfield Village, an array of reconstructed period buildings with costumed inhabitants depicting a living history of town life in the early 1800s. Phone: (636) 798-2005.

Landmarks of Daniel Boone's earlier life in Pennsylvania, North Carolina, and Kentucky are covered under those headings in this book. Around 1799 he followed his son Daniel to what is now called the Daniel Boone region of Missouri—roughly the dozen counties west of St. Louis and north of the Missouri River. Here Boone was given a large land grant at the mouth of Femme Osage Creek and made administrator of the region for the Spanish government. When jurisdiction passed to the United States in 1804,

Boone's land titles were voided, but after many delays Congress confirmed them (1814). His wife had died a year earlier. Boone spent most of his remaining years in the home of his son Daniel, and died in the house.

The grave of Daniel Boone and his wife, Rebecca (1739–1813), is in a cemetery just east of Marthasville, Warren County. The spot is marked by a monument. The cemetery is privately owned but can be visited. Near Matson is the Judgment Tree under which Boone held court. This is a small park located along the 200-mile Katy Trail State Park.

The Boone Society maintains an informative website, www.boonesociety.com. It includes a page describing eighteen Boone sites throughout Missouri commemorating the last twenty years of his life, which was spent mainly in the state.

The Boone Home is on a secondary road (1868 Number 7) about 6 miles northwest of Defiance. It is open daily.

Osage Village Historic Site, east of Nevada, Missouri, off U.S. 54. The Osage were the dominant inhabitants of Missouri during the Revolutionary era. This site offers a history of the Great Osage Village with markers noting its layout in 1777.

Ste. Genevieve, Mississippi River, Ste. Genevieve County. Unlike the British, the French were more interested in hunting and trading in Indian country than in establishing permanent homes. Although the first explorers had come down the Mississippi in 1673 and the Missouri had become a familiar route a few decades later, it was not until 1735 that the French founded their first settlement within the present boundaries of Missouri at Ste. Genevieve. Because of flooding, the site was moved in 1796 to where the present town stands, some 3 miles from the original location. Several French colonial houses of the pre–Revolutionary War era have been preserved. One is the Bolduc House (at 123 South Main, open April through October), which was built in the original settlement in 1770 and moved to the site of the new town before 1790. Four other late-eighteenth-century French houses, all of considerable architectural distinction, are included in the Ste. Genevieve Historic District, a Registered National Historic Landmark. They include the Amoureux House, the Bequette-Ribault House, the Bolduc House Museum, and the Commandant's House. All of them are open to the public at various times. The website, www.ste-genevieve.com, offers a virtual tour and descriptions of the historical district. The Foundation for Restoration of Ste. Genevieve is at 198 South Second Street. Phone: (573) 883-9622.

Bolduc House. *This log house in Ste. Genevieve, Missouri, was built around 1785 (incorporating a smaller house built in 1770) by Louis Bolduc, a miner, merchant, and planter.*

St. Louis. A trading post was established in 1764 on the site of modern St. Louis by Frenchmen from New Orleans. They were joined soon by other Frenchmen moving from the Illinois Country after the Treaty of 1763 gave French territory east of the Mississippi to the British. Spanish sovereignty of the Mississippi Valley west of the river, acquired in 1762, was not a reality in this region until 1770, at which time St. Louis had a population of about five hundred, very few of whom were Spaniards.

Fort San Carlos was built here in 1778, the year George Rogers Clark won control over the predominantly French settlements along the east bank of the Mississippi from Kaskaskia to Cahokia. (The latter was just across the river from St. Louis.)

Spain declared war on Great Britain in June 1779 and began overrunning the isolated British outposts on the Mississippi and along the Gulf Coast in West Florida. The British retaliated by attempting to wipe out all Spanish posts in the Mississippi Valley from St. Louis to Natchez. Success would depend primarily on rallying Indian support en route. The expedition was to start from Fort Michilimackinac (now Mackinaw City, Michigan) under the command of Emanuel Hesse of the Sixtieth Foot, or Royal American Regiment. According to the Spanish report sent to Governor Galvez in New Orleans after the action, Hesse attacked the post of San Luis de

Ylinoises at 1 P.M. on 26 May 1780 with a small contingent of regulars, some two hundred Loyalists, and around six hundred Indian allies.

Captain Don Fernando de Leyba commanded the post. He obviously had plenty of warning, erecting a wooden gun platform for five cannon at one end of the settlement, and digging in others on the opposite side. To defend these works he had thirty-four "veteran soldiers," presumably from his own unit, "the infantry regiment of Luisiana," 281 "countrymen," and artillery. Women and children of the garrison were herded into the commandant's house, guarded by Lieutenant Don Francisco Cartabona and twenty troops. George Rogers Clark is credited with stiffening the resolution of the St. Louis garrison. The Spanish report does not mention his physical presence, but it is known that he was at Kaskaskia around the time of the British attack.

Hesse apparently expected no resistance, and after a brief firefight his effort to take St. Louis collapsed. The invaders did considerable damage in the outlying and undefended farms before withdrawing. Early the next year, in January 1781, a Spanish counteroffensive against Detroit achieved nothing more than the brief occupation of Fort St. Joseph, Michigan.

The original settlement of St. Louis is marked by the 630-foot, stainless steel arch designed by Eero Saarinen and completed in 1965 to symbolize dramatically the city's role as "Gateway to the West." Crowded and obsolescent industrial structures have been cleared from a 91-acre area here as part of the development of the Jefferson National Expansion Memorial, a National Historic Site since 1935. A plaque on the south wall of the Old Courthouse, which is included in the memorial, indicates that Fort San Carlos stood nearby. The site includes the Museum of Westward Expansion, and a thirty-minute documentary film on the making of the Gateway Arch, "Monument to the Dream," is available for visitors to see. The Jefferson National Expansion Memorial is located at 11 North Fourth Street, St. Louis, Mo. 63102. Phone: (314) 655-1700.

NEW HAMPSHIRE

With about eighty thousand inhabitants living mainly along the Atlantic coast when the Revolution started, New Hampshire had a strong Loyalist element. But the Patriots slowly gained control, and New Hampshire led the way in revolutionary activity, capturing Fort William and Mary in December 1774, forcing its native-born royal governor, Sir John Wentworth, to flee in June 1775, and establishing a provisional government in January 1776.

The dramatic victory at Bennington (see BENNINGTON BATTLEFIELD under New York) owed much to the initiative of New Hampshire in raising troops and commissioning John Stark as brigadier general to command them. The Stark House remains standing in Manchester. Prominent in this crisis was John Langdon, whose house is among the many historic landmarks of Portsmouth. Another hero of the Revolution was General John Sullivan, whose memory is preserved in the Sullivan House in Durham. The Strawberry Banke Restoration is a vestige of New Hampshire's original settlement around Portsmouth, and the John Paul Jones House in that city recalls its importance as a shipbuilding center from colonial times until recent years.

New Hampshire's historical marker program was originated in 1955. Texts and locations of markers are given in the pamphlet "New Hampshire Historical Markers," now in its eighth edition (1989). It is published by the New Hampshire Division of Historical Resources, 19 Pillsbury Street, 2nd Floor, Concord, N.H. 03301. Phone: (603) 271-3483 or (603) 271-3558.

Tourist information is available at several state information centers along the New Hampshire Turnpike or by contacting the New Hampshire Division of Travel and Tourism Development. Website: www.visitnh.gov; phone: (603) 271-2665. The address of the New Hampshire Historical Society is 30 Park Street, Concord, N.H. 03301. Phone: (603) 228-6688.

Exeter, Rockingham County. Founded in 1638, Exeter has more Revolutionary landmarks and associations than any other place in the state. New Hampshire's first provincial congress met here on 21 July 1774 and several times in 1775. This same year the capital was moved to Exeter to get away from the powerful Loyalist influences in Portsmouth. Many interesting old buildings have been preserved, and the Exeter Chamber of Commerce offers a walking tour and a booklet describing more than forty sites. Phone (603) 772-2411.

The Ladd-Gilman House, at 1 Governors Lane, was built in 1721. Thirty years later it passed to the Gilman family, which produced two governors and one United States senator, and during the Revolution was the home and office of the state treasurer. The original house was brick, two stories high, with dormer windows. Later modifications included covering the brick with wood siding and making additions that transformed the house into a rambling structure. Furnished in the period of the Revolution, it is part of the American Independence Museum established in 1991, and may be visited by the public from 1 May to 31 October, Wednesday through Saturday from 10 A.M. to 4 P.M. Phone: (603) 772-2622.

The Gilman-Garrison House, 12 Water Street at Clifford Street, started in about 1650 as a "wooden castle" on the Indian frontier. The main part of this rambling structure (for which the Gilman family seemed to have a predilection) was erected by John Gilman as a blockhouse

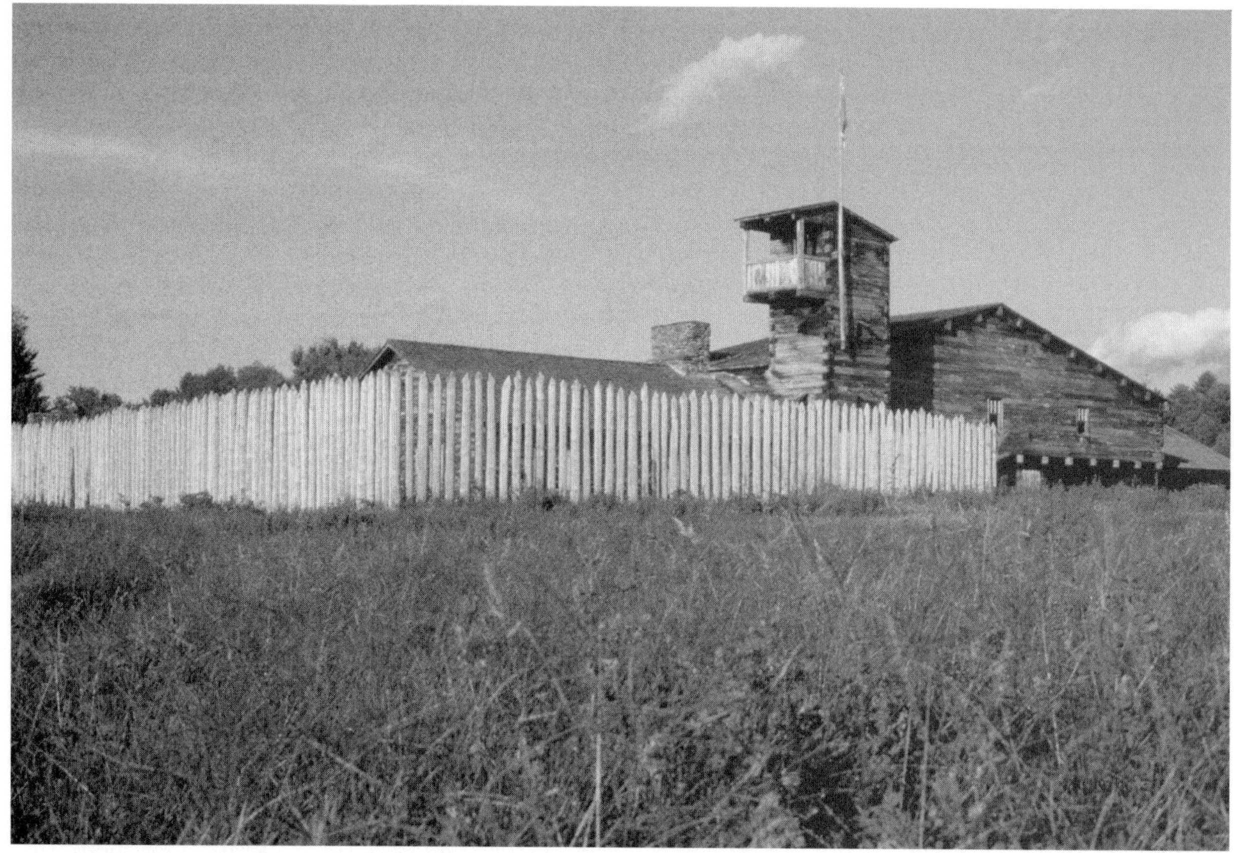

Fort Number Four. *Built near the Connecticut River in Charleston, New Hampshire, during the Colonial Wars, Fort Number Four was a terminus of the Crown Point Military Road, which connected the fort with roads to Boston and Brattleboro, Vermont.* © LEE SNIDER/ PHOTO IMAGES/CORBIS.

of hand-hewn logs, with a second-story overhang and portcullis door. Peter Gilman added the front wing in 1772, when the rustic château fort became an elegant residence in whose elaborately carved and paneled rooms Royal Governor John Wentworth was often entertained. Daniel Webster was a boarder while attending Phillips Exeter Academy in 1796. Furnished in both periods (1650 and 1772), the Gilman-Garrison House is open on a limited schedule. Phone: (603) 436-3205.

Fort Number Four Reconstruction, also known as Fort Stephens, Connecticut River, Charlestown, Sullivan County. On about the same latitude as Fort Edward, New York (start of the portage from the Hudson to Lakes George and Champlain), Fort Number Four was built in 1744 during King George's War. It became a terminus of the Crown Point Military Road (see under VERMONT), which connected here with the road down the west bank to Brattleboro, and another that went southeast through Keene to Boston. The Living History Museum is a reconstruction of the fort and its community in the mid-eighteenth century, with military reenactments and demonstrations of everyday life prior to the Revolution. The fort is open Wednesday to Sunday from June through October. The site is on N.H. 11, 0.5 mile west of N.H. 12 and near Exit 7 of I-91. Phone: (603) 826-5700.

Fort William and Mary Ruins, New Castle. Four months before making his famous ride on the eve of the Battle of Lexington and Concord, Paul Revere rode from Boston to Portsmouth with the news that British authorities had banned the import of military stores by the colonies. The fiery John Sullivan, who had just returned from attending the first Continental Congress, and the Patriot merchant and politician John Langdon, raised a force of four hundred volunteers to take direct action. The next day, 14 December 1774, Captain John Cochran submitted to force majeure, surrendering the fort and its four-man garrison without resistance. Fort William and Mary is therefore remembered as being the scene of one of the first overt acts of armed rebellion leading to the American Revolution, although it is going too far to claim, as some popular writers have, that it was "the first organized fight of the Revolution." It was organized, but there was no fight.

Booty is said to have included about 60 muskets, 16 cannon, and 100 barrels of gunpowder. There seems to be evidence to support the legend that the latter was taken up the frozen Oyster River in gundalows, a channel being cut through the ice, and landed at Sullivan's wharf in Durham. From here it was distributed, some going to other towns and some being hidden under the pulpit of the Durham meeting house (see SULLIVAN HOUSE). Some later went to Boston by oxcart and may have been given back to the British in the Battle of Bunker Hill.

Fort William and Mary was on the site of an earlier earthwork built for protection against pirates. Renamed Fort Constitution, it was manned in 1806 and during the War of 1812. The ruins are officially known as Fort Constitution Historic Site, which is located at Route 1B on the U.S. Coast Guard station. Phone: (603) 436-1552.

New Castle is an attractive little town, its narrow streets lined with houses in the colonial style. In 1873 the town records of 1693 to 1726 were found in Hertfordshire, England, and returned.

Fort Point Lighthouse at the Coast Guard station dates from 1877, but is on the site of the lighthouse built in 1771 to take over as a navigational aid from the improvised system used until that time: a lantern hung from the flagstaff at Fort William and Mary. Opposite the latter fort and part of the defenses of Portsmouth Harbor were the works on Kittery Point mentioned in the article on Kittery (see under MAINE).

Portsmouth, Piscataqua River, Rockingham County. Many houses of great architectural and historic importance remain standing in the present city. Colonial charm survives in the narrow, winding streets of the settlement originally known as Strawberry Banke. The latter community encompassed the territory of Portsmouth, New Castle, Greenland, and most of Rye. The region probably was first settled permanently in 1623 (at Rye), although the date 1630 is also given. In 1653 Strawberry Banke was incorporated as Portsmouth, and in later years portions of the original territory were set apart to form New Castle, Greenland, and Rye.

Portsmouth Navy Yard (1800) evolved from early shipbuilding operations on two islands in the river that are within the township of Kittery, Maine. The sloop *Ranger* was built here, John Paul Jones being appointed its commander on 14 June 1777 and supervising its construction.

Famous men born in Portsmouth include royal governors Benning Wentworth and his son John, the Patriot merchant and postwar governor John Langdon, and Tobias Lear, private secretary to Washington. Five houses in and near Portsmouth are Registered National Historic Landmarks, and most of them are of exceptional architectural importance. The Wentworth-Gardner and Tobias Lear Houses Association operate the sites of those names. Sheafe Warehouse is part of the Prescott Park development, adjacent to the Strawberry Banke Restoration Project.

The major historic sites are:

Governor Benning Wentworth House (Wentworth-Coolidge Mansion), 2 miles south of Portsmouth off U.S. 1A on Little Harbor Road. The oldest part of this rambling frame house was built around 1695. It was enlarged eventually to more than forty rooms, some of which were later removed, so it is of interest in illustrating various periods of construction. Royal Governor Benning Wentworth lived here 1741 to 1766. In the garden are lilacs traced to the first brought to this country. The mansion was given to the state in 1954 by the last owner, J. Templeton Coolidge, who had restored the colonial portions. The entire site encompasses about 65 acres and guided tours are available. It is operated by the State Division of Parks and is open daily from mid-June until Labor day. Phone: (603) 436-6607.

Governor John Langdon House, 143 Pleasant Street. Phone: (603) 436-3205. Built by John Langdon in 1784, this is an elaborately decorated frame mansion within a setting of extensive gardens and flanked by brick gatehouses. Langdon was a wealthy merchant before the Revolution started and held several important political offices during the war. He and John Sullivan led the volunteers who seized Fort William and Mary in 1774, and he commanded militia units at Bennington and Saratoga and in the Newport operations of 1778. He is particularly remembered for organizing and personally financing the militia rally prompted by Burgoyne's advance up Lake Champlain and into the Hudson River Valley in the summer of 1777, the story being told that when New Hampshire authorities could not find the funds, he stepped forth to pledge his personal fortune and to nominate "our friend [John] Stark" to command the forces raised for the emergency. John Langdon was speaker of the state legislature in 1775 and 1777 to 1780, and served in Congress during the years 1775 to 1776, 1786 to 1787, and 1789 to 1801. He declined the post of secretary of the navy (1801) and declined nomination as Republican candidate for vice president (1812), meanwhile being elected governor of New Hampshire every year except 1809 during the years 1805 to 1811. His elder brother, Woodbury Langdon, had a career that was almost as remarkable. The Governor John Langdon Mansion Memorial is open to the public from June through September and operated by the Society for the Preservation of New England Antiquities, whose headquarters is at 141 Cambridge Street, Boston, Mass. 02114. Phone: (617) 227-3956.

John Paul Jones House, 43 Middle Street at State Street. Phone: (603) 436-8420. Captain Gregory Purcell built this frame house in 1758. When he died in 1776 his widow operated it as a "genteel boarding house." John Paul Jones was a paying guest during the period 4 October to 7 November 1782 while supervising the outfitting of the *America.* (Jones lived in Portsmouth while supervising the construction of the sloop *Ranger* in 1777. Many accounts say this was when he stayed with the Widow Purcell, but the more reliable authorities give the later date.) The Portsmouth Historical Society acquired the dignified old gambrel-roofed house in 1920, using it for their headquarters and operating it as a regional museum. The Portsmouth Historical Society can be reached at the phone number previously listed, and through its website: www.portsmouthhistory.org.

Moffat-Ladd House, 154 Market Street. Of considerable architectural importance, this imposing three-story clapboarded mansion was built in 1763 and was once the residence of General William Whipple, a signer of the Declaration of Independence. An unusually large and elegant central hall, rare "Vues d'Italie" wallpaper (printed in Paris during the period 1815–1820), and much original furniture are among the attractions. Home of the New Hampshire Society of Colonial Dames, which also owns the site, it is operated as a house museum from 15 June to 15 October, Monday through Saturday, 11 A.M. to 5 P.M. Phone: (603) 436-8221.

The Richard Jackson House, 76 Northwest Street. Probably the state's oldest frame house, this wooden version of a Stuart-era country house was built about 1664 and occupied by Jackson's descendants for 250 years. The two modern wings were added about 1764. Exterior clapboards are unpainted. (So much for the persistent misconception that painting serves any purpose other than decoration.) Open June through October, the Jackson House is operated by the Society for the Preservation of New England Antiquities. The Jackson House phone is (603) 436-8420.

Strawberry Banke Museum, entrance on Hancock Street. The 10-acre site includes thirty houses, two inns, and a statehouse, and serves as a living history of colonial society. From the Joseph Sherburne House of 1660 to the elegant federal-style Governor Goodwin Mansion of 1811, it is a remarkable museum of early-American architecture. Strawberry Banke was the original name of the English settlement on the Piscataqua River, being derived from the wild strawberries found there. Phone: (603) 433-1100.

Tobias Lear House, 51 Hunking Street. This plain Georgian home was the birthplace of Tobias Lear in 1762. Washington visited it in 1798, when Lear was his private secretary at Mount Vernon and tutor for his two stepchildren. Lear's second and third marriages were to nieces of Martha Washington. In 1935 the Society for the Preservation of New England Antiquities acquired the house, which was then in poor condition. It is now operated by the Wentworth-Gardner and Lear Houses Association. Phone: (603) 436-4406.

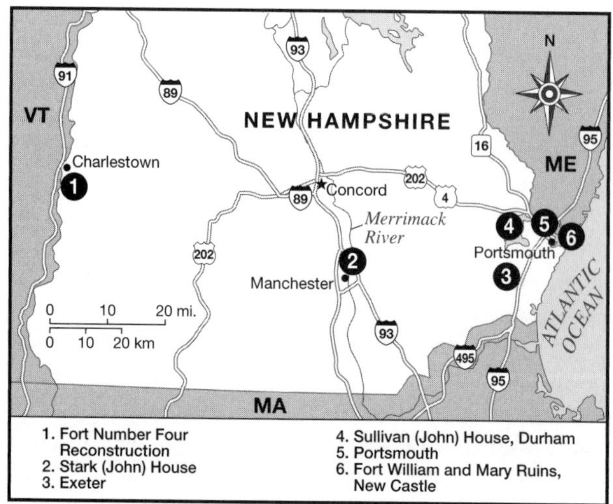

MAP BY XNR PRODUCTIONS. THE GALE GROUP.

Warner House (more precisely called the Macpheadris-Warner House), 150 Daniel Street at Chapel Street. Long classified as a National Historic Landmark, this house was built about 1716 by a wealthy merchant, Archibald Macpheadris. His daughter married Jonathan Warner, who was prominent in town and provincial affairs. The three-story brick mansion has walls 18 inches thick and is considered to be one of the finest early eighteenth-century urban brick dwellings in New England. Many of the furnishings are on loan from outstanding collections, including the Metropolitan Museum of Art in New York. Owned until 1931 by descendants of Captain Macpheadris and Jonathan Warner, the house has undergone no major alteration. It is well maintained by the Warner House Association and open June through October. Website: www.warnerhouse.org; phone: (603) 436-8420.

Wentworth-Gardner House, 140 Mechanic Street at Gardner Street. An exceptionally fine example of Georgian architecture, this house was built in 1760 as a present from his mother to Thomas Wentworth, a brother of the last royal governor. The two-and-a-half-story frame house with hipped roof and rusticated wooden facade of pine clapboards was built by ships' carpenters. Fine carving is featured inside and out. The front door has a gilded pineapple, the symbol of hospitality, in its unusual broken-scroll pediment. Scenic wallpaper and original Dutch tiles accent the splendid paneling and carved woodwork of the interior. The site is operated by the Wentworth-Gardner and Tobias Lear Houses Association, and the touring season begins in June. Phone: (603) 436-1552.

Stark (John) House, Manchester, Hillsborough County. Still standing in what is now the state's largest town is the small frame house in which General John Stark (1728–1822) spent his boyhood and early married life. The one-and-a-half-story Cape Cod structure with central chimney and wing was built about 1737 by John's father, Archibald, who moved his family to this area from Londonderry, New Hampshire. (John's birthplace in the latter town is no longer standing, but the site is marked by a stone on the east side of N.H. 28, 2.3 miles south of the Derry Rotary.) The Stark House has five large rooms on the ground floor, two in the second story, and is a good example of the colonial farmhouses of the region. Originally at 1070 Canal Street but moved to 2000 Elm Street, it was restored in 1969. The house is owned by the Molly Stark chapter of the DAR and is shown by appointment only.

About 1760 John Stark built himself a house in Manchester, where he and Molly raised eleven children on their large farm. This house burned in the 1860s. Its site is on the west side of North River Road, in front of the state industrial school. The "Stark Well" and a plaque on a boulder mark the location. The family cemetery is preserved in Stark Park, on the east side of North River Road and north of the Amoskeag Bridge. One very large stone has replaced the several original headstones of family graves except General Stark's, which has an obelisk monument. In the park is a large equestrian statue of the Revolutionary War hero.

The unmarked location of Stark Fort, believed to have been a small palisaded work built in 1746, is in Manchester near Nutts Pond. About 10 miles northwest of Manchester in Dunbarton, established by General Stark and originally called Starksville, is the Stark Mansion, said to have been built by General Stark for his son Caleb. It is a very handsome and large structure that was occupied by Caleb's descendants until the 1930s. Also in Dunbarton is the surviving childhood home of Elizabeth Page, who became Molly Stark.

Stark was reared as a woodsman and Indian fighter on the New England frontier, where his Scots-Irish father had settled in 1720. During the Seven Years' War he took part in Sir William Johnson's operations around what is now Lake George Village, New York, after which he was an officer in Rogers' Rangers. Coming home a military hero in 1759, he had meanwhile found time to marry. At Bunker Hill, where he showed genius as a commander of militia troops, Stark took another step toward becoming an American legend and one of the country's most widely quoted heroes. Whether he actually used the words attributed to him is unlikely (the "direct quotes" vary considerably in form), but no historian denies that the quotes are in character. "One fresh man in action is worth ten fatigued men," he is quoted as saying when leading his green troops toward Bunker Hill and refusing to hurry them through the frightening but ineffective naval gunfire that was falling on Charles Town Neck. "Boys, aim at their waistbands," he said calmly to his nervous troops as they awaited his order to open fire on the advancing British column along the beach. Whether Stark's troops understood the military wisdom behind those words is doubtful, but the result was not.

Stark is most famous for his victory at Bennington (see BENNINGTON BATTLEFIELD under New York), where he is alleged to have inspired his troops with the words, "There, my boys, are your enemies. . . . We'll beat them before night, or Molly Stark will be a widow." (This combines two of the many versions of what Stark is supposed to have said.) After that battle, Stark cut off Burgoyne's retreat by taking a position on the high ground that has since been called Stark's Knob, New York.

After the Revolution he retired to his large farm and large family, refusing to become involved in public affairs. He died at Manchester a few months before his ninety-fourth birthday.

The Manchester Historic Association, established in 1896, is remarkable for its efficiency and vigor. In its Millyard Museum many of Stark's personal possessions and artifacts are kept. They include furniture, firearms, traps, and other personal belongs. In addition, there hangs a beautiful portrait of the general. The mailing address for the Manchester Historic Association is 129 Amherst Street, Manchester, N.H. 03104. Phone: (603) 622-7531.

Sullivan (John) House, Durham, Strafford County. On 23 New Market Road (N.H. 108) beside the Oyster River in Durham is the substantial country house built in 1716 and bought by John Sullivan (1740–1795) in 1764. The house is privately owned and rarely shown, but the small cemetery of the Sullivan family on a hill east of the house is maintained by the state. In front of General Sullivan's grave and house is a monument erected in 1894 and said to be on the site of the meetinghouse where powder from Fort William and Mary was temporarily stored.

The controversial Sullivan was the son of Irish redemptioners who had come to America some seventeen years before his birth. Educated mainly by his father, a schoolmaster, John studied law with Judge Samuel Livermore of Portsmouth before settling in Durham soon after 1760. Here he became an able and prosperous lawyer, major of militia (1772), and delegate to the first Continental Congress (1774) before playing a leading part in the seizure of Fort William and Mary in December 1774. After taking his seat in the Second Continental Congress, Sullivan was appointed a brigadier general of the Continental army in June 1775. During the siege of Boston he commanded a brigade, later leading reinforcements to Canada, taking over from General John Thomas when the latter died, and storming back to protest to Congress the arrival of General Horatio Gates to supersede him. In August 1776, having been prevailed on to remain in the army, Sullivan was promoted to major general. During the next three years he was prominently engaged in military and political action, showing considerably more aptitude in the latter field.

The final military operation of General Sullivan was his campaign in western New York that virtually destroyed the Iroquois, opening the way for the wave of settlement after the Revolution but failing in its alleged primary purpose of eliminating border raids by the Iroquois. Before leaving the army on grounds of ill health, he secured from as many of his officers as would sign it a statement endorsing his actions during this early-American "search and destroy" operation. (The SULLIVAN-CLINTON EXPEDITION is covered under New York.)

Resigning his military commission on 30 November 1779, Sullivan was promptly reelected to Congress. He was almost immediately in the limelight after his brother Daniel, fatally ill after imprisonment by the British, brought him a peace feeler from the enemy. General Sullivan refused to respond personally, but brought the matter to the attention of Chevalier de Luzerne, who had recently arrived as France's second ambassador to the American government. Because the heavy-spending and usually broke Sullivan had borrowed money from Luzerne, he naturally was suspected of being in the pay of the French, especially after Sullivan suported the French demand that the Americans limit their westward expansion. The charge of bribery has been discredited, but it further reveals the man's character.

Back in New Hampshire politics, the Revolutionary hero was attorney general from 1782 to 1786, when he was elected to the first of two successive one-year terms as governor. In 1789 he was elected for his third term and also appointed United States district judge of New Hampshire. He held the latter position until his death at Durham in 1795.

The Durham Historic Association is at Main Street, Durham, N.H. 03824. Phone: (603) 868-5436.

NEW JERSEY

Little remains in modern New Jersey as a reminder that the region was first colonized by the Dutch and Swedes, who came primarily as traders. But when the British gained suzerainty over New Netherland, they quickly took steps to establish permanent settlements. The Duke of York's Proprietary, granted in 1664 by Charles II to his brother the Duke of York, the future James II, included the present state of New Jersey, which got its name at this time from the Channel island of Jersey, where Charles II had been given refuge in 1650.

Conflicting land claims were long a problem in the new colony, but suffice it to say here that in 1676 a line was drawn dividing it into East and West Jersey. In 1702 "the Jerseys" were united as a royal province though the region continued to have political, social, economic, and cultural differences reflecting its division by the boundary line of the seventeenth century. East Jersey was dominated by New England Puritanism and economically oriented toward the metropolis of New York; West Jersey was dominated by the Quakers, with William Penn and his associates in a controlling role and with an economic orientation toward Philadelphia.

Today's visitor to New Jersey will find many reminders of the state's split personality in the colonial era. There are surviving segments of the Province Line Road. Architectural landmarks and place-names of the Swedish presence are along the Delaware in western New Jersey, whereas their Dutch equivalents are on the other fringe of the state. (Bergen, founded by the Dutch in 1618, is New Jersey's oldest permanent settlement.) In Burlington and Perth Amboy, old capitals of the two Jerseys, vestigial land rights of the original signers of the agreement of 1676 are preserved by the Boards of Proprietors of East and West Jersey.

After a slow start in European settlement, the population of New Jersey grew from about 15,000 in 1702 to about 140,000 at the outbreak of the American Revolution. The state has been called "Cockpit of the Revolution," an apt designation because it was a major theater of military operations as the main American and British armies swept back and forth between New York City and Philadelphia. Late in 1776 the British conquered almost all of the state, only to be driven back by Washington's brilliant actions at Trenton and Princeton. The last major action in the North was on the Monmouth Battlefield in 1778, but before and after this there was serious fighting and much maneuvering when the British advanced from bases in New York, Perth Amboy, and New Brunswick toward Washington's campsites around Morristown and Middlebrook.

Meanwhile, the rich farms of New Jersey had drawn foragers from both armies to regions spared by the main armies (see SALEM), a considerable amount of skirmishing took place between Loyalist and Patriot militia units, and the Jersey coast became a hotbed of privateering (see LITTLE EGG HARBOR MASSACRE SITE). The Raritan River was a base for such "whaleboat warriors," as Adam Hyler and his New Brunswick rivermen armed themselves to conduct raids on British ships around New York.

Much of the terrain that figured so prominently in battles and skirmishes of the Revolution has been paved over by urban development, particularly in the heavily industrialized portion of the state adjacent to New York City. Most landmarks have long since been razed and landforms obliterated so as to make a personal visit unproductive. This guide touches only lightly on this heavily built-up region, but the Bergen County Historical Society is active, and one of its members, Adrian C. Leiby, published *The Revolutionary War in the Hackensack Valley* (Rutgers University Press, 1980). This is an excellent source of information on landmarks in Bergen and Hudson counties.

Many other parts of New Jersey are surprisingly unspoiled. The Pine Barrens, scene of Revolutionary War bushwacking, privateer operations, and skirmishes between foraging parties, still have large areas of wilderness. Hikers will find many historic landmarks that are inaccessible to road-bound travelers. So much of the war in this region having been amphibious, such places as Sandy Hook, the privateering centers, Cape May, and the sites of the Delaware River forts can be seen properly only by boat. Canoeists are fortunate in having available the fourth revised edition of *Exploring the Little Rivers of New Jersey*, by James and Margaret Cawley (Rutgers University Press, 1993).

The state has no published guide to historical markers and no system of official information centers. Individual historians and popular writers have played a greater role in preserving New Jersey's Revolutionary War heritage than government officials. Some of their works are identified above, and others in the articles that follow. One of these came from novelist and historian Alfred Hoyt Bill, who published the 128-page *New Jersey and the Revolutionary War* (Rutgers University Press, 1992). Another, more recent source for this state's Revolutionary War accounts and landmarks is Mark Di Ionno's *A Guide to New Jersey's Revolutionary War Trail: For Families and History Buffs* (Rutgers University Press, 2000).

The New Jersey Historical Commission offices are at 225 West State Street, Trenton, N.J. 08625. Phone: (609) 292-6062; website: www.newjerseyhistory.org. The New Jersey Historical Society is located in the middle of Newark's art district at 52 Park Place. The museum is open Tuesday through Saturday, 10 A.M. to 5 P.M., and the library is open from 12 P.M. to 5 P.M. on the same days. Phone: (973) 596-8500; website: www.jerseyhistory.org.

Basking Ridge Sites, Somerset County. The Widow White's Tavern, where General Charles Lee was captured by a British patrol on Friday, 13 December 1776, had undergone many changes before it was razed about 1950. The site, which remains unmarked, is at the southwest corner of South Finley Avenue and Colonial Drive. A blue state marker on Lord Stirling Road indicates the site of the General William Alexander ("Lord Stirling") estate. Still standing are two small brick buildings, believed to have been slave quarters.

Batsto Historic Site, Mullica River, Batsto, Burlington County. In the Pine Barrens, about 10 miles east of Hammonton on N.J. Route 542, is this recent restoration of a community that produced bog-iron products (including cannon for the Revolution) and glass from 1766 until abandoned in 1848. The Manor House (c. 1750) is all that remains to indicate the wealth of this portion of the huge Joseph Wharton estate, but the restoration includes workmen's cottages, a gristmill, sawmill, blacksmith and wheelwright shops, general store, and the oldest known fully operating post office in America. Batsto Village has been put on the National Register. As of 2004 the entire site, including the Manor House, the museum, and the visitors center underwent renovation. Guided tours are offered three times a day, seven days a week, but it is advisable to call for a reservation. Hours of operation are daily from dawn to dusk. Phone: (609) 561-0024. Website: www.batstovillage.org.

Baylor Massacre Site, Hackensack River, Bergen County. The mass grave and several surviving houses of the so-called Old Tappan Massacre of September 1778 are marked on County Road 53 (Rivervale Road) between Routes 116 (Old Tappan Road) and 90–132 (Prospect and Washington Avenues). The mass grave is in a park on Red Oak Drive a few hundred yards east of Rivervale Road. Bodies of American dragoons had been buried in tanning vats, and the site was long marked by a millstone used in the tanning operation. About the time of the Civil War the stone was dragged away, and in recent years only a few people in the vicinity remembered being told where it had been located. In 1967 Mr. Thomas Demarest of Old Tappan took the initiative in seeing that archaeological work was done to locate the graves before they were permanently lost. After two weeks of digging, the first human remains were found. Uniform buttons with the cipher "LD" (Light Dragoons), silver stock buckles, and other artifacts established beyond doubt that the searchers had found what they were looking for. Parts of six bodies were accounted for when all the vats were found and explored. The official casualty list was eleven Patriots killed outright and four who died of wounds in the area. Either this is wrong, or there are other, undiscovered graves.

Patriot propagandists raised the cry of "massacre" whenever their troops were badly beaten and sustained heavy casualties. At Old Tappan the dragoons commanded by the young and inexperienced Colonel George Baylor had the misfortune of being staked out for attack by forces under Major General Charles Grey, who was famous for his "massacre" of Anthony Wayne's command at Paoli, Pennsylvania. Helped by Loyalist guides, the regulars approached Baylor's position under cover of darkness, killed or captured a twelve-man security outpost at the bridge across the Hackensack just south of the Patriot camp, and caught about one hundred dragoons asleep in three barns along what ironically was then called Overkill Road (now Rivervale Road). Baylor and his second in command, Major Alexander Clough, were among the casualties, only thirty-seven of the 104 enlisted men escaping unhurt. Clough died of wounds several days later; Baylor recovered sufficiently to take command of another dragoon regiment after being exchanged, but he died a few years later of his wounds.

Congress ordered an investigation of the alleged massacre, affidavits collected from survivors indicated that one soldier had received sixteen stab wounds and three others received twelve. The exhumed bodies support the atrocity charges; the skull of one man shows a fracture that almost certainly was caused by the butt stroke of a Brown Bess inflicted when the victim was on the ground.

In 1972 the site of the mass grave was developed into a 2-acre county park. The millstone has been restored to its former position here, after having been donated to the River Vale Board of Education by a descendant of the farmer who had it hauled out of his field and after standing for years on the lawn of the Holdrum School. The exact location of the six barns occupied by the dragoons is not known. Historical markers on Rivervale Road (County Road 53) between Old Tappan Road and Prospect Avenue indicate surviving landmarks. (The Colonel Cornelius house can be seen from the road. A nursing home is on the site of the Haring house where Baylor and Clough were trapped.) Much of the area remains unspoiled by modern construction except just north of the burial site, where a housing development has been planted in the last few years. The county bought three building lots for the park, where the mass gravesite will be preserved in a landscaped area alongside the river. The area where the British formed for their attack is now covered by the Edgewood Country Club.

Historical inquiries may be directed to the Bergen County Historical Society. Phone: (201) 343-9492; website: www.bergancountyhistory.org.

Bound Brook, Raritan River, Somerset County. The present bridge over the Raritan between Bound Brook and South Bound Brook is the site of the important skirmish that took place on 13 April 1777. While the main American army was still in winter quarters at Morristown, an outpost of about five hundred Continentals and militia was here at Bound Brook under the command of General Benjamin Lincoln. About 7 miles southeast at New Brunswick were eight thousand British and German troops. Cornwallis left the latter base with about two thousand regulars on a foraging expedition. The militia outposts around the bridge on the Raritan at Bound Brook were careless, permitting Cornwallis to cross the river and threaten the isolated American position with encirclement by superior forces. Lincoln was able to get away, thanks largely to the personal efforts of Lieutenant Simon Spalding, but he lost his artillery detachment. Cornwallis withdrew with about twenty-five prisoners and the captured guns as General Nathanael Greene approached with a relief column.

An ancient granite monument marking the site of the skirmish has been moved a few feet from its original position in the dangerous intersection just north of the bridge to the side yard of the Pillar of Fire ("Holy Jumper") Temple at 519 Main Street. The inscription says Cornwallis had four thousand troops, but other authorities put the figure at about two thousand. East of the road leading to the bridge from Main Street are markers pertaining to the colonial history of this site, but the entire area is covered with run-down commercial structures. Traffic conditions make sightseeing by car dangerous.

A short distance north of Bound Brook is the site of Washington's Middlebrook Encampment.

Boxwood Hall (Boudinot House), 1073 East Jersey Street, Elizabeth. This mansion, saved from demolition in the late 1930s, restored through a WPA project, and open since 1943 as a historic house museum, was built about 1750 by the mayor of Elizabethtown. It is listed as a National Historic Landmark. During the years 1772 to 1795 it was the home of Elias Boudinot (1740–1821), a man of fine appearance, considerable scholarship, many good works, and great wealth. Alexander Hamilton lived with the Boudinots briefly while getting some schooling in Elizabethtown before entering King's College (Columbia) in 1773. In later years he was a frequent visitor to Boxwood Hall. In June 1777 Boudinot was made commissary general of prisoners, his task being to deal with the British on behalf of American prisoners in enemy hands. The journal he kept during the Revolution was published in 1894 and is an important primary source. Elected to Congress in 1777, he did not attend until July of the next year, but then served until 1784. He was president of that body for a year, starting on 4 November 1782. In June 1783 he became acting secretary of foreign affairs. Back in Congress in 1789, he was a Federalist. He left the House of Representatives to succeed David Rittenhouse as director of the mint, holding this office during the years 1795 to 1805 and leaving Boxwood Hall for a new home in Philadelphia. He then retired to study biblical literature, attempting to prove that the American Indians might be descendants of the Ten Lost Tribes of Israel and taking a leading part in the establishment of the American Bible Society. He became that organization's first president, is credited by some with originating Thanksgiving Day, and was a trustee and benefactor of the College of New Jersey (now Princeton University) from 1772 until his death in 1821.

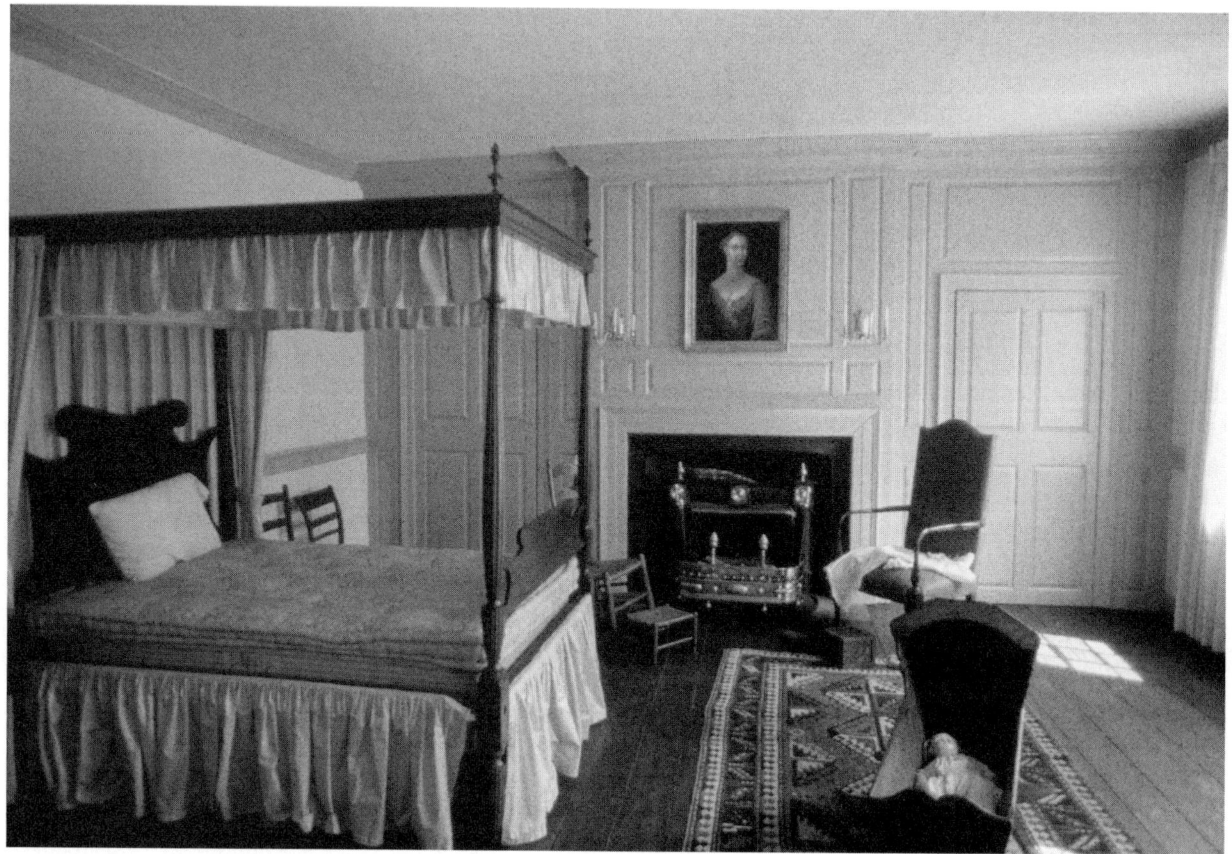

Boxwood Hall, Bedroom. *Boxwood Hall was built around 1750 by the mayor of Elizabethtown, New Jersey, and served for many years as the home of U.S. Congressman Elias Boudinot.* © LEE SNIDER/PHOTO IMAGES/CORBIS.

Boxwood Hall is associated with the controversial story of Reverend and Mrs. James Caldwell. The latter was killed during the British attack on Connecticut Farms in June 1780, and her husband was killed by a sentinel at Elizabethtown Port in January 1782. American patriots then and since have contended that both were martyrs killed by British bullets, but there is evidence that the bullets were fired by Americans. Be that as it may, the body of James Caldwell was publicly displayed before the door of Boxwood Hall, and Elias Boudinot made a speech on the occasion.

Lafayette was an overnight guest in 1824. After having several owners, Boxwood Hall was inherited by William C. DeHart, who undertook to ruin it. In 1870 he demolished the two wings, superimposed two stories, added a rear service wing, and leased it as a boarding house. Later it became the Home for Aged Women of Elizabeth. The restoration has undone much of the damage, but the wings remain clipped and the boxwood-bordered avenue from the river to the front door is gone with the wind. Boxwood Hall is owned and operated by the state of New Jersey. Hours of operation are Wednesday through Saturday from 10 A.M. to 6 P.M. and Sunday from 1 P.M. to 6 P.M.

Burlington, Delaware River, Burlington County. Many colonial buildings remain in this city that for more than a century was the capital of the province of West Jersey. The Revell House, 215213 Wood Street, was built in 1685, making it the oldest in the county; according to tradition this is where Benjamin Franklin stopped on his way to Philadelphia in 1723 and was given gingerbread by an old lady, as recounted in his autobiography. At High and Pearl Streets is the little building where Franklin's print shop was operated in 1728 and where Isaac Collins printed money for the province in 1776. From the site of Burlington Wharf, at the foot of High Street, the strategically important ferry operated from 1685 until the present bridge was built. At the foot of Wood Street was the residence of William Franklin, son of Benjamin Franklin and last royal governor, 1763 to 1774.

Burlington figured prominently in the strategy of the war from December 1776 until June 1778. Justifying his wide dispersal of troops along the Delaware before the

British disaster at Trenton, General Sir William Howe wrote on 20 December 1776: "The chain [of advanced posts], I own, is rather too extensive, but I was induced to occupy Burlington to cover the County of Monmouth, in which there are many loyal inhabitants." But this forced Washington to extend his own defenses of the Delaware down this far on the opposite bank, Burlington being one of the places where the British could cross the river in renewing the offensive against Philadelphia. The German garrison of Burlington was withdrawn after the first Battle of Trenton, and before making his move to Princeton, Washington sent his baggage, stores, and three heaviest guns to Burlington with a strong escort.

When the British evacuated Philadelphia in June 1778, they moved through Burlington en route to Bordentown before striking out for what became the Monmouth Battlefield. New Jersey's first newspaper (excepting *The Plain Dealer*, published for eight weeks in 1775 and 1776 at Matthew Potter's tavern in Bridgeton), the *New Jersey Gazette*, was established at Burlington in 1777 and became influential during the Revolution. In his wild efforts to justify his conduct in the Battle of Monmouth, General Charles Lee used this paper as one of his many channels for taking his case to the public. "A note of [Lee's] to the printer of the Burlington paper savors of insanity or flows from worse sources," wrote General Anthony Wayne in a letter of 16 July 1778.

Further information on other local historic landmarks is available from the Burlington County Historical Society, 451 High Street, Burlington, N.J. 08016. Phone: (609) 386-4773. Guided tours, children's programs, a museum, and a research library are available from 1 P.M. to 5 P.M., Tuesday through Saturday. The Society occupies the James Fenimore Cooper House, where the author was born in 1789. Adjoining is the James Lawrence House, where this naval hero of the War of 1812 was born in 1781.

Camden. *See* COOPER'S FERRY.

Chestnut Neck, Mullica River, Atlantic County. A boatyard covers the ruins of this little village that played such a large part as a center of American privateering during the Revolution. Sir Henry Clinton decided in the fall of 1778 that the time had come to clean out what he called "a nest of rebel pirates," and he gave the job to the remarkable Patrick Ferguson. Then only a captain but famous as inventor of a good breech-loading rifle and as a resourceful commander of independent operations, Ferguson spent three weeks laying waste to a long stretch of the Mullica River, burning ten large vessels and destroying shipyards, storehouses, and Patriot homes. He burned the entire village of Chestnut Neck, which comprised the fort, Payne Tavern, Adams Landing, several storehouses, and about a dozen homes. In the course of his operations he surprised Pulaski's Legion in a raid (see LITTLE EGG HARBOR MASSACRE SITE).

The site of the village of Chestnut Neck is privately owned and access is restricted, but it may eventually be developed as a historic landmark. In 1950 the area of the colonial village was surveyed by Paul C. Burgess, who located the ruins of eleven homes, the fort, and other public structures mentioned above. Some archaeological exploration has been done, and it appears that the ruins have been protected so far from destruction because they lie about 3 feet below ground level. Freak weather in March 1971 exposed much of the river bottom around Chestnut Neck and revealed several sunken ships, tons of English ballast stones, anchors, and other items. The Mullica River from Chestnut Neck to the Batsto Historic Site is one of the few remaining unspoiled waterways in New Jersey, and Great Bay is good for sailing.

Chestnut Neck Battle Monument, erected in 1911 by the General Lafayette Chapter of DAR, is on U.S. 9 near the junction of County Road 575, about 2 miles northeast of Port Republic.

Cooper's Ferry (Camden), Delaware River. First settled in 1679, for the most part by Quakers, this was nothing more than a few houses known variously as Pluckemin, the Ferry, and Cooper's Ferry until after the American Revolution. Jacob Cooper laid out the town in about 1773, naming it in honor of Lord Chancellor Camden, but it was not chartered under that name until 1828. The place was important as the ferry on the main colonial road through Philadelphia.

In the present city there is only one significant vestige of early American architecture, Pomona Hall. This is a handsome house whose early part was begun in 1726 by Joseph Cooper Jr., with a later part built in 1788 by his nephew, Marmaduke Cooper. The two-and-a-half-story house of "tapestry" brickwork (including the builder's initials) is located at 1900 Park Avenue in Camden, and is the home of the Camden Historical Society. Phone: (856) 964-3333. Pomona Hall is open to the public Wednesday through Sunday afternoons and is furnished with some exceptional pieces of furniture, and features a handsome staircase. A modern building adjoining Pomona Hall has a good research library of local history, a museum, and a museum store.

Coryell's Ferry, Delaware River. See under PENNSYLVANIA. The New Jersey end of this strategic crossing was in today's Lambertville.

Cranbury, Middlesex County. One of New Jersey's oldest European settlements and a place mentioned in the military operations of 1776 and 1778 (see MONMOUTH BATTLEFIELD), Cranbury has so far remained an attractive old village at the center of fast-moving industrial and residential construction. On Main Street are several pre-Revolutionary structures, including the Newold House (c. 1750). The old Post House, built during the Revolution and renamed the United States Hotel around 1780, is now the Cranbury Inn. The Cranbury Museum has recently been established in a small frame house dating from the Civil War era. It is located at 4 Park Place East and is open on Sunday afternoons. Phone: (609) 655-2611 or (609) 395-0702.

Crosswicks, Burlington County. Destruction of the bridge and the skirmish here on 23 June 1778, a few days before the Battle of Monmouth, gave Washington valuable intelligence about the route General Clinton was taking in his withdrawal from Philadelphia to New York. Chesterfield Friends Meeting House (1773) was hit three times by American cannon in the course of this delaying action against General Knyphausen's column. A ball remains lodged in the north wall, and scars on the floor at the western end of the interior may have been made by British gun carriages. In December 1776 the church had been occupied by Patriot troops under General John Cadwalader, who crossed the Delaware too late to take part in the Trenton raid but who joined Washington in time for the Princeton campaign.

The little village is exceptionally attractive today, having many interesting buildings that preserve an unreconstructed eighteenth-century appearance. Its famous church is, however, the landmark for which Crosswicks is best known. The large, rectangular structure of aged brick—some of it salvaged from the older structure of 1706—is set in a huge yard. The Crosswicks Oak in the southwest corner of the yard has a plaque proclaiming that the tree was standing when William Penn reached America in 1682. An old wagon shed and other outbuildings are on the grounds.

Dey Mansion, Preakness Valley Park, Passaic County. Washington's headquarters in July and November 1780, this Georgian manor house was built about 1740 for Colonel Theunis Dey by his father, Dirck. Owned by the town of Wayne since 1930, it is a gambrel-roofed, two-and-a-half-story structure of Dutch aspect in which various building materials are combined in an interesting and pleasing manner. The house and garden have been restored. Dey Mansion is located at 199 Totowa Road and is open to the public from 1 P.M. to 4 P.M. on Wednesday, Thursday, and Friday, and from 10 A.M. to 4 P.M. on Saturday and Sunday. Phone: (973) 696-1776.

Elizabeth, Union County. Several important structures of the colonial and Revolutionary War periods have survived in the urban atmosphere that has grown considerably in the past two centuries around Newark Bay. Because of its many Revolutionary War associations, Boxwood Hall (Boudinot House) has been covered separately. The section on SPRINGFIELD gives the story of the two British raids in June 1780 in which Elizabethtown and its "fighting parson," James Caldwell, figured so prominently. His church (the First Presbyterian) and the nearby academy were burned in an earlier raid of January 1780, when record-breaking cold weather permitted the British to cross from Staten Island on the ice. The present structure, dating from 1786, is particularly handsome, and the old burying ground has several graves of famous Americans. The Belcher-Ogden Mansion (c. 1680), 1046 East Jersey Street, is of exceptional importance from the architectural as well as the historical standpoint. Tours are offered by appointment. Phone: (908) 351-2500. Other landmarks, all private, are the Bonnell House, 1045 Jersey Avenue at the northwest corner of Catherine Street; outbuildings of the Crane House, 556 Morris Avenue at Cherry Street; "Liberty Hall," west side of Morris Avenue opposite State Teachers College, open to the public Wednesday to Saturday, 10 A.M. to 4 P.M., and Sunday, noon to 4 P.M. from April through December; and the Wilcox House, 1000 Magie Avenue.

Englishtown, Monmouth County. A few miles northwest of the Monmouth Battlefield and on the Patriot army's line of march to that place, Englishtown has two surviving structures of the Revolution. One is the Village Inn, built in 1726, which was Washington's headquarters after the battle. Well preserved and identified by historical markers in the very center of town (intersection of Water Street and Main Street), the inn is operated by the Battleground Historical Society and features a variety of historical exhibits. A few doors away on N.J. 522 is the two-story frame building that was the home of Moses Laird, Washington's guide before the battle and his host afterward. The building is a private residence.

Five Mile Creek (or Run). This name is frequently applied to the main battle of Colonel Edward Hand's delaying action on the eve of the Battle of Princeton, 2 January 1777. The decisive skirmish actually took place about a mile farther south at Shabakunk Creek.

Fort Lee, community of Fort Lee, Hudson River. The western terminus of the George Washington Bridge and urban development have permanently destroyed most of this historic site. On the 300-foot bluff near the river, the sites of some outer works of Fort Lee are preserved within Palisades Interstate Park. The fortification area west of the ravine is divided among various private owners. Proposals have been made to explore and restore the site, but there is not much left with which to work.

Forts Lee and Washington were built to defend the Hudson River from British naval operations. Work started in the summer of 1776. But Fort Washington was captured with a tremendous loss of personnel and matériel on 16 November 1776, and the Patriots were forced to abandon Fort Lee a few days later, leaving most of their matériel behind to save the two thousand troops stationed there. The British had moved surprisingly fast. Lord Cornwallis with about six thousand regulars landed about 6 miles above Fort Lee at Closter Dock (around modern Alpine in Palisades Park; a historic marker to his scaling of the Palisades is on U.S. 9W). But word of this attempted envelopment reached Washington in time.

The Palisades Interstate Park Commission renovated the Kearney House in 2003. This historic building is listed on the National and State Historic Registries as the "Blackledge-Kearney House" and is sometimes referred to as the Cornwallis Headquarters. It is the oldest surviving structure in Palisades Interstate Park. Phone: (201) 768-1360.

Fort Mercer, Red Bank Battlefield Park, Delaware River near the town of National Park, Gloucester County. Fort Mercer was a large earthwork with fourteen cannon that defended one end of the river barrier extending to Fort Mifflin, Pennsylvania. These two forts were part of a system designed to defend Philadelphia from amphibious assault along the line of the Delaware River. The existence of these river defenses shaped the British strategy of avoiding the direct approach up the Delaware and attacking Philadelphia in 1777 via Head of Elk, Maryland, Cooch's Bridge, Delaware, and the Brandywine, Pennsylvania. After taking Philadelphia on 26 September and repulsing Washington's audacious counteroffensive at Germantown on 4 October, the British had to spend almost two months reducing the Delaware River defenses and establishing a relatively secure line of communications to Philadelphia. Fort Mercer was the last nut the invaders had to crack, and it proved to be a hard one.

Colonel Christopher Greene commanded the garrison of about four hundred Rhode Island troops assigned to the defense of Fort Mercer. New Jersey militia declined to answer the call to reinforce the Continentals, with the result that last-minute changes had to be made in the lines of the earthwork. On the orders of the French engineer assigned to Fort Mercer (Captain, later brevet Lieutenant Colonel, du Plessis), a new wall was built to cut off the northern wing. The attack by two thousand Hessians on 22 October 1777 was brilliantly repulsed by Greene, who had his men hold fire until the Germans were at point-blank range. Colonel Von Donop was fatally wounded and about a third of his 1,200 troops engaged were killed or wounded, whereas Greene had fewer than forty killed and wounded.

Fort Mifflin, across the river, was abandoned about three weeks later, making Fort Mercer no longer tenable. Lord Cornwallis was approaching with two thousand British troops for another assault when Greene successfully evacuated his position the night of 20 to 21 November.

Traces of the moat are preserved in the 20-acre battlefield park, and remnants of Fort Mercer can be found in the northern section of the park. Also standing is the James Whitall House, in whose orchard Fort Mercer was built and where Von Donop and other wounded Hessians were tended. The stone kitchen wing is believed to date from the early 1700s; the main section of the brick house was built in 1748. The park is located at 100 Hessian Avenue and is open from 9 A.M. to 4 P.M., Wednesday through Friday, and 1 P.M. to 5 P.M. on Saturday and Sunday. Phone: (856) 853-5120. The Whitall House is open to the public for tours on Wednesday through Sunday. For further information, contact the Gloucester County Historical Society. Museum phone: (856) 848-8531.

Freehold (Monmouth Courthouse), Monmouth County. When the tired British army in its withdrawal from Philadelphia to New York reached this place on the afternoon of 26 June 1778, they found a village of a few dwellings scattered around a courthouse. The area northeast of Freehold, where Patriot forces under General Charles Lee undertook his mismanaged operations on the morning of the Battle of Monmouth, is covered by modern construction. Some of the preliminary maneuvers, however, may still be traced on the ground. The nearby Monmouth Battlefield, on the other hand, is remarkably well preserved.

Within the present commercial city, best known to visitors for the attraction of its harness-racing events, are several important Revolutionary War sites. The present courthouse is where the original one stood in 1778 and where the British wounded were left. St. Peter's Episcopal Church, occupied by troops of both sides, is still in use and was recently restored. The Craig House survives from the Revolution and has been refurbished to reflect its mid-eighteenth-century style. Guided tours of the farmhouse are available, and interested parties should call for scheduling. Phone: (908) 462-9616.

Hankinson Mansion, known as the Covenhoven House, 150 West Main Street, is the major surviving landmark. It was used by the British commander, Sir Henry Clinton, the night before the Battle of Monmouth. Built

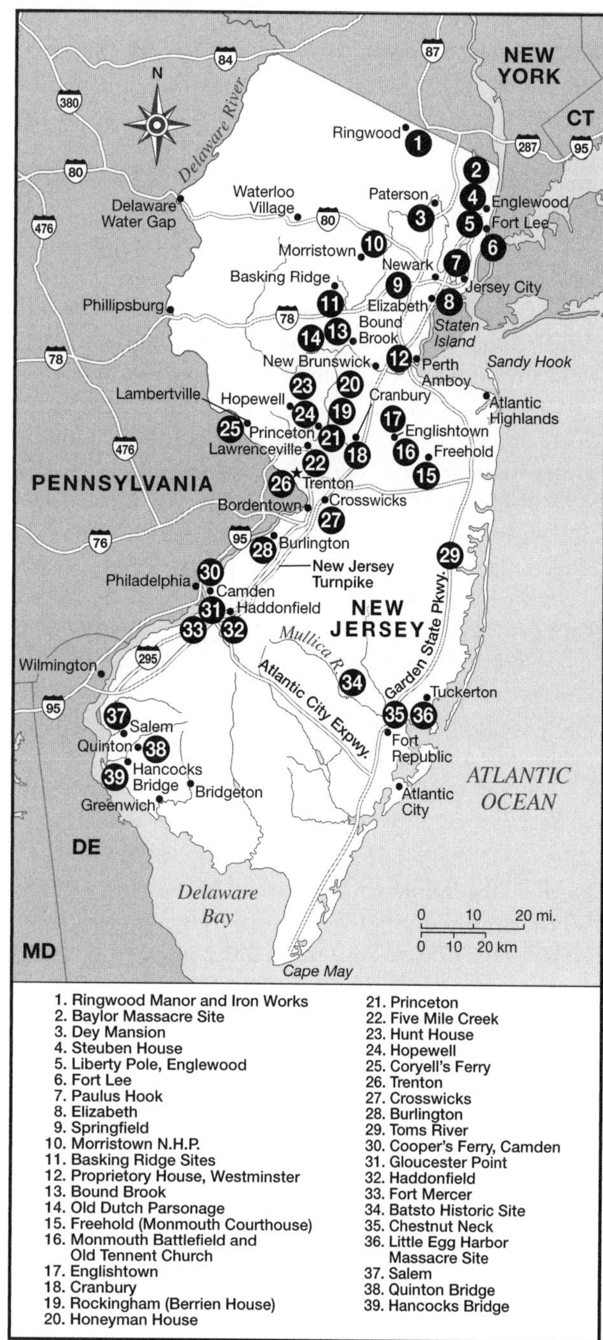

MAP BY XNR PRODUCTIONS. THE GALE GROUP.

between 1690 and 1709, it features fine interior paneling and still has some of its original shingles. It was restored in 1972 to reflect the period after 1740. One of several historic houses maintained by the Monmouth County Historical Association, the Covenhoven House is used for special events. The Association has its headquarters, library, and museum in an attractive modern (1931) building of Georgian design at 70 Court Street. Phone: (732) 462-1466.

Gloucester Point, Delaware River, Gloucester County. The first white settlement on the east bank of the Delaware was established by the Dutch, who built Fort Nassau here in 1623. Not until Irish Quakers arrived in 1682, however, did the village start to grow. Gloucester Point was occupied in November 1777 by five thousand British troops under Cornwallis and supported by the fleet. Gloucester Point Park, at New Jersey Avenue and King Street, is the site of the annual meeting of the Proprietors of West Jersey and of Hugg's Tavern. The latter, razed in 1929, had been used by the local Committee of Correspondence and by Cornwallis.

Remains of the British frigate *Augusta* (sixty-four guns) may be seen here. This ship and the *Merlin* (eighteen) were badly damaged by fire from Fort Mifflin on 22 October 1777 when Washington's forces successfully defended Fort Mercer (Red Bank). In trying to withdraw, both ships ran aground. An explosion wrecked the *Augusta* the next day, and fire destroyed the *Merlin.* During the centennial of the American Revolution an effort was organized to raise the *Augusta* and tow it up the Schuylkill for exhibition in Fairmount Park, and plans were working out until it was discovered that the hull could not be gotten past the bridges on the Schuylkill. Money for the project ran out, and the *Augusta* was abandoned on Gloucester Beach and stripped by souvenir hunters.

Haddonfield. In moving from Philadelphia toward New York City in the summer of 1778, the British army under General Clinton paused here to regroup before marching on to Monmouth Battlefield. Indian King Tavern, located at 233 Kings Highway East, has survived as a significant example of the colonial wayside inn. Built in 1750 and once known as the American House, it was a stopping place for couriers on the Kings Highway before the Revolution, and later a meeting hall for the state legislature and Council of Safety. It is now a state historic site and open to the public for touring on Wednesday through Sunday. Phone: (856) 429-6792. Information on many structures, sites, and programs of historic interest in Haddonfield may be accessed by contacting the Historical Society of Haddonfield, whose home is the acclaimed Greenfield Hall, located at 343 Kings Highway East. Phone: (856) 429-7375.

Hancocks Bridge, Alloway Creek, Salem County. British and Loyalist raids from Salem in March 1778 resulted in so many Patriot casualties at Quinton Bridge and Hancocks Bridge that they are remembered as "massacres." The background of these operations is covered under SALEM.

Major Simcoe was chagrined by his failure to wipe out the entire Patriot force at Quinton Bridge. Colonel

Mawhood decided to commit a larger portion of his command against the Rebel militia around Hancocks Bridge, and entrusted this mission to Simcoe. After a personal reconnaissance, Simcoe planned an elaborate amphibious raid from Salem to the Delaware and up Alloway Creek. Under cover of darkness the attackers landed several miles below the village, waded through swamp to the road south of the creek, and moved stealthily to assigned positions near the houses believed to be occupied by Patriots. One detachment set up a blocking position on the dike along which reinforcements might come from Quinton Bridge. The Twenty-seventh Foot advanced overland from Salem to support the raid from the northwest side of the creek.

It was a dark and stormy night, which made the British movements difficult to control, but helped them achieve complete surprise. As luck would have it, however, all but twenty of the Patriot troops had left the village. The raiders charged through the front and back doors of Judge William Hancock's house and killed everybody in it. Among the victims were the old judge and his brother, both of them well-known Loyalists. Simcoe had been informed that the judge had not lived in his house since the Rebels took control of the village, but what the British did not know was that Hancock returned to his home at night.

(Benson Lossing published Simcoe's sketches of this action and the one at Quinton Bridge. See II, pages 344 and 345 of the original edition, or II, pages 138 and 139 of the 1972 reprint.)

Quite apart from its historic significance, the well-preserved Hancock House is of architectural importance. The brickwork of the two-and-a-half-story structure is remarkable: on one end the initials and date "W S H 1734" are patterned into the "tapestry" design above nineteen zigzag vertical lines of red and blue glazed brick. The initials are for William and Sarah Hancock, the owner and his wife, in accordance with a fairly common custom in this and other regions of colonial America. At the back of the house is a door that appears to be lacking the necessary steps to be reached from ground level. This is a saddle-door, or hearse-door, a common feature in the neighborhood and serving, as the names indicate, for mounting a horse or for a loading platform. In the attic are discolorations said to be bloodstains left from the massacre.

In 1991 the house was closed to the public. It reopened in 1998 after the New Jersey Division of Parks and Services performed a wide array of repairs on the structure, including addition of a cedar-shingle roof.

Adjacent to the Hancock House is the old cabin of cedar planks that was moved to this location from near Salem. Built of beautifully joined planks of local swamp cedar by Swedish pioneers, it is said to date from about 1640. This state historic site is open on Wednesday through Saturday from 10 A.M. to 4 P.M., and on Sunday from 1 P.M. to 4 P.M. Phone (856) 935-4373.

The Quaker Meeting House is on the main street about 100 yards from the above site on land donated by William Hancock. Its oldest portion dates from 1756, an addition from 1784.

(For the local historical society and identification of a useful map of the region, see the end of the section on SALEM.)

Honeyman House, near Griggstown. John Honeyman is credited with giving Washington the information about enemy dispositions in Trenton that led to the great Patriot triumph there on 26 December 1776. One of Washington's most able spies, he kept his secrets so well that he was accused during and after the Revolution of being a British agent. The house where he lived during the period 1776 to 1786 is a well-preserved private home that can be seen from the road. It is 0.7 mile north of the village of Griggstown on the east bank of the canal that parallels the Millstone River.

Hopewell, Mercer County. This old village is famous as the home of John Hart (c. 1711–1779) and as the place where Washington made critical decisions in developing the strategy leading to the Battle of Monmouth. Several historic structures have been preserved in and near Hopewell, which remains a quiet and attractive country town.

John Hart's father had come here from Stonington, Connecticut, about 1712 and had risen to a position of local importance. A good twenty years before the Revolution, John himself had become a successful farmer, "the most considerable man in the community," and a growing power in public affairs. He was elected to the assembly in 1761 and served for the next ten years later, after which he continued in the Provincial Congress of New Jersey until sent to the Continental Congress in June 1776. Two months later he signed the Declaration of Independence, became speaker of the newly created state assembly, and was one of the most prominent Rebels of the region just as it became a theater of war.

John Hart was at this time a man of advanced years with many "hostages to fortune" in addition to his large family, and he was to pay dearly. His farm and mills were devastated by the opposing armies. The elderly Hart and his wife were forced to seek refuge in the woods and hills when the British came to arrest him. Martha Hart died as a result of her hardships as a refugee, and John died about two years later.

The Hart House, at 60 Hart Road, is a private home on a quiet street in modern Hopewell. Not marked, it is

0.6 mile from the traffic light at Greenwood Avenue and West Broad Street (County Road 518). To find it coming from Lambertville, turn left at this light onto Greenwood and look for Hart Road a short distance farther. Turn left onto Hart Road and look for number 60 on the right.

Not until 1865 did the New Jersey Legislature get around to providing for a memorial to its first speaker. Then it managed to botch the job: "Nearly every date on the monument at Hopewell is incorrect," notes the author of the article on John Hart in the *Dictionary of American Biography.* It stands on West Broad Street (County Road 518) next to the easily spotted Old School Baptist Church of 1748. The latter is a simple, two-story brick structure painted bright red, with arched windows and heavy paneled doors. Also known as the Baptist Meeting House, it was a hospital during the Revolution. Hart is buried in the nearby cemetery, as are many Revolutionary War veterans.

Washington reached Hopewell late in the afternoon of 23 June 1778 as his army stalked the British in their withdrawal from Philadelphia to New York. D. S. Freeman writes that Washington opened a headquarters near the Baptist Meeting House and began to get detailed reports that indicated what his enemy was trying to do. An important council of war was held the next day near Hopewell at the Hunt House.

Hunt House, County Line Road near Hopewell, Mercer County. Washington's letters of 23 to 24 June 1778, when critical decisions were being made in the days just before the Battle of Monmouth, were headed "Hunts" or "John Hunt's House." This supports the tradition that this house was the scene of the famous council of war in which most of Washington's generals sided with the veteran Charles Lee in recommending that the British not be seriously molested in their effort to retreat through the Jerseys to New York. Generals Anthony Wayne, Nathanael Greene, and Lafayette went on record with their objections, Alexander Hamilton voicing his off-the-record opinion that the majority decision "would have done honor to the most honorable body of midwives and to them only." (See MONMOUTH BATTLEFIELD.)

Privately owned, unmarked, and screened from the road by high hedges, the well-preserved Hunt House is on a hill roughly midway between Hopewell and Blawenburg, just west of the county line. To reach it from Hopewell, drive toward Blawenburg on County Road 518 and turn left on the unpaved road just short of the county line. The latter is marked on the highway. Drive 1.2 miles, crossing the railroad and making two right-angle turns. This is a section of County Line Road. The Hunt House will be to your right on the crest of the hill and with a commanding view.

The John Woolman Memorial House on 99 Branch Street in Mount Holly commemorates the life and work of John Woolman (1720–1772), one of the first active abolitionists in America, who helped lead the Quakers to their antislavery position, which they adopted in 1776. Construction of the house began in 1771, and it is maintained within Woolman's orchards as it looked in the 1780s. Open Friday, 10 A.M. to 2 P.M., and by appointment by calling (609) 267-3226.

Liberty Pole, Englewood, Bergen County. At Lafayette and Palisade Avenues in Englewood is a liberty pole erected in 1964, presumably on or near the site of the original pole put up in 1766 to celebrate repeal of the Stamp Act. Liberty Pole Tavern, a well-known landmark of the Revolution, stood nearby. The tired troops of "Light Horse Harry" Lee successfully fought off an attack by Loyalists here on 19 August 1779 as the Patriots withdrew to New Bridge from their successful raid on Paulus Hook (Jersey City). The old tavern was one of the few buildings standing when the town of Englewood was laid out in 1859.

Little Egg Harbor Massacre Site, near Tuckerton, Ocean County. When Captain Patrick Ferguson started wiping out American privateering bases along the Mullica River (see CHESTNUT NECK), the newly raised legion of Casimir Pulaski was ordered to oppose his operations. Pulaski's Legion, three light infantry companies, three light horse troops, and an artillery detachment, was too late to interfere seriously with Ferguson's search-and-destroy operations. But its arrival did force the British to discontinue their plan of attacking a major base of the privateers around the Forks of the Mullica and of raiding the nearby Batsto iron works (see BATSTO HISTORIC SITE).

Pulaski's troops included a high percentage of deserters and a good many foreign adventurers of dubious military merit. His legion reached the Little Egg Harbor district around modern Tuckerton and camped a short distance southwest, around a farm. A deserter went over to Ferguson and informed him of Pulaski's location, pointing out that his camp might be surprised because morale was low and security lax.

Ferguson loaded 250 of his best troops in boats and under cover of darkness rowed 10 miles to what is now Osborne's Island. He then moved about 2 miles through salt marshes and bog to reach the place where the infantry of Pulaski's Legion had a fifty-man outpost a short distance from the main camp. It was about an hour before first light on 15 October 1778 when the British moved in to catch their quarry asleep in three houses; only five were taken alive.

Pulaski led his mounted troops up, and Ferguson retreated to his boats with the loss of a few men captured. At a bend in Radio Road on Pulaski Drive, somewhat less than 3 miles from the center of Tuckerton, is the Pulaski Monument. Presumably it stands about where the main American camp was located. What inspired the Society of the Cincinnati to erect this memorial to Pulaski's humiliating defeat is hard to understand, but it is even more difficult to find local authorities who can pinpoint landmarks of the action. Contemporary accounts of the Little Egg Harbor Massacre vary considerably, and modern historians have shown little interest in straightening out the record of exactly when and where it occurred.

Middlebrook Encampment, north edge of Bound Brook, Somerset County, just east of the junction of Routes 22 and 287. The campaign of 1777, which ended with the British capture of Philadelphia, started with a complex sequence of strategic maneuvers between the main British and American armies in north central New Jersey. Anticipating the British offensive, Washington left his winter quarters around Morristown and advanced to a forward position around Middlebrook. Here he covered the passes of the Watchung Mountains while putting his army within 7 miles of the major enemy outpost at New Brunswick. Students of strategy will recognize the Middlebrook encampment as being a classic flanking position that would check a British attempt to advance on Philadelphia via the overland route through New Jersey used the preceding year. General Sir William Howe, who had studied the same basic military textbooks as Washington, consequently undertook to lure his opponent out of this strong position and defeat him. When Howe deployed south of the Raritan between New Brunswick and Somerset Courthouse (now Millstone), Washington left Middlebrook and split his forces, putting a strong detachment under General William Alexander ("Lord Stirling") near modern Metuchen and his main body around the place then called Quibble Town, now New Market. Feigning a strategic withdrawal through New Brunswick to Amboy, Howe then launched an offensive designed to defeat in detail the strong detachment under General Alexander near Metuchen. He hoped to defeat the rest of Washington's weakened army afterwards in a pitched battle after blocking his retreat through the passes to Middlebrook. Washington saw through Howe's strategy as soon as the British advance was detected. Alexander fought a brisk rear guard action against Lord Cornwallis around Metuchen (the Battle of Short Hills), and the main body of the Patriot army withdrew safely to Middlebrook. The British returned to Staten Island, whence they later moved by sea to Head of Elk, Maryland, to start their successful advance on Philadelphia by way of the Brandywine (see under PENNSYLVANIA).

Having used the Middlebrook encampment in May to June 1777, Washington's army was back during the period November 1778 to June 1779. Major military operations in the North had ended with the Battle of Monmouth (see MONMOUTH BATTLEFIELD) in June 1778, so the second season at Middlebrook was less dramatic than the first.

The Washington Camp Ground Association owns 23 acres of the historic site on the north edge of Bound Brook (on Mountain Avenue) and at the foot of First Watchung Mountain. It is undeveloped except for a memorial flagpole flanked by two Civil War cannon (Parrott guns), a painted sign, a speaker's stand, and a Girl Scout cabin. The site is reached by driving north on County Highway 527 (Mountain Avenue) from Bound Brook, proceeding 0.1 mile beyond U.S. 22 (underpass), and turning left (west) onto Middlebrook Avenue. The latter winds through a residential area for 0.5 mile to the Camp Ground, which is easily spotted on the hillside to the right.

The word "Middlebrook," so famous as the name of this encampment, survives locally only as the name of the inconspicuous creek that forms the western boundary of the borough of Bound Brook. The site is open free to the public all year round.

Monmouth Battlefield State Park, west of Freehold, Monmouth County. The colonial crossroads village of Monmouth Courthouse, which gave its name to this major battle of the Revolution, is located approximately 12 miles east of Exit 8 off the N.J. Turnpike on Route 33. From the Garden State Parkway, take Exit 123 to Route 9 south for 15 miles to business Route 33 West. The park is located 1.5 miles on the right, near the present town of Freehold. Here the landmarks of the preliminary skirmishing have virtually disappeared, but a short distance west the terrain of the real battle is remarkably well preserved. Fields have been enlarged, swampy creek beds and ravines have been drained and graded; a railroad and County Road 522 bisect the battlefield, but the state owns about 1,800 acres, including the major terrain features. The site is now a state park and major recreation area that includes a visitors center (located on Comb's Hill), an interpretive center, over 25 miles of hiking and horseback trails, and picnicking areas, and a reenactment of the great battle is held every year during the last week of June. Moving west toward Old Tennent Church (Freehold Meeting House) from modern Freehold on County Road 522, you will initially be following the colonial road along which Lee's disorganized detachment retreated. Between the highway and the railroad embankment is the bogus "Molly Pitcher's Well," constructed by the railroad in modern times and having no true association with history.

A little farther along, and easily spotted, is a railroad underpass. Turn left here and immediately to your right is the site of the hedgerow that figured so prominently in the final phase of the battle. In this immediate area is the surviving Old Tennent Parsonage. The present road leads southwest to Wemrock Brook and the base of Combs Hill, critical terrain from which Patriot guns delivered enfilade fire against the flank of attacking British forces.

Returning to the railroad underpass and the highway, this is where the alignment of the colonial road to Old Tennent Church and the modern highway part company. The old bridge over West Ravine (now Weamacony Creek) was just below the present one. A highway marker indicates that Charles Lee and Washington had their famous encounter just east of the latter point. The high ground due north is where General William Alexander ("Lord Stirling") commanded Washington's left wing. Here the British started their unsuccessful attacks on the last position organized by the Americans. Washington, Von Steuben, and Alexander exhorted the defenders of this flank as the Black Watch, supported by light infantry and field artillery, attempted to penetrate or envelop it.

One problem in the development of Monmouth Battlefield Park was that major disagreement existed among authorities as to what happened where. Mythmakers have already succeeded in creating the impression that Molly Pitcher had an important part in the Patriot victory.

To go back now to an explanation of the Monmouth campaign, the battle took place on 28 June 1778 as General Sir Henry Clinton marched from Philadelphia to New York. The British had been occupying Philadelphia while the Americans shivered at Valley Forge. Lacking shipping to make the move by sea, and also worried about the French fleet, Clinton decided to move overland. Starting on 16 June, he successfully accomplished the difficult task of crossing the Delaware without being caught astride the river. He paused at Haddonfield to embark his sick, his heavy equipment, and some three thousand Loyalists for New York and to organize the rest of his command for the arduous march.

Washington, meanwhile, had reacted quickly to news of the British withdrawal from Philadelphia, ordering his army to cross the Delaware at Coryell's Ferry (now Lambertville). But as Clinton continued up the river toward Bordentown, just below Trenton, the Americans had the perplexing problem of dispersing sufficiently to find and slow up the enemy and at the same time keeping well enough concentrated to avoid "defeat in detail." Bad roads and bad weather (rain alternating with days of record-breaking heat) impeded the operations of friend and foe but caused greatest suffering in the ranks of the British, who were marching with heavy individual loads and escorting 1,500 wagons in addition to their artillery.

From Bordentown the British could have taken any one of several routes north. Not until he reached Hopewell did Washington start to get the detailed reports from which a true picture of enemy intentions emerged. A famous council of war took place on 24 June (probably at the Hunt House) while Washington's troops were given a day's rest. Washington tentatively accepted the "bridge of gold" strategy advocated by General Charles Lee and endorsed by the majority of his generals. Using a term familiar to European strategists of the time, Lee argued that an escape route should be left open to the enemy and that Washington should not risk his amateurs in a major engagement with Clinton, in whose ranks marched some of the finest regiments of the British army.

But Washington and his army had lost their amateur status at Valley Forge, the Trenton-Princeton campaign proving that they were capable of brilliant performance against those professionals who had triumphed so consistently since Bunker Hill. The training directed by General Von Steuben at Valley Forge had already paid off when the young General Lafayette had to extricate his command from Barren Hill, Pennsylvania. The speed and efficiency with which the little Rebel army left its winter quarters at Valley Forge in pursuit of Clinton was further evidence of its new professionalism.

The Monmouth Campaign is therefore fascinating for what it reveals of Washington's generalship, not only in the field of strategic decision making but also in working with the strengths and weaknesses of his major subordinate commanders. Not wanting to abandon hope for bringing on a major engagement but knowing that Lee was not the right man to use, Washington got Lee to waive his seniority so Lafayette could command a special task force organized to put more pressure on the British withdrawal. But just as Washington apparently had finessed this move, Lee decided that he should command this detachment after all.

Thus it came to pass that on the eve of the Battle of Monmouth, five thousand American troops under a general who did not want to fight were 5 miles from Monmouth Courthouse at Englishtown, and the rest of the army was with Washington another 8 miles to the west, at Cranbury.

The British had reached Monmouth Courthouse the afternoon of 26 June after a 19-mile march on roads deep with sand and in a humid heat. Many had died of heat exhaustion, and Clinton let his troops rest on 27 June. The American command and control system, meanwhile, had temporarily broken down. Washington had no further doubt about the general route the British were following, and he had made a night march (25 to 26 June) to reach Cranbury. Colonel Stephen Moylan's thirty dragoons, Colonel Dan Morgan's six hundred riflemen, and General Philemon Dickinson's one thousand New Jersey militia were observing British movements, but their efforts were uncoordinated. Washington was in the dark, not only about enemy movements but also about the location of his own troops at this critical moment.

Shortly before daybreak, at 4 A.M., Clinton's supply train under the escort of Knyphausen's division started north for Middletown while Clinton waited with Cornwallis's division until this forward element had the proper lead. The fatuous Lee got around to resuming his cautious advance at 7 A.M. He had not bothered to send out patrols during the night to make contact with Patriot militia around Monmouth Courthouse or to keep him informed of Clinton's activities, and when he finally did reach the scene of action he proceeded to get into a violent argument with General Dickinson about whether, in fact, Clinton had resumed his retreat or was preparing to attack! But Washington had received a report from Dickinson about the British movement and was leading the rest of his army forward from Cranbury to support Lee.

The true situation at this time was that a strong British rear guard remained around the courthouse, but Clinton and Cornwallis had left. In a confused series of mismanaged efforts Lee succeeded only in warning Clinton that a major portion of the Rebel army was at hand. The British commander in chief, who had been doing everything in accordance with conventional tactical wisdom, ordered back a brigade and some light dragoons from Knyphausen's division to cover his northern flank while Cornwallis turned to eliminate Lee's threat to his rear.

The latter's thoroughly confused troops dropped back and then broke into a panic-stricken retreat. British officers naturally did what they could to encourage this stampede. What happened next is not known with any degree of certainty, except that Washington met Lee on the road and personally took command. The Patriots managed to rally, check the British on successive lines of defense, and hold their final position against a series of heroic but poorly coordinated assaults.

With the temperature reading 100 degrees in the sun, Clinton called a halt to his efforts. Washington ordered a counterattack and planned to pursue, but his own troops were too exhausted to comply. The British regrouped about half a mile east of the Middle Ravine, rested until midnight, and then slipped away. By 10 A.M. the next day they entered Knyphausen's camp at Middletown, and a day later Clinton's entire force was at Sandy Hook waiting for boats to take them to New York.

The Battle of Monmouth was the last major engagement in the North, the longest sustained battle of the Revolution, and perhaps the best one ever fought by the army that Washington personally headed. Strategically and tactically, it showed Washington at his best. Troops and commanders on both sides performed with tremendous proficiency, particularly considering that they had endured great hardships before reaching the battlefield and fought the long battle on one of the hottest days of the Revolutionary period. Monmouth probably witnessed the largest concentration of African American troops on the United States side of the Revolution, an estimated seven hundred serving in the Continental army at the battle.

Monmouth Battlefield State Park is open year-round from dawn to dusk and admission is free. Phone: (732) 462-9616; visitors center phone: (732) 780-5782.

Morristown National Historical Park, 30 Washington Place, Morristown. About 30 miles west of the principal British base of New York City but protected by a series of parallel ranges of hills and small mountains, Morristown was of great military importance to the American cause. Fortunately, the most interesting landmarks have been preserved. In the Jockey Hollow Area a wildlife sanctuary and nature trail have been developed in the unspoiled setting of Washington's army's encampment during the terrible winter of 1779 to 1780. In this area are the Tempe Wick house and gardens and a replica of the crude log hut that served as a military hospital.

The "Fort Nonsense" site is preserved on a hill overlooking Morristown. Reconstructed fortifications once marked this place where Washington is alleged to have ordered construction of earthworks merely to keep his soldiers too busy to get into trouble. This legend has been discredited, no reference to "Fort Nonsense" having yet been discovered in any document written before 1833.

Tours are available daily of the Ford Mansion at 230 Morris Street in the Headquarters Area, which was built during the period 1772 to 1774 by Colonel Jacob Ford Jr., an influential iron manufacturer and powder mill owner. He died early in 1777. During the winter of 1779 to 1780 his widow and their four children occupied two rooms of the mansion while Washington moved in with seventeen other "guests," including his wife, aides, and servants. "Washington's Headquarters" is a splendid example of colonial architecture. Its restoration started in 1939, and another restoration, most of it focused on the Washington's Headquarters Museum, began in January 2005.

Behind it is the Historical Museum, notable for its research library, one of the country's most valuable collections of Washington memorabilia, and other historical exhibits.

The Schuyler-Hamilton House at 5 Olyphant Place dates from about 1765. Here Alexander Hamilton successfully courted Elizabeth Schuyler.

A "living history" program of colonial crafts and military arts has been one of the park's major attractions. Additionally, there is a twenty-minute introductory video and a visitors center where souvenirs and books can be purchased. The entire site encompasses over 1,700 acres. Phone: (973) 539-2016 (visitors' information); (973) 543-4030 (Jockey Hollow Visitors Center).

Old Dutch Parsonage, Somerville, Somerset County. At 65 Washington Place, near the Wallace House and therefore frequented by General and Mrs. Washington during several months in 1778 to 1779, this handsome brick house is the birthplace of Frederick Frelinghuysen (1753–1804). The latter was a young lawyer and Patriot politician before entering military service during the Revolution. First a major of minutemen, then a militia colonel and aide to General Philemon Dickinson, he took part in the campaigns of Trenton, Princeton, and Monmouth. In 1790 he was commissioned a brigadier general in the Indian campaign in the Old Northwest, and during the Whiskey Rebellion he served as a major general of militia. Meanwhile he had held a number of elected offices: congressman for eight months during the Revolution (from November 1778) and for a year starting in 1782, a state legislator for several terms, and a United States senator (5 December 1793–May 1796).

These are the Revolutionary War associations of the Old Dutch Parsonage, but this historic landmark is much more significant for its cultural distinctions. It was built by the congregation of the First Dutch Reformed Church in 1751 for their parson. The first occupant was the father of Frederick, but he died when the boy was only two years old. The bereaved Mrs. Frelinghuysen, daughter of a wealthy East India merchant, was about to take her two small children home to Amsterdam when the young New Yorker who had been living in the household as her husband's divinity student persuaded the widow to marry him.

With this sound secular underpinning the new master of the parsonage, Jacob Rutsen Hardenbergh (1736–1790), went on to become one of the first ministers of the Dutch Reformed faith ordained in America (1758) and a founder of what became Rutgers University (then Queen's College, chartered in 1766). Not until late in 1771 did the school open, however, and at this time the eighteen-year-old Frederick Frelinghuysen was the only member of the faculty. Thus can the Old Dutch Parsonage be called the cradle of Rutgers.

Jacob Hardenbergh preached resistance against England so effectively that the British put a price on his head. The dominie slept with a musket at his bedside and on several occasions had to flee his home to avoid capture. He served in the state legislature during several sessions. When Washington took up residence in the nearby Wallace House, he formed a warm friendship with Hardenbergh. This remarkable man had never been in good health, and he died in 1790 after four years as full-time head of Queen's College. Two other residents of the Wallace House during Washington's stay were the slaves Greg and Phyllis, the latter of whom was admired for her cooking. The original slave quarters above the kitchen have been preserved.

The parsonage was about to be demolished in 1907 but was bought by descendants of the first occupant and moved about 100 yards to the present location. Colonial furnishings include a gilded Dutch mirror brought to this country around 1750 by Dinah Van Bergh when she arrived as the bride of John Frelinguysen. The Frelinghuysen Chapter of the DAR has deeded the house to the state, which administers it as a historic site. Both the Wallace House and the Parsonage are open to the public. Phone: (908) 725-1015.

Old Tennent Church (Freehold Meeting House), 448 Tennent Road, near Route 9, Tennent, Monmouth County. "The new church" is what Washington called it, the simple but imposing white structure having been built in 1751 to replace an earlier one of 1731. The present name was adopted in 1859; before this the church had been known successively as the Old Scots Meeting House and the Old Freehold Meeting House. The Scots Presbyterian congregation was chartered in 1749 and is still vigorous.

On high ground overlooking the West Ravine and alongside the road from Englishtown to Monmouth Courthouse, the tall structure remains as a benchmark of the Battle of Monmouth (see MONMOUTH BATTLEFIELD). The old road past the church has disappeared, the present highway—County Road 522—being a short distance south.

Spectators gathered on the hilltop during the battle of 28 June 1778, some of them watching from the steeple and the roof of the church. One is said to have been mortally wounded by a spent cannonball that left a scar on a gravestone he was using for a seat. Portions of the battlefield are visible from around the church.

Old Tennent is a frame building of two stories with a steeply pitched roof that greatly increases its height. A stubby, octagonal steeple on one end of the high gable is topped by a spire and an early Dutch weathercock. Cedar shingles, with their many layers of white paint, form the siding. The church, which may be visited weekdays between 9 A.M. and noon, has an old-fashioned pulpit with overhanging sounding board, narrow pews with high backs, and a gallery once reserved for slaves. Beneath the center aisle is the grave of William Tennent, former minister and ardent Patriot, who died in 1777. (It is not certain whether the church was named for William, his brother John, or both.)

In the cemetery is the tomb of Lieutenant Colonel Henry Monckton, a British hero of the battle who was mortally wounded in leading his grenadier battalion in the last assault on the hedgerow. He was pulled into the American lines, together with the captured colors of his battalion, and died a prisoner.

Old Tennent Church serves an active congregation today. The venerable building, cemetery, and grounds are beautifully maintained. A modern annex, at a respectful distance, bustles with weekday activity. Phone: (732) 446-6299.

Paulus Hook (Jersey City). The scene of "Light Horse Harry" Lee's triumph on 19 August 1779 has long since been obliterated by the commercial development of Jersey City. The site of the main British fortification is said to be about where Washington and Grand Streets now intersect. Paulus Hook Park has been created at this spot. Elements of Washington's abortive "Flying Camp" are said to have been stationed here in the latter half of 1776, but the main camp, under General Hugh Mercer, was at Amboy. Conceived as a force of ten thousand militia that could move rapidly to threatened areas, the Flying Camp never attained that strength. Some two thousand of Mercer's men helped construct the fortifications of New York City, many were captured in the Battle of Long Island, and most of the troops at Fort Lee were from the Flying Camp. Formally authorized on 3 July 1776, the organization went out of existence on 30 November of the same year, having accomplished little. Yet the romantic name recurs on Revolutionary War monuments. Presently there remains a Paulus Hook Historic District, and a few of the buildings and churches have been preserved.

Princeton, Mercer County. Foreign visitors might well wonder why such great wealth has been expended on the architecture of Princeton University and so little effort has been made to develop the Princeton Battlefield. What happened here in a few minutes on 3 January 1777 brought to a brilliant conclusion "The Nine Days' Wonder," Washington's remarkable counteroffensive with a ragged little army that saved the American Revolution. It was almost five years later that Washington's victory at Yorktown virtually ended the war, but on this occasion Cornwallis said to him: "When the illustrious part that your Excellency has borne in this long and arduous contest becomes a matter of history, fame will gather your brightest laurels rather from the banks of the Delaware than from those of the Chesapeake."

The history of the Trenton-Princeton campaign, the nine days that ended in the Battle of Princeton, has been so well described that it will not be summarized here. Emphasis will be placed instead on what the informed visitor can expect to find on the ground today.

The route of Washington's night march from Trenton to Princeton is marked by twelve stone monuments, the last of which are on County Road 533 leading north to Princeton. U.S. 206 follows the general trace of the main road between Trenton and Princeton that Cornwallis took and along which British reinforcements marched from Princeton toward Trenton. As you approach Princeton on County Road 533, or Quaker Road, the topography is much as it was two centuries ago. It is a region of large farms, with wide, open fields to the right and the unspoiled course of Stony Brook to the left.

But the "Back Road" onto which Washington's main force turned just short of the Quaker Meeting House is gone. The Princeton Pike, which turns into Mercer Street, is a road put in after the Revolution (1807) and is roughly parallel to the old Back Road but some 250 yards to the northwest. (Battle Road, in the residential development just to the southwest of Princeton township, follows a stretch of the old Back Road. Another vestige survives as a declivity just east of the Thomas Clark House, mentioned below.)

Continuing on Quaker Road in the path of General Hugh Mercer's detachment, crossing the Princeton Pike (Mercer Road), the county highway follows Stony Brook to the old stone bridge and ruins of Worth's Mill. Lieutenant Colonel Charles Mawhood had left one regiment behind in Princeton and was leading two others up the steep hill from this bridge toward Trenton (on what is now U.S. 206) when his alert flank guards looked back and discovered the Rebel troop movements to their rear.

Visiting Princeton when the leaves are off the trees, as they were on the day of the battle, makes it possible to appreciate the critical role played by the terrain in providing observation from Mawhood's position on the high ground west of the Stony Brook Bridge.

Mercer's assigned mission was to destroy the heavy wooden flooring of the bridge to block British movement back to Princeton, but his troops were driven off by fire. Mawhood doubled back, retraced his steps up the Post Road (U.S. 206) toward Princeton about one-quarter mile to the vicinity of the Olden House (still standing; see below), then cut south. Mercer, meanwhile, had left the Quaker Road and moved northeast toward the high ground now covered by residential housing. A single modern street, Parkside Drive, starts about where Mercer left Quaker Road and loops up the hill through the general area of the initial skirmish; this street leads to the middle of the battlefield park at Mercer Road.

An important topographical feature of the battlefield was the creek running along the southeast side of the Post Road (U.S. 206) and presenting an obstacle to troop movement from the highway to the high ground that was the initial objective of Mawhood and Mercer. This stream is still there, but its banks have been cleared and smoothed. The orchard in which the first fighting occurred has disappeared.

Battlefield State Park is an open area of about 50 acres astride Mercer Road. For nearly three hundred years, this ground was occupied by a solitary white oak tree famous now as the Mercer Oak. The great tree collapsed in 2001, but it stood near the place where the middle-aged but highly promising Hugh Mercer was mortally wounded. Legend has it that he was carried to the tree after receiving seven bayonet wounds and having been left for dead on the field, but it is much more likely that he was taken straight to the Thomas Clark house.

The battlefield park is unmarked, so the visitor is left to private resources to identify the ground on which Washington rallied his troops for the successful counter-attack against Mawhood. A ceramic tablet beneath a flag-pole on the east edge of the field represents the only "interpretation" that state and local history agencies have managed to come up with so far.

Frog Hollow, where the British tried to make another stand against Washington's army, can still be seen east of the Graduate College in the open ground of the Springdale Golf Course. The positions of American and British troops opposing each other in Frog Hollow were just north of the Back Road, so in terms of present landmarks this portion of the battlefield is not on the golf course but in the residential area bisected by College Road.

The famous "spy map" of Princeton showed the Americans that the Back Road would permit their entering the town without encountering several prepared defenses on the main roads. Mawhood had left the Fortieth Foot to hold Princeton when he headed for Trenton with the Seventeenth and Fifty-fifth Foot. The Fortieth had its main position, one hundred men with eight six-pounders, at the western approach to town, where Stockton and Nassau Streets now join at the Princeton Battle Monument (see below). Another one hundred men were in a fortification in an orchard where Vandeventer Avenue and Wiggins Street now cross. Three or four small cannon were at Vandeventer and Nassau covering the Post Road in the direction of Kingston, and two small guns in front of Nassau Hall covered Witherspoon Street. The latter street led north to John Witherspoon's country house, Tusculum, which was being used by the officers of the Fortieth Foot (see below).

But the British were unable to organize their defense of Princeton. Washington's strategic surprise and his subsequent tactical success against Mawhood in the fierce engagement around the bridge now paid off. The British abandoned their strongpoints in the streets of the village and most of them fled, although they took all but two guns with them. Some took refuge in Nassau Hall and prepared to make a stand. Captain Alexander Hamilton rolled his battery into the Back Campus and a body of infantry prepared to assault the building. The cannon roared, the storming party entered the building, and the British quickly surrendered. Out marched 194 prisoners.

Having so skillfully executed this thrust deep to the British rear, Washington's tired troops had to move fast to escape the larger enemy force under Cornwallis moving north from Trenton. The ragged little Patriot army had been under arms for forty hours in bitter winter weather without time for rest or hot food. Washington marched to Kingston and then up the east side of Millstone River to Somerset Courthouse (now Millstone). Cornwallis pursued to Kingston, then returned to his base at New Brunswick. By 6 January, when Washington reached Morristown, the British had been cleared from all their conquests in New Jersey except the posts at Amboy and New Brunswick, where they presented no offensive threat.

The only Registered National Historic Landmarks in Princeton are Nassau Hall and Princeton Battlefield Park. Morven, the governor's mansion, is among the "Sites Also Noted." Others fail to meet various criteria of the National Survey, mainly that of "integrity," but are nevertheless of great interest. Several excellent guidebooks to the Princeton area are available, but the places associated with the American Revolution are briefly described below. The sequence of the following paragraphs corresponds generally with the route usually followed in visiting the sites. Nassau Hall is the logical starting point, this centrally located structure being Princeton's most important landmark.

The Bainbridge House. Located in the center of Princeton at 158 Nassau Street, this is a handsome little two-story frame structure with a painted brick veneer front. Built about 1765 by Robert Stockton, it was used by General Sir William Howe in late 1776 and by members of Congress in late 1783 (see Nassau Hall, above). William Bainbridge, who became famous as commander of the U.S.S. *Constitution* in the War of 1812, was born in the house in 1774, hence the present name. Owned by Princeton University, the Bainbridge House is leased by the Historical Society of Princeton, which uses it for headquarters and operates it as a house museum. The Society has a good reference library on regional history and genealogy and offers a variety of guided walking tours pertaining to the history, architecture, and ethnicity of the area. Phone: (609) 921-6748.

Morven. Morven is at 55 Stockton Street (U.S. 206), just west of its junction with Nassau Street. It served as the official residence for New Jersey's governors until the late 1980s. The grandfather of Richard Stockton (1730–1781) acquired a large tract around Princeton in 1696, and Morven is believed by some authorities to date from

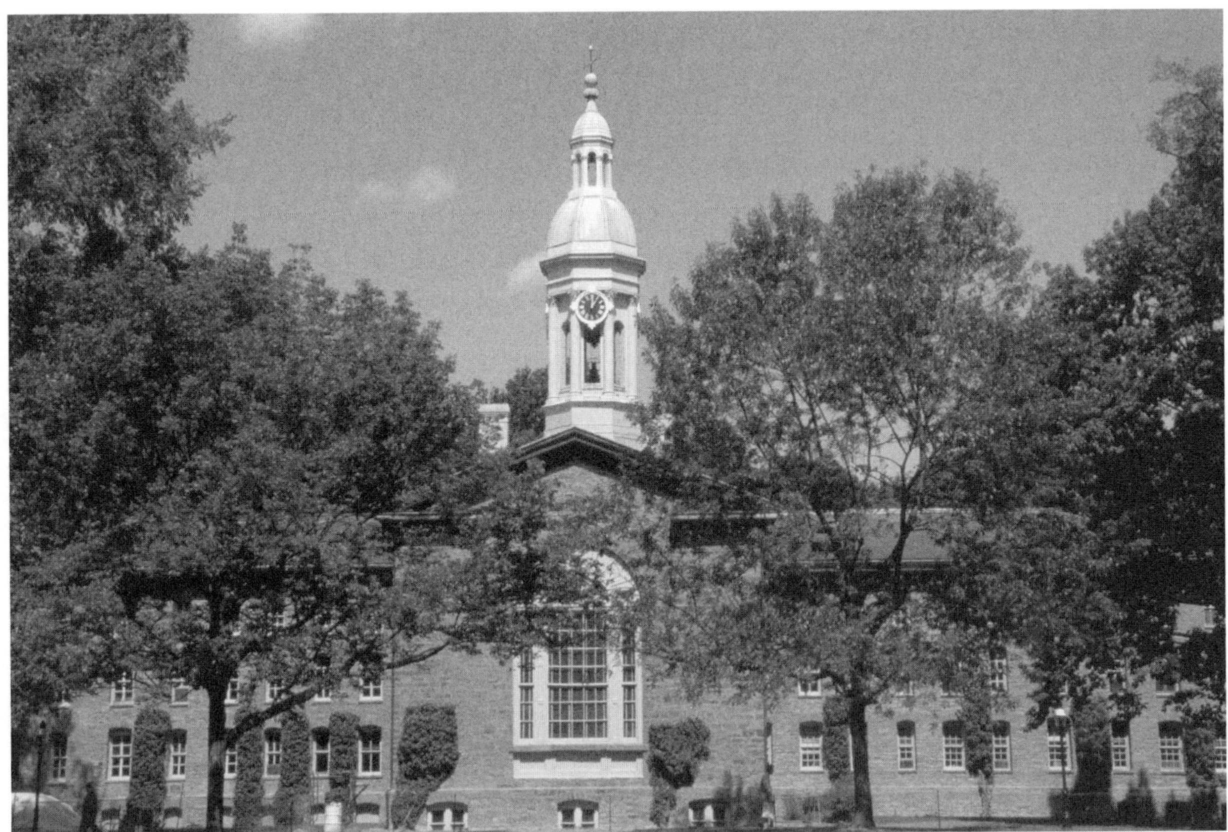

Nassau Hall. *Completed in 1756, Nassau Hall contained classrooms, accommodations, and a chapel for the entire student body of the College of New Jersey (now Princeton University). American and British troops used Nassau Hall during the Revolutionary War as a barracks and hospital.* © ROMAN SOUMAR/CORBIS.

1701. Recent studies (Grieff et al., *Princeton Architecture*) conclude that the structure was completed in 1755. A splendid Georgian manor house of painted brick, with classical columns and detailed pediment on the wide porch of the central section, the mansion has unmatched wings (each the size of a normal house). Two fires were followed by reconstruction, and records are few, so Morven has been a problem for architectural historians. Stockton inherited the mansion and died here a broken man during the Revolution. A graduate of the College of New Jersey eight years before it was moved to Princeton, he had distinguished himself as a lawyer and Patriot politician. As a signer of the Declaration of Independence he was subjected to particularly harsh treatment by the British when they captured him in the winter of 1776. In his weakened condition Stockton signed the amnesty proclamation. He returned to find his estate pillaged by the British, his fortune greatly depleted, his health fatally impaired by neglect of a lip wound during his imprisonment, and his patriotism impugned because he signed the amnesty declaration. A tumor spread from his lip to the throat, and Stockton died early in 1781. His grave was located when the cemetery of the Princeton Friends Meeting (below) was restored in 1912. A memorial stone was erected the next year.

Morven was occupied by senior British officers including Cornwallis. Its library and furniture were looted during the occupation. Washington visited Morven in 1783 while Congress held its sessions in Nassau Hall.

Recently renovated, the Morven House reopened to the public in 2004 from 11 A.M. to 3 P.M. on Wednesday through Friday, and from noon to 4 P.M. on weekends. Phone: (609) 683-4495.

The Nassau Club. This edifice, at 6 Mercer Street near the monument, is on the site of the Jonathan Sergeant house burned to the ground by the British in December 1776, the only house in Princeton to suffer this fate during the Revolution. The present structure dates from 1813.

Nassau Hall. Construction of Nassau Hall was begun in 1754, two years after the College of New Jersey (founded 1746) was formally moved to Princeton from Newark (having been originally at Elizabethtown). Named for King William III of the House of Nassau, the

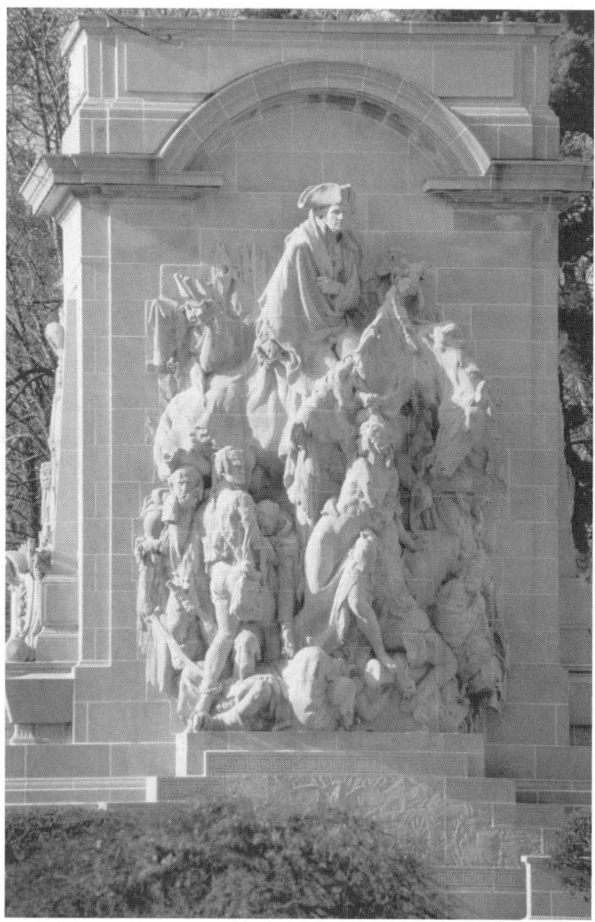

Princeton Battle Monument. *Designed by sculptor Frederick MacMonnies and dedicated by President Warren G. Harding in 1922, this limestone monument commemorates the 1777 Battle of Princeton.* © KELLY-MOONEY PHOTOGRAPHY/CORBIS.

building contained classrooms, eating and sleeping accommodations, and chapel for the entire student body (seventy undergraduates initially). American and British troops used Nassau Hall during the Revolution as barracks and hospital, doing much damage to the building. During the mutiny of the Pennsylvania Line in January 1781 the Board of Sergeants occupied the ruined building. When Congress fled from Philadelphia to escape the threat of three hundred disgruntled war veterans, Nassau Hall was the national capitol during the period 24 June to 3 November 1783.

The simple lines of the solid, long stone building influenced the design of Harvard's Hollis Hall (1762–1763), Brown's University Hall (1770–1771), and Dartmouth Hall (1784–1791), thus helping establish the familiar architectural tradition of so many later college structures. The original character of Nassau Hall was destroyed in the reconstruction following the fire of 1855.

A precious scientific relic exhibited in Nassau Hall is the orrery (planetarium) built by David Rittenhouse and acquired in 1771 by the College. Ironically, it was not damaged by the British (who intended to send it back to England) but was broken by idly curious American troops tampering with the delicate instrument. Most of it could be repaired, but the part showing the phases of the moon never worked properly again. Behind Nassau Hall in the center of the Back Campus, or Cannon Green, is a gun that may have been part of a British battery deployed to defend the village in January 1777. Abandoned by troops of both sides because its carriage was broken, it was taken to New Brunswick during the War of 1812 to be used in the defenses of that town, but was found to be unsafe to fire. A group of Princeton citizens retrieved it about fifteen years later, and in 1838 it was planted, muzzle down, where it has since become an object of various college traditions. Known as the Big Cannon, it is not to be confused with the other one (planted between Clio and Whig Halls a short distance to the south) that figured in the "Cannon War" of 1875 between Princeton and Rutgers.

"***The Old Barracks.***" This edifice at 32 Edgehill Street incorporates part of Princeton's oldest building. It was the original homestead of the Stockton family, started in the early 1700s and evolving into a two-and-a-half-story fieldstone house of eleven rooms. Plain and rectangular in design, it derives its name from the fact that it was used by British troops for barracks. The surviving portion of "the Old Stockton House," as it is labeled on the "spy map" of 1776, was bought in 1908 and restored as a private residence. It remains privately owned and is not open to the public, but presents an interesting view from the street. (Edgehill Street runs between Stockton and Mercer Streets a little less than 0.25 mile west of the Princeton Battle Monument.)

Olden House. The Olden House (private)is marked on the south side of Stockton Street about 0.25 mile east of Stony Brook Bridge. Washington stood on the porch of this little frame house to watch his defeated army march past in its retreat to Trenton in December 1776; exactly a month later he revisited the house to give instructions that British wounded be properly tended there. Architectural historians have disagreed, but an authoritative study concludes that the Olden House stands on its original foundations.

This stretch of Stockton Street is said to preserve its colonial appearance of small houses separated by spaces originally reserved for pastures and gardens. There is evidence that an eighteenth-century blacksmith shop was at number 481 and that the smith's home was at number 487.

In 1996 the Olden House went under a major restoration. It is the gift shop and home of the Drumthwacket Foundation. Reservations are required; phone: (609) 683-0591.

The Princeton Battle Monument. This memorial, conspicuous at the intersection of Nassau and Stockton Streets, was unveiled in 1922 by President Harding. It is a bad imitation of the sculpture on the Arc de Triomphe in Paris.

Princeton Friends Meeting. Commonly known as the Quaker Meeting House, and a landmark of the battle of 1777, this was the center of a Quaker settlement established in 1696. (Captain Henry Greenland was the first white settler, his plantation occupying most of what became Princeton township and dating from 1681.) In 1709 the Quakers built a small frame meetinghouse. The present structure dates from 1758 and is a two-story building with a front porch, stone fireplaces at each end, and a simple interior with a gallery reached by a winding staircase. The window glass and much of the woodwork are original. Wounded men were treated here after the Battle of Princeton. The nearby cemetery, surrounded by a stone wall erected in 1859, has the grave of Richard Stockton (see Morven, above) and of the Olden family. In the late 1800s the Stony Brook Meeting, as this was originally called, fell into disuse. The structure was restored in 1912, and since 1949 it has been used regularly by the Society of Friends formally reestablished in Princeton eight years earlier.

Stony Brook Bridge. The present stone bridge across Stony Brook was built in 1792 to replace the original one of 1738 at this point. Ruins of Worth's Mill rise prominently near the center of the bridge. The mill was bought in 1716 by Joseph Worth and operated until the early part of the twentieth century.

Tusculum. This residence, built by John Witherspoon when he was president of Princeton, remains standing and in excellent condition a short distance north of the town. A great stone structure that looks like a barn, it was built in 1773 and named for the resort where Roman nobles had their summer houses. It was headquarters of the Fortieth Foot during the brief British occupation of Princeton. Little structural damage was done because the invaders left so precipitously on 3 January 1777—leaving their breakfast to be eaten by the Patriots, in fact—but Witherspoon's fine library of rare books and his valuable furniture fell victim to vandalism. Witherspoon lived at Tusculum permanently from 1779 until his death in 1794. As of this writing the house cannot be visited, and in certain seasons is not visible from the road.

The Oliver Cromwell House, located at 114 East Union Street in Burlington City, was built in 1798. Oliver Cromwell (1752–1853) spent much of his long life in this home. Cromwell, a free black, was one of an estimated five thousand African Americans who served on the Patriot side during the Revolution. He was one of the two African Americans to cross the Delaware on 25 December 1776 with George Washington (the other, Prince Whipple, is the one appearing in the famous painting by Emanuel Leutze), taking part in the ensuing Battles of Trenton and Princeton. The following year Washington asked Congress to allow the enlistment of black troops, which it allowed, to the benefit of the Patriot cause. Cromwell went on to see action at the Battles of Brandywine, Monmouth, and Yorktown, and had his discharge papers signed personally by George Washington.

Proprietary House (Westminster), 149 Kearny Avenue, Perth Amboy, Middlesex County. The Council of Proprietors of the Eastern Division of New Jersey had this house built in 1764 for the royal governor's residence. It was occupied by the royal governor, William Franklin, until he was arrested by order of the Provincial Congress of New Jersey in June 1776. During the British occupation of Perth Amboy the house was used by General Sir William Howe. Soon after the Revolution a fire destroyed the interior. The house then became a resort hotel until 1883, when it was taken over by the Presbyterian Board of Relief for Disabled Ministers and Widows and Orphans of Deceased Ministers. At that time it was named Westminster. In 1911 it became a roominghouse. The Proprietary House has gone under significant renovation since being taken over by the state of New Jersey. The house is maintained by the Proprietary House Association and is open to the public during the following hours: 10 A.M. to 4 P.M. on Wednesdays, 1 P.M. to 3 P.M. on Sundays. Phone: (732) 826-5527.

Quinton Bridge, Alloway Creek, Salem County. For reasons explained under Salem, the British were operating in this region in the spring of 1778. Colonel Charles Mawhood and Major John Graves Simcoe, supported by local Loyalists, killed approximately thirty Patriot militia around Quinton Bridge on 18 March by drawing the defenders into an ambuscade. All landmarks have disappeared except the piles of the old bridge, which are a few hundred feet upstream from where N.J. 49 now crosses Alloway Creek into the village of Quinton. About 100 yards farther along this highway and on the north side is a granite marker erected in 1918 to commemorate the Revolutionary War skirmish. About 3 miles away is another granite marker, this one erected in 1928 to mark the graves of men who fought at Quinton Bridge.

Perhaps because the action was a brilliant British victory, local historians have not gone to pains to set the record straight. Even the date of the action and the names of landmarks and principal commanders vary from one account to another. The following reconstruction is as accurate as I have been able to make it.

Captain William Smith was the senior officer with the three hundred Patriot militia around Quinton Bridge when Colonel Mawhood approached from Salem with regulars of the Seventeenth Foot and Simcoe's Loyalist Rangers. Mawhood devised a stratagem to draw the Patriots out of their prepared defenses and across the bridge into an ambuscade. Under cover of darkness the British concealed detachments of the Seventeenth and the Rangers in and around Wetherby's Tavern on the Salem side of the creek and a pistol shot northeast of the highway. The morning of 18 March, Mawhood baited his trap by having an element of the Seventeenth Foot leave the area of the tavern and march away toward Salem.

Falling for the trick, Captain Smith left one hundred troops to man the prepared defenses and led two hundred militiamen across the bridge in a disorganized pursuit. Neglecting to scout their flanks, the Patriots hurried along the road past the tavern. They had gone only a few hundred feet beyond the bridge when a surprise fire was delivered by concealed troops from the front, flanks, and rear. Between thirty and forty Patriots died in the panic-stricken flight back across the creek, many of them drowning in an attempt to cross downstream from the bridge.

Andrew Bacon defied British fire to cut away the draw of the bridge, but this hero received a wound that left him a cripple. Meanwhile, Colonel Elijah Hand arrived with his militia and two cannon to reinforce the defenses on the south bank and check the pursuing British. Disappointed by his lack of greater success, Mawhood withdrew but struck again at Hancocks Bridge.

Although no Revolutionary War structures remain, the terrain over which the main action took place remains undeveloped on the Salem side of Alloway Creek. Simcoe's sketch of the battle can be correlated easily with the modern topographical map of the area. Archaeologists would probably have little difficulty in finding the location of major landmarks on the battlefield.

The cemetery mentioned at the beginning of this section can be found by going east from Quinton on N.J. 49 for about 0.7 mile from the bridge, turning right on Jericho Road (well marked), and proceeding 2.3 miles. The cemetery is in a clump of old trees about 100 yards across an open field to your left (east).

A granite marker there reads: "Honor to the brave American soldiers killed in the skirmish at Quinton's Bridge." The only headstone standing among the stubs of some twenty-five others is that of the commander who blundered so badly: Captain William Smith (1742–1820).

Ringwood Manor and Iron Works, Passaic County. The mines, furnaces, forges, and manor house at Ringwood started becoming a part of American history soon after 1730, when Cornelius Board found iron deposits in the area. He built Sterling Forge sometime before 1740, and sold land to the Ogdens of Newark, whose Ringwood Company started smelting iron in 1741. Peter Hasenclever organized the American Company and developed ironworks at Ringwood and elsewhere as manager for this group of investors (also called the London Company). This German entrepreneur had sold his interest in a mercantile business in Cádiz in 1763 and left Spain for England to become a British citizen. An excellent ironmaster and an energetic manager, he is believed to have lived at Ringwood and to have devoted most of his attention to development of this property. But after becoming overextended in his operations, Hasenclever turned the Ringwood works over to John Jacob Faesch, returned to England, and declared bankruptcy.

Robert Erskine (1735–1780) came to America in 1771 to take over from Faesch, who left to develop highly successful ironworks at Mount Hope and elsewhere. Erskine was educated at Edinburgh and was a fellow of the Royal Society (admitted in 1771 under the sponsorship of Benjamin Franklin) and a qualified engineer in several fields, including hydraulics and topography. He quickly became an excellent ironmaster but was unable to get necessary working capital from London. Erskine struggled along with advances from a New York bank. When the Revolution broke out he lined up with the Patriot cause.

Having thus saved his properties from confiscation, Erskine organized his workers into a militia company. This move not only provided local protection but also kept his men on the job and out of the Continental army. Erskine was commissioned a captain of this company and was promised that his militia would be ordered away only in case of invasion. The Ringwood works furnished the American armies a variety of iron products, from miscellaneous hardware, camp stoves, and ordnance items to major components of the great chains used to obstruct the Hudson. The old manor house, which burned during the Revolution, and the new one built nearby were visited by Washington and his generals. Contemporary journals mention the gracious entertainment for which the ironmaster's manor house was noted.

But the master of Ringwood is better remembered as the mapmaker of the Revolution. In addition to having professional training in topography and unusual skill as a draftsman, Erskine had traveled over much of the region west of the Hudson that became the theater of military operations. Although Washington met Erskine early in the war, knew of his ability as a cartographer and his familiarity with the ground, and was badly handicapped by lack of good maps, Erskine did not become a full-time mapmaker until the summer of 1778. During the next thirty months as geographer and surveyor of the United States, he made 129 maps, some of them having as many as twenty sheets. Most have been preserved by the New-York Historical Society (170 Central Park West, New York,

N.Y. 10024) and many are reproduced in histories of the Revolution.

Erskine caught cold during a field trip and died on 2 October 1780, the day Major John André was executed some 20 miles away at Tappan. The story that Washington attended Erskine's funeral seems to be based on the premise that he did not want to witness André's hanging, but the mythmakers have carelessly overlooked the realities of time, distance, and funeral arrangements.

The tomb of Erskine is in Ringwood Manor State Park. No likeness has yet been found of this major figure in American history, and little mention was made of his work during the Revolution in contemporary writings because so much of it was secret.

Ringwood continued after the Revolution to be a major source of iron products, including heavy ordnance items. The state park preserves little more than the sites that figured in the Revolution. Principal attractions are the elaborate manor house that evolved after 1810, the extensive landscaping and formal gardens, and interesting relics dating mostly from after the Revolution. Ringwood Manor became a National Historic Landmark in 1967. Near the town of Ringwood, the 4,044-acre park is a wildlife sanctuary. Picnicking, hiking, fishing, and other outdoor activities are provided for in the park. 1304 Sloatsburg Road, Ringwood, N.J. 07456-1799; phone: (973) 962-7031.

Rockingham (Berrien House), near Princeton, Somerset County. Located along the Delaware and Raritan Canal on County Route 603 in Franklin Township, this two-story frame house was used by Washington from 23 August to 10 November 1783, before he retired to Mount Vernon. From its second-story porch he read the "Farewell Orders to the Armies of the United States."

The oldest portion of the house is possibly the second-oldest house remaining in the Millstone River Valley. The original structure, a two-story, two-frame house, is believed to have been built between 1702 and 1710. John Berrien bought it about 1764 and expanded it to twenty rooms. In July 1783 the house, its numerous outbuildings, and 360 acres of surrounding farm were offered for sale. Congress had taken refuge in Princeton and was anxious to have Washington handy for final conferences on military matters, so they made the Rocky Hill (Rockingham) house available to him, Mrs. Washington, and his staff. Although the general would have been happier to make a single move from Newburgh to Mount Vernon, his days at Berrien House were exceptionally pleasant. Evidence poured in to prove that he was regarded as a national hero. Congress was expressing its gratitude in a number of ways. Rocky Hill was the scene of much official entertaining (which both of the Washingtons enjoyed), including a dinner for Congress on 5 September that was served under a captured British marquee on the lawn.

After the Revolution the historic house changed hands several times before large-scale quarrying operations started destroying the hill on which it had been built. At one time the abandoned house was a shack for quarry workers. The Washington Headquarters Association was then organized by local citizens to save Rockingham. Moved about 0.25 mile up the hill from the Millstone River, it was restored and opened to the public in 1897. In 1935 the Association presented the house to the state, which has since administered it as a historic site. But the quarry continued its destruction of the hillside, and in 1957 the house was again moved less than a mile from its original site. In 2001 it was moved to the present address. The house is now run by the state of New Jersey within the Department of Parks and Forestry and has been restored to its original state. Visiting hours are from 10 A.M. to 4 P.M. from Wednesday through Sunday, although it is recommended that visitors call first to assure that they are open. Phone: (609) 683-7132.

D. S. Freeman points out in his biography of Washington that the house was known originally as Rocky or Rock Hill, not Rockingham. The latter name may have stemmed from a journalistic error in New York's *Royal Gazette* in August 1783.

Salem, Salem County. The first permanent settlement of English colonists on the Delaware River was established here in 1675 by Quakers under John Fenwick. In 1682 New Salem, as it was originally called, became a port of entry by royal commission. The place prospered as a center of trade and industry.

Foragers under General Anthony Wayne collected 150 head of cattle around Salem in February 1778 for Washington's army at Valley Forge. The British then sent about 1,500 troops to Salem to conduct their own foraging operations and stop those of the Patriots. Loyalist reinforcements joined the British at Salem, increasing the strength of Colonel Charles Mawhood's regulars and the newly raised Queen's Rangers under Major John Graves Simcoe. With intelligence furnished by the local Loyalists, Mawhood and Simcoe surprised and annihilated careless detachments of Patriot militia at nearby Quinton Bridge and Hancocks Bridge.

Salem's decline as a river port started during the Revolution; agriculture in the region became unproductive soon thereafter, and many of its people moved west. In the words of the WPA guide, "Zadock Street left Salem in 1803, founded Salem, Ohio, and then Salem, Indiana, a few years later. His son, Aaron, established Salem, Iowa; the parade ended at the Pacific Ocean with Salem, Oregon."

After an economic revival and the establishment of industry about the time of the Civil War, Salem preserves a considerable amount of small-town charm and a number of historic landmarks. One is the Friends Meeting House on East Broadway opposite the head of Walnut Street. This two-story, red-brick building with two entrances (originally for men and women), was erected in 1772 to replace an earlier structure that stood within the Friends Burial Ground. The latter survives on West Broadway betweenFourth and Fifth Streets. Here is the ancient Salem Oak, beneath which John Fenwick bartered with the Indians for land. At least five hundred years old, the tree is 80 feet tall and measures more than 30 feet in circumference.

The Salem County Historical Society is located at 79–83 Market Street, Salem, N.J. 08079. Phone: (856) 935-5004.

Shabakunk Creek, just south of Lawrenceville on U.S. 206, Mercer County. Washington's brilliant strategy in the Princeton campaign was made possible by the delaying action directed by Colonel Edward Hand against British forces under Cornwallis on the road from Princeton to Trenton. While Washington's main force occupied defensive positions along the Assumpink Creek in Trenton on 2 January 1777, a large covering force was sent north on the Post Road (now U.S. 206) to block the expected British advance. The controversial General Rochedefermoy, whose American *nom de guerre* generally is rendered as Fermoy, had command of the American delaying action, but for reasons that have never been explained he abandoned his troops and returned to Trenton. Colonel Hand assumed command and ordered a slow retreat as superior enemy forces moved south from Lawrence (then called Maidenhead). Wherever a good delaying position could be organized, Hand halted his troops for a stand. Along Shabakunk Creek he held the British for two hours before continuing an orderly withdrawal to Trenton.

The site is marked on U.S. 206 about a mile south of its intersection with County Highway 546 in Lawrenceville.

Springfield, Union County. On 7 and 23 June 1780 the British penetrated to this point in large-scale raids from Staten Island. On both occasions their operations were designed to pull Washington's main army from its strong defensive position around Morristown, and on both occasions they were outfought by American forces. But in the process the British destroyed virtually all of Springfield, Connecticut Farms (now Union), and Elizabethtown (now Elizabeth).

Despite the destruction of 1780 and the subsequent urbanization of this portion of New Jersey, several important structures of the Revolutionary and earlier period remain standing, particularly in Elizabeth. The topography is of more interest to serious students of military history, however, and much of it is still unspoiled. With a current large-scale topographical map of the area and contemporary sketches of the military actions it is possible to trace on the ground the interesting events of June 1780.

From his headquarters at Morristown, Washington had good reason to be perplexed by the British maneuvers that started early in that month. The main British army had shifted its efforts to the South, where they were successfully overrunning South Carolina after having failed to achieve a strategic decision in the North. A large French expeditionary force under Rochambeau was expected in America to support the Patriot cause. One of Washington's finest generals, Benedict Arnold, was commanding the critical defenses of the Hudson Highlands centered around the newly created fortress of West Point.

When a large British expedition from Staten Island landed at De Hart's Point near Elizabethtown and started advancing toward the gaps of the Watchung Mountains around Springfield, Washington suspected that this was a strategic diversion to mask some great strategic plan that the British were unfolding. Actually, General Wilhelm von Knyphausen, the second-highest ranking general in Britain's American forces, was taking advantage of Sir Henry Clinton's absence to exercise his initiative. The veteran Prussian had intelligence indicating that Patriot morale in New Jersey was low and that local Loyalists were eager to rise up and support British military operations in the region.

On 7 June a powerful column of about five thousand British, German, and Loyalist troops advanced west from Elizabethtown through Connecticut Farms. Colonel Elias Dayton's Third New Jersey Regiment (of Maxwell's Brigade) had been outposting Elizabethtown. Reinforced by local militia, Dayton conducted a delaying action to the bridge over the Rahway River at Springfield. Surprised by the effective American resistance, the British withdrew to the high ground just to the northwest of Connecticut Farms and established a defensive position. After burning most of the settlement the raiders retreated in a heavy thunderstorm during the night (7–8 June). The Patriot regulars and militia, both being reinforced, pursued vigorously and effectively. His operation a conspicuous failure, Knyphausen retained his beachhead at De Hart's Point but evacuated part of his force to Staten Island.

Washington had meanwhile moved his main body forward from Morristown to the Short Hills, just to the northwest of Springfield. He was delighted with the performance of Dayton and the Jersey militia but unsure as to what Knyphausen meant to accomplish. The situation became even more confusing when the British marched forth again on 23 June in what appeared to be a repetition of their earlier effort.

Clinton had returned from Charleston on 17 June to learn of Knyphausen's fiasco. But almost immediately, he received a message from the traitor Benedict Arnold that Rochambeau's expeditionary force was on its way across the Atlantic to join the Patriot cause. Clinton therefore ordered a renewal of the advance on Springfield, but this time it really was a strategic diversion. Clinton had good reasons: he wanted to delay Washington's movement to cross the Hudson and join Rochambeau, who was to debark at Newport, Rhode Island, and he wanted to gain time for his troops to return from Charleston, after which he planned to launch an offensive up the Hudson and into Westchester County. The latter maneuver would concentrate British forces, not only to prevent a junction of Washington and Rochambeau but also for the defense of New York City against a French attack from the sea.

The Second Battle of Springfield, 23 June, was a more serious affair than the skirmish on 7 June. Both sides had been reinforced, the British now numbering about six thousand, the Americans having about half that strength in Continentals and local militia. Because of threatening moves of British ships up the Hudson toward West Point on 20 June, Washington had moved his main force to Pompton, but he had left General Greene with about one thousand Continentals at Springfield. He had also detached mounted troops, including the dragoons of "Light Horse Harry" Lee's legion, to screen the country between Springfield and Elizabethtown. In addition, Washington had organized a task force of five hundred men under General Edward Hand to harass the beachhead at De Hart's Point.

So when Knyphausen sallied forth the second time he met a well-organized delaying action. Closing up to the Raritan River just east of Springfield, Knyphausen used half of his strength to continue the advance but sent the rest on a wide envelopment along what is now Vauxhall Road. Lee's dragoons, reinforced by militia, skillfully delayed the British enveloping column while Colonel Israel Angell's Rhode Island Continentals defended the Springfield Bridge (on the Raritan) for forty minutes. Angell then withdrew through the village, a spirited resistance being offered on the high ground around the church (see below), and the Rhode Islanders joined Colonel William Shreve's New Jersey militia around the "Second Bridge," just west of the village.

Greene reinforced Lee with two regiments of New England regulars to block the threatened envelopment and concentrated the rest of his force on high ground just west of Springfield. Knyphausen had had enough. Breaking off the action, he withdrew after burning all but four of the buildings in Springfield. Washington had started moving to support Greene and had ordered the evacuation of supplies from Morristown when he got the news that no help was needed at Springfield. The invaders quickly withdrew to Staten Island, leaving only their dead, wounded, some stragglers, and some prisoners of war. (Casualty figures are very confused, as are many other facts of the two raids.)

The Cannonball House survives in Springfield as the major landmark of the Revolution. Built about 1750 as a simple farm house, it bears the scar of a cannonball said to have been fired during the fighting on 23 June. Open on a very limited schedule as a house museum (the cannonball is among the artifacts on exhibit), it is headquarters for the Springfield Historical Society, located at 166 Milltown Road in Springfield. For an appointment, call (973) 912-4464.

Conspicuous on high ground in the center of modern Springfield is a little white frame church built in 1791 on the site of the one burned in June 1780. By 1778 the latter structure was being used as a public storehouse and the congregation was worshiping in the parsonage a short distance north. Reverend James Caldwell had delivered a memorable series of sermons to the Springfield congregation in 1774. Pastor of the First Presbyterian Church in Elizabeth, Caldwell was known to his Loyalist enemies as the "high priest of the Revolution" and to his admirers as the "fighting parson." When the British landed near Elizabethtown for their first raid, Caldwell's wife Hannah and their children took refuge in the parsonage at Connecticut Farms. Here Mrs. Caldwell was killed during the skirmish on 7 June. Patriot propagandists made her a martyr "killed . . . by a shot from a British soldier, June 25th, 1780, cruelly sacrificed by the enemies of her husband and of her country." Thus reads the inscription on the monument to Reverend Caldwell and his wife in Elizabeth. The date is obviously wrong, but there is evidence that the rest of the statement also is muddled. Nobody can ever know for certain what really happened, but evidence was produced that she was murdered by a former servant who had some motive for revenge. Many believed at the time that she was killed by a stray shot.

Caldwell went to Connecticut Farms after the first skirmish at Springfield, in which he took part as chaplain of Colonel Dayton's regiment, to find this personal tragedy. In the battle of 23 June he is said to have broken into the church at Springfield, emerged with an armful of Watts's hymnals, and flung them to Patriot soldiers who had run out of wadding for their muskets. As they tore pages out for this use the fiery parson is alleged to have exhorted, "Give 'em Watts, boys—give 'em Watts!" Like so many clever sayings of the Revolution, this one is not mentioned by honest historians, probably because it was not mentioned by any primary sources, but it is repeated by civic boosters and popular writers. Bret Harte was inspired to write a poem entitled "Caldwell at Springfield."

Reverend Caldwell was murdered under peculiar circumstances by an American sentry in Elizabethtown. On 24 November 1781 he made the mistake of arguing with a soldier about the latter's strict interpretation of the special orders prescribed for his guard post. The soldier proceeded to shoot the reverend dead, for which lack of good sense the soldier was hanged for murder. Evidence was presented that the soldier, James Morgan, had been bribed to kill Caldwell whenever the opportunity arose.

In Westfield are landmarks associated with the trial and execution of Morgan, the former taking place in a building where the Presbyterian Church now stands at Broad Street and Mountain Avenue, and the latter spot, Morgan's or Gallows Hill, being on Broad Street at the northeast side of town.

Toms River, Ocean County. The Huddy-Asgill Affair started here when Loyalists surprised the blockhouse commanded by Captain Joshua Huddy of the militia, taking him prisoner and burning the small settlement on 24 March 1782. The Loyal Association of Refugees later took Huddy from a prison ship and hanged him on 12 April in revenge for his alleged killing of the Loyalist Philip White. This hanging precipitated a famous episode that figures in most general accounts of the Revolution and is the subject of a book by Katherine Mayo, *General Washington's Dilemma* (1938). (Mayo's book is out of print, but can be purchased through internet venues.) In brief, after failing to have surrendered to them the Loyalist captain, Richard Lippincott, who had been in charge of Huddy's execution, the Patriots selected by lot a British captain to hang in retribution. As luck would have it, the intended victim was the only son of Sir Charles Asgill. Lady Asgill packed off to the French court to intercede with the king and queen for the life of young Captain Charles Asgill, and Congress finally directed that he be released. (Captain Asgill, about twenty years old at the time, succeeded to his father's title and rose to the rank of full general in 1814.)

The crude blockhouse surrendered by Huddy was located on the knoll where the Ocean County Courthouse on Washington Street was built in 1850.

Trenton, at the head of navigation of the Delaware River. New Jersey's capital was first settled by Europeans in 1680. Originally called the Falls, the place was renamed in 1719 for William Trent, who five years earlier had bought the plantation of the original pioneer and who was chief justice of New Jersey in 1724. His house, a red-brick early Georgian structure built in 1719, became the official residence of the first colonial governor and was used by state governors. Restored and furnished in 1936 and again in 1993, it is operated by the Trent House Association and located at 15 Market Street in Trenton. Visiting hours are daily from 12:30 P.M. until 4 P.M. Phone: (609) 989-3027.

To eliminate the odium of billeting British troops during the Colonial Wars, the General Assembly hit on the solution of building five barracks in Burlington, Elizabethtown, Perth Amboy, New Brunswick, and Trenton. Only the Trenton barracks survives. Originally a two-story structure of native, undressed stone, it was started on 31 May 1758 and occupied that December, although it was not completed until the next spring. The central portion was 130 feet long, and 58-foot wings were on the north and south. Officers' quarters were later added to the north wing.

When the Seven Years' War ended (1763), the assembly ordered that the furnishings of all five barracks be sold and the buildings rented. During the Revolution they reverted to their original purpose, being occupied by American, British, and Hessian troops as the tide of war changed. Washington retreated through Trenton, arriving on 3 December 1776 and transporting his army into Pennsylvania four days later. Trenton was garrisoned by the Hessian brigade of Colonel Johann Rall that had distinguished itself at White Plains and Fort Washington, New York.

Having suffered one humiliating defeat after another, and forced to abandon New York City and retreat across New Jersey, Washington astonished friend and foe by the brilliance of his counteroffensive across the storm-lashed Delaware River on Christmas night, 1776. Rall's garrison was surprised the next morning at about 8 A.M., many of the 1,200 Hessians suffering the effects of Christmas festivities. The Germans responded bravely, forming in the streets of Trenton and attempting to assault the guns that had gone into action at the heads of King and Queen Streets. Recoiling in the face of point-blank fire and under increasing musket fire from the west, the Hessians retreated to the open field east of the village. Here they soon surrendered. The elderly Rall was mortally wounded seconds after ordering withdrawal from the village. About 500 Germans escaped, 918 were captured, and 22 were killed. (Authorities disagree wildly on the number who escaped.) Washington did not have a man killed in the skirmish, and only about four Americans were wounded. One was Captain James Monroe, who became the fifth president of the United States. Another was Captain William Washington, kinsman of the commander in chief and later a hero of Nathanael Greene's campaigns in the South. One of the artillery companies that performed such decisive service was commanded by Captain Alexander Hamilton. Washington's force when it crossed the Delaware numbered about 2,400 troops (18 guns); the shooting lasted less than two hours.

Trenton Battle Monument, on the highest ground in modern Trenton, marks the place where the Patriot artillery opened the battle. It is 148 feet high and served by an elevator to an observation deck offering a good view of the surrounding country. On top of the deck's roof is a statue of George Washington. This state and national historic site is at the intersection of North Broad and Warren Streets. The site is open free to the public on Thursdays, 11 A.M. to 3 P.M., Fridays and Saturdays, 9 A.M. to 4 P.M., and Sundays, 1 P.M. to 4 P.M. For further information and details on scheduling private tours, contact the Washington Crossing State Park. Phone (609) 737-0623.

The Old Barracks, from which tumbled the sleepy Hessians on 26 December 1776, has been preserved as Trenton's prize attraction. Of exceptional historical and architectural interest, it also serves as a model and inspiration in the field of conservation. Having been used during the Seven Years' War and the Revolution (hundreds of wounded from Yorktown were cared for here), the barracks were sold in 1786 and made over into private dwellings. In 1813 a 40-foot swath was cut through the northern end of the central section to extend Front Street westward to the State House (built in 1792 and much changed since then). After having served for fifty years as a home for aged women, the remaining L-shaped portion of the barracks was put up for sale in 1899. The Daughters of the American Revolution and others succeeded in saving the historic structure from demolition, later forming the Old Barracks Association to restore it. The northern wing, being used for private housing, was bought by the state. The city later agreed to close the extension of Front Street, making restoration of the entire site possible.

This work was completed in 1917, and since then the Old Barracks has been open to the public. A further restoration began in 1985 and was completed in 1998. The site is owned and maintained by the state but administered by the Old Barracks Association. An interpretation center features large dioramas portraying the three main events in Washington's masterful counteroffensive: his crossing of the Delaware, his raid on Trenton, and his subsequent victory at Princeton. Five smaller dioramas depict significant lesser episodes such as the "capture" of John Honeyman (who is alleged to have given Washington information that contributed to the triumph at Trenton) and the fighting near the Old Barracks. Tape recordings complement the dioramas, and there is a sixteen-minute narrative tied to eighty slides presenting the story of this campaign. An excellent collection of firearms is also on display. The Old Barracks hosts a series of special events, including reenactments. A living-history program, "Camp In," is available.

The Old Barracks is open daily from 10 A.M. to 5 P.M., except on major holidays. Phone: (609) 396-1776. Located near the State Capitol on South Willow Street opposite West Front Street, it may be viewed from the outside at any time. For particulars write Old Barracks Association, South Willow Street, Trenton, N.J. 08608.

Trenton has a number of other sites associated with the Revolution. One is the Friends Meeting House (usually closed to the public) at East Hanover and Montgomery Streets, used by troops on both sides during the war. Others figured in Washington's return to Trenton around New Year's Day 1777 for his campaign to the north around Princeton. Washington's camp was on the south bank of Assumpink Creek. Sandtown Road, which he took from here through Mercerville, is now Route 53. The delaying action north of Trenton that figured so prominently in the events preceding the Battle of Princeton was fought around modern Lawrenceville (see FIVE MILE CREEK).

Von Steuben House, River Edge, Bergen County at the dead end (east) of Main Street. In 1967 it was proved that the oldest portion of this Dutch house was built around 1695 by David Ackerman, whereas previously it had been said to date from Isaac Zabriskie's acquisition of the property about 1738. The Zabriskies enlarged the sandstone and brick structure, which became a mercantile establishment. During the Revolution it was used by American and British forces, Washington being quartered here briefly in 1780. The house was confiscated as Loyalist property, purchased after the war by the state of New Jersey and presented to General Friedrich von Steuben for his services on behalf of the Patriot cause. Steuben never occupied the house (preferring New York City and having been given 16,000 acres in upstate New York), but it has become known popularly as the Von Steuben House. Officially it is the Ackerman–Zabriskie–Von Steuben House. Owned by the state, it is one of the headquarters of the Bergen County Historical Society and open to the public 10 A.M. to 5 P.M., Wednesday through Saturday, and Sunday, 2 P.M. to 5 P.M. Phone: (201) 487-1739.

Wallace House, Somerville, Somerset County. William Wallace had not completed construction of his house when General and Mrs. Washington moved in during the second Middlebrook Encampment. The Washingtons occupied the Wallace House from December 1778 to June 1779. Major operations in the North having ended, Washington's principal military occupation was planning the Sullivan Expedition that wiped out the Iroquois settlements of western New York. Near the Wallace House are several houses still standing that were used by Washington's senior generals. Across the street is the brick house built in 1751 and now known as the Old Dutch Parsonage.

The Wallace House is a white frame structure of two stories with a large attic and a small kitchen wing. Original architectural features survived unchanged when the

Revolutionary Memorial Society acquired the property. In 1946 the Society presented it to the state. The historic house museum is located at 38 Washington Place in Somerville and administered by the New Jersey Division of Parks and Services. Both the Wallace House and the Old Dutch Parsonage are open to the public 10 A.M. to 4 P.M., Wednesday to Saturday, and 1 P.M. to 4 P.M. on Sunday. Phone: (908) 725-1015.

Westminster. *See* PROPRIETARY HOUSE.

NEW YORK

New York has a disproportionately large place in this guide for many reasons that are obvious and a few that should be pointed out. The colony was very active in the events leading up to the Revolution, and remained the main British base during much of the war. Nearly one-third of approximately three hundred battles and engagements took place on New York soil. The border warfare sustained by Loyalist and Indian raiders from Canada is recalled by many landmarks, particularly in the Mohawk Valley. These are the most apparent reasons. A less self-evident one is this: New Yorkers have shown an exceptional interest in preserving their colonial and Revolutionary history, perhaps partly because of their not being diverted by the Civil War interest that predominates in the South.

About 2,800 historic markers were erected in the thirteen years following the first appropriation of state funds for this purpose in 1926. The program was not controlled, typographical and historical errors were common, and proper records were not established. A new historic marker program, managed by the New York State Museum, was established in the 1960s, and the museum published a 129-page guide giving the text and location of approximately 139 large historical markers put up since 1960. The pocket-sized *Historical Area Markers in New York State* is available from the New York State Museum, which is located in Albany, New York on Madison Avenue across the plaza from the State Capitol Building. Phone: (518) 474-5877. To order this and other publications, phone (518) 402-5344 or email:nysmpub@mail.nysed.gov.

Also available through the New York State Museum is the pamphlet "The Hudson Valley in the American Revolution" and an excellent little booklet by David C. Thurheimer, "Landmarks of the Revolution in New York State: A Guide to the [45] Historic Sites Open to the Public." The booklet's value to users of this guide will be its twenty-eight photographs and about the same number of crude sketch maps showing locations of sites in terms of today's roads. Of considerable historical value is the section of Claude Sauthier's map of 1779, used for cover decoration.

A noteworthy pamphlet, "The Mohawk Valley and the American Revolution," once offered for sale, is still available via the internet at http://www.fortklock.com/mvinrevolution.htm. There is one segment of the website, www.fortklock.com, which contains information on American Revolution landmarks in New York's Hudson, Mohawk, and Schoharie Valleys. Another helpful website to look at is www.nysparks.state.ny.us. Click on "Historic Preservation" for detailed descriptions and locations of landmarks.

Albany. In 1609 Henry Hudson ended his exploration of the Hudson River within two months of the time Samuel de Champlain was less than 100 miles to the north, on the lake that now bears his name. The Dutch trading post of Fort Nassau was built in 1614 on an island that now is part of the Albany seaport. Ten years later the first settlers arrived and built Fort Orange. The patroonship of Rensselaerswyck was established in 1630. Centered on Fort Orange, this vast tract straddled the Hudson and was settled by Dutch, Germans, Danes, Norwegians, Scots, and other nationalities. In 1652 the new director general of New Netherland ordered the village of Beverwyck laid out around Fort Orange, and modern

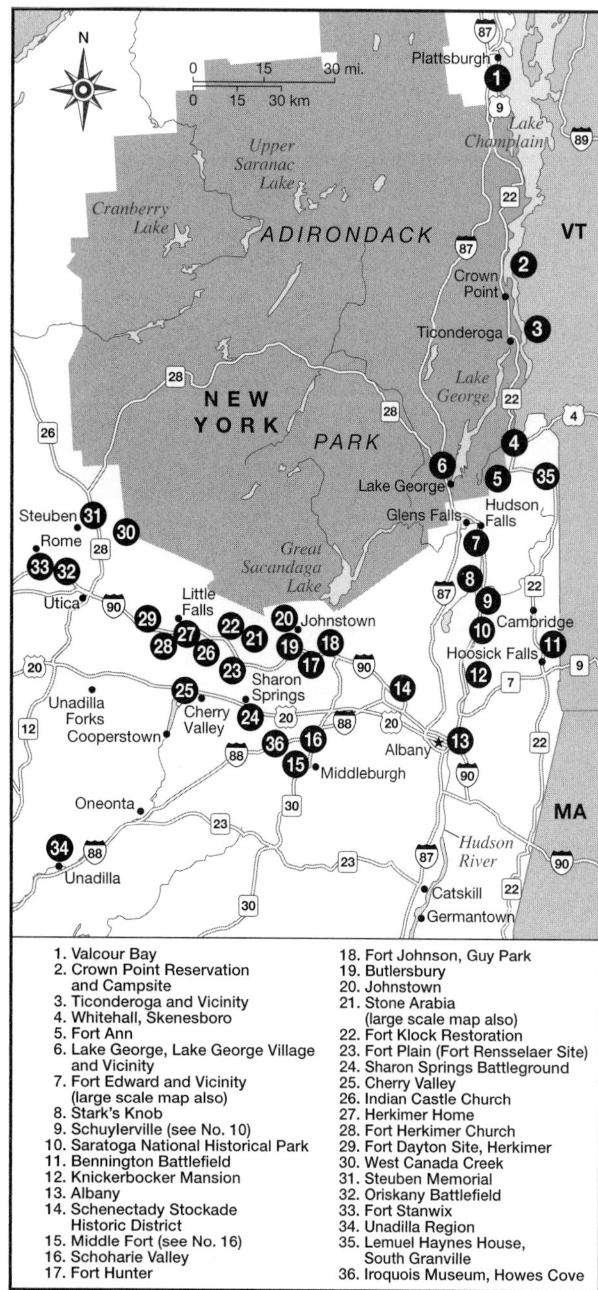

MAP BY XNR PRODUCTIONS. THE GALE GROUP.

Albany got its name when the British took over in 1664. Transition of the colony from one European government to another occurred peacefully, Dutch settlers retaining their language, customs, and local institutions as their leaders—Van Rensselaers, Schuylers, Gansevoorts—mingled with Clintons, Yateses, and Livingstons. Rensselaerswyck became the Manor of Rensselaer and was the only "English" manor to survive the colonial era.

Albany has several important sites from the colonial and Revolutionary period. At the foot of State Street is the place where Henry Hudson landed and where Fort Orange was built. A few blocks up the hill, at the other end of State Street, stood Fort Frederick, the objective of Burgoyne in 1777. At Lodge and Pine Streets is a marker pointing out that near here was the colonial hospital that treated the wounded from Saratoga in 1777, having previously received those from the 1758 attack on Ticonderoga. The body of Lord George Augustus Howe, killed in the latter battle, is said to lie beneath the vestibule floor of St. Peter's Episcopal Church on State Street. This building dates from 1859 but contains important items going back to its origins in 1715.

The home of Colonel Philip Van Rensselaer preserves much of the quality and character dating from its construction in 1787. Located between First and McCarthy Avenues on 523½ South Pearl Street, it is operated by the state-chartered Historic Cherry Hill Association and is open most of the year. Phone: (518) 434-4791; website: www.historiccherryhill.org. Ten Broeck Mansion was built in 1798 by the militia general and Patriot politician Abraham Ten Broeck (1734–1810). Located at 9 Ten Broeck Place, it is furnished in the federal period and is open on a limited schedule. The mansion serves as the headquarters for the Albany County Historical Association. Phone: (518) 436-9826; website: www.tenbroeck.org.

The First Church in Albany (Dutch Reformed) on North Pearl Street at Clinton Square was organized in 1642 and has a pulpit dating from 1656, said to be the oldest in the United States. Sites associated with the Albany Congress of 1754 have been destroyed by streets and buildings of downtown Albany, and both old churches were rebuilt after the Revolution. Across the bridge from Albany is Fort Crailo in Rensselaer.

Located at the corner of Clinton Avenue and Broadway is the Quackenbush House (c. 1730). It is the former home of Colonel Hendrique Quackenbush, who led Albany's Fifth Military Regiment against Burgoyne's army at Saratoga in 1777. Burgoyne was held prisoner at Quackenbush House for a short time after the battle of Saratoga. Privately owned, it is the oldest intact structure in the city of Albany, and is presently an upscale restaurant. Alongside the Quackenbush House is the Albany Visitor Center, wherein visitors can see a variety of maps and drawings of Albany during the American Revolution period. Albany Visitor Center's phone: (800) 258-3582.

Schuyler Mansion (the Pastures). By any criterion, the Schuyler Mansion is among the most noteworthy historic houses in America. Its master, Philip John Schuyler (1733–1804), served the revolutionary cause in a number of capacities. A statue of a stern-faced Philip Schuyler in full general's regalia is located in front of City Hall on Eagle Street.

Philip was born into the fourth generation of the New York Schuylers. His mother was a Van Cortlandt, he married a Van Rensselaer, and one of his daughters married the eighth patroon of the Manor of Rensselaer. Another daughter married Alexander Hamilton.

In 1763, when his father's estate finally was settled, thirty-year-old Philip Schuyler inherited thousands of acres in the Mohawk and Hudson Valleys. In addition, from his Uncle Philip he inherited the old Schuyler homestead where he had spent much of his childhood. This brick manor house, known as the Flats, built in 1666 and only slightly altered in three centuries, stood until burned in 1962 under mysterious circumstances (perhaps as a Halloween prank; the cause has never been determined) just as plans had been made to protect and restore it. The foundations remain (south edge of Watervliet on First Street), archaeology continues to yield important finds on both white and Indian settlements, and a nature trail has been put in near the site along the river. The Schuyler Flats Archeological District was designated a National Historic Landmark in 1993. In 2002 the town of Colonie, which owns the area, created the Schuyler Flatts Cultural Park. Philip also inherited lands in the Saratoga Patent, and here he built his country mansion at the place later called Schuylerville. (See under SARATOGA NATIONAL HISTORIC PARK.)

Schuyler had an excellent education, was commissioned a captain at the start of the Seven Years' War, and gained a reputation as a logistician. In 1761 he started building a mansion on a gentle slope that rose from the Hudson River just south of Albany's communal pasturing grounds. General John Bradstreet loaned him carpenters from British army units camped in the vicinity. While slaves and off-duty soldiers started putting up the mansion, Schuyler went to London with Bradstreet to help the latter settle his War Office accounts and to buy items for his own new house. He named his home the Pastures.

When completed in 1762 the Schuyler Mansion was a Georgian structure of rose-red brick, a building material much favored by the New York Dutch. (Salvaged brick from the Flats, mentioned above, has been used in the restoration of the Herkimer Home.) With a full basement, two stories, and a large attic with dormer windows, the house is 63 feet wide by 48 feet deep. The double-hip roof is enclosed by a wooden parapet of "Chinese" fretwork and is surmounted by twin chimneys. Detracting from the house's original lines is a six-sided vestibule leading to the front door, a tasteless addition of later years (the date not known). Four large rooms (almost 20 by 20 feet) are on each floor, arranged in the common plan of center-hall houses. The halls are 20 feet wide.

Furnishings and decorations of the Schuyler Mansion are particularly noteworthy. The state of New York purchased the building a little more than a century after it had passed out of possession of the family. Public funds were used to restore the building itself, but Schuyler descendants and private benefactors contributed furniture, furnishings, and other eighteenth-century treasures. Others contributed some $20,000 for purchase of period pieces before the mansion was opened to the public in 1917. The state has published a handsome book, *Schuyler Mansion: A Critical Catalogue of the Furnishings and Decorations*, by Anna K. Cunningham (1955). This admirable work includes 114 photographs of items in the collection, from paintings to jewelry, and is available through Willis Monie Books in Cooperstown, New York. Phone: (800) 322-2995.

The home you see today is fundamentally as Philip Schuyler and his many important guests knew it. The Pastures became unofficial headquarters of Patriot political and military affairs in the North. Schuyler was prominent in events leading to the Revolution, having been elected to the Continental Congress in 1775 (again in 1777 and 1779–1780). He was military commander of the Northern Department until relieved of that post shortly before the battles of Saratoga. In October 1778 he was cleared of charges of incompetence in repelling Burgoyne's offensive, having meanwhile had "Gentleman Johnny" as a prisoner-guest at the Pastures. In April 1779 he resigned his commission as major general but held public office continuously until 1798. His daughter Elizabeth married Alexander Hamilton at the Pastures, and Lafayette was a guest at the wedding. Visitors on other occasions included Washington, Franklin, Von Steuben, Rochambeau, and Benedict Arnold.

Schuyler Mansion is in the southern section of modern Albany at 32 Catharine Street. It is open to the public at specified hours. Phone: (518) 434-0834.

Auriesville Shrine, Mohawk Valley, located 3.5 miles east of Fultonville, and 5 miles west of Amsterdam on N.Y. Route 5S. A Catholic shrine was erected in 1930 to 1931 at the place where Father Isaac Jogues and other French Jesuit priests were martyred in the 1640s. Honoring the first North American saints, the shrine is on 600 landscaped acres and provides fine views of the Mohawk Valley. Auriesville is on the site of one of the original Castles of the Mohawk Indians.

Beacon and Mount Beacon. *See* FISHKILL LANDING.

Bear Mountain area, Hudson River, junction of Palisades Interstate Parkway with U.S. 9W and Bear Mountain Bridge. Forts Clinton and Montgomery were captured by the British after a difficult march from Stony Point and a dangerous double envelopment astride Popolopen Creek. Most of the landmarks of this important and

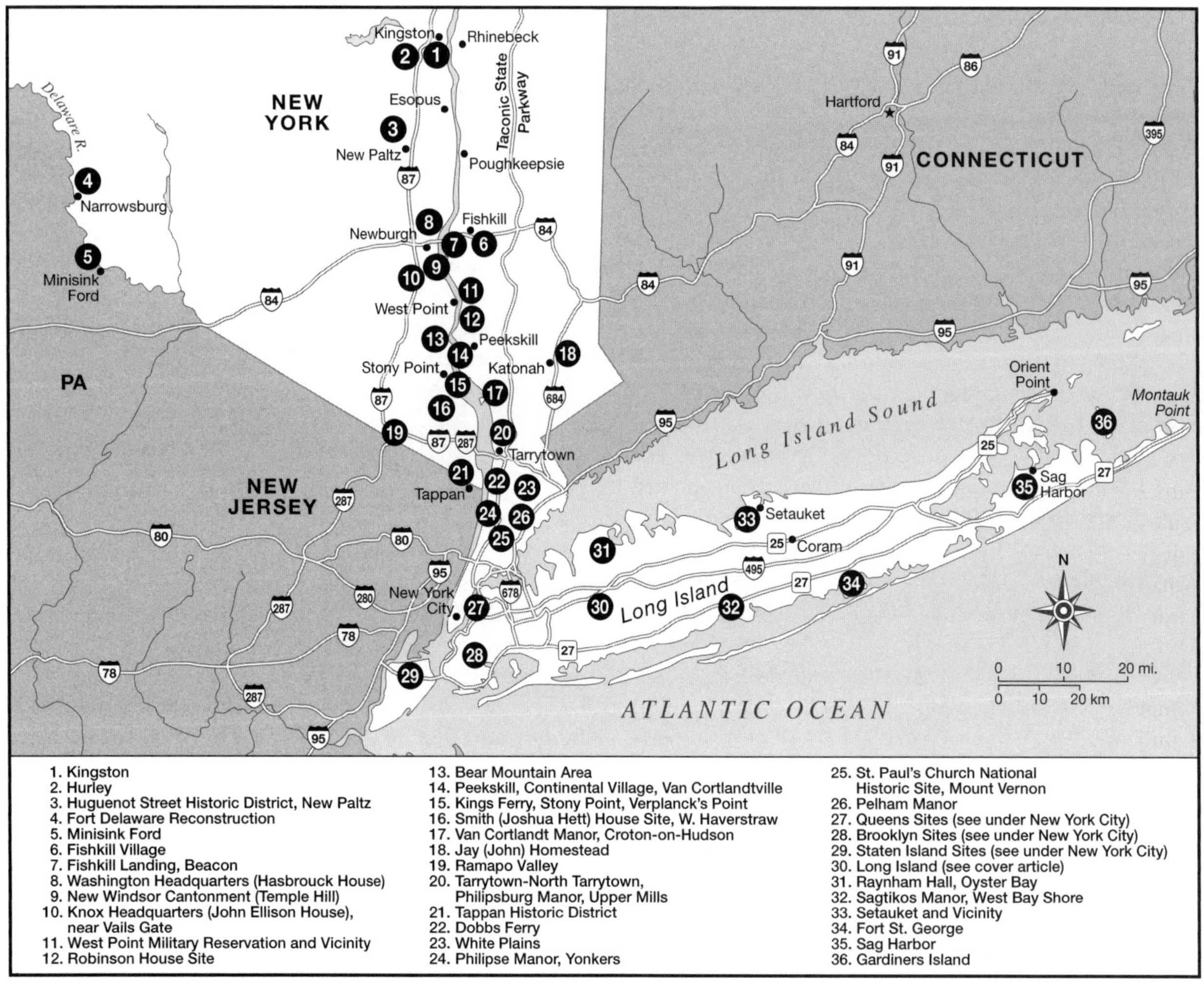

MAP BY XNR PRODUCTIONS. THE GALE GROUP.

interesting operation are preserved within New York's newest historic park, the Fort Montgomery State Historic Site. The outer redoubt of Fort Clinton is in good condition, though a zoo now occupies the site of the main work, and only traces of other fortifications remain here. The site of Fort Montgomery, on the other hand, is free of modern encroachments. The outlines and foundations of this important river fortification have survived. Interpretive signs or an audio tour guide the visitor past the remains of the fort, the powder magazine, and the North Redoubt. There are also occasional Revolutionary War reenactments. Phone: (845) 786-2701, ext. 226.

Beekman Arms, Rhinebeck, mid-Hudson Valley. In about 1700 a two-room stone tavern was built where the Kings Highway crossed the Sepasco Indian trail, 60 miles south of Albany on the east side of the Hudson. The spot is now the intersection of U.S. 9 and N.Y. 308, at the center of Rhinebeck, and the tavern has evolved through two and a half centuries into a large modern inn. Its name comes from the fact that Henry Beekman sold the land on which this, "America's Oldest Operating Inn," was built. The present stone walls of the central portion date from an expansion in 1769. Oak beams measuring 8 by 12 inches support the first floor, which has planks 14 inches wide and 1.5 inches thick. In emergencies the tavern became a community fortress, with field artillery firing from the first floor and noncombatants being sheltered in the large cellar. General Montgomery lived in the inn before marching to his fate in Canada in 1775. Washington and many of his senior officers used the building during the Revolution.

The Beekman Arms retains a great deal of its eighteenth- and nineteenth-century character inside, where some original structural features can still be seen. Phone: (845) 876-2995.

Bemis Heights. *See* SARATOGA.

Bennington Battlefield, north side of Route 67 between Walloomsac, New York and Vermont state line. Phone: (518) 279-1155. The Bennington Battlefield State Historic Site is part of Grafton Lakes State Park, and further information on the Bennington Battlefield site is accessible from that entity. Phone: (518) 686-7109. Although many sites associated with the Battle of Bennington are in Vermont, the battlefield itself is in New York.

"Gentleman Johnny" Burgoyne met so little resistance as he moved along Lake Champlain toward the head of the Hudson Valley in 1777 that he became overconfident. He fatally underestimated the ability of the Patriots to organize an effective resistance. But Burgoyne could see that he would have to live off the country now that his 185-mile-long line of communications with his Canadian bases was being overtaxed. He particularly needed horses to move his artillery and wagons, and to mount the 250 Brunswick dragoons. Inaccurate intelligence convinced him that the Continentals had a large number of horses as well as other military stores at Bennington.

Piling blunder on blunder, Burgoyne selected the Brunswickers to form the nucleus of this eight-hundred-man expedition, because these were the people who most needed the horses. Their commander, Lieutenant Colonel Friedrich Baum, spoke no English, and since one purpose of the operation was to win Loyalist support in the areas overrun, Philip Skene, Loyalist proprietor of some 60,000 acres around modern Whitehall (then called Skenesboro), was sent along as "public affairs advisor." In addition to his own dragoons and other Germans totaling 374 officers and men, Baum had fifty British marksmen and three hundred or so Loyalists, Canadians, and Indians. By 13 August his expedition had reached Cambridge, about 20 miles by road from Bennington, Vermont.

In the few weeks before this operation, however, the Patriots had become sufficiently aroused to start taking action. The present state of Vermont, a wilderness claimed by New York, Massachusetts, and New Hampshire in colonial times, had been known since 1763 as the New Hampshire Grants and was sparsely populated. When the Vermont Council of Safety asked for help, New Hampshire and Massachusetts both said they lacked the necessary funds. The wealthy John Langdon, a Patriot of New Hampshire, allegedly stepped forward in this crisis to offer his personal fortune and credit and to nominate "our friend Stark" as commander of the forces to be raised.

John Stark accepted a commission as a brigadier general from New Hampshire on 17 July and quickly raised a force of about 1,500. The colorful and temperamental hero of Bunker Hill had resigned his commission as a colonel of the Continental army about four months earlier because Congress would not promote him. The "rustic Achilles" agreed to quit sulking in his tent and take the field only when assured that he would be independent of Congressional orders.

When Stark arrived with his brigade at Manchester, Vermont (about 26 miles by road north of Bennington), from which point he intended to attack the flank and rear of Burgoyne's forces in the Hudson Valley, he ran into trouble. A fat major general from Massachusetts, one of the officers previously promoted over Stark's head, was there with orders from Congress to take command of all New England militia raised for the emergency. This individual also had orders from General Schuyler to send Stark's brigade to join the main army on the Hudson. John Stark flat refused. General Benjamin Lincoln tried to make Stark see that such insubordination could be disastrous to the Patriot cause, but when reasoning accomplished nothing, Lincoln showed the character and good sense not to give up in disgust. He reported this problem to Congress, but then proceeded to treat Stark as an ally and to fall in with Stark's strategic notions. Lincoln agreed to his plan of operating against the enemy's flank and rear, and he urged Schuyler to modify his own plans accordingly.

Ironically, Stark's insubordination resulted in his being located, completely by accident, at the very place toward which the enemy raiders were headed: Bennington.

Seth Warner and his Green Mountain Regiment had reassembled at Manchester after their defeat at Hubbardton, Vermont. Here they remained temporarily when Stark moved on to Bennington, some 25 miles south, where he was joined by Vermont's troops, some militia from the Berkshires, and the Stockbridge Indians.

Having camped in Cambridge overnight, Baum resumed his advance on the morning of 14 August, a Thursday. When Stark heard that Indians were ravaging the area around Cambridge, he had sent a two-hundred-man detachment there to chase them off, but on the evening of 13 August he learned that enemy regulars in strength were following the Indians. He therefore ordered Warner to move his men immediately to Bennington. Baum's scouts, meanwhile, reported that the militia force in Bennington was much larger than expected, so the German commander reported back to Burgoyne that he would advance cautiously.

The Battle of Bennington started around 9:00 the morning of Thursday, 14 August 1777 at St. Croix, or Sancoick's Mill, about 12 miles from Bennington, Vermont, on modern Route 67 and 67A (roughly the route Baum was marching). Stark held the bulk of his forces at a crossing of the Walloomsac about 4 miles from town while detachments carried out a delaying action. Baum advanced slowly, and finally decided he had better request reinforcements. When he reached the point where the road crossed the Walloomsac, he secured this critical area with troops on both sides of the river and started deploying the rest of his force in small defensive detachments.

With the idea of establishing a position he could hold until reinforcements arrived, Baum made the fundamental error of scattering his forces. On the Bennington side of the river about 150 of his men, most of them Loyalists, constructed a hasty fortification that became known as the Tory Redoubt. On the other side of the crossing were about seventy-five regulars. Camp followers found and occupied a log cabin between the Tory Redoubt and the river crossing, and other cabins on either side of the river were occupied by Loyalists and Canadians. On the side of a hill overlooking the crossing from the north (his direction of advance), Baum placed 200 officers and men in a position that became known as the Dragoon Redoubt. On top of this hill the Indians encamped. Back along the road to Sancoick's Mill, about 1,000 yards from the vital crossing, Baum posted fifty German infantrymen and some Loyalists to guard his rear. To keep the Americans from infiltrating along the right (north) bank of the river to the crossing site, a detachment of fifty jaegers was posted between the Dragoon Redoubt and the river.

The next day, Friday, 15 August, was so rainy that both sides were content to remain inactive, particularly because both were waiting for their reinforcements to arrive. About 350 of Seth Warner's men left Manchester on Friday morning and made camp that night about two hours' march from Stark's bivouac. Lieutenant Colonel Breymann started marching to Baum's relief on Friday morning with about 650 slow-moving German grenadiers, chasseurs, riflemen, and two cannon. But when he went into camp that night he had covered only 8 miles, and he did not reach the battlefield until 4:30 the next afternoon.

Stark, meanwhile, had reconnoitered the enemy positions and formulated the plan of attack so dear to the hearts of military amateurs—the double envelopment. Splitting his forces into three columns, he planned to have two of these loop wide around the enemy's flanks to join in an attack on his rear, while he himself led the main body in the middle. The rain stopped around noon on Saturday 16 August, and at 3 P.M. the Patriots launched their attack. Two hours later, after what Stark in his report called "the hottest [action] I ever saw in my life—it represented one continued clap of thunder," the first part of the battle was over, and the Patriots had possession of the field. They were preparing to loot the enemy camps when, to their considerable consternation, Breymann's relief column was reported to be only 2 miles away. Breymann had reached Sancoick's Mill around 4:30, half an hour before Baum fell mortally wounded and resistance in the Dragoon Redoubt had collapsed. But because of the phenomenon known as "acoustic shadow," no sound of battle had been heard at Sancoick's Mill, only 4 miles distant. Breymann's troops realized too late that they had marched into a hornets' nest. Warner's Green Mountain Regiment arrived just in time to play the leading role in this final action, which lasted until dark. The Germans then withdrew, leaving Breymann's 2 cannon. Stark reported the capture of 4 cannon (Baum had only 2), 2 brass drums, 250 sabres, 4 ammunition wagons, and several hundred stand of arms. Enemy casualties numbered about 200 dead on the field (others, including Baum, died of wounds) and around 700 prisoners. Only 9 of the 374 Germans of Baum's force returned to Burgoyne's army. Stark reported the loss of 30 of his command killed and 40 wounded, although the generally accepted figure is 40 Americans killed and wounded.

This was one victory the Patriots badly needed. It did much to set the stage for Burgoyne's greater defeat at Saratoga.

Bennington Battlefield State Park encompasses about 276 acres of wooded terrain, and at the battlefield's entrance there is a marker. A map for the entire area is available onsite, and three stone memorials can be found at the top of the hill, in addition to various markers that indicate battlefield positions. From the entrance on the highway a tourist winds up a narrow road through second-growth woods, circles a grassy hill, and can park near the top. This is the site of the Dragoon Redoubt, where the fiercest fighting took place, and there is an excellent map showing troop movements and positions. But even with a good mental picture of what happened at Bennington, it is difficult for visitors to orient themselves. The landmarks of the action are not readily identifiable from this observation point. If a person leaves it and walks back up the road and to the northwest, through a vista cut in that direction can be seen the hill where the Indian auxiliaries of Baum's were positioned on the eve of the battle. Having seen this, one gets a somewhat clearer picture of the total action and can locate the route by which Colonel Moses Nichols enveloped Baum's position. However, until the site is developed further, a visitor will not be able to visualize the action at the Tory Redoubt and the position of the jaegers on the southern slope of the hill below the Dragoon Redoubt. (Sites associated with Stark's approach to the battlefield are covered under BENNINGTON and vicinity, VERMONT.)

Leaving Bennington Battlefield State Park and driving west and north to Cambridge for 10 miles, a tourist will find landmarks of the German advance. Initially, the route is through ugly vestiges of the mill operations that developed in modern times along the Walloomsac River. The site of Breymann's defeat is indicated by a highway marker a little less than a mile west of the entrance to the battlefield park, but there is nothing else to see here except a run-down industrial plant, railroad tracks, and evidence of economic distress. Exactly 2 miles farther west on N.Y. 67 is a highway marker on the left (south) side indicating that St. Croix Church was here, so this is in the vicinity of Sancoick's Mill, where the action started on 14 August (above). The visitor who continues north on N.Y. 22 toward Cambridge (a fine highway through scenic country), will pass the place where Patriot militia skirmished with Baum's advance guard. (Historical marker is on the right [east] of the road .35 mile north of the N.Y. 67–22 road junction, 4 miles south of Cambridge.)

On entering the village of Cambridge, a visitor will learn from a marker on the left (west) that this is the route of the Great Northern War Trail, along which the Indians took their captives from New England to Canada from about 1650 to 1700. Other than an open space at the junction of N.Y. 22 and 327 in Cambridge that was a militia training ground, there are no Revolutionary War sites to see in this attractive little place where Baum camped before marching toward Bennington. (See BENNINGTON under Vermont for the site of Baum's death of wounds and his burial. Here also the landmarks associated with the Patriot advance to the battlefield may be found.)

Boyd-Parker Memorial, site of Little Beard's Town, or Genesee. *See* SULLIVAN-CLINTON EXPEDITION.

Bush Homestead (Putnam's Headquarters), Port Chester, also known as the Bush-Lyon Homestead. Headquarters of General Israel Putnam from May 1777 to March 1778, when he was commander of the Hudson Highlands, this well-preserved Georgian Colonial house was built shortly before the Revolution by Abraham Bush, a sea captain. The original furniture, including the bed and desk used by "Old Put," has been preserved, as have the slave quarters. Listed in the "Sites Also Noted" category by the National Survey of Historic Sites and Buildings (1964), the Bush Homestead is in Lyon Park overlooking King Street and is open only on Thursdays from 1:30 to 4 P.M. Phone: (914) 939-8919.

Butlersbury, Mohawk Valley. On Switzer Hill, near Fonda, overlooking the Mohawk River, the ancient homestead of the much-dreaded Loyalist soldiers John and Walter Butler remains standing despite almost two centuries of local indifference to its historic and architectural significance. The simple frame house built in 1742 by "Old" Walter Butler has survived the modifications of successive farmer-owners, who masked its cherry paneling and hand-hewn beams with lath and plaster, made rambling additions, and covered its clapboard siding with asbestos shingle. The magnificent view over the Mohawk to the west from the 700-foot hill remains virtually unspoiled.

"Old" Walter Butler and his son John were among Sir William Johnson's most valuable subordinates, and their landholdings in the Mohawk Valley—7,800 acres—approached his in magnitude. But the Butlers earned their position in history by military duty far from their comfortable home fires. John spent much of his youth at the exposed outpost of Fort Ontario, where his father was commandant, and he was fifty-three years old when, in the summer of 1778, he led Loyalist and Indian raiders almost 200 miles through the wilderness from Niagara to attack the Wyoming Valley settlement in Pennsylvania. "Young" Walter, John's son and "Old" Walter's grandson, was known as one of the brightest young men in the valley when he was studying law in Albany on the eve of the Revolution. He turned out to be equally talented as a man of military action.

Among the many Loyalists who fled to Canada, John and Walter Butler were the most effective leaders of the raids that subsequently ravaged the Mohawk Valley. Young Walter was captured at the Shoemaker House in 1777 while on one of the boldest missions of the war. Sentenced to death but reprieved because of the intercession of several Patriots, including Philip Schuyler, he escaped to Canada. (There he helped a former neighbor, as outlined in the article on FORT FREY.) After leading the famous raid on Cherry Valley, Major Walter Butler played a key role in the operations of Major Ross in 1781 (see JOHNSTOWN) and was killed in the rear-guard action on West Canada Creek.

Colonel John Butler was active in establishing a settlement of Loyalists in Canada, where he was given 5,000 acres and a pension. Until his death at the age of seventy-one he held important public offices.

The Butler estate was confiscated by the Patriots during the Revolution and later bought by John Fonda. In 1834 his widow and son Jelles sold it to Henry Wilson, whose family occupied the house and farmed the land through the 1940s. For a few years the house remained unoccupied and neglected until bought by Mrs. Eleanore Rockwell in 1959. Extensive restoration of the interior has been completed. When what was believed to be a post-Revolution addition to the back of the house was taken off, an 1826 penny was found, which confirmed the suspicion and eliminated the "saltbox" character of the house. In late 1971, after Mrs. Rockwell's death, her daughter Cynthia moved into Butlersbury with her family. Among the first guests were several busloads of Canadians revisiting the homes of their Loyalist ancestors. Butlersbury has had new owners since that time, and remains privately owned.

The house is reached from Fonda by driving east about 100 yards and turning north on Switzer Hill

Road. At .75 mile, turn right on Old Trail and go 100 yards to Walter Butler Lane on the right. The house is visible on the left (east) side of this short, dead-end road, about 100 yards away. Casual tourists will find the site is well worth visiting for the view. Since ownership is in private hands, tours are not available, but information is available by contacting the Montgomery County Department of History and Archives. Phone: (518) 853-8186.

Castles of the Mohawk Indians. The easternmost tribe of the Iroquois Confederacy, the Mohawks, were responsible for guarding the approaches along the Mohawk Valley. During the period 1580 to 1666 they had approximately sixteen villages known as Indian castles, but all except Auriesville were burned in 1666. The four built to replace these were again destroyed in 1693, and the Mohawks were greatly reduced in numbers. The survivors then planned a separate castle for each clan, and these were in existence from 1700 until 1775, when the Mohawks took the British side in the American Revolution and were finally driven from the valley. Sites of the last three Indian castles are at Fort Hunter (Wolf), Fort Plain (Turtle), and Indian Castle (Bear).

The other Iroquois tribes had castles to the west, most of which were destroyed by the Sullivan-Clinton Expedition of 1779.

Cherry Valley, Otsego County. Walter Butler and Joseph Brant owe their negative reputation as Loyalist and Indian raiders primarily to the fact that they were such good military leaders. They collaborated in a raid on this strategically important settlement and surprised the ineptly commanded garrison ignorant of frontier warfare. The 700 Loyalists and Indians killed some 30 noncombatants and 15 soldiers in an action (11 November 1778) lasting about four hours. The raiders took 71 prisoners but released most of them the next day.

A memorial was erected in the Cherry Valley cemetery on the 100th anniversary of the massacre, and the local museum, at 49 Main Street, has items of historical interest and information on walking tours of historic Cherry Valley. Phone: (607) 264-3098; website: www.cherryvalleymuseum.org.

Clermont, Clermont State Park, Germantown, Hudson River. The first Robert Livingston (1654–1728) reached America in 1673, and by 1686 had by purchase and grant acquired 160,000 acres on the east side of the Hudson. His third son, also named Robert, was bequeathed 13,000 acres in the southwest corner of the Manor of Livingston. This Robert II built Clermont around 1730. His son, Robert III, married Margaret Beekman in 1742, and when the British in their raid of 1777 burned Clermont it was this vigorous lady who undertook immediately to rebuild the mansion. North and south wings were added in 1800.

Robert Livingston IV, statesman and diplomat of the Revolutionary era, retired to Clermont in 1804 after negotiating the Louisiana Purchase in his capacity as minister to France. Here, in addition to work in progressive agriculture, he pursued his earlier interest in steam navigation. He and Robert Fulton produced the first practical steamboat, which was named for the Livingston home and which made a record-setting run up the river to this place.

The steep-pitched roof and dormers of Clermont date from 1878. The state now owns the house with 500 acres, and restoration has been completed. In 1973 it was designated a National Historic Landmark, and the site is a key element to the Hudson River National Landmark District, which was established in 1990. Clermont is the most important of the many structures associated with the remarkable Livingston family, and a local organization, Friends of Clermont, provides tours and maintains an informative website on the house and grounds. Phone: (518) 537-4240; website: www.friendsofclermont.org.

Clinton House, 549 Main Street, Poughkeepsie. Named in honor of the state's first governor and said to have been occupied by him in 1777, this much-reconstructed house of rough fieldstone was built around 1765. It is a state-owned historic site with period furnishings and is open daily to the public for tours. Contact the Dutchess County Historical Society for more information. Phone: (845) 471-1630.

Clove, The. *See* RAMAPO VALLEY.

Constitution Island. *See* WEST POINT MILITARY RESERVATION, which now includes this historic site on the Hudson River.

Continental Village (site), Putnam County, from Van Cortlantville, just north of Peekskill, north about 2 miles on Gallows Hill Road. Here, at the main entrance to the Hudson Highlands east of the river and a few hundred yards south of the junction of the Old West Point Road and the Old Albany Post Road in 1777, the Patriots established a camp and supply center. A few months later (9 October) the small guard detachment was routed by a British force under Governor William Tryon, and the base was destroyed. Maps of Robert Erskine thereafter indicated "Burnt Barracks" at this place on Canopus Hollow Road, but the Patriots reoccupied the area in 1781. This and other Patriot camps in the vicinity have been excavated by the New York Historical Society.

Crown Point Reservation and Campsite, 739 Bridge Road on the west end of the Lake Champlain Bridge. In 1609 Champlain visited this site in his voyage of discovery, and his battle with the Iroquois took place either in this area or at Ticonderoga, about 12 miles farther south. Recent research reveals that the French built a fort across the lake on the Vermont side at Chimney Point before starting the construction of Fort St. Frédéric at Crown Point in 1731. The latter was an outpost for the protection of Canada and also a forward base for their own raids on English settlements. At the approach of Amherst's expedition in 1759 the French garrison blew up their fort and retreated to Canada. (See also TICONDEROGA.)

The English started building a large fort a short distance inland from demolished Fort St. Frédéric, but with French power in North America almost immediately thereafter broken (1763), the plans for making Fort Crown Point a major fortification were curtailed. A fire in 1773 virtually destroyed the outpost, and when Seth Warner occupied the place two years later (after the capture of Ticonderoga) he found a pathetic little garrison of nine men and some camp followers.

During the remainder of the Revolution, Crown Point was important only as an outpost for Ticonderoga. It figured in Arnold's naval operations (see VALCOUR ISLAND) and as a post on the British line of communications in 1776 and 1777.

Now split by the highway leading to the great bridge across Lake Champlain but not disfigured by these modern developments, Crown Point Reservation and Campsite is a picturesque state park. The ruins of the French and English forts are classified as National Historic Landmarks. The French did a thorough job of blowing up Fort Frédéric, which had never been fully developed anyhow: the design was faulty and the construction work had been unsatisfactory. Part of the ruins are fenced off, but the ramparts of this star fort remain.

The English fort, only a few hundred feet away, is a ruin of exceptional beauty and interest. A narrow footpath leads around the top of the ramparts, an earthen mound rising some 30 feet in places from a moat. Portions of this moat were blasted from rock. Inside these high earthen walls are the ruins of two large masonry barracks, their gray walls rising from a green carpet of grass. A spring feeds a rock pool within the parade ground. One would hope that the site will be preserved as a picturesque ruin (like the Loire River chateau of Chinon, where Joan of Arc entered the pages of history).

Across the highway is the campsite. In addition to the vestiges of other fortifications, monuments, historic markers, and a replica of the French trading post, this park includes the Champlain Memorial Lighthouse (1909). On the side facing the lake is a particularly fine bronze by Rodin: a life-size head of a woman symbolizing La France.

The sites are closed during the winter months. Phone: (518) 597-4666 (Crown Point Historic Site); (518) 597-3603 (campsite).

De Wint House. *See* TAPPAN.

Dobbs Ferry Site, Dobbs Ferry, Hudson River. Only the name has survived of this important colonial and Revolutionary War crossing of the lower Hudson River. The site is nevertheless interesting for what remains of the topography. Turning west off U.S. 9, which was originally the Albany Post Road and the extension of Broadway, one winds through the business district of modern Dobbs Ferry and then descends a steep grade to the railroad tracks along the river. The shoreline has been altered beyond recognition, but a park and marina near the railroad station preserve some semblance of its original appearance. At this date there are no historical markers.

Esopus. *See* KINGSTON.

Field of Grounded Arms, Fort Hardy, Schuylerville. Most of the field where Burgoyne's 6,300 troops laid down their arms after surrendering to the Americans is preserved as open ground. Located at the corners of Route 4 and Route 29 is a fully staffed visitors center open to the public seven days a week. Phone: (518) 695-4195. In 2004 the battleground site became the recipient of a grant through the American Battlefield Protection Program to assist in funding nomination into the National Register of Historical Places. (See end of article on SARATOGA NATIONAL HISTORICAL PARK.)

Fishkill Landing, Hudson River opposite Newburgh. Since 1913 incorporated in the town of Beacon, Fishkill Landing was an outpost of the Continental army's defensive system in the Hudson Highlands. Nearby Fishkill Village was a main supply base. In laying plans for letting the British capture the strategic works at West Point, Benedict Arnold found pretexts for weakening its garrison by detaching troops to the Fishkill area for guard duty and to cut wood. In relatively recent years the last vestiges of earthworks have been obliterated, but the site of "Fort Hill" is indicated by a marker on U.S. 9 at the county line.

Mount Beacon (1,640 feet) was once accessible by a renowned inclined railway from 1902 until the railway's closing in 1975. At a point 1 mile by trail to the summit was a signal station during the Revolution, and there rests a 27-foot high monument erected to honor militiamen who were in charge of the beacon fires. The trail continues 2 miles to South Beacon Peak (1,635 feet). Mount Beacon is accessible to hikers, and plans for another railway are continually being proposed.

Fishkill Village, near intersection of U.S. 9 and I-84, in southwest Dutchess County. About 5 miles road distance east of Fishkill Landing (now part of Beacon) and lying pleasantly in the lap of a plain near the foot of the mountains, as Benson Lossing described it, the village of Fishkill is rich in Revolutionary War associations. In 1775 it comprised only a dozen or so houses, a tavern, two churches, and a schoolhouse, although Dutch settlers had been in the area since the start of the century. Wiccopee Pass, just south of the village, was fortified early in the war, with three artillery battery positions there from 1776 to 1783 and a lookout point nearby as the signal relay station to Washington's headquarters in Newburgh. In relatively recent years the last vestiges of earthworks have been obliterated, but the site of "Fort Hill" is indicated by a marker on U.S. 9 at the county line. Barracks and storehouses were constructed in Fishkill, and the place became the principal military depot for the Continental army.

When the British overran the lower Hudson Valley, Fishkill was crowded with refugees. The New York Provincial Congress was in session here during the period 5 September 1776 to 11 February 1777, after being run from New York City to White Plains and before moving on to Kingston. The ambulatory legislators met in the First Reformed, or Dutch, Church, which also served as a prison. A famous inmate of the prison was Enoch Crosby, the model used by James Fenimore Cooper for his character Harvey Birch in *The Spy, A Tale of the Neutral Ground.*

The Dutch Church, 1153 Main Street, dates from 1731, and the exterior of stuccoed stone and brick has been little changed. The interior was radically altered in 1854, and it was after this date that most of the village's surviving houses were built. Phone: (845) 896-9836.

Trinity Episcopal Church, Main Street, east of Route 9, was built around 1769. It was a hospital during the Revolution. Except for removal of the upper part of the tall steeple, which became necessary in 1803 because it was structurally unsound, the exterior of the small frame church is unaltered. Of special architectural interest is its curious cornice. (The hollow concave molding known as cavetto is used rather than the more usual cymatium—a practice common in Etruscan architecture.) Phone: (845) 896-9884.

Because of its association with Fishkill Landing, where a ferry was established in 1743 and where Hudson River traffic stopped, the village of Fishkill was an unusually important stop on the Albany Post Road, or King's Highway. On U.S. 9 about 1.3 miles south of Fishkill is an old red stone marker inscribed "66 Miles to N. York." Although the Albany Post Road dates from 1703, when an act of the colonial assembly started its construction, the more than forty milestones were not set up until after 1797. About half have survived, having been reset in concrete with protective coverings, and can be discovered at various points. The stone markers were erected on the order of the new nation's first postmaster, Benjamin Franklin, to assist mail carriers in navigation.

The Derick Brinkerhoff House, about 3 miles east of Fishkill at the junction of N.Y. 52 and 82, is where Washington stayed whenever he came through. The house is still owned by a family descendant, Todd Brinkerhoff. Across the street, a blue marker was erected to show the Abraham Brinkerhoff store site. Visible from the Derick Brinkerhoff House is a large marker, the Lafayette Memorial informing visitors that the major general lay there many weeks recuperating from a near-fatal fever. Upon his recuperation, subsequent victory over Cornwallis in 1781, and return to France, Lafayette sent, as a token of his gratitude, a large French-made punch bowl. That bowl now rests in the Madam Brett Homestead, 50 Van Nydeck Avenue, in Beacon. The Madam Brett Homestead, maintained and shown by the Melzingah Chapter of the Daughters of the American Revolution, is the oldest building (c. 1709) in Dutchess County. Phone: (845) 831-6533. The Melzingah DAR Chapter is among the most active chapters in the country, and is very helpful in securing additional information. Email: pbarrack-beacon@att.net.

Fort Ann, Washington County, on U.S. 4, about midway between Fort Edward and Whitehall. Colonial and Revolutionary War forts were located at this critical point along the Hudson-Champlain route. From a contour map one can see why: Fort Ann is at the mouth of a defile through which troops moving south along Wood Creek from Skenesboro (now Whitehall) would debouch into flatter country for the rest of their march to the Hudson. The British built a fort here in 1757. The next year about five hundred men under Israel Putnam and Robert Rogers were sent by Abercromby to observe French activity around Ticonderoga. They were returning to Fort Edward from around Skenesboro when they were ambushed in the area of modern Kanesville, about a mile northwest of Fort Ann. Putnam was wounded, taken prisoner, and cruelly treated before being sent to Montreal and eventually exchanged.

A delaying action against Burgoyne's invasion in 1777 was fought on 8 July in the gorge about three-quarters of a mile north of Fort Ann (mentioned earlier). Colonel Pierce Long had fallen back with his 150-man rear guard, and at Fort Ann he was reinforced by about 400 New York militia under Colonel Henry Van Rensselaer. Having fewer than 200 men, the commander of the British advance guard decided to stop and wait for reinforcements. Van Rensselaer and Long sallied forth about 10:30 A.M. One Patriot column crossed to the east bank of the creek (now the barge canal) and threatened the British flank and rear as the other attacked the mouth of the defile. Hard-pressed, the British shifted their position from the bottom of the narrow gorge (now widened out and deforested) to the sharp, 500-foot-high ridge to the north (on the left as one drives from Fort Ann toward Whitehall). The Patriots broke off the engagement after two hours of fierce fighting because their ammunition was running out and the war whoops of enemy reinforcements were heard in the distance. It was later revealed (during the investigation of Burgoyne's operations) that these "Indian war whoops" all emanated from one British captain advancing alone after his troops refused to follow him into the battle.

Although it may be difficult to find, a marker indicating "Battle Hill" is located about one-half mile past the bank on U.S. Route 4. There is a railroad intersection on the right and a large rock cut on the left. Just into the rock cut is the marker. Ownership of the actual battlefield is in flux and a highway runs through it, but visitors can get a sense of the grounds where this significant confrontation took place. For further information contact the town historian, Virginia Parrott. Phone: (518) 639-5375.

Fort Clinton. *See* BEAR MOUNTAIN AREA and WEST POINT.

Fort Constitution (Constitution Island). *See* WEST POINT.

Fort Crailo ("Yankee Doodle House"), 9½ Riverside Avenue, Rensselaer, south of Dunn Memorial Bridge, Rensselaer, 1 mile across the Hudson from Albany. The front portion of this house, designated a National Historic Landmark, is believed to have been built by Hendrick Van Rensselaer, brother of the first patroon of Rennsselaerswyck. Dating from about 1704, the building may be on the site of the 1642 residence of Arent Van Curler, cousin of these Rensselaers and manager of the patroonship from 1637.

The much-restored brick house is maintained by the state as a museum of Dutch culture. The older portion features huge beams, broad floorboards, and large fireplaces, whereas the rear wing (1762) reflects the architectural refinements that came to New Netherland with the intervening years. Like most frontier homes, this one had loopholes in the heavy outside walls.

Some verses for "Yankee Doodle" may have been conceived here in 1758 by British army surgeon Richard Shuckburgh from his impressions of a militia muster. Open Wednesday through Sunday, 11:00 A.M. to 5:00 P.M. Phone: (518) 463-8738.

Fort Dayton Site, Mohawk Valley. In the present village of Herkimer (not to be confused with Fort Herkimer Church or the Herkimer Home), which was settled by Palatines in 1722, is the site of the fort built in 1776 by Colonel Elias Dayton and called Fort Dayton. From here the Patriots under General Nicholas Herkimer started their ill-fated march to Oriskany. The well is the only remaining remnant of Fort Dayton. In Myers Park is a recently refurbished heroic bronze statue depicting the wounded Herkimer directing the final successful stages of the battle. Information on Fort Dayton and other regional areas of interest can be obtained from the Herkimer County Historical Society, 400 North Main Street. Phone: (315) 866-6413.

Fort Delaware Reconstruction, Sullivan County, north of Narrowsburg, on N.Y. Route 97. On the Delaware River a few hundred yards from where the original fort stood before the site was eaten away by the river, this commercial reconstruction includes a stockade, blockhouses, three log cabins, a blacksmith shop, a shed, an armory, an animal yard, and an herb garden. Called the Fort Delaware Museum of Colonial History, it is representative of early forts erected by settlers in this region around 1750. This popular attraction for tourists portrays life for those who settled the upper Delaware Valley in the 1750s. There are a variety of programs and events scheduled all year, including programs tailored for students. The fort is located three-quarters of a mile from Narrowsburg. Phone (845) 726-3869 (September–April); (845) 252-6660 (May–August).

Fort Edward and vicinity, upper Hudson. The town of Fort Edward is located near the Hudson River's end on Route 197. Prior to the 1700s, the Indians named this area the Great Carrying Place because the river's end forced them to portage their canoes over to Lake Champlain. Fort Edward, briefly the third-largest city in British North America, was the site of British works built in 1709, 1731, 1755, and 1757. The famous rangers of Robert Rogers were based here during the colonial wars. The 40-acre site of these early forts and the ranger camps is on Rogers Island, joined to today's village of Fort Edward by N.Y. Route 197. Natural and man-made changes in the Hudson River have vastly altered the island's configuration since colonial times, portions of the original island having become part of the mainland and vice versa. Rogers Island, although still privately owned (at this writing the state is negotiating a purchase) was opened to the public in July 2001. The site is primarily devoted to history of the Seven Years' War and features a visitors center that is open daily from June through August. Admission is free. In September an annual Seven Years' War encampment is presented. Phone: (518) 747-3693; website: www.fortedwardnewyork.net.

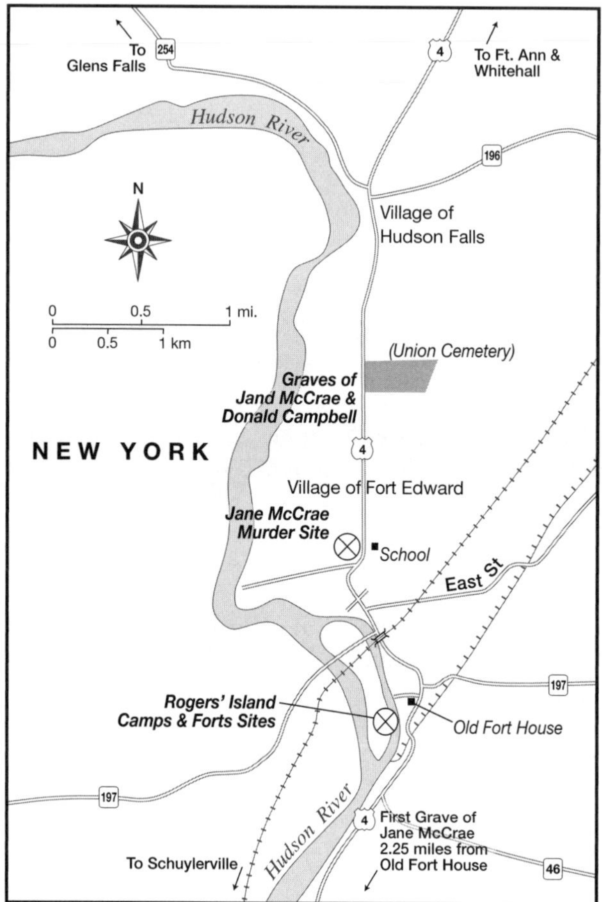

MAP BY XNR PRODUCTIONS. THE GALE GROUP.

If one goes south on U.S. 4 and N.Y. Route 197 through the village of Fort Edward and passes under the railroad, there is a marker on the right (west) that says that the northeast bastion of the old fort was near there. The marker is encompassed within the grounds of the Anvil Inn Restaurant. Continue straight (not bearing left on the highway) and take the first right onto Old Fort Street. On the right (north) is a marker indicating that the low ground there was part of the old moat. Continue a few hundred feet to the dead end at the river, opposite Rogers Island, and there is a boulder with a plaque attached marking the site of Fort Edward, 1775.

If the traveler retraces their route and continues south on the highway, just to the west of U.S. 4 and 0.1 mile beyond the junction with N.Y. 197 is the Old Fort House Museum. Built in 1772 by Patrick Smyth, it was constructed in part with timbers from the ruined Fort Edward. In 1777 Benedict Arnold arrested Smyth and removed him from his home for being a Loyalist. At various historic junctures, the house was used by Generals Schuyler, Arnold, Washington, Burgoyne, and Stark. The two-story white structure has been restored and is a regional museum with Indian relics, furniture, glass, models, and dioramas. It is open to the public daily from June to August, on weekends from September to October, and year-round by appointment. For further information contact the Fort Edward Historical Association, located at 29 Broadway Street. Phone: (518) 747-9600.

Fort Edward is the scene of the Jane McCrae atrocity, which the Patriots, notably General Horatio Gates, skillfully exploited to bring about the great rally of militia that helped to defeat Burgoyne. The episode has been so distorted that the facts will never be certain, but the following outline may be considered reasonably accurate: McCrae was captured by a small patrol of Burgoyne's Indians and killed when another patrol appeared with orders from her Loyalist fiancé to bring word from her. McCrae's captor, a Huron named Le Loup but better known in legend as the Wyandotte Panther, presumably expected a reward for his young female prisoner, and in a fit of rage he ended the argument with the other Indian leader by shooting her. McCrae's scalp was identified by her fiancé in the British camp, and another prisoner filled in what details she could of the episode. Then the propagandists and mythmakers took over.

A marker in front of a privately owned dwelling just north of the high school states that it is the Jane McRae House, supposedly the place of her capture. However, the actual place of her capture was just behind this dwelling, at what used to be Sara McNeil's house. A marker of the actual site where McRae was killed can be found just south of the high school. A highway marker says "The graves of Duncan Campbell and Jane McCrae are just within and to the left of this gateway." Enclosed by a high iron fence, the graves are easy to spot as one drives into the large cemetery. The white stone on McCrae's grave was erected in 1852 by a niece when the remains were moved from their second burial place (in Fort Edward). Her age is given erroneously as seventeen; she probably was twenty-six years old at her death. About 2.2 miles south of the bridge one crosses when leaving Fort Edward on U.S. 4 is the marked site of McCrae's first grave (on the west side of the highway). A Patriot camp was here when the famous atrocity occurred.

Another legend of some renown is connected with Union Cemetery. The story is that Duncan Campbell of Inverawe, major of the Forty-second Regiment of Foot, better known as the Royal Highlanders, or Black Watch, had witnessed a murder but had sworn to keep his knowledge secret. When he later learned that the victim was his own cousin, he still held fast to his oath, whereupon the cousin's ghost appeared in a dream and said, "Farewell, Inverawe, till we meet at Ticonderoga." Campbell tried to rise above his superstitions as his regiment moved on Ticonderoga in 1758 with Abercromby's expedition, but on the eve of battle he is said to have resigned himself to death. He was mortally wounded and died nine days later, 17 July, at Fort Edward. Robert Louis Stevenson knew the story, which was famous in Scottish history, and while spending six months at Saranac Lake (1887–1888) he used it for his ballad "Ticonderoga." The poet errs in the concluding lines: "He sleeps in the place of the name, / As it was doomed to be." At Ticonderoga is a monument to the Black Watch that mentions the above episode. But Campbell does not sleep at Ticonderoga; he sleeps beneath an interesting old brown headstone next to Jane McCrae.

For reference and information on these and other sites, contact the Fort Edward Historical Association listed previously in this section.

Fort Frey, Mohawk Valley. On N.Y. Route 5, exactly a mile west of the junction of N.Y. Route 10 in Palatine Bridge, a state marker identifies the Frey House. Just west of this sign, on the south side of the highway, is the start of a private road that winds 0.3 mile to the house. It is privately owned (1971) but can be viewed from the outside.

Typically Palatine, this long, stone, story-and-a-half house with a gable roof was built in 1739 on the site of a log cabin erected in 1689 by Hendrick Frey, a Swiss. British military posts were located here in 1702 to 1713 and 1755 to 1763.

Hendrick Frey died shortly before the Revolution, but his three sons were active in the war. The most famous, John, was born in the Frey House in 1740 and became chairman of the Tryon County Committee of Safety and major of the Palatine Regiment, Tryon County Militia Brigade. His brothers, Bernard and Philip, became officers on the British side. John was wounded at Oriskany, narrowly escaping death before going to Canada as a prisoner. From the surviving Frey papers it is known that he was well treated. Major Frey's old neighbor, John Butler of Butlersbury, saw that he got the best medical attention available and better food than was the normal lot of prisoners, and on one occasion Butler prescribed an issue of port wine to speed Frey's recovery. When John Frey finally was exchanged, John Butler lent him 20 guineas to get home. When Montgomery County was formed from Tryon County in 1784, John Frey became its first sheriff. He was state senator for twenty years and helped write *Annals of Tryon County.*

Bernard Frey served in Butler's Rangers, was promoted to captain in 1780, and settled in Niagara, upper Canada. He was killed during the War of 1812.

Philip served as an ensign in the Eighth Foot during the Revolution. A surveyor and an attorney, he later returned to the Mohawk Valley and practiced law not far from his birthplace.

Fort Herkimer Church, 2 miles east of Mohawk on N.Y. Route 5S. Construction of this building was started by Palatine settlers about 1730 to replace a log church of 1723, but work was not finished when the Seven Years' War started in 1754 and the walls formed the center of colonial Fort Herkimer. (Another Fort Herkimer, dating from 1775, was the wooden blockhouse that had fallen into ruin and was the site of the Revolutionary War's Fort Dayton. See GERMAN FLATS.) The present structure, altered and enlarged in 1812, dates from 1767. Johan Herkimer (also spelled "Herchheimer" and "Erghemer"), father of Revolutionary War General Nicholas Herkimer, and twelve others established a trading post here after emigrating from the Rhenish Palatinate around 1722, and an inscription on the church indicates that he built it in 1767.

During the Revolution the church was part of a stockaded fort, and here settlers were saved on Sunday, 13 September 1778, from a raid by Loyalists and Indians that ravaged their property in the neighborhood. They had been warned by Adam Helmer, who detected the raiders and stayed ahead of their fastest runners in a dramatic 22-mile race to the settlements.

Later the walls were raised 10 feet to convert the structure from fort to church, and a pitched roof and cupola were added. A picturesque graveyard adjoins the church. The site is open for special occasions and is used for Revolutionary War reenactments. Phone: Don Fenner (607) 547-8490.

Fort Hill, Long Island, westerly end of Lloyd's Neck, overlooking Oyster Bay and Cold Spring Harbor. Here the remains of Fort Franklin (earthworks and barracks) are in the hands of a private owner. In the days of the Revolution, American and French troops made several attempts to capture Fort Franklin. When the British abandoned it at the close of the war, they threw guns into wells and buried others. Some of these have been recovered and placed in spots overlooking the harbor. Nearby, the Lloyd Manor House (1767), an early colonial saltbox of special architectural interest, is owned by the Society for the Preservation of Long Island Antiquities. Phone: (631) 692-4664; website: www.splia.org.

Fort Hunter. Strategically located where the Schoharie Valley joins the Mohawk Valley, this was a well-known place in the early colonial history of New York and during the Seven Years' War. Queen Anne ordered construction of a chapel here in 1712 "for my Mohawk Indians." The chapel is gone, some of its cut stone having been used in 1820 for the lock of the Erie Canal on Schoharie Creek, but the stone parsonage has survived. Still standing as a testimonial to ancient American craftsmanship is the

Dutch Barn (dating from about 1730). Fort Hunter is under the jurisdiction of the New York State Military Museum. Phone: (518) 581-5100.

Fort Johnson, sometimes called Old Fort Johnson, Mohawk Valley, about one mile west of Amsterdam, where N.Y. Route 67 joins N.Y. Route 5. This is the third home of William Johnson, built in 1749 when his personal fortunes had prospered because of his success as an Indian agent and militia colonel in King George's War (1744–1745). Both of his earlier homes have been lost—the small frame building in which he lived near Fort Hunter when he first came to America and the stone house called Mount Johnson, in the area of modern Amsterdam, where he lived during the years 1742 to 1749. When Johnson moved on to Johnson Hall in 1763 (see JOHNSTOWN), Fort Johnson was taken over by his son, Sir John Johnson (1749–1774).

It was during his years at Fort Johnson that Sir William won his baronetcy, gained further fame for his management of Indian affairs, and enlarged his personal estate. During the Seven Years' War (1754–1763) the house was fortified—a palisade was erected, artillery positions were built in the vicinity, and a small garrison was installed. The name Fort Johnson dates from this period. (The French had put a price on Johnson's head.)

Fort Johnson is now a museum maintained by the Montgomery County Historical Society. Phone: (518) 843-0300. Much of the interior woodwork is original, and the house is furnished with a number of pieces that belonged to Sir William. In the attic the hand-hewn, wood-pegged roof timbers are visible, and the construction discredits the myth that it supported a roof of lead sheets (allegedly melted by the Patriots for bullets); the best evidence appears to indicate that wooden shakes were used. Some authorities also challenge the theory that Sir William sent to London for this lead-sheet roofing, interior paneling, hardware, and other fittings and furnishings. But Fort Johnson does have the architectural distinction of departing from the Dutch tradition in the Mohawk Valley and being the first manor house of the English style in the region.

The house is open for tours Wednesday through Sunday from May to September.

Fort Klock Restoration, N.Y. Route 5, is about 2 miles east of St. Johnsville. Of exceptional charm, architectural distinction, and appeal for the casual tourist as well as for serious historical conservationists, Fort Klock deserves to be better known. The large, L-shaped, fortified trading post was built on the bank of the Mohawk in 1750. Its native limestone walls are 2 feet thick and loopholed on all sides. One unique feature is a spring that still flows from the cellar's solid stone floor to form a large pool.

Fort Klock is one of the few surviving fur-trading centers in the Mohawk Valley, and its military and trade room displays a beaver skin, a bark canoe, and the goods that Johannes Klock used for barter. The equipment of colonial troops is also exhibited, reflecting the house's changed role when the Revolution came and its master at that time, John Klock, was on the Tryon County Committee of Safety. (The Klock family retained possession of its ancestral home for almost two centuries and held annual reunions there until recent years.)

Other restored and furnished rooms are a large dining room, a bedroom, and a spinning and weaving room. The kitchen has a sink made from native limestone and a door arrangement through which heavy logs for the fireplace could be dragged by a horse or ox. Several outbuildings have been restored on the site, including a schoolhouse, blacksmith shop, and Dutch barn, forming an attractive setting for the main house.

The Battle of Klock's Field took place on 19 October 1780 just east of Fort Klock. Sir John Johnson's raiders had annihilated one Patriot force earlier in the day at Stone Arabia and were making their way from the present Nelliston westward along the King's Highway (now the railroad tracks). Late in the afternoon they were spotted by the pursuing militia force on the opposite bank of the Mohawk. While militia general Robert Van Rensselaer dined with Governor George Clinton at Fort Plain, his troops improvised a crossing and forced the enemy to turn and fight. Attacking at about sunset, the right flank units under Robert McKean and Chief Louis (with about sixty Oneidas) routed a jaeger company and some Indians under Joseph Brant, but the Loyalists and British regulars held their main position. Van Rensselaer refused to let his men renew the assault, and his officers subsequently charged him with incompetence. He was cleared by a court of inquiry.

Fort Klock was filled with neighborhood families during this action. One of the militia defenders dropped a British officer from the saddle with a long shot, the horse galloped up to the fort, and the officer's camp kettle became a Klock family heirloom.

Fort Klock is open to the public Tuesday through Sunday from May to October, and is maintained by the Fort Klock Historic Restoration Committee. Phone: (518) 568-7779.

Fort Montgomery. *See* BEAR MOUNTAIN.

Fort Neck House (Tryon Hall) Site, Massapequa, Long Island. *See* BRIDGEPORT, CONNECTICUT.

Fort Niagara, at the mouth of the Niagara River on Lake Ontario, near Youngstown. Old Fort Niagara is

Powder Barrels in Old Fort Niagara. *Fort Niagara, on a bluff overlooking Lake Ontario near Niagara Falls, was built by the French in 1726. The British used the fort as a base during the Revolutionary War, and did not relinquish it until 1796, thirteen years after the war ended.* © LEE SNIDER/PHOTO IMAGES/CORBIS.

administered by the Old Fort Niagara Association. Phone: (716) 745-7273. The site is an approved National Historic Landmark in the area of French exploration and settlement. The fortified barracks built by the French in 1726 is the heart of the elaborately restored frontier fortress that figured prominently in four distinct periods of American history. This "French castle" is furnished in the period of the Seven Years' War. It includes the trade room, sleeping quarters, council chamber, military kitchen, prison, dungeon, Jesuit chapel, and gun deck. The "Gate of the Five Nations" features a drawbridge operated by chains, windlasses, and stone counterweights. The British redoubts of 1770 are stone blockhouses with walls 5 feet thick on which cannon are mounted. During the summer months costumed staff play the roles of the British garrison.

Sir William Johnson temporarily assumed command of the British column advancing on Niagara when British General Prideaux was killed in action, and so he had the honor of receiving the surrender of the French post in 1759. During the Revolution, when Johnson's retainers and clansmen from the Mohawk Valley remained loyal to the crown, they used Niagara as their base for bloody raids back into their home territory. The British did not relinquish this post until 1796, thirteen years after the American Revolution ended. In 1813 they recaptured Niagara from the Americans, giving it up after the end of the War of 1812.

The site is now visited by hundreds of thousands annually and has a particular charm for children.

Fort Ontario, 1 East Fourth Street, on Lake Ontario at the mouth of Oswego River, opposite the city of Oswego. Phone: (315) 343-4711. The name "Oswego" occurs often in Revolutionary War accounts of fighting on the northwestern frontier. Strategically located on the Great Lakes waterway and at the end of the Mohawk Valley–Wood Creek–Lake Oneida–Oswego River route from the Hudson Valley at Albany, the British fort was the base for Loyalist-Indian raids into New York and the point of departure for St. Leger's abortive invasion of 1777. (See FORT STANWIX.) In modern Oswego, just across the river from Fort Ontario, is a stone monument marking the site of Fort Oswego, established by the British in 1726 to 1727 as protection for their fur agents. The Pontiac Boulder at West First and Oneida Streets marks the site of Pontiac's submission to Sir William Johnson in July 1765.

Fort Ontario State Historic Site preserves the ramparts of the fort built in 1755 about a quarter of a mile from the Fort Oswego just mentioned. Montcalm destroyed this new fort (1756); the British rebuilt it in 1759 and used it as a base for the capture of Fort Niagara and Montreal. But Oswego continued to be a frontier post. "Old" Walter Butler was Sir William Johnson's representative "at the difficult outpost at Oswego" in the early 1740s and was still there in the early 1750s, his sons being there with him much of the time. (See BUTLERSBURY.)

When the Mohawk Valley Loyalists were forced to flee in the summer of 1775, they went to Oswego and there made contact with the British authorities they would serve so well during the Revolution. In 1777 the British abandoned Fort Ontario, and the next year it was partially burned by Continental troops. In 1782 the British reoccupied the post and rebuilt its defenses, holding the fort until forced to leave in 1796 under the terms of the Jay Treaty.

In the War of 1812 the British captured Fort Ontario and demolished it. Work on restoring it was done during the periods 1839 to 1844 and 1863 to 1872, and in 1946 Fort Ontario became a State Historic Site. Most of the buildings a tourist sees there today are from 1839 to 1844, when the existing scarp wall and casements were built. But the ramparts are original. A museum depicts the ups and downs of Fort Ontario and this strategic site. Open 1 May to 31 October, Tuesday through Sunday, 10 A.M. to 4:30 P.M.

Fort Plain (Fort Rensselaer) Site and Museum, village of Fort Plain, 389 Canal Street, Mohawk Valley. A fortification covering half an acre and built around a stone farmhouse in 1776, it was an important Patriot base during the Revolution. A raid by Joseph Brant in 1780 killed sixteen people in the village and took sixty prisoners. General Robert Van Rensselaer operated from Fort Plain later in 1780 while coping unsuccessfully with Sir John Johnson's raiders at Stone Arabia and Fort Klock. Colonel Marinus Willett had his valley headquarters here in 1781 to 1783, when the place was called Fort Rensselaer. From here he conducted some of the final, successful operations of the Revolution. (See SHARON SPRINGS, JOHNSTOWN, and WEST CANADA CREEK.)

The Fort Plain site and museum features a reconstructed 1848 limestone Greek Revival house, and has exhibits on local history. It is open Wednesday through Sunday from mid-May to September. For the remaining year, tours are available by appointment. Phone: (518) 993-2527.

Fort Putnam. *See* WEST POINT MILITARY RESERVATION.

Fort St. George, Long Island, near Mastic Beach just north of Smith's Point Bridge, off William Floyd Parkway. Colonel William ("Tangier") Smith, so called for his early career in the North African city of that name on the Strait of Gibraltar, came to America with his family in 1686. He acquired large holdings patented in 1693 as the Manor of St. George, and "Tangier" Smith subsequently became the first chief justice of New York. Soon after his death at the manor house near the first family burial ground in modern Setauket, a new manor house was built at Mastic.

When the British occupied Long Island in 1776 they fortified the new house by constructing a 90-foot-square earthwork on the higher ground a little over 100 feet to the west and building a stockade that incorporated this work, the manor house, and another structure. Three barracks within this stockade housed the garrison of Fort St. George.

This became an important British base, the earthwork commanding an inlet into Great South Bay (it survives only as the name of a Fire Island community, Old Inlet), and on the land side Fort St. George was a stronghold in a region where the British gathered valuable supplies (see LONG ISLAND).

In a predawn surprise attack on 23 November 1780 the fort fell quickly to a small force of Continental troops led by Major Benjamin Tallmadge. Having crossed the sound from Fairfield, Connecticut two days earlier and been delayed by a severe storm, the raiders destroyed much of the fort, seized a supply vessel, burned forage at Coram as they withdrew to their boats at Mount Sinai, and returned to Fairfield with about two hundred prisoners. Tallmadge's only loss was one man wounded, and he received commendations from Washington and the Congress for his feat.

The Manor of St. George is now a 127-acre public park and museum, after having been in the Smith family for over 260 years. Eugenie Annie Tangier Smith, the last lineal descendant, died in 1954 and is buried near the manor house with many of those who shared her remarkable heritage. The existing house, a large frame structure, was built in 1810. It is the third on this location, and contains some furniture saved from the fire that destroyed its Revolutionary War predecessor. Part of the house is open to visitors. Thousands of original documents were preserved by the Smiths and were not generally available to scholars until after 1954. Among those exhibited in the museum room are a letter written by General Nathaniel

Woodhull shortly before his death as a British prisoner, letters from Robert R. Livingston and George Clinton, and two deeds of 1691 signed by Indians.

The trace of the British fort (which may be on the site of one built two years earlier) was clearly revealed after a severe drought in 1957. Archaeologists have learned that grass has a distinctive growth pattern on topsoil that has been disturbed, and an aerial photograph taken in 1957 shows the outline of the fort.

As recently as 1928 one authority on Long Island historic homes was able to write that the Manor of St. George was still in a picturesque area of fields and forests little changed since the Revolution. It is now reduced to the status of a large park hemmed in by real-estate developments. The view over Great South Bay remains virtually unspoiled. Open May through October, Wednesday to Sunday, 9:30 A.M. to 5 P.M. Phone: (631) 475-0327.

Fort Stanwix, in Rome, Oneida County. Here a 1-mile portage between the headwaters of the Mohawk River and Wood Creek made the site strategically important on the natural route between the upper Hudson Valley and the Great Lakes. (See FORT ONTARIO.) It also was a frontier post where Iroquois and white leaders held several historic conferences. Starting in 1725 the British kept the site fortified, and in 1758 General John Stanwix built a fort to replace two earlier ones. With the French threat from Canada eliminated in the Seven Years' War, the British fort was abandoned in 1760. Eight years later Sir William Johnson met here with two thousand Indians to negotiate the famous Treaty of Fort Stanwix. In addition to strengthening the British alliance with the Iroquois, Sir William and the Indians agreed to a new boundary that opened vast areas of central New York, western Pennsylvania, and the future states of West Virginia and Kentucky to white settlers. (The earlier Proclamation Line of 1763 is now followed by the Blue Ridge Parkway. See this heading under both NORTH CAROLINA and VIRGINIA.)

In June 1776 a detachment of Continental troops under Colonel Elias Dayton started rebuilding the fort. For a while it was called Fort Schuyler, but the older name clung, and the place continued to be known as Fort Stanwix.

In August 1777 Colonel Peter Gansevoort (1749–1812), a native of Albany and only twenty-eight years old at the time, defended Fort Stanwix with an exceptionally able second in command, Lieutenant Colonel Marinus Willett (1740–1830), and 550 troops. The besiegers under British Lieutenant Colonel Barry St. Leger (1737–1789) numbered about 2,000; about half of these were Indians under Joseph Brant, another 350 were British and German regulars, and the rest were Loyalists and Canadian auxiliaries. Among the Loyalist units were Sir John Johnson's Royal Greens and Colonel John Butler's Rangers, most of them natives of the Mohawk Valley.

An American relief column was ambushed 5 miles short of Fort Stanwix at Oriskany and driven back, but this strategic victory for the British turned out to be the doom of St. Leger's operation. His Indian allies had been recruited with the understanding that they would have lots of looting and scalping but little if any serious fighting. Badly decimated at Oriskany, they came back to find that Willett had made a bold sortie with 250 men and systematically cleaned out the undefended camps of the Indians and the Loyalists.

Willett and another officer slipped out of the fort and reported to General Schuyler at Stillwater (about 11 miles below Saratoga) that Fort Stanwix could not hold out much longer without assistance. Benedict Arnold led eight hundred Continentals to the relief of Stanwix, and news of his approach was enough to send St. Leger's Indians packing. The British commander then had to accept the fact that his expedition was a failure and withdraw to Canada. The heroic defense of Fort Stanwix saved the Mohawk Valley from being invaded and contributed to the greater triumph at Saratoga (see SARATOGA NATIONAL HISTORICAL PARK).

A controversy has raged over whether the first Stars and Stripes flown by ground forces in battle was raised over Fort Stanwix or someplace else. One positive historical gain from this regional controversy is that the Rome Historical Society has been active in bringing about the establishment of the Fort Stanwix National Monument. The National Parks Service reconstructed Fort Stanwix in the center of downtown Rome at the corner of North James Street and Erie Boulevard. The 18-acre site is open every day from April through December and offers an interactive look at eighteenth-century life through a variety of venues. Phone: (315) 336-2090. The Rome Historical Society, located at 200 Church Street, displays exhibits featuring numerous items from the American Revolution, including artifacts from Fort Stanwix. Phone: (315) 336-5870.

Fort Wagner, Mohawk Valley, about 150 yards north of N.Y. 5, 5 miles west of its intersection with N.Y. 10 in Palatine Bridge and half a mile east of its junction with Stone Arabia Road (County Road 34). A highway marker at this point identifies the house built in 1750 by Peter Wagner (or Waggoner), Patriot leader and lieutenant colonel of the Palatine Regiment during the Revolution. Privately owned, the original, two-story stone house has a much larger and unattractive frame house built onto its eastern end. The 1750 house, though long empty and neglected, remains reasonably sound structurally, for the time being.

Gardiner's Island, between the eastern forks of Long Island. An anchorage "where even the largest ships can ride out a storm," as Major Baurmeister of the Hessian forces reported to his superior in Hesse-Cassel (*Revolution in America,* p. 368), Gardiner's Bay and the island are mentioned frequently in naval operations of the Revolution. The place became particularly important for the British when the French fleet was at Newport. Robert David Lion Gardiner, sixteenth "lord of the manor" of Gardiner's Island, successfully fought efforts to turn it into a national monument; he died in 2004. Today the 3,300-acre island remains private and is an important breeding ground of the osprey, an endangered species. Currently the family is divided between holding on to the island or deeding it to the Nature Conservancy or the federal government. Lion Gardiner, first owner of the manor, established in 1639, lies in the Old Burying Ground, East Hampton, Long Island.

German Flats, Mohawk Valley. This designation is usually applied to the entire 10-mile stretch of Palatine settlements that extended, generally on the south side of the Mohawk, to the place now called Herkimer. The latter was the site of Fort Herkimer, erected in the early part of the Seven Years' War and rebuilt in 1776 to 1777 as Fort Dayton. (Two miles to the east was the Fort Herkimer Church of the Revolution.) Some old maps limit the name German Flats (spelled "Flatts" in the original documents) to the spot that is now Herkimer.

The principal reason for encouraging the settlement of Palatines in this region was to provide a buffer against the Iroquois west of the more heavily populated, eastern portion of the Mohawk Valley. German Flats consequently got more than its share of attention from the Indians and Loyalists during the Revolution. The most devastating raid came in September 1778 (authorities disagree as to the precise day), when Joseph Brant and Captain William Caldwell moved against the settlements from Unadilla with 450 Indians and Loyalists. Lieutenant Adam F. Helmer was the sole survivor of a four-man reconnaissance patrol sent out to watch for the expected raid.

A highway marker on N.Y. Route 5S just west of the Shoemaker House indicates where Helmer entered the valley to spread the warning, and a plaque on a boulder at Fort Herkimer Church commemorates this hero. (Walter D. Edmonds has immortalized this American marathon in the novel *Drums Along the Mohawk.*) The settlers had time to gather for protection at Fort Dayton and Fort Herkimer Church. The raiders spared women and children and killed only three men, but inflicted tremendous property damage. Colonel Peter Bellinger said in his report that 63 homes, 57 barns, and 4 mills were burned by the enemy and more than 700 head of livestock captured.

German Flats was raided again in the fall of 1780 when Sir John Johnson withdrew up the valley from his operations in the Schoharie Valley. Small bands of Indians destroyed property in the settlement in early 1781. On 6 August 1781 the settlement of Shell's Bush, 5 miles north of Fort Dayton, was surprised by sixty Indians and Loyalists under Donald McDonald. Most of the Patriots, who had been working in the fields, ran for Fort Dayton, but John Christian Shell (or Schell) made it to his blockhouse with his wife and six sons. They suffered no casualties in successfully defending their position against a determined enemy attack, and McDonald was dragged inside and taken prisoner as he tried to force the door with a crowbar.

Glen-Sanders House (Glen Sanders Mansion, Scotia Mansion), just across the Mohawk River from the Schenectady Stockade in Scotia, on N.Y. 5. Erected in 1713 using stone and other material from a house built in 1658 nearer the river, this large historic structure has recently been restored after having been vacant for many years. Its furnishings were moved long ago to Colonial Williamsburg, Virginia. The historic mansion was originally the home of Alexander Glen, a Scot who bought land here in 1655 and became the first permanent white settler in the Mohawk Valley. Because of Glen's enlightened policies toward the Indians, his house was spared by French and Indian raiders. Scotia was the name Glen gave the settlement in the seventeenth century, and it survives as the name of this suburb of Schenectady.

The Glen Sanders Mansion, as it is now called, has had several additions to the original structure and is an upscale restaurant inn. It is plainly visible at the western end of the Great Western Gateway Bridge at 1 Glen Avenue. Phone: (518) 374-7262.

Groveland Ambush. *See* SULLIVAN-CLINTON EXPEDITION.

Guy Park, at Lock 11 of the Mohawk River on Route 5W at Evelyn Street in Amsterdam (Fort Johnson). The best landmark to watch for here is the lock of the state barge canal. Sir William Johnson built a frame house here in 1766 for his daughter Mary and her husband, Guy Johnson, a nephew of Sir William. This burned in 1774, and the central section of the present stone house was built that same year. Guy succeeded his father-in-law as superintendent of Indian affairs on Sir William's death in July 1774, and exactly a year later fled to Canada with about two hundred Rangers and some Indians; he lived in Guy Park only five months. Colonel Guy Johnson was successful in winning all but two tribes of the Iroquois, the Oneidas and Tuscaroras, entirely to the British side at the outbreak of the Revolution. He has been described as "a short, pursy man, of stern countenance and haughty demeanor." Much more the politician than the field soldier, he spent almost two years with the British army around New York City and then operated from Niagara without personally accompanying any of the raiding parties sent out from there. (He was not at the Battle of Newtown [see NEWTOWN BATTLEFIELD STATE PARK], as some authorities have said.) In March 1782 he was succeeded by Sir John Johnson as superintendent general and inspector general of the Six Nations. After the war he went to England, where he died at about forty-eight years of age.

Guy Park lost much of its Georgian character in 1848 when the roof and cornice were reconstructed, and most of the interior woodwork dates probably from this remodeling. Ten years later the massive central section was given two-story wings, and Guy Park does not meet the criteria for selection as a National Historic Landmark. It is, however, a state-owned historic site, and it houses the current office of the Montgomery County Chamber of Commerce. It is open on weekdays from 8:30 A.M. to 4:30 P.M. Phone: (518) 842-8200.

A highway marker on N.Y. 5 just west of Guy Park says that the Daniel Claus House was nearby. (Its site is about a mile west of Guy Park.) Claus was the other son-in-law of Sir William. He and Ann lived in the stone house on the bank of the Mohawk that had been Sir William's home during the years 1742 to 1749; they called the place Williamsburg during their occupancy. (This structure survived in ruins until the 1920s; no trace now remains.)

Haynes (Lemuel) House, South Granville. Home of one of the most prominent African Americans of the early republic, this house is on the National Register of Historic Places. Haynes, born in 1753 to a black father and white mother, was indentured as a servant until the age of twenty-one. Demonstrating a precocious intelligence, Haynes became a popular lay sermonizer while still a teenager. He served in the Massachusetts militia during the Revolution, seeing action during the siege of Boston. Near the end of the Revolution he was called to the Middle Granville Congregational Church, becoming probably the first black minister of a predominately white congregation in the United States. In 1785 he became the first known ordained African American minister when the Congregational Church recognized his calling. He served mostly white congregations for the next forty years in Connecticut and Vermont, becoming a well-known poet, abolitionist, and Federalist. In 1822 he moved to South Granville and served as minister of the Congregational Church there until his death in 1833. The house is still a private residence, but visitors are welcome to drive by Parker Hill Road off of N.Y. 149; the Haynes House is the second on the right.

Herkimer, Mohawk Valley. *See* FORT DAYTON SITE.

Herkimer Home, 200 State Route 169, Little Falls, Mohawk Valley on N.Y. 5S, 3 miles east of Little Falls between Thruway Exits 29 and 30. Descriptive literature and photographs cannot do justice to this site. Should you come into great wealth and want to build a family mansion, by all means see this one before you get too far along with your plans.

Nicholas Herkimer (1728–1777) was to the Patriot element of the Mohawk Valley what Sir William Johnson's heirs were to the Loyalists. He was born near the present town of Herkimer a few years after his family came to America from the Rhenish Palatinate of modern Germany. By the start of the Revolution he had become the most successful landowner in the Mohawk Valley. The term "farmer-trader" is sometimes used to describe his occupation. Perhaps this is as close as modern Americans can come in tagging Herkimer, but he personally did little farming, and "trader" hardly connotes the large scope of his entrepreneurial activities.

When the Revolution came to the Mohawk Valley and the Johnsons and Butlers took refuge in Canada, Nicholas Herkimer emerged as the most powerful figure in the Whig leadership. His support naturally was strongest among the Palatines in German Flats. In July 1777, as general of the local militia, Herkimer led about four hundred troops to Unadilla for a conference with former neighbor Joseph Brant (see INDIAN CASTLE CHURCH). This chief of the Mohawks had temporarily fallen out with Guy Johnson, Sir William's successor as superintendent of Indian affairs, and was in a mood to bargain with the Patriots. But the conference failed, and only Herkimer's cool handling of the situation kept it from degenerating into a battle.

Later in the year, when he led the militia to the relief of Fort Stanwix, General Herkimer's better judgment was shaken by the dissension of impetuous subordinates. His patriotism as well as his martial ardor assailed by these lesser men, Herkimer put himself at the head of the column and marched into a skillfully planned ambuscade. Then, despite a shattered thigh, he personally directed the defensive battle that eventually saved his force from total annihilation at Oriskany. Eleven days later, after an ineptly performed amputation, he called for the family Bible, read to his assembled family in a clear voice, and died. He is buried in the family cemetery adjoining the home.

There is no other mansion in the Mohawk Valley that so typifies the Germanic style as does this structure. The wide central hall of the two-story brick house is typical of the colonial architecture one finds in all regions. Also typical are the two rooms on one side of this hall. But the German influence is seen on the other side of the central hall, upstairs as well as downstairs, where instead of the expected two rooms are single rooms running the depth of the house. Centered in the outside wall is a large fireplace, built shallow to reflect the maximum heat. The great hall on the ground floor was what we might tritely call the family room today, and the corresponding chamber upstairs was the guest room. The inside dimensions of this room, if one allows for the 2-foot thickness of the outer walls, are about 36 by 23 feet.

Native pine paneling in this house gives a mellow feeling that is lacking in the more elegant colonial mansions of the Georgian style. Dragon's blood stain on the upper floor paneling is as vivid as when it was applied more than two centuries ago.

General Herkimer built this house in 1764 on land given to him by his father, but it did not remain in the family long after his death. The Erie Canal was dug through the backyard of the house, and one owner converted the house into a tavern. Partitions were slapped up to make three rooms out of those great chambers, plaster was smeared on the paneling, and all sorts of other disfigurations were made in the name of commercial enterprise. Then a railroad was put through the backyard, and the tavern keeper went out of business. Now the canal has been filled in and the tracks are silent. The New York State Historic Trust has restored the Herkimer Home and developed the 160-acre tract that surrounds it.

The site is open mid-May through October, 10 A.M. to 5 P.M. Tuesday to Saturday, and 11 A.M. to 5 P.M. on Sunday. Phone: (315) 823-0398.

(Central N.Y. State Parks Commission, Clark Reservation, Jamesville, N.Y. 13078.)

Hinckley Reservoir. *See* WEST CANADA CREEK.

Huguenot Street Historic District, New Paltz, Ulster County, near Thruway between Newburgh and Kingston. Eight stone houses dating from the early eighteenth century preserve the spirit of this unique settlement of plain folk. Each one of the buildings, including the Jean Hasbrouck House, built in 1712, is owned by the Huguenot Historical Society, formerly the Huguenot Patriotic, Historical, and Monumental Society. All of them are included in the Huguenot Historical Society's guided tour, which is available to the public May through October, 10 A.M. to 4 P.M. on every day except Monday. Access inside the houses is available only through the tours. For information, contact the Huguenot Street Historic District, P.O. Box 339, 18 Broadhead Avenue, New Paltz, N.Y. 12561. Phone: (845) 255-1660. The tour begins at the Dubois Fort at Huguenot Street, now the tour's visitors center.

Hurley, U.S. 209 about 4 miles southwest of Kingston. This three-century-old village of almost uniform limestone Dutch houses was the state capital from 18 November to 17 December 1777. The Van Deusen House (1723), in the center of the village, was used by the legislators during this period.

Indian Castle Church. *Indian Castle Church, a simple, white-frame mission church built in 1769, sits on a grassy knoll in New York's Mohawk Valley. The graves of many Mohawk Indians and several early white settlers lie behind it.* © LEE SNIDER/PHOTO IMAGES/CORBIS.

Most of the ten original houses on the main street, all but one privately owned, are open to the public on Stone House Day, held since 1951 on the second Saturday in July. Of special note is the Dumond House, "Spy House" (c. 1685), employed by General Clinton to house prisoners. However, the tour does not allow access through the basement door leading into the actual prison—a deep and inescapable cellar. Hurley is a National Historic District.

Indian Castle Church, Mohawk Valley, on N.Y. 5S about 8 miles west of Fort Plain and roughly the same distance east of Little Falls. On a grassy knoll just south of a particularly scenic stretch of Route 5S sits the simple, white frame mission church built in 1769. Behind it, on slightly higher ground and also visible from the highway, are the graves of many Mohawks and several early white settlers.

The church is on the site of Upper Castle, largest of the last three Castles of the Mohawk Indians and home of Sir William Johnson's principal Indian ally, King Hendrick, uncle of Joseph and Molly Brant. Legend has it that Molly started her liaison with Sir William here, but this is not documented. It is known, however, that she returned to the village after his death in 1774. In August 1777 Molly sent her brother Joseph the intelligence that brought about the Battle of Oriskany. A month later she fled to Canada.

Joseph Brant contributed the land and Sir William put up the money for the church. The entire bill of materials is carefully itemized in the published papers of Sir William. In addition to the timber, stone, nails, paint, plastering, miscellaneous hardware, and a church bell, 80 gallons of rum were budgeted for the project. But the early-American programmers proved to be as fallible as their counterparts today, and an additional 10 gallons and 3 quarts of rum had to be furnished before the job was completed (*Sir William Johnson Papers,* VII, pp. 666–668).

Indian Castle Church is the only surviving structure of the Mohawk Castles. It has been much altered, the present belfry replacing a smaller one and the interior being completely changed. But Joseph and Molly Brant would recognize it today, and the site retains much of its rustic charm. The Indian Castle Church Restoration and Preservation Society owns and maintains the structure and grounds. Phone: (315) 823-2099.

Iroquois Indian Museum, Howes Cave. The main building of this museum devoted to the history and culture of the Iroquois is built in the shape of the traditional longhouse. The Iroquois played a vital role in the American Revolution, dividing between the majority who sided with the British and those who preferred to remain neutral or take the Patriot side. The collection, while devoted to representing all members of the confederation, is strongest on the Mohawk. Located at 324 Caverns Road just north of N.Y. 7. Take the Central Bridge Exit off I-88. Open Tuesday to Saturday, 10 A.M. to 5 P.M., and Sunday noon to 5 P.M. Phone: (518) 296-8949.

Jerseyfield. *See* WEST CANADA CREEK.

John Jay Homestead State Historic Site, Westchester County, on N.Y. 22 between Bedford and Katonah. The large clapboard house, brick cottage, and other outbuildings are preserved here in a beautiful setting of ancient trees essentially as John Jay knew them. Until the 1950s the homestead was occupied by Jay's descendants. Bought by the county in 1958 and deeded to the state, the property has been open to the public since 1964.

John Jay (1745–1829) started his public career in the Continental Congress and ended it as two-term governor of New York. In the interim he was principal author of his state's first constitution, author of several of the Federalist Papers, first chief justice of the United States, and negotiator of the controversial treaty of 1794 known by his name.

Many of the furnishings in the Jay House are original. There is an outstanding collection of eighteenth-century paintings and a display of historical documents. The site's grounds are open all year round and the house is open from April through November, 10 A.M. to 4 P.M. Tuesday to Saturday, and 11 A.M. to 4 P.M. on Sunday. Phone: (914) 232-5651.

Johnson Hall. *See* JOHNSTOWN.

Johnstown, Fulton County, Mohawk Valley. Established in 1760 by Sir William Johnson (1715–1774) as the capital of his vast frontier domain, Johnstown has many important landmarks of the colonial and Revolutionary era.

William Johnson, first baronet of New York, reached the Mohawk Valley in 1737 at the age of twenty-two to manage the estate of his uncle. He quickly revealed talents that made him an outstanding frontier leader. In 1755 all five of the colonies sending troops to northern New York for the expedition against Crown Point commissioned him a major general. At Lake George he defeated a force of French professionals and Indians and was made a hereditary baronet of the British Empire. General Sir William Johnson succeeded to command of the expedition that took Fort Niagara in 1759, and the next year aided Amherst in taking Montreal. As superintendent of Indian affairs north of the Ohio and colonel of the Six Nations, he kept the Iroquois from joining Pontiac's Rebellion in 1763, and negotiated the Treaty of Fort Stanwix in 1768.

For about the last ten years of his life Sir William was in ill health, and in 1774 he died suddenly at Johnson Hall a few hours after making a long address at an Indian council there. Only fifty-nine years old at this time, he left three children from his union in 1739 with a seventeen-year-old indentured servant named Catharine Weisenburg. These children—Ann, John, and Mary—were baptized in their mother's name. But Sir William refers to her in his will as "my beloved wife," a wedding ring engraved with the date "1739 June 26" was found in his grave, and the College of Heralds—which is quite particular in matters of legitimacy—recognized his son John's title as second baronet of New York.

Sir William had eight children by the first of his two "Indian wives" who moved into Johnson Hall after Catharine's death, and in maintaining the intimate relations with the Iroquois for which his services to the crown were so valuable, he undoubtedly sired others. But when his reputation as a "squaw man" became bruited about the coffeehouses of London and prompted an official inquiry, he replied simply that the rumors of his numerous progeny had been grossly exaggerated. (The first "housekeeper" was the famous Mary, or "Molly," Brant, sister of the noted Mohawk Joseph Brant.)

Although Sir William had been dead a year when the American Revolution came to the Mohawk Valley, his dynasty remained a strong Loyalist force. His son had inherited the title and the wealth. His two daughters had married Sir William's principal lieutenants, kinsman Guy Johnson and Daniel Claus. The two Indian mistresses were nieces of Chief Hendrick of the Mohawks, a circumstance which gave the Johnsons "dynastic" ties with the Iroquois. Hundreds of Highland Scots brought to settle Sir William's domain were a further source of Loyalist support.

In the summer of 1775 the principal Loyalists of the valley left for Canada to join the British and organize themselves to reestablish loyal government along the Mohawk by force of arms. Sir John Johnson (1742–1830) had to stay behind temporarily. For one thing, his wife was expecting a baby. Also, Sir John had duties to perform as a judge and as major general of the militia. When the Patriots learned that he was in correspondence with Royal Governor Tryon and was arming his retainers, they marched to Johnson Hall (January 1776) for a showdown. General Philip Schuyler forced Johnson to disband his personal army, to give up three Highlanders as hostages, and to put himself on parole to await orders from Congress. About four months later, after his life had been threatened, Johnson buried his family silver in the cellar of Johnson Hall, his papers in another place, and fled with 170 of his tenants to Montreal, abandoning his wife and the hostages.

The first and greatest battle between the Loyalist exiles and their Mohawk Valley kinsmen and former neighbors was at Oriskany in August 1777. The next spring Sir John led a raid that took the Johnstown settlements by surprise. With four hundred Loyalist Rangers and two hundred Indians under Joseph Brant he had sailed up Lake Champlain to Crown Point, had gone up Lake George, and then had marched overland to continue up the Sacandaga River (now a great reservoir). Killing, burning, taking prisoners, and evacuating families of his Loyalist officers, Johnson destroyed much of Johnstown, and Brant's Indians raided as far south as the Mohawk. After five days, and without meeting the expected Patriot attack, Johnson retraced his steps to Crown Point.

On this first raid Sir John recovered his papers and silver, forty-two pieces of the latter being entrusted to as many of his soldiers and all arriving safely. All but four pieces of the Johnson silver were later put aboard a ship for England and lost in a storm. Sir Colpoys Johnson, the eighth baronet of New York, has a small bowl and salver from this salvaged collection. Sir John's recovered papers had been ruined by dampness.

In the fall of 1780 Johnson and Brant joined forces at Unadilla to ravage the Schoharie Valley. They descended to Fort Hunter and laid waste settlements on both sides of the Mohawk as far up as Fort Plain before the Patriots were able to muster any effective resistance. On 19 October there was fighting in Stone Arabia and near Fort Klock. The raiders then withdrew safely westward to Onondaga Lake (at modern Syracuse) and continued to the site of Fort Ontario.

The Battle of Johnstown was fought on 25 October 1781. Joseph Brant had been ravaging the upper Mohawk since the early part of that year, and in October a force of 570 Loyalists and 130 Indians under Major John Ross had raided to within 12 miles of Schenectady without meeting any real resistance. Sir John was supposed to invade the valley from the direction of Crown Point, but Ross decided to withdraw to Johnstown when this support did not materialize. Colonel Marinus Willett commanded the militia that followed Ross. The weather had been bad for several days, and troops on both sides were tired and wet when the battle started about midafternoon on a dark and gloomy day. The British line was formed generally along the present Johnson Avenue, near Johnson Hall. The Patriots attacked from the southeast, their base being the fortified jail that still stands on South Perry Street. In the early phase of the battle, Patriot militia broke under the attack of Ross's Indians, some seventeen being killed as they tried to escape across Cayadutta Creek near Johnson Hall, and others not stopping until they reached the safety of Old St. John's Church and Fort Johnstown (the stockaded jail). The enemy line then stood fast against an attempt by a reinforcement of one hundred Massachusetts levies to envelop it from the hill about 500 yards to the northeast of Johnson Hall. Ross then maneuvered to counterattack, capturing a small cannon and stripping its ammunition before it could be retaken, and probably would have annihilated the Patriot force if darkness had not fallen early that day.

Foolish claims have been made that the Revolution already was over because Cornwallis had surrendered a few days earlier at Yorktown and that the Battle of Johnstown was fought only because the news had not arrived there. Although there were no more major military operations, the Revolution lasted for two more years.

Today's visitor to Revolutionary War sites in the Mohawk Valley will find historic Johnstown a good place to establish a base for several days. The glove factories, textile mills, and other modern commercial enterprises have made Johnstown and adjoining Gloversville an unattractive specimen of urban development, but the informed sightseer will find more here than he can properly appreciate in a short visit. The following attractions, starting with one of our most important and interesting national landmarks, are all within walking distance in today's Johnstown.

Johnson Hall State Historical Site. On Johnson Avenue just north of its junction with West State Street (N.Y. 29). Completely restored and authentically furnished by state authorities, this white frame mansion stands in a wooded park of some 19 acres. Guided tours are provided May through October. Phone: (518) 762-8712.

Giving nearby Fort Johnson to his son, Sir William built Johnson Hall in 1763. The two-story structure of Georgian Colonial style has a full basement, where the kitchen is located, and an attic. Wooden blocks grooved to simulate stone are used for the siding, as in the central section of Mount Vernon. Samuel Fuller, builder of several other well-known landmarks in the Mohawk Valley, gave Johnson Hall particularly handsome architectural touches in its rooflines, heavy dentiled cornices under the eaves (those added over the windows have, fortunately, been removed), and in the finely detailed little entrance porch.

The floor plan follows the tradition of large central halls upstairs and down, with two rooms on each side. Sir William's study, where he died, is at the head of the cellar stairs on the ground floor, and above it is "Molly Brant's Room." The gigantic upper hall is reproduced in a delightful animated model in the basement museum depicting "a musical evening at Johnson Hall in 1772." With taped music of the period and narrative, the visitor sees Sir William and an assortment of guests playing various instruments as the "faithful housekeeper" Molly Brant sits surrounded by young children. At one point a door opens slightly and briefly to reveal the grinning faces of children in their nightclothes.

The two stone blockhouses were built in 1764 not only for defense but also to provide additional quarters, storage space, office, and study. Only one is original, and it was connected by a narrow underground passageway to the basement. In 1855 this tunnel had to be filled in because it was a safety hazard.

A scale model of the entire complex of buildings around Johnson Hall in Sir William's day is among the exhibits in the blockhouse. A large council house (30 by 100 feet) stood about 300 yards west-southwest of the mansion. The much-reproduced painting by E. L. Henry in 1903 of an Indian council being held between the blockhouses on the back steps of Johnson Hall is wrong in this last detail (although accurate in architectural matters). The painter also has western Indians in his picture, not Sir William's Iroquois.

Lost Grave of Sir William Johnson. A large stone behind new St. John's Church in the center of Johnstown marks the rediscovered grave of the city's founder. He had built St. John's on this site in 1772, and two years later his body was laid to rest beneath the chancel floor. In 1836 the old church burned, and in 1840 the new St. John's was built in a slightly different location. The grave was rediscovered by accident (this same year, 1840), somebody having noticed that dirt kicked into a small hole in the surface of the ground here disappeared into a cavity below. The local Masonic lodge, which Sir William had founded, recovered the remains and reburied them in 1866.

One item of particular historic interest came to light at this time: on Sir William's finger was a wedding ring engraved with the date "1739 June 26." It was a woman's ring enlarged to fit his finger, and the date is that of his union with Catharine Weisenburg. This ring disappeared in 1964, was rediscovered in 1971 (in a Bennington, Vermont, warehouse), and is now exhibited in the cellar museum of Johnson Hall. The search continues for Catharine's grave and her marriage license.

Another item found in Sir William's grave was the lead ball carried in his left hip from his victory at Lake George. It is privately owned and not on exhibit.

Tryon County Courthouse. In the center of the city (West Main between Melcher and William Streets) is the colonial courthouse built in 1772 and still in use. Johnstown became a county seat in this year, and until then the village had comprised only about a dozen houses located a mile away from Johnson Hall. The opening of the first term of court was announced by ringing an improvised device in the cupola that has never been replaced: a large bar of iron bent to form a triangle. The courthouse is a low structure of brick with an interesting cupola. Except for one four-year period, it has been in constant use as a courthouse. Among those said to have argued cases there are Alexander Hamilton and Aaron Burr, but this is not documented.

Other Historic Sites. The Colonial Cemetery on West Green Street contains the graves of Revolutionary War veterans. Fort Johnstown, now the county jail, was built by Sir William in 1772 and fortified by a stockade and two blockhouses; Washington inspected it in 1783. Burke's Tavern, at West Montgomery and South William Streets, was moved to this location in 1788 and is used by the DAR for meetings; it is almost a duplicate of the Miller House in White Plains. The site of Johnson's Free School (1764) is on West Main Street between Market and William Streets. The Drumm House at the intersection of State, William, and Green Streets, near the Colonial Cemetery, is erroneously identified by a state marker as dating from 1763 and being the home of schoolmaster Edward Wall (or Wahl). On this lot was a small frame building used as a church before Old St. John's was built (1772). An official map of 1784 shows an empty lot here, and the Drumm House, moved onto the lot in 1840, has no historical significance other than as an illustration of mythmaking.

St. Patrick's Lodge, No. 4, Free and Accepted Masons, now housed in the Masonic Temple built in 1925 on Perry between East Main and East Green Streets, was founded by Sir William in 1766. The silver jewelry insignia of the officers, furnished by Sir William, are still in the possession of the lodge; those taken away by Sir John when he fled to Canada in 1776 were returned after his death in 1830.

For further information on guided and self-guided tours of Johnstown, contact the following: Fulton County Regional Chamber of Commerce, phone: (518) 725-0641; Bob Gould, phone: (518) 762-8309; the Johnstown Historical Society, 17 North William Street, phone: (518) 762-7076. Internet users should go to: www.johnstown.com.

Jones (Judge Thomas) House Site, Massapequa, Long Island. See under BRIDGEPORT, CONNECTICUT.

Kings Ferry. Crossing the Hudson River between Stony Point and Verplanck's Point, this ferry was of great strategic importance to the Patriots: with the British in control of New York City during most of the war, this was the southernmost crossing of the Hudson that could be safely used. The armies of Washington and Rochambeau used Kings Ferry in August 1781 in their march to Yorktown. No structures have been preserved, but a good view of the site is provided at Stony Point.

Kingston. Here at the principal rendezvous of the Esopus Indians, a fort was established by Dutch traders in 1615. Settlers from Albany arrived in 1653 to live near the protection of Fort Esopus, and in 1661 their village was chartered as Wiltwyck. The present name was bestowed in 1669 by the English governor in honor of his family home in Berkshire. Having had serious Indian troubles from the start, Kingston was a particular target of Indian and Loyalist raids in the early years of the Revolution because it was a center of Patriot sentiment in a region where Loyalism was strong. On the other hand, Kingston became notorious as a Loyalist prison.

During the period 19 February to 7 October 1777 the New York provincial government met at Kingston, having fled ahead of the British invaders from Manhattan to White Plains to Fishkill. At Kingston the first state constitution, primarily the work of John Jay, was adopted and the first state officials took office. General George Clinton was inaugurated as governor in the courthouse on whose site the present Ulster County Courthouse was built in 1818, and he is buried with other Revolutionary War veterans in the graveyard adjoining the Dutch Reformed Church.

The Senate House, at Clinton Avenue and North Front Street, is the important historic landmark in Kingston. It is a one-story house of rock-cut limestone with a rear wall of Holland brick, built about 1676 by Colonel Wessel Ten Broeck. Around 1751 it was acquired by Abraham Van Gaasbeek, who made the south room available to the newly elected state senate. Reconstructed after the British raid on 16 October 1777 (see below), the house continued to be a residence until acquired by the state in 1887 from the Ten Broeck family. Now open year-round to the public from April through October (Monday, Wednesday, and Saturday, 10 A.M. to 5 P.M., and Sunday 11 A.M. to 5 P.M.), it is furnished with items of the colonial period that belonged to early settlers in the region. The adjoining museum (built in 1927) is devoted to regional history and features the paintings of Kingston's John Vanderlyn (1775–1852). Phone: (845) 338-2786.

The British sailed up the Hudson after defeating George Clinton in the vicinity of Bear Mountain, and on 16 October 1777 burned almost every building in Kingston. The government fled to nearby Marbletown and then to Hurley, but the Council of Safety had been meeting in the Conrad Elmendorf Tavern, which survives at 88 Maiden Lane as a privately owned structure. The only house to be entirely spared by the British, the Van Steenbergh House, has survived at Wall Street facing Franklin Street, and is also a private home. The Hoffman House, at 94 North Front and Green Street, was owned by the Hoffman family from about 1707 to the beginning of this century. It has been an upscale restaurant since 1976 and is open for lunch and dinner; phone: (845) 338-2626.

Klock's Field, Battle of. *See* FORT KLOCK.

Knickerbocker Mansion, Rensselaer County, near Schaghticoke. Important in the development of New York as a colony and said (on very doubtful authority) to be the inspiration of many tales by Washington Irving, this site is presently undergoing renovation by the Knickerbocker Historical Society. At the base of a low ridge and about 3 miles off the main highway in a rural setting of rich bottomland, the place has the makings of an exceptionally attractive American landmark. On the grounds is the site of the Tree of Peace planted by Governor Andros in 1676 after a treaty had been made to strengthen the alliance between the River Indians and the Fort Albany militia. Colonel Johannes Knickerbocker arrived here in 1709, built a log cabin, and took command of the fort about a mile away that served as an important patrol base. (It was headquarters for scouts who covered the approaches from Ticonderoga.)

The existing two-story brick house was completed by 1770. A spacious structure with a full basement and attic, its walls have settled in one corner and shoddy work has been done in pointing up the rear wall.

Southwest of Schaghticoke on N.Y. Route 40, 1.6 miles from the junction of N.Y. 40 and 67, a tourist takes Knickerbocker Road westward 2.6 miles and goes north 0.6 mile to the site. The mansion is visible from a great distance as one approaches on an excellent highway through picturesque country. The Knickerbocker Historical Society can be reached by mail at Box 29, Schaghticoke N.Y. 12154; email: Iseman7@aol.com.

Knox Headquarters (John Ellison House), near Vails Gate, 4 miles south of Newburgh on N.Y. Route 94 at Thruway Exit 17. The main two-story stone house was added in 1782 to the single-story frame wing whose original portion dates from 1734. Henry Knox used the house as his headquarters for various periods between the summer of 1779 and the fall of 1782, as did Nathanael Greene and Steuben. Horatio Gates lived here while the army was in the nearby New Windsor Cantonment, and the house was a social center during those months. The "lively and meddlesome but amiable" wife of the gargantuan General Knox lived with him here at one time and enhanced his local reputation as a host.

Well restored and furnished, the house has notable fireplaces, mantels, and woodwork. There is a curious stairway to the attic that will enchant children. State property since 1922, it is open Memorial Day through Labor Day from 10 A.M. to 5 P.M. Wednesday to Saturday, 1 P.M. to 5 P.M. on Sunday. Phone: (845) 561-5498.

Lake George. This narrow, 32-mile-long body of water was a link in the chain of river, lake, and portage connections between the St. Lawrence and the Hudson, and it consequently figured prominently in the Colonial Wars and the Revolution. The short portage to the north into Lake Champlain was dominated by Ticonderoga. From the southern end of the lake, now Lake George Village, the Great Carrying Place extended over about 10 miles to Fort Edward on the Hudson River.

In December 1775 the "Noble Train of Artillery" started south from Ticonderoga along Lake George on its 300-mile trip to the Boston lines. In 1777 Burgoyne made the serious mistake of not using Lake George as the route for his entire invasion force. Instead he sent only his heavy artillery and supplies along the lake, and moved the rest of his expedition from Whitehall (then Skenesboro) along Wood Creek to Fort Edward. The distance was only 22 miles, but the Patriots so obstructed his way that he took twenty days to make the trip.

Two months later the Americans attacked Burgoyne's overextended line of communications. Colonel John Brown had some success in a surprise attack on Ticonderoga; then he moved south on Lake George in captured boats to surprise the British post at Diamond Island. Unfavorable winds slowed his advance, a paroled Loyalist warned the enemy of his approach, and Brown lacked the artillery firepower to attack the British breastworks, so he withdrew after a short bombardment of the island. Located south of Diamond Point and about 3 miles above Lake George Village, Diamond Island is now owned by the state and has a large stone monument dedicated to the armies that passed by between 1666 and 1777.

The Lake George Association was organized in 1885 to protect the lake's natural state, and what Thomas Jefferson called "the most beautiful body of water I ever saw" remains remarkably unspoiled. Of the 155 islands, 48 are state-owned. Lake George Association phone: (518)

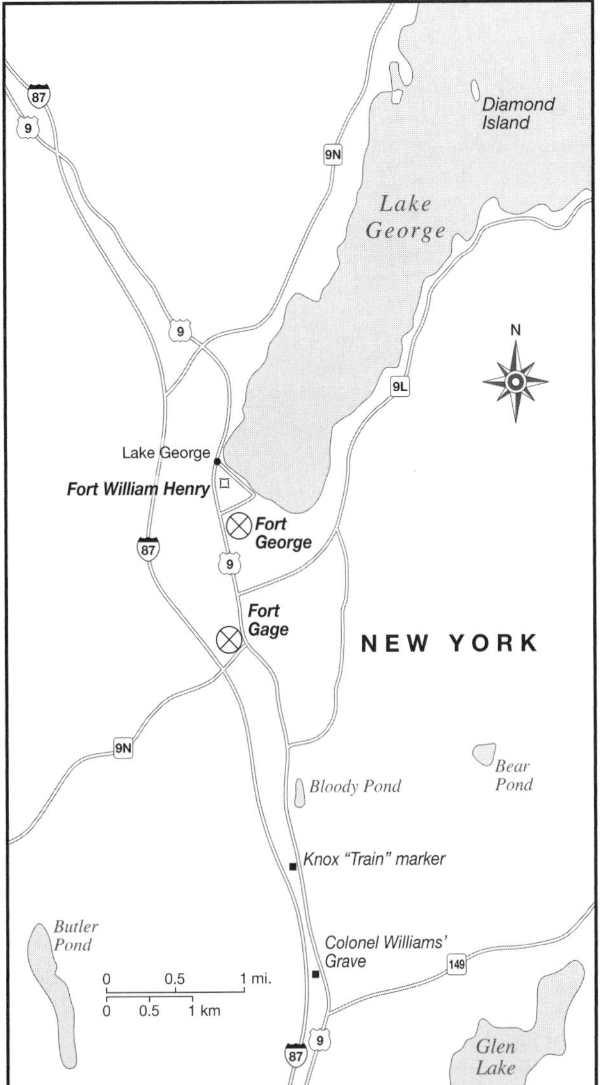

MAP BY XNR PRODUCTIONS. THE GALE GROUP.

668-3558. Lake Shore Drive (N.Y. Route 9N) is a 40-mile scenic route to Ticonderoga.

Lake George Village and vicinity, U.S. 9 and I-87. Just south of Lake George Village (southern tip of the lake) are state parks that include important sites associated more with the Colonial Wars than with the Revolution. In September 1755 William Johnson won his baronetcy (becoming Sir William) by defeating French baron Dieskau. Two days after winning this Battle of Lake George Johnson established Fort William Henry a short distance away to control the portage between the lake and the Hudson River. In March 1757 the new fort easily beat off a French attack, but five months later the garrison surrendered after holding out for almost a week against a well-organized and much larger force under Montcalm. Many hundreds of the Americans were massacred when Montcalm's Indians got out of control and violated the French leader's honorable surrender terms.

The Fort William Henry Corporation (phone: [518] 668-3081), formed in 1953, has reconstructed the fort. A museum displays objects found in archaeological investigations, and there are exhibits with taped explanations. Guided tours, military drills, musket and cannon firing, bullet molding, and the hourly showing of a thirty-minute film, *Last of the Mohicans*, are among the daily attractions during the summer season. (Fort William Henry and the massacre figure prominently in James Fenimore Cooper's *Last of the Mohicans.*) The fort is open May through October, 9 A.M. to 6 P.M.; phone: (518) 668-5471.

Ruins of Fort George (1759) are in the Lake George Battlefield Park, about half a mile south of Fort William Henry and easy to locate. The site of Fort Gage is more difficult to find. It figures in literature of the Seven Years' War (young General Lord George Howe was there just before his death), it is plotted on the U.S. Geological Survey map of the region (Glens Falls quadrangle, 1:62,500), and it is identified in the WPA *Guide* as "Fort Gage Park." But the fort was never more than a fieldwork and was only very briefly occupied, and now there is nothing to find in the ground and not much more to see. The location is the sandy hill behind cabin number 7 of the Fort Gage Motel, just west of U.S. 9 at its junction with U.S. 9N (0.9 mile south of the entrance to Fort William Henry). Within living memory it has never been part of a park.

Bloody Pond is alongside U.S. 9 on the east, just 1.4 miles south of the Fort Gage site (junction of U.S. 9N) and about 3 miles south of the village of Lake George. It is 0.4 mile past Bloody Pond Road (do not be diverted by this promising name). There is a marker noting the pond's name with the date 1755 listed on it. The pond fills to an impressive size—about an acre—during the rainy season, but much of the time it is a stagnant puddle. Digging during a drought failed to reveal evidence that it had been filled with the bodies of men killed in the "Bloody Morning Scout" (see below).

Slightly more than a mile farther south on U.S. 9 is the grave of Colonel Ephraim Williams, just west of the highway. He and the elderly Chief Hendrick were killed in an ambuscade near this point the morning of Johnson's victory at Lake George. His will, made shortly before he led his regiment to join Johnson, left his property to a township on condition that its name be changed to Williamstown and a free school be established. The latter (in 1793) became Williams College, Williamstown, Massachusetts.

One of the handsome bronze markers indicating the route of Knox's "Noble Train of Artillery" from Ticonderoga to the Boston area is west of the highway, about midway between Bloody Pond and Williams's grave.

See LAKE GEORGE for other related sites.

Livingston Manor. *See* CLERMONT.

Long Island. The western end of the 120-mile-long island settled in 1636 by Dutch farmers is part of New York City, and the Revolutionary War sites in Brooklyn (Kings County) and Queens boroughs are listed under the former heading.

The British controlled the entire island after their victory on 27 August 1776 over the Patriot army in what is known generally as the Battle of Long Island but should perhaps be called the Battle of Brooklyn. Long Island was an important source of supplies for the British—cattle, vegetables, hay, salt, and firewood—and the numerous windmills (several of which survive) were commandeered for grinding grain and pumping water. The island was also an important base for amphibious raids across Long Island Sound into Connecticut and for naval operations (see GARDINER'S ISLAND). Active Patriot operations on the island, "whaleboat warfare" in the Sound, dramatic intelligence work centered around Raynham Hall, and the highly successful Patriot raids to Fort St. George and Sag Harbor are remembered today by the physical remains at many historic landmarks.

The cultural and architectural treasures of Long Island deserve special notice. Many are in a remarkably fine state of preservation; others are disappearing as these words are written. The region is unusual also in that its historic and preservationist organizations have been especially effective. The Long Island Historical Society (in Brooklyn; see under NEW YORK CITY) and Society for the Preservation of Long Island Antiquities (in Setauket; see end of this section) have long been venerated by Americans with a serious interest in our heritage. Because up-to-date information on historic sites on Long Island is available from these organizations, the author will here identify only the major landmarks.

The town of Southold covers most of the north fork at the top of Long Island. As the earliest settled portion of the island it is rich in structures of great architectural importance, although many are badly neglected. At the far tip of the island (and a longer drive than it might appear) is Orient Point. Conspicuous near the ferry slip is the great ghost of the Orient Point Inn, used by British troops during the Revolution and (expanded and raised to four stories) as a famous hotel until 1967. Gardiner's Island and Bay may be seen from this area. The ferry trip from Orient Point to New London, Connecticut can be enjoyable and historically profitable in conveying an impression of what Long Island Sound might have been like in the days of "whaleboat warfare" and British raids along the Connecticut coast. For a schedule, contact the Cross Sound Ferry Service. Phone: (631) 323-2525; website: www.longislandferry.com.

The Old House at Cutchogue (1649) has no Revolutionary War associations, but as its National Historic Landmark citation states, it is "one of the most distinguished surviving examples of English domestic architecture in America." The house, in the Village Green Historical Complex on Route 25, can be visited in June and September on Saturdays and Sundays, 2 to 5 P.M., and in July and August on Saturday through Monday, 2 to 5 P.M. Phone: (631) 734-7122.

Rock Hall (c. 1767), 199 Broadway in Lawrence, one of the last great manor houses on Long Island and now the Town of Hempstead Museum, is said to be one of the finest examples of Georgian architecture in America. Open year-round, Wednesday to Saturday 10 A.M. to 4 P.M. Phone: (516) 239-1157.

Fort Hill, Sagtikos Manor, and the several historic landmarks in and around Setauket are covered under those headings.

For information and guide material, write or visit the Society for the Preservation of Long Island Antiquities, 161 Main Street, P.O. Box 148, Cold Spring Harbor, N.Y. 11724. Phone: (631) 692-4664; website: www.splia.org.

McCrae (Jane) Atrocity. *See* FORT EDWARD.

Minisink Ford, Delaware River, Sullivan County, opposite Lackawaxen, Pennsylvania. On a hill overlooking this ancient crossing place is an attractive historical park preserving landmarks of the battlefield where a Patriot force was wiped out on 22 July 1779. Mohawk Chief Joseph Brant had retreated toward the ford with captured cattle, booty, and a few prisoners after raiding the village of Minisink, about 25 miles to the east. His 90 Indians and Loyalists were pursued by 150 militia, most of them from around Goshen. The impetuous Patriots had divided their force, sending an advance party ahead to cut the raiders off at the ford, when they discovered that Brant had safely crossed the river and circled back to cut off their retreat to Goshen. Brant skillfully set up an ambush, cut off a third of the Patriot force from the main body on the hill, and then attacked the latter with superior strength. Around dusk, when the defenders were running out of ammunition, Brant found a weak point and penetrated their position. In the massacre that followed, forty-five Goshen men and a number of others were killed.

In an attractive area developed by the Sullivan County Division of Public Works are marked the two places where the critical action took place at the end of the battle. From a large parking and picnic area a visitor climbs a paved path for about 100 yards to a small plateau where an interesting monument to the battle was erected in 1830. A recorded narrative is provided. About 100 yards to the southwest is a large boulder, "Sentinel Rock," where the Indians made their breakthrough. (Brant saw that the Patriot defender of this point had been killed, and he exploited the opportunity.) About 100 yards west of the old monument is a ledge called Hospital Rock, where Lieutenant Colonel (Doctor) Benjamin Tusten and seventeen other wounded were slaughtered. For information from the Sullivan County Division of Public Works, phone (845) 794-3000 ext. 3066. Another good information source is the Minisink Valley Historical Society. Phone: (835) 856-2375; website: www.minisink.org.

The park is easy to find if a visitor approaches on N.Y. 97 from the west: the junction of County Road 168 and N.Y. 97 has many historical markers and directions to the park entrance, which is 0.8 mile up a steep grade to the north. If approaching on N.Y. 97 from the east, continue past the junction of the Old Minisink Ford Road to the junction of Route 168, just mentioned. (The old road is passable and picturesque, joining Route 168 about 0.1 mile from N.Y. 97 and 0.7 mile below the park entrance.)

N.Y. 97 is along the general trace of the historic Old Mine Road that was built by early colonists along the Minisink Indian route from the Hudson River (around Kingston) to the Delaware (at Port Jervis), then up the Delaware through Minisink Ford and the Delaware Water Gap. The name "Old Mine Road" comes from legends that Dutch prospectors from the Hudson Valley used it to reach copper and silver deposits in New Jersey. It may have the distinction of being the first Indian trail on the east coast to evolve into a true road; by 1756 it was traveled by wagons and stagecoaches. Today it is U.S. 209 from Kingston to Port Jervis, and N.Y. 97—up the Delaware Valley—passes through country that is wild and scenic.

Mount Defiance. *See* TICONDEROGA.

Mount Gulian Reconstruction, just north of Beacon, 145 Sterling Street. Gulian Verplanck and Francis Rombout were partners in acquiring a vast tract around Beacon in 1663, and an old Verplanck house, Mount Gulian, was Steuben's headquarters in the final months of the Revolution. It is remembered primarily as the place where on 13 May 1783 a group of senior officers of Washington's army organized the Society of the Cincinnati. In 1931 this landmark burned to the ground. A small group that includes Verplanck descendants rebuilt the house, which is now open to the public and serves as museum displaying artifacts from the Society of the Cincinnati and the Verplanck family. Mount Gulian is open Wednesday through Friday, 1 P.M. to 5 P.M., and is available Sundays for special events. Phone: (845) 831-8172.

Mount Hope. *See* TICONDEROGA.

Newburgh. *See* WASHINGTON HEADQUARTERS, NEW WINDSOR CANTONMENT, and KNOX HEADQUARTERS.

New Paltz. *See* HUGUENOT STREET.

Newtown Battlefield State Park, near East Elmira, 3 miles east of Elmira, on N.Y. 17.

More than one thousand Indians, Loyalists, and British regulars under Joseph Brant, Major John Butler, and his son Walter were defeated here on 29 August 1779 by four thousand veteran Continental troops under Major General John Sullivan.

The notorious massacres of frontier settlements at Cherry Valley, New York and Wyoming Valley, Pennsylvania took place in 1778, and the American political and military authorities almost simultaneously decided to launch a punitive expedition into the Iroquois territory of upper New York. Washington made Continental troops available for this operation. Major General John Sullivan was selected to lead the expedition, and his orders from Washington were brutal: "total destruction and devastation" of the Iroquois settlements and "the capture of as many prisoners of every age and sex as possible" to be held as hostages for future good behavior of the surviving Indians.

In accordance with the strategic plan, Sullivan's 2,500 troops were joined at Tioga (now Athens, Pennsylvania) by 1,500 who had come south under Brigadier General James Clinton from the Mohawk Valley.

Against the advice of Walter Butler the Indians insisted on making a stand at Newtown, which was only some 15 miles up the Chemung River from the starting point of Sullivan's expedition at Tioga. But here the Indians had found a good place for an ambuscade, and they made elaborate preparations, taking advantage of the time provided by Sullivan's dilatory efforts to get his expedition moving. An elaborately camouflaged breastwork of logs was built along a ridge parallel to the river. Its left flank was anchored on the slope of a steep hill, and the right flank was protected by a defile. After delivering a devastating surprise fire from this position, the defenders planned to sally forth from both flanks and annihilate the Rebel column.

At about 11 A.M. Sullivan's advance guard approached Newtown, and the Virginia riflemen of Dan Morgan's Rangers detected the trap. Morgan's three companies of riflemen were attached to the veteran brigade of General Enoch Poor, and these troops worked their way skillfully through difficult terrain onto the hill the Indians thought would protect their left flank. They were followed by Clinton's division. The Rebel artillery meanwhile took up a position to enfilade the enemy breastworks—that is, to deliver a sweeping fire from one end to the other. The guns opened up and Poor's reinforced brigade charged with the bayonet at about the same time, throwing the defenders into confusion and causing a great many of the Indians to flee in panic. The Loyalists, the fifteen regulars of the British Eighth Regiment, and many of Brant's Indians put up a determined defense, however. Colonel John Reid's Second New Hampshire Regiment on the flank of Poor's column was hit on three sides by a counterattack that would have wiped it out if Colonel Henry Dearborn had not turned back with his Third New Hampshire Regiment and two of Clinton's New York regiments to support Reid.

While this was going on, the brigades of General William Maxwell and Edward Hand, New Jersey and Pennsylvania Continentals, had moved along the riverbank and were on the enemy's other flank. Now outnumbered more than five to one, the defenders withdrew only with difficulty. Sullivan's pursuit was not vigorous, and he therefore threw away his opportunity to annihilate the disorganized enemy force. Casualty reports of this action are unreliable, but Sullivan apparently lost only three men killed, and the enemy had about thirty killed.

This was the only pitched battle of Sullivan's expedition, which proceeded to carry out a ruthless devastation of forty Iroquois towns. During the next two years the Iroquois struck back with greater ferocity and frequency than ever. Sullivan had brought back no hostages.

A portion of the battlefield has been preserved in the 330-acre park, where traces of the earthworks may be seen on high ground overlooking the Chemung River. Newtown Battlefield State Park features a Living History Center and is the sight of large-scale Revolutionary War reenactments. It is open to the public from Memorial Day through mid-October. Phone: (607) 732-6067.

New Windsor Cantonment (Temple Hill), southwest of Newburgh, about 1 mile north of Knox Headquarters on Temple Hill Road. It is a common misconception that the American Revolution ended with the surrender of Cornwallis at Yorktown in October 1781. Actually, hostilities continued for another eighteen months, and the greatest crisis in George Washington's personal leadership came while his army was in its last cantonment here at New Windsor.

Steuben laid out the great camp that held six to eight thousand officers and men during the winter of 1782 to 1783. The troops built some seven hundred huts, each of which accommodated two squads, using trees immediately adjacent to the site. A causeway across Beaver Dam Swamp connected separated portions of the camp. Then a large structure of rough-hewn logs was erected as an all-purpose assembly hall. Originally dubbed "the Temple of Virtue," it was inaugurated with boisterous enthusiasm that "disrobed it of its mantle of purity," as Benson Lossing puts it (*Field Book*, II, p. 118). It became known simply as the Temple, then as the Public Building.

It was used for religious services, for Masonic meetings, and for other assemblies. Here on 15 March 1783 Washington appeared unexpectedly before a tense group of his officers and delivered a dramatic appeal to their sense of duty and patriotism that killed the so-called Newburgh Conspiracy. This was a movement of disgruntled officers to coerce Congress into meeting their demands for long overdue pay and allowances and for a life pension.

In mid-June 1783 most of Washington's troops headed home after learning that Congress was granting them furloughs until the peace treaty was signed and they could be permanently discharged. Their eight months in the Hudson Highlands had been particularly onerous because of shortages in rations and clothing; they were ready to go, and the authorities were happy to be rid of them. On 2 September an auction was held in the Temple to sell off the camp buildings. One of the officers' huts has survived, having been moved a few miles to become somebody's war-surplus home and then having been rescued in 1934 and moved back to the cantonment area.

In a well-qualified sentence that brooks no paraphrasing, the New York State authorities say, "it stands today as the only known existing wooden camp structure built by Revolutionary soldiers." The Temple was demolished soon after its sale, but a representation of the building now stands on the site.

The New Windsor Cantonment is open to the public from Wednesday through Saturday, 10 A.M. to 5 P.M., Sunday from 1 P.M. to 5 P.M. from mid-April through October. Groups are welcome year-round by appointment. There are drills, demonstrations, and museum exhibits (including of Freemasonry of the colonial era); the 120-acre site includes a picnic area. Phone: (845) 561-1765; email: nwc@orn.net.

New York City. The principal nineteenth- and twentieth-century sources for the historic geography and architecture of New York City include Henry Onderdonk's *Revolutionary Incidents of Queens County* (1846 and 1884); Henry P. Johnston's *The Campaign of 1776 around New York and Brooklyn* (1878) and *The Battle of Harlem Heights* (1897); Albert Ulmann's *Landmark History of New York* (1901 and 1939); *Historic Guide to the City of New York* (1909), compiled by F. B. Kelley; *Landmarks of New York* (1923), edited by A. Everett Peterson; *Historical Markers and Monuments in Brooklyn* (Long Island Historical Society, 1952); the six-volume *Iconography of Manhattan Island* (1915–1928), compiled by I. N. Phelps Stokes; Bruce Bliven's *Battle for Manhattan* (1955) and *Under the Guns: New York, 1775–1776* (1972); *The American Revolution in Queens* (1961) by Frank McMaster, the borough historian; and the first volume of Sol Stember's *The Bicentennial Guide to the American Revolution* (1974), covering the war in the North.

More current works include John Gallagher's *The Battle of Brooklyn, 1776* (1999) and Barnet Schecter's *The Battle for New York* (2003), which outlines a walking tour of the five boroughs and Westchester County, with directions at the website TheBattleForNewYork.com. Another self-guided tour, with photographs and maps, is Eric Kramer and Carol Sletten's "New York Freedom Trail" at NYFreedom.com, which can also be accessed through the website of the Sons of the Revolution in the State of New York, SonsOfTheRevolution.org. See also the websites and webpages for individual parks, historic houses, and monuments.

The sites in the five boroughs are arranged alphabetically under Manhattan, Queens, Brooklyn, The Bronx, and Staten Island.

MANHATTAN

Battery Park, southern tip of Manhattan. Most of the 22-acre Battery Park, which includes Castle Clinton National Monument, sits on landfill and has no Revolutionary War associations. In 1693 the British built a fort on the rocky island where Fort Clinton was subsequently constructed (1808–1811). In 1870 the shoreline was moved out to incorporate the present Battery Park with the island. State Street, along the northeastern edge of the park, marks the original waterfront, where a line of cannon faced the harbor in the Dutch and English periods. In August 1775 John Lamb's artillery company, which included Alexander Hamilton, began hauling the British guns up Broadway to the Common (today's City Hall Park) for safekeeping. This provoked a broadside from the man-of-war *Asia*, which spurred the ongoing exodus of New York's residents. Charles Lee's forces completed the capture of the heavy guns when he arrived to fortify the city in February 1776.

Looking south from Battery Park into New York Harbor, one can see the Statue of Liberty, which was dedicated in 1886 as a gift to the United States from France, the ally whose backing ensured the American victory in the Revolutionary War. Closed after 9/11, the statue was reopened to the public in August 2004. This renowned monument sits on the 12-acre Liberty Island and offers panoramic views from its crown that rank among the finest in the world.

Beekman House Site, 51st Street and First Avenue. A tablet on Public School 135 indicates the site of Mount Pleasant, the home of James Beekman, erected in 1763 and used during the British occupation of New York as headquarters for Generals Howe, Clinton, and Carlton in turn. Tradition holds that Nathan Hale was kept in the Beekman greenhouse overnight before his execution on 22 September 1776. The house was demolished in 1874.

Bowling Green, an elliptical park at the south end of Broadway near Battery Park, just north of the United States Custom House, which now houses the National Museum of the American Indian. The Stamp Act Riot of 1765 began on the Common and culminated at Bowling Green, where the mob pounded on the gates of Fort George (now the site of the Custom House), which contained the royal governor's residence. The rioters burned the lieutenant governor's effigy and carriage on the green, using the fence for kindling. On 9 July 1776, after a public reading of the Declaration of Independence on the Common, the crowd marched to Bowling Green and pulled down the gilded lead statue of George III erected six years earlier. The mob also hacked off the crowns on the iron gate around the green. The gate is New York's first designated City Landmark. Most of the statue was reportedly made into bullets, but the horse's tail and bridle have survived and are in the museum of the New-York Historical Society. The site is now occupied by the statue of Mayor Abraham de Peyster (1691–1695).

Central Park. The 843 acres of Central Park are what Bruce Bliven has called "a tidied up sample of what the whole island used to be like." Conservationists see it as a significant inspiration of the nation's park movement. In one corner can be found the vestiges of McGown's Pass.

In 1850 a press campaign launched by William Cullen Bryant and backed by Washington Irving and George Bancroft persuaded the city government to acquire the land. It was then located north of the built-up area, which ended at 42nd Street, and was an unsightly wasteland where squatters raised pigs and goats near their shanties. A largely African American settlement, Seneca Village, covered the area from 81st to 89th Street between Seventh and Eighth Avenues. It was demolished in 1857, and the following year an army of unemployed went to work carrying out the design of Frederick Law Olmsted (who also designed Brooklyn's Prospect Park) and Calvert de Vaux. The work involved the movement of a billion cubic feet of earth, which explains the degree to which the colonial topography was "tidied up." Central Park is enclosed between 59th Street and 110th Street, bordered on the west by Central Park West and on the east by Fifth Avenue.

City Hall Park, between Park Row and Broadway at City Hall. The park was originally part of the Common, also known as the Fields. In the colonial period, City Hall stood at Wall and Nassau Streets, today the site of Federal Hall National Memorial. The Fields is where the Stamp Act protesters gathered in 1765 and where, by some accounts, the first blood of the Revolution was shed on 11 August 1766, when residents clashed with British soldiers who had cut down the first Liberty Pole. The various structures that occupied the Fields are marked today by plaques and architectural footprints. These include the soldiers' barracks, the Liberty Pole, and the provost prison, called the Bridewell, all of which are located to the west of City Hall.

A statue of Nathan Hale faces the front of City Hall's east wing, but he was executed elsewhere. (See HALE EXECUTION SITE.) To the east of City Hall stood the New Gaol, a jail for debtors, which the British used, along with the Bridewell, to confine American prisoners of war. There is also a plaque in honor of Isaac Barre, who proclaimed in Parliament that the colonists were the "Sons of Liberty."

New York patriots met in the Fields on 6 July 1774 and decided to send delegates to the first Continental Congress. Alexander McDougall presided, Alexander Hamilton spoke against British coercion, and the occasion became known in history as the Meeting in the Fields.

Almost exactly two years later the Declaration of Independence was read in the fields to the troops in Washington's presence.

Columbia University (King's College). At the southeast corner of Park Place and West Broadway a tablet indicates the site of King's College during the period 1755 to 1857. The college occupied an area now bounded by Murray, Barclay, Church, and Chapel Streets. Used as a prison during the British occupation (1776–1783), the college reopened in 1784 as Columbia. It moved to Madison Avenue and 49th Street in 1857, and to its current location, at 116th Street and Broadway, in 1897.

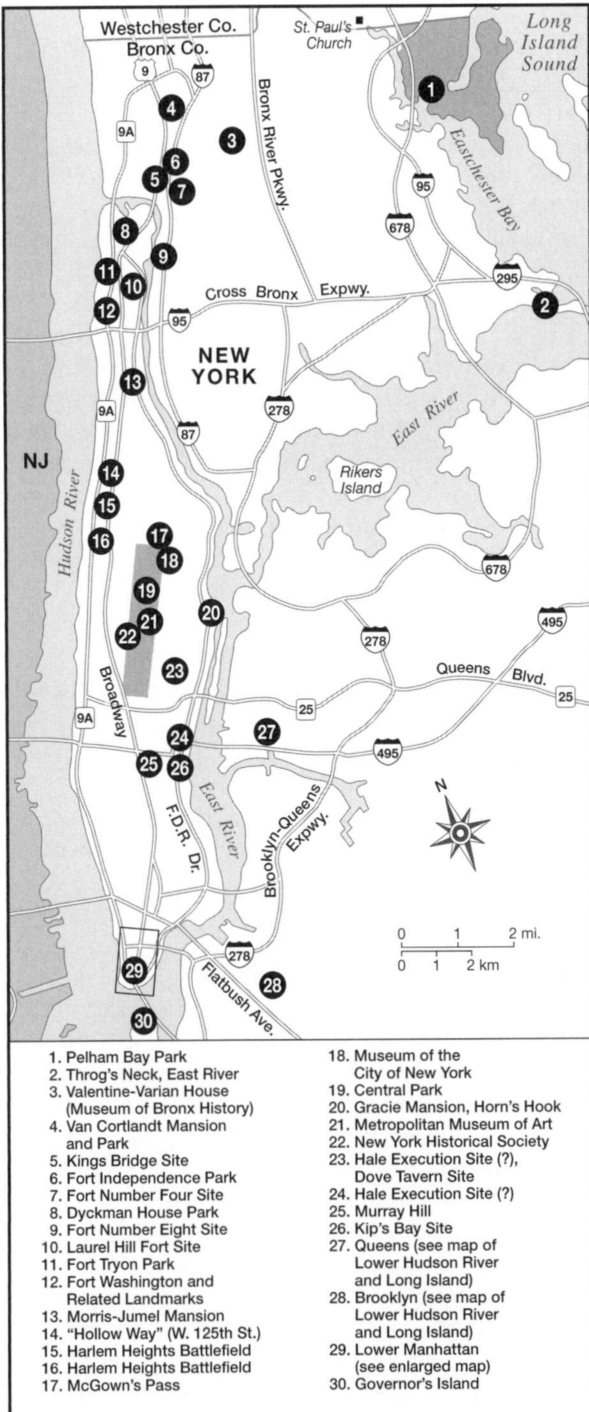

MAP BY XNR PRODUCTIONS. THE GALE GROUP.

Dyckman House, Dyckman House Park, Broadway at 204th Street. The Dyckman House site was once part of a 300-acre Dutch Colonial farm which served as the Patriot bivouac after the Battle of Harlem Heights in 1776 and as a British camp for the rest of the war. One of the fifty Hessian log huts found at another British camp in northern Manhattan has been reconstructed in the garden, where a well and replica of a smokehouse are also to be seen among the boxwood hedges, fruit trees, and grape arbor of the restored farmyard.

The house itself is of fieldstone, brick, and wood. The southern wing probably dates from 1725, but most of the house was built around 1785 by William Dyckman, grandson of a Westphalian immigrant, and his descendants gave the property to the city in 1915. Members of the family have since helped in caring for the house. The restored garden and eight furnished rooms of the house are open to the public. The Relic Room contains artifacts gathered from the Fort Washington battlefield: bullets, cannonballs, explosive shells, guns, bayonets, a uniform, and even a tattered American flag. Although recent construction has resulted in some unexpected closings, under normal circumstances Dyckman House Park is open to the public Tuesday through Sunday from 11 A.M. to 4 P.M. Phone: (212) 304-9422.

Federal Hall National Memorial, Wall and Nassau Streets. The site of the old City Hall has been occupied since 1842 by a Greek Revival structure that is now Federal Hall National Memorial. Here the Stamp Act Congress convened in 1765, Congress sat during the period 1785 to 1790, and the first United States Congress was called (4 March 1789). Washington was inaugurated on the balcony of the old building, and the Departments of State and War, as well as the Treasury and the Supreme Court, were created within its walls. The Bill of Rights was adopted here by Congress. In 1790 Philadelphia had its turn as the seat of the federal government, and the old City Hall fell into ruin. The memorial now exhibits documents and artifacts interpreting the role of old City Hall in early American history.

Fields, Meeting in the. *See* CITY HALL PARK.

Fort Amsterdam Site. Now occupied by the United States Custom House, below Bowling Green at the foot of Broadway. After taking New Amsterdam from the Dutch in 1664, the British built Fort George on the same spot, and it became the focus of American anger during the Stamp Act riot in 1765. The lieutenant governor, Cadwallader Colden, duped New Yorkers by secretly transferring the newly arrived stamps from the British ship to the fort. The rioters threatened to storm the fort, and Colden was prepared to fire on the crowd, but a compromise was reached, and the stamps were moved to City Hall. When Charles Lee fortified the city in 1776 he had the northern wall of the fort torn down and pointed cannons at the interior to prevent the British from using it as a stronghold, as they had in 1765.

Fort Tryon Park. In a 62-acre park of wooded hills on the north end of Manhattan Island overlooking the Hudson, the stone ramparts of Fort Tryon occupy the site of a redoubt where American Patriots put up their most effective resistance before surrendering Fort Washington. The earthworks on the 250-foot hill were manned by Colonel Moses Rawlings and 250 Maryland and Virginia riflemen supported by three small cannon of the Pennsylvania Artillery. An outpost was located on Cock Hill, about a mile north in what is now Inwood Hill Park.

About three thousand German troops under General Knyphausen crossed Kings Bridge and attacked Rawlings in two columns. Because of the rugged, wooded terrain, the narrow front that did not enable them to deploy into their normal linear formations, and the effective American defenses, the Germans made very slow headway and sustained heavy casualties. Margaret Corbin became America's first battlefield heroine by replacing her mortally wounded husband and helping keep his gun in action until she herself was severely wounded. The traffic circle and roadway next to the park are named for her, and she is honored by a bronze tablet mounted on the exterior of the fort. (She is buried at West Point.)

On the site of the American earthworks the British built Fort Tryon. John D. Rockefeller Jr., bought the estate that became Fort Tryon Park and presented it to the city in 1933. A residence on the site of the fort was demolished, and the hilltop now provides a magnificent view of the Hudson, the East River, and Manhattan.

Fort Washington and related landmarks. The George Washington Bridge (between 178th and 179th Streets) crosses the Hudson between Forts Washington and Lee (in New Jersey), almost completely obliterating those two works. But between West 147th Street and the Bronx are many surviving landmarks of the great military disaster suffered by the Americans in November 1776.

On 16 November 1776 the British and Germans attacked in strong columns from the north, east, and south to wipe out the bypassed pocket of American resistance on the high ground in northern Manhattan. From McGown's Pass in today's Central Park came two thousand men under Lord Hugh Percy. About eight hundred Americans under Lieutenant Colonel Lambert Cadwalader opposed them in the three defensive lines established before the Battle of Harlem Heights. These are marked by tablets on Broadway at 147th, 153rd (wall of Trinity Cemetery), and 159th Streets.

Another British attack was from the east across the Harlem River against the defenses of Laurel Hill (192nd Street). On the lawn of George Washington High School at 192nd Street and Audubon Avenue, a boulder at the foot of the flagpole bears a large bronze tablet that reads: "In grateful remembrance of the Patriot Volunteers of the Pennsylvania Flying Camp led by Colonel William Baxter . . . who, with many of his men, fell while defending this height, 16 November 1776, and was buried near this spot." Baxter's position was later the site of the British Fort George, but his troops occupied only field fortifications when he was attacked by the elite Black Watch and overrun after a spirited defense. Highbridge Park, leading down to the Harlem River from Laurel Hill Terrace, between 181st and 188th Streets, displays the steep terrain the British ascended during the attack. The Forty-second Highlanders dropped down the river to make a diversion about where the foot of 152nd Street is now located. The defenders rushed reinforcements to meet this threat from the converging British columns (Lord Percy having resumed his advance), and heavy fighting took place around Trinity Cemetery. Inside the cemetery, in the southeastern corner (east of Broadway), a bronze tablet on a small boulder marks this middle line of defense and points out the remains of an earthen fort.

Meanwhile, the main attack was taking place to the north against the works later called Fort Tryon.

From Fort Lee, across the river, Washington watched helplessly as almost 3,000 of his best officers and men were taken prisoner. Washington also lost a large quantity of valuable matériel, including about 150 cannon.

The British built on the sites of the main American works, Fort Washington becoming Fort Knyphausen, Rawlings's redoubt becoming Fort Tryon, and the Laurel Hill works becoming Fort George. Archaeologists have identified the sites of many other American, British, and German positions on Washington Heights and in the area eastward to the Harlem River. Along the Bronx side are the sites of eight numbered forts.

The site of Fort Washington, chosen because it is the highest natural point on Manhattan (265 feet), is marked by a flagpole in Bennett Park, on Fort Washington Avenue between 183nd and 185th Streets. The battle is commemorated by a marble monument with a granite tablet and bronze letters, built into the wall of rock to the left of the park's entrance. Granite blocks in the ground at the center of the park indicate where part of the fort's walls once stood, but the 4 acres of ground inside the fort extended well beyond the edges of the park. Between Fort Washington and Bennett Avenues, Colonel Robert Magaw Place honors the commander of the fort, as does the plaque on the Fort Washington Collegiate Church on the corner at 181st Street.

Fraunces Tavern, lower Manhattan, 54 Pearl Street at Broad Street. "A 1970 conjectural restoration of [the] earliest 18th century structure remaining in Manhattan" is how this landmark has been characterized by the city's Landmarks Preservation Commission. The National Survey of Historic Sites and Buildings (1964) puts it in the "Other Sites Considered" category, commenting that "it will be considered in more detail in the study of architecture." Authorities agree, however, that Fraunces Tavern is the oldest surviving building in Manhattan and that—"conjectural restoration" or not—it is a particularly fine specimen of Georgian architecture. Historically, it is remembered primarily as the place where Washington said farewell to his senior officers on 4 December 1783 at the end of the American Revolution.

The basic structure of 1719 now known as Fraunces Tavern was built by Stephen (Etienne) De Lancey, a wealthy merchant, as an elegant town house on land he got as a wedding present from his father-in-law, Stephen Van Cortlandt, in 1700. The latter had acquired the land about 1671 and built a cottage in which he lived after his marriage to Gertrude Van Rensselaer. So the site of Fraunces Tavern has as much historical interest as the structure itself.

In 1737 the De Lanceys moved to Broadway and converted their former home into an office and warehouse. The magnificent drawing room, now known as the Long Room (741 square feet), was leased to Henry Holt, who staged pantomimes and America's first puppet show where New York's colonial elite had so recently been entertained. The building was offered for sale in 1759, but it was not until 1762 that a buyer, "Black Sam" Fraunces, was found.

Fraunces had been a caterer at nearby Bowling Green since coming to New York seven years earlier from the French West Indies. He bought the property for £2,000, converted it into a tavern, and called it the Queen's Head. All this happened as the last Seven Years' War ended and the movement toward the American Revolution started developing. The Long Room became popular for social and political meetings not only because of the prime location of the tavern but also because it was the most spacious and elegant public hall available.

When Van Cortlandt built his cottage on this site it fronted on a canal (now Broad Street) and was on the East River shore. Pearl Street derives its name from the abundance of "pearly shells" scattered here in colonial times. The Whitehall Ferry slip to which Washington walked in 1783 was only two long blocks away. The site is in the middle of today's Whitehall Street, about halfway between Pearl Street and the present ferry landings.

"Black Sam" Fraunces leased his tavern a few years after establishing it, and he devoted himself to running a wax museum in the city. In 1770 he took over personal management of the tavern. Five years later, on the eve of the Revolution, he gave up the wax museum and tried to sell the tavern, obviously planning to direct his entrepreneurial talents elsewhere. But he could not find a buyer, which is why the name Fraunces ended up being immortalized in American history. After the Revolution he was rewarded by Congress and commended for his kindness toward American prisoners in the city's notorious jails and for his covert assistance to the cause. After Washington's famous farewell in the Long Room Fraunces again undertook to sell the tavern. In 1785 he succeeded, getting $250 (£50) less than he had paid twenty-three years earlier. When Washington returned to New York in 1789 as president, Fraunces became his steward. Moving with Washington to Philadelphia in this same capacity, Fraunces died there in 1795 and is buried in St. Peter's Churchyard of Christ Church.

Although listed in the New York census of 1790 as white (with a slave in his household), Fraunces probably was of mixed race.

Restoration of Fraunces Tavern has been functional as well as architectural, its public dining room on the first floor carrying on the tradition of "Black Sam." The Sons of the Revolution bought the three-and-a-half-story building in 1904 and completed the initial restoration in 1907. In 1970 the Long Room was stripped to expose its hand-hewn beams and masonry walls, where patches of the original plaster still showed tufts of the red cowhair binding. The restored room is open to the public, ribbon cutting having been performed by a young descendant of Stephen De Lancey. Throughout the large building are paintings, furnishings, relics, and exhibits that preserve the spirit of the Revolution. The first floor is an upscale restaurant; a museum/gift shop is on the second and third floors. The museum's summer hours are 10 A.M. to 5 P.M., Tuesday through Saturday. The hours from October through April are 12 to 5 P.M. except on Saturday, when the museum remains open from 10 A.M. to 5 P.M. Phone: (212) 304-9422.

Golden Hill, "Battle" of. On 19 January 1770 a force of thirty to forty British soldiers used bayonets to quell a riot involving citizens armed with swords and clubs. The disturbance climaxed a series of protests against the Assembly's support of the Quartering Acts of 1765 and 1774. Several rioters were seriously wounded on Golden Hill, and the action has therefore been called "the first significant fighting of the American Revolution." The site is marked by a tablet at William and John Streets, where once a golden field of wheat grew on a hill.

Governors Island. So called because in 1698 the assembly set it aside for the benefit of the royal governors, it was fortified in 1776 by Colonel William Prescott's regiment. These were the famous diggers of Bunker Hill, but their works on Governors Island were not attacked, and the position was abandoned after the American defeat on Long Island. Governors Island, at the mouth of the East River, helped screen the American retreat to

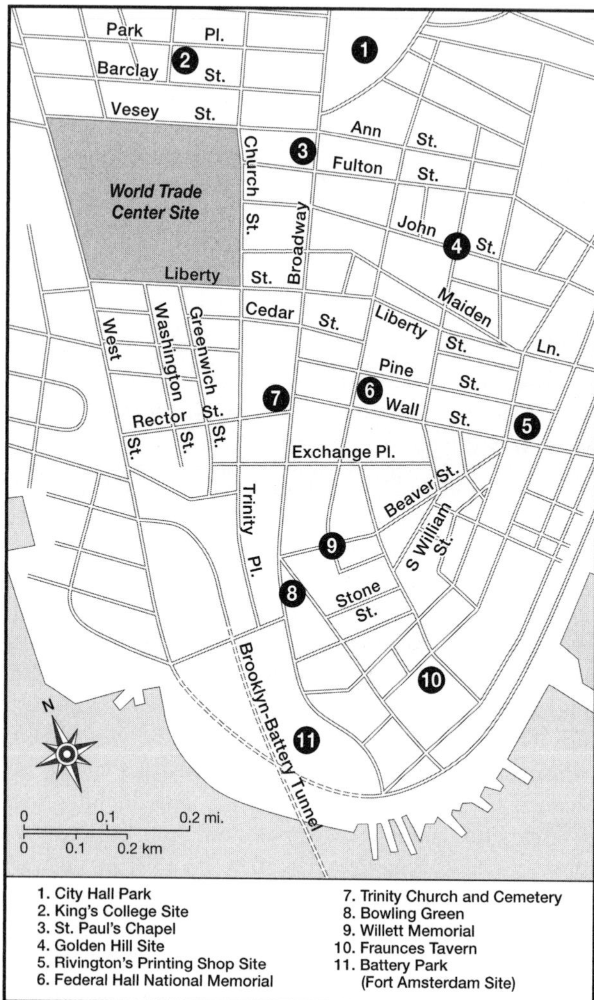

MAP BY XNR PRODUCTIONS. THE GALE GROUP.

Manhattan on the night of 29 August. Castle William was built on Governors Island at the beginning of the nineteenth century, and the old well on the east side is among the few surviving vestiges of the Revolutionary War works.

Gracie Mansion. The mayor's residence. This fine example of Georgian architecture is in Carl Schurz Park. (See HORN'S HOOK.) It was built during the years 1770 to 1774, first owned by Jacob Walton, bought by Archibald Gracie in 1798, and restored. Information about tours of the interior is available from the Gracie Mansion Conservancy, at (212) 570-4751. Excursion boats provide good views of the mansion's exterior.

Greenwich (Village). Before the Revolution two rows of wooden houses belonging mostly to prominent families fronted on Greenwich Street, which was close to the Hudson. Today, an iron bollard, where boats once tied up, marks the old shoreline on the sidewalk in front of the Ear Inn, a nineteenth-century pub on Spring Street between Greenwich and Washington streets. The waterfront has been moved out several hundred yards. When General Israel Putnam and his aide, Aaron Burr, rescued 3,500 American troops by marching them from New York City to Harlem Heights after the Kips Bay invasion on 15 September 1776, their route passed through Greenwich and Chelsea, which were then suburbs. Today there are no Revolutionary War landmarks of significance. Greenwich (pronounced "gren-itch") Village, as this section of the city is called, is a redundancy, for "wich" means "village."

Hale Execution Site. The twenty-one-year-old Nathan Hale of Connecticut stepped forward after no other captain in Knowlton's Rangers would volunteer for the mission of spying on the British. He was captured while returning to his own lines on Harlem Heights. Being in civilian clothes and having incriminating papers on his person, he (like John André) was executed as a spy. As was later the case with André, his death was much lamented by friend as well as foe. His final words were "I only regret that I have but one life to lose for my country."

While the site of his hanging on 22 September 1776 has been a matter of controversy, the best evidence suggests that he died in the vicinity of Third Avenue and 66th Street, where the Dove Tavern was located and near the British artillery park. A plaque on the Chatham apartments on Third Avenue at East 65th Street calls this the "probable" site and refers the reader to the New-York Historical Society's website, www.nyhistory.org, for further details. The statue of Hale in City Hall Park; a plaque on the Beekman condominium apartments on First Avenue and East 51st Street (where Hale was probably held overnight in the Beekman greenhouse); a plaque inside and one on the outside of the Yale Club (on Vanderbilt Avenue, west of Grand Central Terminal) have all added to the uncertainty about the execution site. Similarly, a tablet on a meatpacking plant at the southeast corner of First Avenue and 46th Street claimed that Hale was hanged nearby. That plaque came down when the building was demolished along with many others to make way for the United Nations complex.

Harlem Heights, Battle of. Although the site of this early American victory, on 16 September 1776, has long since been covered by some of the world's most exclusive urban development, many of the most important landmarks can be found. American forces had retreated from southern Manhattan to Harlem Heights, the high ground along the Hudson north of modern 125th Street.

Here they started work on three defensive lines, and before dawn on 16 September Lieutenant Colonel Thomas Knowlton led a reconnaissance to find out what the British were doing. With his elite force of 120 Connecticut Rangers, Knowlton made contact near a slight rise still discernable on 106th Street between West End Avenue and Riverside Drive. After a half-hour firefight Knowlton withdrew when threatened with envelopment by the Forty-second Regiment of Scottish Highlanders, the famous Black Watch.

Skirmishing to the rear in good order, the Americans followed approximately the route now marked by Claremont Avenue and dropped into the valley called the Hollow Way, about where the 125th Street subway station is located. Two British light-infantry regiments pursued to a hill near present-day Grant's Tomb.

Washington left the Morris-Jumel Mansion and reached the advanced American posts near West 135th Street as Knowlton fought his delaying action. An aide reported that the Rangers were doing well and suggested they be reinforced. The commander in chief was considering this when a familiar tune floated from the enemy position—the call sounded by fox hunters at the end of a successful chase!

Washington decided that the moment had come to undertake an offensive action. The plan was for one small force to advance directly against the British around the area of Grant's Tomb while a larger body made an envelopment to trap the British. It was working beautifully, the British charging forward from the hill, when unidentified officers in the enveloping wing prematurely gave the order to fire. The British quickly started withdrawing, the Americans pursued, and Washington sent in reinforcements.

Generally along today's 120th Street the heaviest fighting took place in a buckwheat field. A bronze bas-relief at the Columbia School of Engineering, at Broadway near 118th Street, claims to mark the site of the battle. It is about where the artillery on the British right flank was located after these two 3-pounders had been dragged forward 3 miles by hand. The guns and a company of jaegers may have saved the British from annihilation, but a shortage of ammunition forced another withdrawal. After a brief delaying action along 111th Street, the British made a final stand about where the day's events had started, on 106th Street. Not wanting to fight a major battle, Washington ordered a withdrawal at about 2 P.M.

Success in this skirmish lifted American morale at a time when this was badly needed, and some historians have seen the victory as a turning point in the war. American casualties were about thirty killed and one hundred wounded or captured. Among the dead was the gallant Knowlton, one of Washington's most promising young officers.

Hollow Way. The valley along the bottom of which today's 125th Street runs east from the Hudson to Morningside Avenue was known as the Hollow Way. Here the Battle of Harlem Heights started.

Horn's Hook, a point of land on the East River, at the northern end of today's Carl Schurz Park, at East 88th Street on East End Avenue. This was the site of a nine-gun American battery unsuccessfully shelled by the British before their landing at Kips Bay. Gracie Mansion is in this park.

Jumel Mansion. *See* MORRIS-JUMEL MANSION.

Kings Bridge Site. *See* below under THE BRONX.

King's College. *See* COLUMBIA UNIVERSITY.

Kips Bay Site. At the foot of East 34th Street on the East River, the shoreline has been moved out to obliterate the small inlet where British forces landed on 15 September 1776 to overrun Manhattan. Their initial objective was Murray Hill.

Laurel Hill Fort, 192nd Street and Audubon Avenue, on the west bank of the Harlem River, about half a mile east of the Fort Washington site. See above under FORT WASHINGTON and related landmarks.

McGown's Pass (sometimes spelled McGowan's), near the northeast corner of Central Park, about on line with East 107th Street. A little hill here is crowned with the Fort Clinton Monument—a cannon on a flat boulder to which a plaque is fixed. The marker says the high ground commanded McGown's Pass and was occupied by the British from 15 September 1776 to 21 November 1783.

The Post Road passed between two steep hills here before descending abruptly to Harlem Plains (into the present lake, Harlem Meer, in this corner of Central Park). McGown's Pass was therefore what modern tacticians call "critical terrain," and it figures prominently in contemporary accounts of the war in Manhattan. To protect the American retreat after the British invasion at Kips Bay, Washington posted riflemen just south of the pass with instructions to fall back and ambush the British if they advanced along the road between the hills. McGown's Pass Tavern, which survived into modern times, was on the site of Jacob Dyckman's Tavern, where the provincial assembly met in 1752 while City Hall was being repaired.

Metropolitan Museum of Art, main entrance on Fifth Avenue at 82nd Street. The American Wing (northwest corner) comprises three stories designed especially to illustrate the development of American interior decoration from the seventeenth to the nineteenth centuries. From the museum's collections of three thousand paintings, about three hundred are exhibited in the gallery over the arms and armor room.

Of particular interest to students of colonial and Revolutionary War history are the following rooms: the Parlor, from Ipswich, Massachusetts, dating from the mid-seventeenth century; the Samuel Wentworth Room from Portsmouth, New Hampshire; the reconstitution of the Assembly Room from Gadsby's Tavern in Alexandria, Virginia; the Verplanck Room; and the entry hall from the Van Rensselaer Manor in Albany.

An exhibition in a variety of media, *George Washington: Man, Myth, Monument,* opened in the American Wing on 19 October 2004 and ran until 27 February 2005. The exhibition featured portrayals of Washington through the centuries, including some created during his lifetime. One of the exhibition's purposes was to analyze how the public's changing needs altered depictions of Washington.

Morris-Jumel Mansion, 160th Street and Edgecomb Avenue in Washington Heights. During the Battle of Harlem Heights Washington used this house as his headquarters and lived in a suite of three small rooms on the second floor. The British and Hessians then used the building until their evacuation in 1783.

When Lieutenant Colonel Roger Morris built his mansion in 1765 it was the first in the colonies to have the two-story Greek Revival portico that later was common. Morris reached America in 1746, took part in the Braddock expedition, becoming a friend of Washington's, and fled the country as a Loyalist at the start of the Revolution. His property was confiscated at the end of the war and bought in 1810 by a wine merchant named Stephen Jumel. The latter's widow married Aaron Burr in 1833, when she was about fifty-five and he was seventy-seven, but the two were separated a few months later.

In 1903 the city bought the house and saved it from demolition; it, St. Paul's Chapel, and Fraunces Tavern are the last important structures of the colonial era in Manhattan. The house and grounds have been restored. The spacious rooms are furnished in the periods of their respective owners: the lower floor in the late nineteenth century, and the upstairs in American Federal and French Empire. The basement has servant quarters and the kitchen. Early American household utensils are displayed on the third floor.

Owned by the city, the mansion is operated by a not-for-profit organization, Morris-Jumel Mansion Incorporated, and is open to the public Wednesday through Sunday from 10 A.M. to 4 P.M. Website: www.morrisjumel.org; phone: (212) 923-8008.

Mortier House Site, Sixth Avenue and Spring Street in lower Manhattan. A tablet on the Butterick Building marks it as the site of the original house used by Lord Amherst, Washington (in 1776), Lord Carleton, Vice President John Adams, and Aaron Burr. Built in 1760 by Abraham Mortier, commissary of the British army in North America at the time, the house was originally on Charlton Street between Varick and MacDougal Streets (two blocks north of Spring Street).

Murray Hill. At the southwest corner of Park Avenue and 35th Street is a tablet marking the center of "Inclenberg," the colonial farm on high ground that happened to be an initial objective of the British after their landing at Kips Bay on 15 September 1776. Flaunting all historical evidence, circumstantial as well as factual, the myth has persisted that Mary Lindley Murray (1726–1782), a middle-aged Quaker and mother of twelve children, gave a party for British generals Howe, Clinton, and Cornwallis that delayed their military operations two hours and kept them from trapping General Putman's 3,500 troops and 67 guns in lower Manhattan.

Putnam's column started north at about 4 P.M. Following the Greenwich Road close to the Hudson, it then took farm lanes and footpaths along the axis of today's Eighth Avenue. Around the southwest corner of Central Park the Americans struck the Bloomingdale Road, roughly the route of today's Broadway, as far north as West 86th Street.

Through a gap of less than three-quarters of a mile between the Hudson River and Murray Hill the long American column passed on its 12-mile forced march without seeing an enemy soldier. (Just below today's West 100th Street, the British belatedly tried to intercept the column, but most of the Americans had already passed the intersection, and only one man was killed). But historians point out that Mary Murray's cakes and old Madeira do not deserve the credit for keeping the British inactive at Inclenberg. First, she could not have known that Putnam was slipping away rather than preparing to defend the city. Second, the British were following their plan of waiting on Murray Hill until all their forces had crossed from Long Island.

Yet Mrs. Murray's alleged service to the Patriot cause has been immortalized by painters, playwrights (*A Small War on Murray Hill* was produced in 1956), and patriotic societies (the plaque on 35th Street was put up by the Daughters of the American Revolution in 1926). Another DAR plaque, on the Park Avenue median strip at 37th Street (on the south side), explicitly honors Mary Murray for delaying the British on Murray Hill.

Museum of the City of New York, Fifth Avenue between 103rd and 104th Streets. Devoted to the history of the city, the museum has miniature groups and dioramas that bring to life historic scenes. There are exhibits of costumes, furniture by New York cabinetmakers, prints and photographs, maps, portraits, silver, toys, fire engines, and ship models pertaining to the colonial and Revolutionary War era. From the top of a reconstructed portion of Fort Amsterdam the visitor can see a panorama of the 1660 skyline. Website: www.mcny.org. Phone: (212) 534-1672.

New-York Historical Society, 170 Central Park West and 77th Street. Collections deal with all of American history but are particularly strong on New York State and the city. Since November 2000 the Henry Luce III Center for the Study of American Culture, on the Society's fourth floor, has displayed nearly forty thousand artifacts (including George Washington's camp bed from Valley Forge), many of which were previously in offsite storage. Visitors can take thematic audio tours of the center and learn about the collection through interactive computer ports and mini-exhibition stations. The outstanding reference library on the second floor is also open to the public for research. Website: www.nyhistory.org. Phone: (212) 873-3400.

Point of Rocks, St. Nicholas Avenue at 127th Street. A landmark in the Battle of Harlem Heights, the high ground here was the southernmost defensive position of the Americans overlooking the Hollow Way and the point from which Knowlton's flanking force started forward at about 11 A.M. Knowlton was mortally wounded a short time later about half a mile to the southwest.

Prison Sites. In Manhattan the sites of the notorious British prisons can be identified by today's visitor at the following places:

Livingston's Sugar House is marked by a tablet opposite the entrance to the Federal Reserve Bank, at 28-36 Liberty Street.

Middle Dutch Church was where the Mutual Life Insurance Building now stands on the northeast corner of Cedar and Nassau Streets, and is marked by a plaque.

Rhinelander Sugar House was replaced by the Rhinelander Building, which has also been torn down, and the site, behind the Municipal Building near City Hall, is now occupied by Police Plaza. A window from the original sugar house, preserved in the façade of the Rhinelander Building, was salvaged from the demolition and is now displayed in the side of a brick shed on the edge of Police Plaza. Such windows had iron bars, but no panes of glass to keep out the cold. Another window is in Van Cortlandt Park (see under THE BRONX).

Van Cortlandt's Sugar House stood at the northwest corner of today's Trinity Churchyard. One or more other sugar houses were used as prisons.

Provost Jail, administered by the notorious William Cunningham, was in the present City Hall Park.

Dissenter churches, the hospital, and King's College (see COLUMBIA UNIVERSITY) were also used as prisons. After the fire of September 1776 the prison ships were used for soldiers in addition to the naval prisoners originally held in these death traps. (See PRISON SHIP MARTYRS' MONUMENT under BROOKLYN.)

Rivington's Printing Shop Site, corner of Wall and Pearl Streets. James Rivington's *Royal Gazette* and its successor, published 1773 to 1783, are generally accepted as being the country's first daily newspapers. (A complete file is in the New-York Historical Society Library.) His plant was destroyed in November 1775 by Patriots who objected to his journalistic integrity in presenting both sides of contemporary controversies. Rivington took refuge in England but returned two years later as the king's printer in New York City. In 1781 he started supplying information to the American intelligence service, which enabled him to stay in business after the British left. Renamed *Rivington's New York Gazette and Universal Advertiser,* his paper struggled along despite declining circulation until its final issue of 31 December 1783. The printer tried unsuccessfully to carry on as a bookseller and stationer but ultimately failed and died in poverty. An interesting and important figure, James Rivington deserves more historical recognition than he has received.

St. Paul's Chapel, lower Broadway between Fulton and Vesey Streets. Built in 1764 to 1766 by Trinity Church, whose property it remains, St. Paul's Chapel survived the great fire of September 1776 that destroyed the old Trinity. In addition to being, therefore, the only remaining church of the colonial era in Manhattan, St. Paul's has great architectural interest and merit.

Commencements of King's College (now Columbia University) were held here for twenty-five years, John Jay, Gouverneur Morris, and De Witt Clinton being among those receiving their degrees. British occupation forces used the chapel. A special service was conducted on 30 April 1789 for Congress and George Washington after the latter's first inauguration at nearby (old) City Hall. In the peaceful old cemetery are remains of British officers among the New Yorkers. Against a handsome Palladian window on the Broadway side is the tomb of General Richard Montgomery, originally buried near where he fell in Quebec in 1775 and moved here in 1818.

Trinity Church and Cemetery, Broadway at the beginning of Wall Street. The present structure, for fifty years the tallest in New York, was finished in 1846. The first church burned in the great fire of September 1776. Among the interesting graves in the yard are two secretaries of the Treasury: Alexander Hamilton and Albert Gallatin. The oldest grave dates from 1681. Other famous New Yorkers here are William Bradford Jr., the printer, and Robert Fulton, inventor of the steamboat. (See also ST. PAUL'S CHAPEL.)

Willett Memorial. A tablet at Broad and Beaver Streets is of artistic merit as well as being historically interesting. It marks the spot where the remarkable Marinus Willett (1740–1830) on 6 June 1775 stopped the British from evacuating five cartloads of weapons and ammunition in their withdrawal from New York City. Seizing the bridle of the leading horse, Willett claimed the British had no authority to carry off the arms. He rallied the mob to his side and took possession of the matériel for the Patriot cause.

After graduating from King's College (later Columbia), Willett became a wealthy merchant and property owner. As New Yorkers took sides on the eve of the Revolution, he was a leading firebrand among the Sons of Liberty, and when the war started he quickly became an effective combat commander. He particularly distinguished himself in the defense of Fort Stanwix and as commander of New York troops during the last two years of the murderous border warfare in the Mohawk Valley. (See FORT PLAIN.)

He was a sheriff of New York City and County for many years after the war, mayor from 1807 to 1808, and president of the Electoral College in 1824. At the age of fifty-nine he took for his third wife the twenty-four-year-old Margaret Bancker, by whom he had three sons and a daughter. Willett was buried in Trinity Cemetery in lower Manhattan. One son, William, became a famous author on religious subjects and published *A Narrative of the Military Actions of Colonel Marinus Willett* (1831).

QUEENS

Bowne House, adjoining Weeping Beech Park at 37-01 Bowne Street, Flushing. Built in 1661, this simple colonial frame farmhouse was occupied until 1945 by eight successive generations of the family founded in America by the Quaker John Bowne 284 years earlier. For defying the Dutch ordinance forbidding Quaker meetings, John Bowne was sentenced to a fine (which he did not pay), thrown in jail, deported to Holland, and finally acquitted. A plaque memorializes signers of the Flushing Remonstrance (1657), a little-known document in the history of religious tolerance in America. The Bowne House is the headquarters for the Bowne House Historical Society and is open to the public on Tuesday, Saturday, and Sunday with somewhat limited hours. Tours can be scheduled by reservation. Phone: (718) 359-0528.

Friends Meeting House Graveyard, at 137-16 Northern Boulevard in Flushing, was opened in 1694, and is the burial site of John Bowne (1627–1695).

Grace Church Graveyard, at 155-24 90th Avenue in Jamaica. This is the burial site of Rufus King (see KING MANOR). Opened in 1730, this colonial-era cemetery also contains the graves of Loyalists who served in the various military units supporting the main British army during the Revolution. These include Captain William Dickson of the New York Volunteers, who died in 1780.

King Manor, in King Park, 153rd Street and Jamaica Avenue, Jamaica. In 1805 this Dutch and colonial frame house became the country home of Rufus King (1755–1827), and it remained in his family until 1897. King was a lawyer, delegate to the Continental Congress, United States senator, envoy to Great Britain from 1796 to 1803, and unsuccessful presidential candidate (against James Monroe) in 1816. Sections of King Manor were built in 1730, 1755, and 1806. The house was successively an inn, farmhouse, and parsonage before King acquired it. The furnishings are eighteenth and nineteenth century, some originally in the house. After considerable renovation, the King Manor Museum opened to the public in 1992. The museum room contains hats, silver, and needlework samplers, among other items, to offer a historically accurate look at eighteenth-century Jamaica, Queens. Phone: (718) 206-0545.

Prospect Cemetery, on Beaver Road off Jamaica Avenue, opened in 1640 and holds the graves of two Revolutionary-era Patriots, the Reverend Abraham Keteltas and Judge Egbert Benson.

St. Gabriel's Episcopal Church, at 196-10 Woodhull Avenue in Hollis. A marker on the grounds of the church indicates the approximate site of Increase Carpenter's Tavern, where General Nathaniel Woodhull was taken prisoner by British dragoons on 28 August 1776, the day after the Battle of Long Island. Woodhull and his 200 troops had been driving some 1,500 head of cattle eastward out of the clutches of the British on the night of 26 August, and came within 2 miles of Clinton and Howe's stealthy march around the American left wing. The historian William H. W. Sabine has suggested that Woodhull's failure to discover and disrupt the British plan was a deliberate act of treason that cost the Americans the battle the following day. Woodhull died from wounds reportedly inflicted by his captors after he had surrendered.

BROOKLYN

The name coming from a place near Utrecht in Holland—Breukelen, meaning "broken land"—Brooklyn was settled by Dutch farmers in 1636. They established themselves initially around Wallabout Bay, which was infamous during the Revolution as the place where British prison ships were moored. (See PRISON SHIP MARTYRS' MONUMENT.)

The Battle of Long Island in August 1776 was one of the most important, most complex, and most interesting actions of the Revolution. Although the ground is now covered by one of the world's greatest expanses of urban sprawl, the well-read visitor will find a number of interesting landmarks surviving. Scholars have long been indebted to Henry P. Johnston for his detailed history published in 1878, "The Campaign of 1776 Around New York and Brooklyn . . ." (in *Memoirs of the Long Island Historical Society,* III). Johnston's study included a painstaking examination of the ground and identification of landmarks. Another map of historical value was made by Thomas W. Field, correlating these landmarks with streets existing in 1868 (published in *Memoirs,* II).

As early as 1846, Walt Whitman, as editor of the *Brooklyn Daily Eagle,* urged the nation to celebrate the anniversary of the Battle of Long Island with the same fanfare as the Fourth of July. The effort to establish a "Brooklyn battlefield" was revived sporadically in the early twentieth century, and today the anniversary is marked by "Battle Week," a series of lectures, tours, and ceremonies in late August organized by state and local groups in conjunction with the National Park Service. Information is available from Green-Wood Cemetery, the Old Stone House Historic Interpretive Center, the Fraunces Tavern Museum, the Sons of the Revolution in the State of New York, and local chapters of the Sons of the American Revolution and Daughters of the American Revolution.

Parks and two cemeteries now preserve—at least to the extent that the ground is not covered by buildings and streets—several of the areas of modern Brooklyn associated with the battle of 27 August 1776.

After a large-scale buildup of army and navy forces on Staten Island, General William Howe and his brother, Admiral Lord Richard Howe, launched their amphibious assault on Long Island at dawn on 22 August. An American outpost at Denyse's Point (now Fort Hamilton) withdrew toward Prospect Hill (now Prospect Park). After the initial landing of four thousand British and German troops under Generals Henry Clinton and Charles Cornwallis, their boats returned for an additional five thousand troops; these came ashore in Gravesend Bay between today's Dyker Beach Park and Bensonhurst Park. (The area is now buried under the Shore Parkway of the Belt System and by tall apartment houses.)

As more troops were ferried across Lower Bay, the British established a beachhead line through the villages of New Utrecht (about where the avenue of that name intersects 85th Street), Gravesend (around the present cemetery of that name), and Flatlands (where the avenue of that name crosses what is still called Kings Highway). On Kings Highway just east of Flatbush Avenue, a bronze plaque on the lawn of the Flatlands Reformed Church (formerly the Dutch Reformed Church of Flatlands) marks the path of the British advance on the night of 26 August 1776.

The Americans had long anticipated the British operation and were deployed along a low, densely wooded ridge called Gowanus Heights, not to be confused with Brooklyn Heights. General Howe's strategy was to make a sweeping envelopment (a "turning movement," to be precise) through Jamaica Pass and then advance eastward through the village of Bedford. While ten thousand troops made this main effort under Howe's personal command, two secondary efforts were made: the first along the shore and the other in the center against Flatbush Pass (now in Prospect Park).

The British strategy worked beautifully. (Their lines on the left were formed through today's Green-Wood Cemetery and Prospect Park, extending somewhat to the east of the latter area.) The first contact was made around the Red Lion Inn, at the junction of Martense Lane and the Narrows Road (around 39th Street at Third Avenue). Here on the far western flank the Americans built up their main strength, just as Howe had hoped. Heroic and skillful fighting in this area was under the command of General William Alexander ("Lord Stirling"), culminating at the Vechte House.

In the decisive maneuver, meanwhile, the British had snapped up a five-man American patrol in Jamaica Pass (at Howard's Tavern) and cut behind Washington's main battle position without being detected in time. At 9 A.M. two signal guns were fired by the British in Bedford (about where Nostrand Avenue intersects Fulton Street in today's community of Bedford-Stuyvesant). Some five thousand German auxiliaries under General Leopold Philip von Heister attacked immediately after hearing the signal, pushing through the pass one can see in Prospect Park, fanning right to rout the defenders of Bedford Pass (about where Bedford Avenue intersects Eastern Parkway), moving down the ridge to their left, and pushing north.

The heaviest fighting took place near Baker's Tavern (about where Flatbush Avenue crosses Fulton Street). Caught between the columns of Howe and von Heister,

Americans under General John Sullivan inflicted heavy casualties before being overwhelmed and taken prisoner.

Many Americans had fled at the first sign that the enemy was to their rear, streaming back into the defenses along Brooklyn Heights (following the route of First Avenue across Gowanus Creek to Court Street) while this way was still open. After General Alexander's efforts to dislodge the British from the Vechte House were abandoned, the remaining American forces could escape only by the hazardous route close to the mouth of Gowanus Creek, where salt marshes bordered an 80-foot-wide gap of water. Washington watched the retreat of his shattered army. A tablet marking the Ponkiesburg (Cobble Hill) fort on a building at Court Street and Atlantic Avenue indicates that his observation point was here. This fort stood behind a line of forts and connecting trenches anchored on the American left by the major work, Fort Putnam (whose site is in today's Fort Greene Park).

During the land battle the fort on Red Hook exchanged a few shots with a British warship, one of six trying to sail up the East River and threaten the Americans from this quarter.

General Howe did not follow up his success by assaulting the Brooklyn Heights fortifications, which was a costly error that enabled Washington to save most of his army. After a council of war at the Joralemon House, home of Philip Livingston, Washington executed a secret withdrawal the night of 29 to 30 August. (The site of the Joralemon House is 400 feet south of Joralemon Street on the east side of Hicks Street. A DAR marker on a boulder long and incorrectly identified the house at Montague Street and Pierrepont Place as the site of the council of war. Old Ferry Road is now lower Fulton Street, and the Brooklyn Ferry ran from the foot of Fulton Street westward to Fly Market Slip on Manhattan, now the foot of Maiden Lane.) A tablet on a boulder and plaques in the pavement at the entrance to the Fulton Ferry landing mark this as the spot where Washington embarked his forces during the evacuation from Long Island.

Fort Defiance. *See* RED HOOK.

Green-Wood Cemetery. In the Battle of Long Island, 27 August 1776, the British left wing of about seven thousand troops under Brigadier General James Grant (1720–1806) deployed from the center of today's Green-Wood Cemetery westward to Gowanus Bay. Also within the confines of the present cemetery were Delaware, Pennsylvania, and Connecticut battalions under Colonels Atlee and Haslet and General Parsons. A two-hour action in this sector was restricted to an exchange of artillery and the maneuvering of British light infantry while the envelopment was taking place through Jamaica Pass (see HOWARD'S TAVERN SITE). Grant then advanced and annihilated the American right wing commanded by General Alexander ("Lord Stirling").

Although the battle positions within the present cemetery are not marked, the general topography has been preserved. "Battle Hill," where Parsons and Atlee made a stand against Grant's forces, is the site of an annual wreath-laying ceremony. It is marked by an Altar of Liberty and a statue of Minerva, aligned to gaze and wave at the Statue of Liberty, visible in the distance.

Howard's Tavern Site, at the northeast corner of Atlantic and Alabama Avenues. Here stood Howard's Half Way House or Tavern. It was in front of the Jamaica Pass, which General Howe found guarded by only a five-man patrol as he moved through with his enveloping force of about ten thousand troops in the early hours of 27 August 1776. (Howard's Tavern was torn down in 1902 to make way for the elevated tracks of the Long Island Railroad). The Jamaica Pass was near the southern end of what is now Evergreen Cemetery. In order to inspect the Jamaica Pass for additional defenders, the British forced Howard and his son to lead them along the Rockaway Foot Path, an old Indian trail that skirted the pass. The son's grave is marked by a tombstone in Evergreen Cemetery; the path is indicated by signs in the grass between the graves, and a map is available from the cemetery office.

Jamaica Pass. *See* HOWARD'S TAVERN SITE.

Prison Ship Martyrs' Monument. In Fort Greene Park, at Myrtle Avenue and Cumberland Street, is the imposing monument designed by Stanford White and dedicated in 1908 to the 11,500 American prisoners who died aboard British prison ships in nearby Wallabout Bay (the vestige of which is now Wallabout Channel and Navy Yard Basin). The bones of the estimated 11,500 bodies were collected in the area of the Brooklyn Navy Yard. White's design, featuring a fluted granite shaft 145 feet high, is an important architectural landmark.

Prospect Park. Preserved within the 526 acres of this landscaped park are the Flatbush Road (now East Drive) and Flatbush Pass (now called Battle Pass) that figured in the Battle of Long Island on 27 August 1776. While the British commander directed his main effort in a cleverly executed strategic envelopment through Jamaica Pass (see HOWARD'S TAVERN SITE) and further deceived the Americans by a secondary attack on the other flank (see GREEN-WOOD CEMETERY), his center column pushed toward Flatbush Pass. Most of the American defenders here fled to the rear when they realized their situation was hopeless, but General Sullivan and some of his men tried to fight their way out. Near Baker's Tavern, close to where Fulton and Flatbush Avenues now intersect, Sullivan and most of his men were trapped and captured. A small monument topped by a bronze eagle marks the site of the ancient Dongan Oak, felled to bar the enemy's advance, and two plaques are mounted on boulders in Battle Pass, which is a little north of the zoo.

The Maryland Monument is in the south-central part of the park, between the lake and Lookout Hill. A graceful column surmounted by a ball, it commemorates the gallant performance of Smallwood's Maryland Battalion, commanded that day by Major Mordecai Gist. (See VECHTE HOUSE.)

Prospect Park is on land bought in 1859 from the estate of Edwin C. Litchfield, who had purchased the old Vechte-Cortelyou estate. The development of port facilities on the Gowanus Canal was Litchfield's main activity, and in 1855 he built a showy mansion on the bluff overlooking the harbor. "Litchfield's Castle" has a view of almost a mile to the southeast over the park designed by Frederick Olmsted.

A Quaker cemetery near Lookout Hill dates from 1662.

The Lefferts Homestead, on Flatbush Avenue at Empire Boulevard, is a wooden shingle Dutch Colonial farmhouse. Peter Lefferts salvaged wood and hardware from his family home, accidentally burned by the Americans in their "scorched earth" program to deny the British crops, and built this house during the period 1777 to 1783. His family used it as a residence until 1918, when it was presented to the city and moved from 563 Flatbush Avenue to Prospect Park. Authentically refurnished, it is advertised as a children's historical museum and features a spinning and carding room, a Dutch colonial farmyard with farm animals, crafts, storytelling, and a jam-packed educational program.

Red Hook (Fort Defiance). During the Battle of Long Island, 27 August 1776, six British warships attempted to get up the East River to strike the flank and rear of Washington's forces. They were frustrated primarily by a strong wind, but one ship, the *Roebuck*, got far enough north to exchange a few shots with Fort Defiance. A bronze plaque (1952) on the red-brick building at Dwight and Beard Streets marks the site of the fort. This is in the Erie Basin area of Red Hook.

Vechte House (Old Stone House Historic Interpretive Center), Third Street between Fifth and Fourth Avenues, in J. J. Byrne Park, is the site of the most heroic action in the Battle of Long Island, 27 August 1776. General William Alexander ("Lord Stirling") used the Vechte House (built 1699) as his headquarters in the initial phases of the battle. When the British accomplished their successful envelopment of the American left (east) flank and moved in strength along the Old Jamaica Road behind the main battle positions of the Americans, the only route of escape was across Gowanus Creek. To save what was left of Washington's army, Alexander ordered Major Mordecai Gist to lead diversionary attacks to the north against the British strong point around the Vechte House. Alexander personally took part in the six determined assaults here, which were finally repulsed only after Cornwallis rushed reinforcements up. Almost all of the 250 Maryland Continentals engaged here were captured or killed.

Those who died in this engagement are buried at a place marked by a plaque (1947) on Third Avenue between Seventh and Eighth Streets. The Maryland Monument is near Lookout Hill in Prospect Park. The Vechte-Cortelyou House stood until 1897, and its site was later marked by a tablet. A handsome reconstruction now stands there and is operated by an organization called First Battle Revival Alliance. Hours are 12 to 5 P.M., Thursday through Sunday. Phone: (718) 768-3195.

Wallabout Bay. *See* PRISON SHIP MARTYRS' MONUMENT.

THE BRONX

Fort Independence Park, south end of Jerome Park Reservoir just east of Sedgwick Avenue, at the north end of Giles Place. At the entrance to the park are tablets indicating that on the adjacent hill (now covered by apartment buildings) the Americans under General Washington erected breastworks for the protection of Kings Bridge (see KINGS BRIDGE SITE) and an advanced work, later called Fort Independence, to command Spuyten Duyvil Creek. The positions were abandoned by the Americans in October 1776 when they retreated to White Plains, and the British later incorporated them into their defenses of New York City. In a diversionary effort that turned into a famous fiasco, "Our General" (as he calls himself in his *Memoirs*) William Heath moved on Fort Independence in January 1777, recaptured the Valentine-Varian House, and tried to cannonade the fort into surrender. After five days he withdrew.

Children playing on the site discovered cannonballs; this led to excavation of the ruins in 1914 and the recovery of about five hundred balls, shells, and bar shot. One of the children later gave his finds to the museum in the Valentine-Varian House. (See FORT NUMBER EIGHT.)

Fort Number Eight, New York University campus. A boulder here is inscribed "The Site of Fort Number Eight, 1776–1783." Built by the British, the fort was an artillery base during the attack on Fort Washington. It later figured in the skirmishes of the "Neutral Ground," or "Debatable Ground," between American positions in the Hudson Highlands and the British in New York City. After 1779 the fort was headquarters for Colonel Peter De Lancey's Westchester Light Horse Battalion, the "cowboys" who skirmished with the "skinners" of the Neutral Ground between British and Patriot lines in Westchester County from 1778 until the end of the Revolution.

The site was excavated in 1965, when it was exposed in digging foundations for a new campus building. Numerous artifacts were recovered, much of the material being put in the Valentine-Varian House museum.

Fort Number Four, Old Fort Number Four Park, south end of Jerome Park Reservoir. On a rocky outcropping that faces Reservoir Avenue just west of University Avenue is a plaque erected by the DAR in 1914 stating that the fort was built in 1776 as part of the defenses of Fort Washington and Kings Bridge. Twice attacked, the fort was captured by the British and occupied by British and Hessian troops. Numerous relics, including numbered buttons, were found when the site was explored.

King's Bridge Site, King's Bridge Avenue and West 230th Street. At the place where the Boston Post Road crossed Spuyten Duyvil Creek, the first bridge was built in 1693 under a royal grant to Frederick Philipse and rebuilt in 1713. Broken down by Washington's retreat in October 1776, it was rebuilt by German troops. During the period 1779 to 1782 it was abandoned, being too vulnerable to American raids, and a pontoon bridge was put in farther westward. After the Revolution it was rebuilt with a dike to supply water for Macomb's grist and marble mills. This bend of the creek has subsequently been filled in, and Broadway now passes about 200 yards southeast of the old bridge site, which is marked by a plaque on St. Stephen's Church on West 230th Street.

Pelham Bay Park. After finding his way blocked at Throg's Neck, General Howe reembarked his troops and made another landing a few miles away at Pell's Point. Here, in what has become Pelham Bay Park, was Colonel John Glover's small brigade of Massachusetts troops, including his own Marbleheaders, with three artillery pieces. "Glover's Rock" will be found around the middle of the park, on the old City Island Road, and this marks the place where the Patriots started their well-conducted delaying action on 18 October 1776. Most of the fighting took place near Split Rock, a famous landmark that barely escaped destruction by highway engineers a few years ago; it may be seen on the east side of the New England Thruway near the Hutchinson River Parkway's north entrance to the Thruway (No. 6) at Pelham. For other landmarks associated with the Battle of Pell's Point, see PELHAM MANOR.

Throg's Neck, on the East River. During the period 12 to 18 October 1776 the British under General Howe landed here and made an unsuccessful effort to advance inland. They found the way barred by American defenders at the Westchester Creek Causeway, about where the Bronx and Pelham Bay Parkway crosses the Westchester meadows. Howe made a second amphibious effort at Pell's Point, which is now Pelham Bay Park.

Valentine-Varian House, 3266 Bainbridge Avenue at East 208th Street, adjoining Williamsbridge Park. About 1750 the Valentine family established a farm in the wilderness that has become The Bronx. After living first in a simple cottage, they soon built the large fieldstone structure that has miraculously survived not only the Revolutionary War but also modern urban developers. Peter Valentine may have been the builder and first owner of the house, but it is known that Isaac Valentine bought the property in 1758. His family was forced to flee when Washington's army retreated from Manhattan toward White Plains in the fall of 1776; British and Hessian troops took over the house. When General William Heath undertook his abortive attack on Fort Independence in January 1777, the column under General John Scott overran the outposts on Valentine's Hill and captured the house. The Americans were prepared to use artillery against the house, but this proved to be unnecessary, and later the Valentines moved back in.

In 1791 the property was bought by Isaac Varian, whose son Isaac became mayor of New York in 1839. The Varians owned 260 acres between the Bronx River and today's Jerome Avenue. After passing through various hands, the house was donated to the Bronx County Historical Society by William C. Beller in 1965 and moved at his expense across the street to its present location. The two-story colonial fieldstone farmhouse with an attic is in a good state of preservation. In one room the wall structure has been exposed to show the original chestnut laths and the mud-and-cow-hair mortar.

The historic house is owned and managed by the Bronx County Historical Society. Home to the Museum of Bronx History, it is open on Saturday and Sunday and by appointment on weekdays. Phone: (718) 881-8900.

(Bronx County Historical Society, 3309 Bainbridge Avenue, Bronx, N.Y. 10467.)

Van Cortlandt Mansion and Park, Broadway and 246th Street, near park entrance at 242nd Street. The recently restored manor house and 1,100 acres remain here from an original Dutch grant of the year 1646. The New York City Department of Parks and Recreation touts the mansion as the "oldest house in the Bronx." Frederick Van Cortlandt built this fieldstone-and-brick house in 1748. A full basement lighted by ground-level windows, and an attic with gables, make this a large, four-story structure. Architecturally it is a fine example of Georgian Colonial style, and it has been furnished with seventeenth- and eighteenth-century items of Dutch, English, and American origin. Many of these items belonged to the Van Cortlandt family, which occupied the house until 1889.

During the Revolution the estate was in the Neutral Ground between opposing forces in New York City and the Hudson Highlands. Important public records (the official city archives) were hidden on Vault Hill, the Van Cortlandt burial ground on a hill behind the house. Washington used the house in 1776 when his army was being driven toward the Highlands, and again on the eve of his triumphal reentry into New York City in 1783.

The house and grounds were deeded to the city in 1889. For eight years the historic mansion was a police station, but since then it has been restored and maintained as a museum by the Colonial Dames. Nine rooms open to the public include a Dutch bedroom with cupboard-style bed reached by a ladder, a basement kitchen with cooking fireplace and Dutch oven, a room for spinning and weaving, and a nursery with an eighteenth-century dollhouse. Furnishings are identified as to period, style, and origin, and Colonial Dames in costume are in attendance. The museum includes weapons and documents. Much of the mansion has been restored, but original features are a double Dutch door, high Dutch stoop, a staircase, the floors, and the basic structure.

Near the house is a section of brick wall with a window from the Old Sugar House on Duane Street. (See PRISON SITES in section on MANHATTAN.) The family burial ground also is nearby. Inside the northeastern edge of the park at a place called Indian Field is a DAR marker that reads: "August 31, 1778. Upon this field Chief Nimham and 17 Stockbridge Indians from Massachusetts, as allies of the Patriots, gave their lives for Liberty." The Indians had taken position behind a fence to fire on the flank of an advancing column of troops under the leadership of what one authority calls "the ablest and most dashing partisans of the British army—Simcoe, Tarleton, Emmerick, and De Lancey" (Stephen Jenkins, *The Story of the Bronx*, pp. 162–164). Simcoe spotted the Indians, hit them with a surprise attack on a flank while they were busily engaged in firing on the troops of Emmerick and Tarleton, and killed or seriously wounded about forty. Chief Nimham wounded Simcoe before being killed by the latter's orderly; Tarleton narrowly escaped death while leading the pursuit. Indian dead were buried in the clearing in Van Cortlandt's woods where they fell, and the place has since been known as Indian Field. The Van Cortlandt House Museum is open to the public on Tuesday through Friday from 10 A.M. to 3 P.M., and on the weekend from 11 A.M. to 4 P.M. Phone: (718) 543-3344.

Other sites in New York State associated with this prominent family are the Van Cortlandt Manor and Van Cortlandtville. The family figures also in the early history of Fraunces Tavern (under MANHATTAN) and Sagtikos Manor.

Varian House. *See* VALENTINE-VARIAN HOUSE.

STATEN ISLAND

Early in July 1776 General William Howe started an unopposed landing of British troops from Halifax (Nova Scotia), and on 12 July his brother, Admiral Lord Richard Howe, joined with reinforcements from England. German and more British troops followed, and on 12 August Sir Henry Clinton's expedition returned from Charleston to swell the British ranks to about 42,000 soldiers, seamen, and officers. This was the largest expeditionary force to this date assembled overseas by the British.

On 22 August the first wave of British and Germans started crossing the Narrows and landing at Denyse's Point in the opening moves of the Battle of Long Island.

Staten Island remained a British base for the remainder of the Revolution. Several American raids were conducted, and the British launched their own raids from the island to Springfield and other places in New Jersey.

Conference (Billopp) House. Definitely worth the detour is the Conference House on the southwest tip of Staten Island, easily accessible from the Outerbridge Crossing from New Jersey. Here is the old stone manor house that Christopher Billopp built before 1688 on his 1,163-acre grant. It stands on a hill of well-tended grass at the end of Hylan Boulevard. From the dead end of this boulevard is a view across Raritan Bay that, if one uses a little imagination, is what Benjamin Franklin, John Adams, and Edward Rutledge saw on the day of their polite but pointless "peace conference" with Lord Richard Howe on 11 September 1776. The Conference (Billopp) House has qualified for registry as a National Historic Landmark, and is open to the public Friday to Sunday from 1 P.M. to 4 P.M. Groups are welcome by appointment. Website: www.theconferencehouse.org. Phone: (718) 984-6046. In 1999 the Conference House Association opened a historical research library in connection with the site.

Niagara. *See* FORT NIAGARA.

Old Fort Niagara. *See* FORT NIAGARA.

Old Mine Road. *See* MINISINK FORD.

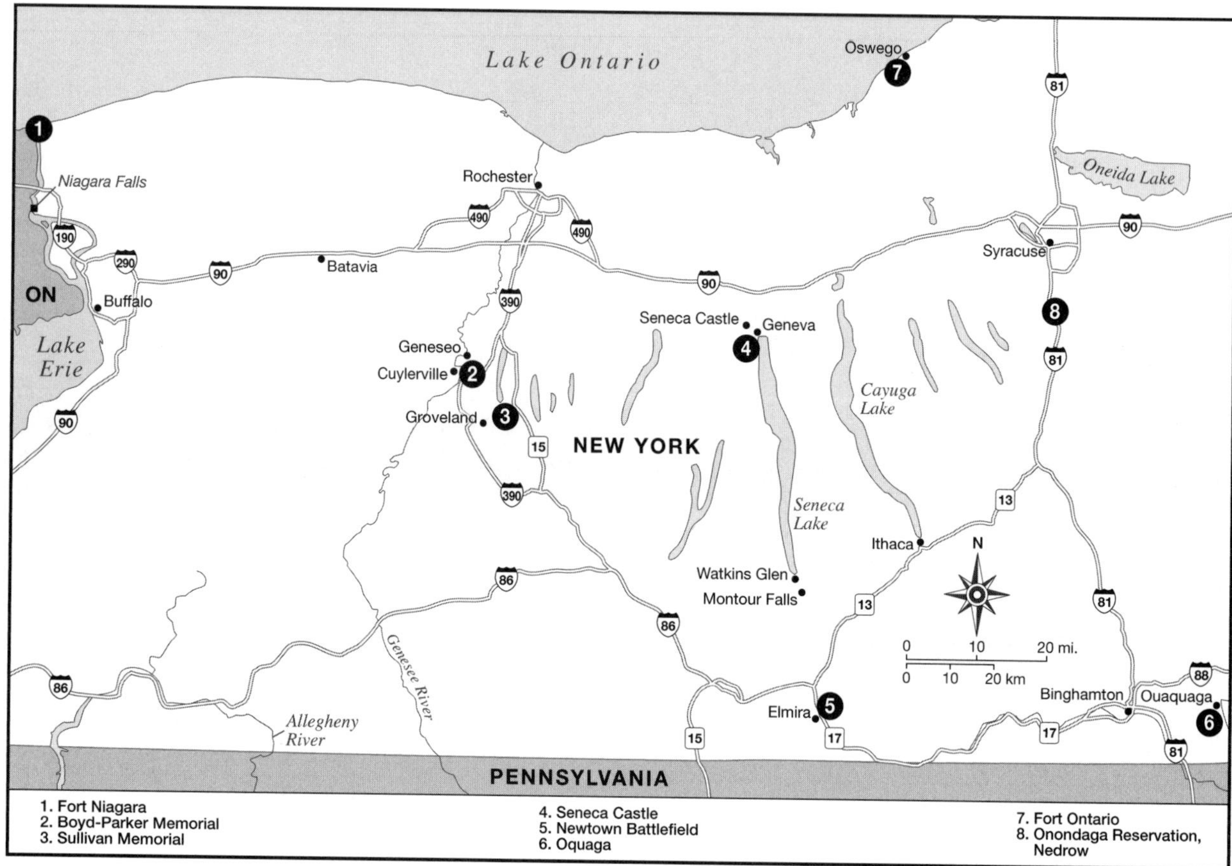

MAP BY XNR PRODUCTIONS. THE GALE GROUP.

Onondaga Reservation, Nedrow. The Onondagas sided with the British during the Revolution and were largely dispossessed after the war ended, the majority of the nation moving to Canada. Visitors are welcome to visit the reservation, which includes the grave of the postwar spiritual leader Handsome Lake, though they should appreciate that it is a sacred site. The reservation is on N.Y. 11A just south of Nedrow and is open daily from dawn to dusk. Phone: (315) 460-8507.

Oquaga, now Ouaquaga, in Broome County east of Binghamton on N.Y. 79. Headquarters of Joseph Brant during St. Leger's expedition of 1777 and for many of his subsequent raids on frontier settlements, this Indian fur-trading post on the Susquehanna (the first one that Sir William Johnson established) was an objective of the Sullivan-Clinton Expedition of 1779. Ten years before the Revolution about 750 Indians, mostly Mohawks, lived here. Remnants of the Esopus, driven from the Kingston area, were around Oquaga by 1775. Brant was away on a raid when Continental troops destroyed his base at Oquaga after burning nearby Unadilla, but both of these places continued to be used by the Loyalists and Indians until the end of the Revolution.

Oriskany Battlefield, state park on N.Y. 69, 5 miles east of Rome. A column of eight hundred Patriot militia under General Nicholas Herkimer was marching to the relief of Fort Stanwix when it was ambushed here on 6 August 1777 by four hundred Indians and Loyalists under the Mohawk war chief Joseph Brant.

When Barry St. Leger's expedition of about two thousand British regulars, Mohawk Valley Loyalists, Canadian auxiliaries, and Indians approached Fort Stanwix (now in Rome, New York), a friendly Oneida reported its advance to General Nicholas Herkimer, commander of militia forces in the Mohawk Valley. Despite considerable reluctance of the settlers to muster for their own defense, Herkimer managed to raise a force of eight hundred men and boys, and on 4 August 1777 he left Fort Dayton (modern Herkimer). Although accompanied by four hundred oxcarts, they were within 10 miles of Fort Stanwix when they made camp at the end of their second day (5 August).

Herkimer sent runners to request that a sortie from the fort be made to provide a diversion as the relief column arrived.

The legendary Molly Brant, Indian mistress of Sir William Johnson and sister of the Mohawk war chief Joseph Brant, brought word to Barry St. Leger the evening of 5 August that Herkimer was 10 miles from Fort Stanwix. The British commander sent Joseph Brant with four hundred Indians and a party of Loyalists to ambush the relief column at the place now known as Battle Brook. Here a ravine 200 yards wide would have to be crossed on a causeway by the enemy, and heavy woods provided cover and concealment for Brant's force.

On the morning of 6 August, Herkimer was adamantly refusing to march on to Fort Stanwix until he heard evidence that the sortie was being made. The regimental commanders were insisting that the expedition press on immediately. Two of them apparently went so far as to impugn Herkimer's courage and loyalty, and the militia general finally gave way to the pressure.

Herkimer's sixty Oneida scouts failed to detect signs of the ambush, and without the rudimentary security precautions of a column marching in hostile territory, the militia plunged into the trap.

More than a dozen officers, including Herkimer, went down in the initial hail of fire. The mile-long column probably had contracted a great deal as the leading elements bunched up to get through this defile, but it is not likely that all of the two hundred–man regiment of Richard Visscher (or Fisher) had gotten within the ambush when the firing started. Apparently this rearguard regiment panicked and ran for home, leaving six hundred men in the other three regiments to their fate.

The latter reacted like veterans. Instead of cowering where they had been hit by the initial volley, they charged toward their hidden attackers and then formed in little groups for defense. The Indians, who were still outnumbered two to one, hesitated to take advantage of their surprise to close in and annihilate Herkimer's force before it could recover sufficiently to organize a defense. After consolidating into a single perimeter, the militia then took advantage of a lull in the battle—a heavy rain that kept both sides from firing for about an hour—to make another important improvement in their position. General Herkimer, bleeding profusely from a leg wound, insisted on being propped up where he could continue to command his men. He had noticed during the first forty-five minutes of the action, before the rain, that individual defenders along the perimeter were being rushed by the Indians and tomahawked as they reloaded. Herkimer issued orders for men to form pairs, and a good many Indians were stopped dead before the others detected this change in tactics.

Although they continued their sniping for about six hours, the Indians could not pry the militia from their defensive positions. Though the exact number of Indian casualties cannot be determined, Oriskany was nevertheless the heaviest engagement fought by St. Leger's expedition.

A force of Royal Greens came from St. Leger's camp to reinforce Brant, and after turning their coats inside out they attempted to get into Herkimer's lines by pretending to be reinforcements sent from Fort Stanwix. The ruse was about to succeed when a sharp-eyed Palatine recognized a Loyalist neighbor, and a spirited little hand-to-hand civil war ensued.

The Indians started drifting off about this time, and the Loyalists had to withdraw also. Herkimer's militia marched back to Fort Dayton carrying fifty wounded. The number of Patriot casualties also remains unknown, though the dead included two of the regimental commanders who had goaded Herkimer into proving his courage and loyalty by pressing on to Fort Stanwix prematurely, without taking normal tactical precautions. Herkimer died of his wound ten days later in his home near modern Little Falls on N.Y. 58 (see HERKIMER HOME).

When Brant and his Indians got back to the siege of Fort Stanwix and discovered that a sortie from the fort had cleaned out their camp, they were more convinced than ever that they had made a bad mistake in joining St. Leger's war party. They were ready to go home, and it was not long before they did so. (See FORT STANWIX.)

Oriskany State Park includes the well-preserved site of the battle, where reenactments are staged at various times throughout the year. The park features guided tours and interpretive signage and is open to the public from May through October, Wednesday to Saturday from 9 A.M. to 5 P.M., Sundays from 1 P.M. to 5 P.M. Phone: (315) 768-7224.

Oswego and Fort Oswego. *See* FORT ONTARIO.

Paine (Thomas) Cottage, in New Rochelle at North and Paine Avenues. Built about 1800 and moved here from its original location nearby, this was Thomas Paine's residence intermittently from 1803 to 1806. Best known for his pamphlet *Common Sense*, which is credited with bringing American public opinion around to demanding independence, Paine had returned to New Rochelle after spending fifteen years in England and France. His last years were spent in poverty, ill health, and virtual ostracism for his deist writings (*The Age of Reason*) and his public criticism of Washington. The Thomas Paine Cottage is a museum and headquarters of the Huguenot and Thomas Paine Historical Association of New Rochelle. The Paine Memorial Building, 983 North Avenue, and adjacent buildings contain memorabilia of the controversial writer and complex man. Open Tuesday through Sunday, 10 A.M. to 5 P.M.

Palatine Church, Mohawk Valley, on N.Y. 5 about 3 miles east of St. Johnsville. For two centuries the most noted landmark on the Old Mohawk Turnpike (now N.Y. 5), this beautifully proportioned church of fine stonework has been preserved on a slight rise alongside the highway. It is in an island of green formed by a loop of old Route 5, so one can turn off the main route and admire it at leisure.

Built in 1770, it was spared by Sir John Johnson's raiders in 1780 and was the Patriot camp after their fight near Fort Klock. Until 1940 it was in continuous use as a church, and summer services were held in it through 1959. The Palatine Society of New York has restored its original appearance by, among other things, moving the door back to the north side from the east end, where it had been relocated in 1870.

Peekskill, on the Hudson River in upper Westchester County. Taking its name from the creek named for Jan Peek, a Dutch trader who settled on its bank in 1665, Peekskill was a trade town for farmers for two centuries. Early in the Revolution there was much military activity here because the Hudson River landing and road approaches to the Hudson Highlands (see CONTINENTAL VILLAGE) made it a transportation hub. Few historic sites of the period exist, but the Memorial Museum of the Field Library, 124 Union Avenue, contains a Patriot cannon that fired on the *Vulture*, thereby setting in train the events that led to Major John André's death as a spy. (See WEST POINT MILITARY RESERVATION, TARRYTOWN, VAN CORTLANDTVILLE, and TAPPAN HISTORIC DISTRICT.)

Drum Hill School, on Ringgold Street past the high school, is on the hill occupied by the British on 23 March 1777 when they made one of their many raids into Peekskill. At 942 South Street is the forty-eighth milestone on the Albany Post Road, placed under Franklin's post-Revolutionary War program of setting up markers. (They were always on the west side, as an aid to land navigation.) Trees where Loyalist spies were hanged have a morbid appeal to some, and a tablet on the grounds of the Peekskill Military Academy immortalizes one of these.

Pelham Manor, Westchester County. The Battle of Pell's Point started at Glover's Rock, proceeded along the line of today's Hutchinson River Turnpike past historic Split Rock (see PELHAM BAY PARK under the section on the Bronx, NEW YORK CITY), then along the old Post Road to end at the bridge over the Hutchinson River. Surviving landmarks in modern Pelham Manor are along Wolf's Lane. The Pell Mansion, or "Pelham Dale," home of Colonel David J. Pell and built sometime before 1776, is standing off Wolf's Lane at 45 Iden Avenue. The "Lord Howe Chestnut," under which the British commander is said to have paused for lunch, survived until the 1940s near Wolf's Lane and not far from the Pell Mansion. (Edgar H. Browne, historian of the town of Pelham, stated that "it stood above the Boy Scout Cabin along the Hutchinson River Parkway, but it died and was taken down a few years before the Scout Cabin was destroyed by fire in 1947.")

At Wolf's Lane and Colonial Avenue is a marker on a rock indicating that at this point on the old Post Road, the British camped while Colonel John Glover's delaying force slipped away.

Philipsburg Manor (Upper Mills), east bank of Hudson on N.Y. 9 at North Tarrytown, 2 miles north of Tappan Zee Bridge. The Lower Mills survive in Yonkers as Philipse Manor. The manor house at Upper Mills was built in 1682. Never the major family residence, the stone building was the center of a trading complex and on several occasions was used as a fort. The original house, mill, and dam have been fully and authentically restored. Like many other manors of the Hudson, it was subject to tenant uprisings in the years surrounding the Revolution. In addition to tenant farmers, Philipsburg relied on slave labor. The excellent tour of the manor draws attention to this little-known history. It is now a National Historic Landmark. The site is open to the public every day except Tuesday from 10 A.M. to 5 P.M. and features guided tours and educational programs. Phone: (914) 631-3993.

Philipse Manor, Warburton Avenue at Dock Street, in downtown Yonkers. Since 1966 under the jurisdiction of the New York State Historic Trust, the Manor Hall of Philipsburg may be looked on as a sacrifice to American democracy. The Manor of Philipsburg was established by a man who came to New Netherlands as a carpenter in the early 1650s. As early as 1672 this Frederick Philipse, a Dutch immigrant, had parlayed his skill as a carpenter into real estate, trade, and shipping, and had started acquiring property along the east bank of the Hudson. Ultimately he held all the land from the Croton River south some 22 miles to Spuyten Duyvil Creek (now the Harlem River). In 1693 this estate was confirmed as the Manor of Philipsburg.

The existing Philipse Manor Hall in Yonkers was started around 1682 (south wing facing Dock Street), and the modern wing was added around 1745. Located on the Albany Post Road, it was one of the great homes of colonial America.

During the Revolution, the third lord of the manor remained loyal to the constituted authority under which his family had prospered, and his estate was confiscated by New York. The land was fragmented, and the Manor Hall passed through various hands. From 1868 to 1872 it was the Yonkers Village Hall; then it was the City Hall. In 1908 the site was purchased by the state with a cash gift from Eva Smith Cochran, and her son contributed his extensive collection of presidential portraits, now exhibited in the mansion. The priceless collection includes five portraits of Washington, three of which depict him with brown eyes and two with blue eyes.

The L-shaped house of weathered brick with white wood trim, hipped slate roof, dormers, and a roof balustrade is furnished in the colonial period. It is open year-round, Wednesday and Thursday from 11 A.M. to 2 P.M., and 2 P.M. to 5 P.M. on Sunday. Admission is free. Phone: (914) 965-4027.

Other vestiges of this early American and most un-American barony are preserved at Philipsburg Manor, North Tarrytown.

Ramapo Valley ("the Clove"), roughly between Thruway Exits 15 (Suffern) and 16 (Harriman). An historical area marker at the Sloatsburg service area on the thruway summarizes the story of this unusual region. From the latter place, now in the vicinity of Monroe (where the Museum Village of Smith's Clove is located on N.Y. 17 Exit 129, 4 miles west of Thruway Exit 16; phone: (845) 782-8247), other passes of the Hudson Highlands lead toward Stony Point, the area that is now Bear Mountain Park, West Point, and the Newburgh area. The Ramapo Valley was the best route between the New Windsor Cantonment and New Jersey.

The Ramapo Furnaces, or Sterling Iron Works, dating from 1751, produced the gigantic chain that obstructed the Hudson River.

Even in very modern times this has been an isolated region where descendants of Loyalist, Hessian, Dutch, African American, and Indian refugees lived in seclusion, becoming known collectively as Jackson Whites. During the Revolution the area was the haunt of the notorious Loyalist highwayman Claudius Smith, who specialized in stealing livestock for sale to the British. On a trail about a mile from the railroad station in Tuxedo are two large caves where Smith's men and stolen animals were hidden. In 1779 a concerted effort was taken to exterminate the Smith gang. Their leader was captured on Long Island, returned in chains, and executed.

In Suffern the tavern and store of the village founder, John Suffern (1741–1836), was located at the important crossroads just south of Ramapo Pass. (The tavern site is at Washington and Lafayette Avenues.) During a five-day stay here in July 1777 Washington wrote the letter to Congress that resulted in Robert Erskine's becoming the famous mapmaker of the Continental army. In August 1780 Washington made his headquarters for sixteen days in the home of Andrew Hopper, a mile below Suffern. Here he learned of the disaster at Camden, South Carolina. He was in this area again when French and American troops marched south from Kings Ferry on their way to Yorktown.

Raynham Hall, Long Island, on 20 West Main Street in Oyster Bay, 7 miles north of Northern State Parkway Exit 35. Addition of the Victorian wing about 1851 and concurrent alterations in that unfortunate style have not destroyed the attraction of this Revolutionary War landmark. The oldest portion dates from the 1730s, before Samuel Townsend bought the farmhouse in 1738 and enlarged it into an eight-room, clapboard, one-and-a-half-story house. Raynham Hall is presently a twenty-room house museum. In 2002 it was named a Revolutionary War Heritage Trail Site by the New York governor, putting it in line for money designated to help preserve New York's Revolutionary War heritage.

During the British occupation of Long Island, from 1776 to the end of the war, Raynham Hall was used as officers' quarters. John Graves Simcoe lived here during the winter of 1778 to 1779 when his famous Loyalist regiment, the Queen's Rangers, was operating in New York and New Jersey. Among the visitors to the house was Major John André, a principal staff officer of the British commander in chief with whom the traitor Benedict Arnold was dealing from May 1779 until André's capture as a spy in September 1780. The fanciful legend has been perpetuated that Sally Townsend overheard a conversation between Simcoe and André, relayed this to her brother Robert, and thus disclosed the plot to surrender West Point. Plausibility is introduced by the fact that Sally's brother was Washington's most valuable secret agent in New York from about the time Arnold started negotiating his betrayal. Robert Townsend succeeded a former agent in Manhattan called Culper Senior and himself had the code name Culper Junior. But the facts are that Arnold's treason was not disclosed until André was accidentally captured at Tarrytown, and Washington's secret service did not have the slightest suspicion that Arnold had been dealing with the enemy for sixteen months.

Raynham Hall has historical and architectural attraction. The National Survey of Historic Sites and Buildings (1964) puts it in the "Sites Also Noted" category. In addition to the aura of romance associated with the names of "the adorable Sally Townsend," the dashing young André and Simcoe, and the Patriot secret service, the house has authentic furnishings, old documents, and a colonial garden. Two links from the great Hudson River chain are in the garden. (The owner of the Sterling Iron Works in the Ramapo Valley was a relative of the Townsends of Raynham Hall.) Public visiting hours are Tuesday through Sunday from 1 P.M. to 5 P.M. Website: www.raynhamhallmuseum.org; phone: (516) 922-6808.

Robert Townsend's grave, enclosed by a fence in 1964, may be reached through a right of way on the property at 51 Simcoe Avenue in Oyster Bay.

Rensselaerswyck (Manor of Rensselaer). *See* ALBANY.

Richmondtown. This is the island's first capital, and it became the county seat in 1727. Now called the Richmondtown Restoration, or Historic Richmond Town, it is a historic village and museum complex on 100 acres of land with twenty-seven original buildings spanning three centuries of Staten Island's history. There are several houses that date from the colonial period, including the Treasure House (c. 1700), where British officers are said to have hidden in the walls the gold coins that were discovered just before the Civil War. The Christopher House (c. 1720) is said to have been a clandestine meeting place for local Patriots, including members of the Mersereau family, who spied for George Washington during the Revolution. Also of interest are the Voorlezer's House (c. 1695), the Moravian Cemetery, the Church of St. Andrew, and the Museum of the Staten Island Historical Society, which displays objects collected from the British fort on nearby Richmond Hill. The last traces of the fort itself are gone. Historic Richmond Town, 441 Clarke Avenue, Staten Island, N.Y. 10306-1125; phone: (718) 351-1611; website: www.historicrichmondtown.org.

Robinson House Site, just south of Garrison, across the river from West Point. The house of Colonel Beverley Robinson (1721–1792) was located at this place until its destruction by fire in 1892. A wealthy Loyalist, he served with distinction as a regimental commander of Loyalist troops (particularly in the capture of Fort Montgomery), but was of most use to the British as an intelligence agent. His fine home was used by the Patriots as a military headquarters and as a hospital. Benedict Arnold and his wife were living here when Arnold's treason was uncovered (see WEST POINT).

The site is a plot of lawn just north of a more recent house and alongside N.Y. 9D, about 5.5 miles north of Bear Mountain Bridge. A highway marker has recently been put up. The original well survives. It had stairs leading to an underground storage room. Now protected by a flat frame covering, it is visible near the base of a large tree between the Robinson House site and a frame barn east of the modern highway. (The road ran to the east of the barn in colonial days.)

Southeast of the Robinson House is Sugarloaf, on the northern slopes of which the Patriots built a fort in 1776 to 1777 as part of the defenses of the Hudson Highlands.

A highway marker about 0.1 mile north of the Robinson House indicates the trail down which Arnold fled to Beverley Dock and thence by barge down the Hudson to the British ship *Vulture.* The trail now winds down a steep hill past modern housing and the village dump to a shoreline reshaped by construction of the railroad. Lossing used the dock and followed this traditional trail of Arnold's flight in visiting and sketching the Robinson House in 1848, when it was in an excellent state of preservation (*Pictorial Field Book,* II, p. 140).

Mandeville's House (1737) is standing just northwest of the road junction, about 0.9 mile north of the Robinson House. Privately owned and in excellent condition, it may be seen from the road that leads down to Garrison. Officers of the West Point garrison used this house as headquarters from 1778 until the end of the Revolution.

Sag Harbor, Long Island. The scene of a famous raid across the Long Island Sound in May 1777, when Colonel Return Jonathan Meigs with 170 men in 13 whaleboats escorted by two armed sloops surprised and badly defeated a large British foraging party (under CONNECTICUT see MEIGS HOUSE SITE and GUILFORD). Now a place of about 2,500 people (although the summer population may be as much as three times that number), Sag Harbor has twelve old structures of architectural importance, the Custom House, Jared Wade House, and Prime House being from the eighteenth century. The Suffolk County Whaling Museum (early 1800s), Main and Garden Streets, has colonial pieces in addition to relics of the nineteenth-century whaling industry for which Sag Harbor was an important center. The Meigs Monument, Union Street, is on the site of the British fort captured by the Patriots.

Sagtikos Manor, West Bay Shore, Long Island. Originally a Van Cortlandt grant (1697), the 1,200 acres were bought by Jonathan Thompson in 1758. The latter's son Isaac acquired the manor as a gift when he married Mary Gardiner, and the house has remained in the same family since that time. (There were two subsequent intermarriages between Thompsons and Gardiners.) The oldest portion of the well-preserved house dates probably from 1692, and today's visitor can see the bedrooms where General Sir Henry Clinton and President George Washington spent the night, the former an unwanted guest during the Revolution (others were Hugh Percy, William Erskine, and William Schaw Cathcart) and the latter in 1790. Wings were added to the house in the late 1890s. The manor's last private owner, Robert David Lion Gardiner, established a foundation for the home and site's preservation. Suffolk County purchased the home from the foundation in November 2002, and it is presently under renovation to make it a public museum. The manor is located approximately one-half mile east of Robert Moses Causeway on Montauk Highway in West Bay Shore. Tours

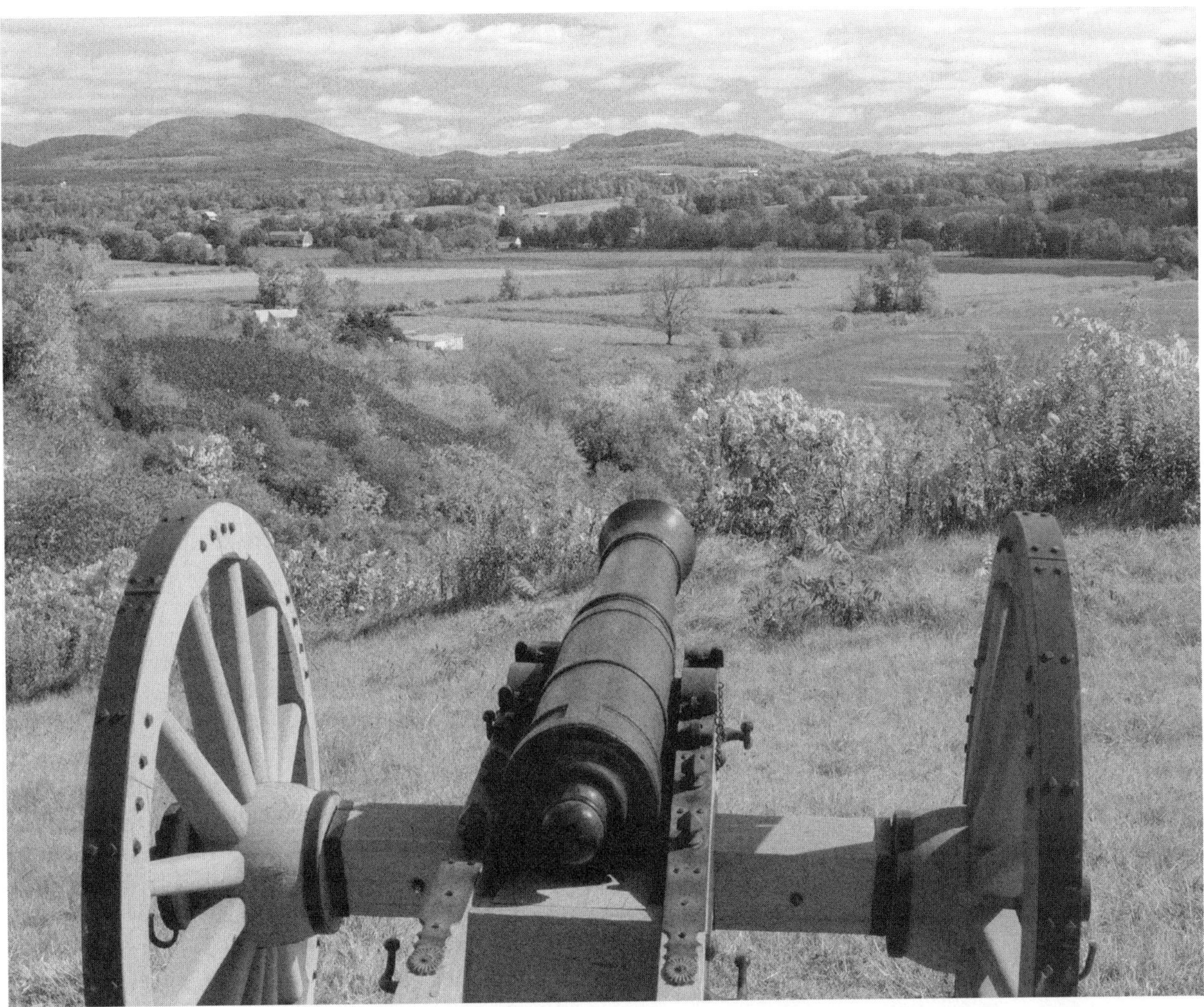

Saratoga National Historic Park. *This large national park on the Hudson River preserves the rolling countryside, terrain features, and principal landmarks of the Saratoga battlefield, where the Americans defeated the British after a series of battles in 1777.*
© DAVID MUENCH/CORBIS.

provided by the Sagtikos Manor Historical Society are available by reservation. Phone: (631) 661-8348.

St. Paul's Church National Historic Site, 897 South Columbus Avenue (Old Boston Post Road) between South Third and Fulton Avenues, Mount Vernon. Take Exit 7 off the Hutchinson Parkway and follow signs. The present structure of stone and brick was started in the 1760s and evidently not completed until after the Revolution. Identifiable graves date from about 1700, and a mass grave contains the bodies of one hundred Hessians, these troops having used the church as a barracks and hospital. In the tower is a bell cast in 1752 by the foundry that made Philadelphia's Liberty Bell. The church was restored in 1942, but the last church service was held in 1977. In 1980 the Episcopal dioceses transferred ownership of the historic church to the National Parks Service. Public visiting hours are 9 A.M. to 5 P.M. Monday through Friday. Guided walking tours are available by appointment. Phone: (914) 667-4116.

Saratoga National Historical Park, on the Hudson River near the village of Bemis Heights, 40 miles north of Albany and 15 miles south of Saratoga; Route 29 east to Schuylerville. Several road signs will indicate specific directions. Modern Schuylersville is the Saratoga of the Revolutionary era, and this is where Burgoyne's army finally laid down its arms. The modern village of Bemis Heights, then known as Bemis Tavern, takes its name from the high ground where the Americans had their field fortifications—their base camp—for the battles of Saratoga. The battles are generally known by the names of Freeman's Farm and Bemis Heights. Sometimes, however, they are given the name of Stillwater, which was (and is) the village 3 miles farther south, where the American forces concentrated before taking up position on Bemis Heights. All these obscure names have become lumped as "Saratoga," a name known today as one of the decisive battles of history.

FIRST SARATOGA

"Gentleman Johnny" Burgoyne, so called by his soldiers because he treated them like human beings and not like hunting dogs, had been moving down from Canada with a force of about eight thousand fighting men. (Another one thousand or so noncombatants and authorized camp followers came along, the latter including Indian women as well as other ladies such as the baroness de Riedesel and her three very young daughters.) Lieutenant Colonel Barry St. Leger led an expedition from Canada that was supposed to move down the Mohawk Valley and join Burgoyne at Albany. Nobody knows for sure even today what sort of British military effort was supposed to be made up the Hudson from New York City in connection with Burgoyne's invasion. The point did not become obviously important until Burgoyne got in trouble at Saratoga.

Burgoyne captured Fort Ticonderoga and pushed on to the southern tip of Lake George and modern Whitehall with such ease that he let optimism blind him to dangers. But it was apparent to experienced military subordinates in Burgoyne's expedition that their supply lines were at the breaking point. Just a week later (23 August 1777) St. Leger had to acknowledge that his expedition had failed, and he withdrew toward Canada after being stopped by the defenders of Fort Stanwix.

Although General Schuyler's Northern army had been forced to retreat before Burgoyne's advance, it was now succeeding in reducing the enemy to a snail's pace. Putting one thousand woodsmen to work felling trees and placing other obstacles in Burgoyne's path from Whitehall to Fort Edward (on the Hudson River), Schuyler forced the British to take twenty days to cover the 22 miles. Burgoyne now had a line of communications stretching 185 miles from Fort Edward to Montreal, with almost 40 miles of portages at both ends of Lake Champlain and near Ticonderoga. But he pressed on toward Albany. Schuyler had sent the Polish military engineer Thaddeus Kosciuszko to select a position for stopping this advance.

Meanwhile, Washington had started sending Schuyler reinforcements. Benedict Arnold, disgusted by the protracted charges that he had misused funds during his Canadian operations, had finally submitted his resignation to Congress, but on that same day (11 July 1777) Congress got a request from Washington that Arnold be assigned to Schuyler's command.

Major General Benjamin Lincoln was sent on Washington's recommendation to command the New England militia being assembled in Vermont to support Schuyler. Both officers proved to be of immediate value, Lincoln at Bennington (see BENNINGTON BATTLEFIELD) and Arnold in leading the relief column to Fort Stanwix. Arnold is also credited with assisting Kosciuszko in laying out the positions at Bemis Heights, and he was a hero of the subsequent Battles of Saratoga.

These two leaders arrived without troops, but Washington also sent Dan Morgan with his five hundred Virginia riflemen and the Massachusetts brigades of John Glover and John Nixon.

Schuyler had the situation under control by this time, but political pressure nevertheless resulted in his being relieved of command and superseded by Major General Horatio Gates. Son of a duke's housekeeper, this unattractive little Englishman was a social radical and sound military professional. He and Arnold were immediately at odds, a personality clash that could easily have given the story of Saratoga a less happy ending. The factionalism between the Gates and the Schuyler parties in the Northern army, New Englanders against New Yorkers, not only weakened the military effort but also led to the so-called Conway Cabal, the objective of which was to have Gates replace Washington as commander in chief. The decisive Battles of Saratoga therefore involved more than a visitor will see from a tour of the site today, and this should make an account of the battles all the more interesting.

On 13 September 1777 Burgoyne started crossing the Hudson from the east bank to Saratoga (now Schuylerville), and four days later he halted his cautious advance and deployed about 3 miles short of Bemis Heights. Abandoned by all but about fifty of his Indians, he was groping in the dark for lack of military intelligence. Rebel patrols had been harassing his now-reduced force of about six thousand rank and file, and Gates was well informed about his movements.

The Battle of Freeman's Farm, or the First Battle of Saratoga, on 19 September, was brought on by Burgoyne's reconnaissance in force by three columns to "develop the situation." Gates was content to sit in his prepared positions, letting Burgoyne take the initiative, but Arnold prevailed on him to use part of his numerical superiority to conduct an "active defense." Dan Morgan and Henry Dearborn therefore moved forward through the rough, wooded terrain on the west side of the battlefield. At 12:30 the advance guard of the British center column had reached Freeman's Farm, where Burgoyne ordered it to halt until the progress of the column on the right was known. Dan Morgan's "turkey shooters" worked their way into position around the unsuspecting enemy regulars, and at 12:45 delivered a surprise fire that knocked out all their officers and drove the others back in blind panic. The Virginians followed up with an enthusiastic but disorganized charge that brought them into collision with the main body of this center column, whose well-disciplined fire sent the Rebels scampering for cover.

The American light infantry rallied, however, and they were reinforced by seven regiments. For three or four hours a heavy engagement was sustained, the Americans charging when the opportunity seemed to be promising and always being driven back to their line of departure by equally determined British regulars.

General Riedesel accepted the risk of leaving a reduced force to guard the position he had taken up near the river to protect Burgoyne's supplies, and sent reinforcements to the center column. After detaching four guns for this purpose as soon as he learned that a general engagement was shaping up around Freeman's Farm, Riedesel also reconnoitered a route to be used if he had to send more support. At about 5 P.M. Riedesel got orders from Burgoyne to head for Freeman's Farm and launch an attack on the American east flank to take pressure off the seriously threatened positions of the center column. When Riedesel threw his German regulars piecemeal against the American flank, Burgoyne attacked around Freeman's Farm and slowly gained ground.

Not only did Gates fail to take advantage of his opportunity to annihilate the reduced forces guarding Burgoyne's vital bateaux and supply train along the river bank, but also, when Arnold returned to Bemis Heights for more reinforcements, he did not let him return to the battlefield. The battle ended with Burgoyne's troops holding the field, but their losses had been exorbitant: 350 dead or wounded out of the 800 who bore the brunt of the fighting. The right-flank column spent most of the day beating its way through the wilderness and was never actively engaged. The Americans lost about 320 killed, wounded, and missing.

SECOND SARATOGA

Burgoyne wanted to resume his offensive the next day, 20 September, but General Simon Fraser, who had led the hard but futile effort of the flank column, convinced him that his grenadiers and light infantry would do much better after a day's rest. Having agreed to this delay, "Gentleman Johnny" then postponed his attack again because he received a message from Sir Henry Clinton offering to make a diversion up the Hudson from New York City to support him. Burgoyne therefore put his troops to work building an extensive system of field fortifications. At Freeman's Farm the Balcarres Redoubt was built, and it was the most important of the forward positions. About 200 yards to the north was the Breymann Redoubt. Between these two key works the Canadian auxiliaries went to work forming a screen of stockaded cabins. An entrenched camp was constructed on the plateau overlooking the North Branch of Mill Creek, between the Balcarres Redoubt and the Hudson. On higher ground to the rear the Great Redoubt and two smaller earthworks were built to cover the Great Ravine and the floating bridge constructed across the Hudson.

American militia under the command of Lincoln were now conducting serious raids against British positions along their vital line of communications to Lake Champlain. Militia reinforcements were swelling the ranks of Gates's force at Bemis Heights, and thanks to General Schuyler's efforts, supplies and ammunition were also coming in. Burgoyne's ranks, on the other hand, were being reduced by desertion and disease. His horses were starving. The troops had been living on salt pork and flour for some time, and on 3 October their rations had to be reduced by one-third. Enemy patrols swarmed around Burgoyne's camp, cutting off foraging parties and keeping his men constantly on the alert against threatened attack.

Rejecting Riedesel's proposal that he withdraw, reestablish communications with Canada, and wait for Clinton's diversion to materialize, Burgoyne insisted on making one more effort to fight his way to Albany. The Second Battle of Saratoga, on 7 October, resulted from another reconnaissance in force, because Burgoyne still had been unable to get information with which to plan a coordinated attack on Bemis Heights.

Using his 600 auxiliaries and Captain Fraser's company of rangers to screen his right flank, Burgoyne sent 1,500 regulars in a southwesterly direction toward high ground that had been his objective in the first battle. About half a mile west of the Neilson House this terrain had been unfortified three weeks earlier, but Gates had taken advantage of the additional time and reinforcements to construct earthworks there.

The British tactics were mysterious. They advanced slowly for less than a mile and then formed on a front of about 1,000 yards on a gentle rise north of Mill Creek. A wheat field to the front permitted good observation and fields of fire from the British line, but the flanks were in the woods.

Benedict Arnold had been relieved of command after a dispute with Gates, but the latter was acting as if he had learned something of Arnold's tactical style, and he ordered Morgan to "begin the game" by the same sort of flank attack the Virginians had made before. Gates ordered the eight-hundred-man brigade of General Enoch Poor to move through the woods and hit the opposite flank.

At about 2:30 P.M. this brigade had deployed at the base of a hill held by Major John Acland's grenadiers, who constituted the left (east) flank of Burgoyne's position. Poor's brigade held its formation in the face of all the artillery and small-arms fire Acland could bring to bear. Outnumbered two to one and worried about this well-disciplined operation to their front, the grenadiers responded eagerly to their commander's shouted order, "Fix bayonets and charge the damned Rebels." The veteran New Hampshire Continentals fired on the order of their officers, stopped the grenadiers in their tracks, and then surged forward to overrun their position.

Morgan's Virginians had meanwhile gone into action, routing the flank security of Captain Fraser and hitting the British line on the flank and rear. Dearborn's light infantry arrived just as the British were changing front to meet this threat, and the right of Burgoyne's line was driven back. Sir Francis Clerke was mortally wounded and captured before he could deliver the order for a general withdrawal, and Riedesel's Germans in the center of the line fought on.

Arnold galloped onto the field at this point, hotly pursued by an officer sent by Gates to order him back to camp.

It is quite true that Burgoyne's line had become untenable before Arnold arrived, and a general withdrawal had already been ordered. The Germans withstood the frontal attack that Arnold led personally in his first heroic act of the afternoon (it was actually about noon, the battle having lasted only an hour so far), and they withdrew only when their flanks were threatened and when ordered to do so. But Burgoyne merely pulled back into those fortifications he had been building. Arnold's achievement was to drive the British from their redoubts, which took an inspired effort on his part and some very heavy fighting. The point overlooked by Arnold's critics is that the Americans could not afford to let the British continue to hold those positions when there was the very real threat that Clinton's expedition could be advancing up the Hudson to hit the Bemis Heights fortifications from the rear. Even the rumor of such a threat would have been dangerous to Gates, whose force of eleven thousand troops included more than eight thousand militia.

Having directed the fighting that drove in the British center, Arnold noticed that there was a hero on the other side who was very conspicuous in his efforts to rally troops to delay the American advance.

"That man on the gray horse is a host in himself and must be disposed of," said Arnold to Dan Morgan. The man was General Simon Fraser, and he was mortally wounded by one of Morgan's riflemen. Legend has it that Tim Murphy picked off Clerke and Fraser that day, firing at a range of about 300 feet from a perch in a tree.

Arnold launched a determined attack on the Balcarres Redoubt that was repulsed. Finding a fresh brigade on the field, he then led an assault that cleared out the line of fortified cabins in the low ground between the Balcarres and Breymann Redoubt. Having thus weakened the latter position, Arnold organized and led the attack that overran the Breymann Redoubt, receiving a serious wound in the same leg that had been hit in the assault on Quebec. (There is a monument to this patriotic leg on the battlefield.)

Burgoyne withdrew in good order to his prepared positions around the Great Redoubt, and two days later he had withdrawn to Schuylerville. Gates was unable to pursue immediately, but by 12 October he had the British surrounded and Burgoyne finally accepted defeat. Negotiations were completed the evening of 16 October, and the formal surrender took place the next day. Playing on the threat of Clinton's appearance to the rear of Gates's army, Burgoyne was able to surrender by convention rather than by capitulation, the significance being that his army would be paroled "upon condition of not serving again in North America during the present contest." Burgoyne and two officers of his staff were eventually allowed to return to England, but his troops ended up as prisoners of war because Congress found various pretexts for not ratifying the convention.

A large national park preserves the rolling countryside, terrain features, and principal landmarks of the Saratoga battlefield. A visitor should try to time a visit for the season of the year when the two battles were fought, not only because the impressions will be more valid historically but also because the fall colors will make the experience particularly memorable. The site superintendent quite rightly points out that three hours should be allowed to do this place justice, and you will need at least an hour to see even briefly the nine major landmarks on the 9-mile automobile route.

Eight miles north on U.S. 4 and to the right as one enters Schuylerville is a 25-acre detached section of Saratoga National Historical Park where the restored country mansion of General Schuyler is located. Built in 1777 after Burgoyne's troops burned it and other buildings on Schuyler's estate for tactical reasons, it is a large white frame structure of two stories and beautifully simple lines.

The Field of Grounded Arms, where Burgoyne's surviving 6,300 troops laid down their weapons in surrender on 17 October 1777, is among the "Other Sites Considered" by the National Survey of Historic Sites (1964). On the west bank of the Hudson in Schuylerville on N.Y. 29, a few hundred feet east of U.S. 4, some 50 acres of this historic site have survived as open ground. A neglected landmark is Stark's Knob, just north of Schuylerville.

The Saratoga Park Battlefield Visitor Center is open year-round, 9 A.M. to 5 P.M. weather permitting, except Thanksgiving, Christmas, and New Year's Day. The Schuyler House is closed in the winter. Phone: (518) 664-9821.

Schenectady Stockade Historic District, just off N.Y. 5 (State Street) on the Mohawk River. The tourist is in for a thrill of discovery when he or she turns from the garish sprawl of modern Schenectady into the narrow, tree-lined streets of this recently created historic district. Several hundred houses in this tidy area of several city blocks constitute not only a unique collection of early and intermediate American styles but also a charming neighborhood. All the houses are private, but descriptive literature is available (see below) and guided tours can be arranged.

The historic district, established legally in 1962, is generally within the area enclosed by a stockade built around the settlement soon after its establishment in 1661. In 1690 this westernmost village in the Mohawk Valley was destroyed by 210 French and Indian raiders. All but five or six houses were burned, and it was with great difficulty that the Mohawks prevailed on the Dutch to reestablish the settlement.

During and after the Revolution, Schenectady was an important shipping center and base for operations to the west. Its shipyards had a virtual monopoly on construction of Durham boats, river craft of 15 to 20 tons developed originally to carry bulk freight on the lower Delaware. Raiders came close on one or two occasions, but Schenectady was not attacked.

St. George's Episcopal Church, on North Ferry Street between Union and Front Streets, was built with the help of Trinity Church in New York City and the benefactions of Sir William Johnson during the years 1759 to 1763 by Samuel Fuller, who was responsible for Johnson Hall in Johnstown and other notable structures. According to some authorities, it is the oldest church in the Mohawk Valley. During the Revolution it was closed (probably because of its Loyalist associations), was used as a barracks, and finally became a haven for stray animals. The legend arose that it was the secret burial place of Walter Butler, killed far away on West Canada Creek. In 1793 the building was renovated, a wooden steeple added, and regular services resumed in 1798. Further alterations and renovations took place through the years, the most recent in 1953 when the colonial atmosphere of the interior was restored. Today St. George's is an attractive structure of gray limestone with a gray slate hipped roof and a tall wooden steeple. It sits within an ancient cemetery and now serves the largest parish in the diocese of Albany.

The many private houses of historic and architectural significance—some dating to about 1700—are described and pictured in an extensive website, www.historicstockade.com. In addition, publications are available from the Schenectady County Historical Society. The society also features many exhibits and archives, and is located at 32 Washington Avenue, Schenectady, N.Y. 12305, in the Stockade District. Phone: (518) 374-0263.

Schoharie Valley. Still a region of great scenic and historic interest, this long, flat, fertile valley a mere half-hour's drive west of the Hudson was a major source of provisions (mainly grain) for the Patriot cause. For this reason it was an objective of Loyalist and Indian raiders from Canada, and a major landmark survives as the Old Stone Fort in the village of Schoharie. Other sites are associated with the legendary Timothy Murphy.

Palatines from Livingston Manor bought land in the Schoharie Valley from Indians and, starting in 1713, established seven villages from Central Bridge to Middleburgh. Many markers indicate historic sites associated with this pioneering effort. The Germans prospered as farmers, maintaining good relations with the local Indians who had inhabited the valley since prehistoric times, but as the Revolution approached they split into Rebel and Loyalist factions. A committee of safety was formed in 1775, five minuteman companies were organized, and three forts were eventually built to protect the valley.

In October 1780 Sir John Johnson and Joseph Brant joined forces at Unadilla and ravaged the valley. Approaching from the southwest and bypassing Upper Fort (the site is in the vicinity of Toepath Mountain), the eight hundred Loyalist and Indian raiders entered the valley at night. The two-hundred-man garrison of Middle Fort (the site is in modern Middleburgh) was alerted by the smoke of burning farms, and the commander was ready to consider surrender terms when Timothy Murphy took matters into his own hands. Already famous for his marksmanship and self-reliance as a scout, Murphy simply drew a bead on the enemy's "flag" each time his craven commander, Major Melancthon Woolsey, tried to receive Sir John's surrender terms. A few stout-hearted fellow soldiers rallied around this insubordinate scout to prevent the officers of the garrison from arresting Murphy, and the raiders, unaware of what was going on inside Middle Fort, moved on for easier pickings.

Murphy had married a local girl when he had been stationed in the valley two years earlier. The site of the house where he lived for several years and where he died is indicated by a highway marker on N.Y. 30 at Watsonville about 4 miles southwest of Middleburgh. It is in pretty, open farm country where deer are still a traffic hazard.

Old Stone Fort is located on the outskirts of the village of Schoharie along Fort Road. Ample signage helps greatly in directing visitors. The Old Stone Fort had been built originally in 1772 as a church, and raiders made an unconvincing effort to capture it in 1780. Parishioners from as far as 15 miles away hauled its native limestone blocks in oxcarts to the construction site, and their names are carved in many of the face stones. Names of Loyalist Christians were obliterated later by Patriots. In 1778 the church was enclosed by a stockade; blockhouses at two corners mounted small cannon. The square tower of the church, once topped by a graceful belfry and spire, was manned by sharpshooters when the fort was defended. A sign on the rear wall of the church points up to a hole in the roof cornice said to have been made by a small cannonball fired by the attackers in 1780.

For almost a century the Schoharie County Historical Society has been collecting relics now displayed in the Old Stone Fort and its cement-block annex. Exhibits include electrified maps and a sound system interpreting Revolutionary War activities of the region. In front of the church is a grave of David Williams, one of the three men who captured Major John André at Tarrytown. The historical society is headquartered on the site and presently maintains six buildings there, including a library that specializes in genealogy dating to the seventeenth century. The site is open to the public from May until the end of October, Tuesday through Saturday from 10 A.M. to 5 P.M., Sunday from 12 A.M. to 5 P.M. The Schoharie County Historical Society can be contacted at (518) 295-7192.

Schuyler Mansion (the Pastures). *See* ALBANY.

Schuylerville. *See* SARATOGA NATIONAL HISTORICAL PARK.

Seneca-Iroquois National Museum, Salamanca. The land of the Seneca was decimated by the troops of Generals Sullivan and Clinton during the Revolution, and then mostly taken from them afterwards. Many Seneca fled to Canada; while those remaining settled mostly around the town of Salamanca, part of which lies within the reservation's grounds. The museum is located on the Allegany Indian Reservation at 814 Broad Street. On Route 17, take Exit 20 and follow the signs. The museum is open April to October, Monday to Saturday 9 A.M. to 5 P.M., and Sunday noon to 5 P.M. Phone: (716) 945-1760.

Setauket and vicinity, Long Island. The only important village in the central portion of the island during the Revolution, Setauket had been settled initially by Puritans from around Boston. The Battle of Setauket took place on 22 August 1777, when the Third Battalion of De Lancey's Loyalists held off a raiding force of five hundred Patriots ferried across the sound in whaleboats by Caleb Brewster. Another raid in the "whaleboat warfare" was led by Brewster on 10 December 1777, and it also was repulsed.

"The Culper Ring" that furnished Washington with valuable intelligence after its creation in August 1778 was centered at Setauket and built around a cell of prominent townsmen: Caleb Brewster, Benjamin Tallmadge, Abraham Woodhull ("Culper Senior"), Robert Townsend (who took over later as "Culper Junior"), and Austin Roe (the local tavernkeeper). All of these men except Tallmadge, who was not a secret agent until later in the war (see RAYNHAM HALL), met at the home of Anna Strong to make their initial plans. She subsequently played a key role in signaling Caleb Brewster on the Connecticut shore when there were messages to be picked up.

A popular but reliable account of the ring's operation is *A Peculiar Service* by Corey Ford (Little, Brown and Company, 1965), a work distinguished by the excellent maps of New York City and the Setauket area during the Revolution. It is still available through internet booksellers.

The Anna Strong House burned many years ago; its unmarked site is on the high ground on the southern portion of Strong's Neck overlooking Little Bay. (Since this is more than 6 miles from the closest point on the Connecticut shore, one wonders about the story that Caleb Brewster watched her clothesline for coded signals.) Roe's Tavern was about half a mile east of the Caleb Brewster House. Built in 1703 and enlarged in 1735, it was moved in the 1930s to a hill off what is now called Old Post Road and is a private residence.

Caleb Brewster's home (c. 1665) stands in a plot of grass on the north side of N.Y. 25A in East Setauket, a few hundred yards east of Old Town Road. Recently restored, it is a simple saltbox house of one and a half stories with shingle siding, two chimneys, and a basement.

Abraham Woodhull's house has disappeared, but its site, overlooking Setauket Harbor, is marked on Dyke Road half a mile north of the Presbyterian Church (1811). Woodhull's grave, including bricks from the foundation of his home, is behind the latter church, which is on the site of two earlier structures, one of which was the Loyalist "fort" during the Battle of Setauket. (To reach the Woodhull house site from the green, drive eastward on Dyke Road from the Caroline Avenue junction and follow Dyke Road as it turns generally north along the edge of the harbor. The highway marker will be on the left, or west, half a mile from the starting point.)

Caroline Church is Setauket's gem. Built in 1729, the severely simple, white frame structure with a twisted steeple is said to be the second-oldest Episcopal Church building in the United States. It and the Presbyterian Church face the triangular village green on Main Street.

The Thompson House (c. 1700) is on North Country Road adjacent to the headquarters of the Society for the Preservation of Long Island Antiquities (SPLIA). The society's museum house is a classic eighteenth-century saltbox featuring unusually high ceilings and fireplaces and exposed framing of heavy timber, and activities such as flax spinning, weaving, and dye-making are demonstrated in season. Of great architectural interest is the Sherwood-Jayne House on Old Post Road, East Setauket, another property of the SPLIA about 3 miles from the Thompson House. This house, another saltbox, is in a rural setting that includes a sheep pasture. SPLIA website: www.splia.org; phone: (631) 692-4664.

Sharon Springs Battleground. U.S. 20 has two markers between Sharon and Sharon Springs indicating the location of the running battle in which about 150 Patriots under Colonel Marinus Willett defeated twice that number of Loyalists and Indians under John Doxtader. The region was a hideout for raiders, who offered a bounty of 50 acres for volunteers and $8 for Patriot scalps. Unable to get through the dense cedar swamp to surprise the enemy camp at night, and finding that Doxtader had moved the next morning (10 July 1781) to a good defensive position on higher ground, Willett resorted to an ancient tactical trick. Taking advantage of the cover provided by the dense woods that limited the enemy's visibility, Willett deployed his smaller forces in a crescent. Initially advancing his forces in the center and then having them fall back, the Patriot commander drew the enemy out of position and hit them with surprise fire from both flanks. He then counterattacked and drove the enemy off the field in confusion.

With a sketch of the battle and a large-scale map a visitor today can reconstruct the action. The terrain is still open farmland, and Cedar Swamp, where the Loyalist camp was located on 9 July 1781, survives a few hundred yards to the northwest of Sharon Center. South of the latter landmark at a distance of a few hundred yards is the draw into which Willett lured the Loyalists.

Shell's (Schell's) Bush, about 5 miles north of modern Herkimer. This settlement was the scene of a heroic defense by a Patriot family in August 1781 (see GERMAN FLATS).

Shoemaker House, Mohawk Valley, in the town of Mohawk on West Main Street, on N.Y. 5S. A large historical marker, conspicuous in the paved parking area in front of a modern tavern, indicates the survival of a two-story frame house with hip roof where Rudolph Shoemaker operated his tavern. The place was known for its hospitality to Loyalists as well as to Patriots. The notorious Walter Butler of Butlersbury was captured here in 1777 while holding a midnight meeting to spark a Loyalist uprising to support St. Leger's siege of Fort Stanwix. In this vicinity 450 Loyalists and Indians under Joseph Brant and Captain William Caldwell are said to have hidden in a ravine before launching their famous raid on German Flats in September 1778.

Skenesboro. Now called Whitehall.

Smith (Claudius) Caves, near Tuxedo. *See* RAMAPO VALLEY.

Smith (Joshua Hett) House Site, West Haverstraw, Rockland County. "The Treason House," as it is identified on the highway marker on U.S. 9W near the entrance to the New York State Rehabilitation Hospital, was the home of the man who played, innocently, a key role in revealing Benedict Arnold's plot to surrender West Point. A successful lawyer from a distinguished family, Smith had directed the Patriot secret service in the Hudson Highlands for Arnold's predecessor and was asked by Arnold to continue these duties. Smith was Arnold's agent in meeting Major John André on the *Vulture* and bringing him to a secret conference with Arnold in the woods about 4 miles from Smith's house. He was supposed to escort André back to the *Vulture.* When the latter became impossible, Arnold and André were put up in Smith's house, within the Patriot lines. From this place they watched the next day as the *Vulture* was forced by Patriot artillery to withdraw. Arnold than gave Smith the mission of escorting André through the American lines on the east side of the Hudson.

Arnold had not taken Smith into his confidence, and Smith did not know the real identity of André or the true nature of his business. Smith left "John Anderson" to complete the last 15 miles of his journey alone, and the unfortunate André was captured at Tarrytown.

Acquitted of being involved in Arnold's treason, Smith was nevertheless jailed by state authorities on suspicion of being a Loyalist. In May 1781 he escaped from Goshen, took refuge with the British, spent eight years in England (1783–1801), and died in 1818 in New York City. His property had not been confiscated, but most of his fortune was lost because he had not been able to attend to his affairs.

The house site is on a steep hill alongside the highway. A visitor can drive onto the large reservation of the state hospital for a view of Haverstraw Bay, where the *Vulture* was supposed to retrieve Major André. The site of the secret meeting in the woods 4 miles from here is not marked.

Smith's Clove, near Monroe. *See* RAMAPO VALLEY.

Springsteel's Farm, about 1.5 miles west of Stony Point, Rockland County. In making their approach march for the storming of Stony Point, Anthony Wayne's troops began to arrive here about 8 P.M. on 15 July 1779. Extraordinary measures were taken to preserve secrecy, with the troops guarded so no traitor could slip away to warn the British. Wayne moved closer to Stony Point for a final reconnaissance, and while he was at Springsteel's he wrote a farewell letter in case he were killed in action. The Patriots resumed their advance about 11:30 P.M., generally following the line of today's Wayne Avenue (Route 77) but dividing into two columns soon after leaving Springsteel's.

The site of Springsteel Farm (as it is called on markers) is opposite the entrance gate to Camp Bullowa, a Boy

Scout camp just 0.15 mile north of the intersection of the Crickettown-Franck Road with Wayne Avenue (Route 77). A direction marker on N.Y. 210 about 0.3 mile west of the junction of N.Y. 210 with U.S. 9W-202 in the village of Stony Point indicates that the site is about a mile north on a narrow road that winds and climbs through country only sparsely developed in modern times. No vestige remains of Springsteel's, but by visiting the spot one will see that it made an ideal "final assembly area." On the highest point along the present Wayne Avenue is the hill from which Wayne is alleged to have made his final reconnaissance; it is now occupied by a private residence.

Stark's Knob, just north of Schuylerville, upper Hudson Valley. The great Patriot victory at Bennington (see BENNINGTON BATTLEFIELD) was due primarily to the fact that John Stark refused to obey orders and join the main American army under Horatio Gates at Saratoga. It is all the more ironic that this same Stark, when he did get around to obeying his orders and joining Gates, was the man who put the cork in the bottle and sealed Burgoyne's fate. This cork was the possession of the hill north of Schuylersville now known as Stark's Knob. Burgoyne had decided to make one last effort to extricate his army when he discovered that his escape route was blocked here.

The site is poorly marked, but a visitor can find it by driving 0.2 mile south from the Mohawk River bridge that is just north of Schuylerville. A dirt road climbs steeply to the west from U.S. 4, and to the right are open fields about where Stark deployed.

Staten Island. *See* NEW YORK CITY.

Steuben Memorial, about 20 miles north of Utica, on Starr Hill Road, about 2.5 miles west of the intersection of Routes 12 and 28, near Remsen, Oneida. This State Historic Site contains a replica of the log house in which Steuben spent his summers and where the old bachelor died. His grave is nearby. The house contains the general's uniform, some of his furniture and other possessions, and a replica of the Ralph Earl portrait.

Friedrich Wilhelm Augustus von Steuben (1730–1794) is credited with transforming the Continental army from an undisciplined crowd into a force of professionals. Of particular significance was his teaching of standards of professionalism to the army's officers.

Steuben is an important and a colorful figure in United States history. With a letter from Benjamin Franklin introducing him to Washington as a "Lieutenant General in the King of Prussia's service," knowing no English and having a limited command of French, Steuben was soon put to work training the army at Valley Forge. When the results were

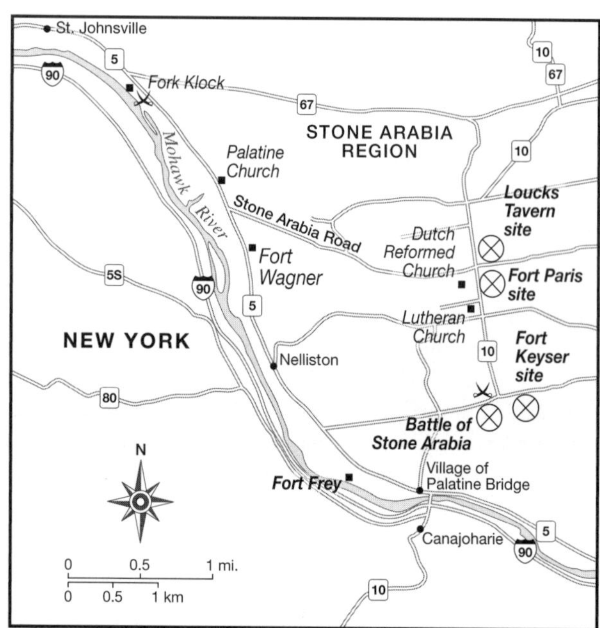

MAP BY XNR PRODUCTIONS. THE GALE GROUP.

proved in battle a few months later, Steuben was made a major general in the Continental army and inspector general. The next winter, 1778 to 1779, he prepared his "Regulations for the Order and Discipline of the Troops of the United States." Later he set up a badly needed system of property accountability for the army.

He took part in the final military operations of the war in Virginia, commanding a division at Yorktown and giving Washington the benefit of his professional knowledge of siege warfare.

General Steuben became an American citizen, established residence in New York City after his discharge from the army in March 1784, and was a prominent social figure. In 1786 New York gave him 16,000 acres in the Mohawk Valley, and the Steuben Memorial is on this land.

Although fairly isolated in a picturesque rural region, the site is easily accessible from a nearby high-speed highway and has great potential as a major historical attraction. In 2004 there were plans in the works for an expansion of the site. There are abundant picnicking facilities, no admission is charged, and the site is open daily from mid-May through Labor Day. Phone: (315) 768-7224.

Stone Arabia, Mohawk Valley, in Montgomery County, bisected by N.Y. 10 north of Palatine Bridge, at Thruway Exit 29. This name was originally applied to the area of some 20,000 acres of rich farmland granted to Palatine settlers in 1723. (In old records it is spelled "Stoneraby," and nobody knows how the picturesque later version evolved.)

The Battle of Stone Arabia, 18 October 1780, took place just to the northeast of Palatine Bridge. Major landmarks have been preserved, but a little prior knowledge is needed for today's visitor to appreciate them.

After devastating the Schoharie Valley, some 1,500 battle-tested raiders under Sir John Johnson were marching up the north bank of the Mohawk, burning settlements and pillaging. General Robert Van Rensselaer had scraped together a force of Patriot militia that was moving some distance to the rear and on the other side of the river. In a position to intercept the raiders was a small body of about 130 Massachusetts levies (and a few others) under Colonel John Brown at the fortified farm of Isaac Paris ("Fort Paris") in the village of Stone Arabia.

Van Rensselaer ordered Brown to march south and attack the head of Johnson's column while the main Patriot force closed up and hit them from the rear. Near the ruins of Fort Keyser the Massachusetts troops were decisively defeated. Brown and about forty of his men were killed, and the rest were routed; the raiders destroyed two old churches and many other buildings in the area before continuing the march toward Fort Klock.

The battlefield and the site of famous old Fort Keyser are indicated by highway markers in the picturesque farmland 2 miles north of Palatine Bridge on N.Y. 10. One sign points out the low, wooded ridge a few hundred yards to the south where the main enemy force was located initially. From the evidence of cannonballs and bullets found throughout the years in neighboring fields, Brown was advancing west along the general line of today's Route 10 when he walked into a well-planned ambuscade.

The site of Fort Keyser—built by Johannes Keyser in 1750—is indicated by a highway marker on Dillenback Road 0.3 of a mile east of Cook Corners (where N.Y. 10 makes its second 90-degree turn after leaving Palatine Bridge). This valley landmark disappeared in 1855, only a few years after a watercolor sketch was made by R. A. Grider; still to be seen is the place where it stood, now a weed-covered mound in a farm field about 300 yards south of the road. An inscribed stone of Fort Keyser has been identified in the foundation of the house nearby.

On N.Y. 10 north of Cook Corners 1.2 miles is the white frame Lutheran church rebuilt in 1792 after the older one was destroyed in 1780 by Sir John's raiders. It is on the site of the first log structure, which was erected in 1729.

About 100 yards farther north is a small architectural gem in a rural setting little despoiled by centuries of American progress. This is the Dutch Reformed Church, of luminous, light gray limestone, built in 1788 on the site of the one destroyed in 1780. Colonel John Brown lies in the ancient cemetery to the rear, and a monument to this colorful character, erected by his son in 1836, is in front of the church.

He was called John Brown of Pittsfield (Massachusetts) to distinguish him from all the others. Only thirty-six years old when killed in action—in fact, on his thirty-sixth birthday—he had packed a full life into those few years. After graduating from Yale (1771) and practicing law briefly in this area of New York, he had returned to his native New England. At the start of the Revolution he volunteered for a secret mission to Canada, charged with feeling out the spirit of rebellion in what the Patriots hoped to make "the fourteenth colony" and setting up an intelligence net. He is among those credited with suggesting that Fort Ticonderoga be captured by a surprise attack, and he took part in the Ethan Allen operation against the fort, though he abandoned Allen during a planned attack on Montreal. Later he was part of General Montgomery's column invading Canada along the Lake Champlain route, and had been promised a promotion to lieutenant colonel when Montgomery was killed at Quebec. Meanwhile, he had clashed with Arnold, who refused to recommend the promotion. Brown became Arnold's most dedicated enemy, using his lawyer's training to press formal charges of malfeasance and incompetence. Failing to remove Arnold, Brown resigned his military commission, returned to his civilian pursuits at Pittsfield, and published a broadside attack on Arnold.

The site of Fort Paris is indicated by a highway marker half a mile north of the stone church. It was on the slight rise about 200 yards east of the road. Colonel Isaac Paris, one of the regimental commanders who goaded General Herkimer into the ambush at Oriskany, was captured there and subsequently murdered by Loyalists.

Another 0.3 mile north is the site of Loucks Tavern, on Stone Arabia Road (County Highway 34). Here the Palatine District Committee of Safety met for the first time on 27 August 1774, "attended by a large number of the inhabitants," writes William W. Campbell in his *Annals of Tryon County* (1831). This spot is approximately the geographic center of the historic region then known as Stone Arabia, and now the Palatine Township of Montgomery County.

Stony Point, near the community of Stony Point on the Hudson River, about 25 miles north of New York City and 12 miles south of West Point, on U.S. 9W and 202.

This was a place of strategic importance, not only for its location at the southern edge of the Hudson Highlands but also because it covered Kings Ferry. A miniature of West Point, it is a rocky promontory protruding half a mile into the river toward Verplanck's Point.

The Americans had concentrated their fortification efforts a few miles farther north, and Sir Henry Clinton's forces easily captured Stony Point and Verplanck's Point on 1 June 1779 when they moved up the Hudson to support Burgoyne's invasion from Canada. Although it quickly became apparent that the enemy was not going to continue his offensive up the Hudson, Washington was worried about the fact that the British were fortifying Stony Point and Verplanck's Point. When he learned from good intelligence reports that the works at Stony Point were not being completed quickly, Washington ordered General Wayne to take them by a *coup de main*—a quick, surprise attack.

The Americans moved from near Fort Montgomery toward their final assembly areas on 15 July 1779, taking elaborate precautions to preserve secrecy along the 15-mile line of march. Wayne received valuable information about the British garrison, which included a number of African American troops, from a slave named Pompey Lamb who spied for the Patriots. Shortly before midnight on 15 to 16 July the "forlorn hopes" of the flank columns started forward from the swampy ground that separates the 150-foot peak of Stony Point from the mainland. A third force, in the middle, made a diversionary attack that accomplished its purpose of drawing about half of the enemy defenders down from the hill and away from the main fortification there.

The fight lasted only fifteen minutes after the two flank columns converged almost simultaneously on the British fort, shortly after midnight. The British commander reported the loss of 20 killed, 74 wounded, 58 missing, and the rest of his 624 officers and men captured. The well-disciplined Americans won praise for taking so many prisoners.

General Wayne, who received a head wound early in the attack but retained command, reported that of 1,350 actually engaged he lost only 15 killed and 83 wounded.

A fiery French officer, scion of a noble family from Provence, won the $500 prize offered by Wayne for being the first man to enter the enemy works. François Louis Teissèdre de Fleury, who had come to America as a volunteer, had immediately distinguished himself and been commissioned a captain of engineers in May 1777. After doing engineering work around Philadelphia he was honored by a resolution of Congress for gallantry at the Brandywine, and was wounded after serving six weeks in the siege of Fort Mifflin (see PHILADELPHIA, under Pennsylvania). He subsequently saw action at Monmouth and Newport before eclipsing all his previous accomplishments at Stony Point. Granted nine months' leave, he went to France, returned to America with Rochambeau, and was decorated by the French for his performance at Yorktown.

Congress voted only eight medals during the Revolution, and three were for Stony Point: a gold one for Wayne and silver ones for Fleury and Major John Stewart, who commanded the advance party of the left column. The French officer did not get his until 1783, when by some bureaucratic alchemy the silver medal had been transformed into gold.

The British reacted swiftly to Wayne's victory, sinking the galley that was taking most of the twelve captured cannon to West Point and securing Verplanck's Point before the planned American attack against that place got going. Washington wisely decided that the defense of Stony Point would not be worth the effort, so he ordered the fortifications destroyed and abandoned. The British reoccupied them on 19 July, the day after Wayne left. The operation had little strategic value, but it was a morale booster, and it was impressive evidence of the military qualities finally being developed within the American army. Edmund Burke's *Annual Register* for 1779 said the action "would have done honor to the most veteran soldiers." The French ambassador to Philadelphia, Gerard, studied reports of the battle carefully and wrote, "I am convinced that this action will . . . elevate the ideas of Europe about the military qualities of the Americans. . . ."

Stony Point Battlefield is unspoiled. Within the state reservation there are extensive remains of the earthworks built during the Revolution, and historical markers identify the main points of interest in "Mad Anthony" Wayne's action. The rugged and heavily wooded promontory can be explored by trail (a road saves a climb to the top), and the view of the Hudson from there is splendid. There is a small but excellent museum. Featured is the oldest lighthouse on the Hudson River. Walking tours are provided, admission is free, and the site is open from 15 April to 31 October from 10 A.M. to 5 P.M. (1 P.M. to 5 P.M. on Sundays). Phone: (914) 786-2521.

Suffern. *See* RAMAPO VALLEY.

Sullivan-Clinton Expedition. Starting at the Newtown Battlefield State Park, one may trace the operations of this punitive force against the Iroquois north into the Finger Lakes and west to the vicinity of Letchworth State Park. The latter place is of interest not only for the great natural beauty of the 15-mile Genesee River gorge but also for the vestiges of Seneca culture preserved there in the museum and the Seneca Council House.

About four thousand Patriot troops under General John Sullivan and James Clinton had the mission of "total destruction and devastation" of the Iroquois settlements. All organized resistance having been broken at Newtown, the invaders were impeded only by their own ponderous supply train. Burning Indian towns, destroying crops, and casting covetous eyes on this new land, the Patriots moved northward to Seneca Lake, westward from the area of modern Geneva to the ancient Indian town of Genesee (near modern Genesco).

Here a patrol of twenty-six men under Lieutenant Thomas Boyd was virtually wiped out on 13 September 1779, and the two survivors were cruelly tortured to death the next day.

Worth mentioning is the Sullivan Memorial between Groveland and East Groveland, southeast of Genesco. It lists the "heroic scouts" killed here in the ambush. The Boyd-Parker Memorial, a few miles west of Genesco on U.S. Alternate 20, is at the site of Little Beard's Town. Here the wounded Thomas Boyd was interrogated and then tortured to death. Although the story persists in patriotic circles that Boyd heroically refused to reveal information, the report of John Butler reads, "The officer who is a very intelligent person says their army consists of near 5,000 Continental troops . . . [who] intend, according to his account, to come no further than Genesee." The memorial indicates that the second prisoner killed here was Sergeant Michael Parker. Another prisoner slaughtered by the Indians, here or earlier, was the celebrated Oneida scout and marksman named Hanyerry.

Sullivan's expedition was supposed to be joined in this area by Colonel Daniel Brodhead's force of six hundred troops that had moved from Fort Pitt up the Allegheny Valley. In an advance of 400 miles this column burned ten villages, collected much booty, defeated the Indians in one skirmish, but turned back 50 miles short of its rendezvous with Sullivan because its guides were inadequate. The projected attack on Niagara was therefore not made, and Sullivan started back after burning Genesee.

Retracing his steps to Seneca Castle, or Kanadesaga, the site of which is covered by modern Geneva, the Patriots continued east to Cayuga Lake, moved south along both shores of this lake, and descended the Susquehanna to the Wyoming Valley (vicinity of modern Wilkes-Barre).

Sullivan had failed in his assigned mission of taking Niagara. He failed to destroy the ability of the Iroquois to continue their border warfare, the raids of 1780 and 1781 being more frequent and more vicious than in previous years. But in burning their crops and villages, Sullivan condemned the Iroquois to a winter of harsh starvation that had serious long-term consequences for their society.

If the Patriots showed little real military aptitude in this expedition, they revealed no lack of genius for real-estate development. Many of the Continental troops involved were New Englanders, who returned to their thin-soil and rocky home states with appetizing reports on the Iroquois country. "The Military Tract" was set aside by New York in 1782 to give bounties for service in the Revolution. It comprised more than 1.5 million acres of Iroquois country—all of the present Onondaga, Cayuga, and Seneca Counties, and portions of Tompkins, Schuyler, Wayne, and Oswego. When drawing for lots started on the first day of 1791, many veterans had sold their claims to speculators. Meanwhile, New York and Massachusetts had settled their differences over control of western lands, and the rest of western New York was taken from the Indians so whites could move in. Today's tourist will find many historical markers and sites associated with post-Revolution land purchases and their development.

Five states participated in an elaborate celebration of the 150th anniversary of the Sullivan-Clinton campaign, locating the forty-eight campsites and erecting handsome bronze plaques along the route of march. The latter remain in place to guide today's tourist. Highway markers pertaining to the expedition have disappeared mysteriously as certain ninety-nine-year leases with the Indians of western New York came due for renegotiation.

Sullivan Memorial (State Historical Site). *See* SULLIVAN-CLINTON EXPEDITION.

Tappan Historic District, Rockland County. Two and a half miles west of the Hudson River landing opposite Dobbs Ferry, about midway between Kings Ferry and New York City, Tappan was an important camping area throughout the Revolution, and Washington's headquarters on several important occasions. The Tappan Patent was settled almost a century before the Revolution, and today it preserves much of its original character. Most of Tappan's historic sites lie within an 85-acre historic district established in 1966.

The little De Wint House at 20 Livingston Street, recently designated as a Washington Masonic Shrine and a National Historic Landmark, is a Dutch brick-and-sandstone structure built about 1700 by Daniel de Clark. John de Windt was a West Indian planter who later owned it. While using this building as his headquarters, Washington gave Benedict Arnold command of the Hudson Highlands, an assignment the turncoat had been angling for, and it was here that Washington made the hard decision that the charming young Major John André would suffer a spy's fate. While back in the De Wint House in May 1783 Washington met with General Sir Guy Carleton to arrange the peaceful British evacuation of New York City. In 1932 the Free and Accepted Masons of the State of New York bought the house and started restoring it.

The 1776 House, or Mabie Tavern, is on Main Street just south of Old Tappan Road. Around 1753 the house was sold to Casparus Mabie, who established a tavern there. The Orangetown Resolutions were signed here on 4 July 1774; this document was hailed by local historians as anticipating the Declaration of Independence by exactly two years, though it is difficult to determine any connection other than the date. The Old 76 House, as it is usually called, is an upscale eatery billed as "New York's Oldest Restaurant." Phone: (845) 359-5476.

John André was a prisoner in Mabie Tavern during his trial in the Dutch Reformed Church a short distance away. (The existing church structure is the third on its site, having been built in 1835; André's trial was in the second.) André's prison room was preserved for more than fifty years, then converted into a ballroom, but in 1897 the entire building was restored. It meets most of the criteria for registration as a National Historic Landmark.

The site of André's hanging and burial is marked by a monument on André Hill just south of Old Tappan Road. (From the Village Green in the center of town go 0.4 mile west on Old Tappan Road and turn south at the highway marker pertaining to the André Monument. Climb half a mile up a rather steep grade, through an attractive residential district, to the large polished stone monument within a circular fence.) André's remains were moved to Westminster Abbey in 1821 and placed near the monument previously erected there by George III (near Poets' Corner). In 1847 a small boulder was placed on the original grave. "A more elegant and durable monument should be erected upon the spot," Lossing commented after sketching it in 1850, and this has been done.

While at Tappan during this distasteful episode, Washington issued the instructions that led to the daring exploit of Sergeant Major John Champe. The plan was for a volunteer from "Light Horse Harry" Lee's legion to take on the role of a deserter, enter the British lines, and kidnap Benedict Arnold from his quarters on lower Broadway in New York City. Champe succeeded in being accepted as a volunteer in Arnold's legion, but was ordered off on an expedition to raid his native Virginia before he could make his attempt to capture Arnold. Unable to effect his escape from the British until Arnold's legion returned from Virginia, Champe eventually rejoined Lee in the Carolinas, and only then could the truth of his "desertion" from the Continental army be told. Tappan was the scene of Sergeant Major Champe's most hazardous feat, that of leaving the American lines. For further information contact the Tappantown Historical Society, P.O. Box 71, Tappan, N.Y. 10983. Phone: (914) 359-7790.

Tappan Massacre. Under New Jersey *See* BAYLOR MASSACRE.

Tarrytown and North Tarrytown, on U.S. 9 just north of Tappan Zee Bridge off Thruway Exit 9 (Tarrytown). Major John André was captured on the creek that separates the two towns, and here in Patriots' Park off U.S. 9 is a monument to his captors. In North Tarrytown is Philipsburg Manor. This is the Sleepy Hollow country made famous after the Revolution by Washington Irving, whose home, Sunnyside, is a mile south of the Tappan Zee Bridge near U.S. 9.

Ticonderoga and vicinity, on Lake Champlain at north end of Lake George. Natural beauty, historic importance, and a superlative reconstruction combine to make Fort Ticonderoga and its associated works a national landmark of the greatest significance and interest. No education is needed to appreciate the natural beauty. But the more one knows about the history of this site and the efforts of a few private citizens to preserve it, the more richly a visit will be rewarded.

"Between the waters" was the meaning of the Indian name for this place, and Ticonderoga is a corruption of their word "Cheonderoga," or "Tyeonderoga." In a position to control the 2-mile portage between Lakes Champlain and George as well as the entrance to Wood Creek (which led to the Great Carrying Place whose Hudson River terminus was Fort Edward), Ticonderoga was a critical spot on the natural route between Canada and the Thirteen Colonies.

During the Colonial Wars the French first fortified Crown Point (1731), about 12 miles north of Ticonderoga. (A visitor viewing the terrain, he might speculate on whether Crown Point is not a better strategic position than Ticonderoga for a fortress to control Lake Champlain.)

When the British built Fort William Henry on the south end of Lake George (see LAKE GEORGE VILLAGE), the French in 1755 started fortifying Ticonderoga. One reason for pushing so far south was that their new fort at Crown Point had been started "on wrong principles." The French first put a military road along the 2-mile portage between the lakes (now Portage Road in the village of Ticonderoga). Then they started building a fort where the present reconstruction stands, first using oak logs and later replacing these with stone.

In the summer of 1758 the fort (named Carillon because water fell from Lake George with a sound like "a chime of bells") was almost finished when it was threatened by the largest British army yet fielded in North America. General James Abercromby was preparing to attack from the direction of Lake George with an expedition that numbered six thousand of Britain's finest regulars and nine thousand provincials.

The marquis de Montcalm reached Fort Carillon on 30 June 1758 to take command. He had fewer than four thousand troops, and reports indicated they would be attacked within a few days by up to six times that number. Montcalm sent strong detachments forward to detect and delay the enemy's approach, but he took another action that revealed his military genius. Instead of passively defending the fort, he deployed the bulk of his command in the woods about three-quarters of a mile to the west.

Here his engineers laid out fieldworks on the forward slopes of a wooded hill, and his troops performed the prodigious labor of erecting abatis and a great wall of logs. All this was done in a few days—from decision to the issue of implementing orders to accomplishment.

Victory was on the side of the smaller battalions and the smarter leaders. Abercromby suffered one of the costliest defeats in British history, losing almost 2,000 in killed and wounded. The French had 377 casualties.

Today a visitor approaches Fort Ticonderoga along a paved road of the 1,000-acre reservation that has several monuments commemorating this French victory and the exceptional gallantry of the British and American battalions involved. The famous Black Watch (Forty-second Highlanders) and Royal Americans (now the King's Royal Rifle Corps of the British army) did the heaviest fighting. The present access road corresponds with the British axis of advance on the fort and gives a visitor an appreciation of Montcalm's wisdom in choosing his defensive position. Those casualty figures prove much more conclusively than any bronze plaques that this was one of the hardest battles ever fought on American soil.

Almost exactly a year later the French were forced to abandon Ticonderoga when its capture by Lord Jeffrey Amherst was imminent. Ethan Allen and Benedict Arnold were among the colonial officers in this operation (and sixteen years later they were to pay Ticonderoga another visit together). Amherst started repairs on the fort, which the French had tried to destroy on their departure by setting fires and leaving a slow match that exploded the powder magazine under the southeast bastion.

When the British won Canada, the military significance of Ticonderoga virtually disappeared. At the start of the American Revolution it was a military depot in the wilderness, guarded by a small garrison whose chief enemy was boredom. Stone forts of this period had the advantage of requiring less upkeep than wooden structures, which would rot away every few years and need rebuilding. But constant repairs are needed to keep up masonry walls in climates where frost works on the mortar. Stone masons were scarce in the American wilderness of two centuries ago, and as early as 1767 Fort Ticonderoga had been reported as being "in a very declining condition."

But a goodly supply of artillery was still there, and when the shooting started in 1775 this was one item the Patriots sorely lacked. Several men are credited with conceiving the plan of capturing this isolated and neglected British post. Massachusetts gave the mission to Benedict Arnold, but Ethan Allen of Vermont organized an expedition that moved out before Arnold's force could get on the scene. Arnold raced on to Castleton, Vermont, accompanied only by a servant, and tried to seize command from Allen. (Historians still disagree as to what command authority Arnold had, if any. None of his own troops were engaged, and Allen's Green Mountain Boys had flatly refused to take any orders from Arnold.)

There were delays in getting boats from Skenesboro (now Whitehall) and other places to Hand's Cove, Vermont. Surprise was essential, so the decision was made to use what boats were available to ferry as many men as possible across Lake Champlain for a dawn attack. With eighty-three men and a number of officers, Allen achieved complete surprise.

The dramatic scene of the surrender has been recreated by innumerable writers and artists. Rudely awakened, an officer appeared at the door of his quarters "with his breeches in his hand," as Allen reported it, and demanded by what authority these rowdies were calling for surrender of the fort. "In the name of the great Jehovah, and the Continental Congress," was the stirring reply. Historians do not deny that an officer could have said this, but they seriously question that he actually did: no contemporary account records the phrase, and it was four years after the event that Allen first entered it into the historical record. Artists and popular writers also have neglected the point that it was not Captain Delaplace who stood trousers in hand to receive this oratorical thunderbolt, but a recently joined subordinate, Lieutenant Jocelyn Feltham. "I asked a number of questions, expecting to amuse them [that is, play for time] till our people fired," he wrote in his report. Delaplace, meanwhile, got dressed, appeared at the head of the stairs, and quite sensibly surrendered the fort.

How to transport all this cumbersome loot to the Boston lines? Colonel Henry Knox, a twenty-five-year-old military amateur, was appointed commander of the Continental Regiment of Artillery and ordered by Washington to go to draw his equipment at Ticonderoga. Knox had previously submitted a plan for this undertaking, which called for the use of sledges hauled over the snow by oxen. (This is one reason why the cannon, captured on 10 May, were not moved sooner.) To summarize the story of his "noble train of artillery," as Knox called it, on 5 December 1775 Knox reached Ticonderoga, and the next day forty-three cannon and sixteen mortars were removed from the fort. By 9 December they had all been taken across the portage and loaded on scows. On 7 January 1776 the 120,000 pounds of matériel were assembled around Lake George Village for what should have been the worst part of the trip. But the 300 miles of difficult terrain were covered in less than three weeks. The route was from Fort Edward to old Saratoga (Schuylerville today), Albany, Kinderhook, and Claverack, then east through steep grades and heavy snows of the Berkshires to Framingham, 20 miles west of Boston. Emplacement of the guns on Dorchester Heights in March forced the British to evacuate Boston.

Ticonderoga was by now of great emotional importance to Patriots—the "Gibraltar of America," "Key to a Continent." Young John Trumbull (1756–1843), later famous as "Painter of the Revolution," and the French-trained Polish military engineer Thaddeus Kosciuszko (1746–1817) were put in charge of the fortification work. But the place fell quickly to Burgoyne's expedition in July 1777. There were charges of gross incompetence and treason. Around campfires of New England troops the story of the "silver bullets of Ticonderoga" was circulated credulously: "Gentleman Johnny" Burgoyne had bought the fort with silver bullets fired over its walls. (In the museum at Ticonderoga there is indeed a silver bullet, but it has quite a different story. Messages were sometimes carried in hollow silver bullets that could be swallowed by the bearer if he were captured. This bullet was purged from the spy carrying Sir Henry Clinton's message of 8 October 1777 about his capture of Forts Clinton and Montgomery in the Bear Mountain area.)

Patriot commanders on the spot knew that Ticonderoga was untenable with the resources at their disposal. Trumbull had warned General Arthur St. Clair, the newly assigned commander at Ticonderoga, that British guns on Mount Defiance could hit the fort. This 800-foot hill had never been occupied in the military history of Ticonderoga, and on some maps it was marked "inaccessible." The defenders knew better. Benedict Arnold and Anthony Wayne walked St. Clair up the hill to show him how the British could emplace guns there. But St. Clair did not have enough troops to defend Mount Defiance. He did not have sufficient men even to defend properly the boom and bridge of boats connecting Ticonderoga to the Mount Independence works on the Vermont shore. He lacked "naval support" to counter the British ships and gunboats.

Faced with these realities, Schuyler and St. Clair decided that Ticonderoga was untenable, but that a show of resistance had to be made. The British forward elements took Mount Hope without any resistance from the outpost there. They wasted little time in getting four 12-pounders up Mount Defiance, and the Americans prepared to withdraw secretly from Fort Ticonderoga to consolidate their defenses around Mount Independence. The significance of the enemy guns on Mount Defiance was not that they could pound the fort into submission: the range was too great for precision fire, and, even more important, not enough ammunition could be supplied over the improvised road for a proper bombardment. The real value of these guns was that they could wreck the floating bridge and boats brought up to evacuate the garrison.

The well-planned American withdrawal turned into a comedy of errors. One of St. Clair's generals was a French volunteer with the splendid name Chevalier Matthias Alexis de Rochefermoy, "a worthless drunkard" in the judgment of at least one close observer. General Fermoy (as he was known in America) not only failed to give his troops on Mount Independence warning orders about the night withdrawal, but also, when he got ready to leave at about 3 A.M., for some reason set fire to his quarters. This illuminated the scene, gave away the plot, and prompted a vigorous reaction from the enemy. Four gunners posted to fire the length of the bridge of boats were found by the British to be in a drunken sleep, so Burgoyne's men crossed the quarter-mile water gap unimpeded.

When the news of Ticonderoga's fall reached King George III, he cried out: "I have beat them! I have beat all the Americans!"

Ticonderoga became a critical post on Burgoyne's overextended line of communications as he blundered farther and farther south to disaster at Saratoga. In late September 1777 a surprise attack on Ticonderoga was led by Colonel John Brown of Pittsfield. Brown achieved surprise, captured three hundred of the enemy, and liberated one hundred American prisoners. (The latter had been used for labor and kept at night in a barn some distance from the fort.) Lacking heavy artillery to attack the fort itself, Brown moved south along Lake George in captured boats with the idea of taking the enemy supply point on Diamond Island. When the wind turned against him and the enemy garrison was alerted before he could launch a surprise attack, Brown made for the east shore, burned his boats, and rejoined the Patriot forces under Benjamin Lincoln in Vermont.

After Burgoyne's surrender at Saratoga the British abandoned Ticonderoga, burning the barracks and buildings on both sides of the lake. The place was never again garrisoned.

RECONSTRUCTION

Historic Fort Ticonderoga and surrounding lands were ceded to Columbia and Union Colleges by the state of New York in 1803. When Benson Lossing visited the spot in 1848 he wrote: "For more than half a century the walls of the fort have been common spoil for all who chose to avail themselves of such a convenient quarry; and the proximity of the lake affords rare facility for builders to carry off the plunder. . . . Year after year the ruins thus dwindle, and, unless . . . government shall prohibit the robbery, this venerable landmark of history will soon have no abiding place among us."

A New York merchant named William Ferris Pell leased the lands in 1816 and bought them four years later. In 1908 a descendant, Stephen Pell, started the remarkable job of reconstruction, which was continued by his son, John H. G. Pell. Today the Fort Ticonderoga Association, a not-for-profit organization, maintains the site, operates a superb historical museum, and publishes an historical quarterly. The Place d'Armes was covered with 6 to 7 feet of rubble, and the west bastions lay under twice that burden. But the debris had preserved the plan of the fort and vital details of its construction. At least 50 percent of the walls were rebuilt by putting back stones that had fallen into the moat. Hardware has been copied from examples found in the ruins. Tiles for the roof and floors have been made by the same methods as in the 1700s, stones have been reset in the same type of mortar as originally, and rough-hewn oak beams have been brought in from the Adirondacks. The wealth of objects found during excavations has been preserved in the fort museum.

The ramparts bristle with a remarkable collection of eighteenth-century artillery of all types. Only two pieces ever saw service at Ticonderoga, but the others were collected in America, from Europe, and from several West Indian islands. Fourteen large 24-pounders were presented by the British government, having been cast for use in America during the Revolution but never shipped.

In the south barracks is a museum on three floors, and the basement of the west barracks has an important gun collection. Highlights of the uncluttered and well-organized museum are: a waterway exhibit (canoes and a bateau); Indian trade goods; sixteen wall cases representing periods of the fort's history; an unusual collection of engraved powder horns, polearms, portraits, and uniforms; two reconstituted Indian graves; and many Indian artifacts. A scale model of Mount Independence includes models of the various vessels built for Arnold's Lake Champlain fleet at Whitehall and fitted out at Mount Independence.

From the previously mentioned model in the south barracks a visitor can see the site's appearance at the time of the Revolution, when most of its timber had been stripped off. The star fort on Mount Independence was more strongly garrisoned than Fort Ticonderoga itself, better provisioned and well outposted. The historic site offers public educational programs and reenactments and is open to the public 10 May to 24 October from 9 A.M. to 5 P.M. Phone: (518) 585-2821.

MOUNT DEFIANCE AND MOUNT HOPE

A toll road to the 853-foot summit of Mount Defiance provides a magnificent panorama for great distances in all directions. On a clear day one can see Mount Marcy, highest point in New York, some 37 miles to the northwest, and sometimes 60 miles down the lake to Westport. "The view from this lofty hill is one of great interest and beauty," wrote Benson Lossing after scrambling up its western slope in August 1848, "including almost every variety of natural scenery, and a region abounding with historical associations." The scene has changed little since his day, except that now one drives up and has the advantage of a taped narrative that explains what one is looking at. Called Sugar Loaf Hill before acquiring its present name, this is where the colorful British General William Phillips emplaced a gun battery within range of Fort Ticonderoga. "Where a goat can go a man can go, and where a man can go he can drag a gun," said this legendary hero of the Royal Artillery—and they went. Already promoted over the heads of many seniors for gallantry and "superlative practice" in Germany, he was Burgoyne's second in command in 1777 and was promoted to major general after the capture of Ticonderoga. Taken prisoner with Burgoyne's army and exchanged in October 1780, he led raids in Virginia and died of typhoid fever in Petersburg. He is buried there.

Mount Hope is owned and managed by the Fort Ticonderoga Association and has the same visiting hours as Fort Ticonderoga. This outpost position of Fort Ticonderoga changed hands many times between its establishment in 1755 by Montcalm and its final occupation by the Patriots in 1781. The existing blockhouse was built in 1776 by Colonel Jonathan Brewer's Massachusetts State Regiment of Artificers. An able artificer himself is the man who began developing the site in 1946, Carroll V. Lonergran. He grew up on a farm that included Fort Mount Hope, and did a great deal of its restoration. Lonergran recovered cannon, cannonballs, bar shot, and the ruins of a gunboat from Lake Champlain.

Unadilla Region. The Unadilla River, now the boundary between Chenango and Otsego Counties, was the dividing line between Iroquois country and the area open to white settlement by the Treaty of Fort Stanwix (1786). When the Revolution started there was a small place known as Unadilla where the river of that name enters the Susquehanna. The site is about 5 miles downstream from modern Unadilla. In June 1777 Joseph Brant showed up with about seventy-five Indian warriors and demanded that the white settlers furnish him with supplies. The Patriot element of the unprotected settlement started packing up, and for the rest of the war years Unadilla was a base for Indian and Loyalist raids against the frontiers of New York and Pennsylvania. The meeting between Brant and Herkimer (see HERKIMER HOUSE) took place on the river flats about a mile and a half east of modern Bainbridge. The historical area marker pertaining to this event ("the Lost Peace") is found on N.Y. 51 between Mount Upton and Gilbertsville, and another marker ("Unadilla Region") is between Bainbridge and Afton on N.Y. 7.

From Unadilla, Joseph Brant launched his raid of 13 September 1778 on German Flats. The Patriots retaliated with a punitive expedition that destroyed Indian castles in the Unadilla area (2–16 October). Brant's base at Oquaga was among the places burned, and the Mohawk chief responded with his notorious Cherry Valley Massacre.

Even after the Sullivan-Clinton Expedition of 1779, which destroyed all major Iroquois settlements, including Unadilla and Oquaga, these places continued to serve as rendezvous points and bases for raids. At Unadilla the Indians under Brant and Cornplanter linked up with Sir John Johnson's forces from Oswego in September 1780 for the raid that devastated Schoharie Valley, and moving up the Mohawk Valley through Stone Arabia and Johnstown, inflicted more damage.

After the Catskill Turnpike was constructed early in the nineteenth century, the modern village of Unadilla began to grow.

Valcour Bay, west shore of Lake Champlain, 7 miles south of Plattsburgh. Benedict Arnold's amazing performance here in 1776 saved the northern frontier from British conquest and delayed Burgoyne's campaign of 1777.

When the American invasion of Canada in 1775 to 1776 failed, General Sir Guy Carleton undertook to gain control of Lake Champlain as the first step in a counter-offensive that could have fatally split the colonies along the line of the Hudson River. But because Arnold was fighting back with the few American ships on the lake and was building more, Carleton had to stop long enough to form a flotilla of his own. This delay probably was fatal because it did not leave him time to take Ticonderoga and push on to Albany before winter set in.

The site of the critical Battle of Valcour Bay has remained virtually unspoiled. Valcour Island is a high, rocky, and wooded island about 2 miles long and 1.25 miles wide. By 1972 the state of New York had purchased most of the island and included it within the Adirondack State Park. In many ways it has changed little in appearance since the October day in 1776 when Carleton's Indian allies climbed its trees to deliver harassing fire onto the decks of Arnold's improvised fleet. The channel between the island and the lake shore is three-quarters of a mile wide, divided into two bays by a high bluff that juts out from the island. The shore of the lake has been built up to some degree, but little damage has been done to the bay as a historical landmark.

In addition to the points already mentioned, the battle is remarkable for several other reasons. Lake Champlain is a most unusual place for a naval battle to take place because it is landlocked and very narrow. Ships were in constant danger of being bottled up and destroyed by attack from the shore. Most lake craft were of the small rowing type, with sails for use only when the wind was from the rear. Nobody knew much about shallow-water sailing craft in those days, and when an ingenious British officer of Carleton's invading force invented a centerboard (or drop keel), his superiors were not smart enough to approve its adoption.

Carleton tried to move schooners and a large gundalow from the St. Lawrence into Lake Champlain by using rollers to bypass the rapids of the Richelieu River, but this otherwise feasible operation was frustrated by soft ground. He therefore had to disassemble these craft, carry the parts overland, and put them back together at St. Johns. Gunboats and provision boats (bateaux) were likewise carried past the rapids, many of them having been received in frame from England. Others were built at St. Johns, including a 422-ton sailing scow, *Thunderer*, 92 feet in length and 33 in beam, carrying a complement of three hundred men and fourteen guns. Being unable to work to windward because of its flat bottom, *Thunderer* did not figure in the action on the lake.

When the Americans withdrew from Canada they had three vessels captured in earlier operations: the schooners *Liberty* and *Royal Savage* and the large sloop *Enterprise*. The schooner *Revenge* was being built at Ticonderoga, and frame timber was evacuated from St. Johns to build the cutter *Lee* at Skenesboro.

Arnold was an experienced seaman, having sailed his own ships to the West Indies and Canada before the Revolution. He was also a human dynamo, and even as he fought the desperate rear-guard action of the American army as the British drove it from Canada in June 1776, Arnold apparently was forming his own plans for building a fleet on Lake Champlain to challenge their further advance. Two months later, on 24 August, he had ten craft ready, and on this date he sailed north from Crown Point to start his own naval war with the British. On 4 October the British started south with a large flotilla, having gotten underway three weeks earlier with land operations.

Although Valcour Bay turned out to be the ideal place for the improvised American fleet to fight the vastly superior British flotilla, Arnold had moved into it on 23 September merely because it was a good anchorage. Carleton was sailing cautiously south when, on 10 October, he learned that the American fleet was somewhere in the vicinity of Cumberland Head. The next day he shot past Valcour Island with a strong wind and had gone 2 miles beyond his quarry before he realized it.

Arnold now had fifteen vessels under his command, three of the captured craft mentioned above (the *Liberty* was off on another mission) and twelve of those built by his superhuman efforts since June. Starting his troops working with available tools in an improvised boatyard at Skenesboro (now Whitehall), Arnold had called for and gotten craftsmen and materials from Albany and the coastal ports. More than two hundred men eventually showed up, commanding exorbitant wages but getting the work done. Critical naval supplies and armament were available because the shipyards in New York and Philadelphia were blockaded.

Knowing that his craft would be manned by inexperienced men, Arnold rigged his four galleys with short masts and lateen sails, giving them the minimum amount of canvas and cordage for his landsmen to fumble with. These galleys, all but one finished in time for the battle, were about 72 feet on deck, 20 feet beam, and a little over 6 feet in the hold. Their complement was eighty men. Although the armament was varied somewhat, the *Washington* mounted two 18-pounders, two 12-pounders, two 9-pounders, four 4-pounders, one 2-pounder, and eight swivel guns.

One of the eight gundalows in action at Valcour Bay was recovered in 1935 and is on display in the Smithsonian Institution in Washington, D.C. Built to carry one 12-pounder and two 9-pounders, the gundalows were essentially rowboats, although they were rigged with two square sails on a single mast and could be very fast in a favoring wind. Pointed at both ends, the gundalow *Philadelphia* as salvaged and now exhibited is 54 feet in length, 15 feet in beam, and approximately 5 feet deep. It was constructed almost entirely of oak, and the hull timbers were still in place when she was lifted 57 feet from the sandy lake bottom near the mid-channel of Valcour Bay. A cannonball remained lodged in the hull, and two shot holes are visible. The mast, nearly 36 feet high, had only the top section missing. In addition to its three cannon, the hull contained shot, cooking utensils, tools, buttons, buckles, and human bones. The *Philadelphia* and the schooner *Royal Savage* were the only American vessels left behind by Arnold at Valcour Bay, and the latter ship, which burned and exploded, was salvaged in 1934. The Lake Champlain Maritime Museum has a working replica of the *Philadelphia* at Basin Harbor, Vermont.

The Battle of Valcour Bay, 11 October 1776, started with the British fleet coming about and heading for Arnold's little fleet in the south bay. Arnold's first concern was to lure the enemy into engaging him from this direction, against the wind, rather than sailing back around the island and entering the channel from the north. Ordering most of his vessels to form a line of battle across the channel just south of the high bluff on Valcour Island, Arnold had sent the schooner *Revenge* out to lure the enemy back. (He was not sure that they had detected the presence of the American fleet in the bay.) Four of his fastest vessels—*Royal Savage* and the galleys *Congress, Trumbull,* and *Washington*—sallied forth to do what damage they could to the British in the initial phase of the action, and also to draw the enemy into attacking from this direction. The stratagem succeeded, but the *Royal Savage* ran aground on the southwest tip of the island and was given a crippling broadside by the British schooner *Carleton.* The latter then got into trouble with the same treacherous winds of the narrow channel that had done in the *Royal Savage,* and to keep from being blown straight into the American line the *Carleton* had to throw out anchors. The other British sailing vessels could not work their way against the wind to support the *Carleton,* which was receiving the massed fire of the American line, but about seventeen British gunboats came up on line with it. At a range of about 350 yards the general engagement lasted from about 12:30 until dusk, which began to fall around 5 P.M. The British ships then withdrew to a line 600 or so yards farther south and continued their firing until dark.

By all rights the British should have been able to destroy the trapped American flotilla the next day, but Benedict Arnold again proved his military genius. Taking advantage of a dark, foggy night and a favoring wind, he slipped out in single file through the British fleet. The wind then turned, however, and, despite ten hours of backbreaking rowing and pumping, the last five of Arnold's battered craft had covered only 8 miles. The *Enterprise, Revenge,* and *Trumbull* made good their escape to Crown Point, where they joined the *Liberty.* The rest of Arnold's fleet was destroyed in a two-day pursuit. He beached his surviving craft, *Congress* and four gundalows, in Buttonmold Bay, near modern Panton, Vermont, and burned them with their colors flying. That night he led his two hundred survivors to Crown Point, about 10 miles away.

Van Alstyne House, Mohawk Valley, in Canajoharie on Moyer Street near N.Y. 5S. Central location and solid construction of this long, low stone house made it a popular meeting place for Patriots throughout the Revolution. At least sixteen meetings of the Tryon County Committee of Safety took place here; Washington was a visitor in 1783. It is now a private clubhouse. Marte Janse (or Martin Gerritse) Van Alstyne built the one-and-a-half-story house in 1749 or 1750. It remained in good structural condition until the Fort Rensselaer Club restored and furnished it. The historic structure can be seen from the street, and the club will make special arrangements for public tours. Phone: (518) 673-3317.

Van Cortlandt Manor, Croton-on-Hudson. Called the most authentic survival of the eighteenth-century Dutch-English manorial house of the Hudson Valley, this is a restoration on 173 acres of the original manor house, ferry house, and ferry-house kitchen. The manor house was built in 1639, remained for two centuries in the family, and is now part of Historic Hudson Valley and serves as a living-history museum. It is open to the public daily except on Tuesday; the hours change depending on the time of year. Phone: (914) 631-8200.

Van Cortlandtville, Westchester County, northeast of Peekskill on Oregon Road about 2 miles from U.S. 9. The village grew up around the Upper Van Cortlandt Manor

House, which still stands, much altered, as the Cortlandt Nursing Home on Oregon Street. Washington often stayed here. St. Peter's Church, an exceedingly simple brick structure built and opened in 1767 for the Van Cortlandt tenants, is a charming example of an eighteenth-century Anglican chapel. The cemetery contains the grave of General Seth Pomeroy, who died 19 February 1777 in Peekskill. This elderly veteran of the Colonial Wars, who had fought as a private on Bunker Hill, was on his way to join the army in New Jersey as a major general of Massachusetts militia when he died of pleurisy. There is a monument to John Paulding, a Peekskill man lionized for his role in the capture of André. The graves of fifty-four Revolutionary soldiers are here, and a monument to these Peekskill men is near St. Peter's. The site of Dusenbury Tavern, where André was put up when en route to Tappan (see TAPPAN HISTORIC DISTRICT), is marked on Oregon Road north of St. Columbanus Church. Gallows Hill Road leads north from the village to the hill where a tablet memorializes the hanging of a Loyalist spy. It continues to Soldier's Spring, where a Patriot was killed by the British on 9 October 1777 when they occupied Peekskill. This road is the colonial route to Albany and leads to the Continental Village Site. The Cortlandt Historical Society organizes tours of local sites if given proper notice. Phone: (914) 734-1110.

Van Schaick Mansion, 1 Van Schaick Avenue, Van Schaick Island, Cohoes. Built in 1735 by Anthony Van Schaick, this house was headquarters during the Seven Years' Wars for Sir William Johnson, Lord Loudoun, General Abercromby, and Lord Jeffrey Amherst. In 1777 it was headquarters for Generals Montgomery, Schuyler, and Gates, and here took place the planning that led to the decisive American victory at Saratoga. In the War of 1812 the house again was a military headquarters. The house has been owned and maintained by the DAR since 2001 and is usually open to the public from 2 P.M. to 4 P.M. on Thursday and Sunday, although that schedule fluctuates for lack of available guides. Calling first is advised. Phone: (518) 235-2699.

Verplanck's Point (Fort Lafayette Site), on Hudson River opposite Stony Point. The eastern end of strategic Kings Ferry, it was defended by Fort Lafayette until the small garrison of that place (one officer and seventy-two troops from North Carolina) surrendered to overwhelming British strength on 3 June 1779. The British built several earthworks on Verplanck's Point and tied them together with an extensive system of abatis. A year later the position was back in American hands.

In the interesting little river town now called Verplanck Point there are no vestiges of Revolutionary War works. The site of Fort Lafayette is covered by modern homes. To reach this spot, continue southwest on Broadway through the center of town and turn right on Third Street. Bear left on Lafayette Street and follow it a short distance to the top of the hill.

Washington Headquarters (Hasbrouck House), 84 Liberty Street, in the center of Newburgh at the intersection of Washington Street. The commanding view of the Hudson is obscured by buildings, but the historic house stands in a 7-acre park that preserves something of its original setting. A two-story museum (1910) adjoins the exceptionally well-preserved house, and the park contains monuments and cannon. The site has special significance for preservationists, its acquisition in 1850 by local citizens having set a precedent for the establishment of historical house museums in America.

The house was used by Washington as a headquarters and residence for almost seventeen months at the end of the Revolution (April 1782–August 1783), longer than he remained anywhere else during the war. During this period he met the greatest challenges to his personal leadership and showed the qualities that earn him the title Father of His Country. First he flatly and candidly rejected the proposal that he head a monarchy in America. Then he met the so-called Newburgh Conspiracy head-on and flattened it (see NEW WINDSOR CANTONMENT). Finally, among the historic documents he drafted at Newburgh, his circular letter to the governors of the states outlined his views on how the new nation should be developed.

Here too he created the first American military award, the Order of the Purple Heart. This has attracted considerable interest, even though only three of the decorations are known to have been given out in Washington's time. The order was not revived until 1932, and it was subsequently awarded to all those wounded in action. (Posthumous award to those killed in action is automatic.)

Construction of the Hasbrouck House was started in 1725. The northeast portion was erected by Jonathan Hasbrouck in 1750, the year after his mother bought the property. Jonathan became a prosperous farmer-merchant and served during the first years of the Revolution as militia colonel. Forced by bad health to resign his commission in 1778, he died two years later. His widow reluctantly agreed to make the house available to Washington in 1782, and she lived temporarily with relatives on Huguenot Street in New Paltz. Having come to the house as a bride, she subsequently lived there until her death in the 1830s. In 1850 the state obtained possession and restored it to what is believed to have been its appearance in 1782.

A large central room has seven doors and a single window, the consequence of piecemeal enlargement of the house. Another curiosity of this room is a fireplace without jambs and with a chimney beginning at the level of the second floor. In the house's exceptionally large attic can be seen the maze of hand-hewn roof timbers.

The house and museum are open year-round for groups with reservations. It is open to the public April through October from Wednesday to Saturday, 10 A.M. to 5 P.M., and Sunday from 1 P.M. to 5 P.M. Phone: (914) 562-1195.

Washington Masonic Shrine. *See* TAPPAN HISTORIC DISTRICT.

West Canada Creek. The site where the notorious Walter Butler of Butlersbury met his death is lost beneath the waters of Hinckley Reservoir, probably where Black Creek entered West Canada Creek. In a rearguard action on 30 October 1781, at a spot known variously by the names Butler's Ford, Jerseyfield, Poland, and West Canada Creek, Captain Walter Butler was left mortally wounded after a six-hour skirmish. Many myths are associated with the death of this remarkable Loyalist leader. What seems reasonably certain is that his scalp was taken to Albany and his body was left near where he died, probably to feed the wolves. The legend that he was secretly buried by Loyalists at Schenectady beneath abandoned St. Paul's Church is more than even the most gullible has ever taken seriously. His executor probably was an Oneida, perhaps the part-African "Colonel Louis." (See FORT KLOCK.)

West Point Military Reservation, Hudson River, on N.Y. 218 off U.S. 9W. A relief map of the northeastern United States will make clear the strategic significance of the Lake Champlain, Mohawk River, Hudson River waterway. Somewhat less evident at first glance is that the major geographical barrier along this natural invasion route is formed by the Hudson Highlands, a mere 45 miles from the Atlantic. The narrow but deep estuary of the Hudson, navigable to oceangoing vessels for 150 miles (to Troy, 6 miles above Albany), winds between steep hills in the Highlands, and West Point is the ideal location for a fortress guarding the northern end of this 12-mile defile.

The first river fortification undertaken by the Patriots in the Highlands was on the island opposite West Point. Called Fort Constitution, it was never fully developed because in 1776 the decision was made to build Forts Clinton and Montgomery, about 10 miles down the river around Bear Mountain. But recent archaeology has discovered interesting remains of Revolutionary War works, and there are ruins of half a dozen or so little forts and redoubts on what is now called Constitution Island (then Martelaers Rock). The Warner House, built after 1836 on remnants of a stone cottage of colonial days, has been restored and preserved.

In the spring of 1778 the Patriots started making West Point into what Washington would later call "the key to America." Work was begun under the direction of General Israel Putnam and his cousin Rufus Putnam. Fort Putnam, the landmark that caps the rocky hill above the United States Military Academy today, was reconstructed in 1907, and extensive development of this picturesque site was started on the eve of the bicentennial. How much the Putnams had to do with designing the West Point fortifications is debatable, but European professionals soon took over. French-trained Thaddeus Kosciuszko, a Pole serving as a colonel of engineers in the Continental army, was in charge from March 1778 until June 1780. Much of the planning was done by Colonel Louis de La Radiere.

Today's visitor to West Point will see many vestiges of the old fortifications. Accessible by trails in the rocky hills are four redoubts and a gun battery to the west and south of Fort Putnam. On lower hills are Redoubts Wyllis and Meigs. Trophy Point, on the north edge of the Plain, has cannon captured during the Revolution and several links of the 180-ton chain that stretched across the Hudson here. Forged at the Sterling Iron Works in the Ramapo Valley, the links are 2 feet, 9 inches long. (The chain was held up by log rafts.)

Kosciuszko's Monument is on the parapet of Fort Clinton, near the northeast corner of the Plain. Designed by a West Pointer, it was erected by the corps of cadets in 1828. (The Polish hero died in 1817, having remained in America until 1798. He spent the rest of his life striving, unsuccessfully, for the revival of Poland.) In 1913 the statue was added to the monument by the Polish Clergy and Laity of the United States.

Washington Monument, just east of Trophy Point, is a replica of the statue in New York City's Union Square.

The West Point Cemetery, off Washington Road and less than half a mile west of the Plain, contains the grave of "Captain Molly" in a prominent spot near the front of the Old Cadet Chapel. This heroine in the defense of Fort Washington (under NEW YORK CITY see FORT TRYON PARK) died in 1800 and was reinterred here in 1926. Inside the chapel (built in 1837 near the site of the present library, and reconstructed here in 1911) are black marble shields inscribed in gold letters with the name, rank, and dates of birth and death of senior American generals in the Revolution. One shield, high in the southeast corner, has all of the inscription chiseled out except "Major General" and "1741."

Major General Benedict Arnold, born in 1741, was one of the best troop leaders this country ever produced. Although General Washington fought to see that Arnold got the recognition he deserved for combat service, the Continental Congress had a way of leaving him off promotion lists. Arnold also was plagued by financial difficulties, and for these and other reasons he finally made up his mind to seek his military fortune on the British side. (See also MOUNT PLEASANT, under PHILADELPHIA, Pennsylvania.) Arnold and the British agreed on a general plan of action. The Rebel general would arrange with his own authorities to get command of a large American force. He would then arrange with the British authorities to surrender this force, and the British would pay him for his services.

Command of the Hudson Highlands impressed Arnold as being the ideal assignment, and in August 1780 he got it. For the preceding fifteen months he had been dealing through intermediaries with Major John André, the talented young aide to the British commander in chief. Now the time had come for a personal meeting to settle final details.

André came up the river on the armed sloop *Vulture* and had a clandestine meeting with Arnold in the woods south of Stony Point. Before he could return to the sloop it was driven off by two cannon that the enterprising Colonel James Livingston moved into position below Peekskill. Arnold then arranged for André to be guided through the American lines on the east side of the Hudson, and the British officer was captured at Tarrytown.

Arnold was having breakfast at the Robinson House and expecting a visit from Washington when he learned that André had been seized with incriminating documents in his possession. Arnold gave his young wife Peggy the news, hurried to his barge on the pretext of rushing to West Point on urgent business, and headed down the river to the *Vulture.* Peggy had been intimately involved in her husband's negotiations with the British from the start, but she put on such a great act that the Patriots never suspected her complicity.

Not until about six hours after Arnold's departure did Washington and his officers learn the essential facts. They then moved hurriedly to reorganize the defenses of the Highlands that Arnold had so carefully weakened and to make sure that reliable officers were in key spots. But these precautions turned out to be needless: none of Arnold's subordinates had been involved in the plot, and no British expedition was en route to attack the Highlands. André was imprisoned, tried, convicted, and hanged as a spy at Tappan (see TAPPAN HISTORIC DISTRICT). In 1821 his remains were moved to Westminster Abbey. Reminders of his tragic story survive in many landmarks throughout the lower Hudson Valley.

Arnold's only monument, which refers to him as "the most brilliant soldier of the Continental Army" but does not mention his name, is the curious one at Saratoga (see SARATOGA NATIONAL HISTORIC PARK). The British gave him pay, pensions, and a field command, but it was not enough for Arnold. After leading a number of destructive raids in Virginia and Connecticut, he went with Peggy and their children to London in December 1781. There he carried on an unsuccessful intrigue against General Sir Henry Clinton for an important military assignment in America. After the war he turned to commerce and died a broken and impoverished man in 1801. Peggy followed him to the grave only three years later. Their children were given British pensions, partly through the interest of Cornwallis, and gained considerable distinction in England. One son became a lieutenant general, and a grandson was a major general in World War I.

The West Point Military Reservation, the oldest United States military post over which the country's flag has flown continuously, is open to the public. Start at the visitors information center near the site of the former Ladycliff College Library. Call for an orientation and for current information on tour schedules. Phone: (845) 938-2638. Over three million people per year visit West Point.

Whitehall, Washington County. In a rocky ravine at the mouth of Wood Creek and at the southern tip of Lake Champlain, this place was called Skenesboro until after the Revolution. Although notoriously unhealthful, the site was perfect as a shipyard. Craft for American fleets on Lake Champlain were built here during the Revolution and the War of 1812, inspiring local boosters to call Whitehall the birthplace of the American navy. "Hardly a vestige of the Revolution is now left there," Benson Lossing found as long ago as 1848. But a detour off U.S. 4 to the grounds of the Skenesborough Museum (which has a model of the 1776 harbor) is recommended. On the grounds, under a long shed, is the giant hulk of the U.S.S. *Ticonderoga* (1814), and there is a picnic area alongside the lock of the Champlain Canal (which is active). Hours vary through the year; phone: (518) 499-1155.

White Plains, Westchester County. A major engagement fought here on 28 October 1776 was another defeat for the Patriots, but Sir William Howe again failed to follow through on his tactical victory and force the showdown that might have ended the Revolution here by annihilating Washington's little army. After their easy successes on Long Island and in Manhattan, British and German regulars had advanced slowly from Pell's Point (now Pelham Bay Park) to reach New Rochelle on 21 October. Colonel Rufus Putnam had made a remarkable ride of more than 50 miles in twenty-eight hours to gather information that indicated the British were headed for White Plains. Vital supplies for the Patriot army were at that place, and Washington therefore put his entire force in march from around Kings Bridge (now in the Bronx) to White Plains. The Americans were moving into the little village (strung out along what now is Broadway, Tibbetts Park being the remnant of the village green) as the enemy occupied New

Rochelle and vicinity. General Howe waited a week before resuming his leisurely advance, and during this time the Patriots dug in.

Chatterton's Hill was not part of their position initially. Washington's forces were deployed from the Bronx River, across Purdy Hill (Church Street and Park Avenue), through the village, over Hatfield Hill to Merritt Hill (in West Harrison on Lake Street, overlooking Silver Lake).

Additional German reinforcements joined General Howe while his army prepared to resume its advance, and on 28 October he massed his thirteen thousand regulars in the open area between today's Mamaroneck Avenue and Rochambeau School on Fisher Avenue.

Chatterton's Hill had been recognized belatedly by Washington as a critical piece of terrain, and it was not until the morning of the battle that Continental regulars started moving to reinforce the Massachusetts militia already on the hill. Howe's military mind told him that this was the key to the battlefield, and here the only real fighting took place. British military historian Sir John Fortescue concludes that Howe lost the Battle of White Plains by failing to execute his planned attack on the main American position simultaneously with the assault on Chatterton's Hill.

In a ridiculous contest between German and British commanders to exhibit the superior courage and discipline of their own regiments, the brightly uniformed European regulars finally took the hill. Two Continental regiments particularly distinguished themselves in repelling the first two attacks and delaying the final assault. These were the Third New York and the Maryland regiments, under Colonels Rudolph Ritzema (who defected to the enemy about a year later) and William Smallwood. Other Continental units withdrew in good order after their right flank was exposed by the panic-stricken flight of the Massachusetts militia. The latter fled along what is now Battle Avenue pursued by dragoons, crossed the wooden bridge where Main Street now spans the Bronx River, and straggled north along the riverbank to Purdy Hill.

Here Washington had watched the battle. It is thought that he had his quarters during the period 23 to 28 October 1776 in the Jacob Purdy House on Spring Street before moving back to the Miller House (below). During the summer of 1778 Washington used the Jacob Purdy House for almost two months. Saved from urban renewal in the 1960s, this wooden farmhouse, built in 1721, has since been restored and made the center of a park. The house, which is owned by the White Plains Historical Society, is located at 60 Park Avenue in White Plains. Tours are by appointment; phone: (914) 428-1776.

Having had to deploy through the village initially to assure evacuation of supplies, Washington now improved his defenses by dropping back from Purdy Hill and Broadway to Miller Hill and Mount Misery (as his cold and hungry troops soon dubbed it). The original positions on Hatfield and Merritt Hills were maintained. When the British moved field guns up to shell Hatfield Hill and Miller Hill, they were driven back by American fire, and Howe made no further effort to find a weak spot. The British withdrew south to capture the bypassed strongpoint of Fort Washington (see under NEW YORK CITY).

Most of the landmarks of this important but neglected battle have been preserved within the highly urbanized area of modern White Plains. Local organizations have collaborated in publishing an excellent guide, in establishing a Heritage Trail that links twenty-four sites, in saving and restoring houses and pieces of the battlefield, and in staging an annual reenactment of the battle.

The Elijah Miller House, on 140 Virginia Road in North White Plains at the foot of Miller Hill, is a story-and-a-half frame structure that Washington used for two weeks after he left the Purdy House (above). It is among the eighty-eight "Sites Also Noted" by the National Survey of Historic Sites and Buildings. The old bake oven is still in working condition, and various housekeeping activities are demonstrated in the kitchen. A table and set of chairs used by Washington and his staff are on display in the council room. Owned by the county and maintained by the DAR, the Miller House is open to the public by appointment. Phone (914) 949-1236.

Miller Hill (the next numbered stop on the Heritage Trail) has restored earthworks, explanatory signs, and a panoramic view. Mount Misery (next stop) has restored earthworks. Merritt Hill, on Lake Street in West Harrison, overlooking Silver Lake, is a picturesque spot where several hundred men from patriotic colonial organizations reenact the battle each year on a Sunday near the 28 October anniversary date.

On Chatterton's Hill a monument marks the crest where Alexander Hamilton's battery of two guns supported the 1,600 Patriot defenders. A private residence on Whitney Avenue occupies the site, and the monument is a cannon of the Spanish-American War.

Other landmarks are along the 3.5-mile drive, which is marked with metal signs.

Contact the White Plains Historical Society (Jacob Purdy House), 60 Park Avenue, White Plains, N.Y. 10603. Phone: (914) 328-1776.

Young's House, Four Corners, Westchester County, in Eastview on N.Y. 100C, in the triangle at the entrance to Grasslands Hospital. A memorial here marks the mass grave of soldiers from both sides killed nearby in a skirmish on the "Neutral Ground" on 3 February 1780. In violation of specific instructions not to remain long in any place with his patrol, a Patriot officer tarried in the vicinity of

Mount Pleasant. The British sent out an expedition of crack troops, many of them mounted, and annihilated the American force in an action that lasted only a few minutes. The 450 Patriots lost 14 killed, 37 wounded, and 76 captured, their commander and 6 other officers being among the prisoners. The 550 attackers—British guards, Hessian infantry and jaegers, and Westchester Loyalists—had 5 killed and 18 wounded.

NORTH CAROLINA

Almost 1,400 markers are included in the *Guide to North Carolina Historical Highway Markers.* Published in a handy pocket-sized format, it provides users with text descriptions and locations of North Carolina's distinctive silver and black markers, photographs of sites, a map, and a helpful index.

The State Department of Archives and History, which issues this guide, also offers a special listing of markers approved since 1990. This was also the year of the most recent edition of the guidebook. These post-1990 markers are viewable on the department's website. Guidebooks can be ordered through their website, by telephone (919-733-7442), or by mailing a request to the State Department of Archives and History, 4622 Mail Service Center, Raleigh, N.C. 27699-4622.

General tourist literature, some of which pertains to the state's colonial history, is mailed out by the Department of Conservation and Development, Travel and Promotion Division. The easiest way to access and/or order the information is via its website, www.visitnc.com, or by calling (919) 733-8372. There is another department within the tourism division that offers better detail, and in addition to the *2005 Official North Carolina Travel Guide*, a variety of other useful publications. Online it is accessible at www.NCCommerce.com (go to the tourism page) and by phone: (919) 733-8302.

Those with a personal or official interest in state and local history programs will find much in North Carolina to inspire them. Land and historic site preservation is a stated priority for the state, and there appears to be a tremendous effort by the state to communicate its extensive historic past. Another important source is the State Historic Preservation Office under the auspices of the Department of Cultural Resources, a division of the Archives and History. Phone: (919) 733-4763.

Some worthy literature is available through the private nonprofit, Historic Preservation Foundation of North Carolina, Incorporated. It offers many books and other publications for sale that lend more than a casual glance at North Carolina's Revolutionary War Landmarks. Website: www.presnc.org; phone: (919) 832-3652. Incidentally, this organization was formed in 1939 and was previously called, until 1974, the North Carolina Society for the Preservation of Antiquities.

Daniel W. Barefoot's *Touring North Carolina's Revolutionary War Sites* (Blair Publishing, 1998) is also a helpful source, especially for anyone planning a backwoods driving tour of the state's eighteenth-century landmarks.

Alamance Battleground State Historic Site, on N.C. 62 South, take Exit 143, 6 miles southwest of Burlington, Alamance County. There is more on the subject of protest and revolution at this site than meets the uninformed eye. Here, the coastal militia under Governor Tryon crushed a backwoods insurgency demanding a more efficient court system and equal recognition before the law.

The Regulators of North Carolina resented a government dominated by and responsive mainly to the desires of the coastal elite. Of particular concern was the Regulators' constituents' lack of representation in the provincial assembly, and the elite's manipulation of the court system to further impoverish those living inland (generally called the "piedmont"). The Regulators' name originated from their goal "to assemble ourselves for conference for regulating public grievances and abuses of power. . . ." They gained ever more popular support and essentially coopted government in the west of the province between 1768 and 1770, becoming more aggressive as the assembly persisted in ignoring their protests. Things came to a head in September 1770 when the Regulators moved into Hillsborough and confronted superior court judge Richard Henderson, demanding that he hear cases without benefit of attorneys. Henderson agreed, adjourning the court after five lawyerless hours, whereupon the Regulators "conducted me with great parade to my lodgings." They assaulted a future signer of the Declaration of Independence, William Hooper, and paraded him through the streets. They brutally whipped Edmund Fanning, a local official, and destroyed his home in Hillsborough.

Governor Tryon called out the coastal militia in March 1771 and prepared to send two columns into Regulator country to demand allegiance to the government. He personally commanded the 1,100 who marched from New Bern to Hillsborough, and General Hugh Waddell led 250 troops from the Cape Fear region to Salisbury. Waddell was moving from the latter place to join Tryon in Hillsborough when he met a small force of rebels at the Yadkin, so he returned to Salisbury. Tryon marched toward Salisbury and found a large body of about two thousand Regulators near Alamance Creek.

Lack of leadership had characterized the Regulator movement from the start. Hermon Husband, a pacifist, was the most prominent but not sole leader of the Regulators. Many Regulators sought to confront Tryon's army in battle, confident that their greater numbers would carry the field. The well-known teacher, preacher, and physician David Caldwell tried to mediate between the two armed forces, but he was unsuccessful.

Governor Tryon had a professional military background and a simple military mind when it came to dealing with armed rebellion. Although his force was outnumbered two to one and was forced to attack rather than defend, it was far better armed than the frontier Regulators. When Tryon sent the rebels the final warning that they must disperse or be fired on, their reply came back: "Fire and be damned."

The royal governor had a little trouble getting his militia to attack, but once the battle started it was more difficult to get them to stop. The Regulators had no artillery, no overall commander to coordinate the efforts of the individual companies of "infantry," and a good many of their men were unarmed. The first command that many Regulators gave themselves when Tryon's artillery dropped in their midst was "Let's get out of here!" When the coastal militia charged, the Regulators broke and ran. Tryon's men then set fire to the woods. The eastern militia suffered nine deaths, the Regulators somewhere between ten and twenty killed and many wounded. Twelve were captured, and one of the prisoners was executed on the field to prove that Governor Tryon was prepared to act forcefully in dealing with armed rebellion. The Regulator movement collapsed.

Tryon issued a proclamation offering pardons for Regulators who would swear allegiance, excluding only a few leaders outlawed under an emergency act. He then marched unopposed through Regulator territory administering the oath of allegiance with great success. The Alamance prisoners were tried at Hillsborough; six were hanged there and the rest were pardoned. At the outbreak of the Revolution all of the outlawed leaders except Hermon Husband were pardoned, but many Regulators had been forced to emigrate in 1772 to the wilder settlements of Tennessee and Kentucky, and others had followed as soon as they could sell their property.

Many former Regulators supported the patriot cause in North Carolina, James Hunter being a member of the legislature during the years 1777 to 1782. Husband, meanwhile, was long gone. With a large price on his head, he abandoned his fine plantation on Sandy Creek in the northeast portion of modern Randolph County. Under an assumed name he lived several years in the wilds of western Pennsylvania at Coffee Springs Farm near modern Somerset. Husband was a leader in the Whiskey Rebellion (1794), and was condemned to death but pardoned. (A highway marker on U.S. 219 east of Somerset says he was the region's first settler. The village of Husband is about 3 miles north-northwest of Somerset, Pennsylvania. In North Carolina is a highway marker on U.S. 421 just south of Siler City, Chatham County, saying Husband's farm was here; presumably this was one he owned before moving to Sandy Creek.)

The 40-acre Alamance Battleground State Historic Site, one of sixteen historic sites administered by the Department of Archives and History, is open throughout the year. It includes the central portion of the battlefield, where there are monuments, markers, a visitors center, field exhibits, an audiovisual program (including a twenty-five minute film, *The War of the Regulation*), and a picnic area. In 1967 the Allen House was opened to the public here after being donated by descendents of the Allen family and moved from Snow Camp, where the interesting log house was built sometime between 1780 and 1782 by John Allen. Husband married John's sister in 1776.

The site of Tryon's Camp on Alamance Creek, 13 to 19 May 1771, is marked on N.C. 62 at the village of Alamance, just north of the battleground. In May, Alamance Battleground Historic Site celebrates the anniversary of the battle. The site is open from 9 A.M. to 5 P.M. every day except Sunday. Phone: (336) 227-4785.

Albemarle, Museum of the, just south of Elizabeth City on at 1116 U.S. 17 South, Pasquotank County. Phone:

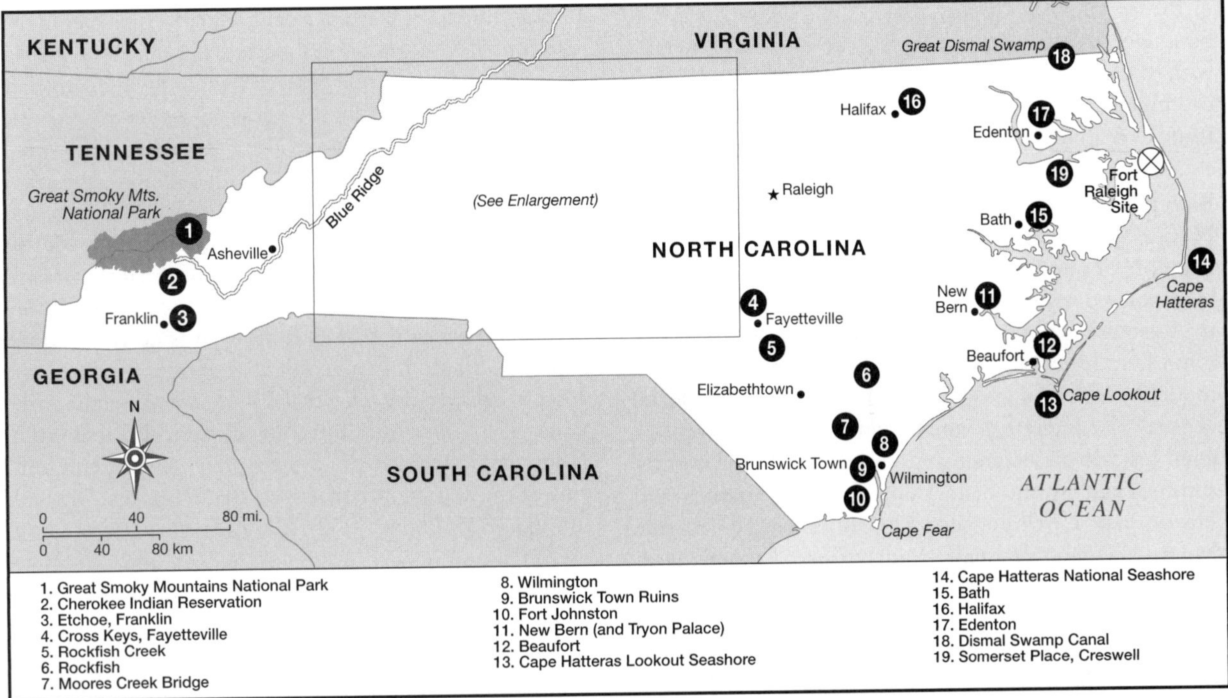

MAP BY XNR PRODUCTIONS. THE GALE GROUP.

(252) 335-1453. This regional museum interprets the history of the ten counties bordering Albemarle Sound. Opened in 1967, it is a remarkable example of how people with an intelligent interest in their history can go about organizing a modern regional museum, and it will appeal primarily to those from other parts of the country who have this concern in their own community. Exhibits are devoted to the geography and culture of the Albemarle area, site of the state's earliest settlements. A museum shop sells work of local craftsmen and publications relating to the exhibits.

Alston House. *See* HOUSE IN THE HORSESHOE.

Balfour Cemetery, near Asheboro Municipal Airport, Randolph County. Colonel Andrew Balfour is remembered primarily as one of David Fanning's most prominent victims. He was killed on 10 March 1782 when about twenty-five Loyalists raided his plantation; Fanning cold-bloodedly put a bullet in Balfour's head as his sister and daughter watched in horror. Balfour's widow became the first woman postmaster in the United States, appointed by Washington to that position in Salisbury.

Andrew Balfour had come to America from Edinburgh in 1772, and in 1779 he acquired a 2,000-acre plantation in newly formed Randolph County. He was a colonel of militia, justice of the peace, member of the General Assembly, and a particularly outspoken enemy of the Loyalists. When David Fanning offered to cease operations if his followers were not required to oppose the British, Balfour went on record as saying: "There is no resting place for a Tory's foot upon the earth." Fanning reacted as we have seen.

Balfour's homesite and the family cemetery are about half a mile off the southern end of the municipal airport runway. On the prosperous hog farm of the Rush family, which acquired the property in the 1840s from the estate of Andrew Balfour, Jr., the neglected Balfour Cemetery of half a dozen headstones survives on a hillside between County Roads 1142 and 1199 (dead end). (The Balfour Cemetery is shown on the Army Map Service topographic map "Asheboro," 1: 50,000, 1964.) In 1997 the Colonel Andrew Balfour Chapter of the National Society Daughters of the American Revolution placed a monument in front of the colonel's headstone.

The site of "Fort Balfour," the fortified farm house from which Colonel Balfour was taken and murdered by Fanning, is near the cemetery on County Road 1142. It may be identified by evergreen trees and metal feed tanks surrounding a house subsequently erected on the spot.

Bettie McGees Creek, which forms the northern boundary of Uwharrie National Forest a few hundred feet from the Balfour Cemetery, is named for a heroine of the Revolution. County Road 1142, the northeastern boundary of the national forest, corresponds generally with the old Salisbury Road, along which lived many prominent Patriot militiamen and which was Fanning's route to Balfour's plantation from his base on Deep River.

Bath Historic Site, Pamlico River. The visitors center is on N.C. Route 92 (Carteret Street) in the town of Bath, Beaufort County. Settled about 1696 and the state's oldest incorporated town (1705), Bath had no important role in the Revolution and is now a quiet little place where several important historical structures fit harmoniously into a modern residential neighborhood. The town should be of particular interest to conservationists as an example of good historic preservation and restoration. In the portion administered by the State Department of Archives and History are a well-designed visitors center (1970), the handsome, architecturally interesting Palmer-Marsh House (1751), the Van Der Veer House (1790s), and the Bonner House (1830s). The Historic Bath Commission has played the key role in acquiring and furnishing these houses in cooperation with the state. The state site is open every day except Monday throughout the year. Phone: (252) 923-3971.

Beattie's Ford (lost site), Catawba River, 4 miles north of Cowan's Ford Dam on Lake Norman. A dramatic moment occurred here shortly after 2 P.M. on Wednesday, 31 January 1781. Dan Morgan's column had beat a retreat from Cowpens, South Carolina, hotly pursued by the main British force under Lord Cornwallis. General Greene had just reached this point after a hurried ride with a small escort from Cheraw, South Carolina, and General William L. Davidson rode up at the head of his North Carolina militia. As the three American generals and Colonel William Washington talked, they saw redcoats of the British advance guard approach the opposite side of the swollen Catawba River. Greene decided to take advantage of the river barrier to make a stand, particularly because this would be a way to use his newly joined militia under Davidson. Cornwallis showed his finest qualities of generalship on the Catawba by making his main crossing at Cowan's Ford, virtually destroying Greene's militia support. The site of Beattie's Ford is flooded by Lake Norman, about where old N.C. 73 used to cross the Catawba River.

Beaufort. One of the state's earliest seaports (surveyed in 1713), the town survives as a picturesque place of narrow, tree-bordered streets and charming architecture in the style of the Bahamas. Beaufort was held by pirates for two days in 1749, and the event is commemorated annually. The place was of little significance during the Revolution but figured in the War of 1812, and a hero of that period, Otway Burns, lies beneath a cannon of his privateer in the Old Burial Ground. A restoration program has helped retain Beaufort's unique character while the modern port of Morehead City and the vacation center of Atlantic Beach—both a few minutes' drive from Beaufort—keep pace with contemporary America. Since 1960 the Beaufort Historic Site has given tours of the historic buildings and burial grounds. Its website, www.beauforthistoricalsite.org, is chocked full of information on what the organization's three tours offer. It is headquartered at 130 Turner Street, just across the street from what is now named the John C. Manson House but was formerly named the Joseph Bell House. The Bell House was thought to be from 1767, but the Beaufort Historical Preservation Commission recently discovered, after some careful scrutiny of the house's infrastructure, that it was actually built around 1825. Phone: (252) 728-5225.

(The pronunciation here, incidentally, is "Bow-furt," whereas in South Carolina it's the Old English "Bew-furt.")

Bell's Mill, Muddy Creek, near its junction with Deep River, about 2 miles northwest of Randleman, Randolph County. This site figures prominently in contemporary accounts of the campaign of Guilford Courthouse. Cornwallis camped near here a few days before the battle and sent his baggage back to this area when he stripped for action on the evening of 14 March 1781. In a region of large-scale dairy farms today, you can see why Cornwallis found this location particularly well suited for a camp. In addition to a mill and other structures, it had several wide stretches of bottomland that furnished his horses excellent grazing and protection. (The mill itself was known after the Revolution by the names of the Walker and Welborn families, and the structure survived until it was demolished about 1967 in connection with development of the Randleman dam and reservoir.) After remaining for two days on the battlefield of Guilford, Cornwallis spent two days marching back to Bell's Mill, where he spent another two days resting and supplying his troops before continuing to Ramsey's Mill.

The plantation and grist mill were the property of William Bell. In 1779 he became the first sheriff of newly formed Randolph County, and the same year married the richest widow in the region, Martha McFarlane McGee. With the reputation of being "a little haughty," perhaps because of her affluence and the many disappointed suitors during the four years of her widowhood, Martha Bell became a heroine during the British occupation of the region. Standing up to Lord Cornwallis, she demanded protection of her property as a condition for its use, threatening otherwise to burn it down herself. Under the pretext of having to see Cornwallis about a grievance against his troops or of having to travel the roads at night

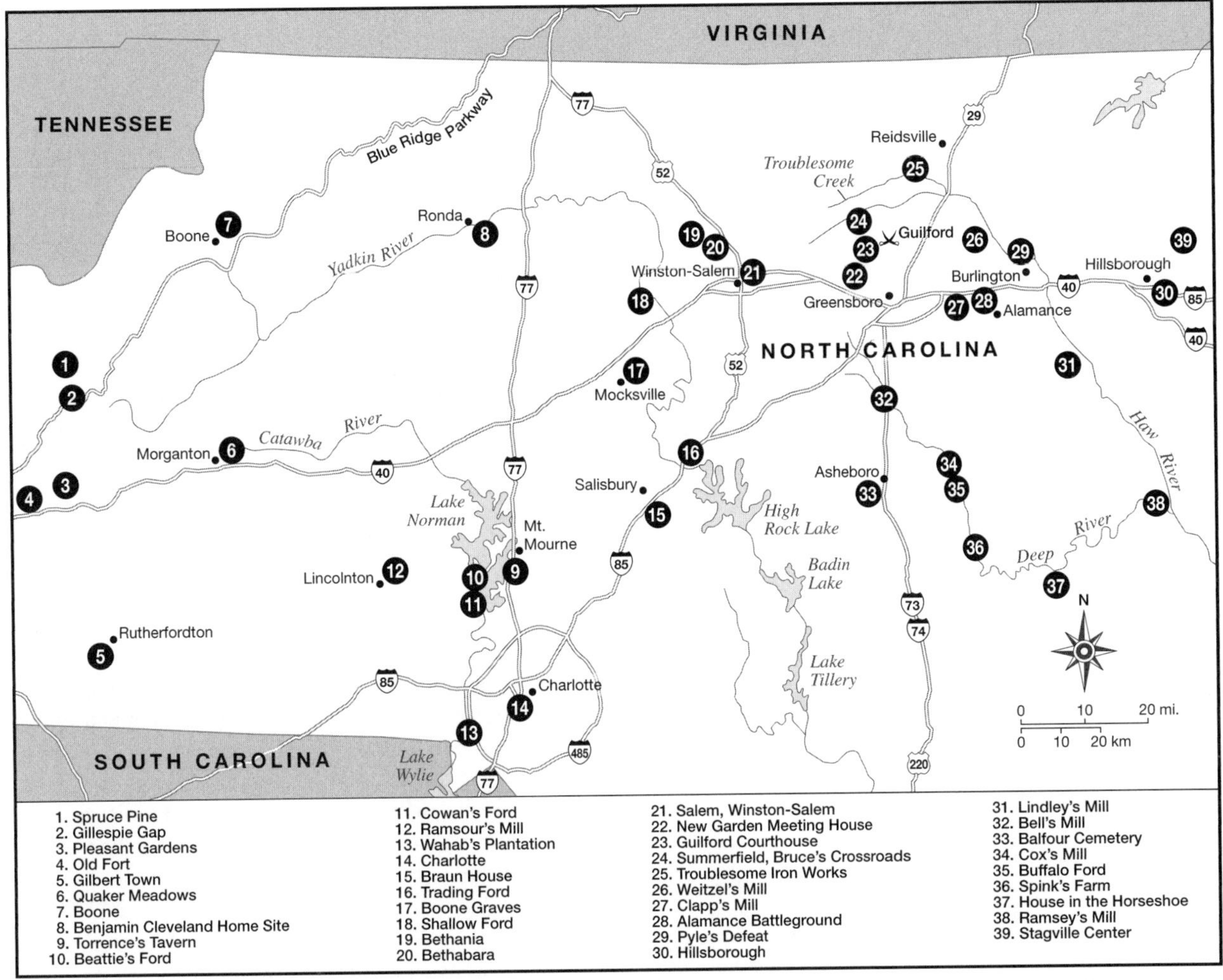

MAP BY XNR PRODUCTIONS. THE GALE GROUP.

on urgent business as a midwife, Martha Bell was a valuable intelligence agent for General Nathanael Greene's army. (Sheriff Bell was off with Greene all this time.) A monument to the heroine was unveiled in 1929 in Guilford Courthouse National Military Park.

The site has been of little interest to modern historians of the region, although Benson Lossing thought it of sufficient importance to locate it on the ground in 1849 (*Pictorial Field Book of the Revolution*, II, pp. 606–14 *passim*). In 2005 a proposal for a Randolph County Historical Park that would include Bell's Mill was put forth by the North Carolina Office of Archaeology. The site is just south of the Muddy Creek bridge of County Road 1939. Proceed west 0.8 mile, continue on County Road 1943 for 0.7 mile to Number 1944, and almost immediately turn south (left) on 1941 to the Bell-Welborn cemetery. It is visible from the road at about 100 yards to your left and can be reached in dry weather by a dirt road. Martha and her husband are buried there.

Bethabara, northwest of Winston-Salem on Bethabara Road about where Oldtown Road joins the latter from S.C. 67. Known during colonial days and during the Revolution as Dutch Fort or Old Town as well as Bethabara, this place was established in 1753 as the first of the "Moravian settlements" in the state. Nothing remains standing but the church built in 1788 (restored 1971) and a few houses, only two of which are older. But excavations in 1964 to 1966 revealed foundations, cellars, and several wells of the original settlement, yielding many important artifacts. The palisade of 1756 has been reconstructed on its original trace, ruins have been stabilized, and interpretive markers placed.

The state has many reminders of the Moravians and their Wachovia Colony, founded by Bishop Augustus Gottlieb Spangenberg (1704–1792) from a purchase of 100,000 acres in Lord Granville's grant. Fifteen unmarried Moravian men went from Bethlehem, Pennsylvania and founded Bethabara in 1753. Bethania was established six years later (it was called New Town), and Salem followed seven years later (1766).

The Moravians, who had left Europe to get away from war, were not having much luck. After surviving the Seven Years' War they went through the War of the Regulation and the Revolutionary War. Governor Tryon marched his army through the Moravian settlements after his victory at Alamance (see ALAMANCE BATTLEGROUND STATE HISTORICAL SITE). Loyalist prisoners from Kings Mountain, South Carolina were brought to Bethabara. Cornwallis passed through Bethania and Salem in 1781.

By 1770 Bethabara had lost its preeminence, overshadowed by Salem (see SALEM RESTORATION). Historic Bethabara Park is an interesting archaeological site dating from a conservation project started in 1964. In addition to the features mentioned above, this National Historic Landmark is a 175-acre wildlife preserve that includes many varieties of birds, a well-marked nature trail, and a vestige of the Old Plank Road. In addition to the restored church, the park's museum displays colonial exhibits, offers tours with costumed guides, and has a reconstructed village, fort, and Moravian gardens. The visitors center shows a video and houses exhibits from some of the recent archeology work done here. Phone: (336) 924-8191.

Bethania. On N.C. 65 between N.C. 67 and U.S. 52, a few miles northwest of Winston-Salem. The first of the Moravian settlements in this region, Bethabara, was known as Old Town after Bethania was settled as the "new town." Both were quickly overshadowed by Salem (see SALEM RESTORATION). The latter place also has eclipsed its two elder sister settlements in drawing funds for restoration, and little of colonial interest remains at Bethania other than its name.

Blue Ridge Parkway. This scenic highway generally follows the Proclamation Line of 1763, established in a vain attempt by British colonial authorities to limit the westward expansion of white settlements into Indian lands. There are numerous overlooks with magnificent panoramas of what once was America's western frontier. The parkway is administered by the National Park Service, and in addition to the scenic overlooks there are campgrounds, trails, picnic areas, interpretive markers, and recreation areas with special exhibits. In 1997 the Blue Ridge Parkway Foundation was initiated primarily to find funding for special projects along the scenic byway. Its website, www.blueridgeparkway.org, offers a wealth of information on the parkway, which turned seventy years old in 2005.

Boone. Now the seat of Watauga County, the site's first white visitor probably was Bishop Spangenberg (see BETHABARA) in 1752. An 18-foot stone monument at Faculty and Newland Streets marks the site of the cabin that Daniel Boone may have used occasionally during the period 1760 to 1769 while he explored the valleys of the New, Watauga, and Holston Rivers. Many of Boone's descendants remain in the area. Each summer the Daniel Boone Wagon Train follows state roads from North Wilkesboro to Boone along the trail blazed by the pioneer hero in 1773 when he led a party of settlers across the mountains. From late June through August a cast of 140 actors, including natives of the area, presents "Horn in the West," an outdoor drama by the late Dr. Kermit Hunter on the contribution of North Carolina's mountaineers to American history. Central characters in addition to Dan Boone are John Sevier, James Robertson, Governor Tryon, and "Butcher" Tarleton. "Horn" has been running since 1952. From 1956 until 1996 actor Glenn Causey played the role of Daniel Boone and never missed a performance in forty-one consecutive years.

Boone Graves, Mocksville, Davie County. The parents of Daniel Boone are buried in old Joppa Cemetery, surrounded by business and industrial development. A historical marker is on N.C. 601 about a mile northwest of the latter town. The graves are marked by a monument that encases the original headstones. Squire and Sarah Boone had established the Boone Homestead in Pennsylvania, where their famous son lived the first sixteen years of his life before the family moved to North Carolina.

Braun House (or Old Stone House). About 4 miles southeast of Salisbury, off U.S. 52 near Granite Quarry, Rowan County.

One of the few remaining Pennsylvania German stone houses in the state and of considerable architectural importance, this structure has a mysterious inscription on the front wall:

michael braun—mrichreda—brau io-pe-me-be-mi-ch-da-1766

Patriot prisoners were once held in the house, and an American officer is said to have escaped pursuers by galloping his horse through the open front door and out the back. The British dragoons were frustrated when the lady of the house slammed the door in their horses' faces.

Quite in addition to these and other charms, the Braun House is a monument to old-fashioned American craftsmanship. Its stone walls are 2 feet thick and rise two stories from a foundation that is 15 feet deep in places. Although most of its mahogany paneling has been stripped off and its beautifully plastered walls defaced by subsequent generations less appreciative of high living standards, the foot-wide floorboards and hand-carved wooden trim of the interior have survived.

On a hill, surrounded by old trees and with the family cemetery nearby, the house has been restored (1966) and furnished. Rowan Museum Incorporated originally purchased it in 1959, and 22 acres of surrounding land was subsequently purchased to protect the area from development. The house is open for tours on most weekends. Phone: (704) 638-3021.

(Rowan Museum, 114 South Jackson Street, Salisbury, N.C. 28144.)

Bruce's Crossroads. *See* SUMMERFIELD.

Brunswick Town Ruins, Cape Fear River below Wilmington. The plan for Brunswick Town (fortunately preserved) was drawn up by 1726, and until overshadowed by Wilmington a decade later, it was probably the most important town in North Carolina. At the start of the Revolution it still was shipping more naval stores than any other colonial town in the British Empire. Meanwhile, Brunswick Town had been the center of Stamp Act resistance in 1766. Two royal governors, Arthur Dobbs and William Tryon, resided at nearby Russellborough ("Old Palace"), and the latter was kept under virtual house arrest there by mobs under the leadership of John Ashe and Hugh Waddell during the Stamp Act disturbances.

In March 1776 British troops started arriving off Cape Fear after the Loyalist defeat at Moores Creek Bridge (see MOORES CREEK BRIDGE NATIONAL MILITARY PARK), the strategy being for expeditionary forces from New York and Ireland to link up and restore royal government in the province. On 12 May Sir Henry Clinton, frustrated by Patriot resistance, declared North Carolina to be in a state of rebellion, shelled Brunswick Town, and sent Lord Cornwallis ashore with nine hundred troops to ravage Rebel property. A principal objective was the plantation of Robert Howe, 2 miles from the town, and it was virtually destroyed. The raiders were stopped when they moved toward Orton's Mill. (Landmarks are now within the restricted area of Sunny Point Army Terminal, which adjoins the ruins of Old Brunswick on the south.) But the British destroyed Russellborough, which had become the home of the well-known Patriot William Dry.

Brunswick Town was so thoroughly wrecked and so vulnerable to further amphibious raids that not more than four families returned after 1776. By 1830 the site was completely abandoned. During the Civil War the Confederates built a huge earthwork, named Fort Anderson, over the northern portion of the old townsite, and in February 1865 it was captured after a heavy bombardment.

Brunswick Town State Historic Site is now a picturesque and exceptionally interesting area of stabilized ruins, nature trails, and the huge earthworks of the Civil War fort. The foundation walls of Russellborough are within the reservation, and the 33-inch-thick brick walls of St. Philips Church (built 1754–1768) still stand in defiance of destruction. Among the old tombs in its shadow are that of Governor Arthur Dobbs, who held office from 1754 until his death at Russellborough in 1765.

The site is about 15 miles by road from Wilmington. From U.S. 17 west of Wilmington, take N.C. 133 south along the Brunswick and Cape Fear Rivers, bearing left after a little more than 12 miles onto Route 1529 past Orton Plantation Gardens. It is open from 10 A.M. to 4 P.M. on Tuesday through Saturday. Phone: (910) 371-6613.

Buffalo Ford, Deep River, Randolph County, just north of County Highway 2628 bridge; about 2.25 miles straight-line distance above Coleridge. As the name implies, Buffalo Ford was a well-worn passage across Deep River long before the Revolution. General Kalb reached this point in late June or early July 1780 with the two Maryland brigades, the Delaware Regiment, and the First Continental Artillery (eighteen guns). He was joined by 120 survivors of Pulaski's Legion (now commanded by "Colonel Armand"). During the two weeks he was camped here Kalb learned that General Gates had been appointed to succeed him. He moved to Spink's Farm, where Gates arrived to assume command on 25 July. (Some authorities say this occurred at Cox's Mill, only about a mile north of Buffalo Ford.) The present highway bridge affords a good view of Deep River and the rocks of the ford about 100 yards upstream.

Cape Hatteras and Cape Lookout National Seashores. The influence of geography on the history of North Carolina has been summed up by William T. Polk in an introductory essay to *The North Carolina Guide*: "The State was not settled from the sea as Virginia and South Carolina were," but by pioneers who came overland. "Its Outer Banks fended off immigration from Britain and Europe," and this same formidable barrier was protection from British amphibious operations to which other colonies were so vulnerable during the Revolution.

These historic Outer Banks are being preserved as well over 100 miles of ocean beach, much of it accessible today only by water or air. The Cape Lookout area is one of the few remaining undeveloped beaches in America. The National Park Service now maintains its 56 miles of beach. The Cape Hatteras National Seashore has 76 miles of ocean beach, campgrounds, nature trails, visitors centers, and museums all linked by a hard surface highway (N.C. 12). A free ferry extends this road to Ocracoke Island. The phone number to the National Park Service headquarters that administers this entire zone is (252) 473-2111.

Carolina Charter (1663), North Carolina Museum of History, Raleigh. The original charter granted by King Charles II on 24 March 1663 was purchased by the state in 1949 after its discovery in England. Now displayed to the public, it is one of eight in the possession of modern American states. (The other charters are those for Connecticut, Delaware, Maryland, Massachusetts, New York, Pennsylvania, and Rhode Island.) As defined in this charter, eight lords proprietors were granted all the land from the Atlantic to the Pacific (the "south seas") lying between the thirty-first and thirty-sixth parallels. This wide swath of the present United States includes all or major portions of thirteen present states and slivers of four others. (At the request of the proprietors, Charles II in 1665 granted another charter, this one extending the boundaries one-half degree north and two degrees south.)

Charlotte. County seat of Mecklenburg County, Charlotte was a center of backcountry dissatisfaction with royal authority from the time the town was chartered in 1768. One particular grievance was royal disallowance of the charter for establishing Queens College for Boys in 1771 (the first college south of Virginia). On 31 May 1775 a committee met at Charlotte and drew up twenty resolutions for the state delegation to present to the Continental Congress. Although adopted, the resolutions were never presented to Congress. For many years the story that a "Mecklenburg Declaration of Independence" passed on 20 May 1775 circulated, but it was later found to be a nineteenth-century fabrication. The dates of these two documents, the real Resolves of 31 May and the contrived "Declaration of Independence" of 20 May, are often confused. The state of North Carolina still features the date of the dubious document in its seal and flag.

Now the largest city in the Carolinas, Charlotte was a village of about twenty homes and a courthouse when Cornwallis approached it on his invasion of North Carolina in 1780. A marker on N.C. 49 indicates the location of a skirmish that took place on 26 September of that year near the courthouse, where a small Rebel force under Colonel William Davie successfully repulsed two charges by Tarleton's legion before being forced to withdraw.

Tarleton had come down with yellow fever, and his legion was temporarily commanded by Major George Hanger. It would be hard to imagine two more similar men than these two, but Hanger had only recently suffered a humiliating defeat at the hands of Davie, who had surprised his bivouac at Wahab's (or Wauchope's) Plantation on 21 September. When Hanger saw Davie's little force of about one hundred men deployed to bar the British advance into Charlotte, the British officer ordered a charge. Hanger personally led the attack against the stone wall near the courthouse where twenty dismounted dragoons were posted. Repulsed, he charged again and was again unsuccessful.

This sort of work was not to the liking of Tarleton's troopers, who preferred their lighter cavalry duties, and Hanger was having trouble organizing a third attack when Cornwallis himself rode up to encourage the van. More significantly, however, the remarkable Lieutenant Colonel James Webster had reached the scene to direct the efforts of the light infantry against the Americans who were defending the fences along the road leading to the courthouse. Having fought off the earlier attacks directed by Hanger, these troops were now forced to fall back on the courthouse, and Davie ordered a withdrawal when Hanger and Webster launched their final assault. The British legion pursued vigorously for several miles, and at Sugaw Creek Presbyterian Church, 13 miles from Charlotte, there is a marker to Captain Joseph Graham (1759–1836), who was wounded in a skirmish at this place. American casualties in all these actions around Charlotte were thirty killed, wounded, and captured; the British lost about half that number.

Cornwallis called the region a "damned hornet's nest," his stay of less than a month in Charlotte being plagued by Rebel forces that chopped up his foragers and intercepted his messengers. Taking advantage of the concentration of grist mills in the area, however, he intended to continue his advance north when news of the Patriot victory at Kings Mountain, South Carolina on 7 October forced Cornwallis to abandon his plans and to march back into South Carolina.

Early in December 1780 Greene reached Charlotte to take command of the Southern army from Horatio Gates. A few days before Christmas the American army left Charlotte, Greene leading one column southeast to Cheraw, South Carolina and Morgan leading another southwest in the operations that ended with his triumph at the Cowpens, South Carolina. When Cornwallis invaded North Carolina in pursuit of Morgan and Greene early in 1781 he passed to the west of Charlotte, so the town was spared a second occupation by the British.

The Hezekiah Alexander House in Charlotte dates from 1774. (Alexander was a member of the Provincial Congress and helped draft the first state constitution in 1776.) Of piedmont stone, it typifies the two-story-and-central-passage plan that later appeared in many variations throughout the state. The house was restored in 1976 and serves as the home for the Charlotte Museum of History. It is located at 3420 Shamrock Drive and is open every day except Monday. Phone: (704) 568-1774.

Cherokee Indian (Qualla) Reservation, in the western tip of the state on U.S. 19 and 441, adjoining Great Smoky Mountains National Park; phone: (800) 438-1601. About forty highway markers in North Carolina identify sites associated with the Cherokee. Major expeditions against these Indians took place in 1761 and 1776, and defiant Cherokee established new towns on Chickamauga Creek in modern Tennessee to continue their resistance to the white invaders of their land until well after the Revolution. The nearly 57,000 acres of today's Qualla Reservation, commonly known as the Cherokee Indian Reservation, were the hideout for those who refused to leave their ancestral homeland during the forced removals of 1838, and these lands eventually were given to the Cherokee as a small recompense for all that had been stolen from them. Several hundred Indians here in the Eastern Band of the Cherokee are under tribal jurisdiction. Today there are twelve thousand Cherokee living on this reservation. The Oconaluftee Indian Village in the town of Cherokee is a re-creation of Cherokee culture. Ancient crafts are demonstrated by modern Cherokee Indians in woven cane and clay structures of the type they built before the arrival of white settlers and in the log cabins they subsequently adopted.

"Unto These Hills" is an open-air drama presented nightly (except Monday) from mid-June through 1 August. Fourteen scenes highlight the history of the Cherokee from De Soto's visit in 1540 to the forced removal of their nation in 1838. The Indian Museum in Cherokee (at Highway 441 and Drama Road) holds the largest collection of Cherokee artifacts. The museum opens every day at 9 A.M. Phone: (828) 497-3481.

Clapps Mill, Beaver Creek, Alamance County. A skirmish here on 2 March 1781 was the first contact between the armies of Greene and Cornwallis in their maneuvers before the Battle of Guilford Courthouse. Tarleton rode into a well-planned ambuscade near Clapps Mill, where Colonel William Campbell's riflemen were deployed behind a rail fence and Lee's mounted troops covered the flanks. The British recovered from the effects of the surprise fire, rallied, and forced Lee to retreat, but they had an officer and twenty men killed and wounded, whereas the Patriots suffered eight casualties.

The site is on Beaver Creek, just 200 feet from the stream's confluence with Big Alamance Creek. In 1992 a marker that commemorates the battle was placed at Huffman Mill Road inside Lake Macintosh Park and Marina.

Cleveland (Benjamin) Homesite, near Ronda, Wilkes County. Before the Revolution Wilkesboro was called Mulberry Fields. In 1779 Benjamin Cleveland was granted 3,400 acres in the horseshoe bend of the Yadkin River about a mile southwest of today's Ronda (N.C. 268). His tract was called Roundabout.

Cleveland had come to this region from Virginia around 1760 as an uneducated man in his early twenties, and he developed into an outstanding frontiersman. After service as a junior officer in the Second North Carolina Continentals for two years he resigned in the summer of 1777 and became a militia colonel, justice of the peace, chairman of the county committee of safety, and (1778) member of the House of Commons. In the fall of 1780 he gained credit as a major hero of Kings Mountain, South Carolina. "Cleveland's Bull Dogs" were the ruthless force of Whig domination in this northwest region of the state, unexcelled in their brutality by David Fanning's Loyalists in the central portion of the state (see DEEP RIVER). On the courthouse lawn in Wilkesboro is a very large tree known locally as the Tory Oak, and tradition has it that Cleveland hanged five men here, including a Loyalist who had previously spared Cleveland's life.

After losing Roundabout in a title dispute, Benjamin Cleveland moved to the portion of South Carolina that is now Oconee County. The site of his house is in open farmland about a quarter of a mile from a brick house built shortly before the Civil War and also called Roundabout. The original house disappeared before 1878.

Cowan's Ford (lost site), Cowan's Ford Dam of Lake Norman, N.C. 73, north of Charlotte. Destroyed by the creation of 32,510-acre Lake Norman in 1963, this is where British valor triumphed over the bad fortune of having a treacherous (or timid) guide in troubled waters. It was 1 February 1781 and the swollen Catawba was a torrent almost 500 yards wide at this place when Lord Cornwallis pushed across after dark to turn General Greene's main defensive positions farther up the river. The principal ford, Beattie's Ford, was a few miles to the north, near the present Iredell-Mecklenburg county line. What the British did not know was that Cowan's Ford split around midstream, the wagon ford continuing straight ahead and the shallower horse ford forking south at a 45-degree angle to exit several hundred yards below the other. General William L. Davidson posted most of his militia at the horse exit. When the British were deserted in midstream by their guide, they floundered forward in the face of enemy fire and naturally took the wagon route. This was harder going insofar as the water was concerned, but it led to the more lightly defended exit, where they secured a foothold before Davidson could shift strength from the horse ford. Davidson was killed as his troops were pushed back. British Generals O'Hara and Leslie were thrown into the water when their horses fell, and Cornwallis's mount collapsed on reaching the bank. There is a memorial near the modern dam to General Davidson, who had been promoted for gallantry at Germantown, Pennsylvania (4 October 1777), and served with distinction in his native state of North Carolina, notably at Ramsour's Mill, before being promoted to general and joining the forces of General Greene.

Lake Norman extends nearly 34 miles up the Catawba and has more than 520 miles of shoreline when filled. A detailed map and other literature, including some historical information on the region, may be had from the Lake Norman State Park. Phone: (704) 528-6350.

Cox's Mill, Mill Creek near junction with Deep River, County Road 2657, between Ramseur and Coleridge, Randolph County. It was Cox's Mill during the Revolution, and today it is operated on about the same scale (but with modern power) by members of the Cox family. About 50 feet east of the elderly frame structure of the present feed mill is a depression about 10 feet deep where the original waterwheel was located. Foundation stones can be seen there. From the bridge near the mill you look upstream at the shoals over which the colonial ford passed. The site is in a narrow, wooded valley into which the road dips from well-tended open farmland.

Marching from Morristown, New Jersey, to the relief of Charleston in the summer of 1780, a tired and hungry column of Continentals under General Kalb reached nearby Buffalo Ford. During the next two weeks they spent some time around Cox's Mill and Spink's Farm. Colonel David Fanning and his Loyalist partisans used Cox's Mill as their principal base in 1781 to 1782 (see DEEP RIVER).

Cross Creek. *See* FAYETTEVILLE.

Deep River, Guilford, Randolph, Moore, Lee, and Chatham Counties. There is a history book to be written some day about all the things that happened along Deep River during the Revolution. Its name crops up repeatedly in three distinct phases of the war. Here we shall merely group Deep River landmarks within these phases and then outline the career of the notorious Loyalist partisan who dominated the last phase.

When Continental army troops were first sent south to challenge the British invaders, the remarkable march led by General Johann Kalb reached Deep River in late June 1780. He moved along an 8-mile stretch during the next month, spending time at Buffalo Ford, Cox's Mill, and Hollingsworth's, or Spink's Farm. At this last place General Horatio Gates assumed command from Kalb and marched his troops off to disaster in South Carolina at Camden.

In the Guilford Courthouse campaign the British had an important base near Deep River at Bell's Mill, and Cornwallis was never far from the river (creek that it is this far up) as he moved through the New Garden Meeting House to Guilford Courthouse. After this major engagement he retraced his steps, and pursuit by the main Patriot army under General Greene ended near the mouth of Deep River at Ramsey's Mill.

With the final departure of the British and the Continentals, Deep River entered its most terrible phase of the Revolution as the domain of David Fanning. Born in Virginia around 1755, he had become a trader among the Catawbas of South Carolina while still in his teens. He served as a scout to Patriot militia in 1779 to 1780, but with the restoration of British rule in South Carolina he joined the the Loyalist militia under William "Bloody Bill" Cunningham. In July 1781 he was given a colonel's commission by the British commandant in Wilmington, Major James H. Craig, and raised troops in North Carolina.

He proved to be shockingly good as a partisan leader. The ink was hardly dry on his commission when Fanning led a surprise attack on Chatham County Courthouse while a court-martial was in session, and many prominent Whigs were among the forty-four prisoners he took away. (The site is the present town of Pittsboro, Chatham County.) Next came his victory at the House in the Horseshoe. But these were merely preliminaries to his greatest coup, the raid on Hillsborough. He then showed his ability as a tactical commander in a real battle at Lindley's Mill. When efforts were initiated by the Whigs to restore peace, Fanning was more than willing to work toward this end, but Patriot leaders made the mistake of refusing to compromise. The Loyalist leader then proceeded to kill one of their most prominent spokesmen, Colonel Andrew Balfour (see BALFOUR CEMETERY).

Deep River is lined with rocks and caves associated with Fanning, one better-known spot being around the mouth of Brush Creek, west of Cheeks (which is on S.C. 22 and 42 in the southeast corner of Randolph County). His main base appears to have been Cox's Mill.

In the spring of 1782 the terrible David Fanning found a bride, sixteen-year-old Sarah Carr. Early in May he moved to a truce area on the lower Pee Dee River in South Carolina, going to East Florida when the British evacuated the South, and then settling in New Brunswick, where he became a leading member of the assembly.

Colonel Tom Presnell, my authority on historic sites in Randolph County, took me to six spots that I had given up for lost. Most of them are unmarked and on private property. There are a few old mill towns along Deep River and some new industrial development, but the region remains generally an attractive rural area of rolling hills.

Dismal Swamp Canal, northeast corner of state on U.S. 17 just 3 miles south of the Virginia–North Carolina border. If Washington could revisit the Dismal Swamp today, he would feel better about his unsuccessful land speculation here as a young man. It remains a wild area of some 750 square miles. The canal for which Washington initiated surveys in 1763 was not started until after the Revolution. U.S. 17 parallels the canal and there are quiet parking spots from which you occasionally spot a beaver and other wildlife. More remote sections of the swamp are accessible by other canals. Information is available through the Dismal Swamp Canal Welcome Center. Phone: (252) 771-8333.

Edenton, head of Albemarle Sound, Chowan County. The region was explored in 1622 by Virginians, who came from Jamestown and its vicinity by 1658 to settle. The Town on Queen Anne's Creek, as it was called for six or seven years before being named for the royal governor who had just died, was surveyed in 1712 and incorporated in 1722. Modern Edenton lacks the colonial charm of such contemporary settlements as Bath (see BATH HISTORIC SITE) and Beaufort, having been more favored by economic progress, but several outstanding architectural treasures have survived. Yet, Edenton is often referred to in state travel guides as "the South's prettiest town."

The Cupola House (1715), 408 South Broad Street, whose pictures do not do it justice, has been called "the best example of an existing wooden house in the Jacobean tradition in all America," the only surviving example in the South of the second-story overhang, and an outstanding example of the transition from colonial to Georgian style. In 1917 the woodwork of the lower hall and two rooms were sold to the Brooklyn Museum of Fine Arts. The Cupola House Association was hastily formed at this time to save the house from destruction, and for the next forty-five years it was the county library. It has since been restored (the lost woodwork reproduced), named a National Historic Landmark, and is open daily as a house museum and as the Edenton Public Library. One curiosity of this venerable structure is that its shoulder is turned to the vulgarity of modern Edenton's main street, South Broad, and the house faces what used to be the waterfront.

The Chowan County Courthouse, 117 East King Street, reopened for public use in 2004. Constructed in 1767, it is one of the most handsome Georgian public buildings in the country. It is a National Historic Landmark. Facing the vestige of the Green, the two-story brick structure is topped by a graceful white cupola, and the warm red of its facade is accented by trim white windows and a small pedimented pavilion at the main entrance. Edenton Green is crowded on both flanks by modern streets so that it is now much smaller than when it was a militia parade, although there is enough room remaining to reinstall the stocks, rack, and pillory that supported law and order in a less sophisticated era. On the waterfront are three French cannon salvaged from a shipment that went down in Albemarle Sound in 1778; others are corner markers in the town, and two are in Capitol Square in Raleigh. On the Green is a monument to a prominent Edentonian, Joseph Hewes, a delegate to the Continental Congress, the one who presented the Halifax Resolves, and chairman of the Committee of Marine. Hewes got John Paul Jones commissioned in the infant navy, signed the Declaration of Independence, and gained the unfortunate distinction of being the only signer to die in Philadelphia (1779). As if to balance such things out, it happened that a Pennsylvania signer, James Wilson, died in Edenton while living as a guest in the James Iredell House in 1798.

The James Iredell House (1751), 105 East Church Street, was bought in 1778 by James Iredell, a distinguished jurist and member of the first United States Supreme Court who lived there the last eleven years of his life. It was also the home of his son James, who became governor of North Carolina and who died in the house when it was occupied by his cousin, the Reverend Samuel I. Johnston, rector of St. Paul's (below). James Iredell, Jr. had been a friend of James Wilson. When the latter was beginning to break under the stress of financial difficulties and threat of impeachment as Supreme Court justice, he moved to the home of his friend in Edenton to recover his health, but he died several months later. Open April through October, Monday to Saturday, 9 A.M. to 5 P.M., and Sunday, 1 to 5 P.M.; November through March, Tuesday to Saturday, 10 A.M. to 4 P.M., and Sunday, 1 to 4 P.M.

The Barker House (1782), 509 South Broad Street, makes a good starting point for your tour. Historic Edenton, Incorporated has exhibits, an audiovisual program, and guidebooks. Moved in 1952 from its original site at 213 Broad Street, this large and impressive white frame house was built for Thomas and Penelope Barker. Thomas had a long career in law and government before becoming a highly successful agent for the colony in London before the Revolution. Penelope figured conspicuously in the mythology of the Edenton Tea Party.

As for the latter, an episode that must be faced by any visitor to Edenton, it is a matter of record that fifty-one women of the town signed and mailed to England a resolution supporting the actions and resolutions of the First Provincial Congress (1774). One part of all this had to do with banning the import and consumption of British tea. A London cartoonist satirized the event by depicting provincial matrons gathered at a tea party to sign the document, and gullible Patriots subsequently pretended that such a tea party, in the literal sense, occurred. They then went on to invent a site, the home of Mrs. Elizabeth King, and to mark this with a bronze teapot on a post. Penelope Barker was picked to pour at this purely conjectural tea party. Responsible historical authorities have long rejected the story of the Edenton Tea Party in the literal sense, but they also have stressed that this resolution signed by the women of Edenton indicates the political activism of American women during the Revolutionary period. At the Barker House are excellent exhibits pertaining to the episode, including wall-size enlargements of London press coverage and the famous cartoon.

St. Paul's Episcopal Church (1736), 100 West Church Street, is another historic structure that deserves special note in this brief sketch. The second-oldest church building in the state, and described as "an ideal in village churches, unrivaled in this country except perhaps by Christ Church, New Castle, Delaware," it has survived neglect and fire to be fully restored.

The five sites mentioned above are included in a tour organized by Historic Edenton Incorporated. Special events are featured throughout the year, along with the tour that includes forty houses or points of interest within walking distance of parking areas at the Barker and Iredell houses. About fifteen more are within a short drive of the town. Historic Edenton's phone: (252) 482-2637 or (800) 775-0111.

Etchoe (or Echoe). Also known as Nikwasi, or Sacred Town, and now occupied by the town of Franklin, seat of Macon County, this was a Cherokee stronghold in the Indians' resolute efforts to stop the encroachment of white settlers. Twice destroyed and rebuilt, it was occupied by the Cherokee until 1819. A large map-marker at the courthouse touches on the highlights of the Cherokee Wars in this area.

The site of the most famous Indian battles in the area, generally called Etchoe Pass in the history books, is today known as Wayah Gap and is preserved in the Nanatahala Gap Campground. This is crossed by the Appalachian Trail, and less vigorous explorers can reach it by car. In this area, 10 miles straight west of Franklin, the Cherokee ambushed and badly mauled a force of British Highlanders and South Carolina militia in June 1760 before finally being defeated. Another expedition of the same general composition marched against the Cherokee the next year, and an untried lieutenant of South Carolina militia named Francis Marion distinguished himself at Etchoe Pass.

Fayetteville, Cumberland County. The colonial village and trading center of Cross Creek merged in 1778 with the settlement of Highland Scots known as Campbeltown. In 1783 Cross Creek became Fayetteville, the first town in America named for Lafayette. The place was important for two different reasons. First, it was the center of Highlander support of the crown in the events leading to the great Patriot victory at Moores Creek Bridge (see MOORES CREEK BRIDGE NATIONAL MILITARY PARK) on 27 February 1776. Second, being at the head of navigation of the Cape Fear River, it could have provided an important inland base for British military operations. Cornwallis retreated to Cross Creek from Guilford Courthouse expecting to find much-needed supplies. But Rebel militia along the riverbanks succeeded in forcing the British supply boats from Wilmington to turn back. Cornwallis therefore had to march on to Wilmington in April 1781.

The Scottish heroine Flora MacDonald (see MOORES CREEK BRIDGE NATIONAL MILITARY PARK) may have lived a few months at the site of Fayetteville in 1774 to 1775, and there is a marker at Green and Bow Streets where her temporary residence supposedly was located. The Market House, erected in 1838, is on the site of the convention hall where Lafayette spoke in 1825.

Fort Johnston, mouth of Cape Fear River in Southport, Brunswick County. The old colonial fort, authorized in 1745 and built from 1748 to 1764 as a defense against privateers, was badly deteriorated when Royal Governor Josiah Martin took refuge here on 2 June 1775. He escaped to a British warship on 18 July just before Patriots Robert Howe, Cornelius Harnett, and John Ashe arrived with a mob to capture him. In burning the fort that day the Patriots performed the first overt act of defiance that brought the American Revolution to North Carolina. Ironically, an act of civil disobedience at the same site on 9 January 1861 is credited with initiating North Carolina into the Civil War.

The wooden fort of 1775 has disappeared. The federal government built a new Fort Johnston in 1794 to 1809 which was seized by the Confederates in 1862 and used during the Civil War. Only the officers' quarters of this later structure remain.

Gilbert Town (now Rutherfordton), Rutherford County. Major Patrick Ferguson of the British army and his Loyalist legion used Gilbert Town as a base of operations off and on from mid-August 1780 until their withdrawal on 27 September to Kings Mountain, South Carolina. On their way to eventual triumph at the latter place the Patriot militia camped at Gilbert Town, and here they later meted out drumhead justice to the vanquished. (Of the thirty Loyalist captives convicted, twelve were condemned to death, and nine were hanged.) Having been the principal settlement of the region before the Revolution, Gilbert Town was the county seat of newly created Rutherford County in 1781 to 1785. It has since disappeared, the highway marker on U.S. 221 just north of Rutherfordton saying it "stood hereabout," but historians generally give Rutherfordton as the site of old Gilbert Town.

Gillespie Gap, intersection of Blue Ridge Parkway with N.C. 226, McDowell-Mitchell county line. The Cherokee Expedition of 1761 moved through here (see ETCHOE), and being at the headwaters of the Catawba River, the pass became a critical point on the Proclamation Line of 1763 (see BLUE RIDGE PARKWAY). The Over Mountain Men came through this pass on 29 September 1780 en route to Quaker Meadows and Kings Mountain, South Carolina. A rock pyramid at Gillespie Pass near the parkway honors these rugged fighters.

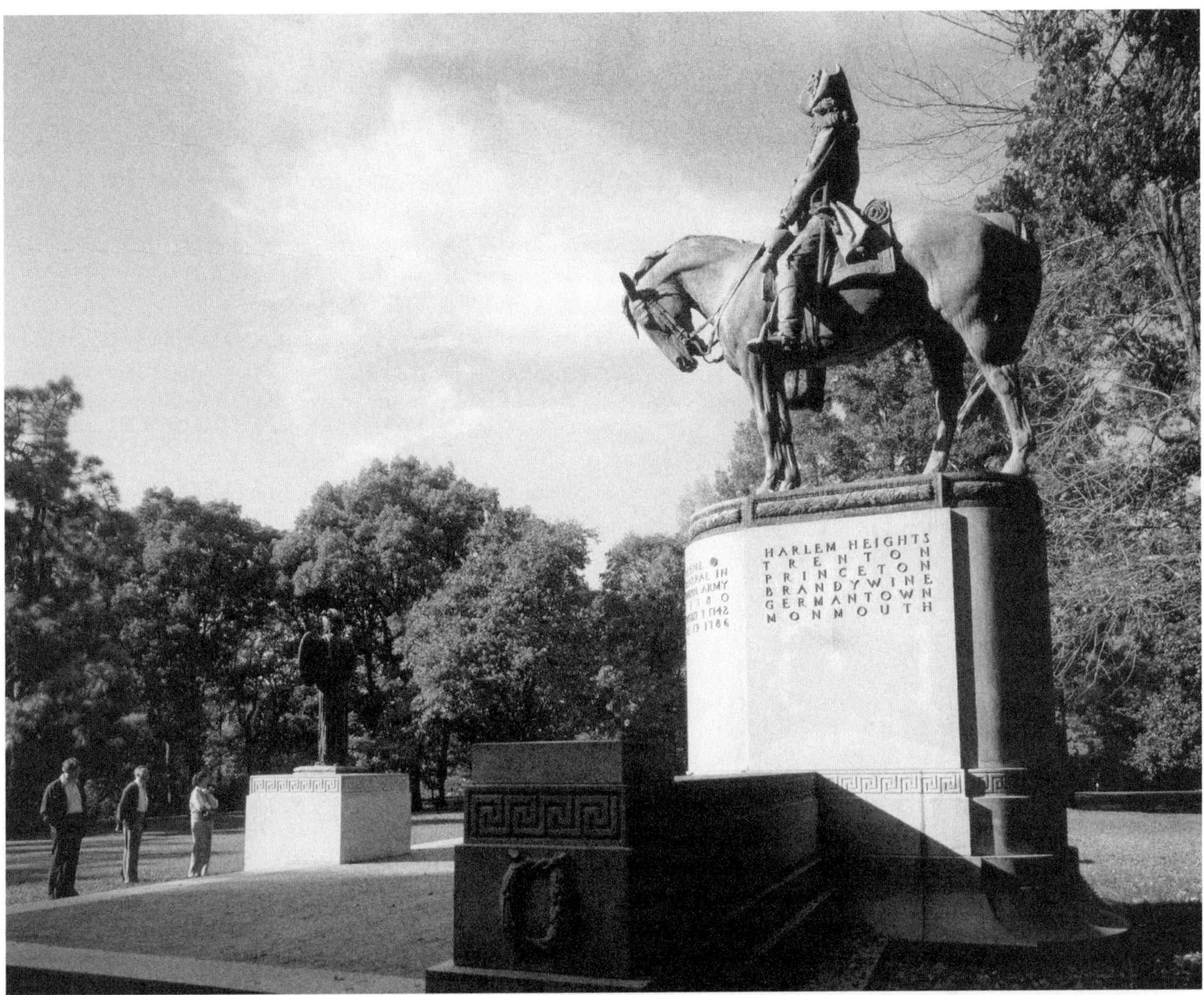

Nathanael Greene. *A large statue of General Nathanael Greene on horseback overlooks Guilford Courthouse National Military Park in North Carolina.* © DAVID MUENCH/CORBIS.

Great Smoky Mountains National Park. The greatest expanse (521,752 acres) of wilderness left in the eastern United States, this 800-square-mile park provides a sense of what this country looked like to the pioneers, though eighteenth-century forests were very different in a number of ways. The main entrance on the North Carolina side is via U.S. 441 near the village of Cherokee at the southern end of the Blue Ridge Parkway. In addition to scenic highways there are campgrounds, 650 miles of scenic trails for hiking and horseback riding, picnic areas, and pioneer exhibits. An observation tower is on top of Clingman's Dome, the highest peak (6,643 feet). The park headquarters is in Tennessee near Gatlinburg on U.S. 441. Phone: (865) 436-1200.

Guilford Courthouse, just north of Greensboro, off U.S. 220 (Battleground Avenue). Phone: (336) 288-1776. In his thirteen-volume *History of the British Army,* Sir John West Fortescue says of Cornwallis's victory over Greene at Guilford on 15 March 1781: "Never perhaps has the prowess of the British soldier been seen to greater advantage than in this obstinate and bloody combat." Yet it was a Pyrrhic victory, brought on by the strategic superiority of the self-taught Nathanael Greene over his professionally trained British opponent, and it can be argued that Cornwallis lost the American Revolution by winning the Battle of Guilford. When Charles Fox saw the casualty figures, he commented, "Another such victory would destroy the British Army." Little did Fox suspect when he said this that Cornwallis had meanwhile decided he would win the American Revolution elsewhere, which is how he got from Guilford to Yorktown.

The military tactics of General Nathanael Greene had succeeded in harassing Cornwallis until the latter was frantic to attack Greene's army anywhere, anytime, and against any odds. The American general had selected the place six weeks earlier. He picked the time, refusing to fight until he maneuvered Cornwallis to this spot and got himself set. And Cornwallis did not consider the numerical odds a bar: although Greene actually had about 4,500 men defending against 2,000 British and Hessians, Cornwallis thought Greene had about 10,000. Of course, most of the Americans had never been in action, and all of the British and Hessians were veterans, but Cornwallis was willing to accept unfavorable odds for the chance to bring Greene to battle.

Having established his base at the place now known as Troublesome Iron Works, Greene marched his army to Guilford Courthouse and deployed to make the best use of the unusual battleground. The first line, consisting of 1,000 North Carolina militia flanked by 600 of Greene's finest troops, was astride the highway a few hundred yards from a defile through which the enemy would approach. Behind each flank were cavalry detachments from the legions of William Washington (on the right) and "Light Horse Harry" Lee.

The second line, manned by about 1,200 Virginia militiamen in the brigades of Robert Lawson and Edward Stevens, was about 300 yards behind the first, also astride the road.

The third line was on high ground about 550 yards to the right rear of the second. Here were the Continental troops, one green Maryland regiment, and the rest veterans from that state, Virginia, and Delaware. They numbered about 1,400. Two of Greene's four guns were posted here, the others being forward with the front line.

In the rich country of the Quaker settlements around the site of modern Greensboro on 14 March Cornwallis got the information he had long been waiting for: the American army was camped 12 miles north at Guilford Courthouse. The next morning, long before dawn and without letting his troops eat breakfast, Cornwallis started north.

He moved slowly, however, with patrols ranging far out on each flank and Tarleton's legion well in advance. "Light Horse Harry" Lee's legion had the mission of screening Greene's front, and had reported the British advance. At sunrise there was a brief but violent encounter between the dragoons of Lee and Tarleton, followed by a little skirmish about 3 miles west of Guilford at a Quaker meetinghouse. Here Lee's infantry reinforced the dragoons, and the British Guards came forward to support Tarleton. The action was inconclusive, but Tarleton received a bad wound that later required amputation of much of his right hand. (He stayed in the saddle and was wounded a second time while leading a charge at the end of the day.)

Cornwallis now was sure he would have his battle on this day, but he had no information about the terrain on which Greene was deployed, nor about the enemy dispositions. He continued his march along the highway until the head of his column came under artillery fire from the two six-pounders in Greene's front line. Cornwallis immediately deployed to attack.

Early in the afternoon the British infantry started advancing across the muddy clearing toward the first American line. The North Carolina militia delivered its first volley at 150 yards, dropping a few Redcoats, but the advance continued. Muskets were useless for accurate, aimed fire, demonstrating their utility in massed fire from a range of 100 feet or less. Such a barrage was generally followed by a bayonet charge, which tended to claim the greater degree of casualties. Cornwallis's troops followed this model as they were trained to do, and the American militia responded as they tended to: as the British charged with fixed bayonets, the North Carolina militia turned tail and ran without letting off another volley. On their flanks the veterans held their positions until driven back.

Cornwallis had to commit his reserves to clear this first line, even though the fleet-footed militia in the center had left him a huge gap.

The American second line performed creditably and conducted an orderly delaying action when forced to fall back. The nine regiments of the British force were now scattered in three groups. While four of them in the middle were dealing with the second American line, two regiments had fanned out to the right in their own private battle with the stubborn Rebel outfits that had originally been on that flank of the first American line. On the opposite side of the field, however, the three British regiments that had pushed back that flank of the first American line found their advance to the third American line unopposed.

At this critical time Lieutenant Colonel James Webster of the Royal Welch Fusiliers raced over to the left and found those three regiments that were sitting right in front of Greene's main position. He undertook to attack here without waiting for Cornwallis to tidy up the middle of the battlefield. Unfortunately for this gallant and resourceful leader, however, he hit two of the finest outfits in the Continental army, the First Maryland and the Delaware Company of Robert H. Kirkwood. These veterans, supported by two cannon, calmly watched Webster organize his attack and held their fire until he was within 40 yards. Then they delivered a devastating volley and counterattacked to drive the British back in disorder. (Webster was mortally wounded leading another attack in this sector.)

Had Greene known then what we know now of Cornwallis's temporary disorganization, and had Greene been a gambler, he might well have followed up on this advantage to win a more brilliant victory at Guilford than Morgan won at Cowpens. But he had previously decided never to risk destruction of his army, and he waited for the next move by Cornwallis.

It was not long in coming, and this time luck was on the other side. General Charles O'Hara commanded the spearhead of the attack on the third American line. The Second Guards Battalion under Lieutenant Colonel James Stewart (or Stuart) led the way, followed by the Grenadier Battalion and supported by the Royal Welch and the Seventy-first Highlanders. Opposite the Guards were the untested troops of the other regiment of Maryland Continentals, on the American left flank. When the latter turned and ran without firing a shot, the Guards rushed forward to exploit this advantage but were hit by two vicious counterattacks. Charging down on their exposed right flank came the dragoons of William Washington's legion, led by the gigantic Peter Francisco wielding the 5-foot sword presented to him by George Washington to match his 260-pound, 6-foot-6-inch frame. He is alleged to have killed eleven men that day, including the one who laid his thigh open with a bayonet when Francisco returned for a second charge. (See also FRANCISCO'S FIGHT under Virginia.)

But the Guards were in much more serious trouble when the First Maryland and Kirkwood's Delawares launched a real counterattack against their other exposed flank. Stewart was killed, and as his Guards fought to avoid annihilation Cornwallis made the cold-blooded decision to fire grapeshot over the heads of his own troops into the American ranks. Despite the protest of his officers that this would hit his own men, Cornwallis issued the order and broke up the American attack.

O'Hara rallied the survivors of the Guards Battalion, whose commander had been killed early in the action, and personally led the final attack although he was suffering from a dangerous wound. As this attack pushed the American main line back and other British units came forward to overlap the flanks, Greene gave the order to withdraw. About 3:30 P.M. he started skillfully extricating himself, and after an all-night march in the rain his army was safely back at Troublesome Creek.

Cornwallis camped on the battleground for the next two days, with his men suffering in the rain because tents had been left behind. Almost 100 of his officers and men had been killed in action, and another 50 died within a few hours of the battle.

The Americans lost about 80 killed and 180 wounded. Expecting Cornwallis to resume his offensive, they wasted no time digging in at Troublesome Creek, but on 18 March Cornwallis withdrew to Bell's Mill and then started his retreat to the coast. Greene caught up at Ramsey's Mill, but then turned the pursuit over to the militia. Finding that Patriot guerrillas had kept British supply boats from getting up the river to Cross Creek (now Fayetteville), Cornwallis led his bedraggled force into Wilmington.

Guilford Courthouse National Military Park comprises about 230 acres in which the main features of the battlefield have been preserved, thanks to local initiative. In 1886 Judge David Schenck of Greensboro, who for six years had studied the battlefield, then a tangled wilderness of old sedgefields, briars, and pines, decided to save the historic site. With friends he formed the Guilford Battleground Company, sold stock to raise funds for buying land piecemeal, and started development of the property. In 1917, after seven years of effort, the company succeeded in getting the federal government to accept the site as a national military park. It was administered until 1933 by the War Department, then taken over by the National Park Service (Interior Department).

Meanwhile, the Battleground Company had undertaken a program of erecting all sorts of "monuments, tombstones, or other memorials" to commemorate participants in this action. Memorials are there today to such deserving heroes as Lieutenant Colonel James Stewart (whose sword was found here in 1866), Peter Francisco, and Kerenhauppuch Turner, who rode from Maryland to care for her wounded son. The most imposing and appropriate monument, an equestrian statue near the center of the American second line, is to Nathanael Greene. (Had the general been there during the battle with better control over his too widely spaced lines he might well have won.) The Delaware and Maryland monuments commemorate the Continental troops who comprised the largest element of Greene's regulars, and a tall white cenotaph marks the center of the third American line.

The precise location of the courthouse itself has not yet been found. However, in 2004 the Battleground Company enlisted the help of a team of archaeologists from the College of William and Mary to determine the location of the courthouse. As of yet, its location remains a mystery. Established in 1771 for the new county of Guilford (named after the first earl of Guilford, father of Lord North), the courthouse became the center of a small settlement that saw much military activity during the Revolution. Guilford Court House, as the settlement was called, was a rallying point, muster ground, and supply depot. Before the Battle of Camden (16 August 1780) the troops of Brigadier Generals William Smallwood and Edward Stephens and those under Colonel William Campbell were assembled at Guilford Court House. Smallwood had twenty British and almost thirty Loyalist prisoners under guard here in late August, and here Brigadier General Isaac Huger's column from Cheraw, South Carolina, and "Light Horse Harry" Lee's legion rejoined Greene on 7 February 1781 in the "Race for the Dan."

At this time the village had only two to three hundred inhabitants. It did not become a town until 1785, when it was renamed Martinville. The courthouse was last used in 1809, after which its functions were moved to Greensboro, and Martinville started dying. The chimney of the dismantled courthouse survived as a landmark until the eve of the Civil War. By 1889 no trace of the settlement could be found except a well (which is still used). The park is north of Greensboro on New Garden Road. Take the Holden Road Exit on I-40 and follow the signs. The visitors center has a small museum and provides self-guided tours along a 2.5-mile walk. Open year-round, 8:30 A.M. to 5 P.M. Phone: (919) 288-1776.

Halifax, Roanoke River, Halifax County. An important political, social, and economic center from its settlement in the early 1720s until the General Assembly moved to Hillsborough in 1783, Halifax is now a small dot on the highway map (east of I-95, near the Virginia line). Extensive restoration of the colonial village has been under way for many years, and part of it is a State Historic Site.

Soon after the Loyalist defeat at Moores Creek Bridge, the Fourth Provincial Congress met and quickly adopted the historic Halifax Resolves (12 April 1776). Authorizing their delegates to the Continental Congress "to concur with the delegates of the other Colonies in declaring Independency," they bestowed on North Carolina this distinction of being the first province to come out officially for independence. The colonial courthouse where this event took place was replaced in 1847, but the site is marked.

Of particular architectural interest is the little Owens House, built by a prominent merchant in about 1760. On a raised brick cellar, the story-and-a-half frame structure had shed dormer windows on two sides of a gambrel roof. The other sides of the house are vertical to the roof line (that is, the structure is gable-ended), and there are small, simple porches front and rear.

The Clerk's Office (1833) and Jail (1838) were once believed to have been built in 1758, but this appears finally to have been disproved. Although post-Revolutionary, they both are interesting, and the former is used as the Historic Halifax Visitors Center. Guided tours begin from there. The visitors center also contains artifact exhibits and an audiovisual tour of the grounds and its history. Constitution-Burgess House, traditionally the place where the state constitution of 1776 was drafted (and proof may yet be discovered), is to be moved into the historic district. A simple frame structure typical of the region, it has a side hall and two very small rooms, each with its separate fireplace and chimney, and furnished as of 1776. Originally behind the Colonial Cemetery (which survives), the house was moved in 1920 to the vicinity of Willie Jones's homesite (see below).

Other landmarks in the historic district are the austere Masonic Lodge of the federal period (the Royal White Hart Lodge, number 2, was established in 1756; the present building is not open to the public); the site of Eagle Tavern (whose guests included Washington in 1791 and Lafayette in 1825; part of the building is incorporated in a private home four blocks south); and Magazine Spring.

The latter was the home of Willie (pronounced "Wylie") Jones, a prominent Patriot also noted for lavish hospitality. Tradition has it that around 1773 a guest was a Scottish sea captain named John Paul who had recently killed a mutinous crewman and been advised to get away from the West Indies until he could be sure of a fair trial. He did not return to the Caribbean, but was later given a lieutenant's commission in the newly established Continental navy thanks to the personal interest of Joseph Hewes (see EDENTON). Historians generally believe that he picked the new name John Paul Jones simply because Jones is so close to being anonymous, but the Jones family of Halifax spawned the legend that he picked it in gratitude for the hospitality extended by Willie and his elder brother, Allen, of nearby Mount Gallant. (The site of the latter place, across the Roanoke River, is indicated by a marker on U.S. 158 between Garysburg and Jackson.) Cornwallis occupied the Grove in May 1781 when passing through on his way to Virginia. Nothing remains of the house but a massive brick chimney. Historic Halifax is open Tuesday through Saturday, 10 A.M. to 4 P.M., and on Sunday, 1 P.M. to 4 P.M. Phone: (252) 583-7191.

Hillsborough, Orange County, off I–85 west of Durham. Until after the Revolution this was the most important town in the western portion of North Carolina and the center of a large farming area. It was laid out on 400 acres of clay hills near the Eno River in 1754 on the site of an ancient Indian village.

In 1766 a name for the place was finally settled on after several others had been tried. Hillsborough comes not from the rolling terrain but from the Irish peer, Wills Hill, earl of Hillsborough, who was secretary of state for the colonies. The final "ugh" got dropped during the years, but was restored by a special act of the General Assembly in 1965.

Hillsborough was closely involved in the War of the Regulation, 1768 to 1771 (see ALAMANCE BATTLEGROUND STATE HISTORIC SITE). Markers on Churton Street (U.S. 70A) indicate the site of Edmund Fanning's house and point to the spot just east of town where the six Regulators were hanged. The Third Provincial Congress met in Hillsborough for three weeks starting on 20 August 1775.

One of the town's attractions was its favorable summer climate in comparison with that along the wealthier coastal region, and planters from the Cape Fear area would annually make the long trek here. This helps explain how this backcountry settlement got so many elegant trappings and why it was such a magnet for military forces during the Revolution. When Continental army forces came south in 1780, Generals Kalb and Gates established headquarters in Hillsborough. After the disaster at Camden, South Carolina, Horatio Gates set some sort of a military equestrian record in getting back to Hillsborough. "One hundred and eighty miles in three days and a half does admirable credit to a man of his time of life," commented Alexander Hamilton in mock admiration.

Cornwallis briefly occupied Hillsborough with his tired troops after his unsuccessful pursuit of General Greene into Virginia (following General Morgan's victory at Cowpens, South Carolina). Two days after his arrival, 22 February 1781, he raised the royal standard in front of the courthouse and pompously proclaimed mission accomplished in this part of North Carolina. But four days later he marched off again because his army had eaten itself out of the local supply of provisions.

When Thomas Burke of Hillsborough was made governor in June 1781 he undertook as his first order of business the suppression of Loyalist raiders in his home district. He had just established headquarters for his antiguerrilla campaign in Hillsborough when his intelligence system informed him that the Whig outpost on the Haw River, some 15 miles southwest, was about to be attacked. It turned out that the enemy objective was Hillsborough, but Governor Burke did not know this until he was captured along with two hundred others including his council, several Continental officers, and about seventy soldiers. The notorious David Fanning with about 750 Loyalists had approached the town undetected, taken advantage of a dark, foggy night to infiltrate from all sides, and bagged all these prisoners with the loss of only one of his own men. About noon of the next day (12 September 1781) Fanning left Hillsborough with his prisoners and thirty Loyalists liberated from the jail. Despite the attempt to cut him off at Lindley's Mill, Fanning evacuated his captives to the British base at Wilmington. The government of the state collapsed and did not recover for another year.

The governor ended up on James Island, near Charleston, on parole. But when he felt he was not getting sufficient protection from Loyalists on the island who were threatening to kill him, Burke broke his parole and late in January 1782 was back home. He refused to stand for reelection in the spring, retired to his estate, Tyaquin, and died there in 1783. His grave is about 3 miles northeast of town (marker on N.C. 86 about a mile north of Hillsborough).

Five General Assemblies met at Hillsborough during and right after the Revolution, in 1778, 1780, 1782, 1783, and 1784. Agitation to make it the state capital continued until 1791, after which it started its decline to its present status of a small but very historic town. At least 116 structures of the late eighteenth and early nineteenth century survive in and around Hillsborough. The courthouse clock has kept time since 1766. The Alliance for Historic Hillsborough, an organization comprised of seven local historical groups, oversees and interprets the town's past. They maintain guided and self-guided walking tours in addition to a bus tour of historic Hillsborough. The Alliance is located at 150 East King Street. Website: www.historichillsborough.org; phone: (919) 732-7741.

"Horn in the West." *See* BOONE.

House in the Horseshoe (Alston House), 324 Alston House Road, Sanford, northeast corner of Moore County in a large horseshoe bend of Deep River. Indicated on official highway map; historical marker on N.C. 27 in Carthage about 10 miles south.

From July 1781 until May 1782 David Fanning consistently outclassed his Patriot opponents in central North Carolina, and one of his earliest successes was at the Alston House. In August he captured Colonel Philip Alston and twenty-five other men here after a spirited skirmish that ended when Alston sent his wife out as the peace emissary. (Alston had killed one of Fanning's close friends, Kenneth Black.)

The large frame house with a large brick chimney on each end and full shed porches front and back was built by Alston around 1772. Implicated in the 1787 murder of Dr. George Glascock, the Revolutionary War surgeon whose mother, Patty Ball, was kin to George Washington, Alston lost his seat in the General Assembly and was forced to leave the state around 1790, his fate remaining unknown. In 1798 Governor Benjamin Williams bought the property and developed it into a large and highly profitable cotton plantation.

The restored house features good woodwork. Bullet holes on the outside have been preserved. The state purchased the house in 1955 and developed it into a state historic site, open every day except Monday, April through October. Encampments and reenactments are staged, and guided tours of the historic grounds and buildings are made available. Phone: (910) 947-2051.

Lindley's Mill (Cane Creek), Alamance County on N.C. 87 about 15 miles south of Burlington. Off Interstate 85/40 at Exit 147, go west on Greensboro–Chapel Hill Road to Lindley Mill Road, then south about a mile to Rock Drive beside Cane Creek Bridge. In a four-hour battle near here on 12 September 1781 there were more than three hundred casualties; yet nothing more than a highway marker commemorates the event. Patriot forces under General John Butler had failed to stop David Fanning's brilliant raid on Hillsborough, but they came close to evening the score here by ambushing the Loyalists on their route of withdrawal. Fanning's second in command, Colonel Hector McNeil, had failed to take the proper military precautions in organizing the vanguard of the Loyalist withdrawal. He and seven other Loyalists were killed when they marched into the ambuscade.

Fanning quickly took control, got his 200 prisoners (including the governor) off the scene, and counterattacked. The action lasted four hours before the Patriots were driven back with the loss of 24 killed, 90 wounded, and 10 captured. Fanning lost 27 killed, 60 seriously wounded, and 30 walking wounded. The Loyalist commander lost so much blood from a ball in the arm that he had to fall behind with the other seriously wounded, but his subordinates successfully evacuated the Patriot prisoners.

Despite the importance and magnitude of this battle, it has generated little interest among historians of the region. The site is just west of Sutphin community with a state marker on the site.

Mocksville. Site of Boone Graves.

Moores Creek National Battlefield near Currie, 20 miles northwest of Wilmington on N.C. 210 in Pender County.

The first battle of the Revolutionary War in North Carolina occurred here on 27 February 1776; through a combination of political and military miscalculations a gallant force of 1,000 Highland Scots and 500 other Loyalists was shattered. The dramatic and decisive Patriot victory killed British hopes of rallying Loyalist support for a conquest of the South. It was not until five years later that the British were able to make a major military effort on North Carolina soil.

Highlanders had started settling the upper stretches of the Cape Fear River soon after their defeat at Culloden Moor in 1746. Pushed out by the Highland Clearances and poverty, they were still arriving in large numbers when the Revolutionary War started in America. By mid-July 1775 Royal Governor Josiah Martin had been forced to seek safety aboard a warship in the Cape Fear River. But he knew there was a strong Loyalist element in the state, and for months he had urged the British authorities in the North and in London to send military forces south to take advantage of this great potential. He finally succeeded to a degree. General Gage ordered General Sir Henry Clinton to take a large expeditionary force south from New York and link up with another large force under General Cornwallis that was leaving from Ireland. Gage also sent two Scots officers to North Carolina to raise the king's standard at Cross Creek, the hub of Highland settlements in the province. Governor Martin, who was meeting all ships, gave these two emissaries promotions of two grades each in the Loyalist militia, so they went to Cross Creek as Brigadier General Donald McDonald and Lieutenant Colonel Donald McLeod. Other ships that the floating royal governor met off Cape Fear were loaded with land-hungry Highlanders, and he succeeded in getting hundreds of these new settlers to take an oath to support the king's cause in return for generous land grants.

The older settlers up at Cross Creek were not rushing to take sides in the third civil war the Highlanders had experienced in the eighteenth century. In the thirty years since Culloden many Highlanders had become genuinely reconciled to British rule, and they were not easily swayed by elaborate arguments about "the rights of Englishmen." Others were not so much for King George as they were against the Lowlanders and Ulstermen and coastal elites who dominated the Rebel element around them. But perhaps the most effective leadership in rallying many of them to the Loyalist camp was provided by the entourage of the legendary Flora MacDonald, who had come to North Carolina in 1774.

As a young woman in her mid-twenties MacDonald had played a key role in the dramatic escape of Bonnie Prince Charlie from Scotland. For five months after his defeat at Culloden, Prince Charles had been a hunted refugee with a price of £30,000 on his head. MacDonald had helped hide him before he was able to make good his escape, and the charming prince had successfully masqueraded as her serving maid. Caught and imprisoned in the Tower of London, MacDonald was released in 1747 as part of a general amnesty. In 1750 she married a distant cousin, Allan MacDonald, son of the laird of Kingsborough and an officer in the British army. Sometime later they emigrated to North Carolina, settling at Cheek's Creek, where Allan had bought 500 acres. A daughter married Alexander McLeod, the illegitimate son of the eighteenth chieftain of McLeod and a former British officer.

Allen MacDonald and his son-in-law had both raised companies before the king's emissaries reached Cross Creek. Although the governor was led to believe that 7,000 loyal Highlanders were mustered for the great uprising that would gain control of the province and put him back in Tryon's Palace, the final head count was about 1,500 Loyalists (see ALAMANCE BATTLEGROUND STATE HISTORIC SITE). On 18 February 1776 General McDonald started his march to the sea, where his force was supposed to meet the incoming expeditions from New York and Ireland. Although most of the men had come in without firearms, and McDonald had had to scour the countryside to get these for his troops, there was no serious shortage of Scottish broadswords and dirks, bagpipes and drums, and kilts and tartans.

The Patriots had been busy during this gathering of the clans. One regiment of Continentals had, unfortunately, been sent to Virginia, but the 650 regulars and five cannon of Colonel James Moore's First North Carolina Regiment were in position at the bridge across Rockfish Creek before the Loyalists reached that point, a mere 7 miles from Cross Creek. Moore was reinforced by about 450 militia under Colonels Alexander Lillington, James Kenan, and John Ashe. Small detachments under Continental Colonels Alexander Martin and James Thackston were approaching from the upcountry (Salisbury and Hillsborough), which would threaten the enemy's rear, and a large force of 800 under Colonel Richard Caswell was marching from New Bern to join Moore.

The opposing commanders exchanged notes across Rockfish Creek, each proposing that the other see the error of his political affiliation and change sides. With a force that was not prepared for a battle, McDonald knew he must reach the coast quickly because the odds against him were mounting with each passing hour. Moore was playing for time as he undertook the difficult task of concentrating the dispersed Patriot forces to block the advance of the Loyalist column.

The elderly McDonald, a man of almost seventy, won the first stage of the campaign by withdrawing undetected, crossing the Cape Fear River back near Cross Creek, and heading for the coast through the rough country between the South River and the Black. This route would require him to cross Corbett's Ferry and Moores Creek Bridge, but the old soldier thought he could move his troops fast enough to make the march unopposed.

Having been outwitted, James Moore reacted quickly. He sent Caswell word to head for Corbett's Ferry, make contact with the enemy, and to do all he could to stop or slow their advance. He detached Lillington and Ashe to reinforce Caswell if possible, otherwise to set up a defensive position at Moores Creek Bridge. Moore planned to cross the river at Elizabeth Town and meet them on their way to Corbett's Ferry or, if he was too late, to surround them there. The final touch of this masterful plan was to order the small detachment under Martin and Thackston to occupy Cross Creek, blocking the enemy's withdrawal to his base.

As the Loyalists approached Corbett's Ferry (the site probably is just west of Ivanhoe, Sampson County) on 23 February, they learned that Caswell was there waiting. General McDonald deceived Caswell into believing he would attempt to force a crossing at the ferry and moved 5 miles upstream to build a bridge. By 8 A.M. on 26 February the entire Loyalist force was across the Black River and racing for Moores Creek Bridge.

Lillington had arrived the night before and was digging in on the south side when Caswell dropped back from Corbett's Ferry. For the third time McDonald found himself blocked by superior forces at a river line. Worn out and sick, the elderly general camped 6 miles from the bridge and called his officers to his bedside for a council of war. They convinced him that the Rebel bivouac on the north side of the stream could be wiped out in a surprise attack before dawn and that the bridge could be captured easily. McDonald put Donald McLeod in command of this enterprise and dropped out of the war.

Leaving their camp at 1 A.M., the Loyalists made an arduous 6-mile march, much of it through swamps. Before dawn they saw the fires of Caswell's camp on the near side of the bridge. As they inched silently forward, there was no sign that the enemy had taken any defensive precautions whatsoever. The Highlanders then discovered that Caswell had left his campfires burning and withdrawn to Lillington's defenses on the far side of the stream.

The creek here was 50 feet wide and 5 feet deep, spanned by a crude bridge—probably two massive logs and a plank flooring. The Highlanders had no choice but to brave the massed fires of muskets, rifles, and cannon from earthworks on the far bank if they insisted on trying to force a crossing at this point. Twice before the wise McDonald had declined far less dangerous a challenge, but now the impetuous McLeod was in command, and he prepared to lead a traditional Highland charge. The screaming, death-defying charge of the Highlanders had terrified defenders for centuries, but failed often, as at Culloden.

It was not yet light enough to see as Donald McLeod made his preparations. Captain John Campbell's elite company of eighty broadswordsmen would make the main attack on the bridge. They would be followed by the main body, and three hundred riflemen would bring up the rear. Three cheers were to signal the start of the attack, and the battle cry was "King George and Broad Swords." The Loyalist commander intended to wait until there was light enough to see, but just before dawn he heard a nervous crackle of firearms near the bridge, and McLeod could not contain himself any longer. The three cheers were followed by the skirl of pipes and the beat of drums.

The light was still too dim for the Rebels to shoot accurately as the Highlanders charged the bridge brandishing their swords, but it probably was too dim also for the attackers to see immediately what the Rebels had done to the bridge. They had created a gap by removing some of the planks, and if some contemporary accounts are to be believed, the Rebels had greased the exposed stringers with soap and tallow. Much more significant was the fact that the defenders were covering the bridge with the fire of a small cannon, a swivel gun, and hundreds of muskets. McLeod and Campbell fell within a few paces of the earthworks, and several others got across the bridge alive, but it was no contest. The firing ended in about three minutes, and it is obvious from the casualty figures that not many of the Highlanders shared the enthusiasm of McLeod and Campbell to do or die. McDonald had had trouble way back on Rockfish Creek in keeping his men from deserting in large numbers at the first sign of armed resistance.

Caswell reported that about thirty Loyalists were killed or mortally wounded. The defenders had two casualties, and only one of these died. Colonel Moore reached the battlefield several hours after the action and organized a vigorous pursuit that netted about 850 prisoners, 13 wagons, 150 rifles, 350 muskets, 150 swords and dirks, and a box containing £15,000 in hard cash (the price of Tryon's Palace!). This haul came not only from the fugitives of the battle but also from Loyalist homes raided by the Patriots.

Moores Creek National Military Park, 88 acres, takes in the site of the battle and has an excellent visitors center with interpretive audiovisual displays. You can see the remains of fortifications, as well as field exhibits and markers. Every year in the last weekend of February the park commemorates the battle with a wreath-laying ceremony preceded by a living-history encampment, including demonstrations and programs that underscore the battle. Guided tours of the grounds are available. The park is 20 miles northwest of Wilmington along N.C. 421 to N.C. 210 and is open daily from 9 A.M. to 5 P.M. The visitors center has a small weapons display. Phone: (910) 283-5591. From the partially restored earthworks the alleged bridge site is 200 feet away. The informed visitor might question whether something is not amiss here—whether in morning twilight and probably with ground haze the Patriots could have stopped a properly conducted Highland charge at a range of 200 feet. Charles East Hatch, Jr., National Park Service historian and author of a monograph *The Battle of Moores Creek Bridge*, has assured me that, contrary to my suspicions, the bridge is correctly sited today. If so, it may be that the valiant McLeod and Campbell were not followed by any substantial number of true Scottish warriors. Perhaps the answer is that the charge was stopped not at the bridge, as artists who have depicted the action would have us believe, but after a handful of Highlanders got close to the earthworks.

A few sites associated with the principal Patriot leaders in the Moores Creek campaign may be found in Pender County. Colonel James Moore's grave has not been found. His plantation was probably just northeast of where U.S. 421 from Wilmington enters Pender County. (The highway marker in Rocky Point says his home was 3 miles southeast of that place, but some regional historians maintain that this is incorrect.) Lillington Hall (1734) was still standing when Benson Lossing visited Alexander Lillington's great-granddaughter there in 1848 and sketched the house (*Pictorial Field Book of the Revolution*, II, p. 587). It has since disappeared, but the location is marked by Lillington's grave, which is near County Highway 1520 about 0.3 mile northeast of the bridge over Lillington Creek. (From U.S. 117 in Rocky Point go east on S.C. 210 across a branch of the Cape Fear River, a little more than 2 miles, and 1.1 miles farther turn left on a secondary road, Number 1520. Lillington Creek Bridge is about 4.5 miles north, and the Lillington graveyard is a short distance to the northeast.)

The grave of John Ashe is near Pike Creek just north of Rocky Point. From the intersection of S.C. 210 and U.S. 117 in the place, go north for 2.7 miles and turn right on 1411. About 1 mile east is the bridge across Pike Creek, and the Ashe graveyard is on the west side of the creek, south of the highway. According to the marker in Rocky Point, Ashe's home was about 3 miles (straight-line distance) from here, near where S.C. 210 now crosses Northeast Cape Fear River.

Alexander McLeod's homesite is 1.5 miles west of a marker on U.S. 15 and 501 about 4 miles south of Carthage in Moore County.

Mountain Gateway Museum (1971). *See* OLD FORT.

Mount Mourne. *See* TORRENCE'S TAVERN SITE.

New Bern, confluence of Trent and Neuse Rivers, Craven County. On a broad estuary and only 35 miles from the open Atlantic, New Bern (pronounced as one word) is North Carolina's second-oldest town. It started as a settlement of Swiss and Germans on a grant received by Baron Christopher de Graffenried in 1710. Here the first Provincial Congress met in 1774 in open defiance of Governor Josiah Martin, and New Bern became the first state capital when Governor Richard Caswell and other state officials were inaugurated in Tryon Palace in January 1777. Otherwise, the town had little direct involvement in the Revolution, although it had sent a contingent to help win the Battle of Moores Creek Bridge, and in 1781 was briefly occupied by a raiding party from the British base at Wilmington. (Major James Craig with 250 regulars and 80 Loyalists arrived on 19 August and destroyed some property before withdrawing.)

It is now a large town lacking the quiet charm of its less commercially favored colonial contemporaries such as Bath, Beaufort, and Brunswick Town, but some 150 historic landmarks are included, as is a notation that New Bern is the birthplace of Pepsi, in a guide map issued by civic boosters. Website: www.visitnewbern.com; Craven County Convention and Visitors Center phone: (800) 437-5767. The principal attraction is the remarkable reconstruction of Tryon Palace and Gardens, website: www.tryonpalace.org; phone: (252) 514-4900. The State Department of Archives and History in collaboration with the Tryon Palace Committee administers several other houses of the decades immediately following the Revolution.

New Garden Meeting House, Guilford County. The two days before the Battle of Guilford Courthouse, Cornwallis was camped at the Deep River Meeting House, between the two branches of Deep River (now a village of that name on N.C. 68, 3.4 miles south of its intersection with U.S. 40). "Light Horse Harry" Lee had the mission of screening the British advance while General Greene organized his position at Guilford Courthouse.

Around sunrise on the day of battle, 15 March 1781, Tarleton's advance guard had a brisk skirmish about 4 miles southwest of Greene's main position with Lee's forces. "Light Horse Harry" should have been an authority on the geography of the region, but he was wrong when he wrote in his *Memoirs* that this skirmish occurred "not at *New Garden meeting-house*, which was twelve miles from Guilford" but probably at "a meeting-house of less notoriety." The skirmish did take place at New Garden Meeting House, according to Dr. Algie I. Newlin, professor emeritus of history at Guilford College, who has attended the New Garden Meeting for more than fifty years and who has written a history of the five meetinghouses built on the tract acquired by the Quakers in 1757. All are within 250 yards of the present Guilford College campus. The one that figured in the Revolution was probably built between 1752 and 1757. It burned in 1784; hence Benson Lossing's ancient informant was wrong in saying the house sketched by Lossing in 1848 was used in 1781 as a hospital for the wounded from Guilford. (Lossing's sketch is on page 613, vol. II, of his *Pictorial Field Book of the Revolution.*)

In 1938 William P. Brandon, park historian at Guilford Courthouse National Military Park, recorded that "the site of the original Meeting House is marked by its foundation stones about 200 yards from the campus [of Guilford College], while the present Meeting House is itself on the campus."

Old Fort, McDowell County on U.S. 70, about 20 miles east of Asheville. The Loyalist force commanded by Patrick Ferguson probed as far west as this point in the operations of September 1780 that led to his annihilation at Kings Mountain, South Carolina. Davidson's Fort, which stood near here and gave the present town its name, was the westernmost outpost of North Carolina. Built in 1776 during the Cherokee War of that year, it was important for more than a decade for security against Cherokee raids from the new towns on Chickamauga Creek (around modern Chattanooga, Tennessee), where British agents had their headquarters. Old Fort Picnic Ground is 3 miles west of the small manufacturing town of Old Fort, on the southern edge of Pisgah National Forest. Old Fort is famous for its Friday evening mountain-music hoedowns. The Mountain Gateway Museum in Old Fort is a recommended place for visitors of Old Fort to start their tour. A fourteen-minute video portrays the town's history, including its mountaineer culture and the coming of the railroad. Website: www.oldfort.org; phone: (828) 668-9259.

Orton Plantation, Cape Fear River on N.C. Highway 133 about 18 miles below Wilmington. Famous for its gardens, the mansion built by "King Roger" Moore sometime after 1734 was the center of an early-eighteenth-century rice plantation. It was closely associated with Brunswick Town (see BRUNSWICK TOWN RUINS), whose site was added to Orton Plantation in 1842 for a price of $4.25. The exquisite Orton Plantation Gardens, about 20 acres in size, are open to the public for self-guided tours from March through November (phone 910-371-6851); the plantation's house is a private residence.

Outer Banks. *See* CAPE HATTERAS.

Pleasant Gardens (McDowell House), near Marion on U.S. 70 just west of its intersection with U.S. 221, McDowell County. "Hunting John" McDowell and his brother Joseph came to this region during the Seven Years' War and settled at points 25 miles apart. Both had sons named Joseph who were famous during the Revolution and whom writers have since had trouble keeping straight. The confusion has been compounded by official highway markers and tourist literature.

John McDowell acquired a grant of "640 acres on the main so. branch of the Catawba . . . including round hill bottom and Pleasant Gardens," as the document of 1768 reads. He bought another 400 acres of adjoining land the same year. Some time before this he had built a two-room cabin on the land and dubbed it Pleasant Gardens. His son Joseph was born in the cabin in 1758. "Pleasant Gardens" Joe, as the latter became known to distinguish him from his cousin "Quaker Meadows" Joe, built the house still standing today as the McDowell House and indicated by a highway marker near the junction of U.S. 70 and 221 that reads: "N-4. Pleasant Gardens. Home of Joseph McDowell, Indian Fighter, hero of King's Mountain."

Visible from the McDowell House is Round Hill, where the family burial ground is preserved. Just across the highway is the site of "Hunting John's" log cabin. Here, then, is the "Pleasant Gardens" of the McDowells, not to be confused with the community of the same name 2 miles to the west. (The latter appears on the official state map as Pleasant Garden [singular], but state and county historical experts assure me that it should be called Pleasant Gardens [plural].) The McDowell House dates from after the Revolution—late 1780s—and in 2005 is considered endangered because the home's owner, enticed by a booming commercial real-estate market, has the house and the remaining 4 acres of land for sale. Adjacent land earmarked for development has been bulldozed within 10 feet of the historic house.

In the community of Pleasant Garden(s) is the Carson House, which local historical authorities have informed me "should not be confused with Pleasant Gardens." But these same authorities acknowledge that the Carson House "was sometimes called 'Second Pleasant Gardens.'" A few words of explanation are therefore in order. Colonel John Carson's first wife was the sister of "Pleasant Gardens" Joe. His second wife was the latter's widow, who is said to have taken along the name of her former house and bestowed it on her new one, the one now called the Historic Carson House. It is maintained by the Carson House Foundation and serves as a museum for the public. Phone: (828) 724-4948.

The final point of confusion to clear up is which Joseph McDowell was the hero of Kings Mountain. Both cousins led troops in the battle. "Pleasant Gardens" Joe commanded a company, whereas his cousin "Quaker Meadows" Joe had the more important role of commanding the local militia regiment (see QUAKER MEADOWS).

Pyle's "Defeat," Haw River, below Graham, Alamance County. When the main Patriot army started back across the Dan River into North Carolina in February 1781, General Greene's advance guard comprised Lee's legion and the South Carolina militia of General Andrew Pickens. Learning that four hundred mounted Loyalists were marching to join Cornwallis at Hillsborough, where "Butcher" Tarleton's green-coated British legion also was based, the Patriots devised a stratagem. Capitalizing on the fact that the uniform of Lee's legion closely resembled that of Tarleton's, and using two captured officers of the latter organization, "Light Horse Harry" Lee tricked the Loyalist commander, Colonel John Pyle, into believing that he (General Lee) was Tarleton. Lee hoped that he could get his dragoons among the Loyalists so that, once the trick was discovered, the enemy would surrender without a fight. The ruse was working perfectly, Pyle and Lee shaking hands and exchanging civilities, when the South Carolina militia exposed themselves prematurely. At least ninety Loyalists were killed in the brief melée that followed. Pyle was badly wounded and left for dead. (He survived, allegedly after hiding in a pond about a quarter-mile to the southeast that was long known as Pyle's Pond.) The charge of "foul massacre" was answered by Lee with the reasoning that the nature of the conflict made it impossible not to kill a large number of Loyalists. The action is therefore of interest in the general consideration of alleged massacres performed by the British. Pyle's "Defeat," as it is called (but comparable British triumphs of Tarleton and "No-flint" Grey were "massacres"), had the important result of denying Cornwallis support from North Carolina Loyalists at a time when he needed all the help he could get.

Quaker Meadows, just west of Morganton, Burke County; marker on N.C. 181 near junction with N.C. 126. After Indians had cleared bottomland here, the area became overgrown with grass and looked like a meadow. Local traders having mistaken the austere Bishop Spangenberg for a Quaker when he came by in 1752 looking for land where the Moravians could settle, the place became known as Quaker Meadows. (This is the origin of the name according to the *WPA Guide*; another explanation is that a real Quaker camped here and traded with the Indians.)

Around 1765 Joseph McDowell moved here from the Valley of Virginia, and his cousin, "Hunting John," stopped 25 miles west at the place he named Pleasant Gardens. At the outbreak of the Revolution, Joseph's eldest son, Charles (c. 1743–1815), was the local militia colonel, and another son, Joseph (1756–1801), was second in command of the regiment. Both were involved in the numerous frontier skirmishes against the Indians and Loyalists that maintained Patriot control of the region, but when the large Loyalist force under the British officer Patrick Ferguson moved up from South Carolina and established its base at Gilbert Town (now Rutherfordton), the Patriots had genuine cause for alarm. Charles McDowell called on the Over Mountain Men for assistance. After an inconclusive series of operations during the summer of 1780 the Patriot leaders decided to assemble their forces in late September at Quaker Meadows and march south for a showdown with Ferguson. The problem of who would have overall command of these forces then arose. Charles McDowell decided to make a trip east to see General Gates, who was operating in the Carolinas with a force of Continentals, and to request that General Daniel Morgan or General William Davidson be sent to take charge. The other militia colonels, happy to be rid of Colonel McDowell (whom one historian has described as being "a rather inactive partisan leader"), named William Campbell as their temporary commander. A week later they had annihilated Ferguson's entire command at Kings Mountain, South Carolina.

The leader of the 160 Burke County militia at Kings Mountain therefore was Major Joseph McDowell of Quaker Meadows and not, as some have argued, the Joseph McDowell of Pleasant Gardens. Nor was Charles McDowell in the action. "Quaker Meadows Joe" commanded a detachment of 190 mounted riflemen at Cowpens, South Carolina, had an active part in operations against the Cherokee in this same year (1781), and commanded the McDowell regiment during his brother's campaign against the Cherokee in 1782. After the war he had a prominent role in politics before dying at the age of forty-five. Charles was a state senator in 1778 and during the period 1782 to 1788. In 1782 he was promoted to brigadier general of militia and given command of the expedition against the Cherokee. Local information is available from the Historic Burke Foundation. Phone: (828) 437-4104.

Ramsey's Mill, Deep River near confluence with Haw (Cape Fear) River, Chatham County. In his withdrawal from Guilford Courthouse to Wilmington, Lord Cornwallis spent several days here in late March 1781 getting across Deep River. He had to build a bridge, and when General Greene arrived with his army the Patriots had the opportunity for hitting the British astride the river. Greene lacked the strength for this promising operation, but Lee's legion succeeded in preventing Cornwallis from destroying his bridge after retreating. This facilitated further pursuit, but Greene decided to hold his main body at Ramsey's Mill for reorganization and then direct his operations into South Carolina. The site of the old mill is 300 yards northwest of a marker on U.S. 1 in Moncure. Some authorities believe the name should be spelled Ramsour's Mill or Mills.

Ramsour's Mill, about half a mile north of Lincolnton (U.S. 321), Lincoln County. Patriot militia under Colonel Francis Locke attacked a larger body of Loyalist militia under Colonel John Moore and defeated them here in a bloody fight at close quarters. This victory on 20 June 1780 deserves more recognition as a turning point in the war. As a prelude to the Battle of Kings Mountain (7 October 1780), it contributed to that famous victory by depriving the British of much-needed Loyalist strength. Ramsour's Mill is remembered also as the place where Lord Cornwallis paused from 25 to 28 January 1781 to burn his wagons and excess baggage before resuming his futile pursuit of General Greene to the Dan.

The battlefield is 400 yards west of a highway marker on U.S. 321, half a mile north of Lincolnton. The top of the hill where much of the fighting occurred has been graded for construction of a school complex, but about two-thirds of the battlefield remains open land. The mill was destroyed years ago, and the mill pond to the north is covered by a football stadium. A mass grave reported to be near the top of the hill has never been discovered. About 30 yards north of the school and marked with a bronze plaque by descendants in 1934 is the grave of Loyalist Captain Nicholas Warlick, his brother Philip, and Israel Sain. Captain Warlick was the most effective Loyalist leader in the bloody battle, and his death was the signal for the Loyalist retreat. Six Patriot leaders are buried on the southern slope of the hill, about 50 yards from the road in an unmarked but easily recognized brick structure. "Tarleton's Tea Table," a large flat rock on the battlefield said to have been used by the famous British dragoon in January 1781, was moved in 1930 to the northeast edge of the Lincoln County Courthouse grounds (about half a mile south).

Rockfish (Rock Creek), near Tin City, Duplin County. In his expedition from Wilmington to New Bern in 1781 Major James H. Craig was opposed here briefly by Patriot militia under Colonel James Kenan, who ran after exhausting their ammunition. British mounted troops took twenty or thirty prisoners in the pursuit. A marker on N.C. 11 at Tin City says the action took place 300 yards to the southeast.

Rockfish Creek, northwest corner of Bladen County, about 15 miles south of Fayetteville. In the opening action of the campaign that ended at Moores Creek Bridge (see MOORES CREEK BRIDGE NATIONAL MILITARY PARK) the Patriot force under Colonel James Moore was camped here from 15 to 18 February 1776. The site is just north of the creek and near the right bank of the Cape Fear River.

Russellborough. *See* BRUNSWICK TOWN RUINS.

Rutherfordton. *See* GILBERT TOWN.

Salem Restoration, Winston-Salem. Off Main Street, just south of U.S. 40, in a modern city, is a meticulously restored village, Old Salem, dating from 1766. The story of the Moravian settlements is sketched in the section on nearby Bethabara. Old Salem is a large-scale historic reconstruction of exceptional charm and merit. Many of the original buildings are open to the public. In the Single Brothers House, built to house apprentice craftsmen, costumed artisans now practice and demonstrate ancient skills in nine craft shops. The chapel, kitchen, and dining room are on display. Other historic buildings are Salem Tavern, the John Vogler House, and the Boys' School (now the Wachovia Museum), all of which date from a few years after the Revolution. The Museum of Early Southern Decorative Arts has four galleries and fifteen period rooms from 1690 to 1820. One intriguing aspect of this Moravian community covered on the tour is the presence of what was surely the largest number of German-speaking African Americans. The church owned slaves (individual Moravians could not), but starting in the Revolutionary period, it manumitted many of them and accepted them into full church membership. A ticket to Old Salem allows access to its four museums: the Historic Town of Salem; the Museum of Early Southern Decorative Arts; the Old Salem Toy Museum; and the Old Salem Children's Museum. Its website, www.oldsalem.org, gives a descriptive virtual tour. Old Salem is closed on Mondays.

Shallow Ford Site, Yadkin River. From Trading Ford there were colonial roads east and west of the Yadkin to the region of the Moravian settlements. (They joined southwest of Bethania.) "Butcher" Tarleton found the ford unguarded and crossed here on 6 February 1781, followed by Lord Cornwallis and the rest of the British army that was pursuing General Greene toward the Dan River. In 1780 the Patriots had won a skirmish with the Loyalists at Shallow Ford, and a Civil War cavalry skirmish occurred here 11 April 1865.

The site is near a place that shows on some maps as Huntsville, but where you will find nothing but rugged terrain dotted with homes. It is reached by driving east from U.S. 601 through Courtney about 8 miles on a road just north of the Yadkin-Davie county line. You will come to a bridge over the Yadkin, which is wide, swift, and beautiful at this point. The right bank is covered with heavy vegetation, but the opposite bank is productive bottomland. You can see from the bridge the site of Shallow Ford about three-quarters of a mile down the river. No road or path remains on the right side, but it can be approached by a wagon road through private property on the Forsythe County side.

Somerset Place State Historic Site, Creswell. One of many Revolutionary era plantations that succeeded because of the knowledge of rice cultivation that African-born slaves brought with them. Archeologists have discovered a number of artifacts illustrative of slave life. Tours of the house and grounds touch honestly on a number of sensitive issues, exploring the lives of both the white and black residents of this plantation. It is worth noting Dorothy Spruill Redford's important and popular book, *Somerset Homecoming: Recovering a Lost Heritage* (1988), which documents her efforts to discover the history of her family back through the time of slavery. Her book also provides a useful description of life on Somerset plantation in the early nineteenth century. Redford currently heads up an effort to continue the restoration and development of this important site. Somerset is 7 miles south of Creswell, in the Pettigrew State Park. It is open year-round, and incredibly, admission is free. Phone: (252) 797-4560.

Speedwell Iron Works. *See* TROUBLESOME IRON WORKS.

Spink's Farm, Deep River, Randolph County. General Horatio Gates took command of the Southern army from General Kalb on 25 July 1780. Some authorities say this occurred at Cox's Mill; others believe it was at Hollingsworth's Farm, which was later known as Spink's Farm. The site is on Deep River in the southeast corner of Randolph County in farmland that has changed little since the Revolution. From County Road 1002 about a mile west of Deep River go north on Road 2873 toward Coleridge for 0.5 mile, then east on a dirt road (Number 2887) to the dead end a little less than a mile away. This is the general location of the Continental camp in July 1780 before the hungry regulars continued their march south. (See CAMDEN, SOUTH CAROLINA.)

Spruce Pine, McDowell County, junction of U.S. 19E and N.C. 226. On the third night of their march from Sycamore Shoals, Tennessee the Over Mountain Men who were en route to Kings Mountain, South Carolina stopped here. The campsite is marked. On their way back the brother of John Sevier, Robert, died of his wounds nearby; his grave is here.

Stagville Center was once a prosperous plantation of nearly 30,000 acres dating back to the Revolutionary era. Some of the buildings on the site have been dated as early as 1776. At one time the plantation was home to nine hundred slaves, and some of their cabins, including a row of very rare two-story structures, are preserved in the Horton Grove section of the plantation. The center, which also works on the preservation of oral traditions, is operated by the North Carolina Division of Archives and History. Located at 5828 Old Oxford Highway, 7 miles northeast of Roxboro Road outside Fairntosh in Durham County, Stagville and Horton Grove are open Tuesday to Saturday, 10 A.M. to 4 P.M. Tours are free, but it is advisable to call in advance: (919) 620-0120.

Summerfield (formerly Bruce's Crossroads). On U.S. 220 a few miles north of Guilford Courthouse National Military Park. On the cold and drizzly morning of 13 February 1781 the American rear guard under Colonel Otho Williams, with "Light Horse Harry" Lee's legion attached, was in this vicinity when informed by an excited countryman that British dragoons were approaching from an unexpected direction. Lee dismounted his young bugler so the countryman could use his horse in accompanying a mounted patrol, and the boy was sent back to camp on foot to inform Williams that no enemy had yet been sighted. Soon after this the Americans drew Tarleton's dragoons into an ambush and killed eighteen of them, but not before they had mortally wounded the unarmed bugler. The latter, James Gillies, was buried nearby in the Bruce family graveyard (his grave may still be seen), and the eighteen British dragoons were buried near the crossroads. A small but strikingly handsome monument to "Bugler Boy" Gillies is in Guilford Courthouse National Military Park.

Charles Bruce was a member of the commission that framed the North Carolina constitution, and his home was a Patriot meeting place before the Revolution. The original house burned and another was erected on its site. A memorial to Bruce and Gillies is in front of the Summerfield public school.

Torrence's Tavern Site. At Mount Mourne, Iredell County, a marker on U.S. 21 indicates that the site is nearby, and the actual spot is indicated by a plaque that has to be emancipated periodically from the surrounding underbrush. Here on 1 February 1781 Tarleton caught up with a body of militia that had withdrawn from its unsuccessful defense of the Catawba River line, 10 miles away. Although outnumbered and far in advance of the British army of Cornwallis, Tarleton ordered his legion to charge. Less than two weeks previously his two hundred dragoons had disgraced themselves at Cowpens, South Carolina, by refusing to follow him in a desperate counterattack. Now he taunted them with "remember the Cowpens," and they showed that they were still good at this sort of work. "They broke through the center" of the milling and disordered militia, he reported, and "with irresistible velocity, killing near 50 on the spot, wounded many in the pursuit and dispersed near 500 of the enemy." These figures apparently are greatly exaggerated, but considering that Tarleton himself lost seven men and twenty horses, this was a serious cavalry charge that undoubtedly inflicted heavy casualties. It quieted the detractors in the British camp who had maintained that Tarleton's military reputation had been irretrievably ruined at Cowpens, and it helps explain why the North Carolina militia did not turn out in masses to oppose the British march through their state.

A dispirited General Nathanael Greene was riding alone from the Catawba toward a point where General Davidson's militia was supposed to rendezvous after covering the fords of that river, and he narrowly escaped capture by Tarleton near Torrence's Tavern.

Mount Mourne, site of the tavern, is one of the oldest white settlements in the region. At the Centre Presbyterian Church (building erected in 1854; church established in 1764), 129 Centre Church Road, is a marble marker to its Revolutionary War members, one of whom was General William L. Davidson, and many are buried in the cemetery across the road.

Trading Ford (lost site), Yadkin River. Now flooded by High Rock Lake but still visible at low water, this ford on the old Trading Path (which ran from Petersburg, Virginia to the Waxhaws) was "critical terrain" in the "Race to the Dan" after the Patriot triumph at Cowpens, South Carolina. Retreating from the Catawba River (see BEATTIE'S FORD), General Dan Morgan's troops found that General Greene had boats waiting to take them across the flooded Yadkin at Trading Ford the night of 2 to 3 February 1781. Lacking boats, the British were unable to follow, so they took the old colonial road north to Shallow Ford (see SHALLOW FORD SITE). Lord Cornwallis hoped to cut Greene off in the vicinity of Salem (see SALEM RESTORATION), assuming that the Patriots lacked boats for crossing the Dan along its lower stretches. But he underestimated his provincial adversary, who had learned a thing or two about military planning since leaving his iron forge to join the Continental army some five and a half years earlier; Greene had boats waiting at the ferries east of today's Danville, Virginia, and escaped with his army intact. The Patriots had gained valuable time by taking the more direct route through Guilford Courthouse.

Sketching Trading Ford in January 1849 (when the water was high, as in February 1781), Benson Lossing wrote: "The river is usually fordable between the island and the stakes seen in the picture; below that point the water is deep" (*Pictorial Field Book* II, p. 601). The Duke Power Company's Buck Steam Plant is now at the site of the ford, a few hundred yards downstream from where I-85 bridges the Yadkin just northeast of Salisbury.

Troublesome Iron Works, Troublesome Creek, 1.5 miles north of Monroeton and about 7 miles southwest of Reidsville, Rockingham County. Referred to also as the Speedwell Iron Works on Troublesome Creek, or Speedwell Furnace, this was where Greene left most of his baggage when he marched off for the decisive Battle of Guilford Courthouse (see GUILFORD COURTHOUSE NATIONAL MILITARY PARK). Returning early on the morning of 16 March 1781 after an all-night march in a steady downpour, Greene immediately put his tired troops to work digging field fortifications in anticipation of a British pursuit. But Cornwallis's army remained at Guilford, too exhausted by its hard-fought victory to follow up.

Cornwallis had used the site as a camp earlier, and Greene had held his main body at Speedwell Furnace when his forward elements skirmished with those of Cornwallis at Weitzel's Mill. Washington visited the place on 3 June 1791 during his southern tour. A water-powered grist mill dating from 1770 has been operating in recent years. The local historical society recently purchased 20 acres of the site. Archaeological digs began in 2005 and it is hoped that the site will end up as a park that not only observes its Revolutionary War significance, but also serves as a place to study the lives of the area's eighteenth-century settlers.

Tryon Palace and Gardens (restoration), in New Bern on Pollack and George Streets, Craven County. Destroyed by fire in 1798 but completely restored (1952–1959) on the basis of careful research, Tryon Palace and Gardens are now a great showplace. The site has qualified as a Registered National Historic Landmark and is open daily. Take the Trent Road/Pembroke Exit off Highway 70 and turn left at the light. Turn right on Broad Street, then right on George Street, and right again onto Pollock Street. The parking lot is on Eden Street to your left. Website: www.tryonpalace.org; phone: (252) 514-4900.

Governor William Tryon (1729–1788) had been commissioned in the British army in 1751, was appointed lieutenant governor of North Carolina in 1764, assumed command of the province on the death of Governor Arthur Dobbs in March 1765, and a few months later was appointed governor. He was just in time to bear the brunt of the Stamp Act resistance, which he had done much to provoke (see BRUNSWICK TOWN RUINS).

Next he was up to his ears in Regulators (see ALAMANCE BATTLEGROUND STATE HISTORIC SITE), and one of the things that caused the trouble was his plan to build himself a provincial palace at a cost of £15,000. The provincials already objected to the taxes being levied by royal officials, many of whom were dishonest, and the news of Tryon's building fund created a furor.

As the local political situation worsened, the English architect John Hawkes came to New Bern and built Tryon's palace during the years 1767 to 1770. His design was late Georgian; a two-story central block with a full basement and attic had two connecting wings. The west wing was stables and the other wing included the secretary's office and the kitchen. In the central portion of the mansion the governor had his residence and held meetings of the assembly.

The back of the building commands an impressive view of the Trent River, and the eighteenth-century formal gardens have been restored to their original grandeur. The palace may well have been the most beautiful building in colonial America during its brief existence. After the precipitous flight of Royal Governor Josiah Martin in 1775 it declined in importance as the center of government, but Richard Caswell, a hero of Moores Creek (see MOORES CREEK BRIDGE NATIONAL MILITARY PARK), established himself in Tryon Palace after his election in November 1776 as the first American governor. (Tryon, meanwhile, became governor of New York soon after his victory over the Regulators at Alamance.)

When Washington visited in 1791 he noted in his diary that "what they call the Pallace [is] . . . now hastening to Ruins." Three years later it ceased to be used by the government, rooms were rented, and in 1798 the main building burned. Only the west wing survived, but it was altered beyond recognition.

Although called a restoration, Tryon Palace and Gardens are a magnificent re-creation. Herein lies its greatest distinction. To the uninformed the site will be "just another Williamsburg" (or Disney fantasy), but it will be an exciting adventure for the person seriously interested in early American culture and historic conservation.

Wahab's Plantation (lost site), Catawba River. Tarleton's legion, temporarily commanded by Major George Hanger, was surprised here and badly defeated by Colonel William R. Davie. The plantation belonged to one of Davie's officers, Captain James Wahab (or Wauchope), and the Patriots were able to achieve their coup because of good information about the enemy's dispositions. With the loss of only one man, wounded accidentally, Davie's 80 mounted partisans and 70 riflemen defeated 300 British, inflicting about 60 casualties (killed and wounded; they took no prisoners), taking off almost 100 fully equipped horses and 120 stands of arms. The action took place around sunrise on 21 September 1780. Wahab's Plantation was burned by the British before they moved toward Charlotte, and the site is not known. Presumably it was just north of the state line on the west bank of the Catawba, and it was flooded by Lake White.

Weitzel's Mill, Reedy Fork Creek, Guilford County. After the skirmish some 10 miles to the south at Clapp's Mill, the screening forces of Generals Greene and Cornwallis made contact here on 6 March 1781. A Patriot rear guard fought a heavy delaying action in which each side lost about twenty killed and wounded. The mill has disappeared, only scattered stones remaining, and the site is unmarked. Near what is now known as Summer's Mill (dating from the Civil War), the site is about 200 yards above the point where N.C. 61 crosses Reedy Fork Creek northeast of Greensboro.

Wilmington, mouth of Cape Fear River, New Hanover County. Wilmington was settled in 1732, about five years later than Brunswick Town (see BRUNSWICK TOWN RUINS), which is farther down the Cape Fear River, and it quickly proved to be a better port. Resistance to the Stamp Act was well organized, reaching a climax on 16 November 1765 when the militia forced the royal stamp master to resign and prevented the unloading of stamped paper. The site of the old courthouse, center of these events and venue for committee of safety meetings in 1775, is beneath the commercial structures at the northeast corner of Front and Market Streets.

When Cornwallis was making his plans to invade North Carolina after gaining control of South Carolina, he ordered Wilmington captured and organized as a supply point to shorten his lines of communications. In addition to being one of the state's few ports, Wilmington could be used for transshipment of supplies by boat up the Cape Fear River to Fayetteville (Cross Creek). Major James H. Craig (1748–1812) had little opposition in capturing the place on 1 February 1781 with about four hundred British regulars. Among his prisoners were the prominent Patriots John Ashe and Cornelius Harnett, both of whom died in captivity. Cornwallis marched his bedraggled army into Wilmington on 7 April, and a little more than two weeks later he started his ill-fated march north to Virginia.

Cornwallis is believed to have used the home of John Burgwin as his headquarters, a belief that has no historical support. It would have been logical, however, for him to take it over; it was one of the finest of the two hundred houses that then comprised the town. Built in 1772, using the town jail for its foundation, it is distinguished by a two-story front porch with superimposed columns. The double cellars are said to have been used as a British military prison, naturally. Now state headquarters for the Colonial Dames at 224 Market Street, and referred to as the Burgwin-Wright Museum House and Gardens, it has an exceptionally good little museum of colonial furnishings and relics. Of particular interest are illustrations of the Venus flytrap and trumpet plant drawn in the Carolinas by a British botanist in the early eighteenth century and found in London after World War II by a Wilmington collector. There is one of the original chairs from Tryon Palace (see TRYON PALACE AND GARDENS) and an unusual little four-poster bed made for a child's room. Phone: (910) 762-0570.

The present St. James Church building, 25 South Third Street, was built in 1839 near the site of the original structure of 1751. It still displays a head of Christ attributed to Francisco Pacheco (1564–1654) taken as part of the loot from a privateer captured at Brunswick Town in 1748. When the British occupied Wilmington they converted the original St. James into the main stronghold of their fortifications. (A contemporary British sketch map is in the state archives; order number MC 193-F.) Materials from the old church were used for the present St. James. In the churchyard are graves of the Patriot Cornelius Harnett (1723–1781) and the pioneer dramatist Thomas Godfrey (1736–1763).

Not until after World War II did Wilmington start on the road to extensive industrial and commercial development that began wrecking its historic district. But in 1961 the old residential part of the city was declared a Historic Area in an effort to preserve its character, and some degree of success has been achieved. The Lower Cape Fear Historical Society has been a major influence in the town's historic conservation. It is located at 126 South Third Street. Phone: (910) 762-0492.

Yellow Mountain Road. On U.S. 19E at Roaring Gap Bridge in Avery County is a highway marker that reads: "Yellow Mountain Road. Along a route nearby the 'Over-Mountain Men' marched to victory at King's Mountain, 1780." The route of the one thousand mounted militia was from Sycamore Shoals (now in Tennessee) to Grassy Bald of Roan Mountain, where they stopped for dinner, and thence to Gillespie Gap. Here the force divided. Colonel William Campbell led his Virginians along the crest of the Blue Ridge, went down the south side, and camped at Turkey Cove. The others camped in North Cove, crossed the south end of Linville Mountain, and followed the old trail down Yellow Mountain Road along Paddie Creek to the Catawba River. The forces reunited at Quaker Meadows. (There are three other Yellow Mountains in North Carolina: in northwest Buncombe County, southeast Clay County, and on the Jackson-Macon line.)

OHIO

French and English colonial ambitions clashed in the Ohio Valley almost from the beginning, but for the Indians it was the Middle Ground, a vast territory used for hunting, trading, settlement, and war. At the time of the Revolution, the Indian town at Mingo Bottom, abandoned about 1779, was the only permanent settlement on the west bank of the Ohio River in what is now Ohio, though there were many seasonal towns along the river and many permanent towns on the east bank and along tributary rivers and streams. Gnadenhutten (see GNADENHUTTEN MONUMENT), Schoenbrunn Village, and Salem were established by the Moravians in the early 1770s but were soon wiped out by the Patriots.

Historic sites of the Revolution are almost all associated with the punitive expeditions sent out in reprisal for long-range raids from Detroit and the Sandusky region against the recently established settlements across the Ohio. Most of the state's historic sites are associated with the Indian wars after the Revolution and with the interesting prehistoric period, but these are outside the scope of this guide.

Tourist information is available from the Ohio Development Department's Division of Travel and Tourism. Website: www.discoverohio.com; phone: (614) 466-8844. The Ohio Division of Parks and Recreation is also a helpful source. The major statewide historical agency is the Ohio Historical Society, 1982 Velma Avenue, Columbus, Ohio 43211. Website: www.ohiohistory.org; phone: (614) 297-2300. The Historical Society publishes a vistors guide that bears information on its Revolutionary War past. It is available free by contacting the organization.

Chillicothe Towns. The Chillicothe division of the Shawnee always called its principal town Chillicothe. Because they distinguished themselves as the Indian nation most hostile to U.S. expansion in the Ohio Valley, being identified with most of the destruction on the Kentucky frontier and therefore the principal objective of punitive expeditions, the Shawnee had their principal town destroyed frequently. Hence three separate places were known at various times during the eighteenth century as Chillicothe.

The first was near the present Chillicothe (founded 1796). This Shawnee town was where the invading white forces under Lord Dunmore linked up in 1774 (after the Battle of Point Pleasant, West Virginia) and forced Chief Cornstalk to make peace. It was destroyed by Kentuckians in 1787.

The new Chillicothe, where Daniel Boone was a captive in 1778 and the place destroyed in George Rogers Clark's expedition of August 1780, was on the Little Miami River around modern Xenia (east of Dayton).

The next Chillicothe, which Clark came back to destroy in another punitive operation in November 1782, was on the Great Miami River where today's Piqua stands. Under the latter name it had previously been burned by Clark, in August 1780. This historic site is covered in more detail under Piqua Towns. Of particular note is the Mound City Group National Monument, 3 miles north of modern Chillicothe on Route 104. Two thousand years ago the Hopewell people built the largest earthwork necropolis in the world, much of which was leveled during World War II to build Camp Sherman. Today the remains are preserved within this park, which is open year-round from dawn to dusk. The visitors center has an excellent introduction to Hopewell culture and is open daily from 8 A.M. to 5 P.M. Phone: (614) 774-1125.

The largest of these Hopewell mounds is at Seip Mound State Memorial, 17 miles west of Chillicothe on U.S. 50; it is open every day, dawn to dusk. Phone: (614) 297-2300. Many of the objects excavated from these mounds can be found at the Ohio Historical Center, 1982 Velma Avenue in Columbus (Exit 111 off I-71), open every day but Monday. Phone: (614) 297-2300. The famous Serpent Mound State Memorial is in the town of Locust Grove on Route 73, 20 miles south of Bainbridge and the I-50. The park's hours are variable, and it is best to call first: (800) 752-2757.

Defiance, Maumee River, Defiance County. Birthplace of Chief Pontiac, this was also the site of a French mission (1650). The present city of sixteen thousand people is named for Fort Defiance, built by "Mad Anthony" Wayne in 1794. Apparently quite a fortress, it is reported by the Ohio History Center that Lieutenant John Boyer, an officer in Wayne's army, claimed "the fort could protect the American soldiers from the English, the Indians, and all the devils in hell." Vestiges of the earthworks are in a city park.

Fort Laurens, Tuscarawas River, near Bolivar, Tuscarawas County. Its site preserved in the 81-acre state memorial park, Fort Laurens, built in the winter of 1778 to 1779 and held with great difficulty through the summer of 1779, is the only Revolutionary War fort erected by United States forces in what is now the state of Ohio. It was designed by a professional military engineer, almost certainly Lieutenant Colonel the Chevalier de Cambray-Digny (1751–1822), who was then assigned temporarily to the American headquarters at Fort Pitt as chief engineer.

In one of several poorly managed Patriot attempts to undertake large-scale "search and destroy" operations from Fort Pitt toward Detroit, the inept General Lachlan McIntosh reached this spot in November 1778 with 1,200 troops. It then being too late in the season to continue, the decision was made to build a fort that would be a forward base for continuing the offensive in 1779 and a strategic outpost on the frontier. The fort was not finished when McIntosh withdrew his main force in early December. Colonel John Gibson remained to garrison the isolated post with 150 men of the Thirteenth Virginia Regiment, who completed the fort a few weeks later.

The supply situation became increasingly critical, until the fort finally was abandoned in August 1779. Meanwhile, Gibson withstood one serious siege undertaken by Wyandots and Mingoes with some support from other tribes, and probably with some leadership supplied by white renegades. The Indians withdrew after twenty-five days of sustained effort. According to some accounts, when both sides had been living for some time on starvation rations, Gibson tricked the Indians into believing he had provisions to spare, and agreed to their proposal to lift the siege in return for a barrel of flour and some meat. On 19 March 1779 a relief column of five hundred troops reached Fort Laurens, but the emergency had passed. Plans for renewing the offensive into the Sandusky region were abandoned; Major Frederick Vernon was left to garrison Fort Laurens with about one hundred Pennsylvania troops, but by the middle of May most of these were sent back because they could not be fed.

The remaining twenty-five troops were on the verge of starvation when saved by a supply column in late May. About two weeks later seventy-five fresh troops reinforced the garrison, Vernon was relieved, and Lieutenant Colonel Campbell took command. (Presumably this was Richard Campbell of the Ninth Virginia, whose colonel at this time was John Gibson.) When Colonel Daniel Brodhead succeeded McIntosh in March as commander of the Western Department, he started planning the evacuation of the untenable fort. It was not destroyed, however, because there were hopes that it could be reoccupied. After the Revolution it was demolished.

Fort Laurens State Memorial is managed by the Friends of Fort Laurens Foundation and is located 0.25 mile south of Bolivar off Ohio 212 where it dead-ends at Fort Laurens Road. It is open from Memorial Day to Labor Day from 9:30 A.M. to 5 P.M., Wednesday through Saturday, and 12 P.M. to 5 P.M. on Sunday. (Closed Monday and Tuesday.) Phone: (330) 874-2059. The Friends of Fort Laurens Foundation was formed in 1994 and aims to further revitalize this site, the only standing Revolutionary War fort in the state. A few miles southeast is Zoar Village State Memorial, commemorating a settlement established in 1817 by German refugees.

Gnadenhutten Monument, Gnadenhutten, Tuscarawas County. A 9-acre state historic memorial is a mile south of where the Moravian mission was established about 1773. Two others, Schoenbrunn Village and Salem, were created about the same time. The Reverend David Zeisberger decided in 1777 that his white missionaries would have to abandon their prospering communities in the no-man's-land of what is now eastern Ohio, but the peaceful Indians tried to remain. In 1781 the Hurons, for various reasons, evacuated these survivors, moving them initially to the Sandusky region and then farther west. Prominently and honorably identified with these actions was the Huron chief of Sandusky, Half King (not the Seneca chief Half King, who collaborated with Washington in 1753 and 1754). About ninety Moravian Indians were revisiting their abandoned settlements in the spring of 1782 to gather corn when they were set upon by the militia of Colonel David Williamson and senselessly

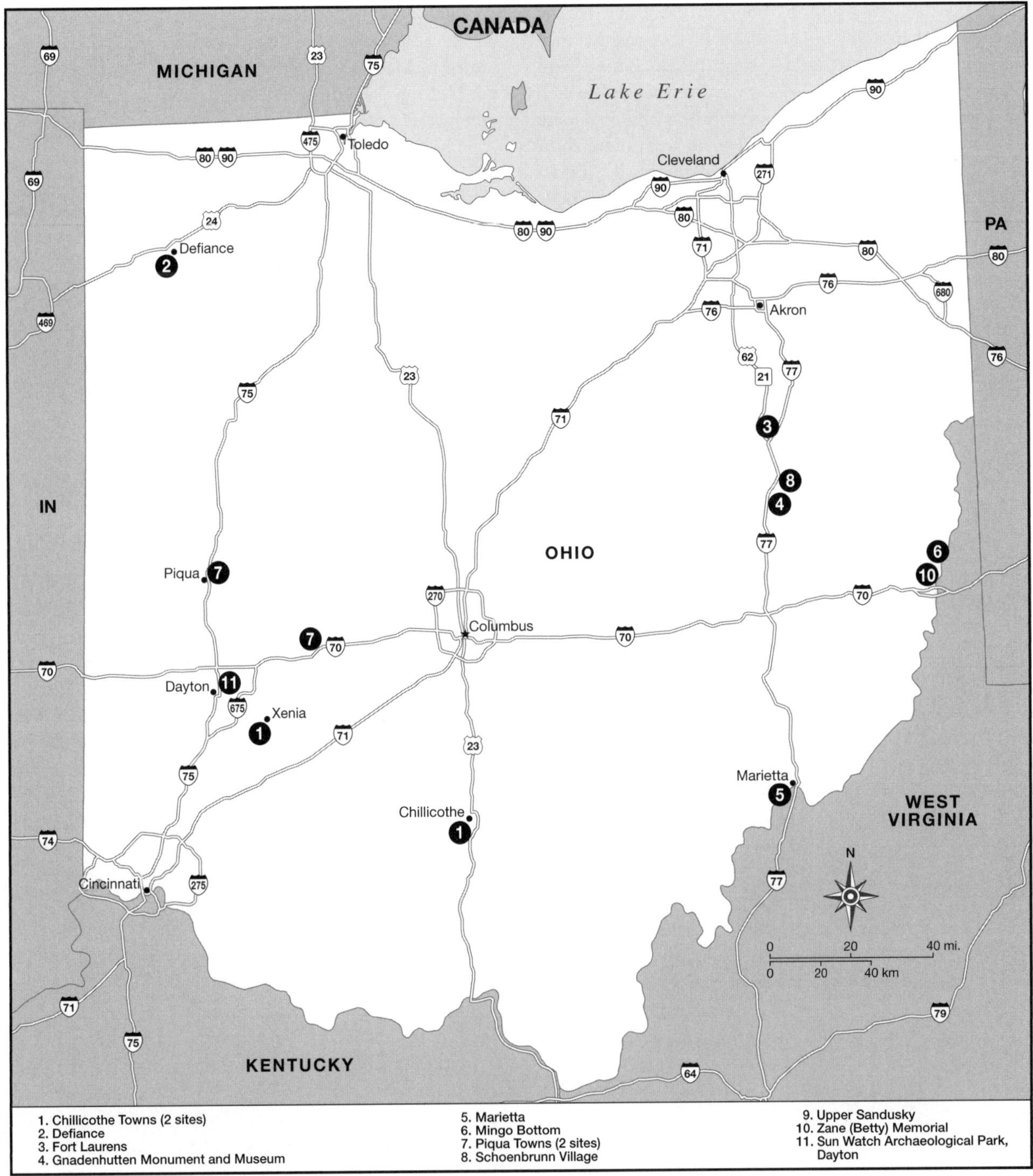

MAP BY XNR PRODUCTIONS. THE GALE GROUP.

massacred, the details of which action mark one of the most horrific scenes in American military history. After luring the unsuspecting, friendly, and, ironically, Christian Indians with talk of protecting them from possible enemies, a quick capture ensued. Williamson and his troops held a trial on the spot. When "guilt" was concluded, another short deliberation took place wherein the troops were asked to vote whether to take the villagers back to Pittsburgh or to kill them. The soldiers assembled in a line and were informed that a vote for leniency could be cast by taking a step forward. A minority of only sixteen troops took a step to spare their lives and the fate of the villagers—none of whom harbored an inkling that they were afoul of anything unlawful or immoral, nor that they would be judged as such—was sealed. Bound and crammed into a building, they were given a day in which to prepare to die. The following morning the men were separated into one house and the woman and children into another. It was decided that the Indians would die by "scalping," a process of killing that involved the hammering of the skull with a mallet, and finally, the cutting and tearing of the scalp (many of the soldiers desired "trophies" to take home). First, the men were killed. Then the soldiers entered the second house and slaughtered the woman and children in the same brutal manner. When an executioner's arm would grow weary of the pounding, another soldier would be waiting earnestly beside to take over. Two young boys escaped and were able to tell their story, further inflaming white settler/Indian relations. In total, 29 men, 27 women, and 34 children were killed. Williamson's militia then destroyed the crops and the Moravian settlements.

These atrocities of 7 to 8 March 1782 set off a new campaign of Loyalist-Indian retaliation against the Kentucky frontier, to which the Patriots responded with the badly bungled Crawford Expedition to Upper Sandusky.

The Gnadenhutten Historical Park and Museum site is a short distance south of modern Gnadenhutten, which is on U.S. 36. Phone: (740) 254-4143. It is open daily from 9 A.M. to 5 P.M. and features many artifacts from the settlement and some authentically reconstructed buildings. A 35-foot high memorial now stands to acknowledge those murdered in the massacre.

Marietta, Ohio River, Washington County. Revolutionary War generals Rufus Putnam and Benjamin Tupper of Massachusetts formed the Ohio Company of Associates in 1787 and, jointly with a group of New York speculators (the Scioto Company of William Duer), arranged to purchase some 1.8 million acres around what became the town of Marietta. (The federal government ended up giving most of this land to the Associates and to individual settlers.) Rufus Putnam arrived with about fifty pioneers in April 1788 to establish the settlement, naming it for Queen Marie Antoinette in recognition of French aid to the American cause during the Revolution. The heart of the settlement was the large fort called Campus Martius, which housed many of the inhabitants until Indian troubles ended with the Treaty of Greenville in 1795. Putnam's home, built around 1788 and used for many years as his office, is the only original structure surviving. It is enclosed in a wing of the imposing Campus Martius State Memorial Museum. Phone: (740) 373-3750. At 326 Front Street is the fifteen-room brick house built in the 1810s by Return Jonathan Meigs, Jr., son of the Revolutionary War hero (see MEIGS HOUSE SITE under Connecticut) and an early governor of Ohio. Many Revolutionary War veterans are buried in Mound Cemetery on Fifth and Scammel Streets not far from downtown Marietta, which contains a perfect example of a prehistoric Indian mound.

Mingo Bottom, Ohio River. A detached band of Iroquois that had left the main body before 1750 was living on the Ohio just before the Revolution. Their town, a well-known landmark, was about where today's Mingo Junction is located, a few miles below Steubenville. In 1766 the town numbered sixty families and was the only permanent settlement—red or white—on the Ohio River between the western area of Pennsylvania and Louisville, Kentucky. The site shows on historical maps as Mingo Bottom.

Piqua Towns. The Piqua division of the Shawnee occupied several towns in Ohio called Piqua. (Like the Chillicothe [see CHILLICOTHE TOWNS], they had the custom of taking this name with them.) According to the *Handbook of American Indians*, the Piqua town in which Tecumseh was born was on the north side of Mad River about 5 miles west of the present Springfield in Clark County. Destroyed by George Rogers Clark in August 1780, it was never rebuilt. The Indians then established Upper and Lower Piqua on the Great Miami River, the latter on the site of modern Piqua and the former about 3 miles to the north. Upper Piqua was on the site of the former Miami town of Pickawillany. Here is the Old Johnson Trading Post, built in 1749, the year Celoron de Blainville passed through on the expedition claiming the Ohio Valley for France. When the French started their move to take physical possession of the Ohio Valley, the first overt act was the capture of Pickawillany, in which all the defenders were killed (1752). Two years later the Seven Years' War started.

No distinction is made in most accounts between the two places on the Great Miami called Upper and Lower Piqua, although old maps clearly indicate that the larger one was at the mouth of Loramie Creek, several miles above today's Piqua (old Lower Piqua). The latter became one of several places called Chillicothe during the Revolutionary era. The present city on the site adopted the old name Piqua in 1823. In the vicinity are the Old Johnson Trading Post and the Clark Monument, said to be on the site of the Indian village destroyed in 1780. The Piqua Historic Indian Museum is part of the Piqua Historical Area, a 200-acre park built on the former farm of John Johnston, United States Indian agent from 1812 to 1829. In addition to a re-creation of the pre-Revolutionary Pickawillany trading post, and an Indian mound, costumed interpreters and craft demonstrators present farm life in the

Log Cabin at Schoenbrunn Village. *A church, school, and about a dozen cabins have been rebuilt in the 190-acre Schoenbrunn Village, the site of a settlement founded in 1772 by Moravian missionaries.* © LEE SNIDER/PHOTO IMAGES/CORBIS.

early Republic. The museum, built to resemble General Anthony Wayne's Fort Piqua, offers displays on eighteenth-century Indian culture. There is also a restored mile-long section of the Miami and Erie Canal off the museum's patio. The Museum is 3 miles northwest of Piqua on Route 66 (take westbound U.S. 36 Exit off of I-75). Hours vary with the season; phone: (800) 752-2619.

Schoenbrunn Village, near New Philadelphia, Tuscarawas County. Moravian missionaries and Christianized Indians from Pennsylvania founded the first permanent white settlement in Ohio at this place in 1772. It prospered until the Revolution, writing Ohio's first civil code and building its first Christian church and schoolhouse. In 1777 military threats from the Patriots forced the town's abandonment. The site was lost and forgotten until members of the surviving Moravian church dug into their archives in Bethlehem, Pennsylvania to find a map from which its location could be determined. In 1923 the Ohio State Archaeological and Historical Society acquired the site and started reconstruction on the original foundations. The church, school, gardens, and seventeen cabins have been rebuilt and furnished in the 190-acre Schoenbrunn Village State Memorial. The cemetery and museum are also open to the public. Every summer the site offers an outdoor pageant, "Trumpet in the Land," retelling the history of Schoenbrunn and Gnadenhutten. Phone: (800) 752-2711.

The site is on Ohio Route 259, 3 miles southeast of New Philadelphia. From I-77 it is reached by using the U.S. 250 bypass to the Schoenbrunn Exit, then driving west on U.S. 250A and Ohio 259 to the park.

Sun Watch Archaeological Park, Dayton, offers a unique and fascinating reconstruction of the Indian culture of the region on one of the most important archaeological sites in Ohio. The park is a National Historic Landmark and is located on West River Road; take the Moses Boulevard Exit from I-75 and turn left onto West River Road. The park is open Monday through Saturday, 9 A.M. to 5 P.M., and Sunday, noon to 5 P.M. Phone: (513) 268-8199.

Upper Sandusky and vicinity, Wyandot County. Colonel William Crawford's Sandusky Expedition in the summer of 1782 was a disaster of the type Americans have come to know better since World War II: a "search and destroy" operation compromised from the start and annihilated by an enemy having the benefit of good military intelligence, in both senses of that term. The fiasco was particularly tragic because of the horribly cruel death of Colonel Crawford, who had been a friend of Washington since their first association on the frontier in 1749, when the latter had started surveying the vast holdings of Lord Fairfax in the Shenandoah Valley (see WASHINGTON'S LANDS and WHEELING under West Virginia).

Crawford had long been urging that Patriot forces invade the Sandusky region to destroy this base of Loyalist-Indian raids. But it was not until 1782 that the expedition finally was authorized. The old frontiersman thought the time was about three years too late insofar as his personal involvement was concerned, but he reluctantly agreed to lead it. The five hundred volunteers assembled at Mingo Bottom, elected leaders, and started their 150-mile advance under the continuous surveillance of the enemy. Their route passed through the Moravian settlements where the Gnadenhutten massacre (see GNADENHUTTEN MONUMENT) had recently taken place. First contact was made on 4 June in the vicinity of today's town of Upper Sandusky.

Enemy forces initially comprised about one hundred of Butler's Rangers under Captain William Caldwell, these famous refugees from New York's Mohawk Valley being then stationed at Detroit. Caldwell was supported by about two hundred Indians with Delaware and Wyandot chiefs and the notorious frontier soldiers Simon Girty, Alexander McKee, and Mathew Elliott. Both sides restricted their action this first day to long-range fire, in which the Patriots appeared to have the advantage. But what Crawford did not realize was that Caldwell was waiting for reinforcements from Detroit. These came in the form of additional Rangers with two cannon. Additional Indians also arrived, about 140 Shawnee plus others. Threatened with envelopment, the Patriots started withdrawing soon after dark, but by this time they were under heavy fire and almost encircled. A panic developed. Most of the Americans managed to extricate themselves. After a harassed retreat of about 20 miles to the southeast, Crawford made a stand near Olentangy Creek in the early afternoon of 6 June. His second in command, Major David Williamson (who had fallen only five votes short of winning Crawford's top leadership post), led most of the troops to safety. Colonel Crawford was captured with his nephew, William Crawford, and his son-in-law, Major William Harrison (of the famous Virginia family). All were tortured to death, the fury of the Indians being particularly savage because of the recent atrocity by white troops at Gnadenhutten.

The details of Colonel Crawford's torture were reported by Dr. John Knight, who was forced to witness the spectacle while waiting his turn, but who then escaped.

Battle Island Monument marks the general location of the initial skirmish between Crawford and Caldwell on 4 June 1782. The monument, enclosed by a metal fence and maintained by the local Lion's Club, is on the southeast side of Ohio 67 about a mile from its intersection just north of Upper Sandusky with U.S. 23 and Ohio 53. On the Sandusky River a short distance to the northeast is the 3-acre Indian Mill (1820) and Park. The Indian Mill State Memorial is located 3 miles northeast of Upper Sandusky on Country Road 47. The first contact between opposing forces on 4 June was made in this area.

The place where Colonel Crawford was tortured to death is marked by a monument on the south side of Tymochtee Creek off County Road 29 about 0.75 mile east of Crawford. On private land but open to the public, the monument is reached by following Ohio 199 north-northeast from Upper Sandusky to Crawford (about 7 miles from the center of the former town), then turning east on County Road 29 to the point where Road T30C comes in from the north. A highway marker helpful for directions and historical information is located on Route 199. A good source of information is the Wyandot County Historical Society located at 130 South 7th Street in Upper Sandusky. Phone: (419) 294-3857.

Upper Sandusky is also home to the Wyandot Mission Church, 200 East Church Street, where the African American minister John Stewart worked with the Wyandot in the aftermath of their devastating defeat at the hands of the United States. The mission is a Methodist historical shrine and can be viewed by appointment; phone: (419) 294-4841.

Zane (Betty) Memorial, Martins Ferry, Belmont County. The heroism of Elizabeth "Betty" Zane, sister of the founder of Wheeling, West Virginia, helped save that place from capture in 1782. Her memorial is at the Fourth Street entrance to Old Walnut Grove Cemetery, where she and many Revolutionary War soldiers are buried. Her brother, Ebenezer Zane (1747–1812), was the first white settler on the site of Wheeling before the Revolution (1769) and a famous pioneer after the Revolution in what is now Ohio. He opened the road from Wheeling to Limestone (now Maysfield, Kentucky) that became famous as Zane's Trace. The settlement he established in 1799 on a section of land where his road crossed the Muskingum River was the state capital from 1810 to 1812. Originally called Westbourne, it was renamed Zanesville. Martins Ferry is said to be the oldest continuously occupied white settlement in Ohio, having been founded before 1785. (See also WHEELING, WEST VIRGINIA.)

PENNSYLVANIA

With the largest city, Philadelphia, which was the principal seat of Patriot government during the Revolution, and with one of the largest land areas, Pennsylvania should have a correspondingly high number of historical sites. There are several reasons why Pennsylvania, like Virginia, takes up fewer pages in this guide than, for example, New York and South Carolina. First, there was considerably less Whig-Loyalist warfare and operations on the frontier. Second, major military operations were limited to the last half of 1777, which ended with the British in possession of Philadelphia for nine months (26 September 1777 to 18 June 1778). Finally, economic prosperity, the greatest enemy of historic preservation, has buried many colonial regions under industrial development.

State historical agencies and many county tourist-historical offices have done an exceptionally thorough job of making available information about colonial and Revolutionary sites.

The *Guide to the Historical Markers of Pennsylvania* is unquestionably the finest publication of this type, a model for other states. The Pennsylvania Historical and Museum Commission (PHMC), as the official agency of the commonwealth for the conservation of its historic heritage, undertook in 1946 a program of erecting and maintaining historical markers at all points associated with "events and personalities of genuine significance to the history of the Commonwealth as a whole." This goal has been achieved with thoroughness. And, of most importance to persons with a mature interest in these sites, the text and location of each marker is included (by county) in the guide mentioned above, and this publication is thoroughly indexed. Revised in 2000, this guide lists over 1,800 markers. It and a variety of other publications that outline the state's colonial past can be purchased by contacting the PHMC. Phone: (800) 747-7790.

Pennsylvania does a remarkable job of maintaining more than fifty state historic properties, state historical museums, National Park Service sites, and landmarks that are administered by independent state commissions. These are listed, briefly described, and plotted in "The Pennsylvania Trail of History," a folder published by the Pennsylvania Historical and Museum Commission. Website:www.phmc.state.pa.us; phone: (866) PA-TRAIL.

Barren Hill, northwest suburbs of Philadelphia. When Washington received information that the British were preparing to evacuate Philadelphia, he sent a strong force under Lafayette from the Valley Forge encampment to establish an outpost between the opposing armies. Lafayette was given three missions: to gather additional information of British preparations, to attack enemy foraging parties, and to protect Valley Forge. With more than two thousand troops and five guns, Lafayette marched from Valley Forge on 18 May 1778, crossed the Schuylkill at Swede's Ford, and moved about 4 miles south to set up a strong position on high ground that has retained the name Barren Hill. Lafayette deployed his command carefully, but came close to being trapped and annihilated by a large British force sent out from Philadelphia with this mission. The young Frenchman kept his head and skillfully retreated by way of Matson's Ford (now Conshohocken), using a route unknown to the enemy.

A stone marker on Ridge Pike at Barren Hill commemorates the encampment of Lafayette in this area. The site of St. Peter's Church, where Lafayette set up a delaying position, is occupied by a more recent structure identified by a highway marker on U.S. 422 on Church Road in Barren Hill.

Battle of the Clouds, Chester County. The action of 16 September 1777 generally associated in the history books with the Admiral Warren and the White Horse Taverns is referred to in markers in Chester County as the Battle of the Clouds. After withdrawing behind the Schuylkill River to the edge of Germantown a few days after his defeat on the Brandywine Battlefield, Washington recrossed the river to contest Lord Howe's advance on Philadelphia. On 15 September he took up positions on what is now called Swedesford Road (Number 15023, running into Pa. 401, then U.S. 30, near Malvern). This was the older and less direct of two "roads to Lancaster." The next day, 16 September, Washington's army ascended hills to the south and set up a line of battle. A major engagement was developing when a record-breaking deluge ruined almost all the forty thousand musket cartridges recently issued to the Patriot army. The British lost little ammunition, being equipped with properly designed cartridge boxes, but Washington had to break off the action and retreat again.

A marker in front of Villa Maria Hall of Immaculata University says the battle took place on or near the 375-acre campus, which occupies the highest ground between Philadelphia and Harrisburg. (The more precise location is given below.) The entrance to the college is on Pa. 352 a little more than a mile south of U.S. 30 (from the junction 3.5 miles west of Paoli).

The Admiral Warren is in good condition and is an upscale eight-suite inn now called the General Warren Inn. It is on a dead-end stretch of the "road to Lancaster" (now the Old Lancaster Highway) near Warren Avenue in Malvern.

White Horse Tavern (established 1721) is now a private residence on Swedesford Road just west of Planebrook Road. Contemporary accounts refer to the taverns as being about 3 miles apart, which squares with the locations given above and refutes the common assumption that another White Horse Tavern, in the modern village of White Horse, some 6 miles southeast, was involved.

Malin Hall, Washington's headquarters during the battle, is standing on a small side road off Swedesford Road about midway between the taverns mentioned above. It is now a private residence. No longer standing are Boot Tavern, where General Knyphausen's advance guard routed the Pennsylvania militia on Washington's right (west flank), and the Three Tuns Tavern and Hershey's Mill, where General Cornwallis's vanguard hit the opposite flank. The present King Road traces the American line of defense. Known in colonial times as the Indian King Road, it is named for the Indian King Tavern, still standing in the village of Indian King.

The house used before the battle by Cornwallis (marked by a plaque) is on the west side of Pa. 352 about 0.2 mile north of Goshenville.

Bethlehem, Northampton County. The Moravians, an evangelical sect of Protestants revived in Saxony by Count Nikolaus van Zinzendorf, started settling in Georgia in 1735. When the War of Jenkins's Ear broke out four years later, they looked to the north for a new home. In 1741 the Moravians from Georgia established Nazareth and Bethlehem. By 1775 these places numbered 2,500 people, becoming a strong and lasting force in America's cultural development. The annual Bach Festival stems from the Moravian "service of song" started in 1742. In the city of 73,000 people now more famous for Bethlehem Steel and other manufacturing industries, twenty-one structures survive from the period 1741 to 1775, the oldest being on West Church Street. The six-story Brothers' House (1748) was used during the Revolution as a military hospital. In the Gemeinhouse (*Gemein* meaning congregation or community), Bethlehem's oldest building (1741), is the Moravian Museum at 66 West Church Street. Phone: (610) 867-0173. The Moravian Archives, a very valuable collection, are on Main Street. For further information on Bethlehem's historic sites call (610) 868-1513.

Brandywine Battlefield, Delaware and Chester Counties. The beautiful name and scenic terrain of the Brandywine came close to acquiring very ugly associations in American history. Here Washington's most devoted admirers had cause for grave doubts about his military competence; D. S. Freeman writes, "Washington conducted the Brandywine operations as if he had been in a daze" (*Washington*, IV, p. 488).

For several months the Americans had been baffled by General Howe's strategic maneuvering from his base in New York City. Washington knew the British would attempt to capture Philadelphia as soon as the weather permitted resumption of military operations in 1777. But would they move overland through New Jersey as they had done the preceding year, or would they take advantage of their naval supremacy to invade from the sea? Late in July 1777 the mystery cleared when the British left New York with a large amphibious force and were subsequently sighted off the Delaware Capes. Washington started moving his army from central New Jersey in the direction of Philadelphia to counter the expected attack, but the British fleet headed back to sea, and its location was unknown to

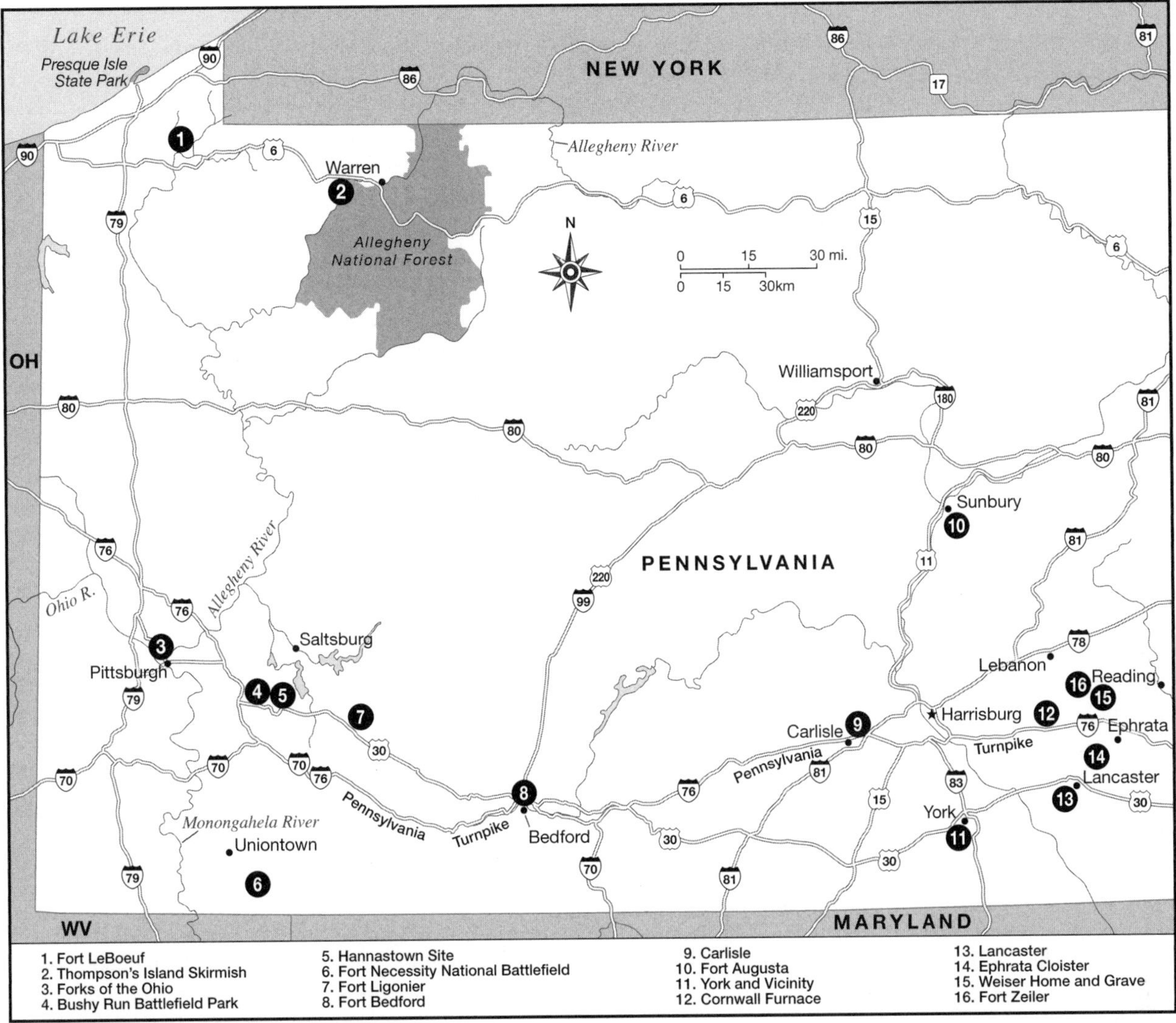

MAP BY XNR PRODUCTIONS. THE GALE GROUP.

the Americans for the next three weeks. On 22 August it appeared in the Chesapeake, and now Washington finally understood what his adversary was up to. On Sunday 24 August the Rebel army marched through Philadelphia and two days later was in position around Wilmington. The British landed at Head of Elk, Maryland.

Having been at sea for so long, the British needed time to get in shape for offensive operations, and several days passed before Washington could decide on his next move. On 9 September the Americans started leaving the Wilmington area to establish a defensive position along Brandywine Creek to bar the British advance on Philadelphia.

Although this was the obvious place to make a stand, the terrain presented problems. The creek was deep enough to require the British to use established fords, but there were many to chose from.

The British professionals used the standard tactics for a river crossing that can be traced back to Alexander the Great. General Howe sent General Knyphausen and his Germans due east to make a secondary attack against the main fords where the Americans had set up their main line of defense around Chadds Ford. Patriot outposts and delaying forces performed well, and by 8 A.M. the American defenses on the east bank of the Brandywine were eagerly awaiting the expected attack across the creek. There was a spirited exchange of musket and cannon fire across Chadds Ford, but when the enemy showed no inclination to advance farther, Washington must have realized that this was a mere diversionary effort.

Around 11 A.M. the Patriot commander began to receive reports of enemy troop movements that threatened his exposed right flank. But the messages were confusing, not only because the Americans had not properly studied the geography of the region but also because the reports were contradictory. Shortly after 2 P.M., however, Washington was convinced that enough of a threat was developing on his north flank to warrant shifting strength in this direction from positions on the Brandywine that had not yet come under fire from Knyphausen's column. The Americans still believed that Howe's main concentration was opposite Chadds Ford and that no more than two enemy brigades (2,000–3,000 men) were attempting the envelopment.

Actually, it was the main British force, and Howe was repeating the strategy that had been so successful against Washington in the Battle of Long Island (see under NEW YORK). Howe personally accompanied this column, which was commanded by Lord Cornwallis and comprised 7,500 of his total force of 12,500 rank and file. Moving north on the Great Valley Road, Howe and Cornwallis led their troops through Trimble's Ford on the west branch of the Brandywine, then eastward across Jeffries' Ford on the east branch, and southeast through Sconnelltown. The British command post was established on Osborne's Hill about 3:30 P.M., line of battle was formed about a mile ahead, generally along Street Road, and an hour later Washington, at his headquarters near Chadds Ford, heard the dreaded sound of enemy cannon far to his flank and rear. At the same time the Germans to his front increased their rate of fire, evidence that their long-expected frontal attack might be starting.

Washington had started the divisions of William Alexander ("Lord Stirling") and Adam Stephen on a march back from the Brandywine toward the Birmingham Meetinghouse after the first reports of an enemy threat in that quarter were received. But he had then sent them orders to halt in place because a new report indicated that no British troops had been seen around the Forks of the Brandywine. At about 2 P.M., however, new intelligence convinced Washington that he should have Alexander and Stephen resume their movement toward the flank and that the division of John Sullivan should also be deployed in this quarter. At 4:30 these three divisions were trying to get their defenses organized when the British attack started. Washington then left the brigades of Anthony Wayne and William Maxwell (with Wayne in overall command) to defend Chadds Ford, ordered Nathanael Greene to move his division cross country toward the Birmingham Meetinghouse from its reserve position around Chadds Ford, and he himself raced to the meetinghouse.

Today a tourist can trace the battle in a driving tour and also, in the spring and fall, a guided van tour sponsored by the PHMC. The driving tour follows a two-lane highway (Birmingham Road) from Sconnelltown, past Osborne's Hill and the Birmingham Meetinghouse through Dilworthtown, down the Old Wilmington Pike to its junction with the new Wilmington Pike (U.S. 202), to the intersection with U.S. 1. All of the driving tour information, as well as all park information, is available by contacting the Brandywine Battlefield Park, which is administered by the PHMC. Park information phone: (610) 459-3342. The battlefield grounds, which make up over 10 square miles, is decimated by development, with the exception of a portion of Sandy Hollow. This area, called Heritage Park, is a designated State Battlefield Site and the grounds of the bloodiest fighting of Brandywine. A considerate local farmer who chose not to sell out to the area's aggressive developers is responsible for this preservation. "The plowed hill" across the highway from the meetinghouse, where the battle started, is now occupied by a large house and crowned by old trees, and most of the ground across which the Guards and Grenadiers attacked is occupied by more of the McMansion-sized, modern-style houses that litter this country's once open fields. A large cemetery covers the area around the meetinghouse, and here a tourist will find the monument to Lafayette and Pulaski. The former was wounded a few hundred yards to the southeast while he was rallying Patriot troops. Young Count Casimir Pulaski had only recently arrived in America when he distinguished himself at the Brandywine while serving as a volunteer aide-de-camp to Washington; four days after the battle he was commissioned a brigadier general by Congress and put in command of the four dragoon regiments recently authorized.

The second position of Washington's was about 0.3 mile southeast of the meetinghouse, on the high ground (now Battle Hill) just beyond today's Wylie Road. Wayne and Maxwell dropped back from the vicinity of Chadds Ford as Knyphausen, pushing forward with overwhelming superiority, joined forces with Cornwallis as night fell. Wayne blocked Knyphausen's attempts to cut off Washington's retreat to Chester, and the shattered Patriot army made good its escape during the night. It had lost eleven cannon and about three hundred men killed; of the six hundred wounded, many were captured. Howe had lost about half that number of men.

A visit to the Brandywine battlefield is interesting to the casual tourist because the region is particularly scenic and rich in associations with the Brandywine School of American art. A personal reconnaissance is rewarding to those who have studied the battle. Many historic points are not marked; except for the previously mentioned van tour, there is no organized self-guided tour of the extensive area over which the opposing forces maneuvered from long before daylight until after dark on that eventful day of 11 September 1777. The PHMC is chiefly concerned with the two historic houses in the 50-acre Brandywine Battlefield State Park; the area encompassed by the battle actually covers more than 30,000 acres. The two houses are the Benjamin Ring House, or "Washington's Headquarters," as it's referred to in the guide; and the Gideon Gilpin House, or "Lafayette's Quarters." The latter has a stunning three hundred-plus-year-old sycamore tree growing so large in the side yard that it takes nine people to reach around it. A reenactment of the battle is held every year in the last week of September (this varies somewhat).

A high-speed, divided highway (U.S. 1) carries a stream of traffic through the southern edge of the battlefield, past the state park in which stand the stone houses used by Washington (burned in 1930 but restored) and Lafayette (original). The houses are open daily for guided tours. The park is about halfway between the village of Chadds Ford and the junction of the Baltimore and Wilmington pikes (now U.S. 1 and U.S. 202) where Washington's army rallied before retreating to Chester. From the village of Chadds Ford the Creek Road (Pa. 100) winds northwest along the foot of the high ground where the Patriots established their main line of defense. This picturesque, two-lane country road provides a view of the bottomland extending a few hundred yards southwest to Brandywine Creek, and a tourist will see clearly why the fords played such a critical role in the strategy of the opposing commanders.

In Kennett Square, on Route 1, 5 miles south of Chapp's Ford, Howe's camp on the eve of battle, the Consolidated School and Presbyterian Home mark the hills on which the British and German troops were bivouacked. Cornwallis and Howe are said to have used the building that survives as Newberrys Store (formerly the Shippen Mansion); Knyphausen's headquarters was in the Unicorn Tavern, Connor's Drugstore in recent years.

The site of Welch's Tavern, where Knyphausen's column made contact with an American patrol about 3 miles east of Kennett Square, is marked at a spot where Pa. 52 turns north from U.S. 1 at Longwood. The Kennett Meetinghouse, where General William Maxwell's light infantry had taken up a delaying position, is standing on U.S. 1, about 1.5 miles west of Chadds Ford and 0.4 mile east of Hammorton, where a marker identifies it.

The Great Valley Road, which Cornwallis followed north, is not today a single road, if it ever was. The British route was initially east on the road to Chadds Ford from Kennett Square for a little more than 3 miles, then north on Schoolhouse Road to Street Road, a few hundred yards east on this road (whose name has been preserved), and then north on the present Red Lion–Northbrook Road. The site of Trimble's Ford on this road is marked on the west branch on County Road 15153, just off Road 15077, and a little more than a mile south of Marshallton.

The latter place is the site of Martin's Tavern, which figures in contemporary accounts of the Battle of the Brandywine. Here Squire Thomas Cheney is alleged to have spent the night before making his legendary ride to warn Washington of the British turning movement. The quiet village of Marshallton dates from the early 1700s. Old buildings, including a Revolutionary War tavern said to be Martin's, have been tastefully restored to form a group of shops and a restaurant.

Taylor's Ford, on the Lancaster Pike east of Marshallton, is now Cope's Bridge, on the outskirts of West Chester. Jeffries' Ford, which Cornwallis reached before 2 P.M., is marked just west of Sconnelltown. From here he moved southeast along the Birmingham Road, as has already been described. In 1915 the major landmarks along this axis of the British advance were marked. Many signs and monuments have since disappeared.

The most useful guide now available is downloadable off the internet at http://www.ushistory.org/brandywine/brandywine.htm. It is also available free at the park. A book on Brandywine is available through the previously mentioned PHMC website. Another good source of information is the Chadds Ford Historical Society, P.O. Box 27, Chadds Ford, Pa. 19317 Website: www.chaddsford-history.org; phone: 610-388-7376.

Brodhead Expedition. *See* THOMPSON'S ISLAND.

Bushy Run Battlefield Park, north of Jeannette and just east of Harrison City, on Pa. 993. On a sultry August day in 1763 a British relief column commanded by Colonel Henry Bouquet (1719–1765) was about 26 miles short of its goal, Fort Pitt, which had been besieged by the Indians. (See FORKS OF THE OHIO). At about 1 P.M. the advance guard was suddenly attacked by a large force of Delawares, Shawnees, Mingoes, and Hurons who had broken off their siege of Fort Pitt to set an ambush. They obviously hoped to repeat the history of Braddock's defeat, which had occurred near this place in 1755.

Two companies of the main body rushed forward to extricate the advance guard, and then the British force hastily organized a perimeter defense on the best ground immediately available. Already tired from a 17-mile march that day, and having covered almost 200 miles from Carlisle, Pennsylvania, in less than twenty days, the British regulars and handful of American volunteers held off the Indians for seven hours, when darkness brought a temporary lull in the fighting. During the night the British unloaded flour bags from the 340 horses in the relief column and stacked these to form a central strong point.

At dawn the Indians resumed their heavy firing and waited for heat and exhaustion to weaken the white soldiers. Around 10 A.M. the Indians could see that enemy troops were being withdrawn from the western side of the defensive perimeter and that a general retreat was obviously under way. Confident of success, the Indians

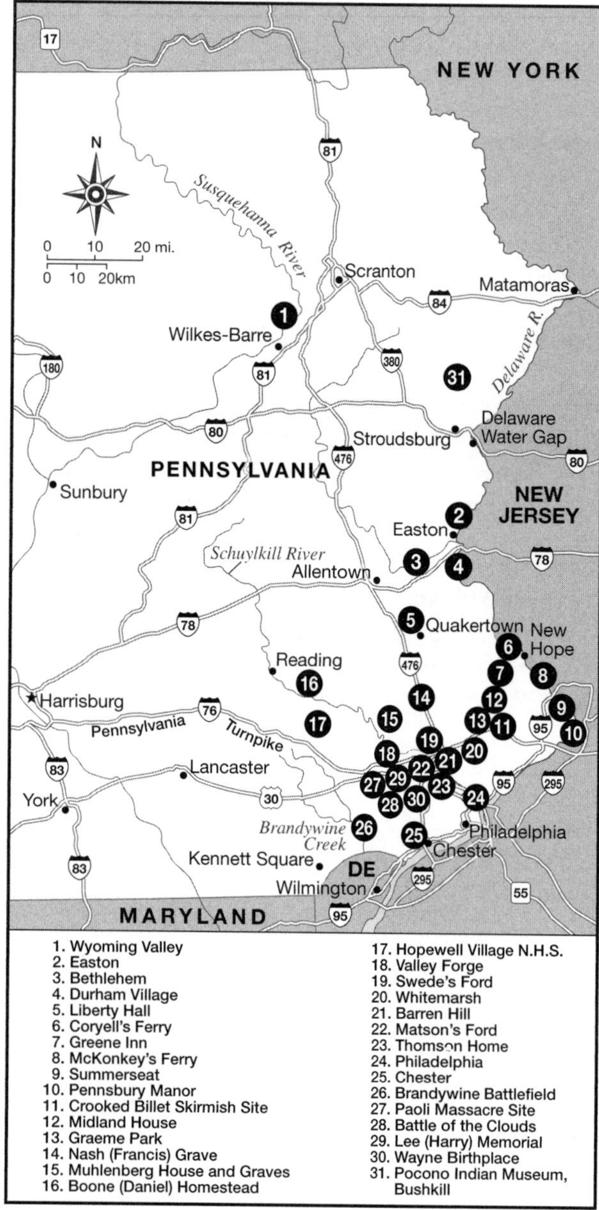

MAP BY XNR PRODUCTIONS. THE GALE GROUP.

attacked the weakened sector, and had penetrated the defensive perimeter when they came in for a series of devastating tactical surprises.

Bouquet had withdrawn two companies to the rear, as if preparing for a withdrawal, but had sent them on a compass course through the heavy woods to attack the south flank of the penetration. The Indians fled in wild confusion from the bayonet attack that followed the surprise fire of these two companies, and then were ambushed by two additional companies of regulars that had infiltrated forward for this purpose.

About sixty dead Indians were counted, but the British had lost eight officers and ninety men killed and wounded in the two days of fighting—a quarter of their total strength. The regulars buried their dead and marched on to Fort Pitt.

The first step in rescuing this site from oblivion was taken in 1918, when schoolchildren of the county donated their pennies to make possible the purchase of 6.5 acres of the battlefield. This became the nucleus of the present 213-acre state park currently managed by the PHMC. A large granite block marks the site of the "flour-bag fort," and trees have been planted to show the first positions taken by the British. There is a museum and a network of drives and walks through the battlefield. The park also has picnic areas and an arboretum. Website: www.bushyrun-battlefield.com; phone: 724-527-5584.

Carlisle, Cumberland county seat. A great amount of small-town charm survives in modern Carlisle despite its location in a region of great economic development. In or just outside the town are sixteen highway historical markers pertaining to the colonial and Revolutionary War periods, and the chamber of commerce has published an admirable map-guide.

Settlers started reaching the area around Carlisle a few years after the first trader, James Letort, arrived in about 1720. The settlement became the center of military activity in Pennsylvania during the Seven Years' War, the jumping-off place from which expeditions made their way along the chain of forts toward the Forks of the Ohio and the Old Northwest.

Carlisle was the place from which John Armstrong's expedition to Kittanning started in 1756, and from which John Forbes's expedition to the Forks of the Ohio started in 1758. In Pontiac's Rebellion, Carlisle was the town where the Swiss colonel Henry Bouquet assembled a relief column of British regulars—men of the Black Watch, the Seventy-seventh Highlanders, and the Royal Americans—to save Fort Pitt, which was being defended by another Swiss mercenary, Captain Simeon Ecuyer. After winning his notable victory at Bushy Run, Bouquet the next year led an expedition into the Old Northwest from Carlisle and decisively defeated the Indians in Pontiac's Rebellion.

Carlisle claims James Wilson as a citizen. Born in Scotland (1742), educated at St. Andrews, Glasgow, and at Edinburgh, Wilson suddenly decided to emigrate to America, and studied law under John Dickinson in Philadelphia. In 1767 he was admitted to the bar, moved to Carlisle, and quickly became its leading lawyer. Rising to prominence as a frontier politician, signer of the Declaration of Independence, statesman, jurist, and large-scale land speculator, he died suddenly (1798) while visiting a friend in Edenton, North Carolina. His body was moved from its grave on a nearby plantation many years later (1906) and reinterred in Christ Church, Philadelphia. The James Wilson Hotel on Pitt Street in central Carlisle is on the site of one of Wilson's many homes (he left for Philadelphia in 1778). The hotel is said to incorporate portions of the original structure.

Dickinson College, at High and West Streets, on Route 11, was founded as a grammar school in 1773 and was named for John Dickinson when chartered as a college in 1783. (The Dickinson School of Law, the oldest law school in Pennsylvania, was not founded until 1834.)

John Armstrong, elderly "hero of Kittanning" (see mention above), served as a brigadier general during the Revolution and was a member of Congress. Although he was at Charleston in June 1776, at the Brandywine in September 1777, at Germantown three weeks later, and with one of the relief columns to the Wyoming Valley in July 1778, he achieved the distinction—quite honorably—of seeing no action at any of these historic places. The site of his home is marked at the northeast corner of High and Bedford Streets, and his grave is two blocks away in the Old Graveyard.

William Irvine's house site (also marked) is across the street from Armstrong's. A British naval surgeon during the Seven Years' War, he resigned and settled in Carlisle (1764). Practicing as a physician, he also became an active Patriot politician and was commissioned in January 1776 to raise a regiment of Pennsylvania Continentals for the invasion of Canada. He was captured with Thompson at Trois Rivières in Canada (see below) and paroled less than two months later, but not exchanged for almost three years (6 May 1778). Made a general a year later, he commanded a brigade under Anthony Wayne in New York and New Jersey before taking command at Fort Pitt in March 1782. On the frontier General Irvine continued his unsuccessful military career, raising volunteers to augment the small garrison of two hundred regulars he found there and sending out the expedition that ended in disaster near modern Upper Sandusky, Ohio (4–5 June 1782). Irvine left Fort Pitt and resigned from the army in the winter of 1783. Remaining active in public life and military affairs, he moved to Philadelphia around 1800, and died there in 1804.

William Thompson, who led the First Regiment of Pennsylvania Riflemen from Carlisle in July 1775 to join Washington's army around Boston, was another famous man of the region, and he is buried in the Old Graveyard. Born in Ireland, Thompson settled near Carlisle and became a surveyor and justice of the peace. He was a captain in Armstrong's expedition to Kittanning (1756). With Edward Hand as his second in command, Thompson led the remarkable march of his frontiersmen to Boston, where they became the terror not only of the besieged British but also of those responsible for discipline in the American camp. Congress promoted Thompson to brigadier general on 1 March 1776, before Washington could express his opinion that this aggressive but otherwise limited leader was not fit for such high command. Leading reinforcements up the Hudson to Canada, General Thompson commanded the disastrous attack on Trois Rivières on 8 June 1776, and was among the 236 taken prisoner there. He was paroled and went to Philadelphia, but was not exchanged (for Baron Riedesel) until four years later. Meanwhile, he became so offensive in agitating for his exchange that Congress censured him and Thomas McKean won a libel suit against him, being awarded almost £6,000 in damages. Thompson died in Carlisle less than a year after being exchanged, and is buried there.

Ephraim Blaine's house site is marked opposite the site of the Green Tree Inn (where Benjamin Franklin stayed in 1753 while making an important treaty with the Indians). Blaine started as commissary of the Eighth Pennsylvania, became commissary of supplies for the Continental army on 1 April 1777, and during the Yorktown campaign was commissary general of Washington's army (with the rank of colonel, not general). The surviving Blaine House, at 4 North Hanover Street, was built in 1794 for a son. It has handsome external features visible from the street and is very well preserved.

The public square has been the center of Carlisle life since it was laid out in 1751. Just to the west is the site of the first fort authorized by Pennsylvania, laid out "in the middle of this town" by Governor Morris in July 1755 after news was received of Braddock's defeat. Later called Fort Lowther by some writers, it is referred to in a revised highway marker as Carlisle Fort. (The map location is between Hanover and Pitt Streets on West High Street. The latter is U.S. 11.) Conspicuous in this vicinity is a stone building known as the Main Magazine, so identified in the National Survey list of "Sites Also Noted" (1964), but for some reason not recognized by a state highway marker or mentioned in chamber of commerce literature.

Many historic or architecturally significant structures still stand in Carlisle. One is the Thomas Butler Gun Shop (1764), a small stone house on the south side of Dickinson Alley and 50 feet west of Pitt Street. Thomas Butler and his five sons served in the Revolution. Just outside Carlisle on U.S. 11 is Carlisle Barracks, on the site of a munitions works erected in 1776 and then called Washingtonburg, the first place in this country named for George Washington. The powder magazine, now called the Hessian Guardhouse, a one-story stone structure built in 1777 by Hessian prisoners, has been restored as a museum (hours limited; phone: [717] 245-4101).

The Old Graveyard, just east of the highway marker on South Hanover between South and Walnut Streets, contains the remains of several important Revolutionary War persons in addition to Armstrong and Thompson, mentioned above.

"Molly Pitcher" is the most publicized attraction of Carlisle today. A German Palatine servant, Mary Ludwig married a barber, John Caspar Hays, who marched off to the war five years later. Like many other women, Ludwig went along. In the Battle of Monmouth, on one of the hottest days since temperatures were recorded in America, Molly Ludwig Hays carried water to the troops. ("Molly" was a common nickname for Margaret, Mary, and other names.) When her husband was wounded, she took his place, manning a ramrod to keep a gun in service. John Hays died shortly after the Revolution, whereupon Ludwig married a wartime comrade of her husband's, George McCauley, who turned out to be a shiftless husband. Ludwig left him, supported herself as a washerwoman and nurse, and received some grants of money. She lived in Carlisle to the ripe old age of seventy-nine. The site of her home is about midway between Bedford and East Streets on the south side of North Street, not far from the army post. Mary Ludwig Hays McCauley, depicted in the heroic statue of Molly Pitcher in the Old Graveyard as the stocky young woman of her prime (she was about twenty-four years old at Monmouth), was in her later years a pipe-smoking, tobacco-chewing, whiskey-drinking "old soldier" who could swear with the best of them. Website: www.visitccpa.com. Carlisle Chamber of Commerce phone: (717) 243-4515.

(Chamber of Commerce, 112 W. High St., Carlisle 17013.)

Chester, Delaware River below Philadelphia, Delaware County. The Swedes called it Upland, and William Penn renamed it Chester. It is the second-oldest white settlement in Pennsylvania (after Tinicum, which was founded in 1643), seat of the colony's government from 1681 to 1682. The colonial courthouse (built in 1724; restored in 1920), said to be the oldest public building in continuous use in the United States, is at Market Street near Fifth. Also standing on Market Street near Mary Street is the Friends Meeting of 1736, remodeled in 1883 and used as a meetinghouse until 1926. The Quaker Burial Ground, on Edgemont Avenue between Sixth and Seventh Streets, established in 1683, contains graves of prominent men of the colonial era.

During the Revolution, Chester figured as the place to which Washington retreated after his defeat at Brandywine and as the place for the encampment for his army on 5 September 1781, after the soldiers had passed through Philadelphia en route to triumph at Yorktown, Virginia. That campsite is marked on U.S. 13 east of the present city line, at Morton and McDowell Streets.

Cornwall Furnace, Lebanon County, on U.S. 322 in the town of Cornwall. Rich sources of iron ore in this area (the "Cornwall Banks" are still being mined and were not surpassed in yield until the Lake Superior ranges were developed) were acquired by Peter Grubb in the 1730s. In 1742 he established the furnace at Cornwall, which remained in operation until 1883. The furnace produced forty-two cannon and other items for the Continental forces during the Revolution. One-third of the workers during the Revolution were slaves or indentured servants. The furnace was bought in 1798 by Robert Coleman and given to the state of Pennsylvania by his great-granddaughter in 1932. It is one of the best preserved of the early ironworks, and today's visitor will see the red sandstone structure that dates from a remodeling of 1856 to 1857. The PHMC manages the site and makes available a thorough interpretive center with guided tours, and a visitors center which serves as a museum. It is open Tuesday through Sunday, 9 A.M. to 5 P.M. Phone: (717) 272-9711. (See HOPEWELL VILLAGE NATIONAL HISTORIC SITE.)

Coryell's Ferry, on the Delaware River where U.S. 202 crosses the river between New Hope, Pennsylvania, and Lambertville, New Jersey. This ferry figures prominently in accounts of military operations of the Revolution. Washington's army used it on four occasions. D. S. Freeman notes in his biography of Washington that "the crossing was a 'base point' in the reckoning of marches. In *Gates Papers*... is a table of distances from 'General Washington's Camp... to Coryell's Ferry' and thence, stage by stage, to Albany. The distance from the ferry to Albany was reckoned at 220 miles" (*Washington*, IV, p. 447n). (It is actually 192 miles.)

Cornwallis marched on the ferry site, hoping to find boats to continue Lord Howe's pursuit of the Patriot army across the Delaware, in early December 1776. Part of Washington's army camped at Coryell's en route to the Brandywine (others crossing at Trenton and Easton), and moved through there from Valley Forge in the maneuvers that led to Monmouth.

Crooked Billet Skirmish Site, Hatboro, Montgomery County. The morning of 1 May 1778 a force of seven hundred British light infantry and mounted troops from occupied Philadelphia surprised the detachment of fewer than sixty Pennsylvania militia under General John Lacey at Crooked Billet. Although virtually surrounded and opposed by two exceptionally able British leaders, Lieutenant Colonel Robert Abercromby and Major John Graves Simcoe, Lacey fought his way out, retreated 2 miles, and shook off pursuit by suddenly changing direction. The Patriots lost twenty-six killed, about ten seriously wounded, and all their baggage. British losses were nine men wounded.

A monument to this battle lies near where the Hatboro elementary school is located.

Daniel Boone Homestead, 1 mile north of Birdsboro in Berks County at 400 Daniel Boone Road. The entrance is marked by a state historical marker. Another marker is on U.S. 422, about 5 miles southeast of Reading, at Baumstown.

The present two-story stone structure, restored and now serving as a museum, was built on the foundations of the log cabin where Daniel Boone was born in 1734. It is believed that Daniel's father built part of the existing house before he took his family to North Carolina in 1750.

America's most famous frontiersman started acquiring his skills at the Boone homestead, where he lived until he was sixteen. The Pennsylvania Historical and Museum Commission has directed the restoration of the house and, in addition to preserving 579 acres of open space, has created a museum of the Pennsylvania pioneer. Near the house are a blacksmith shop, a stone smokehouse, a bank barn, and other structures of the frontier farm and village. A visitors center, picnic facilities, and hiking trails are on the site, which is open Tuesday through Saturday, 9 A.M. to 5 P.M., and Sunday, noon to 5 P.M. (Reduced schedule during January and February.) Phone: 610-582-4900.

Durham Village, near Riegelsville, Bucks County. The foundation of Durham Furnace (1727–1789) survives in the base of an old mill (marked). The furnace in the wilderness was fed ore from Rattlesnake and Mine Hills, making cannon and shot in the Colonial Wars and during the Revolution. Less well remembered but more important, perhaps, than the output of the furnace were the heavy-cargo boats designed and built by Robert Durham at the mouth of Durham Creek. Of shallow draft, 40 to 60 feet long and 8 feet wide, sailed or poled by four or five men, and able to carry as much as 15 tons, Durham boats were for river transportation what the Conestoga wagon was for colonial roads. (Schenectady, New York, became a major center of their construction about the time of the Revolution.) The most famous action of Colonel John Glover's Marbleheaders's amphibious careers came when they manned the unfamiliar Durham boats in subzero weather to put 2,400 Rebel troops, eighteen cannon, and horses of Washington's army across the Delaware and bring them all back within a space of thirty-six hours and without a loss. This was, of course, the famous crossing of the Delaware in December 1776 for the raid on Trenton, New Jersey.

Easton, at the junction of Lehigh River with the Delaware, in Northampton County. Since colonial times the settlement laid out in 1752 at the Forks of the Delaware has been a communications center. A famous Indian treaty was negotiated here in 1758, in which Pennsylvania agreed to limit westward expansion of settlement to the Allegheny Mountains. From Easton principal colonial roads went northwest through the Great Swamp and the Shades of Death to Wilkes-Barre in the Wyoming Valley and northeast to Goshen, New York. The site of David Martin's Ferry, important during the Revolution, is in the park at Front and Ferry Streets. The Sullivan-Clinton Expedition (see under NEW YORK) was organized at Easton. The house of George Taylor, a signer of the Declaration of Independence, built in 1757 by William Parsons, surveyor general, is standing at Fourth and Ferry Streets.

Ephrata Cloisters, Lancaster County. Eleven extensively restored eighteenth-century buildings of this communal religious community of Seventh-Day Baptists founded in 1728 to 1733 are preserved as a state historic shrine by the PHMC. Germanic in culture, Ephrata Cloisters had a significant impact on colonial intellectual life although it numbered only three hundred persons at the height of its prominence in about 1750. In September 1777 several hundred casualties from the Battle of Brandywine were brought here. Two of the three orders at the Cloisters died out in the early 1800s, and the surviving buildings ceased to be used in 1934. A highway marker on U.S. 222 just south of the U.S. 322 underpass gives directions to the nearby site.

Forks of the Ohio, Point State Park, in Pittsburgh's "Golden Triangle." One of America's most important historical sites, Pittsburgh's Golden Triangle is all the more remarkable as a triumph of cultural conservation. The 36-acre Point State Park, where the Monongahela and Allegheny Rivers join to form the mighty Ohio, has been created in recent years by stripping away the overgrowth of steel and concrete of industrial prosperity. Fifteen acres of railroad tracks were removed, commercial structures were blasted, and bridges and traffic arteries were relocated. Archaeological work has established the sites of Forts Duquesne and Pitt and uncovered much valuable historical data. Plaques throughout the park interpret the area's historical significance. The Pennsylvania Department of Conservation and Natural Resources operate Point State Park. Phone: (412) 471-0235.

The Fort Pitt Museum has been built on the site of the Monongahela bastion. It features a model of Fort Pitt, 20 feet in diameter, that is explained to the visitor by a recorded narration coordinated with a system of miniature spotlights. To depict the long history of the Forks of the Ohio there are sixty exhibits in the main museum area, including full-scale replicas of a trader's cabin, a barracks room, and an early Pittsburgh parlor. The flag bastion has been restored, and a small brick blockhouse built in 1763 by Henry Bouquet has survived. A trace of Fort Duquesne is in the center of the park. Promenades have been

The Sisters' House at Ephrata Cloisters. *Originally constructed in 1743, the Sisters' House (also called Saron) is one of eleven restored eighteenth-century buildings at Ephrata Cloisters, a religious community of Seventh-Day Baptists founded around 1728 to 1733.* © LEE SNIDER/PHOTO IMAGES/CORBIS.

constructed along the waterfronts, and stone bleachers for three thousand persons have been erected along the Allegheny side. A modern touch of panache is furnished by the white plume of a water jet in a large circular pond at the tip of the triangle. Phone: (412) 281-9284.

The Forks of the Ohio drew French, British, and American attention like a great magnet from the mid-eighteenth century through the early years of the nineteenth. Not only the European colonial powers but also the American colonists themselves contested possession of this spot in the wilderness, and it was not until 1779 that Virginia agreed that it rightfully belonged to Pennsylvania. Meanwhile, that point was highly academic because there were French and Indian claims to be dealt with.

In 1731 a few Frenchmen tried to establish a settlement at the forks but they were quickly driven off by the Indians. In 1748 the colonies of Pennsylvania and Virginia started a vigorous expansion of trading activities into the upper Ohio that caused the French to react by increasing their own efforts. Within three years the French gained the upper hand by starting construction of a line of posts from the Great Lakes toward the Forks of the Ohio, wiping out British posts along the way. (Among these were Pickawillany, now Piqua, Ohio, and Venango, now Franklin, Pennsylvania.)

The twenty-one-year-old Washington was sent in 1753 by the governor of Virginia to warn the French to withdraw. After an arduous trek through the wilderness, visiting the forks in November, passing through Venango, and finally making contact with the appropriate French authorities at Fort Le Boeuf, where modern Waterford, Pennsylvania, is located, the Virginian was told politely but firmly that the French had no intention of abandoning their claims to the upper Ohio.

In January of the next year (1754) the Virginians of the Ohio Company began building a fort at the Forks of the Ohio. Three months later a five-hundred-man French expedition captured the half-completed works, permitted the Americans to withdraw, and then constructed Fort Duquesne on the site. Washington was leading the vanguard of a Virginia regiment advancing to protect the fort builders when he met them on the trail and learned that he was too late. His subsequent operations, setting the stage for the Seven Years' War, are covered under Fort Necessity

National Battlefield (below). The British and their colonists continued to pyramid their military misadventures at the hands of the French and Indians, the capstone being Braddock's defeat on 9 July 1755, about 8 miles east of Fort Duquesne.

Three years later, on 25 November 1758, General John Forbes reached his objective at the Forks of the Ohio after a remarkable march and found that the French had burned and abandoned their fort the preceding day. The great William Pitt, for whom Forbes now named the place, had recently come to power in England and was sending competent military commanders to lead British regulars and American volunteers against the French. Already feeling the consequences of Pitt's strategy, the French had wisely decided to abandon their far-flung outposts in the Old Northwest.

During the three years of its existence, however, Fort Duquesne had been the base for French and Indian raids on frontier settlements of the English colonies. Having run up an impressive record of "too little and too late," the colonial authorities followed up by doing what turned out to be "too much and too late": they built Fort Pitt in the finest tradition of European military engineering, making it the largest and most sophisticated fort on the American frontier. Pentagonal in trace, surrounded by a ditch, it had walls of earth with bastions at each angle. Inside the wall were buildings of frame and brick. Started in September 1759, the work took two years.

The French threat to the frontier had ended, however. In 1763 the power vacuum resulting from elimination of French military leadership in the Old Northwest caused the great Indian uprising known as Pontiac's War, and Fort Pitt was able to justify its existence.

Pontiac's War began in May 1763 and within a matter of weeks the Indians had wiped out nine British posts and innumerable settlements between Niagara and Detroit. On 29 May they killed two British regulars outside Fort Pitt and attacked several isolated settlements.

The commander of Fort Pitt, Colonel Henry Bouquet, was in Philadelphia when the first reports of Pontiac's War reached the colonial authorities. Captain Simeon Ecuyer, another Swiss adventurer in the British service, was temporarily in command of the frontier post, and he was perfectly suited to the task. The American settlers, panic-stricken and ineffectual in their own self-defense, created a refugee problem that seriously impeded Bouquet's efforts to relieve the siege of the fort.

Ecuyer ordered all settlers into the fort and organized the men into two militia companies to reinforce his own regulars. His garrison numbered 250 regulars and militia initially, and increased as refugees straggled in and decreased as disease took its toll. But Ecuyer maintained his confidence and settled down for a siege while Bouquet organized a relief column of 460 regulars at Carlisle, more than 150 air-line miles away.

A little less than two months after they first appeared around Fort Pitt, the Indians launched an unsuccessful final attack on 27 July and then headed east to deal with the relief column that had reached Fort Ligonier, 45 miles away. At Bushy Run Battlefield, 26 miles east of Fort Pitt, they came very close to repeating their triumph of 1755 by annihilating Bouquet's column. But Bouquet, long a student and practitioner of wilderness warfare, beat the Indians at their own game, and on 10 August he reached Fort Pitt. One of the five outworks subsequently built by Bouquet to strengthen the fort has survived.

As political disturbances on the eve of the Revolution increased the need for British regulars, these were progressively withdrawn from the frontier posts. In 1772 Fort Pitt was abandoned by the British and partially dismantled. Early in 1774 the notorious Dr. John Connolly, agent for Governor Dunmore of Virginia, occupied the fort with an armed band. His purpose initially was to strengthen Virginia's claims to the region, but because of his deliberate efforts to provoke the Indians, the episode known as Dunmore's War occurred. This ended with the victory of the colonists at Point Pleasant, West Virginia.

Meanwhile, the town of Pittsburgh had been laid out in 1764 and had gained the distinction of being the first permanent English settlement west of the Alleghenies. Most of the early settlers were Virginians, and Pittsburgh grew rapidly as a base for traders, backwoodsmen, and pioneers moving westward. A fifth and last fort, named Lafayette, or Fayette, was built during the winter of 1791 to 1792 a quarter of a mile above Fort Pitt. Needed for protection when Indian troubles flamed for the last time in the Old Northwest, it was a base for the campaigns of "Mad Anthony" Wayne that put out the fire. This post furnished troops in the Whiskey Rebellion in 1794 and was used in the War of 1812 as a training center and supply depot. In 1813 the government sold the site, which is identified today by a marker on Ninth Street just north of Pennsylvania Avenue.

Fort Augusta, in Sunbury. The pacifistic policies of Pennsylvania toward the Indians had succeeded for almost three-quarters of a century in preventing hostilities on this colony's western frontier, but the colony divided over the proper strategy in the Seven Years' War. The French were building a chain of forts in the upper Ohio River Valley to protect their communications between Canada and Louisiana. Braddock's defeat in 1755 gave the Pennsylvanians cause for serious alarm, though there was no indication that either the French or the Indians would attack the one colony with which they had always gotten along. Benjamin Franklin led a faction opposed to the pacifist policies of the proprietors of Pennsylvania, and the General Assembly voted to raise troops and establish a string of forts to protect the eastern part of the colony.

The largest and most important of the new outposts was built during the period 1756 to 1757 at the junction of the west and north branches of the Susquehanna, which was also a crossroads of important Indian trails. Presumably named for the mother of the future King George III, Fort Augusta was 204 feet in total length on each of its four sides. An outer stockade encircled a moat, inside which was a bastioned fort of conventional European design. A large model of this portion of Fort Augusta has been skillfully constructed on a scale of 1:6 near the original site. Four blockhouses providing a covered way to the river have not been included in this model. The original well and remains of the underground powder magazine have been preserved.

Because of its large size and strong garrison, Fort Augusta was never attacked, and it became an important base for traders and pioneers. During the Revolution it was a strategic position in the defense of the frontier and was the base for General John Sullivan's punitive expedition (see SULLIVAN-CLINTON EXPEDITION under New York) against the Iroquois in 1779.

The fort was allowed to fall into ruins except for the quarters of Colonel Samuel Hunter, the last commanding officer, who continued to live there and eventually obtained title to the property. This house burned down in 1852, and a grandson of Colonel Hunter built the house that stands near the model of the fort. This now serves as a museum. Also on the grounds are a powder magazine and a reference library.

The site, known as the Hunter House Museum, is administered by the PHMC and is the headquarters of the Northumberland County Historical Society. Located at 1150 North Front Street (Route 147), the museuam is open March to December, Monday, Wednesday, and Friday 1 to 4 P.M. Phone: (570) 286-4083.

Fort Bedford, Bedford Village, in south-central Pennsylvania, off Pa. Turnpike I-76. The fort built here in 1757 and enlarged the next year was an important feature of the wilderness route between the Forks of the Ohio and eastern Pennsylvania. Settled around 1750 and originally known as Raystown, Bedford became a famous health resort in the nineteenth century. It remains an attractive rural village in picturesque country where several important historical sites are identified by markers. The Fort Bedford Museum contains items of frontier life. The restored fort, a blockhouse surrounded by a stockade, is in a park created for the bicentennial celebration of 1958. The museum is open mid-May through mid-October on Wednesday through Sunday, 11 A.M. to 5 P.M. Phone: (814) 623-8891 or (814) 623-2011

Fort LeBoeuf, Waterford. A model of the French fort (1753–1759) is in the Amos Judson House, built on the site of the fort in 1820. The fort, built by Colonel Henry Bouquet in 1760, was destroyed in Pontiac's War, three years later. Foundations of the fort built in 1796 to support "Mad Anthony" Wayne's operations against the Indians are preserved in a small park across the street from the Judson House. There is also a statue commemorating the fruitless visit of Washington to Fort LeBoeuf in 1753 (see FORKS OF THE OHIO). The Amos Judson House was built in 1820 by Judson, owner of the nineteenth-century Eagle Hotel, and is the headquarters for the Fort LeBoeuf Historical Society. The Eagle Hotel, a National Historic Landmark, is across the street at 123 South High Street; it houses the Fort LeBoeuf Museum, which is operated by the Pennsylvania Historical and Museum Commission of Edinboro University. Judson House phone: (814) 796-6030; museum phone: (814) 732-2573.

Fort Ligonier, at the intersection of U.S. 30 and Pa. Route 711 in Ligonier. Named after Sir John Ligonier, commander in chief of the British army until 1767, it was built in 1758 by General John Forbes. Fort Ligonier withstood an attack by the French and Indians the year it was built, and during Pontiac's War it was menaced by a small party of Indians on two occasions. The fort was also called Loyal Hannon, an English corruption of Loyalhanning ("middle stream"), a nearby Delaware Indian village whose site is indicated by a highway marker on U.S. 30 southeast of Ligonier.

The wooden, stockaded inner fort has been reconstructed and furnished. Visitors can visit the site from May through the end of October every day of the week. A fourteen-minute film places the surroundings in its proper historical perspective, and a museum contains artifacts and documents associated with the fort's prominent role in the Seven Years' War. Phone: (724) 238-9701.

Fort Necessity National Battlefield, 11 miles east of Uniontown on U.S. 40. The hasty fortifications erected by Washington at Great Meadows in 1754 were faithfully reconstructed two hundred years later by the National Parks Service. It was not until 1953 that archaeologists finally got their hands on missing documents that enabled them to find the fort's exact location and to establish its outlines.

Today's visitor will see reconstructions on the actual sites of the circular stockade, the storehouse, and the earthworks built by Washington's troops. The park is separated into three different sites that comprise nearly 900 total acres. What is referred to as the "main" unit contains the battlefield and the reconstructed Fort Necessity, in addition to the Mount Washington Tavern and a visitors center. The Braddock Grave is found about 1.5 miles west of there, and the Jumonville Glen section of the park is about 7 miles northwest of the main unit.

The section on the Forks of the Ohio outlines the sequence of events that brought the colony of Virginia into conflict with the French in this region. The twenty-two-year-old Washington, now a lieutenant colonel and second in command of a small regiment of three hundred volunteers raised by Virginia to defend the colony's interests in the upper Ohio Valley, reached Great Meadows with a sixty-man advance guard on 24 May 1754. With great difficulty they had cut a road across the mountains, and their wheeled vehicles and artillery were the first ever to cross the Alleghenies. Meanwhile, the Virginians had met the fort builders driven from their work at the Forks of the Ohio, and Washington proceeded on the assumption—perhaps unwarranted—that the French had committed an act of war.

Learning that a small French force was hiding in the vicinity, Washington launched a surprise attack on the morning of 27 May and killed ten of the enemy, including the French commander, Ensign Joseph Coulon de Villiers, Sieur de Jumonville. One Frenchman got away and made his way back to Fort Duquesne (now Pittsburgh), and Washington's act was subsequently denounced throughout Europe as an "assassination."

Washington wasted no time in preparing for the trouble he expected from the French. On 1 June he noted in his journal that "we are finishing our Fort," and two days later he wrote to Governor Dinwiddie that he was prepared to hold off an attack of five hundred men.

It was a month later, on 3 July, that the attack came. Captain Louis Coulon de Villiers, brother of Jumonville, commanded the force of about five hundred French and four hundred Indians who appeared around Fort Necessity in the early afternoon of a rainy day. Driving in Washington's outposts, they probed the position. After suffering some casualties from small-arms fire and from two swivel guns, the French and Indians encircled the fort and a sniping contest got under way. The rain continued to fall, dampening the ardor of Villiers's Indian allies and filling the American trenches with water.

Governor Dinwiddie had called for assistance from other colonies and from Indian tribes in South Carolina, but only the one hundred regulars of Captain James Mackay's South Carolina Independent Company were present with Washington's Virginians at Fort Necessity. The colonials numbered four hundred men, including one hundred who were sick, and Washington had been abandoned by his former Shawnee and Delaware allies. Even the Mingo chief, Half King, who had participated in the surprise attack on Jumonville, had withdrawn.

But the French were worried about rumors of a large force marching to Washington's assistance, and Villiers's troops, tired and wet, were unenthusiastic about gathering new military laurels in the soggy fields of the Great Meadow. Furthermore, the French had consistently pursued a policy of applying the minimum degree of military force necessary to hold their claims to the Upper Ohio. Villiers was therefore able to get the Americans to sign a surrender document that permitted them to withdraw with the honors of war. What Washington did not realize until later, because he did not read French, was that the document to which he affixed his signature referred to Jumonville's death as an assassination. The French remained one up on the British colonists. Villiers demolished Fort Necessity and returned to Fort Duquesne. Washington's force returned on foot to Wills Creek, harassed on the 50-mile march by the Indians.

Described below are places in the Fort Necessity area of interest to students of the military actions of 1754 to 1755.

Jumonville Glen is a secluded ravine sheltered by a 30-foot ledge of rocks where Half King's scouts found a French force hiding, and where the latter was subsequently attacked by Washington and his Indian allies (see above). Seven miles from Great Meadows, it is now part of the Fort Necessity National Battlefield.

Mount Washington Tavern, built in 1818 as a stage stop on the Old National Pike (now U.S. 40), is now a museum exhibiting relics of Fort Necessity and of Braddock's expedition.

Old Orchard Camp, 1 mile north of Fort Necessity, is the site of General Braddock's ninth encampment in his expedition against Fort Duquesne in 1755 and the first place his shattered forces stopped in their panic-stricken retreat after being ambushed by the French and Indians in the Battle of the Monongahela on 9 July. The wounded Braddock died here on 13 July. To keep his body from being found by the Indians, it was buried secretly on the trail and the expedition marched over it to obliterate signs of the digging. When workmen were repairing the nearby highway half a century later they uncovered a skeleton that, because of the vestiges of a British uniform worn by an officer of high rank, was believed to be Braddock's. The remains were moved 100 yards and reburied where a monument now marks the site.

The Fort Necessity National Battlefield site has been operated since 1933 by the National Park Service. There are parking facilities and a picnic area, as well as the usual historical reenactments in the summer. The park, 11 miles east of Uniontown off U.S. 40, is open daily year-round from sunrise to sunset, except holidays. Phone: (724) 329-5512.

Fort Zeller, 0.5 mile north of Newmanstown, Lebanon County, on the Fort Zeller Road. Pennsylvania's oldest surviving fort, built 1723 and rebuilt in 1745 by pioneers from the Schoharie Valley in New York, it was used for

Jumonville Glen. *This secluded ravine, sheltered by a 30-foot ledge of rocks, was the site where the Indians of Half King discovered a French force hiding in May 1754.* © TED SPIEGEL/CORBIS.

refuge during the Colonial Wars. The National Survey (1964) lists it in the "Sites Also Noted" category. Phone: (610) 589-4301.

Graeme Park, Exit 26 off I-276 to Route 611 and then to County Line Road, Horsham, Montgomery County. The malthouse built in 1722 by Sir William Keith, provincial governor from 1717 until removed from office by the Penns in 1726 (after which it probably was his home for two years), survives as a distinguished example of the stone houses of the region and locality. Sir William's stepdaughter married Dr. Thomas Graeme, who acquired the property in 1739 and converted the plain industrial structure into a mansion with a fine Georgian interior with floor-to-ceiling paneling and an elegant dining-room fireplace. The property was given to the Commonwealth of Pennsylvania in 1958 and has been restored. The 44-acre site, including the Keith House, features a variety of bird life, and is operated by the PHMC. Phone: (215) 343-0965.

Greene Inn, Buckingham, Bucks County. Known during the Revolution as Bogart's Tavern, this was headquarters for General Nathanael Greene in December 1776 before the famous crossing of the Delaware and the attack on Trenton. After this it was renamed the General Greene Inn. Curiously, it is included in the relatively select list of nine Pennsylvania "Sites Also Noted" by the National Survey in 1964, yet not marked by the Pennsylvania Historical and Museum Commission. It has been the site of Edna's Antiques on Durham Road for almost seventy years, and has a yard packed full of old radiators and bathtubs, among other shopworn snippets.

Gulph, The. *See* MATSON'S FORD.

Hannastown Site, near Greensburg, Westmoreland County. When Westmoreland County was created in 1773, Hannastown was the county seat, the first one west of the mountains. It was on the Forbes Road (Raystown Path), about midway between Fort Ligonier and the site of Braddock's defeat on the outskirts of Pittsburgh. Hannastown had the distinction of being burned in the last action of the Revolutionary War in Pennsylvania, a raid by the Seneca that took place on

13 July 1782 (a Saturday). A highway marker is just west of the site, on Pa. 819 north of Greensburg.

Hopewell Furnace National Historic Site, Berks County, 5 miles southeast of Birdsboro on Pa. 23 (via U.S. 422). An iron-making village founded in 1770 by Mark Bird and active until 1883, Hopewell Village was acquired by the federal government in 1935. Restoration of the historic structures started in 1950, and a self-guided tour includes twenty-five important ruins, terrain features, and restored structures. Hopewell furnished cannon and shot to the Continental forces during the Revolution, and Mark Bird served as a colonel of militia in 1776. The furnace owned many slaves and indentured servants during the Revolution, and also employed numerous free blacks, a few of whom attained positions as highly skilled workers in the early nineteenth century. More than fifty structures in Hopewell Furnace National Historic Site can be found on the National Register of Historic Places. The park's museum exhibits an estimated 300,000 artifacts and archival items related to the site's history. (See CORNWALL FURNACE.) The park is open daily from 9 A.M. to 5 P.M. Phone: (610) 582-8773.

Lancaster, Lancaster County Seat. English Quakers and Germans settled on this spot about 1717. Since this town on the Conestoga River was laid out in 1730, it is the oldest inland town in Pennsylvania, and the largest inland town at the time of the Revolution. The Continental Congress met here for one day, 27 September 1777, in its flight from Philadelphia to York; thus Lancaster is entitled to its claim of being the national capital for one day. (It was a serious contender for selection as the permanent site later, and was the state capital from 1799 to 1812.) The "Pennsylvania rifle" was probably developed in Lancaster. The Conestoga wagon, freight carrier of colonial days and ancestor of the prairie schooner, was produced from the mid-eighteenth century in the Conestoga Valley. The mansion of Edward Hand, a leader of Pennsylvania riflemen during the Revolution and eventually adjutant general of the Continental army (1781), is still standing on Conestoga Creek adjoining Williamson Park. (The "Rock Ford" marker is on South Duke Street extended, at the creek, about 0.5 mile northwest of the old house.)

A monument to George Ross, signer of the Declaration of Independence and jurist who practiced law in Lancaster after 1750, is on the site of his house at King and Lime Streets. Edward Shippen, grandfather of Benedict Arnold's wife and a participant in his treason, lived during the years 1751 to 1781 at a spot now occupied by the YWCA on East Orange Street. The old courthouse where Congress met was located (1739–1853) in the southwest portion of the present square.

British and German soldiers of Burgoyne's "Convention Army" were quartered in barracks located on what is now North Duke Street, opposite the Historical Society headquarters. These structures no longer exist, but the military stables used during the Revolution are standing near a highway marker here. At Orange and Shippen Streets is a Georgian house built before 1760 and once occupied by the first mayor of Lancaster. At 418 West King Street is a house built in 1730 that typifies the early architecture of the town. The Historic Preservation Trust of Lancaster County is a primary information source for these sites; it is housed in the Sehner-Ellicott–von Hess House (c. 1787), located on 123 North Prince Street. Phone: (717) 291-5861.

Lee (Harry) Memorial, off Sugartown Road (Number 15112) near Newtown Road (Number 15116), about three-quarters of a mile southwest of U.S. 30 in Berwyn, Chester County. The man who would become famous as "Light Horse Harry" Lee (and whose son was to become considerably more famous as Robert E. Lee) was a twenty-one-year-old captain when his company of Virginia cavalry joined Washington's army in 1777. He had already impressed the commander in chief with his exceptional military qualities when an exploit occurred at the Spread Eagle Tavern on 20 January 1778 that launched Lee on his career as a major figure in the war. The Patriot army was suffering in winter quarters at Valley Forge, and the British army was living high on the hog in occupied Philadelphia. Captain Lee was operating around Philadelphia, attacking foraging parties and causing such general annoyance that the British sent out a force of two hundred light horse to surprise and eliminate him. Surprise him they did, evading his outposts by taking a circuitous route of 20 miles and catching him in an isolated position with only seven companions. But eliminate him they did not: Lee and his little force took refuge in the Spread Eagle Tavern, fought off the British efforts to force the doors, and even succeeded in keeping them from taking his horses from the nearby stable. Lee then routed the attackers by making them believe a Patriot relief force was in sight. (Valley Forge was only 5 miles north.)

The action took place at dawn on 20 January, and Washington's general orders for that same day commended Lee and his seven companions. A congressional resolution of 7 April, occasioned by the affair at the Spread Eagle Tavern, promoted Lee to major commandant and authorized him to raise the separate force that evolved into Lee's Legion (created 30 November 1780 by augmenting his three mounted companies with three infantry companies).

Liberty Hall, Quakertown, Bucks County. This picturesque little two-story stone house on Broad Street, built before 1772, was briefly the hiding place for the Liberty Bell in September 1777 when it was being moved from Philadelphia to Allentown for safekeeping.

Matson's Ford, West Conshohocken. The first mill in this area was built in 1747 (it operated until 1895), and during the Revolution it was an important source of flour. When Washington started his move to winter quarters at Valley Forge from around Whitemarsh, his leading elements ran into a foraging expedition around the Gulph (now Gulph Mills) on the Schuylkill River after crossing the river at Matson's Ford (now West Conshohocken). The Patriots withdrew across the river on 11 December 1777, and Cornwallis returned to Philadelphia the next night with two thousand head of livestock and other provisions foraged by his large force. On 13 December Washington resumed his move toward Valley Forge, camping on hills around the Gulph until 19 December. Several highway markers on Pa. 23 at Gulph Mills, just west of West Conshohocken, pertain to these events. Lafayette used Matson's Ford in his operations around Barren Hill.

McKonkey's Ferry, on the Delaware River. At the time of Washington's famous crossing of the Delaware the ferry-houses and taverns on both sides could properly be called McKonkey's, since they were owned by father and son. But D. S. Freeman concludes from his laborious study of contemporary accounts that "McKonkey's Ferry" was applied to the Pennsylvania side and "Johnson's Ferry" to the New Jersey side. Hessian reports called the latter "John's Ferry" (*George Washington,* IV, p. 307, n. 17). See also WASHINGTON CROSSING STATE PARK, below, and WASHINGTON CROSSING under New Jersey.

Moland House (Washington's Headquarters), near Pa. 263 just north of Warminster, 1641 Old York Road, Warwick Township. On Old York Road (Pa. 263) at one of the main crossroads of Bucks County, about 20 miles north of Philadelphia and the same distance west of Trenton, Washington's tired army camped during the period 10 to 23 August 1777. It was a particularly trying time for Washington, who was coping with many administrative problems in connection with supplying his troops while trying to figure out where he should march them next. Much was made of the difficult administrative and strategic problems at this time (on the eve of the Battle of Brandywine), and this authority is plainly confused as to exactly where Washington's camp was located in terms of modern landmarks. The "Headquarters Farm," as the highway marker calls the Moland House (1713), is also said to be where "Lafayette joined the American Army." Actually, Lafayette had presented his credentials to an unenthusiastic Congress on 28 July, offering to serve at his own expense and start without official rank, after which Congress promptly commissioned him a major general without a command (31 July). The nineteen-year-old French nobleman's first meeting with Washington was in Philadelphia a few days later, and Washington was almost immediately won over by Lafayette's modest, tactful, and admiring manner (ibid., p. 450). At this time, around 5 August, Washington invited Lafayette to visit the American army then deployed in defensive positions around Philadelphia (ibid., p. 448). Lafayette technically "joined the American Army" when Congress commissioned him on 31 July. He undoubtedly visited Washington's army before it encamped around the Moland House, 10 to 23 August. The significance of the house's association with Lafayette is therefore unclear, but it is all the more interesting because of this minor historical mystery.

The Moland House was recently restored, and opened to the public in 2004. It is indicated by a highway historical marker. Some further information is available on the Moland House website, although it is a very difficult site from which to procure clear data. Website: www.moland.org.

Muhlenberg House and Graves, Trappe, Montgomery County. Henry Melchior Muhlenberg (1711–1787) was the single most significant figure in the early history of the Lutheran Church in America, and his son John Peter Gabriel (1746–1807) was a distinguished general during the Revolution as well as a famous clergyman and politician. The house built before the Revolution by the father (who died here) and later owned by the son is still standing, a privately owned structure of three stories, built of stone covered with stucco and having much of its original woodwork. The address is 201 Main Street.

Both of these Muhlenbergs and their wives are buried directly behind the old Augustus Lutheran Church, which is adjacent to the new church and just north of Main Street. The church was founded by Henry Muhlenberg and the surviving structure built in 1743, making it the oldest unchanged Lutheran Church building in continuous use in the United States.

Trappe, first known as New Providence, is located off U.S. 422 (Pottstown Expressway), and is roughly midway between Limerick and Collegeville.

Nash (Francis) Grave, Towamencin Mennonite Meeting, near Kulpsville, Montgomery County. The death of Brigadier General Francis Nash (c. 1742–1777) of a wound received in the Battle of Germantown (see under PHILADELPHIA) was a serious loss to the Patriot cause. He was one of the most promising young generals of the Continental army, his military reputation dating from before the Revolution, when in his native North Carolina he led a company of militia in the Battle of the Alamance (see under NORTH CAROLINA). In addition, Francis Nash had risen to prominence as a merchant, attorney, and Whig politician. His brother Abner, who was about two years older, became governor of North Carolina in the spring of 1780 as his state became an active theater of military operations. Evidence of the fame of the brothers is the fact that Nashville, Tennessee, was named for them from its initial settlement in 1779.

General Nash was leading his North Carolina brigade into action at Germantown on 4 October 1777 when he was hit in the thigh by a cannonball. Three days later he died, far from his home in Hillsborough, North Carolina, and his body has never been moved from its original resting place. The grave has two markers, one erected in 1844 and the other in 1936. Three other officers, also mortally wounded at Germantown, lie beside Nash. The site is at the junction of the Sumneytown Pike and Forty Foot Road, near the Northeast Extension of the Pennsylvania Turnpike.

Paoli Massacre Site, Malvern. On the night of 20 to 21 September 1777, about a week after the Battle of the Brandywine, General Charles Grey surprised and routed General Anthony Wayne's camp about 2 miles southwest of Paoli Tavern (in today's town of Paoli). This was Wayne's home ground (see WAYNE BIRTHPLACE), and he had remained on the south side of the Schuylkill River to harass the British advance. The British learned of his plans and location, surprised his camp shortly after midnight, inflicted many casualties in a brief melee, and scattered Wayne's command before withdrawing with about seventy prisoners. Wayne saved his four cannon and was acquitted of court-martial charges of failing to heed "timely notice" of the attack. As was customary after suffering a humiliating military defeat, the Patriots raised the cry of "massacre." Inscriptions on monuments at the site reiterate the reference to "Patriots who . . . fell sacrificed to British barbarity."

Charles Grey (1729–1807), an experienced tactical commander, achieved at Paoli and later at Old Tappan, New Jersey, what might serve as textbook models of the surprise of detached camps. Acting on superior military intelligence of Wayne's location, Grey made a two-hour night march with several British regiments and achieved surprise. Finally, he solved the difficult problem of maintaining control in a night engagement by restricting his troops to use of the bayonet. This was orthodox doctrine in Grey's day, which saw the bayonet as deadlier than the inaccurate musket, but he became known after Paoli as "No-flint" Grey because he ordered that soldiers remove their flints if they could not draw the charges from muskets previously loaded. Historians have long discredited the patriotic American accusation that Grey's victory at Paoli was an atrocity, and today's visitors should not be deceived by the inscriptions on the monuments.

Near the battle site, in Malvern Memorial Park, is the mass grave of some fifty-three "mangled dead," protected by a low wall of stone. Some of this stone is from the foundation of a log cabin in which a few American officers were quartered at the time of the action. Nearby is a polished granite obelisk commemorating the "massacre." By walking behind this monument a visitor gets a panoramic view of the country to the south. Otherwise the landmarks of the famous skirmish are unidentified, and the ground where Wayne's rear guard was defeated is not part of the park. Privately owned, it is in the glen south of the obelisk mentioned above.

To reach Malvern Memorial Park in the town of Malvern, go 0.5 mile west from Warren Avenue on Monument Avenue The junction of these streets is 0.4 mile east of King Street (in Malvern) and 0.8 mile north of a traffic light on the Paoli Pike near the Malvern Preparatory School. Every year the Upper Main Line Memorial Association sponsors the Memorial Parade to honor those killed in the Paoli massacre.

Pennsbury Manor, on the Delaware River, northeast of Philadelphia, near Tullytown, 400 Pennsbury Memorial Road, in Bucks County. William Penn, founder of Pennsylvania, built a great manor house in the wilderness 25 miles up the Delaware from Philadelphia. He lived there less than two full years before returning to England in 1701, and the property quickly fell into ruin. A re-creation of the estate was completed in 1939 on the foundations of the large manor house and outbuildings. Pennsbury Manor has the largest collection of seventeenth-century furniture in the state, and the reconstructed plantation portrays the world of Pennsylvania's founder almost a century before the American Revolution. The site is managed by the PHMC. Phone: (215) 946-0400.

Philadelphia. The first European settlers on the site of Philadelphia were the Swedes, and their monument—"A jewel in its drab environs" of South Philadelphia—is the Gloria Dei (Old Swedes') Church National Historic Site (see below). The "City of Brotherly Love" was established in 1682 by William Penn as a Quaker colony. It was a "modern" city from the beginning, with an orderly street plan and with such innovations as garbage collection, street-cleaning services, firefighting and fire-insurance companies, a hospital, and street lighting long before such things were known even in Europe. As early as 1751 "law and order" was assured by a body of paid constables, who replaced the traditional night watchmen. There was a rapid growth in population in the decade preceding the Revolution; Philadelphia, with an estimated 38,000 people, was the third-largest city in the British Empire. (London, the largest, then had 750,000 people, the vast majority of them wallowing in squalor; Edinburgh had just over 40,000.)

In addition to having a much larger population than New York City (22,000), Boston (18,000), and Charleston (12,000), Philadelphia was the center of manufacturing in the American colonies. For these and other reasons Philadelphia was the logical place for the first seat of national government. The first Continental Congress met here in 1774. The Second Continental Congress and its successors sat in Philadelphia until the end of the Revolution, except for two periods totaling less than a year. (Congress fled to Baltimore in December 1776, when it looked as if the British were going to capture Philadelphia, and conducted its business as a sort of "rump parliament" of only twenty to twenty-five members until 4 March 1777. When the British occupied Philadelphia, 26 September 1777 to 18 June 1778, it had one meeting in Lancaster, Pennsylvania, and then sat in York, Pennsylvania.)

The sites of greatest Revolutionary War interest are listed below in alphabetical order, but a visit to Philadelphia should start at Independence Hall, which is the heart of the remarkable Independence National Historical Park (see those headings below). Philadelphia "Historical Sites" information is available by phone at (215) 965-7676. The website www.gophila.com is also extremely helpful.

African Methodist Episcopal Church, 419 Richard Allen Avenue. In 1777 an itinerant Methodist preacher spoke to a group of slaves in a clearing in the woods near the Delaware River. One of those slaves was seventeen-year-old Richard Allen, who purchased his freedom three years later and became a Methodist. Refusing to attend a segregated church, Allen joined with several others to form the African Methodist Episcopal Church (AME), the first black church in the United States. Allen was responsible for buying the site for their church. Using his own money, Allen purchased this plot on the corner of Sixth and Lombard. "Mother Bethel," as it was known, opened in 1794, beginning a rich history of involvement in Philadelphia's African American community and participation in many issues of national importance. The current building, dating to 1890, is the fourth on this site. Tours are available by appointment; phone: (215) 925-0616. About the same time that Allen had had enough of segregation, Absalom Jones reached the same conclusion within the Episcopal Church, and organized St. Thomas Episcopal Church. The church moved several times in its history before settling at 401 North 52nd Street. Jones and Allen got together in 1787 to establish an African American Masonic Lodge named to honor Prince Hall, a black Revolutionary veteran who opened the first African American Lodge in Boston. The current Prince Hall Grand Lodge of Pennsylvania is at 4301 North Broad Street.

Afro-American Historical and Cultural Museum, 701 Arch Street. The first municipal museum in the country specifically devoted to the historical experience of black Americans, the museum focuses on the contributions of African Americans to the history of Philadelphia and its region, and includes an exhibit on blacks in the American Revolution. Open Tuesday through Saturday, 10 A.M. to 5 P.M., and Sunday, noon to 6. Phone: (215) 574-0380.

American Women's Heritage Society Museum, 2000 Belmont Mansion. This historic house, built in 1742, played host to Washington, Franklin, and Madison during the Revolution, among many others. Today it houses one of the very few museums devoted to the history of women. Open Tuesday through Saturday, 10 A.M. to 4:30 P.M.; phone: (215) 878-8844.

Bartram (John) House and Botanical Gardens, 54th Street and Lindbergh Boulevard. Phone: (215) 729-5281. A self-educated scientist and pioneer, American botanist John Bartram (1699–1777) built with his own hands the distinctive but remarkably unattractive stone house preserved here. Dating from 1731, the two-and-a-half-story structure has tall Ionic columns that probably were added some years later, when the house was remodeled. Bartram created America's first botanical gardens, which were enlarged by his son and rescued from a subsequent period of neglect. The house is furnished with pieces contemporary with Bartram's period of significant work.

Carpenters' Hall, on 320 Chestnut Street between Fourth and Orianna. Headquarters of the Pennsylvania Committee of Correspondence and seat of the First Continental Congress (1774–1775), this building was constructed in 1770 as a guildhall for the Carpenters' Company of Philadelphia. The basement was used as an ammunition magazine during the Revolution, and it housed the first Bank of the United States during the period 1791 to 1797. Carpenter's Hall is open free to the public. Phone: (215) 925-0167.

Chew House (Cliveden), on Germantown Avenue between Johnson and Cliveden Streets. A famous landmark in the Battle of Germantown, 4 October 1777, this fine Georgian mansion survives as an eighteenth-century island in the urban sprawl of today's world. Privately owned by six generations of the Chew family for 209 years (except for one eighteen-year interval, 1779–1797) and seldom opened to the public during that time, the house and about 6 acres were acquired in 1972 by the National Trust for Historic Preservation. Varieties of events from historical to musical are held on the site in addition to tours and educational programs. It is open to the public from noon to 4 P.M., Thursday through Sunday. Phone: (215) 848-1777.

When Washington found that General Howe had split his forces after taking Philadelphia on 26 September 1777, he decided to mass his entire army of eleven thousand regulars and militia in an attack on the nine thousand British estimated to be in and around Germantown.

As Washington finally evolved his complicated plan, General John Sullivan was to lead his division, Wayne's division, and Conway's brigade down the Shippack Road from Chestnut Hill across Mount Airy and through Germantown. General Alexander ("Lord Stirling") would follow with two brigades, those of Nash and Maxwell. Three miles to the left and operating initially on a parallel line with Sullivan and Alexander would be the powerful force of three divisions under General Nathanael Greene. Militia units were to advance on both flanks of the regulars, and all of Washington's army would converge to annihilate the British around Germantown, after which they would all march against Cornwallis in Philadelphia.

The Americans reached Chestnut Hill at dawn. At 6 A.M., just as the sun was rising over foggy fields in which visibility was sometimes as low as 30 yards, the Rebels made contact with British outposts near Mount Airy. They were already behind schedule, and Greene was not yet in position on the left, but Sullivan decided to press on. Deploying "Mad Anthony" Wayne's division in the fields on the left of the road to narrow the gap on that flank, Sullivan advanced through the buckwheat fields on the other side of the Shippack Road.

Lieutenant Colonel Thomas Musgrave had, meanwhile, led his regiment forward to reinforce the British front lines. Driven back by superior forces, he counterattacked whenever the opportunity arose and conducted a brilliant delaying action. Heavy fog greatly assisted the Americans. Had the British been able to see as far as 100 yards and fire on the Americans as they crossed the numerous fences in their path, "Sullivan's attack would have ended in a slaughter" (Freeman, *Washington,* IV, pp. 513–514). On the other hand, this fog enabled Musgrave to withdraw part of his force (about 120 men) into the Chew House after fighting his delaying action over a stretch of about 2 miles.

Sullivan's wing (see above) swept on without realizing where their resolute opponents had gone, but the rest of Washington's center column quickly found out. General William Maxwell's division of Alexander's command, moving along the Shippack Road, was held up for half an hour by fire from the Chew House.

By the time this center column got moving again, bypassing the battered but still defended Chew House, the battle was turning into a fiasco. One of Greene's divisions (that of Adam Stephen; see STEPHEN HOUSE, WEST VIRGINIA) from the left flank violated orders and marched toward the sound of the fighting around the Chew House. It collided with Wayne's division, which it mistook for the enemy, and shots were exchanged.

Many other things went wrong, and the result was a panic that wrecked Washington's plans just when he and most of his army thought they were about to win a great victory. The Battle of Germantown turned out to have a decisive effect on the outcome of the Revolution because it convinced the French that they should support the Americans openly with military assistance. The French and other European observers were even more impressed by the Germantown defeat than by the Saratoga victory because it showed that the Rebels were determined to keep up their fight for independence. Howe had made Washington look foolish in the Philadelphia campaign; yet Washington snapped back with a powerful and audacious counteroffensive. Whatever historians later decided about Washington's generalship at Germantown, he and his army *thought* they had almost won a great victory, and this was a great boost to their morale; they were eager to try again somewhere else.

Built in 1763 by Benjamin Chew on his country estate of Cliveden, the two-story house is of gray stone quarried near the site. Imported urns ornamenting the gabled roof and marble statuary on the lawn gave Cliveden its most striking and distinctive look, these features being rare for Philadelphia houses. An imposing entrance hall is of particular interest because of its bright natural lighting and the screen of four columns separating it from the stair hall. But one of the most remarkable things about Cliveden is that many original furnishings remain. One outstanding item is a sofa attributed to the workshop of Thomas Affleck and first owned by Governor Penn. Other rare items are American Sheraton and Hepplewhite furniture and Philadelphia Chippendale mirrors. The acquisition also includes paintings of Cliveden, the Chew family, and an extensive collection of documents relating to both. The house joins some fifty other historic eighteenth- and nineteenth-century structures in the Germantown Historic District.

Christ Church, on Second Street between Market and Filbert Streets. This church was founded in 1695 and the present building was erected during the period 1727 to 1754. One of the finest colonial churches in America, it was attended by some of the most famous of the Patriots. Buried there are John Penn (last proprietary governor), General John Forbes, General Charles Lee, James Wilson, and Robert Morris ("The Financier of the Revolution").

Christ Church Cemetery, Fifth and Arch Streets. About a quarter of a mile away from Christ Church, land was purchased here in 1719 as a burial ground. Graves include those of five signers of the Declaration of Independence: Franklin (and his wife), Francis Hopkinson (of New Jersey), Benjamin Rush, Joseph Hewes (of Edenton,

North Carolina), and George Ross. After being closed for twenty-five years, the cemetery reopened to the public in 2003.

Deshler-Morris House, 5442 Germantown Avenue. Built in 1772 to 1773, this was Washington's home during the summers of 1793 and 1794. It is part of the Independence National Historical Park but located in Germantown, far from the main group of buildings. The house has been restored and refurnished, and it is open Friday to Sunday from 1 P.M. to 4 P.M. from April through mid-December, and by appointment only during other months. Phone: (215) 596-1748.

Dilworth-Todd-Moylan House, 343 Walnut Street at Fourth Street. Built in 1776 by Jonathan Dilworth, this house was bought in 1791 by John Todd, Jr., the first husband of Dolly Payne Madison. Between 1796 and 1807 it was the home of Colonel Stephen Moylan, the jolly Irishman who was closely associated with Washington in many varied capacities during the Revolution.

Elfreth's Alley Historical District, north of Arch Street between Front and Second Streets. In a remarkably good state of preservation, the little dwellings of artisans and craftsmen along this narrow street present a scene virtually unchanged in two centuries. It is commonly referred to as "Our Nation's Oldest Residential Street." The Elfreth's Alley Association was established in 1934 to conserve the site; it is using income from the annual fete day to restore Number 126 (built 1741–1762) as a permanent headquarters and museum. Daily guided tours of the district are available. Phone: (215) 574-0560.

Fort Mifflin, on the Delaware River at the foot of Fort Mifflin Road in South Philadelphia, just east of Philadelphia International Airport. Construction of a river fort to bar the water approach to Philadelphia was started in 1772 by the famous Captain John Montresor, a British military engineer. It was completed in 1777 under the direction of Major General Thomas Mifflin, and protected one end of the line of water obstacles stretching across the river to Fort Mercer, New Jersey.

After the British captured Philadelphia on 26 September 1777 by overland operations that avoided the Delaware River forts, General Howe had to open his line of communications with the fleet, or his position in Philadelphia would have become untenable. While the fleet under his brother, Admiral Richard Howe, was battering its way through the defenses farther down the Delaware, General Howe showed unwonted vigor in opening his campaign against the forts from the land side.

Despite the efforts of Washington's troops to stop them, the British succeeded in getting siege artillery emplaced on Providence Island, a swampy region where the United States Naval Depot was later established. At short range the gunners were able to deliver a sustained fire against the land side of the American fort, which had not been properly built for this unexpected threat. The defenders had valiantly fought back against this bombardment and had also inflicted severe damage on warships that tried to force their way past, but British water batteries started closing in. On 10 November, exactly a month after the fire from Providence Island had begun, a floating battery with twenty-two large guns (24-pounders) had closed to within 40 yards of the fort. In succeeding days the Royal Navy moved so close with their ships that their marines were able to fire into the fort from the rigging. Most of the fort's guns had long since been silenced, and the surviving defenders were virtually defenseless.

Major Simeon Thayer, who had succeeded the wounded Lieutenant Colonel Samuel Smith, evacuated his troops the night of 15 to 16 November to Fort Mercer after destroying what was left of his position. (See FORT MERCER, NEW JERSEY.)

Reconstruction of Fort Mifflin was started in the 1790s and modifications were made periodically until 1904. In the 1930s it was restored from the plans drawn by L'Enfant for the construction started in 1798 when war with France was expected. The National Survey of Historic Sites and Buildings notes that "Fort Mifflin preserves much of its character as an example of eighteenth-century military engineering, despite modifications over the years." (The stone wall on the river side is original.) It is of interest also as the scene of one of the bravest defensive fights ever put up by American troops.

Open to the public since 1969, Old Fort Mifflin is restored to its original appearance and features a wide array of historical programs and reenactments. Phone: (215) 685-4167.

Franklin Court, on Orianna Street between Chestnut and Market Streets. A 100-yard section of Orianna Street is one of the federal areas of Independence National Historical Park. Here is the site of the house in which Benjamin Franklin once lived and where he died. Today there is a peculiar "ghost structure" made of steel that outlines Franklin's house. There is an underground museum with historic displays, interactive exhibits, and a twenty-two-minute film, "The Real Ben Franklin." The museum is open daily from 9 A.M. to 5 P.M. Nearby, one can also visit the United States Postal Service Museum at 316 Market Street, open Monday through Saturday 9 A.M. to 5 P.M., and the Franklin Print Shop at 320 Market Street (hours vary, (215) 965-2305).

Gloria Dei (Old Swedes') Church National Historic Site, in South Philadelphia on Delaware Avenue near Christian Street. The existing structure of red brick was dedicated in 1700, and the Swedish accent is preserved in the steep gable roof, square belfry, and small spire. Swedes started settling along the Delaware in 1631. One of their great contributions to what became the American way of life was the log cabin, which was unknown in England. Gloria Dei replaced a small log blockhouse that the church had used since its establishment around 1646. Phone: (215) 389-1513.

Among the church treasures to be seen today are a carved cherubim and baptismal font of 1643 brought over by the first settlers. Silver altar appointments, old Bibles, and other documents comprise a collection of great value and interest.

Betsy Ross married her second husband here in 1777, and Daniel Boone's sister Margaret is among the many people of historical interest buried in the churchyard. Gloria Dei separated from the mother church in 1789, and in 1845 became Episcopalian. It remains the center of an active parish.

Independence Hall, on Chestnut Street between Fifth and Sixth Streets. This is the most important historical site in Philadelphia, if not in America. The city purchased it in 1818 from the Commonwealth of Pennsylvania, taking the first step in a long and sustained process of preservation. By a cooperative agreement between city and federal authorities, the Independence Hall group of buildings has been administered since 1951 as part of Independence National Historical Park (described below). Independence Hall is the heart of this park, and is open daily from 9 A.M. to 5 P.M.

Construction of the building was begun in 1732, and it was originally the statehouse for the colony of Pennsylvania. Here the Second Continental Congress met during the Revolution, except for two periods totaling less than a year when it was not safe to remain in the city. In this building George Washington was chosen to head the Continental army. Washington delivered his acceptance speech here, and in 1787 he started performing his functions as president of the Federal Constitutional Convention. The Declaration of Independence was adopted here in 1776, and four days later, on 8 July, the Liberty Bell (see below) was rung after the Declaration was first read to the citizens of Philadelphia. The bell is displayed here today. The Constitution was signed in this historic building.

Independence National Historical Park, a large area between Chestnut and Walnut Streets and Second and Sixth Streets, in addition to many nearby detached areas and four sites some distance away. The information center is in the west wing of Independence Hall. Covered in alphabetical order in this article on Philadelphia are the sites of Revolutionary War interest within the park. Sites the author has omitted are: Philosophical Hall, Library Hall, the First and Second Banks of the United States, New Hall (a modern reconstruction which houses a museum of early Marine Corps history), the Philadelphia Exchange, and the Bishop White House and Pemberton House (a reconstructed house that features the Army-Navy Museum). Information about all of these places is readily available in tourist guides. Phone: (215) 965-2305.

Jefferson House, officially known as the Graff House, Seventh Street near Market Street. A marker indicates the site of a three-story brick house in which Thomas Jefferson wrote the first draft of the Declaration of Independence in June 1776. He was then thirty-three years old. The house was rebuilt in 1883 and rebuilt years later by the National Park Service, which relied on old photographs for the construction. There is only one item known to be authentic to Jefferson's time in the house: a key to the desk. Open Wednesday through Sunday, 12 P.M. to 2 P.M; phone: (215) 597-8974.

Liberty Bell, in Independence Hall. Construction of the bell tower on Independence Hall was authorized in 1750 and completed in 1753. A bell was ordered from England in 1751 and delivered in 1752. It weighed about 2,000 pounds. The colonial council had prescribed that it should have cast around its crown the words from Leviticus: "Proclaim Liberty throughout all the Land unto all the Inhabitants Thereof." This was intended as a fiftieth anniversary memorial to William Penn's Charter of Privileges (1701). The bell was not known by its current name until 1839, when it was associated with the anti-slavery movement.

The bell cracked while being tested in 1752 in Philadelphia, and was recast twice. Starting in 1753 the bell was rung on public occasions, one of which was the first reading of the Declaration of Independence to the citizens of Philadelphia in Independence Square on 8 July 1776. At least, tradition has it that the bell was rung on this occasion; if true, the scene would have been quite different from that visualized by a modern patriot because nobody paid much attention to the Declaration of Independence until many years later. It merely made a matter of record the course Congress had already set. Few of the men now immortalized as signers mentioned the document in their letters, and although nobody signed the document until 2 August, John Adams and Jefferson were so little impressed by this event that they both insisted many years later that they had signed on 4 July.

The bell was hidden for almost a year in Allentown during the British occupation of Philadelphia, after which it was rung again on public occasions. According to tradition, the bell was strained in tolling during the obsequies of Chief Justice John Marshall in 1835. The final damage, which silenced it forever, occurred in 1846 when it was rung on Washington's birthday. The Liberty Bell Center Museum is open all year and is part of National Independence National Historical Park.

Mikveh Israel Cemetery, Spruce and Ninth Streets. Established in 1738, this is the city's oldest Jewish burial ground, and it is included in the Independence National Historical Park. Graves include those of Haym Salomon, a

Patriot who spent much time in British prisons for subversive activities and performed valuable services as a financier of the Revolution, and of Nathan Levy, whose ship brought the Liberty Bell to America.

Mount Pleasant, in Fairmount Park, between East River Drive and the Columbia Avenue entrance. One of the most beautiful houses in America (one architectural historian, Thomas T. Waterman, calls it the finest colonial house in the North), Mount Pleasant was built during the period 1761 to 1762 by a Scottish sea captain. This probably accounts for the balustraded deck on the hipped roof. From the house's hilltop location there is a magnificent view of the Schuylkill.

The mansion was bought by Benedict Arnold in 1779, when he was military commander of Philadelphia. About this time, the thirty-eight-year-old hero married nineteen-year-old Peggy Shippen. There is no proof that the couple ever lived at Mount Pleasant, but Arnold did install there his devoted sister, Hannah, and his three sons by his first wife. The estate, which Arnold had settled on his wife for life, was confiscated when the hero turned traitor. Arnold secretly repurchased it through his father-in-law for less than the £5,000 ($25,000) he claimed from the British for his loss of the estate, but he subsequently resold it.

The house was leased for a brief period to Baron von Steuben. Eventually it came into the possession of General Jonathan Williams, a kinsman and long-time associate of Benjamin Franklin. The city of Philadelphia bought it in 1868 from the Williams family. Refurnished handsomely by the Philadelphia Museum of Art, it is administered by that institution. It closed for renovation for some time but reopened to the public in the fall of 2005. Phone: (215) 763-8100.

Ross (Betsy) House (c. 1740), 239 Arch Street. The legend of Betsy Ross's making the first Stars and Stripes is based on a story first made public in 1870 by her grandson. But there *was* a Betsy Ross (1752–1836) who rented the house from 1773 to 1786, and there is documentary evidence of her being paid in 1777 for "making ships' colours, etc." She eloped in 1773 with John Ross (the first of her three husbands), who opened an upholsterer's shop on the site of what is now 233 Arch Street. A little brick structure dating from about 1700 has been restored here and furnished with appropriate memorabilia to perpetuate a patriotic myth. The house/museum is open 10 A.M. to 5 P.M. daily from April through September. Phone: (215) 686-1252.

St. George's Church, 235 North Fourth Street. The oldest Methodist church now standing in America, this building has been in continuous use since 1769, except during the British occupation of Philadelphia. Phone: (215) 925-7788.

St. Joseph's Church, on Willings Alley between Third and Fourth Streets. Earlier structures of 1733 and 1757 have been replaced by this one, which was started in 1838. When it opened, St. Joseph's held the only legally allowed Catholic mass in the British Empire. Lafayette and the Comte de Rochambeau both worshiped here, as did a number of other prominent Catholics of the Revolutionary era. Mass has been celebrated here without interruption for more than two centuries. Tours are available by appointment; phone: (215) 923-1733. (See St. Mary's Church, below.)

St. Mary's Church, at 252 South Fourth Street between Locust and Spruce. The principal Catholic church in Philadelphia during the Revolution, it was established in 1763. Thomas Fitz-Simons and Commander John Barry ("Father of the American Navy") are buried here. Phone: (215) 923-7930.

Walnut Street Prison, marker on Sixth Street near Walnut Street. Extending between Walnut and Locust Streets, on the east edge of modern Washington Square, was a notorious prison that stood during the years 1775 to 1838. The Patriots used it as a jail for Loyalists, and during the British occupation of Philadelphia the infamous William Cunningham was in charge of American prisoners there who had been taken at Brandywine and Germantown. The death rate was high, and hundreds of prisoners of war were buried in the potter's field (established in 1704) where Washington Square was subsequently created. The prison was torn down in 1838.

Washington Square, bounded by Sixth, Seventh, Walnut, and Locust Streets, is a beautiful area to walk and view historic buildings. Once known as Congo Square for its use as a meeting place for the city's free blacks, the square was the burial site for hundreds of soldiers during the Revolution.

Pocono Indian Museum, Bushkill. The Delaware, or Lenni Lenapee as they called themselves, were the subject of one of the greatest land frauds in American history, the so-called "Walking Purchase" of 1737. Already crushed by losing most of their land to the proprietors of Pennsylvania, the Delaware were nearly exterminated during the Revolution, with the survivors scattered to regions as far west as Oklahoma and north to Canada. The Pocono Museum, which sits on lands taken from the Delaware, displays artifacts from archaeological excavations as well as information on their history. Located south of town on U.S. 209, the museum is open daily from 9:30 A.M. to 6 P.M. Phone: (717) 588-9338.

Summerseat, Legion and Clymer Avnues, Morrisville, Bucks County. Thomas Barclay built this attractive two-story stone house in 1773. It was the home at later intervals of two signers of the Declaration of Independence, George Clymer and Robert Morris. During the period 8 to 14 December 1776 it was Washington's headquarters (just before his famous crossing of the Delaware). Restored in 1931, it became part of the Morrisville school system until 1976, when it was purchased by the Historic Morrisville Society, and it is now open to the public on a limited basis. For more information phone (215) 295-9287.

Swede's Ford, in modern Norristown on the Schuylkill River. On one of the main avenues of approach to Philadelphia, this crossing figured prominently in maneuvers after the Patriot defeat on the Brandywine (see BRANDYWINE BATTLEFIELD). Washington used it in moving to Valley Forge and in sending the large detachment under Lafayette to Barren Hill.

Thomson Home, officially known as Harriton House, Lower Merion Township, Montgomery County. Charles Thomson came to America from Ireland as an orphan at the age of ten and became a schoolmaster before prospering as a merchant and then becoming active in politics. He is best remembered as the "perpetual secretary" of the Continental Congress, holding this office for almost fifteen years (until 1789). His second marriage was in 1774, to the daughter of the second owner of the estate of Harriton, near Philadelphia, and here he lived until his death in 1824, making "scholarly and felicitous" translations of the Septuagint and the New Testament. The house dates from 1704 and is in the National Survey inventory (1964) under the heading "Sites Also Noted." The house became a museum in 1970. It is located at 500 Harriton Road, west of Bryn Mawr on Montgomery Road to Roberts Road, and then onto Harriton. The house is open Wednesday through Saturday, 10 A.M. to 4 P.M. Phone: (610) 525-0201.

Thompson's Island Skirmish (Brodhead Expedition), Allegheny River, Warren County. The only Revolutionary War engagement in northwestern Pennsylvania occurred here on 15 August 1779. Colonel Daniel Brodhead had left Fort Pitt four days earlier with six hundred troops for a punitive expedition up the Allegheny. (It had been supposed to link up with the Sullivan-Clinton Expedition in New York for an attack on Fort Niagara, but failed to make contact.) Leaving the river at the mouth of Mahoning Creek (around modern Templeton) and moving "through a country almost impassable by reason of stupendous heights and frightful declivities," as described by a participant, the expedition came back to the Allegheny about 15 miles above today's Franklin (then Venango).

From there the going was worse. What shows on modern highway maps as a route recommended for its scenic beauty (U.S. 62) was for the Brodhead Expedition "a continued narrow defile, allowing us only the breadth of an Indian path to march upon" (Commager and Morris, *The Sprit of Seventy Six*, pp. 1023–1024). In the only attempt to bar Brodhead's advance, some thirty to forty Indian warriors landed from canoes at a point opposite Thompson's Island.

The commander of the Patriot advance guard, Lieutenant Jonathan Hardin, attacked before the Indians could get organized. Leaving five dead, and abandoning their canoes, the Indians "fled with the utmost horror and precipitation," some into the woods and others swimming the river (presumably to Thompson's Island). Hardin's only casualties—he had fourteen white soldiers and eight Delawares—were three men slightly wounded.

Brodhead, meeting no further resistance, went on to burn ten towns of the Mingo, Munsey, and Seneca Indians (165 houses) and destroy an estimated 500 acres of corn. Coming back, the expedition found "a creek about 10 miles above Venango, remarkable for an oily liquid which oozes from the sides and bottom of the channel and the adjacent springs, much resembling British oil, and if applied to a woolen cloth, burns instantly" (ibid.). This was, of course, Oil Creek, where the earliest explorers had found the Indians skimming surface oil (used medicinally) and where the petroleum industry was centered during the years 1859 to 1865.

The site of the Thompson's Island Skirmish is marked on U.S. 62, 9 miles southwest of Warren. The latter city is on the site of Conewango, a Seneca village of historical importance on the Iroquois frontier.

Valley Forge National Historical Park, Port Kennedy, off Valley Forge interchange of the Pennsylvania Turnpike. The site of the famous winter quarters of 1777 to 1778 is preserved in a park of 3,466 acres. Although veterans of Washington's miserable little army would have trouble today in recognizing the area that one of them, General Kalb, said was probably selected on the advice of a speculator, a traitor, or a council of ignoramuses, Valley Forge has been transformed into an impressive shrine of American patriotism.

Even when stripped of the myths that have been invented since the Revolution—such as Washington's kneeling to pray in the snow—Valley Forge deserves to be immortalized. It was here that the losers of earlier campaigns were transformed into the winners of Monmouth and Yorktown. Although it was a mild winter (the next one, at Morristown [see MORRISTOWN NATIONAL HISTORICAL PARK under New Jersey], made Valley Forge look like a picnic), an estimated three thousand of the ten thousand troops died there or in various hospitals to which they were removed. Their suffering was caused by administrative incompetence, graft, and

Valley Forge, Soldier's Quarters. *Valley Forge National Historical Park includes reconstructions of the cabins where George Washington's troops resided during the winter of 1777 to 1778.* © JOSEPH SOHM; CHROMOSOHM INC./CORBIS.

war profiteering, however, and the real triumphs of the winter at Valley Forge were the military reforms that Washington was able to bring about. Congress was finally ready to listen to his recommendations on military matters, so Washington was able to strengthen the officer corps, to get more recruits for the Continental infantry, to improve the quality of the cavalry, and to correct weaknesses of army administration. After the miserable failure of Thomas Mifflin as quartermaster general, the supply mess was straightened out by Nathanael Greene, who was prevailed on by Washington to leave his duties as a field commander for this purpose. General Steuben became famous at Valley Forge for his colorful and highly effective performance as the Prussian drillmaster who gave American officers and men the professional training they so sorely needed.

Although Valley Forge had many shortcomings as a campsite—"no village, no plain, and little valley," writes D. S. Freeman in his biography of Washington—it was almost ideal from a tactical and strategic viewpoint. It provided good defensive terrain, it had a good supply of wood for building and for burning, it had good drainage, and water was abundant. Less than 20 miles from Philadelphia, where the British army was living high, it was between that place and the temporary seat of the Continental Congress at York.

Today's visitor will see reconstructed huts, impressive memorials, extensive remains of forts, earthworks, and campsites, the house that served as Washington's headquarters, which now serves as one of the park's museums, and the expected military reenactments. The Mount Joy observatory tower provides a view of the campsite and the surrounding countryside. It stands at the site of Washington's marquee, the field tent he used until he moved into the house of the Quaker preacher Isaac Potts, mentioned above. The tent is preserved in the museum. A visitor will also see the parade ground where Steuben took the troops' minds off their problems of "no pay, no clothes, no provisions, no rum," and where they celebrated with a *feu de joie* the news of the French alliance. Guided tours are available, and visitors can roam the vast grounds while basking in the natural scenery and the site's rich history. The park is open daily from 9 A.M. to 6 P.M. Phone: (610) 783-1077; website: http://www.nps.gov/vafo/home.htm.

Warren Tavern. *See* BATTLE OF THE CLOUDS.

Washington Crossing State Park and New Hope, Delaware River, Bucks County. A highway bridge across the Delaware connects the state parks of Pennsylvania (478 acres) and New Jersey (372 acres) in what the National Survey of Historic Sites and Buildings has called "an outstanding preservation of a key site in the winning of American independence." Operated by the PHMC, this site contains thirteen historic buildings, some of which are noted in this listing. The park is open Tuesday through Saturday, 9:00 A.M. to 5:00 P.M., and Sunday, noon to 5:00 P.M. For further information, call the park at (215) 493-4076.

On the Pennsylvania side the park has two separate sections on the river about 4 miles apart, one at the community of Washington Crossing (Pa. 32) and the other at Bowman's Hill (north of Pa. 32). In New Hope Borough (a little farther north on Pa. 32) are the Coryell and Vansant Houses (see below).

Washington's crossing of the Delaware on the night of 25 to 26 December 1776 to surprise and defeat the Hessian garrison in Trenton is one of the most dramatic events of the American Revolution. There is, however, the danger that the drama of the crossing may obscure Washington's real achievement here in getting this offensive effort out of a ragged and demoralized little band of troops that had taken one beating after another. When there was every reason to assume that the American Revolution had failed militarily, a few individual leaders succeeded in saving it. Washington's personal contribution is evident: knowing that the British could resume their offensive toward Philadelphia when the Delaware froze hard enough to support their crossing, and faced with expiring enlistments that would reduce his army to about 1,400 men on 31 December, Washington decided to make one final military effort. Less well known are the contributions of Thomas Paine and General Thomas Mifflin in whipping up the support Washington needed. The first number of *The Crisis* was published by Paine on 19 December in the *Pennsylvania Journal*, with the opening lines "These are the times that try men's souls. The summer soldier and the sunshine patriot will, in this crisis, shrink from the service of their country." Mifflin undertook a whirlwind tour of Pennsylvania to rally the militia, accomplishing what historian John C. Miller in his *Triumph of Freedom* has called "probably one of the most important missions of the war."

And on the technical side, too often ignored in attempting to appreciate military operations, the role of Colonel John Glover's men and the Durham boats deserve special mention. (For this see the article on Durham Village.)

Of the three separate sites on the Pennsylvania side, the southernmost is around the present community of Washington Crossing. At the landing area is the Old Ferry Inn (1774), on the north side of Pa. 532 near the bridge. A handsome park memorial building here has an important library, but its main attraction is an excellent copy of the painting by the German artist Emanuel Leutze, *Washington Crossing the Delaware.* The less said about the artistic and historical qualities of this famous work the better, but it is only fair to acknowledge that "it constitutes an inspiring interpretation of the event in spirit if not in factual detail" (*Colonials and Patriots*, p. 122). (The original, once on loan here, is in the Metropolitan Museum of Art in New York City.) The Washington Crossing Monument (1916) overlooks the ferry site.

About 4 miles north on Pa. 32 is another section of the park, where the Patriot troops camped during the period 12 to 25 December 1776. On Bowman's Hill, in a 100-acre wildflower preserve, is a fieldstone memorial observation tower where the Patriots had a lookout. Northwest about 2.5 miles away is the Thompson-Neely House, used before the crossing as headquarters of officers including General William Alexander, Captain William Washington, and Lieutenant James Monroe (one of the few wounded at Trenton, where he distinguished himself, and a future president of the United States). The older section of this handsome, two-story stone house was built in 1702; it is furnished and open to the public. The old gristmill owned by Robert Thompson in 1776 is near the house. Just to the south (0.1 mile) is a 17-acre tract of primitive land maintained as a wildlife preserve with restrictions on visiting. Also in this Bowman's Hill section of the park is a memorial flagstaff over the unmarked gravestones of soldiers who died during the encampment.

In the Borough of New Hope, a short distance north, are two historic houses associated with the crossing. (Neither is open to the public.) The home of John Coryell, 105 South Main Street, built around 1750, marks the northern end of the Patriot defensive position along the Delaware in December 1776. Coryell's Ferry was the name of the village during the period 1765 to 1790. (See the separate section on CORYELL'S FERRY.) Near the Town Hall (1790), 0.1 mile away, is the Vansant House on the northwest corner of Mechanic Street. Probably the oldest house in the village, it was built about 1743. The attic walls still show grapeshot from British batteries that fired across the river in 1776. See WASHINGTON CROSSING, NEW JERSEY.

Wayne Birthplace, near Paoli. "Waynesboro," the house where Anthony Wayne was born in 1745 and where he followed his father's trade as a tanner until the start of the Revolution, has remained standing and in the Wayne family. The beautiful house has been carefully restored and is visible from Waynesboro Road, opposite the General Wayne Golf Course (Wayne's Borough Country Club). The fence surrounding the private home has a marker. To reach the site, go a short distance east from Paoli on U.S. 30 to Pa. 252 (Leopard Road), turn right (south), drive about 0.8 mile, and turn right on Waynesboro Road. The house is on the right, near a branch of Crum Creek that runs through the golf course. A few miles away is the Wayne Grave.

Wayne Grave, St. David's (Radnor) Churchyard, near Wayne (see below). Buried first at Fort Presque Isle (site is in Erie at Sixth and Ash Streets), General "Mad Anthony" Wayne was reinterred near his birthplace in 1809. Old St. David's dates from 1715, and the church structure has been well preserved in its ancient and picturesque churchyard. Wayne's grave is about 50 feet north of the small stone structure.

To reach the site, from U.S. 30 (Lancaster Pike) go south from the Devon Horse Show grounds on Dorset Road for 0.5 mile, continue on Sugartown Road for 0.7 mile around two right-angle curves, and continue 0.6 mile south on Valley Forge Road to the entrance on the right. (New St. David's may be seen on the left, 0.2 mile north.)

The official designation of the church is St. David's Radnor, and published literature available on the site gives its location variously as Devon and Wayne, Pennsylvania. Other authorities place it in Radnor. The explanation of this mystery is simply that the church property is split by three township lines.

Weiser Home and Grave, 28 Weiser Road, near Womelsdorf, Berks County. Phone: (610) 589-2934. Conrad Weiser, born in Germany in 1696, came to New York with his family in 1710 and spent the winter of 1712 to 1713 with the Iroquois, becoming a student of Indian culture. Moving to Pennsylvania, he prospered as a farmer and tanner, raised fourteen children, and became a famous trader and treaty maker with the Indians. The site of his trading post, operated from about 1750 to 1760, is marked in Reading in Penn Square between Fifth and Sixth Streets. The property where he built a home in 1729, and where he spent the rest of his life, is preserved as a state park in memory of this enlightened keeper of the peace on the colonial frontier. The park is managed by the PHMC. Another good source of local information is the Historical Society of Berks County. Phone: (610) 375-4375.

White Horse Tavern. *See* BATTLE OF THE CLOUDS.

Whitemarsh, on the Wissahickon Creek, Montgomery County. Before going to Valley Forge for winter quarters in the latter part of December 1777, Washington's army was camped in this area. Although it is now covered by urban development, place-names and some buildings have survived since the Revolution, and much of the terrain is preserved in three separated sections of the 493-acre Fort Washington State Park, other parks, and many country clubs. In Whitemarsh is the George Emlen House, which was Washington's headquarters, and the Hope Lodge State Historic Site, a restored Georgian mansion where General Nathanael Greene was quartered.

When the British were in Philadelphia, General Howe made a night march with most of his army, hoping to catch the Patriots while in a vulnerable situation at Whitemarsh. After pushing in the American outposts, Howe found that Washington's position was too strong, so in mid-afternoon of 7 December he started withdrawing to Philadelphia.

Hope Lodge, 553 South Bethlehem Turnpike in Fort Washington, is a two-story brick mansion with an imposing exterior and a fine interior of molded wainscotings, large fireplaces, and a spacious central hallway. It was built around 1750 and bought not long before the British occupation of Philadelphia by William West, a Philadelphia merchant of the Patriot persuasion whose business sense suggested that this was a good time to acquire property in the suburbs. His nephew and namesake lived in the house as a paroled prisoner, but there is evidence that he did espionage work for the American army. (William West the senior was later involved with General Benedict Arnold in profiteering in Philadelphia.)

In 1784 the mansion was a wedding gift from Henry Hope to his cousin James Watmough, who then gave it its present name. (The Hope Diamond was so called after being acquired by this same international family in 1830.) Hope Lodge was saved from destruction in 1922, restored and refurnished by private owners at that time, and given to the state in 1957. It is maintained by the PHMC and open for tours on Wednesday through Sunday. Forming a crescent around Hope Lodge in Fort Washington State Park are the hills fortified by Washington's army in November to December 1777, since known as Camp Hill, Fort Hill, and Militia Hill. To find Hope Lodge take Exit 339 off the Pennsylvania Turnpike and follow the road past the Holiday Inn. Take a left onto Bethlehem Pike. Hope Lodge will be on the left. Phone: (215) 646-1595.

Wyoming Valley. A 25-mile stretch of the Susquehanna River below the mouth of the Lackawanna River (including modern Wilkes-Barre) was known in colonial times as the Wyoming Valley. (At least a dozen other places were called Wyoming by 1865, when this name was first proposed for the state of Wyoming.) Claimed by Connecticut as well as by Pennsylvania, the valley was the scene of bloody clashes known as the Pennamite Wars. By 1775 the Connecticut element was leading in these intramural contests, but the settlers then started forming new teams for the larger contest, the American Revolution. Loyalists who had come in from the Hudson and Mohawk Valleys were pitted against Whigs (or "Patriots").

In July 1778 the famous Wyoming Valley Massacre occurred. The fifty-three-year-old John Butler led four hundred Loyalists in a remarkable, 200-mile march through the wilderness from Fort Niagara and was joined en route by some five hundred Senecas and Cayugas. The Patriots had been warned of the invasion but were still caught by surprise. In the Battle of Wyoming, 3 July 1778, the raiders wiped out an ineptly led force of three hundred local militia and sixty "regulars." (The latter qualified as such only because Congress had authorized their formation after the best military manpower of the valley had been drained into the Continental army.)

Only sixty Patriots escaped the decisive battle on the afternoon of 3 July. About fourteen captives died that night on "the Bloody Rock" (see below). The raiders ravaged the Wyoming Valley settlements, Loyalists settling old scores and Indians claiming the rewards of victory. More than one thousand houses and other structures were destroyed; more than one thousand head of livestock were carried off. Some two dozen noncombatants were murdered, but perhaps the worst loss of life resulted because panic-stricken fugitives fled without proper provisions over wilderness trails. John Butler reported with "sincerest satisfaction" that his Loyalists and Indians killed no noncombatants.

The major sites figuring in accounts of the massacre are indicated by highway markers. The flat area of pine woods and underbrush where the battle took place is intersected by a wide highway (U.S. 11) in the present town of Wyoming. Here, easily found half a mile south of the traffic light at Eighth Street in the center of Wyoming, is a small park with a 63-foot-high granite monument erected in the 1840s near the scene of the action and "over the bones of the slain." Listed on it are the names of about 45 survivors and 166 slain. Remains of the latter were not collected and buried here in a mass grave until 22 October 1778.

"The Bloody Rock" is about a mile northeast, preserved under a crude grill in a small plot of grass under two large trees between Seventh and Eighth Streets. (From the traffic light mentioned above, go southeast on Eighth Street toward the river for 0.6 mile, then about 100 yards left on Susquehanna Avenue.) Here some fourteen captives were supposedly executed the night of the battle by an Indian woman identified by tradition as "Queen Esther."

Other landmarks, of interest only because their location is marked, are given below in alphabetical order.

Forty Fort, where the town of that name now stands, on U.S. 11, 2 miles below Wyoming. A large cemetery at the principal intersection (Wyoming Avenue, or U.S. 11, and River Street) is about where the first forty settlers from Connecticut built their blockhouse after arriving in 1770. The colony grew, and the Patriots strengthened Forty Fort when they became alarmed about the growing Loyalist activity 2 miles north (now Wyoming) where the fortified house of the Wintermoots was located. It was their base before the Battle of Wyoming, and the place where survivors took refuge with the assembled noncombatants. They all surrendered the next morning with the written stipulation that their lives and property would be protected, fleeing the valley in terror once Butler let them go. The present cemetery, badly damaged in the 1972 flood, has only a few Revolutionary War graves, but one is that of John Jenkins (see Fort Jenkins, below). On River Street and Fort Street rests a huge rock that marks where the fort once stood. A bronze plaque was erected there by the Wyoming Valley DAR Chapter in 1900.

Fort Jenkins, just north of the I-80 bridge, near where U.S. 11 and Pa. 92 now join in West Pittston, about 3 miles above today's Wyoming. It was the home of the Whig John Jenkins, erected in 1776, and almost immediately fortified because the home of the Loyalist Wintermoots was being made into a stronghold. Jenkins's and a smaller "fort" called Exeter were captured and burned by Butler's forces when they first entered the valley on 30 June 1778. The next day the Patriot column advancing from Forty Fort clashed here with Indians who had just killed some men working in a field. Meanwhile, the raiders established themselves around Wintermoot's (see below). Among the three or four Revolutionary graves in the present Forty Fort Cemetery is that of a John Jenkins, most probably the man identified with Fort Jenkins. The highway marker implies that this fort was near the present bridge and the junction of the highways mentioned above, about 3 miles from modern Wyoming. However, after visiting the area in 1848, Benson Lossing put the site 1.5 miles from the battle monument.

Wilkes-Barre Fort (Fort Wyoming), where the public square of today's Wilkes-Barre is located, about 8 miles by road, then and now, from the site of Fort Jenkins. It was first built in 1771 by Pennsylvanians, seized by Connecticut settlers, and rebuilt the year of Butler's raid by enclosing the courthouse. The place was surrendered along with others of the valley the day after the battle. The settlement's twenty-three houses were burned, but enough of the fort survived for it to be the rallying point for the few settlers who did not abandon the valley, and it was the headquarters for the relief column that arrived a month after the Battle of Wyoming. In 1779 the slow-starting punitive expedition under General John Sullivan was at Fort Wyoming for five weeks. In 1784 the fort was destroyed after the postwar garrison was withdrawn.

Wintermoot's Fort, a few hundred yards above "the Bloody Rock," according to Lossing's sketch (op. cit., p. 353). This was where Butler made camp when he entered the valley. Here also he anchored his left flank and stationed himself with his Rangers, while the Indians on the right flank performed the envelopment that led to the Patriot rout on the afternoon of 3 July. (Johnson's Royal Greens were in the center.) The Wintermoots were Loyalists from Minisink Ford, New York who purchased land around the head of the valley before the Revolution, fortified their farm more strongly than the Indian threat appeared to justify, and soon became prominently identified with the Loyalist element in the region.

York and vicinity, York County. Pennsylvania's first two counties were Chester (1682) and Lancaster (1728), after which York County was established in 1748 to comprise the territory west of the broad and then bridgeless Susquehanna River, but York Town had been surveyed and founded in 1741.

When the Continental Congress took refuge in York Town, where they held sessions in the courthouse from 30 September 1777 (with five members present) to 24 June 1778, the town had about 300 houses and 1,800 people.

The historic sites of York have been well identified and most of them have been marked so that a visitor can find them on a walking tour, particularly if starting at the York County Heritage Trust, 250 East Market Street (phone: (717) 848-1587), and the excellent regional museum (see below). The Trust offers guided tours as well as guidebooks to help visitors guide themselves through York's well-preserved historical treasures.

The York County Convention and Visitors Bureau has a very informative website, www.yorkpa.org, and also can be contacted by phone at (717) 849-2217. The historical and architectural gems are the Golden Plough Tavern and the General Gates House, adjoining restorations on West Market Street (U.S. 30E) at Pershing Avenue, two blocks west of the surviving public square.

The Golden Plough Tavern, part of what the York County Trust calls the "Colonial Complex," is believed to date from 1741, when Martin Eichelberger, a native of the Black Forest, secured the lot here. This Germanic half-timber house, using brick in the walls of the second story and large gable end, was an architectural oddity when it was built in colonial Pennsylvania (although the style was standard in the Black Forest), and it is one of the few known to exist in America.

The General Gates House—also located in the Colonial Complex at 157 West Market Street—so called because it was his quarters during the first four months of 1778 when he was in York as president of the newly established Board of War, is a simple, two-story stone structure built in 1751. Much is made locally of the story that here Lafayette destroyed the "Conway Cabal" by proposing a toast to Washington after noting that Gates's other guests had pointedly omitted toasting their commander in chief. Washington's reputation had reached its lowest ebb at this time, after a long series of defeats ending with the British occupation of Philadelphia (26 September 1777). Horatio Gates had at about the same time become famous as the victor of Saratoga, and there naturally was considerable talk about giving him the supreme command. It also is of historical record that Lafayette was one of Washington's staunchest supporters, and it should not be forgotten that Lafayette represented French military aid to the colonists. (The historian Van Tyne points out in his *War of Independence* [Boston, 1929] that 90 percent of the supplies that made the Saratoga victory possible were sent, secretly of course, by France.) But it has never been proved that there was a cabal to oust Washington, much less that Lafayette scuttled it with a French toast.

York can claim to be the first capital of the United States because until the Congress sitting at York adopted the Articles of Confederation (15 November 1777) they had been acting as representatives of the "United Colonies." The printers Hall and Sellers were ordered to York, and from presses set up in a home whose site is marked at Market and Beaver Streets they printed not only the journals of Congress and other publications but also millions of dollars of paper currency. The phrase "not worth a Continental [dollar]" was not coined until the currency collapsed completely in July 1781, but in January 1778, when Hall and Sellers were getting into production, the value of paper money in relation to specie was down 75 percent; a year later it was 90 percent below face value.

Although at least sixty-four delegates attended sessions of Congress at York, not more than half were there at any one time. Yet this rump Congress did some important business, including commissioning a man with false credentials from Benjamin Franklin in Paris (who said he was "a Lieutenant General in the King of Prussia's service," neglecting to point out that this rank equated with brigadier general in the American army). But this deception gave the American cause the invaluable services of a professional military trainer, the Baron von Steuben, whose work at Valley Forge has been well publicized but whose greatest gift was in the more technical business of organizing proper staff procedures and logistical support.

York was the base at one time for the legions of Pulaski and Armand, and was a major center for prisoners of war. Important munitions works were in and around York, including one later called Codorus Furnace that operated until 1850 and has been partially restored. Erected in 1765, and owned for a few years by James Smith, a signer of the Declaration of Independence, it is 2.5 miles northeast of Starview, near the junction of

Codorus Creek with the Susquehanna. Other famous forges or furnaces of York County were Mary Ann Furnace, started in 1762 by George Ross, another signer, and Spring Forge, dating from 1755. The latter was a few miles southwest of York near the present Spring Grove; the former was 4 miles southeast of Hanover.

Modern York is a busy town with heavy traffic, but it preserves the original layout of parallel streets. The surviving center square (Market and George Streets) is the site of the old courthouse (completed 1756, torn down in 1841), a model of which is in the museum. Here also is the original courthouse door and its weathervane in the form of a Pulaski dragoon foolishly nicknamed "the Little General." It was made by a local coppersmith in whose family home the famous Polish volunteer stayed when in York.

Penn Common is about five blocks southwest. Then on the outskirts of York Town, this was where Pulaski's Legion camped during March and April 1779. Anthony Wayne's Pennsylvania Line bivouacked here before starting south on 26 May 1781 to join Lafayette in Virginia. Most of the latter troops had recently been involved in the mutiny of 1 to 10 January. Wayne had been prominently involved in settling this affair, showing a tolerant attitude toward their well-justified demands. But when his troops again started muttering about mutiny, dissatisfied this time about being paid in Continental currency at face value, Wayne had four leaders shot on the commons. He then marched the rest of his command past the corpses, which ended that threat to military discipline. Barracks for prisoners of war were erected on Penn Common in the early years of the war. Starting in the spring of 1781, a large prison camp was built on a hill 4 miles east of York. Prisoners included those from Saratoga and Yorktown.

RHODE ISLAND

It is usual in introducing any discussion of Rhode Island to start by pointing out that it is the smallest of the United States. As historic sites are concerned, however, Rhode Island outclasses many other states that dwarf it in physical size, and there are several reasons why. It was among the earliest to be established as a colony. Because of its port facilities Rhode Island was almost immediately involved more intimately in world affairs than were the other colonies. It prospered quickly as a maritime colony, making its fortune during the Anglo-French wars of the colonial era and being particularly sensitive to Britain's efforts after 1763 to reverse the policy of "salutary neglect" of the Navigation Acts. Rhode Island was therefore more closely attuned than other colonies of British America to the economic and political issues that led to the Revolution. Thus Rhode Island was the scene of the earliest instances of overt resistance to British authority: in 1765 a mob in Newport burning a boat of the British ship *Maidstone* that had been impressing sailors; in 1769 the destruction of the British revenue sloop *Liberty* at Newport; in 1772 the *Gaspee* Affair (see GASPEE POINT).

In the field of art Rhode Island also reached gigantic stature, as any student of American architecture, cabinetmaking, silverware, and decoration can assure you. The tradition of excellence has survived, evidence including the fame of the Rhode Island School of Design (see PROVIDENCE) and the state's many outstanding art museums and programs of historic preservation.

Recreation and tourism being a major industry in Rhode Island, state and local agencies publish an abundance of literature for visitors. Schedules and entrance fees (if any) of all major points of interest are published annually by the Rhode Island Tourism Division in their booklet *Rhode Island Travel Guide.* This agency also distributes the official highway map. The address is 1 West Exchange Street, Providence, R.I. 02903. Other sources of information are identified below.

Battle of Rhode Island Sites, island of Rhode Island. The French Alliance was ratified by Congress in the spring of 1778, a large fleet under Admiral d'Estaing moved across the Atlantic, and Patriot hopes for a swift conclusion of the Revolution ran high. Newport had been a major enemy base since the British occupied this strategic place in December 1776. In the summer of 1778 it was held by a relatively small garrison of about three thousand troops under General Robert Pigot, supported by a small fleet. Congress proposed that a combined operation be undertaken to liberate Newport.

This turned out to be one of the most spectacular fiascos of the American Revolution, botched from the start by the undiplomatic attitude of General John Sullivan of the American army, the supercilious attitude of the French toward their provincial allies, the genius of the Royal Navy for frustrating French naval designs, the undependability of the Patriot militia, and bad luck. But the interesting operation involved some of the most famous names of the American Revolution: Nathanael Greene, John Hancock, Lafayette, James Mitchell Varnum, John Glover, Christopher Greene (with a newly raised regiment of African Americans who distinguished themselves), and one of the greatest admirals ever produced by the French, Pierre André de Suffren de Saint Tropez (1729–1788). "Had he been alive in my time," said Napoleon of Suffren, "he would have been my Nelson."

The plan for the combined operation against Newport was for the French fleet to enter the Middle Channel on 8 August, running the British defenses on Jamestown Island and in Newport. The night of 9 to 10 August, Sullivan would cross from Tiverton with his veteran Continentals and a large contingent of militia raised for the campaign. Early the next morning d'Estaing was to land several thousand of his men for operations ashore, then bombard British fortifications as Sullivan moved south to capture Newport. The Allies had overwhelming odds, and it looked like a sure thing.

A preliminary attack by Suffren on 5 August with two frigates destroyed the little British fleet in the East (or Sakonnet) Channel. The French admiral managed to throw the British into such a panic that they ran aground or scuttled their eight warships and several transports. D'Estaing proceeded successfully according to plan, but things then started going wrong quickly. Instead of waiting for the prearranged time to cross over from Tiverton, Sullivan advanced his schedule by some twelve hours because the British had evacuated their positions on the north end of the island. He did not bother to inform d'Estaing in advance of this improvisation, and as the French admiral was adjusting himself to this modification of the plan, word came that a British fleet was heaving into sight.

D'Estaing reembarked the sick he had landed on Jamestown (Conanicut) Island and headed to sea. Although the French fleet was about a third stronger than that commanded by Admiral Richard ("Black Dick") Howe, d'Estaing spent twenty-four hours maneuvering for the attack. Then came a forty-eight-hour storm of record-breaking magnitude that made both admirals devote their full attention to keeping their fleets afloat. British seamanship proved superior, as usual, and as soon as the gale ended, two of their fifty-gun ships attacked crippled French ships of much greater strength. Howe intended to renew the attack on 14 August but found that his fleet had suffered too much damage, so he withdrew to New York.

The French returned to Newport on 20 August but refused to land the men who were supposed to support the Americans in the land attack on Newport. The next night d'Estaing sailed for Boston to make repairs. Sullivan and his officers signed an intemperate letter of protest, and Lafayette rode to Boston to argue unsuccessfully with d'Estaing to come back.

Sullivan's troops had preserved their morale and momentum despite the first French withdrawal and the storm, but when news of d'Estaing's final departure became known the militia deserted in large numbers. The evening of 28 August, Sullivan started withdrawing from the siege lines he had established around Newport.

East and West Main Road today follow the roughly parallel roads that existed in colonial times and that were the two main axes of military operations as Pigot marched out of Newport to pursue Sullivan. While the main body of the Patriot force headed for Butts Hill, delaying actions were conducted along West Main Road by Colonel John Laurens and by Colonel Henry Beekman Livingston on East Main Road. First contact was made along the line of today's Union Street (see below), with Pigot's leading elements pushing on to Turkey Hill on the west and Quaker Hill on the east. This is roughly the line of today's Cory Lane and Hedley Avenue. Sullivan's troops counterattacked to drive the British back in confusion to this line when Pigot's forward elements tried to push on toward Butts Hill.

The British then closed up to prepare for a final assault, moving first from Quaker Hill, being repulsed by the brigades of Glover and Varnum, then shifting their main effort to the west. But Sullivan was able to move his reserves to meet the latter threat. After making three assaults, the British on this front restricted their efforts to gunfire and waited for reinforcements from Newport. Christopher Greene's newly raised African American regiment (which numbered 197 men at that time) distinguished itself in standing fast against three determined attacks by Hessians. The state awarded freedom to any slave who enlisted in the regiment.

During the night of 30 to 31 August the American army slipped away, not a day too soon because five thousand fresh British troops from New York reached Newport on 1 September and the French fleet was still at Boston. John Glover's Marbleheaders ferried most of Sullivan's troops to Tiverton; the heavy baggage and some troops used Bristol Ferry.

SURVIVING SITES

The Butts Hill Fort, one of eighteen Revolutionary War forts on the island of Rhode Island identified as late as 1896, was where Sprague Street now joins East Main Road (R.I. 138) in Portsmouth. A hill now identified by its crown of power lines and a storage tank was first fortified in 1777 by the British, who abandoned it when d'Estaing's fleet forced the Middle Passage on 8 August 1778. Sullivan's troops hastened to occupy it the next day, fearing that the British might change their minds and come back. The Americans enlarged the fort and made it their base for the subsequent advance south toward Newport. As mentioned above, it was the key to the final American defenses before evacuating the island. This site is part of the Newport County Military Heritage Trail. Open daily dawn to dusk. For more information on this site, contact the Portsmouth Historical Society, phone: (401) 683-9178.

Quaker Hill, to the south astride East Main Road (R.I. 138), is an area that preserves some vestige of rural charm on the verges of commercially exploited areas. Still standing and easy to spot at Hedley Street and Middle Road is the Friends Meeting House, in use since about 1700 by the Quakers and occupied during the Revolution by troops of both sides. This, of course, is the "Quaker Hill" of the eighteenth century, and the place from which the right wing of the British army made its unsuccessful efforts in August 1778 to storm Butts Hill.

About 2.3 miles farther south on East Main Road at Union Street is the former Christian Sabbath Society Meeting House, where the first contact was made between the advancing British troops and the delaying force of Colonel Livingston on 29 August 1778. The house is now the home of the Portsmouth Historical Society. It is still a picturesque spot that provides a view to the east over open fields and over the Sakonnet River to Tiverton and Little Compton. Near the church building, now a museum of the Portsmouth Historical Society, is a small structure dating from about 1716 that is said to be the nation's oldest surviving school building. Long used as a farm building, it stood originally at the eastern end of Union Street before being moved to its present location.

On West Main Road in the Portsmouth area are several surviving landmarks of the Battle of Rhode Island mentioned above. The Memorial to Black Soldiers, in honor of the first African American regiment to fight for the United States, is at a point where high-speed traffic precludes stopping. It is plotted on the official highway map of Rhode Island just west of the fork of R.I. 114 and 24 and marked by a flagpole that can be seen at some distance. The monument is at the place where Christopher Greene's troops made their successful stand against the Hessians. Less than a mile north on R.I. 114, at Willow Lane, is a parking area and scenic overlook on Lehigh Hill. From here you can safely observe several landmarks of the battle just described. To the south are Turkey Hill and the Memorial to Black Soldiers. To the east is Butts Hill. In the opposite direction is the Middle Passage, up which the French fleet advanced to support Sullivan and where the British later sailed to deliver supporting fire for Pigot's attack on 29 August. According to local tradition thirty Hessians were buried in a common grave after being killed in the latter action. The bodies have never been found, but "Hessian Hole" was long a local landmark. According to the *WPA Guide* it is off Cory Lane. Other authorities say it is off Willow Lane in low ground near an old frame house visible from Lehigh Hill.

Down Willow Lane from Lehigh Hill are many old houses and family burial grounds. The site of Arnold's Point Fort, occupied by the Patriots in August 1778, is at the end of an unimproved road that passes the Kaiser cable-manufacturing plant. The latter is built over the old coal mines that long were an important economic feature of this part of Rhode Island.

Bristol Ferry Fort was in the vicinity of the Mount Hope Marina east of the present Mount Hope Bridge, where vestiges of the Revolutionary earthworks were visible until recent years.

Retracing the route south on R.I. 114 toward Newport, you will find several surviving landmarks of the Revolution. At 1596 West Main Street (R.I. 114), 1.4 miles south of the intersection of Cory Lane and Hedley Street, is a frame house of saltbox design painted turquoise that is said to have been used by Lafayette in August 1778; it will be to your left (east) as you drive south toward Newport. About a mile farther south, as you crest the hill near the junction of Union Street near Mail Coach Road, is the site of Redwood Farm. Rows of trees here to the left preserve the image of the few old prints of the Battle of Rhode Island that feature this long-gone landmark where the action against the British left flank started on 29 August. Only in the last few decades have the Revolutionary War earthworks disappeared from this vicinity.

Overing House (1730), a plain, two-and-a-half-story frame structure used by General Richard Prescott until his capture by American raiders there in July 1777, is now the center of the Prescott Farm. The Newport Restoration Foundation purchased and restored the 40-acre farm and offers a number of education programs and nature trails. Phone: (401) 849-7300. The Overing House is privately owned.

Green End Fort, built in 1777 by the British as the eastern anchor of their land defenses of Newport and figuring in the siege of 1778, is also covered separately.

Block Island. When Verrazano discovered this island in 1524 he reported that it had "about the bigness of the Island of the Rhodes." He named it Luisa, for the mother of his patron, King Francis I. After exploration by the Dutchman Adriaen Block in 1614 it was known as Block Island (although he named it Adriaen's Eylandt). According to Samuel E. Morison the name Rhode Island was given to the colony because of Roger Williams's mistaken notion that Verrazano had been referring to Aquidneck Island rather than Block Island when he compared it to the famous island in the Aegean (*European Discovery of America: The Northern Voyages*, p. 303).

Dominating the eastern entrance to Long Island Sound, Block Island was a well-known place in the naval operations of the American Revolution. The defeat near here of five Continental ships under Admiral Esek Hopkins by a single British frigate shortly after midnight on 6 April 1776 is often called the Battle of Block Island.

Strategic location, moderate climate, productive soil (although in sparse quantity), and an abundant supply of

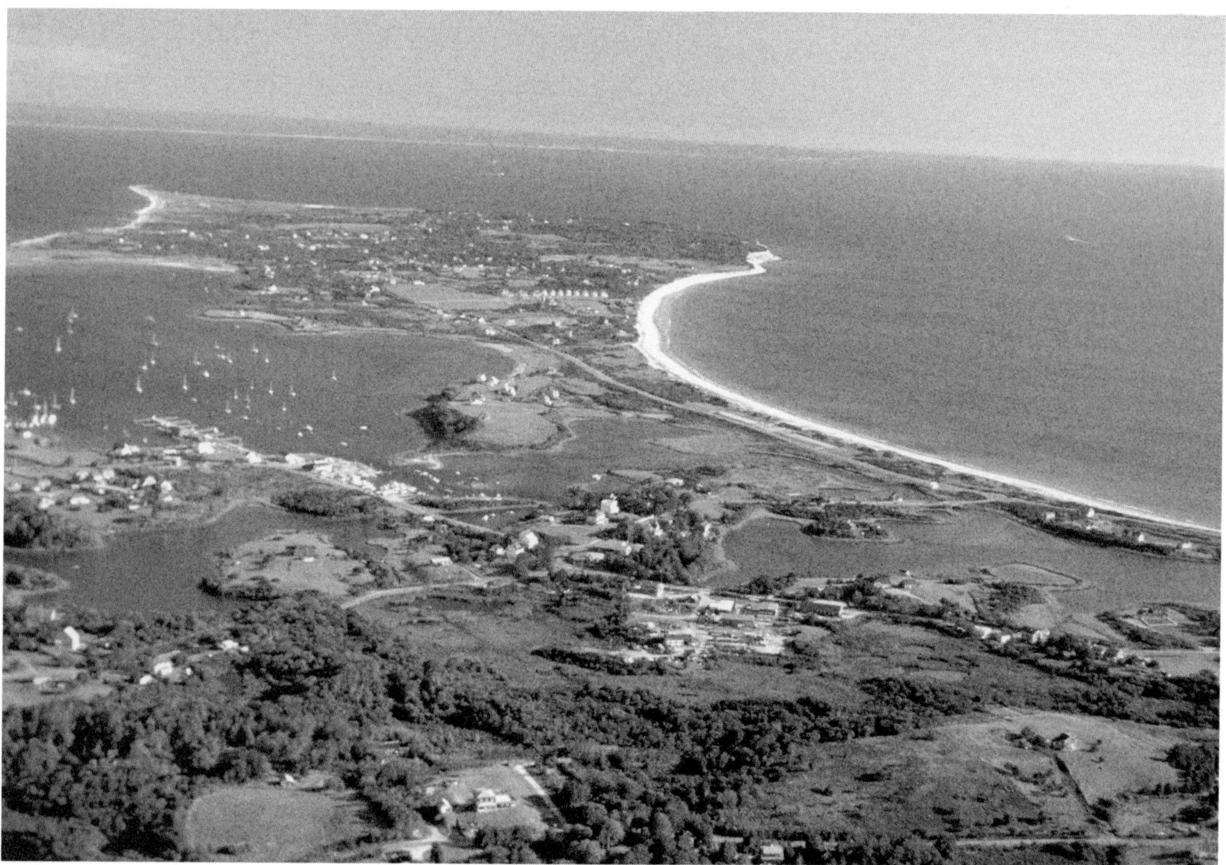

Block Island. *Dominating the eastern entrance to Long Island Sound, Block Island was an important site in the naval operations of the American Revolution.* © KELLY-MOONEY PHOTOGRAPHY/CORBIS.

fresh water from about 365 ponds made Block Island a popular place with privateers during the Colonial Wars. It was a refuge for deserters and criminals during the Revolution. Only its lack of harbors until modern times (the first completed in 1878) protected the islanders from serious war damage.

Now served by automobile ferries and airplanes, Block Island is a popular summer resort and artist colony. Tourist attractions include the spot where the first white settlers in 1661 are believed to have landed, Indian burial grounds, and scenery that has been compared with that of islands off Ireland and Scotland.

(Block Island Chamber of Commerce. Website: www.Blockisland.com; phone: (800) 383-2474. Block Island Historical Society, Box 79, Block Island, R.I. 02807.)

Bristol. Long a key point on the route between Newport and Providence (see BRISTOL FERRY SITES), this old port town was bombarded by the British in October 1775 and raided in May 1778. Many historic houses remain standing, including the one used by Lafayette during his detached service as commanding general of two veteran Continental army brigades during the summer of 1778 (see BATTLE OF RHODE ISLAND SITES). The colonial houses, marked with their date of construction and the names of owners, are the major attraction of the present city. The Herreshoff House (c. 1790), 142 Hope Street, has a fine collection of eighteenth-century furniture that includes cabinetwork of Newport's Goddard and Townsend. The Art Museum on Wardell Street and the Historical Society and Preservation Museum at 48 Court Street have important exhibits. Phone: (401) 253-7223.

But Bristol is perhaps most outstanding for its anthropological associations. The skeleton of an Indian found near Mount Hope inspired Longfellow's poem "The Skeleton in Armor" (under NEWPORT, see *Old Stone Mill*). The Bristol area was headquarters for King Philip (Metacom), who was killed near Mount Hope in 1676 after his Narragansett Indians had lost the Great Swamp Fight (19 December 1675). Brown University's Haffenreffer Museum of Anthropology, 300 Tower Street, near the intersection of Metacom Avenue

(R.I. 136) and Tower Street, is noted for its materials pertaining to the American Indian and other cultures. Phone: (401) 253-8388.

(Bristol Historical and Preservation Society, 48 Court Street, Bristol, R.I. 02809. Phone: (401) 253-7223.)

Bristol Ferry Sites, Portsmouth. Near the present Mount Hope Bridge between Bristol and Portsmouth the remains of the earthworks erected in February 1776 were visible as recently as 1940. They have since disappeared, and their location around the Mount Hope Marina is not marked. The ferry was established in 1680. Its service was disrupted during the Revolution but then resumed until 1865, when the railroad from Fall River to Newport was opened. (See BATTLE OF RHODE ISLAND SITES.)

Butts Hill Fort Site. *See* BATTLE OF RHODE ISLAND SITES.

East Greenwich, Kent County. At the eastern end of Forge Road overlooking the Potowomut River is a granite marker on the site of the forge operated by the family of Nathanael Greene. His birthplace, a large frame house built in 1684 and much remodeled, is in the vicinity. In the yard are several large anchors made at the ford. The armory of the Independent Company of Kentish Guards is on Pierce Street. Chartered in 1774 as the Kentish Light Infantry, this militia unit rejected Nathanael Greene as an officer because of his stiff knee, but he suffered the rebuff and joined as a private. The next year Rhode Island commissioned him a brigadier general to lead the three regiments raised by the state; about a month later he was appointed a brigadier general in the Continental army, and he went on to become one of the most successful troop leaders of the Revolution. At 57 Pierce Street is the restored home of General James Mitchell Varnum, who was made colonel of the Kentish Guards when these fastidious fellows rejected his friend Nathanael Greene in 1774. An honor graduate of the first class of what became Brown University and a highly successful lawyer on the eve of the Revolution, Varnum went on to become an outstanding brigade commander. He took part in the Battle of Rhode Island and is credited with advocating the organization of the African American unit that performed so well in that action. After leaving the army in 1779 he served in Congress (1780 to 1782 and 1786 to 1787) and was appointed judge for the Northwest Territory. In bad health when he reached Marietta, Ohio, in June 1788, he died a few months later at the age of forty-two. The Varnum House is a two-story structure built in 1773 as a town house. With particularly handsome paneling, period furnishings, carriage house, and a garden, the house is owned and administered by the Varnum Continentals and serves as a public museum. It is open June through August. Phone: (401) 884-1776.

The Kent County Courthouse at Main and Court Streets was built in 1750 and enlarged about 1805. The Kentish Guards remain an active historical organization, and they are located in the Kentish Guards Armory at 1774 Armory Street.

Fort Barton Site, Tiverton. On the bluff commanding Howland's Ferry at Tiverton a fort was commissioned on 28 June 1777 and named Tiverton Heights Fort. Its first commander was Major William Barton, who had been there only a week when he undertook his famous raid to capture General Richard Prescott. (For the story of this operation and biographical notes on Barton, see PRESCOTT FARM RESTORATION.)

Renamed Fort Barton, this was General John Sullivan's point of departure for the ill-fated operations that culminated in the Battle of Rhode Island (see BATTLE OF RHODE ISLAND SITES). His ten thousand troops used Howland's Ferry in their advance, and most of them came back this same way in their withdrawal. Fort Barton was lightly held thereafter.

A local committee somewhat restored the site, which was formally opened in 1970. Traces of the old works may be seen in a park and scenic overlook. A newly constructed observation tower provides a fine view, and the park offers 3 miles of nature trails. Fort Barton is on Highland Road at Lawton Avenue and is open daily from dawn to dusk. Phone: (401) 625-6700.

Gaspee Point, about 7 miles below Providence on the west side of Narragansett Bay. The "*Gaspee* Affair" of 1772 was one of the first overt acts of American defiance to British authority. Lieutenant Dudingston had showed more personal interest than the local citizens thought was necessary in commanding the armed revenue schooner *Gaspee* in Narragansett Bay. There is evidence also that he permitted his crew to steal cattle and cut fruit trees for firewood. On 9 June 1772 he was in hot pursuit of Captain Thomas Lindsay when he ran aground after trying to take a shortcut through the shallow water off a spit of land then called Namquit (now Gaspee) Point. Lindsay proceeded to Providence, arriving at about 5 P.M., and informed his friend John Brown that the *Gaspee* would be stuck until high tide refloated it again around 3 A.M. Word was spread that volunteers who cared to join in destroying the hated vessel should rally at Sabin Tavern. Principal instigators of the adventure were John Brown and Captain Abraham Whipple, the latter being given command of the sixty-four men who departed in eight longboats from Fenner's Wharf around 10 P.M. (Under PROVIDENCE see "Sabin Tavern Site.")

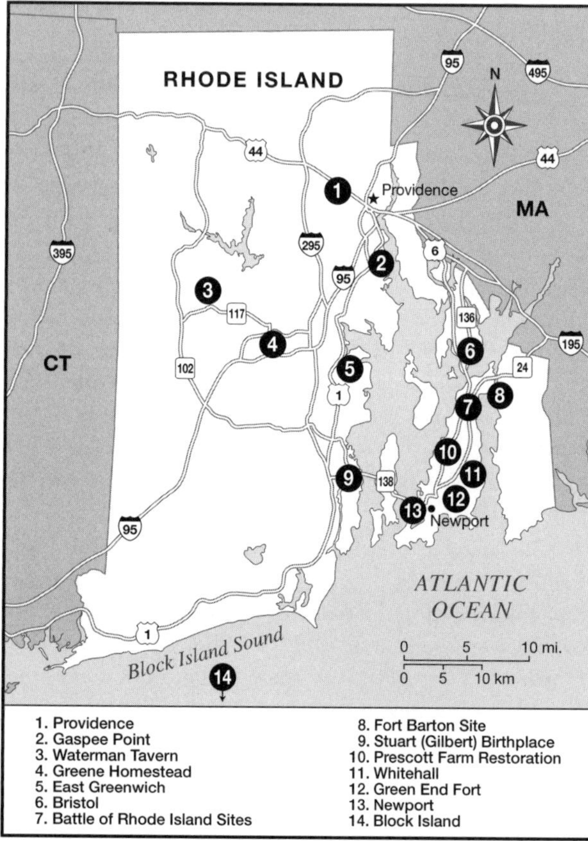

MAP BY XNR PRODUCTIONS. THE GALE GROUP.

The watch called out the alarm as the longboats came close to the *Gaspee.* Dudington and his crew attempted to defend their ship but were overpowered after a hard hand-to-hand fight. The prisoners were taken ashore and put under guard, the *Gaspee* was set on fire—virtually destroyed when the flames exploded the powder stored aboard—and the raiders then rowed back to Providence and dispersed.

A royal commission was appointed to identify the leaders, but after sitting for almost three weeks it could find nobody who knew anything about the affair. John Brown was arrested on suspicion but released for lack of evidence. It was believed that suspects might be taken to England for trial, and the Gaspee Affair loomed large in Patriot minds as they turned toward open rebellion.

Gaspee Point cannot be visited, the historic portion being in private hands with a security guard preventing access, but you can see it from several points on the north side of Passeonkquis Cove. A highway marker is on Narragansett Parkway where it makes a right-angle turn just south of Pawtucket. The official highway map shows a state picnic grove in this area, and the street map shows Gaspee Point Drive leading to the water's edge. The tip of Gaspee Point is submerged at high tide, which local mariners knew but the British revenuer obviously did not. Serious visitors to the historic spot may therefore want to go armed with the appropriate United States Coast and Geodetic Chart (number 278).

Greene (Nathanael) Homestead, 50 Taft Street, Anthony Village, town of Coventry. Nathanael Greene built this handsome frame house in 1770 while managing his family's ironworks in Coventry. When he returned at the end of the Revolution to untangle his personal financial affairs, he lived here while dividing his time between Rhode Island and Mulberry Grove Plantation in Georgia. The substantial white house of fourteen rooms has been carefully restored and furnished in the period of General Greene's residence by the Nathanael Greene Homestead Association. It is open from 1 April through 31 October on Wednesdays and Saturdays from 10 A.M. to 5 P.M. and on Sundays from 12 P.M. to 5 P.M., and by appointment. Phone: (401) 821-8630. (Greene's birthplace is still standing near East Greenwich, not far from the marked site of another forge established by his family.)

Green End (Bliss Hill) Fort, Middletown. Earthen ramparts of the fort built by the British in 1777 remain standing in a little neighborhood park of about half an acre. The site is of interest not only as one of the few Revolutionary War fortifications to have escaped urban development on Aquidneck Island, but also as a historic landmark that helps the visitor relate the present landscape to old maps of the Newport defenses. Green End Fort was the eastern anchor of the British works protecting Newport from land attack. It was the point against which the Americans under Sullivan directed their siege works from Honyman Hill in the operations covered under BATTLE OF RHODE ISLAND SITES. (Honyman Hill was just to the northeast of Bliss Hill, separated by the tip of Green End Pond.)

The site is plotted on the official highway map of Rhode Island, and is difficult to find. Starting from the junction of R.I. 138 and 114 at about the center of the boundary between Newport and Middletown, drive east on Miantonomi Avenue. On the northwest corner of Green End Pond and Miantonomi Avenue is a 7-foot-high granite marker identifying the historic landmark. From the encircling ramparts there is a fairly good view across Green End Point toward Honyman Hill to the northeast.

Newport. Fine natural harbors, favorable climate, and strategic location made Newport a major commercial center of colonial America within a few decades of its settlement in 1639. By 1650 the advantages of bypassing Boston and trading directly with the West Indies were realized. Newport quickly became one tip of the

Triangular Trade, which had various forms but was basically a matter of using New England shipping in trade between America, England or Africa, and the West Indies. Principal cargoes were colonial raw materials such as fish, lumber, and flour; English manufactured goods; slaves from West Africa; and sugar, molasses, and rum from the West Indies. Thus the slave trade was one major source of the wealth evident today in Newport's surviving colonial mansions. Another was privateering: Newport was the smuggling center of the North American colonies from early in the eighteenth century until 1775. Violation of the Navigation Acts became the major maritime enterprise as the colonies moved toward revolution.

Prosperity and the great natural beauty of the site made Newport a cultural center. "In no spot of the . . . colonies was there concentrated more individual opulence, learning, and liberal leisure," wrote a distinguished native son of the period prior to the American Revolution (Dr. Benjamin Waterhouse, quoted in Lossing, I, 639n). The first golden age came from the great fortunes amassed in the Triangular Trade during the period 1739 to 1760. Some of the finest craftsmanship of the eighteenth century, much of it surpassing Old World models, was produced in Newport by men drawn here to execute lucrative commissions for the resident merchant princes.

During the Revolution Newport naturally came in for special attention from British authorities. A small fleet under Captain James Wallace controlled Narragansett Bay from the outbreak of hostilities until driven away in April 1776 by Patriot shore batteries. A large expeditionary force under General Henry Clinton took Newport in early December 1776, and the British garrison occupied the city until late October 1779. Then came the French expeditionary force of some four thousand troops commanded by the Count de Rochambeau and a powerful supporting fleet under Admiral de Ternay, which arrived in July 1780 and remained about a year.

But the British bottled up the French fleet in Newport until the end of August 1781 (when it broke out to take part in the Yorktown Campaign). Newport therefore was neutralized as a port during the Revolution, having no opportunity to continue the activities that had been so profitable in earlier wars, and suffering great material damage from the British occupation. A mass exodus had started in 1775 in anticipation of British occupation (see Stiles House, below).

Having grown from 7,500 in 1760 to 11,000 in 1775, Newport's population dropped to 5,300 in 1776. The city recovered from the effects of the Revolution very slowly, its population in 1870 being no larger than in 1770.

Newport's misfortune in never recovering commercially from British occupation and the subsequent blockade during the Revolution is today's good fortune from the standpoint of historic preservation. An estimated 350 colonial structures have survived, and these are in an area mercifully spared by a subsequent generation of wealthy Americans who built their ostentatious "cottages" during Newport's second age of affluence. Over the last decade efforts have been made by Revolutionary War historians to purge the popular myth that the British burned and ransacked cities during their wartime occupations. Except for peripheral war damage, no sustained efforts by the British to destroy city infrastructure can be proven. The destruction of colonial houses and other sites have been more the result of poor upkeep, post–Revolutionary War development, and city fires. Newport has more colonial buildings standing than all other American cities combined. The city is also unique for never having had a major fire, which is no doubt the main reason for the city's abundance of colonial structures.

Restoration programs have had to cope with nineteenth- and twentieth-century economic development; consequently, Newport is not Colonial Williamsburg. For the visitor with intellectual curiosity about eighteenth-century American life and historic preservation, however, there probably is no more rewarding a place than Newport.

The three major forces of restoration at work are recent creations. Oldest and perhaps most important is the Preservation Society of Newport County, founded in 1945. The major historic landmarks of Newport are exhibited under its auspices; the Society publishes a quarterly, the *Newport Gazette*, and an annual schedule of hours and fees for the buildings open to the public. The Preservation Society of Newport is located at 424 Bellevue Avenue, and has an informative website, www.newport-mansions.org, that gives details on sites that it manages. Phone: (401) 847-1000. Operation Clapboard was conceived in 1963 and was operated until 1970, primarily to assist owners in restoration of colonial homes; it has proved to be more successful than expected. The Newport Restoration Foundation, located at 51 Touro Street, was founded in 1968 by Doris Duke, a lifelong summer resident. It collects funds for buying and restoring old houses, hoping to rent these to suitable tenants or make them into museums. Phone: (401) 849-7300. (Prescott Farm Restoration is one of its projects.)

All of the important architectural attractions of Newport are outlined in a variety of publications obtainable through the Newport Historical Society or at its bookstore located on 82 Touro Street. Website: www.newporthistorical.org; phone: (401) 846-0813. The standard authority is *The Architectural Heritage of Newport, Rhode Island, 1640–1915*, by Antoinette F. Downing and Vincent J. Scully, Jr. (Cambridge University Press, 1952; [Reprinted] Clarkson N. Potter, 1967). Newport is one of the five cities studied by Carl Bridenbaugh in his classic two-volume work on urban life in America from 1625 to 1776. First published in 1938 and 1955, these books were issued in paperback by the Oxford University Press in 1971. They are *Cities in the Wilderness: The First Century of Urban Life in America, 1625–1742* and *Cities in Revolt: Urban Life in America, 1743–1776.* Dealing with Boston, New York, Philadelphia, Charleston, and Newport, they are as fascinating for the intelligent general reader as they are indispensable to the serious scholar. Both of these books are hard to come by; a reader's best chance is in public libraries. In many ways they were superseded by the research of Gary Nash and his students in the later twentieth century.

Below, in alphabetical order, are Newport sites associated with persons or events of the Revolution. Only a brief indication can be given of what to look for in Newport's embarrassment of historical and cultural riches.

Bannister House, 56 Pelham Street. Also known as the Prescott House because the British commander used it, this large, gambrel-roof house was built around 1751. It was one of several owned by John Bannister, a prosperous merchant. In the nineteenth century it was home to the well-known African American painter Edward Mitchell Bannister. It is currently a Bed and Breakfast; phone: (401) 846-0059.

Bowen's Wharf, off Thames Street. This is one of the few remaining wharf complexes where eighteenth-century structures survive. A group of citizens stopped plans for demolishing these. Bowen's Wharf serves Newport as a thriving plaza of shops and restaurants.

Brenton's Point (Fort Adams). Fortification work was started here in May 1776 by Patriots to defend the entrance to Newport Harbor. When the British invaders approached in December of that year, the works were abandoned as untenable. The British burned their barracks on the point when they withdrew from Newport in October 1779. After the French arrived nine months later, the site was fortified to some extent, but not until 1793 was construction started on Fort Adams (dedicated in 1799 and named for President John Adams). The fort fell into disrepair in the years following, but reconstruction of a sturdier granite fort began in 1824, lasting until 1857. Today Fort Adams is owned by the state, and it leases it to the Fort Adams Trust, which serves as steward for the 20-acre site (the fort's parade is 6 acres). Fort Adams is open to the public daily from mid-May through October from 10 A.M. to 4 P.M. Phone: (401) 841-0707.

Brick Market, Thames Street at the foot of Washington Square. One of the few surviving business structures of colonial America, the last work of Newport architect Peter Harrison (probably the country's first professional architect), this National Historic Landmark has a number of other distinctions. It is one of the country's first buildings to have open arcades (later enclosed). The ground floor was intended for use as a market, and the two upper floors (one of them since removed) were used for dry goods stores and offices. All rentals and profits from the building, a civic project of the Proprietors of Long Wharf, went to the town treasury for a public granary. After the Revolution a printing office was housed in the upper floors, which were used from 1793 to 1799 as a theater. In 1842 the building served as the town hall, and from 1853 to 1900 it was Newport's city hall. The Brick Market was built in 1762 to 1763, its details completed in 1772, the third floor removed in an alteration of 1842, and complete restoration (to its present two-story, enclosed-arcade condition) done during the period 1928 to 1930. Owned by the city, it serves as the Museum of Newport History, which is operated by the Newport Historical Society; the museum is open erratically; phone: (401) 846-0813. Brick Market Place is the name of the surrounding area, which includes a plethora of modern shops.

Colonial Burial Ground, Farewell Street. With tombstones from as early as 1660, this cemetery contains the graves of many Revolutionary veterans. There is also a segregated African American section traditionally called "God's Acre." The Burial Ground is a National Historic Site and is open from dawn to dusk.

Fort George Site, Goat Island. A British fort here was one of those that d'Estaing's fleet had to run by in entering Narragansett Bay in August 1779 (see BATTLE OF RHODE ISLAND SITES). Fort Liberty was a Revolutionary War work on Goat Island, presumably the American name for what the British called Fort George. The work disappeared when a naval storage facility was built on the island. Efforts were made to locate the lost site, but as of 2005 there are no visible remnants of Fort George. Goat Island succumbed to unbridled development pressure in the early 1970s, leaving it replete with the effects of modern commercialism.

Fort Greene Site, now Battery Park, between Washington Street and the harbor. A temporary gun emplacement was built here overnight as part of the successful efforts to drive the flotilla of Captain James Wallace from Newport Harbor in April 1776. Fort Greene does not figure as one of the important fortifications of the city, but Battery Park provides an exceptionally fine view of the harbor.

Friends Meetinghouse, 30 Marlborough Street. Dating from 1699, it is the oldest surviving house of worship in Newport and probably the oldest Quaker meetinghouse in America. This structure was once distorted by nineteenth-century additions but is still of great interest. On this site in 1717 John Farmer read one of the earliest antislavery statements in America, for which he was expelled from the meeting. In 1773 the Quakers meeting here voted to oppose slavery and disown those who continued to own slaves. Bequeathed to the Newport Historical Society in the early 1970s, this active organization undertook painstaking efforts to restore the Meetinghouse to its original (1807) appearance. This authentic replica of a Quaker meetinghouse is open to the public on a limited schedule during the summer and by appointment; phone: (401) 846-0813.

Hunter House, 54 Washington Street. A stately mansion of two-and-a-half stories, beautifully restored and furnished with a priceless collection of Goddard and Townsend furniture, the Hunter House is considered one of the finest colonial homes surviving in America. It was built between 1748 and 1754 by Jonathan Nichols, Jr., deputy governor of Rhode Island. Admiral Charles de Ternay, commander of the fleet that escorted the French expeditionary force of Rochambeau to America, died in the house on 15 December 1780 and is buried in the cemetery adjacent to Trinity Church (see below). William Hunter, whose name the house bears, was ambassador to Brazil but more famous locally for marrying the Quaker girl down the street in the Robinson House (see below). A National Historic Landmark, the Hunter House is owned by the Preservation Society of Newport and may be visited by contacting them. Website: www.newportmansions.org; phone: (401) 847-1000.

King Park, North Wellington Avenue, overlooking the harbor. A monument at the west end of this park marks the place where French troops under Rochambeau landed on 12 July 1780 to start their eleven-month stay in the city. The park has a handsome statue of Rochambeau.

Long Wharf Site. A street of this name, extending from America's Cup Avenue southwest to the end of Washington Street, is the only vestige of the busy wharf around which Newport's most lucrative trade centered from about 1685. The cove, long since filled in, extended north from the wharf to what is now Bridge Street, and the Long Wharf had a drawbridge giving access from the harbor to the back doors of the craftsmen's shops and homes on Bridge Street (first called Shipwright Street). The Proprietors of Long Wharf, incorporated in 1702, sponsored many important community services, including construction of the Brick Market (above).

Naval War College Museum, 686 Cushing Road. Devoted primarily to the history of naval warfare and the naval heritage of Narragansett Bay, with exhibits on the American Revolution. The Museum is on the grounds of the Naval War College and open to the public year-round on Mondays through Fridays, 10 A.M. to 4 P.M., and on weekends from June through September, noon to 4 P.M. Phone: (401) 841-4052. Public access is through Gate 1 of the Newport Naval Station.

Newport Artillery Armory and Military Museum, 23 Clarke Street. The handsome stone building dates from 1835, the work of the mason who built much of Fort Adams (above), but the Newport Artillery of the Rhode Island Militia, founded 1741, survives with headquarters here. It is generally accepted as the oldest active military organization in the United States after Boston's Artillery Company. The museum contains uniforms, accoutrements, and military artifacts, and is open Saturday from May through October, 10 A.M. to 4 P.M. and by appointment. Phone: (401) 846-8488.

Newport Historical Society and Sabbatarian Meeting House, 82 Touro Street. One of the three connecting buildings here is the meetinghouse erected in 1729 by a congregation of Seventh-Day Baptists. Particularly fine carving is to be seen on the rail of the pulpit steps. The other two buildings house important collections of pictures, furniture, costumes, marine items, Indian relics, and other objects associated with the history of the city. The Society has added an important local history and genealogy library, and is open Monday through Friday, 9:30 A.M. to 4:30 P.M., and Saturdays, 9:30 A.M. to noon. Phone: (401) 846-0813.

Old State House (Old Colony House), Washington Square. A National Historical Landmark since 1962, this brick assembly house was built in 1739 to 1742. Designed by Richard Munday, it was Newport's first brick building. A gambrel roof topped by a balustraded deck and cupola, a carved wooden balcony above the wide central entrance, and the sandstone trim of the red brick facade give architectural distinction to the historic building. From the balcony came official proclamations of the death of George II, the accession of George III, and the passage of the Declaration of Independence. In 1774 the first law prohibiting the importation of slaves was passed here. In 1776 the first medical lectures in America were given in the council room by Dr. William Hunter. British and French forces used the building as a hospital and barracks, causing considerable damage. In the single huge room of the ground floor are twenty-six flags of the colonial period. On the second floor is a portrait of Washington by Gilbert Stuart. The Historical Society manages the site and the state owns it. Tours are conducted from mid-June until the end of August, Thursday through Saturday, 10 A.M. to 3:30 P.M., and by appointment. Phone: (401) 846-0813.

Old Stone Mill, Touro Park. This picturesque stone tower in the center of Newport was built for a windmill in about 1675 by Governor Benedict Arnold, great-grandfather of the Continental general and traitor. Mythmakers, however, pretend that it was put up by vikings or, later, by Portuguese explorers. Open year-round, dawn to dusk.

Pitts Head Tavern, 77 Bridge Street. A handsome structure that evolved from a much smaller one built in 1726 on Washington Square, where as the very successful Pitts Head Tavern it played host to Patriot, British, and French officers during the Revolution. It has been moved twice. Now a two-and-a-half-story, gambrel-roof, center-chimney frame house, Pitts Head

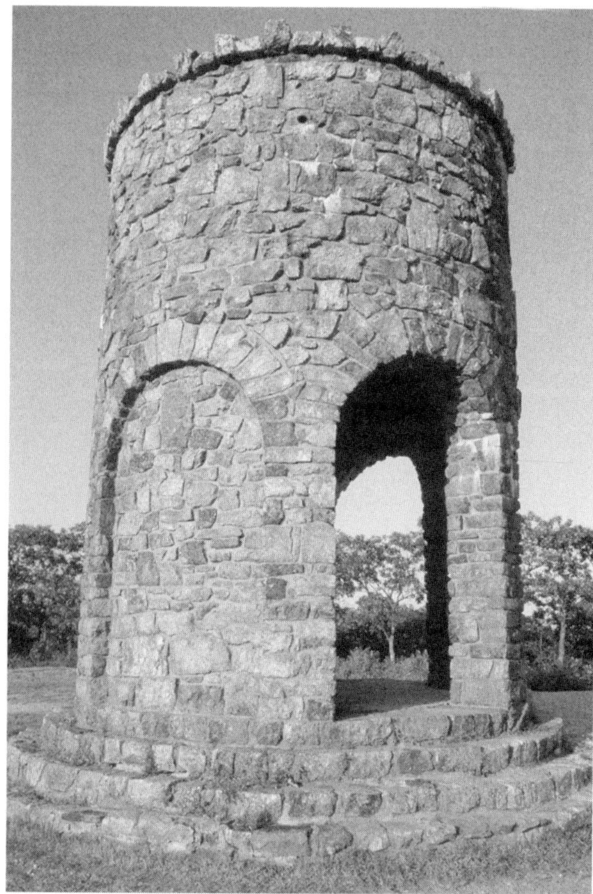

Old Stone Mill. *This picturesque stone tower in the center of Newport, Rhode Island, was built around 1675 by Governor Benedict Arnold, the great-grandfather of the Continental general and traitor.* © NEIL RABINOWITZ/CORBIS.

Tavern is one of the finest restorations of an early Newport house. It is privately owned.

Redwood Library and Athenaeum, 50 Bellevue Avenue. Designed by Peter Harrison, this Georgian adaptation of a Roman temple dates from 1748. Of wood rusticated to resemble stone, it has been called the first example of Palladian architecture in the English colonies. Harrison built the library to house the books of a philosophical society, and Ezra Stiles (see Stiles House, below) was its librarian for twenty years. Today it has a valuable collection of books and early-American paintings, including six by Gilbert Stuart. A statue of George Washington is displayed in front of the building. A National Historic Landmark, it is one of the oldest libraries still used in America. This site closed for renovations in 2005 and is slated to reopen upon completion of the project.

Robinson House, 64 Washington Street. The Quaker Tom Robinson bought this house in 1760 and expanded it to a simple but handsome two-and-a-half-story, gambrel-roof frame residence. During the billeting of the French the viscount de Noailles lived here and became a devoted friend of the Robinsons. (The viscount was Lafayette's brother-in-law, an outstanding combat leader in the siege of Yorktown, and was selected by Rochambeau to be the French peace commissioner to work with John Laurens in negotiating the surrender of Cornwallis at Yorktown.) The Robinsons were considerably less well disposed toward their neighbor at 54 Washington Street when he married a daughter of the family outside her Quaker faith (see Hunter House, above). The Robinson house has remained in the Robinson family and currently (2005) is privately owned. Furnishings include items bought from John Goddard, another neighbor now better known as one of the finest cabinetmakers in colonial America. (John Goddard's house stands at 81 Second Street.) Another treasure is a Sèvres tea service sent by de Noailles to his hostess from France.

Second Congregational Meeting House, 15 Clarke Street. Designed by Cotton Palmer and built in 1733, this structure has suffered from Greek Revival and Victorian modifications. It has long since ceased to be used as a church, and efforts are being made by a local group to buy it for restoration. Ezra Stiles came to Newport in 1755 to be minister of the church, living in the parsonage across the street now known as the Stiles House (see below). During the British occupation the church was used for barracks, and the pews, pulpit, and fixtures were destroyed during this period. The building was sold to the Baptists in 1847. It was recently converted to condominiums.

Stiles House, also known as the Henderson House, 14 Clarke Street. Ezra Stiles (1727–1795), famous colonial scholar and author of a valuable diary, lived here for more than twenty years (1755–1776) as minister of the Second Congregational Church across the street. The two-story, gambrel-roof house was built about 1756 as the parsonage and is now on the National Register and run by the city as a sanatorium. Fear of British occupation caused a mass exodus from Newport long before any soldiers actually landed. In October 1775 Stiles noted in his diary that "three quarters of my beloved Chh (sic) & Congregation are broken up and dispersed." Five months later he left with his family and household goods. In 1778 he became president of Yale College, but his Newport parishioners held him in such high esteem that he remained technically their pastor until May 1786.

Touro Synagogue, 72 Touro Street. America's oldest synagogue, this was designed by Peter Harrison in 1759 and completed in 1763. The austere exterior cloaks one of the finest and most ornate interiors in the country. The synagogue is a National Historic Landmark open to the public and still conducts services, although it is closed for renovations through 2005.

Trinity Church, Queen Anne Square. Richard Munday built this outstanding colonial church in 1725

Touro Synagogue. *Newport's Touro Synagogue, the oldest synagogue in the United States, was designed by colonial architect Peter Harrison and completed in 1763. Its austere exterior cloaks one of the finest interiors in the country.* © BOB KRIST/CORBIS.

on the simple lines of Christopher Wren's examples in England, although it has since been somewhat altered. The church sits on two city blocks wherein all the buildings were cleared in the 1970s to create Queen Anne Square. The site earned a bicentennial dedication by Queen Elizabeth. The adjacent cemetery has the graves of Admiral de Ternay (who died in the Hunter House, noted above) and the chevalier de Fayelle (one of Lafayette's aides-de-camp). It is a National Historic Landmark and offers a number of musical performances in addition to religious services, its organ being widely admired; phone: (401) 846-0660.

Vernon House, 46 Clarke Street. The original part of this handsome Georgian frame house dates from the early 1700s. It was probably enlarged in 1759 by Metcalf Bowler when this wealthy merchant owned the house. (Modern research has revealed that this great "Patriot," chief justice of Rhode Island in 1776, was one of General Henry Clinton's informers. See Carl Van Doren, *Secret History of the American Revolution*, pp. 127–29, 235, 429.) In 1773 the house was bought by William Vernon, who served in Boston as president of the Eastern Navy Board from April 1777 until the end of the Revolution. The British used the Vernon House during their occupation, after which it became the quarters of the count de Rochambeau. Washington stayed here during the second week of March 1781. The two-story house has a hip roof and captain's walk, fine interior trim and stairs, curious murals of Chinese style under some paneling, and a rusticated exterior attributed to Peter Harrison. A National Historic Landmark, it is privately owned.

Wanton-Lyman-Hazard House, 17 Broadway. Newport's oldest house (built 1675) and one of New England's finest specimens of Jacobean architecture, this National Historic Landmark has been carefully restored and furnished by the Newport Historical Society. Rhode Island's last royal governor, Joseph Wanton, owned the house until his death in 1781, after which it was confiscated. Later it was returned to descendants who had been on the winning side. Of architectural interest are the steep roof and its plastered cornice; behind the house is a small colonial garden. A back room on the second floor served as slave quarters. Tours are available from mid-June through the end of August, Thursday to Saturday, 10 A.M. to 3 P.M. Phone: (401) 846-0813.

Warren House, 62 Washington Street. Once known as the Henry Collins House, this two-and-a-half-story, gambrel-roof house was built about 1736 and later enlarged. It was owned by a wealthy Loyalist, George Rome, confiscated during the Revolution, and used briefly by Gilbert Stuart's wife and daughter. The French naval artillery headquarters was in the building while Admiral de Ternay's fleet was blockaded by the British in Newport. The admiral's headquarters were a few doors away at the Hunter House (see above). Warren House is privately owned.

White Horse Tavern, Farewell and Marlborough Streets. America's oldest tavern, built 1673, was has been restored by the Preservation Society. It is privately owned.

Tourist information is available from the Newport County Chamber of Commerce, 45 Valley Road, Middletown, R.I. 02842. Phone: (401) 847-1600. The most important sites open to the public are shown under the auspices of the Preservation Society of Newport County, Washington Square, Newport, R.I. 02840. Another source of current information on schedules and fees is the annual *Rhode Island Tourist Guide*, listed previously at the beginning of the chapter.

Newport County comprises the three towns on the island of Rhode Island (Newport, Middletown, and Portsmouth), Jamestown (Conanicut Island), Little Compton, and Tiverton. More than twenty forts existed in this region during the course of the American Revolution, their locations known as recently as 1896 when Edward Field published *Revolutionary Defences in Rhode Island.* Only three are plotted on the official highway map as points of interest as of this writing: Butts Hill Fort (see under BATTLE OF RHODE ISLAND SITES), Green End Fort, and Fort Barton Site in Tiverton. In the undeveloped southern tip of Conanicut Island (Jamestown) extensive remains of Beaver Head Fort have been found in a lonely spot where trees are growing from earthworks in the middle of a field. Beaver Tail Fort has disappeared, but Beaver Tail Lighthouse stands on the site. The area is remote and picturesque. Vestiges of other Revolutionary War works undoubtedly survive unmarked throughout Newport County. The Newport County Chamber of Commerce is a primary information source.

Portsmouth, Newport County. At one time the village of Portsmouth (established 1638) was the most important one in Rhode Island, but it was soon eclipsed by Newport and Providence. It has many historic landmarks (see BATTLE OF RHODE ISLAND SITES).

Prescott Farm Restoration, 2009 West Main Road (R.I. 114) near Union Street, Middletown. Easy to spot on the east side of the highway is the large, two-and-a-half-story, gambrel-roof, red frame house that has been known since the Revolution as the Overing House (c. 1730). The house was the country estate of Henry Overing. Its present name comes from a once famous episode of the Revolution, the capture here in 1777 of the thoroughly detested commander of the British occupying forces in Newport.

Richard Prescott (1725–1788) was an experienced professional soldier before coming to Canada in 1773 as brevet colonel of the Seventh Foot. He first became unpopular with American Patriots because of his harsh treatment of Ethan Allen after the latter's capture near Montreal on 25 September 1775. Prescott was himself captured less than two months later when he tried to escape from Montreal (see MONTREAL under Canada). By this time he had the local rank of brigadier general, and in September 1776 he was exchanged for Major General John Sullivan, who had been captured in the Battle of Long Island, New York, about a month earlier. In December 1776 Prescott reached Newport with the large force under Sir Henry Clinton that occupied the island. He stayed to command the reduced garrison holding Newport and in this capacity alienated the Americans by his high-handed and contemptuous conduct. The night of 9 to 10 July 1777 he was kidnapped from his country headquarters, the Overing House, by forty raiders under the leadership of Major William Barton.

Commanding the fort at Tiverton that now bears his name (see FORT BARTON), he learned that General Prescott was quartered in the Overing House and that his small guard there might easily be surprised. General Charles Lee, considered by many at this time to be second only to Washington as a Patriot military leader, had been captured at Basking Ridge, New Jersey, by a British patrol under similar circumstances. Barton thought it would be a great triumph to take Prescott and give Congress a general to exchange for Lee. Leaving Tiverton in boats on 4 July, Barton spent several days moving slowly through Mount Hope Bay recruiting volunteers. He visited Bristol and Warren (his home) before reaching his final assembly area across the bay at Warwick Neck. On 9 July the raiders crossed the bay, landed near their objective, and surprised the general in his bedroom. Prescott was taken back to Warwick and held in the Daniel Arnold Tavern, where the final plans for the operation had been made. (Portions of the old tavern are believed to be incorporated in the house standing on the site.)

Barton became a national hero, and his exploit lifted Patriot morale at a time when this was especially needed. Prescott was exchanged in due course and continued to serve in Newport, commanding a brigade in the Battle of Rhode Island and eventually succeeding General Pigot. In October 1779 he evacuated his garrison of about four thousand troops to New York, ending the occupation of Newport. Barton was promoted to lieutenant colonel four months after his famous exploit, having meanwhile been voted thanks by the state and national governments and been given a sword by Congress. When Lafayette visited the United States in 1824 to 1825 he found that Barton had been held a prisoner for fourteen years for refusal to pay a judgment on land he had acquired in Vermont. Lafayette paid the claim; Barton returned to Rhode Island from Danville, Vermont, and died about six years later in Providence. Prescott was a lieutenant general for six years before his death in 1788.

Developed by the Newport Restoration Foundation, this site was opened in 1972. Six of the eleven buildings on the site were brought in from other locations to protect them from urban development. One of the houses here has been moved from the Bristol Ferry Road. The windmill is from Lehigh Hill. Henry Overing's house is on its original site. (See BATTLE OF RHODE ISLAND SITES.) The farm site is open Monday to Friday, 10 A.M. to 4 P.M. Phone: 401-847-6230.

Another "Prescott House" is at 56 Pelham Street in Newport, where it is now known as the John Bannister House. This was the house Prescott used in town during the British occupation.

Providence, Providence River, Providence County. When Roger Williams was banished from Massachusetts for religious nonconformity in 1636, he founded a settlement in the wilderness and named it in commemoration of God's providence. The place is now the second-largest city in New England, but the name is still Providence. Although it was the first settlement in what is now Rhode Island, Providence was overshadowed by Newport until about 1770. But the vigor of Providence's leaders and the advantages of being better situated for land communications with the interior (while having the advantage of being a port only 27 miles from the sea) gave this city the lead over Newport even before the latter was rendered *hors de combat* by the Revolution. Newport never recovered; Providence never stopped growing.

Whereas this may be applauded on the grounds of progress, much of historic Providence has been leveled in the last two centuries. Nothing remains of the nine forts in the area of Providence identified in 1896 by Edward Field in his *Revolutionary Defences in Rhode Island.*

The historic portion of the city lies on the east bank of the river (Exchange Street Exit of I-95). Within a half-mile radius of the First Baptist Meeting House (see below) are more than two hundred well-preserved old houses and public buildings of architectural or historical importance, or both. The Providence Preservation Society, located at 21 Meeting Street, publishes an architectural guide, *PPS/AIAri Guide to Providence Architecture.* Phone: (401) 831-7440.

Rhode Island's colonial heritage of fine craftsmanship and excellence in the arts has been continued into modern times. The famous Rhode Island School of Design, opened in 1878 and now covering more than a city block, is largely responsible for the high standards. Many of the attractions in Providence—houses, museums, and libraries—pertain to the period following the Revolution. Some of these are covered by the Providence Chamber of Commerce's website at www.provodenceri.com. Phone: (401) 421-7740. The following paragraphs are restricted to sites associated with people and events through the eighteenth century.

Brick School House, 24 Meeting Street. The Providence Preservation Society now occupies this structure built in 1769 as a school (on one floor) and a place for town meetings (on the other floor). In 1770 it was the temporary facility of what became Brown University (see below). Munitions were stored in the school during the Revolution, after which it became, in turn, one of the country's first four free public schools (1800), a school for African Americans (before the Civil War), and the first of the country's "fresh air" schools (1908).

Brown (John) House, 52 Power Street. Now the home of the Rhode Island Historical Society and a house museum of ten rooms furnished with a priceless collection of Rhode Island cabinetmakers' work, plus exhibition rooms depicting the history of the state, the John Brown House is one of the country's finest examples of Georgian architecture. It was designed by Joseph Brown in 1786 for his brother John. The latter (1736–1803) is remembered for his leading role in the Gaspee Affair (see GASPEE POINT) and for the prominent part he and his famous brothers had in public affairs. John and his brothers had much to do with relocating Rhode Island College (later Brown University) from Warren to Providence. He laid the cornerstone of University Hall and performed valuable service for twenty years as treasurer of the institution. The John Brown House is a National Historic Landmark. The Rhode Island Historical Society can be found on the internet at www.rihs.org; phone: (401) 273-7507.

Brown University and University Hall. At the end of College Street, the campus covers a large area of downtown Providence in the historic section east of the river. Rhode Island College was chartered at Warren in 1764. In the intense rivalry between Providence and Newport that came to a climax just before the Revolution, the victory of Providence in winning selection as the new site for the college was decisive. (This is the opinion of Carl Bridenbaugh, who touches on the Newport-Providence rivalry in his *Cities in Revolt,* pp. 11, 53, 222, 264, and 378. See NEWPORT.) Renamed Brown University in 1804, this is the seventh-oldest college in America and still one of its finest. Buildings include the Annmary Brown Memorial with its valuable collections of books (some incunabula dating from 1460) and paintings, the John Carter Brown Library, the John D. Rockefeller, Jr., Library, and the John Hay Library. Directly associated with the period of the Revolution is University Hall, a National Historic Landmark. Built in 1770 as the original "college edifice" to accommodate twenty-five students, it was designed by Joseph Brown and probably patterned on Princeton's Nassau Hall. The college had been located temporarily in the Brick School House (see above). Between 1776 and 1782 the building was used by American and French troops as a barracks and hospital, suffering severe damage. Since its reconstruction in 1940 University Hall has housed administrative facilities.

First Baptist Meeting House, 75 North Main Street. The tall, slender spire of this church, one of the most remarkable public buildings in New England (and a National Historic Landmark), is in the center of an exceptionally rich collection of American architecture that spans close to three centuries. Roger Williams founded the congregation in 1638, making it the first Baptist organization in America. The existing church was designed by Joseph Brown, prosperous merchant and amateur architect, who used as his primary source material the *Book of Architecture* by James Gibbs. Started in 1774, construction was completed and the church dedicated in May 1775. Since that time it has been used for commencement ceremonies for Brown University, and it is still a place of religious worship, with guided tours following Sunday services. The Meeting House was rededicated in 1958 after being completely rehabilitated and restored. Phone: (401) 454-3418.

French Barracks, Billets, Campsites, and Graves. Americans seem to have an inordinate interest in houses occupied by Frenchmen. Four such places will be found today on Main Street. The Morris Homestead (1750), North Main Street at Rochambeau Avenue, once stood in the lower corner of a great field "of cold, wet land, rough and rocky," as Lossing described it as late as 1848. In this field the troops of Rochambeau camped for about two weeks in November 1782 before continuing to Boston (thence to the West Indies). A memorial is at Summit Avenue and Brewster Street. The Morris house is opposite the North Burial Ground, where many French soldiers were buried. Some of these graves undoubtedly date from the French encampments of 1781 (see below) and 1782. The Joseph Russell House, 118 North Main Street, was built by this China merchant in 1773 and occupied at one time by the chevalier de Chastellux. Best known today for his valuable *Travels in North America,* the latter was a major general in Rochambeau's army and a principal figure in Franco-American military cooperation during the years 1780 to 1782. Interiors of the Russell House have been moved to museums in Brooklyn, Denver, and Minneapolis, but its handsome external features remain. The Joseph Brown House (1774), 50 South Main Street, was designed by the distinguished amateur architect responsible for Providence's finest colonial structures (above). Joseph Brown's spacious, three-story brick house had been made available to Rochambeau's officers as quarters. Having survived the Revolution, it was for 128 years occupied by the venerable Providence Bank. At 312 South Main Street is a house that was the billet of Count Axel de Fersen (1755–1810). This young Swedish nobleman, persistently identified despite lack of solid evidence as "a lover of Marie Antoinette," had left the French court to be Rochambeau's aide-de-camp in America. In 1791 and 1792 he had a leading role in the unsuccessful attempts to organize the escape of the French royal family from Versailles. French troops were quartered in the Old Market House and, as previously mentioned, in University Hall of Brown University. One of their camps in the march from Newport to Yorktown is in a run-down area on Pine Street just west of the junction of I-95 and I-195. From here the troops marched to the campsite near Potterville.

Hopkins (Esek) House, 97 Admiral Street. This frame house of about 1750 was the home of the first commander in chief of the Continental navy, Esek Hopkins (1718–1802). Younger brother of Stephen Hopkins (see below), Esek had no qualifications for his task other than political influence. He was suspended from command in March 1777 and formally dismissed in January 1778. The partially furnished house is the property of the city and is currently (2005) undergoing renovation.

Hopkins (Stephen) House, Benefit Street at 15 Hopkins Street (its third location). A charming little red house enclosed by a wooden fence and bearing a large bronze plaque, this was the home of the biggest man in Rhode Island during the Revolution. Stephen Hopkins (1707–1785) started as a farmer and surveyor but went on to become chief justice of the colony, governor for ten terms, member of the Continental Congress, and signer of the Declaration of Independence. The oldest part of the simple two-and-a-half-story structure dates from 1707, with additions made in the period 1742 to 1755 and the most recent restoration in 1927. Furnishings include a bed used by George Washington, who was a guest of Hopkins in 1776 and 1781. The property belongs to the state and is open from 1 P.M. to 4 P.M. on Wednesday and Saturday. Phone: (401) 421-0694.

Old Market House, Market Square. A marketplace here in colonial days was also the center of political activity. The surviving market house, now part of the Rhode Island School of Design, was completed in 1774. The third floor was added in 1797 by the local Masonic lodge. In 1939 the building was restored to its appearance of the last century.

Old State House, North Main Street between North Court and South Court Streets. Completed in 1762 to replace one that had burned, this was where the General Assembly met until 1900. (From 1776 to 1900 the assembly held its sessions in various county seats, usually meeting in Providence in January.) This remarkable structure has been the home of the Rhode Island Historical Preservation and Heritage Commission since 1975.

Pendleton House and Collection, 224 Benefit Street. Works of cabinetmakers John Goddard and Job Townsend and a fine collection of silver are exhibited in one room devoted to Rhode Island. The house is a replica (1906) of an early dwelling and was built to display the Pendleton Collection of colonial American decorative arts. It is part of the Rhode Island School of Design Museum. Open Tuesday through Sunday, 10 A.M. to 5 P.M.; phone: (401) 454-6500.

Prospect Terrace, Congdon at Cushing Street. Visiting Providence in the 1840s, Benson J. Lossing commented on "the fine view of the city and surrounding country" as he "passed . . . along the brow of Prospect Hill" toward the site of the French encampment of 1782 "on the western slope of the northern termination of Prospect Hill" (*Pictorial Field Book of the Revolution,* I, p. 624). Prospect Terrace is a vestige of this hill in downtown Providence. The view has changed but is still remarkable. What Lossing called the north end of Prospect Hill is a built-up area east of Old North Burial Ground. (See *French Barracks, Billets,*

Campsites, and Graves, above.) At Prospect Terrace is Leo Friedlander's gallant statue (1939) of Roger Williams.

Rhode Island Black Heritage Society, 460 Aborn Street, traces the history of African Americans in Rhode Island from the seventeenth century on, including information of the First Rhode Island Regiment. Open Monday through Friday, 9 A.M. to 4:30 P.M. Phone: (401) 751-3490.

Sabin Tavern Site and "Gaspee Room." A building on the northeast corner of South Main and Planet Streets has a recently restored plaque indicating the site of Sabin Tavern (1763). Here volunteers assembled for the famous raid on Gaspee Point in 1772, making their final plans in the tavern operated by Joseph Sabin and leaving in boats from nearby Fenner's Wharf. The staircase and much of the tavern's interior woodwork are in the so-called Gaspee Room. This room was reconstructed when Sabin Tavern was demolished during the last century, but is not the one in which the plotters met in 1772. In 1980 the local DAR gave the building to the Rhode Island Historical Society, which sold the building to a private entity in 1983. It is now an apartment house. Winterthur Museum, near Wilmington, Delaware has much of the paneling from the "Gaspee Room" of Sabin Tavern.

State House, 82 Smith Street. A gigantic building of white marble overlooking the city from a hill north of Civic Square, this structure of 1902 contains valuable relics of the Revolution. These objects are moved around from time to time, and it may be necessary to make inquiries at the information desk as to their location if you visit the building. In the Senate lobby is the original charter granted to the colony in 1663 and effective until the present constitution was adopted in 1843. (A copy is in the John Brown House.) In the rotunda are the only two surviving regimental flags of Rhode Island's Continental army units. The governor's reception room on the second floor has a full-length portrait of Washington by Gilbert Stuart (one of the best of many), and Nathanael Greene's field desk, sword, and other items associated with this major figure of the Revolution. Open Monday through Friday, 8:30 A.M. to 4:30 P.M., except holidays; phone: (401) 222-2357; website: www.state.ri.us/.

Smith's Castle,: U.S. 1 near Wickford. On the site of a trading post burned during King Philip's War, this house was built in 1678 using timbers of an earlier structure. The two-and-a-half-story, barn-like building is believed to be the only one surviving where Roger Williams preached to the Indians. Completely restored, it has furnishings of the seventeenth and eighteenth centuries and a garden of the latter period. Smith's Castle also features a museum shop and guided tours. Website: www.smithcastle.org; phone: (401) 294-3521. The site is 1.5 miles north of Wickford on U.S. 1 at Cocumscussoc.

Stuart (Gilbert) Birthplace, near Saunderstown. Between scenic stretches of U.S. 1 and 1A is the restored and furnished house in which the painter Gilbert Stuart was born in 1755, about four years after the little frame house was built by his father. The site, a National Historic Landmark, includes the restored and working snuff mill operated by the painter's father. It is open to the public from April to October, Thursday through Monday from 11 A.M. to 4 P.M. Phone: (401) 294-3001.

Gilbert Stuart (1755–1828) studied in Newport and worked in London (as a pupil of Benjamin West), Dublin, and Paris, achieving great success as a portrait painter during the years 1775 to 1793. Returning to his native country to escape his debts, he is best known today for his two portraits of Washington and the many replicas of these he subsequently executed. He did portraits of Presidents John Adams, Thomas Jefferson, James Madison, James Monroe, John Quincy Adams, and many other prominent people, including Generals Henry Knox and Horatio Gates. Stuart's grasp of character and his technique make him one of the great portrait painters of his time.

Waterman Tavern and Adjacent Campsite, near Potterville. A day's march west of Providence, this was a much-used campground during the Revolution. In an area rapidly being built over are depressions in the ground where wells and fireplaces once served the village of sod huts. Across the road on the north side is Waterman Tavern. Rochambeau and his officers stayed here on at least one occasion when their troops were marching through. The site is about 0.7 mile east of Potterville on Town Farm Road.

Whitehall,: Middletown. Rescued by the Colonial Dames and beautifully restored along with its garden, this ancient frame house of 1729 had fallen into such disrepair that it had become a barn. The two-story house with hipped roof and central chimney was the home of George Berkeley during the three years he spent in Newport (1729–1731). The philosopher and Anglican dean stimulated the cultural development of Newport before moving on to Bermuda. Whitehall is 2 miles southeast of Middletown on 311 Berkeley Avenue at the head of Paradise Avenue. Furnished in the period of Dean Berkeley's occupancy, it is operated by the Colonial Dames and included among the houses of Newport shown by appointment during the months of June, July, and August under the auspices of the Preservation Society. Phone: (401) 846-3116.

SOUTH CAROLINA

South Carolina's experience of the Revolution was particularly bitter and complex. In 1976 the South Carolina Department of Archives and History published a list of 180 military engagements that took place over a seven-year period (November 1775 to November 1782) in the state, though the majority of these were minor skirmishes. Of that number, the exact location of nine engagements cannot be determined, and sixteen engagements occurred without any overt hostilities.

So many military actions took place in South Carolina not only because it was a principal theater of British operations in 1780 but also because it was the scene of exceptionally virulent civil war between Whigs and Loyalists, as well as the country of the guerrilla leaders Andrew Pickens, Thomas ("Gamecock") Sumter, and Francis ("Swamp Fox") Marion. This "irregular warfare" and its colorful leaders generated an inordinate number of historic sites. In addition, South Carolina was the scene of some of the Revolution's biggest battles.

The interest in the American Revolution in South Carolina is exceeded only by the obsession with the Civil War, though it can take a number of peculiar local forms, such as commemorating "the 225th Anniversary of the American Revolution" in 2005 rather than 2000. A great number of significant books explore many aspects of the Revolution in South Carolina. Especially helpful guides are John W. Gorden's *South Carolina and the American Revolution: A Battlefield History* (University of South Carolina Press, 2003) and Daniel W. Barefoot's *Touring South Carolina's Revolutionary War Sites* (Blair Publishing, 1999).

South Carolina unfortunately has no published guide to highway historical markers, although the state-sponsored Historical Marker Program offers some information on individual markers. Another good source of the state's Revolutionary War history is through the South Carolina Department of Parks, Recreation and Tourism. Its official website is www.discoversouthcarolina.com. Phone: (803) 734-1700. The state's Department of Archives and History is also helpful. It is located at 8301 Parklane Road, Columbia, S.C. 29223. Phone: (803) 896-6100.

Beaufort and vicinity. *See* PORT ROYAL ISLAND.

Beckhamville (Beckham's Old Field), northwest corner of Great Falls, Chester County. The "Battle of Beckhamville" may have historical significance as the first Patriot victory after the fall of Charleston in May 1780. It was a surprise attack by Captain John McClure and thirty-two other Patriots on a much larger force of Loyalists assembled to support British efforts to administer oaths of loyalty at Beckham's Old Field. Without the loss of a man and with a minimum of shooting, the Patriots routed the entire force of about two hundred Loyalists.

On the edge of an open field northeast of the junction of S.C. 97 and 99 is the granite marker to the event. The date is erroneously given as "May 1780." The exact day of the action probably will never be determined, though it is known that it came after Buford's Defeat (29 May) and is variously given as falling between 2 and 6 June. A similar action took place at Mobley's Meeting House.

Beech Island, Savannah River just south of Augusta, Georgia. When the Patriots undertook their final siege of

Augusta, Georgia, Colonel Elijah Clark sent the horses to Beech Island with a six-man guard. Learning of this, Colonel Thomas Brown ordered out a body of regulars, militia, and Indians that killed the guards, took the horses, and headed back to Augusta. Over Mountain Men under Colonel Isaac Shelby and Georgia militia under Major Patrick Carr routed Brown's force as it returned, the action taking place probably on the Georgia side of the river. The date was about a week before the Patriot victory at Fort Galphin, approximately 15 May 1781. The present town of Beech Island, Aiken County, South Carolina, is just east of the old horseshoe bend of the Savannah in which Beech Island lay. The explanation available as to the derivation of Beech Island's name, since it is not an island, comes from the Beech Island Historical Society. It informs that the area's plentiful beech trees provided the impetus. The Society is a good source of local information and is located at 144 Old Jackson Highway, Beech Island, S.C. 29842. Phone: (803) 827-0184. (The topographic feature now called Beech Island is listed in Georgia.)

Bee's Plantation, Edisto River just below Jacksonboro, Colleton and Charleston counties. In a skirmish here on 23 March 1780 Lieutenant Colonel Banastre Tarleton killed ten Patriot militia, captured four, and picked up a few desperately needed horses for his troopers. The plantation of 1,500 acres, no vestiges of which have survived, was owned by Lieutenant Governor Thomas Bee. Some authorities give the site of this skirmish the name "Pon Pon," which is what the Indians called the Edisto River.

Belleville Plantation (Midway Plantation) and associated sites, Santee River, just east of U.S. 601 bridge in Calhoun County. Colonel William Thomson's Belleville Plantation here was occupied by the British in 1780 and became a fortified post and supply depot. General Thomas Sumter surprised the defenders in February 1781 but had to withdraw when British troops approached from Camden (see FORT WATSON). Belleville changed hands several times but presumably was permanently liberated by the Patriots when they took nearby Fort Motte in May 1781.

It is a National Historic Site but apparently not highly treasured by state authorities. The notice in *Colonials and Patriots* (1964) says: "Among the historic remains at and near the plantation are earthwork fortifications overlooking the Santee; the Thomson Cemetery, said to contain the remains of troops who died in the area; a camp and hospital site; McCord's Ferry, a strategic crossing of the Camden Road over the river; and Gillon's Retreat, plantation of Alexander Gillon, a commodore of the South Carolina Navy during the War for Independence."

The spot on Thomson's Plantation where Sumter's action of 22 February 1781 took place is on the east side of S.C. 151 just north of its junction with S.C. 80.

Biggin Bridge and Church, Cooper River, opposite Moncks Corner. The church whose brick ruins and ancient cemetery stand today alongside S.C. 44 less than a mile south of U.S. 17A and 52 was founded in 1706. The first structure was built in 1712 and replaced in 1756; its vestrymen later included William Moultrie and Henry Laurens (see MEPKIN PLANTATION). The church was burned in a forest fire during the first year of the Revolution, rebuilt, and its interior burned by the British in the summer of 1781 after they had made it into a military stronghold (see QUINBY BRIDGE AND QUINBY PLANTATION). A little more than a year earlier the Patriots under General Isaac Huger had been deployed around Biggin Bridge and were defeated in the action remembered by the name of Moncks Corner. The reconstructed church was again destroyed by a forest fire in 1886, but its ruined brick walls survive as a monument to this embattled site in a neighborhood of Revolutionary War skirmishes.

Black Mingo Creek, Georgetown-Williamsburg counties, about 20 miles north-northwest of Georgetown near Rhems (junction of S.C. 41 and 51). One of Marion's hottest fights took place in this area, which has a number of other important historical associations. Beautiful Black Mingo winds through coastal swamps to join Black River, and Willtown was settled on its bank near modern Rhems in 1750. Although the town has disappeared, in 1800 it was the largest in the region. The British set up an outpost of about fifty men under Loyalist Colonel John Coming Ball at Shepherd's Ferry, about where S.C. 41–51 now crosses the Black Mingo and somewhat less than a mile downstream from Willtown. In September 1780 Marion attempted to surprise Ball in a night attack.

Loyalist sentinels heard the Patriot horsemen crossing the bridge at Willtown around midnight, and Ball formed his men quietly in the open. The Patriots suffered heavy casualties when their center column was hit by surprise fire at short range, but they rallied to rout the Loyalists in a brisk skirmish that lasted only fifteen minutes. Only fifty men were engaged on each side, but Marion had ten men killed or wounded and the Loyalist losses were almost twice as heavy. One prize was Colonel Ball's fine mount, which Marion renamed Ball and rode for the rest of the war.

Sparsely inhabited today but sprinkled with signs of real-estate developers, this region was the home of many of Marion's partisans, and they were at their best in this skirmish known by the name of Black Mingo Creek.

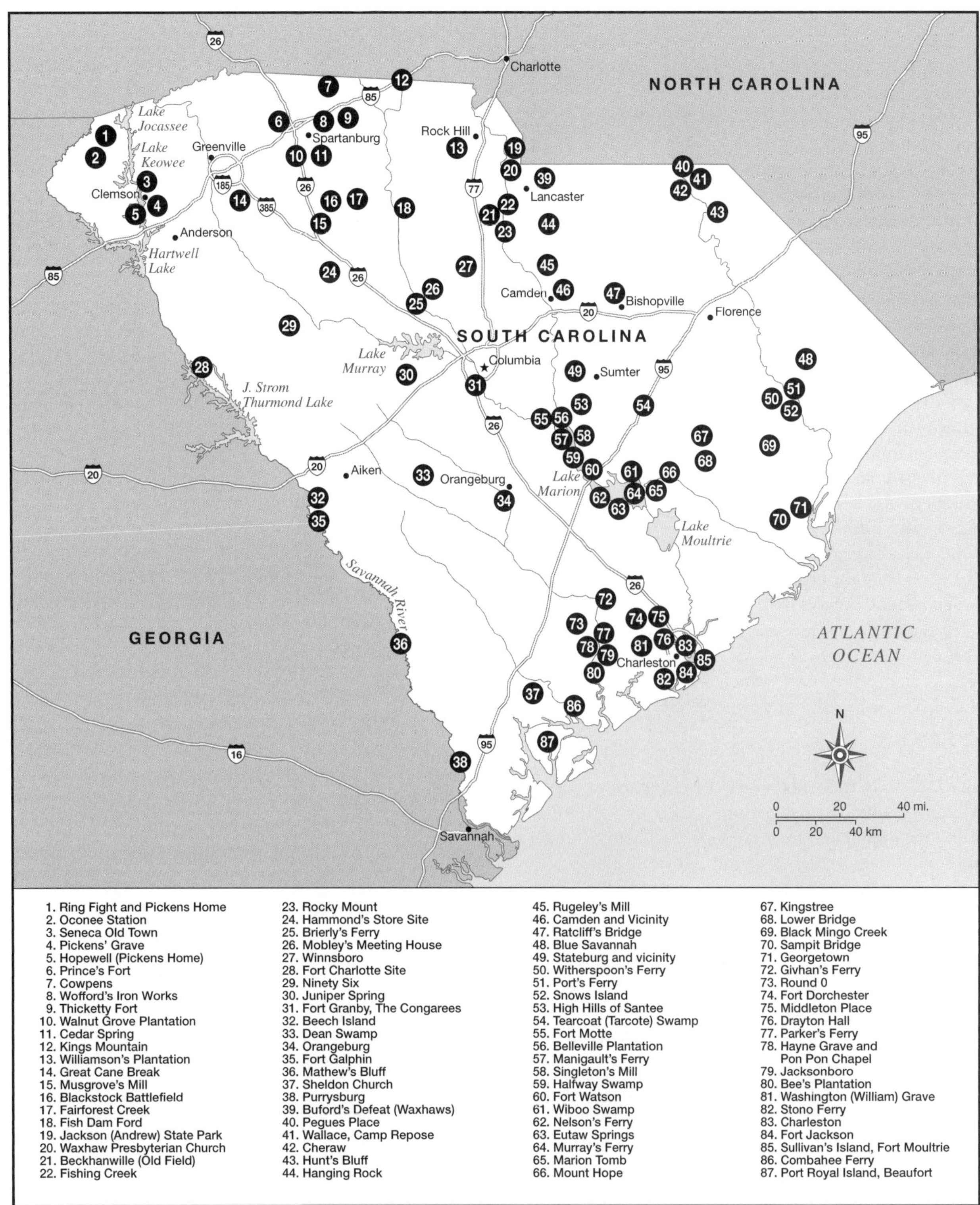

NORTH CAROLINA
SOUTH CAROLINA
GEORGIA
ATLANTIC OCEAN
Charlotte
Rock Hill
Spartanburg
Greenville
Clemson
Anderson
Lancaster
Camden
Bishopville
Florence
Columbia
Sumter
Aiken
Orangeburg
Charleston
Savannah
Lake Jocassee
Lake Keowee
Hartwell Lake
Lake Murray
J. Strom Thurmond Lake
Lake Marion
Lake Moultrie
Savannah River
N
0 20 40 mi.
0 20 40 km
1. Ring Fight and Pickens Home
2. Oconee Station
3. Seneca Old Town
4. Pickens' Grave
5. Hopewell (Pickens Home)
6. Prince's Fort
7. Cowpens
8. Wofford's Iron Works
9. Thicketty Fort
10. Walnut Grove Plantation
11. Cedar Spring
12. Kings Mountain
13. Williamson's Plantation
14. Great Cane Break
15. Musgrove's Mill
16. Blackstock Battlefield
17. Fairforest Creek
18. Fish Dam Ford
19. Jackson (Andrew) State Park
20. Waxhaw Presbyterian Church
21. Beckhanwille (Old Field)
22. Fishing Creek
23. Rocky Mount
24. Hammond's Store Site
25. Brierly's Ferry
26. Mobley's Meeting House
27. Winnsboro
28. Fort Charlotte Site
29. Ninety Six
30. Juniper Spring
31. Fort Granby, The Congarees
32. Beech Island
33. Dean Swamp
34. Orangeburg
35. Fort Galphin
36. Mathew's Bluff
37. Sheldon Church
38. Purrysburg
39. Buford's Defeat (Waxhaws)
40. Pegues Place
41. Wallace, Camp Repose
42. Cheraw
43. Hunt's Bluff
44. Hanging Rock
45. Rugeley's Mill
46. Camden and Vicinity
47. Ratcliff's Bridge
48. Blue Savannah
49. Stateburg and vicinity
50. Witherspoon's Ferry
51. Port's Ferry
52. Snows Island
53. High Hills of Santee
54. Tearcoat (Tarcote) Swamp
55. Fort Motte
56. Belleville Plantation
57. Manigault's Ferry
58. Singleton's Mill
59. Halfway Swamp
60. Fort Watson
61. Wiboo Swamp
62. Nelson's Ferry
63. Eutaw Springs
64. Murray's Ferry
65. Marion Tomb
66. Mount Hope
67. Kingstree
68. Lower Bridge
69. Black Mingo Creek
70. Sampit Bridge
71. Georgetown
72. Givhan's Ferry
73. Round 0
74. Fort Dorchester
75. Middleton Place
76. Drayton Hall
77. Parker's Ferry
78. Hayne Grave and Pon Pon Chapel
79. Jacksonboro
80. Bee's Plantation
81. Washington (William) Grave
82. Stono Ferry
83. Charleston
84. Fort Jackson
85. Sullivan's Island, Fort Moultrie
86. Combahee Ferry
87. Port Royal Island, Beaufort

MAP BY XNR PRODUCTIONS. THE GALE GROUP.

Willtown prospered for several decades after the Revolution, and Aaron Burr stayed in its tavern when traveling to visit his beloved daughter Theodosia near Georgetown.

The town site can be found in a region of cut-over pine by following an unimproved road about a mile from the historical marker ("Skirmish at Black Mingo Creek") on S.C. 41–51, 1.6 miles northeast of Rhems. A shorter route is over this same unimproved road from its intersection with County Road 24 about 1.6 miles north of Rhems. Either way you will come to Black Mingo Baptist Church. A woods road just north of the large frame church and its chain-link-fenced cemetery leads eastward a short distance to several old graves on the edge of a large pond. These are said to be "British" graves.

About half a mile north of the church is the overgrown site of Willtown. Black Mingo Creek will be seen here, but unless the weather has been dry this is no place to try to drive an ordinary passenger car. The picturesque creek can also be viewed from the highway bridge of S.C. 41–51 and from several spots to the east in this vicinity. One such place is Tara Hall, a boys' home on the creek 0.7 miles from the highway, the entrance being marked by a sign about 0.7 miles north of Rhems.

Another way to explore Black Mingo Creek is through the services of a local outfitter, one of which is Blackwater Adventures, which provides guided canoe and kayak trips up and down the creek. Phone: (843) 761-1850.

Blackstock Battlefield, Tyger River, western edge of Union County. A small granite marker on a prominent hill is the monument to one of General Thomas Sumter's most important battles, a National Historic Site.

Reinforced by Georgia troops under Elijah Clark and John Twiggs, Sumter was threatening Loyalist posts just north of Ninety Six. Cornwallis ordered Tarleton to break off his operations against Marion along the lower Pee Dee and disperse this Rebel partisan force under Sumter. Warned by a British deserter, Sumter started a hasty retreat north to avoid being caught between Tarleton and the strong Loyalist force at Ninety Six. Tarleton pursued with his entire force until he realized that Sumter was gaining, so Tarleton pushed ahead with his mounted troops and ordered his infantry and artillery to follow. The Patriots had reached the Tyger River as the light was failing on 20 November 1780, and the Carolina Gamecock decided to take advantage of a good defensive position around Blackstock Plantation to make a stand.

The Patriot force of about 1,000 was deployed when Tarleton made contact with his advance element of 190 dragoons of his legion and 80 mounted infantry of the Sixty-third Regiment. Sumter had learned that the rest of the enemy force was still to the rear, so he undertook an attack to destroy Tarleton's advance piecemeal. With a numerical superiority of almost four to one, Sumter had reason to expect success from the bold but completely orthodox tactical decision. The plan was for the Patriot center to hold its defensive positions on high ground around five log houses and along a rail fence. Clark was to lead 100 Georgians in an encirclement of the British right flank and block the advance of Tarleton's reinforcements. Sumter himself led the main effort, an attack by 400 Patriot militia against the 80 regulars of the Sixty-third Regiment, who had dismounted to take up a position on Tarleton's right overlooking a creek.

The 400 were routed by the 80 British soldiers and driven back through the plantation houses of the American center. Sumter ordered a detachment of mounted infantry under Colonel Lacey to attack the dragoons on the British left. Lacey got close enough to deliver a surprise fire that inflicted 20 casualties among Tarleton's troopers (who had been distracted by the remarkable performance of the British infantry), but he was then driven back. Sumter was returning to the center of his line when he was badly wounded and forced to relinquish command to Twiggs. Colonel Wade Hampton's South Carolina riflemen and the Georgia sharpshooters stood fast, stopping the 80 British regulars and forming a strong point around which the rest of Sumter's troops rallied. Tarleton had to lead a desperate charge of cavalry into the center to break contact and withdraw his infantry.

The statistics tell a curious story. Of 1,000 engaged, the Patriots lost 3 killed and 5 wounded, whereas Tarleton lost about 50 killed and wounded out of 270 engaged.

A dirt road named Monument Road that goes on to follow the track of the original Blackstock Road leads for about 1.5 miles to the hill where the battlefield marker is located. Vandals repeatedly removed the bronze plaques originally set there by the local DAR, so now an unadorned engraved concrete monument commemorates the spot. The Palmetto Conservation Foundation has recently acquired and given to the state 110 acres of the Blackstock Battlefield area. The state is in the process (2005) of developing this into a historic site, complete with hiking trails and interpretive panels outlining the history of the area.

The village of Blackstock, about 40 miles east of the battlefield and near the southern boundary of Chester County, was settled after the Revolution.

Blue Savannah, Little Pee Dee River, near U.S. 501 south of Ariel Cross Roads in Marion County, or south of Galivants Ferry Bridge. Francis Marion moved 60 miles east to Port's Ferry after his triumph at Nelson's Ferry. Having escaped pursuit from that direction, he learned that Major Micajah Ganey was moving down the Little Pee Dee with a large Loyalist force. Marion advanced with his small band, only fifty-two mounted partisans, to cope with this new threat. In a clash between advance guards, Major John James routed forty-five men under Ganey's personal command. When Marion saw the remaining two hundred Loyalists forming he withdrew to Blue Savannah, he circled back to set up an ambuscade, and surprised his pursuers with a sudden attack. The Loyalists under Captain Jesse Barfield delivered one volley (three Patriots wounded) before scattering. Important as this action of 4 September 1780 is—it broke Loyalist morale east of the Pee Dee and doubled Marion's strength by bringing him sixty volunteers—the location has never been fixed. That it took place on a swampy island just south of Galivants Ferry appears to be certain, but the authoritative WPA *Guide* of 1941 refers to the site as being unmarked, as being east of the river, and as taking place on 16 August. One of Marion's more recent biographers, Robert D. Bass, places the action just west of the river and south of Ariel (intersection of U.S. 501 and S.C. 41). State historical authorities favor the latter location.

Brierly's Ferry (or Ford), Broad River. This critical point on the British line of communications between Ninety Six and Camden, frequently mentioned in accounts of operations in 1780 to 1781, is about where S.C. 213 crosses the Broad between Parr Shoals Dam and Peak. The exact site has not yet been fixed. Here Tarleton on 18 November 1780 drew fire from 150 mounted militia as he tracked Sumter to Blackstock. About this time the Seventy-first Highlanders under Major McArthur from Cheraw and eighty survivors of Major Wemyss's engagement at Fish Dam Ford established a post on orders from Cornwallis, who was worried about the security of Ninety Six. From Brierly's Ferry, McArthur and his Highlanders marched with Tarleton in pursuit of Dan Morgan to Cowpens.

Buford's Defeat (Waxhaws), 9 miles east of Lancaster, 0.15 miles south on S.C. 522 from S.C. 9, Lancaster County. Known also as the Battle of the Waxhaws and Buford's Massacre, 29 May 1780, this Patriot defeat ended organized military resistance in South Carolina for many long months. When Charleston surrendered on 12 May 1780 the only American military force left in the field was the Third Virginia Continental Regiment commanded by Colonel Abraham Buford. They had been joined by a few cavalry troops who had survived the skirmishes at Moncks Corner and Leneud's Ferry. Buford was ordered to retreat to Hillsborough, North Carolina, and he had a ten-day lead when Cornwallis started up the Santee in pursuit. Seeing that Buford would get away, and being particularly anxious to capture the rebel governor, John Rutledge, who was being escorted by Buford, Cornwallis ordered Colonel Banastre Tarleton to take over the pursuit.

The stocky little redhead had already impressed his British superiors with his exceptional abilities as a commander of mobile troops. Since the end of 1778 he had commanded the British Legion, Loyalists who qualified before the end of the Revolution for official acceptance as regulars. For this mission the 130 cavalry and 100 infantry of Tarleton's legion were reinforced by forty British dragoons, and on 27 May they left Nelson's Ferry. In the next fifty-four hours Tarleton covered 105 miles to pick up the tail of the Patriot column. Governor Rutledge had left Buford's column at Rugeley's Mill, and the 350 Virginia Continentals were double-timing to escape when Tarleton sent Buford a "flag" demanding surrender.

It was early afternoon, and for several days the weather had been oppressively hot. Many of Tarleton's horses had died of exhaustion and the British column was badly strung out. But the British advance guard badly chopped up Buford's rear guard after the Continental commander defied the surrender summons, and at around 3 P.M. the Americans turned to fight.

When it was all over a very short time later, the American casualties were 113 killed and 203 captured. Of the 200 British and Loyalists on hand, Tarleton reported 19 killed or wounded. Patriot propagandists cried "massacre" because Tarleton's troops killed several Patriots who had surrendered (inspiring the phrase "Tarleton's quarter"—that is, no quarter), but the brilliance of Tarleton's accomplishment and the tactical errors of Buford's command remain apparent.

Most of the battlefield remains in open land just south of a main highway and intersected by a secondary road. In a grove of hardwood trees on a low knoll alongside the latter road (S.C. 522) is the common grave of Buford's dead, encircled by a 2-foot wall of white rocks. A weathered obelisk about 7 feet tall serves as the common headstone, and its almost illegible inscription is copied on a newer monument of 1955. With the long view of a blue ridge line to the west and good observation south and east, it is easy to visualize the battle from a sketch map. Unfortunately, contemporary Patriots of the region have not seen fit to develop the site by providing interpretive exhibits on the well-preserved battlefield. However, the Andrew Jackson State Park sponsored a complete weekend of festivities on the battlegrounds in 2005 to commemorate the 225th anniversary of the battle.

Authorities have long confused this site with that of the Waxhaw Presbyterian Church, probably because the church is where the wounded from the battle were brought for care.

Camden and vicinity, Kershaw County. On U.S. 1 and just off I-20, modern Camden retains its antique charm and historic interest. Fortunately, the site of the original settlement has been preserved because newer construction after the Revolution was to the north. Hobkirk Hill, a major battlefield, is completely taken over by a residential area, and the Logtown of the Revolution is the business district, but the 1780 to 1781 town site is being explored, and a main portion of it restored. About 5 miles north of Camden in country that has changed little since the Revolution is the battlefield where Lord Cornwallis inflicted a decisive and demoralizing defeat on a large American army under General Horatio Gates.

To outline quickly the history of this region, it was one of several picked by colonial authorities for settlement in the early 1730s. Until then only the coastal areas had been developed, and King George II ordered the creation of nine townships on major rivers well back in the interior. Camden quickly evolved from Fredericksburg Township, whereas most of the others died out, and it claims to be the oldest inland town of South Carolina.

Because Camden was a natural communications hub at the head of navigation on the Wateree River and near the intersection of important Indian trails, it prospered and became a strategic location during the Revolution.

When Lord Cornwallis assumed command of all British forces in the South after the capture of Charleston in May 1780, he ignored his instructions to pursue a passive defense of the conquered territory. Instead, he sent young Lord Rawdon to establish a forward base at Camden with strong outposts at Cheraw, Hanging Rock, and Rocky Mount. Congress selected General Horatio Gates, the victor of Saratoga, as the man to liberate the Carolinas, and on the moonless night of 15 to 16 August, two armies were advancing, each intending to attack the other the next morning. Around 2:30 A.M. they collided a few miles north of Camden.

Cornwallis had the disadvantage of being less than a mile north of Saunders Creek, with insufficient depth of position to deploy his reserves properly and no opportunity for maneuver initially. Gates had slightly higher ground on which to form for battle, but no natural protection for his flanks. On the other hand, he had about twice as many troops as Cornwallis, even though 80 percent of these were unseasoned militia.

But Gates had brought his army to the battlefield in a weakened and dispirited condition. Unfortunately, his militia were on the east flank where, as it turned out, Cornwallis had put his regulars and one of the war's most remarkable troop leaders, Lieutenant Colonel James Webster. At the age of thirty-two Webster had succeeded Cornwallis as commander of the Thirty-third Foot ("West Riding"), a regiment that was to figure prominently in the American Revolution. Webster came to America in early 1776 as part of Cornwallis's force and led his regiment with great distinction. He was cited by General Clinton for his performance at Monmouth, New Jersey in June 1778, given the temporary rank of brigadier less than a year later, and entrusted with command of a vital British post in the Hudson Highlands (Verplanck's, opposite Stony Point); and in December 1779 he sailed south with the forces that overran the Carolinas. Seven months after the Battle of Camden, having meanwhile been conspicuous in the operations against General Nathanael Greene in North Carolina and defying death on many battlefields, he was mortally wounded in the final stages of the Battle of Guilford Courthouse, North Carolina.

This was the man who commanded on the British right at Camden, and the foregoing summary of his career may make it somewhat easier to understand why the American militia opposite him did not distinguish itself for martial valor on this day.

Gates seems to have had no plan other than to deploy as best he could and let Cornwallis take the initiative. Webster formed his line as the artillery exchanged volleys with little effect other than to shroud the battlefield with dust and smoke. Colonel Otho Williams, a brilliant officer of the Maryland Line who was serving as principal staff officer to Gates on this occasion, prevailed on the Virginia militia to advance and hit the British before they could complete their deployment. He then led about fifty volunteers forward to disrupt the enemy.

Deploying with drill-field precision from march column into line of battle and then advancing with volley fire and the traditional cheering, Brigadier Webster's wing inspired such terror that the Virginia militia fled panic-stricken to the rear. Few tarried long enough to fire a shot, most threw their loaded weapons to the ground, and only three are known to have been wounded. Their flight inspired the North Carolina militia in the center to follow suit, leaving the Second Maryland Brigade unsupported on the American right flank.

Webster wheeled left to roll up the American flank rather than pursuing the militia. Cornwallis then turned Webster's efforts toward the American reserves, which is why the First Maryland Brigade was unable to fight its way forward to support the Second Brigade.

General Johann Kalb commanded the Continentals on the right, and the Marylanders stood fast initially against the wing led by Lord Rawdon. Despite several wounds and the loss of his horse, the huge Bavarian, fifty-eight years old and a professional officer since 1743, refused to retreat without orders from Gates. As the British closed in with overwhelming numbers the heroic Kalb went down bleeding from eleven wounds.

The miserable Horatio Gates had long since quit the battlefield. Swept back to Rugeley's Mill with the militia, he covered 60 miles on the day of the battle to reach Charlotte. (Camden being famous horse country even today, it must be mentioned that Gates was mounted on no ordinary steed for this ride.) Two days later, using relays of horses, Gates had covered another 120 miles to Hillsborough, North Carolina, where he planned to reorganize his shattered army. Only seven hundred of his original four thousand troops rejoined him. There is almost hopeless disagreement among authorities as to numbers engaged in the Battle of Camden and losses sustained on the Patriot side. According to some computations the Americans did not have as many as two hundred men killed in this tremendous defeat. Gates himself did not know how many men he had on the battlefield after sending large detachments off earlier on secondary missions, but only about one thousand Patriot troops did any real fighting in the Battle of Camden. And this action lasted only about an hour. Cornwallis's claim of one thousand Americans killed seems absurdly high, but it is credited by respectable authorities. About one thousand were captured, including almost all the wounded. The British lost 324 officers and men killed and wounded out of about two thousand engaged.

General Kalb died in Camden three days after the battle, and his grave was moved to its present location in front of the Bethesda Presbyterian Church at 502 DeKalb Street. The cornerstone for his monument, designed by Robert Mills, was laid by Lafayette in 1825.

Johann Kalb was the son of Bavarian peasants. He left home at the age of sixteen (in 1737) and six years later entered the pages of history as Lieutenant Jean de Kalb of the French army. After reaching the rank of major and further distinguishing himself as a soldier, he married a wealthy woman and retired from the army in 1765 to live near Paris. Three years later he traveled in America as a secret agent with the mission of reporting to the minister of foreign affairs on the colonists' attitude toward their mother country. In 1775 Kalb returned to the army; he was commissioned a brigadier general the next year, but meanwhile had decided to seek his military fortune in America. With a contract from Silas Deane he came to America with Lafayette in the summer of 1777 (see GEORGETOWN), but it was two years before Congress gave him an assignment commensurate with his rank of major general in the Continental army.

In April 1780 he was ordered to lead the Maryland and Delaware Continentals south to the relief of Charleston, but on 25 July he was superseded by Gates. General Kalb remained as a subordinate to Gates and tried vainly to prevent him from making the blunders that led to disaster at Camden. As we have seen, he died a hero's death here.

The Camden Battlefield is 5 miles north of the town of Camden on a county road just west of U.S. 521 and 601. The site has changed little from the time of the battle, consisting of open fields and pine woods bordered by small streams. The DAR put up a marker approximately where Kalb fell. In 2000 a group of local residents set up a nonprofit group to protect the site, which remains privately owned, from development.

The British fortified the town of Camden after the battle of 16 August 1780. An outer perimeter of six redoubts incorporated the stockaded house and outbuildings of Camden's founder, Joseph Kershaw. The latter had arrived from Charleston in 1758 and built a store. His large new home was still unfinished when the British occupied Camden but became their headquarters and has been known since as the Cornwallis House. Other structures incorporated into the fortifications were the civil jail and the Patriot powder magazine.

Lord Rawdon had been the British commander at Camden when the base was first established. He was twenty-six years old when he led the left wing of Cornwallis's army in the defeat of Gates, and only a year older when entrusted with command of eight thousand troops for the control of South Carolina and Georgia while Cornwallis undertook to win the American Revolution in North Carolina. After Cornwallis's subsequent departure for Virginia, Rawdon was supreme commander of British field forces in the South. (This point is disputed, particularly in connection with the Isaac Hayne Affair—see HAYNE GRAVE AND HOMESITE. But major military operations of the British after Cornwallis left South Carolina were directed by Rawdon.)

Of a noble Irish family (he succeeded his father as earl of Moira in 1793, having added his mother's surname of Hastings to his own when his mother succeeded to the barony of Hastings in 1789), Francis Rawdon had distinguished himself in his baptism of fire at Bunker Hill. Tall and athletic, with a fine military bearing, he also was known as the "ugliest man in England." This distinction is not supported by his portraits, but he proved to be an ugly opponent to Nathanael Greene in the Battle of Hobkirk Hill on 25 April 1781.

When Greene undertook the reconquest of South Carolina he advanced on Camden from the northeast in hopes of surprising its defenders. But Rawdon kept himself well informed of Greene's movements and of his logistic problems. Marion the "Swamp Fox" and Sumter the Carolina "Gamecock" had been his greatest problems before the American regulars entered the arena, and as Greene approached Camden about half of Rawdon's fighting forces were detached under Lieutenant Colonel John Watson to wipe out Marion's partisans in the Pee Dee swamps. Meanwhile, Greene had detached the legion of "Light Horse Harry" Lee to support Marion. The Gamecock had his own ideas of how the war should be prosecuted, and refused to cooperate with Greene, but the latter did not know this and was expecting Sumter to join the team around Camden.

While the sideshow between Watson and the Lee-Marion combination progressed (see FORT WATSON),

Greene reached the outskirts of Camden. He had failed to achieve surprise, and although Rawdon's garrison had been reduced to only nine hundred men, Greene was not strong enough to take the fortified British position by assault. Greene therefore went into camp on Hobkirk Hill to await suppplies and reinforcements.

Although he could scrape together only eight hundred combatants, including convalescents, Rawdon decided to attack Greene's army of almost twice that number. His audacity paid off, largely because he was able to catch the Americans off guard and because they made a number of tactical mistakes. Captain Robert Kirkwood's Delaware Company effectively delayed the British advance once it was detected, but the crack First Maryland Regiment for some unaccountable reason collapsed, followed by the Fifth Maryland and the Fourth Virginia. Only the Fifth Virginia stood firm; otherwise Greene's entire force might have been destroyed. The Patriots fell back in good order to Rugeley's Mill.

Highway markers on U.S. 521 and 601 (Broad Street) point to the locations of Greene's headquarters and the American line (just north of Greene Street) in the handsome residential area that now covers Hobkirk Hill. (Signs tell you to keep your horse off the sidewalks.) Markers are also visible on I-20 heading west from Florence and heading east out of Columbia toward Camden. Lots on Hobkirk Hill started being sold in 1817 for summer cottages, and some of these original structures are incorporated in the mansions built after 1840 in Camden's golden era. Nearly all the houses of historic interest have numbered markers keyed in with a guidebook available at various places in Camden. The battlefield in the center of the residential Hobkirk Hill, now named Kirkwood Commons, has been preserved, and there are several commemorative monuments to both Patriot and Loyalist soldiers.

Restoration of Historic Camden, the fortified village of the Revolution, is an all-too-rare example of what can be accomplished by an intelligent group of local citizens who, in this case, formed the aptly named Historic Camden Foundation.

The Foundation owns and operates Historic Camden, a 107-acre outdoor museum complex with nature trails, a gift shop, picnic areas, and its most spectacular presentation—a number of historic houses that were reproduced or moved into the park from the surrounding area. They include: Bradley House (c.1800), moved from 9 miles east of Camden to the park in the late 1970s; Craven House (c.1789), moved in 1979 from Mill Street; Cunningham House (1840), which serves as the executive offices and gift shop, moved from Market and Dekalb Streets; Drakeford House (c.1812), moved from the farthest location of them all—about 12 miles in the early 1970s; and the Kershaw-Cornwallis House, which is a reproduction of the original home owned by Camden founder Joseph Kersaw. Historic Camden is open to the public every day but Monday. Website: www.camden-sc.org; phone: (803) 432-9841.

Although modern building construction continues to obliterate some of the Revolutionary War fortifications, developers of Historic Camden are striving to acquire additional acreage that includes much of the eighteenth-century town site that has not yet been destroyed.

The visitor to modern Camden will find his way well marked to the area's many historic attractions. Literature is available at the clearly identified information center on the north side of U.S. 1 in the quiet business district. Historic Camden is just off U.S. 521 (Broad Street), on the south edge of town, and the way is marked. The route north to Hobkirk Hill, the Camden Battlefield, and Rugeley's Mill (U.S. 521 and 601 for about 6 miles, then left on County Road 58) is marked by the "Washington Coach" silhouette signs posted by the state.

Cedar Spring, junction of S.C. 56 and 295 on southeast edge of Spartanburg. Alongside the highway, at the foot of the hill on which the South Carolina Deaf and Blind School is located, is a pipe spewing forth the waters of old Cedar Spring. Only about 2 miles from Wofford's Iron Works, this spring gave its name to two little battles of the Revolution. In July 1780 Mrs. Jane Thomas left her home near here to visit her husband at Ninety Six, where the militia colonel was imprisoned for parole violation. Overhearing two Loyalist women mention a proposed raid to surprise the Rebel camp at Cedar Spring, Jane raced back to warn her son, who commanded the sixty Patriots. She arrived in the evening after a nonstop ride of 60 miles. The Patriots left their fires burning and withdrew to set up an ambuscade that routed the 150-man raiding party. On 8 August, three weeks later, there was a drawn battle in this vicinity known variously as the Second Battle of Cedar Springs, the Peach Orchard Fight, and the Old Iron Works Engagement. It was a running battle, with most of the action taking place about halfway between the spring and the iron works. Although indecisive, it was followed by gradually increasing Whig supremacy in the region.

Charleston. In 1670 a permanent English settlement was established at Albemarle Point on the west bank of the Ashley River about 3.5 miles from where that river joins the Cooper to form Oyster Point. The site remained in private ownership for three centuries, unspoiled by developers, and is part of the 200-acre Charles Towne Landing State Historic Site. Phone: (843) 852-4200. No trace of the old settlement survives, but the palisade, redoubt, and trenches have been rebuilt. In Old Town Creek is a reproduction of a seventeenth-century trading ship. Nearby is an exhibition of the crops grown experimentally by the original settlers. Other attractions are a "forest" with animals indigenous to the state (including bison) and a landscaped park of almost 100 acres. Routes to the site are marked.

Oyster Point quickly proved to be a better location than Albemarle Point, despite its greater vulnerability to naval attack. Settlement soon started here on the tip of the peninsula formed by the Ashley and Cooper Rivers, and in 1680 the seat of government was moved to the new Charles Town. French Protestants started arriving this same year. Around 1719 the name of the growing settlement was changed to Charlestowne, and the current spelling was not adopted until British occupation ended in 1783 and the town was incorporated.

As the colonists moved toward revolution the population of Charleston (to use its present name) grew to 12,000. Only Philadelphia (with 38,000), New York City (22,000), and Boston (18,000) were larger in 1775. Although Charleston was not a chartered city and did not even have a township government until the end of the Revolution, it was by far the most important settlement south of Philadelphia, and was the political and social center of South Carolina. In the immediate vicinity were many prosperous plantations. Charleston was therefore intimately involved in the political and commercial controversies that started in 1763. But the city enjoyed many years of immunity from serious warfare while the British made their main effort in the North.

This immunity was bought early in 1776 when a major British attempt to take Charleston and the southern provinces was repulsed on nearby Sullivan's Island, primarily because of the gallant resistance at the place later named Fort Moultrie. But with the next threat, a mere feint made by General Augustine Prevost to relieve General Benjamin Lincoln's counteroffensive toward Augusta, Georgia in May 1779, Charlestonian civic leaders wanted to surrender. While Governor John Rutledge and General William Moultrie carried out uncoordinated and ineffectual efforts to manage the defense of the city, the terrified citizenry tried to work out a deal with the enemy to spare Charleston in return for a promise of the city's neutrality. The white citizens of Charleston were not only anxious to avoid battle, they also feared that a British attack, which would likely come with promises of freedom to the state's slaves, would permanently disrupt their "way of life." Given that the majority of South Carolina's population was enslaved, it is easy to understand their fear. Negotiations broke down because Prevost foolishly insisted that the armed garrison of the city be surrendered—the very garrison which the whites of Charleston relied upon for protection from slave uprisings. Having achieved much more success in this strategic diversion than he could have hoped for, Prevost shifted his force to Johns Island to reestablish his lines of communication by sea with his base in Georgia. (He had advanced on Charleston overland from Ebenezer, Georgia, marching along the general line of today's U.S. 17.) When he learned that Lincoln was racing back to "save" Charleston, precisely what the British strategy had sought to achieve, Prevost left a large rear guard on the islands south of Charleston and withdrew the rest of his troops along the coast to Savannah. About a month later this rear guard repulsed a mismanaged American attack at Stono Ferry.

Early in 1780 the British were able to launch a major expedition into the Carolinas. Meanwhile, a combined force of French and Americans had suffered a costly defeat in trying to recapture Savannah, Georgia (9 October 1779). The British expedition from New York under General Henry Clinton was so buffeted by storms that it could not come into North Edisto Inlet, just south of Charleston, as planned, but had to reorganize at Savannah. In a plodding campaign Clinton forced the surrender of Charleston on 12 May 1780 after the citizens of Charleston informed General Lincoln that they would not act to defend their city. The decisive military action took place along the Patriot lines of communications into Charleston, particularly around Moncks Corner; within the city itself there are no significant landmarks associated with the siege. A block of tabby construction in Marion Square, just north of Calhoun Street, is a vestige of the "horn work" that was roughly in the center of the main defensive line. Forts Moultrie and Johnson had no significant role in the defense or the city in 1780. The surrender was a major disaster to the Patriot cause. A vigorous pursuit by "Butcher" Tarleton destroyed the last organized Patriot armed force in the action known as Buford's Defeat, more than 100 miles from Charleston, and South Carolina was a conquered province for almost a year before the tide of war turned again. Forced slowly back to Charleston, the British finally evacuated their last stronghold here on 11 July 1782. General Nathanael Greene maintained his headquarters in Charleston until August 1783, when he received news that the preliminary peace treaty had been negotiated.

About 550 buildings of the eighteenth and first half of the nineteenth century survive in the two historic areas of Charleston. Concentrated in the southeast corner of the city, they may be found on maps and literature furnished without charge by the well-organized tourist agencies of the state and city. One of the most helpful and active is the Historic Charleston Foundation, founded in 1947. Phone: (843) 723-1623. Following is a discussion of the highlights.

The report of the National Survey of Historic Sites and Buildings names twenty-seven structures "worthy of special notice." Of these, the following are listed in the order of a walking tour that requires a minimum of backtracking:

Miles Brewton House, 27 King Street. Built in 1765 to 1769 for the prominent citizen and slave trader from which it takes its name, probably the best example of the Charleston "double-house," and perhaps the "finest town house of the colonial period," it is a brick structure, almost square in design, with a two-story white portico and a formidable barbed fence put up in 1822 in response to the alleged Denmark Vesey slave insurrection. The exterior and interior are richly ornamented. As the National Survey points out, "such historical interest as the house possesses springs directly from its architectural distinction." It naturally became headquarters for the British, and is now a private residence.

Heyward-Washington House, 87 Church Street. Built in 1772 on a street where several other noteworthy eighteenth-century houses survive, this was the home of a signer of the Declaration of Independence, Thomas Heyward, Jr. The city rented it for George Washington to stay in for a week in May 1791; hence it is called the Heyward-Washington House. The house was recognized as a National Historic Landmark in 1976 and is owned and operated by the Charleston Museum, which has opened it to the public. Phone: (843) 722-2996.

St. Michael's Episcopal Church, 80 Meeting Street at Broad Street. Called "one of the great Georgian churches of the Colonies," it features a two-story portico of gigantic proportions and a spire that rises from a square base in a series of three diminishing octagons to a conical tip which is 185 feet high. The architect may have been Peter Harrison, whose King's Chapel in Boston is marred by the absence of the lofty spire he intended it to have. Dedicated in 1761, St. Michael's is a memorial to the culture and wealth of Charleston in the early days of the colony.

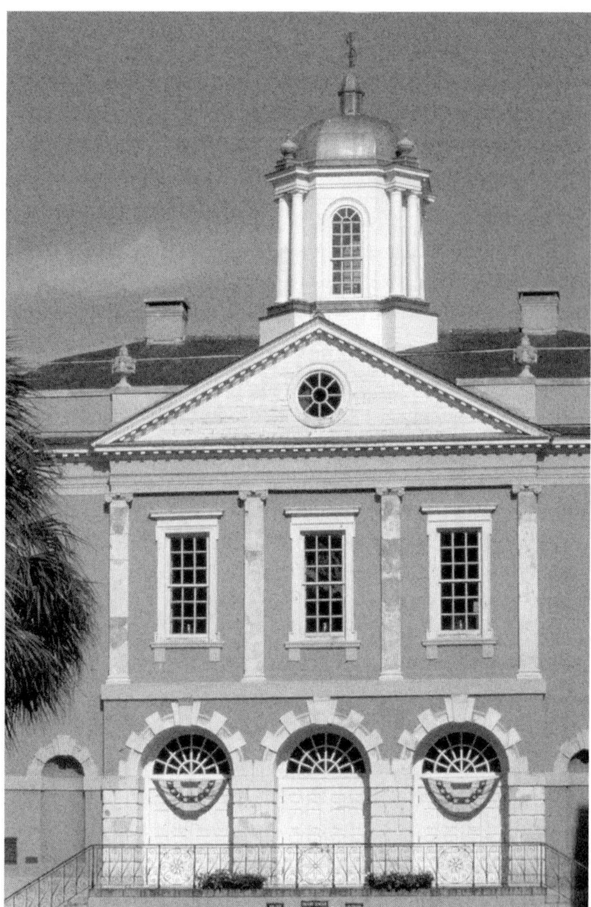

The Exchange and Provost Dungeon. *Charleston's Exchange was built in 1767 to 1771 after the adoption of the Townshend Acts, which mandated duties on imports of glass, lead, painters' colors, tea, and paper. The Exchange had commodious cellars for customs storage; during the British occupation, American prisoners were held there.* © JAN BUTCHOFSKY-HOUSER/CORBIS.

The Exchange (Custom House) and Provost Dungeon, 122 East Bay Street, east end of Broad Street. Built in 1767 to 1771 after adoption of the Townshend Acts (duties on imports of glass, lead, painters' colors, tea, and paper by the colonists were imposed to pay expenses of British government in America), the Exchange had commodious cellars for customs storage. American opposition to the Townshend Acts led to the elimination of all products but tea from the duty list before Charleston's new customhouse was finished. In 1773 the cellars held British tea seized by the colonists, and in 1780 they were used by the Patriots for storing powder. During the British occupation American prisoners were held here, including Colonel Isaac Hayne (see HAYNE GRAVE AND HOMESITE). When renovations were undertaken in 1965 a portion of the old city seawall of 1690 and a gun battery were uncovered. The "Provost Dungeon" is a DAR museum with a model of the Half Moon Battery that stood on the site before the Revolution, artifacts from recent excavations, a representation of the Patriot powder cache that remained undetected during the British occupation, and life-size wax figures of prisoners and guards. The Exchange has undergone extensive modification throughout the years and was badly damaged during the Civil War, but much of the original structure has survived. It was renovated again in 1981 by the Friends of the Old Exchange, who raise money and awareness on the building's behalf. Open daily, 9 A.M. to 5 P.M. Museum phone: (843) 727-2165.

Colonial Powder Magazine, 79 Cumberland Street. The oldest public building in the city, this low, single-story structure of stuccoed brick with a heavy tile roof was authorized in 1703 and completed several years later. Of architectural note are the unusually small bricks used in its construction and a massive arch supporting the central portion of the roof. Located near the northwest bastion of the walled city, the magazine was used until the British besieged Charleston in the spring of 1780. The public powder supply was then moved to the Exchange. Owned by the Colonial Dames until they entrusted it to the Historic Charleston Foundation in 1993, the Powder Magazine is a museum open to the public daily from mid-March through October, 10 A.M. to 5 P.M., except on Sunday, when it is open from 2 P.M. to 5 P.M. Phone: (843) 722 3767.

William Rhett House, 54 Hasell Street. The oldest dwelling in Charleston and still a private residence, it was completed by 1716 as a plantation house just outside the fortified walls of the city. Major alterations have been made on the exterior of this National Historic Landmark. William Rhett was an outstanding leader in the early days of the colony, commanding the flotilla that repulsed a Franco-Spanish attack in 1706 and leading the expedition that captured Stede Bonnet, the pirate. Confederate General Wade Hampton (1818–1902), grandson of the Colonel Wade Hampton who served under Thomas Sumter, was born in the Rhett House.

Charleston Museum, 360 Meeting Street. Established in 1773, this claims to be the oldest museum in the United States. Devoted to the life and environment of Charleston and its region, the museum contains a number of historical displays, including a permanent exhibit on slavery. Open Monday through Saturday, 9 A.M. to 5 P.M., and Sunday 1 to 5 P.M. Phone: (843) 722-2996.

Old Bethel United Methodist Church, 222 Calhoun Street. Though construction did not start until 1797, Old Bethel is the oldest extant Methodist Church in Charleston, and provides interesting insights to racial relations under slavery. The church was built by whites, free blacks, and slaves at a time when the Methodist Church still encouraged interracial worship. All that changed in the 1840s when the Methodist Church divided between North and South, with the latter supporting slavery and segregating services. Old Bethel, which is listed on the National Register of Historic Places, currently serves a largely African American congregation. Phone: (803) 722-3470.

Old Slave Mart, 6 Chalmers Street. Nothing about the South, including the American Revolution, makes sense without integrating slavery into the story. The Old Slave Mart, where people were bought and sold, was slated for demolition in 1960 when the Wragg sisters, Judith and Louise, realized the importance of preserving this vestige of African American history. It took these white women twenty years to pay for the Mart, and they never realized their dream of an African American museum on the site. The city now owns the site and there are plans to fulfill the Wraggs's vision of a museum. The Wraggs also collected more than twenty thousand books and documents relevant to African American history. This library is on Sullivan's Island and can be seen by appointment only; phone: (803) 883-3797.

Many of the historic homes and sites in and around Charleston are open all year; many others are open for tours from mid-March to mid-April. Schedules and fees (if any) being subject to change, you should check on these in advance through tourist agents or the Historic Charleston Foundation; phone: (843) 723-1623.

Cheraw, Great Pee Dee River, Chesterfield County. Because of its location on a navigable stream about 100 miles above the major port of Georgetown and covering the northeastern approaches to the state from North Carolina, Cheraw was of considerable strategic importance during the Revolution. It had been settled around 1752 by Welsh from Pennsylvania, and the church they completed in 1773 is the major architectural attraction in modern Cheraw.

A British punitive expedition under the notorious Major James Wemyss came up the Pee Dee as far as Cheraw soon after the coastal region was overrun in May 1780. When the enemy base was established at Camden, a major outpost was created at Cheraw in June. Major Archibald McArthur with his First Battalion, Seventy-first Highlanders, garrisoned the place until moved to Brierly's Ferry five months later. Meanwhile, hopes of the region's Patriots had been raised briefly when General Gates came by in August on his way toward Camden.

When General Greene succeeded Gates after the Camden disaster and adopted the unorthodox strategy of splitting his forces into two widely separated wings, he himself came with the larger force to the vicinity of Cheraw. His camp was selected by Colonel Thaddeus Kosciuszko 2 miles from the settlement, where modern Wallace is located. Here about one thousand troops camped during the period 20 December 1780 to 28 January 1781 while Lord Cornwallis tore his hair trying to figure out Greene's strategy. That strategy worked out beautifully, with General Dan Morgan winning a major victory at Cowpens, way off on the other side of the state, and both wings of Greene's army then running for Virginia with the British in hot but unsuccessful pursuit. Greene himself had reached the Cheraw encampment with Huger's Division on 26 December and had left with a small escort on 28 January.

When Cornwallis withdrew from Guilford Court House toward the port of Wilmington, North Carolina and Greene moved to attack Camden, Cheraw again became a critical point. Should Cornwallis turn and seek battle with Greene in South Carolina he would have to do so around Cheraw. Lee's Legion had the mission of screening against this threat, and when it did not materialize, the legion came through Cheraw to join up with Francis Marion's command along the Pee Dee.

The Heritage and Beauty Trail links the places of interest in modern Cheraw, which has an attractive district of old homes and a number of historic buildings. Most of these date from after the Revolution, but the notable exception, previously mentioned, is St. David's Episcopal Church. This is a simple but impressive white frame structure with a high belfry. The British used it as a hospital during a smallpox epidemic, and fifty patients are buried in a common grave in the churchyard. The Greater Cheraw Chamber of Commerce, located at 221 Market Street, is a good source of local historic information. Phone: (843) 537-7681.

Cherokee Ford, Savannah River. *See* under Georgia.

Combahee Ferry and Tar Bluff (Chehaw Point), Combahee River. The light brigade under General Mordecai Gist, which had been created to cope with strong foraging expeditions sent out by the British to supply their remaining garrisons at Savannah and Charleston in 1782, was ordered to destroy one of these forces in the Combahee River.

Gist set up a howitzer position at Chehaw Point, 12 miles down the meandering river from Combahee Ferry, where the British expedition of about eighteen sailing craft and five hundred troops was located. When he learned that the British were dropping down the river under cover of darkness, Gist moved his entire brigade toward Chehaw Point. Colonel John Laurens, ordered to move ahead quickly with an advance guard and secure the howitzer position, started from Gist's camp near the ferry and stopped briefly at the Stock Plantation, about 6 miles from his destination. At 3 A.M. on 27 August he resumed his march and walked into an ambuscade.

The skirmish that followed is well-known only because it cost the life of John Laurens, a fine young officer (see MEPKIN PLANTATION) who had distinguished himself not only as a combat leader on many major battlefields of the Revolution but also in a diplomatic assignment in Paris with Benjamin Franklin (spring 1781). Laurens was also notorious in his time for opposing slavery and proposing that slaves be offered their freedom in return for serving in the Continental army. With a reputation for "intrepidity bordering on rashness," as Washington put it, "and a love of military glory [that] made him seek it upon occasions unworthy of his rank," as General Greene said of him, the twenty-seven-year-old Colonel Laurens had left a sickbed to follow Gist from the Charleston area and plead for this assignment. He was killed in leading a charge against impossible odds because he had no alternative but surrender.

But all this should not obscure the superior military ability of the British in this clash. Learning of Gist's maneuver, they had landed three hundred regulars undetected on Chehaw Point and deployed to surprise the Patriot column on its line of march. After shattering the advance guard, the British rose from their positions in the tall grass and drove the survivors back onto the main body that followed. The regulars then formed a defensive line in rough, wooded terrain where the American cavalry could not operate to support Gist's infantry elements. Without the loss of a man, the British finally withdrew and carried on with their foraging. One Patriot in addition to Laurens was killed, about twenty were wounded, and the howitzer was captured along with its crew.

Old Chehaw Point remains unspoiled on the bank of the wide and picturesque Combahee River. To reach it from the U.S. 17 bridge over the Combahee (the site of Combahee Ferry; remains of an old fort are at the southwest end of the bridge), drive east for 2.2 miles and turn south on S.C. 162. Continue for 6.5 miles to the junction with S.C. 161. This is the site of the Stock Plantation, where Laurens spent several hours with Mrs. Stock and her family. He was buried just east of this road junction. "A small inclosure, without a stone, marks his grave," wrote Benson Lossing in 1849. (Laurens's cenotaph is on the site of Mepkin Plantation.)

Continue south, on S.C. 161, about 3 miles and turn right on the unimproved road that goes about 3 miles southwest to the river. The action took place along this route.

Congarees, The. *See* FORT GRANBY.

Cowpens. This national battlefield site is about 20 miles west of Kings Mountain, 11 miles northwest of Gaffney, and 2 miles southeast of Chesnee at intersection of S.C. 11 and 221. Take Exit 78 from the I-85.

Daniel Morgan (1736–1802) won a little masterpiece of a battle here on 17 January 1781, whipping the redoubtable Banastre Tarleton (1754–1833) and raising Patriot morale at a time when it badly needed raising. The battle is remarkable for the critical role played by terrain, and the site has been sufficiently well preserved and marked for a visitor to appreciate Morgan's tactical genius in selecting and using this unusual piece of ground.

The temperamental and irascible Morgan had come out of retirement and offered his services to Horatio Gates after that misguided general had led the Americans to a humiliating defeat at Camden. Shortly thereafter, Morgan was promoted to brigadier general, and he took command of a little force of light troops comprising 320 Continentals of the Maryland and Delaware line, 200 Virginia riflemen, and about 80 light dragoons. When

Nathanael Greene arrived on 3 December 1780 to replace Gates, this southern army had a handful of superb military leaders. Greene was probably second only to Washington as a combat leader. Morgan had established his record long before as a formidable leader of light troops, but even more important, he had two outstanding subordinate commanders: Colonel John Eager Howard (1752–1827), who led the foot elements, and Colonel William Washington (1752–1810), a distant cousin of the commander in chief, who led the dragoons. (A dragoon was a mounted infantryman. That is to say, he did not normally fight from horseback, but rode into battle and dismounted to fight on foot.)

Furthermore, to complete this all-star roster, militia general Andrew Pickens (1739–1817) arrived on the field on the eve of battle, and to his leadership is due most of the credit for the remarkably good performance of the militia at Cowpens.

The day before this great Patriot victory, however, nobody would have predicted such an outcome. Morgan had led his command from Charlotte, North Carolina, in a deep penetration of the territory supposedly under the control of Cornwallis and the Loyalists. (About three weeks after Morgan was detached, Greene further confounded his enemy by moving the rest of his little army to Cheraw, arriving there a few days before Christmas 1780.) On New Year's Day Cornwallis got alarming reports that Morgan was approaching the Loyalist stronghold at Ninety Six with three thousand men, and Tarleton was dispatched to that place to counter the American threat. The report was, of course, grossly exaggerated. Morgan had only one-fifth the strength reported to Cornwallis, and he was hampered by lack of supplies. William Washington had raided to within 15 miles of Ninety Six, but the Patriots were not about to try assaulting that place.

Cornwallis had the main body of his four-thousand-man field army at Winnsboro and was anxious to undertake a major offensive into North Carolina, but he could not start this until the threat of Morgan was eliminated. He therefore accepted the strategy proposed by Tarleton: with his legion and a reinforcement of supporting troops, Tarleton would take off through the rugged country of backwoods South Carolina and destroy Morgan or drive him toward Kings Mountain; Cornwallis would move toward the same point with the main body to trap the Americans who got away from Tarleton.

Morgan confounded this plan by not following the obvious and shorter route through Kings Mountain to rejoin Greene. Taking advantage of the numerous streams as delaying positions, the American commander withdrew in a more westerly direction. On 15 January, however, Morgan learned that Tarleton was on his track with a force that outnumbered him two to one. During the day Tarleton probed unsuccessfully for an unguarded ford on the Pacolet River. That night he faked a march up the stream, went silently into bivouac, and then moved downstream to make an unopposed crossing 6 miles below Morgan. The Americans were about to have breakfast at 6:00 the morning of 16 January when scouts clattered in with the reports of Tarleton's approach. Half an hour later Morgan was hurrying north to put the Broad River between him and the British, and Tarleton was eating Morgan's breakfast.

The peculiar piece of terrain called "Hannah's Cowpens" was known to some of the officers with Morgan as he moved northward that day. Not far off their route, this was relatively high, open ground where a wealthy Loyalist had owned extensive enclosures used for wintering cattle. It was a place where the Americans could stop and make a stand, and it had the additional advantage of being well-known to local guides because the Patriots had used it as an assembly point before the Battle of Kings Mountain. Bodies of militia were moving to reinforce Morgan, so this would be an ideal rendezvous. By mid-afternoon 16 January, when he was still 10 miles from the safety of the Broad River and 5 miles from Hannah's Cowpens, Morgan decided to head for that place and make a stand.

Looking at the prospective battlefield from the south, the direction from which Tarleton would approach it, Morgan saw a tree-dotted meadow rising gradually to a height of about 70 feet in total elevation. About 300 yards forward of this peak and 400 yards from the edge of the woods was a break in the ground known to tacticians as the "military crest" of the hill. That is to say, troops deployed along this crest would have a view of the lower slope and could cover it by fire. On the other hand, troops on the top of the hill would have their fire masked by such a military crest until the enemy reached it.

Morgan's unusual plan of battle called for three lines. The veteran Virginia riflemen and Continentals, under the command of John Eager Howard, would form the main line near the top of the hill. The bulk of the militia, under Andrew Pickens, would be deployed along the military crest, some 150 yards forward of Howard and at a lower elevation. Out in front of Pickens about 200 yards and well concealed in the grass and behind trees would be 150 picked riflemen of the militia.

Knowing that militia would not stand and fight like veteran regulars, Morgan devised unorthodox tactics to make use of the terrain so as to capitalize on their presence in large numbers. In so doing he showed the all-too-rare leadership quality of shaping his plans to the *weaknesses* of troops rather than exhorting them to make efforts of which they were incapable.

The 200-pound, 6-foot veteran of Braddock's massacre, Arnold's march to Quebec, and the two battles of Saratoga moved around his noisy bivouac the night before the battle and made sure that everybody understood what he wanted them to do the next day. He carefully explained to the militiamen that he wanted them to run, but that he first wanted them to actually fire their guns. The picked riflemen in the line closest to the enemy were to hold their fire until the last possible minute and then deliver only two shots. But Morgan wanted these to be two hits; then these men were free to drop back to Pickens's line. This stronger militia line was to do about the same thing: fire one or two shots from their muskets and then fall back. But they were to withdraw along a prescribed route, around the left (east) flank of the Continentals, and re-form in reserve.

While Morgan's troops were making careful preparations for the battle and getting a good night's rest, Tarleton's were making an exhausting night march through the brush. British scouts drew scattered shots from Morgan's forward riflemen when they reached the battlefield around dawn. Loyalist guides told Tarleton about this well-known clearing in the wilderness, but the British commander saw no need to waste time in reconnaissance.

Forming his infantry in line of battle on the southern edge of the clearing, and holding the Seventy-first Highlanders and 250 horsemen in reserve, Tarleton started the engagement in the standard European fashion: he ordered a wave of fifty troopers to charge forward to drive in the enemy skirmishers. The Georgia and North Carolina militia of Morgan's forward line squeezed off their two shots from hidden positions at close range and emptied fifteen saddles.

Even a horse cavalryman should have had enough sense to change his plans for a frontal attack. But not Tarleton. He led his infantry forward, Pickens held his fire until the range was closed to 100 paces, and then 450 militiamen fired on order. Many of the 100 British killed at Cowpens fell in this phase of the battle. Almost half of these were officers and noncommissioned officers, in accordance with Morgan's instructions to fire at the epaulettes and the crossbelts.

But when the militia withdrew, the British thought they had won the field and had only to mop it up. Tarleton re-formed his line and started for the crest of the hill. His men were cheering in triumph when the first volley hit them. While his line continued to press forward, Tarleton rode to the rear and ordered his reserve of two hundred kilted Highlanders and fifty attached dragoons to attack the American right (west) flank. To meet this new threat, Howard issued orders for the unit on the right of the line to withdraw slightly and face the enveloping force—a maneuver known as "refusing the flank."

The rest of the line misunderstood this maneuver and thought Howard had ordered a general withdrawal, with the result that the entire line started to the rear, although in good order. This accident was turned into a final triumph because Howard had the good sense to let the withdrawal continue, but he also kept it under control, and Morgan himself selected a new position to the rear. As the British rushed forward for the kill, the retreating Americans stopped, turned, fired a volley at point-blank range, and counterattacked with the bayonet.

William Washington had been watching all this from the flank, and led a well-timed cavalry attack against the British right and rear. Then to compound British misfortunes of the day, Pickens showed up at the head of the militia to attack the other flank.

Most of the British tried to fight their way out, but the battle was lost. Tarleton's final humiliation, which he richly deserved for his lack of mature military leadership in this action, was the refusal of his 200 legion cavalry to follow him in a final effort to save the day.

The fighting had lasted only an hour, but the British had 100 killed and about 830 captured. American losses were 12 killed and 60 wounded. Morgan wasted no time leaving the scene of his triumph, marching north at about noon and making camp on the other side of the Broad River. He rejoined Greene in North Carolina at Beattie's Ford.

In April 1972 Congress passed legislation creating the Cowpens National Battlefield Park. Formerly known as Cowpens National Battlefield Site, which comprised a mere 1.25 acres, it has been enlarged to 842 acres that include the major features of the battlefield. This national full-service park includes many hiking trails, including an interpretive Battlefield Trail that takes the visitor around the battle site. There is camping, a museum, and a visitors center with interactive panels and other educational media. The Battlefield is open daily except holidays, 9 A.M. to 5 P.M. Phone: (864) 461-2828.

Dean Swamp, just northwest of Salley, Aiken County. In May 1782 Captains Michael Watson and William Butler went to disperse a body of Loyalists here and were lured into an ambush. Watson and a sergeant were mortally wounded. Butler rallied the survivors in a farmhouse, and a rescue column came out from Orangeburg. Historians have long been confused about the date and place of this action. Heitman's *Register* says Michael Watson was killed at Sharon, Georgia, on 24 May 1782. But the death date on Watson's grave in Orangeburg is 5 May 1782. The site of the skirmish is said to be within a few hundred yards south of the S.C. 394 highway bridge over Dean Creek, about a mile northwest of Salley (once Johntown). A new marker is on S.C. 394.

Drayton Hall, 3380 Ashley River Road, Charleston County. "The best surviving example in South Carolina of the colonial plantation house," says the National Survey of this "monumental brick structure of two stories over a high basement, [with an interior] distinguished by spacious rooms with magnificent paneling and richly ornamented ceilings." "Especially impressive are the stair halls," this authority goes on to say, "with its double flight of stairs, and the entrance hall, with fireplace after a design by the great British architect Inigo Jones. The other rooms are almost equally fine" (*Colonials and Patriots*, pp. 161–162).

A landmark in the British military operations around Charleston in 1780, it was the birthplace of the fiery Patriot William Henry Drayton (1742–1779), whose father built Drayton Hall when he acquired the property around 1738.

In 1973 the National Trust for Historic Preservation and the Historic Charleston Foundation jointly leased the mansion and 633 acres with an option to purchase it for $680,900 (the appraised value of the property for tax assessment). Long unoccupied, the mansion is unique in that it remains unmarred by the addition of modern plumbing, heat, or electricity. It is one of only three mansions on the Ashley River not destroyed by General William T. Sherman's troops during the Civil War, spared because it was being used as a hospital for smallpox victims. Unusually, the plantation has a well-preserved slave cemetery and an excellent tour that discusses the role of slaves in building this plantation and investing their labor to create its prosperity. Important archaeological excavations are currently being conducted at this site. It has remained in the Drayton family for seven generations and is open daily, 9:30 A.M. to 4 P.M. Phone: (843) 769-2600.

Its grounds adjoin Magnolia Gardens. The property is about 2 miles north of the village of Drayton Hall (junction of S.C. 57 and 61) and is reached via S.C. 61.

Eutaw Springs Battlefield (lost site), village of Eutaw Springs on an arm of Lake Marion, Orangeburg County. A pretty little park maintained by the state on a curve of a country highway is the monument to the last major engagement in the South (8 September 1781), one of the hardest-fought battles of the Revolution and one of the most interesting. The British hero of the battle, Major John Marjoribanks (pronounced Marshbanks), is buried in the park, his remains having been moved there after Lake Marion overtook his original burial spot. Several historical markers summarize the action, and although the battlefield has not been preserved except for the park, it remains on firm ground—reports of its being submerged and lying underneath Lake Marion are greatly exaggerated. Take Exit 98 off I-95 and head east on S.C. 6 for 12 miles. Open daily, dawn to dusk.

Fairforest Creek ("the Forest"), Spartanburg and Union Counties. A picturesque battleground in the civil war between Whigs and Loyalists, the valley of this creek was known as "the Forest." The stream runs through Spartanburg, then generally midway between the Pacolet and Tyger Rivers before entering the latter at a point due south of modern Union. Colonel Thomas Fletchall was a principal Loyalist leader of the Forest until taken prisoner in the Snow Campaign of 1775. His impressive home overlooking Fairforest Creek has not survived, but the site is known. (It is on private property, a few miles south of Union near U.S. 176.)

Fish Dam Ford, Broad River, Chester County. Major James Wemyss with his one hundred mounted troops of the Sixty-third Foot and forty dragoons of Tarleton's Legion undertook to surprise the camp of General Thomas Sumter about 30 miles northwest of Cornwallis's base at Winnsboro. Five British dragoons had the special mission of capturing Sumter dead or alive, and the leader of this enterprise, Wemyss, was second only to Tarleton as an object of Patriot hatred and fear.

The British expected to surprise Sumter at dawn, 9 November 1780, at a place called Moore's Mill. But the Patriots had moved 5 miles south, to the east end of Fish Dam Ford. Here Wemyss rode into Sumter's outposts around 1 A.M., there was a quick volley of shots before the security detachment fell back, and the British commander toppled from the saddle with a broken arm and a wounded knee. Tarleton's troopers charged blindly ahead and were badly shot up. The British infantry went into action on foot, but finally withdrew after sustaining heavy losses.

As at Fishing Creek, Sumter escaped by making a run for it, but because it was dark he hid in the vicinity. About noon the next day he returned to his camp, where his troops had started reassembling a few hours after dawn and where a British sergeant had been left to tend the wounded. The story is that Sumter was handed a paper taken from Wemyss's pocket that listed the Patriots he had hanged and the houses he had burned on his expedition to Cheraw. Sumter allegedly threw the incriminating document in the fire. (Wemyss was paroled with the other wounded, presumably exchanged, was promoted to lieutenant colonel of the Sixty-third Foot in 1787, and left the British army two years later. But he does not reappear in the history of the Revolution.)

Fish Dam Battleground Monument is just east of the Broad River bridge on the north side of S.C. 72 and 121, more easily seen when the trees are bare. Visible when water is low during the summer, the "fish dam" is a zigzag chain of rocks built by the Cherokee as a dual-purpose ford and fish trap.

Fishing Creek (Catawba Ford), just north of Great Falls, Chester County. The loss of historic sites is usually lamented, but in the case of the Fishing Creek battlefield modern Patriots must secretly be happy. A granite marker on U.S. 21 just north of Great Falls indicates the general area of General Thomas Sumter's defeat on 18 August 1780. Sumter was retreating from Wateree Ferry and Fort Carey to escape British forces pursuing the survivors of the Camden disaster. Early on 17 August, Tarleton got on Sumter's trail. The next morning he pushed on with 100 dragoons and 60 infantry (riding double), cut down two scouts, and caught Sumter's command lolling around camp unprepared for action. With a loss of 16 killed and wounded, Tarleton killed 150 Patriots, captured 300, liberated 100 British prisoners, and recovered more than 40 loaded supply wagons. Sumter escaped by leaping bareback on a horse, and reports of this skirmish made Tarleton a hero in England.

The exact location of the action is not known. Most of the battlefield, if not all of it, is beneath Fishing Creek Reservoir near the dam. A granite marker is on the east side of U.S. 21 just north of Great Falls, on a dangerous hilltop curve. Just south of this marker is a loop of the older highway, and from this stretch of road the waters that cover Sumter's unfortunate campsite can be viewed.

Fletchall (Thomas) Estate Site. *See* FAIRFOREST CREEK.

Fort Charlotte (lost site), Savannah River, McCormick County. About 50 miles up the Savannah River from Augusta was Fort Charlotte of the colonial era. The first overt act of rebellion in the state took place when Patriots seized the fort on 12 July 1775 by order of the Council of Safety. After this the place was mentioned frequently in accounts of military operations across the Savannah River, so its map location is of historical importance. Opposite the mouth of Georgia's Broad River and covering Cowens Ford, the site is under the waters of J. Strom Thurmond Lake. S.C. 91, running southwest from Mount Carmel in the western tip of McCormick County, ends at the aforementioned body of water officially named J. Strom Thurmond Lake and Dam at Clarks Hill, which is in the general vicinity of the lost site.

Fort Dorchester, Ashley River, Dorchester County. At the start of the Revolution Patriot forces rebuilt Fort Dorchester on the site of a settlement that had existed here from 1696 (see MIDWAY under Georgia). Dorchester was a British base from April 1780 until retaken by General Greene's forces on 1 December 1781. The British garrison of 850 made the mistake of assuming that Greene's presence in the approaching column meant that he had his entire army with him, so they destroyed their supplies, threw their artillery into the river, and without a fight abandoned the last outpost around Charleston. The truth was that Greene had only two hundred infantry and two hundred cavalry, having sent the main body of his army to Round O, more than 20 miles to the west.

In Old Dorchester State Park, on S.C. 642 about 6 miles south of Summerville, the picturesque tabby ruins mark the site of the old town that was finally abandoned by 1788. (Do not confuse this place with the present town of Dorchester, about 20 miles to the northwest on U.S. 78.)

Fort Galphin (Dreadnought), Savannah River about 12 miles below Augusta (beeline) on Silver Bluff, extension of S.C. 32. A small stockaded place, home of George Galphin, deputy superintendent of Indian affairs, it was garrisoned by two Loyalist companies in May 1781 when the final siege of Augusta was undertaken. After Elijah Clark and Andrew Pickens had attacked boats bringing the annual royal presents for the Indians, driving their guard into Fort Galphin, Lee's Legion arrived from Augusta to capture the position on 21 May. With the loss of only one man, Lee took supplies and arms badly needed by the Rebels.

To reach the site, drive north from Jackson on S.C. 5 about 2 miles from the center of town (junction of S.C. 62 and 299 with 5). Turn west on the unimproved road that is joined by the extension of S.C. 32 a little more than a mile farther west, and continue about a mile to Silver Bluff. The site is now part of the Audubon Society's Silver Bluff Center and sanctuary. For the last several years, the Savannah River Archeological Research Program has been exploring and unearthing many noteworthy artifacts on the Fort Galphin site. Phone: (803) 725-3623.

Fort Granby (the Congarees), Congaree River below Columbia. A graveyard and historical marker just south of Cayce in Lexington County identify the site of Granby, once known as the Congarees. Here an Indian trading post was built in 1718. By 1754 this had grown into an important river depot and the seat of old Lexington District. The Cayce House, built in 1765 and surviving until modern times, was fortified during the Revolution and served as a major British stronghold from 1780 until its capture on 15 May 1781 by Lee's Legion.

Fort Johnson, James Island, Charleston. The principal fort guarding Charleston from naval attack in colonial times, Fort Johnson protected royal officials and papers during the Stamp Act crisis. When the Provincial Congress seized all authority in South Carolina after

Lexington and Concord, one of its first acts was to order the capture of Fort Johnson. The royal governor learned of this and started dismantling the fort, and the Patriots found only five British guards when they occupied Fort Johnson on 15 September 1775. No resistance was put up by the British; the twenty heavy guns of the fort were soon back in battery and they took part (ineffectually) in repulsing the attack nine months later on Sullivan's Island. The first flag of South Carolina was designed by Colonel William Moultrie and flown here after his troops occupied Fort Johnson. Maintenance was not kept up, and the fort was easily captured by the British from the land side when they attacked Charleston in early 1780. The brick powder magazine remains standing on the site of Fort Johnson, whose grounds are presently occupied by the Marine Laboratory of the College of Charleston. To visit the site, phone (843) 953-9200.

Fort Motte, on the Congaree River near its junction with the Wateree. The fortified mansion of the widow Rebecca Brewton Motte at this point on the old trail from Charleston to the backcountry was the principal British supply depot during their occupation of South Carolina. Motte was living in a nearby farmhouse when Patriot forces under Francis Marion and Harry Lee arrived on 8 May 1781 from their victory at Fort Watson to besiege the British garrison of 150 infantry and a few visiting dragoons. The Americans had started digging trenches for a formal siege when they learned that Lord Rawdon was abandoning Camden, and there was danger that he would rescue the Fort Motte garrison on his way south to the Charleston area.

Lee conceived the plan of quickly capturing the fort by using fire arrows to ignite the shingle roof of Motte's home, whereupon the patriotic lady not only granted her permission but also produced a fine East Indian bow and a bundle of arrows. When the approach trenches were within range, one of Marion's men lobbed two flaming arrows onto the roof, American artillery prevented the British firefighters from knocking burning shingles to the ground, and the defenders put up the white flag. The fire was then extinguished, and Motte served dinner to the British and American officers.

A village grew up around the Revolutionary War post, and the name Fort Motte survives on the highway map and in the Southern Railway system. Patriotic ladies of the twentieth century erected a granite marker on the site of Rebecca Motte's home in 1909, but this has since been abandoned in an overgrown area 1.5 miles straight-line distance northeast of Fort Motte village. The monument is shown on the Calhoun County highway map, but as of this writing is buried in the brush about half a mile from the nearest road. A DAR chapter is named for this prolific woman, and recent scholars of the American Revolution, intent on directing more attention toward women from this era, have done extensive research on Rebecca Motte's role in the war. Fort Motte is also known as the Mount Joseph Plantation, and is privately owned.

Fort Moultrie. *See* SULLIVAN'S ISLAND.

Fort Watson, Santee River (now Lake Marion). Preserved in a small, fenced park on the edge of Lake Marion near the northeast end of the highway bridges (I-95; U.S. 15 and 301) is the Indian mound where the British constructed a fort on their line of communications from Charleston to Camden. Named for the British Guards officer John Watson Tadwell Watson (1748–1826), who became a full colonel in 1783 and a full general in 1808, it was this officer's base of operations to defend the British supply lines against raids by American partisans. The fort comprised a small but strong stockade on top of the 30-foot-high mound (whose flat top is today a rough oval about 75 feet long and 50 feet wide), with three rings of abatis. Known earlier as Wright's Bluff, the site was on the edge of Scott's Lake, then part of the swamp-lined Santee River, and it had a commanding view over the bare plain by which an enemy would approach.

In mid-February 1781 General Thomas Sumter ordered General Francis Marion to join him for a campaign that was supposed to touch off a great uprising of patriotic militia along the Santee. The operation was premature; the British were at this time reinforcing security detachments along their extended line of communications, and Sumter was forced to scurry northward after failing in his efforts around Fort Granby, Belleville Plantation, and Fort Watson. His mismanaged attack against the last place on 28 February 1781 cost him heavy losses, and he suffered another reverse on Lynches River near modern Bishopville (see RATCLIFF'S BRIDGE) before temporarily calling off his private war to liberate South Carolina. (See CAMDEN for his negative role in the Battle of Hobkirk Hill.)

When General Nathanael Greene's regulars pushed into South Carolina after forcing Cornwallis to abandon his offensive in North Carolina, the time had come to start reducing British outposts between Charleston and Camden. The British, meanwhile, were making their last major effort to wipe out the partisan bands that had given them so much trouble, and Watson was given about half of Lord Rawdon's available field forces—some five hundred regulars and Loyalists—to run the "Swamp Fox" to ground and wipe him out. But Marion had been reinforced by the legion of "Light Horse Harry" Lee, and the fox turned against the hounds.

Lee linked up with Marion on 14 April 1781, and the next evening they invested the British garrison of eighty regulars and forty Loyalists under Lieutenant McKay at Fort Watson. Colonel Watson, meanwhile, had run himself ragged in trying to catch Marion, and had then been forced to take refuge at the British base of Georgetown. But the British and Americans around Fort Watson did not know that Colonel Watson would move from Georgetown to rejoin Rawdon at Camden (instead of coming to the relief of Fort Watson), and there was the very real threat that he might appear over the horizon.

Lieutenant McKay heroically declined the traditional surrender demand. When the besiegers seized his water point on the lake he quickly improvised a system whereby water from the lake filled a newly dug well. Lacking artillery and fearing the intervention of a British relief column, the Americans were becoming worried when Colonel Hezekiah Maham came up with the suggestion for building a type of siege tower that subsequently bore his name. Used successfully here and in later sieges, the Maham Tower was a fabricated crib of notched logs, rectangular in plan and topped by a protected platform from which fire could be delivered into a fort. Of flexible design, it could be made of varying heights and could serve as a platform for small cannon (see AUGUSTA under Georgia).

It took five days to prepare the logs, but a company of riflemen started delivering plunging fire into the fort at dawn on 23 April. When two assault parties attacked the abatis and the marksmen on the tower kept the defenders pinned down behind their stockade, Lieutenant McKay surrendered his garrison. Patriot losses were only two killed and six wounded.

Fort Watson was the first important British post retaken in the liberation of South Carolina. Rawdon abandoned Camden on 10 May and withdrew to Moncks Corner as the Patriots took Orangeburg, Fort Motte, and Fort Granby during the period 11 to 15 May.

To reach Fort Watson, take Exit 102 on I-95, look for the sign on U.S. 15 and 301 (named "Highway to Southern Living") about 8 miles southwest of Summerton and a little less than a mile short of the Lake Marion bridge. This highway also features the "Swamp Fox Murals Trail," a series of viewable, artful murals that demonstrate and honor the exploits of General Francis Marion. Drive northwest for about a mile to the site, passing the patrol station of the Santee National Wildlife Refuge. Plainly visible on the edge of the lake and indicated by a historical marker is the Indian mound with several flights of wooden stairs leading up one side.

Francis Marion and Sumter National Forest, northeast of Charleston, Berkeley, and Charleston Counties. These two parks make up nearly 600,000 acres. Although this remarkable reservation is not especially identified with the heroes for whom it is named, it deserves special mention in this guide for two reasons. First, it includes the following sites: Biggin Bridge and Church, Wadboo Bridge and Plantation (proposed Waterhorn Historic Area), Quinby Bridge and Plantation, a stretch of the King's Highway, St. James Santee Church, Hampton Plantation, and Leneud's Ferry (now Jamestown Bridge). Second, an exceptionally fine map is available through normal tourist information channels that shows not only these sites within the national forest but also the important historic landmarks to the west, along the Cooper River. These include Goose Creek (St. James) Church, Strawberry (the ferry site, the settlement itself, and the chapel), Moncks Corner, and Mepkin Plantation. For further information on this vast area call or write to the park itself. USDA Forest Service, 4931 Broad River Road, Columbia, S.C. 29212; phone: (803) 561-4000.

Georgetown, Winyah Bay, Georgetown County. The Pee Dee and three other rivers empty into the bay here to form one of the state's three major harbors. Georgetown was founded in 1735, became a busy port, and was surrounded by prosperous indigo and rice plantations. Parallel streets, most of them retaining such old royal names as Prince, Duke, King, Queen, and Orange, divide a quiet residential district of some thirty blocks in the center of Georgetown, where many eighteenth- and early-nineteenth-century homes, churches, and public buildings are preserved. Visitors may find remnants of the wharves along the Sampit River behind Front Street, where planters pulled in during colonial days to do their shopping, including for slaves, and where until not long ago the merchants of Front Street did as much business out of their back doors as on the street.

When the British occupied South Carolina in 1780 they established a small garrison in Georgetown. Francis Marion raided the town on 15 November 1780 and, supported by Lee's Legion, on 24 January 1781. In late July 1781 a body of General Sumter's irregulars plundered Loyalists in Georgetown, and the British retaliated by virtually destroying the town on 2 August.

Near Georgetown on S.C. 45 is the site of Belle Isle Plantation, where Francis Marion's family may have come to live when he was about six years old, and which his brother Gabriel owned at the time of the Revolution. Its handsome gardens are open to the public. Featured there is the Marion family cemetery, containing the remains of General Marion and his wife, among other descendents. Across the bay from here you can see North Island, where Lafayette and Kalb landed on 13 June 1777 to join the Patriot cause as volunteers.

Prince George Winyah Church, on Broad Street at Highmarket, about in the center of historic Georgetown, is a charming little brick structure of 1750 with a huge but graceful belfry dating from 1824. Phone: (843) 546-4358.

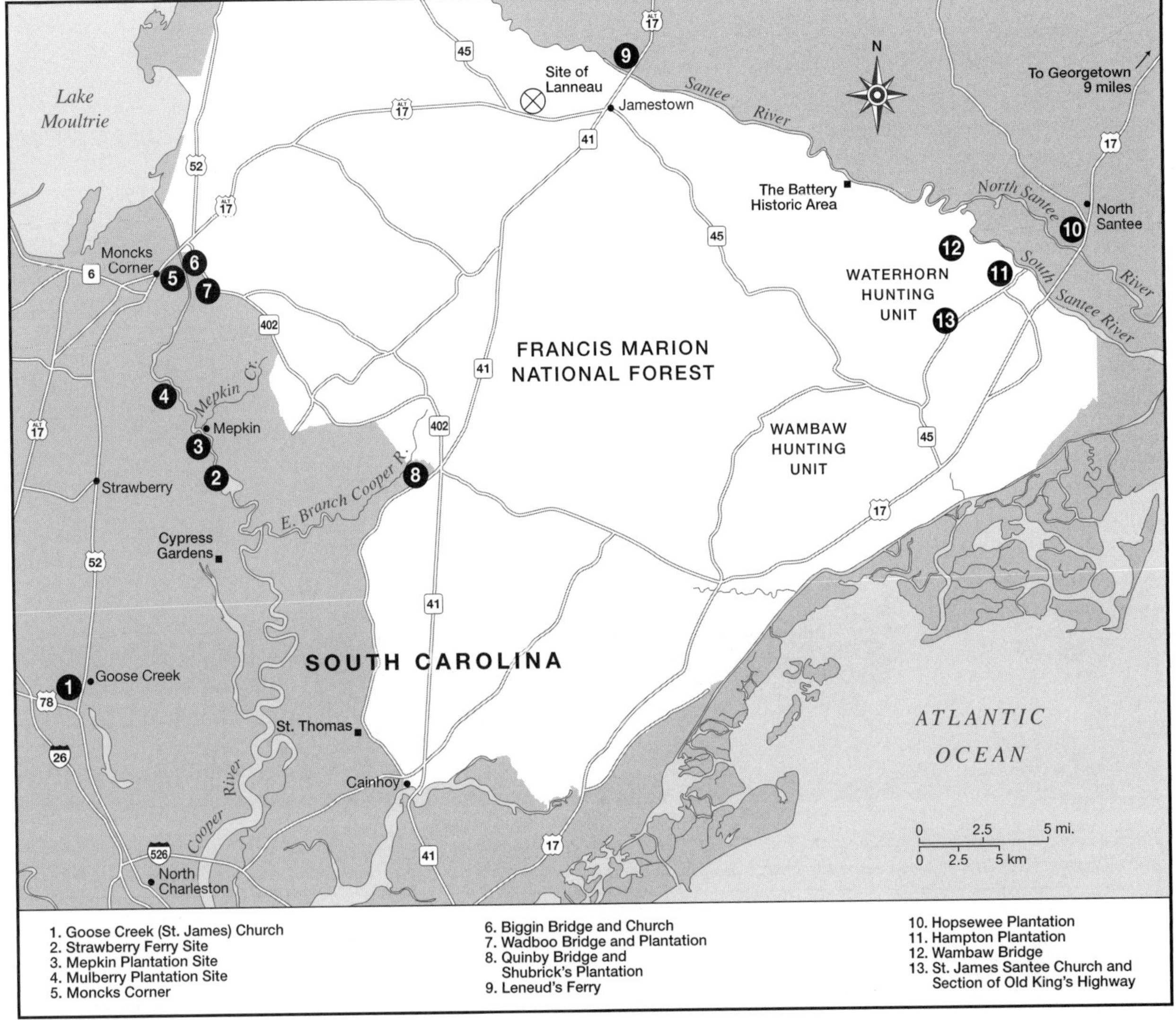

MAP BY XNR PRODUCTIONS. THE GALE GROUP.

British occupation troops used it as a stable. Annual tours of private plantations and town houses are sponsored in the spring by the Women of Prince George Winyah Episcopal Church. Phone: (843) 543-8291.

The Masonic Temple at Prince and Screven Streets was built in 1740 and long used as an inn. Washington addressed the Masons here in 1790.

The Georgetown Chamber of Commerce provides local historic site information through its website, newsletter, and pamphlets. Website: www.georgetownchamber.com; phone: (843) 546-8436.

Givhan's Ferry State Park, Edisto River, Colleton and Dorchester Counties, about 35 miles northwest of Charleston. One of the principal ferry sites on the Edisto from prehistoric times, Givhan's Ferry is mentioned frequently in literature of the American Revolution. It is preserved as a picturesque place of moss-draped oaks on high bluffs overlooking the dark waters of the Edisto. Fishing, hiking, camping, and picnicking are available. Phone: (843) 873-0692.

Goose Creek (St. James) Church, Berkeley County, Vestry Lane, off U.S. 52, about 15 miles northwest of Charleston. Built in 1719 in a prosperous region of old plantations, this parish church was the center of many skirmishes during the Revolution. According to tradition it was spared by the British because local Patriots had not vandalized the royal coat of arms, a re-creation of which may still be seen above the pulpit (the original having been destroyed in the earthquake of 1886). Wade Hampton raided the town on Sunday 15 July 1781, surrounding the

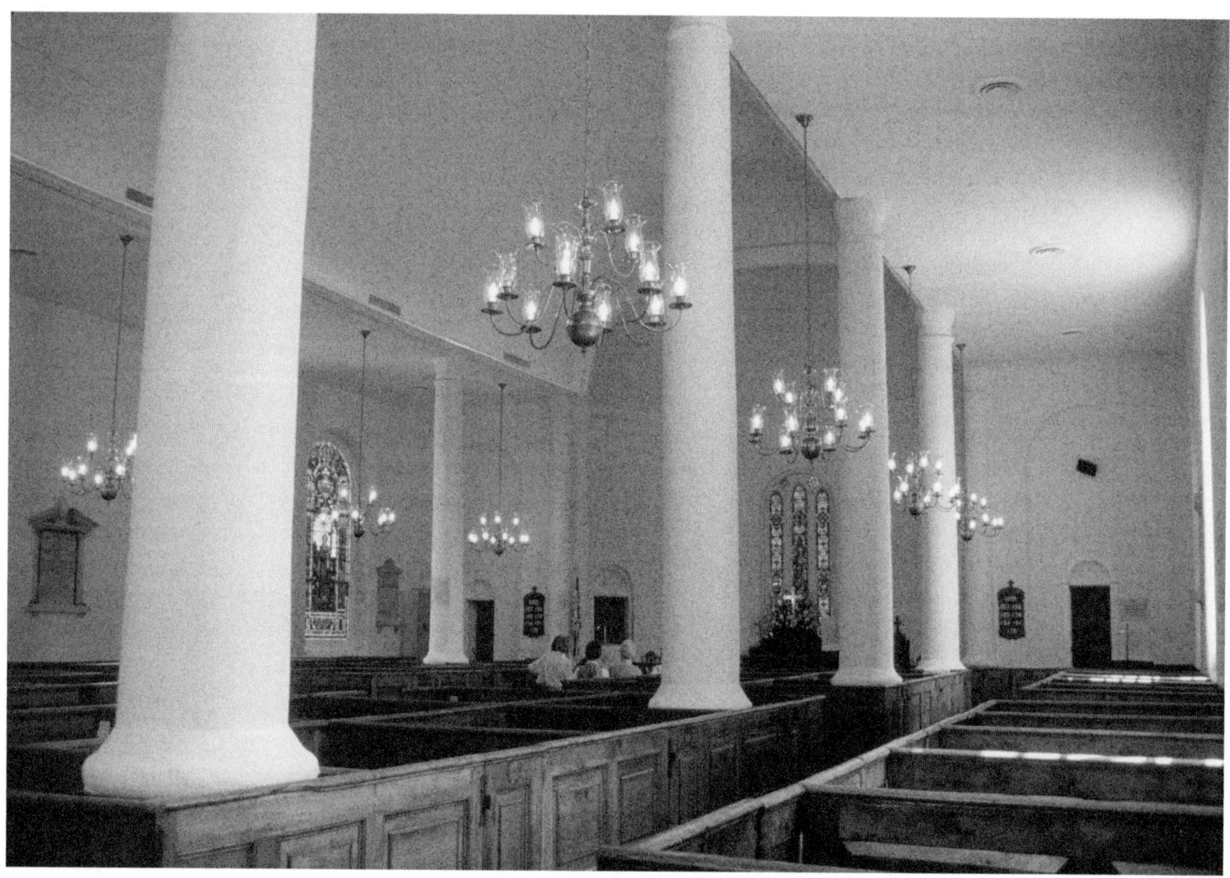

Prince George Winyah Church. *This small Episcopal church in Georgetown, South Carolina, was built in 1750, with the graceful belfry dating from 1824. British troops used the church as a stable during the Revolutionary War.* © LEE SNIDER/PHOTO IMAGES/CORBIS.

church during services and taking several Loyalists prisoners. The pretty little pink-stuccoed brick chapel, which closed in the nineteenth century for lack of parishioners, is well preserved and of exceptional interest. Its cemetery has twenty-seven graves dating back to the mid-eighteenth century.

Great Cane Brake, Reedy River, about 6 miles southwest of Fountain Inn, Greenville County. The successful conclusion of Colonel Richard Richardson's "Snow Campaign" to break up Loyalist mobilization in this backcountry region took place here in late 1775. Reinforced by militia from North Carolina, Richardson had more than four thousand Patriot troops by December, and Loyalist strength started fading away. Only Patrick Cunningham's band of about two hundred men remained in the field. At dawn on 22 December a force under Colonel William Thompson surprised the Loyalists in camp about 4 miles east of the Cherokee boundary line. Cunningham and a few others escaped, but five Loyalists were killed and about 130 captured at a cost of one Patriot wounded.

The "great cane brake" still covers the area, and a highway marker indicates the traditional location of the battle nearby. To find the highway marker, start at Fountain Inn on S.C. 418 and from its intersection with U.S. 276 drive southwest 5.5 miles (just short of the bridge across Reedy River). Turn right on the blacktopped road for a little more than half a mile, and the marker is at a house on the left. The battlefield supposedly is about 500 yards to the northwest, on the south side of the creek that feeds into Reedy River.

Great Savannah. *See* NELSON'S FERRY.

Halfway Swamp. About 10 miles downstream from where the Congaree and Wateree Rivers join to form the Santee there was a "Halfway Swamp" on each side of the Santee. Each was about halfway from Moncks Corner to the Congarees and Camden on main colonial routes. The name survives for the swamp on the right (west) bank, but the Halfway Swamp astride the Old Santee Road to Camden is now Spring Grove Creek. This is the place where Marion had the skirmish in December 1780 that is covered under SINGLETON'S MILL.

Hammond's Store (lost site), Laurens County. On 28 December 1780 Colonel William Washington led his 80 dragoons and 200 mounted militia on a 40-mile ride to Hammond's Store, where they found and brutally cut up a force of 250 Loyalist raiders, killing or wounding 150 and taking 40 prisoner. The next day Colonel Joseph Hayes rode westward and forced Patrick Cunningham to abandon a little fort at Williams' Plantation, only 15 miles north-northeast of Ninety Six. This caused Cornwallis to send Tarleton in pursuit of Morgan, which led ultimately to the dramatic American victory at Cowpens. The sites of Williams' Plantation and Hammond's Store (house) have been lost. If the former was 15 miles north-northeast of Ninety Six, its location would be around where S.C. 72 is intersected 2 miles northeast of Mountville by S.C. 49. Hammond's Storehouse was probably the site of the village of Huntsville that existed in the 1820s about 3 miles due south of the center of modern Clinton.

Hampton Plantation State Historic Site, lower Santee River, Charleston County. Heretofore open only on special occasions, this stately home is known to millions from its photographs. The home of South Carolina's first poet laureate (1934), Archibald Rutledge, a descendant of the original owners, Hampton House and the adjoining 322 acres were purchased by the state for development into a park. The surrounding grounds feature garden-lined paths, and a picnic shelter is included. A gift shop is located inside the house; a special feature there are the poetry books of Mr. Rutledge.

The existing mansion evolved from a small frame structure built in 1735 by Noë Serré. This passed in 1757 to his son-in-law, Daniel Huger Horry, who added a two-story ballroom on one end and a lofty bedchamber on the other. This Horry (there were many famous members of the family) was commissioned in the Second South Carolina Regiment at the start of the Revolution and commanded a company in the defense of Charleston in 1776, but took the oath of allegiance to the crown after the fall of Charleston to the British in May 1780. Little as we may admire his patriotism, we must acknowledge Colonel Horry as a pioneer conservationist, because his political agility is probably what saved Hampton House from destruction by the British.

Daniel Horry's successors, notably Eliza Lucas Pinckney (famous for developing the indigo industry in the South), gave Hampton House its present magnificence, the dominant feature being the six-column portico and pediment. Final touches were added in preparation for the visit of President George Washington in 1791.

Near St. James Santee Church and Wambaw Bridge, Hampton Plantation is on the beaten tourist track of U.S. 17 and 701 16 miles southwest of Georgetown. About a mile west of the Santee River bridge, turn north from the latter highway on S.C. 857 and go about 2.5 miles to the entrance of the plantation; from here a road leads about .75 mile eastward to the mansion. It is open year-round with special limited winter hours. Phone: (843) 546-9361.

Hanging Rock, just south of Heath Springs in Lancaster County. A huge boulder on a knob overlooking the creek has given its name to a landmark in this region since before the white man's arrival. The rock does not "hang" in the sense of being precariously balanced. It is a firmly planted boulder of spherical shape, about 25 feet in diameter, with what Benson Lossing in 1849 described as a "concavity . . . in the form of the quarter of an orange paring, and capacious enough to shelter fifty men from rain."

When the British occupied the backcountry after capturing Charleston in May 1780, they established a major base at Camden and pushed outposts north to Rocky Mount and Hanging Rock. In August, General Thomas Sumter moved simultaneously against both enemy positions, which had been stripped of British regulars and were held by Loyalists. Repulsed at Rocky Mount, Sumter concentrated his forces against the Loyalists at Hanging Rock. The Patriots had considerable success in preliminary skirmishes, but on 6 August were forced to withdraw after a fierce four-hour engagement and leave the Loyalists in possession of the battlefield. Sumter inflicted about four times as many casualties as he himself sustained, but victory was snatched from his grasp because his troops abandoned their military duties to loot the enemy camp and were unable to wipe out the hollow square formed by the Loyalists in the center of their camp.

The site is shown on the highway map of Lancaster County, but the route to the picturesque park around Hanging Rock is somewhat poorly marked. If you follow north from Camden on S.C. 58 you may find this "side trip" marked just south of Heath Springs. Look for a road junction about a mile south of Heath Springs and go east on S.C. 467 for 6 miles; cross the creek and follow a dirt road to the right that leads a few hundred feet to a DAR monument at the base of Hanging Rock. Across the creek to the right is the site of the Loyalist camp and the battle that took place in August 1780. This dirt road circles a collection of large boulders and continues to the famous "hanging rock." The site is comparatively unspoiled by human beings and affords a good view of the surroundings if the trees have shed their leaves.

To find the place from the main highway between Camden and Lancaster, follow S.C. 521 into Heath Springs. In the downtown area, US-521 makes a 90-degree left turn. At this point, SC-15 (Flat Rock Road) continues straight. Take Flat Rock Road about 2.5 miles to Hanging Rock Road, where a historical roadside marker is located. Turn left onto Hanging Rock Road, and Hanging Rock is located on the right immediately after crossing the bridge over Hanging Rock Creek.

Hayne Grave and Homesite, near Jacksonboro, Colleton County. On S.C. 64 about 1.3 miles north of its junction with U.S. 17 in the settlement of Jacksonboro is a marker to the Isaac Hayne tomb, a mile away at the end of a dirt road. Here at the site of a prosperous plantation, now an undeveloped region of timber operations and hunting camps, is a pathetic family cemetery where vandals have pried off the tops of tombs to look for skeletons.

Isaac Hayne was thirty years old when the Revolution started. Planter, breeder of fine horses, civic leader, slave-owner, joint owner of ironworks in the northern part of the colony (York district), Hayne was also a captain in the militia. He was taken prisoner at Charleston in May 1780 and paroled to his plantation, but when the British subsequently ordered him to join their armed forces, he considered his parole invalidated and took the field as a militia colonel. In July 1781 he was captured, charged with espionage and stirring up insurrection, brought before a court of inquiry (the British later cited the precedent of Major John André), and sentenced to death. On 4 August he was hanged in Charleston. Hayne's "martyrdom" was exploited to accelerate the recruiting of Patriot militia, and "the Hayne affair" was hotly debated in memoirs and histories of the Revolution. (See particularly the analysis by "Light Horse Harry" Lee in his *Memoirs* and the lengthy rebuttal of Lord Rawdon included in later editions of Lee's work.)

About half a mile across the fields from Hayne's grave, but now about 2.5 miles by road, was Pon Pon Chapel. About 6 miles to the east is Parker's Ferry Battleground, and one participant in the battle at that place mentions seeing the fresh grave of Colonel Hayne.

The skirmish in which Hayne was captured on 7 July within 5 miles of his home was in the Horse Shoe. Formed by Horse Shoe Creek and Chessey Creek, this is astride S.C. 199 and is intersected by S.C. 64 midway between Jacksonboro and Walterboro. Here Major Thomas Fraser with ninety dragoons surprised Hayne's camp, killed fourteen Patriots on the spot, captured Hayne, and liberated the turncoat militia general Andrew Williamson.

High Hills of Santee, Sumter County. Along the east side of the Wateree River is a narrow ridge extending about 40 miles, well known during the Revolution as the High Hills of Santee. The name probably comes from the French *santé,* health, rather than from the Indian name of the river to the south. To General Nathanael Greene the region was important for its healthful qualities. He withdrew his army into the High Hills for six weeks ending 22 August 1781, after the siege of Ninety Six and before the Battle of Eutaw Springs.

Greene headed for the Hills again after this major engagement on 8 September. Early in December he established a new base at Round O.

In modern times the High Hills have been depopulated, and in this scenic region of good climate and fertile fields there are the ruins of many fine old homes. Manchester State Forest and Poinsett State Park preserve most of the southern half of the High Hills but, curiously, their historic and picturesque name has virtually disappeared. Hikers and mountain bikers can enjoy the Palmetto Trail that runs for 14 miles through this part of the High Hills. Information on the trail and on the area's history is obtainable from the Palmetto Conservation Foundation. Phone: (803) 771-0870. The Borough House, a major landmark of the Revolution, is at Stateburg.

Hopewell (Pickens Home), about a mile and a half west and south of the Old Stone Church (see PICKENS GRAVE), on the Clemson University campus grounds, Pickens County. The house built on a knoll here in 1785 by General Andrew Pickens was later the home of his son and grandson, both of whom became governors of South Carolina. Across the highway north of the house is the site of the oak where Pickens negotiated the Treaty of Hopewell with the Cherokee (28 November 1785), confirming rights of these Indians to most of their land held in 1777.

Hopsewee Plantation, lower Santee River, Georgetown County. Birthplace and home of Thomas Lynch, Jr., who was sent as an additional delegate to the Continental Congress in 1776 to assist his ailing father. Young Lynch signed the Declaration of Independence, but he himself was suffering the effects of a fever caught while recruiting a company about a year earlier. Father and son started home to Hopsewee in the fall of 1776, but the father died at Annapolis. The son never recovered his health. In late 1779 he and his wife sailed for better climate and were lost at sea. Hopsewee was built of black cypress around 1740. The mansion has been little altered, and although it lacks the magnificence of nearby Hampton Plantation, it is of great architectural interest. The plantation is open to the public from 10 A.M. to 4 P.M., Monday through Friday from March through October, but only on Thursday and Friday during the winter months. Phone: (843) 546-7891.

Horse Shoe. Skirmish in which Colonel Issac Hayne was captured and General Andrew Williamson was liberated. See HAYNE GRAVE AND HOMESITE.

Hunt's Bluff, Great Pee Dee River, west of Blenheim 5 miles on S.C. 57. (This road makes a right angle turn to the north at this point; do not turn, but continue on an unimproved road a few hundred yards to the bluff.) In the sharp bend of the river, a group of local Patriots under Major Tristram Thomas captured several British supply boats by using the "Quaker gun trick": making a fake cannon from a log and bluffing the enemy into surrendering. The date was about 26 July 1780. Hunt's Bluff is a picturesque spot high above the Great Pee Dee, an important commercial and military route at the time of the Revolution.

Jacksonboro, near Edisto River, U.S. 17, Colleton County. An unattractive stretch on the main coastal highway is all that remains to commemorate the name of the place founded around 1735 and the provincial capital of the state in January to February 1782. The "Jacksonboro Assembly" was historic in that it was the first meeting of the General Assembly after the British overran South Carolina.

Jackson (Andrew) State Historical Park, Lancaster County. On U.S. 521, 8 miles north of Lancaster. A five-room log house, similar to the one in which Andrew Jackson was born (1767) at this place, is a museum of the rugged frontier settlement of the Waxhaws. In his early teens, when Loyalist raiders and British regulars battled Patriot partisans and Continental troops throughout this region, several members of Jackson's family took part in several actions. During the Battle of Hobkirk Hill near Camden in April 1781, Jackson and his brother Robert were imprisoned in Camden for having been present at a Patriot gathering. When a British officer told young Andrew to clean his boots, the boy refused on the grounds that such service was demeaning. The officer swung his sword, and in warding off the blow Andrew was cut on the left hand and head. His father had died just before Andrew's birth, his brother Hugh was killed in 1779, Robert died of wounds or the effects of disease contracted in the Camden jail (where the boys were held two months and where Andrew almost died of smallpox and mistreatment), and his mother died soon after moving to Charleston to serve as a nurse. Only fourteen at this time, having known war in the Waxhaws since he was nine, Jackson went on to become the seventh president of the United States.

The reconstructed blockhouse-home and the museum give an indication of what life was like on the Carolina frontier at the time of the Revolution. There is an equestrian statue of a young Andrew Jackson, and the 360-acre park also has recreational facilities. Phone: (803) 285-3344.

Juniper Spring, near Gilbert, Lexington County. Colonel Charles Mydeltons's force of 150 men from Sumter's command with the mission of harassing the British column enroute to save Ninety Six was ambushed and routed by Major John Coffin. The action took place about 18 June 1781 just northwest of Gilbert, where Juniper Creek begins. (The latter name survives.)

Kings Mountain. This national military park is just south of the North Carolina–South Carolina line off Interstate 85.

A murderous, bushwacking civil war was waged in the backcountry of the Carolinas between bands of Patriots and Loyalists. After the British captured Charleston (12 May 1780), Major Patrick Ferguson was given the mission of organizing Loyalist militia, and by June he had an army of about four thousand.

Ferguson had a flair for this work. Born into a good Scottish family (1744), he had been appointed a cornet in the Scots Greys at the age of fourteen. In 1768 he purchased a captaincy in the Seventieth Foot and served with it in putting down a slave uprising in the West Indies at Tobago. Impressed by the reputation gained by American riflemen in the early stages of the Revolution, Ferguson made an abortive attempt to introduce a new type of rifle into the British army. He invented an excellent repeating military rifle that was a century ahead of its time, and was doing well with an experimental body of riflemen when his right arm was permanently crippled at the Brandywine in September 1777. Although his force was disbanded and most of his rifles put in permanent storage (only two are known to still exist), Ferguson continued to impress his superiors with his "partisan abilities." In the summer of 1780 he was an officer marked for a long and illustrious career.

With his army of southern Loyalists and a few handpicked veterans from northern militia units, Patrick Ferguson then undertook operations in the western portions of the two Carolinas.

A number of important raids and skirmishes occurred, and in July a force of six hundred "Over Mountain Men" arrived on the scene under the command of Colonel Isaac Shelby (see SYCAMORE SHOALS AND FORT WATAUGA SITES under Tennessee). Patriot militia from Georgia and South Carolina were also in the area, commanded by Colonel Elijah Clark. The two Whig leaders had some success and were considering an attack on Ferguson's base at Ninety Six when the American disaster at Camden forced them to retreat hastily toward Gilbert Town (now Rutherfordton), North Carolina. Ferguson was in hot pursuit and only thirty minutes behind them when he got orders to attend an important conference.

Cornwallis told Ferguson he was preparing to invade North Carolina. The strategy was for the main British force under Cornwallis to overrun the centers of Rebel strength at Charlotte and Salisbury. Then the British could link the two Loyalist strongholds around Cross Creek (Fayetteville) and Gilbert Town, and the rebellion in the South would be crushed. Ferguson had already been as far north as Gilbert Town, and he assured Cornwallis that he had enough Loyalist support there to dominate the entire region.

With little opposition, Ferguson entered Gilbert Town and quickly convinced himself that his pacification program was a complete success. About the only organized militia resistance left was some 30 miles north, where Colonel McDowell's Burke County militia had not proved to be particularly troublesome. Even farther north were other backcountry militia, and way over the Blue Ridge Mountains were some scattered white settlements.

Before withdrawing temporarily from Gilbert Town on 10 September, Ferguson sent a warning to Colonel Shelby that if the mountaineers did not cease rebellion he would invade their territory, hang their leaders, and "lay their country waste with fire and sword." The addressees of this communication and a few other local chiefs had already decided to take care of Ferguson before he became more of a threat. The Loyalists had raided as close to them as Old Fort, in North Carolina, and having recently returned from a successful expedition against the Indian Confederation of the Ohio, the frontiersmen believed that this was a good time to attack the troublesome Loyalists on their eastern front.

Sycamore Shoals (now in Tennessee) was the place for the rendezvous of Patriot forces on 25 September. In response to the call for help, four hundred Virginia militiamen reported under the command of their gigantic leader, William Campbell. (The National Park Service pamphlet on Kings Mountain says, in eighteenth-century cadences, "As William Campbell reached maturity, he stood 6 ½ feet tall, was amiable when not enraged, and devoted to the cause of liberty.") There were five hundred Tennessee volunteers, and, strictly speaking, these were the only true "Over Mountain Men" at Kings Mountain; they were equally divided between the commands of Colonels Isaac Shelby and John Sevier.

Snow lay ankle-deep on the crest of the Blue Ridge when the column passed Gillespie Gap, North Carolina, but the 90-mile march to Quaker Meadows, North Carolina, was covered in five days. Here the forces of Campbell, Shelby, and Sevier were joined by North Carolina militia under Colonel Charles McDowell (160 strong), Benjamin Cleveland, and Major Joseph Winston (another 350 men from Wilkes and Surry Counties in the upper Yadkin region).

The Patriots thought that Ferguson was still at Gilbert Town, about 30 miles southwest, and on 1 October they started cautiously in that direction. But agents had informed Ferguson of the Patriots' departure from Sycamore Shoals, and he had withdrawn south on 27 September. The Loyalist leader had also been informed that Clark might be moving north to cooperate with the other Whigs in getting him, and on 30 September two deserters from the Sycamore Shoals column joined Ferguson and gave him further information. After moving due south toward Ninety Six to deceive his pursuers and also to intercept Clark, Ferguson then turned east toward Charlotte. He took his time, however, because the Patriots were moving with great caution, and he was expecting reinforcements from all quarters—from the Loyalists in his "pacified" province, from Ninety Six, and from Cornwallis. None of this help arrived, however. When he stopped for two days at the plantation of the Loyalist Tate, 50 miles from Charlotte, Ferguson sent Cornwallis a message on 5 October saying, "I am on my march towards you, by a road leading from Cherokee Ford, north of Kings Mountain." He sent a message the next day saying: "I arrived today at Kings Mountain & have taken a post where I do not think I can be forced by a stronger enemy than that against us."

As the Loyalists established their camp on top of a ridge that rose some 60 feet from the surrounding countryside, the Patriot force was camped 21 miles to the west at a place called "Hannah's Cowpens." Here their total strength was raised to about 1,800 by the arrival of 400 South Carolina militia under Colonel James Williams.

The future heroes of Kings Mountain had succeeded in mustering a remarkably large militia force, holding it in some semblance of order, and getting within striking distance of their quarry. Initially fooled by Ferguson's movement due south from Gilbert Town (see above), the Patriots eventually picked up Ferguson's trail. On 6 October, when they made camp at "the Cowpens," a spy confirmed earlier reports that their quarry was at Kings Mountain. But now there was a real danger that he would escape. If they waited until morning to move, Ferguson could leave Kings Mountain at the same time and be halfway to Charlotte when they reached Kings Mountain. They could not assume that the Loyalists planned to stand fast where they were, and as a matter of fact historians have since wondered how Ferguson could have made this mistake. The Patriot leaders therefore decided to march forward after dark. About nine hundred of the best horsemen started at 8 P.M., followed by the rest of the mounted men and the "footmen" as quickly as possible.

The night was dark and rainy. The path led through rough country, and there was the danger of bumping into enemy patrols or of being detected by Loyalists who would alert Ferguson. Men got lost during the night and had to be rounded up the next morning. Having followed Ferguson's route during the night, the Patriots made a detour around Tate's Plantation on the Broad River to avoid the possibility of finding a delaying force there, and they crossed the river 2.5 miles downstream at Cherokee Ford. The rain had stopped but a light drizzle kept up, and the riflemen had to take precautions to keep their weapons dry. Some of the leaders recommended calling a temporary halt to rest the flagging horses and men, but Shelby kept them going.

About a mile from their objective the Patriot troops dismounted, hitched their horses, and made their final preparations. Their opponents on the ridge ahead were totally unaware of their predicament.

The Scotsman Ferguson was the only non-American among the 1,100 officers and men gathered on Kings Mountain. Ferguson's second in command was a captain of the Fourth ("King's") American Regiment, Abraham De Peyster. He was from an illustrious and wealthy New York family, and his uncle (Arent Schuyler De Peyster) and two brothers were Loyalist officers.

The plan of attack adopted by the Americans was simplicity itself: to infiltrate into assault positions around the base of the ridge, completely encircling the enemy before he detected their presence, and attack simultaneously from all directions. Skill and luck were both on the side of the Patriots this day. The militia officers got their men into their assigned positions, and they achieved surprise in the military sense of "accomplish your purpose before the enemy can effectively react." As for luck, the Loyalists were incredibly lax in outposting their camp to prevent surprise, and the expected reinforcements from Cornwallis did not arrive

Kings Mountain is shaped like the sole of a giant foot. Ferguson's camp was on the front portion. At about 3 P.M. a Loyalist detachment fired on a column of troops that was advancing toward the heel of the foot, but other Patriot forces had already moved undetected toward the places where they would start working their way to the top of the ridge. Sevier and Campbell were the first to become heavily engaged, and their attack was against the back of the heel. Then Shelby attacked on their left, and the three Rebel forces converged toward the high ground at the heel. The fight seesawed back and forth as Loyalist counterattacks hit one threatened point after another, but the attackers won the high ground. As the surviving defenders fought a delaying action across the narrow part of the foot toward their camp, the other Patriot forces started their attack on all sides of the front end of the foot. Well thinned out by the fire of the Patriots, many of whom were at pistol range and just could not miss, the surviving Loyalists tried to make a stand behind the wagons in their bivouac. White flags popped up here and there, but Ferguson and his officers raced around, cutting them down and shouting encouragement to their troops.

When it finally stopped, 157 Loyalists lay dead and 163 were too seriously wounded to be evacuated. All the rest of Ferguson's corps, about 700 officers and men, were prisoners. The attackers are said to have had 28 killed (which is probably an accurate figure) and 62 wounded. (This last figure does not square with the normal ratio of about three wounded for each man killed in this sort of an engagement.) Dr. Uzal Johnson, the New Jersey Loyalist who was the surgeon for the "British," tended all the wounded.

The Patriot army started disintegrating when the battle ended. On Sunday, the day after the battle, the militia who had not already left for home and the prisoners who had not already escaped left Kings Mountain and headed for Gilbert Town. Near here they held a court-martial, convicting thirty Loyalists of various crimes, sentencing twelve to death, and hanging nine. The rest of the prisoners were marched north, many escaping from the careless Patriot militia guards, and the rest being eventually exchanged.

The Kings Mountain battlefield was long avoided, even by the morbidly curious. It was in an area that was inaccessible as late as 1849, when Benson J. Lossing beat his way there gathering material for his monumental *Pictorial Field Book of the Revolution.* In 1815, however, a veteran of the battle organized an effort to bury the scattered bones left by wolves and to mark the common grave of Major William Chronicle and three others. Patriot organizations eventually got national recognition of the site, and in 1931 the National Military Park was established. This now includes nearly 4,000 acres, and it adjoins Kings Mountain State Park, where there are camping and other recreational facilities. The park is open daily from 9 A.M. to 5 P.M. Phone: (864) 936-7921.

The site of the battle is well organized. The museum has displays and exhibits explaining the strategy and tactics of the historic American battle. A self-guiding walking tour starts near the museum, where the first shot was fired, and leads to where the first heavy action took place. The trail then passes the peak first captured by the Patriots and follows their route along the ridge to where the battle ended. The spot where Ferguson is believed to have been mortally wounded is marked. A handsome monument, dedicated in 1930 by President Hoover, stands by the traditional rock cairn of Ferguson's grave. Farther along the trail are the Chronicle markers of 1815 and 1914, the spring used by the Loyalists before the battle and later by the wounded of both sides, and the positions from which the Tennessee Over Mountain Men began their attack.

Kingstree, Black River, Williamsburg County. Where the bridge now crosses the river on the southwest edge of Kingstree, there once stood a white pine blazed with the broad arrow that meant it was reserved for the king's use, destined to become a mast for the Royal Navy. Around this great tree in 1732 a body of Irish Calvinists built their clay shelters to establish Williamsburg Township, one of the first nine inland settlements. With Camden and Orangeburg it remains among the survivors of this abortive program.

After the fall of Charleston (May 1780), paroled Patriots of this region became enraged by British depredations and formed four militia companies under Major John James. In August 1780, at what is now the head of Academy Street, they made a stand against raiders led by the notorious Major Wemyss (see FISH DAM FORD). After sustaining heavy losses—some accounts say thirty killed—they rallied and drove the larger force back into Georgetown County. A few months later they became part of the nucleus for Marion's Brigade, forming a company under Major James. A large British raiding force was heading for Kingstree in March 1781 when blocked by Marion at Lower Bridge.

Lafayette-Kalb Landing Site, North Island, Winyah Bay, Georgetown County. On 13 June 1777 Lafayette landed here with Johann Kalb and other volunteers to seek their military fortunes with the Continental army. They selected this remote spot to elude the British blockade, and North Island remains accessible only by boat today.

Leneud's Ferry, Santee River on U.S. 17A. Here on 6 May 1780 Tarleton with 150 dragoons decimated a much larger force of Continental dragoons from New Jersey and Virginia under Colonels Anthony Walton White and Abraham Buford. White was falling back on Buford's position around the ferry after a successful raid to the rear of the British expedition that had recently taken Moncks Corner. Unaware that Tarleton was on his trail, White had reached the ferry and was preparing to evacuate his eighteen British prisoners when Tarleton struck. Taken completely by surprise, the Patriots lost about one hundred men killed, wounded, and captured.

The place gets its name from the Lanneau family, Acadians who came here with other refugees from Nova Scotia after their eviction in 1755. Their settlement was about 5 miles west of the present-day Jamestown bridge on U.S. 17A, but because of yellow fever it had not prospered, and many of the Acadians had left before the Revolution. Many variations of Lanneau (now generally "Lenud") are used as the name for this site, but all are mispronounced "Lenoo."

Lower Bridge, Black River, 5.5 miles south of Kingstree, Williamsburg County. In the third engagement between Marion and Watson in March 1781 (see WIBOO SWAMP), Marion blocked the British drive toward Kingstree. The battle took place where S.C. 377 now crosses Black River.

Lynches River, 6 March 1781. *See* RATCLIFF'S BRIDGE.

Manigault's Ferry, Santee River just below junction of Congaree and Wateree Rivers, Calhoun County. On 23 February 1781, the day after his abortive attack at Belleville Plantation, Sumter captured a supply train here on its way to Fort Motte.

Marion Tomb, Belle Isle Plantation site, Berkeley County. North of Lake Moultrie and east of Lake Marion, about a mile north of S.C. 45, is the simple but handsome tomb of General Francis Marion, the legendary "Swamp Fox." There is no proof that Marion's parents lived at this Belle Isle Plantation, or at the one near Georgetown, as one reads in tourist guides. But Francis did live at various times in the house built by his brother Gabriel at this first-mentioned "Belle Isle." The house survived until modern times. Francis built his own home, Pond Bluff, a few miles to the southwest (see below).

Marion's reputation as a partisan leader was established at numerous places identified throughout this book's section on South Carolina. When all organized military resistance had been destroyed by the British in the spring of 1780, Marion raised and led the band of irregulars in the coastal region who kept Patriot hopes alive until Continental troops could be sent south to drive the invaders out. What should be said here about General Marion, because it is not apparent from considering his exploits individually, is that he had the capacity for subordinating his operations to the overall strategy directed by his superiors. Brilliant as he was in independent actions, he was the rare partisan who could cooperate with other military commanders in operations not of his own conception and not to his own liking. In this he stands in sharp contrast to General Thomas Sumter.

Elected to the state senate for the session starting at Jacksonboro in early January 1782, Marion had to return almost immediately to resume command of his brigade because his principal subordinates let their personal jealousies stand in the way of their military duties. Moody, introverted, and semiliterate, Sumter had all the military qualities demanded of the situation when he started his career as an unexcelled partisan leader. After the Revolution he held various honorific offices, served off and on in the state senate, and married a wealthy cousin about eight years before his death at the age of sixty-three.

The tomb of Marion is reached by taking S.C. 45 west from Pineville about 3.5 miles and going north 1 mile on a blacktop road. In the bend of the Santee about 3.5 miles beeline to the northwest is Gaillards Island, where Marion had a base for about a month. Running generally south from here into Lake Moultrie is Old Canal, dating from the late eighteenth or early nineteenth century. Near Eadytown, reached by S.C. 45 continuing west and near the mouth of the Diversion Canal, was Pond Bluff, acquired by Marion in 1773. The house burned in 1816, but some of the original furniture is preserved in the present structure built in that year.

Mathew's Bluff, Savannah River, Allendale County. On 3 March 1779 General Griffith Rutherford was crossing with eight hundred North Carolina militia from this position into Georgia to join General John Ashe when the latter was surprised at Brier Creek and his force annihilated (see this last site in the section on Georgia). In April 1781 a skirmish took place around Mathew's Bluff in which Lieutenant Kemp of the King's Rangers was killed while trying to disperse Patriots who were attacking British boats on the river. The site is at the end of S.C. 41, accessible by road only from the South Carolina side. From U.S. 301 take S.C. 26 south (from the road junction of S.C. 3, 5.7 miles east of the Georgia line). A little less than 9 miles south is the intersection of S.C. 41. Go right (southwest) for 1.4 miles to the boat ramp. (Georgia authorities put Mathew's Bluff about 3 miles farther north on the Savannah, around the place now called Red Bluff Point.)

Mepkin Plantation, Cooper River about 30 miles above Charleston. Now a Trappist monastery and tree farm, 3,000-acre Mepkin Plantation was the principal holding of Henry Laurens (1724–1792). He was a highly successful merchant and planter (owning several plantations on the Georgia coast and a large tract around Ninety Six), and in the events leading to the American Revolution he became increasingly involved in politics. In 1777 he was elected to the Continental Congress, and in November of that year he started a one-year term as its president during a period of particularly bitter factionalism. Resigning this office in protest, he was elected to negotiate a treaty with the Netherlands, and in September 1780 was captured at sea. The British recovered incriminating documents thrown overboard by Laurens and used these as a pretext for declaring war on the Dutch. Laurens unsuccessfully pleaded diplomatic immunity, was held for treason in the Tower of London for fifteen months, and finally was released on heavy bail and exchanged four months later for Cornwallis. He was indirectly involved in peace negotiations while recuperating at Bath, and took part in the last two days' work in Paris before the preliminary articles were signed. For the next eighteen months he had a semi-official diplomatic role in negotiations between the French and British on the final peace treaty, finally returning to America on the fourth anniversary of his capture. Early the next year, 1785, he retired to spend the last seven years of his life at Mepkin.

Henry's son John had been killed in the skirmish at Combahee Ferry (see COMBAHEE FERRY AND TAR BLUFF) in the final phases of the war. The elder Laurens was in bad health after his own exertions during the Revolution, and he suffered heavy property losses. He stipulated that his body be cremated, a highly unusual practice in eighteenth-century America.

Mepkin's plantation house, long since destroyed, was on one of three fingers of high ground overlooking the river. Simple gateposts on the highway, the mile-long avenue of live oaks, other ancient trees, and the general landscaping of the magnificent site survive, and the Laurens cemetery is preserved. The burial plot has the cenotaph of John Laurens. The chapel and gardens of what is now called Mepkin Abbey are open to the public daily from 9 A.M. to 4:30 P.M. Phone: (843) 761-8509. Mepkin Plantation was the last home of dramatist and diplomat Clare Booth Luce and her husband Henry, who was editor of *Time* and *Life* magazines. The couple donated the home to the Catholic Church.

Middleton Place Gardens, Ashley River, 14 miles northwest of Charleston. In 1741 Henry Middleton built his mansion (destroyed by fire at the end of the Civil War) and started developing the magnificent landscaped gardens that can be seen today. Henry Middleton (1717–1784) was one of the colony's greatest owners of land and slaves. He became leader of the opposition in 1770, was sent to the first Continental Congress, and served as president of that body for about seven months (to May 1775). He resigned his seat in 1776 and was succeeded by his son Arthur, who became a signer of the Declaration of Independence. Arthur Middleton (1742–1787) declined the governorship of South Carolina in 1778, took an active part in the defense of Charleston in 1780, and was a prisoner at St. Augustine for more than a year. Exchanged in July 1781, he returned to Congress. After the war he lived at Middleton Place, which had been partially destroyed by the British in 1780, and his granite tomb is in the gardens.

An English landscape architect and one hundred men spent ten years creating the gardens conceived by Henry Middleton. French botanist André Michaux planted America's first camellias here in 1783; three of the original four still flourish in the midst of their proliferation and other plantings. A link with prehistory in this highly sophisticated landscaping is an Indian trail tree, the Middleton Oak, whose age is nearing one thousand years. The Middleton Place museum official described it in 2005 as the "largest specimen in the garden." The restored south wing was a private residence until 1975, and is now part of the site's house museum tour. The unusual charm of this large Georgian structure in its setting of lush American vegetation can be seen from near and far as you tour the estate. The plantation has an excellent section devoted to slave life, including artisan crafts mastered by some of the fifty slaves on the plantation during the Revolution. Eliza's House, named for its last occupant, Eliza Leach, was the home of a group of freed slaves who stayed on the plantation after emancipation. Many activities are provided in the plantation stableyards, including crafts demonstrations, guided tours, and outdoor activities including mule-drawn wagon rides. The Middleton Place Foundation, formed in 1974, preserved and maintains the site. Website: www.middletonplace.org; phone: (843) 556-6020. It is open year-round and is located at 4300 Ashley River Road, 14 miles north of Charleston.

Mobley's (or Gibson's) Meeting House, northeast of Jenkinsville, Fairfield County. Patriot militia under Colonel William Bratton, Major Richard Winn, and Captain John McClure dispersed a body of Loyalists at a Baptist meetinghouse in Mobley's settlement. The date probably was in June 1780, the Patriot uprising (as at Beckhamville) being inspired by alarm over Buford's Defeat. Documentary evidence (Winn's supported by British accounts) indicates that the action took place not at Mobley's Meeting House but at Gibson's Meeting House. State historical authorities say the site is on S.C. 247 just north of the bridge over a branch of Little River. (S.C. 247 goes southeast from S.C. 213 at a point .6 mile east of where S.C. 213 joins S.C. 215 about 3 miles north of Jenkinsville.)

Moncks Corner, Cooper River about 30 miles north of Charleston. This place, scene of several Revolutionary War skirmishes, takes its name from Thomas Monck, who bought a plantation here in 1735 and established a store on the "corner" formed by the main roads from Charleston north to Murray's Ferry and northwest to the Congarees. When the Revolution started it was an important commercial center, and when the British surrounded Charleston on three sides in April 1780 the Rebels were able to keep open a tenuous line of communications up the Cooper to supply depots at Moncks Corner and Cainhoy (on the Wando River). General Isaac Huger had the mission of protecting these critical points, and was stationed near Moncks Corner with about five hundred Patriot troops.

The British formed a task force to cut the Charleston garrison's last links with the interior. Tarleton's Legion, who were badly in need of horses to replace those lost in the rough passage south from New York, and a force of about 150 British rangers under Patrick Ferguson were the vanguard of this expedition. But the real power was supplied by the Thirty-third Foot, commanded since 1775 by Lieutenant Colonel James Webster. An acting brigadier after distinguishing himself in the northern theater against Washington's army, Webster had overall command of the 1,400 troops in this important operation.

On the evening of 13 April, Tarleton and Ferguson were approaching Moncks Corner from Goose Creek when they captured a slave messenger who revealed the disposition of Patriot forces and became a guide for the British. Tarleton advanced undetected by Patriot patrols and at about 3 A.M. attacked the ineptly organized defenses around Biggin Bridge. The British had only three casualties in overrunning the position, killing about 20 Patriots, capturing approximately 70, taking more than 40 loaded wagons, and picking up between 300 and 400 horses. Webster arrived on 15 April with two regiments to consolidate Tarleton's gains, and the fate of Charleston was sealed.

Moncks Corner of the Revolution was about a mile northeast of the place that perpetuates the name. The site is just south of the U.S. 52 bridge over the canal connecting Lake Moultrie with the Cooper, and this place is opposite the ruins of Biggin Church (see BIGGIN BRIDGE AND CHURCH).

Motte's Plantation. *See* FORT MOTTE.

Mount Hope Swamp, often referred to as the Battle of Wyboo Swamp, near Santee River, south of Greeleyville, Williamsburg County. About 15 miles eastward on the Old Santee Road from his losing encounter with Marion at Wiboo Swamp on 6 March 1781, Colonel John Watson's column was again stopped. Colonel Hugh Horry of Marion's command had destroyed the bridge across Mount Hope Swamp and established a defensive position. Watson had to deploy and use his artillery to drive the Patriots back. Striking toward Kingstree, Watson was blocked next at Lower Bridge.

To trace the line of operations from Wiboo Swamp to Mount Hope Swamp, follow the route of the Old Santee Road. From I-95 Exit 115 take Historic U.S. 301 north. Turn south (right) onto S.C. 260, then turn right on Patriot Road (Secondary Road 410). The site is at the end of the road.

Mulberry Plantation, Cooper River about 30 miles above Charleston. Privately owned and not open to the public, Mulberry Plantation qualifies as a National Historic Landmark. Its ricefields, dikes, and canals survive in a good state of preservation. The mansion, part of it dating from 1714 and major alterations from 1800, is in excellent condition and of considerable architectural importance. During the Yamassee War of 1715 to 1716 the plantation house was fortified, and British commanders used it as a headquarters during the Revolution.

A sign to Mulberry Plantation is on U.S. 52, 3 miles south of the Moncks Corner town line, and the mansion is a little more than 2 miles due east.

Murray's Ferry, Santee River, Berkeley-Williamsburg County lines. Between Moncks Corner and Kingstree, a long causeway takes U.S. 52 over the Santee Swamp, following the trace of the colonial road. The modern bridge marks the site of Murray's Ferry, where the British established a post after taking Charleston during May 1780. Marion's part-time home, Belle Isle Plantation (see MARION TOMB), was within 7 miles of this ferry (beeline distance); in the latter part of the Revolution he had a base nearby at Cantey's Plantation. According to some sources, Marion captured the British base at Murray's Ferry on 23 August 1780.

Musgrove's Mill State Historic Site, Enoree River, about 27 miles south of Spartanburg near the bridge on S.C. 56. From 56, go approximately 7 miles northeast of Exit 52 on I-26. An important skirmish around Musgrove's Mill, particularly significant because it was one of the few times the untrained American militia defeated professional British troops, took place on 18 August 1780. The National Survey puts "Musgrove's Mill Battlefield, Union County," in the category of "Sites Also Noted."

The fight came about because Colonel Isaac Shelby and Lieutenant Colonels Elijah Clark and James Williams were sent to break up a concentration of Loyalists at Musgrove's Mill. A large expedition of Loyalists under Major Patrick Ferguson had advanced through this region from Ninety Six into North Carolina, and the Patriots were rallying to stamp out what could have developed into a large-scale Loyalist uprising in the backcountry of the Carolinas. The Patriots discovered that the Loyalists around the mill had been reinforced by British regulars, so instead of carrying out their original plan of launching a surprise attack, the Americans took up a defensive position just north of the Enoree and near the mouth of Cedar Creek. They then succeeded in luring the enemy into an ambuscade, killing 63, wounding 90, and capturing 70 with the loss of only 4 Patriots killed and 8 wounded.

The triumph was due primarily to the success of Captain Shadrack Inman and 25 volunteers who drew the British regulars and Loyalist militia into the main Patriot position organized on a ridge just north of the ford. Although outnumbered 500 to 200, the troops of Shelby, Clark, and Williams waited coolly behind a hasty breastwork until the unsuspecting enemy had charged within point-blank range. Inman was fatally wounded by a retreating Loyalist.

Inman's grave is on the ridge just north of the river and alongside S.C. 56. It is generally agreed that this is where the action ended. The county to the south, in which the mill itself was located and where the Loyalists camped, has tried to claim the battlefield, and a historical marker established north of the river in Union County was improperly moved south of the river into Laurens County. The Patriot camp on the eve of the battle was along Cedar Creek in the southeast tip of Spartanburg County, roughly 3 miles from where Captain Inman was buried. It is possible that the Patriot defensive lines were in Spartanburg County, perhaps between Cedar Creek and the Enoree. The old frame house of the Musgroves, used as headquarters by the British during the battle, was burned by vandals in late 1971. The state purchased the property and developed the attractive grounds into a park in the early 2000s. The battlefield has been preserved, and a series of interpretive panels in the park's visitors center chronicle the battle. The park offers picnicking, fishing, and hiking, and is open 9 A.M. to 6 P.M. all days except Tuesday and Wednesday. Phone: (864) 938-0100.

Nelson's Ferry (lost site), Santee River (now Lake Marion). The major crossing place of the upper Santee River, about 9 miles downstream from Fort Watson, Nelson's Ferry is mentioned frequently in Revolutionary War literature of South Carolina. In the same area, and also lost beneath the waters of Lake Marion, was Great Savannah, where Thomas Sumter's plantation was located. (Some sources indicate that this plantation, burned by Tarleton's men in the summer of 1780, was 6 miles above Nelson's Ferry. Others say it was just north of the ferry. But the names Nelson's Ferry and Great Savannah are used synonymously in many accounts.) As a newly commissioned brigadier of state militia, Francis Marion on 20 August 1780 surprised a guard of British regulars at Sumter's abandoned plantation and liberated 150 Maryland Continentals who had been captured four days earlier at Camden.

The flooded site is on the county line due north of Eutawville.

Ninety Six, Greenwood County. Astride S.C. 248 about 2 miles south of the present village of Ninety Six and identified by historical markers on the highway are extensive remains of the settlement and fortifications of Old Ninety Six.

The place-name derives from the erroneous idea that the distance to Fort Prince George, the frontier outpost on the end of the Charleston Path, was 96 miles. In 1730 a trading post was established at Ninety Six. This formed the nucleus for a sizable fortified settlement that grew up during the next two decades, and in 1769 it was selected as the first place for construction of an upcountry courthouse. When the split with England evolved, Loyalist

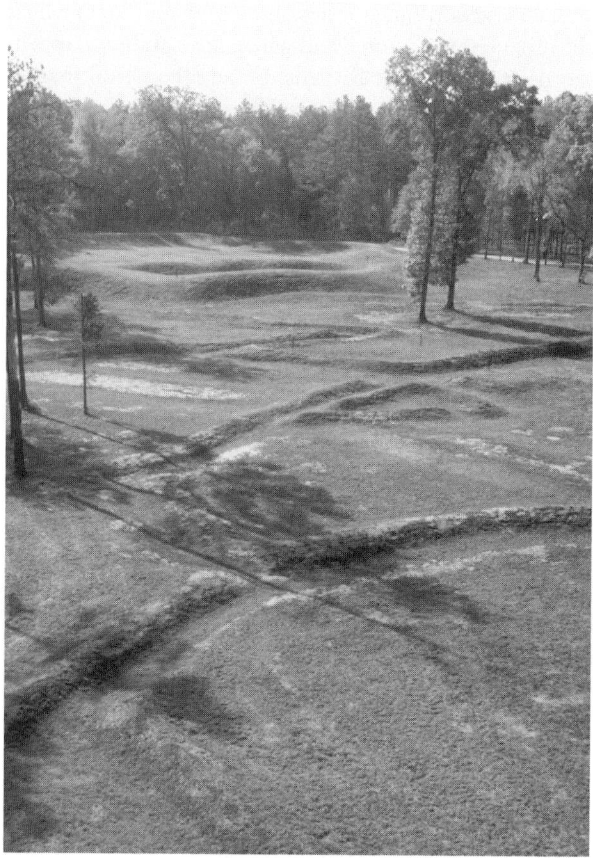

Siege Trenches at Ninety Six. *The unusual name of this site in Greenwood County, South Carolina, derives from the erroneous idea that the distance to Fort Prince George, the frontier outpost at the end of the Charleston Path, was ninety-six miles. Ninety Six was the scene of several battles during the American Revolution.* © WILLIAM A. BAKE/CORBIS.

sentiments prevailed in this region as they did in Augusta and the backcountry of Georgia, some 45 miles due south; close military ties existed throughout the Revolution between these two Loyalist strongholds.

Between August and November 1775 there were three confrontations between Patriots and Loyalists that brought opposing factions to Ninety Six. In each case the Patriots were forced to back off in the face of superior Loyalist strength before there was any significant bloodshed, but these uprisings are interesting because they involved leaders who became well-known in the history of the Revolution. On the Patriot side were William H. Drayton, the Reverend William Tennent, and Major Andrew Williamson. Loyalist leaders were Thomas Fletchall, Moses Kirkland, Robert and Patrick Cunningham, and Thomas Brown.

When the British shifted their main military effort to the South, they established principal Loyalist strongholds at Augusta and Ninety Six. In the summer of 1780, after the fall of Charleston, a force of about four thousand Loyalists was raised at Ninety Six by Majors Patrick Ferguson and George Hanger to rally Loyalist supporters in the backcountry of the two Carolinas. Ferguson's advance toward the Blue Ridge Mountains of North Carolina intensified the bloody warfare between Whigs and Loyalists in this spacious frontier region, but led to the great Patriot victory at Kings Mountain. Fear for the security of Ninety Six a few months later caused General Cornwallis to send Tarleton in pursuit of General Dan Morgan, which ended with another American triumph, the Battle of Cowpens. Meanwhile, a relief column from Ninety Six enabled Colonel Thomas Brown to hold Augusta.

In May 1781 the Rebel field army under General Nathanael Greene besieged Augusta and Ninety Six simultaneously, forcing the British to abandon Camden because their lines of communication to Charleston were being destroyed by Greene's operations. Augusta fell because no outside help could be furnished, and Ninety Six then bore the full weight of Greene's efforts.

The defenses of Ninety Six at this time consisted of the stockaded village of that name, a strong redoubt shaped like a star and encircled by abatis and a ditch, and a detached work called Fort Holmes off the opposite corner of the fortified village. A ravine separated Fort Holmes from the village, but a covered way permitted the defenders to shift forces safely between the outwork and the main defensive position. The post had a garrison of 550 Loyalist troops: Colonel Andrew Devaux's South Carolina militia (200 strong), the New Jersey Volunteers (200), and De Lancey's New York Volunteers (the Third Battalion, numbering 150 officers and men). Their commander was Colonel John Harris Cruger, scion of a prominent New York family, who had come south with the British expedition that took Savannah. After leading the First Battalion, De Lancey's Volunteers (Cruger was a son-in-law of the senior Oliver De Lancey), in the capture and subsequent defense of Savannah, Colonel Cruger had succeeded Colonel Nisbet Balfour as commander at Ninety Six in August 1780. (See also AUGUSTA, under Georgia.)

General Greene reached Ninety Six on 21 May 1781 to undertake the siege of this bastion. Having detached Lee's Legion to reinforce General Andrew Pickens's siege of Augusta, Greene had about one thousand Continentals and an unknown number of ineffective militia troops initially. When the siege was into the nineteenth day (8 June), Lee and Pickens joined Greene to play a major role at Ninety Six.

Meanwhile, Greene's operations were along lines recommended by his engineer officer, Colonel Thaddeus Kosciuszko, a Lithuanian-born and French-trained officer who had joined his staff after serving four years in the North. He had distinguished himself as a military engineer in planning the defenses of the Delaware River in 1776, in stopping Burgoyne's offensive in New York, and in fortifying West Point. In North Carolina he had played a key role in planning Greene's operations. But the siege of Ninety Six was his first experience in formal siegecraft, and he made two errors: instead of giving first priority to cutting off the defenders' water supply in the ravine to the west, Kosciuszko started digging regular approaches toward the star redoubt, and he also began these works too close to the enemy's positions.

Cruger had only three small cannon (3-pounders), but he mounted them on an elevated platform, and under cover of a surprise fire of artillery and small arms, sent out a raiding party that destroyed Kosciuszko's initial work. The Rebels backed off, and it took them eleven days to complete the second leg of their zigzag approach and regain the point from which they had first started. Loyalist raiding parties had continued to interrupt the work, but Greene was now able to bring his light artillery to bear. (He had no proper siege guns.)

When Lee arrived, he began siege operations against Cruger's water supply in the ravine west of the village. Kosciuszko had meanwhile put men to work on a tunnel north of the star redoubt and was getting along well until the defenders started getting vibrations and sent patrols out to check. They not only found the tunnel, overrunning a gun battery on the way, but they also found and wounded Kosciuszko—in "the seat of honor," as one contemporary British writer put it.

The Americans erected a Maham Tower (see FORT WATSON), but the Loyalists countered by raising the parapets with sandbags. The attackers used fire arrows (see FORT MOTTE), but the defenders stripped the shingle roofs from their buildings. When Lee's siege works got so close on the west side that Loyalist guards had to be withdrawn from the water supply, naked African American Loyalists sneaked out at night to get water. The defenders dug a 40-foot well through heavy clay within the star redoubt, but they did not find water. (Vestiges of the hole have survived.)

Cruger's food supply was adequate, but his soldiers and the refugees at Ninety Six suffered from the scorching sun, lack of water, and the artillery bombardment. Greene's troops had started the fourth week of their siege when word came from General Sumter that a British relief column from Charleston was coming his way. Sending General Andrew Pickens and Colonel William Washington with all the American cavalry to reinforce Sumter, and calling on Marion to do the same, Greene hoped to block the force from Charleston until he could force Cruger to surrender. Simultaneous assaults were launched against the star redoubt and Fort Holmes at noon on 18 June. Captain Michael Rudolph of Lee's Legion fought his way into the latter position, but the 150 New York Loyalists in the redoubt repulsed the attack and then sallied forth to drive the Patriots back with heavy losses before they could reorganize for a renewed effort. The next day Greene withdrew, and on 21 June, Lord Rawdon reached Ninety Six with two thousand British regulars.

The twenty-eight-day siege cost Greene about 150 men (killed, wounded, and missing), and Cruger lost about half that number. But the best indication of the effort made by the defenders is that fifty of Lord Rawdon's men died of sunstroke during their withdrawal to Charleston, and Rawdon was invalided back to England. (A young officer of twenty-seven at this time, he recovered to become a full general, governor-general of India, the first marquess of Hastings, and in his declining years, governor and commander in chief at Malta. See CAMDEN.)

Although Greene had suffered another tactical defeat at Ninety Six, he had taken another step toward strategic victory. The British abandoned this last backcountry post and consolidated their forces along the coast. Greene rested his army in the High Hills of Santee before resuming operations that achieved the final liberation of the South in December 1782, when the British evacuated Charleston.

Fortunately for historic preservation, the village of Ninety Six was displaced 2 miles due north when the railroad came through in 1855. The ruins of old Ninety Six are therefore in country that has been spared urbanization. Benson Lossing quotes a letter he received in 1849 from a gentleman in old Cambridge, a village very near old Ninety Six: "The trees and shrubbery on the battle-ground are considered by the inhabitants too sacred to be molested." The major landmarks are remarkably well preserved by the federal government, which implemented a National Historic Site on the grounds in 1976. Outlines of the star redoubt are covered by scattered trees and bushes, but the earthworks, 4 to 5 feet high, are clearly discernible. Within their perimeter is a great depression, the vestige of the 40-foot well dug by the Loyalists. Part of Kosciuszko's abortive tunnel is still there. Other identifiable landmarks are the ravine where the defenders got their water (a creek named Springs Branch), the level area where 582 Patriots under Major Andrew Williamson had a three-day battle with about three times as many Loyalists in November 1775 (around Fort Holmes, see below), the site of the old brick jail used as a stronghold by Cruger's Loyalists, and the site of the courthouse completed in 1772 and used as barracks in 1780 to 1782. Also to be seen on a one-mile walking tour are vestiges or locations of the defenses and siege works of 1781, the village, and the wooded area where a large burial ground rests, although the origin of its inhabitants is yet to be determined.

Rumored to be a slave burial ground, it is located along Gouedy Trail. This preserved trail was originally the work of Robert Gouedy, who established a trading post here in 1753. Another significant trail within the park is Cherokee Trail. Visitors can walk the grounds on a self-guided tour where informative panels offer insight into the 989-acre park's history. The memorial to James Birmingham, the first South Carolina soldier to die in the American Revolution, is located along this trail. Inside the visitors center a ten-minute film outlines the military significance of the area, and Ninety Six National Historic Site maintains numerous hiking trails and opportunities to picnic.

The Star Fort Historical Commission was established in 1969 to develop and administer the site before the commission turned it over to the federal government and then dissolved. The site is open daily 8 A.M. to 5 P.M. Phone: (846) 543-4068.

Ninety Six was added to the National Register of Historic Sites in 1974. It claims the distinctions of being the site of the first battle of the Revolution in the South, the strongest fortification in the South, and the scene of the longest siege conducted by the Continental army.

Oconee Station State Historic Site, on S.C. 95, about 5.5 miles due north of Walhalla, Oconee County. This 210-acre state park contains a stone fort (1792) named Oconee Station and a two-story brick house known as the William Richards House. The fort, one of three erected around 1760 as fortified outposts on the Cherokee border, was probably used successively as a haven for frontier families, a military base during the Revolution, and an Indian trading post. On S.C. 95, where the Ring Fight and Andrew Pickens Homesites are located, it is a few miles southeast of Oconee State Park and is reached by paved road from Picket Post on U.S. 271. Phone: (864) 638-0079.

Old Iron Works. *See* WOFFORD'S IRON WORKS.

Orangeburg, Edisto River, Orangeburg County. One of the first nine inland townships established in the 1730s to develop the interior regions of the colony, Orangeburg is one of the few that survive as places of any significance. The first permanent settlers were Germans and Swiss, who named it for the Prince of Orange. When South Carolina mobilized in early 1779 to meet the threat created by the British invasion of Georgia, Orangeburg became the center of military operations, and Governor John Rutledge established headquarters in the Donald Bruce House.

The British established a post at Orangeburg in 1780. When Lord Rawdon started regrouping his forces in the spring of 1781 to meet the major counteroffensive conducted by General Nathanael Greene to liberate the South, the British commander at Orangeburg did not receive the order to abandon his position. On 11 May 1781 he surrendered his garrison of fifteen regulars and an undetermined number of Loyalists to General Thomas Sumter.

But because of its central location, almost equidistant from Augusta, Ninety Six, and Charleston, Orangeburg continued to be used as a British base. Rawdon massed his field forces here in July 1781 after forcing Greene to abandon the siege of Ninety Six. Lieutenant Colonel Alexander Stewart held Orangeburg with his regiment, the famous Third Foot ("Buffs"), until he succeeded Rawdon as commander of troops opposing Greene in the field. With the last British outpost withdrawn to Charleston in December 1781 and Greene's army gaining in strength, the role of Orangeburg in the Revolution was ended.

The Donald Bruce House has survived. Moved to a new location on Route 301, two miles north of the Orangeburg town limits, the two-story frame building remains structurally sound and has been developed into a historical site.

Information on other Revolutionary War landmarks in Orangeburg is available through the Orangeburg Historical Society. Phone: (803) 535-0022. Another source is the town's Chamber of Commerce. Phone: (803) 534-6821.

Parker's Ferry Battleground, Edisto River, Colleton County. Not to be confused with modern Parker's Ferry on U.S. 17 in Charleston County, some 6.5 miles due south of the Revolutionary War site, old Parker's Ferry was 6 miles due east of Pon Pon Chapel. Here, in a desolate area of hunting and fishing camps, is the site of Marion's brilliant victory in mid-August 1781. Of perhaps more interest to students of the Revolution are the extensive earthworks rediscovered in recent years and not yet understood by historians.

Old Parker's Ferry was on the main highway in colonial times, although it is now approached by an unimproved road through lonely country. In the summer of 1781 the civil war between Patriots and Loyalists rose to a crescendo, the unfortunate Isaac Hayne being summarily executed by the British on charges of treason (see HAYNE GRAVE AND HOMESITE) and some 450 Loyalists taking up arms. From Dorchester the British sent a force of regulars, including Hessians, under Major Thomas Fraser to forage south toward the Georgia border and to support the Loyalists. General Nathanael Greene's Patriot army was resting in the High Hills of Santee when he received an appeal for help from Colonel William Harden. Greene relayed the call to Francis Marion, asking him to do what he could.

Covering about 100 miles by night marches, the one hundred picked partisans under Marion's command reached Parker's Ferry shortly before Fraser approached that place on the return toward Dorchester. He camped at Hayne's plantation the night after the unfortunate colonel was brought home for burial. Alerted to Marion's presence, the British commander started off the next afternoon with his infantry and artillery in the lead and his cavalry following. About a mile west of the ferry, where a long causeway crossed a swamp, a small party of Rebel horsemen suddenly appeared and then turned tail. The British cavalry took off in hot pursuit.

This was precisely what Marion had hoped for, but the results were greater than he could have expected. When hidden marksmen blasted the first wave of British riders with a surprise fire of buckshot at 50 yards' range, Fraser rallied his troops and led them in another charge that caught two more volleys. Marion counted twenty-seven dead horses and estimated his men had killed or wounded one hundred enemy dragoons, but a British participant wrote: "We lost 125 killed." The Patriots withdrew because they were low on ammunition, but not a man was wounded, and Marion promptly rejoined Greene. It was a masterpiece of partisan warfare.

The substantial earthworks at Parker's Ferry are something of a mystery. Large trees growing from the embankment and brickwork in the vicinity indicate that the works date from the Revolution. The American army camped at Parker's Ferry on 17 May 1779 with several wagon loads of entrenching tools, and the Continentals were supposed to fortify their camp whenever they halted. (General Augustine Prevost's diversionary raid on Charleston in the first half of May 1779 probably took the British through Parker's Ferry, after which they withdrew along the coast to Savannah. It would therefore be logical for the Patriots to see the need for fortifying Parker's Ferry later in May 1779, and the surviving earthworks may date from then.) The site is located a few miles north of Jacksonboro, off S.C. 64, nearly 2 miles past Hayne's tomb. At that point, turn right on a dirt road noticeable by a Parker's Ferry historical marker. The ruins are off to the right. Call (843) 717-3090 for more information.

Visitors to the site should be sure to continue another mile north on the road from Pon Pon Chapel, where they will find a much more rewarding view of the Edisto River. Here to the north the banks are higher and afford a better picture of what the ferry site of the colonial era probably looked like. Casual tourists with low-slung cars and skittish families may find that the site of Parker's Ferry is too far from the beaten track, and even the most adventurous should be warned that the road is not passable during rainy periods.

Pegues Place, Pee Dee River just north of Cheraw in Marlboro County. An important cartel for the mass exchange of prisoners was signed in the home of Claudius Pegues (pronounced "puh-GEEZ") on 3 May 1783. The house is in excellent condition and is occupied by descendants of the original owners. It is open to visitors on special occasions, but its location makes it easy to find and see from the outside. From U.S. 1 just 0.6 mile south of the state line, turn west on S.C. 266 and go one mile. Pegues Place is to the right front, a two-story, white frame, clapboarded house with a raised porch and chimneys on each end.

Pendleton District. Created in 1800 to encompass the area later organized into the counties of Anderson, Pickens, and Oconee (established 1826–1868), this is Andrew Pickens country. It also is exceptionally scenic and rich in facilities for outsdoorsmen. The Pendleton District Historical and Recreational Commission provides a number of tri-state brochures detailing historic sites and walking tours.

These guides are normally available at welcome centers on main routes leading into the state. They are also available by contacting the commission and requesting that they be mailed. Website: www.pendleton-district.org; phone: (864) 646-3782.

Pickens Grave, Old Stone Church, southeast edge of Clemson on U.S. 76. General Andrew Pickens (1739–1817) ranks with Marion and Sumter as a Revolutionary War hero in South Carolina. Born in Pennsylvania, he moved with his family as they lived successively in the Shenandoah Valley of Virginia and in the Waxhaws of South Carolina. While in his late teens he took part in an expedition against the Cherokee (1761). Two years later he and his brother settled in the Pendleton District, where Andrew started a long career as a public figure. He was for this region what Marion and Sumter were for the piedmont and coastal areas. For his part in the victory at Cowpens, Congress presented him with a sword that has been preserved by his descendants. A representative of the Ninety Six District from 1782, he was in Congress for the 1793 to 1795 session and then served as a state major general. In 1785 he built Hopewell, and his last home was near the site of his legendary Ring Fight.

Old Stone Church, where he is buried with men who followed him at Ninety Six, Cowpens, and Eutaw Springs, was built during the years 1797 to 1802. Austere as the major American hero who lies in its yard, the barnlike structure of natural fieldstone is an interesting historical and architectural landmark.

See PENDLETON DISTRICT for visitor information.

Pon Pon. The Yuchi Indians had a village in southwest South Carolina called Pon Pon, and this was also their name for the Edisto River. The name survives in Pon Pon Chapel, and the skirmish at Bee's Plantation is listed by some authorities as Pon Pon.

Pon Pon Chapel, old Parker's Ferry Road, near Hayne Grave and Homesite, Colleton County. From U.S. 17 in Jacksonboro take the road north toward Round O, following S.C. 64 for 2.2 miles, then County Road 40 for .6 mile to its intersection with the dirt road to Parker's Ferry Battleground. To the south (right) about .1 mile east of the blacktop road to Round O is a chain-link fence encircling the ruins of this old brick chapel. Through the locked gate at a distance of about 100 yards can be seen the brick corners of the ruined structure rising to a height of about 20 feet, with a narrow, arched window preserved. The church was established here in 1725, and John Wesley preached on this spot in 1737. The brick chapel was built in 1754 and destroyed by fire in 1801.

Port Royal Island, Beaufort County. Between Charleston and Savannah is a cluster of coastal islands forming a great natural harbor. The Spanish and French were attracted to the region, making landings and establishing missions in the sixteenth century. In 1710 the British laid out Beaufort (still pronounced "Bewfort," in the British fashion), making it the oldest city in the state after Charleston. The first in a long series of man-made and natural disasters struck almost immediately: the Yamassee Indian uprising of 1715 killed several settlers and forced the rest to escape to a ship in the harbor.

When the British captured Savannah, and Patriot forces started massing along the lower Savannah River, Beaufort was picked as the place for the invaders to strike next. Taking advantage of their naval supremacy, they sent two hundred regulars under Major Gardiner to Beaufort. This was supposed to be a strategic envelopment or turning movement to force General Benjamin Lincoln to abandon his positions along the Savannah and retreat to protect his line of communications to Charleston. Instead, Lincoln ordered General William Moultrie to meet the threat by turning out the militia.

With three hundred Charleston militia and twenty Continentals, the Patriot column under Moultrie marched south from Gardens Corner to cross Whale Branch at Port Royal Ferry and make contact with the enemy about 3 miles farther south (historical markers on U.S. 21 at Grays Hill). Here on 3 February 1779 the inexperienced Patriot militia got the best of the British regulars in a hot little skirmish lasting about forty-five minutes. The British had the advantage of being deployed with some cover and concealment in the sparsely wooded patch of higher ground and bordering swamps, but their single artillery piece was disabled early in the action. Moultrie was running out of ammunition for his infantry and two guns, but shortly after ordering a withdrawal he discovered that the enemy had already started a retreat. Moultrie was unable to pursue vigorously, but the British took to their ships and returned to Savannah. The Americans lost about thirty killed and wounded in this highly creditable performance, and enemy casualties (exact numbers unknown) were much higher. More than a strategic triumph for the southern Patriots, it was a morale builder that stimulated recruiting.

For the last three years of the Revolution, a British base was maintained at Beaufort. Lieutenant Colonel John Maitland established this in June 1779 when he withdrew from the Charleston area after his rear-guard victory at Stono Ferry. About three months later he led his large command in a remarkable movement through coastal waterways to elude the Franco-American forces that should have prevented him from reinforcing the garrison of Savannah.

Today one can follow U.S. 21 between Gardens Corner and Beaufort to trace Moultrie's route. A highway bridge arches high over Whale Branch where Port Royal Ferry once operated. The battlefield around Grays Hill is an unattractive scene of commercial development and highway construction at this writing. Once the visitor passes through the crust of contemporary civilization, they will find historic Beaufort preserved in an exceptionally attractive district of well-maintained old homes on large lots. Many eighteenth-century town houses and plantations have survived, but most of Beaufort's architectural charm dates from its prosperity (rice and Sea Island cotton) on the eve of the Civil War. The broad expanse of river to the south and east, unspoiled by progress, is a beautiful natural setting for the little town.

St. Helena's Episcopal Church is Beaufort's most important survival of the colonial and Revolutionary era. Established in 1712, the parish has remained in continuous religious activity and is one of the oldest functioning churches in the United States. The building dates from 1724, with two subsequent modifications. A high brick wall of early construction encloses the churchyard, which takes up a large city block near the center of the historic district. Among the oldest graves is that of Colonel John ("Tuscarora Jack") Barnwell, hero of the early Indian wars, who died in 1724. His remains are under the enlarged church, but his name is on one of the many picturesque family plots in the yard. Markers were placed in 1970 on the graves of two British officers buried by the Patriots after the skirmish in 1779, described above. It was a Captain Barnwell who recovered the bodies on the battlefield, read the burial service, and wrote in a letter that has been preserved: "We have shown the British we not only can best them in battle, but that we can also give them a Christian burial." The officers' regiment in England has corresponded with St. Helena's about the graves. (Markers are on the right of the brick walk on the west side of the churchyard.)

The ruins of Sheldon Church are maintained by St. Helena's. Tours of houses and gardens in and around Beaufort are sponsored annually by the Women of St. Helena's. Walking tours of Beaufort are also organized through the Spirit of Old Beaufort Walking Tour; phone: (843) 525-0459.

Tourist facilities in Beaufort County are well organized. The Beaufort County Chamber of Commerce, Beaufort, S.C. 29902, has well-prepared literature on historical attractions, including a map for self-guided tours. Website: www.beaufortsc.org; phone: (843) 986-5400.

Prince's Fort (Blackstock Road), Spartanburg County. The Loyalist expedition from Ninety Six that met its first defeat at Cedar Spring, 12 July 1780, was defeated the next day, and most of its surviving troops were captured, in the action known by the name of Gowen's Old Fort. The prisoners were taken just across the North Carolina line to the camp of Colonel Charles McDowell, "a rather inactive partisan leader" who had been joined recently by forces under the very active Colonel Isaac Shelby and Colonel Elijah Clark. When the Loyalists attacked "McDowell's Camp" on 16 July they were repulsed. (The location of this action is controversial. Some authorities say "McDowell's Camp" was just north of the state line. Others say the action of 16 July took place at Earle's Ford on the Pacolet River just south of the state line.) The next day a pursuit force under Edward Hampton overtook the Loyalists as they headed south on the Old Black-stock Road, routed them, and drove the survivors into Prince's Fort. A DAR marker on the site of this Loyalist post, near Zion Chapel, erroneously says the Patriots captured the position. To find the site, go west from Spartanburg on I-85 and turn north toward Inman at the exit 2.4 miles west of the I-26 interchange. Go north about 0.5 mile to S.C. 123, turn left (toward Inman), and a little more than 0.5 mile farther is a road junction in the vicinity of the Prince's Fort site.

Purrysburg Site, Savannah River, Jasper County. Although the village had disappeared by the early 1800s, the abortive Purrysburg Township, one of the first nine townships created in the 1730s to develop the inland regions, figured prominently in Revolutionary War operations in the South. In 1777 it was a Patriot base, and in December 1778 the forces under General Benjamin Lincoln massed here to face the main British camp across the Savannah in Ebenezer, Georgia. General Augustine Prevost pushed through the American screening force at Purrysburg to make his diversionary raid against Charleston in May 1779. Only a cemetery remains where the town was established in 1732 (junction of S.C. 31 and 34, 2.6 miles from U.S. 17 in Hardeeville). Jean-Jacques Rousseau's *Confessions* has a description of the methods used by Colonel Jean Pierre Purry to inveigle six hundred of his fellow Swiss into settling the malaria-ridden site.

Quinby Bridge and Shubrick's Plantation, Huger Crossroads, Berkeley County. In mid-July 1781, when Greene's army was recuperating in the High Hills of Santee, General Thomas Sumter got authority from General Greene to undertake a major offensive against the British post at Moncks Corner. Lee's Legion and Marion's Brigade were attached to Sumter, and the veteran militia outfit of Colonel Thomas Taylor had been with Sumter for some time.

When Sumter maneuvered to cut off the enemy force at Moncks Corner, Lieutenant Colonel John Coates won the first round by withdrawing into his stronghold at Biggin Church (see BIGGIN BRIDGE AND CHURCH). Three days later, before dawn on 17 July, he again slipped away with his entire force, burning the historic church and heading southeast for Quinby Bridge. Here he could be reinforced from Charleston by way of Cainhoy, or he could continue his retreat to that place. Coates was a military commander who knew what he was doing.

Sumter, on the other hand, was piling error on error. He headed on down the road for another go at annihilating the elusive Coates and permanently clearing the British from this prosperous region.

The cavalry of "Light Horse Harry" Lee's Legion almost accomplished this. Leaving the slower-moving infantry of Lee, Marion, Taylor, and Sumter to follow as fast as they could walk, three cavalry sections formed the Patriot advance guard. They succeeded in gobbling up the British rear guard and charging across Quinby Bridge with two sections before Coates knew what was happening. The British had covered the 18 miles to Quinby Creek in a rapid march and by afternoon of 17 July were holding a strong defensive position behind it. They had loosened the plank flooring of the bridge with the idea of removing it when their rear guard got across. As you can see today, the creek here is wide and deep—a good defensive barrier if covered by fire and if that bridge is fixed so cavalry cannot charge over it.

The first two sections of Lee's cavalry crossed the bridge, but in so doing they loosened the flooring, and the third section was unable to repair it in time to join the fray on the opposite bank. Meanwhile, the surprise attack by Captain James Armstrong and Lieutenant George Carrington Jr. routed all the defenders but a small body that formed around Coates. But the British rallied, and Armstrong and Carrington escaped by finding a ford upstream. Here they were joined by Lee and Marion, who had come up with the foot troops of their commands, and these two leaders wisely decided not to renew the action.

But when Sumter arrived with the rest of the infantry, at about 5 P.M., he overruled this decision and formed for an attack. Coates, meanwhile, reoriented his defenses to face this new threat. Using the rail fences and outbuildings of Captain Thomas Shubrick's plantation (now Quinby Plantation), he formed a hollow square. A single howitzer covered his front, but Sumter had left all the American artillery behind.

Taylor's infantry opened the attack by charging across an open field and forming a line along a fence. The British counterattacked and regained the position. Marion's infantrymen cut across from their initial position on the left flank and retook the fence line, but were then driven back with heavy losses and ammunition almost used up. Sumter's troops fired from the protection of buildings.

The Gamecock had failed again, and his subordinates now rebelled at the price they were paying with the lives of their men. Taylor informed Sumter on the spot that he would no longer take his commands, and the next morning Lee and Marion marched away with their troops. British reinforcements were meanwhile coming up to join Coates, so Sumter had to withdraw his remaining forces.

The battlefield is not marked, but the terrain has changed little in two centuries. Open, well-tended fields surround a modern house on the site of Quinby Plantation, a little to the west of the bridge. Tourist literature says that "bones of the hastily buried dead are still occasionally unearthed here." The Quinby Plantation House, also known as the Halidon Hill House, was added to the National Register of Historic Places in 1985. Quinby Bridge survives as a small bridge approached by dipping down from the high banks of Quinby Creek. The latter feeds into the east branch of the Cooper River about a mile below the bridge, and is an edge of the remarkable Francis Marion National Forest. Quinby Bridge is on S.C. 98 just west of Huger.

Ratcliff's Bridge, Lynches River, Lee County. General Thomas Sumter's defeat on 6 March 1781 by Major Thomas Fraser's Loyalist South Carolina battalion has never had a convenient name. On the classic list of engagements compiled by Edward McCrady it is called "Lynches Creek, Kershaw County." This is unfortunate because there is a *Little* Lynches Creek in Kershaw County (formed 1791) and because Lee County (formed 1902) was not in existence when McCrady was doing his research.

The action took place after Sumter's abortive campaign that reached Fort Watson before he was forced to start retreating. He went by his plantation at Great Savannah (see NELSON'S FERRY), picked up his young son and his paralytic wife, and moved about 40 miles northeast in hope of still being joined by Marion. On 6 March he finally resumed his retreat and was attacked this same day by Fraser. Sumter escaped with the loss of about ten killed and forty wounded.

The action took place along Stirrup Branch, which runs through today's Bishopville to the site of Ratcliff's Bridge. The latter is just south of the present bridge on U.S. 15 and S.C. 34 over Lynches River. Ratcliff's Bridge is listed as a "battle site" on the state historical markers program.

Ring Fight and Andrew Pickens Homesites, near Tamassee, Oconee County. Firmly entrenched in legend if unsupported by any documentary evidence is Andrew Pickens's victory here in the far west corner of the state. The Cherokees had taken advantage of their opportunity to attack frontier settlements when the backcountry militia were supporting Patriot operations along the coast during the spring and summer of 1779. Colonel Andrew Pickens and his militia returned to launch one of their many punitive expeditions. Surprised and surrounded by Indians, Pickens claimed later to have saved his force by setting fire to a cane brake, causing loud popping noises as the joints of cane exploded from the heat. The Cherokees fled, mistaking these sounds for gunfire from reinforcements. So goes the story. But Pickens was so impressed by the natural beauty of the region that he returned many years later to build his "Red House" on Tamassee Creek. A small stone marks the house site on the creek and appears on large-scale maps as "General Pickens Monument." It is on S.C. 95, .75 mile from its junction with S.C. 375. A few yards north of the latter road junction is another stone (not shown on maps) marking the site of the legendary Ring Fight (July 1779?).

Rocky Mount, Catawba River, Fairfield County, just south of Great Falls. As part of their strategy to dominate the backcountry the British established outposts here, at Hanging Rock and Cheraw. When Continental troops started south from Virginia to challenge the enemy in the Carolinas, General Thomas Sumter rallied South Carolina militia and by the end of July 1780 had sufficient strength to attack British outposts. On 30 July he personally led one force of about six hundred men against Rocky Mount as Major William Davie advanced on Hanging Rock. About 150 New York Volunteers held a strong position around Rocky Mount that for eight hours defied all Sumter's efforts to force their surrender. The Patriots withdrew to Land's Ford (preserved in Landsford Canal State Park), crossed the river, and reinforced Davie at Hanging Rock.

Round O, Colleton County. Surviving as little more than a place-name on the highway map (U.S. 17A, 11 miles east of Walterboro), this is where the southern army under Greene was concentrated during the final months of the war when the British held only Charleston and Savannah. Greene joined his troops here on 9 December 1781 after his easy victory at Fort Dorchester, and a little less than a month later he welcomed the two thousand Continentals who had marched south under General Arthur St. Clair from Yorktown.

One curious thing about Round O is that a circle drawn around it on the map with a 30-mile radius (one day's forced march) passes through Nelson's Ferry, Moncks Corner, Charleston, and Beaufort (see PORT ROYAL ISLAND), all of them places of exceptional strategic importance.

Rugeley's Mill (Clermont), Kershaw County, on County Road 58 near the bridge over Grannies Quarter Creek, about 10 miles north of Camden and 4 miles north of the Camden Battlefield site.

Henry Rugeley was a Loyalist who kept a foot in the Patriot camp. His estate, variously known as Clermont, Rugeley's Fort, and (most commonly) Rugeley's Mill or Mills, was the scene of several historic events during the Revolution, having the attraction not only of his home and mill but also of a large barn adaptable to many military uses.

When the British invaded the South, Rugeley was commissioned a colonel and had good prospects of becoming a brigadier. He is nevertheless credited with saving Governor John Rutledge from capture by Tarleton in May 1780, just before the skirmish remembered as Buford's Defeat. Tarleton was out to get the governor, who paused during his flight at Rugeley's home and was warned by his host in time to get away safely.

Colonel William Washington brought Colonel Rugeley's military career to an abrupt end a few months later (4 December 1780) by using the Quaker gun trick. Washington and his dragoons found Rugeley with well over one hundred Loyalist troops in his fort here, a log barn encircled by a ditch and abatis. Not having artillery, unable to inflict any serious harm with small-arms fire, and not foolish enough to attempt an assault, Washington made a fake cannon, moved it into view of the defenders, and told them they would be blown to bits if they did not surrender. The ancient stratagem succeeded once again, and the Loyalists were marched off as prisoners of war.

Gates camped at Rugeley's Mill before marching on Camden in August 1780, and Cornwallis marched from Camden with the intention of attacking Gates here. Gates retreated to Rugeley's with his panic-stricken militia. In his pursuit from the Camden battlefield, Tarleton encountered some stiff resistance at Rugeley's from a handful of officers who were attempting to protect the baggage train from Patriot looters.

The site is not one for casual tourists to visit, but remains have been found of Rugeley's house, barn, mill, and pond.

St. James Santee Church, a few miles west of Hampton Plantation, Charleston County. An architectural gem dating from 1768 and locally known as the Brick Church, it is on a dirt road that was the Old King's Highway and the main coastal road when President Washington made his grand tour in 1791. From U.S. 17 and 701 go north toward Hampton Plantation for about 1.5 miles, turning left on Old King's Highway shortly after crossing a creek; the church is about 2 miles west on this road on the north side.

Sampit Bridge, Georgetown County. The campaign that started at Wiboo Swamp on 6 March 1781 was supposed to be a British search-and-destroy operation to annihilate the pesky guerrilla band commanded by General Francis Marion. It ended with the British fleeing for safety within their fortified camp at Georgetown. The final action was at Sampit Bridge, where Marion caught the retreating enemy astride the river and killed about twenty of them with accurate musketry. "I have never seen such shooting before in my life," said the British commander, Colonel John Watson, whose horse was killed under him. The action occurred around the present village of Sampit, which is on U.S. 17A and 521, exactly 10 miles from the center of Georgetown.

Seneca Old Town Site, Clemson University campus, Pickens County. A Cherokee attack in July 1776 was answered by a punitive expedition led by Major Andrew Williamson. The Patriots walked into an ambuscade as they approached Essenecca, or Seneca Old Town, the evening of 31 July, their advance guard being suddenly fired on from the fences alongside the road leading into the town. After rallying his troops, Williamson finally captured the village and destroyed it.

Killed in the action was Francis Salvador, a Jewish Patriot who had brought Williamson the first report of the Cherokee threat and who was riding alongside the major with the advance guard. A diorama in the B'nai B'rith Klutznick Exhibit Hall, 1640 Rhode Island Avenue, Washington, D.C., shows Salvador being shot from his horse and about to be scalped.

After destroying Cherokee towns and burning crops throughout a wide area east of the Blue Ridge, Williamson returned to the ruins of Essenecca and built Fort Rutledge, naming it for the president of the General Assembly.

On the shore of modern Lake Hartwell is a rock with a bronze plaque marking the site of the Cherokee town. Back in the bushes is a miniature fort of dressed stone and fanciful design that marks the site of the Patriot fort.

Sheldon Church, near Sheldon, Beaufort County. From U.S. 17 and 21 in Sheldon go northeast about 2 miles on S.C. 235 to its junction with S.C. 21, where the site is located; or take S.C. 21 at its junction with U.S. 17 and 21 just 0.5 mile west of Gardens Corner (1.6 miles east of S.C. 235 in Sheldon) and go north 1.7 miles. In lonely isolation and framed by gigantic oaks, the tall brick walls stand in a fenced yard where a few old tombs remain. One of South Carolina's most elegant churches when built in 1746, Sheldon Church was burned by the British in 1779. Rebuilt, it was burned by Sherman's troops in late 1864, or in early 1865. The site is maintained by St. Helena's Episcopal Church in Beaufort (see PORT ROYAL ISLAND), 15 miles away. On the second Sunday after Easter the congregation of St. Helena's holds a service at the ruins, using that day's collection for their preservation. For more information, contact the St. Helena's Episcopal Church. Phone: (843) 522-1712.

Shubrick's Plantation. *See* QUINBY BRIDGE.

Singleton's Mill, southwestern tip of Sumter County, exact site undetermined. About where the Old Santee Road to Camden crossed Fullers Earth Creek was this mill, an important point on the British line of communications. Its seizure by Marion as the British withdrew into winter quarters in late October 1780 was the final irritation that convinced Lord Cornwallis to let Tarleton take most of his legion on a campaign to eradicate Marion's band. Without ever getting in sight of his quarry, however, Tarleton finally turned back for a go at Sumter, allegedly saying to his men that "as for this damned old fox, the devil himself could not catch him."

About six weeks later the "Swamp Fox" was back, this time to intercept a column of two hundred British recruits being escorted from Charleston by regulars of the Sixty-fourth Regiment under Major Robert McLeroth. On 12 December the partisans hit the rear guard of McLeroth's escort just north of Halfway Swamp in modern Clarendon County, less than a mile short of Rimini.

McLeroth played for time by proposing a proper battle in the open. Marion responded with the suggestion that twenty picked men from each side fight it out on a mutually agreeable field. The British accepted, but then ordered their men off the field at the last moment and took up a defensive position under cover of darkness. Marion had numerical superiority—about 700 mounted men—but 140 Loyalist dragoons under Captain John Coffin were within supporting distance of the British. Waiting for daylight to resume his attack, Marion learned shortly after midnight that the British had slipped away.

Major John James cut behind the British and was waiting for them on the high ground near Singleton's Mill. A curious thing then happened: the Rebels delivered a single volley and for no apparent reason abandoned their position without offering any further resistance. They had suddenly and belatedly discovered that the Singleton family had smallpox. Marion withdrew. McLeroth, reinforced by Coffin, went on with his business, reaching Winnsboro on 16 December.

Old Santee Road between Fort Watson and Rimini followed the route of modern S.C. 76, but its course is unknown north of there in the Singleton's Mill area. It is a safe assumption, however, that the site is on the unimproved road about a mile south of Poinsett State Park or near the crossroads about 2 miles east on S.C. 261.

Snows Island, southeast tip of Florence County. In the latter part of December 1780 (after his action at Halfway Swamp), General Francis Marion established his famous base here, using it during the most critical months of his career as a partisan. The place was found and destroyed in March 1781 (exact day unknown), but by then it had lost its importance because General Greene's forces were starting their liberation of South Carolina, and Marion was no longer the only major enemy of the British in the low country.

The successful search-and-destroy mission in 1781 was conducted by Colonel Welbore Doyle and his New York Loyalists while Marion was away executing the most brilliant campaign of his career (see WIBOO SWAMP). Coming down Lynches River, Doyle surprised the defenders of Snows Island under Marion's second in command, Colonel John Ervin, and killed seven Patriots and wounded fifteen, forcing Ervin to dump his supplies into Lynches River and retreat.

Marion sent Colonel Hugh Horry to the scene, following with the rest of his command. Horry killed or wounded nine Loyalists and captured sixteen before inflicting two more casualties on Doyle's rear guard at Witherspoon's Ferry.

Snows Island remains very much as Marion's men knew it two centuries ago. Loggers put a rail line across to the extreme western tip, but it has long since been abandoned, and the island is still accessible only by boat. But it shows up well on the modern topographic map distributed by the United States Geological Survey (Johnsonville Quadrangle, fifteen-minute series, 1946). Labeled "Snow Island," it shows as a piece of swamp bounded on the north and east by the Great Pee Dee River, on the south by the wide stretch of lower Clark's Creek, and on the west by the upper part of this creek and the mouth of Lynches River.

Several meandering streams intersect the island, which measures roughly 4.5 by 1.5 miles. Maximum elevation shown on the map is 14 feet, but the island is not so waterlogged as cartographers make it appear. In conjunction with Dunham Bluff (see PORT'S FERRY), it provided more than enough dry ground for a partisan hideout.

You can drive to two points from which a worthwhile view of this historic and picturesque site is provided. The first is on the north side at Dunham Bluff. The other is on Clark's Creek, to the south. From Hemingway (S.C. 41, 51, and 261) go east 0.2 mile, turn north on S.C. 34 and continue 5.7 miles; turn left on S.C. 488 to its dead end, a distance of 1.7 miles. You will have arrived.

Stateburg and vicinity, near U.S. 76 and 378 between Columbia and Sumter. Founded by General Sumter, this town in the High Hills of the Santee was vigorously promoted in 1786 as the site for the state capital.

The Borough House in Stateburg, an impressive structure built in 1758 with rammed-earth walls, was used by Lord Cornwallis and General Greene. Open to the public on special occasions, it is owned and beautifully maintained by the descendants of the original family. Borough House was named a National Historic Landmark in 1988. Near the Borough House is Greene Spring, built on orders of the general when his army was in the High Hills, and still in use. Borough House is located on Route 261 nearly a mile north of the intersection of 261 and U.S. Highways 76 and 376.

Stono Ferry, near Rantowles, Charleston County. An ill-conceived and poorly conducted operation by 1,500 American troops under Generals Benjamin Lincoln and William Moultrie against 900 British on Johns Island culminated in the Battle of Stono Ferry, 20 June 1779. It was one of the war's hardest battles and one of its most pointless.

Lieutenant Colonel John Maitland commanded the large rear guard left by General Prevost when he withdrew to Savannah after his May 1779 raid on Charleston. A bridgehead to cover Stono Ferry was established on the northern side of what is now called New Cut Church Flats. Three strong redoubts circled by an abatis were manned by Highlanders and Hessians, and it was this point against which Lincoln led the main attack while Moultrie commanded a secondary effort against Johns Island, to the east.

After a night march of 8 miles from the Ashley Ferry (modern village of Drayton Hall where the railroad bridge crosses), Lincoln's column deployed and his troops started struggling through dense woods for an attack at dawn. The Americans advanced in two wings. Carolina militia under General Jethro Sumner were on the right with two guns, and their right flank was covered by a light-infantry company under the marquis de Malmady. The left wing was made up of Continental troops with four guns and commanded by General Isaac Huger. Light infantry under John Henderson were with Huger, and these troops made the first contact shortly before sunrise.

After engaging the British positions with small arms and cannon fire for an hour, the Patriots advanced to the abatis. Two companies of Highlanders resisted until only eleven men were left standing, but a Hessian battalion finally broke. Maitland shifted his forces to meet the more dangerous threat by Huger's wing, the Hessians rallied and went back into action, and reserves were brought across the bridge, at which point Lincoln ordered a withdrawal. Patriot losses had been heavy: about 150 killed or wounded and the same number "missing." The heat was severe (Andrew Jackson's brother Hugh died of heat and exhaustion), and most of the American "missing" were deserters (the British claimed no prisoners). General Huger was severely wounded. The British lost 130 officers and men, only one of whom was reported missing.

Maitland had decided almost a week before the battle to withdraw, but was delayed by lack of water transportation. On 23 June he started moving to Beaufort, but Lincoln's costly attack had little to do with hastening his departure.

Stono Ferry has retained no Revolutionary War vestiges other than its topography. To reach the site drive a mile south from Rantowles to the end of S.C. 318.

Strawberry Ferry, Cooper River, Berkeley County. Because of its strategic location at a natural crossing place of land and water routes about 25 miles up the Cooper River from Charleston, Strawberry Ferry was the center of much military activity during the Revolution. The site is now marked by an exceptionally attractive little church, Strawberry Chapel (1725), and its interesting cemetery. Easily found in a region of numerous historic landmarks, Strawberry Chapel is at the end of S.C. 44, just off Highway 402 along the Cooper River, a little less than 2 miles from the entrance to Mepkin Trappist Monastery (see MEPKIN PLANTATION).

Sullivan's Island, Charleston Harbor. The mismanaged British expedition against Charleston in 1776 culminated here on 28 June and left South Carolina free of major military operations for another three years. Sullivan's Island is fairly heavily populated today, but the major landmarks of 1776 survive. These are the Cove, across which the Patriots maintained their line of communications to Colonel Moultrie's fort of palmetto logs and sand; the Breach, between the eastern end of Sullivan's Island and Long Island (now Isle of Palms), where warning signs of "deep holes, fallouts, and strong currents" were posted too late to spare the British the disastrous mistake of trying to ford this gap at low tide; and the site of Fort Sullivan, later renamed for William Moultrie.

This controversial fort was a square redoubt with bastions on each corner. For lack of stone with which to build to the specifications of conventional military wisdom, the Patriots put up retaining walls of palmetto logs about 16 feet apart and filled in with sand. Only the half of the fort facing the sea was finished when the British attack was expected, so Moultrie emplaced most of his guns to cover the harbor. He did the best he could to meet the threat from Long Island against the rear of his fort by putting a strong detachment to defend the Sullivan's Island side of the Breach and by constructing hasty breastworks on the unfinished side of Fort Sullivan.

At 11 A.M. on 28 June the long-expected British bombardment finally started. More than one hundred pieces of artillery massed their fire on Moultrie's fort from the south and southeast while three ships sailed into the harbor to attack from the west flank and rear. Fortunately for the Patriots, all three ships ran onto the Middle Ground, where Fort Sumter was later built. Many historians believe that this accident was decisive, and perhaps it was, but the British had already made an incredible number of errors. The first was in electing to destroy the harbor forts instead of running past them to strike straight at Charleston itself. The second was to waste time in leisurely operations against Sullivan's Island. The third was to count on getting troops across the Breach by fording. (The author's authority is Professor W. B. Willcox, who has written extensively since 1945 on British strategy in the American Revolution. See specifically his introduction to *The American Rebellion: Sir Henry Clinton's Narrative* . . . , p. xx and n.)

Moultrie and the 431 men of his Second South Carolina Regiment plus 22 men of the Fourth Artillery nevertheless had a hot day's work. It turned out that their palmetto and sand fort was ideally suited to withstanding bombardment because palmetto does not splinter like ordinary wood and the sand filling of the walls further cushioned the impact of cannonballs. But the enemy fire did not stop until 9:30 P.M., and the Patriots had about forty men killed or wounded. When Moultrie's flag was knocked down by one barrage, Sergeant William Jasper ran outside the walls to replace it on the parapet. (Before the days of telephone and radio a commander had to keep his flag flying to show friendly troops and headquarters that he had not surrendered.)

The present Fort Moultrie dates from 1809 but retains its importance as a Revolutionary War site because the view from its walls provides an appreciation of the 1776 battle from the defenders' vantage point. The more recent fort is said to occupy the site of Fort Sullivan (renamed after the battle for Moultrie), but at least one authority says the site of the Revolutionary War fort is about 100 yards out in the harbor (WPA *Guide*, p. 282). Fort Moultrie is administered as part of Fort Sumter National Monument by the National Park Service. It is on West Middle Street, reached via U.S. 17B and S.C. 703. Camping and picnicking facilities are 4 miles east on Isle of Palms. Phone: (843) 883-3123.

Sumter's Tomb and Homesite. *See* STATEBURG.

Tearcoat (Tarcote) Swamp Skirmish, Black River, Clarendon County. With instructions from General Gates to continue harassing the British lines of communications, Marion left Port's Ferry with 150 newly raised partisans to break up a Loyalist force being assembled by Colonel Samuel Tynes. After a swift advance he surprised the enemy camp shortly after midnight on 25 October 1780 and scored one of his most impressive triumphs: about forty Loyalists killed, wounded, or captured; eighty good horses and eighty new muskets taken; and a number of recruits won over from the Loyalist cause. Marion apparently had no losses, and he killed only three Loyalists in the engagement. The site is near S.C. 50 just south of Tearcoat Branch, which enters Black River about a mile farther east, just above the bridge of U.S. 301. I-95 passes under S.C. 50 about a mile northwest of the battle site.

Thicketty Fort (Fort Anderson), Cherokee County. In July 1780 Colonel Isaac Shelby with six hundred militia attacked the Loyalist post at this place and secured surrender of the garrison without firing a shot. Dates for the action are given variously as 13 and 30 July. Also called Fort Anderson, the place was probably where the village of Thicketty is located, on U.S. 29 about 4.5 miles southwest of Gaffney.

Thomson's Plantation. *See* BELLEVILLE PLANTATION.

Wadboo Bridge and Plantation, near the junction of Wadboo Swamp with the Cooper River and in the vicinity of Moncks Corner and Biggin Bridge and Church. Revolutionary War skirmishes took place around here in January and July 1781, and Marion fought his last battle here on 29 August 1782. Sometimes designated incorrectly by the name of Fairlawn Plantation, the estate of Sir John Colleton about half a mile east of the bridge, this action pitted Marion against his old adversary, Major Thomas Fraser, British commander at the battle of Parker's Ferry. Marion again drew Fraser into an ambuscade, inflicting twenty casualties on a force of two hundred dragoons, but the British captured an ammunition wagon and Marion was forced to withdraw. Wadboo Plantation, about a half-mile east of Wadboo Bridge, is where Marion said goodbye to his troops.

Wallace, Marlboro County. General Nathanael Greene's "Camp Repose" (see CHERAW) was where S.C. 9 joins U.S. 1 in the center of this town. A granite marker indicates the spot.

Walnut Grove Plantation (Moore House), 1200 Otts Shoals Road south of Spartanburg. When built in 1765, the two-story, white frame house of Charles Moore near the North Tyger River was one of the finest in the upcountry. It has been restored and authentically furnished by the Spartanburg County Historical Society. Phone: (864) 596-3501. The oldest graves in the family cemetery are those of a Captain Steadman, murdered in his sickbed by "Bloody Bill" Cunningham, and two other Patriots killed by Cunningham as they ran from the house. Another grave is that of "Kate" Moore Barry, Revolutionary scout and heroine. The house is at I-26 and U.S. 221. Phone: (864) 576-6546.

Wambaw Bridge, near junction of Wambaw Creek with the South Santee River, southeast tip of Berkeley County. When Marion left his brigade early in January 1782 to serve as state senator in Jacksonboro, his two principal lieutenants found various pretexts to delegate their command duties to subordinates. At this critical period the British sallied forth from Charleston with a large foraging party and scattered Marion's disorganized forces. The Swamp Fox left his legislative duties and rallied survivors of his brigade. At Wambaw Bridge his troops suffered another reverse when untrained horsemen improperly executed their part of an attack on the British.

The Charleston County highway map shows a modern bridge at the site of the Revolutionary War structure. Unidentified by any name, it is on a private road in prolongation of State Highway 857 a little less than 5 miles north of U.S. 17 and 701.

Colonel Elias Ball's Wambaw Plantation was more than 30 miles to the west, about 6 miles south of Moncks Corner. Colonel Anthony White captured a British officer and seventeen men here on 6 May 1780 and was pursued to Leneud's Ferry.

Washington's Grave, near Rantowles, Charleston County. Colonel William Washington (1752–1810) was a distant kinsman of George Washington and a Virginian by birth. When the Revolution started he gave up studying for the ministry and launched an active and successful career as a commander of Continental dragoons. He and Tarleton clashed on a number of occasions in South Carolina, and the honors were about even. Their personal encounter on the battlefield of Cowpens is the subject of a painting frequently reproduced in histories of the Revolution. Wounded and captured at Eutaw Springs, he met and married a young lady in Charleston and settled in this area.

A historic marker on an open and flat stretch of U.S. 17 about 1 mile east of Rantowles (and almost exactly 11 miles from Charleston's Ashley River Bridge) indicates the location nearby of Washington's grave on what once was Live Oak Plantation, and of his country home, then Sandy Hill Plantation, 7 miles northwest.

Washington's grave is preserved in an isolated burial yard enclosed by an ancient brick wall about 4 feet high. A bronze plaque on the iron gate says the cemetery, which has about ten graves, including those of about four Washingtons, was rehabilitated (recently) by the Washington Light Infantry of Charleston. Colonel Washington's wife, Jane Riley Elliott (1763–1830), is buried at his side.

The gravesite is located and marked by a state highway marker on U.S. 17 at Rantowles just short of a mile north of the Live Oak Plantation. On U.S. Highway 17, leaving Charleston, look for a marker on the right and turn there. A white sign with an arrow points right; follow that on to a narrow path at the end of which lies the monument. A brick wall surrounds the picturesque site.

Wateree Ferry and Fort Carey, Kershaw County, just south of Camden where the I-20 bridge crosses the Wateree River. During construction of the new highway bridge here in recent years, portions of the riverbank were washed away to expose remains of Revolutionary works. One of the numerous mistakes made by General Horatio Gates before the Battle of Camden in August 1780 was to approve of the detachment of General Sumter for a secondary effort against the British line of communications to Charleston. Reinforced by 100 Maryland Continentals, 300 North Carolina militia, and 2 cannon, all under the command of Lieutenant Colonel Thomas Woolford of the Fifth Maryland Regiment, Sumter surprised the British defenders of Fort Carey, a small redoubt guarding the west side of Wateree Ferry, capturing Colonel Carey, 30 troops, and 36 loaded supply wagons. Later the same day, 15 August, Sumter captured a supply train of 6 baggage wagons and several hundred head of livestock. Attempting to escape north after Gates's defeat on 16 August, Sumter was surprised at Fishing Creek and his force was wiped out.

Waxhaw Presbyterian Church, 8100 Old Waxhaw Monroe Road on Route 16 about 37 miles east of U.S. 521. The Waxhaws Meeting House, a log structure built here around 1755, was a regional landmark during the Revolution. Patriots wounded in Buford's Defeat (about 12 miles east-southeast as the crow flies) were tended here, and several are buried in the adjoining cemetery. Among their nurses was the mother of young Andrew Jackson. Her husband was buried at the church just before Andrew's birth in 1767.

Another grave is that of General William Richardson Davie (1756–1820). Born in England, he came to the Waxhaws with his father, graduated from Princeton with first honors in 1776, distinguished himself as a militia officer during the Revolution, moved to North Carolina in 1782, and had a prominent role in state and national politics thereafter. Phone: (704) 843-4685.

Wiboo Swamp, Santee River, Clarendon County. Colonel John Watson Tadwell Watson was given the mission in March 1781 of leading a force of five hundred Loyalists down the Santee to wipe out the partisans commanded by Marion, who had been cutting up the British line of communications to Camden from Charleston. On 5 March the operation started with Watson's departure from Fort Watson. Four engagements and about three weeks later the British expedition took refuge in their camp at Georgetown, Colonel Watson admitting failure and complaining that Marion "would not fight like a gentleman or a Christian." The first of these actions, and the only one for which an exact date is known, took place on 6 March at Wiboo Swamp. (The next three engagements were at Mount Hope Swamp, Lower Bridge, and Sampit Bridge.)

Wiboo Swamp is now a branch of Lake Marion, due south of Manning and west of the intersection of S.C. 260 and 410. But the latter road follows the trace of the Old Santee Road, astride which Marion blocked Watson's advance before falling back to Mount Hope Swamp.

Williamson's Plantation (Huck's Defeat), Historic Brattonsville, Brattonsville, York County. In a surprise attack at dawn on 12 July 1780 a Patriot force slaughtered a band of Loyalist raiders and killed its leader, the notorious Captain Huck. The event lifted Patriot morale at a time when the British were trying to consolidate their conquest of the state, and it greatly assisted the recruiting efforts of Thomas Sumter.

Christian Huck was one of the Loyalists who had come south in Tarleton's Legion, and in a short time he had made himself particularly detested in the Catawba district. From the forward base at Rocky Mount, Captain Huck with a hard core of northern Loyalists and support from indigenous Loyalists had ravaged the Scotch-Irish settlements. He reached the area of modern Brattonsville on 11 July. The homes of Colonel William Bratton and Captain John McClure were high on his list of official calls, and the wives of these famous Patriot chiefs were roughed up and their houses looted. Captain McClure's son and son-in-law were taken prisoner and scheduled for hanging the next day.

Huck and his ruffians settled down for the night on the plantation of James Williamson, less than half a mile from the Bratton house. They were surprised at dawn by about ninety militiamen under Colonels Bratton and Edward Lacey, who had been told of the raid by Captain McClure's daughter. Because Huck had neglected security precautions, his men were camped on a lane whose rail fences formed a slaughter pen. The Patriots blocked the ends of the lane, cutting the raiders off from their horses, and opened fire at 75 yards. Huck died game. Only about twelve of the legion cavalry and the same number of Huck's mounted infantry escaped; the rest of his 115-man expedition was wiped out. (About thirty-five were killed; most of the rest were captured.) The Patriots had only one man killed, and they liberated the two men captured the preceding day by Huck.

The Bratton house, a simple frame structure, stands weathered and forlorn on the edge of some woods in the place later named Brattonsville. At the site of Williamson's Plantation is a DAR marker to Huck's Defeat with a newer inscription that reads: "On this date, Sept. 30, 1953, there stands 200 feet to the north of this stone the Revolutionary home of Col. William Bratton and his wife Martha. The land was a grant under George the Third." In 1971 it came under the care of the Brattonsville Historic District, which maintains the entire 775-acre grounds as a living museum. Phone: (803) 329-2121.

The site is on S.C. 322 about 4 miles east of McConnells (on U.S. 321) and a little less than 2 miles west of S.C. 324. Rock Hill is about 9 miles east.

Williams' Plantation, Laurens County. *See* HAMMOND'S STORE.

Winnsboro, Fairfield County, 28 miles north of Columbia on U.S. 321. Lord Cornwallis withdrew to this place with about half of his field forces after the disaster at Kings Mountain forced abandonment of his first attempt to invade North Carolina. Here he stayed from late October 1780 to early January 1781, receiving reinforcements and building his strength to about four thousand troops before launching his second offensive into North Carolina. Although its settlement dated from only 1775, Winnsboro was centrally located between Ninety Six and Camden and the main British line of communications down the Santee River to Charleston. Further, it was an excellent base for foraging, the land to the south being particularly rich in farms.

The so-called Cornwallis House (private) at 8 Zion Street is presumed to have been quarters for the British general. The original portion of the well-preserved and little-altered structure has massive masonry walls and partitions coated with a hard plaster. The wooden wing was added later and became the home of a Revolutionary soldier, Captain John Buchanan. The latter's slave, Pompey Fortune, was Lafayette's body servant during the war, and his name is commemorated in Fortune Springs Garden near Lafayette Heights in the northwestern portion of Historic Winnsboro.

The Old Muster Ground (unmarked as such, but easily spotted) is near the Cornwallis House and opposite the site of the Mount Zion Academy or Institute (marked). This is where British troops camped in 1780 to 1781.

Winnsboro is an attractive little town with some fifty places of historic interest marked and keyed to a tour guide published by the town and the Fairfield Historical Society. The most important landmarks date from the early 1800s, including the courthouse designed by Robert Mills (built 1823) and the famous Old Town Clock (installed 1837 and still running).

Literature is available from the Fairfield County Chamber of Commerce, phone: (803) 635-4242, and the Fairfield County Historical Society, Hudson and Walnut Streets, Winnsboro, S.C. 29180. Phone: (803) 635-9811.

Witherspoon's Ferry, Lynches River about 5 miles above Snows Island, near modern Johnsonville, Florence County. After a rear-guard action here against Colonel Hugh Horry, the hard-pressed New York Loyalists under Colonel Doyle burned their baggage and hastened toward Camden (see SNOWS ISLAND). The ferry was where the S.C. 41 and 51 bridge crosses Lynches River.

Wofford's Iron Works (lost site), probably on Lawson Fork Creek between Spartanburg and Glendale. Its precise site is not known because the works were burned down during the Revolution and the area subsequently was industrialized. Wofford's Iron Works (often called simply the Old Iron Works) was built in 1773 and was the first of its type in the state. Several important events took place here and at nearby Cedar Spring during the Revolution. Colonel William Washington had his horses shod at Wofford's as the Patriots under General Dan Morgan retreated from Tarleton. Tarleton outmaneuvered Morgan the night of 15 to 16 January 1780 by faking a march west toward the ironworks and going secretly into camp as the Patriots shifted up the far bank of the Pacolet River to block him. Tarleton then countermarched to cross 6 miles below Morgan, at Easterwood Shoals (today's Pacolet Mills). With enemy scouts a mere 5 miles behind him, Morgan hastily resumed his retreat before turning to make a stand.

The modern town of Cowpens, near the Pacolet and about 10 miles northeast of Spartanburg, is about where Morgan was camped when the British made their unopposed crossing downstream. The Battle of Cowpens took place about 10 miles farther north. The site of the ironworks, according to some authorities, was covered after the Revolution by a mill pond. One educated guess as to its precise map location (see Spartanburg County General Highway Map) is on Lawson Fork Creek at the end of a short dead-end road running north from S.C. 47, about midway between Glendale and the "enlargement inset" line of Spartanburg. See CEDAR SPRING, a site closely identified with the ironworks during the Revolution.

TENNESSEE

The Tennessee Historical Commission has published a 404-page illustrated guide, *Tennessee Historical Markers,* that can be purchased by contacting the Commission by mail at 2941 Lebanon Road, Nashville, Tenn. 37243 (located in the historic Clover Bottom Mansion). Phone: (615) 532-1550. Another source of assistance for Tennessee history is the Tennessee Department of Tourist Development, 312 Eighth Avenue North, 25th floor, Nashville, Tenn. 37243. Phone: (617) 741-2159. This state agency publishes a travel guide obtainable free by calling (800) GO2-TENN.

Bean Station (lost site), Grainger County. William Bean started the first permanent white settlement in eastern Tennessee. He and Robert Bean arrived in 1776, according to the historical marker, but the National Survey gives 1769 as the date he built a rude cabin on Boone's Creek near its junction with the Watauga River (*Colonials and Patriots,* p. 228); the later date being generally accepted by scholars. At the junction of the Knoxville-Abingdon road and the road through Cumberland Gap, the station was used by westbound settlers and (after the Revolution) by eastbound stock drovers. Whiteside Tavern was established here in 1801. Boone's Lake has flooded the site, but its location is indicated by a highway marker on U.S. 11W, 8 miles east of Rutledge. A monument is on the lakeshore above the site. Bean Station incorporated as its own town in 1996.

Cragfront, Castalian Springs. Home to General James Winchester. After serving with distinction as a captain in the Maryland line of the Continental army, Winchester and his brother George moved to this site in 1785, building a log cabin. Active in Tennessee politics and a general of militia, Winchester would lead these troops to their disastrous defeat at the Raisin River during the War of 1812. The current house dates to 1802 and is well furnished in the frontier mode. Take Route 25 west from Carthage to Route 49 and then follow the signs. Open to the public 15 April to 1 November, Tuesday through Saturday, 10 A.M. to 5 P.M., and Sunday, 1 to 5 P.M. Phone: (615) 452-7070.

Cumberland Gap National Historical Park. *See* under KENTUCKY.

Eaton's Station and Fort, Sullivan County. A highway marker on U.S. 11W about 9 miles southwest of Blountville is at the site of the fortified frontier station that figured decisively in the action of 1776 (see under LONG ISLAND OF THE HOLSTON), a few miles to the west. Eaton's Station was one of the first post offices on the frontier. Here also was the first and only mint of the Southwest Territory.

Fort Loudoun Reconstruction, Little Tennessee River, Monroe County. The colony of South Carolina built this isolated fort in 1756 to 1757, deep in Indian country, to challenge French expansion into the Mississippi Valley and to support the Cherokee alliance. But the Cherokee continued to be victimized by white settlers, and there were frequent clashes. The Cherokee laid siege to the fort during the winter of 1759 to 1760. With his food supply exhausted, the fort commander surrendered on 7 August 1760 with assurance that the garrison and its families

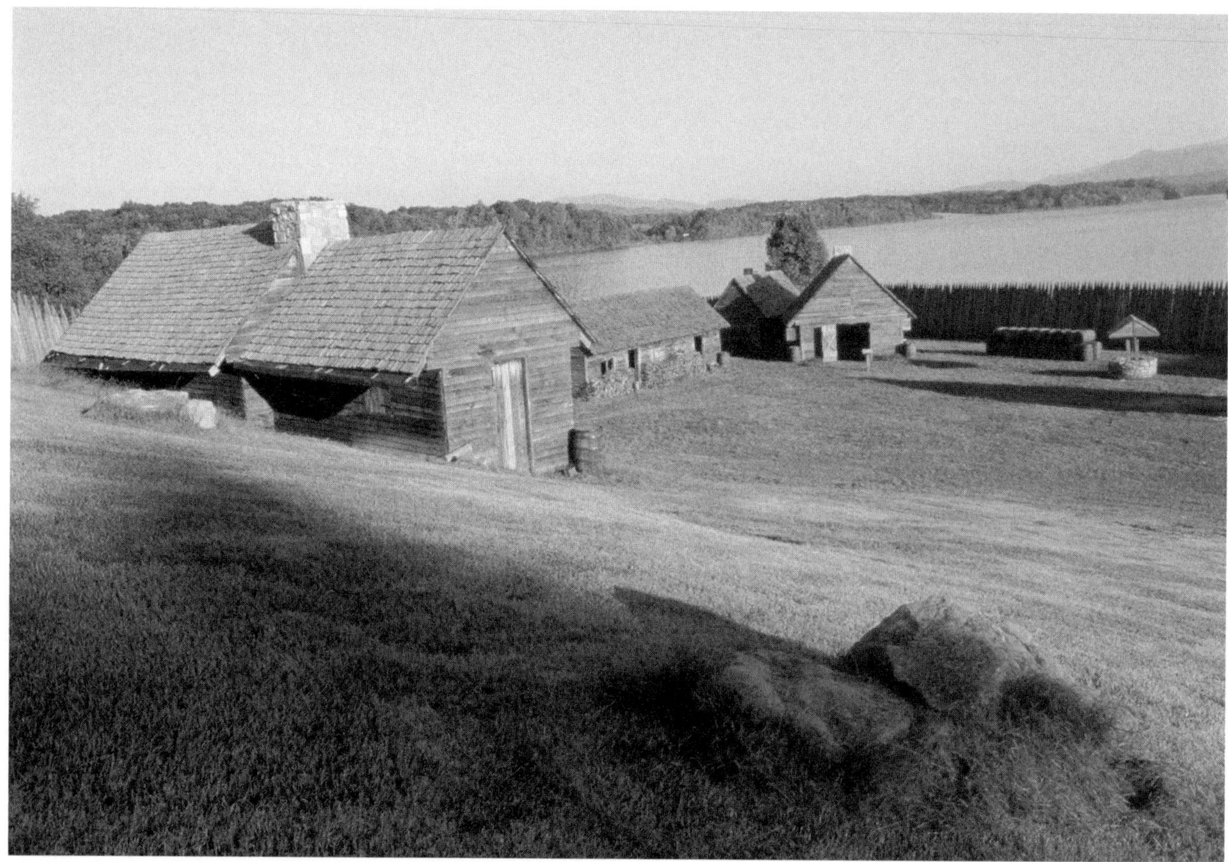

Fort Loudoun. *The colony of South Carolina built this isolated fort near Vonore, Tennessee, in 1756 to 1757 to challenge French expansion into the Mississippi Valley and to support the Cherokee alliance.* © RAYMOND GEHMAN/CORBIS.

could return safely to Charleston. About 15 miles from the fort, the Indians attacked the column on 10 August, killing twenty-five officers and men, and taking most of the rest prisoner. Some of these were later killed, the others ransomed. After occupying the fort briefly, the Cherokee burned it. (The massacre site is at the junction of Cane Creek and Tellico River. Four miles southwest is a highway marker on Tenn. 68, near Mount Vernon, about 8 miles south of Madisonville, Monroe County.)

The 5.6-acre site of Fort Loudoun has been archaeologically explored, and the fort of 1760 is is being reconstructed. In 1978 the Fort Loudoun Association, after having cared for the site since 1933, gave over maintenance responsibilities to the state, and it is now a piece of the Tennessee parks system. As the most southwesterly outpost of the thirteen British colonies, it has the distinction of having been the first English structure in the Tennessee Valley. It was diamond-shaped in plan, a palisaded earthwork inside a honey locust hedge, with barracks, officers' quarters, storehouses, magazine, guardhouse, and blacksmith shop. All of this is beautifully restored into a living-history museum. The visitors center is open daily 8:00 A.M. to 4:30 P.M., and the park is open 8 A.M. to sunset. The Fort Loudoun State Historical Area is at 338 Fort Loudoun Road, Vonore, Tenn. 37885. Phone: (423) 884-6217.

Great Smoky Mountains National Park. Headquarters of this 800-square-mile wilderness preserve are near the junction of U.S. 441 and Tenn. 73 about 40 miles southeast of Knoxville, near Gatlinburg. See the entry on this park under NORTH CAROLINA for additional details.

Long Island of the Holston, south fork of the Holston River, south edge of Kingsport, Sullivan County. About 4 miles long by half a mile wide, and strategically located just east of the junction of the north and south forks of the Holston, near the crossing of major Indian trails, Long Island figured prominently in the early struggles of the colonists with the Cherokee. Colonel William Byrd of Virginia built Fort Robinson at the river junction in 1761 and tried to establish a settlement, but soon withdrew it. Earlier discovery of Cumberland Gap in 1750 (see under KENTUCKY) could not be exploited until the Seven Years' War and Pontiac's Uprising ended in 1763 and 1764. In 1769 William Bean was a pioneer settler in this region (see BEAN STATION and SYCAMORE SHOALS AND FORT WATAUGA SITES), and in 1775 Daniel Boone's opening of the Wilderness Road from Long Island increased Cherokee apprehension. In July 1776 the Indians attacked the settlements in this area, but from Eaton's Fort (see EATON'S STATION AND FORT) on high ground near Long Island, frontiersmen sallied forth to defeat the Cherokee in a hard-fought action on Long Island Flats. This was the most serious of several attacks that started the Cherokee War of 1776, which British agents had tried to head off. Congress aided South Carolina in getting a large-scale punitive expedition started. Three forces totaling more than six thousand militia overran the Cherokee, destroying their villages and driving them into Florida and west to the vicinity of modern Chattanooga. The Indians paid a heavy price for their attack. In the Treaties of De Witt's Corner, South Carolina, and the Long Island of the Holston (20 May and 20 July 1777), the Cherokee ceded all their lands east of the Blue Ridge and relinquished claims to the land occupied by settlers in east Tennessee.

Long Island increased in importance as a terminus and starting point for settlement of Kentucky as the Revolution progressed and as Indian resistance waned. Colonel James Robertson had led a party through Cumberland Gap in the fall of 1779 to establish the first permanent settlement in middle Tennessee, now Nashville. In late 1779 a flotilla left Long Island with the families of the settlers, Colonel John Donelson leading the boats on the long, arduous voyage down the Holston into the Tennessee, up the Ohio to the mouth of the Cumberland, then up that river to the new settlement. A boatyard was established opposite the west end of Long Island to support the island's new role as a base for water movement. The site is marked on U.S. 11W south of Kingsport.

Today the western third of Long Island is much as it was two centuries ago, under single ownership and virtually undeveloped. The eastern third is covered by housing and industrial development. The central third is largely undeveloped except for a railroad.

Nashville, Cumberland River, Davidson County. A Frenchman from New Orleans had operated a trading post here as early as 1710, and his successor, Charles Charleville, died on the job in 1780 at the age of eighty-four. The place was called French Lick because of the salt and sulfur spring that attracted an abundance of game. Old maps show the Chickasaw-Choctaw trail from Natchez ending in this point of hills and bluffs about 200 miles up the Cumberland River from its junction with the Ohio. (The Natchez Trace is covered under MISSISSIPPI.)

James Robertson, a founder of the Watauga settlements (see SYCAMORE SHOALS AND FORT WATAUGA SITES), had heard about French Lick from traders and explorers. Remembered for the phrase "We are the Advanced Guard of Civilization; Our way is across the Continent," he was determined to push west from Watauga. In the spring of 1779 he reached French Lick with eight men, having come 300 miles through the wilderness. Robertson made the long trip to Illinois to get "cabin rights" from George Rogers Clark, returned to French Lick, retraced his steps through Cumberland Gap to Watauga, and led 260 men back to the site of his proposed settlement before the end of 1779.

Fort Nashborough was built on the arid bluff named for General Francis Nash, who had recently been mortally wounded in the Battle of Germantown, Pennsylvania, where he led the North Carolina brigade of Washington's army. (A brother, Abner Nash, was elected governor of North Carolina in the spring of 1780, and older histories say Nashborough was named for him. If Robertson had the ulterior motive of securing the special patronage of the governor for his isolated settlement, the hope was empty; North Carolina had too many problems at home to be able to send Robertson the men and military supplies he quickly needed.)

Families of the first settlers came by water from the Long Island of the Holston, led by Colonel John Donelson. After a voyage of extreme hardship that lasted four months, they arrived on 24 April 1780. A few days later the Cumberland Compact was signed (1 May) by 242 men, setting up a local government much like that of the Watauga settlement (see SYCAMORE SHOALS AND FORT WATAUGA SITES).

Eight stations comprised the isolated Cumberland settlements, and the going was rough. The winter of 1779 to 1780 was the coldest recorded in America at that time. Some sixty men were killed by Indian raiders during the first year. Supplies ran low. The Battle of the Bluffs, 2 April 1781, followed an earlier Indian raid of 15 to 16 January that caused Robertson to consolidate all the settlers in Fort Nashborough. The Indians were finally driven off by war dogs of the fort. ("Let slip the dogs of war" had a literal meaning in ancient warfare. The Spaniards had found war dogs to be very effective in America, and so did the founders of Nashville.)

It was not until 1794 that Indian attacks on Nashville finally ceased, and this was due largely to two retaliatory campaigns led by Robertson. After its initial difficulties as "the Advanced Guard of Civilization," Robertson's settlement began to flourish. It had acquired its present name when incorporated as a town in 1784. In 1843 Nashville became the capital of Tennessee.

A replica of Fort Nashborough is on the bluff a few blocks south of the actual site. Much smaller than the

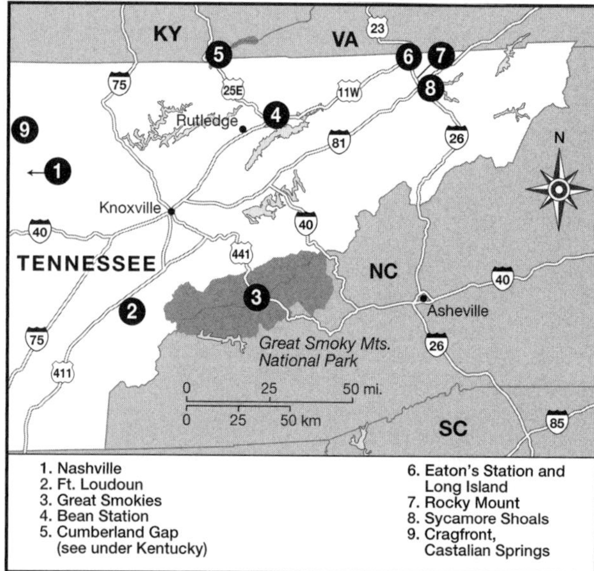

MAP BY XNR PRODUCTIONS. THE GALE GROUP.

original (which covered 2 acres), the interesting and authentic reconstruction of 1930 is on First Avenue North and Church Street.

The grave of James Robertson is in the old City Cemetery at Fourth Avenue South and Oak Street. He died at Chickasaw Bluffs in 1814 while serving as Indian agent to keep the Chickasaw tribe from joining the British in the War of 1812. In 1825 his remains were reinterred in Nashville.

The site of Freeland's Station is marked at 1400 Eighth Avenue North. Here on 11 January 1781 in one of the principal stations of the Cumberland settlements Felix Robertson was born, four days before his father returned from a trip to the Kentucky settlements for much-needed ammunition and salt. Colonel Robertson reached Freeland's just in time to help fight off an Indian attack (mentioned above). Felix was one of Charlotte Robertson's eleven children, and the first white child born in Nashville.

The French trading post of 1710 was located where Fifth Avenue North and Jefferson Street now intersect, and Great French Lick was about 300 yards southwest.

Rocky Mount, 200 Hyder Hill Road, Piney Flatts, Sullivan County. This two-story log house was built about 1770 by the pioneer William Cobb two years before the Watauga settlement was established at Sycamore Shoals (see next entry). It was ten years old when it sheltered frontiersmen moving east to the latter place for their rendezvous before the Battle of Kings Mountain, and twenty years old when it became the first seat of government of the Southwest Territory. Andrew Jackson lived here for six weeks while waiting for his license to practice law. The historic house was later a stop on the stagecoach road from Baltimore to Memphis, and a United States post office from 1838 to 1847.

The simple old pioneer house was acquired by the state in 1959 and has been restored to its original appearance. An outdoor kitchen has been rebuilt. The frontier history of east Tennessee is depicted in a living-history museum as actors portray members of the Cobb family and present life as it was in 1791. Farm animals roam the property and seasonal crops grow abundantly. Phone: (423) 538-7396.

On U.S. 11E, 5 miles south of Bluff City and northeast of Johnson City, is a highway marker a few hundred yards from the site.

Sycamore Shoals and Fort Watauga Sites, just west of Elizabethton (Tenn. 91), Carter County. Sycamore Shoals was the capital of the Watauga settlements along the Watauga, Nolichucky, and Holston Rivers. The first permanent white settlement of the area dates from 1769, when William Bean arrived from Virginia and built a primitive cabin at a site now at the bottom of Boone's Lake. He was followed by a few others from Virginia who formed a tiny community. In 1772 a group of sixteen families from North Carolina established the Watauga settlement under the leadership of James Robertson, with John Sevier as his second in command. They immediately agreed to a lease of the land from the Cherokee and then established local government, the Watauga Association, signed by 113 settlers to indicate their unanimous agreement to abide by its provisions.

It was, of course, completely illegal, violating (among other things) the Proclamation of 1763 prohibiting settlement west of the headwaters of the rivers running into the Atlantic, and Lord Dunmore, governor of Virginia, condemned it as "a dangerous example." The Transylvania Purchase of March 1775, by which the Watauga Association purchased the right to more than 20 million acres from the Cherokee for £10,000 in cash and trade goods, was even more illegal. This deal was consummated in a meeting at Sycamore Shoals, where 1,200 Cherokee met with settlers under the leadership of Richard Henderson, John Williams, and Thomas and Nathanael Hart. Daniel Boone moved out quickly as agent of the Transylvania Company to establish their first settlement in Kentucky at Boonesborough.

At the time of the Revolution there were very few white settlers in the Over Mountain, Back Water, or Black Water region, as it was commonly called, but they came across the Blue Ridge on several occasions to reinforce militia of the Carolina backcountry when the Loyalist threat became critical. Colonels Isaac Shelby and John

Sevier were their most famous military leaders. The historic rally at Sycamore Shoals in September 1780 for the march to Kings Mountain, South Carolina, is covered under the latter heading.

Meanwhile, the settlement had withstood the Cherokee attack of July 1776, some two hundred pioneer men, women, and children holding Fort Watauga for two weeks against three hundred Indians. In so doing they not only saved the backcountry of the southern colonies from serious Indian raids but they also preserved the base from which effective punitive expeditions were launched (see LONG ISLAND OF THE HOLSTON).

The Over Mountain Men were understandably reluctant to undertake sustained military operations that would keep them too long from their own settlements, where they perceived a continuing Indian threat.

Shelby and Sevier checked into Nathanael Greene's headquarters after the Battle of Eutaw Springs but faded away when asked to help out in subsequent operations by reinforcing Francis Marion. Their great victory was at Kings Mountain, which is remembered as a triumph of the Over Mountain Men despite the fact that they constituted only a quarter of the total Patriot militia mustered for that campaign, and not much more than half of the force engaged in the battle.

Sycamore Shoals and the lost site of Fort Watauga qualify as Registered National Historic Landmarks. The traditional site of Fort Watauga is about half a mile southwest of the lower end of Sycamore Shoals on a low ridge beside Tenn. Route 67. A residential development covers the area, but a marker has been erected. The Sycamore Shoals State Historic Area is a 60-acre state park that includes a reconstructed Fort Watauga and a museum. Visitors are encouraged to take part in a variety of colonial crafts. Picnicking and hiking are among the other activities available, and Tennessee's official outdoor drama, "The Wataugans," is performed in the park. This show has been running since 1978. Phone: (423) 543-5808.

VERMONT

The region that became the fourteenth state in 1791 was a battlefield of conflicting land claims during the colonial and Revolutionary War periods. New York fought to maintain possession of the New Hampshire Grants, not giving up until 1789. And local leaders, notably Ethan Allen and his brother Ira, engaged in highly questionable negotiations with British authorities in Canada to secure Vermont's survival. The American Revolution in Vermont was therefore a matter of continuing the struggle for local independence against New York while participating in the war against the British. Vermonters revealed considerably more aptitude in the former arena. After their capture of Fort Ticonderoga, New York, the Green Mountain Boys fell far short of distinguishing themselves in the invasion of Canada and in their subsequent rear-guard action at Hubbardton (see HUBBARDTON BATTLEFIELD). The latter was the only battle of the Revolution in Vermont, though there were a number of skirmishes. The Vermonters succeeded at securing a fragile truce on the northern frontier in the last four years of the war and in producing the most democratic constitution of its age, the first to establish universal male suffrage and to end slavery.

The Battle of Bennington took place in New York, and credit for the victory is appropriately shared with New Hampshire and Massachusetts. The town of Bennington figured conspicuously in the strategy of the campaign, the Vermont militia played an active role in the battle, and Seth Warner arrived with his Green Mountain Regiment to clinch the victory. It is no poor reflection on the Green Mountain State that it was too thinly populated during the Revolution (approximately thirty thousand people in 1780) to play a central role in the winning of American independence.

Because so much of Vermont's natural beauty remains unspoiled, however, visiting its few historic landmarks of the colonial and Revolutionary periods is exceptionally enjoyable. There are great opportunities for boaters, campers, and hikers who are willing to do their historical homework in advance. You can see the Hubbardton Battlefield from a car seat, but the Crown Point Military Road and the sites along the Vermont shore of Lake Champlain from Button Mold Bay to Chimney Point offer highly rewarding opportunities for outdoorsmen and -women.

A good starting place for information on Vermont's Revolutionary War history is the Vermont Division for Historic Preservation. A branch of the Department of Housing and Community Affairs, this state-operated agency is located in the National Life Building at 6 National Life Drive in Montpelier. (Mailing address: Drawer 20, Montpelier, Vt. 05602.) Phone: (802) 828-3211. The department demonstrates Vermont's commitment to its rich past by offering particulars on a wide range of themes, including a series of historical enrichment programs that cover Revolutionary War topics. The Vermont Historical Society's main office and library are located at 60 Washington Street, Barre, Vt. 05641. Website: www.vermonthistory.org; phone: (802) 479-8500. Its museum is located in the Pavilion Building at 109 State Street in Montpelier. Phone: (802) 828-2291. Both are excellent sources for the history of Vermont in the Revolutionary period.

Allen (Ethan) Farm Site and Grave, Burlington, Lake Champlain, Chittenden County. Vermont's largest city is Burlington, an industrial and communications center of nearly 40,000 people. Burlington was chartered in 1763 but not permanently settled until 1783. The armed schooner *Liberty*, which figured prominently in Revolutionary War events on Lake Champlain, was built on the Winooski River at Burlington in 1772. Settlers arrived the next year, but most of them left in 1775 to join Ethan Allen's Green Mountain Boys, and most of the rest retreated with Patriot forces before the British counter-offensive of 1776 from Canada. The pioneers returned in 1783 to establish the present city.

Ethan Allen and his brother Ira were landowners in the adjacent town of Colchester. Ethan Allen died (1789) only two years after permanently establishing his home in the latter town. A granite shaft, a statue representation of Allen, was erected in 1855 near his grave in Green Mountain Cemetery on Colchester Avenue. Winooski Park, on Vt. Route 127 about 2.5 miles from the center of Burlington, includes the farmhouse that he had built for his second wife, Fanny, in 1785. It is the place of Allen's death. The site is now the Ethan Allen Homestead Museum. Open Monday through Saturday, 10 A.M. to 4 P.M., and Sunday, 1 to 4 P.M. Phone (802) 865-4556. A stone tower offers commanding panoramic views of the area from the bluff on which Ethan Allen Park is located.

A helpful online source for this listing is www.historiclakes.org. Another pertinent historical authority is the Chittenden County Historical Society. Phone: (802) 658-1047. The Society has published a three-volume set, *Historic Guide to Burlington Neighborhoods.*

American Precision Museum, Windsor. An unusual museum located in the original Robbins and Lawrence Armory, this museum has historic guns and machinery on display. Open daily late May through October, 10 A.M. to 5 P.M. Take Exit 9 off I-91 and turn left onto Route 5, which becomes Windsor's Main Street. The museum is at 196 Main Street. Phone: (802) 674-5781.

Bennington and vicinity, Bennington County. The Bennington Battlefield is in New York, but in and around the present town of Bennington, Vermont, are several significant landmarks associated with that important Patriot victory. Other sites pertain to Vermont history before and after the Revolution.

The ***Bennington Battle Monument*** is classified among the "Sites Also Noted" by the National Survey of 1964. It stands on a hill in Old Bennington where the Patriots had erected a small building that was the objective of the British raiders who came to grief in the Battle of Bennington. When built in 1887 to 1891, the 306-foot granite obelisk was the tallest battle monument in the world, and three states are viewable from its observation deck. Elevator service has been added, and the upper lookout chamber provides a beautiful view over country mostly unspoiled by modern development. An excellent diorama of the battle is in the base of the monument, near the door to the elevator. The road (Monument Avenue) leading to the monument from Vt. 9 is lined by handsome houses on large lots. On the northeast corner of Monument Avenue and Vt. 9 is a polished granite pedestal topped by a large bronze statue of an animal that is supposed to pass for a catamount, Vermont's extinct state animal (the last of which is stuffed in the Vermont Historical Society's Museum on State Street). It marks the site—45 feet to the east—of the Catamount Tavern. In this structure, built about 1769 and destroyed by fire in 1871, the local Council of Safety held its meetings (1777–1778), and Ethan Allen met with the Green Mountain Boys to plan their skirmishes with New York authorities (1770–1781) and their capture of Fort Ticonderoga (1775). Known simply as Landlord (Stephen) Fay's House, later as the Green Mountain Tavern, it was not called Catamount Tavern until about the time of the Civil War, after it had long been converted to a private residence.

North of the battle monument, directly across from the granite monument to Seth Warner, is a bronze statue of General Stark. The statue, designed in 1889 by American sculptor Jon Rogers, portrays the general in an aggressive fighting pose. The statue was donated and erected in 2000.

Old First Church, "Vermont's Colonial Shrine," is on Monument Avenue (Vt. 9) a short distance southeast of the Catamount Tavern marker. The present structure (1805), one of the most beautiful in New England, is on the site of the first meetinghouse in which the territory's first church was organized. To the rear are graves of Patriots and their enemies (British, Canadian, and German) who died of wounds after the Battle of Bennington. Also buried in the cemetery is poet Robert Frost, whose wishes were "to be placed in surroundings that would never change." Members of the First Congregational Church, as it was then called, were early advocates of abolition and equality. They demonstrated that they were more than just talk in 1780 when they invited the Revolutionary War veteran Reverend Lemuel Haynes to be their minister. Haynes thus became the first African American minister to a white congregation in American history. He was also the first African American awarded an honorary degree when Vermont's Middlebury College awarded him an M.A. in 1804. (Middlebury awarded the first degree to a black student in 1823 when Alexander Twilight earned his B.A. Twilight became the nation's first black legislator in 1836.) The church is still in use as a house of worship. Phone: (802) 447-1223.

The Bennington Museum, just down the hill from the church and highly conspicuous on the south side of Vt. 9

Bennington Battle Monument. *A statue of Seth Warner, who led the Green Mountain Regiment in the 1777 Battle of Bennington, stands near the Bennington Battle Monument. When completed in 1891, the 306-foot granite obelisk was the tallest battle monument in the world.* © LEE SNIDER/PHOTO IMAGES/CORBIS.

(West Main Street), has a number of important Revolutionary War items and a disturbing statue of Abraham Lincoln out front. In a class by itself, and considered to be the most precious item in this outstanding regional museum, is the Bennington Flag. Once believed by many authorities to be the oldest surviving Stars and Stripes, it allegedly was used by the Bennington militia in the historic battle just over the border. Tradition further holds that it was raised by the grandfather of President Millard Fillmore. The last Fillmore owner presented it to the local historical association in 1926. The majestic flag remained inside its carry box until 1995, when it was examined for authentic age. Experts discovered that the Bennington Flag was constructed of machine-spun fibers, making its earliest possible date of origin 1810. The Bennington Flag is 10 by 5.5 feet with a white "76" in the union. It is exhibited dramatically in a frame at the end of the long hall that houses the museum's military collection. Also exhibited is the field of General Stark's personal flag that he took into battle. Near it is one of the four brass cannon of French origin captured from the Germans. These little 3-pounders were captured by Wolfe at Quebec in 1759, taken by the Patriots at Bennington (where only John Stark himself knew how to shoot them), surrendered by General William·Hull at Detroit in 1812, and retaken by the Americans the next year at Niagara. The museum's Battle of Bennington Gallery has a number of important firearms and historical relics of the Revolutionary era. (American glass, Bennington pottery, toys and dolls, household items, furniture, and paintings comprise the bulk of the collection. The Grandma Moses exhibit draws visitors in by the transcontinental busloads.)

It is not easy for the informed visitor to trace the route of Patriot forces from Old Bennington Battlefield, some 8 miles to the northwest. Although much of the route is along the Walloomsac River, once disfigured by industrial development but now reclaimed by nature, you will find it well worthwhile to pick your way along it.

The best point of departure is the entrance to Bennington College on Vt. 67A, about a mile from this highway's junction with U.S. 7 northwest of modern Bennington. A drive up the winding road that zigzags through the college grounds will provide a fine panorama of the ground covered by the Patriots in their march to the battlefield, but you will need to know what to look for.

The Silk Road runs along the eastern base of the high ground on which Bennington College is located. (By following this southeast from the entrance to the College on Vt. 67A for 0.9 mile you will hit Vail Road and circle eastward to the Bennington Battle Monument.) From east to west are three historic covered bridges along the Walloomsac that figured in the preliminaries of the battle of 1777. The Silk Road bridge (called Robinson Bridge) is near the entrance to the college. Continue 0.3 mile southwest on Vt. 67A from the latter entrance and turn left to reach the Paper Mill Bridge. Cross this and bear right, along the line of the river, for 1.3 miles through somewhat undeveloped country to the Bert Henry Bridge. En route look for a virtually hidden marker on the right (0.4 mile short of the Henry Bridge) that indicates the site of the Breakenridge home, "Birthplace of Vermont." Destroyed in 1889—only the cellar hole remains—this was the scene of the successful and bloodless resistance of Vermont settlers in July 1771 to an attempt by three hundred New Yorkers to evict them. (This marker is hard to see until you are right on it.)

The ***Seth Warner House*** site, indicated by a highway marker, is now occupied by a modern frame house of colonial style (saltbox). It is midway between the Henry Bridge and the "birthplace" site. Seth Warner was a leader of the Green Mountain Boys, having settled in this area in 1763 as a young man of twenty. He took part in the capture of Ticonderoga in 1775. Warner and Ethan

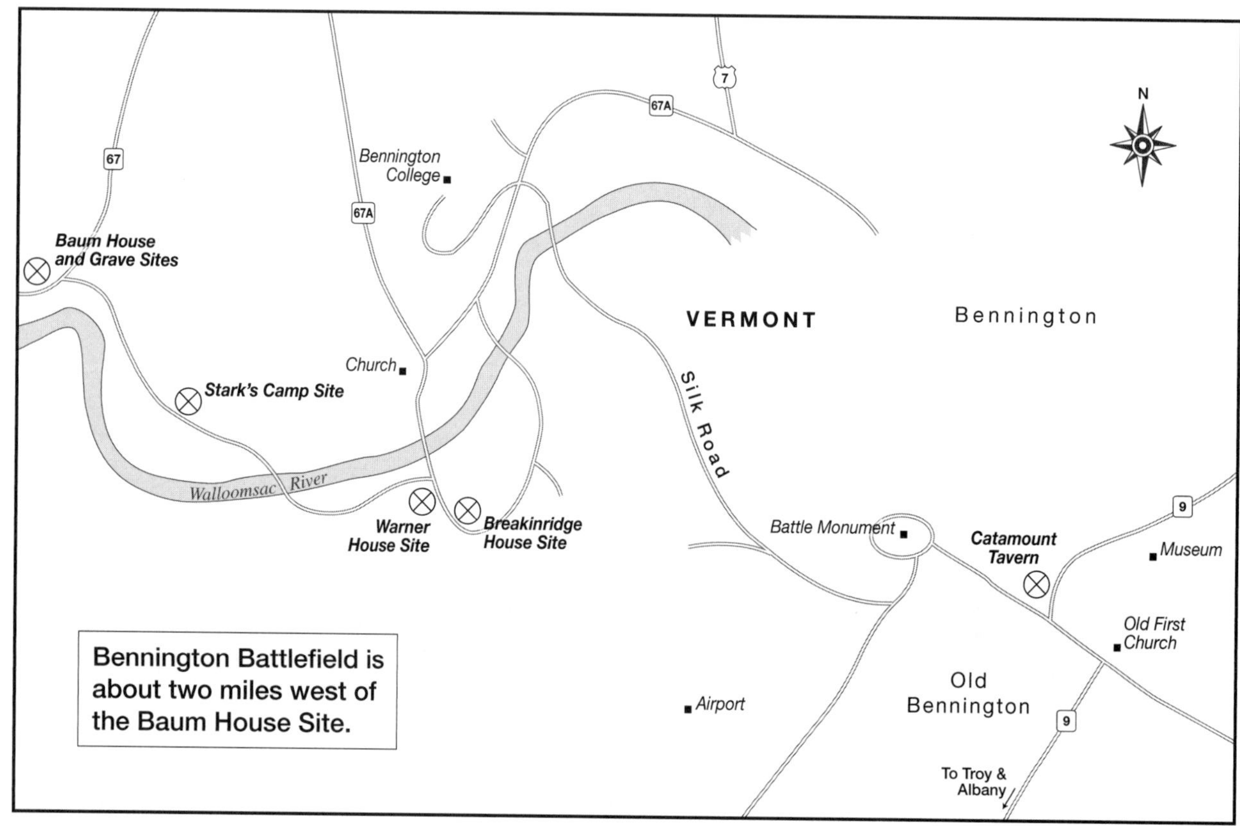

MAP BY XNR PRODUCTIONS. THE GALE GROUP.

Allen then arranged for incorporation of their band into the Continental army as a battalion of seven companies under Warner's command. As a lieutenant colonel he took part in the Canada operations, in which his regiment was decimated. Promoted to colonel, Warner and a few of his officers raised a new force to replace the original Green Mountain Regiment. Surprised and badly defeated at Hubbardton Battlefield (7 July 1777), the rough-and-ready Green Mountain Regiment under Warner reinforced General Stark in the final phase of the Battle of Bennington, clinching the victory. Warner became a militia general (March 1778) and remained in the Continental army as a regimental commander, but because of failing health saw little active service after 1777. He retired in January 1783 at the age of forty and died the day after Christmas 1784.

The site of Stark's encampment during the period 14 to 16 August, before the battle, is now an open hillside in picturesque farm country on a secondary road midway between the Warner House site (near Henry Bridge) and the junction of this road with Vt. 67. (It is exactly 1 mile from the latter point.) A simple monument is inscribed with the dubious quotation: "There are the redcoats and they are ours or this night Molly Stark sleeps a widow." (See also STARK HOUSE under New Hampshire.) A splendid panorama to the west is provided by the site, which is undeveloped.

From the junction of this country road on the left bank of the river and Vt. 67 you will find the site of the Baum House by driving toward the New York–Vermont state line and the battlefield. The house site is marked on a dangerous curve in the highway just 0.2 mile from the road junction previously mentioned, and 0.35 mile from the state line. Here the German commander Lieutenant Colonel Friedrich Baum died of his wounds and was buried. The location of his grave is not known.

There are many interesting landmarks associated with the Battle of Bennington, and the area surrounding the battlefield remains largely undeveloped. The entire site is under the management of the Division for Historical Preservation. Phone: (802) 447-0550.

Bennington Battlefield. *See* under NEW YORK.

Button Mold Bay and Arnold Bay, Lake Champlain, Addison County. The place where Benedict Arnold abandoned the major surviving portion of his fleet after the Battle of Valcour Bay, New York, is a tiny cove in what today is called Button Bay. Generally unspoiled, it survives in the 253-acre Button Bay State Park. But no effort has so far been made to mark or interpret the history of the site where Arnold ran the *Congress* and four smaller vessels aground on 13 October 1776 and burned them with their colors flying. From here Arnold and two hundred men made their way to Crown Point, ending one of the most gallant military exploits of the Revolution.

The park is most easily reached by taking the highway from Vergennes toward Basin Harbor and then going south on the road to Panton. Phone: (802) 475-2377.

Chimney Point, Lake Champlain, Addison County. So called because only chimneys of the old settlement remained standing after the Mohawk raid in 1760, Chimney Point was a well-known landmark during the colonial and Revolutionary War eras. Champlain visited the promontory after his fight with the Iroquois in 1609. Jacobus De Warm built a small fort here as early as 1690, having headed a French expedition to this point from Albany. De Warm's fort was rebuilt in 1730 by a small group of French settlers, but the site was abandoned in 1759 on threat of Indian attack and the houses were destroyed the next year. The Barnes House (open) is on the site of the French fort and incorporates one 2.5-foot-thick wall of that structure. The house's great oven is believed to be another vestige of Fort de Pieux. The keel and ribs of Benedict Arnold's *Congress* galley are exhibited along with other relics.

The ***John Strong Mansion*** is on Vt. 17 about 1 mile north of Chimney Point. John Strong built a house here that was burned by General von Riedesel's left wing of Burgoyne's offensive in 1777. Strong, a militia general, put up a fine federal mansion in 1795 on the site of his original house. The brick house has interesting interiors: a beautiful entrance hall spanned by a wide arch, a great kitchen fireplace, and corkscrew hinges on some doors. The massive chimney has a hiding place that would accommodate half a dozen people. Five generations of the family lived in the Strong Mansion before the DAR acquired it in 1934 and restored it as a house museum, which is open on Saturday and Sunday from Memorial Day through Labor Day, 10 A.M. to 5 P.M. Phone: (802) 759-2309. The house is conspicuous from the highway.

During the Seven Years' War, Chimney Point was fortified by the British as the terminus of the Crown Point Military Road. Near the Champlain Bridge are markers to this effect.

Colchester. *See* ALLEN (ETHAN) FARM SITE AND GRAVE.

Crown Point Military Road, Springfield to Chimney Point. When the British under Lord Jeffery Amherst drove the French from Ticonderoga and Crown Point in 1759 it was not foreseen that the strategic importance of those places in the Colonial Wars had ended. With the British conquest of Canada, sealed by the Treaty of 1763, Lake Champlain was no longer a military avenue of approach for enemy expeditions into the thirteen British colonies to the south. But Amherst could not count on this when he took the French positions on Lake Champlain, and he consequently planned major military construction to strengthen the British position in the region. Part of this was the road from the vicinity of Chimney Point, opposite Crown Point, diagonally across the Hampshire Grants (now Vermont) to Fort Number Four (now Charlestown, New Hampshire) in the Connecticut River Valley. The valley was an abundant source of provisions (even more important during the Revolution than during the Colonial Wars), and the new road opened a new line of communications with the port of Boston.

Like so many military projects, the Crown Point Road turned out to be relatively unimportant militarily but of tremendous value economically. It opened large regions for settlement. Curiously, the trace of the road finished in 1760 was not followed by subsequent builders, and most of this pioneer highway can be traced only because it has been mapped in an admirable program now directed by the Crown Point Road Association. Their work has followed that of others, notably the DAR, who placed markers earlier. Some sections of the old road are hiking trails. Other portions are barely discernible paths through the woods, some sections have been plowed under or built over, and a few short stretches are town roads.

A second edition of the pamphlet "Historical Markers on the Crown Point Road" was published by the Association. In addition to brief historical data, old and modern maps, and photographs of many markers, the pamphlet gives the location and text of the sixty-six markers in place as of 1965.

Copies of the booklet and information about the Association are available by contacting the Association at 51 Eden Street in Proctor, Vt. 05765, or by calling (802) 459-2837.

Fort Drummer (lost site), near Brattleboro, Connecticut River, Windham County. The first permanent English settlement in Vermont was established by Massachusetts in 1724 when Fort Drummer was built just south of today's Brattleboro. The first commander was Captain Timothy Dwight, whose son became president of Yale. Forty-three English soldiers and twelve Mohawk Indians formed the fort's initial garrison. Contemporary drawings have survived of the 180-foot-square fort of yellow pine. It was dismantled in 1763 and the site was covered by the backed-up waters of the river after the Vernon Dam was constructed. A granite marker, giving the history of the

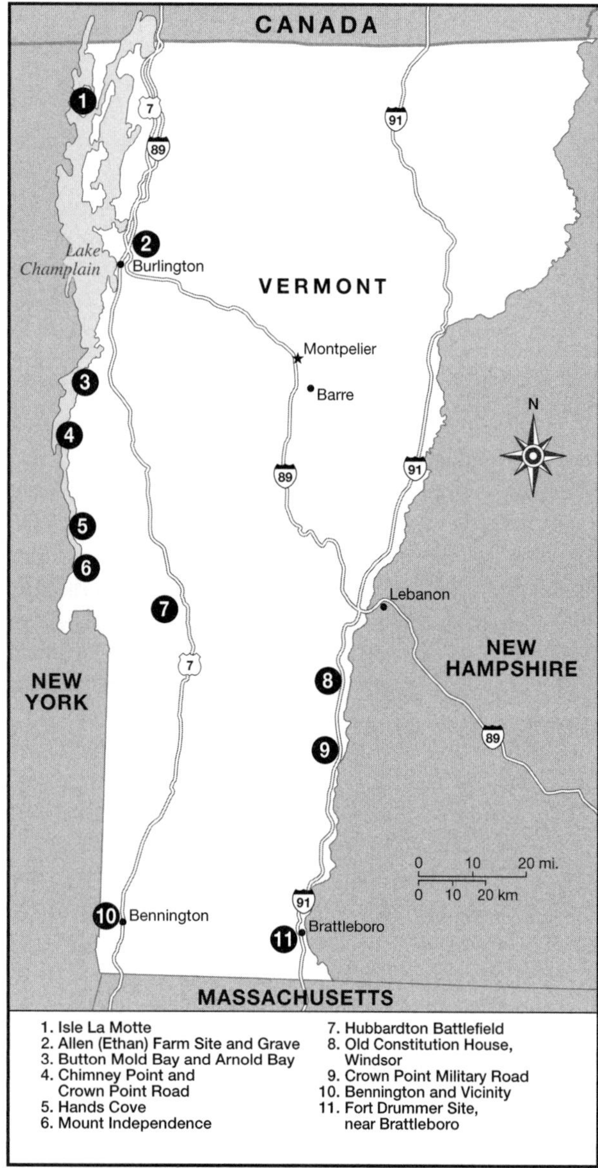

MAP BY XNR PRODUCTIONS. THE GALE GROUP.

fort, is 2,200 feet northwest of the site flooded in 1928. Fort Dummer State Park overlooks the site. The park is on Old Guilford Road outside Brattleboro and can be reached by taking Exit 1 from I-91 and following the signs. Phone: (802) 254-2610.

Hands Cove, Lake Champlain, Addison County. Figuring in the Patriot capture of Fort Ticonderoga, New York, in 1775 (under New York see TICONDEROGA), Hands Cove shows on modern topographical maps about 0.5 mile north of Larrabees Point, a terminus of the ancient Ticonderoga Ferry. Four miles in a straight line northeast is the Hands Cove Monument in Shoreham village (intersection of Vt. 74 and 22A).

Hubbardton Battlefield, near Hubbardton, 18 miles northwest of Rutland, Rutland County. About one thousand Americans under Colonels Seth Warner, Nathan Hale (not the same as the Nathan Hale who was hanged as a spy), and Ebenezer Francis, covering the rear of General Arthur St. Clair's column in the retreat from Ticonderoga, were surprised and beaten in an action here on 7 July 1777.

After a hard march through rugged country in oppressively hot weather, St. Clair passed the two-house settlement of Hubbardton (now East Hubbardton) and marched another 6 miles south to bivouac at Castleton. From here he intended to continue with the 2,500 men in his column to Skenesboro (now Whitehall, New York), where he hoped to find that his remaining 400 to 500 troops and heavy equipment had been successfully moved by boat from Ticonderoga.

Lieutenant Colonel Seth Warner, controversial leader of the Green Mountain Regiment, was ordered to wait at Hubbardton with his 150 men until the rear-guard regiments caught up, and then to lead them to Castleton. The troops had covered about 25 miles that day over primitive trails and hilly country in midsummer weather, and they were demoralized about their defeat at Ticonderoga. Probably Warner and the other two regimental commanders figured everybody needed a good night's sleep and that this was no time to harass the troops about being good combat soldiers. When night fell on the American camp at Hubbardton on 6 July the regiments of Francis and Hale had joined Warner's regiment.

Burgoyne had detected the American departure from Ticonderoga and had quickly taken up the pursuit. He himself led the chase by water to Skenesboro, and he ordered General Simon Fraser to march quickly to overtake St. Clair's column. Fraser's advance corps of 750 elite troops left Mount Independence (opposite Ticonderoga) at 4 A.M. on 6 July, only two hours after St. Clair. He was followed by General Riedesel, who brought his own regiment and Breymann's advance corps. Riedesel caught up with Fraser at about 1 P.M., and the two commanders agreed that Fraser should move a few more miles and camp at the site of modern Hubbardton. The Germans would bivouac a short distance to the rear, and both would resume the advance at 3:00 the next morning.

During the night Indian scouts found Warner's camp, which turned out to be just over the next range of hills from where Fraser had stopped. The British made plans for an attack at dawn. Hale's New Hampshire regiment was having breakfast when Fraser hit it at 4:40 A.M. This body of troops was routed, apparently without firing a shot in its own defense, and Hale himself was captured with seventy of his men.

Warner's men and the Massachusetts regiment of Colonel Francis had little time to react, but they dropped twenty-one of the enemy with their first volley. The British and Americans formed their lines of battle in the rocky, wooded terrain. The American left flank was anchored on the slopes of a 1,200-foot rise now known as Zion Hill, and the British commander quickly identified this as key terrain. Fraser therefore started building up strength on this flank for an envelopment, and to do this he thinned out his own left flank.

Inexperienced in frontier warfare (and not having such a good night's sleep, perhaps), the British were getting the worst of the battle when up came Riedesel with his Germans. Best remembered as the husband of the lady who followed him to America with their three daughters and wrote the famous memoirs of their six years' experience, this General Baron von Riedesel (1738–1800) was somebody to write about. Hearing the sound of battle, he had rushed forward with the faster-moving jaegers and grenadiers of his column, sending the jaegers straight against the American right flank, starting the grenadiers on an envelopment of that flank, and ordering his main body to come up on the double. As an Old World touch, he sent his own regiment forward singing to the music of its band. This was too much for the Massachusetts regiment. They held their own against the jaegers for about ten minutes, but then their colonel, Francis, was killed, the grenadiers came crashing through the brush toward their flank, and they started giving ground.

The Green Mountain Regiment was left to face the onslaught alone. Hit by a bayonet attack, it responded with alacrity to Colonel Warner's order to "Scatter and meet me at Manchester."

In his *War of the Revolution*, Christopher Ward says that the two-hour action at Hubbardton was as bloody as Waterloo in proportion to the forces engaged. Almost one-third of the Americans were captured, and more than 40 were killed. The other side lost about 35 killed and 150 wounded. Most of the remaining two-thirds of the American forces were able to regroup at Manchester, from where Warner led his regiment to action at the Battle of Bennington.

The site of the battle, the only one fought during the Revolution on Vermont soil, is preserved in the Hubbardton Battlefield Sate Park, which is open from Memorial Day to Columbus Day, 10:30 A.M. to 5:30 P.M., Monday through Friday. Phone: (802) 273-2282. A diorama of the battle is available in the park's visitors center, and a path across the field brings visitors to benches on a ridge above the valley where the military road came through. Looking east, there are wonderful views of the Green Mountains, and to the west one can see the Taconic Mountains of New York.

Hyde Log Cabin, on U.S. Route 2 just north of the town of Grand Isle. The home of the two Jedediah Hydes, father and son. The elder, Captain Jedediah Hyde, fought at Bunker Hill and served in Captain William Coit's Connecticut Grenadiers. His son, Jedediah Hyde, Jr., was a member of Captain Rufus Putnam's Corps of Engineers. After the Battle of Bennington, Hyde the younger picked up a surveyor's compass and a theodolite from the spoils captured from the German troops. He used these tools when he surveyed Grand Isle after he and his father moved to this cabin in 1783. The house reamined in the Hyde family for 150 years. Today it is owned by the state and contains numerous items from the Revolutionary period. Open 4 July through Labor Day, Thursday through Monday, 11 A.M. to 5 P.M. Phone: (802) 828-3051.

Isle La Motte, Lake Champlain, Grand Isle County. Strategically situated on the Lake Champlain–Lake George waterway, this place is named for Captain La Mothe, who built a shrine here in 1665 or 1666 and established a settlement that proved to be short-lived. The site of the French Fort Ste. Anne, built in 1666 for a garrison of three hundred men but soon abandoned, is marked by cedars and rock mounds that trace its outline. The Shrine of Ste. Anne survives as a small chapel in a grove of pines. The island of about 11,000 acres is accessible by highway and is of exceptional interest geologically (fossil coral reef).

Lake Champlain Maritime Museum, Basin Harbor. A unique museum devoted to the naval history of Lake Champlain, which devotes particular attention to the Revolutionary era. Visitors can explore a working replica of Benedict Arnold's 1776 54-foot square-rigged gunboat, the *Philadelphia.* In addition to exhibits on eighteenth-century shipbuilding and demonstrations by artisans, the museum has a display on the naval defense of Lake Champlain and another on "The Revolutionary War in the Champlain Valley." The museum is located 7 miles west of Vergennes off Route 22A on Basin Harbor Road. Open May through October daily, 10 A.M. to 5 P.M. Phone: (802) 475-2022.

Montpelier. With just eight thousand people, Montpelier is the nation's least populous state capital. It is also the only one without a single fast-food restaurant. The State Capitol on State Street is hard to miss, with its gold dome dominating the beautiful setting. In addition to the famous statue of Ethan Allen, the capitol building boasts two brass cannon captured from the Germans at the Battle of Bennington in 1777. As you face the capitol, the Vermont Historical Society Museum is to your immediate right. For the serious scholar, it is hard to surpass the Vermont State Archives, which are probably the best run in the nation; the Redstone Building, 26 Terrace Street; phone: (802) 828-2363.

Mount Independence Site, Lake Champlain opposite Fort Ticonderoga, New York, Addison County. At the time of the Revolution it was not covered by the heavy vegetation there now, and Mount Independence was quite bare. Clearing had been done to provide better fields of observation and to furnish timber for the important ship-fitting operations at the site.

In the article on Ticonderoga (see under NEW YORK) is a sketch of Mount Independence's role in the Revolution and a mention of the exceptionally fine model to be seen in the museum of Fort Ticonderoga. The Mount Independence site is operated by the state, which maintains several hiking trails through the remains of the old military grounds. The National Historic Landmark encompasses the remains of the fort built by an estimated ten to twelve thousand American troops in 1776, which some claim was the largest built by the Patriots during the Revolution. The fort was named in honor of the recent Declaration of Independence. In addition to the fortification ruins, there are remains and explanatory displays of the stockade, blockhouse, barracks, gun batteries, and hospital scattered over this 300-acre site. In 2005 the state added a wheelchair accessible trail. The visitors center's museum examines military life at the fort and includes many artifacts recovered during recent archaeological excavations. Special events, including military reenactments, are scheduled throughout the season that runs from late May until October. It is open from late May through the end of October daily from 9:30 A.M. to 5:30 P.M. Phone: (802) 759-2412. Take Route 73 west from Orwell, turning at the first left. A marker on Route 22A in Orwell notes the route of the Mount Independence Military Road built during the construction of the fort on Mount Independence. In nearby Shoreham one can take the MV *Carillon* for a cruise on Lake Champlain with narration about the several Revolutionary War sites on the lake. Phone: (802) 897-5331.

Old Constitution House, Windsor, Windsor County. Delegates met at Windsor starting on 4 June 1777 to adopt a constitution for the "free and independent state of Vermont." (Settlers of the Hampshire Grants had declared their independence earlier in the year.) For the final phase of their deliberations the delegates met in the frame house dating from about 1760 and operated as a tavern by Elijah West. Tradition has it that the news of Seth Warner's defeat at Hubbardton Battlefield arrived just as the final reading of the new constitution was taking place on 8 July, and that only a violent thunderstorm kept the legislators together long enough to vote on the document. The final product of their labor was a document startling for its democratic clarity: outlawing slavery, establishing the right of all adult men to vote, and creating a public school system. (The first of these schools was built in 1785 in Norwich, where there is a historical marker on Route 5.) The pub has since been dubbed the Old Constitution House and, naturally, "the Birthplace of Vermont." (Another "birthplace" is near Bennington.) The site, including its museum artifacts, is owned and operated by the state's Division of Historic Sites. It is a house museum with a good collection pertaining to Vermont's early history. (A republic until 1791 because of New York's refusal to acknowledge the loss of this territory, Vermont finally joined the Union as the fourteenth state in that year.) Take Exits 8 or 9 off I-91 and drive into Windsor. The house is at 16 North Main Street (U.S. 5) and is open Wednesday through Sunday from late May into October. Phone: (802) 672-3773.

Royalton Raid Site, Route 14 in the town of Royalton. On 16 October 1780 more than two hundred Indians (primarily Mohawk) led by a British officer surprised the town of Royalton on Vermont's remote northern frontier. They killed two people and took thirty-two prisoners before setting fire to Royalton. The Indians took their captives back to Canada, where they were ransomed for $8 a head.

VIRGINIA

An excellent system of historical markers on Virginia's principal highways was conceived in 1927. Today there are more than 2,000 tall, silver markers pertaining to a wide range of topics that help tell the state's history. The Department of Historic Resources (once the Historic Landmarks Commission) provides an impressive list of books dealing with Virginia's history, some of which it publishes and others that are distributed by various publishing companies. All of the books, including the newest editions of *A Guidebook to Virginia's Historical Markers* (1994) and *The Virginia Landmarks Register* (2000), are available for purchase from its website, www.dhr.virginia.gov or by calling University of Virginia Press at (800) 831-3406. A visitor to the state's Department of Historic Resources website will also find a wealth of information on historic preservation and state landmarks.

The Virginia State Tourism Corporation is located at 901 East Byrd Street, Richmond, Va. 23219. They distribute an assortment of travel guides and maps, some of which pertain directly to colonial landmarks. However, similar to the states to Virginia's south, the Civil War receives more focus than the American Revolution. Website: www.virginia.org; phone: (800) 847-4882.

The Virginia Historical Society (1831) has a museum illustrating the early history of the state and a library open to approved users without charge. It is located at 428 North Boulevard, Richmond, Va. 23220 (mailing address: P.O. Box 7311, Richmond, Va. 23221). Website: www.vahistorical.org; main phone: (804) 358-4901; museum phone: (804) 342-9671.

Albemarle Old Courthouse, James River, Albemarle County. The first seat of Albemarle County was at the sharp hook in the James River near the present town of Scottsville. In 1761 the county seat was moved to Charlottesville. Albemarle Old Courthouse nevertheless remained an important landmark during the Revolution, being an important depot for Patriot supplies until their evacuation to Charlottesville and Staunton was forced by Cornwallis's raid in June 1781. See POINT OF FORK and MECHUNK CREEK.

Alexandria. Captain John Smith passed the site of Alexandria during his explorations of 1608. Land was first patented here in 1657, a grant was made in 1669, and the next year John Alexander bought and surveyed 6,000 acres that included the area where the city would later be built. Alexander's tract was just north of the one later called Mount Vernon. A few white settlers started appearing around 1670, and by 1695 there was something resembling a village near the mouth of Great Hunting Creek. A warehouse was built there in 1731, and a public ferry established. The settlement was called Belhaven.

Not surprisingly, the local Indians resisted this invasion. John Washington, George's great-grandfather, led the Virginia contingent that joined up with Marylanders to battle the Susquehannocks for control of this region, and many of the local settlers joined in Bacon's Rebellion, which aimed to exterminate the Indians. The end of Queen Anne's War in 1713 marked the start of an era of prosperity for the white elite, founded on tobacco, and the port of Alexandria eventually became second only to Boston in colonial America in the value of exports. As settlement moved west into the Shenandoah, export of flour to England and the West Indies became nearly as important as tobacco. Ships coming for these products brought cargoes of manufactured goods and luxuries from England and the Caribbean.

Meanwhile, the town of Alexandria had been established. In 1748 the seventeen-year-old George Washington, then living at Mount Vernon, assisted the county surveyor in laying out the town of 84 half-acre lots. Some of these were bought by his half-brothers, Lawrence and Augustine. Alexandria became the seat of Fairfax County in 1752 and was incorporated in 1779. To create the District of Columbia, in 1789 Virginia contributed Alexandria and the portion of Fairfax County that now is Arlington County. The towering Washington Masonic Memorial (see below) is on a site proposed for the national capitol. In 1846 Alexandria petitioned Congress successfully for return to Virginia. Meanwhile, the city's commercial importance had been eclipsed by Washington, and it has retained a quaint, old-fashioned character.

In a historic district of nearly 100 blocks, many buildings of the colonial period survive. These are appealing from an architectural and cultural standpoint, but they also furnish the "third dimension" for a significant portion of American history.

Alexandria Black History Resource Center, 902 Wythe Street. Covers the history of African Americans in Alexandria from the mid-eighteenth century to today. Open Tuesday through Saturday, from 10 A.M. to 4 P.M. Phone: (703) 838-4356.

Gadsby's Tavern, 132 Royal Street. Alexandria was important as the only major settlement on the main colonial highway between Baltimore and Fredericksburg, this segment being a part of the route between the northern and southern colonies. Colonial taverns played a vital role as focal points for news and political activity, and Gadsby's was more important than most because it was fed foreign news and political opinion by customers coming into the port as well as by those who traveled the highway. The older portion of the brick building you see in modern Alexandria was built around 1792 and long known as City Tavern. In November 1799 Washington reviewed the local militia from the tavern steps, ending his military activities where they had started forty-five years earlier. A gigantic reception was held here for Lafayette in 1824. John Gadsby became host of the tavern in 1796. Today, the Gadsby's Tavern Restaurant is privately owned, while the Gadsby's Tavern Museum is operated by the city. Phone: (703) 838-4242.

Carlyle House. Entrance at 121 North Fairfax Street. Phone: (703) 549-2997. Here Braddock planned his ill-fated expedition of 1755, met with governors of four colonies to discuss the strategy for driving the French from the Forks of the Ohio, and commissioned Washington as his aide-de-camp. The house was built in 1752 by John Carlyle, one of Alexandria's many Scottish merchants. This site is called Carlyle House Historic Park and serves as a museum that organizes guided tours and many historical special events. There is also a museum gift shop.

Ramsay House, King and Fairfax Streets. Home of Alexandria's first and only lord mayor, William Ramsay, this rather odd building was long thought to date from the period 1749 to 1751. In the process of reconstruction after the house had been almost totally destroyed by fire in 1942, evidence was uncovered to indicate that it had been put up around 1725. The experienced historical architect in charge of reconstruction also came to the conclusion that the house had been moved from a former location closer to the mouth of Hunting Creek (Jones Point). Another theory is that it was built at Dumfries, some 25 miles down the Potomac from Alexandria, and moved by barge. Quite apart from the fact that William Ramsay would have been less than ten years old in 1725, there is strong evidence that these recent revelations are misguided, that instead the house was not started before 1749, and that it has always stood at its present location. As for the claim of being Alexandria's oldest house, it must be reiterated that the structure is a reconstruction, not a restoration.

The Information Center for Old Town Alexandria is in the Ramsay House, whose mail address is 221 King Street, Alexandria, Va. 22314. Here the out-of-town visitor can pick up brochures that detail a walking tour and other information on the area. It is open daily from 9 A.M. to 5 P.M. Phone: (703) 838-4200.

Stabler-Leadbeater Apothecary Shop, 107 South Fairfax Street. One of the country's oldest drugstores, in continuous operation during the years 1792 to 1933, it has prescription files which record sales to the Washington, Lee, Custis, and Fairfax families, and to Henry Clay, John C. Calhoun, and Daniel Webster. It is now a private museum. Phone: (703) 836-3713.

Craik House (private), 210 Duke Street. Built about 1790, this was the home and office of Dr. James Craik (1730–1814), chief physician and surgeon of the Continental army. (It should be noted that this title did not signify the top position in the medical department, as might be assumed. At 212 South Fairfax Street is the house of another man with the similarly misleading title of physician general of the Continental army, Dr. William Brown. The actual top doctor of the American army during the Revolution held a variety of titles incorporating the operative word "director.") James Craik was the son of a Scottish squire whose gardener was the father of John Paul Jones. After studying medicine at Edinburgh, Craik practiced successively in the West Indies, Norfolk, Virginia, and Winchester, Virginia, where he was physician of the fort. Having become surgeon of a Virginia regiment, he was with Washington at Great Meadows, tended the mortally wounded Braddock, and became

Friendship Fire Engine House. *This small brick building in Alexandria, Virginia, dates to about 1775. It housed the volunteer fire company to which George Washington donated a fire engine in 1774, the year the company was formally organized.* © LEE SNIDER/PHOTO IMAGES/CORBIS.

Washington's chief medical officer when the latter was named head of the state's military forces in August 1755. Thereafter he was closely associated with Washington, tending him in his final illness (1799) and leaving an account of this event, which he hastened.

Coryell House (private), 208 Duke Street. A "flounder" house, long and narrow with a lean-to roof and without windows on the taller side, this is a specimen of an architectural tax-evasion device probably brought to Alexandria by Philadelphia Quakers. The owner of such a house could claim that it was unfinished, thereby dodging the tax due on completed houses. Although "flounder" is the local term in Alexandria, many houses of this type can be seen in the older sections of Philadelphia. The unpainted frame Coryell House, which leans against the brick house of Dr. Craik and was built about the same year, was the home of George Coryell, who in 1776 had assisted his father, Cornelius, in ferrying Washington across the Delaware to attack the Hessians in Trenton.

Christ Church, Cameron and North Washington Streets. Washington was a vestryman here for three months in 1765, and his box pew is marked. Construction on the existing structure started two years later, and features such as the tower and cupola were added in 1818. Pohick Church was the one regularly attended by Washington. The church is open to the public. Phone: (703) 549-1450.

Friendship Fire Engine House, 107 South Alfred Street. A small brick building dating from about 1775, this housed the fire company to which Washington gave a fire engine brought from Philadelphia in 1774, the year the company was formally organized. This is the first volunteer fire department in Alexandria. Tours and educational programs are scheduled here. Among the early fire-fighting equipment on display is a model of this man-powered machine. Museum phone: (703) 838-3891.

Washington Masonic National Memorial, King Street and Russell Road. Dominating the landscape and visible for many miles in all directions, this monstrous edifice (333 feet high) on Shooter's Hill houses relics and important portraits in the possession of the Alexandria-Washington Lodge of Masons. Open daily. Phone: (703) 683-2007.

Tourist information is available from the Ramsay House (see above).

Belvoir Ruins, Fort Belvoir Military Reservation, 9 miles south of Alexandria and near Mount Vernon, U.S. 1. The manor house of William Fairfax figured prominently in the early life of George Washington (see MOUNT VERNON). Construction was started in 1741 of a nine-room brick house 36 by 60 feet in size, with a full basement, a large central hall and four rooms on the ground floor, and five large bedrooms upstairs. When completed in 1743, Belvoir included brick "dependencies"—offices, stables, and a coach house. The eccentric Thomas, Sixth Lord Fairfax (1693–1781), who had inherited proprietary rights to 5 million acres in Virginia, lived at Belvoir for several years before establishing his home near Winchester. William's son, George William Fairfax (1724–1787), a close friend of George Washington, inherited Belvoir in 1757. He was a Loyalist, and at the outbreak of the Revolution he returned to England. The mansion was gutted by fire in 1783. Despite repeated urgings by Washington to come back and rebuild Belvoir, the Fairfaxes remained in England. Belvoir was completely demolished by the British in 1814.

Berkeley Plantation, James River, 7 miles west of Charles City and just off Va. 5. Quite aside from the architectural charms of the brick mansion and its two large dependencies, Berkeley has a long list of historical distinctions. It was the site of the first Thanksgiving service in America, held more than a year before the more famous one in New England. It was the ancestral home of a signer of the Declaration of Independence and two presidents, and it was visited by every president from Washington to James Buchanan—fifteen presidents during the period 1789 to 1861. During the Civil War it served in 1862 as McClellan's headquarters, and it was here that the famous American bugle call, "Taps," originated.

The estate, eventually known as Harrison's Landing, was part of the grant made in 1619 to Sir George Yeardley, Richard Berkeley, and others; settlers landed there on 4 December 1619 with instructions from the proprietors that "the day of our ships arrival . . . shall be yearly and perpetually kept as a day of Thankgsiving."

Abandoned after the Indian massacre of 1622, the place was repatented in 1636 and acquired by John Bland. The latter's son, Giles, was executed for his part in Bacon's Rebellion (1676). The estate was confiscated by the governor and later sold to Benjamin Harrison III (1673–1710), who was the colony's attorney general, treasurer, and speaker of the House of Burgesses. (This Harrison was the third of his name in Virginia; hence the designation III, which is a genealogical convenience only—the men did not so sign their names.) The eldest son, Benjamin IV, started building the present mansion in 1726. Benjamin V (1726–1791), who inherited the place in 1745 when his father and two sisters were killed by lightning, was a signer of the Declaration of Independence and three-time governor of Virginia. Benjamin VI installed the handsome interior woodwork; his brother, William Henry, and the latter's grandson, Benjamin, became presidents of the United States.

The mansion, whose restoration was started in 1937, is a plain two-story brick building of early Georgian style with two tall chimneys. Flanked by dependencies, it was altered around 1800 to two stories. The site is open to the public daily from 9 A.M. to 5 P.M. Phone: (804) 829-6018.

Boswell's Tavern, South Anna River, Louisa County. At the present village of this name (intersection of U.S. 15 and Va. 22) a tavern was kept by a large Scot named Boswell. Here Lafayette stayed on 11 June 1781 while en route from Raccoon Ford to Mechunk Creek. The locality is referred to also in Revolutionary War history as Mumford's (Bridge). Now a private residence, Boswell's is one of the most complete colonial taverns surviving in Virginia: a story-and-a-half frame building with large end chimneys.

Carter's Grove Plantation, six miles southeast of Williamsburg on U.S. 60. From the standpoint of the original craftsmanship and the expert restoration, this is a superb example of colonial Virginia architecture. Carter's Grove is unquestionably one of the most beautiful places in America. Historically, it is of minor interest: the ubiquitous saber marks of Banastre Tarleton on the balustrade; the "Refusal Room" in which Washington and Jefferson are said to have been turned down by ladies they wanted to marry. The eighteenth-century slave quarters have been reconstructed and located on the site as the Winthrop Rockefeller Archeology Museum. Carter Grove is managed by Colonial Williamsburg. Website: www.history.org; phone: (757) 229-1000. See CHRIST CHURCH for biographical data on the Carter family.

Castle Hill, Cobham, Albemarle County, 9 miles northeast of Charlottesville on Va. 231. Its earlier section built in 1764 by Dr. Thomas Walker (1715–1794), whose achievements included discovery of Cumberland Gap, Castle Hill has a "modern," two-story addition dating from 1824. It was the site of a delaying action that probably kept Thomas Jefferson from being captured by Tarleton. Captain John Jouett of the Virginia militia had gotten ahead of Tarleton's raiders and ridden through the night of 3 to 4 June 1781 toward Monticello and Charlottesville to warn Jefferson and the state legislators. Given a fresh mount at Castle Hill, he hastened on. When Tarleton reached Castle Hill, where he captured a number of prominent Patriots, he could not resist the offer of a sumptuous breakfast. His delay of an hour to rest his tired troopers (who had left Louisa Courthouse at 2 A.M.) gave Jefferson time to escape from Monticello a mere ten minutes ahead of the British. It is a private residence.

Chiswell Lead Mines, Austinville, Wythe County. Colonel John Chiswell discovered lead deposits here in 1756 (allegedly while hiding in a cave to escape pursuit by Indians), and numerous small industrial developments at this place were important during the Revolution. These included furnaces and forges in addition to lead and zinc mines. The settlement that grew up in the neighborhood became the capital of far-flung Fincastle County, which from 1772 to 1776 comprised southwestern Virginia and Kentucky. At Chiswell Lead Mines (as the settlement originally was called) the famous Fincastle Resolves were adopted.

In July 1775 the Fincastle Committee of Safety was directed by the Virginia Assembly to contract with the mines for lead and to take over the mines if not satisfied with production. Loyalists naturally attempted to put the mines out of business, and several skirmishes were fought in the region. In 1780 Colonel Charles Lynch, then superintendent of the mines, used extralegal methods in suppressing Loyalist efforts to stop production, thereby perhaps contributing his name as a new term to the vocabulary; there are many possible origins for the phrase "lynch law." (It is to be noted that "lynch law" acquired its more sinister connotations later. Lynch's court did not hand down sentences more severe than whipping.)

Colonel Chiswell died suddenly in his Williamsburg home after being charged with the murder of Robert Routledge at Effingham Tavern in 1766. Chiswell had been regaling guests with fabulous accounts of his lead mines when Routledge impugned his veracity and was run through by Chiswell's sword. Although a physician testified that the famous prospector, miner, and promoter died of natural causes, it was universally believed that he committed suicide to escape trial.

In the out-of-the-way and forlorn little town of Austinville on the bank of New River is a monument marking the site of the Chiswell lead mines. Approaching the town from U.S. 52 on County Road 619 over a narrow, winding road, you drop into bottomland and enter the portion of Austinville on the northern bank of the river. Do not cross the bridge and railroad tracks to the main section of town, but continue west from the bridge half a mile and the monument will be to the south, opposite a cemetery.

The Chiswell lead mines (Austinville) site is not to be confused with Fort Chiswell, 6 miles to the north. Although built after the Revolution, about 1820, the Old Shot Tower is worth visiting when you leave Austinville. It is visible from the historical marker on U.S. 52 about 8 miles southeast of Fort Chiswell and about 5 miles from Austinville via County Road 619 and U.S. 52. (I-77 will pass within a few hundred yards.)

Christ Church, 3 miles south of Kilmarnock on Route 646 just off Route 200. On the site of a church dating from 1669 to 1675, this Greek-cruciform brick building was erected in 1732 by "King" Carter. Although the latter's magnificent home on the Rappahannock has not survived, the church of the Carters remains almost as it was when completed 273 years ago. From an architectural standpoint it is remarkable not only for a combination of typical early Georgian features, with several that are unique, but also for the integrity of its interior furnishings.

John Carter settled at Corotoman about 1650 and laid the foundations of a family that, primarily through the female line, would produce eight governors of Virginia, three signers of the Declaration of Independence, two famous fighting generals (Robert E. Lee and his father, "Light Horse Harry" Lee) and a chief justice. John's second son, Robert (1663–1732), pyramided the estate inherited from his father in 1669 and older brother (1690) into holdings that earned him the sobriquet of "King." Most of his wealth came from two periods during which he was agent for the Fairfaxes, who held the royal patent for 5 million acres (see GREENWAY COURT). He left his descendants about 300,000 acres, 1,000 slaves, £10,000 in cash, and the family seat of Corotoman. As an indication of the value of money left by Carter, his grandson built Carter's Grove Plantation for a total of £500, of which £150 was the contractor's fee. Whereas English visitors and French aristocrats could comment that even the famous Mount Vernon was a simple place in comparison with the stately houses of Europe, Corotoman "rivaled the splendor of many an English noble's estate" (Louis B. Wright, *The First Gentlemen of Virginia*, p. 248).

Tombs of the early Carters are at Christ Church. The church grounds are open daily and the Carter Reception Center Museum is open daily from April through November. Tours are by appointment. Phone: (804) 438-6855.

Colonial Heights, Appomattox River opposite Petersburg. George Archer acquired property here in 1665, and it was to Archer's Hill that Patriot forces withdrew in good order after unsuccessfully opposing the British capture of Petersburg on 25 April 1781. Lafayette marched south from Richmond and on 10 May started a cannonade of Petersburg from behind the boxwood hedge on the lawn of Oak Hill. The house, known also as Archer's Hill, and the hedge are still standing on Carroll Avenue of modern Colonial Heights (see below).

Violet Bank (named for a bank of violets, not a financial operation) was Lafayette's headquarters. The first mansion was built in 1770 and burned in 1810. The surviving structure, dating from 1814, was General Robert E. Lee's headquarters during the siege of Petersburg in 1864. Presently it is owned by the city and serves as a Civil War museum. Still standing in front of Violet Bank is the gigantic Cucumber Tree (a species of magnolia), said to have been brought back by one of Governor Alexander Spotswood's "Knights of the Golden Horseshoe" from their exploration of the Shenandoah Valley in 1716. This is just one of the numerous stories surrounding the tree's origin. (Others, including the gigantic hero Peter Francisco, have been credited with planting the tree.)

The sites are indicated by highway markers on U.S. 1 and 301 in Colonial Heights a short distance north of the bridge from Petersburg. The city of Colonial Heights maintains an informative website on its colonial history, www.colonial-heights.com.

Cuckoo Tavern Site, Louisa County. In the triangle where U.S. 33 and 522 intersect (which shows on the highway map as the village of Cuckoo) is a marker indicating the site of the tavern from which the proprietor's son, Jack Jouett, rode over the Old Mountain Road through Castle

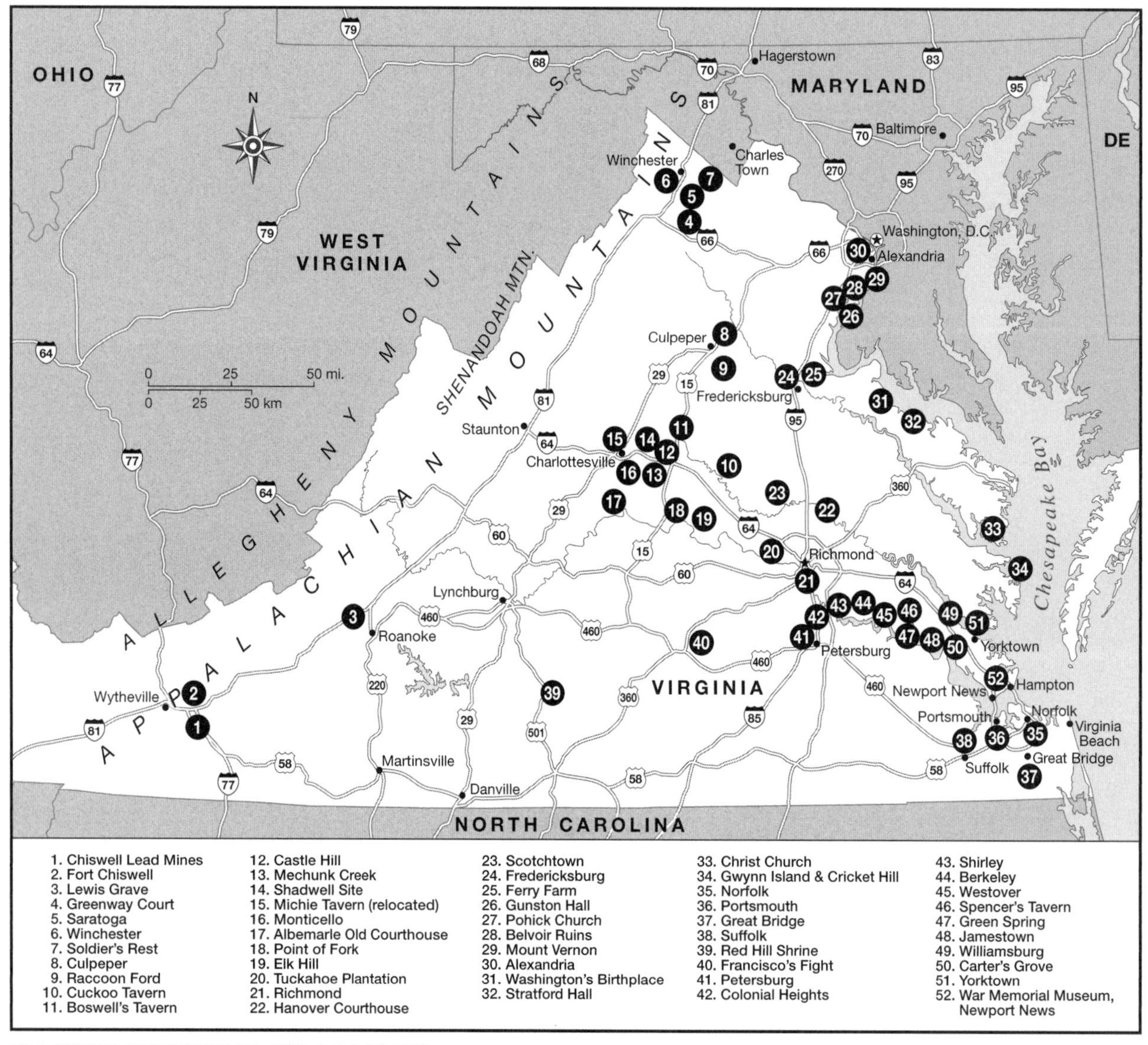

MAP BY XNR PRODUCTIONS. THE GALE GROUP.

Hill to warn Thomas Jefferson at Monticello that Tarleton was coming.

Culpeper, seat of Culpeper County. On U.S. 522, half a mile west of the traffic light in the center of modern Culpeper and opposite a very large cemetery, is a highway marker saying that the Culpeper Minutemen were organized on the hill to the south in 1775. Following Glazier Street south from the vicinity of this sign on U.S. 522 (Sperryville Pike), you will find a region of unpretentious modern homes and several small hills, but no particular landmarks or signs identifying "the hill." A 10-foot stone obelisk inscribed "Virginia's First Minutemen—Great Bridge Their First Battle" (erected by the DAR in 1938) is in Culpeper on U.S. 522, 0.8 mile south of the traffic light mentioned above.

John Marshall, later chief justice of the Supreme Court, marched as a lieutenant in his father's company from Fauquier County to join the Culpeper Minutemen, which included volunteers from Orange County as well (see GREAT BRIDGE). The old courthouse that gave this place its name has been succeeded by one built in 1870.

Cumberland Gap. *See* under KENTUCKY.

Elk Hill, James River. Thomas Jefferson's estate here was occupied by Cornwallis during the period 7 to 15 June 1781 and was virtually destroyed by the British raiders. It was again sacked by an invading army in 1865. The gray-stucco brick house has survived on its high hill among ancient elms and box bushes. Privately owned and hard to find, it is reached by taking Va. 6 west from Georges Tavern for 1 mile, at which point a highway marker indicates that the site is 2 miles south; the entrance to the estate is actually 1.6 miles south on County Road 608.

Ferry Farm Site, opposite Fredericksburg, on State Route 3 in Stafford County near the Rappahannock River. George Washington spent much of his boyhood, from late 1738 to 1747, at this place. It was his share of the estates of his father, who died here in 1743. His mother lived at Ferry Farm until she moved across the river in 1772 to Fredericksburg. If the young Washington ever cut down a paternal cherry tree (which he didn't) or threw a Spanish dollar across the river (highly improbable), Ferry Farm would have been the scene.

In 1996 the George Washington's Fredericksburg Foundation purchased the Ferry Farm and preserved it for generations to come. Visitors should start their tour of George Washington's boyhood home at the visitors center, where a map for a self-guided tour of the grounds is available. The visitors center features a museum gallery, "George Washington—Boy before Legend." Open daily from 10 A.M. to 5 P.M. Phone: (540) 370-0732.

Fort Chiswell, Wythe County. A pyramid of boulders in the present village of Fort Chiswell north of the junction of interstates I-81 and I-77 about 6 miles east of Wytheville is all that remains to mark the site of the fort built by William Byrd III in the fall of 1760. Byrd named the frontier post for his friend Colonel John Chiswell, who had recently started developing the nearby Chiswell Lead Mines. It may have been at Fort Chiswell that Dan Morgan, then a twenty-year-old wagoner and veteran of Braddock's Defeat, was sentenced to receive five hundred lashes for hitting back at a British officer who slapped him with the flat of a sword. Wherever this actually happened, in later years the famous leader of riflemen used to bare his back to his followers, showing them why he so hated the British and bragging that he owed them one more stripe because they miscounted.

Francisco's Fight (Ward's Tavern) Site, Nottoway County. Although the site of this heroic episode is not plotted on the official highway map of Virginia, it does appear—a little flag with the legend "Spot Signalized by Francisco's Gallantry"—in, of all places, plate CXXXVII of the *Atlas to Accompany the Official Records of the Union and Confederate Armies, 1861–1865.* On modern highway maps there is no such nod to history, only the symbol for an airport. A state highway marker on U.S. 360, 6 miles northeast of Burkeville and approximately 3 miles due west of the site, reads: "FRANCISCO'S FIGHT. A few miles east [at Ward's Tavern] Peter Francisco . . . defeated, singlehanded, nine of Tarleton's British dragoons, July, 1781. Francisco weighed 260 pounds and was considered the strongest man in Virginia. . . ." Some historians credit the claim that he killed eleven dragoons on this occasion.

Peter Francisco (c. 1760–1836) appeared mysteriously in Virginia as an abandoned baby, possibly of Portuguese origin. He was raised by an uncle of Patrick Henry's, grew to a 6'6" giant, and joined a regiment of Virginia Continentals at the age of fifteen. Seriously wounded on several occasions, he distinguished himself on many famous battlefields (Brandywine, Germantown, Fort Mifflin, Monmouth, Stony Point, Paulus Hook, Camden, and Guilford) and was truly a legend in his own time. After the war he prospered as a businessman and undertook a highly successful program of self-education.

On 15 March many states celebrate Peter Francisco Day. The United States Postal Service produced a stamp (18-cent) in his honor in 1975. He is buried in Richmond in Shockoe Hill Cemetery.

Fredericksburg. Important as a tidewater port and trading center in colonial days, Fredericksburg was settled in 1671, legally founded in 1727 and named for the father of George III, and incorporated in 1781. The town figured prominently in Washington's life; he lived for a while at Ferry Farm, a family estate across the Rappahannock from Fredericksburg, attended school in town for four months, frequented the Masonic Lodge and the Rising Sun Tavern, and visited the homes of his mother and sister. Other prominent Virginians and associates of Washington are identified with the town, which furnished leaders for the Revolution, maintained a "gunnery" and a military hospital, and was the site of a German prison camp. Most of the sites identified with these activities have been preserved and can be visited. Some points of interest are described below.

Masonic Lodge, 803 Princess Anne Street at Hanover Street. Portions of the old lodge building are preserved in this newer one, which was erected in 1815. Washington was initiated into Lodge No. 4 in Fredericksburg (1752), and the Masonic Bible on which he took his oath as president is displayed here along with the minute book recording the three degrees conferred. The lodge also has a Gilbert Stuart portrait of Washington. (It has been said that every major general of the American army during the Revolution was a Master Mason except one: Benedict Arnold.) Phone: (540) 373-5885.

Masonic Cemetery, Charles at George Street. One of the oldest Masonic burial grounds in America (1784), this half-acre includes an impressive collection of ancient tombstones, including that of Basil Gordon (1768–1817), one of the country's first millionaires. In one corner of the cemetery is the grave of Lewis Littlepage (1762–1802), whose career included military service with his townsman John Paul Jones on the Russian side against the Turks, and with Kosciuszko on the Polish side against the Russians (1794).

James Monroe Law Office, Museum, and Memorial Library, 908 Charles Street between William and George Streets. Phone: (504) 654-1043. Dating from 1758, this brick building has been little altered since Monroe practiced in it from 1786 to 1790. Monroe left the College of William and Mary to join the Continental army and became a second lieutenant in Hugh Mercer's regiment in September 1775. After a little more than three years' service, seeing action in most of the principal engagements in the North and reaching the grade of major, he resigned his commission. During the period 1780 to 1783 he studied law under Thomas Jefferson and started his career in politics. The law office contains the furniture Monroe bought while minister to France (1794–1796) and used in the White House when he was president (1816–1825). Also on display is the desk on which Monroe wrote the message to Congress of 2 December 1823 setting forth the principles embodied in the Monroe Doctrine. Monroe's Revolutionary War weapons are on display with many other subjects associated with his life and his wife's. A thirty-minute guided tour is provided, and visitors are invited to linger over the self-guided galleries. In 1998 the James Monroe Presidential Center was created as an alliance institution with the museum. In the garden behind the museum is an impressive sculpture of Madison.

Hugh Mercer Apothecary Shop, 1020 Caroline Street at Amelia. Phone: (540) 373-1776. Shelves, drawers, and pigeonholes of an old apothecary shop were uncovered when lath and plaster were removed in this small, clapboarded building. The handwriting on some of the drawer labels is thought to be that of Hugh Mercer, so this is believed to be the shop he is known to have operated in Fredericksburg. Mercer (c. 1725–1777) had been a doctor in the army of Bonnie Prince Charlie and had come to America after the defeat at Culloden. (See MOORES CREEK BRIDGE NATIONAL MILITARY PARK, NORTH CAROLINA for the story of his fellow refugees of "the Forty-Five.") He settled in Pennsylvania around 1748 and practiced medicine in the vicinity of modern Mercersburg, and during the Seven Years' War he rose from captain to colonel in four years of active campaigning (1755–1759). During these years on the frontier he came to know George Washington, who may have been instrumental in bringing about Mercer's change of residence to Fredericksburg. As a doctor and apothecary, Mercer kept up his friendship with Washington and became well established in the community. He had reached the relatively mellow age of fifty when the Revolutionary War started, but he was beaten by only a slim margin in the competition for command of the First Virginia Regiment. This coveted post went to a politician of some reputation in Virginia named Patrick Henry. About six months later, however, Mercer was commissioned a colonel, and four months after this he became a brigadier general. After commanding the Third Virginia Regiment and the "Flying Camp," Mercer led a column in the decisive battle at Trenton and was mortally wounded at Princeton. His monument, at Washington Avenue and Faquier Street, was erected by Congress in 1906 and features a bronze figure of the heroic Scot. The Hugh Mercer Apothecary is open to the public daily, and group tours are available by appointment. The Association for the Preservation of Virginia Antiquities (APVA) owns and maintains this site.

Rising Sun Tavern, 1304 Caroline Street between Faquier and Hawke Streets (another APVA property). Phone: (540) 373-1776. Like all colonial taverns, the Rising Sun was a focus of political activity. But because of its famous host, George Weedon, who was to become a general known to his troops as "Joe Gourd" (because he used a gourd to serve punch at his tavern), this particular tavern was especially well-known to travelers. One of these, an Englishman, commented five years before the Revolution started that Weedon was "very active in blowing the seeds of sedition." Washington and Lafayette celebrated here with their officers after the victory at Yorktown. Weedon fought in the Seven Years' War before settling in Fredericksburg and becoming host of the tavern believed to have been built about 1760 by Washington's brother Charles. As the lieutenant colonel of the Third Virginia Regiment he was second in command to his brother-in-law Hugh Mercer (see preceding paragraph), and he led a force of about six hundred men in Washington's campaigns in New York and New Jersey before becoming acting adjutant general to Washington and being promoted to brigadier general (February 1777). Weedon quit the army in 1778 in a common dispute over seniority but returned for the Virginia campaign in 1781 as commander of Virginia militia. He died in 1793 at the age of fifty-nine. This site is open to the public daily, with special summer hours.

Mary Washington's Town House, 1200 Charles Street, Lewis Street at Charles. Open to the public (APVA property). Three blocks from her daughter Betty's mansion (see Kenmore, below), George Washington's not-too-doting mother lived in this simple frame house during the years 1772 to 1789. Having moved here at his urging, presumably because he felt the management of Ferry Farm was too much for her and that she would not be happy at Mount Vernon, Mary Washington caused her son much embarrassment by complaining that she had "never lived so poore." She regularly visited her daughter at Kenmore (then a large plantation called Millbank), and although she apparently never went to Mount Vernon, she was frequently visited in Fredericksburg by her son George. The two-story middle portion of the house was built by Washington in 1772, the year his mother moved in from Ferry Farm. The interior has been restored and furnished as it might have been when occupied by Mary Washington. In the yard are box bushes she planted two centuries ago and her personal sundial still stands in the garden and keeps perfect time.

Kenmore, 1201 Washington Avenue between Lewis and Fauquier Streets. Phone: (540) 373-3381. George Washington's only sister to survive infancy, Betty, married Fielding Lewis, who started building this brick mansion in 1752 for his nineteen-year-old bride. (Oil portraits of both hang in the mansion.) Although not completed until fifteen years later, it was occupied long before then and was a center of social and political life. Originally called Millbank, the house was erected with its "dependencies" on a plantation of nearly 1,300 acres surveyed by young George Washington. (Note for suburban homeowners: there are 640 acres in a square mile.) Fielding Lewis was a Patriot who put his money where others put only their mouths: he furnished the funds for three regiments and a ship during the Revolution, and as chief commissioner for the "gunnery" (see next paragraph) used his own money to keep up manufacturing when public funds were exhausted. He died in 1782, leaving a debt of £7,000 and a mortgage on Millbank. His widow sold the house in 1796. A few years later it was bought by the Gordon family, who changed its name to Kenmore. In 1922 an association was formed to save the mansion and the remaining three acres of land from approaching oblivion. The house is an architectural jewel and is filled with furniture and relics of the Washington and Lewis families. Among these is the only weapon from the Fielding Lewis gunnery known to survive. The plantation house's dependencies have been reconstructed on the original foundations, and the grounds have been restored. Further renovations and restorations were going on at Kenmore in 2005, but the site remains open daily for tours. Period furniture, portraits, historical documents, and lush gardens are some of what is displayed here.

Gunnery Springs, off Gunnery Lane in back of Old Walker Grant School, an extension of Ferdinand Street. On the south end of Old Fredericksburg and in what was an open field at the base of a steep hill are the springs where small arms and ammunition were to be manufactured during the Revolution, though very few guns were made. Colonel Fielding Lewis and Major Charles Dick were appointed commissioners by the Virginia Convention of 1775 to establish and operate the factory and were given £2,500 of state funds for this purpose. When this money was exhausted, Lewis raised capital by pledging his own property, and for his patriotic pains his family lost title to it (see preceding paragraph). The site is marked by the local DAR and by a masonry covering over the slow trickling springs.

John Paul Jones House (private), Caroline Street at Lafayette Boulevard. The elder brother of the naval hero was a tailor named William Paul who emigrated from Scotland in 1758 and established a business in Fredericksburg. He was visited here about a year later by his brother John, who was a twelve-year-old apprentice to a shipowner of Whitehaven, England. (This was the first place Jones later raided during the Revolution when he got into foreign waters, "the only American operation of war on English soil.") Although brother William's house has been called the only place in America the naval-hero-to-be could call home, it is improbable that he spent much time here. It is likely that he fled to this house in 1773 from the West Indies after killing the ringleader of his mutinous crew, but it was after this incident that he changed his name by adding the final "Jones," and it would not make sense for him to then reestablish family ties that would help authorities in the West Indies bring him to trial there. But in the years of obscurity before John Paul Jones emerged to become a famous naval commander, he probably stayed closer to the homes of his North Carolina benefactors, Allen and Willie (pronounced "Wylie") Jones. That he spent time in this Fredericksburg house is, however, unquestionable.

Slave Auction Block, corner of William and Charles Streets. Slaves were sold and rented from this spot in the century before the Civil War.

Great Bridge, Intracoastal Canal, city of Chesapeake, Norfolk County. Governor Dunmore had fled from Williamsburg in June 1775, and on 7 November he started assembling an army of Loyalists and freed slaves (thus his nickname "Dunmore the Liberator") around a small core of regulars. When a Patriot column advanced on Norfolk, Dunmore picked Great Bridge as the place to stop it. A long causeway and a 120-foot bridge spanned a tidal swamp at this point. The British had an ideal defensive position, but on 9 December Dunmore made the error of attacking. (The legend is that a servant of John Marshall's father entered the enemy camp pretending to be a deserter and reported that only a few riflemen were defending the south end of the causeway.)

The British suffered a bloody repulse in a brief action that cost the Patriots only one casualty. Dunmore crowded his Loyalist refugees and troops aboard ships and fled to Gwynn Island.

The topography around the present community of Great Bridge has been altered beyond recognition since the Revolution. It is not an attractive area, although the historic spot is worth the detour if you are driving between the Norfolk area and colonial sites in the Albemarle region of North Carolina. Highway markers at Great Bridge (intersection of Va. 165 and 168) indicate the general location of the British and American works at the northern and southern ends of the causeway that no longer exists.

Green Spring Battlefield, between Williamsburg and Jamestown, near the junction of Va. 5 and County Road 614. After withdrawing down the peninsula to Williamsburg, followed cautiously by Lafayette, Cornwallis moved to cross the James and establish a base around Portsmouth. Lafayette was alert to the possibility of catching the British in a vulnerable position astride the river, but the experienced Cornwallis was thinking ahead of his young adversary. When General Anthony Wayne pressed forward with an advance guard of about five hundred men (later reinforced), thinking he would have to deal only with a British rear guard around Green Spring, he suddenly found himself under counterattack. Cornwallis had his main force of some seven thousand troops immediately available. Lafayette had been concerned about this possibility and made a reconnaissance that confirmed his suspicions, but he could not get to Wayne in time to keep that fiery warrior from becoming heavily engaged. Cornwallis, on the other hand, made the mistake of hoping he could draw the major portion of Lafayette's force into battle before delivering a decisive counterblow.

Wayne retrieved the situation masterfully, surprising the British by continuing to attack, and then extricating the bulk of his command before the enemy could recover. Patriot losses were high—some 140 killed, wounded, and captured out of 900 engaged—but disaster was averted. Cornwallis had delayed his attack so long that he had only an hour of daylight remaining; thus, he could not exploit his advantage by undertaking a pursuit.

The action was fought around the estate that Governor Sir William Berkeley had established more than a century earlier. The great mansion of Green Spring had been used by the insurgents in Bacon's Rebellion (1676). The architect Benjamin Latrobe made a sketch of the house before demolishing it in 1796 to construct a new one of his design. All that remains standing aboveground today are the ruined walls of what may be the seventeenth-century jail and an unattractive brick structure over the bubbling spring for which the place was named. The site was thoroughly excavated in 1954 to 1955 by the National Park Service, results recorded in detail, and the extensive ruins recovered with sod. In 1967 Green Spring's house site and surrounding land was acquired by the federal government and made part of Colonial National Historical Park. Included is Berkeley's seventeenth-century plantation home and the Cape Henry Memorial, put up to honor the arrival of the first settlers to Jamestown in 1607. This memorial consists of a white concrete cross to commemorate the wooden one that the settlers placed after landing. It was erected in 1935 by the DAR. Information is available by calling the Colonial National Historical Park at (757) 898-2410.

The battlefield of 1781 has been little affected by time; the action may be traced on the ground, but there are no markers.

Greenway Court (Private), one mile south of White Post, near Va. 277. Frontier home for thirty years (1752–1781) of the only British peer resident in America, Thomas, Sixth Lord Fairfax of Cameron, this place was never built in the style one might expect from the man who was proprietor of more than 5 million acres in Virginia. The manor house was never constructed. The lord of Greenway was content to live in crude simplicity in what had been planned as the hunting lodge. This has been replaced by a two-story brick farmhouse dating from 1828. The Fairfax land office has survived, a 28-by-18-foot structure of thick limestone walls and narrow windows built probably in 1762 and restored in 1930.

In 1649 Charles II had made a grant of more than 5 million acres of Virginia lands to establish a refuge for Cavaliers who had forfeited their estates to support his father. Thomas Fairfax inherited this property through his mother, the heiress of Lord Thomas Culpeper. The grant comprised the Northern Neck, between the Potomac and Rappahannock, and extended westward to include the northern portion of the Shenandoah Valley, between the North Branch of the Potomac and the Rapidan. Largely because Culpeper agents had antagonized Virginians, there was a long-lived effort to reduce the size of the lands claimed under the grant from Charles II, particularly when westward expansion made the frontier property more valuable. But in 1745 the Privy Council upheld the Fairfax claims to all the land in northwest Virginia, and two years later Thomas came to America to live.

A dumpy little man of democratic outlook, he lived during the Revolutionary period with all the privileges of a Virginia citizen and without molestation. While staying briefly at Belvoir, the home of his cousin and agent, he became a patron of young George Washington of nearby Mount Vernon and charged him with surveying Fairfax lands in the Shenandoah Valley. He was a confirmed woman hater, having been jilted for a duke, and it is said that no woman was ever permitted at Greenway Court. His passions were fox hunting and real estate.

Lord Fairfax died at Greenway Court in his eighty-ninth year. He was buried under the altar of the parish church in Winchester, and his remains were moved later to Christ Church. The exact location of the second grave was found in 1926, and the bones reburied beneath the floor of the church.

Gunston Hall, near Lorton, about 20 miles south of Washington, D.C., off Interstate 90 and Route 1. A particularly attractive little Georgian house, this was the home of a Virginia statesman who played an important offstage role in the founding of America. The fourth of his name in Virginia, George Mason (1725–1792) was a lifetime associate of Washington, and had a relationship with George Rogers Clark (1752–1818) that was as father to son. He is remembered for drafting the Virginia Resolves (1769), the Fairfax Resolves (1774), the Virginia Bill of Rights, and the Virginia Constitution. His statement of the constitutional position of the American colonists in the Fairfax Resolves was adopted by the Continental Congress. His Virginia Bill of Rights was drawn on by Jefferson in drafting the first part of the Declaration of Independence, was copied by many states, formed the basis for the first ten amendments to the United States Constitution, and even had an influence in the French Revolution. Gunston Hall was built in 1755 to 1758. The architect was a skilled draftsman from Oxford under indenture to Mason's brother.

Gunston Hall was eventually bought by the state and today is a 550-acre historic landmark open 9:30 A.M. to 5 P.M. daily. Visitors can visit Mason's home and/or walk the grounds to learn about eighteenth-century plantation life. Website: www.gunstonhall.org.

Gwynn Island and Cricket Hill, Chesapeake Bay, Mathews County. On 2,000-acre Gwynn Island the last royal governor of Virginia made his last stand before being driven off by artillery fire from Cricket Hill, on the mainland about 500 yards away. From Va. 14 a little more than 2 miles north of Mathews, follow Va. 198 North 1 mile to Va. 223 and go right for 2.3 miles to Fort Cricket Hill. Secondary Highway 633 leads on to Gwynn Island.

In 1991 the community established the Gwynn Island Museum. Much of the two-floor museum is dedicated to the Civil War, but there is a very interesting exhibit concerning the Battle of Cricket Hill and colonial artifacts. Phone: (804) 725-7949.

Hanover Courthouse and Tavern, 18 miles north of Richmond on U.S. 301. Here in 1763 Patrick Henry argued for the defense in the Parson's Cause, winning the fame as a lawyer and advocate of local government that launched his political career. In a radical and well-reasoned speech he challenged the long-established prerogative of the British government to veto ("disallow") acts of local American legislatures. Although the judges had to rule that the local Anglican clergy had been damaged by the Two Penny Acts of the Virginia Assembly, when Parson James Maury subsequently sued for damages he was awarded only 1 d. (one British penny).

Still used as the county courthouse, the single-story, T-shaped brick structure with its arcaded piazza is set serenely in a rectangle of grass and trees. Quite apart from its great historic associations (it was a scene of action during the Civil War), Hanover Courthouse is a sight of exceptional charm.

Across the road is Hanover Tavern, a rambling, two-story frame building that was used by the Barksdale Theater from 1953 to 1996. Started in 1723 and built over a high basement, it was acquired in 1760 by the father-in-law of Patrick Henry. Having turned to the law in 1760, Patrick Henry lived at the tavern for some time during the next few years. Cornwallis stayed there briefly during the summer of 1781, when he was playing hounds and hare with Lafayette. The tavern recently underwent renovation by an organization called the Hanover Tavern Foundation, and plans are to use it as a place of education and entertainment.

Hite's Fort and Springdale (not open), about 2 miles north of Stephens City on U.S. 11. The two-story house of gray stone is Springdale, built in 1753 by John Hite. Just to the south are the broken stone walls that probably are the ruins of Hite's Fort, the house built around 1734 by John's father. The latter was an Alsatian whose first name probably was spelled Jost; it is rendered as Joist by local authorities, but this sounds more Virginian than Alsatian. Hite settled in Pennsylvania in 1710 and in 1731 obtained contracts for about 140,000 acres in the Shenandoah Valley. The next year he settled sixteen families on Opequon Creek, starting the German immigration into the valley.

Jamestown Site, James River near Williamsburg. By the time of the Revolution, the site of the first permanent settlement in English America had become farmland that was on its way to being reclaimed by the wilderness. The place was nevertheless important strategically. A major engagement occurred around the nearby ruins of Green Spring (see GREEN SPRING BATTLEFIELD), and the French expedition from the West Indies debarked at Jamestown for the Yorktown campaign.

Since 1934 some 1,500 acres around Jamestown have been developed as part of Colonial National Historical Park. Phone: (757) 229-1733. The visitors center offers a seventeen-minute audiovisual program, and foundations of the settlement are exposed. The picturesque Old Church Tower of 1639 is standing. The nearby Jamestown Festival Park has a fine museum, a reconstruction of the Powhatan village, Jamestown's palisaded fort, and full-scale sailing models of the three tiny ships that brought the first 104 settlers to Virginia. The first slaves in the British colonies were sold here on 20 August 1619 (though there is some evidence that a few slaves were brought here even earlier). The Association for the Preservation of Virginia Antiquities began excavating the site in 1994, uncovering thousands of artifacts dating back to the first half of the seventeenth century. One big discovery was that James Fort was not washed into the James River as previously believed; rather, the APVA has unearthed over 250 feet of foundation for two distinct walls of the fort's triangular shape.

Lewis (Andrew) Grave, Salem. A frontier leader before the Revolution, Andrew Lewis served with Washington at Fort Necessity, with Braddock in the expedition of 1755, and with Forbes three years later against Fort Duquesne. (Under Pennsylvania, see FORT NECESSITY and FORKS OF THE OHIO). He was captured in the latter operation and taken to Montreal. After being released he took part in important Indian negotiations, including the one ending with the Treaty of Fort Stanwix, New York. In Dunmore's War he won the decisive Battle of Point Pleasant (see POINT PLEASANT BATTLEFIELD under West Virginia). At the outbreak of the Revolution the Continental Congress was slow in commissioning Lewis a brigadier general (not until 1 March 1776), and he was not considered qualified for further promotion even after successfully commanding the action against Gwynn Island (see GWYNN ISLAND AND CRICKET HILL) that drove the royal governor, Dunmore, from Virginia. Lewis resigned in April 1777 from the Continental army but continued to serve in the militia and on the governor's executive council until his death in 1781 at the age of sixty-two. The once famous pioneer, statesman, and military leader is buried on part of his 625-acre estate near Main Street (U.S. 460) and Park Avenue.

Mechunk Creek, Albemarle County. Six miles east of Shadwell a highway marker on Va. Route 22 about a half-mile from the county line says that Lafayette's defenses were established 2 miles south. Here on the morning of 12 June 1781 the young French general started digging in between the British army under Lord Cornwallis (around Elk Hill) and the Shenandoah Valley. Stores had been evacuated from Albemarle Old Courthouse, and after Tarleton's raid on Charlottesville the Patriots had every reason to expect that Cornwallis would follow with his main force. To accomplish the dangerous mission of reaching this position along the Mechunk without being exposed to attack by Cornwallis on the Patriots' eastern flank, Lafayette had secretly reopened a long abandoned road from Boswell's Tavern. A marker at the latter place now explains that "The road has ever since been known as 'The Marquis Road.'" When Cornwallis started retreating from Elk Hill on 15 June, Lafayette left his position on Mechunk Creek and followed the British cautiously on a parallel course down the South Anna, gathering strength as he went. He then got on the tail of Cornwallis's column as the British retreated down the peninsula toward Jamestown.

Michie Tavern, 683 Thomas Jefferson Parkway, Charlottesville. Phone: (434) 977-1234. In 1927 this large colonial structure was moved from its "inaccessible" location northwest of Charlottesville to the beaten tourist track less than half a mile from the gate to Monticello. Although cheapened by development as a tourist attraction and its architectural integrity degraded, Michie (pronounced "Micky") Tavern has legitimate historical significance. The oldest portion dates from before 1740 and has fine interior woodwork. In 1746 the house was sold by Patrick Henry's father to John Michie, who enlarged it about seven years later and whose descendants owned it until 1910. The Michie family operated a tavern catering to guests whose names are today famous: Jefferson, Madison, Monroe, and Lafayette. Many of the furnishings are original. Today it continues to serve guests whose needs are attended by a staff attired in period clothing. There is also a variety of shops available.

Monticello, about 32 miles southeast of Charlottesville. The hilltop home of Thomas Jefferson is a monument, self-built, to a giant of American history who also happened to be the country's first original architect. After the marquis de Chastellux visited Monticello in 1782 he wrote: "We may safely aver that Mr. Jefferson is the first American who has consulted the fine arts to know how he should shelter himself from the weather."

Jefferson also had a scientific bent, and Monticello is full of inventions and gimmicks to delight the heart of the most blasé modern houseowner: the dumbwaiter, the bed with no wrong side to get out of, the hall clock with cannonball weights to mark the days, the revolving chair that becomes a chaise lounge. Monticello, which means "little mountain," is approached by a winding road from either side, with distant vistas unscarred by modern earthmovers. The familiar view on the American nickel is from an angle that does not convey the picture of a mansion on a high hill.

It was up one of the winding roads to Monticello that a British raiding party rode on 4 June 1781 to seize the author of the Declaration of Independence. They were just ten minutes late, thanks to the delay at nearby Castle Hill. It is a tribute to the military discipline of their leader, Tarleton, that they did little damage to the abandoned house, limiting themselves to a binge in Jefferson's wine cellar.

America's first Thomas Jefferson was living in Henrico County (which would include Richmond) in 1677. Three generations later the subject of this sketch was born near the site of Monticello at Shadwell, a frontier farm his father, Peter, had bought from William Randolph of Tuckahoe Plantation. The price of the 400-acre parcel shows in the deed as "Henry Weatherburn's biggest bowl of Arrack punch to him delivered." (See Wetherburn Tavern, WILLIAMSBURG.) What does not show in the deed is that Peter Jefferson (1705–1757) had married the nineteen-year-old Jane Randolph, a first cousin of William and the eldest surviving child of Isham Randolph of Dungeness.

The Randolphs were probably Virginia's most distinguished family, and this connection gave Thomas Jefferson the social and cultural background that contributed so much to his later achievements. From his father, a frontiersman who made the first accurate map of Virginia and went on to become a burgess and county lieutenant, he inherited 2,750 acres, an established position in the community, a love of the frontier, and a fondness for science.

Jefferson started building Monticello, whose site he had picked as a boy, in 1770, having lived at Shadwell since 1752. He moved into the first completed pavilion at Monticello in 1771, a year after Shadwell burned. On 1 January 1772 he married the twenty-four-year-old widow of Bathurst Skelton at her home 15 miles southeast of Richmond and took her to Monticello, reaching his pavilion on horseback in a snowstorm.

When his wife died after almost eleven years of devoted marriage (September 1782), Jefferson returned to public life. He was in Europe for many years, and this experience broadened his outlook so that when he enlarged Monticello during the period 1796 to 1809 he was able to make it a remarkable example of classical design adapted to its environment and function (WPA *Guide*, p. 624)

The last seventeen years of Jefferson's life were spent without venturing more than a few miles from Monticello. During this period he finally succeeded in getting the University of Virginia established, and he was its architect in the literal as well as the figurative sense. Despite careful management, Jefferson spent large sums of money on luxuries and was plagued with financial difficulties throughout most of his life. Like many Americans, he was badly hurt by the Embargo of 1807, that daring measure by which he hoped to avoid war with Britain and France. In 1815 he sold his ten-thousand–volume library to the government at a low price and was temporarily relieved of his financial distress. (The books became the nucleus of the Library of Congress.) But four years later he suffered a fatal financial blow when a friend failed to cover a note Jefferson had endorsed. He was trying to find a buyer for his lands—some 10,000 acres—when public sympathy was aroused and voluntary contributions protected Monticello during the last year of his life. Jefferson believed to the end that he would be able to pay off his debts, but his heirs were not able to hold the place long.

There is reason to believe that Jefferson's commitment to slavery actually undermined his financial position, though scholars continue to debate such points. His heirs held a public sale of furnishings in early 1827, and the last member of the family moved out in 1829. Two years later the estate, reduced to 552 acres, was bought for about $7,000 by a Charlottesville apothecary, James T. Barclay, who undertook to use its mulberry trees to establish a silkworm culture. The project failed within two years, with much damage being done to Jefferson's gardens in the meantime and the rest of the property being ravaged by vandals and curiosity seekers.

In 1836 the estate was bought, sight unseen, by Uriah Phillips Levy (1792–1862). His family held Monticello for eighty-nine years, never using it as a full-time residence but maintaining it extremely well. In 1923 the newly organized Thomas Jefferson Memorial Foundation bought Monticello for $500,000 and undertook the difficult task of raising funds to make it a national shrine. A major difficulty was that Americans had almost forgotten Thomas Jefferson. Not until 1930 did the Foundation have sufficient funds to guarantee the survival of Monticello. Major work was done on the house in 1954, and the beautifully maintained estate of nearly 2,000 acres is now a major tourist attraction open to the public year-round.

Leaving the mansion by road, a visitor passes the little family burial ground, still used by Jefferson's descendants, where a simple obelisk of Jefferson's design bears the epitaph he himself wrote: "Here was buried Thomas Jefferson / Author of the Declaration of American Independence / Of the Statute of Virginia for religious freedom / And Father of the University of Virginia."

In recent years Monticello has moved to come to terms with Jefferson's attitudes toward slavery and to one slave in particular, Sally Heming. The story of Jefferson's affair with Heming, who was his wife's half-sister, encapsulates so much of the sordid nature of America's racial relations. No visit to Monticello is complete without asking a tour guide for a consideration of this story, which was denied and avoided for nearly two centuries. The plantation's slave quarters no longer exist, and there are no plans to restore them. More information is available through the Thomas Jefferson Foundation. Monticello is open daily, 1 March to 31 October, 8 A.M. to 5 P.M., and 1 November to the end of February, 9 A.M. to 4:30 P.M. Website: www.monticello.org; phone: (434) 984-9800.

Mount Vernon, Potomac River, 7 miles south of Alexandria. The home of George Washington, and part of a family grant dating from 1669, Mount Vernon is second only to the White House as a famous American residence. The 500-acre estate has been restored in accordance with plans drafted by Washington before the Revolution. In addition to the famous mansion, which is furnished with original items retrieved from widely scattered sources, a visitor will see the numerous outbuildings that supported life on a colonial plantation, including, of course, the slave quarters. George and Martha Washington are buried near the main house.

In 1669 George Washington's great-grandfather and Nicholas Spencer applied for a 5,000-acre grant some 40 miles up the Potomac (as the crow flies) from the former's first holdings on Pope's Creek (see WASHINGTON'S BIRTHPLACE). John Washington's half of this grant, called (Little) Hunting Creek, was left to his son Lawrence, who left it to his daughter. She sold it in 1726 to her brother Augustine, father of George Washington, who was three years old when his family moved from Pope's Creek to the site of the Mount Vernon mansion. Augustine had built a house here on the site of an older one, and the Washingtons lived in it until George was six years old.

The year 1743 was a landmark in the fortunes of the Washington family. Augustine died, Washington's elder half-brother Lawrence inherited Mount Vernon (as he was to call it), built a simple house on the foundations of the one put up by his father and destroyed by fire, and moved in with a bride. He had lifted the Washingtons from the middle ranks of Tidewater society by marrying Anne Fairfax, daughter of Lord Fairfax's kinsman and agent. The Fairfax mansion, Belvoir, was within distant eyesight of Mount Vernon, and it became a second home to young George. Although Belvoir lacked the magnificence of the country seats of the aristocracy back in England, Lord Fairfax had inherited a grant of more than 5 million acres between the Potomac and the Rappahannock, and Belvoir was the seat of power for administration of this land empire.

George was sixteen years old when he came to live permanently at Mount Vernon with Lawrence and Anne, and he was looked on by the Fairfaxes of Belvoir as a member of the family.

Lawrence had shown signs about this time of having consumption, and he died three years later of this disease, in 1752. His will made George executor and residuary heir should his infant daughter, Sarah, die without issue, and subject to dower rights for Anne. The latter remarried within a few months of becoming a widow, moved away with Sarah, and left George as virtual master of Mount Vernon. Two years later he bought Anne's dower rights. Sarah Washington died in 1761, and George fell heir to the house and land that had for all practical purposes been his since his half-brother's death nine years earlier.

Meanwhile, he had married in 1759 and before bringing his bride to Mount Vernon had started the changes that would gradually transform the house from a one-and-a-half-story structure to the odd but attractive architectural creation it finally became. During the summer of 1758 he had the roof raised to provide for a second story and made other modifications. Later he would extend the ends of the house (1774 and 1776), build the colonnaded porch on the river side (1780s), add the pediment and cupola after the Revolution, and throughout this period make numerous other architectural modifications.

During his lifetime Washington increased the acreage of Mount Vernon to more than 8,000. In 1786 there were about 240 people on the place; at its peak, the Mount Vernon plantation was home to 317 slaves. But although he tried hard, Washington never could make the place pay. The soil was not good enough for high-quality tobacco; wheat, flax, and hemp production were unsuccessful; and many economic historians now argue that slavery was a counterproductive economic system. Although the river was teeming with shad and herring, Washington could not make a profit from them. But he had the one thing needed in his day (and in this) to maintain a country home that could not support itself: a rich wife.

Martha Washington was an extremely wealthy woman. About a year older than George, she had been left a widow at the age of twenty-six, with two surviving children from her marriage with Daniel Parke Custis and an estate tentatively appraised at well over $100,000. It was in all ways a happy marriage, although the Washingtons had no children of their own.

Martha Washington, hardly 5 feet tall beside her 6-foot, 2-inch husband, was a born hostess. Although she brought no luxuries with her except the Custis coach, her money enabled the Washingtons to import furniture, furnishings, and all manner of good things from England, and Mount Vernon became famous for its hospitality. With more than a dozen house slaves, the manor house had hundreds of visitors a year. Intimate friends and total strangers came for a meal or for a week (there being no public accommodations closer than Alexandria), and the Washingtons complained to each other of boredom when bad weather kept guests away.

Mount Vernon now draws more than a million visitors a year.

Unlike many slave owners, Washington provided medical care to his slaves, recognized their marriages, refused to break up families, and arranged for their eventual freedom upon his death. Washington sought to train numerous slaves in a variety of artisan skills and put a few in positions of responsibility. Just 50 yards from his tomb is the old slave burial ground.

Washington died at Mount Vernon on 14 December 1799. Martha followed about eighteen months later, the mansion and 4,000 acres then passing to Bushrod Washington, the son of George's brother John Augustine Washington. Bushrod was an associate justice of the Supreme Court whose duties kept him away from Mount Vernon. The estate passed to his nephew John Augustine Washington in 1829, to the latter's wife three years later, then in 1850 by conveyance to their son, John Augustine Washington, Jr. The latter tried unsuccessfully to interest the state and federal government in acquiring what was left of the Mount Vernon estate, and Ann Pamela Cunningham of South Carolina then marched forth to organize the Mount Vernon Ladies' Association. In a remarkable pioneering effort in the field of historic preservation, the Ladies' Association raised funds in a nationwide campaign, and in 1858 acquired a 200-acre tract that included the mansion. This initial acquisition has since been expanded to just under 500 acres, about the area of Washington's Mansion House Farm. Second in importance only to preservation of the property has been the remarkable effort to find and return the mansion's contents that were widely scattered after Washington's death. Mount Vernon's principal sources of income are admission fees, retail and dining sales, and donations from private organizations and corporations. Over 450 individuals are employed at Mount Vernon, and another estimated 400 volunteers round out the workforce needed to maintain the site. The Mount Vernon Ladies' Association is proud that no tax dollars are used to support this beloved site, and that it boasts over a million visitors a year. Hours vary seasonally, though they are open daily; check their website for specifics and directions: http://www.mountvernon.org. Phone: (707) 780-2000.

Norfolk. At the start of the Revolution this city, laid out in 1682, was the largest in Virginia. Its population was about six thousand. The ruling element was made up of English and Scottish merchants who tended toward Loyalism, being much more interested in continuing their profitable trade with Britain than in revolution. Royal Governor Dunmore came here when driven from Williamsburg in 1775, a major reason being that he could be supported by the Royal Navy while organizing Loyalist militia. After his defeat at Great Bridge, Dunmore and the Loyalists crowded aboard ships off Norfolk. In exasperation over the Patriots' refusal to let him send foraging parties ashore, and seeing no prospect of reaching any terms with the rebels, Dunmore announced he was going to bombard the town. Less than twenty-four hours later, starting at 4 A.M. on New Year's Day 1776, naval guns opened fire and landing parties burned warehouses near the waterfront. The ill-disciplined Patriot militia, who had done much to provoke Dunmore into this act of retribution, started setting fires in the homes of prominent Loyalists, and a wind helped spread the flames. Militia officers finally got control of their troops and stopped the senseless destruction of valuable property, but then decided to destroy what remained of the town to deny its use to the British. (The militia withdrew from Norfolk a few weeks later.) Dunmore moved back among the ashes, built barracks to ease the crowding aboard ship, but then abandoned this beachhead because he was unable to provision it from the surrounding countryside. After the Revolution, Norfolk was rebuilt, but a disastrous fire swept the town in 1799 and the War of 1812 was a further setback to the reviving commercial prosperity. A yellow-fever epidemic in 1855, followed closely by the Civil War, were the next disasters, but Norfolk slowly recovered and is now a thriving maritime city, thanks largely to the U.S. Navy

Distinctive blue "Norfolk Tour" signs lead visitors from the numerous highways into the urban sprawl of the modern city. There is tourist material available at the information center at Gardens-by-the-Sea on Azalea Garden Road. The website www.historicnorfolk.org is another good source.

St. Paul's Church, 201 St. Paul's Boulevard, the only structure to survive the destruction of early 1776, is in the original 50-acre tract of the colonial settlement. One of the country's oldest churches still in use, the present edifice was built in 1739 on the site of a chapel that had been there almost a century. The last renovation (1913) restored St. Paul's to its colonial style. In the south wall is a cannonball with a stone tablet saying it was fired by Lord Dunmore on 1 January 1776. Ancient oaks shade the churchyard, where the oldest headstone dates from 1673. Phone: (757) 627-4353.

The Moses Myers House (c. 1792), East Freemason Street at Bank Street, one of the first brick houses built after the destruction of Norfolk in 1776, is nearby. It is one of the South's most elegant townhouses, open as a museum and containing authentic furnishings of the prosperous merchant's period. Phone: (757) 333-6283.

The Willoughby-Baylor House (1794), 601 East Freemason Street, is another survivor, restored starting in 1963, and adjacent to the Myers House. It also is a house museum with eighteenth-century furnishings. The museum was closed for most of 2005 as it underwent renovation.

The Adam Thoroughgood House, believed to date from 1636, is the oldest brick home in America. Thoroughgood came to America in 1621 as an indentured servant and later brought in a group of settlers that included Augustine Warner, an ancestor of George Washington. The charming house is preserved in an attractive setting of gardens and old trees about 8 miles from the historic district of Old

Norfolk (Northhampton Boulevard) at 1636 Parish Road in Virginia Beach. Phone: (757) 431-4000.

Pamunkey Indian Museum, King William County. The Pamunkey were the largest group within the Powhatan confederation at the time of the English invasion. They lived primarily along the banks of the York River. Pocahontas's uncle led the Pamunkey and their allies in the final attempt to force back the English in 1644. In 1781 the surviving Pamunkey were collected onto a reservation near Lanesville. The Pamunkey Museum, located on this reservation, is devoted to their history and culture. The museum is near the intersection of Routes 30 and 633, and open Monday through Saturday, 10 A.M. to 4 P.M., and Sunday 1 to 5 P.M. Phone: (804) 843-4792.

Petersburg, Appomattox River. Modern Petersburg was created after the Revolution (1784) by the combination of four settlements. Colonial Petersburg, in the northwestern portion of today's city, is neglected in Chamber of Commerce map-guides encouraging the tourist to "Visit Historic Petersburg." But *The Virginia Guide* of 1940 locates three Revolutionary sites in this older section of today's Petersburg that historians consider important.

The first is a brick residence called ***Mountain View,*** on McKenzie Street opposite the north end of South Street. This may be the site of Fort Henry, whose construction at the head of navigation of the Appomattox was directed by the General Assembly in 1645, and around which Abraham Wood developed a trading post. Wood's son-in-law, Peter Jones, later took over this enterprise, after which the locality became known as Peter's Point. A stone building some distance to the east and included in current tourist literature as Peter Jones's Trading Station is alleged to have been "the center of his flourishing Indian trade."

Of better-established historical authenticity, and west of the alleged site of Fort Henry, is ***Battersea.*** Built before the Revolution by John Banister, friend of Thomas Jefferson, ardent Patriot, and first mayor of modern Petersburg (1784), this has been called one of Virginia's finest Palladian houses. Visiting it in 1781, the marquis de Chastellux commented that "the house is decorated in the Italian rather than the British or American style, having three porticoes at the three principal entrances, each of them supported by four columns." (Palladian architecture is named after Andrea Palladio, a sixteenth-century architect who was very Italian.) The British treated Banister's mansion badly in 1781, and until recent years it was in shabby condition. Now a well-maintained private residence at the north end of Battersea Lane, it may be seen from the street. (A highway marker is on U.S. 1 and 460 in the western end of Petersburg at Battersea Lane, four blocks south of the site.) In 1992 the city of Petersburg began hosting a reenactment of the battle of 25 April 1781. The reenactment is at Battersea Plantation, located at the west end of Washington Street, less than 2 miles off the Washington Street Exit on Interstate-95.

On North West Street, near the railroad tracks and roughly midway between Battersea and Mountain View, is a group of red-brick buildings, including Pride's Tavern. Pride's Race Track was nearby, and his tavern was one of the many for which Colonial Petersburg was famous. The ***Golden Ball Tavern***, built about 1750, remained standing until razed in 1944. An unpainted frame building with brick ends and dormers along its gabled roof, it was a lunchroom when described in *The Virginia Guide* of 1940. The site is the southeast corner of Grove Avenue and North Market Street, a short distance south of Peter Jones's Trading Station. Niblo's Tavern, where Lafayette was entertained in 1824, stood at the northeast corner of modern Second and Boilingbrook Streets.

The site of ***Bollingbrook,*** the colonial mansion built by Robert Bolling on East Hill after 1725 and the last portion surviving until razed in 1915, is a knoll between North Jefferson Street and the railroad tracks. (It may be located on the city map as being in the block formed by Franklin, Jefferson, Bank, and Madison Streets, about 700 feet due east of the Center Hill Mansion Museum and roughly the same distance north-northeast of the Information Center.) Here the British had their headquarters in 1781 (see below). Lossing visited and sketched Bollingbrook a few years before the larger part burned in 1855, commenting that the Widow Bolling, "one of the largest land-holders in Virginia . . . owned the tobacco warehouses at Petersburg, and nearly one half of the town" (*Pictorial Field Book of the Revolution,* II, pp. 544n. and 545).

Blandford Church and the adjacent Blandford Cemetery, located at 111 Rochelle Lane and marked in 1914 by a DAR monument, is where Major General William Phillips is buried. The church cemetery contains headstones dated to 1702. The church and cemetery is open daily to the public and guided tours are available. Phone: (804) 733-2396.

Petersburg on the eve of the Revolution was what the French call a "*ville étape*," a term with no English counterpart but meaning a place with exceptional facilities for catering to travelers. In addition to the fine homes, many taverns, and race track, there was a theater. But the place was more important as a center in the all-important tobacco business; here at the head of navigation were the warehouses of the trade, and this is what drew the British raiders in 1781.

In May of that year the British artillery general William Phillips advanced from City Point on Petersburg with two thousand crack regulars he had just brought south from New York and the one-thousand-man force that the traitor Benedict Arnold had brought down a few months earlier. General von Steuben, Prussian trainer of Washington's army at Valley Forge, had been in Virginia a very short time with the mission of doing what he could to help mobilize the military resources of the region.

The important depot of military supplies and tobacco at Petersburg was guarded by about one thousand militia under the command of von Steuben's deputy, Brigadier General John Peter Gabriel Muhlenberg. The Patriots had organized a good position near the village of Blandford, on the eastern edge of modern Petersburg. In an action that lasted several hours, Muhlenberg's militia delayed a numerically superior force of particularly high-quality British regulars, dropping back in an orderly fashion to the high ground around Blandford Church before withdrawing under cover of its artillery to what is now Colonial Heights, across the river from Petersburg.

Phillips then occupied Petersburg and had the local people remove some four thousand hogsheads of tobacco from the warehouses for burning. The British destroyed several small vessels and one warehouse but did little other damage. Phillips then was stricken with typhoid fever, and as he lay dying in the Bollingbrook House (mentioned earlier), the Patriot force under Lafayette started shelling Petersburg from Colonial Heights. The hero of the Royal Artillery, who had first become famous at Minden in 1759 before distinguishing himself in New York at Ticonderoga and Saratoga, is said to have complained that the Americans wouldn't even let him die in peace. He was buried in Blandford Church Cemetery on 13 May 1781. For what the distinction is worth, Phillips is the highest-ranking British officer of the Revolution buried in America.

Several other Revolutionary War legends and historic claims are associated with Petersburg. One is that when the traitor Benedict Arnold asked a Patriot prisoner what the Americans would do if they captured him, the soldier said they would bury with military honors the leg wounded at Quebec and Saratoga, "and hang the remainder of you upon a gibbet," or words to this effect. (There are several variations of this dubious story, and several localities challenge Petersburg's claim to being the scene of the dialogue.)

Lord Cornwallis reached Petersburg from North Carolina a week after Phillips's death, took over from Benedict Arnold, who had been temporarily in command, and four days later (24 May 1781) headed for Westover and his frustrating attempt to trap and wipe out Lafayette's force. (See RACCOON FORD and its cross-references.)

A visitors center is open daily from 9 A.M. to 5 P.M. and located at 425 Cockade Alley. Phone: (800) 368-3595. In addition to that, a second visitors center, to accommodate motorists, is located just off Interstate-95 at the Carson Rest Area. Phone: (434) 246-2145. The city website, www.petersburg-va.org, is another helpful source.

Pohick Church, 9301 Richmond Highway, on U.S. 1, 10 miles south of Alexandria. Washington, George Mason, and George William Fairfax were on the building committee, and Mason was contractor after the original "undertaker" died. Construction started in 1769, and the first services were held in 1774. Washington kept two adjacent pews for family and guests and attended services here until the Revolutionary War started. The church was badly damaged during the Civil War, but the walls are original and the interior is a close reproduction. Three services are held on Sunday to accommodate a large modern congregation. Tours are available daily, but not offered on Sunday until after 12:30 P.M. so as not to interrupt the regular church services. Phone: (703) 339-6572.

Point of Fork, James River, Fluvanna County. An important arsenal and supply depot, Point of Fork was selected by General von Steuben as the principal base for training recruits for Greene's Southern army. When the powerful column of raiders under Cornwallis approached in the summer of 1781, von Steuben evacuated some of the supplies, but then abandoned a large quantity on the approach of a force under Colonel John Graves Simcoe. Burned by the British, the arsenal was rebuilt and stored weapons for the militia until the new arsenal was built in Richmond in 1801. It is now a significant archaeological site a little less than a mile west of Columbia on Va. 6. A highway marker commemorating the site is on Route 6 near Columbia.

Pope's Creek. *See* WASHINGTON'S BIRTHPLACE.

Poplar Forest, Bedford County. In 1806 Jefferson started work on this remarkable octagonal house, which he finished in 1819. He inherited this 4,000-acre plantation from his wife, Martha Wayles Skelton, and generally spent parts of each summer here, originally in a cottage, and then later in the current house. Like Jefferson's other houses, Poplar Forest is extremely well sited on beautiful grounds. Take Route 29 south to 501 North, avoiding the business routes, taking Exit 11, Graves Mill Road (Route 1425). Keep turning left onto Routes 221, 811, and 661. The entrance is on the right of 661. The house is open 10 A.M. to 4 P.M. every day but Tuesday, April through November. Phone: (434) 525-1806.

Portsmouth, Hampton Roads. The only vestige of an early townscape in historic Hampton Roads is in the Olde Town Portsmouth, a place that has been called "a significant assemblage of late-eighteenth- and nineteenth-century urban architecture" (Virginia Landmarks Commission).

After the destruction of nearby Norfolk, Portsmouth and Suffolk were crowded with refugees. Fort Nelson, on Windmill Point, was abandoned when British raiders under Admiral Sir George Collier and General Edward Mathew arrived from New York in May 1779, doing tremendous damage in the area. Portsmouth was subsequently a base for the British expeditions under Alexander Leslie (headed for the Carolinas to reinforce Cornwallis), Benedict Arnold, and William Phillips (see PETERSBURG). Cornwallis reached Portsmouth in July 1781 before moving to his fate at Yorktown.

Highway markers in Portsmouth refer to these events, and several colonial and Revolutionary War landmarks exist in addition to the structures mentioned above. The site of Fort Nelson is marked by a monument on the grounds of the United States Naval Hospital, on the peninsula at the north end of Green Street. (The hospital dates from 1827.) Trinity Church (1762) at Court and High Streets is a remodeled brick structure in the city's first public cemetery.

Raccoon Ford, Rapidan River, Orange County. "I am not strong enough even to get beaten," the young marquis de Lafayette wrote Washington the day a large British force under Lord Cornwallis left Petersburg with precisely this objective in mind. As the British advanced from Westover through White Oak Swamp and Hanover Courthouse (see HANOVER COURTHOUSE AND TAVERN) as far north as Cook's Ford on the Pamunkey (about where I-95 now crosses the river), Lafayette led his little command north to safety behind the Rapidan. He crossed Ely's Ford, circled northwest through the muster ground of the Culpeper Minutemen, and then recrossed the Rapidan at Raccoon Ford (on 6 June 1781). He had been joined by General Anthony Wayne, whose column of reinforcements from Washington's main army was a few days' march to the rear, and Lafayette now had the strength to go back and oppose the British raiders (see MECHUNK CREEK).

Raccoon Ford today appears on some highway maps. On the northern edge of the Wilderness and a quiet place of considerable natural beauty in picturesque Orange County, the general location of the old ford may be identified by an antique suspension bridge. The most direct route is from U.S. 522 just south of the Rapidan: from the junction here of the secondary road, No. 611, drive east 1.3 miles. The place can be reached also by driving north from Va. 20 at Locust Grove.

Red Hill, also known as the Patrick Henry National Memorial, 1250 Red Hill Road (Route 2), near Brookneal, Charlotte County. Open daily, 9 A.M. to 4 P.M. Phone: (434) 376-2044. Patrick Henry's last home and burial place are located in a remnant of his Red Hill Plantation, where he spent the last few years of his life. The law office and cook's cabin are original; the main house, kitchen, smokehouse, and stables are reconstructions on original foundations. Visitors can view a fifteen-minute film on the life of Patrick Henry before browsing the museum and grounds that feature seven period-authentic buildings, including the slave quarters and Henry's law office and library. Patrick Henry and other family members are buried in the cemetery on this site. This is most comprehensive museum in the country regarding information on Patrick Henry.

Richmond. At the head of navigation on the James River and ideally situated for a frontier post and trading center, "the Falls of the Potomac" were explored by a party from Jamestown on 27 May 1607. A settlement was started on the site of modern Richmond two years later, but because of hostile Indians it was almost immediately abandoned. Thomas Stegg established a trading post in 1637. He later received a grant around the falls, to which his son added land purchased on both sides of the river. William Byrd I (1652–1704) inherited these holdings through his mother, a sister of Thomas Stegg II.

The Indians continued to resist this penetration of what had been the center of the Powhatan confederation. Nathaniel Bacon, who had settled at Curies Neck, a series of bends in the James about 9 miles southeast of Richmond, became the champion of settlers who took Indian affairs into their own hands when they became convinced that the colonial governor (Berkeley) was indifferent to their problems. Leading a punitive expedition against the surviving natives, he started by killing about 150 Indians on a hill just east of Richmond, an action remembered as the Battle of Bloody Run. Bacon did not distinguish between friendly and hostile, insuring that the Indians themselves abandoned this distinction.

In 1737 the village of Richmond was laid out on the orders of William Byrd II by William Mayo, who surveyed thirty-two "squares" in the area that would become called Church Hill, which has recently been designated a historic district (see ST. JOHN'S EPISCOPAL CHURCH below). Named presumably for the site's resemblance to Richmond on the Thames, the town was incorporated in 1742. Growth continued to be slow; the population of only 250 people in 1742 had increased to fewer than two thousand at the time of the Revolution, and half of these were slaves. As settlement moved westward, however, the location of Richmond made it a more logical place than Williamsburg for the capital, particularly because it was less vulnerable to British sea power. Three significant Virginia conventions were held in Richmond in 1775, the public records were moved there in 1777, and after earlier attempts had failed, the place was made the state capital in May 1779.

As fate would have it, this date coincided with the first of a devastating series of British raids that lasted until 1781. Richmond became an important military depot and also a port for the shipment of tobacco, which constituted an important basis of foreign credit. It was not until 1781 that the raiders got as far inland as Richmond, but in January of that year Benedict Arnold occupied the capital for three days, burning tobacco warehouses and other buildings. Governor Thomas Jefferson, who lived there in a rented house, could muster only two hundred men to oppose the eight hundred raiders. Simcoe's Rangers figured prominently as a force in Arnold's expedition.

When the cries of Virginia Patriots who would not themselves turn out to defend their state finally forced Washington to send regulars to defend them, Lafayette led a force of New England and New Jersey light infantry (one regiment commanded by his compatriot and former aide-de-camp, Jean-Joseph Sourbader de Gimat). The Continentals arrived after a series of forced marches just in time to save Richmond from another raid, but too late to help defend Petersburg. (See COLONIAL HEIGHTS.) Remaining there during the period 29 April to 27 May 1781, Lafayette then retreated north to evade a superior force under Lord Cornwallis, who had come up from the Carolinas to do some serious raiding in Virginia. The British passed through Richmond three weeks later on their withdrawal down the peninsula.

Following are some of Richmond's principal points of interest to students of the Revolution:

St. John's Episcopal Church. The church, at 2401 East Broad and 24th Streets, is the most famous site in Richmond pertaining to the colonial era, drawing about fifty thousand visitors a year to the scene of Patrick Henry's most famous oration. In the third great speech of his life, on 23 March 1775, he said: "I know not what course others may take, but as for me, Give me liberty or give me death!"

Patrick Henry's political career had been launched by his performance in the Parson's Cause (see HANOVER COURTHOUSE AND TAVERN). As a newly elected member of the House of Burgesses, two years later, on 29 May 1765, he had spoken the other lines that played such an important part in rousing Patriot spirits against colonial oppression: "Caesar had his Brutus—Charles the first, his Cromwell—and George the third—may profit by their example.... If *this* be treason, make the most of it." However, he apologized for these words when challenged by his fellow legislators.

The Richmond church now called St. John's was built during the years 1740 to 1741 on land given by William Byrd II, and for almost seventy-five years it was the only church in town. The original 25-by-40-foot building was enlarged in December 1772 by an addition on the north side, and the interior was rearranged to make this new part the nave. A belfry was added at the same time. The "New Church" or the "Church on Richmond Hill" was being used by the Virginia Assembly in 1775, when Henry made his famous speech, because it was the largest building available for the 120 or so members of the assembly. (Governor Dunmore had dissolved this body, so it could not meet in the capitol in Williamsburg.)

St. John's churchyard has the graves of George Wythe (whose house is covered under WILLIAMSBURG), and Dr. James McClurg (c. 1746–1823). The latter was a distinguished physician who had served during the Revolution as a surgeon and as director general of military hospitals in Virginia. He was proposed by James Madison to be Livingston's successor as secretary of foreign affairs, but not appointed. In 1787 he was selected as a member of the Virginia delegation to the Constitutional Convention in Philadelphia, where he was influential in promoting the principle that the legislative branch of the government should exercise minimum influence on the executive. He also urged that the president serve for life.

Several city blocks around St. John's known as Church Hill and containing an extraordinary variety of nineteenth-century structures are now a historic district. Extensive restoration was completed in the 1970s. Reenactments of the Second Virginia Convention began in 1976 as part of the bicentennial, and have now become a regular fixture at the church. Today thousands of viewers see the show every year, and for a healthy fee, one can even schedule a private showing of the reenactment. St. John's possesses beautiful gardens, and a museum gift shop is accessible. Phone: 804-649-7938.

Capitol Square. This 12-acre plot set aside for public buildings by the act establishing the state capital in Richmond is now a pretty area of walks and large trees. In one corner is a sculptural group of famous Virginians of the Revolution: Washington, Mason, Henry, Lewis, Marshall, Nelson, and Jefferson.

The State Capitol. The famous statue of Washington by Houdon (in the rotunda) and a copy of his bust of Lafayette, the original of which was a gift to the city of Paris from the state of Virginia, are both here.

John Marshall House. This landmark is at Ninth and East Marshall Streets. Designed and built by Marshall shortly after 1789, this was the home of the famous chief justice of the Supreme Court until his death in 1835. Although his reputation rests on his legal career after the Revolution, John Marshall had just reached manhood when that war started. He was a lieutenant in the Patriot force that defeated the British at Great Bridge in December 1775. After serving with the Culpeper Minutemen, in July 1776 he became a first lieutenant in the Third Virginia Continentals. Marshall was later made deputy judge advocate, and in February 1781 he retired as a captain. He had seen action at the Brandywine, Germantown, Monmouth, and Stony Point.

Having been raised on the frontier, he moved to Richmond in 1783 and quickly became successful as a lawyer. In 1801 he became chief justice, serving thirty-four years and establishing the prestige of the Supreme Court. Phone: (804) 648-7998.

The Site of Powhatan's Village. This historic spot is said to be in Chimborazo Park, on East Broad between 32nd and 35th Streets, and the place is indicated by a stone that once marked the chief's grave. Authorities agree that Powhatan's power was originally centered in the region north and east of Richmond, so they undoubtedly would have had one of their villages here at some time. However, their main "capital"—the one visited by John Smith and other Jamestown settlers—was on the north bank of the York River, probably at Purton Bay, near Gloucester. (It is important to note that the first settlers were confused and thought that the chief Wahunsonacock, Pocahontas's father, was named Powhatan.)

Shockoe Hill Cemetery. Peter Francisco, known as the Hercules of the American Revolution, is buried in this cemetery, a 12.5-acre tract of ancient trees and graves of the period 1825 to 1875 located at the north end of Third Street. As a child of about five years, he had been put ashore from a strange ship and abandoned near the present Hopewell, Virginia. Recent research discovered that a Pedro Francisco was born in the Azores in 1760 and disappeared five years later. An uncle of Patrick Henry raised the boy. In 1776 he joined the Tenth Virginia Regiment and during the war he distinguished himself in a number of hard-fought battles, including Brandywine, Germantown, Fort Mifflin, Monmouth, Stony Point, Paulus Hook, Camden, Guilford Courthouse, and Yorktown. He moved to Richmond in 1823 and became sergeant at arms in the House of Delegates. Having survived at least five serious wounds during the war, he died in 1831 of an intestinal ailment. (See FRANCISCO'S FIGHT in this article, and also GUILFORD COURTHOUSE, under North Carolina.)

Virginia Historical Society Headquarters. The Society's collections at 428 North Boulevard include the gigantic broadsword presented to Peter Francisco by Washington. Here you can also see Charles Willson Peale's portrait of Lafayette and Thomas Sully's Pocahontas and many other items and exhibits relevant to the colonial and Revolutionary periods. Phone: (804) 358-4901.

Ampthill (private). This historic residence at the south end of Ampthill Road off Cary Street was moved to this location in 1929 to 1930 from Falling Creek, on the south bank of the James. Built long before 1732 by one of the Henry Carys, and moved to Richmond by a member of the family, it was the home of Colonel Archibald Cary. The latter was chairman of the committee that directed the Virginia delegates to the Continental Congress to move for independence.

Wilton. Located at the south end of Wilton Road off Cary Street Road, this brick mansion of remarkably beautiful proportions was moved to its present site in 1935. It was built around 1750 by William Randolph III on the north bank of the James, 6 miles below Richmond.

Saratoga (Daniel Morgan's Home), near Boyce, Clarke County. Privately owned, this large, austere, two-story stone house on a rocky elevation is one of the best preserved mansions of the Revolutionary period in the Shenandoah. Morgan built it in 1781 to 1782, probably with German prisoner of war labor. The "Old Wagoner" had resigned for "ill health" on 10 February 1781, having done this once before, on 18 July 1779, before joining General Gates at Hillsborough, North Carolina, and then winning his brilliant victory at Cowpens, South Carolina. Extremely proud of Saratoga, he lived there until about 1798, when lameness forced him to move to one of his smaller farms, Soldier's Rest.

Scotchtown, in Hanover County, 11 miles northwest of Ashland off Route 54. Probably built around 1719, this unusually large frame house was Patrick Henry's home during the years 1771 to 1777, although as the first Revolutionary governor of Virginia he moved into the governor's mansion in Williamsburg soon after his election at the end of June 1777, and before this had been in Philadelphia as a member of the Continental Congresses. He sold the house, which he had bought for £600, to a wealthy planter. The next owner was the father of the future Dolley Madison, who wrote vividly of Scotchtown in her *Memoirs.* The house has been restored and has particularly noteworthy paneling. It also has more than its share of legends: Indian raids, duels, a wife chained in a "dungeon," and one of the many stories about Tarleton riding around the second floor on his horse.

Acquired in 1958 by Hanover County, it is now owned by the Association for the Preservation of Virginia Antiquities (APVA). The site is a National Historic Landmark and is open from April through October, Thursday through Sunday. Phone: (804) 227-3500.

Shadwell. About 3 miles east of Charlottesville on U.S. 250 and within sight of Monticello is a highway marker near the entrance to the farmland on which Thomas Jefferson was born in 1743. He lived at Shadwell until 1745, when he went to Tuckahoe Plantation, and again during the period 1752 to 1770. In the latter year the house built by Peter Jefferson in about 1737 was destroyed by fire and his son started constructing Monticello.

Although the general location of Shadwell was always known, the foundations were not discovered until 1955. A conjectural reconstruction of the house was built in 1960 as a tourist attraction but removed after the Thomas Jefferson Memorial Foundation acquired the property. A "No Trespassing" sign bars visitors from the site where Jefferson's father had bought 400 acres from his wife's cousin William Randolph in exchange for a bowl of Henry Wetherburn's arrack punch. (See MONTICELLO and its cross-reference for particulars.)

Shirley Plantation, James River, 25 miles southeast of Richmond on Va. Route 5. The unique distinction of this estate is that it is still owned and operated by the family that acquired it in 1660. The property has been reduced somewhat from the 170,000-acre complex it comprised in the early 1800s, and the two hundred slaves are no longer employed, but the eleventh generation of the Hills and Carters make do on the 800 acres remaining in their agricultural operation.

Edward Hill II acquired the property in 1660, but it had been settled in 1613 and was producing tobacco for export in 1616. The present house, a large Georgian, three-story brick edifice with two-story white porticos on both main facades, was begun around 1723 by Edward Hill III. His great-granddaughter, Ann Hill Carter, married "Light Horse Harry" Lee and was the mother of Robert E. Lee. Carter portraits and original furnishings are in the mansion, which is still a private home but is open daily from 9 A.M. to 5 P.M. to visitors. Museum exhibits and educational programs highlight a visit to Shirley Plantation, as does a relaxed stroll on the sprawling grounds. Phone: (804) 829-5121.

Soldier's Rest (Daniel Morgan's Home), Berryville, Clarke County. About 1762, when Dan Morgan married Abigail Bailey, he started building this T-shaped frame house. He moved to Saratoga when this house was completed in 1782, but returned briefly to Soldier's Rest before the need for regular medical attention made him take up residence in Winchester in 1800. (Here he died in 1802.) A private home, Soldier's Rest is listed by the National Survey in the "Sites Also Noted" category (1964), whereas Saratoga is not mentioned.

Spencer's Tavern, near Williamsburg, James City County. After Cornwallis had reached Williamsburg in his withdrawal down the peninsula he detached Lieutenant Colonel John Graves Simcoe westward to destroy Patriot supplies on the Chickahominy. Lafayette had halted his cautious pursuit at New Kent Courthouse, but from here he sent his advance elements to cut Simcoe off as he returned. Before dawn on 26 June 1781 the forces of Butler and Simcoe clashed in the vicinity of Spencer's Ordinary (tavern). It was a classic meeting engagement, both commanders committing their units piecemeal as they caught up with their advance echelons. Simcoe was getting the better of it, but broke off the action because he was afraid that Lafayette's main column might be closing up. Each side had about thirty casualties and each commander claimed the victory, but Butler retained possession of the field. The site is about a mile north of Green Spring Battlefield and 4 miles south of a highway marker on U.S. 60 at Lightfoot. It is undeveloped, but with a contemporary sketch of the action you can find the principal landmarks. (The sketch from Simcoe's *Military Journal* is reproduced by Lossing in *Field Book of the American Revolution* , II, p. 464.)

Stratford Hall Plantation, Potomac River, 3 miles north of Lerty on Va. 214. In 1716 Thomas Lee (1690–1750) bought 16,000 acres here that were part of lands patented in 1651 by George Washington's great-great grandfather, Nathaniel Pope (see WASHINGTON'S BIRTHPLACE). In 1722 he married Hannah Ludwell of Green Spring; they had eleven children, of whom four became famous during the Revolution: Richard Henry, Francis Lightfoot, William, and Arthur.

Thomas built the great mansion during the period 1725 to 1730, and under his son Philip Ludwell Lee "Stratford exemplified the pinnacle of colonial cultural, social, and plantation life" (Virginia *Guide*, 546). Philip's daughter Matilda married her cousin "Light Horse Harry" Lee in 1782, having inherited Stratford in 1775. She died in 1790. Harry Lee became governor of Virginia the next year, and in 1793 brought a new wife to Stratford; their son Robert E. Lee was born there in 1807 and remained until the family moved to Alexandria in 1811. "Light Horse Harry" had been a great cavalry commander, but he and his son Henry, who inherited Stratford from his mother, allowed the family estate to run down. Much to the chagrin of his half-brother, the future Confederate commander, Henry Lee became involved in moral and financial difficulties that forced him to sell Stratford in 1828 for a paltry $11,000.

The Lee Memorial Foundation, organized in 1929, has bought and restored the estate as a model colonial plantation with characteristic industries. The site is billed as "the birthplace of Robert E. Lee." The mansion is a notable example of early Georgian architecture, and has many unique features, including a monumental hall and unusual chimney stacks. The vista onto the river has been cleared of the trees that long obscured it, and the formal gardens have been restored. Stratford Hall Plantation is open daily to the public. Phone: (804) 493-8038.

Suffolk, Nansemond River, Nansemond County. The Widow Constance's tobacco warehouse, established in 1730, was in a settlement pioneered by Edward Waters in 1618, only ten years after Captain John Smith explored the Nansemond River. Some three hundred Puritans, the first to reach Virginia, were expelled from this area by Governor Berkeley. (They established Providence, Maryland.) In the operations that eventually drove Governor Dunmore from Norfolk in early 1776, North Carolina and Virginia troops under General Robert Howe occupied Suffolk, which was crowded with refugees. The place was burned on 13 May 1779 by British raiders who had landed at Portsmouth. Cornwallis camped at Suffolk in mid-July 1781 when he maneuvered his army from Green Spring to Portsmouth in the operations leading to Yorktown.

Suffolk's colonial church of 1753 survived the Revolution but fell into ruin and was demolished by 1802. The site is marked on Western Avenue about 200 feet west of Church Street. The Widow Constance's house has been carefully restored in Suffolk Cemetery, at the east end of Mahan Street.

Tuckahoe Plantation (private), 7 miles west of Richmond, take Interstate 64 to Gaskin Road. Thomas Jefferson spent seven of his first nine years here at the home of his Randolph cousins, receiving the cultural foundations of his later achievements. It is designated a National Landmark. Notable for its H-shaped plan, the house was built between 1712 and 1730. The interior has not been significantly changed. Among the original outbuildings that remain is the little brick schoolhouse attended by Jefferson, and his boyish autograph has survived on its plastered walls. (Jefferson's other homes were Poplar Forest, Shadwell, and Monticello.) Individuals or groups wishing to tour Tuckahoe are advised to make an appointment. Phone: (804) 749-4000.

War Memorial Museum of Virginia, Newport News. Covers the military history of Virginia from the colonial period to today, with more than fifty thousand artifacts. Take Exit 263A, Warwick Boulevard, off Route 258. The Museum is at 9285 Warwick Boulevard. Open Monday through Saturday, 9 A.M. to 5 P.M., and Sunday 1 to 5 P.M. Phone: (757) 247-8523.

Washington's Birthplace (Pope's Creek), Potomac River 38 miles east of Fredericksburg. George Washington was born here (1732) in a house completed a few years earlier by his father on property lying between Pope's and Bridges Creeks. This house was destroyed by fire about 1779. A memorial house has been built in the style of the period, and a working plantation of the eighteenth century has been developed by the National Park Service on the land settled by the Washington family. Take Route 204 from Route 3. Open weekdays, 9 A.M. to 5 P.M. Phone: (804) 224-1732.

George Washington's father, Augustine, added to property purchased by Colonel John Washington, George's great-grandfather. The family cemetery, a mile from the memorial house, has the tombs of thirty-one Washingtons, including George's father, grandfather, and great-grandfather. (The route is marked from the house and may now be reached by car.)

The future president lived his first three years at Pope's Creek (as the family place was known). His family then spent about three years on the property that would later be called Mount Vernon, and late in 1738 they moved to Ferry Farm (see FERRY FARM SITE), opposite Fredericksburg. After the death of his father, Augustine, in 1743, young George spent time at all three of these family places, and according to some evidence he lived at Pope's Creek part of the period 1744 to 1746.

The original family place had been willed to George's half-brother Augustine. Lawrence, the other half-brother, inherited the place that he would later name Mount Vernon and pass on to George, and George was left Ferry Farm in his father's will.

John Washington was a young Englishman in the transatlantic shipping trade when he reached the little river landing of Mattox, close to the site we are discussing. Here he was befriended by Colonel Nathaniel Pope, who had built the wharf and warehouse at Mattox. John decided to remain in Virginia, staying in the Pope house, and eventually marrying Pope's daughter Anne (around 1658). Colonel Pope gave the young couple 700 acres that included Mattox. In 1664 they moved to a 150-acre tract John had bought on Bridges Creek, their new home being built 50 yards east of the place where the family burial lot was later established.

The Mattox property descended through John's older son, Lawrence, to a grandson, Augustine, who was George's father. In 1717 to 1718 Augustine bought land adjoining the Bridges Creek property that had passed down to his cousins from the second son of the original John Washington.

The U-shaped house in which George was born was completed by his father around 1726. Its foundation survived the fire of 1779, and its outline and basement design have been traced; the site is marked near the memorial house. Until recent years research failed to uncover any information about the design and appearance of the house other than that it resembled the Christian House at Providence Forge. With only these two clues, the memorial mansion was built, and now it serves to portray a typical plantation house of the Northern Neck at the time when George Washington was born. A monument, about

Birthplace of George Washington, Kitchen. *Although the house where George Washington was born in 1732 was destroyed by a fire in 1779, this period-style memorial house was built in the 1930s near Washington's original birthplace.* © DAVE BARTRUFF/CORBIS.

one-tenth the size of the Washington Monument but an otherwise somewhat exact replica, was erected here in honor of the birthplace of Washington. The name Wakefield, by which Washington's birthplace has long been known, apparently was not associated with the property until after the Revolution.

Westover, James River, 7 miles west of Charles City Courthouse off Route 5. Land here was settled in 1619 by Francis, John, and Nathaniel West, who were killed in the Indian massacre of 1622. The first William Byrd (1652–1704) bought 1,200 acres from the family of Theodoric Bland in 1688 for £300 and 10,000 pounds of tobacco. This Byrd built an impressive wooden mansion in 1690 and established the tradition of abundant and cultured living at Westover while pursuing wealth in business and land speculation. His son, William II, who would leave a reputation as a distinguished writer of the colonial period in addition to being a highly successful man in politics and commerce, built the present brick mansion in 1730 to 1734. His only son, William III, dissipated the family fortune and committed suicide in 1777.

The Byrds of the Revolutionary era were sympathetic to the British. Westover was the place where Benedict Arnold landed in January 1781 on his raid to Richmond and where Cornwallis landed four months later to chase Lafayette (see RICHMOND).

The famous Byrd mansion is rarely open to the public, but the garden and grounds are open to visitors daily from 9 A.M. to 6 P.M. The mansion is open to the public for four days in the last week of April and for one day in September. Westover is one of the finest Georgian houses in America. A number of once prominent men are buried at the site of the first Westover Church, 400 yards from the mansion. (The present Westover Church was built in 1737 on a site several miles away, donated by the Byrd family according to tradition because they got tired of always having the congregation for Sunday dinner.) Phone: (804) 829-2882.

Williamsburg, on I-64, 50 miles east of Richmond. Colonial Williamsburg is an amazing restoration and reconstruction of the large provincial village that was Virginia's capital during the years 1699 to 1780. Its appeal is on several levels. The first, unfortunately, is that of the amusement park, and Williamsburg's colonial charm can be overwhelmed by hordes of bus-borne children (many of whom would rather be at nearby Busch Gardens) and older citizens unprepared intellectually for the experience. If spared this shattering contrast between contemporary American culture and its idealized origins, one can spend many full days enjoying and learning from Williamsburg's architectural treasures, collections, gardens, exhibitions of colonial craftsmen at work, and from its preservation research—the work of historians, architects, and archaeologists.

The 130-acre Historic Area contains more than eighty original structures, most of them extensively restored. Hundreds of others have been reconstructed after exhaustive archaeological and documentary research. Almost one hundred gardens have been reconstructed with the plans and plants of the eighteenth century. At the time of the Revolution, half of Williamsburg's population was enslaved, and many looked to the royal governor, Lord Dunmore, as a liberator for offering them freedom if they joined the British forces to fight the rebels. Few sites at Williamsburg acknowledge this history, which is difficult to address. In the 1990s a reenactment of a slave auction created a major controversy, and the practice was abandoned. The park has attempted to be sensitive to these concerns and interests by establishing a Department of African American Interpretation and Presentations which offers a number of creative programs to introduce the visitor to numerous aspects of black daily life in the colonial period.

A number of interesting books and other publications pertaining to the eighteenth century, from history to house design, are sold at Williamsburg shops or over the internet via their website, www.history.org. The general phone for information on Williamsburg is (757) 229-1000.

Discordant modern elements have been eliminated almost entirely from Colonial Williamsburg, or, as in the case of telephone and electrical wires, they are hidden.

The most important of the original eighteenth-century buildings in Williamsburg are:

The Public Magazine. Built in 1715 to 1716 for the public arms and ammunition, this building figured in the early phases of the Revolution when Governor Dunmore secretly had the gunpowder removed the night of 20 to 21 April 1775. Patrick Henry marched on Williamsburg with the Hanover County militia and demanded that the public powder be restored. The governor roared at this legalistic insolence, but backed down and reimbursed the province. He explained that he took the powder because a slave uprising was rumored. (He should have known. He was threatening to instigate such a revolt.)

Bruton Parish Church. Built in 1710 to 1715, this was restored early in the twentieth century by the Reverend W. A. R. Goodwin, who later inspired John D. Rockefeller, Jr., to restore all of Williamsburg. Presidents Washington, Jefferson, Monroe, and Tyler attended this church as young men.

The George Wythe House. Built about 1750 by the distinguished amateur architect Richard Taliaferro (pronounced "tah-liver"!), it was left twenty years later to his son-in-law, George Wythe (pronounced "with"). The latter was a signer of the Declaration of Independence, statesman, jurist, law professor, and the close associate of more famous men who were friends in early life or his students in later years. Among the latter were Jefferson, John Marshall, James Monroe, and Henry Clay. Born in 1726, Wythe was poisoned by his nephew in 1806 and is buried outside St. John's Church in Richmond. Ironically, the nephew was acquitted because the only witness, a black servant (Wythe freed all his slaves) was not allowed to testify in a court of law because he was black.

Wetherburn Tavern. Formerly known as the Bland-Wetherburn House, the tavern has only recently been restored and refurnished. Almost 200,000 artifacts were found in the archaeological exploration of the site. The house belonged originally to a branch of the famous Bland family and is believed to be the birthplace of Richard Bland (1710–1776), a distinguished colonial statesman. About 1716 the house was sold to Henry Wetherburn, a former operator of the Raleigh Tavern (across the street). The enterprising Wetherburn was famous for his "Arrack punch," a bowl of which was the price paid by Thomas Jefferson's father to William Randolph of Tuckahoe Plantation for 400 acres of prime land (see under MONTICELLO).

Most notable of the reconstructed buildings are the Capitol, the Governor's Palace, and Raleigh Tavern.

Within modern Williamsburg and at the opposite end of Duke of Gloucester Street from the colonial Capitol is the *Wren Building* of the College of William and Mary. The Wren Building is flanked by the President's House and the Brafferton (see below).

Designed by Sir Christopher Wren, but in the words of a contemporary, "adapted to the Nature of the Country by the *Gentlemen* there," this is the oldest academic building in the United States. Construction was started in 1695 and finished in 1702. Three years later it burned, and reconstruction was completed in 1732. There were fires again in 1859 and 1862, and alterations were made with each reconstruction. When restoration was about to start in 1927, a last-minute discovery was made at Oxford University of a copper engraving plate showing several Williamsburg buildings, including this one. With this and a plan drawn by Jefferson it was possible to reconstruct the Wren Building fairly accurately.

The President's House has been used by every president of the college. It was built in 1732 to 1733 and has been restored. Cornwallis occupied it briefly in 1781. Facing it is the Brafferton, built in 1723 as the first permanent Indian school in the colonies. The English scientist Robert Boyle died in 1691, leaving instructions that revenue from his English estate, Brafferton, be used for charity. The fund was divided between Harvard and William and Mary for the education of Indians.

Winchester, Frederick County seat. From prehistoric times this place has grown as an important hub of activity in the region. Major east-west highways still intersect in the center of the old town, taking heavy traffic through streets where important historic sites are marked, and where many interesting buildings still stand.

Settlement of the Shenandoah Valley, whose throat (if not its mouth) is the site of Winchester, was predominately by Englishmen from Virginia and Germans from Pennsylvania. The region was part of the Fairfax Grant. The sixth Lord Fairfax made his home here in the wilderness at Greenway Court and is buried in Winchester (Christ Episcopal Church, on Washington Street near Boscawen Court).

George Washington worked in the area as a surveyor for Lord Fairfax, a simple little building now called Washington's Office surviving at 32 West Cork Street. In front of it is a small cannon mounted on a masonry base, one of the monuments erected to mark the route of Braddock's March in 1755 to defeat on the Monongahela (Battle of the Wilderness). After this disaster Washington took command of frontier defenses, building works that included Fort Loudoun, whose site is marked in Winchester at Peyton and Loudoun Streets. In the course of his long acquaintance with this region Washington and his family staked out a number of choice land claims, particularly around nearby Charlestown, West Virginia. In 1999, after a tremendous effort on the part of volunteers, Washington's Office reopened as a renovated museum, and now is maintained by the Winchester-Frederick County Historical Society.

Dan Morgan's memory also is alive in the area. At the age of nineteen he accompanied Braddock's expedition as a teamster, rendering good service and becoming acquainted with Washington. It may have been at Fort Chiswell, up the Shenandoah Valley, where Morgan got his famous lashing from the British. In 1762 he settled near Winchester on a small grant, and from here he left at the head of a major contingent of frontiersmen to launch his career as the most famous rifleman of the Revolution. The temperamental Morgan, who also was plagued by recurring bouts of bad health that seemed to coincide with his military career plans, spent much time tending his personal affairs near home. He is believed to have used German prisoner's of war to build Saratoga.

Prospering in many enterprises after the Revolution, eventually acquiring a tremendous amount of land, he lived at Soldier's Rest until about two years before his death in 1802. His last two years were spent in Winchester, where the house survives, privately owned, at 226 West Amherst Street. Morgan's grave is southeast of the ruins of the Old Lutheran Church (1764–1864), near the entrance to Mount Hebron Cemetery, at the east end of Boscawen Street. Near Morgan lie five of the six men known as his "Dutch Mess," who were his bodyguards during the Revolution. (The word "mess" in military parlance means a group of men who eat together regularly.)

The first Pennsylvania German pioneer of the region was Jost Hite, his monument being the ruins of Hite's Fort. Winchester's architecture reflects the German influence as well as the English.

Today's boosters of Winchester are focused on its industrial attractions and the annual Shenandoah Apple Blossom Festival. But the modern city and the surrounding region have much to recommend them to visitors interested in the colonial and Revolutionary eras. The best source of information on the area's history is the Winchester-Frederick County Historical Society, located at 1340 South Pleasant Valley Road in Winchester. Phone: (540) 662-6550.

Yorktown, on U.S. 17 and a short distance off Interstate 64, about 13 miles east of Williamsburg, 106 miles south of Fredericksburg, and 32 miles north of Norfolk. Open daily, 9 A.M. to 5 P.M. Phone: (757) 898-2410. Only a few months before the decisive Franco-American victory at Yorktown (October 1781), it looked as if the American cause was hopeless. The war had dragged on five years, the British land and sea forces could take and hold vital places at will, and Patriot finances had collapsed. The French alliance was three years old, but it had not brought any results. A French expeditionary force under Rochambeau was sitting in Newport with nothing to do because the French fleet had been unable to achieve the naval supremacy needed for decisive operations.

Then several things happened to brighten the scene. In May 1781 Admiral de Barras reached Newport, Rhode Island, to command the French fleet blockaded there by the Royal Navy. Although he proved to be a problem to Rochambeau and Washington because of his independent and uncooperative outlook, he brought good news: Admiral Comte de Grasse was heading for the West Indies with a powerful fleet, and six hundred recruits were on the way to reinforce the four French regiments in Rhode Island.

Washington and Rochambeau met in Wethersfield, Connecticut to make plans for immediate employment of their forces. Agreeing on a strategic diversion against New

York City to draw British forces from Virginia and the Carolinas, they left in abeyance the matter of what might be done if de Grasse appeared. They did agree, however, to send word to de Grasse that he should come north as soon as possible for combined operations.

Thanks largely to a series of British blunders, things worked out better than the Allies could have hoped. Cornwallis decided that Virginia was the decisive theater and that he would abandon his frustrating operations against Nathanael Greene in the Carolinas and march north. The neurotic Sir Henry Clinton, British commander in chief in North America with headquarters in New York City, overreacted to the Franco-American threat against that city and called on Cornwallis for reinforcements. The politically powerful Cornwallis was reporting directly to Lord Germain in London, receiving seriously delayed orders and instructions from New York and London, and interpreting these in accordance with his own strategic lights.

The end result was that after chasing Lafayette's small Continental force around Virginia for about two months, he selected Yorktown as the place to make camp and wait for developments. About a week before Cornwallis completed his concentration at Yorktown and Gloucester Point (across the river), Washington got the news that shaped the final strategy of the war: de Grasse was sailing for the Chesapeake with about thirty warships and three thousand soldiers, and would remain for combined operations until 15 October. Continuing to make feints against New York City, the Franco-American army marched for Virginia.

De Grasse slipped away from the British in the West Indies with an alacrity for which Americans must eternally be grateful, and sailed into Chesapeake Bay unimpeded. Admiral Hood made such good time in pursuit that he lost sight of the French, reaching the Virginia Capes ahead of them. Finding no enemy naval forces in Chesapeake Bay, Hood assumed de Grasse had continued north to New York, Boston, or Newport, and headed that way himself. On 31 August the combined fleets of Hood and Graves left New York for the Virginia Capes to fight the French—wherever they might be—and reinforce Cornwallis at Yorktown. This same day de Barras left Rhode Island with siege artillery and provisions for the allied forces concentrating outside Yorktown. On 5 September de Grasse left the Chesapeake to fight Graves and Hood off the Capes. In a long, running naval engagement on 5 September the French were unable to score a clean victory, but inflicted such damage that the British withdrew to New York for repairs. While this was taking place, de Barras entered the Chesapeake. De Grasse soon followed, and the cork was in the bottle Cornwallis had picked for himself at Yorktown.

When French troops from the West Indies were landed at Jamestown by de Grasse on 5 September, Cornwallis still had a chance to fight his way out. But he let himself fall for what classical military scholars know as "the fatal fascination of a fortress," and continued to fortify his positions at Yorktown and Gloucester Point. The forces of Washington and Rochambeau left Williamsburg early on 28 September and by dark had started closing in on Yorktown.

So long as de Grasse could hold off British naval efforts to relieve the siege, the defeat of Cornwallis was simply a matter of time, although the Allies would have to shed a certain amount of blood and much sweat. Alexander Hamilton's assault of Redoubt No. 10 was a brilliant success, the more satisfactory because the Americans accomplished their task in a manner the French veterans had to admire. The French had simultaneously attacked Redoubt No. 9, and before the operation the French commander had annoyed Lafayette by intimating that his Americans might not be up to their task. The Americans, unimpeded by the formal doctrine of using pioneer troops to clear a path for the assault troops in attacking a fortified position, had merely scrambled through the abatis, ditch, and fraises, and taken their redoubt with relatively light losses, some minutes before the French took theirs. Lafayette sent an officer to ask his compatriots whether they would like any help.

On 17 October Cornwallis asked for terms, and two days later his army marched out to lay down their arms. Cornwallis himself pleaded sick, and had a subordinate represent him.

The battlefield is beautifully preserved, and several of the earthworks, including Redoubt No. 9, have been reconstructed. Two self-guided tour routes are marked, and you can easily spend an hour following these by car. One, about 7-miles long, is called the Battlefield Tour Road, and the other, 2 miles longer, is the Encampment Tour Road. An excellent orientation film is shown free at the visitors center, where a truly admirable little museum is located. Visitors may also pick up maps and brochures, and there is a variety of interpretive programs to explore. In addition to exhibits characteristic of these National Park Service museums there is a full-scale reconstruction of a section of the gun deck and captain's cabin of the British frigate *Charon*, which was sunk during the siege.

Yorktown itself, first settled about 1631 and established as a town when eighty-five lots were laid out in 1691, remains a quiet, picturesque little place. Several colonial houses remain and others have been reconstructed. The most famous is that of General Thomas Nelson, Jr., a signer of the Declaration of Independence who, as Virginia's war governor after Thomas Jefferson, was commander of Virginia militia during the siege. He is reported to have directed that his own house be shelled because Cornwallis was believed to be using it. There is a cannonball still embedded in one wall. Built before 1745 by "Scotch Tom" Nelson of Penrith, the general's grandfather, it is well preserved (although the roof has been altered). The Nelson House was a private residence until acquired by the National Park Service in 1968 and made part of the Colonial National Historical Park.. The house is open daily mid-June to mid-August, from 10 a.m. to 4:30 p.m., and in the spring and fall from 1 p.m. to 4:30 p.m. Phone: (757) 898-2409.

The site of another Thomas Nelson home is nearby. He was "Secretary" Nelson, uncle of General Nelson, and secretary of the governor's council for thirty years. His was the finest house in Yorktown, and therefore the first headquarters of Cornwallis, and it was destroyed during the siege.

Grace Church has been active since its construction around 1697, and much of the original marl walls are incorporated in the present structure. Nelson family tombs are in the churchyard.

Other noteworthy buildings are the reconstructed Swan Tavern and its kitchen, stable, smokehouse, and privy; a reconstructed medical shop; the restored Somerwell House (built before 1707); the Thomas Pate House (early eighteenth century); the Customhouse (c. 1720); the Edmund Smith House (c. 1750); and the Thomas Sessions House, which is the oldest of them all, having been built before 1699. Other colonial houses are the Ballard House, the frame structure near the Sessions House called the Dudley Dibbes House, and parts of the small frame Archer House below the bluffs and nearly opposite the site of the town wharf. Remains of the latter can be seen at exceptionally low tide.

WEST VIRGINIA

To get the proper historical perspective on West Virginia in the colonial era and the Revolution, it is helpful to start with a map. The present boundary between West Virginia and Pennsylvania was agreed to in 1779. West Virginia separated from Virginia during the Civil War, and its northeastern panhandle includes the lower end of the strategic Shenandoah Valley.

Hence the colonial history of West Virginia is the history of the Virginia, Maryland, and Pennsylvania frontiers. Its people were involved in the disputes over the Forks of the Ohio (see under PENNSYLVANIA), the Seven Years' War of 1754 to 1763 that followed, and Pontiac's War of 1763 to 1764. All these events were important to West Virginia not only because of the fighting but also because of the direct bearing these events had on settlement (see FORT ASHBY RESTORATION and WASHINGTON'S LANDS for further background).

Dunmore's War of 1774 can be considered to have started at the Logan Massacre Site and to have ended at the Point Pleasant Battlefield.

When the Revolution started in 1775 there were approximately twenty to thirty thousand white men, women, and children in what became West Virginia. These men had informal training in border warfare, and during the Revolution the "Berkeley [County] Riflemen" became famous as rangers along with their counterparts from Pennsylvania, Maryland, and Virginia.

Homes of three prominent generals of the Revolution, Charles Lee, Horatio Gates, and Adam Stephen, have survived in the lower Shenandoah (see PRATO RIO, STEPHEN HOUSE, and TRAVELER'S REST). Landmarks associated with other major figures are identified by highway markers, many of which are mentioned in the following sections.

Like other border regions, during the Revolution western Virginia performed the useful function of absorbing the raids of Indians and Loyalists from British bases in Canada. In the Ohio Valley these came primarily from Detroit, and most of them hit the Kentucky settlements, but several major attacks were repulsed at Wheeling.

The state has many associations with George Rogers Clark, who explored the Ohio and Great Kanawha Rivers in 1772. At the Little Kanawha in 1774 he was preparing to move into Kentucky with a party of about ninety men recruited for the most part in western Virginia when his plans were delayed by Dunmore's War. After serving as a captain in this conflict he was a surveyor for the Ohio Company in Kentucky. In 1778 he stopped at Point Pleasant on his way down the Ohio to conquer the Old Northwest (see FORT KASKASKIA under Illinois and VINCENNES under Indiana).

Daniel Boone was a scout for the Virginia militia moving down the Great Kanawha to the Point Pleasant Battlefield in 1774. After the Revolution he suffered a series of heartbreaking personal reverses, eventually losing all his large holdings in Kentucky because the titles were found to be defective. During part of this period (1788–1795), he lived near Charleston and at Point Pleasant, operating a trading post at the latter place around 1790 to 1791 and representing Kanawha County in the Virginia assembly. (See also BOONE HOME under Missouri.)

In the period of Indian resistance that persisted long after the Revolution, the settlers of western Virginia continued to build frontier fortifications and fight off serious raids. Many highway markers, not included in this guide, pertain to these actions.

The West Virginia Department of Archives and History publishes an excellent guide to the state's nearly one thousand historical highway markers. It is titled Marking Our Past. Last updated in 2002, this 210-page book gives locations arranged by county, full inscriptions of the markers, more than one hundred photographs, and a history of the state's highway marker program, which began in 1937. This book can be purchased from the website or by mail ($15) from West Virginia Archives and History, The Cultural Center, 1900 Kanawha Boulevard East, Charleston, W.V. 25305. Phone: (304) 558-0230. The Department of Archives and History is part of West Virginia's Division of Culture and History and its website, www.wvculture.org, is extremely informative regarding the state's colonial past. The department encompasses almost every aspect of history and landmark preservation within the state, including the State Historical Society. The department's general phone number for information is (304) 558-0220.

West Virginia has a very rich history concerning the travel, property ownership, and family tree of George Washington. A website that merits exploration is www.washingtonheritagetrail.org. This site furnishes information on numerous self-guided tours, including the 112-mile scenic Washington Trail Tour. In addition, it gives details on many noteworthy colonial and Revolutionary-era landmarks.

Charles Town and vicinity, Jefferson County. A few miles west of Harpers Ferry, this picturesque region is remarkable for the surprisingly large concentration of historic colonial homes that survive in a fine state of preservation. Close to Charles Town are (these are each outlined separately later in the chapter) Prato Rio (off State Route 48) and Traveler's Rest (off County Route 1). Both of these were designated National Historic Landmarks in 1972. In nearby Martinsburg is the Stephen House (309 East John Street, open weekends, 2 P.M. to 5 P.M. for tours). These three places were the homes (albeit briefly) of Major Generals Charles Lee, Horatio Gates, and Adam Stephen.

The Charles Town racetrack has grown from its colonial origins into two flourishing modern facilities. The courthouse stands on land donated by Charles Washington, and the present structure incorporates the original one-room house of 1801. John Brown, captured at nearby Harpers Ferry, was tried here in 1859. The Jefferson County Museum Building (1965) houses the old Charles Town library, the county chamber of commerce, and a collection of exhibits pertaining primarily to the Civil War era.

The area has many homes of George Washington's brothers and their descendants. Surviving Washington houses are private, but they may be viewed from the outside. The most famous ones have been opened for the annual house and garden tour. These are:

Harewood, 3 miles west of Charles Town on W.Va. 51. Built by George Washington's brother Samuel around 1770, this large, two-story, limestone structure of Georgian style is noted for the plain dignity of its exterior and interior. The native pine paneling of the drawing room is exceptionally fine. While Lucy Payne Washington was mistress of Harewood, her sister Dolley and James Madison were married in this drawing room. A wing on the north is a modern addition that matches the original wing on the south. Samuel Washington's office and the family graveyard are on the grounds. This is a private residence and is still owned by a descendent of the Washington family.

Happy Retreat (Mordington), in Charles Town on Mordington Avenue at Blakeley Place. Charles Town is named for another brother of George Washington, Charles, who laid the town out in 1786 on 80 acres of his land. In 1780 he built the two wings of the house he called Happy Retreat, but the stone kitchen and adjoining smokehouse probably are older. The house was completed in 1837 by Judge Isaac Douglas and renamed Mordington, for his home in Scotland. (Since 1945 it has been known by the original name.) On the grounds is an octagonal schoolhouse resembling the one at Mount Vernon, but the stone slave quarters and barn have disappeared. Charles Washington was buried on the estate in 1799, and a DAR marker is on the supposed location of his grave. Privately owned.

Blakeley, 2.5 miles southwest of Charles Town. This fine house was built in 1820 by John Augustine Washington II, grandson of George Washington's brother John Augustine. John II moved to Mount Vernon (see under VIRGINIA) when he inherited it from Bushrod Washington. (John III sold Mount Vernon in 1858.) Blakeley is a private home in a beautiful rural setting. It is reached from Charles Town by driving south on U.S. 350 for about 2.5 miles, then west for about 1.5 miles. The house will be on your left (south). Privately owned.

St. George's Chapel ruins are marked on W.Va. 51 about 1.5 miles west of Charles Town near the entrance to another old estate, Piedmont. The chapel was completed in 1769 and used by local families, including the Washingtons.

Local information is available through the Jefferson County Chamber of Commerce. Phone: (304) 725-2055. Another good source is the small but informative Jefferson County Museum, 200 East Washington Street. Phone: (304) 725-8628. The museum is also the starting point and information area for a self-guided walking tour of Historic Charles Town.

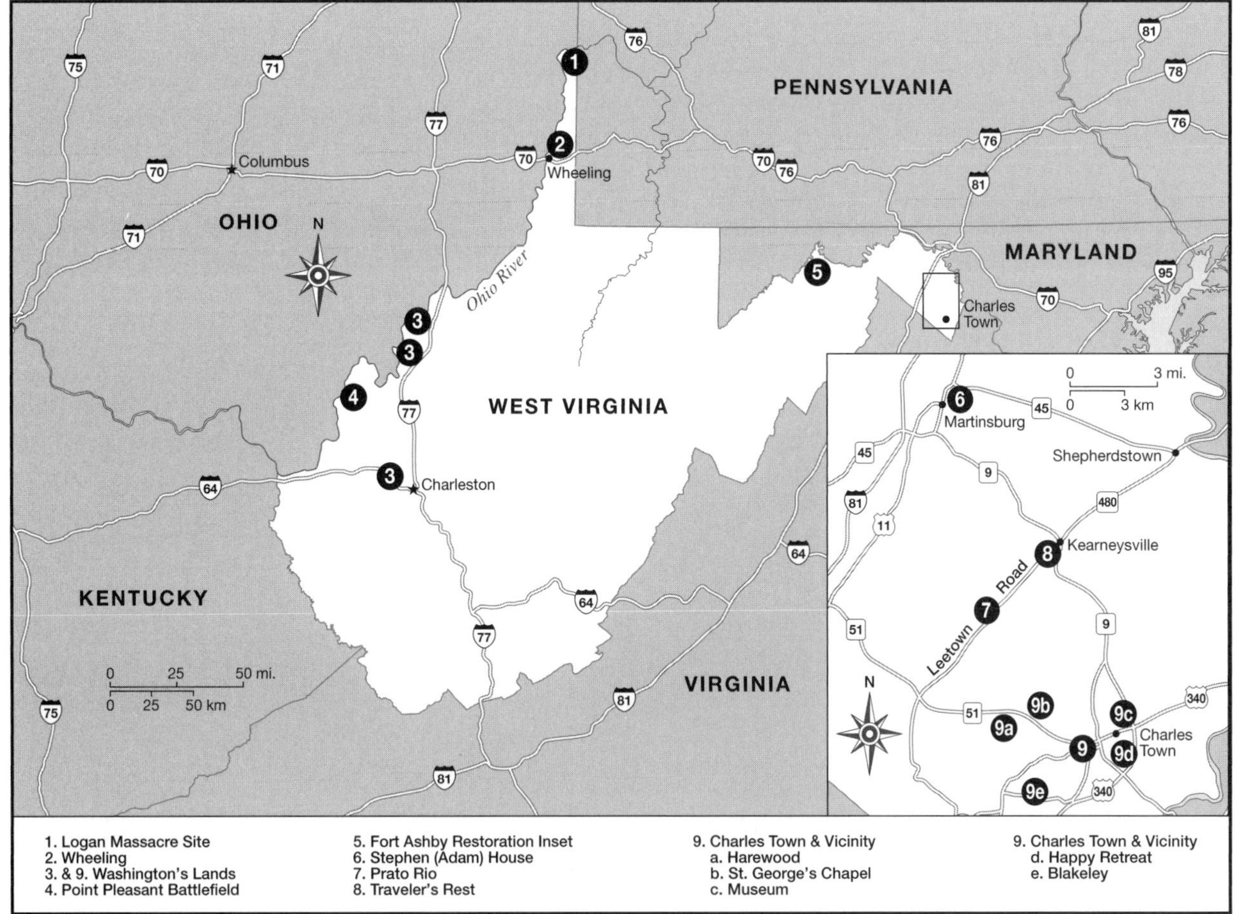

MAP BY XNR PRODUCTIONS. THE GALE GROUP.

Fort Ashby Restoration, town of Fort Ashby, Mineral County. Frontiersmen flowed across the Alleghenies into Indian territories after 1750 in such numbers that a wave of resistance was unleashed. Virginia authorities, concerned about maintaining their claim to this region and halting French expansion into the Ohio country, first sent George Washington to warn the French to pull back. Then they started building a system of fortifications and raising additional troops to protect the fort builders. After Braddock's Defeat in July 1775, the twenty-three-year-old Washington spent two years as commander of some seven hundred militia attempting to defend a frontier about 350 miles long. In 1755 and 1756 a chain of nearly one hundred forts existed. These varied from simple blockhouses to more elaborate military works; they stretched from Fort Cumberland on the Potomac (see under MARYLAND) through the South Branch and Greenbrier Valleys. Many of these forts were manned during the Revolution and later. The booklet West Virginia Highway Markers (see West Virginia introduction) names more than seventy forts in the state, most of them associated with the period through the Revolution.

Fort Ashby is the only one of those structures that has survived. It was built in 1755 by Lieutenant John Bacon and garrisoned with twenty-one men. In August 1756 the place was attacked by French and Indians, who defeated a ranger company under Lieutenant Robert Rutherford. The fort is named for Colonel John Ashby, a frontier soldier who commanded here during and after the Revolution. Troops under General Morgan camped here in 1794 during the Whiskey Rebellion.

As restored in 1939 by the WPA, Fort Ashby is a large log cabin on a stone foundation with a ridged roof providing a commodious attic. Its most striking feature is a huge chimney built 14 feet wide and 4 feet thick. Well-marked, the site is at the junction of W.Va. 28 and 46 in the town of Fort Ashby. The fort is owned by the Daughters of the American Revolution.

Logan Massacre Site, Ohio River opposite the mouth of Yellow Creek (Ohio), Hancock County. The Indian war that ended on the Point Pleasant Battlefield was touched off by the treacherous murder of thirteen unsuspecting Mingo Indians by white frontiersmen led by Daniel Greathouse at "Logan's Camp," or "Baker's Cabin," on 30 April 1774. In a famous speech, Soyechtowa, generally known as Chief Logan, concluded with the words "Who is there to mourn for Logan? Not one!" Logan satisfied himself by personally killing thirteen settlers in retaliation, but the violence between whites and Indians persisted. Controversy over the slaughter continues to this day.

Yellow Creek survives as a geographical name in Ohio, so there is no problem in locating the massacre site on the map. But the area has been devastated by floods in recent years, and it is difficult to locate this site on the ground today. The state highway marker is not much help, being about 6 miles east of the river on W.Va. 2 near U.S. 30 and stating that the massacre was "at this point." The map in Scribner's *Atlas of American History* places "Baker's Cabin Massacre, April 30" on the east bank of the Ohio River directly opposite the mouth of Yellow Creek. The National Survey has "Logan Massacre Site" among its "Sites Also Noted," but puts it in Ohio County. This is almost certainly an error.

Point Pleasant Battlefield, city of Point Pleasant. The victory of the Virginians over the Indians in the pitched battle at this place on 10 October 1774 in Dunmore's (or Cresap's) War accelerated the settlement of Kentucky. Provoked by a series of atrocities that culminated in the Logan Massacre, the Shawnee moved to defend themselves in June 1774. Governor Dunmore of Virginia established headquarters at Pittsburgh, prepared to move down the Ohio with about two thousand militia, and ordered Colonel Andrew Lewis to lead a column of militia from southwest Virginia down the Kanawha River to its junction with the Ohio at Point Pleasant.

About 1,000 Shawnee, Miami, Wyandot (Huron), and Ottawa under Shawnee Chief Cornstalk attacked the 1,100 Virginians under Lewis at Point Pleasant early in the morning of 10 October. The battle raged until late afternoon before the Indians withdrew and left the Virginians in possession of the bloody field. Burying a brother and about fifty others, Lewis linked up with Lord Dunmore near the location of modern Chillicothe, Ohio. Chief Cornstalk sued for peace.

Most of the battlefield is covered by the modern city, but a portion is included in the 4-acre Tu-Endie-Wei Point Pleasant Battle Monument State Park. (Tu-Endie Wei means "the point between two rivers.") The park is located a mile north of the intersection of U.S. 35 and State Route 2, and is open dawn to dusk. Phone: (304) 675-0869. A tavern dating from 1796 is maintained here as a museum, and an 84-foot granite shaft commemorates the battle. There are graves of:

Ann Bailey (1742–1825). A frontier heroine, she was born in Liverpool and came to America in 1761. Her first husband survived Braddock's Massacre and was killed in the Battle of Point Pleasant. Ann thereupon assumed male garb and became a noted scout and messenger. Her second husband was John Bailey. The legend of "Mad Ann" grew as she performed amazing feats along the frontier and had narrow escapes from the Indians. Her most famous exploit was in making a solitary ride of 200 miles in three days from Fort Lee, on the site of Charleston, West Virginia, to Fort Savannah, on the site of Lewisburg, West Virginia, to get a supply of gunpowder that saved the fort in 1791. (The site of Fort Lee in Charleston is marked by a plaque in front of 1202 East Kanawha Boulevard.)

Charles Lewis. Youngest son of the founder of Staunton, Virginia, he was killed under his brother's command at Point Pleasant. He is identified as a colonel. The site of Fort Lewis, his stockaded home more vulgarly known as "Lewis' Hog Pen," is in the vicinity of Hot Springs and Warm Springs, Virginia, both of which are within his former frontier holdings (Va. Guide, 512).

Chief Cornstalk (c. 1720–1777). He returned to Point Pleasant with his son three years after the battle to warn the settlers that he might be forced by his tribe to renew hostilities. Held hostage, he and his son were then killed in retribution for the death of a white settler.

Another interesting burial is marked in the park. It is where Céloron de Blainville in 1749 buried one of the lead plates claiming the Ohio Valley for France.

The ***Point Pleasant*** historic site is near the bridges that span the Ohio River and the mouth of the Great Kanawha. It was here that the final phase of the all-day battle took place; other landmarks of the battle are obscured by the city of Point Pleasant.

Point Pleasant was visited by Washington in 1770 (see WASHINGTON'S LANDS). George Rogers Clark explored the region in 1772 and was here two years later when Dunmore's War disrupted his plans to lead a large party into Kentucky. Clark served as a militia captain in the operations that followed. In 1778 he stopped at Point Pleasant before continuing down the Ohio to become the conqueror of the Old Northwest. The site of Daniel Boone's trading post of 1790 is marked at City Park on U.S. 35 (see introduction).

Prato Rio (Charles Lee Home), Leetown, Jefferson County. As the home of General Charles Lee (1731–1782), a major figure in the Revolution and one of its most colorful personalities, this primitive stone house will be of exceptional interest to serious students of early-American history.

Charles Lee attended school in England and Switzerland before joining his father's regiment as an ensign in 1747. He knew the American frontier well.

After taking part in Braddock's Expedition of 1755 he went to the Mohawk Valley, purchased a captain's commission, married the daughter of a Seneca chief, and was badly wounded at Ticonderoga in 1758 but recovered sufficiently to take part in the capture of Fort Niagara and Montreal (1759–1760). Before being retired on half-pay in November 1763 he served with distinction in Portugal under Burgoyne. During much of the period 1765 to 1771 he was a soldier of fortune with the Polish army, becoming intimate with King Stanislaus Poniatowski, advancing to the grade of major general, and fighting the Turks.

In 1773 Lee came to America, immediately aligned himself with the rebel element, and went to work setting himself up for high military command in the coming war with England. As part of this program, Lee bought an estate in what was then Berkeley County in Virginia, now Jefferson County, West Virginia. On 17 June 1775 he became a major general in the new Continental army, subordinate in rank only to Washington and Artemas Ward. The latter faded quickly into obscurity, and Lee appeared to be a strong contender for Washington's position.

By amazing coincidence, another candidate, also an Englishman, had settled a few miles from Lee's estate and at about the same time. This was Horatio Gates (see TRAVELER'S REST).

Lee ruined himself in the Battle of Monmouth, New Jersey, in June 1778. This was his first real test as a combat commander, and he failed spectacularly. But it was his subsequent conduct that resulted in his conviction by a court-martial, suspension from duty for a year, and subsequent dismissal. During his suspension he lived at Prato Rio from July 1779 to mid-January 1780. He then moved to Philadelphia, where he died in 1782.

The name Prato Rio harks back to Lee's service in Portugal and means "near the river." Lee bought the property from Jacob Hite, and the simple little stone cottage—typically Pennsylvania German with its stoop and two front doors—is believed to have been built by the first white settler of the Shenandoah Valley, Joist Hite, for one of his sons. The original portion is one and a half stories with small-paned windows and outside end chimneys. Lee bought it in 1775 at the urging of Horatio Gates, and it is said that the three suspended generals, Lee, Gates, and Adam Stephen (see STEPHEN HOUSE), met frequently at Prato Rio. In the WPA's *West Virginia: A Guide to the Mountain State*, the story is told of their toasting each other as "Lee, who was cashiered ... because when he should have advanced he retreated," "Gates, who was cashiered because when he should have retreated he advanced," and "Stephen, who was cashiered because when he might have advanced or retreated he did neither." (References are to Lee at Monmouth, New Jersey, Gates at Camden, South Carolina, and Stephen at Germantown, near Philadelphia, Pennsylvania.) This story is certainly apocryphal, especially as Gates was not cashiered from the Continental army.

At Prato Rio, Lee cultivated his famous eccentricities, living in seclusion with his Italian bodyguard, slaves, hounds, and horses. The unpartitioned ground floor of his house was divided by chalk lines into quarters (quite literally), one for the kitchen, one for guns and riding equipment, one for his library, and the other for his bed.

Prato Rio is easy to spot, being on a slight rise alongside the road (Route 48) from Leetown to Middleway and a few hundred feet southwest of Leetown. The latter is on most highway maps. A national fish hatchery near Leetown occupies land that was part of Lee's estate. The historic house is currently a private residence.

Stephen House, 309 East John Street, Martinsburg, Berkeley County. On a rocky hill of the town he founded in 1778 (after being court-martialed out of the Continental army) is the severely rectilinear and unadorned stone house built by General Adam Stephen in 1789.

Born in Scotland in 1718, Stephen had been educated at the Universities of Aberdeen and Edinburgh before serving in the Royal Navy as a surgeon (1746–1747). He came to America and practiced medicine in Fredericksburg, Virginia until 1754. After this he fought on the frontier in the Seven Years' War, achieving the rank of brigadier general of militia and being closely associated with Washington.

As early as 1750 Stephen had bought land in what is now Jefferson County, West Virginia, and in 1770 he acquired 255 acres farther west on the site of Martinsburg, with the intention of establishing a town. In 1773 he added 563 acres to his homesite, but during the next four years he spent most of his time as a military commander in Dunmore's War of 1774 and in the Continental army.

All the evidence indicates that Stephen was a highly unreliable combat commander. D. S. Freeman in his biography of Washington points out that when Washington discovered that Stephen had almost ruined his plans for surprising the Hessians at Trenton, New Jersey the day after Christmas 1776, "it was almost as if Fate had brought Stephen to the Delaware to mock him—Stephen, his one-time political rival, who had been suspected in the old days [of 1763] of making theatrical moves of no military value" (*Washington*, III, 98; and IV, 313 and 313n).

Nevertheless promoted to major general (an exalted rank during the Revolution), Stephen continued to build a reputation for sending his troops on misguided missions and then submitting false reports of their successes. The end came when his brigade collided with that of General Anthony Wayne in order to precipitate the debacle at

Germantown, Pennsylvania on 4 October 1777. A court-martial convicted Stephen of conduct unbecoming an officer, including drunkenness, and he was dismissed from the service in November 1777.

Back on the frontier, however, he continued to be a major force until his death in 1791, shortly after completing the house that stands today as an important historic landmark. Now restored (open 2 P.M. to 5 P.M. on weekends for tours), the house is of native limestone with four rooms on each of the two main floors. The grounds slope to Tuscarora Creek. In 1959 the property was acquired by the city, and various organizations have since collaborated in its development.

Traveler's Rest (Horatio Gates Home), near Kearneysville, Jefferson County. Now being restored as a private home and not open to the public, this historic house was occupied off and on for eighteen years by General Horatio Gates (1728–1806).

A British professional soldier, Gates had become a close friend of Washington's during the disastrous expedition under Braddock toward Fort Duquesne in 1755. He was badly wounded in the decisive action. After more service in North America and the West Indies, he retired on half-pay in England (1765–1772) rather than accept further assignment in the colonies. In 1772 he returned with his wife and son after receiving a letter from Washington about land being available on the Virginia frontier, where Washington's brothers had settled.

Gates considered himself a victim of English society. Technically he belonged to the upper class, but was not at ease there because of his servant-class antecedents. He apparently saw in becoming an American the opportunity to gain social stature as a member of the landed gentry while striking back at the system he resented. Be that as it may, Gates became an early hero of the Patriot cause and was tremendously valuable because of his professional military ability as an administrator. His good fortune in his new world hit its peak when he got command of the Northern Department just as the tide was turning against Burgoyne's offensive in 1777. Horatio Gates thus became the victor of Saratoga when Washington's military record was approaching a near-fatal low. A growing sentiment that Gates should replace Washington as commander in chief did not lead to anything other than an intensification of partisan politics.

Gates blundered at Camden, South Carolina, one of the worst American defeats of the Revolution (the fall of Charleston costing the Americans far more). The general withdrew to Traveler's Rest in December 1780. Here he received a distinguished delegation from the Virginia House of Delegates, Patrick Henry, Richard Henry Lee, and Thomas Nelson being in the committee sent to inform him that the House had voted unanimously that no reverse could obliterate the glory of his previous services.

Throughout 1781 Gates kept up a correspondence with Washington and Congress, requesting an official inquiry. He spent most of April and May in Philadelphia on the same business. In August 1782 Congress finally informed Gates that it had dropped all plans of making the inquiry previously directed (5 October 1780), and ordered him to report to Washington at Newburgh, New York. Thus Gates was able to rehabilitate himself in the last days of the Revolution, rendering loyal and valuable support to Washington in the "Newburgh Conspiracy."

He returned home in 1783 and remained there until 1790. But the problem of slavery became too great for his inbred feelings of social equality, and he then moved to a farm on Manhattan. On the plot of land now bounded by Second and Park Avenues between 23rd and 30th Streets, he lived the last sixteen years of his life.

Traveler's Rest is a two-and-one-half-story limestone house with end chimneys and center porch. The "ground floor" is more a raised basement, and a flight of about ten steps leads to the porch and the fortresslike front door with its iron-strap hinges and gigantic lock.

To reach the site from Kearneysville (W.Va. 9), drive 0.6 mile southwest on the prolongation of Route 48 (toward Leetown and Middleway), turn right on the unimproved road, and continue 0.4 mile to the driveway leading to Traveler's Rest. It is currently a private residence.

Washington's Lands. Seven state highway markers refer to the large pieces of choice land acquired by Washington between 1750 and 1784. Three tracts are below Charleston on the Great Kanawha River, with markers at Dunbar Bridge (the Mouth of Tyler Creek Tract of 2,950 acres, extending more than 6 miles along the river), at St. Albans (the Cole River Tract of 2,000 acres, extending more than 5 miles along the Cole and Kanawha Rivers), and at Bancroft (the Poca River Tract of 7,276 acres, extending more than 12 miles along the Kanawha).

Three other tracts along the Ohio River are marked on W.Va. 2 at Pleasant View (the Millwood Tract of 4,395 acres, stretching more than 5 miles along the river), at Lubeck (3 miles east of Washington's Bottom, 2,314 acres with a river frontage of 5 miles), and at Round Bottom (587 acres patented by Washington in 1784).

Washington's first acquisition in West Virginia, surveyed by him in 1750, was where his brother later founded Charles Town. At this place is a marker referring to this "Bullskin," or Rock Hall Tract, which he eventually expanded to 2,233 acres.

Washington's appetite for land speculation was remarkable even for that time in American history. It developed early, when he became a surveyor for Lord Fairfax (1748), but was enhanced by military service on the frontier and the custom of granting land to veterans. William Crawford (1732–1782) remained a close friend and associate of Washington's after their first meeting on the frontier in 1749. He became Washington's agent in scouting for "valuable lands" in the Ohio Valley in defiance of the Proclamation of 1763 that prohibited settlement west of the mountains. As restrictions were lifted on the eve of the American Revolution, Washington made a canoe trip down the Ohio late in 1770. Starting off with his old friend and associate Dr. James Craik (1730–1814) and picking up Crawford at Fort Pitt, Washington drifted 250 miles through an extensive wilderness, carefully avoiding any notice of Indian habitation.

The region that struck Washington as being the Eldorado he sought was the peninsula formed by the lower 50 miles of the Great Kanawha River and the wide loop of the Ohio above the mouth of that river (now Point Pleasant). Washington and Craik carefully selected the specific parcels they personally wanted when the promised land grants were made. Although Washington was eventually to receive 30,000 acres here, he never saw the lands again. But many scholars now suggest that a number of his political decisions were guided by an interest in protecting his vast western land claims.

Wheeling (Fort Henry), Ohio River, Ohio County. When Captain Pierre-Joseph Céloron de Blainville led his expedition down the Ohio in 1749 to claim this vast region officially for France, he buried lead plates at a number of strategic points. One such place, later known as the Forks of Wheeling Creek (a highway marker is at the intersection of U.S. 40 and W.Va. 88), is now the manufacturing center of Wheeling (an Indian name). The Treaty of Fort Stanwix (see under NEW YORK) opened this territory for settlement. Ebenezer Zane and his brothers had already explored along the Ohio, and in 1769 they became the first permanent white settlers on the site of Wheeling. Their families arrived the next year from the vicinity of what is now Moorefield, on the south branch of the Potomac in Hardy County, West Virginia. Later in 1770 George Washington came through the infant settlement, with Dr. James Craik and William Crawford, prospecting for land speculations. Washington described the area of Zane's settlement in his journal before continuing on down the Ohio to the mouth of the Great Kanawha River (see WASHINGTON'S LANDS).

William Crawford was back at the site of Wheeling in 1774, this time to build a fort during Dunmore's War. Initially called Fort Fincastle in honor of Lord Dunmore (one of whose titles was viscount Fincastle), it was renamed in 1776 for Patrick Henry.

Fort Henry was the primary objective of many raids during the Revolution from the British base at Detroit. The first major attack, 31 August to 1 September 1777, was by about 400 Indians and Loyalists. Before settlers could take refuge in the fort, 23 of its 42-man garrison were killed. Reinforcements from nearby Fort Van Meter fought their way through and forced the raiders to withdraw, but the settlement of 25 cabins was burned. The noted Indian fighter Major Samuel McCulloch made his famous "leap" down a high bank into Wheeling Creek to escape pursuers after he was cut off from the relief column he was leading.

The last attack, which may technically be called the last battle of the Revolution, was the successful defense of Fort Henry during the period 11 to 13 September 1782. Some 250 Indians and 40 Loyalists participated in this operation, which was commanded by British officers. During one of these sieges the sister of Ebenezer Zane, Betty, volunteered to leave the fort and get a keg of powder from her brother's cabin. Taking advantage of the Indians' astonishment at seeing a woman stroll from the fort to the cabin, some 60 yards away, she then raced safely back with the powder.

Wheeling is an industrial city where no colonial charm remains. It extends a better effort of preservation toward its Civil War past. Highway markers at 12th and Chapline Streets (W.Va. 2 and U.S. 40 and 250) summarize the actions of 1777 and 1782. The site of the fort is marked by a bronze plaque on a stone nearby, on Main Street between 11th and Ohio Streets. The site of Fort Van Meter is marked northwest of Oglebay Park on the Consolidated School Grounds (Greggsville, Clinton, and Potomac Road). For information on these sites and on Wheeling's Civil War history, contact the Wheeling Convention and Visitors Bureau. Phone: (800) 828-3097.

Index

Page numbers in **bold** *indicate the main article on a subject. Page numbers in italics indicate illustrations. This index is sorted letter by letter.*

C

G

H

N

O

Q

R

S

W

Y

Z